OPERATIONS MANAGEMENT
Processes and Value Chains

EIGHTH EDITION

LEE J. KRAJEWSKI
University of Notre Dame

LARRY P. RITZMAN
Professor Emeritus at
The Ohio State University
and Boston College

MANOJ K. MALHOTRA
University of South Carolina

PEARSON
Prentice
Hall

Upper Saddle River, New Jersey 07458

Library of Congress Cataloging-in-Publication Data

Krajewski, Lee J.
    Operations management processes and value chains / Lee J. Krajewski, Larry
P. Ritzman, Manoj K. Malhotra.—8th ed.
        p. cm.
    Includes bibliographical references and index.
    ISBN 0-13-187294-X
    1. Production management.   I. Ritzman, Larry P.   II. Malhotra, Manoj K.   III.
Title.
    TS155.K785 2007
    658.5—dc22

                                                                        2005058688

AVP/Executive Editor: Mark Pfaltzgraff
Editorial Director: Jeff Shelstad
Senior Project Manager: Alana Bradley
Editorial Assistant: Barbara Witmer
Developmental Editor: Amy Ray
Media Product Development Manager: Nancy Welcher
AVP/Executive Marketing Manager: Debbie Clare
Marketing Assistant: Joanna Sabella
Senior Managing Editor (Production): Cynthia Regan
Production Editor: Melissa Feimer
Permissions Supervisor: Charles Morris
Manufacturing Buyer: Diane Peirano
Design Manager: Christy Mahon
Art Director: Janet Slowik
Interior Design: Amanda Kavanagh
Cover Design: Ray Cruz
Illustrator (Interior): ElectraGraphics, Inc.
Director, Image Resource Center: Melinda Reo
Manager, Rights and Permissions: Zina Arabia
Manager, Visual Research: Beth Brenzel
Image Permission Coordinator: Debbie Latronica
Photo Researcher: Teri Stratford
Manager, Print Production: Christy Mahon
Composition/Full-Service Project Management: BookMasters, Inc.
Printer/Binder: Quebecor

Credits and acknowledgments borrowed from other sources and reproduced, with permission, in this textbook appear on appropriate page within text (or on page 709)

Microsoft® and Windows® are registered trademarks of the Microsoft Corporation in the U.S.A. and other countries. Screen shots and icons reprinted with permission from the Microsoft Corporation. This book is not sponsored or endorsed by or affiliated with the Microsoft Corporation.

Pearson Education LTD.
Pearson Education Singapore, Pte. Ltd
Pearson Education, Canada, Ltd
Pearson Education—Japan

Pearson Education Australia PTY, Limited
Pearson Education North Asia Ltd
Pearson Educación de Mexico, S.A. de C.V.
Pearson Education Malaysia, Pte. Ltd

10 9 8 7 6 5 4 3 2 1
ISBN 0-13-187294-X

DEDICATED with love to our families.

Judie Krajewski

Gary

Lori and Dan; Aubrey, Madeline, and Amelia

Carrie and Jon; Jordanne and Alaina

Selena and Jeff

Virginia and Jerry

Virginia and Larry

Barbara Ritzman

Karen and Matt; Kristin and Alayna

Lisa and Todd; Cody, Cole, Taylor, and Clayton

Kathryn and Paul

Mildred and Ray

Maya Malhotra

Vivek, Pooja, and Neha

Santosh and Ramesh Malhotra

Indra and Prem Malhotra; Neeti and Deeksha

Sadhana Malhotra

Leela and Mukund Dabholkar

Aruna and Harsha Dabholkar; Aditee

Mangala and Pradeep Gandhi; Priya and Medha

BRIEF CONTENTS

CONTENTS

CONTENTS

CONTENTS

CONTENTS

CONTENTS

CONTENTS

CONTENTS

CONTENTS

CD-ROM SUPPLEMENTS

The Eighth Edition of *Operations Management* by Lee Krajewski, Larry Ritzman, and new co-author **Manoj Malhotra** has many exciting changes. Highlights of these changes are as follows:

NEW! Co-Author: Manoj Malhotra, the Jeff B. Bates chair at the University of South Carolina, was asked to join this team because of his teaching ability, his active research record, and his success as a consultant to such top firms as John Deere, Metso Corporation, Phelps Dodge, Sonoco, Milliken, and Verizon among others. Above all, Manoj is a master teacher who knows how to teach operations management creatively and effectively at both the undergraduate and MBA level. He has taught from the book since the first edition and brings new energy and ideas to this edition. Examples of his many contributions to the pedagogical quality of the eighth edition include:

- *Chapter 7, "Constraint Management."* He elevates the discussion of the theory of constraints, explains how to identify and manage bottlenecks, and introduces bottleneck-based product-mix selection techniques that dovetail with the Min-Yo Garment Company Experiential Learning Exercise.

- *Chapter 9, "Lean Systems,"* moved forward in the book, includes fresh Managerial Practice examples, and connects lean systems with poka-yoke methods, the Five S concept, and value stream mapping. These changes help tie together the first nine chapters of the book and reinforce the notion of viewing operations from a process management perspective, which then transitions to managing value chains in Part 3 of the book.

- *Chapter 11, "Location,"* is more contemporary and practically-oriented with a strong decision-making focus. Manoj introduces such innovations as GIS-based location methods using Microsoft MapPoint 2004. There are videos on its use, along with new location examples and a new end-of-chapter case.

NEW! Starwood Case and Video Integration: Another notable change to the eighth edition is the introduction of six Managerial Challenge cases based on Starwood Hotels and Resorts. This case material, and the accompanying video footage, illustrates chapter topics through the eyes of Starwood, one of the world's largest hotel companies.

NEW! Design and Organization: The book is streamlined, with fewer pages and an attractive design that lends a much different "look and feel" to the eighth edition. The art is completely redone to correspond with the design, and it has many innovative features. However, the innovations go far beyond cosmetics. Substantive changes have been made in almost every chapter and supplement, without losing the main themes that have been so valued in the past editions. For example:

- **Theme:** The two dominant themes of processes and value chains have been further reinforced with considerable attention being paid to service providers. A central figure in the margin of each chapter's introduction makes the point, as do the brief discussions on how the chapter relates to both processes and value chains and to the firm's various functional areas.

- **Part 1:** Chapter 1, "Operations As a Competitive Weapon," presents China and India as two notable countries affecting global competition and introduces the first of six Managerial Challenges. Chapter 2, "Operations Strategy," has a new a section on order winners

PREFACE

and qualifiers, plus a new example of closing the gap in performance using operations strategy, and cuts tangential discussion. Chapter 3, "Project Management," is earlier in the book to show how projects can be used to implement operations strategy. It enhances the discussion of project risk, adds a new section on the critical chain, and has new material on the concept of earned value in projects.

■ **Part 2:** Chapter 4, "Process Strategy," identifies the strategic issues in designing processes and describes how to embed strategy into processes. Chapter 5, "Process Analysis," streamlines the flowchart presentations and describes the many metrics that can be measured. Chapter 6, "Process Performance and Quality," describes quality measures in the health care industry and expands the discussion of the six sigma process. Chapter 7, "Constraint Management," brings Theory of Constraints principles to life and shows how they can be exploited to manage bottlenecks. Chapter 8, "Process Layout," demonstrates activity settings in offices and streamlines the discussion of line balancing. Chapter 9, "Lean Systems," connects poka-yoke methods, Five S concepts, and value stream mapping to lean approaches.

■ **Part 3:** Chapter 10, "Supply Chain Strategy," benefits from major revisions guided by faculty reviews, including detailed new material on mass customization, lean supply chains, outsourcing/offshoring, and virtual supply chains. Chapter 11, "Location," has exciting new additions such as MS MapPoint 2004–based GIS to make real-world location decisions, complete with three new instructional videos and Solver files that facilitate calculation. Chapter 12, "Inventory Management," brings out the cost of capital concept relative to holding inventory. Chapter 13, "Forecasting," describes the forecasting process and showcases the new POM for Windows software with regression analysis. Chapter 14, "Sales and Operations Planning," renamed to fit the terminology actually used in practice (instead of "aggregate planning"), shows how to balance supply with demand and simplifies the pure planning strategies. Chapter 15, "Resource Planning," brings in Drum-Buffer-Rope and lean systems as part of the portfolio of resource planning systems. Chapter 16, "Scheduling," has two new Managerial Practices addressing current scheduling approaches in service and manufacturing organizations.

ACKNOWLEDGMENTS

We wish to thank various people at Prentice Hall who make up the publishing team. Those most closely involved with the project and for whom we hold the greatest admiration include Mark Pfaltzgraff, executive editor of decision sciences, who supervised the overall project; Barbara Witmer, the editorial assistant who kept the manuscript moving through to production; Nancy Welcher, the media project development manager, who managed the production of the Student CD-ROM materials and the course management and Companion Website assets; Melissa Feimer, production editor, who kept us on schedule and helped assemble the book into the final product; Janet Slowik, art director, who delivered on a sleek new design of the book; Amy Ray, who seamlessly meshed three author voices into one; Debbie Clare, executive marketing manager, and Joanna Sabella, marketing assistant, whose marketing insights and promotional efforts make all the work of the publishing team worthwhile; and Richard Bretan and Avik Karmaker for helping make possible our media supplements while coordinating these projects through the production process. Annie Puciloski contributed her expertise to checking the text, Solutions Manual, and Test Item File for accuracy. We also express our warm gratitude to Pedro Reyes of Baylor University for writing the Instructor's Resource Manual; Lew Hofmann of the College of New Jersey for the creation of the Lecture PowerPoint materials; Geoff Willis of Central Oklahoma University, who revised the Test Item File and the Online Study Guide; and Don Knox of Wayland Baptist University for revising the Instructor's Solutions Manual. This year we have several new additions to our video library and for that we owe special thanks to Beverly Amer and her colleagues at Aspenleaf Productions, Inc., as well as the folks at Starwood Hotels, Inc., who allowed us to feature their fine hotels in our new segments. We especially appreciate the creations of Howard Weiss, who updated the Active Models and the OM Explorer software materials, and who made POM for Windows available in a new version.

We also thank our colleagues at other universities who provided extremely useful guidance for all our revisions. For this edition they include the following:

Robert H. Burgess	Georgia Institute of Technology
Karen C. Eboch	Bowling Green State University
Mike Godfrey	University of Wisconsin, Oshkosh
Marilyn Helms	Dalton State University
Vijay R. Kannan	Utah State University
Dennis Krumwiede	Idaho State University
Ajay K. Mishra	State University of New York
Ken Paetsch	Cleveland State University
Taeho Park	San Jose State University
Madeleine E. Pullman	Colorado State University
Gyula Vastag	Indiana University–Purdue University, Indianapolis
Rohit Verma	University of Utah

Kudos go to Larry Meile, of Boston College, for his contributions to the Internet Exercises. Brooke Saladin's cases continue to make it easy for instructors to add interest and excitement to their classes.

At the University of Notre Dame, we want to thank Deb Coch for her Internet research and assistance in file preparation. Likewise, Jerry Wei, Dave Hartvigsen, Hojung Shin, Sarv Devaraj, and Jennifer Ryan—all of Notre Dame—were a constant source of encouragement and ideas for improvement. Patrick Philipoom, from the University of South Carolina, made stellar contributions to many of the GIS-related ideas and videos in Chapter 11 and also wrote a related end-of-chapter case. Daniel Steele, also from the University of South Carolina, served as a great sounding board and friend throughout this process. Doctoral students Alan Mackelprang and Jeff Smith at the University of South Carolina also provided valued inputs.

Finally, we thank our families for not abandoning us during our days of seclusion even when the weather for fishing or golf was perfect. Our wives, Judie, Barb, and Maya, have provided love, stability, encouragement, and a sense of humor that were needed when we were transforming the seventh edition into the eighth.

PART 1

USING OPERATIONS
TO COMPETE

LEARNING GOALS

*After reading this chapter,
you should be able to:*

1. Define the decisions operations
   managers make.

2. Identify the trends and
   challenges facing operations
   management.

3. Describe operations in terms of
   inputs, processes, outputs,
   information flows, suppliers, and
   customers.

4. Describe operations as a
   function alongside finance,
   accounting, marketing,
   management information
   systems, and human resources.

5. Explain how operations can be
   used as a competitive weapon.

A FedEx employee scans a package for
ground delivery. Because the Internet
makes it easy for people to send
documents to one another instantly,
FedEx is now focusing more on its
ground service.

FEDEX

FedEx is a $26-billion-a-year delivery service company that thrives on speed and reliability. FedEx delivers 5.5 million packages each day. Because 60 percent of the packages go by plane, FedEx can charge premium prices for the service. For 25 years, companies traditionally chose FedEx because of its on-time delivery and technological superiority in tracking packages. The Internet, however, changed things drastically. Many businesses use complex Web-based processes designed to eliminate much of the unpredictability in their operations by communicating directly with customers and suppliers. E-mail delivers documents instantaneously, and low-cost truck lines, discount air carriers, and even ocean vessels can now track shipments via the Internet.

These technological advances cut into the demand for FedEx's traditional services. The growth potential now lies in ground transportation, presently dominated by United Parcel Service. This demand is fueled by Internet companies such as Amazon.com, which relies on ground transportation services to deliver packages directly to the customer's door, and by the vast business-to-business supply networks created by Web-based purchasing systems. To remain competitive, FedEx created two new services: FedEx Ground and FedEx Home Delivery. FedEx Ground focuses on business-to-business deliveries via a recently procured trucking company. FedEx Home Delivery specializes in deliveries to residences. The goals are now low-cost operations and dependable delivery—a change from past operations goals that stressed speed. In addition, FedEx invested $100 million in processes

>

Helping you understand how to make operations a competitive weapon is a primary goal of this book. Operations management deals with processes—those fundamental activities that organizations use to do work and achieve their goals—to produce goods and services that people use every day. A **process** is any activity or group of activities that takes one or more inputs, transforms them, and provides one or more outputs for its customers. For example, FedEx must receive packages from customers, sort them by destination, move them to their destination by air or ground transportation, keep track of progress, and bill the customer for the service. The changes at FedEx provide one example of designing processes for competitive operations. Major new processes created for the ground delivery services involved the coordination of processes from all areas of the firm. By selecting appropriate techniques and strategies, managers can design processes that give companies a competitive edge.

process
Any activity or group of activities that takes one or more inputs, transforms them, and provides one or more outputs for its customers.

> OPERATIONS MANAGEMENT ACROSS THE ORGANIZATION <

operations management
The systematic design, direction, and control of processes that transform inputs into services and products for internal, as well as external, customers.

The term **operations management** refers to the systematic design, direction, and control of processes that transform inputs into services and products for internal, as well as external, customers. Broadly speaking, operations management underlies all departments in a business because departments carry out many processes. If you aspire to manage a department or a particular process in your discipline, or if you just want to understand how the process you are a part of fits into the overall fabric of the business, you need to understand the principles of operations management. From this perspective, at least a little bit of operations management lives in all of us.

Figure 1.1 shows operations as one of several functions within an organization. Each function specializes by having its own knowledge and skill areas, primary responsibilities, processes, and decision domains. Regardless of how lines are drawn, departments and functions are always linked together through processes. Consequently, operations managers need to build and maintain solid relationships both inside and outside the organization. Too often, managers allow various barriers between functional areas and departments. Jobs or tasks move sequentially from marketing to engineering to operations, often resulting in slow or poor decision making because each department bases its decisions on its own limited perspective, not the organization's overall goals.

Cross-functional coordination is essential to effective management. Consider how other functional areas interact with operations. Perhaps the strongest connection is with the marketing function, which determines the need for new services and products and the demand for existing ones and focuses on customer satisfaction. Operations managers must bring together human and capital resources to meet demands to the customers' satisfaction. Marketing and sales make delivery promises that depend on current operations capabilities. Marketing demand forecasts guide the operations manager in planning output rates and capacities.

The operations manager also needs feedback from the accounting and finance functions to understand current performance. Financial measures help the operations manager assess labor costs, the long-term benefits of new technologies, and quality improvements. Accounting can help the operations manager monitor the production system's vital signs with multiple tracking methods. Finance influences decisions about investing the company's capital assets in new technology, layout redesign, capacity expansion, and even inventory levels. Similarly, human resources interacts with operations to hire and train work-

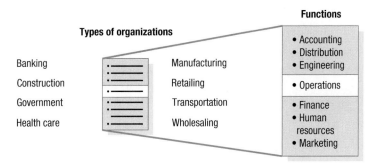

FIGURE **1.1**

Operations Management As a
Function

ers and aids in changeovers related to new process and job designs. Engineering can also
have a big impact on operations. In designing new services or products, engineering needs
to consider technical trade-offs and to ensure that the designs do not create costly specifications or exceed capabilities.

Business and government leaders increasingly recognize the importance of involving
the whole organization in making strategic decisions. Operations plays an important role in
meeting global competition. Foreign competition and the explosion of new technologies
increase the awareness that a firm competes not only by offering new services and products,
creative marketing, and skillful finance, but also through its unique competencies in operations and sound management of core processes. The organization that offers superior services and products at lower prices is a formidable competitor.

> A PROCESS VIEW <

You might wonder why we choose to look at processes as the unit of analysis rather than at
departments or even the firm. The reason is that a process view of the firm provides a much
more relevant picture of the way firms actually work. Departments typically have their own
set of objectives, set of resources with capabilities to achieve those objectives, and managers
and employees responsible for their performance. Some processes, such as billing, may be
contained wholly within a department, such as accounting.

The concept of a process, however, can be much broader. A process can have its own set
of objectives, involve a work flow that cuts across departmental boundaries, and require
resources from several departments. Product development, for example, may involve coordination between engineering, marketing, and operations. You will see examples throughout
the text of companies that discovered they can use their processes to competitive advantage.
You will notice that the key to success in many organizations is a keen understanding of how
their processes work.

HOW PROCESSES WORK

An organization is only as effective as its processes. Let's take a look at what happens at an ad
agency. Suppose a client contacts her account executive (AE) about her need for a memo-
rable ad for the next Super Bowl football game. The AE gathers the pertinent information and
passes it along to a creative design team and a media planning team that prepare an ad layout and a media exposure plan acceptable to the client. The AE also gives the information to
the accounting department, which prepares an account for billing purposes. The creative
design team passes the layout design to a production team, which prepares the final layout
for publication and delivers it to the selected media outlets according to the schedule developed by the media team and approved by the client. The design team, media team, and production team send their billable hours and expense items to the accounting department,
which prepares an invoice that is approved by the AE and then sent to the client for payment.

Figure 1.2 shows a process view of the ad agency at two levels. The red-outlined box represents the ad agency as an aggregate process. Viewed at this level, the ad agency requires
inputs from external sources and produces outputs, which are advertisements for external
clients. The inputs from external sources are resources used by the ad agency's processes and
include employees, managers, money, equipment, facilities, materials, services, land, and

A design team discusses an ad campaign for a new Ortho product at an ad agency. The design team must coordinate with the media planning team to produce an ad that satisfies the client.

energy. The output is the Super Bowl ad for its client. However, inside the red box we see a more detailed process view: The client interface process includes the AE and her interactions with the client. The advertisement design and planning process creates the ad and plans its exposure during the Super Bowl and subsequent showings. The production process acquires the actors and actresses, prepares the production set and props, coordinates the schedules of all involved in the production of the ad, films the content, prepares a video, and delivers the ad to the media outlets on time. The arrows in the diagram indicate information and work flows between the processes along with feedback on performance.

Each process has inputs and each has outputs. At the process level, we see that the inputs could be the resources from external sources mentioned earlier, or they may be very specific to the tasks of the process received from other processes. For example, the advertisement design and planning process receives detailed information about the ad requirements from the client interface process, and the production process receives the ad layout and media plan from the advertisement design and planning process. Billable hours for the ad are an output of the production process, and a complete invoice for the client is an output of the accounting process. Among primary and supporting processes, the output of one process is the input of another. It follows that performance failures in one process can significantly influence other processes.

NESTED PROCESSES

Our process view of the ad agency is helpful; however, even at this level of detail, we may not have a clear enough picture of what is going on. If we peel away a few more layers, we can consider the advertisement design and planning process. Figure 1.3 shows that two separate processes are involved. The creative design process starts with a work request from the AE, after which the creative design director assembles the team. The work request includes the ad's objective, the overall message, the evidence supporting the claims, and the intended audience. The design team comes up with several designs, gets feedback from the AE, prepares a final design, gets feedback from the client through the client interface process, and revises the design as needed. This process consists of its own set of inputs and outputs, separate from the media planning process. The work request for the media planning process, which includes the information in the creative design director's work order plus information about the size of the

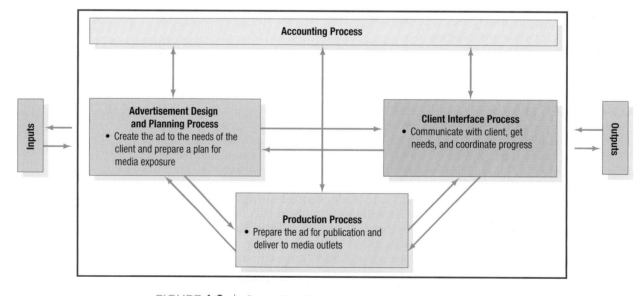

FIGURE 1.2 | Process View of an Ad Agency

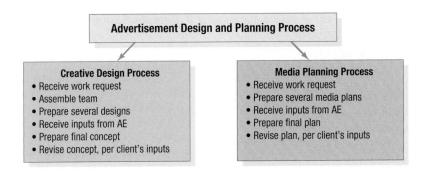

FIGURE **1.3**

Nested Processes

ad and the intended duration of the campaign, goes to the media director, who selects a media planner. The media planner prepares several plans, gets feedback from the AE, prepares a final plan, gets feedback from the client, and revises the plan as needed.

Any process, such as the advertisement design and planning process, can be broken down into subprocesses, which in turn can be broken down further. For example, "preparing an ad design" is a process within the creative design process. We refer to this concept of a process within a process as a **nested process**. It may be helpful to separate one part of a process from another for several reasons. One person or one department may be unable to do all parts of the process, or different parts of the process may require different skills. The skills needed for creative ad designs are quite different from the skills needed for effective media planning; one part of the process provides services requiring considerable customer contact, which requires special employee skills and attitudes, whereas another part is hidden from the customer. Finally, some parts of the process may be designed for routine work while other parts may be geared for customized work. The nested process concept reinforces the need to understand the interconnectivity of activities within a business and the nature of each process's inputs and outputs.

nested process

The concept of a process within a process.

CUSTOMER–SUPPLIER RELATIONSHIPS

Processes provide outputs—often services (which can take the form of information)—to customers. Every process and every person in an organization has customers. Some are **external customers**, who may be end users or intermediaries (such as manufacturers, financial institutions, or retailers) buying the firm's finished services or products. The client of the ad agency is an external customer. Others are **internal customers**, who may be employees or processes that rely on inputs from other employees or processes in order to perform their work. The production process is an internal customer of the advertisement design and planning process.

In similar fashion, every process and every person in an organization relies on suppliers. **External suppliers** may be other businesses or individuals who provide the resources, services, products, and materials for the firm's short-term and long-term needs. The ad agency needs bank loans, office supplies, computer equipment, software, and new personnel to support its processes over time. Processes also have **internal suppliers**, who may be employees or processes that supply important information or materials. In the ad agency, the advertisement design and planning process supplies an ad design and media plan to the production process.

external customers

A customer who is either an end user or an intermediary (i.e., manufacturers, financial institutions, or retailers) buying the firm's finished services or products.

internal customers

One or more employees or processes that rely on inputs from other employees or processes in order to perform their work.

external suppliers

The businesses or individuals who provide the resources, services, products, and materials for the firm's short-term and long-term needs.

internal suppliers

The employees or processes that supply important information or materials to a firm's processes.

SERVICE AND MANUFACTURING PROCESSES

Two major types of processes are service and manufacturing. Service processes pervade the business world. Statistics from the major industrialized countries in the world indicate that more than 80 percent of the jobs in business are in services. Service processes have a prominent place in our discussion of operations management. Manufacturing processes are also important; without them the products we enjoy as part of our daily lives would not exist. In addition, manufacturing gives rise to service opportunities.

Differences Why do we distinguish between service and manufacturing processes? The answer lies at the heart of the design of competitive processes. The two key differences between service and manufacturing processes are (1) the nature of their output and (2) the degree of customer contact.

Manufacturing processes convert materials into goods that have a physical form we call products. For example, an assembly line produces a 350 Z sports car, and a tailor produces an outfit for the rack of an upscale clothing store. The transformation processes change the materials on one or more of the following dimensions:

1. Physical properties
2. Shape
3. Fixed dimension
4. Surface finish
5. Joining parts and materials

The outputs from manufacturing processes can be produced, stored, and transported in anticipation of future demand.

If a process isn't changing the properties of materials on at least one of those five dimensions, it is considered a service (or nonmanufacturing) process. Service processes tend to produce intangible, perishable outputs. For example, the output from the auto loan process of a bank would be a car loan, and an output of the order fulfillment process of the U.S. Postal Service is the delivery of your letter. The outputs of service processes typically cannot be held in finished goods inventory to insulate the process from erratic customer demands.

A second key difference between service processes and manufacturing processes is degree of customer contact. Service processes tend to have a higher degree of customer contact. Customers may take an active role in the process itself, as in the case of shopping in a supermarket, or they may be in close contact with the service provider to communicate specific needs, as in the case of a medical clinic. Manufacturing processes tend to have less customer contact. For example, washing machines are ultimately produced to meet retail forecasts. The process requires little information from the ultimate consumers (you and me), except indirectly through market surveys and market focus groups.

The distinction between service and manufacturing processes on the basis of customer contact is not perfect. Some service processes have nested subprocesses with low customer contact. The central offices of an insurance provider where insurance products and policies are designed and produced may have little contact with customers. By contrast, its branch offices where insurance agents deal directly with the public may have high customer contact. Some manufacturing processes require high customer contact, as in the case of the production of unique engine parts for a specific model of automobile. The important point is that managers must recognize the degree of customer contact required when designing processes.

Similarities At the level of the firm, service providers do not just offer services and manufacturers do not just offer products. Patrons of a restaurant expect good service and good food. A customer purchasing new computers expects a good product as well as good warranty, maintenance, replacement, and financial services.

Further, even though service processes do not use finished goods inventories, they do inventory their inputs. For example, hospitals need to keep inventories of medical supplies and materials needed for day-to-day operations. Some manufacturing processes, on the other hand, do not inventory their outputs because they are so costly. Such would be the case with low-volume customized products (e.g., tailored suits) or products with short shelf lives (e.g., daily newspapers).

When you look at what is being done at the process level, it is much easier to see whether the *process* is providing a service or manufacturing a product. But this clarity is lost when the whole company is classified as either a manufacturer or a service provider, because it often performs both types of processes. For example, the process of cooking the meat at a McDonald's is a manufacturing process, because it changes the material's physical properties (dimension 1), as is the process of assembling the hamburger with the bun (dimension 5). However, most of the other processes visible or invisible to McDonald's customers are service processes. You can debate whether to call the whole McDonald's organization a service provider or a manufacturer, whereas classifications at the process level are much less ambiguous.

> ADDING VALUE: THE VALUE CHAIN <

value chain

An interrelated series of processes that produces a service or product to the satisfaction of customers.

Most services or products are produced through a series of interrelated business activities. Our process view of a firm is helpful for understanding how services or products are produced and why cross-functional coordination is important, but it does not shed any light on the strategic benefits of the processes. The missing strategic insight is that processes must add value for customers. The cumulative work of the processes of a firm is a **value chain**, which is the interrelated series of processes that produces a service or product to the satisfaction of customers. Each activity in a process should add value to the preceding activities; waste and unnecessary cost should be eliminated.

The concept of value chains reinforces the link between processes and performance, which includes a firm's internal processes as well as those of its external customers and suppliers. A need registered by an internal or external customer jump-starts a value chain. These needs may be actual work orders (as in the work request from the AE at the ad agency to the director of the creative design process) or they may be forecasts of future needs. Many of these needs may be present in any process at any time, making for a complicated management challenge. The concept of value chains also focuses attention on the types of processes in the value chain. For example, a **core process** is a chain of activities that delivers value to external customers. Managers of these processes and their employees interact with external customers and build relationships with them, develop new services and products, interact with external suppliers, and produce the service or product for the external customer. Examples include a hotel's reservation handling, new car design for an auto manufacturer, or Web-based purchasing for an online retailer like Amazon.com. A **support process** provides vital resources and inputs to the core processes and is essential to the management of the business. Examples include budgeting, recruiting, and scheduling.

CORE PROCESSES

Figure 1.4 shows the links between the core and support processes in a firm and a firm's external customers and suppliers. In this text we focus on four core processes:

1. *Customer Relationship Process,* sometimes referred to as *customer relationship management.* Employees involved in the **customer relationship process** identify, attract, and build relationships with external customers, and facilitate the placement of orders by customers. Traditional functions, such as marketing and sales, may be a part of this process. The client interface process for the ad agency is an example.

2. *New Service/Product Development Process.* Employees in the **new service/product development process** design and develop new services or products. The services or products may be developed to external customer specifications or conceived from inputs received from the market in general. The advertisement design and planning process for the ad agency is an example.

3. *Order Fulfillment Process.* The **order fulfillment process** includes the activities required to produce and deliver the service or product to the external customer. The production process in the ad agency is an example.

4. *Supplier Relationship Process.* Workers in the **supplier relationship process** select the suppliers of services, materials, and information and facilitate the timely and efficient flow of these items into the firm. Working effectively with suppliers can add significant value to the services or products of the firm. For example, negotiating fair prices, scheduling on-time deliveries, and gaining ideas and insights from critical suppliers are just a few of the ways to create value.

core process

A chain of activities that delivers value to external customers.

support process

A process that provides vital resources and inputs to the core processes and therefore is essential to the management of the business.

customer relationship process

A process that identifies, attracts, builds relationships with external customers, and facilitates the placement of orders by customers, sometimes referred to as *customer relationship management.*

new service/product development process

A process that designs and develops new services or products from inputs received from external customer specifications or from the market in general through the customer relationship process.

order fulfillment process

A process that includes the activities required to produce and deliver the service or product to the external customer.

supplier relationship process

A process that selects the suppliers of services, materials, and information and facilitates the timely and efficient flow of these items into the firm.

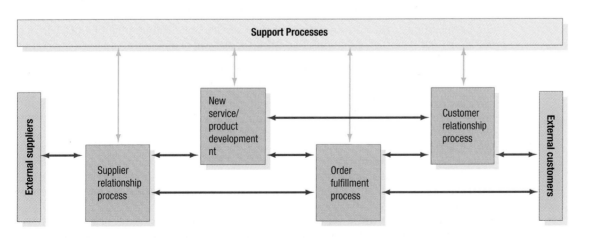

FIGURE 1.4 | Value-Chain Linkages Showing Work and Information Flows

TABLE 1.1 | Examples of Support Processes

Capital acquisition	The provision of financial resources for the organization to do its work and to execute its strategy
Budgeting	The process of deciding how funds will be allocated over a period of time
Recruitment and hiring	The acquisition of people to do the work of the organization
Evaluation and compensation	The assessment and payment of people for the work and value they provide to the company
Human resource support and development	The preparation of people for their current jobs and future skill and knowledge needs
Regulatory compliance	The processes that ensure that the company is meeting all laws and legal obligations
Information systems	The movement and processing of data and information to expedite business operations and decisions
Enterprise and functional management	The systems and activities that provide strategic direction and ensure effective execution of the work of the business

Source: Peter S. Pande, Robert P. Neuman, and Roland R. Cavanagh, *The Six Sigma Way* (New York: McGraw-Hill, 2000), p. 161.

We discuss the concept of core processes further in Chapter 2, "Operations Strategy." Of course, each of the core processes has nested processes within it. We will explore some of these processes in later chapters.

SUPPORT PROCESSES

Firms also have many support processes. We used accounting (actually, invoice preparation) as an example in the ad agency. Support processes provide key resources, capabilities, or other inputs that allow the core processes to function. Table 1.1 provides some examples of support processes.

ADDING VALUE WITH PROCESSES

Examining processes from the perspective of the value they add is an important part of a successful manager's agenda. Managerial Practice 1.1 shows how value chain innovation can make a big difference in a low-growth industry.

> OPERATIONS MANAGEMENT AS A SET OF DECISIONS <

Operations serves as an excellent career path to upper management positions in many organizations. The reason is that operations managers are responsible for key decisions that affect the success of the organization. In manufacturing firms, the head of operations usually holds the title chief operations officer (COO) or vice president of manufacturing (or production or operations). The corresponding title in a service organization might be COO or vice president (or director) of operations. Reporting to the head of operations are the managers of departments, such as customer service, production and inventory control, quality assurance, and check processing.

Decision making is an essential aspect of all management activity, including operations management. Although the specifics of each situation vary, decision making generally involves the same basic steps: (1) recognize and clearly define the problem, (2) collect the information needed to analyze possible alternatives, (3) choose the most attractive alternative, and (4) implement the chosen alternative. Some decisions are strategic, while others are tactical. Strategic decisions are less structured and have long-term consequences; tactical decisions are more structured, routine, and repetitive and have short-term consequences. What sets operations managers apart, however, are the types of decisions they make or participate in making.

In this text we cover the major decisions operations managers make in practice. At the strategic level, operations managers are involved in the development of new capabilities and the maintenance of existing capabilities to best serve the firm's external customers.

MANAGERIAL **PRACTICE**   1.1

MANAGERIAL **PRACTICE**   1.1   OPERATIONAL INNOVATION IS A COMPETITIVE WEAPON AT PROGRESSIVE INSURANCE

Progressive Insurance, an automobile insurer that started business in 1937, had approximately $1.3 billion in sales in 1991. By 2004 it had more than $11 billion in sales. How did it accomplish this amazing growth rate in a 100-year-old industry that traditionally grows with the gross domestic product, which certainly did not experience that sort of growth rate? You might think that Progressive diversified into new businesses, or that it sought sales in global markets. The growth in sales might have been generated through aggressive marketing campaigns or low prices that undercut profit margins. None of these tactics is the secret. In fact, profit margins are quite healthy. A key financial performance measure in the insurance industry is the "combined ratio," which is expenses plus claims payouts, divided by premiums. A typical auto insurer has a ratio of 102 percent, which implies a 2 percent loss on their underwriting activities that must be covered by their investment income. Progressive, however, has a ratio of 96 percent.

So, how did Progressive do it? The answer is simple but the implementation was challenging: offer low prices and better service through operational innovation. That is, provide more value to customers by dramatically changing the way work is done. *Operational innovation* means designing entirely new processes to do work. For example, Progressive reinvented claims processing to lower costs and increase customer satisfaction and retention. Progressive's agency-dedicated Web site, ForAgentsOnly.com (FAO), lets agents quickly, easily, and securely access payments; view policy, billing, and claims information; and send quote information directly to customers through e-mail. Customers are encouraged to go online to perform routine tasks such as address changes or simple billing inquiries. In addition, a value chain called Immediate Response Claims Handling allows a claimant to now reach a Progressive representative by phone 24 hours a day. The representative immediately sends a claims adjuster to inspect the damaged vehicle. The adjuster drives to the vehicle accident site in a mobile claims van, examines the vehicle, prepares an on-site estimate of damage, and writes a check on the spot, if possible (a change to the order fulfillment process). It now takes only 9 hours to complete the cycle, compared with 7–10 days before the changes.

Via operational innovations that add value to its services, Progressive Insurance has been able to achieve amazing growth in a low-growth industry. Under the company's Immediate Response Claims Handling program, for example, claims adjusters are quickly dispatched to the scene of an accident to examine the vehicle and process claims.

The operational innovations to the processes in the customer relationship–order fulfillment value chain for claims processing produced several benefits. First, claimants received faster service with less hassle, which helped retain them as customers. Second, the shortened cycle time significantly reduced costs. The costs of storing a damaged vehicle and providing a rental car can often wipe out the expected underwriting profit for a six-month policy. This cost becomes significant when you realize that the company processes more than 10,000 claims a day. Third, the new value chain design requires fewer people for handling the claim, which reduces operational costs. Finally, the operational innovations improved Progressive's ability to detect fraud by arriving on the accident scene quickly and helped to reduce payouts because claimants often accept less money if the payout is quick and hassle free. Progressive Insurance found a way to differentiate itself in a low-growth industry without compromising profitability, and it accomplished that feat with operational innovation.

Source: Michael Hammer, "Deep Change: How Operational Innovation Can Transform Your Company," *Harvard Business Review* (April 2004), pp. 85–93; http://pressroom.progressive.com, 2005.

Operations managers design new processes that have strategic implications, and they are deeply involved in the development and organization of value chains linking external suppliers and external customers to the firm's internal processes. Operations managers are often responsible for key performance measures such as cost and quality. These decisions have strategic impact because they affect the processes the firm uses to gain a competitive edge.

Great strategic decisions lead nowhere, however, if the tactical decisions that support them are wrong. Operations managers are also involved in tactical decisions, including process improvement and performance measurement, managing and planning projects, generating production and staffing plans, managing inventories, and scheduling resources. You will find numerous examples of these decisions, and the implications of making them, throughout the text. You will also learn about the decision-making tools practicing managers use to recognize and define the problem and then choose the best solution.

DECISION-MAKING TOOLS

The Student CD-ROM contains a unique set of decision tools we call OM Explorer. This package contains 41 powerful Excel-based computer routines to solve problems often encountered in practice. Figure 1.5 shows the drop-down menu and how to access the solvers. OM Explorer also has 63 tutors that provide coaching for all of the difficult analytical techniques in the text, and can be accessed from the drop-down menu.

The Student CD-ROM also contains POMS for Windows, which is an extensive set of useful decision-making tools to complete your arsenal for solving operations problems, many Active Models (spreadsheets designed to help you learn more about important decision-making techniques), and a spreadsheet-based simulation package called SimQuick, and Extend, a powerful simulation tool.

SUPPORTING THE FIRM'S GOALS

The operations manager's decisions should reflect corporate strategy. Plans, policies, and actions should be linked to those in other functional areas to support the firm's goals and objectives. These links are facilitated by taking a process view of a firm. Regardless of whether you aspire to be an operations manager, or you just want to use the principles of operations management to be a more effective manager, remember that effective management of people, capital, information, and materials is critical to the success of any process and any value chain.

As you study operations management, keep two principles in mind.

1. Each part of an organization, not just the operations function, must design and operate processes that are part of a value chain and deal with quality, technology, and staffing issues.

2. Each part of an organization has its own identity and yet is connected with operations.

> TRENDS IN OPERATIONS MANAGEMENT <

Several trends are currently having a great impact on operations management: productivity improvement; global competition; rapid technological change; and ethical, workforce diversity, and environmental issues. In this section, we look at these trends and their challenges for operations managers.

FIGURE 1.5

OM Explorer Menu

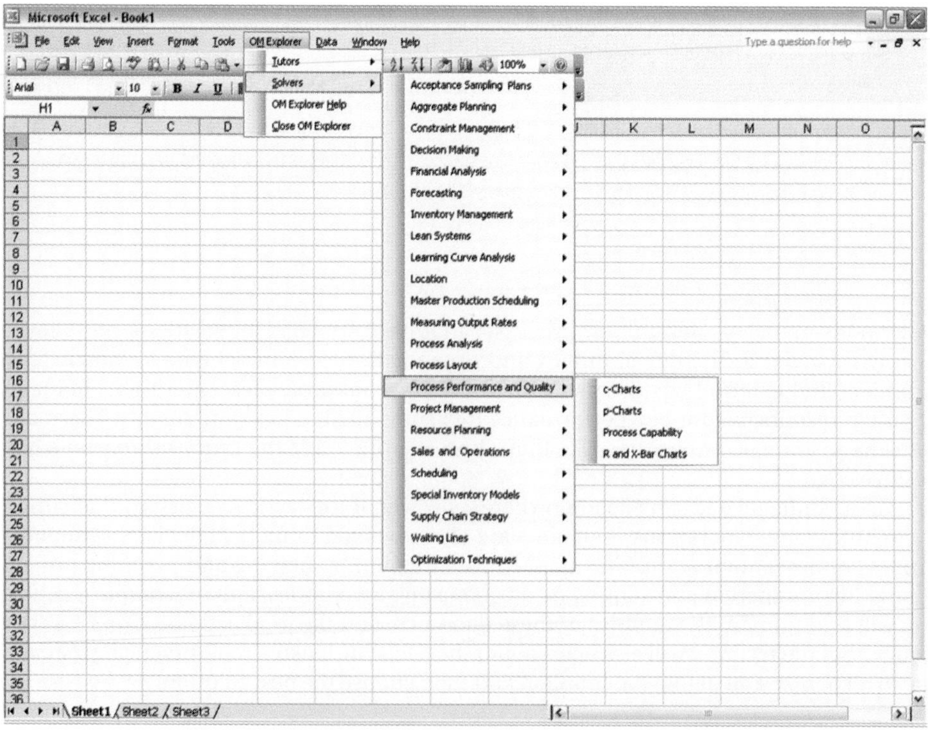

PRODUCTIVITY IMPROVEMENT

Productivity is a basic measure of performance for economies, industries, firms, and processes. **Productivity** is the value of outputs (services and products) produced divided by the values of input resources (wages, cost of equipment, and the like) used:

$$\text{Productivity} = \frac{\text{Output}}{\text{Input}}$$

productivity

The value of outputs (services and products) produced divided by the values of input resources (wages, costs of equipment, etc.).

It is interesting, and even surprising, to compare productivity improvements in the service and manufacturing sectors. In the United States, employment in the service sector has grown rapidly, outstripping the manufacturing sector, but service-sector productivity gains have been much lower. If productivity growth in the service sector stagnates, so does the overall standard of living regardless of which part of the world you live in. Other major industrial countries, such as Japan and Germany, experienced the same problem. Yet, signs of improvement are appearing. The surge of investment across national boundaries can stimulate productivity gains by exposing firms to greater competition. Increased investment in information technology by service providers will also increase productivity.

Measuring Productivity As a manager, how do you measure the productivity of your processes? Many measures are available. For example, value of output can be measured by what the customer pays or simply by the number of units produced or customers served. The value of inputs can be judged by their cost or simply by the number of hours worked.

Managers usually pick several reasonable measures and monitor trends to spot areas needing improvement. For example, a manager at an insurance firm might measure office productivity as the number of insurance policies processed per employee per week. A manager at a carpet company might measure the productivity of installers as the number of square yards of carpet installed per hour. Both measures reflect *labor productivity*, which is an index of the output per person or per hour worked. Similar measures may be used for *machine productivity*, where the denominator is the number of machines. Accounting for several inputs simultaneously is also possible. *Multifactor productivity* is an index of the output provided by more than one of the resources used in production; it may be the value of the output divided by the sum of labor, materials, and overhead costs. Here is an example.

Productivity Calculations	EXAMPLE 1.1

Calculate the productivity for the following operations:

a. Three employees process 600 insurance policies in a week. They work 8 hours per day, 5 days per week.

b. A team of workers makes 400 units of a product, which is valued by its standard cost of $10 each (before markups for other expenses and profit). The accounting department reports that for this job the actual costs are $400 for labor, $1,000 for materials, and $300 for overhead.

SOLUTION

a.

$$\text{Labor productivity} = \frac{\text{Policies processed}}{\text{Employee hours}}$$

$$= \frac{600 \text{ policies}}{(3 \text{ employees})(40 \text{ hours/employee})} = 5 \text{ policies/hour}$$

b.

$$\text{Multifactor productivity} = \frac{\text{Quantity at standard cost}}{\text{Labor cost} + \text{Materials cost} + \text{Overhead cost}}$$

$$= \frac{(400 \text{ units})(\$10/\text{unit})}{\$400 + \$1,000 + \$300} = \frac{\$4,000}{\$1,700} = 2.35$$

Decision Point These measures must be compared with performance levels in prior periods and with future goals. If they do not live up to expectations, the process should be investigated for improvement opportunities.

Foreign companies opened 60,000 new factories in China between 2000 and 2003. Labor costs are low in China, and its workforce is educated and disciplined.

The Role of Management The way processes are managed plays a key role in productivity improvement. Managers must examine productivity from the level of the value chain because it is the collective performance of individual processes that makes the difference. The challenge is to increase the value of output relative to the cost of input. If processes can generate more output or output of better quality using the same amount of input, productivity increases. If they can maintain the same level of output while reducing the use of resources, productivity also increases.

GLOBAL COMPETITION

Businesses accept the fact that, to prosper, they must view customers, suppliers, facility locations, and competitors in global terms. Most products today are composites of materials and services from all over the world. Your Gap polo shirt is sewn in Honduras from cloth cut in the United States. Sitting in a Cineplex theater (Canadian), you munch a Nestle's Crunch bar (Swiss) while watching a Columbia Pictures movie (Japanese). Five developments spurred the need for sound global strategies: (1) improved transportation and communications technologies, (2) loosened regulations on financial institutions, (3) increased demand for imported services and goods, (4) reduced import quotas and other international trade barriers, and (5) comparative cost advantages.

Improved Transportation and Information Technologies Improvements in information technology and transportation break down the barriers of time and space between countries. Air transportation can move goods quickly from Kansas City to New York or even from Osaka, Japan, to Kansas City. Telecommunications (voice and data) technology—including e-mail, fax machines, the Internet, and sophisticated toll-free telephone arrangements—allows facilities to serve larger market areas and lets firms centralize some operations and provide support to branches located near customers. It also permits managers around the world to communicate quickly, increasing the opportunities for cooperation and coordination.

Loosened Regulations on Financial Institutions During the 1980s, U.S. banking regulators removed interest rate ceilings, which allowed banks to attract more foreign investors by offering higher rates. At the same time, foreign banks removed barriers to entry. As a result, the world's financial systems became more open, making it easier for firms to locate where capital, supplies, and resources are cheapest.

Increased Demand for Imported Services and Goods As political barriers to international trade crumble, market penetration of the major economies increases. Imported services and goods now are the equivalent of about 13 percent of total output in the United States and 14 percent in Japan, up considerably from earlier decades. Firms have found that they can increase their market penetration by locating their production facilities in foreign countries because it gives them a local presence that reduces customer aversion to buying imports. For example, Elasticos Selectos, a Mexico City–based elastics concern, built a plant in the United States primarily to gain customers who demand a "made-in-the-USA" label.

Reduced Import Quotas and Other International Trade Barriers Producing services or goods where one's customers live circumvents quotas and other trade barriers designed to restrict imports. Regional trading blocks, such as the European Union (EU) and the North American Free Trade Agreement (NAFTA), also make trade between countries easier, as does the General Agreement on Tariffs and Trade (GATT), a tariff-cutting world trade agreement. The U.S.–China Trade Relations Act of 2000 helped restore normal trade relations with China. Japanese and Chinese markets are far more open to foreign entrants than in the past, creating an explosion of partnership opportunities unthinkable just a decade ago. Lastly, the World Trade Organization (WTO) facilitates free trade. Created in 1995 after massive negotiations over new trade rules among 123 nations, the WTO has powers to hear trade disputes and to issue binding rulings. WTO's goals are free trade, open markets, and an unrestricted flow of capital.

Comparative Cost Advantages Wages for comparable skills can vary dramatically throughout the world. China and India recently became the sources for low-cost, but skilled, labor.[1] In China, for example, a project manager with seven years of experience would be billed at less than one-third that of a U.S. project manager with similar experience. Service as well as manufacturing companies might save as much as 30 to 50 percent in labor costs by locating facilities in these countries. In the late 1990s, companies produced in China to avoid high-tariff barriers, to grab a foothold in a huge market, or to get cheap labor to produce low-tech products despite doubts about the quality of the workforce and shoddy roads and rail systems. Today, however, China's new factories, such as those in the Pudong industrial zone in Shanghai, produce high-value, top-quality sophisticated products. China's labor force is not only vast and cheap, it is educated and disciplined.

Foreign companies opened as many as 60,000 new factories in China from 2000 to 2003. As much as 55 percent of the goods the United States imports from China now come from foreign-owned companies with operations there. These companies include telephone makers such as Nokia and Motorola, computer companies such as IBM, and nearly all of the big footwear and clothing brands. Many more major manufacturers are there as well. The implications for competition are enormous. Companies without operations in China are finding it difficult to compete on the basis of low prices with companies that do. These companies are finding other ways to compete, such as speed to market and small production runs.

What China is to manufacturing, India is to service. As with the manufacturing companies, the cost of labor is a key factor. A programmer in India may get one-sixth the wages of a programmer in the United States with comparable skills and experience. Indian software companies have grown sophisticated in their applications and offer a big advantage in costs. The computer services industry is also affected. To remain competitive, Electronic Data Systems increased its staff in India by almost tenfold in three years. Back-office operations are affected for the same reason. Many firms are using Indian companies for accounting and bookkeeping, preparing tax returns, and processing insurance claims. Many tech companies such as Intel and Microsoft are opening significant research and development (R&D) operations in India.

Disadvantages of Globalization Of course, operations in other countries can have disadvantages. A firm may have to relinquish proprietary technology if it turns over some of its component manufacturing to offshore suppliers or if suppliers need the firm's technology to achieve desired quality and cost goals. Political risks may also be involved. Each nation can exercise its sovereignty over the people and property within its borders. The extreme case is nationalization, in which a government may take over a firm's assets without paying compensation. Further, a firm may actually alienate customers back home if jobs are lost to offshore operations.

Employee skills may be lower in foreign countries, requiring additional training time. South Korean firms moved much of their sports shoe production to low-wage Indonesia and China, but they still manufacture hiking shoes and in-line roller skates in South Korea because of the greater skills required. In addition, when a firm's operations are scattered, customer response times can be longer. Effective cross-functional connections also may be more difficult. We discuss these issues in more depth in Chapter 10, "Supply Chain Strategy," because they should be considered when making decisions about outsourcing.

Strong global competition affects industries everywhere. For example, U.S. manufacturers experienced declining shares of the domestic and international markets in steel, appliances and household durable goods, machinery, and chemicals. With the value of world trade in services now at more than $1.5 trillion per year, banking, law, data processing, airlines, and consulting services are beginning to face many of the same international pressures. Regional trading blocs, such as the European Union (EU) and North American Free Trade Agreement (NAFTA), further change the competitive landscape in both services and manufacturing. Regardless of which area of the world you live in, if you face international competition, the challenge is to produce services or products that can compete in a global market, and to design the processes to back them up.

RAPID TECHNOLOGICAL CHANGE

Accelerating *technological change* affects the design of new services and products and a firm's processes. Many new opportunities come from advances in computer technology,

[1]For additional information on global issues involving India and China, see Neil King Jr., "A Whole New World," *Wall Street Journal* (September 27, 2004); and Bill Powell, "It's All Made in China Now," *Fortune* (March 4, 2002), pp. 121–128.

Leading companies find that workforce diversity can provide a forum for unique perspectives and solutions.

USING OPERATIONS TO COMPETE

↓

Operations As a Competitive Weapon
Operations Strategy
Project Management

MANAGING PROCESSES

↓

Process Strategy
Process Analysis
Process Performance and Quality
Constraint Management
Process Layout
Lean Systems

MANAGING VALUE CHAINS

↓

Supply Chain Strategy
Location
Inventory Management
Forecasting
Sales and Operations Planning
Resource Planning
Scheduling

FIGURE **1.6**

Managing Processes and Value Chains

such as robots and various forms of information technology. E-commerce is dramatically changing sales and purchasing processes. U.S. firms alone spend billions of dollars each year on information technology. The Internet provides a vital tool linking firms internally and externally with customers, strategic partners, and critical suppliers. The exploding rate of technological opportunities offers enormous potential, but also many challenges. How can new technology be used to greatest advantage? How must processes be redesigned? Introducing any new technology involves risk, and employee attitudes depend on how the change is managed. The right choices and the effective management of technology can give a firm a competitive advantage.

ETHICAL, WORKFORCE DIVERSITY, AND ENVIRONMENTAL ISSUES

Businesses face more ethical quandaries than ever before, intensified by an increasing global presence and rapid technological change. As companies locate new operations and acquire more suppliers and customers in other countries, potential ethical dilemmas arise when business can be conducted by different rules. Some countries are more sensitive than others about lavish entertainment, conflicts of interest, bribery, discrimination against minorities and women, poverty, minimum-wage levels, unsafe workplaces, and workers' rights. Managers must decide whether to design and operate processes that do more than just meet local standards. In addition, technological change brings debates about data protection and customer privacy. In an electronic world, businesses are geographically far from their customers, so a reputation of trust may become even more important.

In the past, many people viewed environmental problems such as toxic wastes, poisoned drinking water, air quality, and global warming as quality-of-life issues; now, many people see them as survival issues. Industrial nations face a particular burden because their combined populations, representing only 25 percent of the total global population, consume 70 percent of all resources. Just seven nations, including the United States and Japan, produce almost half of all greenhouse gases. The United States and some European nations now spend 2 percent of their gross domestic products on environmental protection. Managerial Practice 1.2 shows how one company created a successful recycling business by designing a high-tech value chain.

The challenge is clear: Issues of ethics, workforce diversity, and the environment are becoming part of every manager's job. When designing and operating processes, managers should consider integrity, respect for the individual, and customer satisfaction along with more conventional performance measures such as productivity, quality, cost, and profit.

> ADDRESSING THE CHALLENGES IN OPERATIONS MANAGEMENT <

How can firms meet challenges today and in the future? One way is to recognize challenges as opportunities to improve existing processes and value chains or to create new, innovative ones. The management of processes and value chains goes beyond designing them; it requires the ability to ensure they achieve their goals. Firms should manage their processes and value chains to maximize their competitiveness in the markets they serve. We share this philosophy of operations management, as illustrated in Figure 1.6. We use this figure at the start of each chapter to show how the topic of the chapter fits into our philosophy of operations management.

The figure shows that all effective operations decisions follow from a sound operations strategy. Consequently, our text has three major parts: "Using Operations to Compete," "Managing Processes," and "Managing Value Chains." The flow of topics reflects our approach of first understanding how a firm's operations can help provide a solid foundation for competitiveness before tackling the essential process design decisions that will support its strategies. Each part begins with a strategy discussion to support the decisions in that part. Once it is clear how firms design and improve processes, and how they implement those

| MANAGERIAL **PRACTICE** | 1.2 | HIGH-TECH OPERATIONS HELP RECYCLE HIGH-TECH EQUIPMENT |

Have you ever wondered what happens to your old computer after you purchase a new one? You may have given it to the store where you purchased your new one, or merely slipped it into the household trash. Twenty-seven percent of retired computers in the United States are dumped in landfills, while only 13 percent are recycled. Old computers contain electronics components with materials that can be recycled. However, they also have toxins that leach into the soil if these components are left unprocessed: lead and cadmium in computer circuit boards, lead oxide and barium in computer monitors and TV cathode-ray tubes, mercury in switches and flat screens, and fire retardant on printed circuit boards and plastic casings.

Many recycling processors are located in developing countries and are typically low tech. Recyclable material is collected and processed. Workers, who usually do not wear protective gear, often toss the chemicals that come out during the processing into nearby streams and rivers. Other materials not processed often are left in the dumps, allowing the toxins to leak out. This disregard for the environment prompted a backlash in developed countries. The European Union passed a law requiring electronics manufacturers to take back and recycle 75 percent of the products they sell in the European Union (EU). Some states in the United States banned e-waste from landfills and are considering making electronics manufacturers responsible for managing e-waste.

The growing need to be environmentally responsible in the electronics manufacturing industry provided a unique opportunity to deliver a service to both the manufacturers and the countries in which they do business. Citiraya Industries Ltd, a company based in Singapore, commands a 70 percent share of the corporate market for scrapped electronics. The reason for the high market share is that Citiraya created a value chain that includes high-tech processes and a sophisticated tracking system that allows manufacturers to prove their compliance with environmental laws.

Citiraya's recycling value chain begins with its collection centers in 11 countries, including China, India, and the United Kingdom. These centers ship the electronic trash to its premier processing plant in Singapore. Workers wearing thick boots, gloves, and breathing apparatus use heavy cutters to break up integrated-circuit chips, which are moved to a furnace designed to melt special plastics. In another section, workers use chemicals to strip out materials such as gold, copper, and plastic resins. Monitoring devices analyze the air discharged by the plant as well as the water discharged into the city's sewage system. The plant has 60 cameras to allow customers to witness the destruction of their products via the Internet. The value chain developed by Citiraya recycles 90 percent of the products manufacturers send it, while its competitors recover only 65 percent. It is clear that environmentally friendly operations can be a competitive niche.

Source: Cris Prystay, "Recycling 'E-Waste'," *Wall Street Journal* (September 23, 2004); www.citiraya.co.uk, 2005.

designs, we examine the design and operation of value chains that link processes, whether they are internal or external to the firm. The performance of the value chains determines the firm's outcomes, which include the services or products the firm produces, the financial results, and feedback from the firm's customers. These outcomes, which are considered in the firm's strategic plan, are discussed throughout the text.

PART 1: USING OPERATIONS TO COMPETE

In the remainder of this part we continue the discussion of processes and value chains begun in this chapter by presenting the big picture of what an operations strategy is and how it links to the firm's corporate strategy. We present a framework that links the operating characteristics of processes at all levels to the strategies and objectives of the firm, thereby defining the way processes add value to services or products. An *operations strategy* is the means by which firms develop the capabilities to compete successfully in the marketplace. BMW, for example, takes operations strategy seriously. The German auto maker is using the Internet to allow customers to custom-order cars without destroying production line efficiency. Buyers can select from 350 model variations, 500 options, 90 exterior colors, and 170 interior trims. Dealers submit the customer's order and receive a delivery date in 5 seconds; delivery typically occurs 12 days later. If the car must come to the United States, 12 more days are added to delivery. To accomplish this feat, BMW completely overhauled its entire value chain from sales to suppliers. It created a market niche that is difficult for competitors to match.[2]

We conclude this part with a discussion of the methods and tools of project management. Project management is an effective approach to implementing operations strategy through the introduction of new services or products as well as any changes to a firm's processes or value chains.

[2]See "Web Smart 50," *Business Week* (November 24, 2003), pp. 82–106, for the examples mentioned in this section as well as many others demonstrating the use of the Internet to improve business processes.

PART 2: MANAGING PROCESSES

In this part we focus on analyzing processes and how they can be improved to meet the goals of the operations strategy. We begin by addressing the strategic aspects of process design and then present a six-step systematic approach to process analysis: (1) identify the opportunity, (2) define the scope, (3) document the process, (4) evaluate performance, (5) redesign the process, and (6) implement the changes. Each chapter in this part deals with some aspect of that approach. We discuss the tools that help managers analyze processes, and we reveal the methods firms use to measure process performance and quality. These methods provide the foundation for programs such as Six Sigma and total quality management.

Determining the best process capacity with effective constraint management, designing the appropriate layout of the process's activities, and making processes "lean" by eliminating activities that do not add value while improving those that do are also key decisions in the redesign of processes. The activities involved in managing processes are essential for providing significant benefits to the firm. Take, for example, HIP Health Plan of New York, which completely reengineered its claims processing system to allow its 1.1 million members to view claims and refill prescriptions online. Doctors can use the system to authorize CAT scans and visits to specialists. Effective management of its processes provides HIP Health Plan of New York with annual savings of $10 million in claims processing.

PART 3: MANAGING VALUE CHAINS

The management of value chains is based upon process management and operations strategy. In Part 2 we focus on individual processes. The focus of Part 3, however, is on value chains involving processes both internal and external to the firm and the tools that enhance their execution. We begin this part with a look at the strategic dimensions of supply chain designs and how major decisions such as outsourcing and inventory placement affect performance. We follow that with chapters focused on six key planning activities that are useful for the effective operation of value chains: (1) location, (2) inventory management, (3) forecasting, (4) sales and operations planning, (5) resource planning, and (6) scheduling.

It's important to note that the effective operation of a value chain is as important as its design. Yellow Transportation, Inc., found out its importance when it completely redesigned its aggregate planning and scheduling processes to cut costs in its value chain. Every day the $2.6 billion company receives 60,000 orders over the Internet or at its call centers. The new planning process determines down to the person how many drivers the company will need during the four shifts at each of its terminals the next day. Drivers who are not needed are told to take the day off—without pay—which is quite a feat, considering that the process includes 19,300 Teamsters, 8,250 trucks, and 335 facilities across the United States. Orders vary 15 to 20 percent from Monday to Friday; having this capability to match resources to requirements shaves $100 million a year in operating costs. Who says operations management does not make a difference?

The topics in this text will help you meet operations challenges regardless of your chosen career path. We conclude this chapter with a managerial challenge faced by managers of Starwood hotels. Meeting planners bring significant business to the hotels each year. However, the meeting planning process was inconsistent across the company's properties around the world, which frustrated meeting planners who needed to organize meetings at different locations.

> STUDENT CD-ROM AND INTERNET RESOURCES <

The Student CD-ROM and the Companion Website at **www.prenhall.com/krajewski** contain many tools, activities, and resources designed for this chapter.

> KEY EQUATION <

Productivity is the ratio of output to input:

$$\text{Productivity} = \frac{\text{Output}}{\text{Input}}$$

MANAGERIAL **CHALLENGE**	OPERATIONS AS A COMPETITIVE WEAPON AT STARWOOD

DVD

Starwood is one of the world's largest hotel companies, with more than 750 owned, managed, and franchised properties in more than 80 countries. The company's lodging brands include The Luxury Collection, St. Regis, Sheraton, Westin, Four Points, and W Hotels. Its hotels regularly appear on lists of top hotels around the world. On any given night, guests in the hotels may be individual leisure travelers, independent business guests, or part of a meeting or convention.

When guests stay at a Starwood property as part of a meeting or convention, arrangements are typically made by a meeting planner. The meeting planner works with a location to arrange meeting facilities, banquet rooms, lodging, and events for participants. Prior to 2002, the company's individual properties had their own approaches to convention planning, yet no consistent, coordinated program within or across brands made it easy for meeting planners to do business with Starwood. For example, paperwork for confirming program details, rooms, and food and beverage requirements differed between properties and brands. Some hotels had diagrams of meeting space, while others did not. Technology available for meeting rooms varied widely, and a hotel liaison was not always immediately available during the event in case a need arose.

Recognizing that Starwood's future growth and success relied heavily on its relationships with meeting planners, the company held focus groups to gather information about their needs and expectations. One clear priority emerged: consistency in the meeting planning process, whether that meeting was held at the Sheraton New York, the Westin Kierland in Phoenix, or the W. Hotel Lakeshore Chicago. Such a program could create consistency across all brands, and generate loyalty and increased revenues from those meeting planners who drive large volumes of business to Starwood properties annually.

As a result of the meetings, Starwood created the Starwood Preferred Planner program. Every hotel property now has the same paperwork for the meeting planning process, and can share that paperwork electronically across properties and brands. Contracts were standardized and new standards created to recognize and reward frequent VIP meeting planners. Each meeting is assigned a "Star Meeting Concierge" whose sole responsibility is to anticipate and fulfill any needs of the meeting planner during the event. Handheld Nextel radio phones are now issued at check-in to the meeting planner at no extra charge so that they have 24-hour access to the concierge.

To measure the performance of the new process, Starwood set high internal targets for scores on the surveys given to meeting planners after their events concluded. For instance, at the Luxury Collection and St. Regis brands, individual meeting scores must be 4.55 on a 5-point scale. At the Westin and W Hotels, scores must be above 4.35 on the 5-point scale.

In 2002, Starwood standardized its operating processes so that it could measure, improve, and ultimately grow its convention business. Each meeting is assigned a Star Meeting Concierge who works closely with meeting planners.

Scores from Sheraton properties must exceed 4.30, and Four Points hotels have a target of 4.25 on the 5-point scale. Because the expectations for an airport location one-day meeting (not held at the St. Regis or Luxury Collection) differ from a multiday resort experience, the targets reflect those expectations.

Managerial Challenges for Starwood

1. What are the key inputs and outputs associated with Starwood's new meeting planning process?

2. How does the meeting planning process at Starwood interact with the following core processes in their hotels?

   a. Customer relationship (internal and external)

   b. New service or product development

   c. Order fulfillment

   d. Supplier relationship

> KEY TERMS <

core process 9
customer relationship process 9
external customers 7
external suppliers 7
internal customers 7
internal suppliers 7

nested process 7
new service/product development
   process 9
order fulfillment process 9
operations management 4

process 4
productivity 13
supplier relationship process 9
support process 9
value chain 8

> SOLVED PROBLEM 1 <

Student tuition at Boehring University is $100 per semester credit hour. The state supplements school revenue by matching student tuition dollar for dollar. Average class size for a typical three-credit course is 50 students. Labor costs are $4,000 per class, materials costs are $20 per student per class, and overhead costs are $25,000 per class.

a. What is the *multifactor* productivity ratio for this course process?

b. If instructors work an average of 14 hours per week for 16 weeks for each three-credit class of 50 students, what is the *labor* productivity ratio?

SOLUTION

a. Multifactor productivity is the ratio of the value of output to the value of input resources.

$$\text{Value of output} = \left(\frac{50 \text{ students}}{\text{class}}\right)\left(\frac{3 \text{ credit hours}}{\text{student}}\right)\left(\frac{\$100 \text{ tuition} + \$100 \text{ state support}}{\text{credit hour}}\right)$$

$$= \$30,000/\text{class}$$

$$\text{Value of inputs} = \text{Labor} + \text{Materials} + \text{Overhead}$$

$$= \$4,000 + (\$20/\text{student} \times 50 \text{ students/class}) + \$25,000$$

$$= \$30,000/\text{class}$$

$$\text{Multifactor productivity} = \frac{\text{Output}}{\text{Input}} = \frac{\$30,000/\text{class}}{\$30,000/\text{class}} = 1.00$$

b. Labor productivity is the ratio of the value of output to labor hours. The value of output is the same as in part (a), or $30,000/class, so

$$\text{Labor hours of input} = \left(\frac{14 \text{ hours}}{\text{week}}\right)\left(\frac{16 \text{ weeks}}{\text{class}}\right) = 224 \text{ hours/class}$$

$$\text{Labor productivity} = \frac{\text{Output}}{\text{Input}} = \frac{\$30,000/\text{class}}{224 \text{ hours/class}}$$

$$= \$133.93/\text{hour}$$

> SOLVED PROBLEM 2 <

Natalie Attire makes fashionable garments. During a particular week employees worked 360 hours to produce a batch of 132 garments, of which 52 were "seconds" (meaning that they were flawed). Seconds are sold for $90 each at Attire's Factory Outlet Store. The remaining 80 garments are sold to retail distribution, at $200 each. What is the *labor* productivity ratio of this manufacturing process?

SOLUTION

$$\text{Value of output} = (52 \text{ defective} \times \$90/\text{defective}) + (80 \text{ garments} \times \$200/\text{garment})$$

$$= \$20,680$$

$$\text{Labor hours of input} = 360 \text{ hours}$$

$$\text{Labor productivity} = \frac{\text{Output}}{\text{Input}} = \frac{\$20,680}{360 \text{ hours}}$$

$$= \$57.44 \text{ in sales per hour}$$

> DISCUSSION QUESTIONS <

1. Consider your last (or current) job.

    a. What activities did you perform?

    b. Who were your customers (internal and external), and how did you interact with them?

    c. How could you measure the customer value you were adding by performing your activities?

    d. Was your position in accounting, finance, human resources, management information systems, marketing, operations, or other? Explain.

2. Make a list of possible endings to this sentence: "The responsibility of a business is to . . ." (e.g., ". . . *make money*" or ". . . *provide health care for its employees*"). Make a list of the responsibilities that you would support and a list of those that you would not support. Form a small group, and compare your lists with those of the others in the group. Discuss the issues and try to arrive at a consensus. An alternative discussion question: "The responsibility of a student is to . . ."

3. Multinational corporations are formed to meet global competition. Although they operate in several countries, workers do not have international unions. Some union leaders complain that multinationals are in a position to play off their own plants against each other to gain concessions from labor. What responsibilities do multinational corporations have to host countries? To employees? To customers? To shareholders? Would you support provisions of international trade treaties to address this problem? Form a small group, and compare your views with those of the others in the group. Discuss the issues and try to obtain a consensus.

> PROBLEMS <

Software, such as OM Explorer, Active Models, and POM for Windows, is packaged with every new copy of the textbook. Check with your instructor on how best to use it. In many cases, the instructor wants you to understand how to do the calculations by hand. At most, the software provides a check on your calculations. When calculations are particularly complex and the goal is interpreting the results in making decisions, the software replaces entirely the manual calculations. The software also can be a valuable resource well after your course is completed.

1. (Refer to Solved Problem 1.) Coach Bjourn Toulouse led the Big Red Herrings to several disappointing football seasons. Only better recruiting will return the Big Red Herrings to winning form. Because of the current state of the program, Boehring University fans are unlikely to support increases in the $192 season ticket price. Improved recruitment will increase overhead costs to $30,000 per class section from the current $25,000 per class section. The university's budget plan is to cover recruitment costs by increasing the average class size to 75 students. Labor costs will increase to $6,500 per three-credit course. Material costs are about $25 per student for each three-credit course. Tuition will be $200 per semester credit, which is matched by state support of $100 per semester credit.

   a. What is the productivity ratio? Compared to the result obtained in Solved Problem 1, did productivity increase or decrease for the course process?

   b. If instructors work an average of 20 hours per week for 16 weeks for each three-credit class of 75 students, what is the *labor* productivity ratio?

2. Suds and Duds Laundry washed and pressed the following numbers of dress shirts per week.

Week	Work Crew	Total Hours	Shirts
1	Sud and Dud	24	68
2	Sud and Jud	46	130
3	Sud, Dud, and Jud	62	152
4	Sud, Dud, and Jud	51	125
5	Dud and Jud	45	131

   a. Calculate the *labor* productivity ratio for each week.

   b. Explain the labor productivity pattern exhibited by the data.

3. Compact disc players are produced on an automated assembly line process. The standard cost of compact disc players is $150 per unit (labor, $30; materials, $70; and overhead, $50). The sales price is $300 per unit.

   a. To achieve a 10 percent multifactor productivity improvement by reducing materials costs only, by what percentage must those costs be reduced?

   b. To achieve a 10 percent multifactor productivity improvement by reducing labor costs only, by what percentage must those costs be reduced?

   c. To achieve a 10 percent multifactor productivity improvement by reducing overhead costs only, by what percentage must those costs be reduced?

4. The output of a process is valued at $100 per unit. The cost of labor is $50 per hour including benefits. The accounting department provided the following information about the process for the past four weeks:

	Week 1	Week 2	Week 3	Week 4
Units Produced	1,124	1,310	1,092	981
Labor ($)	12,735	14,842	10,603	9,526
Material ($)	21,041	24,523	20,442	18,364
Overhead ($)	8,992	10,480	8,736	7,848

   a. Use the multifactor productivity ratio to see whether recent process improvements had any effect and, if so, when the effect was noticeable.

   b. Has labor productivity changed? Use the labor productivity ratio to support your answer.

ADVANCED PROBLEM

5. The Big Black Bird Company (BBBC) has a large order for special plastic-lined military uniforms to be used in an urgent military operation. Working the normal two

shifts of 40 hours, the BBBC production process usually produces 2,500 uniforms per week at a standard cost of $120 each. Seventy employees work the first shift and 30 the second. The contract price is $200 per uniform. Because of the urgent need, BBBC is authorized to use around-the-clock production, six days per week. When each of the two shifts works 72 hours per week, production increases to 4,000 uniforms per week but at a cost of $144 each.

a. Did the productivity ratio increase, decrease, or remain the same? If it changed, by what percentage did it change?

b. Did the labor productivity ratio increase, decrease, or remain the same? If it changed, by what percentage did it change?

c. Did weekly profits increase, decrease, or remain the same?

> ACTIVE MODEL EXERCISE <

This Active Model appears on the Student CD-ROM. It allows you to evaluate the important elements of labor productivity.

QUESTIONS

1. If the insurance company can process 60 (10%) more policies per week, by what percentage will the productivity measure rise?

2. Suppose the 8-hour day includes a 45-minute lunch. What is the revised productivity measure, excluding lunch?

3. If an employee is hired, what will be the weekly number of policies processed if the productivity of five policies per hour is maintained?

4. Suppose that, during the summer, the company works for only four days per week. What will be the weekly number of policies processed if the productivity of five policies per hour is maintained?

ACTIVE MODEL 1.1

Labor Productivity Using Data from Example 1.1

Chad's Creative Concepts

Chad's Creative Concepts designs and manufactures wood furniture. Founded by Chad Thomas on the banks of Lake Erie in Sandusky, Ohio, the company began by producing custom-made wooden furniture for vacation cabins located along the coast of Lake Erie and on nearby Kelly's Island and Bass Island. Being an "outdoors" type himself, Chad Thomas originally wanted to bring "a bit of the outdoors" inside. Chad's Creative Concepts developed a solid reputation for creative designs and high-quality workmanship. Sales eventually encompassed the entire Great Lakes region. Along with growth came additional opportunities.

Traditionally, the company focused entirely on custom-made furniture, with the customer specifying the kind of wood from which the piece would be made. As the company's reputation grew and sales increased, the sales force began selling some of the more popular pieces to retail furniture outlets. This move into retail outlets led Chad's Creative Concepts into the production of a more standard line of furniture. Buyers of this line were much more price sensitive and imposed more stringent delivery requirements than did clients for the custom line. Custom-designed furniture, however, continued to dominate sales, accounting for 60 percent of volume and 75 percent of dollar sales. Currently, the company operates a single manufacturing process in Sandusky, where both custom furniture and standard furniture are manufactured. The equipment is mainly general purpose in nature to provide the flexibility needed for producing custom pieces of furniture. The layout puts together saws in one section of the facility, lathes in another, and so on. The quality of the finished product reflects the quality of the wood chosen and the craftsmanship of individual workers. Both custom and standard furniture compete for processing time on the same equipment by the same craftspeople.

During the past few months, sales of the standard line steadily increased, leading to more regular scheduling of this product line. However, when scheduling trade-offs had to be made, custom furniture was always given priority because of its higher sales and profit margins. Thus, scheduled lots of standard furniture pieces were left sitting around the plant in various stages of completion.

As he reviews the progress of Chad's Creative Concepts, Chad Thomas is pleased to note that the company has grown. Sales of custom furniture remain strong, and sales of standard pieces are steadily increasing. However, finance and accounting indicate that profits are not what they should be. Costs associated with the standard line are rising. Dollars are being tied up in inventory, both of raw materials and work in process. Expensive public warehouse space has to be rented to accommodate the inventory volume. Thomas also is concerned with increased lead times for both custom and standard orders, which are causing longer promised delivery times. Capacity is being pushed, and no space is left in the plant for expansion. Thomas begins a careful assessment of the overall impact that the new standard line is having on his manufacturing process.

QUESTIONS

1. What types of decisions must Chad Thomas make daily for his company's operations to run effectively? Over the long run?

2. How did sales and marketing affect operations when they began to sell standard pieces to retail outlets?

3. How has the move to producing standard furniture affected the company's financial structure?

4. What might Thomas have done differently to avoid some of the problems he now faces?

Source: This case was prepared by Dr. Brooke Saladin, Wake Forest University, as a basis for classroom discussion.

> SELECTED REFERENCES <

Bowen, David E., Richard B. Chase, Thomas G. Cummings, and Associates. *Service Management Effectiveness.* San Francisco: Jossey-Bass, 1990.

Buchholz, Rogene A. "Corporate Responsibility and the Good Society: From Economics to Ecology." *Business Horizons* (July–August 1991), pp. 19–31.

Collier, David A. *The Service Quality Solution.* Milwaukee: ASQC Quality Press, and Burr Ridge, IL: Irwin Professional Publishing, 1994.

Green, Heather. "The Web Smart 50." *Business Week* (November 24, 2003), pp. 82–106.

Hayes, Robert H., and Gary P. Pisano. "Beyond World-Class: The New Manufacturing Strategy." *Harvard Business Review* (January–February 1994), pp. 77–86.

Heskett, James L., W. Earl Sasser Jr., and Christopher Hart. *Service Breakthroughs: Changing the Rules of the Game.* New York: Free Press, 1990.

"The Horizontal Corporation." *Business Week* (December 20, 1993), pp. 76–81.

Kaplan, Robert S., and David P. Norton. *Balanced Scoreboard.* Boston, MA: Harvard Business School Press, 1997.

King Jr., Neil. "A Whole New World." *Wall Street Journal* (September 27, 2004).

Pande, Peter S., Robert P. Neuman, and Roland R. Cavanagh. *The Six Sigma Way.* New York: McGraw-Hill, 2000.

Porter, Michael. *Competitive Advantage.* New York: The Free Press, 1987.

Post, James E. "Managing As If the Earth Mattered." *Business Horizons* (July–August 1991), pp. 32–38.

Powell, Bill. "It's All Made in China Now." *Fortune* (March 4, 2002), pp. 121–128.

Roach, Stephen S. "Services Under Siege—The Restructuring Imperative." *Harvard Business Review* (September–October 1991), pp. 82–91.

Rummler, Geary A., and Alan P. Brache. *Improving Performance.* San Francisco: Jossey-Bass, 1995.

Schmenner, Roger W. *Service Operations Management.* Englewood Cliffs, NJ: Prentice Hall, 1995.

Skinner, Wickham. "Manufacturing—Missing Link in Corporate Strategy." *Harvard Business Review* (May–June 1969), pp. 136–145.

"Time for a Reality Check in Asia." *Business Week* (December 2, 1996), pp. 58–66.

van Biema, Michael, and Bruce Greenwald. "Managing Our Way to Higher Service-Sector Productivity." *Harvard Business Review* (July–August 1997), pp. 87–95.

Womack, James P., Daniel T. Jones, and Daniel Roos. *The Machine That Changed the World.* New York: HarperPerennial, 1991.

SUPPLEMENT
Decision Making

LEARNING GOALS

After reading this supplement, you should be able to:

1. Explain break-even analysis, using both the graphic and algebraic approaches.

2. Define a preference matrix.

3. Identify the maximin, maximax, Laplace, minimax regret, and expected value decision rules.

4. Explain how to construct a payoff table.

5. Describe how to draw and analyze a decision tree.

Operations managers make many decisions as they manage processes and value chains. Although the specifics of each situation vary, decision making generally involves the same basic steps: (1) recognize and clearly define the problem, (2) collect the information needed to analyze possible alternatives, and (3) choose and implement the most feasible alternative.

Sometimes, hard thinking in a quiet room is sufficient. At other times, reliance on more formal procedures is needed. Here, we present four such formal procedures: break-even analysis, the preference matrix, decision theory, and the decision tree.

- Break-even analysis helps the manager identify how much change in volume or demand is necessary before a second alternative becomes better than the first alternative.

- The preference matrix helps a manager deal with multiple criteria that cannot be evaluated with a single measure of merit, such as total profit or cost.

- Decision theory helps the manager choose the best alternative when outcomes are uncertain.

- A decision tree helps the manager when decisions are made sequentially—when today's best decision depends on tomorrow's decisions and events.

> BREAK-EVEN ANALYSIS <

break-even quantity

The volume at which total revenues equal total costs.

break-even analysis

The use of the break-even quantity; can be used to compare processes by finding the volume at which two different processes have equal total costs.

To evaluate an idea for a new service or product, or to assess the performance of an existing one, determining the volume of sales at which the service or product breaks even is useful. The **break-even quantity** is the volume at which total revenues equal total costs. Use of this technique is known as **break-even analysis**. Break-even analysis can also be used to compare processes by finding the volume at which two different processes have equal total costs.

EVALUATING SERVICES OR PRODUCTS

We begin with the first purpose: to evaluate the profit potential of a new or existing service or product. This technique helps the manager answer questions, such as the following:

- Is the predicted sales volume of the service or product sufficient to break even (neither earning a profit nor sustaining a loss)?
- How low must the variable cost per unit be to break even, based on current prices and sales forecasts?
- How low must the fixed cost be to break even?
- How do price levels affect the break-even volume?

variable cost

The portion of the total cost that varies directly with volume of output.

fixed cost

The portion of the total cost that remains constant regardless of changes in levels of output.

Break-even analysis is based on the assumption that all costs related to the production of a specific service or product can be divided into two categories: variable costs and fixed costs.

The **variable cost**, c, is the portion of the total cost that varies directly with volume of output: costs per unit for materials, labor, and usually some fraction of overhead. If we let Q equal the number of customers served or units produced per year, total variable cost $= cQ$. The **fixed cost**, F, is the portion of the total cost that remains constant regardless of changes in levels of output: the annual cost of renting or buying new equipment and facilities (including depreciation, interest, taxes, and insurance); salaries; utilities; and portions of the sales or advertising budget. Thus, the total cost of producing a service or good equals fixed costs plus variable costs times volume, or

$$\text{Total cost} = F + cQ$$

The variable cost per unit is assumed to be the same no matter how small or large Q is, and thus, total cost is linear. If we assume that all units produced are sold, total annual revenues equal revenue per unit sold, p, times the quantity sold, or

$$\text{Total revenue} = pQ$$

If we set total revenue equal to total cost, we get the break-even point as

$$pQ = F + cQ$$
$$(p - c)Q = F$$
$$Q = \frac{F}{p - c}$$

We can also find this break-even quantity graphically. Because both costs and revenues are linear relationships, the break-even quantity is where the total revenue line crosses the total cost line.

EXAMPLE A.1	Finding the Break-Even Quantity

ACTIVE MODEL A.1

Active Model A.1 on the Student CD-ROM provides additional insight on this break-even example and its extensions.

A hospital is considering a new procedure to be offered at $200 per patient. The fixed cost per year would be $100,000, with total variable costs of $100 per patient. What is the break-even quantity for this service? Use both algebraic and graphic approaches to get the answer.

SOLUTION

The formula for the break-even quantity yields

$$Q = \frac{F}{p - c} = \frac{100,000}{200 - 100} = 1,000 \text{ patients}$$

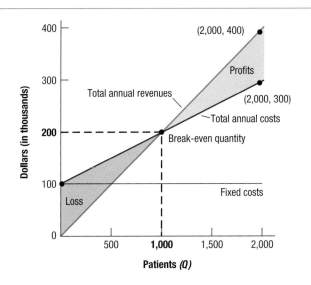

FIGURE **A.1**

Graphic Approach to
Break-Even Analysis

To solve graphically we plot two lines: one for costs and one for revenues. Two points determine a line, so we begin by calculating costs and revenues for two different output levels. The following table shows the results for $Q = 0$ and $Q = 2,000$. We selected zero as the first point because of the ease of plotting total revenue (0) and total cost (F). However, we could have used any two reasonably spaced output levels.

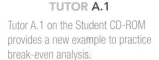

TUTOR A.1

Tutor A.1 on the Student CD-ROM
provides a new example to practice
break-even analysis.

Quantity (patients) (Q)	Total Annual Cost ($) ($100,000 + 100Q$)	Total Annual Revenue ($) ($200Q$)
0	100,000	0
2,000	300,000	400,000

We can now draw the cost line through points (0, 100,000) and (2,000, 300,000). The revenue line goes between (0, 0) and (2,000, 400,000). As Figure A.1 indicates, these two lines intersect at 1,000 patients, the break-even quantity.

Decision Point Management expects the number of patients needing the new procedure will exceed the 1,000-patient break-even quantity but first wants to learn how sensitive the decision is to demand levels before making a final choice.

Break-even analysis cannot tell a manager whether to pursue a new service or product idea or drop an existing line. The technique can only show what is likely to happen for various forecasts of costs and sales volumes. To evaluate a variety of "what-if" questions, we use an approach called **sensitivity analysis**, a technique for systematically changing parameters in a model to determine the effects of such changes. The concept can be applied later to other techniques, such as linear programming. Here we assess the sensitivity of total profit to different pricing strategies, sales volume forecasts, or cost estimates.

sensitivity analysis

A technique for systematically changing
parameters in a model to determine the
effects of such changes.

Sensitivity Analysis of Sales Forecasts	EXAMPLE **A.2**

If the most pessimistic sales forecast for the proposed service in Figure A.1 were 1,500 patients, what would be the procedure's total contribution to profit and overhead per year?

SOLUTION

The graph shows that even the pessimistic forecast lies above the break-even volume, which is encouraging. The product's total contribution, found by subtracting total costs from total revenues, is

$$pQ - (F + cQ) = 200(1,500) - [100,000 + 100(1,500)]$$
$$= \$50,000$$

Decision Point Even with the pessimistic forecast, the new procedure contributes $50,000 per year. After having the proposal evaluated by the present value method, management added the new procedure to the hospital's services.

EVALUATING PROCESSES

Often, choices must be made between two processes or between an internal process and buying services or materials on the outside. In such cases, we assume that the decision does not affect revenues. The manager must study all the costs and advantages of each approach. Rather than find the quantity at which total costs equal total revenues, the analyst finds the quantity for which the total costs for two alternatives are equal. For the make-or-buy decision, it is the quantity for which the total "buy" cost equals the total "make" cost. Let F_b equal the fixed cost (per year) of the buy option, F_m equal the fixed cost of the make option, c_b equal the variable cost (per unit) of the buy option, and c_m equal the variable cost of the make option. Thus, the total cost to buy is $F_b + c_bQ$ and the total cost to make is $F_m + c_mQ$. To find the break-even quantity, we set the two cost functions equal and solve for Q:

$$F_b + c_bQ = F_m + c_mQ$$
$$Q = \frac{F_m - F_b}{c_b - c_m}$$

The make option should be considered, ignoring qualitative factors, only if its variable costs are lower than those of the buy option. The reason is that the fixed costs for making the service or product are typically higher than the fixed costs for buying. Under these circumstances, the buy option is best if production volumes are less than the break-even quantity. Beyond that quantity, the make option becomes best.

EXAMPLE A.3	Break-Even Analysis for Make-or-Buy Decisions

ACTIVE MODEL A.2

Active Model A.2 on the Student CD-ROM provides additional insight on this make-or-buy example and its extensions.

The manager of a fast-food restaurant featuring hamburgers is adding salads to the menu. For the two new options, the price to the customer will be the same for each. The make option is to install a salad bar stocked with vegetables, fruits, and toppings and let the customer assemble the salad. The salad bar would have to be leased and a part-time employee hired. The manager estimates the fixed costs at $12,000 and variable costs totaling $1.50 per salad. The buy option is to have preassembled salads available for sale. They would be purchased from a local supplier at $2.00 per salad. Offering preassembled salads would require installation and operation of additional refrigeration, with an annual fixed cost of $2,400. The manager expects to sell 25,000 salads per year.

What is the break-even quantity?

SOLUTION

The formula for the break-even quantity yields

$$Q = \frac{F_m - F_b}{c_b - c_m}$$
$$= \frac{12,000 - 2,400}{2.0 - 1.5} = 19,200 \text{ salads}$$

TUTOR A.2

Tutor A.2 on the Student CD-ROM provides a new example to practice break-even analysis on make-or-buy decisions.

Figure A.2 shows the solution from OM Explorer's *Break-Even Analysis* Solver. The break-even quantity is 19,200 salads. As the 25,000-salad sales forecast exceeds this amount, the make option is preferred. Only if the restaurant expected to sell fewer than 19,200 salads would the buy option be better.

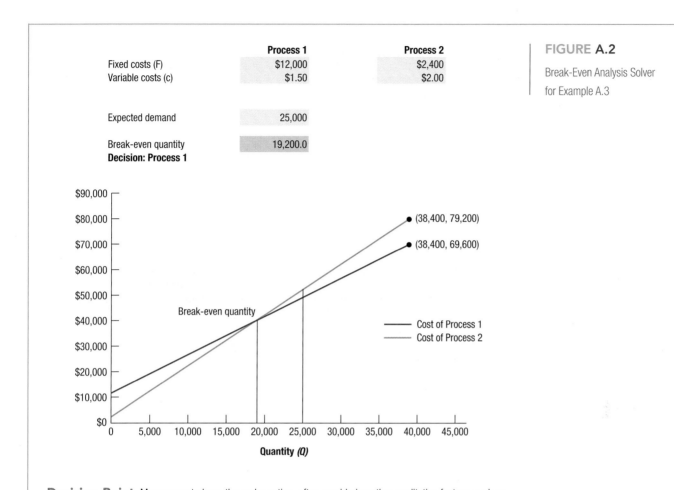

	Process 1	**Process 2**
Fixed costs (F)	$12,000	$2,400
Variable costs (c)	$1.50	$2.00
Expected demand	25,000	
Break-even quantity	19,200.0	

Decision: Process 1

FIGURE A.2

Break-Even Analysis Solver
for Example A.3

Decision Point Management chose the make option, after considering other qualitative factors, such as customer preferences and demand uncertainty. A deciding factor was that the 25,000-salad sales forecast is well above the 19,200-salad break-even quantity.

> PREFERENCE MATRIX <

Decisions often must be made in situations where multiple criteria cannot be naturally merged into a single measure (such as dollars). For example, a manager deciding in which of two cities to locate a new plant would have to consider such unquantifiable factors as quality of life, worker attitudes toward work, and community reception in the two cities. These important factors cannot be ignored. A **preference matrix** is a table that allows the manager to rate an alternative according to several performance criteria. The criteria can be scored on any scale, such as from 1 (worst possible) to 10 (best possible) or from 0 to 1, as long as the same scale is applied to all the alternatives being compared. Each score is weighted according to its perceived importance, with the total of these weights typically equaling 100. The total score is the sum of the weighted scores (weight × score) for all the criteria. The manager can compare the scores for alternatives against one another or against a predetermined threshold.

preference matrix

A table that allows the manager to rate an alternative according to several performance criteria.

Evaluating an Alternative with a Preference Matrix	**EXAMPLE A.4**

The table at the top of page 30 shows the performance criteria, weights, and scores (1 = worst, 10 = best) for a new product: a thermal storage air conditioner. If management wants to introduce just one new product and the highest total score of any of the other product ideas is 800, should the firm pursue making the air conditioner?

TUTOR A.3

Tutor A.3 on the Student CD-ROM provides a new example to practice with preference matrixes.

Performance Criterion	Weight (A)	Score (B)	Weighted Score (A × B)
Market potential	30	8	240
Unit profit margin	20	10	200
Operations compatibility	20	6	120
Competitive advantage	15	10	150
Investment requirement	10	2	20
Project risk	5	4	20
			Weighted score = 750

SOLUTION

Because the sum of the weighted scores is 750, it falls short of the score of 800 for another product. This result is confirmed by the output from OM Explorer's *Preference Matrix* Solver in Figure A.3.

FIGURE A.3

Preference Matrix Solver for Example A.4

Insert a Criterion	Add a Criterion	Remove a Criterion

	Weight (A)	Weight (B)	Weighted Score (A x B)
Market potential	30	8	240
Unit profit margin	20	10	200
Operations compatability	20	6	120
Competitive advantage	15	10	150
Investment requirement	10	2	20
Project risk	5	4	20
	Final Weighted Score		750

Decision Point Management should drop the thermal storage air-conditioner idea. Another new product idea is better, considering the multiple criteria, and management only wanted to introduce one new product at the time.

Not all managers are comfortable with the preference matrix technique. It requires the manager to state criteria weights before examining the alternatives, although the proper weights may not be readily apparent. Perhaps only after seeing the scores for several alternatives can the manager decide what is important and what is not. Because a low score on one criterion can be compensated for or overridden by high scores on others, the preference matrix method also may cause managers to ignore important signals. In Example A.4, the investment required for the thermal storage air conditioner might exceed the firm's financial capability. In that case, the manager should not even be considering the alternative, no matter how high its score.

> DECISION THEORY <

decision theory

A general approach to decision making when the outcomes associated with alternatives are often in doubt.

Decision theory is a general approach to decision making when the outcomes associated with alternatives are often in doubt. It helps operations managers with decisions on process, capacity, location, and inventory because such decisions are about an uncertain future. Decision theory can also be used by managers in other functional areas. With decision theory, a manager makes choices using the following process.

1. List the feasible *alternatives*. One alternative that should always be considered as a basis for reference is to do nothing. A basic assumption is that the number of alternatives is finite. For example, in deciding where to locate a new retail store in a certain part of the city, a manager could theoretically consider every grid coordinate on the city's map. Realistically, however, the manager must narrow the number of choices to a reasonable number.

2. List the *events* (sometimes called *chance events* or *states of nature*) that have an impact on the outcome of the choice but are not under the manager's control. For example, the demand experienced by the new facility could be low or high, depending not only on whether the location is convenient to many customers but also on what the competition does and general retail trends. Then group events into reasonable categories. For example, suppose that the average number of sales per day could be anywhere from 1 to 500. Rather than have 500 events, the manager could represent demand with just 3 events: 100 sales/day, 300 sales/day, or 500 sales/day. The events must be mutually exclusive and exhaustive, meaning that they do not overlap and that they cover all eventualities.

3. Calculate the *payoff* for each alternative in each event. Typically, the payoff is total profit or total cost. These payoffs can be entered into a **payoff table**, which shows the amount for each alternative if each possible event occurs. For 3 alternatives and 4 events, the table would have 12 payoffs (3×4). If significant distortions will occur if the time value of money is not recognized, the payoffs should be expressed as present values or internal rates of return. For multiple criteria with important qualitative factors, use the weighted scores of a preference matrix approach as the payoffs.

4. Estimate the likelihood of each event, using past data, executive opinion, or other forecasting methods. Express it as a *probability*, making sure that the probabilities sum to 1.0. Develop probability estimates from past data if the past is considered a good indicator of the future.

5. Select a *decision rule* to evaluate the alternatives, such as choosing the alternative with the lowest expected cost. The rule chosen depends on the amount of information the manager has on the event probabilities and the manager's attitudes toward risk.

Using this process, we examine decisions under three different situations: certainty, uncertainty, and risk.

payoff table

A table that shows the amount for each alternative if each possible event occurs.

DECISION MAKING UNDER CERTAINTY

The simplest situation is when the manager knows which event will occur. Here the decision rule is to pick the alternative with the best payoff for the known event. The best alternative is the highest payoff if the payoffs are expressed as profits. If the payoffs are expressed as costs, the best alternative is the lowest payoff.

Decisions Under Certainty	EXAMPLE A.5

A manager is deciding whether to build a small or a large facility. Much depends on the future demand that the facility must serve, and demand may be small or large. The manager knows with certainty the payoffs that will result under each alternative, shown in the following payoff table. The payoffs (in $000) are the present values of future revenues minus costs for each alternative in each event.

Alternative	Possible Future Demand	
	Low	High
Small facility	200	270
Large facility	160	800
Do nothing	0	0

What is the best choice if future demand will be low?

SOLUTION

In this example, the best choice is the one with the highest payoff. If the manager knows that future demand will be low, the company should build a small facility and enjoy a payoff of $200,000. The larger facility has a payoff of only $160,000. The "do nothing" alternative is dominated by the other alternatives; that is, the outcome of one alternative is no better than the outcome of another alternative for each event. Because the "do nothing" alternative is dominated, the manager does not consider it further.

Decision Point If management really knows future demand, it would build the small facility if demand will be low and the large facility if demand will be high. If demand is uncertain, it should consider other decision rules.

DECISION MAKING UNDER UNCERTAINTY

Here, we assume that the manager can list the possible events but cannot estimate their probabilities. Perhaps a lack of prior experience makes it difficult for the firm to estimate probabilities. In such a situation, the manager can use one of four decision rules.

1. *Maximin.* Choose the alternative that is the "best of the worst." This rule is for the *pessimist,* who anticipates the "worst case" for each alternative.

2. *Maximax.* Choose the alternative that is the "best of the best." This rule is for the *optimist* who has high expectations and prefers to "go for broke."

3. *Laplace.* Choose the alternative with the best *weighted payoff.* To find the weighted payoff, give equal importance (or, alternatively, equal probability) to each event. If there are n events, the importance (or probability) of each is $1/n$, so they add up to 1.0. This rule is for the *realist.*

4. *Minimax Regret.* Choose the alternative with the best "worst regret." Calculate a table of regrets (or opportunity losses), in which the rows represent the alternatives and the columns represent the events. A regret is the difference between a given payoff and the best payoff in the same column. For an event, it shows how much is lost by picking an alternative to the one that is best for this event. The regret can be lost profit or increased cost, depending on the situation.

EXAMPLE A.6	Decisions Under Uncertainty

TUTOR A.4

Tutor A.4 on the Student CD-ROM provides a new example to make decisions under uncertainty.

Reconsider the payoff matrix in Example A.5. What is the best alternative for each decision rule?

SOLUTION

a. *Maximin.* An alternative's worst payoff is the *lowest* number in its row of the payoff matrix, because the payoffs are profits. The worst payoffs ($000) are

Alternative	Worst Payoff
Small facility	200
Large facility	160

The best of these worst numbers is $200,000, so the pessimist would build a small facility.

b. *Maximax.* An alternative's best payoff ($000) is the *highest* number in its row of the payoff matrix, or

Alternative	Best Payoff
Small facility	270
Large facility	800

The best of these best numbers is $800,000, so the optimist would build a large facility.

c.   *Laplace.* With two events, we assign each a probability of 0.5. Thus, the weighted payoffs ($000) are

Alternative	Weighted Payoff
Small facility	0.5(200) + 0.5(270) = **235**
Large facility	0.5(160) + 0.5(800) = **480**

The best of these weighted payoffs is $480,000, so the realist would build a large facility.

d.   *Minimax Regret.* If demand turns out to be low, the best alternative is a small facility and its regret is 0 (or 200 − 200). If a large facility is built when demand turns out to be low, the regret is 40 (or 200 − 160).

	Regret		
Alternative	Low Demand	High Demand	Maximum Regret
Small facility	200 − 200 = **0**	800 − 270 = **530**	**530**
Large facility	200 − 160 = **40**	800 − 800 = **0**	**40**

The column on the right shows the worst regret for each alternative. To minimize the maximum regret, pick a large facility. The biggest regret is associated with having only a small facility and high demand.

Decision Point   The pessimist would choose the small facility. The realist, optimist, and manager choosing to minimize the maximum regret would build the large facility.

DECISION MAKING UNDER RISK

Here we assume that the manager can list the events and estimate their probabilities. The manager has less information than with decision making under certainty, but more information than with decision making under uncertainty. For this intermediate situation, the *expected value* decision rule is widely used. The expected value for an alternative is found by weighting each payoff with its associated probability and then adding the weighted payoff scores. The alternative with the best expected value (highest for profits and lowest for costs) is chosen.

This rule is much like the Laplace decision rule, except that the events are no longer assumed to be equally likely (or equally important). The expected value is what the *average* payoff would be if the decision could be repeated time after time. Of course, the expected value decision rule can result in a bad outcome if the wrong event occurs. However, it gives the best results if applied consistently over a long period of time. The rule should not be used if the manager is inclined to avoid risk.

Decisions Under Risk	EXAMPLE A.7

Reconsider the payoff matrix in Example A.5. For the expected value decision rule, which is the best alternative if the probability of small demand is estimated to be 0.4 and the probability of large demand is estimated to be 0.6?

SOLUTION

The expected value for each alternative is

Alternative	Expected Value
Small facility	0.4(200) + 0.6(270) = **242**
Large facility	0.4(160) + 0.6(800) = **544**

Decision Point Management would choose a large facility if it used this expected value decision rule, because it provides the best long-term results if consistently applied over time.

> DECISION TREES <

The decision tree method is a general approach to a wide range of OM decisions, such as product planning, process analysis, process capacity, and location. It is particularly valuable for evaluating different capacity expansion alternatives when demand is uncertain and sequential decisions are involved. For example, a company may expand a facility in 2007 only to discover in 2010 that demand is much higher than forecasted. In that case, a second decision may be necessary to determine whether to expand again or build a second facility.

decision tree

A schematic model of alternatives available to the decision maker, along with their possible consequences.

A **decision tree** is a schematic model of alternatives available to the decision maker, along with their possible consequences. The name derives from the tree-like appearance of the model. It consists of a number of square *nodes*, representing decision points, that are left by *branches* (which should be read from left to right), representing the alternatives. Branches leaving circular, or chance, nodes represent the events. The probability of each chance event, *P(E)*, is shown above each branch. The probabilities for all branches leaving a chance node must sum to 1.0. The conditional payoff, which is the payoff for each possible alternative-event combination, is shown at the end of each combination. Payoffs are given only at the outset, before the analysis begins, for the end points of each alternative-event combination. In Figure A.4, for example, payoff 1 is the financial outcome the manager expects if alternative 1 is chosen and then chance event 1 occurs. No payoff can be associated yet with any branches farther to the left, such as alternative 1 as a whole, because it is followed by a chance event and is not an end point. Payoffs often are expressed as the present value of net profits. If revenues are not affected by the decision, the payoff is expressed as net costs.

After drawing a decision tree, we solve it by working from right to left, calculating the *expected payoff* for each node as follows:

1. For an event node, we multiply the payoff of each event branch by the event's probability. We add these products to get the event node's expected payoff.

2. For a decision node, we pick the alternative that has the best expected payoff. If an alternative leads to an event node, its payoff is equal to that node's expected payoff (already calculated). We "saw off," or "prune," the other branches not chosen by marking two short lines through them. The decision node's expected payoff is the one associated with the single remaining unpruned branch.

FIGURE A.4

A Decision Tree Model

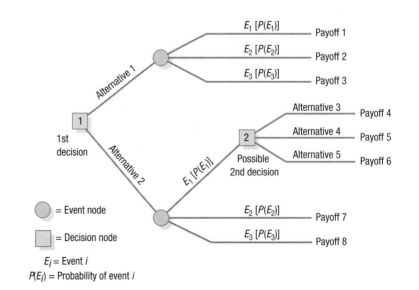

E_i = Event i
$P(E_i)$ = Probability of event i

We continue this process until the leftmost decision node is reached. The unpruned branch extending from it is the best alternative to pursue. If multistage decisions are involved, we must await subsequent events before deciding what to do next. If new probability or payoff estimates are obtained, we repeat the process.

Various software is available for drawing decision trees. PowerPoint can be used to draw decision trees, although it does not have the capability to analyze the decision tree. More extensive capabilities, in addition to OM Explorer, are found with SmartDraw (**www.smartdraw.com**), PrecisionTree decision analysis from Palisade Corporation (**www.palisade.com/html/ptree.html**), and TreePlan (**www.treeplan.com/treeplan.htm**).

Analyzing a Decision Tree	EXAMPLE A.8

A retailer must decide whether to build a small or a large facility at a new location. Demand at the location can be either small or large, with probabilities estimated to be 0.4 and 0.6, respectively. If a small facility is built and demand proves to be high, the manager may choose not to expand (payoff = $223,000) or to expand (payoff = $270,000). If a small facility is built and demand is low, there is no reason to expand and the payoff is $200,000. If a large facility is built and demand proves to be low, the choice is to do nothing ($40,000) or to stimulate demand through local advertising. The response to advertising may be either modest or sizable, with their probabilities estimated to be 0.3 and 0.7, respectively. If it is modest, the payoff is estimated to be only $20,000; the payoff grows to $220,000 if the response is sizable. Finally, if a large facility is built and demand turns out to be high, the payoff is $800,000.

Draw a decision tree. Then analyze it to determine the expected payoff for each decision and event node. Which alternative—building a small facility or building a large facility—has the higher expected payoff?

ACTIVE MODEL A.3

Active Model A.3 on the Student CD-ROM provides additional insight on this decision tree example and its extensions.

SOLUTION

The decision tree in Figure A.5 shows the event probability and the payoff for each of the seven alternative-event combinations. The first decision is whether to build a small or a large facility. Its node is shown first, to the left, because it is the decision the retailer must make now. The second decision node—whether to expand at a later date—is reached only if a small facility is built and demand turns out to be high. Finally, the third decision point—whether to advertise—is reached only if the retailer builds a large facility and demand turns out to be low.

Analysis of the decision tree begins with calculation of the expected payoffs from right to left, shown on Figure A.5 beneath the appropriate event and decision nodes.

1. For the event node dealing with advertising, the expected payoff is 160, or the sum of each event's payoff weighted by its probability [0.3(20) + 0.7(220)].

2. The expected payoff for decision node 3 is 160 because *Advertise* (160) is better than *Do nothing* (40). Prune the *Do nothing* alternative.

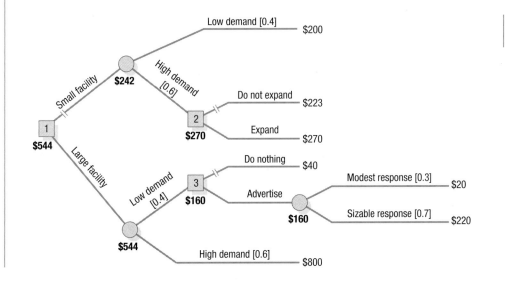

FIGURE **A.5**

Decision Tree for Retailer (in $000)

3. The payoff for decision node 2 is 270 because *Expand* (270) is better than *Do not expand* (223). Prune *Do not expand.*

4. The expected payoff for the event node dealing with demand, assuming that a small facility is built, is 242 [or 0.4(200) + 0.6(270)].

5. The expected payoff for the event node dealing with demand, assuming that a large facility is built, is 544 [or 0.4(160) + 0.6(800)].

6. The expected payoff for decision node 1 is 544 because the large facility's expected payoff is largest. Prune *Small facility.*

Decision Point   The retailer should build the large facility. This initial decision is the only one made now. Subsequent decisions are made after learning whether demand actually is low or high.

> STUDENT CD-ROM AND INTERNET RESOURCES <

The Student CD-ROM and the Companion Website at **www.prenhall.com/krajewski** contain many tools, activities, and resources designed for this supplement.

> KEY EQUATIONS <

1. Break-even volume: $Q = \dfrac{F}{p-c}$

2. Evaluating processes, make-or-buy indifference quantity: $Q = \dfrac{F_m - F_b}{c_b - c_m}$

> KEY TERMS <

break-even analysis 26
break-even quantity 26
decision theory 30

decision tree 34
fixed cost 26
payoff table 31

preference matrix 29
sensitivity analysis 27
variable cost 26

> SOLVED PROBLEM 1 <

The owner of a small manufacturing business has patented a new device for washing dishes and cleaning dirty kitchen sinks. Before trying to commercialize the device and add it to her existing product line, she wants reasonable assurance of success. Variable costs are estimated at $7 per unit produced and sold. Fixed costs are about $56,000 per year.

a. If the selling price is set at $25, how many units must be produced and sold to break even? Use both algebraic and graphic approaches.

b. Forecasted sales for the first year are 10,000 units if the price is reduced to $15. With this pricing strategy, what would be the product's total contribution to profits in the first year?

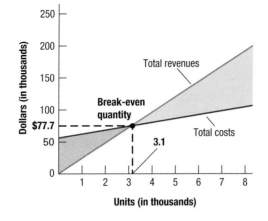

SOLUTION

a. Beginning with the algebraic approach, we get

$$Q = \frac{F}{p-c} = \frac{56,000}{25-7}$$
$$= 3,111 \text{ units}$$

Using the graphic approach, shown in Figure A.6, we first draw two lines:

$$\text{Total revenue} = 25Q$$
$$\text{Total cost} = 56,000 + 7Q$$

The two lines intersect at $Q = 3,111$ units, the break-even quantity.

b. Total profit contribution = Total revenue − Total cost

$$= pQ - (F + cQ)$$
$$= 15(10,000) - [56,000 + 7(10,000)]$$
$$= \$24,000$$

> SOLVED PROBLEM 2 <

Binford Tool Company is screening three new product ideas, A, B, and C. Resource constraints allow only one of them to be commercialized. The performance criteria and ratings, on a scale of 1 (worst) to 10 (best), are shown in the following table. The Binford managers give equal weights to the performance criteria. Which is the best alternative, as indicated by the preference matrix method?

	Rating		
Performance Criterion	**Product A**	**Product B**	**Product C**
1. Demand uncertainty and project risk	3	9	2
2. Similarity to present products	7	8	6
3. Expected return on investment (ROI)	10	4	8
4. Compatibility with current manufacturing process	4	7	6
5. Competitive advantage	4	6	5

SOLUTION

Each of the five criteria receives a weight of 1/5 or 0.20.

Product	Calculation	Total Score
A	$(0.20 \times 3) + (0.20 \times 7) + (0.20 \times 10) + (0.20 \times 4) + (0.20 \times 4)$	= 5.6
B	$(0.20 \times 9) + (0.20 \times 8) + (0.20 \times 4) + (0.20 \times 7) + (0.20 \times 6)$	= 6.8
C	$(0.20 \times 2) + (0.20 \times 6) + (0.20 \times 8) + (0.20 \times 6) + (0.20 \times 5)$	= 5.4

The best choice is product B. Products A and C are well behind in terms of total weighted score.

> SOLVED PROBLEM 3 <

TUTOR A.6

Tutor A.6 on the Student CD-ROM examines decisions under uncertainty for a location example.

Adele Weiss manages the campus flower shop. Flowers must be ordered three days in advance from her supplier in Mexico. Although Valentine's Day is fast approaching, sales are almost entirely last-minute, impulse purchases. Advance sales are so small that Weiss has no way to estimate the probability of low (25 dozen), medium (60 dozen), or high (130 dozen) demand for red roses on the big day. She buys roses for $15 per dozen and sells them for $40 per dozen. Construct a payoff table. Which decision is indicated by each of the following decision criteria?

  a. Maximin

  b. Maximax

  c. Laplace

  d. Minimax regret

SOLUTION

The payoff table for this problem is

Alternative	Demand for Red Roses		
	Low (25 dozen)	Medium (60 dozen)	High (130 dozen)
Order 25 dozen	$625	$625	$625
Order 60 dozen	$100	$1,500	$1,500
Order 130 dozen	($950)	$450	$3,250
Do nothing	$0	$0	$0

  a. Under the maximin criteria, Weiss should order 25 dozen, because if demand is low, Weiss's profits are $625, the best of the worst payoffs.

  b. Under the maximax criteria, Weiss should order 130 dozen. The greatest possible payoff, $3,250, is associated with the largest order.

  c. Under the Laplace criteria, Weiss should order 60 dozen. Equally weighted payoffs for ordering 25, 60, and 130 dozen are about $625, $1,033, and $917, respectively.

  d. Under the minimax regret criteria, Weiss should order 130 dozen. The maximum regret of ordering 25 dozen occurs if demand is high: $3,250 − $625 = $2,625. The maximum regret of ordering 60 dozen occurs if demand is high: $3,250 − $1,500 = $1,750. The maximum regret of ordering 130 dozen occurs if demand is low: $625 − (−$950) = $1,575.

> SOLVED PROBLEM 4 <

White Valley Ski Resort is planning the ski lift operation for its new ski resort. Management is trying to determine whether one or two lifts will be necessary; each lift can accommodate 250 people per day. Skiing normally occurs in the 14-week period from December to April, during which the lift will operate seven days per week. The first lift will operate at 90 percent capacity if economic conditions are bad, the probability of which is believed to be about a 0.3. During normal times the first lift will be utilized at 100 percent capacity, and the excess crowd will provide 50 percent utilization of the second lift. The probability of normal times is 0.5. Finally, if times are really good, the probability of which is 0.2, the utilization of the second lift will increase to 90 percent. The equivalent annual cost of installing a new lift, recognizing the time value of money and the lift's economic life, is $50,000. The annual cost of installing two lifts is only $90,000 if both are purchased at the same time. If used at all, each lift costs $200,000 to operate, no matter how low or high its utilization rate. Lift tickets cost $20 per customer per day.

Should the resort purchase one lift or two?

SOLUTION

The decision tree is shown in Figure A.7. The payoff ($000) for each alternative-event branch is shown in the following table. The total revenues from one lift operating at 100 percent capacity are $490,000 (or 250 customers $\times$ 98 days $\times$ \$20/customer-day).

Alternative	Economic Condition	Payoff Calculation (Revenue – Cost)
One lift	Bad times	$0.9(490) - (50 + 200) = 191$
	Normal times	$1.0(490) - (50 + 200) = 240$
	Good times	$1.0(490) - (50 + 200) = 240$
Two lifts	Bad times	$0.9(490) - (90 + 200) = 151$
	Normal times	$1.5(490) - (90 + 400) = 245$
	Good times	$1.9(490) - (90 + 400) = 441$

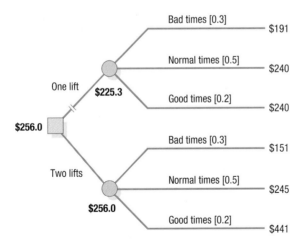

| FIGURE **A.7**

> PROBLEMS <

Software, such as OM Explorer, Active Models, and POM for Windows, is packaged with every new copy of the textbook. Check with your instructor on how best to use it. In many cases, the instructor wants you to understand how to do the calculations by hand. At most, the software provides a check on your calculations. When calculations are particularly complex and the goal is interpreting the results in making decisions, the software replaces entirely the manual calculations. The software also can be a valuable resource well after your course is completed.

BREAK-EVEN ANALYSIS

1. Mary Williams, owner of Williams Products, is evaluating whether to introduce a new product line. After thinking through the production process and the costs of raw materials and new equipment, Williams estimates the variable costs of each unit produced and sold at $6 and the fixed costs per year at $60,000.

   a. If the selling price is set at $18 each, how many units must be produced and sold for Williams to break even? Use both graphic and algebraic approaches to get your answer.

   b. Williams forecasts sales of 10,000 units for the first year if the selling price is set at $14.00 each. What would be the total contribution to profits from this new product during the first year?

   c. If the selling price is set at $12.50, Williams forecasts that first-year sales would increase to 15,000 units. Which pricing strategy ($14.00 or $12.50) would result in the greater total contribution to profits?

   d. What other considerations would be crucial to the final decision about making and marketing the new product?

2. A product at the Jennings Company enjoyed reasonable sales volumes, but its contributions to profits were disappointing. Last year, 17,500 units were produced and sold. The selling price is $22 per unit, c is $18, and F is $80,000.

   a. What is the break-even quantity for this product? Use both graphic and algebraic approaches to get your answer.

   b. Jennings is considering ways to either stimulate sales volumes or decrease variable costs. Management believes that sales can be increased by 30 percent or that c can be reduced to 85 percent of its current level. Which alternative leads to higher contributions to profits, assuming that each is equally costly to implement? (*Hint:* Calculate profits for both alternatives and identify the one having the greatest profits.)

   c. What is the percent change in the per-unit profit contribution generated by each alternative in part (b)?

3. An interactive television service that costs $10 per month to provide can be sold on the information highway for $15 per client per month. If a service area includes a potential of 15,000 customers, what is the most a company could spend on annual fixed costs to acquire and maintain the equipment?

4. A restaurant is considering adding fresh brook trout to its menu. Customers would have the choice of catching their own trout from a simulated mountain stream or simply asking the waiter to net the trout for them. Operating the stream would require $10,600 in fixed costs per year. Variable costs are estimated to be $6.70 per trout. The firm wants to break even if 800 trout dinners are sold per year. What should be the price of the new item?

5. Gabriel Manufacturing must implement a manufacturing process that reduces the amount of toxic by-products.

Two processes have been identified that provide the same level of toxic by-product reduction. The first process would incur $300,000 of fixed costs and $600 per unit of variable costs. The second process has fixed costs of $120,000 and variable costs of $900 per unit.

   a. What is the break-even quantity beyond which the first process is more attractive?

   b. What is the difference in total cost if the quantity produced is 800 units?

6. A news clipping service is considering modernization. Rather than manually clipping and photocopying articles of interest and mailing them to its clients, employees electronically input stories from most widely circulated publications into a database. Each new issue is searched for key words, such as a client's company name, competitors' names, type of business, and the company's products, services, and officers. When matches occur, affected clients are instantly notified via an online network. If the story is of interest, it is electronically transmitted, so the client often has the story and can prepare comments for follow-up interviews before the publication hits the street. The manual process has fixed costs of $400,000 per year and variable costs of $6.20 per clipping mailed. The price charged the client is $8.00 per clipping. The computerized process has fixed costs of $1,300,000 per year and variable costs of $2.25 per story electronically transmitted to the client.

   a. If the same price is charged for either process, what is the annual volume beyond which the automated process is more attractive?

   b. The present volume of business is 225,000 clippings per year. Many of the clippings sent with the current process are not of interest to the client or are multiple copies of the same story appearing in several publications. The news clipping service believes that by improving service and by lowering the price to $4.00 per story, modernization will increase volume to 900,000 stories transmitted per year. Should the clipping service modernize?

   c. If the forecasted increase in business is too optimistic, at what volume will the new process break even?

7. Hahn Manufacturing purchases a key component of one of its products from a local supplier. The current purchase price is $1,500 per unit. Efforts to standardize parts succeeded to the point that this same component can now be used in five different products. Annual component usage should increase from 150 to 750 units. Management wonders whether it is time to make the component in-house, rather than to continue buying it from the supplier. Fixed costs would increase by about $40,000 per year for the new equipment and tooling needed. The cost of raw materials and variable overhead would be about $1,100 per unit, and labor costs would be $300 per unit produced.

   a. Should Hahn make rather than buy?

   b. What is the break-even quantity?

   c. What other considerations might be important?

8. Techno Corporation is currently manufacturing an item at variable costs of $5 per unit. Annual fixed costs of

manufacturing this item are $140,000. The current selling price of the item is $10 per unit, and the annual sales volume is 30,000 units.

a. Techno can substantially improve the item's quality by installing new equipment at additional annual fixed costs of $60,000. Variable costs per unit would increase by $1, but, as more of the better-quality product could be sold, the annual volume would increase to 50,000 units. Should Techno buy the new equipment and maintain the current price of the item? Why or why not?

b. Alternatively, Techno could increase the selling price to $11 per unit. However, the annual sales volume would be limited to 45,000 units. Should Techno buy the new equipment and raise the price of the item? Why or why not?

9. The Tri-County Generation and Transmission Association is a nonprofit cooperative organization that provides electrical service to rural customers. Based on a faulty long-range demand forecast, Tri-County overbuilt its generation and distribution system. Tri-County now has much more capacity than it needs to serve its customers. Fixed costs, mostly debt service on investment in plant and equipment, are $82.5 million per year. Variable costs, mostly fossil fuel costs, are $25 per megawatt-hour (MWh, or million watts of power used for one hour). The new person in charge of demand forecasting prepared a short-range forecast for use in next year's budgeting process. That forecast calls for Tri-County customers to consume 1 million MWh of energy next year.

a. How much will Tri-county need to charge its customers per MWh to break even next year?

b. The Tri-County customers balk at that price and conserve electrical energy. Only 95 percent of forecasted demand materializes. What is the resulting surplus or loss for this nonprofit organization?

10. Earthquake, drought, fire, economic famine, flood, and a pestilence of TV court reporters have caused an exodus from the City of Angels to Boulder, Colorado. The sudden increase in demand is straining the capacity of Boulder's electrical system. Boulder's alternatives have been reduced to buying 150,000 MWh of electric power from Tri-County G&T at a price of $75 per MWh, or refurbishing and recommissioning the abandoned Pearl Street Power Station in downtown Boulder. Fixed costs of that

project are $10 million per year, and variable costs would be $35 per MWh. Should Boulder build or buy?

11. Tri-County G&T sells 150,000 MWh per year of electrical power to Boulder at $75 per MWh, has fixed costs of $82.5 million per year, and has variable costs of $25 per MWh. If Tri-County has 1,000,000 MWh of demand from its customers (other than Boulder) what will Tri-County have to charge to break even?

PREFERENCE MATRIX

12. The Forsite Company is screening three ideas for new services. Resource constraints allow only one idea to be commercialized at the present time. The following estimates have been made for the five performance criteria that management believes to be most important.

	Rating		
Performance Criterion	Service A	Service B	Service C
Capital equipment investment required	0.6	0.8	0.3
Expected return on investment (ROI)	0.7	0.3	0.9
Compatibility with current workforce skills	0.4	0.7	0.5
Competitive advantage	1.0	0.4	0.6
Compatibility with EPA requirements	0.2	1.0	0.5

a. Calculate a total weighted score for each alternative. Use a preference matrix and assume equal weights for each performance criterion. Which alternative is best? Worst?

b. Suppose that the expected ROI is given twice the weight assigned to each of the remaining criteria. (Sum of weights should remain the same as in part (a).) Does this modification affect the ranking of the three potential services?

13. You are in charge of analyzing five new product ideas and have been given the information shown in Table A.1 (1 = worst, 10 = best). Management has decided that criteria 2 and 3 are equally important and that criteria 1 and 4 are each four times as important as criterion 2. Only two new

TABLE A.1	Analysis of New Product Ideas				
	Rating				
Performance Criterion	Product A	Product B	Product C	Product D	Product E
Compatibility with current manufacturing	8	7	3	6	9
Expected return on investment (ROI)	3	8	4	7	7
Compatibility with current workforce skills	9	5	7	6	5
Unit profit margin	7	6	9	2	7

products can be introduced, and a product can be introduced only if its score exceeds 70 percent of the maximum possible total points. Which product ideas do you recommend?

14. Accel Express, Inc., collected the following information on where to locate a warehouse (1 = poor, 10 = excellent).

Location Factor	Factor Weight	Location Score	
		A	B
Construction costs	10	8	5
Utilities available	10	7	7
Business services	10	4	7
Real estate cost	20	7	4
Quality of life	20	4	8
Transportation	30	7	6

a. Which location, A or B, should be chosen on the basis of the total weighted score?

b. If the factors were weighted equally, would the choice change?

DECISION THEORY AND DECISION TREE

15. Build-Rite Construction has received favorable publicity from guest appearances on a public TV home improvement program. Public TV programming decisions seem to be unpredictable, so Build-Rite cannot estimate the probability of continued benefits from its relationship with the show. Demand for home improvements next year may be either low or high. But Build-Rite must decide now whether to hire more employees, do nothing, or develop subcontracts with other home improvement contractors. Build-Rite has developed the following payoff table.

	Demand for Home Improvements		
Alternative	Low	Moderate	High
Hire	($250,000)	$100,000	$625,000
Subcontract	$100,000	$150,000	$415,000
Do nothing	$ 50,000	$ 80,000	$300,000

Which alternative is best, according to each of the following decision criteria?

a. Maximin

b. Maximax

c. Laplace

d. Minimax regret

16. Analyze the decision tree in Figure A.8. What is the expected payoff for the best alternative? First, be sure to infer the missing probabilities.

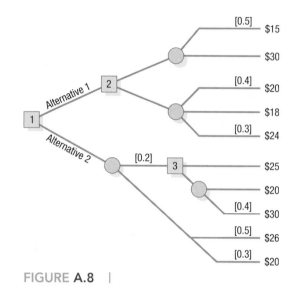

FIGURE A.8

17. A manager is trying to decide whether to buy one machine or two. If only one is purchased and demand proves to be excessive, the second machine can be purchased later. Some sales will be lost, however, because the lead time for producing this type of machine is 6 months. In addition, the cost per machine will be lower if both are purchased at the same time. The probability of low demand is estimated to be 0.20. The after-tax net present value of the benefits from purchasing the two machines together is $90,000 if demand is low and $180,000 if demand is high.

If one machine is purchased and demand is low, the net present value is $120,000. If demand is high, the manager has three options. Doing nothing has a net present value of $120,000; subcontracting, $160,000; and buying the second machine, $140,000.

a. Draw a decision tree for this problem.

b. How many machines should the company buy initially? What is the expected payoff for this alternative?

18. A manager is trying to decide whether to build a small, medium, or large facility. Demand can be low, average, or high, with the estimated probabilities being 0.25, 0.40, and 0.35, respectively.

A small facility is expected to earn an after-tax net present value of just $18,000 if demand is low. If demand is average, the small facility is expected to earn $75,000; it can be increased to average size to earn a net present value of $60,000. If demand is high, the small facility is expected to earn $75,000 and can be expanded to average size to earn $60,000 or to large size to earn $125,000.

A medium-sized facility is expected to lose an estimated $25,000 if demand is low and earn $140,000 if demand is average. If demand is high, the medium-sized facility is expected to earn a net present value of $150,000; it can be expanded to a large size for a net payoff of $145,000.

If a large facility is built and demand is high, earnings are expected to be $220,000. If demand is average for the large facility, the present value is expected to be $125,000; if demand is low, the facility is expected to lose $60,000.

   a. Draw a decision tree for this problem.

   b. What should management do to achieve the highest expected payoff?

19. A manufacturing plant has reached full capacity. The company must build a second plant—either small or large—at a nearby location. The demand is likely to be high or low. The probability of low demand is 0.3. If demand is low, the large plant has a present value of $5 million and the small plant, $8 million. If demand is high, the large plant pays off with a present value of $18 million and the small plant with a present value of only $10 million. However, the small plant can be expanded later if demand proves to be high, for a present value of $14 million.

   a. Draw a decision tree for this problem.

   b. What should management do to achieve the highest expected payoff?

20. Benjamin Moses, chief engineer of Offshore Chemicals, Inc., must decide whether to build a new processing facility based on an experimental technology. If the new facility works, the company will realize a net profit of $20 million. If the new facility fails, the company will lose $10 million. Benjamin's best guess is that there is a 40 percent chance that the new facility will work.

What decision should Benjamin Moses make?

> SELECTED REFERENCES <

Bonini, Charles P., Warren H. Hausman, and Harold Bierman, Jr. *Quantitative Analysis for Management*. Burr Ridge Parkway, IL: Irwin/McGraw-Hill, 1996.

Clemen, Robert T. *Making Hard Decisions: An Introduction to Decision Analysis*. Boston: PWS-Kent, 1991.

2

LEARNING GOALS

*After reading this chapter,
you should be able to:*

1. Define an operations strategy.

2. Identify the nine different
   competitive priorities used in
   operations strategies.

3. List the steps in the new
   service/product development
   process.

4. Describe the role of operations
   strategy as a source of
   competitive strength in a global
   marketplace.

5. Explain how to link marketing
   strategy to operations strategy
   through competitive priorities.

6. Explain how a pattern of
   decisions about processes and
   value chains is used to develop
   the capabilities to achieve
   competitive priorities.

A customer selects songs for burning
to CD as another orders coffee at a
Starbucks in Santa Monica, California.

STARBUCKS

Want to go for a coffee? You say that you want something special, such as espresso or cappuccino? Perhaps, then, we should go to Starbucks as millions of others do. Who would have thought that someone could turn a pedestrian product like coffee into an upscale consumer accessory? Entrepreneur Howard Schultz did, 15 years ago, when he purchased the 17-store Seattle chain and turned it into a global success. In 2005 the chain had 9,571 outlets in 28 countries. Average growth in profits reached a phenomenal 30 percent per year. Apparently something special is going on here.

What is the secret to this outstanding performance? Much of it has to do with the Starbucks service strategy. Consider what you get when you shop at a Starbucks. Certainly you get your choice of exotic coffees, lattes, cappuccino, or espresso. You can also buy a sandwich, dessert, a CD of your favorite pop artist, or even packaged coffee for a special occasion. To speed up your service, you may choose to use an automated espresso machine or a prepaid Starbucks card. At some stores, you may even wish to use Starbucks Express, which uses Web technology to provide faster service. Customers can order and pay for beverages and pastries via phone or Starbucks' Website, and the order will be available for pickup. In about 1,200 locations in North America and Europe, you can access the Internet while enjoying your java. You also get upscale, or "hip" surroundings (as some customers say) that are conducive to conversation and socializing and friendly service from a cadre of baristas.

Starbucks' strategy goes beyond the actual services and goods it offers customers. The company likes to cluster stores in a good market to increase total revenue and market share

For additional chapter resources check the Student CD-ROM or the Companion Website at
www.prenhall.com/krajewski

because it is cheaper to manage stores located closely together. For example, you find a Starbucks store for every 9,400 people in Seattle. Manhattan's 24 square miles has 124 Starbucks stores or about one store for every 12,000 people. Starbucks is capable of designing and opening a new store in 16 weeks or less and recouping the initial investment in three years.

Even though the Starbucks business model has been successful, it faces a number of challenges. For example, to maintain its growth in a saturated home market, Starbucks must look to international markets. Global expansion poses risks, not the least of which is lower profitability per store. Most of the international stores are operated by partners, thereby reducing the share Starbucks gets.

Also, the profile of customers is changing. The chain's successes were largely built on baby boomers. A new generation of younger potential customers is more averse to the power and image of the Star-

bucks brand and is turned off by the image of latte-sipping sophisticates and piped-in soft rock music. Three-dollar cups of coffee are not an attraction, and they feel unwanted in Starbucks stores, where the only other people in the store like them are behind the counter. The business model also relies on employing lots of low-wage workers. Keeping them happy is a key to the successful delivery of the services provided at the Starbucks stores—a significant challenge in an environment that traditionally has low pay and long, hard hours.

Many of the innovations Starbucks is adding at selected stores are designed to attract the new generation of customers. Successful companies must constantly evaluate their strategies and update the goods and services they offer to reflect changes in demographics and customer desires.

Source: Stanley Holmes, "Planet Starbucks," *Business Week* (September 9, 2002), pp. 100–110; www.starbucks.com, 2004.

Starbucks' amazing growth is an example of a customer-driven operations strategy in action. Its core processes focus on critical activities, ranging from the acquisition of select coffee beans to the delivery of a variety of goods and services to delight customers. Managerial challenges abound as customers desire change, requiring managers to revisit the strategy that historically brought them success and to redesign processes to support the new directions.

operations strategy

The means by which operations implements the firm's corporate strategy and helps to build a customer-driven firm.

In this chapter we focus on **operations strategy**, which specifies how operations implements corporate strategy and helps to build a customer-driven firm. Operations strategy links long-term and short-term operations decisions to corporate strategy and develops the capabilities the firm needs to be competitive. As we will see throughout the text, it is the core of managing processes and value chains. A firm's internal processes are only building blocks: They need to be organized to ultimately be effective in a competitive environment. Operations strategy is the linchpin that brings these processes together to form value chains that extend beyond the walls of the firm, encompassing suppliers as well as customers.

No firm understands the value of operations strategy better than Dell, Inc. As the personal computer (PC) became more of a commodity, Dell understood that customers wanted a product that was reliable, inexpensive, and delivered with short lead times. How can you get fast deliveries without generating mountains of inventories waiting for the next order to arrive? If you have large inventories, how can you keep costs low? Dell's answer was to recreate its customer relationship, order fulfillment, and supplier relationship processes to be an integrated and agile value chain.

At Dell's plant in Nashville, online orders go directly to assembly-line robots, which find all the parts to create a custom-built PC. The system automatically loads software onto hard drives and tests the machines before another bank of robots boxes them up for shipping. Such a feat could not be accomplished without redesigning the customer relationship process (particularly the order entry subprocess) and the supplier relationship process (particularly the logistical processes that enable close coordination of inbound component shipments and outbound customer deliveries). Prices, promotional packages, product features, and the like can provide a short-term advantage for a firm; it is the firm's operations that produce a long-term advantage because they are difficult to copy, as Dell—and Starbucks—found out.

> OPERATIONS STRATEGY ACROSS THE ORGANIZATION <

In implementing operations strategy, continuous cross-functional interaction is necessary. For example, a Starbucks operations manager needs feedback from marketing to determine how much capacity should be planned for a new store, and the operations manager must work with finance regarding the timing and funding of the new store. In identifying the operational capabilities needed for the future, operations managers must work closely with the managers of other functional areas.

Corporate strategy views the organization as a system of interconnected parts, or functional areas, each working in concert with the others to achieve desired goals. Operations strategy, which supports corporate strategy, also requires a close connection among the functional areas. A key area is *management information systems,* which designs the systems that provide market data and competitor information in a global environment. Operations strategy specifies the overall service or manufacturing strategy and involves a pattern of decisions that affect the processes, systems, and procedures of the firm. Consequently, when marketing wants to add a new service or product, it should coordinate with operations to ensure that the firm has the ability to support the new endeavor. Adding new services or products without the ability to produce them can lead to poor performance.

Often, new investments are required to support new endeavors or to improve existing operations. An operations strategy that requires investments in new equipment and other financial support for improvements must be coordinated with finance. In addition, finance is interested in the operations strategy because it affects the ability of the firm to generate revenues and contribute to company performance.

Invariably, operations strategies involve the design of new processes or the redesign of existing ones. Engineering works with operations to arrive at the designs that achieve the appropriate competitive priorities. Engineering also is heavily involved in the design of new services and products and must do so in light of the ability of the firm to produce them.

> DEVELOPING A CUSTOMER-DRIVEN OPERATIONS STRATEGY <

Developing a customer-driven operations strategy begins with *corporate strategy,* which coordinates the firm's overall goals with its core processes (see Figure 2.1). It determines the markets the firm will serve and the responses the firm will make to changes in the environment. It provides the resources to develop the firm's core competencies and core processes, and it identifies the strategy the firm will employ in international markets. Based on corporate strategy, a *market analysis* categorizes the firm's customers, identifies their needs, and assesses competitors' strengths. This information is used to develop *competitive priorities.* These priorities help managers develop the services or products and the processes needed to be competitive in the marketplace. Competitive priorities are important to the design of new services or products, the processes that will deliver them, and the operations strategy that will develop the firm's capabilities to fulfill them. Developing a firm's operations strategy is a continuous process because the firm's capabilities to meet the competitive priorities must be periodically checked and any gaps in performance must be addressed in the operations strategy. We will discuss market analysis and competitive priorities in greater detail later in this chapter.

CORPORATE STRATEGY

Corporate strategy provides an overall direction that serves as the framework for carrying out all the organization's functions. It specifies the business or businesses the company will pursue, isolates new opportunities and threats in the environment, and identifies growth objectives.

USING OPERATIONS TO COMPETE

Operations As a Competitive Weapon
Operations Strategy
Project Management

MANAGING PROCESSES

Process Strategy
Process Analysis
Process Performance and Quality
Constraint Management
Process Layout
Lean Systems

MANAGING VALUE CHAINS

Supply Chain Strategy
Location
Inventory Management
Forecasting
Sales and Operations Planning
Resource Planning
Scheduling

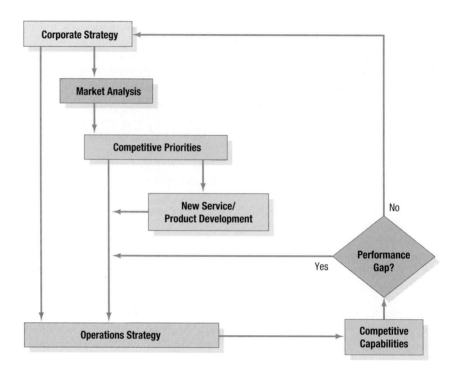

Developing a corporate strategy involves three considerations: (1) monitoring and adjusting to changes in the business environment, (2) identifying and developing the firm's core competencies, and (3) developing the firm's core processes.

Environmental Scanning The external business environment in which a firm competes changes continually, and an organization needs to adapt to those changes. Adaptation begins with *environmental scanning,* the process by which managers monitor trends in the environment (i.e., the industry, the marketplace, and society) for potential opportunities or threats. A crucial reason for environmental scanning is to stay ahead of the competition. Competitors may be gaining an edge by broadening service or product lines, improving quality, or lowering costs. New entrants into the market or competitors that offer substitutes for a firm's service or product may threaten continued profitability. Other important environmental concerns include economic trends, technological changes, political conditions, social changes (e.g., attitudes toward work), and the availability of vital resources. For example, car manufacturers recognize that dwindling oil reserves will eventually require alternative fuels for their cars. Consequently, they have designed prototype cars that use hydrogen or electric power as supplements to gasoline as a fuel.

Core Competencies Good managerial skill alone cannot overcome environmental changes. Firms succeed by taking advantage of what they do particularly well—that is, the organization's unique strengths. **Core competencies** are the unique resources and strengths that an organization's management considers when formulating strategy. They reflect the collective learning of the organization, especially in how to coordinate processes and integrate technologies. These competencies include the following:

core competencies

The unique resources and strengths that an organization's management considers when formulating strategy.

1. *Workforce.* A well-trained and flexible workforce allows organizations to respond to market needs in a timely fashion. This competency is particularly important in service organizations, where customers come in direct contact with employees.

2. *Facilities.* Having well-located facilities (offices, stores, and plants) is a primary advantage because of the long lead time needed to build new ones. In addition, flexible facilities that can handle a variety of services or products at different levels of volume provide a competitive advantage.

3. *Market and Financial Know-How.* An organization that can easily attract capital from stock sales, market and distribute its services or products, or differentiate them from similar services or products on the market has a competitive edge.

4. *Systems and Technology.* Organizations with expertise in information systems will have an edge in industries that are data intensive, such as banking. Particularly advantageous is expertise in Internet technologies and applications, such as business-to-consumer and business-to-business systems. Having the patents on a new technology is also a big advantage.

Core Processes A firm's core competencies should determine its core processes. In Chapter 1, we discussed four core processes: customer relationship, new service/product development, order fulfillment, and supplier relationship. Many companies have all four processes. Many other companies focus on a subset of them to better match their core competencies. In the newspaper industry, for example, all four processes were once tightly integrated.

A newspaper typically attracted its own customers—both readers and advertisers (customer relationship). It developed most of its product—the news stories printed on its pages (new service/product development). It also managed its own production, delivery, and supply processes (order fulfillment and supplier relationship). Many newspaper companies found it difficult to be good at all four processes and still be competitive. Today, much of the typical newspaper's product is outsourced to wire services, syndicated columnists, and publishers of specialty magazine inserts. In addition, many newspapers have divested themselves of the order fulfillment process, leaving the capital-intensive printing and delivery processes to specialty printers. All of this outsourcing allows the newspapers to focus on the customer relationship process (helping to connect readers to advertisers), and a portion of the new service/product development process (editing the daily newspaper and developing stories of local interest).

A similar situation exists in the banking industry, particularly in the credit card business. Companies specialize in finding customers and maintaining relationships with them. For example, American Airlines' credit card program reaches out and achieves a special affinity to customers through its marketing database. Specialized credit card companies, such as CapitalOne, focus on service innovation by creating new features and pricing programs. Finally, many companies are taking over the order fulfillment process by managing the processing of credit card transactions and call centers. The important point is that every firm must evaluate its core competencies and choose to focus on those processes that provide the greatest competitive strength.

GLOBAL STRATEGIES

Identifying opportunities and threats today requires a global perspective. A global strategy may include buying foreign services or parts, combating threats from foreign competitors, or planning ways to enter markets beyond traditional national boundaries. Although warding off threats from global competitors is necessary, firms should also actively seek to penetrate foreign markets. Two effective global strategies are strategic alliances and locating abroad.

Strategic Alliances One way for a firm to open foreign markets is to create a *strategic alliance*. A strategic alliance is an agreement with another firm that may take one of three forms. One form of strategic alliance is the *collaborative effort,* which often arises when one firm has core competencies that another needs but is unwilling (or unable) to duplicate. Such arrangements commonly arise out of buyer–supplier relationships.

Another form of strategic alliance is the *joint venture,* in which two firms agree to produce a service or product jointly. This approach often is used by firms to gain access to foreign markets. For example, to get access to the large Chinese market, GM and VW each developed joint ventures with Shanghai Automotive Industry Corp. or SAIC.[1] The Chinese partner is a large manufacturer of automobiles, producing more than 600,000 cars with GM and VW.

Finally, *technology licensing* is a form of strategic alliance in which one company licenses its service or production methods to another. Licenses may be used to gain access to foreign markets.

Locating Abroad Another way to enter global markets is to locate operations in a foreign country. However, managers must recognize that what works well in their home country might not work well elsewhere. The economic and political environment or customers' needs may be significantly different. For example, McDonald's is known for the consistency of its products—a Big Mac tastes the same anywhere in the world. By contrast, the family-owned chain Jollibee Foods Corporation has become the dominant fast-food chain in the

[1]Alex Taylor, "Shanghai Auto Wants to Be the World's Next Great Car Company," *Fortune* (October 4, 2004), pp. 103–110.

Philippines. Jollibee caters to a local preference for sweet-and-spicy flavors, which it incorporates into its fried chicken, spaghetti, and burgers. Jollibee's strength is its understanding of local tastes and claims that its burger is similar to the one a Filipino would cook at home. McDonald's responded by introducing its own Filipino-style spicy burger, but competition is stiff. McDonald's experience demonstrates that, to be successful, corporate strategies must recognize customs, preferences, and economic conditions in other countries.

Locating abroad is a key decision in the design of value chains because it affects the flow of materials, information, and employees in support of the firm's core processes. See Chapter 10, "Supply Chain Strategy," and Chapter 11, "Location," for an in-depth discussion of these other implications.

MARKET ANALYSIS

One key to success in formulating a customer-driven operations strategy for both service and manufacturing firms is understanding what the customer wants and how to provide it. A *market analysis* first divides the firm's customers into market segments and then identifies the needs of each segment. In this section, we examine the process of market analysis and we define and discuss the concepts of market segmentation and needs assessment.

Market Segmentation *Market segmentation* is the process of identifying groups of customers with enough in common to warrant the design and provision of services or products that the group wants and needs. To identify market segments, the analyst must determine the characteristics that clearly differentiate each segment. The company can then develop a sound marketing program and an effective operating strategy to support it. For instance, The Gap, Inc., a major provider of casual clothes, targets teenagers and young adults and, for its GapKids stores, the parents or guardians of infants through 12-year-olds. At one time, managers thought of customers as a homogeneous mass market. Managers now realize that two customers may use the same product for different reasons. Identifying the key factors in each market segment is the starting point in devising a customer-driven operations strategy.

Needs Assessment The second step in market analysis is to make a *needs assessment,* which identifies the needs of each segment and assesses how well competitors are addressing those needs. Each market segment's needs can be related to the service or product and its value chain. Market needs, which should include both the tangible and the intangible service or product attributes and features that a customer desires, may be grouped as follows:

- *Service or Product Needs.* Attributes of the service or product, such as price, quality, and degree of customization.
- *Delivery System Needs.* Attributes of the processes and the supporting systems and resources needed to deliver the service or product, such as availability, convenience, courtesy, safety, accuracy, reliability, delivery speed, and delivery dependability.
- *Volume Needs.* Attributes of the demand for the service or product, such as high or low volume, degree of variability in volume, and degree of predictability in volume.
- *Other Needs.* Other attributes, such as reputation and number of years in business, after-sale technical support, ability to invest in international financial markets, and competent legal services.

Once it makes this assessment, the firm can incorporate the needs of customers into the design of the service or product and the value chain that must deliver it. We will discuss these market needs further when we explore new service or product development.

> COMPETITIVE PRIORITIES AND CAPABILITIES <

competitive priorities

The critical dimensions that a process or value chain must possess to satisfy its internal or external customers, both now and in the future.

A customer-driven operations strategy requires a cross-functional effort by all areas of the firm to understand the needs of the firm's external customers and to specify the operating capabilities the firm needs to outperform its competitors. Such a strategy also addresses the needs of internal customers because the overall performance of the firm depends upon the performance of its core and supporting processes. **Competitive priorities** are the critical operational dimensions a process or value chain must possess to satisfy internal or external customers, both now and in the future.

We focus on nine broad competitive dimensions, which fall into four groups:

Cost	1. Low-cost operations
Quality	2. Top quality
	3. Consistent quality
Time	4. Delivery speed
	5. On-time delivery
	6. Development speed
Flexibility	7. Customization
	8. Variety
	9. Volume flexibility

Competitive priorities are planned for processes and the value chain created from them. They are abilities that must be present to maintain or build market share or to allow other internal processes to be successful. Not all nine dimensions are critical for a given process; management selects those that are most important. **Competitive capabilities** are the cost, quality, time, and flexibility dimensions that a process or value chain actually possesses and is able to deliver. When the capability falls short of the priority attached to it, management must find ways to close the gap or else revise the priority. We will have more to say about closing the gap later in this chapter.

A firm is composed of many processes that must be coordinated as a value chain to provide the overall desirable outcome for the external customer. To link to corporate strategy, management assigns selected competitive priorities to each process (and the value chain created from them) that are consistent with the needs of external as well as internal customers. Management thus communicates the level of importance it attaches to certain capabilities for each value chain or process.

competitive capabilities

The cost, quality, time, and flexibility dimensions that a process or value chain actually possesses and is able to deliver.

COST

Lowering prices can increase demand for services or products, but it also reduces profit margins if the service or product cannot be produced at lower cost. **Low-cost operations** deliver a service or produce a product at the lowest possible cost to the satisfaction of the external or internal customers of the process or value chain. To reduce costs, processes must be designed and operated to make them efficient using rigorous process analysis that addresses workforce, methods, scrap or rework, overhead, and other factors to lower the cost per unit of the service or product. Often, lowering costs requires a completely new process, which may require investment in new automated facilities or technology. Managerial Practice 2.1 shows how Costco uses the low-cost operations priority (along with other competitive priorities) to strategic advantage.

low-cost operations

Delivering a service or producing a product at the lowest possible cost to the satisfaction of the external or internal customers of the process or value chain.

QUALITY

Quality is a dimension of a service or product that is defined by customers. Two important competitive priorities deal with quality: top quality and consistent quality.

Top Quality **Top quality** is delivering an outstanding service or product. This priority may require a high level of customer contact, and high levels of helpfulness, courtesy, and availability of servers from a service process. Alternatively, it may require superior product features, close tolerances, and greater durability from a manufacturing process. Processes delivering top quality need to be designed to more demanding requirements. For example, Club Med and a no-frills motel both provide a room, bed, and bath for their guests. However, the processes at Club Med (the all-inclusive resorts with entertaining, dining, recreation, and hotel processes) have much more demanding requirements for customer service than does the no-frills motel. Ferrari and Isuzu both provide vehicles that will get you from one location to another; however, the difference in the ride is eye-popping. Will anyone debate the claim that Ferrari's processes have to deal with superior product features and more demanding requirements?

top quality

Delivering an outstanding service or product.

Looking for bargains on items ranging from watermelons to baby grand pianos? One company addressing those needs is Costco, a wholesale club with 446 stores that generate $47 billion in annual revenue. Its closest competitor is Wal-Mart's Sam's Club, whose 170 more stores generate $13 billion less in annual revenue. Individual and business customers pay Costco from $45 to $100 a year for a membership and the privilege of buying staple items in bulk quantities and other select items at big discounts.

What makes Costco so successful? It links the needs of its customers to its operations by developing an operations strategy that supports its retailing concept. Costco's competitive priorities are low-cost operations, quality, and flexibility. A visit to a Costco store shows how these competitive priorities manifest themselves.

Low-Cost Operations

Costco's low prices are possible because processes are designed for efficiency. The store is actually a warehouse. Products are stacked on pallets with little signage. New products can easily replace old products. In addition, Costco managers are tough price negotiators with suppliers because they buy in such high quantity. Suppliers are expected to change factory runs to produce specially built packages that are bigger but cheaper per unit. Costco's profit margins are low, but annual profits are high because of the volume.

Quality

Customers are not looking for customer service, but they are looking for high value. In addition to low prices, Costco backs everything it sells with a return-anything-at-any-time guarantee. Customers trust Costco, which generates an 86 percent membership renewal rate—the highest in the industry. To support the need for high value, operations must ensure that products are of high quality and undamaged when placed in the store.

Costco has been able to achieve a competitive advantage by designing an operation that is flexible and low-cost but that still offers customers high-quality products.

Flexibility

One of the key aspects of Costco's operations is the fact that it carries only 4,000 carefully selected items in a typical store, while a Wal-Mart Superstore carries 125,000 items. However, items change frequently to provide return customers with a "surprise" aspect to the shopping experience. Processes must be flexible to accommodate a dynamic store layout. In addition, the supply chain must be carefully managed because the products are constantly changing.

Source: "Inside the Cult of Costco," *Fortune* (September 6, 1999), pp. 184–190; www.hoovers.com (2004); www.costco.com (2004); www.samsclub.com (2004).

consistent quality

Producing services or products that meet design specifications on a consistent basis.

Consistent Quality **Consistent quality** is producing services or products that meet design specifications on a consistent basis. External customers want services or products that consistently meet the specifications they contracted for, have come to expect, or saw advertised. For example, bank customers expect that the bank's accounting process will not make errors when recording transactions. Customers of a foundry expect castings to meet tolerances for length, diameter, and surface finish. Internal customers also want consistency in the outputs of internal or external suppliers. The payroll department needs the correct hours each employee worked from each of the other departments, and the purchasing department needs consistent quality materials from suppliers. To compete on the basis of consistent quality, managers need to design and monitor processes to reduce errors.

TIME

As the saying goes, "Time is money." Some companies do business at "Internet speed," while others thrive on consistently meeting delivery promises. Three competitive priorities deal with time: delivery speed, on-time delivery, and development speed.

delivery speed

Quickly filling a customer's order.

lead time

The elapsed time between the receipt of a customer order and filling it.

Delivery Speed **Delivery speed** is quickly filling a customer's order. Delivery speed is often measured by the elapsed time between the receipt of a customer order and filling it, often referred to as **lead time**. You increase delivery speed by reducing lead times. An acceptable lead time can be minutes for an ambulance, hours for a report from the legal department, several weeks for scheduling elective surgery, and a year for a complex, customized machine. A cushion of backup capacity is one way to reduce lead times. Manufacturing processes sometimes have another way: storing inventory.

On-Time Delivery   **On-time delivery** is meeting delivery promises. An airline, for example, might measure on-time delivery as the percent of flights that arrive at the gate within 15 minutes of the scheduled arrival. Manufacturers may measure on-time delivery as the percent of customer orders shipped when promised, with 95 percent often considered the goal. On-time delivery is important for many processes, especially just-in-time processes where inputs are required at specific times (see Chapter 9, "Lean Systems").

Development Speed   **Development speed** is quickly introducing a new service or product. Development speed is measured by the elapsed time from idea generation through the final design and introduction of the service or product. Achieving a high level of development speed requires a high level of cross-functional coordination. Sometimes critical external suppliers are asked to participate in the process. Getting the new service or product to market first gives the firm an edge on the competition that is difficult to overcome, and it may involve international connections. For example, The Limited can get a new product idea for a sweater, design the sweater, transmit the design to Hong Kong where it is produced, ship the sweater back to the United States, and put the sweater on the store shelves in less than 25 weeks.

Time-Based Competition   Many companies focus on the competitive priorities of delivery speed and development speed for their processes, a strategy called **time-based competition**. To implement the strategy, managers carefully define the steps and time needed to deliver a service or produce a product and then critically analyze each step to determine whether they can save time without hurting quality. In Part 2, "Managing Processes," we provide the framework and tools to analyze processes to improve performance for any of the competitive priorities, including those relating to time.

FLEXIBILITY

Flexibility is a characteristic of a firm's processes that enables them to react to customers' needs quickly and efficiently. Some processes require one or more of the following types of flexibility: customization, variety, and volume flexibility.

Customization   **Customization** is satisfying the unique needs of each customer by changing service or product designs. For example, the advertisement design and planning process in an ad agency must be able to satisfy customers needing ads, where requests can range from selling cat litter featuring a wandering herd of cats in a commercial to informing the public of the dangers of secondhand smoke via a public-service announcement.

Customization typically implies that the service or product has low volume. However, some exceptions can be made to that generalization. For example, a customized plastic bottle design for a shampoo manufacturer may be produced in large volumes until the design of the bottle is changed. Nonetheless, processes with a customization priority must be able to work closely with their customers (external or internal) and then devote their resources to their unique needs. Managerial Practice 2.2 shows how one company's need for high degrees of customization in its processes involves modifications caused by product design changes and long lead times.

Variety   **Variety** is handling a wide assortment of services or products efficiently. Variety differs from customization in that the services or products are not necessarily unique to specific customers and may have repetitive demands. For example, Amazon.com has a customer relationship process that allows customers access to thousands of services and products through the Internet. A manufacturing process that produces an assortment of parts for tables, chairs, and cabinets has a variety priority. Processes with a variety priority must focus on the needs of internal or external customers and efficiently shift focus across a variety of predefined services or products.

Volume Flexibility   **Volume flexibility** is accelerating or decelerating the rate of production of services or products quickly to handle large fluctuations in demand. Volume flexibility often supports other competitive priorities, such as delivery speed or development speed. The need for this priority is driven by the severity and frequency of demand fluctuations. For

on-time delivery

Meeting delivery-time promises.

development speed

Quickly introducing a new service or product.

time-based competition

A strategy that focuses on the competitive priorities of delivery speed and development speed.

customization

Satisfying the unique needs of each customer by changing service or product designs.

variety

Handling a wide assortment of services or products efficiently.

volume flexibility

Accelerating or decelerating the rate of production of services or products quickly to handle large fluctuations in demand.

Arguably the most technically challenging and toughest product to manufacture is a nuclear-powered aircraft carrier. Consider the newest addition to the U.S. Navy's *Nimitz*-class carriers, the USS *Ronald Reagan,* which measures a fifth of a mile from bow to stern, has 4.5 acres of flight deck, can plow through the ocean at more than 35 miles per hour, and can carry 85 aircraft. Each ship in the *Nimitz* class (nine at present) costs more than $4 billion, and involves 47,000 tons of precision-welded steel up to 4 inches thick, more than 1 million different parts, 900 miles of wire and cable, about 40 million skilled-worker hours, thousands of engineers, and more than seven years to build. Such a product requires an enormous amount of technological skill and coordination and processes that can be efficient with low volumes.

The world's only producer of full-sized aircraft carriers, nuclear or otherwise, is Northrup Grumman Newport News, situated along the James River in Virginia. The shipyard has 550 acres of sheds, cranes, dry docks, and piers and employs 17,800 employees, many of them from families that have worked in the yard for generations. Over the years, Newport News designed processes with high degrees of flexibility to handle the changes in carrier design. Each aircraft carrier differs significantly in design from its predecessors, has tons of specialized equipment, houses munitions lockers and nuclear reactors, must provide quarters for 6,000 people, and more than 18,000 meals a day.

The design changes can be dramatic. For example, two years of planning before construction began on the *Reagan* resulted in 1,362 major changes from its predecessor, including a new bow and an expanded flight control tower. The need for flexibility required Newport News to redesign its processes. The first carriers in the *Nimitz* class were largely hand-built in dry dock by skilled craftsmen. Pipes, ducts, and cables were run only after large sections of the superstructure were constructed. Major sections of the *Reagan* were designed using 3-D computer drafting software, constructed from huge prebuilt modules built indoors, and then taken to the building site and hoisted into place. The software avoided the need for mock-ups because the designer could actually simulate the use of various compartments or the operation of equipment with computer-generated mannequins.

The long lead time associated with the construction of an aircraft carrier also poses problems for Newport News. For example, one of the first

Newport News Shipbuilding

jobs in the construction schedule is to order the long lead time equipment, such as major nuclear reactor components. However, after seven years, the equipment could be outdated. Modifications must be made to the superstructure of the aircraft carrier to accommodate the new specifications. Processes must be capable of handling these changes.

A key resource for a manufacturing operation focusing on customization is the workforce, which must be highly skilled. While 2,700 employees may have been working on the *Reagan* at any one time, the individuals and the jobs changed over time. There was lots of work for welders early on, but toward the end it was the painters who were in demand. Welders can wield a paintbrush, but painters typically cannot operate a blowtorch. Newport News has managed to get a flexible United Steelworkers labor contract and it is the sole contractor for the refurbishing of the entire nuclear aircraft carrier fleet. Both of these advantages help to mitigate the problem.

The USS *Ronald Reagan* was commissioned on July 12, 2003, 8.5 years after the contract was awarded.

Source: Philip Siekman, "Build to Order: One Aircraft Carrier," *Fortune* (July 22, 2002), pp. 180(B)–180(J); www.nn.northropgrumman.com (2005); http://united-states-navy.com (2005).

example, the time between demand peaks might be hours, as with the swings in demand at a large postal facility where processes are required for receiving, sorting, and dispatching mail to numerous branch locations. It may be months, as with processes at ski resorts or processes used to manufacture lawn fertilizers. It may even be years, as with political campaigns or home construction.

ORDER WINNERS AND QUALIFIERS

order winner

A criterion customers use to differentiate the services or products of one firm from those of another.

Competitive priorities focus on what operations can do to help a firm be more competitive. Another useful way to examine a firm's ability to be successful in the marketplace is to identify the order winners. An **order winner** is a criterion that customers use to differentiate the services or products of one firm from those of another.[2] Order winners can include price (which is supported by low-cost operations) and most of the dimensions of quality, time, and flexibility already discussed. However, order winners also include criteria not directly related to the firm's operations, such as after-sale support (Are maintenance service contracts available? Is there a return policy?); technical support (What help do I get if something goes wrong? How knowledgeable are the technicians?); and reputation (How long has this company been in business? Have other customers been satisfied with the service or product?). It may take good performance on a subset of the order-winner criteria, cutting across operational as well as nonoperational criteria, to make a sale.

Order winners are derived from the considerations customers use when deciding which firm to purchase a service or product from. Sometimes customers demand a certain level of demonstrated performance before even contemplating a service or product. In these cases an order winner becomes an **order qualifier**, which is a requirement for doing business in a particular market segment. Fulfilling the order qualifier will not ensure competitive success; it will only position the firm to compete in the market. From an operations perspective, understanding which competitive priorities are order qualifiers is important for the design and management of processes and value chains.

Order winners and qualifiers are often used in competitive bidding. For example, before a buyer considers a bid, suppliers may be required to document their ability to provide consistent quality as measured by adherence to the design specifications for the service or component they are supplying (order qualifier). The buyer will select the supplier on the basis of low prices and the reputation of the supplier (order winners).

order qualifier

A demonstrated level of performance of an order winner that is required for a firm to do business in a particular market segment.

USING COMPETITIVE PRIORITIES: AN AIRLINE EXAMPLE

Competitive priorities are a useful tool for translating the goals of corporate strategy to the level of actual processes. The key word here is *priorities* because these are targets the firm's operations must hit to win not only current business but also future business. Appropriate competitive priorities that reflect the needs of internal customers must also be assigned to core and supporting processes.

To get a better understanding of how companies use competitive priorities, let us look at a major airline. We will consider two market segments: first-class passengers and coach passengers. Core services for both market segments are ticketing and seat selection, baggage handling, and transportation to the customer's destination. The peripheral services are quite different. A needs assessment of both market segments would reveal that first-class passengers require separate airport lounges; preferred treatment during check-in, boarding, and deplaning; more comfortable seats; better meals and beverages; more personal attention (cabin attendants who refer to customers by name); more frequent service from attendants; high levels of courtesy; and low volumes (adding to the feeling of being special). Coach passengers are satisfied with standardized services (no surprises), courteous flight attendants, and low prices. Both market segments expect the airline to hold to its schedule. Consequently, we can say that the competitive priorities for the first-class segment are *top quality* and *on-time delivery*, whereas the competitive priorities for the coach segment are *low-cost operations, consistent quality,* and *on-time delivery.*

The airline knows what its collective capabilities must be as a firm, but how does that get communicated to each of its core processes? Let us focus on four core processes: customer relationship, new service/product development, order fulfillment, and supplier relationship. Competitive priorities are assigned to each core process to achieve the service required to provide complete customer satisfaction. Here are some possible assignments, just to give you an idea of how this works.

One of the competitive priorities of airline companies is on-time delivery of their services. Being able to repair and maintain planes rapidly to avoid delays is a crucial aspect of this.

[2]Terry Hill, *Manufacturing Strategy: Text and Cases,* 3rd ed. (Burr Ridge, IL: Irwin/McGraw-Hill, 2000).

Customer Relationship This process involves high levels of customer contact through ticketing (both electronic and telephone), elite lounge service, and boarding. It also has marketing and sales functions. Possible competitive priorities include the following:

- *Top Quality.* High levels of customer contact and lounge service for the first-class passengers.
- *Consistent Quality.* The information and service must be error free.
- *Delivery Speed.* Customers want immediate information regarding flight schedules and other ticketing information.
- *Variety.* The process must be capable of handling the service needs of all market segments and promotional programs, such as frequent-flier services.

New Service Development New services must continually be developed to stay ahead of the competition. Such services include tours to the world's vacation paradises, new routes, or new dinner service. Competitive priorities might include the following:

- *Development Speed.* It is important to get to market fast to preempt the competition.
- *Customization.* The process must be able to create unique services.
- *Top Quality.* New services must be carefully designed because the future of the airline depends on them.

Order Fulfillment This process is responsible for delivering the service to the customer's satisfaction. It is a huge process in an airline, involving scheduling, gate operations, maintenance, cabin service, pilot operations, and baggage handling. It has many nested processes, and many competitive priorities, which might include the following:

- *Low-Cost Operations.* Airlines compete on price and must keep costs in check.
- *Top Quality.* The service provided to first-class passengers must be top notch. To a large extent, this service aspect involves well-trained and experienced cabin attendants and high-quality meal and beverage service.
- *Consistent Quality.* Once the quality level is set, it is important to achieve it every time.
- *On-Time Delivery.* The airline strives to arrive at destinations on schedule, otherwise the passengers might miss connections to other flights.
- *Variety.* Maintenance operations are required for a variety of aircraft models.

Supplier Relationship This process is responsible for acquiring all of the inputs the airline requires to do business, which range from human resources to capital goods. Competitive priorities might include the following:

- *Low-Cost Operations.* The cost of acquiring inputs must be kept to a minimum to allow for competitive pricing.
- *Consistent Quality.* The quality of the inputs must adhere to the required specifications. In addition, the information provided to the suppliers must be accurate.
- *On-Time Delivery.* Inputs must be delivered to tight schedules, particularly meal services.
- *Variety.* Many different inputs must be acquired, including maintenance items, meals and beverages, and even aircraft.
- *Volume Flexibility.* The process must be able to handle variations in supply quantities efficiently.

> NEW SERVICE OR PRODUCT DEVELOPMENT <

Competitive priorities help managers develop services and products that customers want. New services or products are essential to the long-term survival of the firm. Times change, people change, technologies change, and so services or products change. *New* refers to both brand new services or products or major changes to existing services or products. The new service/product development process is often a core process in a firm. As we discuss the nature and importance of the new service/product development process, we will occasionally refer to a firm's services or products as its "offerings." We begin with the various strategies firms use to compete with new offerings.

DEVELOPMENT STRATEGIES

Firms use a number of ways to bring value to customers beyond low prices and good quality. Here are several strategies that proved successful:

- *Product Variety.* Amazon.com and Wal-Mart in retail, Dell in computers, Honda in motorcycles, and Campbell in soups are just a few companies that have established their niches in part through product variety. This strategy requires processes that have the flexibility to offer a wide band of offerings without compromising cost, quality, or speed.

- *Design.* eBay in Web auctions, Saks Fifth Avenue in retailing, Ralph Lauren in clothes, Stickley in furniture, and Kenwood in electronic equipment are examples of companies that use design as a competitive edge. Aesthetic appeal, safety, ease of use, ease of maintenance, and service or product features distinguish a firm's services or products from those of competitors. Competing on the basis of design often requires an emphasis on top quality and development speed to ensure that the firm stays ahead of the competition.

- *Innovation.* Firms that compete with innovative offerings must have the capability to develop new technologies and then to translate them into new products. LASIK surgery, virtual CAT scans, handheld computers, cell phones, global positioning systems, and digital cameras are examples of innovative offerings that have opened new markets. Innovation requires significant research and development and the ability to get the new offerings to market fast. With innovative services or products, the firm that is a "first mover" often obtains a strong competitive advantage.

- *Service.* Manufacturers can win orders by providing value-added services to complement their products, such as financial services, repair contracts, consulting, and delivery services. Dell, for example, helps customers design their information infrastructure. Automobile manufacturers consider car dealerships as part of the total process that begins with the construction of an automobile and ends by delivering it to the ultimate consumer. Through the dealership, the manufacturers offer assistance in product selection and delivery, financing, warranty repairs, and maintenance services. The customer's total experience includes the comfort feeling that lingers after the transaction is completed, which is affected by the helpfulness and courtesy of the salesperson, the design of the showroom, and the personal attention received before, during, and after the purchase.

Development strategies go beyond specifying the variety, design, innovation, or service thrust. Firms must also define their market position relative to competitors and the type of relationship the firm wishes to pursue with customers. Market positioning decisions entail choosing to be a *leader* (the first to introduce a service or product, consistent with an innovation thrust); *middle-of-the-road* (wait until the leaders introduce a service or product); or *laggard* (wait and see whether the service or product idea catches on in the market). The market position decision determines when the firm will initiate the new service/product development process.

Customer relationship decisions, at the extremes, entail choosing to build long-term partnerships with customers or to have an encounter-by-encounter transactional relationship. Long-term relationships involve services or products specific to a particular customer, while an encounter-by-encounter relationship involves services or products with appeal to a broader range of customers. The customer relationship decision determines the nature of the firm's offerings.

SERVICE AND PRODUCT DEFINITION

New services and products are important to any developed economy, especially for services, given that more than half of the gross domestic product of developed economies is in the service sector. Globalization, technological advancement, and changing customer requirements increase the need for firms to compete on a widening array of new service and product offerings. The benefits from providing new services and products include the following:

- Enhancing the profitability of existing offerings
- Attracting new customers to the firm
- Improving the loyalty of existing customers
- Opening markets of opportunity

New services and products provide the foundation for future growth in the dynamic business environment firms face today.

service package

A collection of goods and services provided by a service process to its external or internal customers.

Service Package One of the more difficult aspects of managing a service process is defining what it is the process provides to its customers. Recall the last time you had a pleasurable experience at a hotel. What did the hotel building, lobby area, and your room look like? Was the meal you ordered from room service tasty and in ample proportions? Did the hotel have a swimming pool, restaurant, and concierge? Was it easy to park at the hotel and was the bellhop friendly and informative?

Your experience at the hotel was a collection of goods and services delivered by the hotel's many processes. We call this collection a **service package**, and it consists of the following four features.

1. *Supporting Facility.* The physical resources that must be in place before a service can be offered are known as the supporting facility. The hotel building, the lobby, and your room would be considered supporting facilities. Other examples include a bus, a golf course, and a movie theater. Supporting facilities include bricks and mortar (e.g., buildings and rooms), machines and equipment, and human resources.

2. *Facilitating Goods.* The material purchased or consumed by the customer or the items provided by the customer to receive a service are known as facilitating goods. The food you ordered from room service is a facilitating good. Other examples include your own golf clubs for a round of golf, popcorn and condiments at the movie theater, and your tax records for a tax accountant. These items are not the service; however, they are needed to provide the service.

3. *Explicit Services.* The benefits that are readily observable by the senses and consist of essential features of the service are known as explicit services. The explicit services you received from room service included the preparation of the food by the chef and the delivery of the meal to your room by the bellhop. Taking a swim in the swimming pool, experiencing a prepared meal and the table service at the restaurant, and getting advice on tours from the concierge are additional examples of explicit services at the hotel. Other examples of explicit services include the delivery of a package to your home, a washed car, and the preparation of a tax-deferred annuity portfolio.

4. *Implicit Services.* Psychological benefits that the customer may sense only vaguely or nonessential features of the service are known as implicit services. A jovial bellhop may provide a sense of warmth and comfort, and just sitting in the hotel lobby absorbing the glamour of lavish surroundings may provide a vague sense of well-being. Other examples include the use of an appointment system in a doctor's office (fairness and control); a well-lighted parking area (safety); and entertainment while waiting in a line, as at Disney World (to make the time delays seem shorter).

Designing the service package requires a careful analysis of customer requirements and a good understanding of competitive priorities. Compare the service package of the hotel you visited to that of a bargain motel, which has a stucco facade and a small lobby, no room service, no swimming pool, and no bellhop. The motel is attractive to guests who want consistent quality and low prices, while the upscale hotel is attractive to guests who want top quality and a variety of services. The motel's service package is much less complex than the upscale hotel's service package. In each case, the processes must be designed with the service package and competitive priorities in mind.

quality function deployment (QFD)

A means of translating customer requirements into the appropriate technical requirements for each stage of service or product development and production.

Quality Function Deployment A key input into the definition of services and products is the customer's needs and wants. This input can be used to define new services and products or refine existing ones. A technique used by manufacturing companies and by some service companies to refine existing offerings is **quality function deployment (QFD)**. This process is a means of translating customer requirements into the appropriate technical requirements for each stage of service or product development and production. Bridgestone Tire and Mitsubishi Heavy Industries originated QFD in the late 1960s and early 1970s when it used charts that took customer requirements into account in the product design process. In 1978, Yoji Akao and Shigeru Mizuno published the first work on this subject, showing how design considerations could be "deployed" to every element of competition. Since then, more than 200 U.S. companies have used the approach, including Digital Equipment, Texas Instruments, Hewlett-Packard, AT&T, ITT, Ford, Chrysler, General Motors, Procter & Gamble, Polaroid, and Deere & Company.

The QFD approach seeks answers to the following six questions.

1. *Voice of the Customer.* What do our customers need and want?
2. *Competitive Analysis.* In terms of our customers, how well are we doing relative to our competitors?
3. *Voice of the Engineer.* What technical measures relate to our customers' needs?
4. *Correlations.* What are the relationships between the voice of the customer and the voice of the engineer?
5. *Technical Comparison.* How does our service or product performance compare to that of our competition?
6. *Trade-Offs.* What are the potential technical trade-offs?

The competitive analysis is a place to start looking for ways to gain a competitive advantage. Then the relationships between customer needs and engineering attributes need to be specified. Finally, planners must recognize that improving one performance measure may detract from another.

The QFD approach provides a way to set targets and debate their effects on quality. Engineering uses the data to focus on significant service or product design features. Marketing uses this input to determine marketing strategies. Operations uses the information to identify the processes that are crucial to improving quality as perceived by the customer. As a result, QFD encourages interfunctional communication for the purpose of improving the quality of services and products.

DEVELOPMENT PROCESS

The new service/product development process begins with consideration of the development strategy and ends with the launch of the new offering. Figure 2.2 shows the four stages of the process.

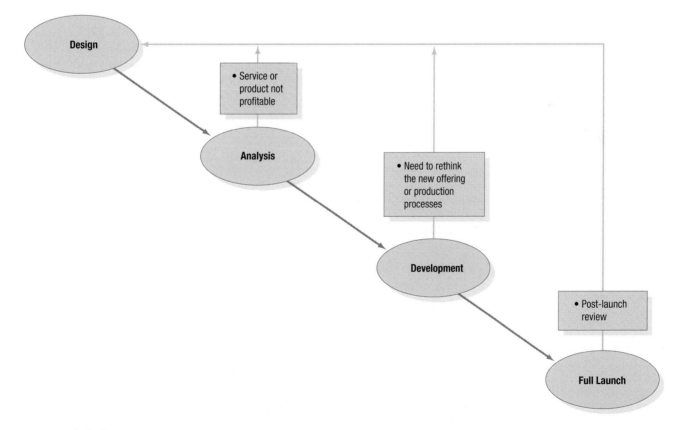

FIGURE 2.2 | New Service/Product Development Process

Design   The *design* stage is critical because it links the creation of new services or products to the corporate strategy of the firm. As we have already noted, the corporate strategy specifies the long-term objectives and the markets the firm wishes to compete in. Within that framework, the development strategy specifies the direction the firm wants to take with its offerings. Ideas for new offerings are generated and screened for feasibility and market worthiness. For services, these ideas specify how the customer connects with the service provider, the service benefits and outcomes for the customer, the value of the service, and how the service will be delivered. A specific service package is then formulated for the best idea, the competitive priorities are assigned to the processes, and the manner in which the service package will be delivered is proposed and checked for feasibility. We will have more to say about how the service is delivered when we address the topic of service process design in Chapter 4, "Process Strategy."

For manufactured products, the new ideas include a specification of the product's architecture, which is either modular or integrated. With a modular architecture, the product is an assembly of components. Several varieties of products can be made quickly using the same standardized components. This approach supports competitive priorities of product variety and delivery speed; however, it may cause lower product performance because of the pressure to use existing components in new products. In addition, such designs may be easier for competitors to copy. With the integrated product architecture, the product's functions are performed by only a few components that are specifically designed for it. Integrated product structures often lead to higher product performance and are not easily imitated; however, the design lead time is high and the ability to produce a variety of products is limited.

The most promising new product idea is selected for more detailed attention, which includes diagramming assembly, providing specifications for the product's performance dimensions, and investigating the manufacturability and cost of the new product. In this stage, firms engage the inputs of their manufacturing engineers in an activity referred to as *design for manufacturing*. Even though the detailed specifics of the product and process have not yet been developed, this interaction of designers and manufacturing engineers can avoid costly mistakes.

Analysis   The second stage, *analysis,* involves a critical review of the new offering and how it will be produced to make sure that it fits the corporate strategy, is compatible with regulatory standards, presents an acceptable market risk, and satisfies the needs of the intended customers. The resource requirements for the new offering must be examined from the perspective of the core capabilities of the firm and the need to acquire additional resources or form strategic partnerships with other firms. If the analysis reveals that the new offering has good market potential and that the firm has the capability (or can acquire it), the authorization is given to proceed to the next stage.

Development   The third stage, *development,* brings more specificity to the new offering. The required competitive priorities are used as inputs to the design (or redesign) of the processes that will be involved in delivering the new offering. The processes are analyzed; each activity is designed to meet its required competitive priorities and to add value to the service or product. Once the new offering is specified and the processes have been designed, the market program can be designed. Finally, personnel are trained and some pilot runs can be conducted to iron out the kinks in production. At this stage in the development process, it is possible that some unforeseen problems may arise, forcing a reconsideration of the service or product or the processes required to produce it.

For example, a new service package for an airline may include adding a new route from South Bend, Indiana, to Columbus, Ohio, at 5 P.M. on weekdays. It would be delivered with a Boeing 737 because of the space and comfort such a plane offers. But suppose the airline's fleet of 737s was already being used to capacity and shifting the schedules would affect an entire network of flights and schedules. The new flight could be offered if the airline contracted with a regional provider that uses smaller commuter aircraft. Passenger comfort and service delivery costs would be affected. Such a change to the service package and the processes required to deliver it would require further analysis.

To avoid costly mismatches between the design of a new offering and the capability of the processes required to produce it, many firms engage in a concept called **concurrent engineering**, which brings product engineers, process engineers, marketers, buyers, information specialists, quality specialists, and suppliers together to design a product and the processes that will meet customer expectations. For example, Ford Motor Company gives full responsibility for each new product to a program manager who forms a product team representing every relevant part of the organization. Each department can raise concerns or anticipate

concurrent engineering

A concept that brings product engineers, process engineers, marketers, buyers, information specialists, quality specialists, and suppliers together to work jointly to design a service or product and the required processes that will meet customer expectations.

problems in time to alter the product or the manufacturing processes. Changes are much simpler and less costly at this stage. However, problems with the product design or the capability to deliver the product may be discovered during this stage. The product proposal may have to be scrapped or completely rethought.

Full Launch The final stage, *full launch,* involves the coordination of many processes. Promotions for the new offering must be initiated, sales personnel briefed, distribution processes activated, and old services or products that the new offering is to replace withdrawn. A particular strain is placed on the processes needed to produce the offering during a period referred to as *ramp-up,* when the production processes must increase volume to meet demands while coping with quality problems and last-minute design changes.

Apple CEO Steve Jobs rallies the sales force during Apple Computer's launch of its online music store and iPod. Downloadable songs on the site cost 99 cents apiece.

Competitive priorities may change over time. For example, consider a high-volume standardized product, such as color ink-jet desktop printers. In the early stages of the ramp-up period, when the printers had just entered the mass market, the manufacturing processes required consistent quality, delivery speed, and volume flexibility. In the later stages of the ramp-up, when demand was high, the competitive priorities became low-cost operations, consistent quality, and on-time delivery. A postlaunch review will compare the competitive priorities of the processes with their competitive capabilities and may signal a need to rethink the original product idea. The review also gets inputs from customers, who will divulge their experiences and may share ideas for new offerings.

> OPERATIONS STRATEGY AS A PATTERN OF DECISIONS <

Operations strategy translates service or product plans and competitive priorities for each market segment into decisions affecting the value chains that support those market segments. Figure 2.3 shows how corporate strategy provides the umbrella for key operations management decisions. The operations manager must select a service or manufacturing strategy for each process in the value chain. This strategy determines how the firm's processes are organized to handle the volume and variety of services or products for each specific market segment. This initial choice sets in motion a series of other decisions that govern the design of the processes, systems, and procedures that support the operations strategy. These decisions are not static; they must be constantly reevaluated according to the dynamics of the marketplace. We cover these decisions in detail throughout this text.

From a strategic perspective, operations managers are responsible for making the decisions that ensure the firm has the capability to address the competitive priorities of new and existing market segments as they evolve. Furthermore, because of differences in core competencies, market segments served, and degree of Web integration, the pattern of decisions for one organization may be different from that of another, even if they are both in the same industry. Each process must be analyzed from the perspective of the customers it serves, be they external or internal.

The operations management decisions contribute to the development of the firm's ability to compete successfully in the marketplace. Once managers determine the competitive priorities for a process, it is necessary to assess the *competitive capabilities* of the process. Any gap between a competitive priority and the capability to achieve that competitive priority must be closed by an effective operations strategy.

Developing capabilities and closing gaps is the thrust of operations strategy. To demonstrate how this works, suppose the management of a bank's credit card division decided to embark on a marketing campaign to significantly increase its business, while keeping costs low. A key process in this division is billing and payments. The division receives credit transactions from the merchants, pays the merchants, assembles and sends the bills to the credit card holders, and processes payments. The new marketing effort is expected to significantly increase the volume of bills and payments. In assessing the capabilities the process must have

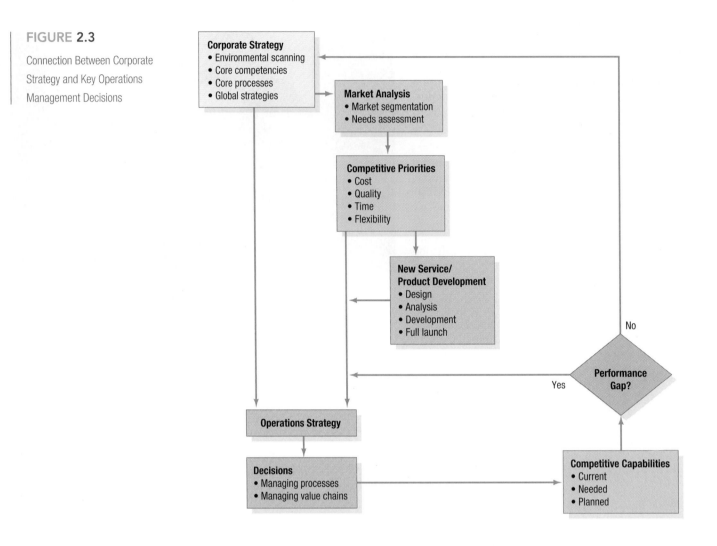

to serve the bank's customers, and to meet the challenges of the new market campaign, management assigned the following competitive priorities for the billing and payments process:

- *Low-Cost Operations.* It is important to maintain low costs in the processing of the bills because profit margins are tight.

- *Consistent Quality.* The process must consistently produce bills, make payments to the merchants, and record payments from the credit card holders accurately.

- *Delivery Speed.* Merchants want to be paid for the credit purchases quickly.

- *Volume Flexibility.* The marketing campaign is expected to generate many more transactions in a shorter period of time.

Management assumed that customers would avoid doing business with a bank that could not produce accurate bills or payments. Consequently, consistent quality is an order qualifier for this process.

Is the billing and payment process up to the competitive challenge? Table 2.1 shows how to match capabilities to priorities and uncover any gaps in the credit card division's operations strategy. The procedure for assessing an operations strategy begins with identifying good measures for each priority. The more quantitative the measures are, the better. Data are gathered for each measure to determine the current capabilities of the process. Gaps are identified by comparing each capability to management's target values for the measures, and unacceptable gaps are closed by appropriate actions.

The credit card division shows significant gaps in the process's capability for low-cost operations. Management's remedy is to redesign the process in ways that reduce costs but will not impair the other competitive priorities. Likewise, for volume flexibility, management realized that a high level of utilization is not conducive for processing quick surges in vol-

TABLE 2.1	Operations Strategy Assessment of the Billing and Payment Process			
Competitive Priority	**Measure**	**Capability**	**Gap**	**Action**
Low-cost operations	• Cost per billing statement	• $0.0813	• Target is $0.06	• Eliminate microfilming and storage of billing statements
	• Weekly postage	• $17,000	• Target is $14,000	• Develop Web-based process for posting bills
Consistent quality	• Percent errors in bill information	• 0.90%	• Acceptable	• No action
	• Percent errors in posting payments	• 0.74%	• Acceptable	• No action
Delivery speed	• Lead time to process merchant payments	• 48 hrs	• Acceptable	• No action
Volume flexibility	• Utilization	• 98%	• Too high to support rapid increase in volumes	• Acquire temporary employees • Improve work methods

umes while maintaining delivery speed. The recommended actions will help to build a capability for meeting more volatile demands.

To make these priorities work, you have to know how to improve capabilities to reduce the gaps. The chapters in Part 2 will provide you with the tools to assess performance, determine the capability of a process, and redesign processes to close the gaps. Part 3 will show you how to design value chains and how to achieve the needs of the customers they serve.

> STUDENT CD-ROM AND INTERNET RESOURCES <

The Student CD-ROM and the companion Web site at **www.prenhall.com/krajewski** contain many activities and resources designed for this chapter.

> KEY TERMS <

competitive capabilities 51
competitive priorities 50
concurrent engineering 60
consistent quality 52
core competencies 48
customization 53
delivery speed 52

development speed 53
lead time 52
low-cost operations 51
on-time delivery 53
operations strategy 46
order qualifier 55
order winner 54

quality function deployment (QFD) 58
service package 58
time-based competition 53
top quality 51
variety 53
volume flexibility 53

> DISCUSSION QUESTIONS <

1. The onset of exponential growth in the development of information technologies has encouraged the birth of many dot-com companies. The Internet enabled these companies to reach customers in effective ways. Consider Amazon.com, whose Web site enjoys millions of "hits" each day and puts customers in touch with more than 18 million services and products. What are Amazon.com's competitive priorities and what should its operations strategy focus on?

2. A local hospital declares that it is committed to provide *care* to patients arriving at the emergency unit in less than 15 minutes and that it will never turn away patients who need to be hospitalized for further medical care. What implications does this commitment have for strategic operations management decisions (e.g., decisions relating to capacity and workforce)?

3. FedEx built its business on quick, dependable delivery of items being shipped by air from one business to another. Its early advantages included global tracking of shipments using Web technology. The advancement of Internet technology enabled competitors to become much more sophisticated in order tracking. In addition, the advent of dot-com business put pressure on increased ground transportation deliveries. Explain how this change in the environment

could affect FedEx's operations strategy, especially relative to UPS, which has a strong hold on the business-to-consumer ground delivery business.

4. Understanding the service package enables management to identify ways to gain competitive advantage in the marketplace. What do you consider to be the components of the service package in the provision of the following?

   a. An automobile insurance policy

   b. Dental work to install a crown

   c. An airline flight

5. Suppose that you were conducting a market analysis for a new textbook about technology management. What would you need to know to identify a market segment? How would you make a needs assessment? What should be the collection of services and products?

6. Although all nine of the competitive priorities discussed in the chapter are relevant to a company's success in the marketplace, explain why a company should not necessarily try to excel in all of them. What determines the choice of the competitive priorities that a company should emphasize?

7. Choosing which processes are core to a firm's competitive position is a key strategic decision. For example, Nike, a popular sports shoe company, focuses on the customer relationship, new product development, and supplier relationship processes and leaves the order fulfillment process to others. Edmonds, a top-quality shoe company, considers all four processes to be core processes. What considerations would you make in determining which processes should be core to your manufacturing company?

8. A local fast-food restaurant processes several customer orders at once. Service clerks cross paths, sometimes nearly colliding, while they trace different paths to fill customer orders. If customers order a special combination of toppings on their hamburgers, they must wait quite some time while the special order is cooked. How would you modify the restaurant's operations to achieve competitive advantage? Because demand surges at lunchtime, volume flexibility is a competitive priority in the fast-food business. How would you achieve volume flexibility?

9. Kathryn Shoemaker established Grandmother's Chicken Restaurant in Middlesburg five years ago. It features a unique recipe for chicken, "just like grandmother used to make." The facility is homey, with relaxed and friendly service. Business has been good during the past two years, for both lunch and dinner. Customers normally wait about 15 minutes to be served, although complaints about service delays have increased. Shoemaker is currently considering whether to expand the current facility or open a similar restaurant in neighboring Uniontown, which has been growing rapidly.

   a. What types of strategic plans must Shoemaker make?

   b. What environmental forces could be at work in Middleburg and Uniontown that Shoemaker should consider?

   c. What are the possible distinctive competencies of Grandmother's?

10. For 20 years, Russell's Pharmacy has been located on the town square of River City, the only town for 20 miles in any direction. River City's economy is dominated by agriculture and generally rises and falls with the price of corn, but Russell's Pharmacy enjoys a steady business. Jim Russell is on a first-name basis with the entire town. He provides friendly, accurate service; listens patiently to health complaints; and knows the family health history of everyone. He keeps an inventory of the medicines required by regular customers, but sometimes has a one-day delay to fill new prescriptions. However, he cannot obtain drugs at the same low price as the large pharmacy chains can. There's trouble right here in River City. Several buildings around the town square are now abandoned or used as storerooms for old cars. The town is showing signs of dying off right along with the family farm. Twenty miles upstream, situated on a large island in the river, is the growing town of Large Island. Russell is considering a move to the Conestoga Mall in Large Island.

    a. What types of strategic plans must Russell make?

    b. What environmental forces could be at work that Russell should consider?

    c. What are the possible core competencies of Russell's Pharmacy?

11. Wild West, Inc., is a regional telephone company that inherited nearly 100,000 employees and 50,000 retirees from AT&T. Wild West has a new mission: to diversify. It calls for a 10-year effort to enter the financial services, real estate, cable TV, home shopping, entertainment, and cellular communication services markets—and to compete with other telephone companies. Wild West plans to provide cellular and fiber-optic communications services in markets with established competitors, such as the United Kingdom, and in markets with essentially no competition, such as Russia and former Eastern Bloc countries.

    a. What types of strategic plans must Wild West make? Is the "do-nothing" option viable? If Wild West's mission appears too broad, which businesses would you trim first?

    b. What environmental forces could be at work that Wild West should consider?

    c. What are the possible core competencies of Wild West? What weaknesses should it avoid or mitigate?

12. You are in the process of choosing a bank to open a checking with interest account. Several banks in your community offer competitive checking services with the same interest payment. Identify the nature of the service package that would guide your choice.

13. You are designing a grocery delivery business. Via the Internet, your company will offer staple and frozen foods in a large metropolitan area and then deliver them within a customer-defined window of time. You plan to partner with two major food stores in the area. What should be your competitive priorities and what capabilities do you want to develop in your operations?

BSB, Inc., The Pizza Wars Come to Campus

Renee Kershaw, manager of food services at a medium-sized private university in the Southeast, just had the wind taken out of her sails. She had decided that, owing to the success of her year-old pizza service, the time was right to expand pizza-making operations on campus. However, yesterday the university president announced plans to begin construction of a student center on campus that would house, among other facilities, a new food court. In a departure from past university policy, this new facility would permit and accommodate food-service operations from three private organizations: Dunkin' Donuts, Taco Bell, and Pizza Hut. Until now, all food service on campus had been contracted out to BSB, Inc.

Campus Food Service

BSB, Inc., is a large, nationally operated food-services company serving client organizations. The level of service provided varies, depending on the type of market being served and the particular contract specifications. The company is organized into three market-oriented divisions: corporate, airline, and university or college. Kershaw, of course, is employed in the university or college division.

At this particular university, BSB, Inc., is under contract to provide food services for the entire campus of 6,000 students and 3,000 faculty, staff, and support personnel. Located in a city of approximately 200,000 people, the campus was built on land donated by a wealthy industrialist. Because the campus is somewhat isolated from the rest of the town, students wanting to shop or dine off campus have to drive into town.

The campus itself is a "walking" campus, with dormitories, classrooms, and supporting amenities such as a bookstore, sundry shop, barbershop, branch bank, and food service facilities—all within close proximity. Access to the campus by car is limited, with peripheral parking lots provided. The university also provides space, at a nominal rent, for three food-service facilities. The primary facility, a large cafeteria housed on the ground floor of the main administration building, is located in the center of campus. This cafeteria is open for breakfast, lunch, and dinner daily. A second location, called the Dogwood Room, on the second floor of the administration building, serves an upscale luncheon buffet on weekdays only. The third facility is a small grill located in the corner of a recreational building near the dormitories. The grill is open from 11 A.M. to 10 P.M. daily and until midnight on Friday and Saturday nights. Kershaw is responsible for all three operations.

The Pizza Decision

BSB, Inc., has been operating the campus food services for the past 10 years—ever since the university decided that its mission and core competencies should focus on education, not on food service. Kershaw has been at this university for 18 months. Previously, she was assistant manager of food services at a small university in the Northeast. After 3 to 4 months of getting oriented to the new position, she had begun to conduct surveys to determine customer needs and market trends.

An analysis of the survey data indicated that students were not as satisfied with the food service as Kershaw had hoped. A large amount of the food being consumed by students, broken down as follows, was not being purchased at the BSB facilities:

Percent of food prepared in dorm rooms	20
Percent of food delivered from off campus	36
Percent of food consumed off campus	44

The reasons most commonly given by students were (1) lack of variety in food offerings and (2) tight, erratic schedules that did not always fit with cafeteria serving hours. Three other findings from the survey were of concern to Kershaw: (1) the large percentage of students with cars, (2) the large percentage of students with refrigerators and microwave ovens in their rooms, and (3) the number of times students ordered food delivered from off campus.

Percent of students with cars on campus	84
Percent of students with refrigerators or microwaves in their rooms	62
Percent of food that students consume outside BSB, Inc., facilities	43

In response to the market survey, Kershaw decided to expand the menu at the grill to include pizza. Along with expanding the menu, she also started a delivery service that covered the entire campus. Now students would have not only greater variety, but also the convenience of having food delivered quickly to their rooms. To accommodate these changes, a pizza oven was installed in the grill and space was allocated to store pizza ingredients, to make cut-and-box pizzas, and to stage premade pizzas that were ready to cook. Existing personnel were trained to make pizzas, and additional personnel were hired to deliver them by bicycle. In an attempt to keep costs down and provide fast delivery, Kershaw limited the combinations of toppings available. That way a limited number of "standard pizzas" could be preassembled and ready to cook as soon as an order was received.

The Success

Kershaw believed that her decision to offer pizza service in the grill was the right one. Sales over the past 10 months steadily increased, along with profits. Follow-up customer surveys indicated a high level of satisfaction with the reasonably priced and speedily delivered pizzas. However, Kershaw realized that success brought with it other challenges.

The demand for pizzas had put a strain on the grill's facilities. Initially, space was taken from other grill activities to accommodate the pizza oven, preparation, and staging areas.

As the demand for pizzas grew, so did the need for space and equipment. The capacities of existing equipment and space allocated for making and cooking pizzas now were insufficient to meet demand, and deliveries were being delayed. To add to the problem, groups were beginning to order pizzas in volume for various on-campus functions.

Finally, a closer look at the sales data showed that pizza sales were beginning to level off. Kershaw wondered whether the capacity problem and resulting increase in delivery times were the reasons. However, something else had been bothering her. In a recent conversation, Mack Kenzie, the grill's supervisor, had told Kershaw that over the past couple of months requests for pizza toppings and combinations not on the menu had steadily increased. She wondered whether her on-campus market was being affected by the "pizza wars" off campus and the proliferation of specialty pizzas.

The New Challenge

As she sat in her office, Kershaw thought about yesterday's announcement concerning the new food court. It would increase competition from other types of snack foods (Dunkin' Donuts) and fast foods (Taco Bell). Of more concern, Pizza Hut was going to put in a facility offering a limited menu and providing a limited selection of pizzas on a "walk-up-and-order" basis. Phone orders would not be accepted nor would delivery service be available.

Kershaw pondered several crucial questions: Why had demand for pizzas leveled off? What impact would the new food court have on her operations? Should she expand her pizza operations? If so, how?

QUESTIONS

1. Does BSB, Inc., enjoy any competitive advantages or core competencies?

2. Initially, how did Renee Kershaw choose to use her pizza operations to compete with off-campus eateries? What were her competitive priorities?

3. What impact will the new food court have on Kershaw's pizza operations? What competitive priorities might she choose to focus on now?

4. If she were to change the competitive priorities for the pizza operation, what are the gaps between the priorities and capabilities of her processes? How might that affect her operating processes and capacity decisions?

5. What would be a good service strategy for Kershaw's operations on campus to meet the food court competition?

Source: This case was prepared by Dr. Brooke Saladin, Wake Forest University, as a basis for classroom discussion.

> SELECTED REFERENCES <

Berry, W. L., C. Bozarth, T. Hill, and J. E. Klompmaker. "Factory Focus: Segmenting Markets from an Operations Perspective." *Journal of Operations Management,* vol. 10, no. 3 (1991), pp. 363–387.

Blackburn, Joseph. *Time-Based Competition: The Next Battle-Ground in American Manufacturing.* Homewood, IL: Business One-Irwin, 1991.

Collier, David A. *The Service Quality Solution.* Milwaukee: ASQC Quality Press, and Burr Ridge, IL: Irwin Professional Publishing, 1994.

Fitzsimmons, James A., and Mona Fitzsimmons. *Service Management for Competitive Advantage.* New York: McGraw-Hill, 2001.

Gilmore, James H., and B. Joseph Pine II. "The Four Faces of Mass Customization." *Harvard Business Review,* vol. 75, no. 1 (1997), pp. 91–101.

Goldstein, Susan Meyer, Robert Johnson, JoAnn Duffy, and Jay Rao. "The Service Concept: The Missing Link in Service Design Research?" *Journal of Operations Management,* vol. 20 (2002), pp. 121–134.

Hammer, Michael, and Steven Stanton. "How Process Enterprises Really Work." *Harvard Business Review* (November–December 1999), pp. 108–120.

Hayes, Robert H., and G. P. Pisano. "Manufacturing Strategy: At the Intersection of Two Paradigm Shifts." *Production and Operations Management,* vol. 5, no. 1 (1996), pp. 25–41.

Hayes, Robert H., Gary P. Pisano, David M. Upton, and Steven C. Wheelwright. *Operations, Strategy, and Technology: Pursuing the Competitive Edge.* New York: Wiley, 2004.

Heim, Gregory R., and Kingshuk K. Sinha. "Service Process Configurations in Electronic Retailing: A Taxonomic Analysis of Electronic Food Retailers." *Production and Operations Management,* vol. 11, no. 1 (Spring 2002), pp. 54–74.

Heskett, James L., and Leonard A. Schlesenger. "The Service-Driven Service Company." *Harvard Business Review* (September–October 1991), pp. 71–81.

Hill, Terry. *Manufacturing Strategy: Text and Cases,* 3d ed. Homewood, IL: Irwin/McGraw-Hill, 2000.

Jack, Eric P., and Thomas L. Powers. "Volume Flexible Strategies in Health Services: A Research Framework." *Production and Operations Management,* vol. 13, no. 3 (2004), pp. 230–244.

Kellogg, Deborah L., and Winter Nie. "A Framework for Strategic Service Management." *Journal of Operations Management,* vol. 13 (1995), pp. 323–337.

Menor, Larry J., Mohan V. Tatikonda, and Scott E. Sampson. "New Service Development: Areas for Exploitation and Exploration." *Journal of Operations Management,* vol. 20 (2002), pp. 135–157.

O'Reilly, Brian. "They've Got Mail!" *Fortune* (February 7, 2000), pp. 101–112.

Prahalad, C. K., and Venkatram Ramaswamy. "Co-opting Customer Competence." *Harvard Business Review* (January–February 2000), pp. 79–87.

Rayport, Jeffrey F., and Bernard J. Jaworski. "Best Face Forward." *Harvard Business Review,* vol. 82, no. 12 (2003), pp. 47–58.

Roth, Aleda V., and Marjolijn van der Velde. "Operations As Marketing: A Competitive Service Strategy." *Journal of Operations Management,* vol. 10, no. 3 (1993), pp. 303–328.

Safizadeh, M. H., L. P. Ritzman, D. Sharma, and C. Wood. "An Empirical Analysis of the Product–Process Matrix." *Management Science,* vol. 42, no. 11 (1996), pp. 1576–1591.

Skinner, Wickham. "Manufacturing Strategy on the 'S' Curve." *Production and Operations Management,* vol. 5, no. 1 (1996), pp. 3–14.

Stalk, George, Jr., P. Evans, and P. E. Schulman. "Competing on Capabilities: The New Rules of Corporate Strategy." *Harvard Business Review* (March–April 1992), pp. 57–69.

Vickery, S. K., C. Droge, and R. E. Markland. "Production Competence and Business Strategy: Do They Affect Business Performance?" *Decision Sciences,* vol. 24, no. 2 (1993), pp. 435–456.

Ward, Peter T., and Rebecca Duray. "Manufacturing Strategy in Context: Environment, Competitive Strategy and Manufacturing Strategy." *Journal of Operations Management,* vol. 18 (2000), pp. 123–138.

Ward, Peter T., Deborah J. Bickford, and G. Keong Leong. "Configurations of Manufacturing Strategy, Business Strategy, Environment and Structure." *Journal of Management,* vol. 22, no. 4 (1996), pp. 597–626.

Wheelwright, Steven C., and H. Kent Bowen. "The Challenge of Manufacturing Advantage." *Production and Operations Management,* vol. 5, no. 1 (1996), pp. 59–77.

Womack, J. P., D. T. Jones, and D. Roos. *The Machine That Changed the World.* New York: Rawson Associates, 1990.

3

LEARNING GOALS

*After reading this chapter,
you should be able to:*

1. Define the major activities
    associated with defining,
    organizing, planning,
    monitoring, and controlling
    projects.
2. Identify the sequence of critical
    activities that determines the
    duration of a project.
3. Define the options available to
    project managers to alleviate
    resource problems.
4. Diagram the network of
    interrelated activities in a
    project.
5. Describe the considerations
    managers make in assessing the
    risks in a project and calculate
    the probability of completing a
    project on time.
6. Explain how to determine a
    minimum-cost project schedule.

Bechtel workers go about constructing a
Motorola semiconductor manufacturing
plant in Tianjin, China. Bechtel was the
first U.S. company ever granted a
construction license in China.

CHAPTER 3
Project Management

BECHTEL GROUP, INC.

Bechtel Group, Inc., is a $16.3-billion-a-year construction contractor that specializes in large projects. In business for more than a century, the venerable company led the Six Companies consortium that built Hoover Dam early in the twentieth century and has built scores of rail systems, refineries, airports, and power plants since then. Bechtel led the rebuilding of Kuwait's oil and gas infrastructure after Desert Storm and became the first U.S. company to be granted a construction license in China. This enabled it to work with Motorola on a number of projects including the construction of a $650 million state-of-the-art semiconductor manufacturing complex at Tianjin.

Bechtel's customers choose the company because of its ability to deliver projects on time. They also choose the company because of its capability for delivery speed. For example, Wis-consin's Kewaunee nuclear power plant needed to replace its two steam generators, a common problem with aging nuclear power plants. Bechtel's crews cut the domes off the two generators, refurbished the domes, brought in new lower assemblies, and welded everything into place in just 71 days, thereby minimizing the time that Kewaunee would be out of service. Many of Bechtel's customers want to set up facilities nationwide or around the world with short lead times and do not have the time to deal with local contractors. Bechtel satisfies their needs.

For each major project it undertakes, Bechtel must organize a project team and provide it with the supporting information systems and resources with on-time delivery and short delivery lead times in mind. Because of the complexity of many ongoing projects with diverse needs, teams must be flexible enough to

>

respond to changes in schedules or requirements. Communication is a major issue; it takes an average of five days to get a piece of paper from Bechtel's Singapore office to a project in Thailand. Paperwork ranging from routine requests for information to detailed architectural drawings can suffer unnecessary delays when it must be copied and faxed or sent by mail, thereby delaying decisions and lengthening a project.

Bechtel initiated a Web-based communications system that provides access to project information electronically. Members of the project team can access schedules, progress reports, drawings, and messages at one Web site without relying on faxes. Decisions on various issues can be made quickly, thereby reinforcing Bechtel's competitive priorities.

Source: The Bechtel Report 2003; Bechtel Global Report 2002; www.bechtel.com, 2005.

project

An interrelated set of activities with a definite starting and ending point, which results in a unique outcome for a specific allocation of resources.

USING OPERATIONS TO COMPETE

Operations As a Competitive Weapon
Operations Strategy
Project Management

MANAGING PROCESSES

Process Strategy
Process Analysis
Process Performance and Quality
Constraint Management
Process Layout
Lean Systems

MANAGING VALUE CHAINS

Supply Chain Strategy
Location
Inventory Management
Forecasting
Sales and Operations Planning
Resource Planning
Scheduling

Companies such as Bechtel are experts at managing projects. They master the ability to schedule activities and monitor progress within strict time, cost, and performance guidelines. A **project** is an interrelated set of activities with a definite starting and ending point, which results in a unique outcome for a specific allocation of resources.

Projects are common in everyday life as well as in business. Planning weddings, remodeling bathrooms, writing term papers, and organizing surprise parties are examples of small projects in everyday life. Conducting company audits, planning mergers, creating advertising campaigns, reengineering processes, developing new services or products, and establishing a strategic alliance are examples of large projects in business.

The three main goals of any project are (1) complete the project on time or earlier; (2) do not exceed the budget; and (3) meet the specifications to the satisfaction of the customer. When we must undertake projects with some uncertainty involved, it does not hurt to have flexibility with respect to resource availability, deadlines, and budgets. Consequently, projects can be complex and challenging to manage.

Projects often cut across organizational lines because they need the skills of multiple professions and organizations. Furthermore, each project is unique, even if it is routine, requiring new combinations of skills and resources in the project process. For example, projects for adding a new branch office, installing new computers in a department, or developing a sales promotion may be initiated several times a year. Each project may have been done many times before; however, differences will arise with each replication. Uncertainties, such as the advent of new technologies or the activities of competitors, can change the character of projects and require responsive countermeasures. Finally, projects are temporary because personnel, materials, and facilities are organized to complete them within a specified time frame and then are disbanded.

Projects can be used to implement changes to processes as well as value chains. For example, projects involving the implementation of major information technologies may affect all of a firm's core processes and supporting processes as well as some of their suppliers' and customers' processes. As such, projects are a useful tool for improving processes and value chains.

> PROJECT MANAGEMENT ACROSS THE ORGANIZATION <

The use of projects to make changes to processes and value chains is pervasive across all types of organizations and disciplines. Managers often find themselves collaborating with counterparts from other departments on strategic initiatives as well as working on smaller projects within their own departments.

USING PROJECTS TO IMPLEMENT OPERATIONS STRATEGY

Consider a financial services firm that was experiencing a loss of clientele to its major competitors. After a careful examination of the situation, the top management team recommended to the board that the firm improve its customer service by reducing the errors in the reports it generates, increasing the variety of the reports it offers, and speeding up the delivery of the services. The strategy, called the Customer Service Initiative, was intended to win customers by providing improved services more quickly than competitors. The new services department head was given the task of developing the new reports and the other department heads were told to find ways to reduce report errors and reduce the lead time of developing the client reports within the purview of their respective departments. After two years the Customer Service Initiative was abandoned.

Reasons for Failure Why did the initiative fail? Strategic initiatives tend to dissipate as they are implemented by line managers and staff because of the organization's inertia to implement strategic change.[1] Implementation of strategic initiatives can be hampered because each department assesses its own way to contribute to the strategy, which is often incremental, when a more risky, radical change in the way the department does work is required. Such change requires managers to conceive and accept new practices, something difficult to do because the current practices have been developed over time and reflect the organization's current way of doing business. As the financial services firm discovered, doling out the responsibilities for the implementation of a strategy to each department is likely to result in failure.

Implementing Operations Strategy What is the best way to implement operations strategy? The challenge is to manage the required changes to processes and value chains outside of the traditional organizational bureaucracy, procedures, and norms. **Project management**, which is a systemized, phased approach to defining, organizing, planning, monitoring, and controlling projects, is one way to overcome that challenge. In the remainder of this chapter, you will see that project management provides an unbiased methodology for planning and undertaking the necessary activities to implement a strategic initiative. Cross-functional teams are organized, responsibilities are assigned, schedules are developed, and controls put in place, all of which can help to overcome the problems of dissipation.

project management

A systemized, phased approach to defining, organizing, planning, monitoring, and controlling projects

Projects, and the application of project management, facilitate the implementation of operations strategy. However, the power of this approach goes beyond the focus on one project. Operations strategy initiatives often require the coordination of many interdependent projects. In the financial services example, the Customer Service Initiative might have projects such as (1) determining what the competition offers in the way of financial reports, (2) designing and developing new reporting services, (3) analyzing, redesigning, and implementing changes to the report generation process to reduce errors and improve delivery speed, and (4) developing and implementing a new Web interface to outreach to new customers and to facilitate the delivery of reports. Such a collection of projects is called a **program**, which is an interdependent set of projects with a common strategic purpose. As new project proposals come forward, management must assess their fit to the current operations strategy and ongoing initiatives and have a means to prioritize them because funds for projects are often limited.[2]

program

An interdependent set of projects that have a common strategic purpose.

CROSS-FUNCTIONAL INTERACTION

Even though a project may be under the overall purview of a single department, other departments likely should be involved in the project. For example, consider an information systems project to develop a corporate customer database at a bank. Many of the bank's customers are large corporations that require services spanning several departments at the bank. Because no department at the bank knew exactly what services a corporate customer was receiving from the other departments, the project would consolidate information about

---

[1]See the article by Sergio Pellegrinelli and Cliff Bowman, "Implementing Strategy Through Projects," *Long Range Planning*, vol. 27, no. 4 (1994), pp. 125–132, for more information on the topic of this section.
[2]This approach is referred to as the *project portfolio process*. See Samuel J. Mantel, Jr., Jack R. Meredith, Scott M. Shafer, and Margaret M. Sutton, *Project Management in Practice*, 2d ed. (New York: John Wiley & Sons, 2005), pp. 26–30.

corporate customers from many areas of the bank into one database. From this information, corporate banking services could be designed not only to better serve the corporate customers but also to provide a basis for evaluating the prices that the bank charges. Marketing is interested in knowing all the services a customer is receiving so that it can package and sell other services that the customer may not be aware of. Finance is interested in how profitable a customer is to the bank and whether the provided services are appropriately priced. The project team, led by the information systems department, should consist of representatives from the marketing and finance departments who have a direct interest in corporate clients. All departments in a firm benefit from sound project management practices, even if the projects remain within the purview of a single department.

> DEFINING AND ORGANIZING PROJECTS <

Successful projects begin with a clear definition of scope, objectives, and tasks. A clear understanding of its organization and how personnel are going to work together to complete the project is also important. In this section, we will address three important activities in this initial phase of planning and managing projects: (1) defining the scope and objectives, (2) selecting the project manager and team, and (3) selecting the organizational structure.

DEFINING THE SCOPE AND OBJECTIVES OF A PROJECT

A thorough statement of a project's scope, time frame, and allocated resources is essential to managing the project. This statement is often referred to as the *project objective statement*. The scope provides a succinct statement of project objectives and captures the essence of the desired project outcomes in the form of major deliverables, which are concrete outcomes of the project. These deliverables become the focus of management attention during the life of the project. For example, suppose a firm wants to reengineer its billing process. Major deliverables for the project might include a list of all affected processes in both the firm and entities exterior to the firm; redesign of the billing process; an implementation plan; a staffing plan; and a new, fully operational billing process. Each of the deliverables requires activities to achieve it; therefore, it is important to avoid many changes to the scope of the project once it is underway.

Changes to the scope of a project inevitably increase costs and delay completion. For example, adding a requirement to recommend an e-commerce software solution to the reengineering project after it has started might require a reanalysis of the recommended changes to the existing internal processes and a consultant to recommend a software package. Such a change will not only delay the completion of a project but will add to the needed resources to complete it. Collectively, changes to scope are called *scope creep* and, in sufficient quantity, are primary causes of failed projects.

The time frame for a project should be as specific as possible. For example, "by the first quarter, 2008," is too vague for most purposes. Some people could interpret it as the beginning and others the end. Even though it should be considered only as a target at this early stage of the project plan, the time frame should be much more specific as in "the billing process reengineering project should be completed by January 1, 2008."

Although specifying an allocation of resources to a project may be difficult at the early stages of planning, it is important for managing the projects. The allocation could be expressed as a dollar figure or as full-time equivalents of personnel time. For example, in the billing process reengineering project, the allocated resources might be $250,000. Avoid statements such as "with available resources" because they are too vague and imply that there are sufficient resources to complete the project when there may not be. A specific statement of allocated resources makes it possible to make adjustments to the scope of the project as it proceeds.

SELECTING THE PROJECT MANAGER AND TEAM

Once the project is selected, a project manager must be chosen. The qualities of a good project manager should reflect the roles a project manager must play.

- *Facilitator.* The project manager often must resolve conflicts between individuals or departments to ensure that the project has the appropriate resources for the job to be completed. It helps to have a "big picture" framework and still be a good negotiator. Successful project managers have a *systems view,* which encompasses the interaction of the project, its resources, and its deliverables with the firm as a whole. Good project managers exhibit *leadership* so that team members and department heads work toward completion of the project as a whole as opposed to optimizing their own parts of the project.

- *Communicator.* The project manager is responsible to senior management and other stakeholders in a project. Project progress and requests for additional resources must be clearly communicated. In addition, the project manager must communicate with the project team to get the best performance. Good project managers are *credible* from the perspective of technical knowledge as well as administrative knowledge. It also helps if the project manager is *sensitive* to organizational politics as well as aware of interpersonal conflicts between team members.

- *Decision Maker.* The project manger must organize the team meetings, specify how the team will make decisions, and determine the nature and timing of reports to senior management. Decisions can be made by consensus, majority, or by the project manager. Good project managers will be sensitive to the way the team will perform best and be ready to make tough decisions if necessary.

Selecting the project team is just as important as the selection of the project manager. Several characteristics should be considered.

- *Technical Competence.* Team members should have the technical competence required for the tasks they will be assigned to.

- *Sensitivity.* All team members should be sensitive to interpersonal conflicts that may arise. Senior team members should be politically sensitive to help mitigate problems with upper level management.

- *Dedication.* Team members should feel comfortable solving project problems that may spill over into areas outside their immediate expertise. They should also be dedicated to getting the project done, as opposed to maintaining a comfortable work schedule. Major projects may require extra effort to maintain schedules.

ORGANIZATIONAL STRUCTURE

The relationship of the project manager to the project team is determined by the firm's organizational structure. Each of the three types of organizational structure has its own implications for project management.

- *Functional.* The project is housed in a specific functional area, presumably the one with the most interest in the project. Assistance from personnel in other functional areas must be negotiated by the project manager. However, reliance on other departments leaves the project manager with minimal control over the timing of the project because those departments may place a low priority on the project. Nonetheless, resource usage within the project manager's department is maximized because team members not working on one project can be assigned to another project in the same department.

- *Pure Project.* The team members work exclusively for the project manager on a particular project. This structure is particularly effective for large projects that consist of enough work for each team member to work full time. Although this structure simplifies the lines of authority for the project manager, for small projects it could result in significant duplication of resources across functional areas. Small projects typically do not include enough work to keep all team members busy all of the time. It would be better for the firm if those members could work on other projects to fill their slack time.

- *Matrix.* The matrix structure is a compromise between the functional and pure project structures. The project managers of the firm's projects all report to a "program manager" who coordinates resource and technological needs across the functional boundaries. The matrix structure allows each functional area to maintain control over who works on a project and the technology that is used. Team members are never displaced from their departments, as may be the case in the pure project structure. Most of the resource duplication problems are eliminated. However, team members in effect have two bosses: the project manager and the department manager. The project manager has control over which activities the team member performs; the department manager has control over performance evaluations and salary. Resolving these "line of authority" conflicts requires a strong program manager.

Managerial Practice 3.1 shows that defining and organizing projects takes on critical importance when dealing with global teams.

| MANAGERIAL **PRACTICE** | 3.1 | VIRTUAL GLOBAL TEAMING AT BAXTER INTERNATIONAL |

Baxter international is an $8 billion company that produces services and products for the health care industry in facilities located in 22 countries worldwide. Baxter produces thousands of services and products, such as online continuing education courses for a wide variety of health care professionals, products and technologies for blood centers, transfusion services, intravenous therapy services, and vaccines for serious infectious diseases. One product, however, provided the vehicle for Baxter to learn some interesting lessons in the management of projects.

BaxHealth is a software package produced by Baxter that is used by companies to manage their environmental, health, and safety initiatives. When management decided to develop the next generation of the software package, the assignment to the software development team was to develop a top-quality product at the lowest cost possible and to get the product to the market in a compressed time frame. The software development team would have normally had the capability to deliver the project on time and within budget; however, a recent merger placed a heavy load on software development. Shortly after the BaxHealth project began, it became clear that the project team was not going to be able to deliver the project on time.

In a bold move, the team decided to enlist the help of a software development firm in India. Now, part of the project team was in Deerfled, Illinois, and the other part was in Bangalore, India. Steps were taken to transform the two separate international teams into a single, high-performing team.

- Establishing planning at all levels of the project, not just at the aggregate level.

- Establishing the processes that would foster consistent and open communication among team members, so as to minimize biases and finger-pointing.

- Defining a rigorous development process, establishing discipline, and providing leadership throughout the project, so as to ensure that the same planning and management procedures were being employed everywhere.

- Setting clear and measurable team and individual goals.

- Developing an integrated project plan and schedule that reflected all time demands placed on team members, even those outside the BaxHealth project.

Communications became a critical element of the project success. Language, international regulations, culture, and different time zones had to be taken into consideration. Each week, the project management team communicated the status of the project with respect to goals, risks, and progress to all team members. Since the team was spread out Internationally, walking

Baxter International produces products for the health care industry worldwide. The company has learned to use virtual global teaming to manage projects involving team members located in different parts of the world.

down the hall to discuss problems was not an option. E-mail, fax, Web pages, and the phone had to fill the need to communicate. In many regards, the BaxHealth project team was a virtual team.

The BaxHealth software package was reengineered and launched in 18 months, which was on schedule. Baxter learned that the management of virtual, global project teams requires solid project management principles, excellent communication with the entire global team, and an agreement by all to follow the same process. The approach requires patience and personal accountability from all team members. Nonetheless, after the project was over, Baxter examined the product development process for improvements. For example, the team learned that it would have been better to have the Bangalore development team work with the Deerfield team in Illinois in the early stages of the project, so as to reduce the time it takes to achieve a "one team" spirit. Many other improvements were identified that will be incorporated in future development projects.

Source: Robert J. Seguy, Mary Ann Latko, Jay Balma, and Errol Jones, "Virtual Global Teaming: Baxter International Builds a Successful Model," *Target* (Second Quarter 2002), pp. 23–31; www.baxter.com (2003).

> PLANNING PROJECTS <

After the project is defined and the project organized, the team must formulate a plan that identifies the specific tasks to be accomplished and a schedule for their completion. Planning projects involves five steps: (1) *defining the work breakdown structure,* (2) *diagramming the network,* (3) *developing the schedule,* (4) *analyzing cost–time trade-offs,* and (5) *assessing risks.*

DEFINING THE WORK BREAKDOWN STRUCTURE

The **work breakdown structure (WBS)** is a statement of all work that has to be completed. Perhaps the single most important contributor to delay is the omission of work that is germane to the successful completion of the project. The project manager must work closely with the team to identify all work tasks. Typically, in the process of accumulating work tasks, the team generates a hierarchy to the work breakdown. Major work components are broken down to smaller tasks by the project team. Figure 3.1 shows a WBS for the start of a new business. The level 1 activities are major work components that can be broken down into smaller tasks. For example, "proceed with start-up plan" can be divided into three tasks at level 2, and "establish business structure" can be further divided into five tasks at level 3. It is easy to conclude that the total WBS for starting a new business may include more than 100 tasks. Regardless of the project, care must be taken to include all important tasks in the WBS to avoid project delays. Often overlooked are the tasks required to plan the project, get management approval at various stages, run pilot tests of new services or products, and prepare final reports.

An **activity** is the smallest unit of work effort consuming both time and resources that the project manager can schedule and control. Each activity in the WBS must have an "owner" who is responsible for doing the work. *Task ownership* avoids confusion in the execution of activities and assigns responsibility for timely completion. The team should have a defined procedure for assigning tasks to team members, which can be democratic (consensus of the team) or autocratic (assigned by the project manager).

work breakdown structure (WBS)

A statement of all work that has to be completed.

activity

The smallest unit of work effort consuming both time and resources that the project manager can schedule and control.

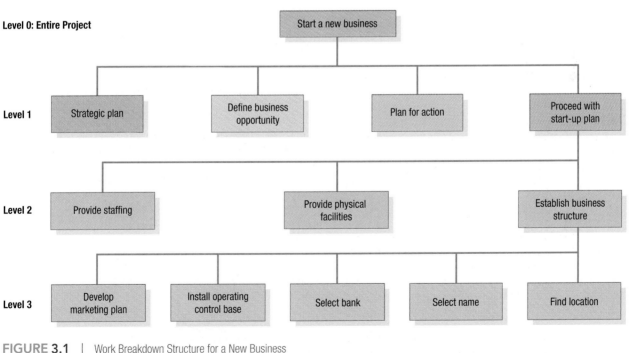

FIGURE 3.1 | Work Breakdown Structure for a New Business

Source: Abstracted from MS Project 2000 template for a new business.

DIAGRAMMING THE NETWORK

network diagram

A network planning method, designed to depict the relationships between activities, that consists of nodes (circles) and arcs (arrows).

program evaluation and review technique (PERT)

A network planning method created for the U.S. Navy's Polaris missile project in the 1950s, which involved 3,000 separate contractors and suppliers.

critical path method (CPM)

A network planning method developed in the 1950s as a means of scheduling maintenance shutdowns at chemical-processing plants.

Network planning methods can help managers monitor and control projects. These methods treat a project as a set of interrelated activities that can be visually displayed in a **network diagram**, which consists of nodes (circles) and arcs (arrows) that depict the relationships between activities. Two network planning methods were developed in the 1950s. The **program evaluation and review technique (PERT)** was created for the U.S. Navy's Polaris missile project, which involved 3,000 separate contractors and suppliers. The **critical path method (CPM)** was developed as a means of scheduling maintenance shutdowns at chemical-processing plants. Although early versions of PERT and CPM differed in their treatment of activity time estimates, today the differences between PERT and CPM are minor. For purposes of our discussion, we refer to them collectively as PERT/CPM. These methods offer several benefits to project managers, including the following.

1. Considering projects as networks forces project teams to identify and organize the data required and to identify the interrelationships between activities. This process also provides a forum for managers of different functional areas to discuss the nature of the various activities and their resource requirements.

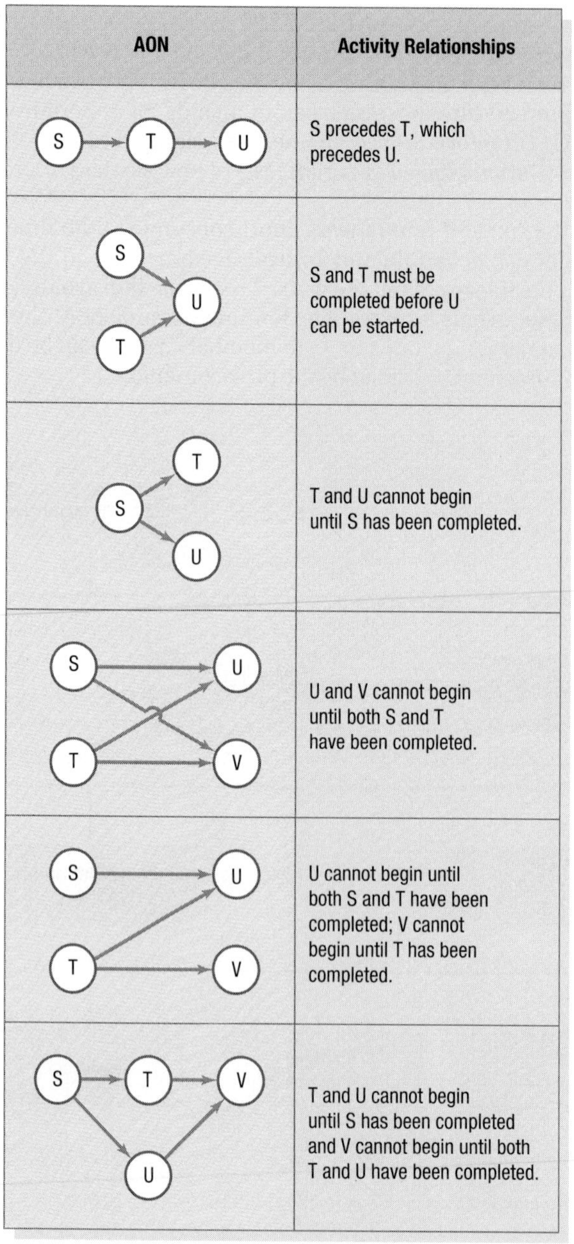
AON
Activity Relationships
S precedes T, which precedes U.
S and T must be completed before U can be started.
T and U cannot begin until S has been completed.
U and V cannot begin until both S and T have been completed.
U cannot begin until both S and T have been completed; V cannot begin until T has been completed.
T and U cannot begin until S has been completed and V cannot begin until both T and U have been completed.

FIGURE 3.2

Diagramming Activity Relationships

2. Networks enable project managers to estimate the completion time of projects, an advantage that can be useful in planning other events and in conducting contractual negotiations with customers and suppliers.

3. Reports highlight the activities that are crucial to completing projects on schedule. They also highlight the activities that may be delayed without affecting completion dates, thereby freeing up resources for other, more critical activities.

4. Network methods enable project managers to analyze the time and cost implications of resource trade-offs.

Establishing Precedence Relationships Diagramming the project as a network requires establishing the precedence relationships between activities. A **precedence relationship** determines a sequence for undertaking activities; it specifies that one activity cannot start until a preceding activity has been completed. For example, brochures announcing a conference for executives must first be designed by the program committee (activity A) before they can be printed (activity B). In other words, activity A must *precede* activity B. For large projects, this task is essential because incorrect or omitted precedence relationships will result in costly delays. The precedence relationships are represented by a network diagram.

Using the Activity-on-Node Approach The approach we use in this text is referred to as the **activity-on-node (AON) network**, in which nodes represent activities and arcs represent the precedence relationships between them. Precedence relationships require that an activity not begin until all preceding activities have been completed. Some diagramming conventions must be used for AON networks. In cases of multiple activities with no predecessors, it is usual to show them emanating from a common node called *start*. For multiple activities with no successors, it is usual to show them connected to a node called *finish*. Figure 3.2 (p. 76) shows how to diagram several commonly encountered activity relationships.

precedence relationship

A relationship that determines a sequence for undertaking activities; it specifies that one activity cannot start until a preceding activity has been completed.

activity-on-node (AON) network

An approach used to create a network diagram, in which nodes represent activities and arcs represent the precedence relationships between them.

Diagramming a Hospital Project	EXAMPLE 3.1

St. Adolf's Hospital is a private hospital that first started serving the community 30 years ago. Judy Kramer, executive director of the board of St. Adolf's, initiated a strategic assessment of the hospital's service package, so as to identify the gaps in its capability to provide top-quality service. The study revealed a gap in the hospital's capability to provide the level of service required by the community, particularly because of the lack of bed space and small, inefficient lab facilities. However, expansion at its present location was impossible.

In the interest of better serving the public in Benjamin Country, the board of St. Adolf's Hospital decided to relocate from Christofer to Northville. The move to Northville will involve constructing a new hospital and making it operational. Judy Kramer must prepare for a hearing, scheduled for next week, before the Central Ohio Hospital Board (COHB) on the proposed project. The hearing will address the specifics of the total project, including time and cost estimates for its completion.

With the help of her team, Kramer has developed a WBS consisting of 11 major project activities. Each team member was assigned the responsibility for certain activities, with Kramer taking overall responsibility as project manager. The team also has specified the immediate predecessors (those activities that must be completed before a particular activity can begin) for each activity as shown in the following table.

Activity	Description	Immediate Predecessor(s)	Responsibility
A	Select administrative and medical staff	—	Johnson
B	Select site and do site survey	—	Taylor
C	Select equipment	A	Adams
D	Prepare final construction plans and layout	B	Taylor
E	Bring utilities to the site	B	Burton
F	Interview applicants and fill positions in nursing, support staff, maintenance, and security	A	Johnson

(continued)

Activity	Description	Immediate Predecessor(s)	Responsibility
G	Purchase and take delivery of equipment	C	Adarns
H	Construct the hospital	D	Taylor
I	Develop an information system	A	Simmons
J	Install the equipment	E, G, H	Adams
K	Train nurses and support staff	F, I, J	Johnson

Draw the network diagram for the hospital project.

SOLUTION

The network diagram for the hospital project, based on Kramer's 11 activities and their precedence relationships, is shown in Figure 3.3. It depicts activities as circles, with arrows indicating the sequence in which they are to be performed. Activities A and B emanate from a *start* node because they have no immediate predecessors. The arrows connecting activity A to activities C, F, and I indicate that all three require completion of activity A before they can begin. Similarly, activity B must be completed before activities D and E can begin, and so on. Activity K connects to a *finish* node because no activities follow it. The start and finish nodes do not actually represent activities. They merely provide beginning and ending points for the network.

FIGURE 3.3

Network Diagram for the St. Adolf's Hospital Project

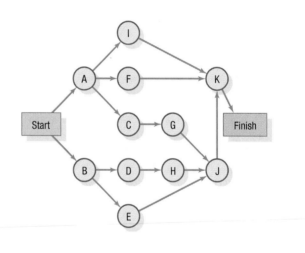

DEVELOPING THE SCHEDULE

Next, the project team must make time estimates for activities. When the same type of activity has been done many times before, time estimates are apt to have a relatively high degree of certainty. Several ways can be used to get time estimates in such an environment. First, statistical methods can be used if the project team has access to data on actual activity times experienced in the past (see Supplement H, "Measuring Output Rates," on the Student CD-ROM). Second, if activity times improve with the number of replications, the times can be estimated using learning curve models (see Supplement G, "Learning Curves Analysis," on the Student CD-ROM). Finally, the times for first-time activities are often estimated using managerial opinions based on similar prior experiences (see Chapter 13, "Forecasting"). If the estimates involve a high degree of uncertainty, probability distributions for activity times can be used. We discuss two approaches for incorporating uncertainty in project networks when we address risk assessment later. For now, we assume that the activity times are known with certainty. Figure 3.4 shows the estimated time in weeks for each activity of the St. Adolf's Hospital project.

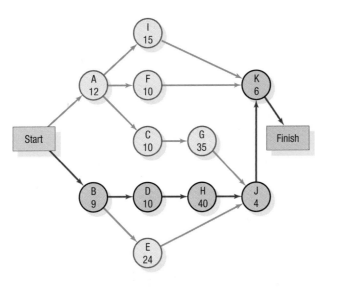

FIGURE **3.4**

Network Showing Activity Times for the St. Adolf's Hospital Project

A crucial aspect of project management is estimating the time of completion. If each activity in relocating the hospital were done in sequence, with work proceeding on only one activity at a time, the time of completion would equal the sum of the times for all the activities, or 175 weeks. However, Figure 3.4 indicates that some activities can be carried on simultaneously given adequate resources. We call each sequence of activities between the project's start and finish a **path**. The network describing the hospital relocation project has five paths: A–I–K, A–F–K, A–C–G–J–K, B–D–H–J–K, and B–E–J–K. The **critical path** is the sequence of activities between a project's start and finish that takes the longest time to complete. Thus, the activities along the critical path determine the completion time of the project; that is, if one of the activities on the critical path is delayed, the entire project will be delayed. The estimated times for the paths in the hospital project network are

path
The sequence of activities between a project's start and finish.

critical path
The sequence of activities between a project's start and finish that takes the longest time to complete.

Path	Estimated Time (wk)
A–I–K	33
A–F–K	28
A–C–G–J–K	67
B–D–H–J–K	69
B–E–J–K	43

The activity string B–D–H–J–K is estimated to take 69 weeks to complete. As the longest, it constitutes the critical path and is shown in red in Figure 3.4.

Because the critical path defines the completion time of the project, Judy Kramer and the project team should focus on these activities. However, projects can have more than one critical path. If activity A, C, or G were to fall behind by two weeks, the string A–C–G–J–K would become a second critical path. Consequently, the team should be aware that delays in activities not on the critical path could cause delays in the entire project.

Manually finding the critical path in this way is easy for small projects; however, computers must be used for large projects. Computers calculate activity slack and prepare periodic reports, enabling managers to monitor progress. **Activity slack** is the maximum length of time that an activity can be delayed without delaying the entire project. Activities on the critical path have zero slack. Constantly monitoring the progress of activities with little or no slack enables managers to identify activities that need to be expedited to keep the project on schedule. Activity slack is calculated from four times for each activity: (1) earliest start time, (2) earliest finish time, (3) latest start time, and (4) latest finish time.

activity slack
The maximum length of time that an activity can be delayed without delaying the entire project.

Earliest Start and Earliest Finish Times The earliest start and earliest finish times are obtained as follows.

earliest finish time (EF)

An activity's earliest start time plus its estimated duration, t, or $EF = ES + t$.

earliest start time (ES)

The earliest finish time of the immediately preceding activity.

1. The **earliest finish time (EF)** of an activity equals its earliest start time plus its estimated duration, t, or $EF = ES + t$.
2. The **earliest start time (ES)** for an activity is the earliest finish time of the immediately preceding activity. For activities with more than one preceding activity, ES is the latest of the earliest finish times of the preceding activities.

To calculate the duration of the entire project, we determine the EF for the last activity on the critical path.

Latest Start and Latest Finish Times To obtain the latest start and latest finish times, we must work backward from the finish node. We start by setting the latest finish time of the project equal to the earliest finish time of the last activity on the critical path.

latest finish time (LF)

The latest start time of the activity that immediately follows.

latest start time (LS)

The latest finish time minus its estimated duration, t, or $LS = LF - t$.

1. The **latest finish time (LF)** for an activity is the latest start time of the activity that immediately follows. For activities with more than one activity that immediately follow, LF is the earliest of the latest start times of those activities.
2. The **latest start time (LS)** for an activity equals its latest finish time minus its estimated duration, t, or $LS = LF - t$.

EXAMPLE 3.2	Calculating Start and Finish Times for the Activities

Calculate the ES, EF, LS, and LF times for each activity. Which activity should Kramer start immediately? Figure 3.4 contains the activity times.

SOLUTION

To compute the early start and early finish times, we begin at the start node at time zero. Because activities A and B have no predecessors, the earliest start times for these activities are also zero. The earliest finish times for these activities are

$$EF_A = 0 + 12 = 12 \text{ and } EF_B = 0 + 9 = 9$$

Because the earliest start time for activities I, F, and C is the earliest finish time of activity A,

$$ES_I = 12, ES_F = 12, \text{ and } ES_C = 12$$

Similarly,

$$ES_D = 9 \text{ and } ES_E = 9$$

After placing these ES values on the network diagram (see Figure 3.5), we determine the EF times for activities I, F, C, D, and E:

$$EF_I = 12 + 15 = 27, EF_F = 12 + 10 = 22, EF_C = 12 + 10 = 22$$
$$EF_D = 9 + 10 = 19, \text{ and } EF_E = 9 + 24 = 33$$

The earliest start time for activity G is the latest EF time of all immediately preceding activities. Thus,

$$\begin{array}{ll} ES_G = EF_C & ES_H = EF_D \\ \quad = 22 & \quad = 19 \\ EF_G = ES_G + t & EF_H = ES_H + t \\ \quad = 22 + 35 & \quad = 19 + 40 \\ \quad = 57 & \quad = 59 \end{array}$$

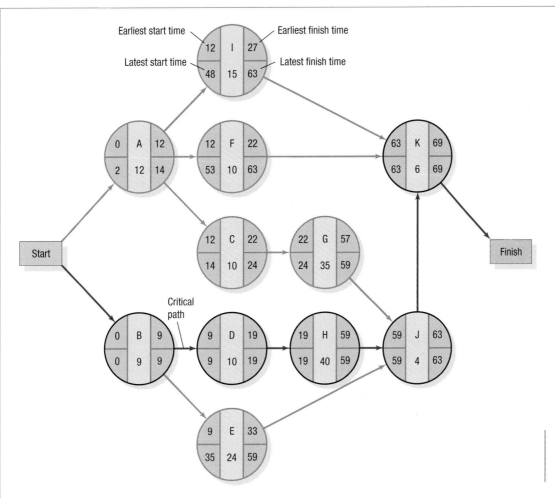

FIGURE 3.5

Network Diagram Showing
Start and Finish Times

The project team can now determine the earliest time any activity can be started. Because activity J has several predecessors, the earliest time that activity J can begin is the latest of the EF times of any of its preceding activities: EF_G, EF_H, EF_E. Thus $EF_J = 59 + 4 = 63$. Similarly, $ES_K = 63$ and $EF_K = 63 + 6 = 69$. Because activity K is the last activity on the critical path, the earliest the project can be completed is week 69. The earliest start and finish times for all activities are shown in Figure 3.5.

To compute the latest start and latest finish times, we begin by setting the latest finish activity time of activity K at week 69, which is its earliest finish time as determined in Figure 3.5. Thus, the latest start time for activity K is

$$LS_K = LF_K - t = 69 - 6 = 63$$

If activity K is to start no later than week 63, all its predecessors must finish no later than that time. Consequently,

$$LF_I = 63, LF_F = 63, \text{ and } LF_J = 63$$

The latest start times for these activities are shown in Figure 3.5 as

$$LS_I = 63 - 15 = 48, LS_F = 63 - 10 = 53, \text{ and } LS_J = 63 - 4 = 59$$

After obtaining LS_J, we can calculate the latest start times for the immediate predecessors of activity J:

$$LS_G = 59 - 35 = 24, LS_H = 59 - 40 = 19, \text{ and } LS_E = 59 - 24 = 35$$

Similarly, we can now calculate the latest start times for activities C and D:

$$LS_C = 24 - 10 = 14 \text{ and } LS_D = 19 - 10 = 9$$

Activity A has more than one immediately following activity: I, F, and C. The earliest of the latest start times is 14 for activity C. Thus,

$$LS_A = 14 - 12 = 2$$

Similarly, activity B has two immediate followers, D and E. Because the earliest of the latest start times of these activities is 9,

$$LS_B = 9 - 9 = 0$$

Decision Point The earliest or latest start dates can be used for developing a project schedule. For example, Kramer should start activity B immediately because the latest start date is 0; otherwise, the project will not be completed by week 69. When the LS is greater than the ES for an activity, that activity could be scheduled for any date between ES and LS. Such is the case for activity E, which could be scheduled to start anytime between week 9 and week 35, depending on the availability of resources. The earliest start and earliest finish times and the latest start and latest finish times for all activities are shown in Figure 3.5.

Gantt chart

A project schedule, usually created by the project manager using computer software, that superimposes project activities, with their precedence relationships and estimated duration times, on a time line.

Project Schedule The project manager, often with the assistance of computer software, creates the project schedule by superimposing project activities, with their precedence relationships and estimated duration times, on a time line. The resulting diagram is called a **Gantt chart**. Figure 3.6 shows a Gantt chart for the hospital project created with Microsoft Project, a popular software package for project management. The critical path is shown in red. The chart clearly shows which activities can be undertaken simultaneously and when they should be started. You perhaps noticed that the number of calendar days between the start and finish dates for an activity is greater than the expected duration in weeks. The reason is that Microsoft Project's default setting is to schedule Saturdays and Sundays as off days. Also, Figure 3.6 shows the earliest start schedule for the project. Both the calendar and the schedule priority can be changed as needed. Gantt charts are popular because they are intuitive and easy to construct.

Activity Slack Information on slack can be useful because it highlights activities that need close attention. In this regard, activity slack is the amount of schedule slippage that can be tolerated for an activity before the entire project will be delayed. Activities on the critical path have zero slack. Slack at an activity is reduced when the estimated time duration of an activity is exceeded or when the scheduled start time for the activity must be delayed because of resource considerations. For example, activity G in the hospital project is estimated to have 2 weeks of slack. Suppose that the orders for the new equipment are placed in week 22, the activity's earliest start date. If the supplier informs the project team that it will have a 2-week delay in the normal delivery time, the activity time becomes 37 weeks, consuming all the slack and making activity G critical. Management must carefully monitor the delivery of the equipment to avoid delaying the entire project.

Sometimes managers can manipulate slack to overcome scheduling problems. Slack information helps the project team make decisions about the reallocation of resources. When resources can be used on several different activities in a project, they can be taken from activities with slack and given to activities that are behind schedule until the slack is used up.

total slack

Slack shared by other activities; calculated as S = LS − ES or S = LF − EF.

Two types of activity slack are possible. **Total slack** for an activity is a function of the performance of activities leading to it. It is shared by other activities. Total slack can be calculated in one of two ways for any activity:

$$S = LS - ES \quad or \quad S = LF - EF$$

free slack

The amount of time that an activity's earliest finish time can be delayed without delaying the earliest start time of any activity that immediately follows.

Free slack is the amount of time that an activity's earliest finish time can be delayed without delaying the earliest start time of any activity that immediately follows. To demonstrate the calculation of free slack, refer to Figure 3.5. Notice that activity A has an earliest finish time of 12 weeks and a total slack of 2 weeks. Now look at the three activities that immediately follow

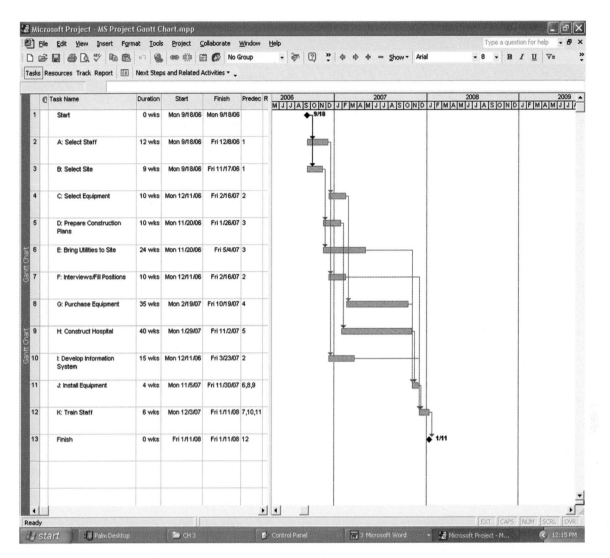

FIGURE 3.6 | MS Project Gantt Chart for the St. Adolf's Hospital Project Schedule

activity A. All of those activities have earliest start times of 12 weeks. If activity A experiences any delays at all, it will force a change in the earliest start times of the three following activities even though it may still have total slack. Activity A has no free slack. In contrast, look at activity G. It also has two weeks of total slack. However, its early finish time of 57 weeks is less than the earliest start time of its only following activity, J, at 59 weeks. Consequently, G has two weeks of free slack. It could experience up to two weeks of delay without affecting the earliest start schedules of any other activity. The distinction between the two types of slack is important for making resource allocation decisions. If an activity has total slack but no free slack, any slippage in its start date will affect the slack of other activities. However, the start date for an activity with free slack can be delayed without affecting the schedules of other activities.

Calculating Activity Slack	EXAMPLE **3.3**

Calculate the slack for the activities in the St. Adolf's Hospital project. Use the data provided in Figure 3.5.

SOLUTION

The following table from Microsoft Project shows the total slack and the free slack for each activity. Figure 3.7 shows activities B, D, H, J, and K have zero slack because they are on the critical path.

	Task Name	Start	Finish	Late Start	Late Finish	Free Slack	Total Slack
1	Start	Mon 9/18/06	Mon 9/18/06	Mon 9/18/06	Mon 9/18/06	0 wks	0 wks
2	A: Select Staff	Mon 9/18/06	Fri 12/8/06	Mon 10/2/06	Fri 12/22/06	0 wks	2 wks
3	B: Select Site	Mon 9/18/06	Fri 11/17/06	Mon 9/18/06	Fri 11/17/06	0 wks	0 wks
4	C: Select Equipment	Mon 12/11/06	Fri 2/16/07	Mon 12/25/06	Fri 3/2/07	0 wks	2 wks
5	D: Prepare Construction Plans	Mon 11/20/06	Fri 1/26/07	Mon 11/20/06	Fri 1/26/07	0 wks	0 wks
6	E: Bring Utilities to Site	Mon 11/20/06	Fri 5/4/07	Mon 5/21/07	Fri 11/2/07	26 wks	26 wks
7	F: Interviews/Fill Positions	Mon 12/11/06	Fri 2/16/07	Mon 9/24/07	Fri 11/30/07	41 wks	41 wks
8	G: Purchase Equipment	Mon 2/19/07	Fri 10/19/07	Mon 3/5/07	Fri 11/2/07	2 wks	2 wks
9	H: Construct Hospital	Mon 1/29/07	Fri 11/2/07	Mon 1/29/07	Fri 11/2/07	0 wks	0 wks
10	I: Develop Information System	Mon 12/11/06	Fri 3/23/07	Mon 8/20/07	Fri 11/30/07	36 wks	36 wks
11	J: Install Equipment	Mon 11/5/07	Fri 11/30/07	Mon 11/5/07	Fri 11/30/07	0 wks	0 wks
12	K: Train Staff	Mon 12/3/07	Fri 1/11/08	Mon 12/3/07	Fri 1/11/08	0 wks	0 wks
13	Finish	Fri 1/11/08	Fri 1/11/08	Fri 1/11/08	Fri 1/11/08	0 wks	0 wks

FIGURE **3.7** | Schedule Table Showing Activity Slacks for the St. Adolf's Hospital Project

ACTIVE MODEL 3.1

Active Model 3.1 on the Student CD-ROM provides additional insight on Gantt charts and their uses for the St. Adolf's Hospital project.

Decision Point The total slack at an activity depends on the performance of activities leading to it. If the project team decides to schedule activity A to begin in week 2 instead of immediately, the total slack for activities C and G would be zero. Thus, total slack is shared among all activities on a particular path. The table also shows that several activities have free slack. For example, activity G has two weeks of free slack. If the schedule goes as planned to week 22 when activity G is scheduled to start, and the supplier for the equipment asks for a 2-week extension on the delivery date, the project team knows that the delay will not affect the schedule for the other activities. Nonetheless, activity G would be on the critical path.

Now that we have discussed the fundamentals of project management it is time to test your understanding of what you learned. What should the management of The Phoenician in the Managerial Challenge do to meet the challenges of planning a renovation program?

ANALYZING COST–TIME TRADE-OFFS

Keeping costs at acceptable levels is almost always as important as meeting schedule dates. In this section, we discuss the use of PERT/CPM methods to obtain minimum-cost schedules.

The reality of project management is that there are always cost–time trade-offs. For example, a project can often be completed earlier than scheduled by hiring more workers or running extra shifts. Such actions could be advantageous if savings or additional revenues accrue from completing the project early. *Total project costs* are the sum of direct costs, indirect costs, and penalty costs. These costs are dependent either on activity times or on project completion time. *Direct costs* include labor, materials, and any other costs directly related to project activities. Managers can shorten individual activity times by using additional direct resources, such as overtime, personnel, or equipment. *Indirect costs* include administration, depreciation, financial, and other variable overhead costs that can be avoided by reducing total project time: The shorter the duration of the project, the lower the indirect costs will be. Finally, a project may incur penalty costs if it extends beyond some specific date, whereas a bonus may be provided for early completion. Thus, a project manager may consider *crashing,* or expediting, some activities to reduce overall project completion time and total project costs.

DVD

The Phoenician in Phoenix, Arizona, is part of Starwood's Luxury Collection and its only AAA 5 Diamond Award resort in the Southwestern United States. Sophistication, elegance, and excellence only begin to describe the guest experience at the hotel. Guests can dine in one of nine restaurants, relax poolside, play tennis, take in 27 holes of golf on three 9-hole courses, or relax with a variety of soothing spa treatments at the 22,000-square-foot Centre for Well-Being.

The Phoenician recently embarked on an ambitious $38 million spa and golf renovation program. The resort's golf and spa programs historically earned high marks from surveys in their industries over the years, but the environment was changing. Evidence of this change was seen in the explosive growth of new golf courses and spas in the Southwest region. Phoenix alone has over 275 golf courses, and the Southwest boasts the largest concentration of new luxury spas anywhere. The Phoenician's facilities, while world-class and highly rated, were more than 15 years old. The hotel's recently awarded 5 Diamond status renewed emphasis on bringing every process and service at the property up to 5 Diamond level.

The decision to renovate the golf course and existing spa became not a question of *whether* to undertake the projects, but *to what degree* they needed to be pursued. Key considerations centered on (1) whether to build basic facilities or commit to the grandiose luxury level, (2) having a domestic versus international reputation, and (3) developing creative packaging of the new facilities to attract loyal guests, such as through a spa and golf "country club-like" membership program. Such a program would be limited to about 600 spa/golf memberships, with a one-time fee of $65,000 each.

The company's senior management considered three options for the "Centre for Well-Being" spa. First, the existing space in the heart of the resort could be renovated. This option would require relocating the spa to another part of the resort and offering limited treatments during this time, thereby reducing spa revenues significantly. With option 2, hilly terrain directly behind the resort could be carved out to create a new mountainside facility with sweeping vistas. This option meant the closure of one of the hotel's buildings housing 60 guest rooms and suites during the construction period. The existing spa could remain open, however. Under option 3, a parking structure on existing hotel property could be used, having the least impact on revenues. The first option was seen as a short-term fix, while the remaining two were viewed as having longer-term potential.

Additional discussion centered on the type of spa to be built. Recent acquisition of the Bliss spa brand for Starwood's W Hotels was an option, offering day spa amenities and an indulgence atmosphere. The second option was to remain a holistic resort spa with an emphasis on health and restoration. The third option was to become a destination spa with dedicated guest stays and week-long programs. Day spas are the fastest-growing category, with few destination spas.

The Phoenician management team, with assistance from Starwood Field Operations and Corporate offices, prepared an extensive analysis of strengths, weaknesses, opportunities and threats to better understand the environment. The result of this analysis was used by the team to identify the set of activities necessary for each option. The Corporate Design and Construction group developed architectural and engineering plans, as well as the work breakdown structure and diagrams showing the critical path for the possible project options. The work breakdown structure, activity times, and activity precedence relationships are shown in the table.

When the Phonoecian, a luxury hotel in Phoenix, Arizona, sought to redesign its spa facilities, its management team created a work breakdown structure in order to compare different project options and choose the best one.

Work Breakdown Structure	Activity Time (days)	Activity Precedence Relationships
Project Conception		
A. Kick-off meeting	2	
B. Creation of spa specifications	30	A
Geotechnical Investigation		
C. Preliminary site characterizations	10	B
D. Subsurface investigation	10	C
E. Laboratory testing	5	D
F. Geologic hazard assessments	10	E
Design Development		
G. Initial designs	70	B
H. Preliminary zoning compliance plan	15	C, G
I. Final designs	18	H
J. Owner approval of designs	5	I
Documentation and Cost Estimation		
K. Construction documentation and landscape package	80	F, I
L. Acquisition of contractor estimates and bids	90	J, K
Decision		
M. Owner approval of one of the three projects	60	L

(continued)

Managerial Challenges for Selecting a Spa Alternative

1. Coordinating departments in a major project is always a challenge. Which departments within the Starwood organization likely played a role in each of the following project related activities?

   a. Defining and organizing the project

   b. Planning the project

   c. Monitoring and controlling the project

2. Many times, project decision makers do not rely solely on financial hurdles, such as return on investment or internal rates of return, but put a lot of weight on intangible factors. Which are the salient intangible factors associated with selecting one of the three options for the spa?

3. Timing is always a challenge in managing projects. Construct a network diagram for the spa selection process. How soon can The Phoenician management make a decision on the spa?

Cost to Crash To assess the benefit of crashing certain activities—from either a cost or a schedule perspective—the project manager needs to know the following times and costs.

normal time (NT)

The time necessary to complete an activity under normal conditions.

normal cost (NC)

The activity cost associated with the normal time.

crash time (CT)

The shortest possible time to complete an activity.

crash cost (CC)

The activity cost associated with the crash time.

1. The **normal time (NT)** is the time necessary to complete an activity under normal conditions.

2. The **normal cost (NC)** is the activity cost associated with the normal time.

3. The **crash time (CT)** is the shortest possible time to complete an activity.

4. The **crash cost (CC)** is the activity cost associated with the crash time.

Our cost analysis is based on the assumption that direct costs increase linearly as activity time is reduced from its normal time. This assumption implies that for every week the activity time is reduced, direct costs increase by a proportional amount. For example, suppose that the normal time for activity C in the hospital project is 10 weeks and is associated with a direct cost of $4,000. If, by crashing activity C, we can reduce its time to only 5 weeks at a crash cost of $7,000, the net time reduction is 5 weeks at a net cost increase of $3,000. We assume that crashing activity C costs $3,000/5 = $600 per week—an assumption of linear marginal costs that is illustrated in Figure 3.8. Thus, if activity C were expedited by 2 weeks (i.e., its time reduced from 10 weeks to 8 weeks), the estimated direct costs would be $4,000 + 2($600) = $5,200. For any activity, the cost to crash an activity by one week is

$$\text{Cost to crash per period} = \frac{CC - NC}{NT - CT}$$

Table 3.1 contains direct cost and time data, as well as the costs of crashing per week for the activities in the hospital project.

FIGURE 3.8

Cost–Time Relationships in Cost Analysis

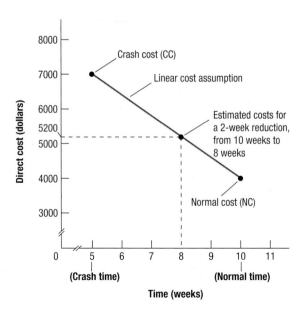

	TABLE 3.1		Direct Cost and Time Data for the St. Adolf's Hospital Project			
Activity	Normal Time (NT)	Normal Cost (NC)	Crash Time (CT)	Crash Cost (CC)	Maximum Time Reduction (wk)	Cost of Crashing per Week
A	12	$ 12,000	11	$ 13,000	1	$ 1,000
B	9	50,000	7	64,000	2	7,000
C	10	4,000	5	7,000	5	600
D	10	16,000	8	20,000	2	2,000
E	24	120,000	14	200,000	10	8,000
F	10	10,000	6	16,000	4	1,500
G	35	500,000	25	530,000	10	3,000
H	40	1,200,000	35	1,260,000	5	12,000
I	15	40,000	10	52,500	5	2,500
J	4	10,000	1	13,000	3	1,000
K	6	30,000	5	34,000	1	4,000
	Totals	$1,992,000		$2,209,500		

Minimizing Costs The objective of cost analysis is to determine the project schedule that minimizes total project costs. Suppose that project indirect costs are $8,000 per week. Suppose also that, after week 65, the Central Ohio Hospital Board imposes on St. Adolf's a penalty cost of $20,000 per week if the hospital is not fully operational. With a critical path completion time of 69 weeks, the hospital faces potentially large penalty costs unless the schedule is changed. For every week that the project is shortened—to week 65—the hospital saves one week of penalty *and* indirect costs, or $28,000. For reductions beyond week 65, the savings are only the weekly indirect costs of $8,000.

The minimum possible project duration can be found by using the crash times of each activity for scheduling purposes. However, the cost of that schedule could be prohibitive. Project managers are most interested in minimizing the costs of their projects so that budgets are not exceeded. In determining the **minimum-cost schedule**, we start with the normal time schedule and crash activities along the critical path, whose length equals the length of the project. We want to determine how much we can add in crash costs without exceeding the savings in indirect and penalty costs. The procedure involves the following steps:

Step 1. Determine the project's critical path(s).
Step 2. Find the activity or activities on the critical path(s) with the lowest cost of crashing per week.
Step 3. Reduce the time for this activity until (a) it cannot be further reduced, (b) another path becomes critical, or (c) the increase in direct costs exceeds the savings that result from shortening the project. If more than one path is critical, the time for an activity on each path may have to be reduced simultaneously.
Step 4. Repeat this procedure until the increase in direct costs is larger than the savings generated by shortening the project.

minimum-cost schedule
A schedule determined by starting with the normal time schedule and crashing activities along the critical path, in such a way that the costs of crashing do not exceed the savings in indirect and penalty costs.

Find a Minimum-Cost Schedule	EXAMPLE 3.4

Determine the minimum-cost schedule for the St. Adolf's Hospital project. Use the information that was provided in Table 3.1 and Figure 3.5.

ACTIVE MODEL 3.2

Active Model 3.2 on the Student CD-ROM provides additional insight on cost analysis for the St. Adolf's Hospital project.

SOLUTION

The projected completion time of the project is 69 weeks. The project costs for that schedule are $1,992,000 in direct costs, 69($8,000) = $552,000 in indirect costs, and (69 − 65) ($20,000) = $80,000 in penalty costs, for total project costs of $2,624,000. The five paths in the network have the following normal times.

A–I–K:	33 weeks
A–F–K:	28 weeks
A–C–G–J–K:	67 weeks
B–D–H–J–K:	69 weeks
B–E–J–K:	43 weeks

It will simplify our analysis if we can eliminate some paths from further consideration. If all activities on A–C–G–J–K were crashed, the path duration would be 47 weeks. Crashing all activities on B–D–H–J–K results in a duration of 56 weeks. Because the *normal* times of A–I–K, A–F–K, and B–E–J–K are less than the minimum times of the other two paths, we can disregard those three paths; they will never become critical regardless of the crashing we may do.

Stage 1

Step 1: The critical path is B–D–H–J–K.

Step 2: The cheapest activity to crash per week is J at $1,000 which is much less than the savings in indirect and penalty costs of $28,000 per week.

Step 3: Crash activity J by its limit of 3 weeks because the critical path remains unchanged. The new expected path times are

A–C–G–J–K: 64 weeks and B–D–H–J–K: 66 weeks

The net savings are 3($28,000) − 3($1,000) = $81,000. The total project costs are now $2,624,000 − $81,000 = $2,543,000.

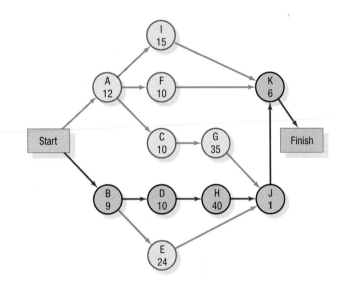

Stage 2

Step 1: The critical path is still B–D–H–J–K.

Step 2: The cheapest activity to crash per week now is D at $2,000.

Step 3: Crash D by 2 weeks. The first week of reduction in activity D saves $28,000 because it eliminates a week of penalty costs, as well as indirect costs. Crashing D by a second week saves only $8,000 in indirect costs because, after week 65, no more penalty costs are incurred. These savings still exceed the cost of crashing D by 2 weeks. Updated path times are

A–C–G–J–K: 64 weeks and B–D–H–J–K: 64 weeks

The net savings are $28,000 + $8,000 − 2($2,000) = $32,000. Total project costs are now $2,543,000 − $32,000 = $2,511,000.

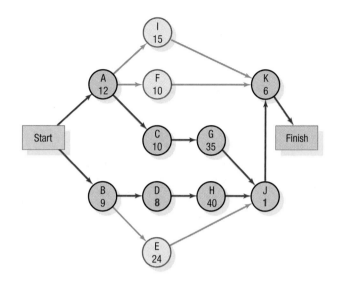

Stage 3

Step 1: After crashing D, we now have two critical paths. *Both* critical paths must now be shortened to realize any savings in indirect project costs. If one is shortened and the other is not, the length of the project remains unchanged.

Step 2: Our alternatives are to crash one of the following combinations of activities—(A, B); (A, H); (C, B); (C, H); (G, B); (G, H)—or to crash activity K, which is on both critical paths (J has already been crashed). We consider only those alternatives for which the cost of crashing is less than the potential savings of $8,000 per week. The only viable alternatives are (C, B) at a cost of $7,600 per week and K at $4,000 per week. We choose activity K to crash.

Step 3: We crash activity K to the greatest extent possible—a reduction of one week—because it is on both critical paths. Updated path times are

A–C–G–J–K: 63 weeks and B–D–H–J–K: 63 weeks

The net savings are $8,000 − $4,000 = $4,000. Total project costs are $2,511,000 − $4,000 = $2,507,000.

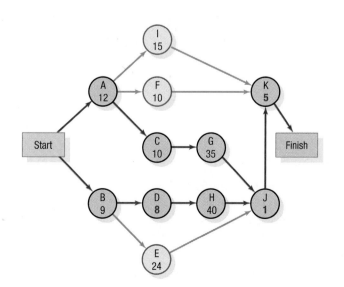

Stage 4

Step 1: The critical paths are B–D–H–J–K and A–C–G–J–K.

Step 2: The only viable alternative at this stage is to crash activities B and C simultaneously at a cost of $7,600 per week. This amount is still less than the savings of $8,000 per week.

Step 3: Crash activities B and C by 2 weeks, the limit for activity B. Updated path times are

A–C–G–J–K: 61 weeks and B–D–H–J–K: 61 weeks

Net savings are 2($8,000) − 2($7,600) = $800. Total project costs are $2,507,000 − $800 = $2,506,200.

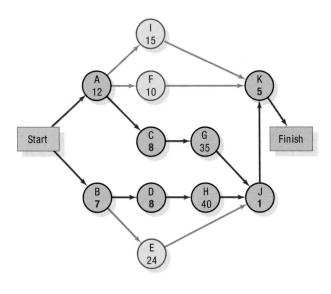

The following table summarizes the analysis.

Stage	Crash Activity	Time Reduction (wks)	Resulting Critical Path(s)	Project Duration (wks)	Project Direct Costs, Last Trial (000)	Crash Cost Added (000)	Total Indirect Costs (000)	Total Penalty Costs (000)	Total Project Costs (000)
0	—	—	BDHJK	69	1,992.0	—	552.0	80.0	2,624.0
1	J	3	BDHJK	66	1,992.0	3.0	528.0	20.0	2,543.0
2	D	2	BDHJK ACGJK	64	1,995.0	4.0	512.0	0.0	2,511.0
3	K	1·	BDHJK ACGJK	63	1,999.0	4.0	504.0	0.0	2,507.0
4	B,C	2·	BDHJK ACGJK	61	2,003.0	15.2	488.0	0.0	2,506.2

Decision Point Because the crash costs exceed weekly indirect costs, any other combination of activities will result in a net increase in total project costs. The minimum-cost schedule is 61 weeks, with a total cost of $2,506,200. To obtain this schedule, the project team must crash activities B, D, J, and K to their limits and activity C to 8 weeks. The other activities remain at their normal times. This schedule costs $117,800 less than the normal-time schedule.

ASSESSING RISKS

Risk is a measure of the probability and consequence of not reaching a defined project goal. Risk involves the notion of uncertainty as it relates to project timing and costs. Often, project teams must deal with uncertainty caused by labor shortages, weather, supply delays, or the outcomes of critical tests. A major responsibility of the project manager at the start of a project is to develop a **risk-management plan**. Team members should have an opportunity to describe the key risks to the project's success and prescribe ways to circumvent them, either by redefining key activities or by developing contingency plans in the event problems occur. A good risk-management plan will quantify the risks and predict their impact on the project. For each risk, the outcome is either acceptable or unacceptable, depending on the project manager's tolerance level for risk. Project risks can be grouped into four categories: strategic fit, service/product attributes, project team capability, and operations.

risk-management plan
A plan that identifies the key risks to a project's success and prescribes ways to circumvent them.

Strategic Fit Projects should be carefully evaluated from a strategic perspective. Regardless of the size of the project, it should have a purpose that supports the strategic goals of the firm. If the connection to the overall strategy is unclear, the project runs the risk of funding falling short of needs as priorities are shifted over time. Using the concept of the project *program*, discussed earlier, is useful for demonstrating the strategic importance of a collection of smaller projects.

Service/Product Attributes If the project involves the introduction of a new service or product, a *market risk* comes from competitors for the service or product. The presence of this risk puts pressure on the market analysis and demand projections that become the basis for the decision to proceed on the project. *Technological risk* may arise from technological advances made once the project has started and render obsolete the technology chosen for the service or product. This risk is prevalent in the telecommunications industry where cell phone technology, for example, is rapidly changing. The danger is that a cell phone product under development may be usurped by a new technology developed by a competitor. *Legal risk*, such as liability suits or environmental legislation, may require change in the design of services or products after development has begun.

Project Team Capability Risks are also associated with the project team itself. We already discussed the selection of the project manager and team and some of the considerations that should be made. Poor selections can compromise the completion of a project. Other factors that affect the riskiness of projects from the perspective of team capability include *project size*, relative to what the team (or the firm) has ever attempted before measured in terms of the budget, *project complexity*, relative to the number of different entities (internal and external) that must be coordinated, and *technological experience*, relative to the technologies required to design a service or product or to implement the project.

Operations The risks associated with operations are affected by *information accuracy*, relative to the completeness of the work breakdown schedule and all data required for assessing progress, completion times of activities, and costs; *communication*, relative to timely reporting of progress and action items and issues that need to be resolved to project stakeholders and team members; and *activity completion and timing*, relative to the challenge of managing the project with uncertainty in the estimates for the activity times.

These risks should be identified and the significant ones should have contingency plans in case something goes wrong. The more risky a project is, the more likely the project will experience difficulties as Managerial Practice 3.2 shows.

PERT/CPM networks can be used to quantify risks associated with project timing. Often, the uncertainty associated with an activity can be reflected in the activity's time duration. For example, an activity in a new product development project might be developing the enabling technology to manufacture it, an activity that may take from eight months to a year. To incorporate uncertainty into the network model, probability distributions of activity times can be calculated using two approaches: computer simulation and statistical analysis. With simulation, the time for each activity is randomly chosen from its probability distribution (see Supplement B, "Simulation"). The critical path of the network is determined and the completion date of the project computed. The procedure is repeated many times, which results in a probability distribution for the completion date.

Boston, Massachusetts, has many noteworthy attractions: the world champion Boston Red Sox baseball team, the Freedom Trail, depicting many historic buildings and sights dating back to the 1600s, and the most ambitious road infrastructure project attempted in the United States. The six-lane elevated highway that ran through the center of town was designed for 75,000 cars per day but was forced to accommodate close to 200,000 cars per day. The highway was congested for 10 hours a day; it was expected to increase to 16 hours a day by 2010. It was costing residents and businesses $500 million a year in accidents, fuel, and late delivery charges.

Solving the traffic problem would take more than adding a few more lanes to the existing highway, which was built in 1953 and whose elevated superstructure was rapidly deteriorating. Rather than fixing the old highway, the decision was made to build an eight-to-ten-lane underground highway directly beneath the existing road, culminating at the north end of town in a 14-lane, two-bridge crossing of the Charles River. On the south end, a four-lane tunnel was built under South Boston and the Boston Harbor to Logan Airport, leaving no doubt how the project got its "Big Dig" nickname; the project spans 7.8 miles of highway with half in tunnels under a major city and harbor!

To get some perspective of the size and complexity of this project, it required 3.8 million cubic yards of concrete, enough to cover 2,350 acres, 1 foot thick. Over 16 million cubic yards of dirt were excavated, enough to fill the New England Patriots' football stadium 16 times. The undertaking required 109 construction contracts involving many of New England's biggest construction firms. More than 5,000 construction employees were employed at its peak. To control traffic once the project was completed, a highly advanced Smart Highways system was installed that included 1,400 loop detectors to measure traffic density and identify traffic patterns, 430 TV cameras, 130 electronic message signboards, and 300 control signals and carbon monoxide detectors. To add to the complexity, the city had to remain open for business during the project; traffic capacity had to be maintained and businesses and residences had to remain accessible. The project had to work around subway tunnels and underground steam pipes. Planning for the project began in 1983, construction began in 1991, and in 2005 almost the entire project was complete, except for repair work.

Was the project successful? The answer might depend on whom you ask. The residents of Boston have a much more efficient transportation network that will allow for growth for many years into the future. The project makes downtown Boston much more aesthetically pleasing, with 150 acres of prime land, freed up with the demolition of the old elevated highway system, that can be used for cultural events, gathering places, and parks. However, from a project management perspective, it missed the three goals of every project: on time, under budget, and meet the specifications. The Big Dig was five years late (originally scheduled for completion in 1998), more than $10 billion over the budget (originally projected to be about $4 billion in today's dollars), and required significant repairs for leaks shortly after the tunnels were opened. Since the project was funded with

A great deal of controversy surrounds the "Big Dig," a massive highway tunnel built under the city of Boston and Boston Harbor. By the time the Big Dig was completed, it was over budget, late, and did not meet the specification—in part, because no one had ever undertaken such a complex project before.

taxpayer dollars, it is no wonder that the project is the subject of much debate and controversy.

Why did this project experience problems? The Big Dig is an example of a risky project, not because of doubt that it would ever be finished, but because it was huge and complex. It was called one of the most complex and controversial engineering projects in human history, rivaling the likes of the Panama Canal, the English Channel Tunnel, and the Trans-Alaska Pipeline. The project included two major tunnels and the world's largest ventilation system, four major highway interchanges, a two-bridge 14-lane crossing of the Charles River, the world's most advanced traffic management system, and the development of parks and open space. Project managers held many meetings with environmental and permitting agencies, community groups, businesses, and political leaders to gain consensus on how the project would be built. Because of meetings such as these the project scope was modified over time, thereby causing the project plan to change. From an operational perspective, most of the construction companies involved in the project had never done anything of this size and scope before and had difficulty providing good time estimates for their pieces of the project. Delays and cost overruns were inevitable. Further, quality was difficult to achieve because so many contractors were involved in such a complex project. Projects of this size and complexity are inherently risky; contingency plans should cover the most likely disruptions. Schedule and budget problems are not unusual; however, the job of project managers is to manage the risks and minimize the deviations.

Source: www.massturnpike.com/bigdig/updates (2005); Seth Stern, "$14.6 Billion Later, Boston's Big Dig Wraps Up," *Christian Science Monitor* (December 19, 2003); "The Big Dig, Boston, MA, USA," www.roadtraffic-technology.com (2005); "Big Dig Tunnel Is Riddled with Leaks," *Associated Press,* http://abcnews.go.com (November 19, 2004); Michael Roth, "Boston Digs the Big Dig," *Rental Equipment Register* (November 1, 2000), http://rermag.com/ar (2005).

The statistical analysis approach requires that activity times be stated in terms of three reasonable time estimates:

1. The **optimistic time (*a*)** is the shortest time in which an activity can be completed, if all goes exceptionally well.
2. The **most likely time (*m*)** is the probable time required to perform an activity.
3. The **pessimistic time (*b*)** is the longest estimated time required to perform an activity.

In the remainder of this section, we will discuss how to calculate activity statistics using these three time estimates and how to analyze project risk using probabilities.

Calculating Time Statistics   With three time estimates—the optimistic, the most likely, and the pessimistic—the project manager has enough information to estimate the probability that an activity will be completed on schedule. To do so, the project manager must first calculate the mean and variance of a probability distribution for each activity. In PERT/CPM, each activity time is treated as though it were a random variable derived from a beta probability distribution. This distribution can have various shapes, allowing the most likely time estimate (*m*) to fall anywhere between the pessimistic (*b*) and optimistic (*a*) time estimates. The most likely time estimate is the *mode* of the beta distribution, or the time with the highest probability of occurrence. This condition is not possible with the normal distribution, which is symmetrical, because the normal distribution requires the mode to be equidistant from the end points of the distribution. Figure 3.9 shows the difference between the two distributions.

Two key assumptions are required. First, we assume that *a*, *m*, and *b* can be estimated accurately. The estimates might best be considered values that define a reasonable time range for the activity duration negotiated between the project manager and the team members responsible for the activities. Second, we assume that the standard deviation, σ, of the activity time is one-sixth the range *b* − *a*. Thus, the chance that actual activity times will fall between *a* and *b* is high. Why does this assumption make sense? If the activity time followed the normal distribution, six standard deviations would span approximately 99.74 percent of the distribution.

Even with these assumptions, derivation of the mean and variance of each activity's probability distribution is complex. These derivations show that the mean of the beta distribution can be estimated by using the following weighted average of the three time estimates:

$$t_e = \frac{a + 4m + b}{6}$$

optimistic time (*a*)

The shortest time in which an activity can be completed, if all goes exceptionally well.

most likely time (*m*)

The probable time required to perform an activity.

pessimistic time (*b*)

The longest estimated time required to perform an activity.

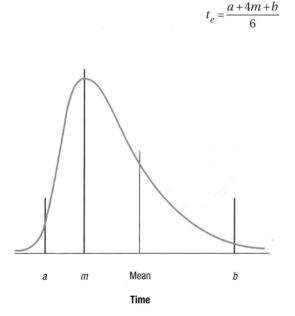

(a) Beta distribution: The most likely time (*m*) has the highest probability and can be placed anywhere between the optimistic (*a*) and pessimistic (*b*) times.

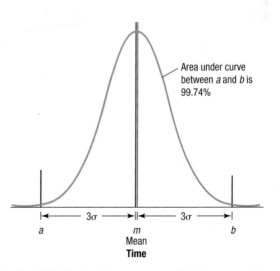

(b) Normal distribution: The mean and most likely times must be the same. If *a* and *b* are chosen to be 6σ apart, there is a 99.74% chance that the actual activity time will fall between them.

FIGURE 3.9 | Differences Between Beta and Normal Distributions for Project Analysis

Note that the most likely time has four times the weight of the pessimistic and optimistic estimates.

The variance of the beta distribution for each activity is

$$\sigma^2 = \left(\frac{b-a}{6} \right)^2$$

The variance, which is the standard deviation squared, increases as the difference between b and a increases. This result implies that the less certain a person is in estimating the actual time for an activity, the greater will be the variance.

EXAMPLE 3.5	**Calculating Means and Variances**

Suppose that the project team has arrived at the following time estimates for activity B (site selection and survey) of the St. Adolf's Hospital project:

$$a = 7 \text{ weeks}, \; m = 8 \text{ weeks, and } b = 15 \text{ weeks}$$

a. Calculate the expected time for activity B and the variance.

b. Calculate the expected time and variance for the other activities in the project.

SOLUTION

a. The expected time for activity B is

$$t_e = \frac{7 + 4(8) + 15}{6} = \frac{54}{6} = 9 \text{ weeks}$$

Note that the expected time (9 weeks) does not equal the most likely time (8 weeks) for this activity. These times will be the same only when the most likely time is equidistant from the optimistic and pessimistic times. We calculate the variance for activity B as

$$\sigma^2 = \left(\frac{15-7}{6} \right)^2 = \left(\frac{8}{6} \right)^2 = 1.78$$

b. The following table shows expected activity times and variances for the activities listed in the project description.

	Time Estimates (wk)			Activity Statistics	
Activity	**Optimistic** **(a)**	**Most Likely** **(m)**	**Pessimistic** **(b)**	**Expected** **Time (t_e)**	**Variance** **(σ^2)**
A	11	12	13	12	0.11
B	7	8	15	9	1.78
C	5	10	15	10	2.78
D	8	9	16	10	1.78
E	14	25	30	24	7.11
F	6	9	18	10	4.00
G	25	36	41	35	7.11
H	35	40	45	40	2.78
I	10	13	28	15	9.00
J	1	2	15	4	5.44
K	5	6	7	6	0.11

Decision Point The project team should notice that the greatest uncertainty lies in the time estimate for activity I, followed by the estimates for activities E and G. These activities should be analyzed for the source of the uncertainties and actions should be taken to reduce the variance in the time estimates. For example, activity I, developing an information system, may entail the use of a consulting firm. The availability of the consulting firm for the time period scheduled for activity I may be in doubt because of the firm's other commitments. To reduce the risk of delay in the project, the project team could explore the availability of other reputable firms or scale down the requirements for the information system and undertake much of that activity themselves.

Analyzing Probabilities Because time estimates for activities involve uncertainty, project managers are interested in determining the probability of meeting project completion deadlines. To develop the probability distribution for project completion time, we assume that the duration time of one activity does not depend on that of any other activity. This assumption enables us to estimate the mean and variance of the probability distribution of the time duration of the entire project by summing the duration times and variances of the activities along the critical path. However, if one work crew is assigned two activities that can be done at the same time, the activity times will be interdependent. In addition, if other paths in the network have small amounts of slack, one of them might become the critical path before the project is completed. In such a case, we should calculate a probability distribution for those paths.

Because of the assumption that the activity duration times are independent random variables, we can make use of the central limit theorem, which states that the sum of a group of independent, identically distributed random variables approaches a normal distribution as the number of random variables increases. The mean of the normal distribution is the sum of the expected activity times on the path. In the case of the critical path, it is the earliest expected finish time for the project:

$T_E = \Sigma$ (Expected activity times on the critical path) = Mean of normal distribution

Similarly, because of the assumption of activity time independence, we use the sum of the variances of the activities along the path as the variance of the time distribution for that path. That is, for the critical path,

$\sigma^2 = \Sigma$ (Variances of activities on the critical path)

To analyze probabilities of completing a project by a certain date using the normal distribution, we use the z-transformation formula:

$$z = \frac{T - T_E}{\sqrt{\sigma^2}}$$

where

$T =$ due date for the project

Given the value of z, we use the Normal Distribution appendix to find the probability that the project will be completed by time T, or sooner. An implicit assumption in this approach is that no other path will become critical during the time span of the project.

The procedure for assessing the probability of completing any activity in a project by a specific date is similar to the one just discussed. However, instead of the critical path, we would use the longest time path of activities from the start node to the activity node in question.

Near-Critical Paths A project's duration is a function of its critical path. However, paths that are close to the same duration as the critical path may ultimately become the critical path over the life of the project. In practice, at the start of the project managers typically do not know the activity times with certainty and may never know which path was the critical path until the actual activity times are known at the end of the project. Nonetheless, this uncertainty does not reduce the usefulness of identifying the probability of one path or another causing a project to exceed its target completion time; it helps to identify the activities that need close management attention. To assess the chances of near critical paths delaying the project completion, we can focus on the longest paths in the project network keeping in mind that both duration and variance along the path must be considered. Shorter paths with high variances could have just as much a chance to delay the project as a longer paths with smaller variances. We can then estimate the probability that each path will exceed the project target completion time. We demonstrate that approach using statistical analysis in Example 3.6. Alternatively, simulation can be used to estimate the probabilities. The advantage of simulation is that you are not restricted to the use of the beta distribution for activity times. Also, activity or path dependencies, such as decision points that could involve different groups of activities to be undertaken, can be incorporated in a simulation model much more easily than with the statistical analysis approach. Fortunately, regardless of the approach used, it is rarely necessary to evaluate every path in the network. In large networks, many paths will have both short durations and low variances, making them unlikely to affect the project duration.

EXAMPLE 3.6	Calculating the Probability of Completing a Project by a Given Date

Calculate the probability that St. Adolf's Hospital will become operational in 72 weeks, using (a) the critical path and (b) path A–C–G–J–K.

ACTIVE MODEL 3.3

Active Model 3.3 on the Student CD-ROM provides additional insight on probability analysis for the St. Adolf's Hospital project.

SOLUTION

a. The critical path B–D–H–J–K has a length of 69 weeks. From the table in Example 3.5, we obtain the variance of path B–D–H–J–K: $\sigma^2 = 1.78 + 1.78 + 2.78 + 5.44 + 0.11 = 11.89$. Next, we calculate the z-value:

$$z = \frac{72-69}{\sqrt{11.89}} = \frac{3}{3.45} = 0.87$$

Using the Normal Distribution appendix, we go down the left-hand column until we arrive at the value 0.8, and then across until we arrive at the 0.07 column, which shows a tabular value of 0.8078. Consequently, we find that the probability is about 0.81 that the length of path B–D–H–J–K will be no greater than 72 weeks. Because this path is the critical path, there is a 19 percent probability that the project will take longer than 72 weeks. This probability is shown graphically in Figure 3.10.

b. From the table in Example 3.5, we determine that the sum of the expected activity times on path A–C–G–J–K is 67 weeks and that $\sigma^2 = 0.11 + 2.78 + 7.11 + 5.44 + 0.11 = 15.55$. The z-value is

$$z = \frac{72-67}{\sqrt{15.55}} = \frac{5}{3.94} = 1.27$$

The probability is about 0.90 that the length of path A–C–G–J–K will be no greater than 72 weeks.

Decision Point The project team should be aware of the 10 percent chance that path A–C–G–J–K will cause a delay in the project. Although the probability is not high for that path, activities A, C, and G bear watching during the first 57 weeks of the project to make sure no more than 2 weeks of slippage occurs in their schedules. This attention is especially important for activity G, which has a high time variance.

FIGURE 3.10

Probability of Completing the St. Adolf's Hospital Project on Schedule

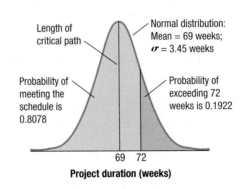

> CRITICAL CHAIN <

Cost–time trade-offs and project uncertainties are two important issues project managers must address, but resource availability is an underlying factor that drives cost and performance to promised due dates. Human resources, in particular, bring a behavioral dimension to the management of projects that affect schedules and performance. Eliyahu Goldratt, in his book *Critical Chain* (1997), addresses the problem of constrained resources and how project managers can overcome the common problems of poor project performance.[3]

RESOURCE-RELATED PROBLEMS

Goldratt identifies six problems related to resource limitations and human behavior that are not addressed adequately by traditional project management techniques.

1. *Excessive Activity Duration Estimates.* When asked how long their activity will take, most people reply with an estimate that gives them a high chance of beating. The problem is that each activity will have a built-in cushion that management will not realize until after the activity has been completed.

2. *Latest Date Mentality.* Employees tend to wait until the last moment before initiating the work to complete an activity. Sound familiar? Goldratt calls this mentality the *student syndrome* after students who wait until the end of the semester to do all of their term papers. The student syndrome coupled with the excessive time estimates unduly causes projects to take longer than they should.

3. *Failure to Deliver Early.* Even if work is completed before the latest finish date, it is often not passed on to the next activity until the scheduled date. Many possible reasons explain why employees do not like to finish early, including not being able to charge all of their scheduled time to the project or taking more time to make sure everything is in order. The problem is that slack time is consumed and late finishes on some activities are not counterbalanced against early finishes elsewhere. The whole project slips behind schedule.

4. *Path Mergers.* A path merger occurs when two or more activity paths combine at a particular node in a project network. Suppose that two paths converge on node 10, which initiates the start of another series of activities. All merging paths of work must be completed before the activities starting with node 10 can begin. The merging of paths reduces any built-up slack in the paths because the path with the longest delay dominates the schedule of the activities at node 10. Path mergers are another source of project delay.

5. *Multitasking.* Managers are rarely fortunate enough to be working on only one project at a time. Most managers must allocate their time across several ongoing projects. Multitasking is the performance of multiple project activities at the same time. Intuitively, multitasking is thought to be a way to keep all projects going forward. What manager would want to be blamed for a project delay because they were not working on it? However, multitasking can actually contribute to project delay. Suppose a manager is involved in four projects and that each project will take 1 day of his time if he devotes his full attention to it. Consider one of those projects. With multitasking, the manager's time estimate for that activity would be four days, rather than one day, to account for the multitasking. If the manager had focused on that activity for one day, the project could have moved forward rather than waiting for the added three days. In this example, all four project durations are extended because of multitasking.

6. *Loss of Focus.* Projects can also be delayed when the project manager loses focus, which can happen if the critical path changes frequently. Standard project scheduling methods allow the project critical path to change as actual activity times deviate from estimated times.

---

[3]The *Critical Chain* applies an approach called the Theory of Constraints (TOC) to project management. We address TOC in Chapter 6 when we discuss the issue of bottlenecks in processes. See also the informative article by Larry P. Leach, "Critical Chain Project Management Improves Project Performance," *Project Management Journal* (June 1999), pp. 39–51.

THE CRITICAL CHAIN APPROACH

The critical chain approach addresses these six problems by improving the time estimates for activities, redefining the concept of a critical path to include resources, incorporating time buffers in the project work breakdown structure, scheduling activities according to the latest start schedule, and controlling the behavioral aspects of the project.

Time Estimates The critical chain approach asks activity time estimators to first provide a "low risk" time estimate for the project activity, which would be akin to the "pessimistic" time estimate (b) we used in our analysis of time estimates earlier. Next, the estimator is asked for the "most likely" time estimate (m), assuming everything went as they hoped it would and they were able to devote 100 percent of their time once they started on the activity. Use the *most likely* time estimates to build the critical chain project plan and use the difference ($b - m$) to develop the project time buffers.

critical chain
The sequence of dependent events that prevents the project from completing in a shorter interval and recognizes resource as well as activity dependencies.

Critical Chain Goldratt defined the **critical chain** to be the sequence of dependent events that prevents the project from completing in a shorter interval and recognizes resource as well as activity dependencies. Identifying the critical chain requires good activity time estimates as well as an assignment of resources to activities. During this analysis resources that are overloaded can be identified. The resource constraints most often are people; however, they could also be physical limitations or policies. The critical chain extends the concept of the critical path by recognizing resource limitations and provides the focus for applying project time buffers.

Buffers Once the critical chain and all of the paths feeding the critical chain are identified, time buffers can be added to the network to protect the critical chain. The difference in activity time estimates, ($b-m$), can be used to develop *feeder buffers* at the point where each feeder path interfaces with the critical chain. Likewise, at the end of the critical chain, a *project buffer* can be added. The time buffers can be treated as "activities" in the project network. The advantage of this approach is that the time buffers, which are an accumulation of the slack along a path, are located in isolated places in the network rather than at individual activities as activity slack. Management can focus on these time buffers to monitor project progress.

Latest Start Schedules Using latest start schedules has the advantages of delaying project cash outlays and recognizing the "student syndrome" in the planning of projects. The feeder and project time buffers provide the protection project managers need to avoid delays because of activities taking longer than their most likely time estimate.

Project Control Managers using the critical chain approach must control the behavioral aspects of their projects. First, managers should seek to minimize the practice of multitasking because it affects the estimates of the activity times and can delay projects. The manager must develop an environment where date-driven behavior is eliminated. That is, employees should not be criticized for time overruns if they started the activity on schedule, worked 100 percent on it, and passed on the output as soon as it was ready. The project buffers should cover the overruns. Second, managers should focus on the management of the feeder and project buffers on a periodic basis. Management can set critical buffer levels that, when they are reached, initiate action to remedy any problems. Finally, indiscriminately adding more projects to the portfolio can cause problems. Projects should be added and scheduled on the basis of the load on the critical resources.

> MONITORING AND CONTROLLING PROJECTS <

Once project planning is over, the challenge becomes keeping the project on schedule within the budget of allocated resources. In this section, we discuss how to monitor project status and resource usage. In addition, we identify the features of project management software useful for monitoring and controlling projects.

MONITORING PROJECT STATUS

A good tracking system will help the project team accomplish its project goals. Often, the very task of monitoring project progress motivates the team as it sees the benefits of its planning efforts come to fruition. It also focuses attention on the decisions that must be made as the project unfolds. Effective tracking systems collect information on three topics: open issues, risks, and schedule status.

Open Issues and Risks One of the duties of the project manager is to make sure that issues that have been raised during the project actually get resolved in a timely fashion. The tracking system should remind the project manager of due dates for open issues and who was responsible for seeing that they are resolved. Likewise, it should provide the status of each risk to project delays specified in the risk management plan, so that the team can review them at each meeting. The project manager should also enter new issues or risks into the system as they arise. To be effective, the tracking system requires team members to update information periodically regarding their respective responsibilities. Although the tracking system can be computerized, it can also be as simple as using e-mail, voice mail, or meetings to convey the necessary information.

Schedule Status Even the best laid project plans can go awry. Monitoring slack time in the project schedule can help the project manager control activities along the critical path. Suppose in the hospital project that activity A is completed in 16 weeks rather than the antici-pated 12 weeks and that activity B takes 10 weeks instead of the expected 9 weeks. Table 3.2 shows how these delays affect slack times as of the sixteenth week of the project. Activities A and B are not shown because they have already been completed.

Negative slack occurs when the assumptions used to compute planned slack are invalid. Activities C, G, J, and K, which depend on the timely completion of activities A and B, show negative slack because they have been pushed beyond their planned latest start dates. The activities at the top of Table 3.2 are more critical than those at the bottom because they are the furthest behind schedule and affect the completion time of the entire project. To meet the original completion target of week 69, the project manager must try to make up two weeks of time somewhere along path C–G–J–K. Moreover, one week will have to be made up along path D–H. If that time is made up, two critical paths are the result: C–G–J–K and D–H–J–K. Many project managers work with computer scheduling programs that generate slack reports like the one shown in Table 3.2.

MONITORING PROJECT RESOURCES

The principles of the critical chain have shown that the resources allocated to a project are consumed at an uneven rate that is a function of the timing of the schedules for the project's activities. Projects have a *life cycle* that consists of four major phases: (1) definition and orga-nization, (2) planning, (3) execution, and (4) close out. Figure 3.11 shows that each of the four phases requires different resource commitments.

We have already discussed the activities associated with the project definition and orga-nization and project planning phases. The phase that takes the most resources is the *execution phase,* during which managers focus on activities pertaining to deliverables. The project schedule becomes very important because it shows when each resource devoted to a given activity will be required. Monitoring the progress of activities throughout the project is

TABLE 3.2	Slack Calculations After Activities A and B Have Been Completed			
Activity	**Duration**	**Earliest Start**	**Latest Start**	**Slack**
C	10	16	14	−2
G	35	26	24	−2
J	4	61	59	−2
K	6	65	63	−2
D	10	10	9	−1
H	40	20	19	−1
E	24	10	35	25
I	15	16	48	32
F	10	16	53	37

FIGURE **3.11**

Project Life Cycle

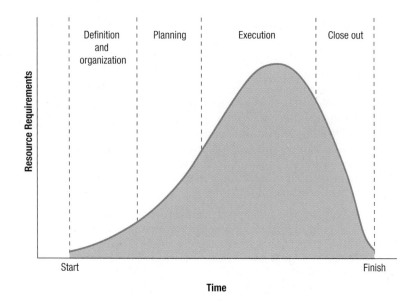

important to avoid potential overloading of resources. Problems arise when a specific resource, such as a construction crew or staff specialist, is required on several activities with overlapping schedules. Project managers have several options to alleviate resource problems, including the following:

■ *Resource Leveling.* The attempt to reduce the peaks and valleys in resource needs by shifting the schedules of conflicting activities within their earliest and latest start dates. Software packages such as MS Project have algorithms that move activities to avoid violating resource constraints. However, if an activity must be delayed beyond its latest start date, the completion date of the total project will be delayed unless activities on the critical path can be reduced to compensate. The crashing techniques or the project buffering approaches we have discussed might help to bring the project in on time, but the possibility of added costs must be considered.

■ *Resource Allocation.* The assignment of resources to the most important activities. Most popular project management software packages have a few priority rules that can be used to decide which activity a critical resource should be scheduled to perform when conflicts arise. For example, for all the activities requiring a given resource, assign the resource to the one with the earliest start time. Other priority rules are available, such as the "latest start time," which is recommended by Eliyu Goldratt to recognize the "student syndrome." The project manager could also move employees to other tasks even if they were not originally assigned to them. A slack report, such as the one in Table 3.2, identifies potential candidates for resource shifting. However, efficiency can be compromised if shifted employees do not have all the skills required for their new assignments.

■ *Resource Acquisition.* The addition of more of an overloaded resource to maintain the schedule of an activity. Obviously, this tactic is constrained by the project budget.

CONTROLLING PROJECTS

Project managers have the responsibilities of accounting for the effective use of the firm's resources as well as managing the activities to achieve the time and quality goals of the project. The firm's assets include the physical assets, human resources, and financial resources. Physical assets are controlled by the timely maintenance of machines and equipment so that their failure does not delay the project. Inventories must be received, stored for future use, and replenished. Project managers are also responsible for human resource development. Projects provide a rich environment to develop future leaders; project managers can take advantage of the situation by assigning team members important tasks to aid in their managerial development. Last, but not least, project managers must control the expenditures of the firm's financial resources. Most project management software packages contain accounting reports, budget reports, capital investment controls, and cash flow reports. Deviations from the project plan, often referred to as variances, must be periodically reported and analyzed for their causes.

Project managers can exert control over the achievement of the project's time and quality goals by monitoring the project status and project resources, as we have discussed. Unacceptable project progress can trigger leveling, allocation, or acquisition decisions. A key is knowing when to take action. Three measures can be used to guide project managers.[4] *Earned value* (EV) of a project is the budgeted cost of the work actually completed to date. It is calculated by multiplying the budgeted cost of each activity by its percentage of completion and summing all activities in the project. *Actual cost* (AC) is the actual cost of the work performed to date. Finally, *planned cost* (PC) is the budgeted cost of the work that was scheduled to have been completed to date in the original project plan. These measures can be used to calculate two indices for assessing project progress as of a particular date:

$$\text{Cost Performance Index (CPI)} = EV/AC$$

$$\text{Schedule Performance Index (SPI)} = EV/PC$$

The CPI tells you how actual project expenditures relate to the original project budget. The SPI tells you whether progress on the project's many activities is ahead or behind the project plan. The critical value for each index is 1.0. Values less than 1.0 are undesirable and, if low enough, would trigger action.

For example, suppose that as of today your project has EV = $14,000, AC = $20,000, and PC = $19,000. Consequently,

$$CPI = \$14,000/\$20,000 = 0.70$$

$$SPI = \$14,000/\$19,000 = 0.74$$

The indices tell you that you have spent more than the original project plan allowed and, for the amount that you have spent so far, you have not progressed very well in the project schedule. This revelation would prompt you to reexamine your resource decisions to see why the schedule has slipped and review the expenditure history to see why project costs are exceeding the planned costs for the progress so far.

Monitoring and controlling projects are ongoing activities throughout the execution phase of the project life cycle. The project **close out**, however, is an activity that many project managers forget to include in their consideration of resource usage. The purpose of this final phase in the project life cycle is to write final reports and complete remaining deliverables. An important aspect of this phase, however, is compiling the team's recommendations for improving the project process of which they were a part. Many team members will be assigned to other projects where they can apply what they learned.

close out
An activity that includes writing final reports, completing remaining deliverables, and compiling the team's recommendations for improving the project process.

> STUDENT CD-ROM AND INTERNET RESOURCES <

The Student CD-ROM and the Companion Website at **www.prenhall.com/krajewski** contain many tools, activities, and resources designed for this chapter.

> KEY EQUATIONS <

1. Start and finish times:

ES = max (EF times of all activities immediately preceding activity)

EF = ES + t

LS = LF − t

LF = min (LS times of all activities immediately following activity)

2. Activity slack:

S = LS − ES or S = LF − EF

[4]For more information on controlling projects, see Samuel J. Mantel et al., *Project Management in Practice,* 2d ed. (Hoboken, NJ: John Wiley & Sons, 2005).

3. Project costs:

$$\text{Crash cost per unit of time} = \frac{\text{Crash cost} - \text{Normal cost}}{\text{Normal time} - \text{Crash time}}$$

$$= \frac{CC - NC}{NT - CT}$$

4. Activity time statistics:

$$t_e = \frac{a + 4m + b}{6} \text{ (Expected activity time)}$$

$$\sigma^2 = \left(\frac{b - a}{6}\right)^2 \text{ (Variance)}$$

5. z-transformation formula:

$$z = \frac{T - T_E}{\sqrt{\sigma^2}}$$

where

T = due date for the project

T_E = (expected activity times on the critical path)

= mean of normal distribution

$\sigma^2 = \Sigma$(variances of activities on the critical path)

> KEY TERMS <

activity 75
activity-on-node (AON) network 77
activity slack 79
close out 101
crash cost (CC) 86
crash time (CT) 86
critical chain 98
critical path 79
critical path method (CPM) 76
earliest finish time (EF) 80
earliest start time (ES) 80

free slack 82
Gantt chart 82
latest finish time (LF) 80
latest start time (LS) 80
minimum-cost schedule 87
most likely time (m) 93
network diagram 76
normal cost (NC) 86
normal time (NT) 86
optimistic time (a) 93
path 79

pessimistic time (b) 93
precedence relationship 77
program 71
program evaluation and review technique (PERT) 76
project 70
project management 71
risk-management plan 91
total slack 82
work breakdown structure (WBS) 75

> SOLVED PROBLEM 1 <

Your company has just received an order from a good customer for a specially designed electric motor. The contract states that, starting on the thirteenth day from now, your firm will experience a penalty of $100 per day until the job is completed. Indirect project costs amount to $200 per day. The data on direct costs and activity precedence relationships are given in Table 3.3.

a. Draw the project network diagram.

b. What completion date would you recommend?

TABLE 3.3		Electric Motor Project Data			
Activity	**Normal Time (days)**	**Normal Cost ($)**	**Crash Time (days)**	**Crash Cost ($)**	**Immediate Predecessor(s)**
A	4	1,000	3	1,300	None
B	7	1,400	4	2,000	None
C	5	2,000	4	2,700	None
D	6	1,200	5	1,400	A
E	3	900	2	1,100	B
F	11	2,500	6	3,750	C
G	4	800	3	1,450	D, E
H	3	300	1	500	F, G

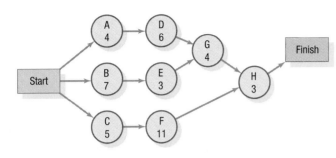

FIGURE **3.12**

Network Diagram for the Electric
Motor Project

SOLUTION

a. The network diagram, including normal activity times, for this procedure is shown in Figure 3.12. Keep the following points in mind while constructing a network diagram.

1. Always have start and finish nodes.

2. Try to avoid crossing paths to keep the diagram simple.

3. Use only one arrow to directly connect any two nodes.

4. Put the activities with no predecessors at the left and point the arrows from left to right.

5. Be prepared to revise the diagram several times before you come up with a correct and uncluttered diagram.

b. With these activity durations, the project will be completed in 19 days and incur a $700 penalty. Determining a good completion date requires the use of the minimum-cost schedule procedure. Using the data provided in Table 3.3, you can determine the maximum crash-time reduction and crash cost per day for each activity. For example, for activity A

$$\text{Maximum crash time} = \text{Normal time} - \text{Crash time} =$$
$$4\,\text{days} - 3\,\text{days} = 1\,\text{day}$$

$$\frac{\text{Crash cost}}{\text{per day}} = \frac{\text{Crash cost} - \text{Normal cost}}{\text{Normal time} - \text{Crash time}} = \frac{CC - NC}{NT - CT} =$$
$$\frac{\$1,300 - \$1,000}{4\,\text{days} - 3\,\text{days}} = \$300$$

Activity	Crash Cost per Day ($)	Maximum Time Reduction (days)
A	300	1
B	200	3
C	700	1
D	200	1
E	200	1
F	250	5
G	650	1
H	100	2

Table 3.4 summarizes the analysis and the resultant project duration and total cost. The critical path is C–F–H at 19 days, which is the longest path in the network. The cheapest of these activities to crash is H, which costs only an extra $100 per day to crash. Doing so saves $200 + $100 = $300 per day in indirect and penalty costs. If you crash this activity two days (the maximum), the lengths of the paths are now

A–D–G–H: 15 days, B–E–G–H: 15 days, and C–F–H: 17 days

The critical path is still C–F–H. The next cheapest critical activity to crash is F at $250 per day. You can crash F only two days because at that point you will have three critical paths. Further reductions in project duration will require simultaneous

---

TABLE 3.4 | Project Cost Analysis

Stage	Crash Activity	Time Reduction (days)	Resulting Critical Path(s)	Project Duration (days)	Project Direct Costs, Last Trial	Crash Cost Added	Total Indirect Costs	Total Penalty Costs	Total Project Costs
0	—	—	C–F–H	19	$10,100	—	$3,800	$700	$14,600
1	H	2	C–F–H	17	$10,100	$200	$3,400	$500	$14,200
2	F	2	A–D–G–H B–E–G–H C–F–H	15	$10,300	$500	$3,000	$300	$14,100

crashing of more than one activity (D, E, and F). The cost to do so, $650, exceeds the savings, $300. Consequently, you should stop. Note that every activity is critical. The project costs are minimized when the completion date is day 15. However, some goodwill costs may be associated with disappointing a customer who wants delivery in 12 days.

> SOLVED PROBLEM 2 <

An advertising project manager developed the network diagram shown in Figure 3.13 for a new advertising campaign. In addition, the manager gathered the time information for each activity, as shown in the accompanying table.

	Time Estimates (wk)			
Activity	**Optimistic**	**Most Likely**	**Pessimistic**	**Immediate Predecessor(s)**
A	1	4	7	—
B	2	6	7	—
C	3	3	6	B
D	6	13	14	A
E	3	6	12	A, C
F	6	8	16	B
G	1	5	6	E, F

a. Calculate the expected time and variance for each activity.

b. Calculate the activity slacks and determine the critical path, using the expected activity times.

c. What is the probability of completing the project within 23 weeks?

SOLUTION

a. The expected time and variance for each activity are calculated as follows:

$$t_e = \frac{a+4m+b}{6}$$

Activity	Expected Time (wk)	Variance
A	4.0	1.00
B	5.5	0.69
C	3.5	0.25
D	12.0	1.78
E	6.5	2.25
F	9.0	2.78
G	4.5	0.69

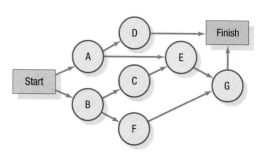

FIGURE **3.13** | Network Diagram for an Advertising Project

b. We need to calculate the earliest start, latest start, earliest finish, and latest finish times for each activity. Starting with activities A and B, we proceed from the beginning of the network and move to the end, calculating the earliest start and finish times:

Activity	Earliest Start (wk)	Earliest Finish (wk)
A	0	0 + 4.0 = 4.0
B	0	0 + 5.5 = 5.5
C	5.5	5.5 + 3.5 = 9.0
D	4.0	4.0 + 12.0 = 16.0
E	9.0	9.0 + 6.5 = 15.5
F	5.5	5.5 + 9.0 = 14.5
G	15.5	15.5 + 4.5 = 20.0

Based on expected times, the earliest finish for the project is week 20, when activity G has been completed. Using that as a target date, we can work backward through the network, calculating the latest start and finish times (shown graphically in Figure 3.14):

Activity	Latest Start (wk)	Latest Finish (wk)
G	15.5	20.0
F	6.5	15.5
E	9.0	15.5
D	8.0	20.0
C	5.5	9.0
B	0.0	5.5
A	4.0	8.0

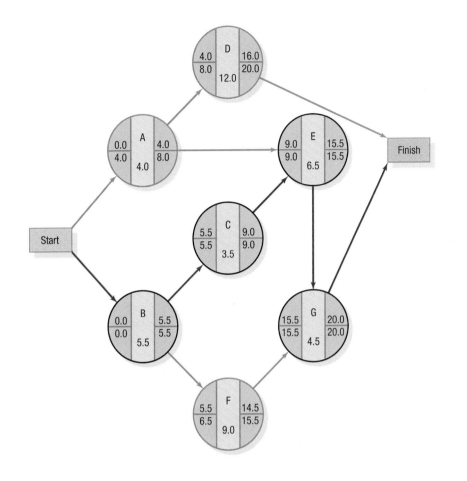

FIGURE **3.14**

Network Diagram with All Time
Estimates Needed to Calculate Slack

We now calculate the activity slacks and determine which activities are on the critical path:

Activity	Start Earliest	Start Latest	Finish Earliest	Finish Latest	Total Slack	Free Slack	Critical Path
A	0.0	4.0	4.0	8.0	4.0	0.0	No
B	0.0	0.0	5.5	5.5	0.0	0.0	Yes
C	5.5	5.5	9.0	9.0	0.0	0.0	Yes
D	4.0	8.0	16.0	20.0	4.0	4.0	No
E	9.0	9.0	15.5	15.5	0.0	0.0	Yes
F	5.5	6.5	14.5	15.5	1.0	1.0	No
G	15.5	15.5	20.0	20.0	0.0	0.0	Yes

The paths, and their total expected times and variances, are

Path	Total Expected Time (wk)	Total Variance
A–D	4 + 12 = 16	1.00 + 1.78 = 2.78
A–E–G	4 + 6.5 + 4.5 = 15	1.00 + 2.25 + 0.69 = 3.94
B–C–E–G	5.5 + 3.5 + 6.5 + 4.5 = 20	0.69 + 0.25 + 2.25 + 0.69 = 3.88
B–F–G	5.5 + 9 + 4.5 = 19	0.69 + 2.78 + 0.69 = 4.16

The critical path is B–C–E–G, with a total expected time of 20 weeks. However path B–F–G is 19 weeks and has a large variance.

c. We first calculate the z-value:

$$z = \frac{T - T_E}{\sqrt{\sigma^2}} = \frac{23 - 20}{\sqrt{3.88}} = 1.52$$

Using the Normal Distribution appendix, we find that the probability of completing the project in 23 weeks or less is 0.9357. Because the length of path B–F–G is close to that of the critical path and has a large variance, it might well become the critical path during the project.

> DISCUSSION QUESTIONS <

1. One of your colleagues comments that software is the ultimate key to project management success. How would you respond?

2. When a large project is mismanaged, it makes news. Form a discussion group and identify penalties associated with a mismanaged project in your experience or in recent headlines. Identify the cause of the problem, such as in- accurate time estimates, changed scope, unplanned or improperly sequenced activities, inadequate resources, or poor management–labor relations.

3. Describe a project in which you participated. What activities were involved and how were they interrelated? How would you rate the project manager? What is the basis of your evaluation?

> PROBLEMS <

Software, such as OM Explorer, Active Models, and POM for Windows is packaged with every new copy of the textbook. Check with your instructor on how best to use it. In many cases, the instructor wants you to understand how to do the calculations by hand. At most, the software provides a check on your calculations. When calculations are particularly complex and the goal is interpreting the results in making decisions, the software replaces entirely the manual calculations. The software also can be a valuable resource well after your course is completed.

1. Consider the following data for a project.

Activity	Activity Time (days)	Immediate Predecessor(s)
A	2	—
B	4	A
C	5	A
D	2	B
E	1	B
F	8	B, C
G	3	D, E
H	5	F
I	4	F
J	7	G, H, I

a. Draw the network diagram.
b. Calculate the critical path for this project.
c. How much total slack is in activities G, H, and I?
d. How much free slack is in activities G, H, and I?

2. The following information is known about a project.

Activity	Activity Time (days)	Immediate Predecessor(s)
A	7	—
B	2	A
C	4	A
D	4	B, C
E	4	D
F	3	E
G	5	E

a. Draw the network diagram for this project.
b. Determine the critical path and project duration.
c. Calculate the free slack for each activity.

3. A project has the following precedence relationships and activity times.

Activity	Activity Time (wks)	Immediate Predecessor(s)
A	4	—
B	10	—
C	5	A
D	15	B, C
E	12	B
F	4	D
G	8	E
H	7	F, G

a. Draw the network diagram.

b. Calculate the total slack for each activity. Which activities are on the critical path?

4. The following information is available about a project.

Activity	Activity Time (days)	Immediate Predecessor(s)
A	3	—
B	4	—
C	5	—
D	4	—
E	7	A
F	2	B, C, D
G	4	E, F
H	6	F
I	4	G
J	3	G
K	3	H

a. Draw the network diagram.

b. Find the critical path.

5. The following information has been gathered for a project.

Activity	Activity Time (wks)	Immediate Predecessor(s)
A	4	—
B	7	A
C	9	B
D	3	B
E	14	D
F	10	C, D
G	11	F, E

a. Draw the network diagram.

b. Calculate the total slack for each activity and determine the critical path. How long will the project take?

c. What is the free slack for activities D and E?

6. Consider the following project information.

Activity	Activity Time (wks)	Immediate Predecessor(s)
A	4	—
B	3	—
C	5	—
D	3	A, B
E	6	B
F	4	D, C
G	8	E, C
H	12	F, G

a. Draw the network diagram for this project.

b. Specify the critical path.

c. Calculate the total slack for activities A and D.

d. What happens to the total slack for D if A takes five weeks?

e. Which activity has the most free slack?

7. Barbara Gordon, the project manager for Web Ventures, Inc., compiled a table showing time estimates for each of the company's manufacturing activities of a project, including optimistic, most likely, and pessimistic.

a. Calculate the expected time, t_e, for each activity.

b. Calculate the variance, σ^2, for each activity.

Activity	Optimistic	Most Likely	Pessimistic
A	3	8	19
B	12	15	18
C	2	6	16
D	4	9	20
E	1	4	7

8. Recently, you were assigned to manage a project for your company. You have constructed a network diagram depicting the various activities in the project (Figure 3.15). In addition, you have asked your team to estimate the amount of time that they would expect each of the

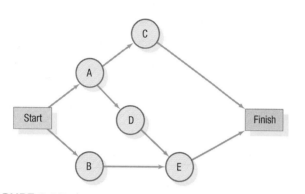

FIGURE 3.15 | Network Diagram for Your Project

activities to take. Their responses are shown in the following table.

Time Estimates (days)			
Activity	**Optimistic**	**Most Likely**	**Pessimistic**
A	5	8	11
B	4	8	11
C	5	6	7
D	2	4	6
E	4	7	10

a. What is the expected completion time of the project?

b. What is the probability of completing the project in 21 days?

c. What is the probability of completing the project in 17 days?

9. In Solved Problem 2, estimate the probability that the noncritical path B–F–G will take more than 20 weeks. *Hint:* Subtract from 1.0 the probability that B–F–G will take 20 weeks or less.

10. Consider the following data for a project never before attempted by your company.

Activity	Expected Time t_e(wk)	Immediate Predecessor(s)
A	5	—
B	3	—
C	2	A
D	5	B
E	4	C, D
F	7	D

a. Draw the network diagram for this project.

b. Identify the critical path and estimate the project's duration.

c. Calculate the total slack for each activity.

11. The director of continuing education at Bluebird University just approved the planning for a sales training seminar. Her administrative assistant identified the various activities that must be done and their relationships to each other, as shown in Table 3.5.

   Because of the uncertainty in planning the new course, the assistant also has supplied the following time estimates for each activity.

Time Estimates (days)			
Activity	**Optimistic**	**Most Likely**	**Pessimistic**
A	5	7	8
B	6	8	12
C	3	4	5
D	11	17	25
E	8	10	12
F	3	4	5
G	4	8	9
H	5	7	9
I	8	11	17
J	4	4	4

   The director wants to conduct the seminar 47 working days from now. What is the probability that everything will be ready in time?

TABLE 3.5		Activities for the Sales Training Seminar
Activity	**Description**	**Immediate Predecessor(s)**
A	Design brochure and course announcement	—
B	Identify prospective teachers	—
C	Prepare detailed outline of course	—
D	Send brochure and student applications	A
E	Send teacher applications	B
F	Select teacher for course	C, E
G	Accept students	D
H	Select text for course	F
I	Order and receive texts	G, H
J	Prepare room for class	G

12. Table 3.6 contains information about a project. Shorten the project three weeks by finding the minimum-cost schedule. Assume that project indirect costs and penalty costs are negligible. Identify activities to crash while minimizing the additional crash costs.

13. Information concerning a project is given in Table 3.7. Indirect project costs amount to $250 per day. The company will incur a $100 per day penalty for each day the project lasts beyond day 14.

   a. What is the project's duration if only normal times are used?

   b. What is the minimum-cost schedule?

   c. What is the critical path for the minimum-cost schedule?

14. You are the manager of a project to improve a billing process at your firm. Table 3.8 contains the data you will need to conduct a cost analysis of the project. Indirect costs are $1,600 per week, and penalty costs are $1,200 per week after week 12.

   a. What is the minimum-cost schedule for this project?

   b. What is the difference in total project costs between the earliest completion time of the project using "normal" times and the minimum-cost schedule you derived in part (a)?

15. Table 3.9 contains data for the installation of new equipment in a manufacturing process at your customer's plant. Your company is responsible for the project. Indirect costs are $10,000 per week, and a penalty cost of $10,000 per week will be incurred for every week the project is delayed beyond week 9.

   a. What is the shortest time duration for this project regardless of cost?

   b. What is the minimum total cost associated with completing the project in 12 weeks?

   c. What is the total time of the minimum-cost schedule?

16. Jason Ritz, district manager for Gumfull Foods, Inc., is in charge of opening a new fast-food outlet in the college town of Clarity. His major concern is the hiring of a manager and a cadre of hamburger cooks, assemblers, and dispensers. He also has to coordinate the renovation of a building that was previously owned by a pet supplies retailer. He has gathered the data shown in Table 3.10.

TABLE 3.6			Project Activity and Cost Data	
Activity	Normal Time (wks)	Crash Time (wks)	Cost to Crash ($ per week)	Immediate Predecessor(s)
A	7	6	200	None
B	12	9	250	None
C	7	6	250	A
D	6	5	300	A
E	1	1	—	B
F	1	1	—	C, D
G	3	1	200	D, E
H	3	2	350	F
I	2	2	—	G

TABLE 3.8				Data for the Billing Process	
Activity	Immediate Predecessor(s)	Normal Time	Crash Time	Normal Cost	Crash Cost
A	—	4	1	5,000	8,000
B	—	5	3	8,000	10,000
C	A	1	1	4,000	4,000
D	B	6	3	6,000	12,000
E	B, C	7	6	4,000	7,000
F	D	7	6	4,000	7,000

TABLE 3.7					Project Activity and Cost Data
Activity	Normal Time (days)	Normal Cost ($)	Crash Time (days)	Crash Cost ($)	Immediate Predecessor(s)
A	5	1,000	4	1,200	—
B	5	800	3	2,000	—
C	2	600	1	900	A, B
D	3	1,500	2	2,000	B
E	5	900	3	1,200	C, D
F	2	1,300	1	1,400	E
G	3	900	3	900	E
H	5	500	3	900	G

TABLE 3.9				Data for the Equipment Installation Project	
Activity	Immediate Predecessor(s)	Normal Time	Crash Time	Normal Cost	Crash Cost
A	—	3 weeks	2 weeks	7,000	10,000
B	—	1	1	3,000	3,000
C	A	4	2	12,000	40,000
D	B	2	1	12,000	28,000
E	C	1	1	8,000	8,000
F	D, E	4	2	5,000	15,000
G	E	2	1	9,000	18,000

			Time (wk)		
Activity	Description	Immediate Predecessor(s)	a	m	b
A	Interview at college for new manager	—	2	4	6
B	Renovate building	—	5	8	11
C	Place ad for employees and interview applicants	—	7	9	17
D	Have new manager prospects visit	A	1	2	3
E	Purchase equipment for new outlet and install	B	2	4	12
F	Check employee applicant references and make final selection	C	4	4	4
G	Check references for new manager and make final selection	D	1	1	1
H	Hold orientation meetings and do payroll paperwork	E, F, G	2	2	2

TABLE 3.10 | Data for the Fast-Food Outlet Project

Top management told Ritz that the new outlet is to be opened as soon as possible. Every week that the project can be shortened will save the firm $1,200 in lease costs. Ritz thought about how to save time during the project and came up with two possibilities. One was to employ Arctic, Inc., a local employment agency, to locate some good prospects for the manager's job. This approach would save three weeks in activity A and cost Gumfull Foods $2,500. The other was to add a few workers to shorten the time for activity B by two weeks at an additional cost of $2,700.

Help Jason Ritz by answering the following questions.

a. How long is the project expected to take?

b. Suppose that Ritz has a personal goal of completing the project in 14 weeks. What is the probability that it will happen this quickly?

c. What additional expenditures should be made to reduce the project's duration? Use the expected time for each activity as though it were certain.

17. The diagram in Figure 3.16 was developed for a project that you are managing. Suppose that you are interested in finding ways to speed up the project at minimal addi-

tional cost. Determine the schedule for completing the project in 25 days at minimum cost. Penalty and project-overhead costs are negligible. Time and cost data for each activity are shown in Table 3.11.

18. Paul Silver, owner of Sculptures International, just initiated a new art project. The following data are available for the project.

Activity	Activity Time (days)	Immediate Predecessor(s)
A	4	—
B	1	—
C	3	A
D	2	B
E	3	C, D

TABLE 3.11 | Project Activity and Cost Data

	Normal		Crash	
Activity	Time (days)	Cost ($)	Time (days)	Cost ($)
A	12	1,300	11	1,900
B	13	1,050	9	1,500
C	18	3,000	16	4,500
D	9	2,000	5	3,000
E	12	650	10	1,100
F	8	700	7	1,050
G	8	1,550	6	1,950
H	2	600	1	800
I	4	2,200	2	4,000

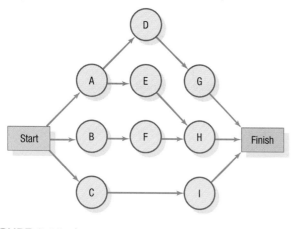

FIGURE 3.16 | Network Diagram for Problem 17

a. Draw the network diagram for the project.

b. Determine the project's critical path and duration.

c. What is the total slack for each activity?

19. Reliable Garage is completing production of the J2000 kit car. The following data are available for the project.

Activity	Activity Time (days)	Immediate Predecessor(s)
A	2	—
B	6	A
C	4	B
D	5	C
E	7	C
F	5	C
G	5	F
H	3	D, E, G

a. Draw the network diagram for the project.

b. Determine the project's critical path and duration.

c. What is the total slack for each activity?

20. The following information concerns a new project your company is undertaking.

Activity	Activity Time (days)	Immediate Predecessor(s)
A	10	—
B	11	—
C	9	A, B
D	5	A, B
E	8	A, B
F	13	C, E
G	5	C, D
H	10	G
I	6	F, G
J	9	E, H
K	11	I, J

a. Draw the network diagram for this project.

b. Determine the critical path and project completion time.

ADVANCED PROBLEMS

21. The project manager of Good Public Relations gathered the data shown in Table 3.12 for a new advertising campaign.

a. How long is the project likely to take?

b. What is the probability that the project will take more than 38 weeks?

c. Consider the path A–E–G–H–J. What is the probability that this path will exceed the expected project duration?

22. Michaelson Construction builds houses. Create a network showing the precedence relationships for the activities listed in Table 3.13.

23. Fronc is a wedding coordinator. Beatrice Wright and William Bach have asked Fronc to help them organize their wedding. Create a network showing the precedence relationships for the activities listed in Table 3.14.

24. The information in Table 3.15 is available about a large project.

a. Determine the critical path and the expected completion time of the project.

b. Plot the total project cost, starting from day 1 to the expected completion date of the project, assuming the earliest start times for each activity. Compare that result to a similar plot for the latest start times. What implication does the time differential have for cash flows and project scheduling?

TABLE 3.12	Activity Data for Advertising Project

	Time Estimates (days)			
Activity	Optimistic	Most Likely	Pessimistic	Immediate Predecessor(s)
A	8	10	12	—
B	5	8	17	—
C	7	8	9	—
D	1	2	3	B
E	8	10	12	A, C
F	5	6	7	D, E
G	1	3	5	D, E
H	2	5	8	F, G
I	2	4	6	G
J	4	5	8	H
K	2	2	2	H

TABLE 3.13	Michaelson Construction Building Activities		
Activity	**Description**	**Activity**	**Description**
Start			
A	Appliance installation	M	Roughing-in plumbing
B	Building permit	N	Outside painting
C	Carpets and flooring	O	Interior painting
D	Dry wall	P	Roof
E	Electrical wiring	Q	Siding
F	Foundation	R	Final wood trim
G	Framing	S	Pouring sidewalks, driveway, basement, and garage floors
H	Heating and air conditioning	T	Doors
I	Insulation	U	Windows
J	Kitchen and bath cabinets	V	Bath fixtures
K	Lighting fixtures	W	Lawn sprinkler system
L	Moving in	X	Landscaping

TABLE 3.14	Will and Bea Wright-Bach Wedding Activities		
Activity	**Description**	**Activity**	**Description**
Start	Accept proposal	O	Order cake, mints, cashews
A	Select and print announcements	P	Photographer
B	Blood tests	Q	Reserve reception hall
C	Color theme selection	R	Rings
D1	Wedding dress	S	Bachelor party
D2	Bridesmaids' dresses	T	Tuxedo rental
D3	Bride's mother's dress	U	Ushers
D4	Groom's mother's dress	V	Reserve church
E	Establish budget and net worth of parents	W	Wedding ceremony
F	Flowers	X	Select groomsmen, ring bearer
G	Gifts for wedding party	Y	Select bridesmaids, flower girls
H	Honeymoon planning	Z	Rehearsal and prenuptial dinner
I	Mailed invitations	AA	Prenuptial agreement
J	Guest list	BB	Groom's nervous breakdown
K	Caterer	CC	Register for china, flatware, gifts
L	Marriage license	DD	Dance band
M	Menu for reception	EE	Thank you notes
N	Newspaper photograph, society page announcement	FF	Finish

TABLE 3.15	Activity and Cost Data		
Activity	**Activity Time (days)**	**Activity Cost ($)**	**Immediate Predecessor(s)**
A	3	100	—
B	4	150	—
C	2	125	A
D	5	175	B
E	3	150	B
F	4	200	C, D
G	6	75	C
H	2	50	C, D, E
I	1	100	E
J	4	75	D, E
K	3	150	F, G
L	3	150	G, H, I
M	2	100	I, J
N	4	175	K, M
O	1	200	H, M
P	5	150	N, L, O

> ACTIVE MODEL EXERCISE <

This Active Model appears on the Student CD-ROM. It allows you to evaluate the sensitivity of the project time to changes in activity times and activity predecessors.

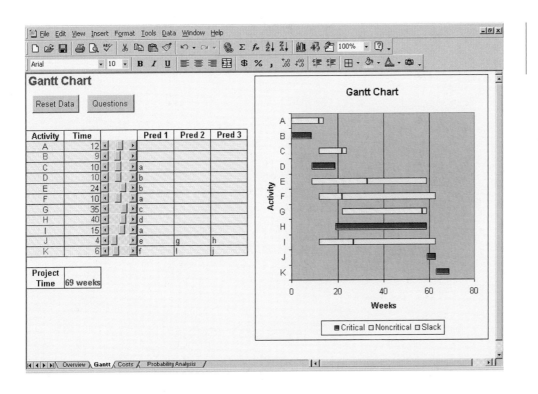

ACTIVE MODEL 3.1

Gantt Chart Using Data from Example 3.2

QUESTIONS

1. Activity B and activity K are critical activities. Describe the difference that occurs on the graph when you increase activity B versus when you increase activity K.

2. Activity F is not critical. Use the scroll bar to determine how many weeks you can increase activity F until it becomes critical.

3. Activity A is not critical. How many weeks can you increase activity A until it becomes critical? What happens when activity A becomes critical?

4. What happens when you increase activity A by one week after it becomes critical?

5. Suppose that building codes may change and, as a result, activity C would have to be completed before activity D could be started. How would this affect the project?

The Pert Studebaker

The new director of service operations for Roberts Auto Sales and Service (RASAS) started work at the beginning of the year. It is now mid-February. RASAS consists of three car dealerships that sell and service several makes of American and Japanese cars, two auto parts stores, a large body shop and car painting business, and an auto salvage yard. Vikky Roberts, owner of RASAS, went into the car business when she inherited a Studebaker dealership from her father. The Studebaker Corporation was on the wane when she obtained the business, but she was able to capitalize on her knowledge and experience to build her business into the diversified and successful mini-empire it is today. Her motto, "Sell 'em today, repair 'em tomorrow!" reflects a strategy that she refers to in private as "Get 'em coming and going."

Roberts has always retained a soft spot in her heart for Studebaker automobiles. They were manufactured in South Bend, Indiana, from 1919 to 1966, and many are still operable today because of a vast number of collectors and loyal fans. Roberts has just acquired a 1963 Studebaker Avanti that needs a lot of restoration. She has also noted the public's growing interest in the restoration of vintage automobiles.

Roberts is thinking of expanding into the vintage car restoration business and needs help in assessing the feasibility of such a move. She also wants to restore her 1963 Avanti to mint condition, or as close to mint condition as possible. If she decides to go into the car restoring business, she can use the Avanti as an exhibit in sales and advertising and take it to auto shows to attract business for the new shop.

Roberts believes that many people want the thrill of restoring an old car themselves but they do not have the time to run down all the old parts. Still, others just want to own a vintage auto because it is different and many of them have plenty of money to pay someone to restore an auto for them.

Roberts wants the new business to appeal to both types of people. For the first group, she envisions serving as a parts broker for NOS ("new old stock"), new parts that were manufactured many years ago and are still packaged in their original cartons. It can be a time-consuming process to find the right part. RASAS could also machine new parts to replicate those that are hard to find or that no longer exist.

In addition, RASAS could assemble a library of parts and body manuals for old cars to serve as an information resource for do-it-yourself restorers. The do-it-yourselfers could come to RASAS for help in compiling parts lists, and RASAS could acquire the parts for them. For others, RASAS would take charge of the entire restoration.

Roberts asks the new director of service operations to take a good look at her Avanti and determine what needs to be done to restore it to the condition it was in when it came from the factory more than 40 years ago. She wants to restore it in time to exhibit it at the National Studebaker Meet in Springfield, Missouri. If the car wins first prize in its category, it will be a real public relations coup for RASAS—especially if Roberts decides to enter this new venture. Even if she does not, the car will be a showpiece for the rest of the business.

Roberts asks the director of service operations to prepare a report about what is involved in restoring the car and whether it can be done in time for the Springfield meet in 45 working days using PERT/CPM. The parts manager, the body shop manager, and the chief mechanic have provided the following estimates of times and tasks that need to be done, as well as cost estimates.

- Order all needed material and parts (upholstery, windshield, carburetor, and oil pump). Time: 2 days. Cost (phone calls and labor): $100.

- Receive upholstery material for seat covers. Cannot be done until order is placed. Time: 30 days. Cost: $250.

- Receive windshield. Cannot be done until order is placed. Time: 10 days. Cost: $130.

- Receive carburetor and oil pump. Cannot be done until order is placed. Time: 7 days. Cost: $180.

- Remove chrome from body. Can be done immediately. Time: 1 day. Cost: $50.

- Remove body (doors, hood, trunk, and fenders) from frame. Cannot be done until chrome is removed. Time: 1 day. Cost: $150.

- Have fenders repaired by body shop. Cannot be done until body is removed from frame. Time: 4 days. Cost: $200.

- Repair doors, trunk, and hood. Cannot be done until body is removed from frame. Time: 6 days. Cost: $300.

- Pull engine from chassis. Do after body is removed from frame. Time: 1 day. Cost: $50.

- Remove rust from frame. Do after the engine has been pulled from the chassis. Time: 3 days. Cost $300.

- Regrind engine valves. Have to pull engine from chassis first. Time: 5 days. Cost: $500.

- Replace carburetor and oil pump. Do after engine has been pulled from chassis and after carburetor and oil pump have been received. Time: 1 day. Cost: $50.

- Rechrome the chrome parts. Chrome must have been removed from the body first. Time: 3 days. Cost: $150.

- Reinstall engine. Do after valves are reground and carburetor and oil pump have been installed. Time: 1 day. Cost: $150.

- Put doors, hood, and trunk back on frame. The doors, hood, and trunk must have been repaired. The frame also has to have had its rust removed. Time: 1 day. Cost: $80.

- Rebuild transmission and replace brakes. Do so after the engine has been reinstalled and the doors, hood, and trunk are back on the frame. Time: 4 days. Cost: $700.

- Replace windshield. Windshield must have been received. Time: 1 day. Cost: $70.

- Put fenders back on. The fenders must already have been repaired and the transmission rebuilt and the brakes replaced. Time: 1 day. Cost: $60.

- Paint car. Cannot be done until the fenders are back on and windshield replaced. Time: 4 days. Cost: $1,700.

- Reupholster interior of car. Must have first received upholstery material. Car must also have been painted. Time: 7 days. Cost: $1,200.

- Put chrome parts back on. Car has to have been painted and chrome parts rechromed. Time: 1 day. Cost: $50.

- Pull car to Studebaker show in Springfield, Missouri. Must have completed reupholstery of interior and have put the chrome parts back on. Time: 2 days. Cost: $500.

Roberts wants to limit expenditures on this project to what could be recovered by selling the restored car. She has already spent $1,500 to acquire the car.

In addition, she wants a brief report on some of the aspects of the proposed business, such as how it fits in with RASAS's other businesses and what RASAS's operations task should be with regard to cost, quality, customer service, and flexibility.

According to *Turning Wheels,* a publication for owners and drivers of Studebakers, and other books on car restoration, there are various categories of restoration. A basic restoration gets the car looking great and running, but a mint condition restoration puts the car back in original condition—as it was "when it rolled off the line." When restored cars compete, a car in mint condition has an advantage over one that is just a basic restoration. As cars are restored, they can also be customized. That is, something is put on the car that could not

have been on the original. Customized cars compete in a separate class. Roberts wants a mint condition restoration, without customization. (The proposed new business would accept any kind of restoration a customer wanted.)

The total budget cannot exceed $8,500 including the $1,500 Roberts has already spent. In addition, Roberts cannot spend more than $1,700 in any week given her present financial position. Even though much of the work will be done by Roberts's own employees, labor and materials costs must be considered. All relevant costs have been included in the cost estimates.

QUESTIONS

1. Using the information provided, prepare the report that Roberts requested, assuming that the project will begin immediately. Assume 45 working days are available to complete the project, including transporting the car to Springfield before the meet begins. Your report should briefly discuss the aspects of the proposed new business, such as the competitive priorities that Roberts asked about.

2. Construct a table containing the project activities, with a letter assigned to each activity, the time estimates, and the precedence relationships from which you will assemble the network diagram.

3. Draw a network diagram of the project similar to Figure 3.5. Determine the activities on the critical path and the estimated slack for each activity.

4. Prepare a project budget showing the cost of each activity and the total for the project. Can the project be completed within the budget? Are there any cash flow problems? If so, how might Roberts overcome them?

Source: This case was prepared by and is used by courtesy of Professor Sue Perrott Siferd, Arizona State University.

> SELECTED REFERENCES <

Bloom, R. "Software for Project Management." *Transportation & Distribution,* vol. 34 (1993), pp. 33–34.

Branston, Lisa. "Construction Firms View the Web As a Way to Get Out from Under a Mountain of Paper." *The Wall Street Journal* (November 15, 1999).

Caland, D. I. *Project Management: Strategic Design and Implementation.* New York: McGraw-Hill, 1994.

Day, P. J. *Microsoft Project 4.0 for Windows and the Macintosh: Setting Project Management Standards.* New York: Van Nostrand Reinhold, 1995.

Goldratt, E. M. *Critical Chain.* Great Banington, MA: North River, 1997.

Hartvigsen, David. *SimQuick: Process Simulation with Excel.* 2nd ed. Upper Saddle River, NJ: Prentice Hall, 2004.

IPS Associates. *Project Management Manual.* Boston: Harvard Business School Publishing, 1996.

Kerzner, Harold. *Advanced Project Management: Best Practices on Implementation,* 2nd ed. New York: John Wiley & Sons, 2004.

Kerzner, Harold. *Project Management: A Systems Approach to Planning, Scheduling, and Controlling,* 6th ed. New York: John Wiley & Sons, 1998.

Leach, Larry P. "Critical Chain Project Management Improves Project Performance." *Project Management Journal* (June 1999), pp. 39–51.

Lewis, J. P. *Mastering Project Management.* New York: McGraw-Hill, 1998.

Littlefield, T. K., and P. H. Randolph. "PEAT Duration Times: Mathematical or MBO." *Interfaces,* vol. 21, no. 6 (1991), pp. 92–95.

Mantel Jr., Samuel J., Jack R. Meredith, Scott M. Shafer, and Margaret M. Sutton. *Project Management in Practice,* 2nd ed. New York: John Wiley & Sons, 2005.

Meredith, Jack R., and Samuel J. Mantel, *Project Management: A Managerial Approach,* 5th ed. New York: John Wiley & Sons, 2003.

Nichols, John M. *Managing Business and Engineering Projects.* Englewood Cliffs, NJ: Prentice Hall, 1990.

Pellegrinelli, Sergio, and Cliff Bowman. "Implementing Strategy Through Projects." *Long Range Planning,* vol. 27, no. 4 (1994), pp. 125–132.

"Project Management Body of Knowledge." Available from the Project Management Institute at www.pmi.org.

"Project Management Software Buyer's Guide." *Industrial Engineering* (March 1995), pp. 36–37.

Srinivasan, Mandyam, Darren Jones, and Alex Miller. "CORPS Capabilities." *APICS Magazine* (March 2005), pp. 46–50.

PART 2

MANAGING PROCESSES

LEARNING GOALS

*After reading this chapter,
you should be able to:*

1. Discuss the four major process decisions.

2. Position a process on the customer-contact matrix or product-process matrix.

3. Relate process choice with inventory strategy.

4. Identify the pros and cons of customer involvement.

5. Explain automation, capital intensity, economies of scope, and focus.

6. Discuss how process decisions should fit together.

7. Define process reengineering and process improvement.

The new structure at Duke Power
requires collaboration between process
managers and the regional VPs.
Teamwork is essential in the design
and operation of processes.

DUKE POWER

Duke Power is a true pioneer of the enterprise process. The electric utility arm of Duke Energy, Duke Power serves nearly 2 million customers in North and South Carolina. In 1995, with deregulation looming, the company realized that its processes had to do a much better job of customer service. But the existing organizational structure of Customer Operations, the business unit responsible for delivering electricity to customers, was getting in the way of process improvements. The unit was divided into four regional profit centers, and regional vice presidents had little time for wrestling with process improvements for customer service.

To resolve the problem, Duke Power identified the five core processes that together encompassed the essential work of Customer Operations: developing market strategies, maintaining customers, providing reliability and integrity, delivering products and services, and calculating and collecting revenues. Each process was assigned an owner, and the five process owners, like the four existing regional vice presidents, now report directly to the head of Customer Operations.

With the new structure, regional vice presidents continue to manage their own workforces—the process owners have only small staffs—but process owners have been given vast authority over the design and operation of the processes. They decide how work will proceed at every step. Then they establish performance targets and set budgets among regions. In other words, while regions have authority over people, they are evaluated on how well they meet goals set by process owners. This structure requires a new collaborative style of management, in which the process managers and regional vice presidents

For additional chapter resources check the Student CD-ROM or the Companion Website at
www.prenhall.com/krajewski

act as partners rather than rivals. Teams are composed of individuals with broad process knowledge, and they are measured on performance. They take over most of the managerial responsibilities usually held by supervisors. Supervisors, in turn, become more like coaches. Because the same employees are often involved in several processes, sometimes simultaneously, processes overlap.

Improvements continue to be made. The Customer Service Center now is available 24 hours a day, every day, to assist customers with billing inquiries or service requests. An electronic billing and payment service was launched in 2003. Duke Power's electric rates are ranked among the lowest in the nation, its customer service is ranked first or second among electric utilities, and the U.S. Environmental Protection Agency recognized it with the 2004 Clean Air Excellence Award.

Source: Steven Stanton, "How Process Enterprises Really Work," *Harvard Business Review* (November–December 1999), pp. 108–117; www.duke-energy.com/ (February 17, 2005).

---

process strategy

The pattern of decisions made in managing processes so that they will achieve their competitive priorities.

USING OPERATIONS TO COMPETE

↓

Operations As a Competitive Weapon
Operations Strategy
Project Management

MANAGING PROCESSES

↓

Process Strategy
Process Analysis
Process Performance and Quality
Constraint Management
Process Layout
Lean Systems

MANAGING VALUE CHAINS

↓

Supply Chain Strategy
Location
Inventory Management
Forecasting
Sales and Operations Planning
Resource Planning
Scheduling

Process decisions are strategic in nature: As we saw in Chapter 2, they should further a company's long-term competitive goals. In making process decisions, managers focus on controlling such competitive priorities as quality, flexibility, time, and cost. Process management is an ongoing activity, with the same principles applying to both first-time and redesign choices. Thus, the processes at Duke Power are in constant change.

In this chapter we focus on **process strategy**, which specifies the pattern of decisions made in managing processes so that they will achieve their competitive priorities. Process strategy guides a variety of process decisions, and in turn is guided by operations strategy and the organization's ability to obtain the resources necessary to support them. We begin by defining four basic process decisions: process structure, customer involvement, resource flexibility, and capital intensity. We discuss these decisions for both service and manufacturing processes, and also methods of focusing operations. We pay particular attention to ways in which these decisions fit together, depending on factors such as competitive priorities, customer contact, and volume. We conclude with two basic change strategies of analyzing and modifying processes: process reengineering and continuous process improvement. A coherent process strategy, however, is also a key to managing value chains effectively (Part 3). Each process in the chain must be designed to achieve its competitive priorities and add value to the work performed.

> PROCESS STRATEGY ACROSS THE ORGANIZATION <

As we explained in Chapter 1, processes are everywhere and are the basic unit of work. They are found in accounting, finance, human resources, management information systems, marketing, and operations. Managers in all departments must make sure that their processes are adding as much customer value as possible. They must understand that many processes cut across organizational lines, regardless of whether the firm is organized along functional, product, regional, or process lines.

The customer operations unit at Duke Power had five core processes that cut across boundaries between its four regions. The "calculate and collect revenues process" is most closely aligned with accounting, the "deliver products and services process" with operations, the "develop market strategies process" and "maintain customers process" with marketing, and the "provide reliability and integrity process" with quality assurance. Cross-functional coordination paid off in better performance. This payoff came in part by reorganizing to create process owners but also by creating a new collaborative style of management. The process owners and regional vice presidents acted as partners rather than rivals.

> PROCESS STRATEGY <

A process involves the use of an organization's resources to provide something of value. No service can be provided and no product can be made without a process, and no process can exist without at least one service or product. One recurring question in managing processes is deciding *how* to provide services or make products. Many different choices are made in selecting human resources, equipment, outsourced services, materials, work flows, and methods that transform inputs into outputs. Another choice is which processes are to be done in-house, and which processes are to be outsourced—that is, done outside the firm and purchased as materials and services. This decision helps to define the value chain, and is covered in subsequent chapters.

Process improvement decisions are most likely when:

- A gap exists between competitive priorities and competitive capabilities.
- A new or substantially modified service or product is being offered.
- Quality must be improved.
- Competitive priorities have changed.
- Demand for a service or product is changing.
- Current performance is inadequate.
- The cost or availability of inputs has changed.
- Competitors are gaining by using a new process.
- New technologies are available.
- Someone has a better idea.

The impact on the environment is another increasingly important consideration, especially in Europe and the United States. A good example is McDonald's. McDonald's made subtle changes in the processes used to package food, reducing waste by more than 30 percent since 1990 and becoming one of the country's leading buyers of recycled materials. This entailed replacing "clamshell" boxes with special lightweight paper; introducing shorter napkins; and relying less on plastics in straws, dining trays, and playground equipment. McDonald's is now looking at a plan to turn waste into fertilizer, so that eating out could generate less waste than eating at many homes.

Concerns for ecology in process decisions are also increasing in the manufacturing sector. General Motors found in 1991 that it was generating 88 pounds of waste and trash for each car assembled. By examining its processes with a particular focus on waste, the amount of solid waste dropped to only 15 pounds. A focus on pollution and waste gained momentum internationally when the International Organization of Standards adopted ISO 14001 in 1996. **ISO 14001** is a set of standards on how a company goes about eliminating pollution, such as setting up a formal system and database for monitoring environmental performance. Since 1996, more than 250,000 firms have been certified in more than 50 countries, with the rate of certification growing at least 50,000 each year.

ISO 14001

A set of standards on how a company goes about eliminating pollution.

Three principles concerning process decisions are particularly important.

1. The key to successful process decisions is to make choices that fit the situation and that make sense together. They should not work for cross-purposes, with one process optimized at the expense of other processes. A more effective process is one that matches key process characteristics and has a close *strategic fit*.

2. Although this section of the text focuses on individual processes, they are the building blocks that eventually create the firm's whole value chain. The cumulative effect on customer satisfaction and competitive advantage is huge.

3. Whether processes in the value chain are performed internally or by outside suppliers, management must pay particular attention to the interfaces between processes. Having to deal with these interfaces underscores the need for cross-functional coordination.

> MAJOR PROCESS DECISIONS <

Process decisions directly affect the process itself and indirectly the services and the products that it provides. Whether dealing with processes for offices, service providers, or manufacturers, operations managers must consider four common process decisions.

FIGURE **4.1**

Major Decisions for Effective Processes

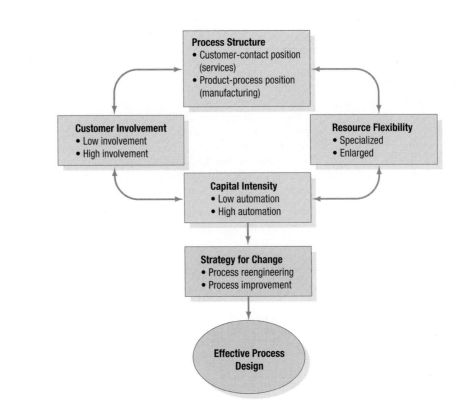

Figure 4.1 shows that they are all important steps towards an effective process design.

process structure

A process decision that determines how processes are designed relative to the kinds of resources needed, how resources are partitioned between them, and their key characteristics.

- **Process structure** determines how processes are designed relative to the kinds of resources needed, how resources are partitioned between them, and their key characteristics. Beginning points for making these decisions for services are the desired amount and type of customer contact and the competitive priorities that the process design must achieve. Beginning points for manufacturing are the volume level and amount of customization and once again the competitive priorities. Understanding these connections helps the manager detect possible misalignments in processes, paving the way for reengineering and process improvements.

customer involvement

The ways in which customers become part of the process and the extent of their participation.

- **Customer involvement** reflects the ways in which customers become part of the process and the extent of their participation.

resource flexibility

The ease with which employees and equipment can handle a wide variety of products, output levels, duties, and functions.

- **Resource flexibility** is the ease with which employees and equipment can handle a wide variety of products, output levels, duties, and functions.

capital intensity

The mix of equipment and human skills in a process.

- **Capital intensity** is the mix of equipment and human skills in a process. The greater the relative cost of equipment, the greater is the capital intensity.

These four decisions are best understood at the process or subprocess level, rather than at the firm level. Process decisions act as building blocks that are used in different ways to achieve effective processes.

> PROCESS STRUCTURE IN SERVICES <

One of the first decisions a manager makes in designing a well-functioning process is to choose a process type that best achieves the relative importance of quality, time, flexibility, and cost for that process. Strategies for designing processes can be quite different, depending on whether a service is being provided or a product is being manufactured. We begin with service processes, given their huge share of the workforce in industrialized countries.

NATURE OF SERVICE PROCESSES: CUSTOMER CONTACT

An effective service process strategy in one situation can be a poor choice in another. A process strategy that gets customers in and out of a fast-food restaurant quickly would not

be the right process strategy for a five-star restaurant, where customers seek a leisurely dining experience. Further, a good strategy for the servers at a restaurant might be totally in-
appropriate for a process back in the restaurant's business office. Economists sometimes put
service organizations into different industry classifications, such as financial services, health
services, education, and the like. Such distinctions help in the understanding of aggregate
economic data and perhaps even some general tendencies on process decisions within a
firm. However, the classifications are not as helpful when it gets down to designing an individual process. For example, no standard blueprint shows how work should be done in the
banking industry. To get insights, we must start at the process level and recognize key contextual variables associated with the process. Only by doing so can we recognize appropriate
patterns and see how decisions should be grouped together.

A good process strategy for a service process depends first and foremost on the type and
amount of customer contact. **Customer contact** is the extent to which the customer is present,
is actively involved, and receives personal attention during the service process. In contrast
with a manufacturing process, the customer can be a significant part of the process itself.
Figure 4.2 shows several dimensions of customer contact. The nested-process concept
applies to customer contact, because some parts of a process can have low contact and other
parts of a process can have high contact. Further, even a subprocess can be high on some
dimensions and low on others.

Figure 4.2 shows only the two extremes of customer contact, but they really represent a
continuum. Thus, many levels are possible on each of the five dimensions. Only when they
are taken together can you truly measure the kind and extent of customer contact. For example, the customer may not be physically present, but may still have high contact by being
actively involved in the process, such as with eBay and other forms of Internet interactions
that are managed without any face-to-face contact.

The first dimension of customer contact is whether the customer is physically present at
the process. Customer contact is important for all types of processes. The amount of contact
can be approximated as the percentage of the total time the customer is at the process, relative to the total time to complete the service. The higher the percentage of time that the customer is present, the higher the customer contact. Face-to-face interaction, sometimes
called a *moment of truth* or *service encounter,* brings the customer and service providers
together. At that time, customer attitudes about the quality of the service provided are
shaped. Many processes requiring *physical presence* are found in health care, hospitality services, and manufacturing customized products that require customer inputs. When physical
presence is required, either the customer comes to the service facility, or the service providers and equipment go to the customer. Either way allows the customer to be present
while the service is being created.

customer contact

The extent to which the customer is
present, is actively involved, and receives
personal attention during the service
process.

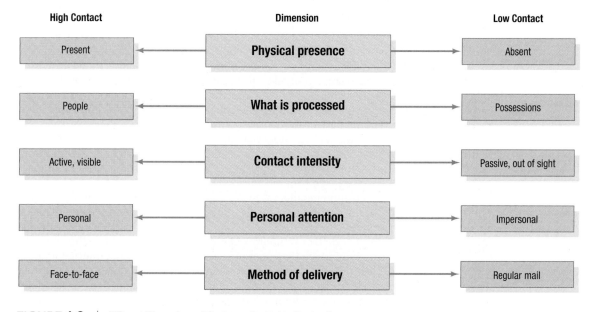

High Contact	Dimension	Low Contact
Present	**Physical presence**	Absent
People	**What is processed**	Possessions
Active, visible	**Contact intensity**	Passive, out of sight
Personal	**Personal attention**	Impersonal
Face-to-face	**Method of delivery**	Regular mail

FIGURE 4.2 | Different Dimensions of Customer Contact in Service Processes

A bank's branch manager talks with a customer at his desk. The customer at this high-contact process is not only present but also is actively involved and receiving personal attention.

A second dimension is *what is being processed* at the service encounter. *People-processing services* involve services provided *to* the person, rather than *for* the person, and so it requires a physical presence. Customers become part of the process, making the service's production simultaneous with its consumption. *Possession-processing services* (many such processes are found in e-commerce, freight transportation, equipment installation, maintenance and repair, and warehousing) involve tangible actions to physical objects that provide value to the customer. The object must be present during the processing, but not the customer. The service is consumed after the process is finished, rather than simultaneously with the service's creation. Customer contact is also established with *information-based services*, which collect, manipulate, analyze, and transmit data that have value to the customer. Such processes are common in insurance, news, banking, education, and legal services.

The *intensity of customer contact* goes one step beyond physical presence and what is processed. It deals with the extent to which the process accommodates the customer, and it involves considerable interaction and service customization. **Active contact** means that the customer is very much part of the creation of the service and affects the service process itself. The customer can personalize the service to suit her particular needs and even might decide in part how the process is performed. Active contact usually means the process is visible to the customer. Many processes for dental services, hair dressing, or psychiatric services involve active contact. **Passive contact** means that the customer is not involved in tailoring the process to meet special needs or in how the process is performed. Even if the customer is present, he may simply be sitting in a waiting room, standing in line, or perhaps lying in a hospital bed. Many processes where the customer is present but the contact is passive can be found in public transportation or theaters. Interaction with service personnel is limited.

A fourth dimension is the extent of *personal attention* provided. High-contact processes are more intimate, and they exhibit mutual confiding and trust between the service provider and the customer. They also can mean a richer interchange of information between the customer and the service provider. For example, the concierge at The Ritz-Carlton Hotel gives you more personal attention than received at a Days Inn. When contact is more personal, the customer often *experiences* the service rather than just receiving it. The customer is changed in some way. Impersonal contact lies at the other end of the customer-contact continuum. At a less intimate process, for example, the customer might move through a standardized work flow or stand in line at a ticket counter.

A final dimension of customer contact is the *method of delivery*. A high-contact process would use face-to-face or the telephone, assuring more clarity in identifying customer needs and in delivering the service. A low-contact process would likely use a less personable means to deliver the service. Regular mail or standardized e-mail messages would be the preferred way to exchange information for a low-contact process. The advent of the Internet and the widening channels of electronic distribution channels allow processes that traditionally had high customer contact to be converted into low-contact processes. Retail banking is a good example. Customers can go to the traditional branch bank or they now can do their banking online.

active contact

The customer is very much part of the creation of the service and affects the service process itself.

passive contact

The customer is not involved in tailoring the process to meet special needs or in how the process is performed.

CUSTOMER-CONTACT MATRIX

The customer-contact matrix, shown in Figure 4.3, brings together three elements: the degree of customer contact, the service package, and the process. It synchronizes the service to be provided with the delivery process. The matrix is the starting point for evaluating and improving a process.

Customer Contact and Service Package The horizontal dimension of the matrix represents the service provided to the customer in terms of customer contact, the service package, and the competitive priorities. A key competitive priority is how much customization is needed. Positions on the left side of the matrix represent high customer contact and highly customized services. The customer is more likely to be present and active, with competitive priorities calling for more customization. The process is visible to the customer, who receives more personal attention. The right side of the matrix represents low customer contact, passive involvement, less personalized attention, and a process out of the customer's sight.

Process Complexity, Divergence, and Flow The vertical dimension of the customer-contact matrix deals with three characteristics of the process itself: (1) complexity, (2) divergence, and (3) flow. Each process can be analyzed on these three dimensions.

Process complexity is the number and intricacy of the steps required to perform the process. Complexity depends in part on how broadly the process is defined. At a bank, for example, the *auto finance* process is complex because it involves many steps. One of the subprocesses nested within auto finance is *credit application*. It is not as complex because it is just one part of the auto finance process, and thus involves fewer steps. Nested within credit application, in turn, is the *loan documentation* process. It is even less complex because it represents just one small part of the overall auto finance process. Focusing on a more narrowly defined nested process reduces the number of steps to be performed if they are all to be completed by the same service provider (or team). However, even just a few steps can still be complex.

Process divergence is the extent to which the process is highly customized with considerable latitude as to how it is performed. If the process changes with each customer, virtually every performance of the service is unique. Examples of highly divergent service processes where many steps in them change with each customer are found in consulting, law, and architecture. For an architect's nested processes, completing the home design can take on a different character for each customer, even if many activities are common to all designs.

process complexity
The number and intricacy of the steps required to perform the process.

process divergence
The extent to which the process is highly customized with considerable latitude as to how it is performed.

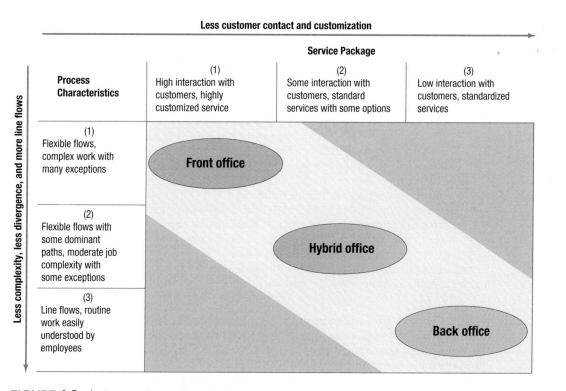

FIGURE 4.3 | Customer-Contact Matrix for Service Processes

They involve much judgment and discretion, depending on what the situation and customer dictate. Services that involve interpretative skills, as with creating art works, also are highly divergent because the execution of the process is individualized. A service with low divergence, on the other hand, is repetitive and standardized. The work is performed exactly the same with all customers. Certain hotel services and telephone services are highly standardized to assure uniformity. At many hotels, every step from room cleaning to checkout is standardized with documentation and rules governing how the process is performed.

Closely related to divergence is how the customer, object, or information being processed flows through the service facility. Work progresses through the sequence of steps in a process, which could range from highly diverse to linear. When divergence is considerable, the work flow is flexible. A **flexible flow** means that the customers, materials, or information move in diverse ways, with the path of one customer or job often crisscrossing the path that the next one will take. Each one can follow a carefully preplanned path, even though the first impression is one of disorganized, jumbled flows. Such an appearance goes naturally with high process divergence. A **line flow** means that the customers, materials, or information move linearly from one operation to the next, according to a fixed sequence. When diversity is low and the process standardized, line flows are a natural consequence. With line flows, the work invariably goes from one workstation to the next in the same sequence for every customer or job.

A process can be analyzed with respect to its complexity, divergence, and work flow. A physician's service, for example, can be complex. It can also be divergent, as the doctor defines the steps performed based on the information collected during the diagnosis and then takes one or more actions. The patient may be routed to testing areas that vary with the patient, creating flexible flows rather than line flows. Some services are low in complexity, but high in divergence. For example, a teacher simply transmits knowledge, but the actual ways used can be highly individualized and can vary with each topic covered.

SERVICE PROCESS STRUCTURING

Figure 4.3 shows several desirable positions in the matrix that effectively connect the service product with the process. The manager has three process structures, which form a continuum, to choose from: (1) *front office,* (2) *hybrid office,* and (3) *back office.* Figure 4.4 illustrates each type of service process position with an example from the financial services industry. It is unlikely that a process can be a top performer if a process lies too far from one of these diagonal positions, occupying instead one of the extreme positions represented by the light blue triangles in the matrix (refer to Figure 4.3). Such positions represent too much of a disconnect between the service package and process characteristics. A much more likely position is somewhere within the light-colored area, or band, that stretches down from the front-office position to the back-office position. Some deviation from the diagonal is expected and even desirable, allowing for special niches. However, the extreme positions are to be avoided.

Front Office A **front-office** process has high customer contact where the service provider interacts directly with the internal or external customer. Because of the customization of the service and variety of service options, the process is more complex and many of the steps in it have considerable divergence. Work flows are flexible, and they vary from one customer to the next. More freedom is allowed or inherent in the steps and sequence of the process. The work involves many exceptions to the usual work pattern.

Not only does the process include more steps, but employees find them more difficult to understand. There is more service variety and services are more customized. The high-contact service process tends to be adapted or tailored to each customer. The customer has more choice in how each step of the service process is carried out and sometimes even where the service encounter occurs. An example of a front office, as illustrated by the first column in Figure 4.4, is the process of the sale of financial services to municipalities. This process is highly customized to meet specific customer needs, with customer contact, complexity, and divergence all quite high. The process flow is flexible, depending on customer requirements.

Hybrid Office A hybrid office tends to be in the middle on the five dimensions in Figure 4.2, or perhaps high on some contact measures and low on others. A **hybrid-office** process has moderate levels of customer contact and standard services, with some options available from which the customer chooses. The work flow progresses from one workstation to the next, with some dominant paths apparent. The work is reasonably complex, and some customization exists in how the process is performed.

Front Office	**Hybrid Office**	**Back Office**
Sale of financial services to municipalities	*Creation of quarterly performance reports*	*Production of monthly client fund balance reports*
• Research customer finances • Work with customer to understand customer needs • Make customized presentation to customer addressing specific customer needs • Involve specialized staff offering variety of services • Continuing relationship with customer, reaction to changing customer needs	• Data obtained electronically • Report calculated using standardized process • Report reviewed using standardized diagnostic systems • Manager provides written analysis and recommendations in response to individual employee performance • Manager meets with employee to discuss performance	• Data obtained electronically • Report run using standardized process • Results checked for "reasonableness" using well-established policies • Hard copies and electronic files forwarded to analysts • Process repeated monthly with little variation

FIGURE 4.4

Service Process Structures in the Financial Services Industry

An example of a hybrid office, as illustrated by the second column in Figure 4.4, is the process of evaluating employee performance on a quarterly basis. This portion of the process is not particularly complex, in that the reports are fairly standardized and the process is repeated periodically according to a well-established process. Some parts of the performance analysis are even computerized. On the other hand, this portion of the process aggregates information from a variety of sources, both quantitative and qualitative, and is therefore more complex than the back-office process discussed next. Furthermore, the manager's written analyses and meetings with employees are highly customized and tailored to the individual.

Back Office A **back-office** process has low customer contact and little service customization. The work is standardized and routine, with line flows from one service provider to the next until the service is completed. An example of a back-office process, as illustrated by the third column of Figure 4.4, is the monthly production of client fund balance reports. The process is almost completely standardized, repeated frequently, and requires little variation. When completed, and checked for reasonableness, the reports are sent to the analysts. Customer contact is quite low, as are process complexity and divergence. The process has a line flow.

back office

A process with low customer contact and little service customization.

EMBEDDING STRATEGY INTO SERVICE PROCESSES

After analyzing a process and determining its position on the matrix, it may be apparent that it is improperly positioned, either too far to the left or right, or too far to the top or bottom. Opportunities for improvement can become apparent. Maybe the service package calls for more customization and customer contact than the process currently provides. Perhaps, instead, the process is too complex and divergent, with unnecessarily flexible flows. Reducing divergence and complexity might reduce costs and improve productivity.

The process should reflect its desired competitive priorities. Front offices generally emphasize top quality and customization, whereas back offices are more likely to emphasize low-cost operation, consistent quality, and on-time delivery. But many exceptions to this pattern do and should exist. Managerial Practice 4.1 demonstrates that even the back-office processes (not just their front-office processes) at The Ritz-Carlton place an extraordinary emphasis on top quality. However, processes at the same service facility can have different competitive priorities.

An employee uses a FedEx computer in a back-office process. The work being performed is standardized and repeated frequently, with no direct customer contact.

The Ritz-Carlton Hotel Company targets the top 1 to 3 percent of luxury travelers, and so gives top quality a huge emphasis as a competitive priority. The goal is to not just exceed guests' expectation, but also staff expectations. Every employee, whether in the front office or back office, carries a card with eight business-card-sized panels describing Ritz-Carlton's Gold Standards, which include an elegant and simple motto: "We are ladies and gentlemen serving ladies and gentlemen." The company emphasizes a passion to have its people and processes behave in extraordinary ways, both towards guests (external customers) and toward each other (often internal customers). They pay remarkable attention to every opportunity (or "customer touch point") to delight customers or disappoint them. By one calculation, the average guest represents 1,100 touch points each day. Not all of those touch points involve the customer's physical presence with an employee. Many of those points occur in back offices, such as the kitchen, offices, or garage. These points eventually affect a guest—positively or negatively.

Emphasis on top quality is codified and integrated into processes at each touch point. The Ritz-Carlton manages details like few other organizations do. It is strongly process-driven, and sophisticated systems measure virtually every aspect of performance. It has an almost fanatical determination to drive quality improvements through all of its operations. It begins with hiring the right people for the 120 hotel-specific job positions. Current employees are involved in the interviewing process of new employee applicants, so everyone feels responsible.

After finding the right people, employees go through an extensive orientation and continuing education. Job certification is task-specific, depending on the processes that a person will perform. All senior property leaders attend orientation sessions for new employees, seeking to impart a genuine service mind-set with all. New employees undergo 310 hours of training in their first year, and a minimum of 125 hours in subsequent years. Everyone is also expected to attend a "daily lineup" everyday. They feature typical announcements on new policies, announcements of employees' anniverary dates or birthdays, recognitions, and so on. Most interesting are the stories of exceptional behavior toward guests. In every daily lineup, employees are encouraged to share stories of exceptional customer care. The great stories are remembered and repeated, communicating not only what is possible but what is expected.

The Ritz-Carlton's sophisticated processes allow it to manage details like few other hotels do. Employees are encouraged to treat not only guests graciously, but each other, too.

Source: © 2004 The Ritz-Carlton Hotel Company. All rights reserved. Reprinted with permission of the Ritz-Carlton Hotel Company, L.L.C. The Ritz-Carlton is a federally registered trademark of the Ritz-Carlton Hotel Company L.L.C.

When any employee encounters a situation where guests' needs are not being met, they are expected to take charge of the problem and follow it through to resolution. They are empowered to spend up to $2,000 per guest to resolve complaints or problems. Customers with complaints are not passed along to "the person who can help you." Part of the job is to take responsibility for getting such problems fixed. Housekeepers (in the back office) who discover a broken lamp would enter the defect into a computer, so that it is fixed before customers even find it. Employees, and the processes performed in both the front and back offices, seek to "enliven the senses, instill well-being, and fulfill even the unexpressed wishes of their guests."

Sources: Terry R. Bacon and David G. Pugh, "Ritz-Carlton and EMC: The Gold Standards in Operational Behavioral Differentation," *Journal of Organizational Excellence* (Spring 2004), pp. 61–76; www.ritzcarlton.com.

Processes for McDonald's walk-in customers must be more personal than for its drive-through customers. There must be a real person behind the counter. By contrast drive-through customers, who want even faster delivery speed and an efficient transaction, are likely to be less concerned about getting personal attention.

> PROCESS STRUCTURE IN MANUFACTURING <

Many processes at a manufacturing firm are actually services to internal or external customers, and so the previous discussion on services applies to them. Here we focus instead on the manufacturing processes themselves. Because of the differences between service and manufacturing processes, we need a different view on process structure.

PRODUCT-PROCESS MATRIX

The product-process matrix, shown in Figure 4.5, brings together three elements: (1) volume, (2) product design, and (3) process. It synchronizes the product to be manufactured with the manufacturing process itself.

A good strategy for a manufacturing process depends first and foremost on volume. Customer contact, a primary feature of the customer-contact matrix for services, normally is not a consideration for manufacturing processes (although it *is* a factor for the many service processes throughout manufacturing firms). For many manufacturing processes, high product customization means lower volumes for many of the steps in the process. If customization, top quality, and product variety are strongly emphasized, the likely result is lower volume for any particular step in the manufacturing process.

The vertical dimension of the product-process matrix deals with the same three characteristics in the customer-contact matrix: complexity, divergence, and flow. Each manufacturing process should be analyzed on these three dimensions, just as was done for a service process.

MANUFACTURING PROCESS STRUCTURING

Figure 4.5 shows several desirable positions (often called *process choices*) in the product-process matrix that effectively connect the manufactured product with the process. **Process choice** is the way of structuring the process by organizing resources around the process or organizing them around the products. Organizing around the process means, for example, that all milling machines are grouped together and process all products or parts needing that kind of transformation. Organizing around the product means bringing together all the

process choice

A way of structuring the process by organizing resources around the process or organizing them around the products.

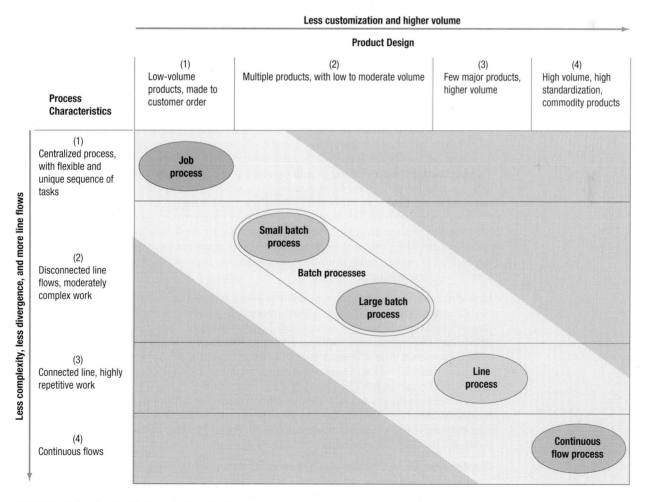

FIGURE 4.5 | Product-Process Matrix for Processes

different human resources and equipment needed for a specific product and dedicating them to producing just that product. The manager has four process choices, which form a continuum, to choose from: (1) *job process*, (2) *batch process*, (3) *line process*, and (4) *continuous process*. As with the customer-contact matrix, it is unlikely that a manufacturing process can be a top performer if its position is too far from the diagonal. The fundamental message in Figure 4.5 is that the best choice for a manufacturing process depends on the volume and degree of customization required of the process. The process choice might apply to an entire manufacturing process or just one subprocess nested within it. For example, one step of the process might be a job process where a specific part is machined (along with parts for many different products), whereas another step might be a line process where the part is assembled with other parts and materials to create the final product. We now concentrate on the differences among the four choices for manufacturing processes.

Job Process Examples are machining a metal casting for a customized order or producing customized cabinets. A **job process** creates the flexibility needed to produce a wide variety of products in significant quantities, with considerable complexity and divergence in the steps performed. Customization is high and volume for any one product is low. The workforce and equipment are flexible to handle considerable task divergence. Companies choosing job processes often bid for work. Typically, they make products to order and do not produce them ahead of time. The specific needs of the next customer are unknown, and the timing of repeat orders from the same customer is unpredictable. Each new order is handled as a single unit—as a job.

A job process primarily organizes all like resources around itself (rather than allocating them out to specific products); equipment and workers capable of certain types of work are located together. These resources process all jobs requiring that type of work. Because customization is high and most jobs have a different sequence of steps, this process choice creates flexible flows through the operations rather than a line flow. Even though considerable variability may exist in the flows through a job process, some line flows may occur within it as well, due to identical nested processes and repeat orders from customers.

Batch Process The batch process is by far the most common process choice found in practice, leading to terms such as *small batch* or *large batch* to further distinguish one process choice from another. Examples of a batch process are making standard components that feed an assembly line or some processes that manufacture capital equipment. A **batch process** differs from the job process with respect to volume, variety, and quantity. The primary difference is that volumes are higher because the same or similar products or parts going into them are produced repeatedly. Some of the components going into the final product may be processed in advance. Another difference is that a narrower range of products is provided. A third difference is that production lots are handled in larger quantities (or *batches*) than are with job processes. A batch of one product (or component part going into it or perhaps other products) is processed, and then production is switched to the next one. Eventually the first product is produced again. A batch process has average or moderate volumes, but process divergence is still too great to warrant dedicating a separate process for each product. The process flow is flexible, with no standard sequence of steps throughout the facility. However, more dominant paths emerge than at a job process, and some segments of the process have a line flow.

Line Process Products created by a line process include the assembly of computers, automobiles, appliances, and toys. A **line process** lies between the batch and continuous processes on the continuum; volumes are high and products are standardized, which allows resources to be organized around particular products. Divergence is minimal in the process or line flows, and little inventory is held between the processing steps. Each step performs the same process over and over, with little variability in the products manufactured. Production and material handling equipment is specialized.

Production orders are not directly linked to customer orders, as is the case with job processes. Standard products are produced in advance of their need and held in inventory so that they are ready when a customer places an order. Product variety is possible by careful control of the addition of standard options to the main product.

Continuous Flow Process Examples of a continuous flow process are petroleum refining; chemical processes; and processes making steel, soft drinks, and food (such as Borden's huge pasta-making plant). A **continuous flow process** is the extreme end of high-volume standardized production, with rigid line flows. Process divergence is negligible. Its name

job process
A process with the flexibility needed to produce a wide variety of products in significant quantities, with considerable complexity and divergence in the steps performed.

batch process
A process that differs from the job process with respect to volume, variety, and quantity.

line process
A process that lies between the batch and continuous processes on the continuum; volumes are high and products are standardized, which allows resources to be organized around particular products.

continuous flow process
The extreme end of high-volume standardized production and rigid line flows, with production not starting and stopping for long time intervals.

derives from the way materials move through the process. Usually, one primary material (such as a liquid, a gas, or a powder) moves without stopping through the process. The process seems more like a separate entity by itself. The process is often capital-intensive and operates around the clock to maximize utilization and to avoid expensive shutdowns and start-ups. A continuous flow process differs from a line process in one important respect. Materials (be they undifferentiated or discrete) flow through the process without stopping until the whole batch is finished. The time span can be several shifts or even several months. Line processes, on the other hand, can be started and stopped with each shift or day, even if the batch is not finished.

PRODUCTION AND INVENTORY STRATEGIES

Strategies for manufacturing processes differ from those in services, not only because of low customer contact and involvement, but also because of the ability to use inventories. Make-to-order, assemble-to-order, and make-to-stock strategies are three approaches to inventory that should be coordinated with process choice.

Make-to-Order Strategy   Manufacturers that make products to customer specifications in low volumes tend to use the **make-to-order strategy**, coupling it with job or small batch processes. It is a more complex process than assembling a final product from standard components, such as assembling a Dell computer to customer order. Many different types of manufacturing processes might be used, other than primarily "assembly or joining parts and materials." The process is viewed with a make-to-order strategy as a set of subprocesses that can be used in many different ways to satisfy the unique needs of customers. This strategy provides a high degree of customization and typically uses job or small batch processes. The processes are complex, with high divergence. Because most products, components, and assemblies are custom-made, the manufacturing process must be flexible to accommodate the variety. Specialized medical equipment, castings, and expensive homes are suited to the make-to-order strategy. The assemble-to-order strategy is another possibility.

Assemble-to-Order Strategy   The **assemble-to-order strategy** is an approach to producing a wide variety of products from relatively few assemblies and components after the customer orders are received. Typical competitive priorities are variety and fast delivery times. The assemble-to-order strategy often involves a line process for assembly and a batch process for fabrication. Because they are devoted to manufacturing standardized components and assemblies in high volumes, the fabrication processes focus on creating appropriate amounts of inventories for the assembly processes. Once the specific order from the customer is received, the assembly processes create the product from standardized components and subassemblies produced by the fabrication processes.

Stocking finished products would be economically prohibitive because the numerous possible options make forecasting relatively inaccurate. Thus, the principle of *postponement* is applied. For example, a manufacturer of upscale upholstered furniture can produce hundreds of a particular style of sofa, with no two alike, to meet customers' selections of fabric and wood. Other examples include paint (any color can be produced at the paint store by mixing standard pigments) and prefabricated homes for which the customer chooses among color and trim options.

Make-to-Stock Strategy   Manufacturing firms that hold items in stock for immediate delivery, thereby minimizing customer delivery times, use a **make-to-stock strategy**. This strategy is feasible for standardized products with high volumes and reasonably accurate forecasts. It is the inventory strategy of choice for line or continuous flow processes. For example, in Figure 4.6, which depicts a final automobile assembly process, both the midsized 6-cylinder and the compact 4-cylinder models are assembled on the same line. Their volumes are sufficient to warrant a make-to-stock strategy. The process flow for the two products is straightforward, with four nested processes devoted to the two products.

This strategy is also applicable to situations in which the process produces a unique product for a specific customer if the volumes are high enough. For example, a company producing a sensor for the transmission of the Ford Explorer would have enough volume to operate a production line specifically for that sensor and would carry a stock of the finished product for the scheduled shipments to the factory. Other examples of products produced with a make-to-stock strategy include garden tools, electronic components, soft drinks, and chemicals.

make-to-order strategy

A strategy used by manufacturers that make products to customer specifications in low volumes.

assemble-to-order strategy

A strategy for producing a wide variety of products from relatively few assemblies and components after the customer orders are received.

make-to-stock strategy

A strategy that involves holding items in stock for immediate delivery, thereby minimizing customer delivery times.

FIGURE **4.6**

Automobile Assembly Process

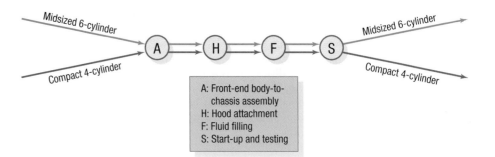

A: Front-end body-to-
   chassis assembly
H: Hood attachment
F: Fluid filling
S: Start-up and testing

mass production

A term sometimes used in the popular
press for a line process that uses the
make-to-stock strategy.

Combining a line process with the make-to-stock strategy is sometimes called **mass production**. It is what the popular press commonly envisions as the classical manufacturing process, because the environment is stable and predictable, with workers repeating narrowly defined task with low divergence. However, a line process is only one of four process choices.

EMBEDDING STRATEGY INTO MANUFACTURING PROCESSES

Just as a service process can be repositioned in the customer-contact matrix, so can a manufacturing process be moved in the product-process matrix. Changes can be made either in the horizontal direction of Figure 4.5 by changing the degree of customization and volume, or they can be moved in the vertical direction by changing process complexity or divergence. Process flows can be made more linear by dedicating human and capital resources to a specific product or perhaps a group of similar products. In that way, the sequence of tasks becomes the same. Little divergence is present because, essentially, the same product is made repetitively with no deviations. The production and inventory strategy can also be changed.

Competitive priorities must be considered when translating strategy into specific manufacturing processes. Figure 4.7 shows some usual tendencies found in practice. Job and small batch processes are usual choices if top quality, on-time delivery, and flexibility (customization, variety, and volume flexibility) are given primary emphasis. Large batch, line, and continuous flow processes match up with an emphasis on low-cost operations, consistent quality, and delivery speed.

FIGURE **4.7**

Links of Competitive Priorities
with Manufacturing Strategy

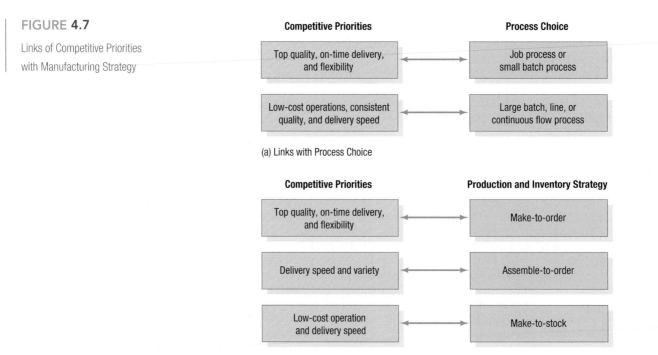

(a) Links with Process Choice

(b) Links with Production and Inventory Strategy

For production and inventory strategies, the make-to-order strategy matches up with flexibility (particularly customization) and top quality. Because delivery speed is more difficult, meeting due dates and on-time delivery get the emphasis on the time dimension. The assemble-to-order strategy allows delivery speed and flexibility (particularly variety) to be achieved, whereas the make-to-stock strategy is the usual choice if delivery speed and low-cost operations are emphasized. Keeping an item in stock assures quick delivery because it is generally available when needed, without delays in producing it. High volumes open up opportunities to reduce costs.

Having covered the various dimensions of process structure decisions, we now turn to a second major decision—customer involvement—shown in Figure 4.1.

> CUSTOMER INVOLVEMENT <

Customer involvement reflects the ways in which customers become part of the process and the extent of their participation. It is especially important for many service processes, particularly if customer contact is (or should be) high.

A good place to begin increasing customer involvement is making more of the process visible to the customer. Letting customers see what normally is hidden from them is part of the service design at Harvey's, a Canadian fast-food chain. There you can see workers in a sanitary and neat workplace broiling your meat, and you can pick the kinds of additional ingredients desired. An even bolder step is to let your customers participate in selected back-office processes, in effect converting them into front offices.

POSSIBLE DISADVANTAGES

Customer involvement is not always a good idea. In some cases giving the customer more active contact in a service process will just be disruptive, making the process less efficient. Dealing with the unique needs of each customer can make the process more complex and divergent. Managing the timing and volume of customer demands becomes more challenging if the customer is physically present and expects prompt delivery. Quality measurement also becomes more difficult and exposing the facilities and employees to the customer can have important quality implications (favorable or unfavorable). No longer buffered from external influences, service provider productivity can drop, and costs can increase. Such changes make interpersonal skills a prerequisite to the service provider's job, but higher skill levels come at a cost. Revising the facility layout might be a necessary investment, now that managing customer perceptions becomes an important part of the process.

If customer involvement requires physical presence, customers may determine the time and location that the service is to be provided. If the service is delivered to the customer, decisions involving the location become part of the process strategy. Will the customer be

A college student is waiting for his meal at a restaurant in the UCLA food court in Los Angeles, California. A good place to begin increasing customer involvement is making the process more visible to the customer.

served only on the service provider's premises, will the service providers go to the customer's premises, or will the service be provided at a third location? Having many smaller decentralized facilities closer to the various customer concentration areas may be required if the customer comes to the service providers. Otherwise, the service capability must be mobile. Either approach increases costs. Although certified public accountants frequently work on their clients' premises, both the time and the place are likely to be known well in advance, and travel becomes a cost consideration.

POSSIBLE ADVANTAGES

Despite these possible disadvantages, the advantages of a more customer-focused process might increase the net value to the customer. Some customers seek active participation in and control over the service process, particularly if they will enjoy savings in both price and time. The manager must assess whether advantages outweigh disadvantages, judging them in terms of the competitive priorities and customer satisfaction. The manager must also be aware of the possible use of emerging technologies in facilitating more customer involvement.

Improved Competitive Capabilities Depending on the situation, more customer involvement can mean better quality, faster delivery, greater flexibility, and even lower cost. Customers can come face-to-face with the service providers, where they can ask questions, make special requests on the spot, provide additional information, and even offer advice. Such a change creates a more personal relationship with the service provider and makes the customer part of assuring the competitive priority of consistent quality.

If customization and variety are highly valued, customer involvement might help. Some processes can be designed to allow the customers to come up with their own service or product specifications or even become involved in the design of the product. A good example is in the custom-designed and custom-built home industry: The customer is heavily involved in the design process and inspects the work in process at various times. If a wide variety of services or products are available, the customers can make their own selections to fit their own preferences. In effect, they "pick their own groceries."

Just as active customer contact and personalized attention can increase costs, in other ways it can reduce costs. Self-service is the choice of many retailers, such as gasoline stations, supermarkets, and bank services. Sometimes referred to as the "salad-bar approach" to productivity, it substitutes customer efforts for those of the service provider. Manufacturers of products (such as toys, bicycles, and furniture) may also prefer to let the customer perform the final assembly because product, shipping, and inventory costs frequently are lower, as are losses from damage. The savings are passed on to the customers as lower prices. Of course, some customers prefer a more passive role, such as full-service at a gasoline station during a wintry day, despite the higher cost.

Emerging Technologies In a market where customers are technology enabled, companies can now engage in an active dialogue with customers and make them partners in creating value. Customers are a new source of competence for such processes. To harness customer competencies, companies must involve customers in an ongoing dialogue. They must also revise some of their traditional processes, such as pricing and billing systems, to account for their customers' new role. For example, in business-to-business relationships, the Internet changes the roles that companies play with other businesses. Ford's suppliers now are close collaborators in the process of developing new vehicles and no longer are passive providers of materials and services. The same is true for distributors. Wal-Mart does more than just distribute Procter & Gamble's products: It shares daily sales information and works with Proctor & Gamble in managing inventories and warehousing operations.

> RESOURCE FLEXIBILITY <

Just as managers must account for customer contact when making customer involvement decisions, so must they account for process divergence and diverse process flows when making resource flexibility decisions in Figure 4.1. High task divergence and flexible process flows require more flexibility of the process's resources—its employees, facilities, and equipment. Employees need to perform a broad range of duties, and equipment must be general purpose. Otherwise, resource utilization will be too low for economical operations.

WORKFORCE

Operations managers must decide whether to have a **flexible workforce**. Members of a flexible workforce are capable of doing many tasks, either at their own workstations or as they move from one workstation to another. However, such flexibility often comes at a cost, requiring greater skills and thus more training and education. Nevertheless, benefits can be large: Worker flexibility can be one of the best ways to achieve reliable customer service and alleviate capacity bottlenecks. Resource flexibility helps to absorb the feast-or-famine workloads in individual operations that are caused by low-volume production, divergent tasks, flexible routings, and fluid scheduling.

   The type of workforce required also depends on the need for volume flexibility. When conditions allow for a smooth, steady rate of output, the likely choice is a permanent workforce that expects regular full-time employment. If the process is subject to hourly, daily, or seasonal peaks and valleys in demand, the use of part-time or temporary employees to supplement a smaller core of full-time employees may be the best solution. However, this approach may not be practical if knowledge and skill requirements are too high for a temporary worker to grasp quickly. Controversy is growing over the practice of replacing full-time workers with temporary or part-time workers.

EQUIPMENT

Low volumes mean that process designers should select flexible, general-purpose equipment. Figure 4.8 illustrates this relationship by showing the total cost lines for two different types of equipment that can be chosen for a process. Each line represents the total annual cost of the process at different volume levels. It is the sum of fixed costs and variable costs (see Supplement A, "Decision Making"). When volumes are low (because customization is high), process 1 is the best choice. It calls for inexpensive general-purpose equipment, which keeps investment in equipment low and makes fixed costs (F_1) small. Its variable unit cost is high, which gives its total cost line a relatively steep slope. Process 1 does the job, but not at peak efficiency. However, volumes are not high enough for total variable costs to overcome the benefit of low fixed costs.

   Conversely, process 2 is the best choice when volumes are high and customization is low. Its advantage is low variable unit cost, as reflected in the flatter total cost line. This efficiency is possible when customization is low because the equipment can be designed for a

Technicians in the Parts Repair Department of this ABB facility, a global leader in power and automation technologies, must be flexible enough to repair many different parts for automation equipment installed at customer locations in the field. This service facility has 30 different workstations configured to perform different types of processes. Workers are cross-trained to move from one station to another, depending on what needs to be done.

flexible workforce

A workforce whose members are capable of doing many tasks, either at their own workstations or as they move from one workstation to another.

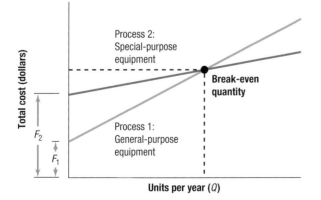

FIGURE 4.8

Relationship Between Process Costs and Product Volume

TUTOR 4.1

Tutor 4.1 on the Student CD-ROM demonstrates how to do break-even analysis for equipment selection.

narrow range of products or tasks. Its disadvantage is high equipment investment and, thus, high fixed costs (F_2). When annual volume produced is high enough, spreading these fixed costs over more units produced, the advantage of low variable costs more than compensates for the high fixed costs.

The break-even quantity in Figure 4.8 is the quantity at which the total costs for the two alternatives are equal. At quantities beyond this point, the cost of process 1 exceeds that of process 2. Unless the firm expects to sell more than the break-even amount, which is unlikely with high customization and low volume, the capital investment of process 2 is not warranted.

> CAPITAL INTENSITY <

Capital intensity is the mix of equipment and human skills in the process; the greater the relative cost of equipment, the greater is the capital intensity. As the capabilities of technology increase and its costs decrease, managers face an ever-widening range of choices, from operations utilizing very little automation to those requiring task-specific equipment and little human intervention. **Automation** is a system, process, or piece of equipment that is self-acting and self-regulating. Although automation is often thought to be necessary to gain competitive advantage, it has both advantages and disadvantages. Thus, the automation decision requires careful examination.

automation

A system, process, or piece of equipment that is self-acting and self-regulating.

AUTOMATING MANUFACTURING PROCESSES

Substituting labor-saving capital equipment and technology for labor has been a classic way of improving productivity and quality consistency in manufacturing processes. If investment costs are large, automation works best when volume is high, because more customization typically means reduced volume. Gillette, for example, spent $750 million on the production lines and robotics that gave it a capacity to make 1.2 billion razor cartridges a year. The equipment is complicated and expensive. Only with such high volumes could this line process produce the product at a price low enough that consumers could afford to buy it.

One big disadvantage of capital intensity can be the prohibitive investment cost for low-volume operations (see Figure 4.8). Generally, capital-intensive operations must have high utilization to be justifiable. Also, automation does not always align with a company's competitive priorities. If a firm offers a unique product or high-quality service, competitive priorities may indicate the need for skilled servers, hand labor, and individual attention rather than new technology. A case in point is Gillette's downstream processes that package and store the razor cartridges. It customizes the packaging for different regions of the world, so that volumes for any one type of package are much lower. As a result of the low volumes, Gillette does not use expensive automation for these processes. In fact, it outsources them.

fixed automation

A manufacturing process that produces one type of part or product in a fixed sequence of simple operations.

Fixed Automation   Manufacturers use two types of automation: fixed and flexible (or programmable). Particularly appropriate for line and continuous flow process choices, **fixed automation** produces one type of part or product in a fixed sequence of simple operations. Until the mid-1980s, most U.S. automobile plants were dominated by fixed automation—and some still are. Chemical processing plants and oil refineries also utilize this type of automation.

Operations managers favor fixed automation when demand volumes are high, product designs are stable, and product life cycles are long. These conditions compensate for the process's two primary drawbacks: large initial investment cost and relative inflexibility. However, fixed automation maximizes efficiency and yields the lowest variable cost per unit if volumes are high.

flexible (or programmable) automation

A manufacturing process that can be changed easily to handle various products.

Flexible Automation   **Flexible** (or **programmable**) **automation** can be changed easily to handle various products. The ability to reprogram machines is useful for both low-customization and high-customization processes. In the case of high customization, a machine that makes a variety of products in small batches can be programmed to alternate between products. When a machine has been dedicated to a particular product or family of products, as in the case of low customization and a line flow, and the product is at the end of its life cycle, the machine can simply be reprogrammed with a new sequence of operations for a new product.

Managerial Practice 4.2 describes how R.R. Donnelley benefits from more flexible automation, allowing for quick changeovers from one customer order to the next.

AUTOMATING SERVICE PROCESSES

Using capital inputs as a labor-saving device is also possible for service processes. In educational services, for example, long-distance learning technology now can supplement or even replace the traditional classroom experience by using books, computers, Web sites, and videos as facilitating goods that go with the service. Justifying technology need not be limited to cost reduction. Sometimes it can actually increase complexity and task divergence by making available a wide menu of choices to the customer. Technology in the future surely will make possible even a greater degree of customization and variety in services than currently only human providers can now deliver. Beyond cost and variety

---

| MANAGERIAL **PRACTICE** | 4.2 | FLEXIBLE AUTOMATION AT R.R. DONNELLEY |

R.R. Donnelley is the largest commerical printer in the United States and the number one printer of books. The industry makes huge capital investments in its printing presses to help drive down the variable unit cost of a book (see Figure 4.8). Its uses a make-to-order strategy, with customers such as book publishers placing new orders as their inventories became too low. However, the "make-ready" time to prepare for the new order and change over the presses for the next customer order was time consuming. Keeping such expensive equipment idle for changeovers is costly. These high costs force customers such as book publishers to make large, infrequent orders for their books. They often ordered 100,000 copies of a new work—and sometimes winding up with 50,000 unsold books in their warehouses. All too often, they ended up either being out of stock or having too much stock. They also placed orders well in advance of their desired delivery dates, because lead times were so long. R.R. Donnelley carefully allocated its production schedule well into the future, and the total time to run large batches (including preparation time) was large.

Flexible automation at its Roanoke, Virginia, plant allows R.R. Donnelley to take a different course, and it is reaping big rewards. The new process begins when the contents of a book arrive via the Internet as a PDF (portable document format) and go to the plant's prepress department. The intricate manual operations required to prepare text and pictures for printing traditionally caused the biggest bottlenecks. Roanoke now makes its plates digitally instead of from photographic film. With the elimination of steps such as duplicating and cleaning the file, a job that once took hours can now be completed in 12 minutes. The all-digital workflow also makes possible the creation of electronic instructions, known as ink presets, that improve productivity and quality. Cleaner and sharper plates are created for the presses because, unlike film, electronic type does not have to be repeatedly handled.

Quick, efficient press changeovers along with new types of automation make it possible to profitably print 50 copies of a single-color book or 2,500 copies of a four-color book. The publisher can then gradually increase the batch size after testing the market. The rise of book sales through Amazon.com also boosted demand for small editions, and the new flexibility allows publishers to reprint classics and other books in manageable quantities. At the other extreme, Donnelley can still manufacture mil-

R.R. Donnelly has been able to achieve flexible automation by receiving books digitally and preparing them to go on press electronically. This allows the company to put books on press more quickly and print smaller, more manageable quantities in a single print run.

lions of copies of a single book, as it did when it turned out most of the 8 million copies of the latest Harry Potter book.

With more flexible automation, the Roanoke plant produces 75 percent of its titles in two weeks or less, compared with four to six weeks for a four-color book using traditional technology. Management created a culture of continous improvement at the plant, home of some 300 workers. Overall, Roanoke increased throughput 20 percent without having to buy an additional press and binding line, a savings of $15 million. Its presses run around the clock producing 3.5 million books a month; productivity rose 20 percent, and service improved. Book publishers now enjoy a just-in-time product when they want it.

considerations, the process designer must understand the customer and how much close contact is valued. If the customers seek a visible presence and personal attention, technologies reduced to sorting through a variety of options on the Internet or over the telephone might be a poor choice.

The need for volume to justify expensive automation is just as valid for service processes as for manufacturing processes. Increasing the volume lowers the cost per dollar of sales. Volume is essential for many capital-intensive processes in the transportation, communications, and utilities industries. A jetliner idled because of low demand is very expensive, a reality reflected in recent income statements of airline companies. Managers must carefully assess both volume and investment dollars in deciding how much automation makes sense. While buying larger, more standardized equipment might be tempting, it may not provide a good strategic fit.

It is often correctly assumed that volumes are higher in back-office processes, where customer contact is low. Physical contact, personalized treatment, and face-to-face communication often create divergent tasks and low volume, but not always. A recent study of financial services shows that high volumes are just as likely in front offices as in back offices. As a result, automation is not concentrated in the back office, but is just as likely found in front-office processes. Automation of financial services comes primarily from information technology, which can flexibly handle a wide array of processes at multiple locations. Another factor allowing technology in both the front offices and back offices of financial services is the low investment cost. For example, the typical capital cost might be $300,000 per employee in a manufacturing process. In financial service processes, it might be only in the range of $50,000 per employee. In terms of Figure 4.8, the break-even volume for introducing the technology in services is much lower.

ECONOMIES OF SCOPE

economies of scope

Economies that reflect the ability to produce multiple products more cheaply in combination than separately.

If capital intensity is high, resource flexibility is low. King Soopers produces a high-volume product (loaves of bread) efficiently on an automated (high-capital-intensity) bread line, with few people monitoring its operation; but the process has low resource flexibility. In contrast, the custom cake line produces a low volume of product because it requires high customization. To complete the unique customer orders, resources must be flexible, and because the process requires hand work, capital intensity is low.

In certain types of manufacturing operations, such as machining and assembly, programmable automation breaks this inverse relationship between resource flexibility and capital intensity. It makes possible both high capital intensity and high resource flexibility, creating economies of scope. **Economies of scope** reflect the ability to produce multiple products more cheaply in combination than separately. In such situations, two conflicting competitive priorities—customization and low price—become more compatible. However, taking advantage of economies of scope requires that a family of parts or products have enough collective volume to utilize equipment fully.

Economies of scope also apply to service processes. Consider, for example, Disney's approach to the Internet. When the company's managers entered the volatile Internet world, their businesses were only weakly tied together. Disney's Infoseek business, in fact, was not even fully owned. However, once its Internet markets became more crystallized, managers at Disney moved to reap the benefits of economies of scope. They aggressively linked their Internet processes with one another and with other parts of Disney. A flexible technology that handles many services together can be less expensive than handling each one separately, particularly when the markets are not too volatile.

> STRATEGIC FIT <

The process strategist should understand how the four major process decisions tie together, so as to spot ways of improving poorly designed processes. The choices should fit the situation and each other. When the fit is more *strategic*, the process will be more effective. We examine services and manufacturing processes, looking for ways to test for strategic fit.

DECISION PATTERNS FOR SERVICE PROCESSES

The common denominator for decisions on service processes is primarily customer contact. Figure 4.9 shows how the process structure and the other key process decisions are tied to customer contact. High customer contact at a front-office service process means:

1. *Process Structure.* The customer (internal or external) is present, actively involved, and receives personal attention. These conditions create processes with high complexity, high divergence, and flexible process flows.

2. *Customer Involvement.* When customer contact is high, customers are more likely to become part of the process. The service created for each customer is unique.

3. *Resource Flexibility.* High process divergence and flexible process flows fit with more flexibility from the process's resources—its workforce, facilities, and equipment.

4. *Capital Intensity.* When volume is higher, automation and capital intensity are more likely. Even though higher volume is usually assumed to be found in the back office, it is just as likely to be in the front office for financial services. Information technology is a major type of automation at many service processes, which brings together both resource flexibility and automation.

Of course, this list provides general tendencies rather than rigid prescriptions. Exceptions can be found, but these relationships provide a way of understanding how process decisions can be linked coherently.

DECISION PATTERNS FOR MANUFACTURING PROCESSES

The common denominator for decisions on manufacturing processes is volume. Figure 4.10 summarizes the relationships between volume and the four key process decisions. High volumes at a manufacturing process typically mean

1. *Process Choice.* The high volumes at King Soopers' bread line, combined with a standard product, make a line flow possible. It is just the opposite with the King Soopers' custom cakes, where a job process produces cakes to specific customer orders.

2. *Customer Involvement.* Customer involvement is not a factor in most manufacturing processes, except for choices made on product variety and customization. Less discretion is allowed with line or continuous flow processes in order to avoid the unpredictable demands required by customized orders.

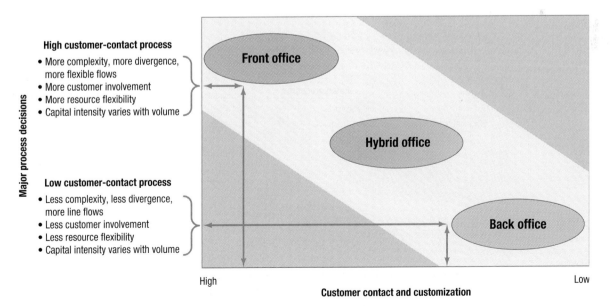

FIGURE 4.9 | Decision Patterns for Service Processes

3. *Resource Flexibility.* When volumes are high and process divergence is low, flexibility is not needed to utilize resources effectively, and specialization can lead to more efficient processes. King Soopers' bread line can make just one product: bread.

4. *Capital Intensity.* High volumes justify the large fixed costs of an efficient operation. The King Soopers bread line is capital-intensive. It is automated from dough mixing to placement of the product on shipping racks. Expanding this process would be expensive. By way of contrast, the King Soopers' custom cake process is labor-intensive and requires little investment to equip the workers.

GAINING FOCUS

In the past, new services or products often were added to a facility in the name of better utilizing fixed costs and keeping everything under the same roof. The result was a jumble of competitive priorities, process structures, and technologies. In the effort to do everything, nothing was done well.

Focus by Process Segments A facility's process often can neither be characterized nor actually designed for one set of competitive priorities and one process choice. King Soopers had three processes under one roof, but management segmented them into three separate operations that were relatively autonomous. At a services facility, some parts of the process might seem like a front office and other parts like a back office. Such arrangements can be effective, provided that sufficient focus is given to each process.

plants within plants (PWPs)

Different operations within a facility with individualized competitive priorities, processes, and workforces under the same roof.

Plants within plants (PWPs) are different operations within a facility with individualized competitive priorities, processes, and workforces under the same roof. Boundaries for PWPs may be established by physically separating subunits or simply by revising organizational relationships. At each PWP, customization, capital intensity volume, and other relationships are crucial and must be complementary. The advantages of PWPs are fewer layers of management, greater ability to rely on team problem solving, and shorter lines of communication between departments.

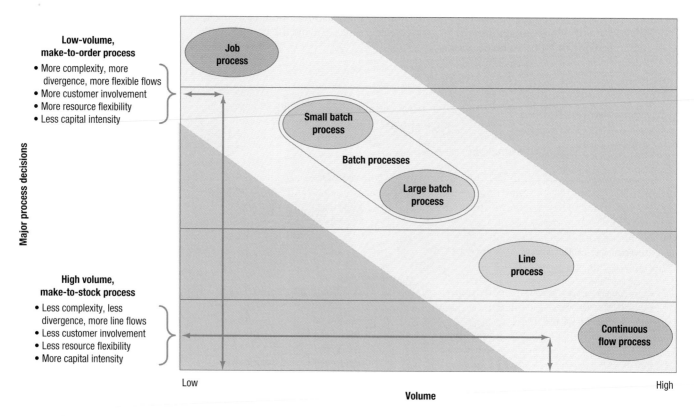

FIGURE 4.10 | Decision Patterns for Manufacturing Processes

Focused Service Operations Service industries also implement the concepts of focus and PWPs. Specialty retailers, such as Gap and The Limited, opened stores with smaller, more accessible spaces. These focused facilities generally chipped away at the business of large department stores. Using the same philosophy, some department stores now focus on specific customers or products. Remodeled stores create the effect of many small boutiques under one roof.

Focused Factories Hewlett-Packard, S. C. Johnson and Sons, Japan's Ricoh and Mitsubishi, and Britain's Imperial Chemical Industries PLC are some of the firms that created **focused factories,** splitting large plants that produced all the company's products into several specialized smaller plants. The theory is that narrowing the range of demands on a facility will lead to better performance because management can concentrate on fewer tasks and lead a workforce toward a single goal. In some situations, a plant that used to produce all the components of a product and assemble them may split into one that produces the components and one that assembles them, so that each can focus on its own individual process technology.

focused factories

The result of a firm's splitting large plants that produced all the company's products into several specialized smaller plants.

> STRATEGIES FOR CHANGE <

The four major process decisions represent broad, strategic issues. Decisions that are made must be translated into actual process designs or redesigns. We conclude with two different but complementary philosophies for process design: (1) process reengineering and (2) process improvement. Let us first examine process reengineering and the considerable attention it received in management circles during the last decade.

PROCESS REENGINEERING

Reengineering is the fundamental rethinking and radical redesign of processes to improve performance dramatically in terms of cost, quality, service, and speed. Process reengineering is about reinvention, rather than incremental improvement. It is strong medicine and not always needed or successful. Pain, in the form of layoffs and large cash outflows for investments in information technology, almost always accompanies massive change. However, reengineering processes can have big payoffs. For example, Bell Atlantic reengineered its telephone business. After five years of effort, it cut the time to connect new customers from 16 days to just hours. The changes caused Verizon to lay off 20,000 employees, but the company is decidedly more competitive.

reengineering

The fundamental rethinking and radical redesign of processes to improve performance dramatically in terms of cost, quality, service, and speed.

A process selected for reengineering should be a core process, such as a firm's order-fulfillment activities. Reengineering then requires focusing on that process, often using cross-functional teams, information technology, leadership, and process analysis. Let us examine each element of the overall approach.

Critical Processes The emphasis of reengineering should be on core business processes, rather than on functional departments, such as purchasing or marketing. By focusing on processes, managers may spot opportunities to eliminate unnecessary work and supervisory activities, rather than worry about defending turf. Because of the time and energy involved, reengineering should be reserved for essential processes, such as new-product development or customer service. Normal process-improvement activities can be continued with the other processes.

Strong Leadership Senior executives must provide strong leadership for reengineering to be successful. Otherwise, cynicism, resistance ("we tried that before"), and boundaries between departments can block radical changes. Managers can help overcome resistance by providing the clout necessary to ensure that the project proceeds within a strategic context. Executives should set and monitor key performance objectives for the process. Top management should also create a sense of urgency, making a case for change that is compelling and constantly refreshed.

Cross-Functional Teams A team, consisting of members from each functional area affected by the process change, is charged with carrying out a reengineering project. For instance, in reengineering the process of handling an insurance claim, three departments should be represented: customer service, adjusting, and accounting. Reengineering works best at high-involvement workplaces, where self-managing teams and employee empowerment are the rule rather than the exception. Top-down and bottom-up initiatives can be combined—top-down for performance targets and bottom-up for deciding how to achieve them.

Information Technology   Information technology is a primary enabler of process engineering. Most reengineering projects design processes around information flows, such as customer order fulfillment. The process owners who will actually be responding to events in the marketplace need information networks and computer technology to do their jobs better. The reengineering team must determine who needs the information, when they need it, and where.

Clean-Slate Philosophy   Reengineering requires a "clean-slate" philosophy—that is, starting with the way the customer wants to deal with the company. To ensure a customer orientation, teams begin with internal and external customer objectives for the process. Often, teams first establish a price target for the service or product, deduct profits desired, and then find a process that provides what the customer wants at the price the customer will pay. Reengineers start from the future and work backward, unconstrained by current approaches.

Process Analysis   Despite the clean-slate philosophy, a reengineering team must understand things about the current process: what it does, how well it performs, and what factors affect it. Such understanding can reveal areas in which new thinking will provide the biggest payoff. The team must look at every procedure involved in the process throughout the organization, recording each step, questioning why it is done, and then eliminating everything that is not necessary. Information on standing relative to the competition, process by process, is also valuable.

Reengineering has led to many successes and will continue to do so. However, it is not simple or easily done, nor is it appropriate for all processes or all organizations. Many firms cannot invest the time and resources to implement a radical, clean-slate approach. Significant process improvements that have nothing to do with information technology can be realized. Finally, the best understanding of a process, and how to improve it, often lies with the people who perform the work each day, not cross-functional teams or top management.

PROCESS IMPROVEMENT

process improvement

The systematic study of the activities and flows of each process to improve it.

Process improvement is the systematic study of the activities and flows of each process to improve it. Its purpose is to "learn the numbers," understand the process, and dig out the details. Once a process is really understood, it can be improved. The relentless pressure to provide better quality at a lower price means that companies must continually review all aspects of their operations. As the chief executive of Dana Corporation, a $7.9 billion producer of automotive parts, put it, "You have to get productivity improvements forever." Process improvement goes on, whether or not a process is reengineered.

Each aspect of the process is examined. An individual or a whole team examines the process, using the tools described in the next chapter. One must look for ways to streamline tasks, eliminate whole processes entirely, cut expensive materials or services, improve the environment, or make jobs safer. One must find the ways to trim costs and delays and to improve customer satisfaction.

> STUDENT CD-ROM AND INTERNET RESOURCES <

The Student CD-ROM and the Companion Website at **www.prenhall.com/krajewski** contain many tools, activities, and resources designed for this chapter.

> KEY TERMS <

active contact 124
assemble-to-order strategy 131
automation 136
back office 127
batch process 130
capital intensity 122
continuous flow process 130
customer contact 123
customer involvement 122
economies of scope 138
fixed automation 136
flexible (or programmable) automation 136

flexible flow 126
flexible workforce 135
focused factories 141
front office 126
hybrid office 126
ISO 14001 121
job process 130
line flow 126
line process 130
make-to-order strategy 131
make-to-stock strategy 131

mass production 132
passive contact 124
plants within plants (PWPs) 140
process choice 129
process complexity 125
process divergence 125
process improvement 142
process strategy 120
process structure 122
reengineering 141
resource flexibility 122

> DISCUSSION QUESTIONS <

1. What processes at manufacturing firms are really service processes that involve considerable customer contact? Can customer contact be high, even if the process only has internal customers?

2. Consider this sign seen in a local restaurant: "To-go orders do NOT include complimentary chips and salsa. If you have any questions, see our management, NOT our employees." What impact does this message have on its employees, their service processes, and customer satisfaction? Contrast this approach with the one taken by The Ritz-Carlton hotels. Are the differences primarily due to different competitive priorities?

3. Medical technology can outfit a patient with an artificial heart, or cure vision defects with the touch of a laser. However, hospitals still struggle with their back-office processes, such as getting X-ray files from radiology on the fourth floor to the first-floor view boxes in the emergency room without having to send a runner. More than 90 percent of the estimated 30 billion health transactions each year are conducted by phone, fax, or mail. To what extent, and how, can information technology improve productivity and quality for such processes? Remember that some doctors are not ready to give up their pads and pencils, and many hospitals have strong lines drawn around its departments such as pharmacy, cardiology, radiology, and pediatrics.

4. To give utilities an incentive to spend money on new pollution-control technology, the EPA proposes that flue gas emission limits be changed to require slightly cleaner stacks than the older technology is capable of producing. To comply, some utilities will install the new technology. Some will not. Utilities that reduce emissions below the new requirements will receive "credits," which they can sell to utilities that choose not to install the pollution-control technology. These utilities can then continue business as usual, so long as they have purchased enough credits to account for the extra pollution they create. The price of the credits will be determined by the free market.

    Form sides and discuss the ethical, environmental, and political issues and trade-offs associated with this proposition.

5. The Dewpoint Chemical Company is deciding where to locate a fertilizer plant near the Rio Grande. What are the ethical, environmental, and political issues and trade-offs associated with locating a fertilizer plant on the north bank versus the south bank of the Rio Grande?

> PROBLEMS <

Software, such as OM Explorer, Active Models, and POM for Windows is packaged with every new copy of the textbook. Check with your instructor on how best to use it. In many cases, the instructor wants you to understand how to do the calculations by hand. At most, the software provides a check on your calculations. When calculations are particularly complex and the goal is interpreting the results in making decisions, the software replaces entirely the manual calculations. The software also can be a valuable resource well after your course is completed. Problems 3 and 4 apply break-even analysis (discussed in Supplement A, "Decision Making") to process decisions.

1. Rate a service process with which you are familiar on each of the five dimensions of customer contact. Use a

seven-point scale, where 1 = very low and 7 = very high. Explain your ratings, and then calculate a combined score for the overall customer contact. Did you use equal weights in calculating the combined score? Why or why not? Where is your process positioned on the customer-contact matrix? Is it properly aligned? Why or why not?

2. Select one of the three processes shown in the video for King Soopers (bread, pastry, or customer cake). What kind of transformation process, process choice, and inventory strategy are involved? Is the process properly aligned? Explain.

3. Dr. Gulakowicz is an orthodontist. She estimates that adding two new chairs will increase fixed costs by $150,000, including the annual equivalent cost of the capital investment and the salary of one more technician. Each new patient is expected to bring in $3,000 per year in additional revenue, with variable costs estimated at $1,000 per patient. The two new chairs will allow her to expand her practice by as many as 200 patients annually. How many patients would have to be added for the new process to break even?

4. Two different manufacturing processes are being considered for making a new product. The first process is less capital-intensive, with fixed costs of only $50,000 per year and variable costs of $700 per unit. The second process has fixed costs of $400,000 but varible costs of only $200 per unit.

   a. What is the break-even quantity, beyond which the second process becomes more attractive than the first?

   b. If the expected annual sales for the product is 800 units, which process would you choose?

CASE | **Custom Molds, Inc.**

Custom Molds, Inc., manufactures custom-designed molds for plastic parts and produces custom-made plastic connectors for the electronics industry. Located in Tucson, Arizona, Custom Molds was founded by the father and son team of Tom and Mason Miller in 1987. Tom Miller, a mechanical engineer, had more than 20 years of experience in the connector industry with AMP, Inc., a large multinational producer of electronic connectors. Mason Miller had graduated from the University of Arizona in 1986 with joint degrees in chemistry and chemical engineering.

The company was originally formed to provide manufacturers of electronic connectors with a source of high-quality, custom-designed molds for producing plastic parts. The market consisted mainly of the product design and development divisions of those manufacturers. Custom Molds worked closely with each customer to design and develop molds to be used in the customer's product development processes. Thus, virtually every mold had to meet exacting standards and was somewhat unique. Orders for multiple molds would arrive when customers moved from the design and pilot-run stage of development to large-scale production of newly designed parts.

As the years went by, Custom Molds' reputation grew as a designer and fabricator of precision molds. Building on this reputation, the Millers decided to expand into the limited manufacture of plastic parts. Ingredient-mixing facilities and injection-molding equipment were added, and by the mid-1990s Custom Molds developed its reputation to include being a supplier of high-quality plastic parts. Because of limited capacity, the company concentrated its sales efforts on supplying parts that were used in limited quantities for research and development efforts and in preproduction pilot runs.

Production Processes

By 1997, operations at Custom Molds involved two distinct processes: one for fabricating molds and one for producing plastic parts. Although different, in many instances these two processes were linked, as when a customer would have Custom Molds both fabricate a mold and produce the necessary parts to support the customer's research and design efforts. All fabrication and production operations were housed in a single facility. The layout was characteristic of a typical job shop, with like processes and similar equipment grouped in various places in the plant. Figure 4.11 shows a schematic of the plant floor. Multiple pieces of various types of high-precision machinery, including milling, turning, cutting, and drilling equipment, were located in the mold-fabrication area.

Fabricating molds is a skill-oriented, craftsman-driven process. When an order is received, a design team, comprising a design engineer and one of 13 master machinists, reviews the design specifications. Working closely with the customer, the team establishes the final specifications for the mold and

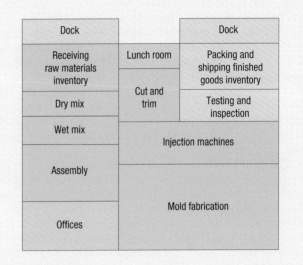

FIGURE 4.11 | Plant Layout

gives them to the master machinist for fabrication. It is always the same machinist who was assigned to the design team. At the same time, the purchasing department is given a copy of the design specifications, from which it orders the appropriate raw materials and special tooling. The time needed to receive the ordered materials is usually three to four weeks. When the materials are received for a particular mold, the plant master scheduler reviews the workload of the assigned master machinist and schedules the mold for fabrication.

Fabricating a mold takes from two to four weeks, depending on the amount of work the machinist already has scheduled. The fabrication process itself takes only three to five days. Upon completion, the mold is sent to the testing and inspection area, where it is used to produce a small number of parts on one of the injection molding machines. If the parts meet the design specifications established by the design team, the mold is passed on to be cleaned and polished. It is then packed and shipped to the customer. One day is spent inspecting and testing the mold and a second day cleaning, polishing, packing, and shipping it to the customer. If the parts made by the mold do not meet design specifications, the mold is returned to the master machinist for retooling and the process starts over. Currently, Custom Molds has a published lead time of nine weeks for delivery of custom-fabricated molds.

The manufacturing process for plastic parts is somewhat different from that for mold fabrication. An order for parts may be received in conjunction with an order for a mold to be fabricated. In instances where Custom Molds has previously fabricated the mold and maintains it in inventory, an order may be just for parts. If the mold is already available, the order is reviewed by a design engineer, who verifies the part and raw material specifications. If the design engineer has any questions concerning the specifications, the customer is contacted and any revisions to specifications are mutually worked out and agreed upon.

Upon acceptance of the part and raw material specifications, raw material orders are placed and production is scheduled for the order. Chemicals and compounds that support plastic-parts manufacturing are typically ordered and received within one week. Upon receipt, the compounds are first dry-mixed and blended to achieve the correct composition. Then the mixture is wet-mixed to the desired consistency (called *slurry*) for injection into molding machines. When ready, the slurry is transferred to the injection molding area by an overhead pipeline and deposited in holding tanks adjacent to the injection machines. The entire mixing process takes only one day.

When the slurry is staged and ready, the proper molds are secured—from inventory or from the clean and polish operation if new molds were fabricated for the order—and the parts are manufactured. Although different parts require different temperature and pressure settings, the time to produce a part is relatively constant. Custom Molds has the capacity to produce 5,000 parts per day in the injection-molding department; historically, however, the lead time for handling orders in this department has averaged one week. Upon completion of molding, the parts are taken to the cut and trim operation, where they are disconnected and leftover flashing is removed. After being inspected, the parts may be taken to assembly or transferred to the packing and shipping area for shipment to the customer. If assembly of the final parts is not required, the parts can be on their way to the customer two days after being molded.

Sometimes the final product requires some assembly. Typically, this entails attaching metal leads to plastic connectors. If assembly is necessary, an additional three days is needed before the order can be shipped. Custom Molds is currently quoting a three-week lead time for parts not requiring fabricated molds.

The Changing Environment

In early 2006, Tom and Mason Miller began to realize that the electronics industry they supplied, along with their own business, was changing. Electronics manufacturers had traditionally manufactured their own component parts to reduce costs and ensure a timely supply of parts. By the 1990s, this trend had changed. Manufacturers were developing strategic partnerships with parts suppliers to ensure the timely delivery of high-quality, cost-effective parts. This approach allowed funds to be diverted to other uses that could provide a larger return on investment.

The impact on Custom Molds could be seen in sales figures over the past three years. The sales mix was changing. Although the number of orders per year for mold fabrication remained virtually constant, orders for multiple molds were declining, as shown in the following table:

	Number of Orders		
Order Size	Molds 2003	Molds 2004	Molds 2005
1	80	74	72
2	60	70	75
3	40	51	55
4	5	6	5
5	3	5	4
6	4	8	5
7	2	0	1
8	10	6	4
9	11	8	5
10	15	10	5
Total orders	230	238	231

The reverse was true for plastic parts, for which the number of orders per year had declined but for which the order sizes were becoming larger, as illustrated in the following table:

	Number of Orders		
Order Size	Parts 2003	Parts 2004	Parts 2005
50	100	93	70
100	70	72	65
150	40	30	35
200	36	34	38
250	25	27	25
500	10	12	14
750	1	3	5
1,000	2	2	8
3,000	1	4	9
5,000	1	3	8
Total orders	286	280	277

During this same period, Custom Molds began having delivery problems. Customers were complaining that parts orders were taking four to five weeks instead of the stated three weeks and that the delays were disrupting production schedules. When asked about the situation, the master scheduler said that determining when a particular order could be promised for delivery was difficult. Bottlenecks were occurring during the production process, but where or when they would occur could not be predicted. They always seemed to be moving from one operation to another.

Tom Miller thought that he had excess labor capacity in the mold-fabrication area. So, to help push through those orders that were behind schedule, he assigned one of the master machinists the job of identifying and expediting those late orders. However, that tactic did not seem to help much. Complaints about late deliveries were still being received. To add to the problems, two orders had been returned recently because of the number of defective parts. The Millers knew that something had to be done. The question was "What?"

QUESTIONS

1. What are the major issues facing Tom and Mason Miller?

2. What are the competitive priorities for Custom Molds' processes and the changing nature of the industry?

3. What alternatives might the Millers pursue? What key factors should they consider as they evaluate these alternatives?

Source: This case was prepared by Dr. Brooke Saladin, Wake Forest University, as a basis for classroom discussion.

> SELECTED REFERENCES <

Alster, Norm. "What Flexible Workers Can Do." *Fortune* (February 13, 1989), pp. 62–66.

Bowen, John, and Robert C. Ford. "Managing Service Organizations: Does Having a 'Thing' Make a Difference?" *Journal of Management,* vol. 28, no. 3 (2002), pp. 447–469.

Collier, D. A., and Meyer, S. "An Empirical Comparison of Service Matrices." *International Journal of Operations and Production Management,* vol. 20, no. 5–6 (2000), pp. 705–729.

Collier, D. A., and Meyer, S. "A Positioning Matrix for Services." *International Journal of Operations and Production Management,* vol. 18, no. 12 (1998), pp. 1223–1244.

Collins, Jim. *Good to Great: Why Some Companies Make the Leap . . . and Others Don't.* New York: HarperCollins, 2001.

Cook, David P., Chon-Huat Goh, and Chen H. Chung. "Service Typologies: A State of the Art Survey." *Production and Operations Management,* vol. 8, no. 3 (1999), pp. 318–338.

Dixon, J. Robb, Peter Arnold, Janelle Heineke, Jay S. Kim, and Paul Mulligan. "Business Process Reengineering: Improving in New Strategic Directions." *California Management Review* (Summer 1994), pp. 1–17.

Fitzsimmons, James A., and Mona J. Fitzsimmons. *Service Management: Operations, Strategy, and Information Technology.* New York: McGraw-Hill, 1998.

Goldhar, J. D., and Mariann Jelinek. "Plan for Economies of Scope." *Harvard Business Review* (November–December 1983), pp. 141–148.

Grover, Varun, and Manoj K. Malhotra. "Business Process Reengineering: A Tutorial on the Concept, Evolution, Method, Technology and Application." *Journal of Operations Management,* vol. 15, no. 3 (1997), pp. 194–213.

Hall, Gene, Jim Rosenthal, and Judy Wade. "How to Make Reengineering Really Work." *Harvard Business Review* (November–December 1993), pp. 119–131.

Hammer, M. "Reengineering Work: Don't Automate, Obliterate." *Harvard Business Review,* vol. 68, no. 4 (1990), pp. 104–112.

Hammer, Michael. "Deep Change: How Operational Innovation Can Transform Your Company." *Harvard Business Review,* vol. 82, no. 4 (April 2004), pp. 85–93.

Hammer, M. *Beyond Reengineering.* New York: Harper Business, 1996.

Hammer, Michael, and James Champy. *Reengineering the Corporation: A Manifesto for Business Revolution.* New York: HarperBusiness, 1993.

Hill, Terry. *Manufacturing Strategy: Text and Cases,* 3d ed. Homewood, IL: Irwin/McGraw-Hill, 2000.

Hill, Terry. *The Strategy Quest.* Coventry, Great Britain: AMD Publishing (UK), 1998.

Kelliher, Clare, and Michael Riley. "Beyond Efficiency: Some By-Products of Functional Flexibility." *Service Industries Journal,* vol. 23, no. 4 (2003), pp. 98–114.

Kellogg, Deborah L., and Winter Nie. "A Framework for Strategic Service Management." *Journal of Operations Management,* vol. 13, no. 4 (1995), pp. 323–337.

Klassen, R. D., and C. P. McLauglin. "The Impact of Environmental Management on Firm Performance." *Management Science,* vol. 42, no. 8 (1990), pp. 1100–1214.

Leibs, Scott. "A Little Help from Their Friends." *Industry Week,* February 2, 1998.

Lovelock, Christopher H., and George S. Yip. "Developing Global Strategies for Service Businesses." *California Management Review,* vol. 38, no. 2 (1996), pp. 64–86.

"Making It by the Billions." *The Boston Globe,* August 9, 1998.

Makowe, J. *Beyond the Bottom Line.* New York: Simon & Schuster, 1994.

Malhotra, Manoj K., and Larry P. Ritzman. "Resource Flexibility Issues in Multistage Manufacturing." *Decision Sciences,* vol. 21, no. 4 (1990), pp. 673–690.

Melnyk, S. A., Robert P. Sroufe, and Roger Calantone. "Assessing the Impact of Environmental Management Systems on Corporate and Environmental Performance." *Journal of Operations Management,* vol. 21, no. 3 (2003), pp. 329–351.

Mersha, Tigineh. "Enhancing the Customer Contact Model." *Journal of Operations Management,* vol. 9, no. 3 (1990), pp. 391–405.

Metters, Richard, Kathryn King-Metters, and Madeleine Pullman. *Successful Service Operations Management.* Mason, OH: South-Western, 2003.

Narasimhan, Ram, and Jayanth Jayaram. "Reengineering Service Operations: A Longitudinal Case Study." *Journal of Operations Management,* vol. 17, no. 1 (1998), pp. 7–22.

Port, Otis. "The Responsive Factory." *Business Week,* Enterprise 1993, pp. 48–51.

"Process, Process, Process." *Planning Review* (special issue), vol. 22, no. 3 (1993), pp. 1–56.

Quinn, J. B. "The Productivity Paradox Is False: Information Technology Improves Services Performance." *Advances in Services Marketing and Management,* vol. 5 (1996), pp. 71–84.

Rayport, Jeffrey F., and Bernard J. Jaworski. "Best Face Forward." *Harvard Business Review,* vol. 82, no. 12 (2003), pp. 47–58.

Roth, Aleda V., and Marjolijn van der Velde. *The Future of Retail Banking Delivery Systems.* Rolling Meadows, IL: Bank Administration Institute, 1988.

Safizadeh, M. Hossein, Joy M. Field, and Larry P. Ritzman. "An Empirical Analysis of Financial Services Processes with a Front-Office or Back-Office Orientation." *Journal of Operations Management*, vol. 21, no. 5 (2003), pp. 557–576.

Safizadeh, M. Hossein, Larry P. Ritzman, and Debasish Mallick. "Revisiting Alternative Theoretical Paradigms in Manufacturing." *Production and Operations Management*, vol. 9, no. 2 (2000), pp. 111–127.

Schmenner, Roger W. *Service Operations Management.* Englewood Cliffs, NJ: Prentice Hall, 1998.

Shostack, G. Lynn. "Service Positioning Through Structural Change." *Journal of Marketing*, vol. 51, no. 1 (1987), pp. 34–43.

Silvestro, R. L. Fitzgerald, R. Johnston, and Chris Voss. "Toward a Classification of Service Processes." *International Journal of Service Industry Management*, vol. 3 (1992), pp. 62–75.

Skinner, Wickham. "Operations Technology: Blind Spot in Strategic Management." *Interfaces*, vol. 14 (January– February 1984), pp. 116–125.

Wemmerlöv, U. "A Taxonomy for Service Processes and Its Implications for System Design." *International Journal of Service Industry Management*, vol. 1, no. 1 (1990), pp. 20–40.

Wheelwright, Steven C., and Robert H. Hayes. "Competing Through Manufacturing." *Harvard Business Review* (January– February 1985), pp. 99–109.

5

LEARNING GOALS

*After reading this chapter,
you should be able to:*

1. Explain a systematic way to analyze processes.
2. Define flowcharts, service blueprints, and process charts.
3. Identify metrics for process evaluation.
4. Describe Pareto charts, cause-and-effect diagrams, and process simulation.
5. Describe using benchmarking to create better processes.
6. Identify keys for effective process management.

Omgeo devised a better way to communicate its product release schedule. Here, employees discuss this aspect of their overall straight-through processing operation, which allows stock trades to move through its system in 3 hours versus 20.

OMGEO

When a Hong Kong investment manager buys stock from a broker in Tokyo, chances are the deal passes through Omgeo LLC. Omgeo's name (pronounced OM-gee-oh) combines the Latin word omni, meaning "in all ways or places" with the Greek word geo, meaning "earth." Omgeo is the leading provider of complete global trade management services. In 2005, it processed more than 1 million trades per day and serviced 6,000 broker-dealers, custodian banks, and investment managers in more than 40 countries. The Depository Trust & Clearing Corporation (DTCC) and Thomson Financial created Omgeo in 2000 as a new joint venture. DTCC is an institution set up and owned by financial services firms to settle their trades. A unit of Thomson Financial originally marketed this posttrade, presettlement service in the late 1980s as a money saver for institutional investors.

The dozens of scribbled faxes, telexes, and phone calls made for the typical trade cost from $10 to $12, but Thomson's process allowed it to charge only 20 cents to $1 per trade—and investment managers essentially got the service free. Its behind-the-scenes service was an improvement over previous processes for making trades, but it was still a tangle of communications between brokers (such as Goldman Sachs), big investors (such as Royal London Asset Management), and banks (such as the Deutsche Bank) every time a trade was placed. It took three to five days to settle a trade in the United States, when money and securities officially changed hands.

But every process can be improved, in part by critically analyzing the current process. Omgeo made a major improvement, with the goal of completing the whole process in potentially just

>

one day. A key factor was the Internet and new information technology solutions. With the revised process, steps 1 through 3 were done the same way. However, steps 4 through 9 were replaced by entering all of the information into a central database that the broker, investment manager, and custodian banks all have access to in real time (e.g., central matching). The revised process ended the need to tack message after message onto a cumbersome file. It cut some of the grinding monotony of processing trades and saved employees' time. It also saved vast amounts of money by reducing human errors. Royal London Asset Management, currently using Omgeo Central Trade Manager (CTM), is able to move a trade through to step 8 (settlement notification) in 3 hours. Before, when using Omgeo's old process, it took 20 hours to move one trade that far along the trade cycle. Now, they have 17 extra hours to identify and fix trade errors and get them done on the same day.

Central trade matching information technology replaces many of the steps that were performed sequentially. With central matching, the allocations from the institutional investment manager and trade details from the broker are submitted into a central engine, and the details of the trades are automatically compared to eliminate errors. The CTM engine provides straight-through processing of the work flow in back-office operations.

Sources: Beth Healy, "One Day, Not Three: A Push to Trade Faster." *The Boston Globe* (July 19, 2000); www.omgeo.com, March 2005.

The changes leading to the creation of Omgeo involved processes with considerable customer contact, and they reflect a process strategy favoring more automation and "process reengineering" (rather than "process improvement"). The process was so totally revamped that a new company was formed to implement it, and information technology was a primary enabler of the new process.

Processes are perhaps the least understood and managed aspect of a business. No matter how talented and motivated people are, a firm cannot gain competitive advantage with faulty processes. Just as Mark Twain said of the Mississippi River, a process just keeps rolling on—with one big difference. Most processes can be improved if someone thinks of a way and implements it effectively. Indeed, companies will either adapt processes to the changing needs of customers or cease to exist. Long-term success comes from managers and employees who really understand their businesses. But all too often, highly publicized efforts that seem to offer quick-fix solutions fail to live up to expectations over the long haul, be they programs for conceptualizing a business vision, conducting culture transformation campaigns, or providing leadership training.

Within the field of operations management, many important innovations over the past several decades include work-simplification or better-methods programs, statistical process control, optimization techniques, statistical forecasting techniques, material requirements planning, flexible automation, lean manufacturing, total quality management, reengineering, Six Sigma programs, enterprise resource planning, and e-commerce. We cover these important approaches in the following chapters because they can add significant customer value to a process. However, they are best viewed as just part of a total system for the effective management of work processes, rather than cure-alls.

Of course, process analysis is needed for both reengineering and process improvement, but it is also part of monitoring performance over time. In this chapter, we first analyze a process in detail and determine exactly how each step will be performed. We begin with a systematic approach for analyzing a process that identifies opportunities for improvement, documents the current process, evaluates the process to spot performance gaps, redesigns the process to eliminate the gaps, and implements the desired changes. The goal is continual improvement.

Three supporting techniques—flowcharts, service blueprints, and process charts—can give good insights into the current process and the proposed changes. Data analysis tools, such as checklists, bar charts, Pareto charts, and cause-and-effect diagrams, allow the analyst to go from problem symptoms to root causes. Simulation is a more advanced technique to evaluate process performance. We conclude with some of the keys to managing processes effectively, to ensuring that changes are implemented and an infrastructure is set up for making continuous improvements.

Process analysis, however, extends beyond the analysis of individual processes. It is also a tool for improving the operation of value chains. Consider Zara, one of Europe's most profitable apparel brands. Zara thrives on bringing new apparel designs to the market fast. It was able to accomplish this speed by creating an agile new product development process that allows it to quickly go from sketches to preliminary designs and then, after reliable demand data are available, quickly finalizing designs. It also designed an agile order fulfillment process that manufactures and distributes garments quickly and efficiently even under extreme conditions of demand fluctuations. The capability of the order fulfillment process had to support the capability of the new product development process to be effective. Clearly, process analysis enabled Zara to design a competitive value chain.

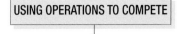

> ## PROCESS ANALYSIS ACROSS THE ORGANIZATION <

All parts of an organization need to be concerned about process analysis simply because they are doing work, and process analysis focuses on how work is actually done. Are they providing the most value to their customers (internal or external), or can they be improved? Operations and sales are often the first areas that come to mind because they are so closely connected with the core processes. However, support processes in accounting, finance, and human resources are crucial to an organization's success, too. Top management also gets involved, as do other departments. During these handoffs of the "baton," disconnects are often the worst and opportunities for improvement the greatest.

> ## A SYSTEMATIC APPROACH <

Figure 5.1 shows a six-step blueprint for process analysis. **Process analysis** is the documentation and detailed understanding of how work is performed and how it can be redesigned. Process analysis begins with identifying a new opportunity for improvement and ends with implementing a revised process. The last step goes back to the first step, thus creating a cycle of continual improvement.

STEP 1: IDENTIFY OPPORTUNITIES

In order to identify opportunities, managers must pay particular attention to the four core processes: supplier relationship, new service/product development, order fulfillment, and the customer relationship. Each of these processes, and the subprocesses nested within

process analysis
The documentation and detailed understanding of how work is performed and how it can be redesigned.

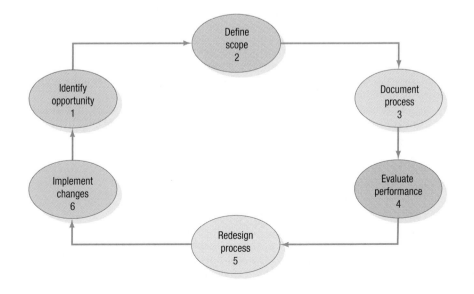

FIGURE 5.1
Blueprint for Process Analysis

them, are involved in delivering value to external customers. Are customers currently satisfied with the services or products they receive, or is there room for improvement? How about internal customers? Customer satisfaction must be monitored periodically, either with a formal measurement system or with informal checks or studies. Managers sometimes develop an inventory of their core and support processes that provide a guide for what processes need scrutiny.

Another way to identify opportunities is by looking at the strategic issues. Do gaps exist between a process's competitive priorities and its current competitive capabilities? Do multiple measures of cost, top quality, quality consistency, delivery speed, and on-time delivery meet or exceed expectations? Is there a good *strategic fit* in the process? If the process provides a service, does its position on the customer-contact matrix (see Figure 4.3) seem appropriate? How does the degree of customer contact match up with process structure, customer involvement, resource flexibility, and capital intensity (see Figure 4.9)? Similar questions should be asked about manufacturing processes regarding the strategic fit between process choice, volume, and customization (see Figure 4.10).

Employees who actually perform the process or internal suppliers or customers should be encouraged to bring their ideas to managers and staff specialists (such as industrial engineers), or perhaps pass on their ideas through a formal suggestion system. A **suggestion system** is a voluntary system by which employees submit their ideas on process improvements. Usually, a specialist evaluates the proposals, makes sure worthy suggestions are implemented, and provides feedback to those who make the suggestions. Sometimes the person or team making a good suggestion is rewarded with money or special recognition.

STEP 2: DEFINE THE SCOPE

Step 2 establishes the boundaries of the process to be analyzed. Is it a broad process that stretches across the whole organization, involving many steps and many employees, or a more narrowly bracketed nested subprocess that is just part of one person's job? A process's scope can be too narrow or too broad. For example, a broadly defined process that outstrips the resources available, sometimes called trying to "boil the ocean," is doomed because it will increase employee frustration without producing any results.

The resources that management assigns to improving or reengineering a process should match the scope of the process. For a small nested process involving only one employee, perhaps the employee is asked to redesign the process herself. For a project that deals with a major core process, managers typically establish one or more teams. A **design team** consists of knowledgeable, team-oriented individuals who work at one or more steps in the process, do the process analysis, and make the necessary changes. Other resources may be full-time specialists called internal or external *facilitators*. Facilitators know process analysis methodology, and they can guide and train the design team. If the process cuts across several departmental lines, it may benefit from a *steering team* of several managers from various departments, headed by a project manager who oversees the process analysis.

STEP 3: DOCUMENT THE PROCESS

Once scope is established, the analyst should document the process. Documentation includes making a list of the process's inputs, suppliers (internal or external), outputs, and customers (internal or external). This information then can be shown as a diagram, with a more detailed breakdown given in a table.

The next part of documentation is understanding the different steps performed in the process, using one or more of the diagrams, tables, and charts described later in this chapter. When breaking down the process into steps, the analyst notes the degrees and types of customer contact, process complexity, and process divergence along the various steps in the process. He or she also notes what steps are visible to the customer and where in the process work is handed off from one department to the next.

STEP 4: EVALUATE PERFORMANCE

It is important to have good performance measures to evaluate a process for clues on how to improve it. **Metrics** are performance measures for the process and the steps within it. A good place to start is with competitive priorities, but they need to be specific. The analyst creates

suggestion system

A voluntary system by which employees submit their ideas on process improvements.

design team

A group of knowledgeable, team-oriented individuals who work at one or more steps in the process, do the process analysis, and make the necessary changes.

metrics

Performance measures that are established for a process and the steps within it.

multiple measures of quality, customer satisfaction, time to perform each step or the whole process, cost, errors, safety, environmental measures, on-time delivery, flexibility, and the like.

Once the metrics are identified, it is time to collect information on how the process is currently performing on each one. Measurement can be as simple as making a reasoned guess, asking a knowledgeable person, or taking notes while observing the process. More extensive studies involve collecting data for several weeks, consulting cost accounting data, or checking data recorded in information systems. In addition, techniques for analyzing wait times and delays can provide important information (see Supplement B, "Simulation" and Supplement C, "Waiting Lines"). Other valuable techniques include work sampling, time studies, and learning curve analysis (see Supplement G, "Learning Curve Analysis" and Supplement H, "Measuring Output Rates" on the Student CD-ROM). Managerial Practice 5.1 describes how McDonald's evaluates performance to spot ways to improve processes and restore customer satisfaction.

STEP 5: REDESIGN THE PROCESS

A careful analysis of the process and its performance on the selected metrics should uncover *disconnects,* or gaps, between actual and desired performance. Performance gaps can be caused by illogical, missing, or extraneous steps. They can be caused by metrics that reinforce the silo mentality of individual departments when the process spans across several departments. The analyst or design team should dig deep to find the root causes of performance gaps.

Using analytical and creative thinking, the design team generates a long list of ideas for improvements. These ideas are then sifted and analyzed. Ideas that are justifiable, where benefits outweigh costs, are reflected in a new process design. The new design should be documented "as proposed." Combining the new process design with the documentation of the current process gives the analysts clear before and after pictures. The new documentation should make clear how the revised process will work and the performance expected for the various metrics used.

STEP 6: IMPLEMENT CHANGES

Implementation is more than developing a plan and carrying it out. Many processes have been redesigned effectively, but never get implemented. People resist change: "We have always done it that way" or "we tried that before." Widespread participation in process analysis is essential, not only because of the work involved but also because it builds commitment. It is much easier to implement something that is partly your own idea. In addition, special expertise may be needed, such as for developing software. New jobs and skills may be needed, involving training and investments in new technology. Implementation brings to life the steps needed to bring the redesigned process online. Management or the steering committee must make sure that the implementation project goes according to schedule.

In the remainder of the chapter, we examine steps in process analysis in detail.

> DOCUMENTING THE PROCESS <

Three techniques are effective for documenting and evaluating processes: (1) flowcharts, (2) service blueprints, and (3) process charts. They allow you to lift the lid and peer inside to see how an organization does its work. You can see how a process operates, at any level of detail, and how well it is performing. Trying to create one of these charts might even reveal a lack of any established process. It may not be a pretty picture, but it is how work actually gets done. Techniques for documenting the process lend themselves to finding performance gaps, generating ideas for process improvements, and documenting the look of a redesigned process.

FLOWCHARTS

A **flowchart** traces the flow of information, customers, equipment, or materials through the various steps of a process. Flowcharts are also known as flow diagrams, process maps, relationship maps, or blueprints. Flowcharts have no precise format and typically are drawn

flowchart

A diagram that traces the flow of information, customers, equipment, or materials through the various steps of a process.

MANAGERIAL **PRACTICE**   5.1   EVALUATING PERFORMANCE AT MCDONALD'S

With the growth in system sales reaching $41.5 billion in 2002, up 4.3 percent per year since 1998, why would executives lose sleep over a few complaints? In just the prior year, McDonald's launched a five-year, $1 billion initiative to overhaul its information systems to enhance customer services at its more than 30,000 restaurants around the world. Like many customer relationship management (CRM) systems, it was intended to track and respond to shifting customer desires. The new, Internet-based data management structure would cover everything from software for tracking customer purchasing patterns to electronic links with suppliers to sensors for monitoring the temperature of fat in french-fry vats. The goal was to scrutinize every detail of its business in real time, ensuring that each outlet fine-tuned its operations to serve customers flawlessly.

In reality, reams of sales data were not what McDonald's needed when customers were upset with lousy food, slow service, and surly employees. McDonald's never realized—until it was too late—that customer complaints were growing more frequent and bitter. Tinkering with recipes for basic products such as the Big Mac special sauce saved pennies but turned off loyal Big Mac fans. Worse, McDonald's was opening stores too fast, with each new one eating into the sales of existing outlets. Even though system sales were rising, the average store gross fell 12 percent to $1.6 million from 1995 to 2002.

McDonald's is now listening to the customers again, and changing its processes to reflect it. The board brought on a new CEO who had spent 20 years on the operational side of the business. With a zeal for measuring customer satisfaction and sharing the data freely with operators, he pulled off a turnaround that stunned everyone in the business with its speed and scope. A million more diners flocked daily to the arches in 2003 than in 2002.

This turnaround began by pulling the plug on installing the massive new CRM system. Instead, other initiatives were launched to collect performance measures and revamp McDonald's processes to meet customer expectations. McDonald's sends mystery shoppers to restaurants to conduct anonymous reviews using a hard-number scoring system. Mystery diners from outside survey firms jot down on a paper checklist their grades for speed of service; food temperature; presentation and taste; cleanliness of the counter, tables and condiment islands; even whether the counter crewperson smiles at diners. Trailing 6-month and year-to-date results are posted on an internal McDonald's Web site so owners can compare their scores with regional averages. Operators could now pinpoint lingering problems, and performance measures focus operators' attention on needed process changes.

Another initiative was to send 900 operations missionaries into the field, each visiting stores multiple times to fine-tune processes while also

Instead of a CRM system, McDonald's uses mystery shoppers to evaluate its stores. It also sends operations "emissaries" to its stores to help managers fine-tune their processes.

conducting day-long seminars where store managers could share tips from corporate kitchen gurus—such as where to place staff—that would shave previous seconds off average service times. McDonald's restored the more expensive ingredients in the Big Mac sauce and changed the salt-and-pepper seasoning in the beef patties. The process was changed back to toasting buns rather than microwaving them, and lengthened the toasting time by 6 seconds, giving them an even sweeter caramelized flavor.

Other initiatives are being taken on McDonald's fast lane. Every 6 seconds shaved off the wait time adds a percentage point to sales growth. Outdoor menu boards now have more pictures and fewer words. An LED display confirms what customers say, reducing confusion later on. Premium sandwiches are put in boxes rather than paper wrappers, saving a few seconds, and boxes are color coded by sandwich to improve speed and accuracy. When cars start to stack up in line, a crew member may sally forth, PDA in hand, to take orders. A small number of restaurants are testing another process improvement, using professional order takers with strong communication skills located at remote call centers to handle drive-through orders. The orders might be taken better and the on-site McDonald's employees can focus on delivering better customer service.

When customers stopped going to McDonald's, so did investors. Now that sales are on the rise, the stock has regained its sizzle. By the start of 2005, the stock had more than doubled in two years. Performance measurement and improving processes to increase customer value pays off.

Sources: Daniel Kruger, "You Want Data with That?" *Forbes,* vol. 173, no. 6 (March 2004), pp. 58–60; Darrell K. Rigby and Dianne Ledingham, "CRM Done Right," *Harvard Business Review,* vol. 82, no. 11 (November 2004), pp. 118–129; The Associated Press, "McDonald's Testing Use of Call Centers," March 12, 2005.

with boxes (with a brief description of the step inside), and with lines and arrows to show sequencing. The rectangle (□) shape is the usual choice for a box, although other shapes (○, ◯, ◇, ▽, or ▱) can differentiate between different types of steps (operation, delay, storage, inspection, and the like). Colors and shading can also call attention to different types of steps, such as those particularly high on process complexity or on process divergence. Divergence is also communicated when an outgoing arrow from a step splits into two or more arrows that lead to different boxes. Although many representations are acceptable, there must be agreement on the conventions used. They can be given as a key somewhere in the flowchart, or described in accompanying text. It is also important to communicate *what* (information, customer order, customer, materials, or the like) is being tracked.

You can create flowcharts with several programs. Microsoft Power-Point offers many different formatting choices for flowcharts (see the Flowchart submenu under Auto-Shapes). The "Flowcharting Tutor in Excel" (see Student CD-ROM) offers another option. Other powerful software packages for flowcharting and drawing diagrams (such as organization charts and decision trees) are SmartDraw (www.smartdraw.com), Microsoft Visio (www.microsoft.com/office/visio), and Micrografx (www.micrografx.com). Often, free downloads are available at such sites on a trial basis.

A consultant discusses the proposal for a new organizational development program with clients during a follow-up meeting. The use of flowcharts can help in understanding this step as just one part of the overall sales process for a consulting company.

Flowcharts can be created for several levels in the organization. For example, at the strategic level, they could show the core processes and their linkages, as in Figure 1.4. At this level, the flowcharts would not have much detail; however, they would give a bird's eye view of the overall business. Just identifying a core process is often helpful. Let us now turn to the process level, where we get into the details of the process being analyzed. Figure 5.2 shows such a process, which consists of many steps that have subprocesses nested within them.

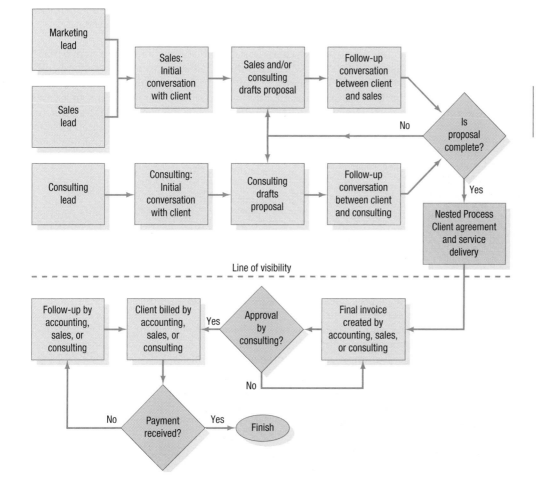

FIGURE 5.2

Flowchart of the Sales Process for a Consulting Company

FIGURE **5.3**

Flowchart of the Nested Subprocess
of Client Agreement and Service
Delivery

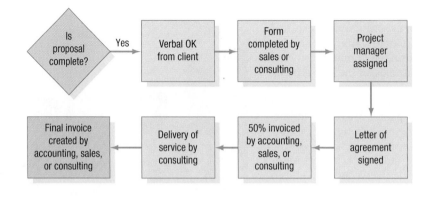

Rather than representing everything in one flowchart, Figure 5.2 presents an overview of the whole process. It describes the sales process for a consulting firm that specializes in organizational development and corporate education programs. Four different departments (accounting, consulting, marketing, and sales) interact with the external customer (client). The process goes through three main phases: generating business leads, client agreement and service delivery, and billing and collection.

Figure 5.2 illustrates one other feature. The diamond shape (◇) represents a yes/no decision or outcome, such as the results of an inspection or a recognition of different kinds of customer requirements. In Figure 5.2, it represents three yes/no decision points: (1) whether the proposal is complete, (2) whether consulting approves the invoice, and (3) whether payment is received. These yes/no decision points are more likely to appear when a process is high in divergence.

Nested processes can then be created for steps that were more aggregated. For example, Figure 5.3 flowcharts a nested process within the client agreement and service delivery step in Figure 5.2. Figure 5.3 brings out more details, such as invoicing the customer for 50 percent of the total estimated cost of the service before the service is delivered, and then putting together a final invoice after the service is finished. This nesting approach often becomes a practical necessity because only so much detail can be shown in any single flowchart.

Figure 5.4 shows still another format that is most appropriate when the process spans several department boundaries. This flowchart illustrates the order-filling process of a manufacturing company. The process starts when an order is generated by a customer and ends when payment is received by the company. All functions contributing to this process are included in the flowchart. The rows represent different departments or functional areas, and the steps appear in the department row where they are performed. This approach shows the *handoffs* from one department to another when the outgoing arrow from a step goes to another row. Special arrows are another way to show handoffs. Handoffs are points where cross-functional coordination is at particular risk due to the silo mentality. Misunderstandings, backlogs, and errors are more likely at these points.

Flowcharts allow the process analyst and managers to look at the horizontal organization, rather than the vertical organization and departmental boundaries implied by a typical organizational chart. Flowcharts show how organizations produce their outputs through cross-functional work processes, and allow the design team to see all the critical interfaces between functions and departments.

SERVICE BLUEPRINTS

service blueprint

A special flowchart of a service process
that shows which steps have high
customer contact.

A good design for service processes depends first and foremost on the type and amount of customer contact. A **service blueprint** is a special flowchart of a service process that shows which steps have high customer contact. Consider Figure 5.2 once again. It actually qualifies as a service blueprint because it shows a line of visibility. This special feature identifies which steps are visible to the customer (and thus more of a front-office process) and those that are not (back office process).

Of course, visibility is just one aspect of customer contact, and it may not adequately capture how actively the customer is involved or how much personal attention is required. A service blueprint can use colors, shading, or box shapes, instead of the line of visibility, to show the extent and type of customer contact. Another approach to service blueprinting is to tag each step with a number, and then have an accompanying table that describes in detail the customer contact for each numbered step.

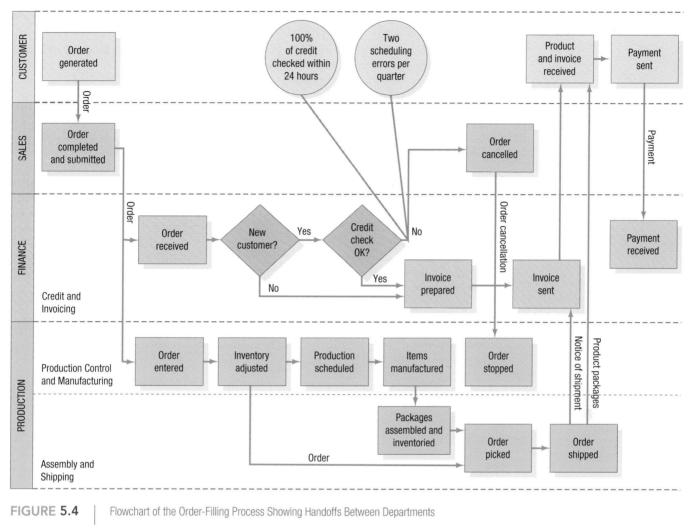

FIGURE 5.4 | Flowchart of the Order-Filling Process Showing Handoffs Between Departments

Source: Geary A. Rummler and Alan P. Brache, *Improving Performance,* 2nd ed. (San Francisco: Jossey-Bass, 1995).

PROCESS CHARTS

A **process chart** is an organized way of documenting all the activities performed by a person or group of people at a workstation, with a customer, or working with certain materials. It analyzes a process using a table, and can provide information about each step in the process. Often it is used to drill down to the job level for an individual person, a team, or a focused nested process. It can have many formats. Here we group the type of activities for a typical process into five categories:

- *Operation.* Changes, creates, or adds something. Drilling a hole or serving a customer are examples of operations.
- *Transportation.* Moves the study's subject from one place to another (sometimes called *materials handling*). The subject can be a person, a material, a tool, or a piece of equipment. A customer walking from one end of a counter to the other, a crane hoisting a steel beam to a location, and a conveyor carrying a partially completed product from one workstation to the next are examples of transportation.
- *Inspection.* Checks or verifies something but does not change it. Getting customer feedback, checking for blemishes on a surface, weighing a product, and taking a temperature reading are examples of inspections.
- *Delay.* Occurs when the subject is held up awaiting further action. Time spent waiting for a server, time spent waiting for materials or equipment; cleanup time; and time that

process chart

An organized way of documenting all the activities performed by a person or group of people, at a workstation, with a customer, or on materials.

workers, machines, or workstations are idle because they have no work to complete are examples of delays.

■ *Storage.* Occurs when something is put away until a later time. Supplies unloaded and placed in a storeroom as inventory, equipment put away after use, and papers put in a file cabinet are examples of storage.

Depending on the situation, other categories can be used. For example, subcontracting for outside services might be a category, or temporary storage and permanent storage might be two separate categories. Choosing the right category for each activity requires taking the perspective of the subject charted. A delay for the equipment could be inspection or transportation for the operator.

To complete a chart for a new process, the analyst must identify each step performed. If the process is an existing one, the analyst can actually observe the steps and categorize each step according to the subject being studied. The analyst then records the distance traveled and the time taken to perform each step. After recording all the activities and steps, the analyst summarizes the steps, times, and distances data. Figure 5.5 shows a process chart prepared using OM Explorer's *Process Chart* solver. It is for a patient with a twisted ankle being treated at a hospital. The process begins at the entrance and ends with the patient exiting after picking up the prescription.

After a process is charted, the analyst sometimes estimates the annual cost of the entire process. It becomes a benchmark against which other methods for performing the process can be evaluated. Annual labor cost can be estimated by finding the product of (1) time in hours to perform the process each time, (2) variable costs per hour, and (3) number of times the process is performed each year, or

$$\begin{array}{l} \text{Annual} \\ \text{labor cost} \end{array} = \left(\begin{array}{c} \text{Time to perform} \\ \text{the process in hours} \end{array}\right)\left(\begin{array}{c} \text{Variable costs} \\ \text{per hour} \end{array}\right)\left(\begin{array}{c} \text{Number of times process} \\ \text{performed per year} \end{array}\right)$$

FIGURE 5.5

Process Chart for Emergency Room Admission

Process:	Emergency room admission
Subject:	Ankle injury patient
Beginning:	Enter emergency room
Ending:	Leave hospital

Insert Step

Append Step

Remove Step

Summary

Activity		Number of Steps	Time (min)	Distance (ft)
Operation	●	5	23.00	
Transport	➡	9	11.00	815
Inspect	■	2	8.00	
Delay	▶	3	8.00	
Store	▼	—	—	

Step No.	Time (min)	Distance (ft)	●	➡	■	▶	▼	Step Description
1	0.50	15.0		X				Enter emergency room, approach patient window
2	10.00		X					Sit down and fill out patient history
3	0.75	40.0		X				Nurse escorts patient to ER triage room
4	3.00				X			Nurse inspects injury
5	0.75	40.0		X				Return to waiting room
6	1.00					X		Wait for available bed
7	1.00	60.0		X				Go to ER bed
8	4.00					X		Wait for doctor
9	5.00				X			Doctor inspects injury and questions patient
10	2.00	200.0		X				Nurse takes patient to radiology
11	3.00		X					Technician x-rays patient
12	2.00	200.0		X				Return to bed in ER
13	3.00					X		Wait for doctor to return
14	2.00		X					Doctor provides diagnosis and advice
15	1.00	60.0		X				Return to emergency entrance area
16	4.00		X					Check out
17	2.00	180.0		X				Walk to pharmacy
18	4.00		X					Pick up prescription
19	1.00	20.0		X				Leave the building

For example, if the average time to serve a customer is 4 hours, the variable cost is $25 per hour, and 40 customers are served per year, then the labor cost is $4,000 per year (or 4 hrs/customer × $25/hr × 40 customers/yr).

In the case of the patient in Figure 5.5, this conversion would not be necessary, with total patient time being sufficient. What is being tracked is the patient's time, not the time and costs of the service providers.

You can design your own process chart spreadsheets to bring out issues that are particularly important for the process you are analyzing, such as categories for customer contact, process divergence, and the like. You can also track performance measures other than time and distance traveled, such as error rates. In addition, you can also create a different version of the process chart spreadsheet that examines processes much as done with flowcharts, except now in the form of a table. The columns that categorize the activity type could be replaced by one or more columns reporting different metrics of interest, rather than trying to fit them into a flowchart. Although it might not look as elegant, it could be just as informative—and easier to create.

TUTOR 5.1

Tutor 5.1 on the Student CD-ROM provides a new example to practice creating process charts.

> EVALUATING PERFORMANCE <

Metrics and performance information complete the documentation of a process (see step 4 in Figure 5.1). Metrics can be displayed in various ways. Sometimes they can be added directly on the flowchart or process chart. Figure 5.4 shows metrics with circled entries. They establish the goals for the credit check: (1) all credit checks completed within 24 hours and (2) no more than two instances of inadvertently continuing the process without a credit check. When the number of metrics gets unwieldy, another approach is to create a supporting table for the chart. Its rows are the steps in the flowchart, service blueprint, or process charts. The columns are the current performance, goals, and performance gaps for various metrics.

The specific metrics analysts choose depends on the process being analyzed and on the competitive priorities. Good starting points are the per-unit processing time and cost at each step, and the time elapsed from beginning to end of the process. Capacity utilization and customer (or job) waiting times reveal where in the process delays are most likely to occur. Customer satisfaction measures, error rates, and scrap rates identify possible quality problems. We introduce many such metrics in subsequent chapters. Figure 5.6 shows the chapter or supplement that relates with some basic ones. Only when these subsequent chapters are understood do we really complete our discussion of process analysis.

DATA ANALYSIS TOOLS

Metrics may reveal a performance gap. Various tools are available to help you understand the causes of the problem. Here we present six tools: (1) checklists, (2) histograms and bar charts, (3) Pareto charts, (4) scatter diagrams, (5) cause-and-effect diagrams, and (6) graphs. Many of them were developed initially to analyze quality issues, but they apply equally well to the full range of performance measures.

Checklists Data collection through the use of a checklist is often the first step in the analysis of a metric. A **checklist** is a form used to record the frequency of occurrence of certain service or product characteristics related to performance. The characteristics may be measurable on a continuous scale (e.g., weight, customer satisfaction on a 1-to-7 scale, unit cost, scrap loss percentage, time, or length) or on a yes-or-no basis (e.g., customer complaint, posting error, paint discoloration, or inattentive servers).

Histograms and Bar Charts The data from a checklist often can be presented succinctly and clearly with histograms or bar charts. A **histogram** summarizes data measured on a continuous scale, showing the frequency distribution of some quality characteristic (in statistical terms, the central tendency and dispersion of the data). Often the mean of the data is indicated on the histogram. A **bar chart** is a series of bars representing the frequency of occurrence of data characteristics measured on a yes-or-no basis. The bar height indicates the number of times a particular quality characteristic was observed.

Pareto Charts When managers discover several process problems that need to be addressed, they have to decide which should be attacked first. Vilfredo Pareto, a nineteenth-century Italian scientist whose statistical work focused on inequalities in data, proposed that

checklist

A form used to record the frequency of occurrence of certain service or product characteristics related to performance.

histogram

A summarization of data measured on a continuous scale, showing the frequency distribution of some quality characteristic (in statistical terms, the central tendency and dispersion of the data).

bar chart

A series of bars representing the frequency of occurrence of data characteristics measured on a yes-or-no basis.

The features and layout of The Phoenician property of Starwood Hotels and Resorts at Scottsdale, Arizona, are shown below. Starwood Hotels and Resorts is no stranger to process improvement. In fact, the president's letter in a recent annual report stated that through ". . . benchmarking, Six Sigma, and recognition of excellence, [Starwood is] driving results in a virtual cycle of self-improvement at all levels of the Company." Recognizing that improved processes in one department of a single hotel, if rolled out across the organization, could lead to significant improvements, the company recently created a program called the "Power of Innovation," or POI.

The Power of Innovation program in Starwood seeks to capture best practices that exist throughout hotels across all brands in North America. An internal team with expertise in kitchen preparation and production, laundry, stewarding, front office, and housekeeping works with individual properties to build upon and maximize the existing knowledge of local property management teams. The team usually spends about a week on property entrenched in operations to really see day-to-day activity over an extended period. Of particular interest is scheduling the workforce to meet the demand of each hotel's individual operations while streamlining operations processes.

At the Westin Galleria-Oaks in Houston, Texas, for example, the POI team helped management achieve a 6 percent productivity improvement in the kitchen preparation and production job, with a reduction of 2,404 hours used and $23,320 in annual payroll savings alone. At the same time, other POI projects at the hotel generated an additional $14,400 in annual payroll savings.

The Phoenician in Scottsdale also had a visit from the POI team. One area the team focused on was stewarding. The typical stewarding process includes the following duties: dishwashing, kitchen trash removal, polishing

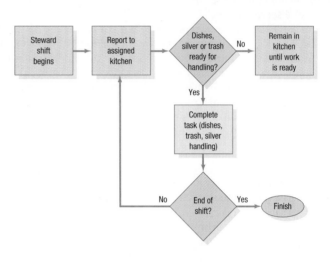

silver, and assisting with banquet meal food prep lines. Stewards support eight kitchens and two bakeries, and work with housekeeping in keeping public areas such as restrooms and pool cabanas clean.

A flowchart that diagrams the existing stewarding process that the team documented is shown above. In any given day, a particular steward may provide support to more than one kitchen, and be called upon to do a variety of tasks.

Before the POI Team arrived, stewards were dedicated to a particular kitchen or area during their shift. Each kitchen required stewarding coverage as outlined by the Executive Chef, so more than one steward may be assigned to an area. A certain amount of stewarding work could be

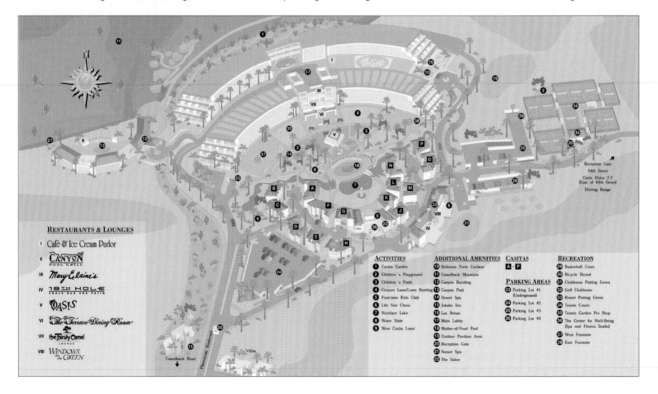

forecast by the Food and Beverage Manager, based on scheduled banquets, afternoon teas, conference buffets, and restaurant reservations. Considerable uncertainty also arose from traffic generated by leisure travelers and local clientele, meaning that stewards assigned to designated areas periodically did not have a steady flow of work.

On a weekly basis, activity levels for the dedicated stewarding staff were determined, based on Executive Chef input. Other factors considered in the weekly planning included prior year activity, special events and holidays, and children. With this information, the executive steward created a summary of all meals, called covers, by location, date, and time of day. Then, an Excel spreadsheet template was used to create the schedule for deployment of stewarding staff throughout the resort's kitchens and restaurants.

In performing its analysis, the POI team examined staff availability, banquet events, restaurants, occupied room counts, and other drivers of business to areas supported by stewards. Time studies were done to determine how far stewards were traveling throughout the property, and how long it took to perform each stewarding task. Some restaurants and kitchens didn't require full-time coverage by a steward, so the steward would be assigned multiple kitchens to fill a work shift. In the case of coverage between the 19th Hole restaurant on one side of the resort, and the Canyon Building on the other side, that steward would walk one-half mile, one way, to take care of duties in both locations because they lacked enough work for a dedicated steward in each location.

Often, stewards had downtime as they waited for banquet dishes to be cleared, or kitchen pots and utensils to be brought in for cleaning. Some restaurants had china with special cleaning requirements, meaning those dishes had to be handwashed instead of being placed in an automated sanitizing dishwasher. This situation required a dedicated steward to perform that task.

Time studies revealed how long it took stewards to move from one kitchen to the next. The studies also helped the POI team understand how long it took to wash dishes in the 5-star restaurant versus the casual poolside dining area's kitchen. Additionally, the studies uncovered building design and landscaping limitations that prevented staff from moving between kitchens quickly. In some cases, a maze of corridors added miles to the distances covered each day, and thick privacy hedges barred entry to sidewalk shortcuts.

Managerial Challenges for the Power of Innovation Program at Starwood

1. How can the management specifically improve the stewarding process at the Phoenician? Using the information provided, create a flowchart illustrating the new process.

2. What are the benefits that the POI program can bring to Starwood? Can these benefits be extended to other processes and properties within the Starwood system?

3. Of the seven mistakes organizations can make when managing processes (see last section of this chapter), which ones might Starwood be most at risk of making? Why?

Chapter 6 Process Performance and Quality

- Customer satisfaction measures
- Error rate
- Rework or scrap rate
- Internal failure cost

Chapter 7 Constraint Management; Supplement C, Waiting Lines; Supplement H, Measuring Output Rates

- Processing time
- Total time from start to finish (throughput time)
- Setup time
- Operating expenses
- Capacity utilization
- Average waiting time
- Average number of customers or jobs waiting in line

Chapter 8 Process Layout

- Distance traveled
- Cycle time
- Idle time

Chapter 9 Lean Systems

- Setup time
- Average waiting time
- Total time from start to finish (throughput time)

FIGURE 5.6

Metrics for Flowcharts, Process Charts, and Accompanying Tables

most of an "activity" is caused by relatively few of its factors. In a restaurant quality problem, the activity could be customer complaints and the factor could be "discourteous waiter." For a manufacturer, the activity could be product defects and a factor could be "missing part." Pareto's concept, called the 80–20 rule, is that 80 percent of the activity is caused by 20 percent of the factors. By concentrating on the 20 percent of the factors (the "vital few"), managers can attack 80 percent of the quality problems. Of course, the exact percentages vary with each situation, but inevitably relatively few factors cause most of the performance shortfalls.

The few vital factors can be identified with a **Pareto chart**, a bar chart on which the factors are plotted in decreasing order of frequency along the horizontal axis (see Figure 5.8). The chart has two vertical axes, the one on the left showing frequency (as in a histogram) and the one on the right showing the cumulative percentage of frequency. The cumulative frequency curve identifies the few vital factors that warrant immediate managerial attention.

Pareto chart

A bar chart on which factors are plotted in decreasing order of frequency along the horizontal axis.

EXAMPLE 5.1	Pareto Chart for a Restaurant

ACTIVE MODEL 5.1

Active Model 5.1 on the Student CD-ROM provides additional insights on this Pareto chart example and its extensions.

TUTOR 5.2

Tutor 5.2 on the Student CD-ROM provides a new example on creating Pareto charts.

The manager of a neighborhood restaurant is concerned about the smaller numbers of customers patronizing his eatery. Complaints have been rising, and he would like to find out what issues to address and present the findings in a way his employees can understand.

SOLUTION

The manager surveyed his customers over several weeks and collected the following data:

Complaint	Frequency
Discourteous server	12
Slow service	42
Cold dinner	5
Cramped tables	20
Smoky air	10

Figure 5.7 is a bar chart and Figure 5.8 is a Pareto chart, both created with OM Explorer's *Bar, Pareto, and Line Charts* solver. They present the data in a way that shows which complaints are more prevalent (the vital few). These charts are set up for a quality metric, but you can reformat them for other "yes-or-no" metrics. Just click on "unprotect sheet" under the spreadsheet's Tools menu, and then make your revisions. Another approach is to create your own spreadsheets from scratch. More advanced software with point-and-click interfaces include Minitab (www.minitab.com/index.htm), SAS (www.sas.com/rnd/app/qc.html), and Microsoft Visio (www.microsoft.com/office/visio).

FIGURE 5.7

Bar Chart

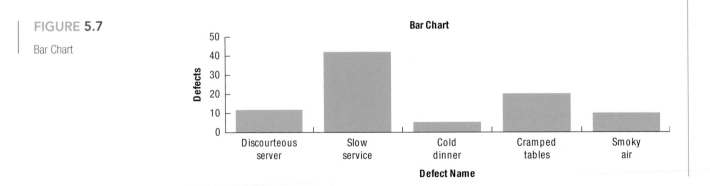

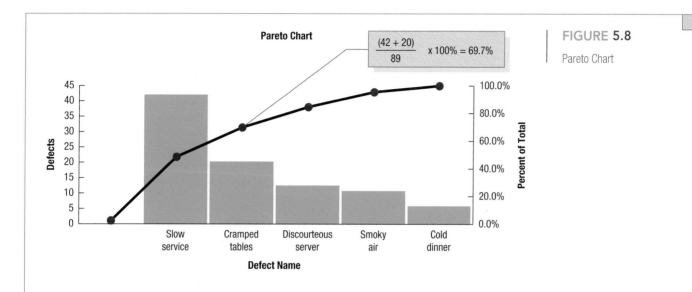

FIGURE **5.8**

Pareto Chart

Decision Point It was clear to the manager (and all employees) which complaints, if rectified, would cover most of the quality problems in the restaurant. First, slow service will be addressed by training the existing staff, adding another server, and improving the food preparation process. Removing some decorative furniture from the dining area and spacing the tables better will solve the problem with cramped tables. The Pareto chart shows that these two problems, if rectified, will account for almost 70 percent of the complaints.

Scatter Diagrams Sometimes managers suspect that a certain factor is causing a particular quality problem. A **scatter diagram**, which is a plot of two variables showing whether they are related, can be used to verify or negate the suspicion. Each point on the scatter diagram represents one data observation. For example, the manager of a castings shop may suspect that casting defects are a function of the diameter of the casting. A scatter diagram could be constructed by plotting the number of defective castings found for each diameter of casting produced. After the diagram is completed, any relationship between diameter and number of defects will be clear.

scatter-diagram

A plot of two variables showing whether they are related.

Cause-and-Effect Diagrams An important aspect of process analysis is linking each metric to the inputs, methods, and process steps that build a particular attribute into the service or product. One way to identify a design problem is to develop a **cause-and-effect diagram** that relates a key performance problem to its potential causes. First developed by Kaoru Ishikawa, the diagram helps management trace disconnects directly to the operations involved. Operations that have no bearing on a particular problem are not shown on the diagram.

cause-and-effect diagram

A diagram that relates a key performance problem to its potential causes.

The cause-and-effect diagram sometimes is called a *fishbone diagram*. The main performance gap is labeled as the fish's "head," the major categories of potential causes as structural "bones," and the likely specific causes as "ribs." When constructing and using a cause-and-effect diagram, an analyst identifies all the major categories of potential causes for the problem. These might be personnel, machines, materials, and processes. For each major category, the analyst lists all the likely causes of the performance gap. Under personnel might be listed "lack of training," "poor communication," and "absenteeism." Creative thinking helps the analyst identify and properly classify all suspected causes. The analyst then systematically investigates the causes listed on the diagram for each major category, updating the chart as new causes become apparent. The process of constructing a cause-and-effect diagram calls management and worker attention to the primary factors affecting product or service quality. Example 5.2 demonstrates the use of a cause-and-effect diagram by an airline.

EXAMPLE 5.2	Analysis of Flight Departure Delays

The operations manager for Checker Board Airlines at Port Columbus International Airport noticed an increase in the number of delayed flight departures.

SOLUTION

To analyze all the possible causes of that problem, he constructed a cause-and-effect diagram, shown in Figure 5.9. The main problem, delayed flight departures, is the "head" of the diagram. He brainstormed all possible causes with his staff, and together they identified several major categories: equipment, personnel, materials, procedures, and "other factors" that are beyond managerial control. Several suspected causes were identified for each major category.

Decision Point   The operations manager, having a good understanding of the process, suspected that most of the flight delays were caused by problems with materials. Consequently, he had food service, fueling, and baggage-handling operations examined. He learned that the number of tow trucks for the baggage-transfer operations was insufficient and that planes were delayed waiting for baggage from connecting flights.

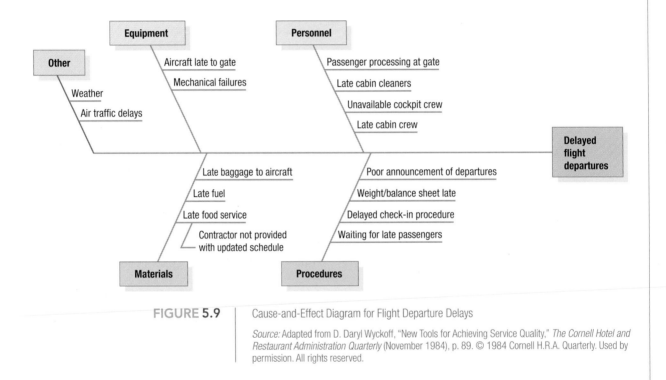

FIGURE **5.9** | Cause-and-Effect Diagram for Flight Departure Delays

Source: Adapted from D. Daryl Wyckoff, "New Tools for Achieving Service Quality," *The Cornell Hotel and Restaurant Administration Quarterly* (November 1984), p. 89. © 1984 Cornell H.R.A. Quarterly. Used by permission. All rights reserved.

graphs

Representations of data in a variety of pictorial forms, such as line charts and pie charts.

Graphs   **Graphs** represent data in a variety of pictorial formats, such as line charts and pie charts. *Line charts* represent data sequentially with data points connected by line segments to highlight trends in the data. Line charts are used in control charts (see Chapter 6, "Process Performance and Quality") and forecasting (see Chapter 13, "Forecasting"). Pie charts represent process factors as slices of a pie; the size of each slice is in proportion to the number of occurrences of the factor. Pie charts are useful for showing data from a group of factors that can be represented as percentages totaling 100 percent.

DATA SNOOPING

Each of the tools for improving quality may be used independently, but their power is greatest when they are used together. In solving a process-related problem, managers often must act as detectives, sifting data to clarify the issues involved and deducing the causes. We call this process *data snooping.* Example 5.3 demonstrates how the tools for improving quality can be used for data snooping.

Identifying Causes of Poor Headliner Quality	EXAMPLE 5.3

The Wellington Fiber Board Company produces headliners, the fiberglass components that form the inner roof of passenger cars. Management wanted to identify which defects were most prevalent and to find the cause.

SOLUTION
Figure 5.10 shows the sequential application of several tools for improving quality.

Step 1. Checklist

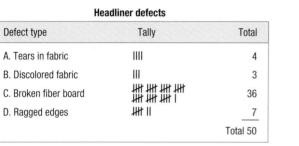

Headliner defects

Defect type	Tally	Total
A. Tears in fabric	IIII	4
B. Discolored fabric	III	3
C. Broken fiber board	IIII IIII IIII IIII IIII IIII IIII I	36
D. Ragged edges	IIII II	7
		Total 50

Step 2. Pareto Chart

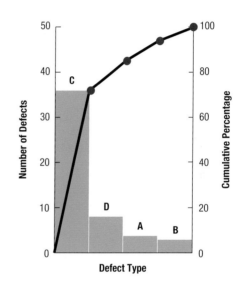

Step 3. Cause-and-Effect Diagram

Step 4. Bar Chart

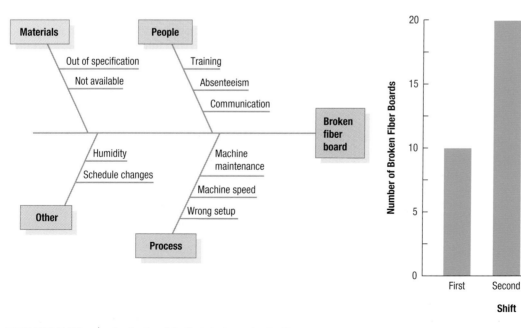

FIGURE 5.10 | Application of the Tools for Improving Quality

Step 1: A checklist of different types of defects was constructed from last month's production records.

Step 2: A Pareto chart prepared from the checklist data indicated that broken fiber board accounted for 72 percent of the quality defects.

Step 3: A cause-and-effect diagram for broken fiber board identified several potential causes for the problem. The one strongly suspected by the manager was employee training.

Step 4: The manager reorganized the production reports into a bar chart according to shift because the personnel on the three shifts had varied amounts of experience.

Decision Point The bar chart indicated that the second shift, with the least experienced workforce, had most of the defects. Further investigation revealed that workers were not using proper procedures for stacking the fiber boards after the press operation, which caused cracking and chipping. The manager set up additional training sessions focused on board handling. Although the second shift was not responsible for all the defects, finding the source of many of the defects enabled the manager to improve the quality of her operations.

SIMULATION

process simulation

The act of reproducing the behavior of a process, using a model that describes each step.

A simulation model goes one step further than data analysis tools, because it can show how the process dynamically changes over time. **Process simulation** is the act of reproducing the behavior of a process, using a model that describes each step. Once the process is modeled, the analyst can make changes in the model to measure the impact on certain metrics, such as response time, waiting lines, resource utilization, and the like. To learn more about how simulation works, see Supplement B, "Simulation," which follows this chapter. More advanced capabilities are possible using software packages such as SimQuick (www.nd.edu/~dhartvig/simquick/top.htm), Extend (www.imaginethatinc.com), SIMPROCESS (www.caciasl.com), ProModel (www.promodel.com), and Witness (www.lanner.com/corporate).

Here we illustrate process simulation with the SimQuick software (provided on the Student CD-ROM). Consider the following process within a small bank: Customers enter the bank, get into a single line, are served by a teller, and finally leave the bank. Currently, this bank has one teller working from 9 A.M. to 11 A.M. Management is concerned that the wait in line seems to be too long. Therefore, it is considering two process improvement ideas: adding an additional teller during these hours or installing a new automated check-reading machine that can help the single teller serve customers more quickly.

A first step in using SimQuick is to draw a flowchart of the process using SimQuick's building blocks. Figure 5.11(a) shows that the one-teller bank (both the original and the variation with a check-reading machine) can be modeled with four building blocks: an entrance (modeling the arrival of customers at the bank), a buffer (modeling the waiting line), a workstation (modeling the teller), and a final buffer (modeling served customers). The two-teller variation can be modeled with five building blocks, as shown in Figure 5.11(b).

FIGURE 5.11(a)

Flowchart of Bank

Flowchart for a one-teller bank

FIGURE 5.11(b)

Flowchart for a two-teller bank

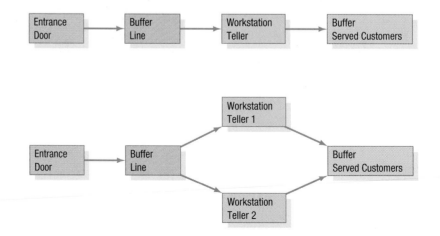

Element Types	Element Names	Statistics	Overall Means
Entrance(s)	Door	Service level	0.90
Buffer(s)	Line	Mean inventory	4.47
		Mean cycle time	11.04

FIGURE **5.12**

Simulation Results of Bank

Information describing each building block is entered into SimQuick tables. Three key pieces of information need to be entered: when people arrive at the door, how long the teller takes to serve a customer, and the maximum length of the line. The first two pieces of information are described by statistical distributions. Each of the three models is run 30 times, simulating the hours from 9 A.M. to 11 A.M. Statistics are collected by SimQuick and summarized. Figure 5.12 shows the key results for the model of the original one-teller process as output by SimQuick (many other statistics are collected, but they are not displayed here).

The numbers shown in Figure 5.12 are averages across the 30 simulations. The service level for Door tells us that 90 percent of the simulated customers who arrived at the bank were able to get into Line (hence 10 percent found Line full and immediately left). The mean inventory for Line tells us that, on average, 4.47 simulated customers were standing in line. The mean cycle time tells us that simulated customers waited an average of 11.04 minutes in line.

When we run the model with two tellers, we find that the service level increases to 100 percent, the mean inventory in Line decreases to 0.37 customers, and the mean cycle time drops to 0.71 minutes. All dramatic improvements. When we run the one-teller model with the faster check-reading machine we find that the service level is 97 percent, the mean inventory in Line is 2.89 customers, and the mean cycle time is 6.21 minutes. These statistics, together with cost information, should help management select the best process. All the details for this model (as well as many others) appear in the book *SimQuick: Process Simulation with Excel,* which is included, along with the SimQuick software, on the Student CD-ROM that comes with this text.

> REDESIGNING THE PROCESS <

A doctor pinpoints an illness after a thorough examination of the patient, and then the doctor recommends treatments based on the diagnosis; so it is with processes. After a process is documented, metrics data collected, and disconnects identified, the process analyst or design team puts together a set of changes that will make the process better. At this step, people directly involved in the process are brought in to get their ideas and inputs.

Managerial Practice 5.2 describes how various people at a hospital came together to improve their processes, avoiding the need to add expensive capacity.

GENERATING IDEAS: QUESTIONING AND BRAINSTORMING

Sometimes ideas for reengineering or improving a process become apparent after documenting the process and carefully examining the areas of substandard performance, hand-offs between departments, and steps where customer contact is high. Example 5.3 illustrates how such documentation pointed to a better way of handling the fiber boards through better training. In other cases, the better solution is less evident. Ideas can be uncovered (because there is always a better way) by asking six questions about each step in the process, and about the process as a whole.

1. *What* is being done?
2. *When* is it being done?
3. *Who* is doing it?
4. *Where* is it being done?
5. *How* is it being done?
6. *How well* does it do on the various metrics of importance?

| MANAGERIAL **PRACTICE** | 5.2 | REDESIGNING PROCESSES AT BAPTIST MEMORIAL HOSPITAL |

Baptist Memorial Hospital–Memphis, the flagship of the Baptist Memorial Health Care system, is a 706-bed tertiary care hospital. It had a capacity problem, or so it seemed, with occupancy routinely exceeding 90 percent. Process improvement efforts for more than five years led to the centralization of bed assignments and adding a new bed-tracking system to provide bed information in real time. These improvements reduced turnaround time (TAT) for bed assignments but demand continued to exceed capacity. In March 2002, Memphis hospitals were diverting ambulances an average of 70 percent of the time. Ambulance services were exhausted daily, and ambulance crews waited at the local emergency departments (EDs) for as long as 90 minutes. Memphis's hospital leadership and the Emergency Medical Service Council decided to eliminate diversion, instead allowing patients to go to the preferred hospital. This change solved the ambulance crisis, but the larger crisis related to patient flow shifted to the ED.

Administration, nurses, and physicians adopted a zero-tolerance philosophy for barriers to flow and bottlenecks. The first initiative was to open the express admission unit (EAU) with no additional labor being used to staff it. The EAU is a 21-bed dedicated area that processes direct and emergency department admissions. By relieving unit nurses of work associated with admissions, it removed responsibility for a particularly time-intensive activity from busy unit nurses. The new processes had more of a line flow, with less complexity and divergence. All initial paperwork and diagnostics were completed in the express admission unit with a projected turnaround time of only 60 to 70 minutes. Physicians no longer sent patients to get their workup in ED, because it was done expeditiously in the EAU. The ED holding hours for admitted patients were cut by 50 percent.

The next process redesign effort was with *rapid process improvement,* a technique of testing ideas for change on a small scale, altering processes to improve them, and spreading the processes to other areas when they are successful. The first test was faxing reports from the ED to the receiving unit, which eliminated time spent holding and returning calls. Three months later, this process spread to the entire facility. Other changes included shifting more medic and triage nurses to work during peak periods, beginning with lab and X-ray diagnostic procedures at triage when the EU was at capacity, and taking patients directly to a room when one became available with bedside registration. One of the highest-leverage changes was seg-

Baptist Memorial Hospital in Memphis, Tennessee, holds "huddle meetings" at least three times a day. The meetings bring together the hospital's house supervisor, housekeeping supervisor, and key nurses to improve bed-flow planning.

menting the urgent care population within the ED by creating a fast-track area that essentially provided a minor medical unit within the ED. Patients with nonemergency needs previously waited the longest and required the least amount of time for treatment, leading to great dissatisfaction. *Huddle meetings* are now held at least three times a day. These meetings bring together the house supervisor, housekeeping supervisor, and key charge nurses to improve bed-flow planning and provide more information to all concerned. The discharge process was also improved.

Redesigned processes reduced delays in placing ED patients in an inpatient bed, and transferring patients from the inpatient facility to long-term care facilities. TAT for the overall ED was reduced by 9 percent, even while the ED volume was increasing. Length of stay was reduced by two days, the equivalent of building 12 ICU beds. The mortality rate decreased, volume increased by 20 percent, and patient satisfaction improved from the 10th percentile to the 85th percentile according to a survey conducted by the Gallup Organization. What first appeared to be a capacity problem was resolved without adding staff or the number of beds—it was solved with redesigned processes.

Sources: Suzanne S. Horton, "Increasing Capacity While Improving the Bottom Line," *Frontiers of Health Services Management,* vol. 20, no. 4 (Summer 2004), pp. 17–23; Richard S. Zimmerman, "Hospital Capacity, Productivity, and Patient Safety—It All Flows Together," *Frontiers of Health Services Management,* vol. 20, no. 4 (Summer 2004), pp. 33–38.

brainstorming

Letting a group of people, knowledgeable about the process, propose ideas for change by saying whatever comes to mind.

Answers to these questions are challenged by asking still another series of questions. *Why* is the process even being done? *Why* is it being done where it is being done? *Why* is it being done when it is being done?

Creativity can also be stimulated by **brainstorming**, letting a group of people knowledgeable about the process propose ideas for change by saying whatever comes to mind. A facilitator records the ideas on a flipchart, so that all can see. Participants are discouraged from evaluating any of the ideas generated during the session. The purpose is to encourage creativity and to get as many ideas as possible, no matter how far-fetched the ideas may seem. The participants need not be limited to the design team as long as they have seen or heard the process documentation. A growing number of big companies, such as Sun Life Financial and Georgia-Pacific, are taking advantage of the Internet and specially designed software to run brainstorming sessions that allow people at far-flung locations to "meet" online and hash out solutions to particular problems. The technology lets employees see, and build on, one another's ideas, so that one person's seed of a notion can grow into a practical plan.

After the brainstorming session is over, the design team moves into the "get real" phase: They evaluate the different ideas. The team identifies the changes that give the best payoffs for process redesign. The redesign could involve issues of capacity, layout, technology, or even location, all of which are discussed in more detail in the following chapters.

The redesigned process is documented once again, this time as the "after" view of the process. Expected payoffs are carefully estimated, along with risks. For changes involving investments, the time value of money must be considered (see Supplement J, "Financial Analysis," on the Student CD-ROM). The impact on people (skills, degree of change, training requirements, and resistance to change) must also be factored into the evaluation of the new design.

BENCHMARKING

Benchmarking can be another valuable source for process redesign. **Benchmarking** is a systematic procedure that measures a firm's processes, services, and products against those of industry leaders. Companies use benchmarking to better understand how outstanding companies do things so that they can improve their own processes.

Benchmarking focuses on setting quantitative goals for improvement. *Competitive* benchmarking is based on comparisons with a direct industry competitor. *Functional* benchmarking compares areas such as administration, customer service, and sales operations with those of outstanding firms in any industry. For instance, Xerox benchmarked its distribution function against L.L.Bean's because Bean is renowned as a leading retailer in distribution efficiency and customer service.

Internal benchmarking involves using an organizational unit with superior performance as the benchmark for other units. This form of benchmarking can be advantageous for firms that have several business units or divisions. All forms of benchmarking are best applied in situations where you are looking for a long-term program of continuous improvement.

Typical measures used in benchmarking include cost per unit, service upsets (breakdowns) per customer, processing time per unit, customer retention rates, revenue per unit, return on investment, and customer satisfaction levels.

Benchmarking consists of four basic steps.

1. *Planning.* Identify the process, service, or product to be benchmarked and the firm(s) to be used for comparison; determine the performance metrics for analysis; collect the data.

2. *Analysis.* Determine the gap between the firm's current performance and that of the benchmark firm(s); identify the causes of significant performance gaps.

3. *Integration.* Establish goals and obtain the support of managers who must provide the resources for accomplishing the goals.

4. *Action.* Develop cross-functional teams of those most affected by the changes; develop action plans and team assignments; implement the plans; monitor progress; recalibrate benchmarks as improvements are made.

Collecting benchmarking data can sometimes be a challenge. Internal benchmarking data is surely the most accessible. One way of benchmarking is always available—tracking the performance of a process over time. Functional benchmarking data are often collected by professional associations or consulting firms. Several corporations and government organizations have agreed to share and standardize performance benchmarks. The American Productivity and Quality Center, a nonprofit organization, created thousands of measures, as Figure 5.13 illustrates. The full range of metrics can be explored at www.apqc.org.

benchmarking

A systematic procedure that measures a firm's processes, services, and products against those of industry leaders.

FIGURE 5.13

Illustrative Benchmarking Metrics by
Type of Process

Customer Relationship Process

- Total cost of "enter, process, and track orders" per $1,000 revenue
- System costs of process per $100,000 revenue
- Value of sales order line item not fulfilled due to stockouts, as percentage of revenue
- Percentage of finished goods sales value that is returned
- Average time from sales order receipt until manufacturing or logistics is notified
- Average time in direct contact with customer per sales order line item

Order Fulfillment Process

- Value of plant shipments per employee
- Finished goods inventory turnover
- Reject rate as percentage of total orders processed
- Percentage of orders returned by customers due to quality problems
- Standard customer lead time from order entry to shipment
- Percentage of orders shipped on time

New Service/Product Development Process

- Percentage of sales due to services/products launched last year
- Cost of "generate new services/products" process per $1,000 revenue
- Ratio of projects entering the process to projects completing the process
- Time to market for existing service/product improvement project
- Time to market for new service/product project
- Time to profitability for existing service/product improvement project

Supplier Relationship Process

- Cost of "select suppliers and develop/maintain contracts" process per $1,000 revenue
- Number of employees per $1,000 of purchases
- Percentage of purchase orders approved electronically
- Average time to place a purchase order
- Total number of active vendors per $1,000 of purchases
- Percentage of value of purchased material that is supplier certified

Support Process

- Systems cost of finance function per $1,000 revenue
- Percentage of finance staff devoted to internal audit
- Total cost of payroll processes per $1,000 revenue
- Number of accepted jobs as percentage of job offers
- Total cost of "source, recruit, and select" process per $1,000 revenue
- Average employee turnover rate

> MANAGING PROCESSES <

Failure to manage processes is failure to manage the business. Implementing a beautifully redesigned process is only the beginning to continually monitoring and improving processes. Metrics goals must be continually evaluated and reset to fit changing requirements. Avoid the following seven mistakes when managing processes.[1]

1. *Not Connecting with Strategic Issues.* Is particular attention being paid to core processes, competitive priorities, impact of customer contact and volume, and strategic fit during process analysis?

2. *Not Involving the Right People in the Right Way.* Does process analysis closely involve the people performing the process, or those closely connected to it as internal customers and suppliers?

3. *Not Giving the Design Teams and Process Analysts a Clear Charter, and Then Holding Them Accountable.* Does management set expectations for change and maintain pressure for results? Does it allow paralysis in process improvement efforts by requiring excessive analysis?

---

[1]Geary A. Rummler and Alan P. Brache, *Improving Performance,* 2nd ed. (San Francisco: Jossey-Bass, 1995), pp. 126–133.

4. *Not Being Satisfied Unless Fundamental "Reengineering" Changes Are Made.* Is the radical change from process reengineering the expectation? If so, the cumulative effect of many small improvements that could be made incrementally could be lost. Process management efforts should not be limited to downsizing or to reorganization only, even though jobs may be eliminated or the structure changed. It should not be limited to big technological innovation projects, even though technological change occurs often.

5. *Not Considering the Impact on People.* Are the changes aligned with the attitudes and skills of the people who must implement the redesigned process? It is crucial to understand and deal with the *people side* of process changes.

6. *Not Giving Attention to Implementation.* Are processes redesigned, but never implemented? A great job of flowcharting and benchmarking is of only academic interest if the proposed changes are not implemented. Sound project management practices are required.

7. *Not Creating an Infrastructure for Continuous Process Improvement.* Is a measurement system in place to monitor key metrics over time? Is anyone checking to see whether anticipated benefits of a redesigned process are actually being realized?

Managers must make sure that their organization spots new performance gaps in the continual search for process improvements. Process redesign efforts need to be part of periodic reviews and even annual plans. Measurement is the particular focus of the next chapter. It covers how a performance tracking system is the basis for feedback and improvement efforts. The essence of a learning organization is the intelligent use of such feedback.

> STUDENT CD-ROM AND INTERNET RESOURCES <

The Student CD-ROM and the Companion Website at **www.prenhall.com/krajewski** contain many tools, activities, and resources designed for this chapter.

> KEY TERMS <

bar chart 161	flowchart 155	process chart 159
benchmarking 171	graphs 166	process simulation 168
brainstorming 170	histogram 161	scatter diagram 165
cause-and-effect diagram 165	metrics 154	service blueprint 158
checklist 161	Pareto chart 164	suggestion system 154
design team 154	process analysis 153	

> SOLVED PROBLEM 1 <

Create a flowchart for the following telephone-ordering process at a retail chain that specializes in selling books and music CDs. It provides an ordering system via the telephone to its time-sensitive customers besides its regular store sales.

First, the automated system greets customers and identifies whether they have a tone or pulse phone. Customers choose 1 if they have a tone phone; otherwise, they wait for the first available service representative to process their request. If customers have a tone phone, they complete their request by choosing options on the phone. First, the system checks to see whether customers have an existing account. Customers choose 1 if they have an existing account or choose 2 if they want to open a new account. Customers wait for the service representative to open a new account if they choose 2.

Next, customers choose between the options of making an order, canceling an order, or talking to a customer representative for questions and/or complaints. If customers choose to make an order, then they specify the order type as a book or a music CD, and a specialized customer representative for books or music CDs picks up the phone to get the order details. If customers choose to cancel an order, then they wait for the automated response. By entering the order code via phone, customers can cancel the order. The automated system says

FIGURE 5.14

Flowchart of Telephone Ordering Process

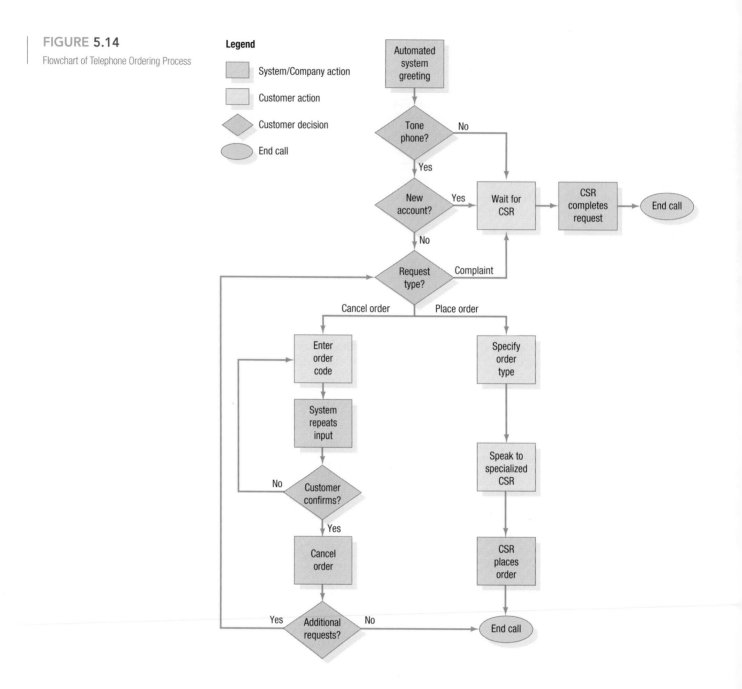

the name of the ordered item and asks for the confirmation of the customer. If the customer validates the cancellation of the order, then the system cancels the order; otherwise, the system asks the customer to input the order code again. After responding to the request, the system asks whether the customer has additional requests; if not, the process terminates.

SOLUTION

Figure 5.14 shows the flowchart.

> **SOLVED PROBLEM 2** <

An automobile service is having difficulty providing oil changes in the 29 minutes or less mentioned in its advertising. You are to analyze the process of changing automobile engine oil. The subject of the study is the service mechanic. The process begins when the mechanic directs the customer's arrival and ends when the customer pays for the services.

SOLUTION

Figure 5.15 shows the completed process chart. The process is broken into 21 steps. A summary of the times and distances traveled is shown in the upper right-hand corner of the process chart.

The times add up to 28 minutes, which does not allow much room for error if the 29-minute guarantee is to be met and the mechanic travels a total of 420 feet.

Process:	Changing engine oil
Subject:	Mechanic
Beginning:	Direct customer arrival
Ending:	Total charges, receive payment

Insert Step

Append Step

Remove Step

Summary

Activity	Number of Steps	Time (min)	Distance (ft)
Operation ●	7	16.50	
Transport ➡	8	5.50	420
Inspect ■	4	5.00	
Delay ❭	1	0.70	
Store ▼	1	0.30	

FIGURE 5.15

Process Chart for Changing Engine Oil

Step No.	Time (min)	Distance (ft)	●	➡	■	❭	▼	Step Description
1	0.80	50.0		X				Direct customer into service bay
2	1.80		X					Record name and desired service
3	2.30				X			Open hood, verify engine type, inspect hoses, check fluids
4	0.80	30.0		X				Walk to customer in waiting area
5	0.60		X					Recommend additional services
6	0.70					X		Wait for customer decision
7	0.90	70.0		X				Walk to storeroom
8	1.90		X					Look up filter number(s), find filter(s)
9	0.40				X			Check filter number(s)
10	0.60	50.0		X				Carry filter(s) to service pit
11	4.20		X					Perform under-car services
12	0.70	40.0		X				Climb from pit, walk to automobile
13	2.70		X					Fill engine with oil, start engine
14	1.30				X			Inspect for leaks
15	0.50	40.0		X				Walk to pit
16	1.00				X			Inspect for leaks
17	3.00		X					Clean and organize work area
18	0.70	80.0		X				Return to auto, drive from bay
19	0.30						X	Park the car
20	0.50	60.0		X				Walk to customer waiting area
21	2.30		X					Total charges, receive payment

> SOLVED PROBLEM 3 <

What improvement can you make in the process shown in Figure 5.15?

SOLUTION

Your analysis should verify the following three ideas for improvement. You may also be able to come up with others.

a. **Move Step 17 to Step 21.** Customers should not have to wait while the mechanic cleans the work area.

b. **Store Small Inventories of Frequently Used Filters in the Pit.** Steps 7 and 10 involve travel to the storeroom. If the filters are moved to the pit, a copy of the reference material must also be placed in the pit. The pit will have to be organized and well lighted.

c. **Use Two Mechanics.** Steps 10, 12, 15, and 17 involve running up and down the steps to the pit. Much of this travel could be eliminated. The service time could be shortened by having one mechanic in the pit working simultaneously with another working under the hood.

> SOLVED PROBLEM 4 <

Vera Johnson and Merris Williams manufacture vanishing cream. Their packaging process has four steps: mix, fill, cap, and label. They have had the reported defects analyzed, which shows the following.

Defect	Frequency
Lumps of unmixed product	7
Over- or underfilled jars	18
Jar lids did not seal	6
Labels rumpled or missing	29
Total	60

Draw a Pareto chart to identify the vital defects.

SOLUTION

Defective labels account for 48.33 percent of the total number of defects:

$$\frac{29}{60} \times 100\% = 48.33\%$$

Improperly filled jars account for 30 percent of the total number of defects:

$$\frac{18}{60} \times 100\% = 30.00\%$$

The cumulative percent for the two most frequent defects is

$$48.33\% + 30.00\% = 78.33\%$$

Lumps represent $\frac{7}{60} \times 100\% = 11.67\%$ of defects; the cumulative percentage is

$$78.33\% + 11.67\% = 90.00\%$$

Defective seals represent $\frac{6}{60} \times 100\% = 10\%$ of defects; the cumulative percentage is

$$10\% + 90\% = 100.00\%$$

The Pareto chart is shown in Figure 5.16.

> DISCUSSION QUESTIONS <

1. Continuous improvement recognizes that many small improvements add up to sizable benefits. Will continuous improvement take a company at the bottom of an industry to the top? Explain.

2. The Hydro-Electric Company (HEC) has three sources of power. A small amount of hydroelectric power is generated by damming wild and scenic rivers; a second source of power comes from burning coal, with emissions that create acid rain and contribute to global warming; the third source of power comes from nuclear fission. HEC's coal-fired plants use obsolete pollution-control technology, and an investment of several hundred million dollars would be required to update it. Environmentalists urge HEC to promote conservation and purchase power from suppliers that use the cleanest fuels and technology.

However, HEC is already suffering from declining sales, which have resulted in billions of dollars invested in idle equipment. Its large customers are taking advantage of laws that permit them to buy power from low-cost suppliers. HEC must cover the fixed costs of idle capacity by raising rates charged to its remaining customers or face defaulting on bonds (bankruptcy). The increased rates motivate even more customers to seek low-cost suppliers, the start of a death spiral for HEC. To prevent additional rate increases, HEC implements a cost-cutting program and puts its plans to update pollution controls on hold.

Form sides and discuss the ethical, environmental, and political issues and trade-offs associated with HEC's strategy.

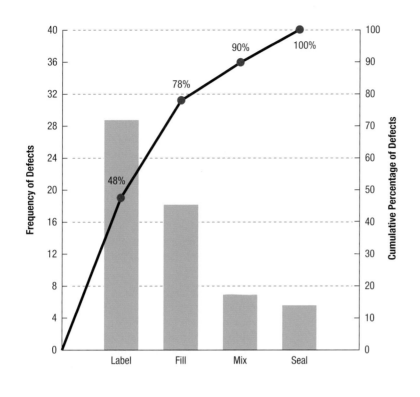

FIGURE **5.16**

Pareto Chart

> PROBLEMS <

Software, such as OM Explorer, Active Models, and POM for Windows is packaged with every new copy of the textbook. Check with your instructor on how best to use it. In many cases, the instructor wants you to understand how to do the calculations by hand. At most, the software provides a check on your calculations. When calculations are particularly complex and the goal is interpreting the results in making decisions, the software replaces entirely the manual calculations. The software also can be a valuable resource well after your course is completed.

1. Consider the Custom Molds, Inc., case at the end of Chapter 4, "Process Strategy." Prepare a flowchart of the mold fabrication process and the parts manufacturing process, showing how they are linked. For a good tutorial on how to create flowcharts, see www.hci.com.au/ hcisite2/toolkit/flowchar.htm. Also check out the Flowcharting Tutor in Excel on the Student CD-ROM.

2. Do Problem 1 using a process chart spreadsheet of your own design, one that differs from the Process Chart solver in OM Explorer. It should have one or more columns to record information or metrics that you think are relevant, be it external customer contact, time delays, completion times, percent rework, costs, capacity, and demand rates. Your entries should show what information you would collect, even though only part of it is available in the case.

3. Founded in 1970, ABC is one of the world's largest insurance companies with locations in 28 countries. Given the following description, flowchart the new policy setup process as it existed in 1970.

Individual customers who wanted to set up a new policy would visit one of ABC's 70 branch offices or make contact with an agent. They would then fill out an application and sometimes attach a check. The branch office then sent the application package through company mail to the XYZ division in London. In addition, a customer might also fill out the application at home and send it directly to a number of ABC locations, which would then transfer it to the London operation. Once received, XYZ separated the various parts of the application, then scanned it and digitized it. The electronic image was then retrieved from a server and delivered to an associate's desktop client computer. The associate was responsible for entering the information on the form into the appropriate database. If the information supplied on the application was complete, a confirmation notice was automatically printed and sent to the customer. If the information was incomplete, then another associate, trained to deal with customers on the phone, would call the customer to obtain the additional information. If the customer noticed something wrong on the confirmation notice she received, she would either call a toll-free number or send in a letter describing the problem. The Customer Problem Resolution division dealt with problems arising at this point. An updated confirmation notice was sent to the customer. If the information was correct, the application transaction was complete.

4. Do Problem 3 using a process chart spreadsheet of your own design, one that differs from the Process Chart solver in OM Explorer. It should have one or more columns to

record information or metrics that you think should be collected to analyze the process (see Problem 2).

5. Prepare a flowchart of the field service division process at DEF, as described here. Start from the point where a call is received and end when a technician finishes the job.

   DEF was a multibillion dollar company that manufactured and distributed a wide variety of electronic, photographic, and reprographic equipment used in many engineering and medical system applications. The Field Service Division employed 475 field service technicians who performed maintenance and warranty repairs on the equipment sold by DEF. Customers would call DEF's National Service Center (NSC), which received about 3,000 calls per day. The NSC staffed its call center with about 40 call-takers. A typical incoming service call was received at the NSC and routed to one of the call-takers who entered information about the machine, caller's name, and type of problem into DEF's mainframe computer. In some cases, the call-taker attempted to help the customer fix the problem. However, call-takers were currently only able to avoid about 10 percent of the incoming emergency maintenance service calls. If the service call could not be avoided, the call-taker usually stated the following script, "Depending upon the availability of our technicians, you should expect to see a technician sometime between now and (now + X)." ("X" was the target response time based on the model number and the zone.) This information was given to the customer because many customers wanted to know when a tech would arrive on site.

   Call-takers entered service call information on DEF's computer system, which then sent the information electronically to the regional dispatch center assigned to that customer location. (DEF had four regional dispatch centers with a total of about 20 dispatchers.) Service call information was printed on a small card at the dispatch center. About every hour, cards were ripped off the printer and given to the dispatcher assigned to that customer location. The dispatcher placed each card on a magnetic board under the name of a tech that the dispatcher believed would be the most likely candidate for the service call, given the location of the machine, the current location of the tech, and the tech's training profile. After completing a service call, techs called the dispatcher in the regional dispatch center, cleared the call, and received a new call assigned by the dispatcher. After getting the service call from a dispatcher, a tech called the customer to give an expected time of arrival, drove to the customer site, diagnosed the problem, repaired the machine if parts were available in the van, and then phoned the dispatcher for the next call. If the tech did not have the right parts for a repair, the tech informed the NSC and the part was express mailed to the customer; the repair was done the next morning.

6. Do Problem 5 using a process chart spreadsheet of your own design, one that differs from the Process Chart solver in OM Explorer. It should have one or more columns to record information or metrics that you think should be collected to analyze the process (see Problem 2).

7. If you have seen the *Process Choice at the King Soopers Bakery* video in class, prepare a flowchart for the three processes at King Soopers. For additional information on the processes, see the *Big Picture* for Chapter 4 on the Student CD-ROM.

8. Your class has volunteered to work for Referendum 13 on the November ballot, which calls for free tuition and books for all college courses except operations management. Support for the referendum includes assembling 10,000 yard signs (preprinted water-resistant paper signs to be glued and stapled to a wooden stake) on a fall Saturday. Construct a flowchart and a process chart for yard sign assembly. What inputs in terms of materials, human effort, and equipment are involved? Estimate the amount of volunteers, staples, glue, equipment, lawn and garage space, and pizza required.

9. Suppose that you are in charge of a large mailing to the alumni of your college, inviting them to contribute to a scholarship fund. The letters and envelopes have been individually addressed (mailing labels were not used). The letters are to be folded and stuffed into the correct envelopes, the envelopes are to be sealed, and a large commemorative stamp is to be placed in the upper right-hand corner of each envelope. Make a process chart for this activity, assuming that it is a one-person operation. Estimate how long it will take to stuff, seal, and stamp 2,000 envelopes. Assume that the person doing this work is paid $8.00 per hour. How much will it cost to process 2,000 letters, based on your time estimate? Consider how each of the following changes individually would affect the process:

   ■ Each letter has the greeting "Dear Alumnus or Alumna," instead of the person's name.

   ■ Mailing labels are used and have to be put on the envelopes.

   ■ Prestamped envelopes are used.

   ■ Envelopes are stamped by a postage meter.

   ■ Window envelopes are used.

   ■ A preaddressed envelope is included with each letter for contributions.

   a. Given your time estimates, which of these changes would reduce the time and cost of the process?

   b. Would any of these changes be likely to reduce the effectiveness of the mailing? If so, which ones? Why?

   c. Would the changes that increase time and cost be likely to increase the effectiveness of the mailing? Why or why not?

   d. What other factors need to be considered for this project?

10. Diagrams of two self-service gasoline stations, both located on corners, are shown in Figure 5.17(a) and (b). Both have two rows of four pumps and a booth at which an attendant receives payment for the gasoline. At neither station is it necessary for the customer to pay in advance. The exits and entrances are marked on the diagrams. Analyze the flows of cars and people through each station.

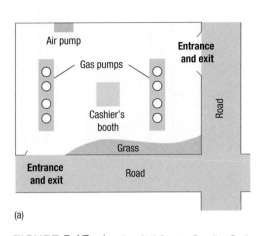
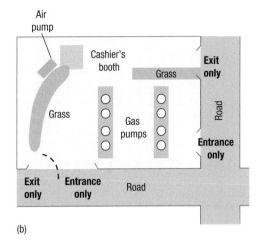

FIGURE 5.17 | Two Self-Service Gasoline Stations

a. Which station has the more efficient flows from the standpoint of the customer?

b. Which station is likely to lose more potential customers who cannot gain access to the pumps because another car is headed in the other direction?

c. At which station can a customer pay without getting out of the car?

11. The management of the Just Like Home restaurant has asked you to analyze some of its processes. One of these processes is making a single-scoop ice cream cone. Cones can be ordered by a server (for table service) or by a customer (for takeout).

Figure 5.18 illustrates the process chart for this operation.

- The ice cream counter server earns $10 per hour (including variable fringe benefits).
- The process is performed 10 times per hour (on average).
- The restaurant is open 363 days a year, 10 hours a day.

a. Complete the summary (top-right) portion of the chart.

b. What is the total labor cost associated with the process?

c. How can this operation be made more efficient? Make a process chart of the improved process. What are the annual labor savings if this new process is implemented?

| FIGURE **5.18**

Process:	Making one ice cream cone
Subject:	Server at counter
Beginning:	Walk to cone storage area
Ending:	Give it to server or customer

Insert Step

Append Step

Remove Step

Summary

Activity	Number of Steps	Time (min)	Distance (ft)
Operation ●			
Transport ➡			
Inspect ■			
Delay ◗			
Store ▼			

Step No.	Time (min)	Distance (ft)	●	➡	■	◗	▼	Step Description
1	0.20	5.0		X				Walk to cone storage area
2	0.05		X					Remove empty cone
3	0.10	5.0		X				Walk to counter
4	0.05		X					Place cone in holder
5	0.20	8.0		X				Walk to sink area
6	0.50					X		Ask dishwasher to wash scoop
7	0.15	8.0		X				Walk to counter with clean scoop
8	0.05		X					Pick up empty cone
9	0.10	2.5		X				Walk to flavor ordered
10	0.75		X					Scoop ice cream from container
11	0.75		X					Place ice cream in cone
12	0.25				X			Check for stability
13	0.05	2.5		X				Walk to order placement area
14	0.05		X					Give server or customer the cone

12. As a graduate assistant, your duties include grading and keeping records for operations management course homework assignments. Five sections for 40 students each are offered each semester. A few graduate students attend sections 3 and 4. Graduate students must complete some extra work to higher standards for each assignment. Every student delivers (or is supposed to deliver) directly to (under) the door of your office one homework assignment every Tuesday. Your job is to correct the homework, record grades, sort the papers by class section, sort by student last name in alphabetical order, and return the homework papers to the appropriate instructors (not necessarily in that order). There are some complications. A fair majority of the students sign their names legibly, others identify their work with the correct I.D. number, and a few do neither. Rarely do students identify their section number or graduate status. Prepare a list of process chart steps and place them in an efficient sequence.

13. At the Department of Motor Vehicles, the process of getting license plates for your car begins when you enter the facility and take a number. You walk 50 feet to the waiting area. During your wait, you count about 30 customers waiting for service. You notice that many customers become discouraged and leave. When a number is called, if a customer stands, the ticket is checked by a uniformed person, and the customer is directed to the available clerk. If no one stands, several minutes are lost while the same number is called repeatedly. Eventually, the next number is called, and more often than not, that customer has left too. The DMV clerk has now been idle for several minutes but does not seem to mind.

An unkempt man walks over to the ticket dispenser, picks up several tickets from the floor, and returns to his seat. A new arrival, carrying a stack of paper and looking like a car dealer, walks directly to the unkempt man. Some sort of transaction takes place. A few more numbers are called and it is the car dealer's number! After 4 hours, your number is called and checked by the uniformed person. You walk 60 feet to the clerk, and the process of paying city sales taxes is completed in 4 minutes. The clerk then directs you to the waiting area for paying state personal property tax, 80 feet away. With a sinking heart, you take a different number and sit down with some different customers who are just renewing licenses. You notice the same unkempt man. A 1-hour, 40-minute wait this time, and after a walk of 25 feet you pay property taxes in a process that takes 2 minutes. Now that you have paid taxes you're eligible to pay registration and license fees. That department is 50 feet away, beyond the employees' cafeteria. As you walk by the cafeteria, you notice the unkempt man having coffee with a uniformed person.

The registration and license customers are called in the same order in which personal property taxes were paid. There is only a 10-minute wait and a 3-minute process. You receive your license plates, take a minute to abuse the license clerk, and leave exactly 6 hours after arriving.

Make a process chart to depict this process, and suggest improvements.

14. Refer to the process chart for the automobile oil change in Solved Problem 2. Calculate the annual labor cost if:

   ■ The mechanic earns $40 per hour (including variable fringe benefits).

   ■ The process is performed twice per hour (on average).

   ■ The shop is open 300 days a year, 10 hours a day.

   a. What is the total labor cost associated with the process?

   b. If steps 7, 10, 12, and 15 were eliminated, estimate the annual labor savings associated with implementing this new process.

15. The manager of Perrotti's Pizza collects data concerning customer complaints about delivery. Pizza is arriving late, or the wrong pizza is being delivered.

Problem	Frequency
Topping stuck to box lid	17
Pizza is late	35
Wrong topping or combination	9
Wrong style of crust	6
Wrong size	4
Pizza is partially eaten	3
Pizza never showed up	6

   a. Use a Pareto chart to identify the "few vital" delivery problems.

   b. Use a cause-and-effect diagram to identify potential causes of late pizza delivery.

16. Smith, Schroeder, and Torn (SST) is a short-haul household furniture moving company. SST's labor force, selected from the local community college football team, is temporary and part-time. SST is concerned with recent complaints, as tabulated on the following tally sheet.

Complaint	Tally
Broken glass	JHT JHT III
Delivered to wrong address	JHT IIII
Furniture rubbed together while on truck	JHT JHT JHT JHT
Late delivery	JHT
Late arrival for pickup	JHT JHT JHT III
Missing items	JHT JHT JHT JHT JHT I
Nicks and scratches from rough handling	JHT JHT
Soiled upholstery	JHT III

   a. Draw a bar chart and a Pareto chart to identify the most serious moving problems.

   b. Use a cause-and-effect diagram to identify potential causes of complaints.

17. Rick DeNeefe, manager of the Golden Valley Bank credit authorization department, recently noticed that a major competitor was advertising that applications for equity loans could be approved within two working days. Because fast credit approval was a competitive priority, DeNeefe wanted to see how well his department was doing relative to the competitor's. Golden Valley stamps each application with the date and time it is received and again when a decision is made. A total of 104 applications were received in March. The time required for each decision, rounded to the nearest hour, is shown in the following table. Golden Valley's employees work 8 hours per day.

Decision Process Time	Frequency
7–9 hours	8
10–12 hours	19
13–15 hours	28
16–18 hours	10
19–21 hours	25
22–24 hours	4
25–27 hours	10
Total	104

a. Draw a bar chart for these data.

b. Analyze the data. How is Golden Valley Bank doing with regard to this competitive priority?

18. Last year, the manager of the service department at East Woods Ford Instituted a customer opinion program to find out how to improve service.

One week after service on a vehicle was performed, an assistant would call the customer to find out whether the work had been done satisfactorily and how service could be improved. After a year of gathering data, the assistant discovered that the complaints could be grouped into the following five categories.

Complaint	Frequency
Unfriendly atmosphere	5
Long wait for service	17
Price too high	20
Incorrect bill	8
Need to return to correct problem	50
Total	100

a. Draw a bar chart and a Pareto chart to identify the significant service problems.

b. Use a cause-and-effect diagram to identify potential causes of complaints.

19. Oregon Fiber Board makes roof liners for the automotive industry. The manufacturing manager is concerned about product quality. She suspects that one particular defect, tears in the fabric, is related to production-run size. An assistant gathers the following data from production records.

Run	Size	Defects (%)	Run	Size	Defects (%)
1	1,000	3.5	11	6,500	1.5
2	4,100	3.8	12	1,000	5.5
3	2,000	5.5	13	7,000	1.0
4	6,000	1.9	14	3,000	4.5
5	6,800	2.0	15	2,200	4.2
6	3,000	3.2	16	1,800	6.0
7	2,000	3.8	17	5,400	2.0
8	1,200	4.2	18	5,800	2.0
9	5,000	3.8	19	1,000	6.2
10	3,800	3.0	20	1,500	7.0

a. Draw a scatter diagram for these data.

b. Does there appear to be a relationship between run size and percent defects? What implications do these data have for Wellington's business?

20. Grindwell, Inc., a manufacturer of grinding tools, is concerned about the durability of its products, which depends on the permeability of the sinter mixtures used in production. Suspecting that the carbon content might be the source of the problem, the plant manager collected the following data.

Carbon Content (%)	Permeability Index
5.5	16
3.0	31
4.5	21
4.8	19
4.2	16
4.7	23
5.1	20
4.4	11
3.6	20

a. Draw a scatter plot for these data.

b. Is there a relationship between permeability and carbon content?

c. If low permeability is desirable, what does the scatter plot suggest with regard to the carbon content?

21. The operations manager for Superfast Airlines at Chicago's O'Hare Airport noticed an increase in the number of delayed flight departures. She brainstormed possible causes with her staff:

- Aircraft late to gate

- Acceptance of late passengers

- Passengers arrive late at gate

- Passengers processing delays at gate

- Late baggage to aircraft

- Other late personnel or unavailable items

- Mechanical failures

    Draw a cause-and-effect diagram to organize the possible causes of delayed flight departures into the following major categories: equipment, personnel, material, procedures, and "other factors" beyond managerial control. Provide a detailed set of causes for each major cause identified by the operations manager, and incorporate them in your cause-and-effect diagram.

22. Plastomer, Inc., specializes in the manufacture of high-grade plastic film used to wrap food products. Film is rejected and scrapped for a variety of reasons (e.g., opacity, high carbon content, incorrect thickness or gauge, scratches, etc.). During the past month, management collected data on the types of rejects and the amount of scrap generated by each type. The following table presents the results.

Type of Defect	Amount of Scrap (lbs.)
Air bubbles	500
Bubble breaks	19,650
Carbon content	150
Unevenness	3,810
Thickness or gauge	27,600
Opacity	450
Scratches	3,840
Trim	500
Wrinkles	10,650

    Draw a Pareto chart to identify which type of defect management should attempt to eliminate first.

23. Management of a shampoo bottling company introduced a new 13.5-ounce pack and used an existing machine, with some modifications, to fill it. To measure filling consistency by the modified machine (set to fill 13.85 ounces), an analyst collected the following data (volume in ounces) for a random sample of 100 bottles.

13.0	13.3	13.6	13.2	14.0	12.9	14.2	12.9	14.5	13.5
14.1	14.0	13.7	13.4	14.4	14.3	14.8	13.9	13.5	14.3
14.2	14.1	14.0	13.9	13.9	14.0	14.5	13.6	13.3	12.9
12.8	13.1	13.6	14.5	14.6	12.9	13.1	14.4	14.0	14.4
13.1	14.1	14.2	12.9	13.3	14.0	14.1	13.1	13.6	13.7
14.0	13.6	13.2	13.4	13.9	14.5	14.0	14.4	13.9	14.6
12.9	14.3	14.0	12.9	14.2	14.8	14.5	13.1	12.7	13.9
13.6	14.4	13.1	14.5	13.5	13.3	14.0	13.6	13.5	14.3
13.2	13.8	13.7	12.8	13.4	13.8	13.3	13.7	14.1	13.7
13.7	13.8	13.4	13.7	14.1	12.8	13.7	13.8	14.1	14.3

  a. Draw a histogram for these data.

  b. Bottles with less than 12.85 ounces or more than 14.85 ounces are considered to be out of specification. Based on the sample data, what percent of the bottles filled by the machine will be out of specification?

ADVANCED PROBLEMS

24. This problem should be solved as a team exercise.

    Shaving is a process that most men perform each morning. Assume that the process begins at the bathroom sink with the shaver walking (say, 5 feet) to the cabinet (where his shaving supplies are stored) to pick up bowl, soap, brush, and razor. He walks back to the sink, runs the water until it gets warm, lathers his face, shaves, and inspects the results. Then, he rinses the razor, dries his face, walks over to the cabinet to return the bowl, soap, brush, and razor, and comes back to the sink to clean it up and complete the process.

  a. Develop a process chart for shaving. (Assume suitable values for the time required for the various activities involved in the process.)

  b. Brainstorm to generate ideas for improving the shaving process. (Do not try to evaluate the ideas until the group has compiled as complete a list as possible. Otherwise, judgment will block creativity.)

25. At Conner Company, a custom manufacturer of printed circuit boards, the finished boards are subjected to a final inspection prior to shipment to its customers. As Conner's quality assurance manager, you are responsible for making a presentation to management on quality problems at the beginning of each month. Your assistant has analyzed the reject memos for all the circuit boards that were rejected during the past month. He has given you a summary statement listing the reference number of the circuit board and the reason for rejection from one of the following categories:

       A = Poor electrolyte coverage

       B = Improper lamination

       C = Low copper plating

       D = Plating separation

       E = Improper etching

For 50 circuit boards that had been rejected last month, the summary statement showed the following:

C B C C D E C C B A D A C C C B C A C D C A C C B

A C A C B C C A C A A C C D A C C C E C C A B A C

a. Prepare a tally sheet (or checklist) of the different reasons for rejection.

b. Develop a Pareto chart to identify the more significant types of rejection.

c. Examine the causes of the most significant type of defect, using a cause-and-effect diagram.

> ACTIVE MODEL EXERCISE <

This Active Model appears on your CD-ROM. It allows you to evaluate the structure of a Pareto chart.

QUESTIONS

1. What percentage of overall defects does discourteous service account for?

2. What percentage of overall defects do the three most common complaints account for?

3. How does it affect the chart if we could eliminate discourteous service?

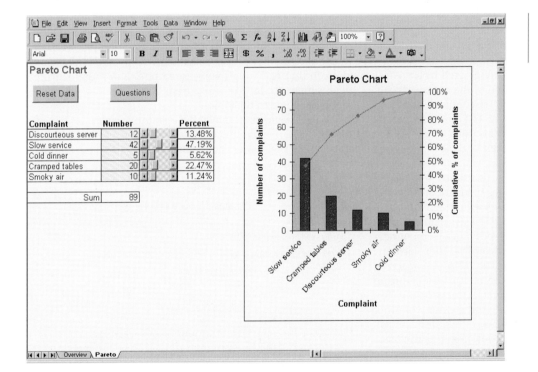

ACTIVE MODEL 5.1

Pareto Chart Using Data from Example 5.1

CASE	José's Authentic Mexican Restaurant

"Two bean tacos, a chicken burrito grande, and a side order of Spanish rice, please." Ivan Karetski called his table's order into the kitchen as he prepared the beverage orders. Business was brisk. Karetski liked it that way. Lots of customers meant lots of tips and, as a struggling graduate student, the extra income was greatly appreciated. Lately, however, his tips had been declining.

José's is a small, 58-seat restaurant that offers a reasonably broad range of Mexican food prepared and presented in a traditional Mexican style. It is located in New England in a mature business district on the edge of a large metropolitan area. The site is adjacent to a central artery and offers limited free off-street parking. The restaurant's interior decoration promotes the Mexican theme: The walls appear to be made of adobe and are draped with serapes, the furniture is Spanish-Mexican style, and flamenco guitar and mariachi alternate as background music.

Patrons enter the restaurant through a small vestibule that opens directly into the dining area; there is no separate waiting area. Upon arrival, patrons are greeted by a hostess and either seated directly or apprised of the expected wait. Seating at José's is usually immediate except for Friday and Saturday nights when waits of as long as 45 minutes can be encountered. Because space inside for waiting is very limited patrons must remain outside until their party is called. José's does not take reservations.

After seating patrons, the hostess distributes menus and fills glasses with water. If standards are being met, the waiter assigned to the table greets the patrons within one minute of their being seated. (Being a traditional Mexican restaurant, all its waitstaff are male.) The waiter introduces himself, announces the daily specials, and takes the beverage orders. After delivering the beverages, the waiter takes the meal orders.

The menu consists of 23 main entrees assembled from eight basic stocks (chicken, beef, beans, rice, corn tortillas, flour tortillas, tomatoes, and lettuce) and a variety of other ingredients (fruits, vegetables, sauces, herbs, and spices). Before the dining hours begin, the cook prepares the basic stocks so that they can be quickly combined and finished off to complete the requested meals. The typical amount of time needed to complete a meal once it has been ordered is 12 minutes. A good portion of this time is for final cooking, so several meals may be in preparation at the same time. As can be imagined, one of the skills a good cook needs is to be able to schedule production of the various meals ordered at a table so that they are ready at approximately the same time. Once all the meals and any side dishes have been completed by the cook, the waiter checks to see that all meals are correct and pleasing to the eye, corrects any mistakes, and adds any finishing touches. When everything is in order, he assembles them on a tray and delivers them to the table. From this point on, the waiter keeps an eye on the table to detect when any additional service or assistance is needed.

When the diners at the table appear to be substantially finished with their main meal, the waiter approaches, asks if he can clear away any dishes, and takes any requests for dessert or coffee. When the entire meal has been completed, the waiter presents the bill and shortly thereafter collects payment. José's accepts cash or major credit card but no checks.

Karetski feels that his relationship with the cook is important. As the cook largely controls the quality of the food, Karetski wants to stay on good terms with him. He treats the cook with respect, tries to place the items on his order slip in the sequence of longest preparation time, and makes sure to write clearly so that the orders are easy to read. Although it is not his job, he helps out by fetching food stocks from the refrigerator or the storage area when the cook is busy and by doing some of the food preparation himself. The cook has been irritable lately, complaining of the poor quality of some of the ingredients that have been delivered. Last week, for example, he received lettuce that appeared wilted and chicken that was tough and more bone than meat. During peak times, it can take more than 20 minutes to get good meals delivered to the table.

Karetski had been shown the results of a customer survey that management conducted last Friday and Saturday during the evening mealtime. The following table shows a summary of the responses.

Customer Survey Results		
Were you seated promptly?	Yes 70	No 13
Was your waiter satisfactory?	Yes 73	No 10
Were you served in a reasonable time?	Yes 58	No 25
Was your food enjoyable?	Yes 72	No 11
Was your dining experience worth the cost?	Yes 67	No 16

As Karetski carried the tray of drinks to the table, he wondered whether the recent falloff in tips was due to anything that he could control.

QUESTIONS

1. How should quality be defined at this restaurant?
2. What are the restaurant's costs of poor quality?
3. Use some of the tools for process analysis to assess the situation at José's.

Source: This case was prepared by Larry Meile, Boston College, as a basis for classroom discussion.

> **SELECTED REFERENCES** <

Anderson, Merrill C. "Transforming Human Resources: Maximizing Value While Increasing Productivity." *National Productivity Review,* vol. 17, no. 3 (Autumn 2000), pp. 75–80.

Anupindi, Ravi, Sunil Chopra, Sudhakar D. Deshmukj, Jan A. Van Mieghem, and Eitan Zemel. *Managing Business Process Flows.* Upper Saddle River, NJ: Prentice Hall, 1999.

Banker, R. D., J. M. Field, R. G. Schroeder, and K. K. Sinha. "Impact of Work Teams on Manufacturing Performance: A Longitudinal Field Study." *Academy of Management Journal,* vol. 39, no. 4 (1996), pp. 867–890.

Collier, D. A. *The Service/Quality Solution.* Burr Ridge, IL: Irwin Professional Publishing, 1993.

Deming, W. Edwards. "Improvement of Quality and Productivity Through Action by Management." *National Productivity Review,* vol. 1, no. 1 (Winter 1981–1982), pp. 12–22.

Drucker, Peter F. "The Discipline of Innovation." *Harvard Business Review,* vol. 80, no. 8 (August 2002), pp. 95–101.

Ellis, Christian M., and Lea A. P. Tonkin. "Mature Team Rewards and the High-Performance Workplace: Change and Opportunity." *Target,* vol. 11, no. 6 (1995).

Fisher, Anne. "Get Employees to Brainstorm Online." *Fortune,* vol. 150, no. 11 (November 2004), p. 72.

Fitzsimmons, James A., and Mona J. Fitzsimmons. *Service Management: Operations, Strategy, and Information Technology,* New York: McGraw-Hill, 1998.

Hartvigsen, David. *SimQuick: Process Simulation with Excel,* 2d ed. Upper Saddle River, NJ: Prentice Hall, 2004.

Iakovou, Eleftherios T., and Olga L. Oritz. "Reengineering of the Laundry Service at a University Campus: A Continuous-Improvement Quality-Management Methodology." *Quality Engineering,* vol. 16, no. 2 (2004), pp. 245–255.

Karmarkar, Uday. "Will You Survive the Services Revolution?" *Harvard Business Review,* vol. 82, no. 6 (June 2004), pp. 100–107.

Katzenbach, Jon R., and Douglas K. Smith. "The Discipline of Teams." *Harvard Business Review* (March–April 1993), pp. 111–120.

Kingman-Brundage, Jane. "Technology, Design, and Service Quality." *International Journal of Service Industry Management,* vol. 2, no. 3 (1991), pp. 47–59.

La Ferla, Beverly. "Mapping the Way to Process Improvement." *IEE Engineering Management* (December 2004–January 2005), pp. 16–17.

Lee, Hau L. "The Triple-A Supply Chain." *Harvard Business Review* (October 2004), pp. 102–112.

Liebs, Scott. "A Little Help from Their Friends." *Industry Week* (February 2, 1998).

Lovelock, Christopher H., and George S. Yip. "Developing Global Strategies for Service Businesses." *California Management Review,* vol. 38, no. 2 (1996), pp. 64–86.

Melnyk, Steven A., Douglas M. Stewart, and Morgan Swink. "Metrics and Performance Measurement in Operations Management: Dealing with the Metrics Maze." *Journal of Operations Management,* vol. 22, no. 3 (June 2004), pp. 209–217.

Metters, Richard, Kathryn King-Metters, and Madeleine Pullman. *Successful Service Operations Management.* Mason, OH: South-Western, 2003.

Pande, Peter S., Robert P. Neuman, and Roland R. Cavanagh. *The Six Sigma Way.* New York: McGraw-Hill, 2000.

"Process, Process, Process." *Planning Review* (special issue), vol. 22, no. 3 (1993), pp. 1–56.

Pullman, Madeleine E., and William L. Moore. "Optimal Service Design: Integrating Marketing and Operations Perspectives." *International Journal of Service Industry Management,* vol. 10, no. 2 (1999), pp. 239–260.

Rampersad, Hubert K. *Total Performance Scorecard.* New York: Butterworth-Heinemann, 2003.

Rummler, Geary A., and Alan P. Brache. *Improving Performance,* 2nd ed. San Francisco: Jossey-Bass Inc., 1995.

Schmenner, Roger W. *Service Operations Management.* Englewood Cliffs, NJ: Prentice Hall, 1998.

Senge, P. *The Fifth Discipline: The Art and Practice of the Learning Organization.* New York: Doubleday, 1990.

Shapiro, Benson R., V. Kasturi Rangan, and John J. Sviokla. "Staple Yourself to an Order." *Harvard Business Review,* vol. 82, no. 7/8 (July–August 2004), pp. 162–171.

SUPPLEMENT
Simulation

LEARNING GOALS

After reading this supplement, you should be able to:

1. Identify problems best suited for simulation models.
2. Describe the Monte Carlo simulation process.
3. Explain how to create a simulation model and use it to help make a decision.
4. Create a simple simulation model with an Excel spreadsheet.
5. Describe the advanced capabilities of SimQuick and Extend.

The act of reproducing the behavior of a system using a model that describes the processes of the system is called **simulation**. Once the model has been developed, the analyst can manipulate certain variables to measure the effects of changes on the operating characteristics of interest. A simulation model cannot prescribe what should be done about a problem. Instead, it can be used to study alternative solutions to the problem. The alternatives are systematically used in the model, and the relevant operating characteristics are recorded. After all the alternatives have been tried, the best one is selected.

Simulation can be used in managing processes as well as value chains. Various simulation models can help in understanding how a process performs dynamically over time and how well revised processes will work. Some of the changes that simulation can be used to assess include quality improvement ideas, capacity changes aimed at relieving bottlenecks, the layout of the process, or even changes that come from implementing lean systems ideas—in effect, all of the decision areas covered in Part 2. Simulation can also be used for many of the decisions related to managing value chains (Part 3), such as where to position inventory and in what quantities, or how different scheduling procedures work.

Waiting-line models (see Supplement C, "Waiting Lines") are not simulation models because they describe the operating *characteristics with known equations. With simulation, the equations describing the operation characteristics are unknown. Using a simulation model, the analyst actually generates customer arrivals, puts customers into waiting lines, selects the next customer to be served by using some priority discipline, serves that customer, and so on. The model keeps track of the number in line, waiting time, and the like during the simulation and calculates the averages and variances at the end.*

simulation

The act of reproducing the behavior of a system using a model that describes the processes of the system.

> REASONS FOR USING SIMULATION <

Simulation is useful when waiting-line models become too complex. Using simulation for analyzing processes may be based on other reasons as well. First, when the relationship between the variables is nonlinear or when the situation involves too many variables or constraints to handle with optimizing approaches, simulation models can be used to estimate operating characteristics or objective function values and analyze a problem.

Second, simulation models can be used to conduct experiments without disrupting real systems. Experimenting with a real system can be costly. For example, a simulation model can be used to estimate the benefits of purchasing and installing a new flexible manufacturing system without first installing such a system. Also, the model could be used to evaluate different configurations or processing decision rules without disrupting production schedules.

Third, simulation models can be used to obtain operating characteristic estimates in much less time than is required to gather the same operating data from a real system. This feature of simulation is called **time compression**. For example, a simulation model of airport operations can generate statistics on airplane arrivals, landing delays, and terminal delays for a year in a matter of minutes on a computer. Alternative airport designs can be analyzed and decisions made quickly.

Finally, simulation is useful in sharpening managerial decision-making skills through gaming. A descriptive model that relates managerial decisions to important operating characteristics (e.g., profits, market share, and the like) can be developed. From a set of starting conditions, the participants make periodic decisions with the intention of improving one or more operating characteristics. In such an exercise, a few hours' "play" can simulate a year's time. Gaming also enables managers to experiment with new ideas without disrupting normal operations.

time compression

The feature of simulation models that allows them to obtain operating characteristic estimates in much less time than is required to gather the same operating data from a real system.

> THE SIMULATION PROCESS <

The simulation process includes data collection, random-number assignment, model formulation, and analysis. This process is known as **Monte Carlo simulation**, after the European gambling capital, because of the random numbers used to generate the simulation events.

DATA COLLECTION

Simulation requires extensive data gathering on costs, productivities, capacities, and probability distributions. Typically, one of two approaches to data collection is used. Statistical sampling procedures are used when the data are not readily available from published sources or when the cost of searching for and collecting the data is high. Historical search is used when the data are available in company records, governmental and industry reports, professional and scientific journals, or newspapers. Example B.2 provides the data that Specialty Steel collected.

Monte Carlo simulation

A simulation process that uses random numbers to generate simulation events.

| Data Collection for a Simulation | EXAMPLE B.1 |

The Specialty Steel Products Company produces items, such as machine tools, gears, automobile parts, and other specialty items, in small quantities to customer order. Because the products are so diverse, demand is measured in machine-hours. Orders for products are translated into required machine-hours, based on time standards for each operation. Management is concerned about capacity in the lathe department. Assemble the data necessary to analyze the addition of one more lathe machine and operator.

SOLUTION

Historical records indicate that lathe department demand varies from week to week as follows:

Weekly Production Requirements (hr)	Relative Frequency
200	0.05
250	0.06
300	0.17
350	0.05
400	0.30
450	0.15
500	0.06
550	0.14
600	0.02
Total	1.00

To gather these data, all weeks with requirements of 175.00–224.99 hours were grouped in the 200-hour category, all weeks with 225.00–274.99 hours in the 250-hour category, and so on. The average weekly production requirements for the lathe department are

$$200(0.05) + 250(0.06) + 300(0.17) + \cdots + 600(0.02) = 400 \text{ hours}$$

Employees in the lathe department work 40 hours per week on 10 machines. However, the number of machines actually operating during any week may be less than 10. Machines may need repair, or a worker may not show up for work. Historical records indicate that actual machine-hours were distributed as follows:

Regular Capacity (hr)	Relative Frequency
320 (8 machines)	0.30
360 (9 machines)	0.40
400 (10 machines)	0.30

The average number of operating machine-hours in a week is

$$320(0.30) + 360(0.40) + 400(0.30) = 360 \text{ hours}$$

The company has a policy of completing each week's workload on schedule, using overtime and subcontracting if necessary. The maximum amount of overtime authorized in any week is 100 hours, and requirements in excess of 100 hours are subcontracted to a small machine shop in town. Lathe operators receive $10 per hour for regular time. However, management estimates that the cost for overtime work is $25 per hour per employee, which includes premium-wage, variable-overhead, and supervision costs. Subcontracting costs $35 per hour, exclusive of materials costs.

To justify adding another machine and worker to the lathe department, weekly savings in overtime and subcontracting costs should be at least $650. These savings would cover the cost of the additional worker and provide for a reasonable return on machine investment. Management estimates from prior experience that with 11 machines the distribution of weekly capacity machine-hours would be

Regular Capacity (hr)	Relative Frequency
360 (9 machines)	0.30
400 (10 machines)	0.40
440 (11 machines)	0.30

RANDOM-NUMBER ASSIGNMENT

Before we can begin to analyze this problem with simulation, we must specify a way to generate demand and capacity each week. Suppose that we want to simulate 100 weeks of lathe operations with 10 machines. We would expect that 5 percent of the time (5 weeks of the 100) we would have a demand for 200 hours. Similarly, we would expect that 30 percent of the time (30 weeks of the 100) we would have 320 hours of existing capacity with the 10 machines. However, we cannot use these averages of demand in our simulation because a real system does not operate that way. Demand may be 200 hours one week but 550 hours the next.

We can obtain the effect we want by using a random-number table to determine the amount of demand and capacity each week. A **random number** is a number that has the same probability of being selected as any other number (see the Table of Random Numbers in Appendix 2 for five-digit random numbers).

The events in a simulation can be generated in an unbiased way if random numbers are assigned to the events in the same proportion as their probability of occurrence. We expect a demand of 200 hours 5 percent of the time. If we have 100 random numbers (00–99), we can assign 5 numbers (or 5 percent of them) to the event "200 hours demanded." Thus, we can assign the numbers 00–04 to that event. If we randomly choose numbers in the range of 00–99 enough times, 5 percent of the time they will fall in the range of 00–04. Similarly, we can assign the numbers 05–10, or 6 percent of the numbers, to the event "250 hours demanded." In Table B.1 we show the allocation of the 100 random numbers to the demand events in the same proportion as their probability of occurrence. We similarly assigned random numbers to the *capacity* events for 10 machines. The capacity events for the 11-machine

random number

A number that has the same probability of being selected as any other number.

TABLE B.1	Random-Number Assignments to Simulation Events

Event					
Weekly Demand (hr)	Probability	Random Number	Existing Weekly Capacity (hr)	Probability	Random Numbers
200	0.05	00–04	320	0.30	00–29
250	0.06	05–10	360	0.40	30–69
300	0.17	11–27	400	0.30	70–99
350	0.05	28–32			
400	0.30	33–62			
450	0.15	63–77			
500	0.06	78–83			
550	0.14	84–97			
600	0.02	98–99			

simulation would have the same random-number assignments, except that the events would be 360, 400, and 440 hours, respectively.

MODEL FORMULATION

Formulating a simulation model entails specifying the relationships among the variables. Simulation models consist of decision variables, uncontrollable variables, and dependent variables. **Decision variables** are controlled by the decision maker and will change from one run to the next as different events are simulated. For example, the number of lathe machines is the decision variable in the Specialty Steel Products problem in Example B.1. **Uncontrollable variables**, however, are random events that the decision maker cannot control. At Specialty Steel Products, the weekly production requirements and the *actual* number of machine-hours available are uncontrollable variables for the simulation analysis. Dependent variables reflect the values of the decision variables and the uncontrollable variables. At Specialty Steel Products, operating characteristics such as idle time, overtime, and subcontracting hours are dependent variables.

The relationships among the variables are expressed in mathematical terms so that the dependent variables can be computed for any values of the decision variables and uncontrollable variables. For example, in the simulation model for Specialty Steel Products, the methods of determining weekly production requirements and actual capacity availability must be specified first. Then the methods of computing idle-time hours, overtime hours, and subcontracting hours for the values of production requirements and capacity hours can be specified.

decision variables

Variables that are controlled by the decision maker and will change from one run to the next as different events are simulated.

uncontrollable variables

Random events that the decision maker cannot control.

Formulating a Simulation Model	EXAMPLE B.2

Formulate a simulation model for Specialty Steel Products that will estimate idle-time hours, overtime hours, and subcontracting hours for a specified number of lathes. Design the simulation model to terminate after 20 weeks of simulated lathe department operations.

SOLUTION

Let us use the first two rows of random numbers in the random number table for the demand events and the third and fourth rows for the capacity events (see the Table of Random Numbers in Appendix 2). Because they are five-digit numbers, we use only the first two digits of each number for our random numbers. The choice of the rows in the random-number table was arbitrary. The important point is that we must be consistent in drawing random numbers and should not repeat the use of numbers in any one simulation.

To simulate a particular capacity level, we proceed as follows:

Step 1: Draw a random number from the first two rows of the table. Start with the first number in the first row, then go to the second number in the first row, and so on.

Step 2: Find the random-number interval for production requirements associated with the random number.

Step 3: Record the production hours (PROD) required for the current week.

Step 4: Draw another random number from row 3 or 4 of the table. Start with the first number in row 3, then go to the second number in row 3, and so on.

Step 5: Find the random-number interval for capacity (CAP) associated with the random number.

Step 6: Record the capacity hours available for the current week.

Step 7: If CAP ≥ PROD, then IDLE HR = CAP − PROD.

Step 8: If CAP < PROD, then SHORT = PROD − CAP.
   If SHORT ≤ 100, then OVERTIME HR = SHORT and SUBCONTRACT HR = 0.
   If SHORT > 100, then OVERTIME HR = 100 and SUBCONTRACT HR = SHORT − 100.

Step 9: Repeat steps 1–8 until you have simulated 20 weeks.

ANALYSIS

Table B.2 contains the simulations for the two capacity alternatives at Specialty Steel Products. We used a unique random-number sequence for weekly production requirements for each capacity alternative and another sequence for the existing weekly capacity to make a direct comparison between the capacity alternatives.

Based on the 20-week simulations, we would expect average weekly overtime hours (highlighted in orange) to be reduced by $41.5 - 29.5 = 12$ hours and subcontracting hours (highlighted in gray) to be reduced by $18 - 10 = 8$ hours per week. The average weekly savings would be

$$\text{Overtime:} \quad (12 \text{ hours})(\$25/\text{hours}) = \$300$$

$$\text{Subcontracting:} \quad (8 \text{ hours})(\$35/\text{hour}) = \underline{\quad 280}$$

$$\text{Total savings per week} = \$580$$

This amount falls short of the minimum required savings of \$650 per week. Does this outcome mean that we should not add the machine and worker? Before answering, let us look at Table B.3 which shows the results of a *1,000-week* simulation for each alternative. The costs (highlighted in lavender) are quite different from those of the 20-week simulations. Now the savings are estimated to be $\$1,851.50 - \$1,159.50 = \$692$ and exceed the minimum

TABLE B.2	20-Week Simulations of Alternatives

				10 Machines				**11 Machines**			
Week	**Demand Random Number**	**Weekly Production (hr)**	**Capacity Random Number**	**Existing Weekly Capacity (hr)**	**Idle Hours**	**Overtime Hours**	**Subcontract Hours**	**Existing Weekly Capacity (hr)**	**Idle Hours**	**Overtime Hours**	**Subcontract Hours**
1	71	450	50	360		90		400		50	
2	68	450	54	360		90		400		50	
3	48	400	11	320		80		360		40	
4	99	600	36	360		100	140	400		100	100
5	64	450	82	400		50		440		10	
6	13	300	87	400	100			440	140		
7	36	400	41	360		40		400			
8	58	400	71	400				440	40		
9	13	300	00	320	20			360	60		
10	93	550	60	360		100	90	400		100	50
11	21	300	47	360	60			400	100		
12	30	350	76	400	50			440	90		
13	23	300	09	320	20			360	60		
14	89	550	54	360		100	90	400		100	50
15	58	400	87	400				440	40		
16	46	400	82	400				440	40		
17	00	200	17	320	120			360	160		
18	82	500	52	360		100	40	400		100	
19	02	200	17	320	120			360	160		
20	37	400	19	320		80		360		40	
				Total	490	830	360		890	590	200
				Weekly average	24.5	41.5	18.0		44.5	29.5	10.0

TABLE B.3	Comparison of 1,000-Week Simulations	
	10 Machines	**11 Machines**
Idle hours	26.0	42.2
Overtime hours	48.3	34.2
Subcontract hours	18.4	8.7
Cost	$1,851.50	$1,159.50

required savings for the additional investment. This result emphasizes the importance of selecting the proper run length for a simulation analysis. We can use statistical tests to check for the proper run length.

Simulation analysis can be viewed as a form of hypothesis testing, whereby the results of a simulation run provide sample data that can be analyzed statistically. Data can be recorded and compared with the results from other simulation runs. Statistical tests also can be made to determine whether differences in the alternative operating characteristics are statistically significant.

Even though a difference between simulation experiments may be statistically significant, it may not be *managerially* significant. For example, suppose that we developed a simulation model of a car-wash operation. We may find, by changing the speed of the car wash from 3 to 2.75 minutes per car, that we can reduce the average waiting time per customer by 0.20 minute. Even though this may be a statistically significant difference in the average waiting time, the difference is so small that customers may not even notice it. What is managerially significant often is a judgment decision.

> COMPUTER SIMULATION <

The manual simulation of the lathe process in Examples B.1 and B.2 demonstrates the basics of simulation. However, the simulation involves only one step in the process, two uncontrollable variables (weekly production requirements and the actual number of machine-hours available), and 20 time periods. It is important to simulate a process long enough to achieve **steady state**, so that the simulation is repeated over enough time that the average results for performance measures remain constant. Manual simulations can be excessively time-consuming, particularly if they include many subprocesses, many services or products with unique flow patterns, many uncontrollable variables, complex logic for releasing new jobs and assigning work, and the like.

Simulating these real-world situations manually can become too time-consuming and therefore requires a computer instead. Simple simulation models, say with one or two uncontrollable variables, can be developed using Excel. Its ability to generate random numbers—coupled with adding formulas elsewhere in the worksheet to specify relations between demand, customer served, inventory, and output—allow the Monte Carlo simulation approach to be implemented. Even more computer power comes from commercial, prewritten simulation software.

steady state

The state that occurs when the simulation is repeated over enough time that the average results for performance measures remain constant.

SIMULATION WITH EXCEL SPREADSHEETS

The starting point in creating an Excel simulation is generating random numbers, the computer equivalent of using Appendix 2 for manual simulations. Equally important is random-number assignment, which translates a random number into a value for an uncontrollable variable.

Generating Random Numbers Random numbers can be created from 0 to 1 by entering the formula = RAND() into a cell of the Excel spreadsheet. This formula then can be copied to other cells in the spreadsheet as needed. Figure B.1 shows a table of 100 random numbers generated with the RAND() function in the range A3:J12. They were formatted to show four-digit numbers, although the format can be changed as desired. These random numbers are

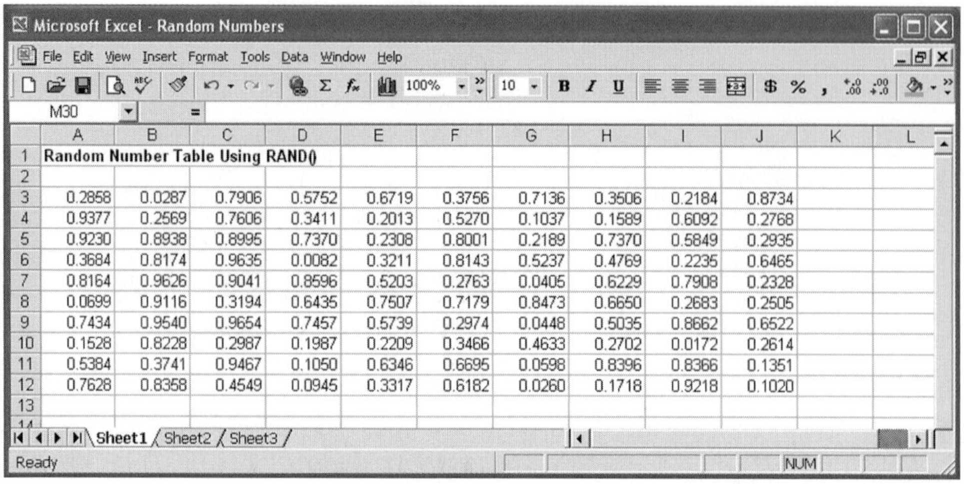

Random Number Table Using RAND()

	A	B	C	D	E	F	G	H	I	J
3	0.2858	0.0287	0.7906	0.5752	0.6719	0.3756	0.7136	0.3506	0.2184	0.8734
4	0.9377	0.2569	0.7606	0.3411	0.2013	0.5270	0.1037	0.1589	0.6092	0.2768
5	0.9230	0.8938	0.8995	0.7370	0.2308	0.8001	0.2189	0.7370	0.5849	0.2935
6	0.3684	0.8174	0.9635	0.0082	0.3211	0.8143	0.5237	0.4769	0.2235	0.6465
7	0.8164	0.9626	0.9041	0.8596	0.5203	0.2763	0.0405	0.6229	0.7908	0.2328
8	0.0699	0.9116	0.3194	0.6435	0.7507	0.7179	0.8473	0.6650	0.2683	0.2505
9	0.7434	0.9540	0.9654	0.7457	0.5739	0.2974	0.0448	0.5035	0.8662	0.6522
10	0.1528	0.8228	0.2987	0.1987	0.2209	0.3466	0.4633	0.2702	0.0172	0.2614
11	0.5384	0.3741	0.9467	0.1050	0.6346	0.6695	0.0598	0.8396	0.8366	0.1351
12	0.7628	0.8358	0.4549	0.0945	0.3317	0.6182	0.0260	0.1718	0.9218	0.1020

FIGURE B.1

A Spreadsheet with 100 Random Numbers Generated with RAND( )

fractions from 0 to 1, rather than the two-digit integer numbers from 0 through 99 in Table B.1. If you attempt to replicate Figure B.1, or reopen an Excel file that was created earlier and saved, you will see a different set of random numbers. To use the same exact set or *stream* of random numbers, such as for experiments that compare the effectiveness of different policies, you should *freeze* the random numbers. First, select with your mouse the cells holding the random numbers that you wish frozen. For example, cover A3:J12 in Figure B.1. Next, click on Edit/Copy in the menu at the top of your spreadsheet. Click next on Edit/Paste Special and choose the Values option. When you click on OK, a copy of the numbers in these cells is pasted over the same cells with the =RAND() formulas in them. The result is that they are fixed in place and will not change from one use of the spreadsheet to the next. Each simulation is conducted with the same stream of random numbers. In fact, the numbers in Figure B.1 were frozen using this procedure.

Random-Number Assignment A second capability that is needed for Excel simulations is to translate random numbers into values for the uncontrollable variables. It is equivalent to identifying the random-number interval in which a random number falls and then selecting the value of the uncontrollable variable assigned to that interval (see Table B.1 for the demand or capacity variables). In an Excel spreadsheet, the Lookup feature serves this purpose. Read about the VLOOKUP() function under Excel's Help Topics and check out the function by selecting Insert/Function/Lookup & Reference/VLOOKUP. Example B.3 demonstrates the use of both the VLOOKUP() and RAND() functions.

EXAMPLE B.3 Excel Simulation Model for BestCar Auto Dealer

The BestCar automobile dealership sells new automobiles. The BestCar store manager believes that the number of cars sold weekly has the following probability distribution:

Weekly Sales (cars)	Relative Frequency (probability)
0	0.05
1	0.15
2	0.20
3	0.30
4	0.20
5	0.10
Total	1.00

The selling price per car is $20,000. Design a simulation model that determines the probability distribution and mean of the weekly sales.

SOLUTION

Figure B.2 simulates 50 weeks of sales at BestCar. A longer run length, say 500 or 1,000 weeks, would be prudent, but here we keep it small for demonstration purposes. The bottom right of the spreadsheet shows that the average weekly sales is 2.88 cars, for $57,600 per week. The distribution of the simulated weekly demand is shown in cells B17:E22. For example, 13 of the 50 weeks experienced a demand for 3 cars, which translates into 26 percent of the weeks (see cell D20). The chance that sales are not more than 3 cars is 60 percent (see cell E20).

The first step in creating this spreadsheet is to input the probability distribution, including the cumulative probabilities associated with it. These inputs values are highlighted in yellow in cells B6:B11 of the spreadsheet, with corresponding demands in D6:D11. The lower range of cumulative probabilities is calculated in cells C6:C11 by entering 0 in C6 and then entering the formula "=C6+B6" into cell C7 and copying it to cells C8:C11. The cumulative values provide a basis to associate random numbers to the corresponding demand, using the VLOOKUP() function. For example, the first random number for week 1 has the value 0.5176 and will result in a demand of 3 cars, because 0.5176 is greater than the lower range for a demand of 3 cars, but smaller than the lower range for demand of 4 cars. In a similar way, any random number with a value greater than 0.70 but smaller than 0.90 will correspond to a demand of 4 cars.

The next step is to create a table with four columns. Column G identifies each of the 50 weeks to be simulated in cells G6:G55. Column H generates the random numbers, one for each of the 50 weeks. To create the random numbers, we enter the formula "=RAND()" into cell H6 of our spreadsheet and then copy it to the cells H7:H55. After generating the random numbers, we need to match these numbers with the corresponding demand values. We can do this by using the VLOOKUP function. We enter the formula "=VLOOKUP(H6,$C$6:$D$11,2)" into cell I6 and copy it through I7:I55. With this use of the VLOOKUP function, Excel's logic identifies (or "looks up") for each week's random number (in column H) which demand it corresponds to in the lookup array defined by $C$6:$D$11. Once it finds the probability range (defined by column C) in which the random number fits, it posts the car demand (in column D) for this range back into the week's sales (in column I). When searching the

FIGURE B.2

BestCar Simulation Model

Microsoft Excel - BestCar Simulation

File Edit View Insert Format Tools Data Window Help

BestCar Simulation

Probability of Weekly Demand

	Probabilty of Demand	Lower Range Probability	Car Demand
	0.05	0.00	0
	0.15	0.05	1
	0.20	0.20	2
	0.30	0.40	3
	0.20	0.70	4
	0.10	0.90	5
	1.00		

Results

Demand	Frequency	Percentage	Cumulative
0	3	6%	6%
1	6	12%	18%
2	8	16%	34%
3	13	26%	60%
4	17	34%	94%
5	3	6%	100%
Totals	50	100%	

Simulation of 50 Weeks

Week	Random Number	Simulated Sales (Cars)	Revenue
1	0.5176	3	$60,000
2	0.7665	4	$80,000
3	0.2134	2	$40,000
4	0.1822	1	$20,000
5	0.1659	1	$20,000
6	0.9094	5	$100,000
7	0.6448	3	$60,000
8	0.7032	4	$80,000
9	0.0356	0	$0
10	0.7906	4	$80,000
11	0.4109	3	$60,000
12	0.9407	5	$100,000
13	0.4683	3	$60,000
14	0.8326	4	$80,000
15	0.4208	3	$60,000
16	0.1243	1	$20,000
17	0.4481	3	$60,000
18	0.0629	1	$20,000
19	0.8345	4	$80,000
48	0.1776	1	$20,000
49	0.8761	4	$80,000
50	0.5297	3	$60,000
Average		2.88	$57,600

Generate random numbers for cells H6:H55 with the formula "=RAND()".

Enter =VLOOKUP(H6,$C$6:$D$11,2) into cell I6 and copy it through I7:I55.

Cells are frozen at row 25 to show first and last weeks.

Enter {=FREQUENCY(I6:I55,B17:B22)} into cells C17:C22 as an array formula.

Sheet1 / Sheet2 / Sheet3

Ready

NUM

lookup array, it moves down through column C until it finds a cell that has a value greater than the random number. It goes back to the previous cell, gets the corresponding demand value from column D, and returns it to the cell in column I. The weekly revenue column is the fourth column in the simulation table, created in cells J6:J55 by multiplying the weekly demand values (column I) by average selling price ($20,000). The average car sales is calculated in cell I56 using the =AVERAGE(I6:I55) function, and the average revenue in cell J56 using the = AVERAGE(J6:J55) function. Note that Figure B.2 only shows the first 19 weeks and the last 3 weeks. This compression is possible using the Window/Freeze Panes option. Here, the window is frozen up through week 19 (at start of row 25). You can scroll down or up to show just a few of the last weeks or most of them, depending on how much you want to display.

Finally, the results table is created at the lower left portion of the spreadsheet to summarize the simulation output. By entering the FREQUENCY function into cells C17:C22, we calculate the number of observations in each demand category out of a total of 50 observations. The function looks through the simulated demand values in cells I6:I55 and compares them to the demand categories in cells B17:B22, which are defined as the bin array of the FREQUENCY function. Percentage and cumulative columns next to the frequency column show the frequencies in percentage and cumulative percentage terms.

SIMULATION WITH MORE ADVANCED SOFTWARE

Simulation programming can be done in a variety of computer languages, including general-purpose programming languages such as VISUAL BASIC, FORTRAN, or C++. The advantage of general-purpose programming languages is that they are available on most computer systems. Special simulation languages, such as GPSS, SIMSCRIPT, and SLAM, are also available. These languages simplify programming because they have macroinstructions for the commonly used elements of simulation models. These macroinstructions automatically contain the computer instructions needed to generate arrivals, keep track of waiting lines, and calculate the statistics on the operating characteristics of a system.

Simulation is also possible with powerful PC-based packages, such as SimQuick (www.nd.edu/~dhartvig/simquick/top.htm), Extend (www.imaginethatinc.com), SIMPROCESS (www.caciasl.com), ProModel (www.promodel.com), and Witness (www.lanner.com/corporate). Here we illustrate process simulation with the SimQuick software (provided on the Student CD-ROM).

SimQuick   SimQuick is an easy-to-use package that is simply an Excel spreadsheet with some macros. Models can be created for a variety of simple processes, such as waiting lines, inventory control, and projects. Here we consider the passenger security process at one terminal of a medium-sized airport between the hours of 8 A.M. and 10 A.M. The process works as follows. Passengers arriving at the security area immediately enter a single line. After waiting in line, each passenger goes through one of two inspection stations, which involves walking through a metal detector and running any carry-on baggage through a scanner. After completing this inspection, 10 percent of the passengers are randomly selected for an additional inspection, which typically involves a more thorough search of the person's carry-on baggage. Two stations handle this additional inspection, and selected passengers go through only one of them. Management is interested in examining the effect of increasing the percentage of passengers who undergo the second inspection. In particular, they want to compare the waiting times for the second inspection when 10 percent, then 15 percent, and then 20 percent of the passengers are randomly selected for this inspection. Management also wants to know how opening a third station for the second inspection would affect these waiting times.

A first step in simulating this process with SimQuick is to draw a flowchart of the process using SimQuick's building blocks. SimQuick has five building blocks that can be combined in a wide variety of ways. Four of these types are used to model this process. An *entrance* is used to model the arrival of passengers at the security process. A *buffer* is used to model each of the two waiting lines, one before each type of inspection, as well as the passengers that have finished the process. Each of the four inspection stations is modeled with a *workstation*. Finally, the random selection of passengers for the second inspection is modeled with a *decision point*. Figure B.3 shows the flowchart.

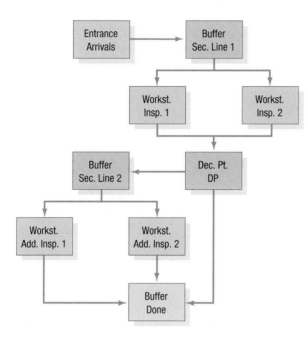

Information describing each building block is entered into SimQuick tables. In this model, three key types of information are entered: (1) when people arrive at the entrance, (2) how long inspections take at the four stations, and (3) what percentage of passengers are randomly selected for the additional inspection. All of this information must be entered into SimQuick in the form of statistical distributions. The first two types of information are determined by observing the real process from 8 A.M. and 10 A.M. The third type of information is a policy decision (10 percent, 15 percent, or 20 percent).

The original model is run 30 times, simulating the hours from 8 A.M. to 10 A.M. Statistics are collected by SimQuick and summarized. Figure B.4 provides some key results for the model of the present process as output by SimQuick (many other statistics are collected, but not displayed here).

The numbers shown are averages across the 30 simulations. The number 237.23 is the average number of passengers that enter line 1 during the simulated two hours. The two mean inventory statistics tell us, on average, 5.97 simulated passengers were standing in line 1 and 0.10 standing in line 2. The two mean cycle time statistics tell us that the simulated passengers in line 1 waited an average of 3.12 minutes, while those in line 2 waited 0.53 minutes. The final inventory statistic tells us that, on average, 224.57 simulated passengers passed through the security process in the simulated two hours. The next step is to change the percentage of simulated passengers selected for the second inspection to 15 percent, and then to 20 percent, and rerun the model. Of course, these process changes will increase the average waiting time for the second inspection, but by how much? The final step is to rerun these simulations with one more workstation and see its effect on the waiting time for the

Element Types	Element Names	Statistics	Overall Means
Entrance(s)	Door	Objects entering process	237.23
Buffer(s)	Line 1	Mean inventory	5.97
		Mean cycle time	3.12
	Line 2	Mean inventory	0.10
		Mean cycle time	0.53
	Done	Final inventory	224.57

second inspection. All the details for this model (as well as many others) appear in the book *SimQuick: Process Simulation with Excel*, which is included, along with the SimQuick software, on the CD-ROM that comes with this textbook.

> STUDENT CD-ROM AND INTERNET RESOURCES <

The Student CD-ROM and the Companion Website at **www.prenhall.com/krajewski** contain many tools, activities, and resources designed for this supplement.

> KEY TERMS <

decision variables 191
Monte Carlo simulation 188
random number 190

simulation 188
steady state 193
time compression 188

uncontrollable variables 191

> SOLVED PROBLEM <

A manager is considering production of several products in an automated facility. The manager would purchase a combination of two robots. The two robots (named Mel and Danny) in series are capable of doing all the required operations. Every batch of work will contain 10 units. A waiting line of several batches will be maintained in front of Mel. When Mel completes its portion of the work, the batch will then be transferred directly to Danny.

$$\boxed{\text{Waiting line}} \rightarrow \text{Mel} \rightarrow \text{Danny}$$

Each robot incurs a setup before it can begin processing a batch. Each unit in the batch has equal run time. The distributions of the setup times and run times for Mel and Danny are identical. But because Mel and Danny will be performing different operations, simulation of each batch requires four random numbers from the table. The first random number determines Mel's setup time, the second determines Mel's run time per unit, and the third and fourth random numbers determine Danny's setup and run times, respectively.

Setup Time (min)	Probability	Run Time per Unit (sec)	Probability
1	0.10	5	0.10
2	0.20	6	0.20
3	0.40	7	0.30
4	0.20	8	0.25
5	0.10	9	0.15

Estimate how many units will be produced in an hour. Then simulate 60 minutes of operation for Mel and Danny. The random numbers have already been selected in Table B.4 for each of the four uncontrolled variables. For example the third column provides the random numbers for determining Mel's setup time for each batch, and the fifth column provides the random numbers for determining Mel's processing times.

SOLUTION

Except for the time required for Mel to set up and run the first batch, we assume that the two robots run simultaneously. The expected average setup time per batch is

$$[(0.1 \times 1 \text{ min}) + (0.2 \times 2 \text{ min}) + (0.4 \times 3 \text{ min}) + (0.2 \times 4 \text{ min}) + (0.1 \times 5 \text{ min})] = 3 \text{ minutes} \quad \text{or} \quad 180 \text{ seconds per batch}$$

The expected average run time per batch (of 10 units) is

$$[(0.1 \times 5 \text{ sec}) + (0.2 \times 6 \text{ sec}) + (0.3 \times 7 \text{ sec}) + (0.25 \times 8 \text{ sec}) + (0.15 \times 9 \text{ sec})] = 7.15 \text{ seconds/unit} \times 10 \text{ units/batch} = 71.5 \text{ seconds per batch}$$

Thus, the total of average setup and run times per batch is 251.5 seconds. In an hour's time we might expect to complete about 14 batches (3,600/251.5 seconds = 14.3). However, this estimate is probably too high.

Keep in mind that Mel and Danny operate in sequence and that Danny cannot begin to do work until it has been completed by Mel (see batch 2 of Table B.4). Nor can Mel start a new batch until Danny is ready to accept the previous one. Refer to batch 6, where Mel completes this batch at time 25:50 but cannot begin the seventh batch until Danny is ready to accept the sixth batch at time 28:00.

Mel and Danny completed only 12 batches in one hour. Even though the robots used the same probability distributions and therefore have perfectly balanced production capacities, Mel and Danny did not produce the expected capacity of 14 batches because Danny was sometimes idle while waiting for Mel (see batch 2) and Mel was sometimes idle while waiting for Danny (see batch 6). This loss-of-throughput phenomenon occurs whenever variable processes are closely linked, whether those processes are mechanical, such as Mel's and Danny's, or functional, such as production and marketing. The simulation shows the need to place between the two robots sufficient space to store several batches to absorb the variations in process times. Subsequent simulations could be run to show how many batches are needed.

| TABLE B.4 | Simulation Results for Mel and Danny |

	Mel						Danny					
Batch No.	Start Time	Random No.	Setup	Random No.	Process	Cumulative Time	Start Time	Random No.	Setup	Random No.	Process	Cumulative Time
1	0:00	71	4 min	50	7 sec	5 min 10 sec	5:10	21	2 min	94	9 sec	8 min 40 sec
2	5:10	50	3 min	63	8 sec	9 min 30 sec	9:30	47	3 min	83	8 sec	13 min 50 sec
3	9:30	31	3 min	73	8 sec	13 min 50 sec	13:50	04	1 min	17	6 sec	15 min 50 sec
4	13:50	96	5 min	98	9 sec	20 min 20 sec	20:20	21	2 min	82	8 sec	23 min 40 sec
5	20:20	25	2 min	92	9 sec	23 min 50 sec	23:50	32	3 min	53	7 sec	28 min 0 sec
6	23:50	00	1 min	15	6 sec	25 min 50 sec	28:00	66	3 min	57	7 sec	32 min 10 sec
7	28:00	00	1 min	99	9 sec	30 min 30 sec	32:10	55	3 min	11	6 sec	36 min 10 sec
8	32:10	10	2 min	61	8 sec	35 min 30 sec	36:10	31	3 min	35	7 sec	40 min 20 sec
9	36:10	09	1 min	73	8 sec	38 min 30 sec	40:20	24	2 min	70	8 sec	43 min 40 sec
10	40:20	79	4 min	95	9 sec	45 min 50 sec	45:50	66	3 min	61	8 sec	50 min 10 sec
11	45:50	01	1 min	41	7 sec	48 min 00 sec	50:10	88	4 min	23	6 sec	55 min 10 sec
12	50:10	57	3 min	45	7 sec	54 min 20 sec	55:10	21	2 min	61	8 sec	58 min 30 sec
13	55:10	26	2 min	46	7 sec	58 min 20 sec	58:30	97	5 min	31	7 sec	64 min 40 sec

> PROBLEMS <

The SimQuick simulation software is on the Student CD-ROM packaged with every new copy of the textbook, along with its user's manual. Exercises also are provided on how to use SimQuick to simulate various problems encountered in managing processes and value chains. SimQuick can be a valuable resource well after your course is completed.

1. Comet Dry Cleaners specializes in same-day dry cleaning. Customers drop off their garments early in the morning and expect them to be ready for pickup on their way home from work. The risk is, however, that the work needed on a garment cannot be done that day, depending on the type of cleaning required. Historically, an average of 20 garments have had to be held over to the next day. The outlet's manager is contemplating expanding to reduce or eliminate that backlog. A simulation model was developed with the following distribution for garments per day:

Number	Probability	Random Numbers
50	0.10	00–09
60	0.25	10–34
70	0.30	35–64
80	0.25	65–89
90	0.10	90–99

With expansion, the maximum number of garments that could be dry-cleaned per day is

Number	Probability	Random Numbers
60	0.30	00–29
70	0.40	30–69
80	0.30	70–99

In the simulation for a specific day, the number of garments needing cleaning (NGNC) is determined first. Next, the maximum number of garments that could be dry-cleaned (MNGD) is determined. If MNGD ≥ NGNC, all garments are dry-cleaned for that day. If MNGD < NGNC, then (NGNC − MNGD) garments must be added to the number of garments arriving the next day to obtain the NGNC for the next day. The simulation continues in this manner.

a. Assuming that the store is empty at the start, simulate 15 days of operation. Use the following random numbers, the first determining the number of arrivals and the second setting the capacity:

(49, 77), (27, 53), (65, 08), (83, 12), (04, 82), (58, 44), (53, 83), (57, 72), (32, 53), (60, 79), (79, 30), (41, 48), (97, 86), (30, 25), (80, 73)

Determine the average daily number of garments held overnight, based on your simulation.

b. If the cost associated with garments being held over is $25 per garment per day and the added cost of expansion is $200 per day, is expansion a good idea?

2. The Precision Manufacturing Company is considering the purchase of an NC machine and has narrowed the possible choices to two models. The company produces several products, and batches of work arrive at the NC machine every six minutes. The number of units in the batch has the following discrete distribution:

Number of Units in Batch	Probability
3	0.1
6	0.2
8	0.3
14	0.2
18	0.2

The distributions of the setup times and processing times for the two NC models follow. Assume that the work in a batch shares a single setup and that each unit in the batch has equal processing time. Simulate two hours (or 10 batch arrivals) of operation for the two NC machines. Use the following random numbers, the first one for the number of units in a batch, the second one for setup times, and the third one for run times:

(71, 21, 50), (50, 94, 63), (96, 93, 95), (83, 09, 49), (10, 20, 68), (48, 23, 11), (21, 28, 40), (39, 78, 93), (99, 95, 61), (28, 14, 48)

Which one would you recommend if both machines cost the same to purchase, operate, and maintain?

NC Machine 1

Setup Time (min)	Probability	Run Time per Unit (sec)	Probability
1	0.10	5	0.10
2	0.20	6	0.20
3	0.40	7	0.30
4	0.20	8	0.25
5	0.10	9	0.15

NC Machine 2

Setup Time (min)	Probability	Run Time per Unit (sec)	Probability
1	0.05	3	0.20
2	0.15	4	0.25
3	0.25	5	0.30
4	0.45	6	0.15
5	0.10	7	0.10

3. In Problem 2, what factors would you consider if the initial cost of NC Machine 1 was $4,000 less than that of NC Machine 2?

4. The 30 management professors at Omega University (ΩU) find out that telephone calls made to their offices are not being picked up. A call-forwarding system redirects calls to the management office after the fourth ring. A department office assistant answers the telephone and takes messages. An average of 90 telephone calls per hour are placed to the management faculty, and each telephone call consumes about one minute of the assistant's time. The calls arrive to a Poisson distribution, as shown in Figure B.5(a), with an average of 1.5 calls per minute. Because the professors spend much of their time in class and in conferences, there is only a 40 percent chance that they will pick up a call themselves, as shown in Figure B.5(b). If two or more telephone calls are forwarded to the office during the same minute, only the first call will be answered.

a. Without using simulation, make a preliminary guess of what proportion of the time the assistant will be on the telephone and what proportion of the telephone calls will not be answered.

b. Now use random numbers to simulate the situation for one hour starting at 10:00 A.M. Table B.5 will get you started.

c. What proportion of the time is the office assistant on the telephone? What proportion of the telephone calls are not answered? Are these proportions close to what you expected?

5. The management chair at ΩU is considering installing a voice-mail system. Monthly operating costs are $25 per voice-mailbox, but the system will reduce the amount of time the office assistant spends answering the telephone by 60 percent. The department has 32 telephones. Use the results of your simulation in Problem 4 to estimate the proportion of the assistant's time presently spent answering the telephone. The office assistant's salary (and overhead) is $3,000 per month. Should the management chair order the voice-mail system?

6. Weekly demand at a local E-Z Mart convenience store for 1-gallon jugs of low-fat milk for the past 50 weeks varied between 60 and 65 jugs, as shown in the following table. Demand in excess of stock cannot be backordered.

Demand (jugs)	Number of Weeks
60	5
61	7
62	17
63	11
64	6
65	4
Total	50

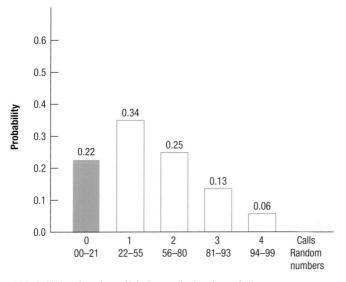

(a) Probabilities of numbers of telephone calls placed per minute

(b) Probability of forwarding a call

FIGURE B.5 | Probability Distributions for Omega University

a. Assign random numbers between 00 and 99 to simulate the demand probability distribution.

b. E-Z Mart orders 62 jugs every week. Simulate the demand for this item for 10 weeks, using the random numbers 97, 2, 80, 66, 99, 56, 54, 28, 64, and 47. Determine the shortage or excess stock for each week.

c. What is the average shortage and the average excess stock for the 10 weeks?

7. The Brakes-Only Service Shop promises its customers same-day service by working overtime if necessary. The shop's two mechanics can handle a total of 12 brake jobs a day during regular hours. Over the past 100 days, the

number of brake jobs at the shop varied between 10 and 14, as shown in the following table:

Demand (jobs)	Number of Days
10	10
11	30
12	30
13	20
14	10
	Total 100

TABLE B.5 | Office Assistant Simulation

Time	RN	Number of Calls Made	RN	1st Call Forwarded? (Yes/No)	RN	2d Call Forwarded? (Yes/No)	RN	3d Call Forwarded? (Yes/No)	RN	4th Call Forwarded? (Yes/No)	Number of Calls Not Answered	Assistant Idle (✓)
10:00	68	2	30	Yes	54	Yes					1	
10:01	76	2	36	Yes	32	Yes					1	
10:02	68	2	04	Yes	07	Yes					1	
10:03	98	4	08	Yes	21	Yes	28	Yes	79	No	2	
10:04	25	1	77	No							0	✓
10:05	51	1	23	Yes							0	
10:06	67	2	22	Yes	27	Yes					1	
10:07	80	2	87	No	06	Yes					0	
10:08	03	0									0	✓
10:09	03	0									0	✓
10:10	33	1	78	No							0	✓

a. Assign random numbers between 00 and 99 to simulate the demand probability distribution for brake jobs.

b. Simulate the demand for the next 10 days, using the random numbers 28, 83, 73, 7, 4, 63, 37, 38, 50, and 92.

c. On how many days will overtime work be necessary? On how many days will the mechanics be underutilized?

d. What percent of days, on average, will overtime work be necessary?

8. A machine center handles four types of clients: A, B, C, and D. The manager wants to assess the number of machines required to produce goods for these clients. Setup times for changeover from one client to another are negligible. Annual demand and processing times are uncertain; demand may be low, normal, or high. The probabilities for these three events are shown in the following tables:

Client A			
Demand (units/yr)	Probability	Processing Time (hr/unit)	Probability
3,000	0.10	10	0.35
3,500	0.60	20	0.45
4,200	0.30	30	0.20

Client B			
Demand (units/yr)	Probability	Processing Time (hr/unit)	Probability
500	0.30	60	0.25
800	0.50	90	0.50
900	0.20	100	0.25

Client C			
Demand (units/yr)	Probability	Processing Time (hr/unit)	Probability
1,500	0.10	12	0.25
3,000	0.50	15	0.60
4,500	0.40	20	0.15

Client D			
Demand (units/yr)	Probability	Processing Time (hr/unit)	Probability
600	0.40	60	0.30
650	0.50	70	0.65
700	0.10	80	0.05

a. Explain how simulation could be used to generate a probability distribution for the total number of machine hours required per year to serve the clients.

b. Simulate one year, using the following random numbers. Use random number 88 for client A's demand, 24 for client A's processing time, etc.

88, 24, 33, 29, 52, 84, 37, 92

9. The sales activity at BestCar (see Example B.3) has changed. Weekly sales are now estimated to be distributed as follows:

Weekly Sales (cars)	Relative Frequency (probability)
0	0.02
1	0.03
2	0.05
3	0.10
4	0.15
5	0.30
6	0.20
7	0.10
8	0.05
Total	1.00

Create an Excel model that simulates 500 weeks at BestCar. It should calculate from the simulated experience the average number of cars and revenue per week and also a frequency table on car sales.

10. Keep the same weekly sales distribution for BestCar as in Example B.3, but assume that the price of cars is distributed as follows:

Sales Price (price/car)	Relative Frequency (probability)
$18,000	0.15
$20,000	0.35
$22,000	0.35
$24,000	0.10
$26,000	0.05
Total	1.00

Create an Excel model that simulates 500 weeks at BestCar. It should calculate from the simulated experience the average number of cars and revenue per week and also a frequency table on car sales.

> SELECTED REFERENCES <

Abdou, G., and S. P. Dutta. "A Systematic Simulation Approach for the Design of JIT Manufacturing Systems." *Journal of Operations Management*, vol. 11, no. 3 (1993), pp. 25–38.

Brennan, J. E., B. L. Golden, and H. K. Rappoport. "Go with the Flow: Improving Red Cross Bloodmobiles Using Simulation Analysis." *Interfaces*, vol. 22, no. 5 (1992), p. 1.

Christy, D. P., and H. J. Watson. "The Application of Simulation: A Survey of Industry Practice." *Interfaces*, vol. 13, no. 5 (October 1983), pp. 47–52.

Conway, R., W. L. Maxwell, J. D. McClain, and S. L. Worona. *XCELL & Factory Modeling System Release 4.0.* San Francisco: Scientific Press, 1990.

Ernshoff, J. R., and R. L. Serson. *Design and Use of Computer Simulation Models.* New York: Macmillan, 1970.

Hartvigsen, David. *SimQuick: Process Simulation with Excel,* 2d ed. Upper Saddle River, NJ: Prentice Hall, 2004.

Imagine That! (www.imaginethatinc.com). *Extend Simulation Package.* San Jose, CA.

Law, A. M., and W. D. Kelton. *Simulation Modeling and Analysis,* 2d ed. New York: McGraw-Hill, 1991.

Meier, R. C., W. T. Newell, and H. L. Pazer. *Simulation in Business and Economics.* Englewood Cliffs, NJ: Prentice Hall, 1969.

MicroAnalysis and Design Software Inc. "Hospital Overcrowding Solutions Are Found with Simulation." *Industrial Engineering* (December 1993), p. 557.

Naylor, T. H., et al. *Computer Simulation Techniques.* New York: John Wiley & Sons, 1966.

Pritsker, A. A. B., C. E. Sigal, and R. D. Hammesfahr. *SLAM II: Network Models for Decision Support.* Upper Saddle River, NJ: Prentice Hall, 1989.

Solomon, S. L. *Simulation of Waiting Lines.* Englewood Cliffs, NJ: Prentice Hall, 1983.

Swedish, Julian. "Simulation Brings Productivity Enhancements to the Social Security Administration." *Industrial Engineering* (May 1993), pp. 28–30.

Winston, Wayne L. *Simulation Modeling Using @RISK.* Belmont, CA: Wadsworth Publishing Company, 1996.

6

LEARNING GOALS

After reading this chapter, you should be able to:

1. Define the four major costs of poor process performance and quality.

2. Identify *quality* from the customer's perspective.

3. Explain the differences between common causes and assignable causes of variation in process performance and why the distinction is important.

4. Describe how to construct control charts and use them to determine whether a process is out of statistical control.

5. Describe how to determine whether a process is capable of producing a service or product to specifications.

6. Explain the basic principles of TQM or Six Sigma programs.

CROWNE PLAZA CHRISTCHURCH

The Crowne Plaza Christchurch, a luxury hotel in Christchurch, New Zealand, has 298 guest rooms, three restaurants, two lounges, and 260 employees to serve 2,250 guests each week who purchase an average of 2,450 meals. Even though the operation is complex, service performance and quality get top priority at the Crowne Plaza because customers demand it. Customers have many opportunities to evaluate the quality of service they receive. For example, prior to the guest's arrival, the reservation staff gathers a considerable amount of information about the guest's particular likes and dislikes. This information (e.g., preference for firm pillows or extra towels) is distributed to housekeeping and other hotel functions and is used to customize the service that each guest receives. Upon arrival, a guest is greeted by a porter who opens the car door and unloads the luggage. Then the guest is escorted to the receptionist who registers the guest and assigns the room. Finally, when the guest goes to dinner, servers and cooks must also live up to the high standard of quality that distinguishes the Crowne Plaza from its competitors.

How can such a level of quality be sustained? The Crowne Plaza empowers employees to take preventive and, if necessary, corrective actions without management's approval. Also, management and employees use line charts, histograms, and other graphs to track performance and identify areas needing improvement. In the hotel's kitchens, for example, photos of finished dishes are posted to remind chefs about how the dishes should be presented and their content. Finally, in this service business with high customer contact, superior employee recruiting,

>

For additional chapter resources check the Student CD-ROM or the Companion Website at
www.prenhall.com/krajewski

training, and motivation are essential for achieving and sustaining high levels of service quality.

Source: The name of the hotel was changed from Parkroyal Christchurch to Crowne Plaza Christchurch in 2005. See also *Operations Management 8e Video Library* (Upper Saddle River, NJ: Prentice Hall, 2005): www.crowneplaza.co.nz,2005.

USING OPERATIONS TO COMPETE

↓

Operations As a Competitive Weapon
Operations Strategy
Project Management

MANAGING PROCESSES

↓

Process Strategy
Process Analysis
Process Performance and Quality
Constraint Management
Process Layout
Lean Systems

MANAGING VALUE CHAINS

↓

Supply Chain Strategy
Location
Inventory Management
Forecasting
Sales and Operations Planning
Resource Planning
Scheduling

The challenge for businesses today is to satisfy their customers through the exceptional performance of their processes. The Crowne Plaza Christchurch is one example of a company that met the challenge by designing and managing processes that provide customers with total satisfaction. Evaluating process performance is important if this is to happen. It is the fourth step in the Blueprint for Process Analysis, Figure 5.1.

Evaluating process performance is also necessary for managing value chains. For example, at the Crowne Plaza Christchurch, the restaurant process might be measured on the consistency of its presentation and content of the meal and the timeliness of the service provided. The procurement process, which involves selecting the suppliers for the restaurant and how they deliver their products, might be measured in terms of the quality of the products delivered to the restaurant, the on-time delivery performance of the suppliers, and the cost of the food. Ultimately, the evaluation of the value chain consisting of these two processes will depend on how well they satisfy the customers of the restaurant, who consider the value of the meal and how well the dining experience meets or exceeds expectations. The performance of these individual processes must be consistent with the performance measures for the value chain.

> PROCESS PERFORMANCE AND QUALITY ACROSS THE ORGANIZATION <

Process performance and quality should be everybody's concern. Take for example QVC, a $4.9 billion televised shopping service. QVC airs 24 hours a day, all year round except on Christmas.[1] QVC sells some 60,000 items ranging from jewelry, tools, cookware, clothing, and gourmet food to computers.

QVC's operations spring into action with a customer order: Order taking, a promised delivery date, billing, and order delivery all ensue once an order is placed. QVC operates four call centers that handle 3 million calls each month from customers who want to order something, complain about a problem, or just get product information. In this process, the call center representative's demeanor and skill are critical to achieving a successful customer encounter. QVC management keeps track of productivity, quality, and customer satisfaction measures for this process. When the measures slip, problems are addressed aggressively. Knowing how to assess whether the process is performing well and when to take action are key skills QVC managers must have. Chapter 6 first addresses the costs of poor process performance and quality and then focuses on the philosophies and tools that many companies embrace to evaluate and improve it.

> COSTS OF POOR PROCESS PERFORMANCE AND QUALITY <

defect

Any instance when a process fails to satisfy its customer.

When a process fails to satisfy a customer, it is considered a **defect**. For example, according to the California Academy of Family Physicians, defects for the processes in a doctor's practice are defined as "anything that happened in my office that should not have happened, and

[1]Anne Schwarz, "Listening to the Voice of the Customer Is the Key to QVC's Success," *Journal of Organizational Excellence* (Winter 2004), pp. 3–11.

that I absolutely do not want to happen again." Obviously, this definition covers process failures that the patient sees, such as poor communication and errors in prescription dosages. It also includes failures the patient does not see, such as incorrect charting.

Many companies spend significant time, effort, and expense on systems, training, and organizational changes to improve the performance and quality of their processes. They believe that it is important to be able to gauge current levels of performance so that any process gaps can be determined. Gaps reflect potential dissatisfied customers and additional costs for the firm. Most experts estimate that the losses due to poor performance and quality range from 20 to 30 percent of gross sales. These costs can be broken down into four major categories: prevention, appraisal, internal failure, and external failure.

PREVENTION COSTS

Prevention costs are associated with preventing defects before they happen. They include the costs of redesigning the process to remove the causes of poor performance, redesigning the service or product to make it simpler to produce, training employees in the methods of continuous improvement, and working with suppliers to increase the quality of purchased items or contracted services. In order to improve performance, firms must invest additional time, effort, and money.

prevention costs
Costs associated with preventing defects before they happen.

APPRAISAL COSTS

Appraisal costs are incurred when the firm assesses the level of performance of its processes. As preventive measures improve performance, appraisal costs decrease because fewer resources are needed for quality inspections and the subsequent search for causes of any problems that are detected.

appraisal costs
Costs incurred when the firm asseses the performance level of its processes.

INTERNAL FAILURE COSTS

Internal failure costs result from defects that are discovered during the production of a service or product. Defects fall into two main categories: *rework*, which is incurred if some aspect of a service must be performed again or if a defective item must be rerouted to some previous operation(s) to correct the defect; and *scrap*, which is incurred if a defective item is unfit for further processing. For example, an analysis of the viability of acquiring a company might be sent back to the mergers and acquisitions department if an assessment of the company's history of environmental compliance is missing. Likewise, if the final inspector at an automobile paint shop discovers that the paint on a car has a poor finish, the car may have to be completely resanded and repainted. The additional time spent correcting such a mistake results in lower productivity. In addition, the car may not be finished by the date on which the customer is expecting it.

internal failure costs
Costs resulting from defects that are discovered during the production of a service or product.

EXTERNAL FAILURE COSTS

External failure costs arise when a defect is discovered after the customer receives the service or product. For instance, suppose that you have the oil changed in your car and that the oil filter is improperly installed, causing the oil to drain onto your garage floor. You might insist that the company pay for the car to be towed and restore the oil and filter immediately. External failure costs to the company in this case include the towing and additional oil and filter costs, as well as the loss of future revenue because you decide never to take your car back there for service.

external failure costs
Costs that arise when a defect is discovered after the customer receives the service or product.

Dissatisfied customers talk about bad service or products to their friends, who in turn tell others. If the problem is bad enough, consumer protection groups may even alert the media. The potential impact on future profits is difficult to assess, but without doubt external failure costs erode market share and profits. Encountering defects and correcting them after the product is in the customer's hands is costly.

External failure costs also include warranty service and litigation costs. A **warranty** is a written guarantee that the producer will replace or repair defective parts or perform the service to the customer's satisfaction. Usually, a warranty is given for some specified period. For example, television repairs are usually guaranteed for 90 days and new automobiles for five years or 50,000 miles, whichever comes first. Warranty costs must be considered in the design of new services or products.

warranty
A written guarantee that the producer will replace or repair defective parts or perform the service to the customer's satisfaction.

> TOTAL QUALITY MANAGEMENT <

total quality management (TQM)

A philosophy that stresses three principles for achieving high levels of process performance and quality: customer satisfaction, employee involvement and continuous improvement in performance.

Total quality management (TQM) is a philosophy that stresses three principles for achieving high levels of process performance and quality. These principles are related to customer satisfaction, employee involvement, and continuous improvement in performance. As Figure 6.1 indicates, TQM also involves a number of important elements that are covered in other chapters and supplements in this text: service/product design (see Chapter 2, "Operations Strategy"); process design (see Chapter 4, "Process Strategy"); purchasing (see Chapter 10, "Supply Chain Strategy"); and benchmarking and problem-solving tools (see Chapter 5, "Process Analysis," and Supplement A, "Decision Making"). Here we focus on the three main principles of TQM.

CUSTOMER SATISFACTION

quality

A term used by customers to describe their general satisfaction with a service or product.

Customers, internal or external, are satisfied when their expectations regarding a service or product have been met or exceeded. Often, customers use the general term **quality** to describe their level of satisfaction with a service or product. Quality has multiple dimensions in the mind of the customer, which cut across the nine competitive priorities we introduced in Chapter 2, "Operations Strategy." One or more of the following definitions apply at any one time.

Conformance to Specifications Although customers evaluate the service or product they receive, it is the processes that produced the service or product that are really being judged. In this case, a process failure would be the process's inability to meet certain advertised or implied performance standards. Conformance to specifications may relate to consistent quality, on-time delivery, or delivery speed.

Bell Canada measures the performance of its call center process by the length of time it takes to process a call (called "handle time"). If the average time exceeds the standard of 23 seconds, managers work with the employees to reduce the time. Customers become agitated if they cannot get access to an operator quickly. Seagate, however, advertises that its high-performance Cheetah disk drives have a mean time between failures of 1.2 million hours. All of the components of the disk drive must conform to Seagate's individual specifications to achieve the desired performance of the complete product. Consistent quality is important because customers measure quality by the performance of the product. However, each of the manufacturing processes at Seagate and its suppliers are being evaluated, too.

Value Another way customers define quality is through value, or how well the service or product serves its intended purpose at a price customers are willing to pay. The service/

FIGURE 6.1

TQM Wheel

product design process plays a role here, as do the firm's competitive priorities relating to top quality versus low-cost operations. The two factors must be balanced to produce value for the customer. How much value a service or product has in the mind of the customer depends on the customer's expectations before purchasing it. A complicated trust set up by a reputable law firm may cost $3,000; however, if the trust is flexible enough so that it will not have to be changed over time, the price may be worth it. Likewise, purchasing a Honda Civic for $13,000 may have more value for a customer than purchasing a Jaguar for $45,000 because the intended purpose for the car is to provide a student with transportation while attending school.

Fitness for Use When assessing how well a service or product performs its intended purpose, the customer may consider the convenience of a service or the mechanical features of a product. Other aspects of fitness for use include appearance, style, durability, reliability, craftsmanship, and serviceability. For example, you might evaluate your dentist's quality of service on the basis of the age of her equipment because new dental technology greatly reduces the discomfort associated with visits to the dentist. Or you may define the quality of the entertainment center you purchased on the basis of how easy it was to assemble and how well it housed your equipment.

Support Often the service or product support provided by the company is as important to customers as the quality of the service or product itself. Customers get upset with a company if its financial statements are incorrect, responses to its warranty claims are delayed, or its advertising is misleading. Good product support can reduce the consequences of quality failures, however. For example, if you just had a brake job done, you would be upset if the brakes began squealing again a week later. If the manager of the brake shop offers to redo the work at no additional charge, the company's intent to satisfy the customer is clear.

Psychological Impressions People often evaluate the quality of a service or product on the basis of psychological impressions: atmosphere, image, or aesthetics. In the provision of services, where the customer is in close contact with the provider, the appearance and actions of the provider are especially important. Nicely dressed, courteous, friendly, and sympathetic employees can affect the customer's perception of service quality. For example, rumpled, discourteous, or grumpy waiters can undermine a restaurant's best efforts to provide high-quality service. In manufacturing, product quality often is judged on the basis of the knowledge and personality of salespeople, as well as the product image presented in advertisements.

Attaining quality in all areas of a business is a difficult task. To make things even more difficult, consumers change their perceptions of quality. In general, a business's success depends on the accuracy of its perceptions of consumer expectations and its ability to bridge

An employee at a hard disk factory wears a special suit and a mask to avoid contaminating the product. Maintaining a dust-free environment is critical to the quality of disk drives.

the gap between those expectations and operating capabilities. Good quality pays off in higher profits. High-quality services and products can be priced higher and yield a greater return. Poor quality erodes the firm's ability to compete in the marketplace and increases the costs of producing its service or product. For example, by improving its conformance to specifications, a firm can increase its market share *and* reduce the cost of its services or products, which in turn increase profits. Management is better able to compete on both the basis of price and quality.

EMPLOYEE INVOLVEMENT

One of the important elements of TQM is employee involvement, as shown in Figure 6.1. A program in employee involvement includes changing organizational culture and encouraging teamwork.

Cultural Change   The challenge of quality management is to instill an awareness of the importance of quality in all employees and to motivate them to improve it. With TQM, everyone is expected to contribute to the overall improvement of quality—from the administrator who finds cost-saving measures, to the salesperson who learns about a new customer need, to the engineer who designs a product with fewer parts, to the manager who communicates clearly with other department heads. In other words, TQM involves all the functions that relate to a service or product.

One of the main challenges in developing the proper culture for TQM is to define *customer* for each employee. In general, customers are internal or external. External customers are the people or firms who buy the service or product. In this sense, the entire firm is a single unit that must do its best to satisfy external customers. However, communicating external customers' concerns to everyone in the organization is difficult. Some employees, especially those having little contact with external customers, may have difficulty seeing how their jobs contribute to the whole effort.

It is helpful to point out to employees that each employee also has one or more internal customers—employees in the firm who rely on the output of other employees. For example, a machinist who drills holes in a component and passes it on to a welder has the welder as her customer. Even though the welder is not an external customer, he will have many of the same definitions of quality as an external customer, except that they will relate to the component instead of a complete product. All employees must do a good job of serving their internal customers if external customers ultimately are to be satisfied. They will be satisfied only if each internal customer demands value be added that the external customer will recognize and pay for. The notion of internal customers applies to all parts of a firm and enhances cross-functional coordination. For example, accounting must prepare accurate and timely reports for management, and purchasing must provide high-quality materials on time for operations.

In TQM, everyone in the organization must share the view that quality control is an end in itself. Errors or defects should be caught and corrected at the source, not passed along to an internal or external customer. For example, a consulting team should make sure its billable hours are correct before submitting them to the accounting department. This philosophy is called **quality at the source**. In addition, firms should avoid trying to "inspect quality into the product" by using inspectors to weed out unsatisfactory services or defective products after all operations have been performed. By contrast, in some manufacturing firms, workers have the authority to stop a production line if they spot quality problems.

Teams   Employee involvement is a key tactic for improving processes and quality. One way to achieve employee involvement is by the use of **teams**, which are small groups of people who have a common purpose, set their own performance goals and approaches, and hold themselves accountable for success. Teams differ from the more typical "working group" in the following ways:

- Members have a common commitment to an overarching purpose that all believe in and that transcends individual priorities.
- Leadership roles are shared rather than held by a single, strong leader.
- Performance is judged not only by individual contributions but also by collective "work products" that reflect the joint efforts of all the members.

quality at the source

A philosophy whereby defects are caught and corrected where they were created.

teams

Small groups of people who have a common purpose, set their own performance goals and approaches, and hold themselves accountable for success.

- Open-ended discussion, rather than a managerially defined agenda, is prized at meetings.
- Members of the team do real work together, rather than delegating it to subordinates.

The three approaches to teamwork most often used are problem-solving teams, special-purpose teams, and self-managed teams. All three use some amount of **employee empowerment**, which moves responsibility for decisions further down the organizational chart—to the level of the employee actually doing the job.

First introduced in the 1920s, problem-solving teams, also called **quality circles**, became popular in the late 1970s after the Japanese used them successfully. Problem-solving teams are small groups of supervisors and employees who meet to identify, analyze, and solve process and quality problems. The philosophy behind this approach is that the people who are directly responsible for providing the service or making the product will be best able to consider ways to solve a problem. Also, employees take more pride and interest in their work if they are allowed to help shape it. A quality circle typically consists of 5 to 12 volunteers drawn from a department or from a group of employees assigned to a particular task, such as credit application processing or automobile assembly. The teams meet several hours a week to work on quality and process problems and make suggestions to management. Such teams are used extensively by Japanese-managed firms in the United States. The Japanese philosophy is to encourage employee input while maintaining close control over their job activities. Although problem-solving teams can successfully reduce costs and improve quality, they die if management fails to implement many of the suggestions they generate.

An outgrowth of the problem-solving teams, **special-purpose teams** address issues of paramount concern to management, labor, or both. For example, management may form a special-purpose team to design and introduce new work policies or new technologies or to address customer service problems. Essentially, this approach gives workers a voice in high-level decisions. Special-purpose teams first appeared in the United States in the early 1980s.

The **self-managed team** approach takes worker participation to its highest level: A small group of employees work together to produce a major portion, or sometimes all, of a service or product. Members learn all the tasks involved in the operation, rotate from job to job, and take over managerial duties such as work and vacation scheduling, ordering supplies, and hiring. In some cases, team members design the process and have a high degree of latitude as to how it takes shape. Self-managed teams essentially change the way work is organized because employees have control over their jobs. Some self-managed teams increased productivity by 30 percent or more in their firms.

CONTINUOUS IMPROVEMENT

Continuous improvement, based on a Japanese concept called *kaizen,* is the philosophy of continually seeking ways to improve processes. Continuous improvement involves identifying benchmarks of excellent practice and instilling a sense of employee ownership in the process. The focus can be on reducing the length of time required to process requests for loans at a bank, the amount of scrap generated at a milling machine, or the number of employee injuries at a construction site. Continuous improvement also can focus on problems with customers or suppliers, such as external customers who request frequent changes in shipping quantities or internal suppliers who fail to maintain high quality. The bases of the continuous improvement philosophy are the beliefs that virtually any aspect of a process can be improved and that the people most closely associated with a process are in the best position to identify the changes that should be made. The idea is not to wait until a massive problem occurs before acting.

Getting Started Instilling a philosophy of continuous improvement in an organization may be a lengthy process, and several steps are essential to its eventual success.

1. Train employees in the methods of statistical process control (SPC) and other tools for improving quality and performance. (We discuss SPC later in this chapter.)
2. Make SPC methods a normal aspect of daily operations.
3. Build work teams and encourage employee involvement.

employee empowerment

An approach to teamwork that moves responsibility for decisions further down the organizational chart—to the level of the employee actually doing the job.

quality circles

Another name for problem-solving teams; small groups of supervisors and employees who meet to identify, analyze, and solve process and quality problems.

special-purpose teams

Groups that address issues of paramount concern to management, labor, or both.

self-managed team

A small group of employees who work together to produce a major portion, or sometimes all, of a service or product.

continuous improvement

The philosophy of continually seeking ways to improve processes based on a Japanese concept called *kaizen.*

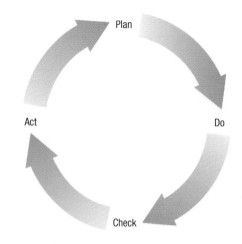

4. Utilize problem-solving tools within the work teams.

5. Develop a sense of operator ownership in the process.

Note that employee involvement is central to the philosophy of continuous improvement. However, the last two steps are crucial if the philosophy is to become part of everyday operations. A sense of operator ownership emerges when employees feel a responsibility for the processes and methods they use and take pride in the quality of the service or product they produce. It comes from participation on work teams and in problem-solving activities, which instill in employees a feeling that they have some control over their workplace and tasks.

plan-do-check-act cycle

A cycle, also called the Deming Wheel, used by firms actively engaged in continuous improvement to train their work teams in problem solving.

Problem-Solving Process Most firms actively engaged in continuous improvement train their work teams to use the **plan-do-check-act cycle** for problem solving. Another name for this approach is the Deming Wheel. Figure 6.2 shows this cycle, which lies at the heart of the continuous improvement philosophy. The cycle comprises the following steps.

1. *Plan.* The team selects a process (an activity, method, machine, or policy) that needs improvement. The team then documents the selected process, usually by analyzing related data; sets qualitative goals for improvement; and discusses various ways to achieve the goals. After assessing the benefits and costs of the alternatives, the team develops a plan with quantifiable measures for improvement.

2. *Do.* The team implements the plan and monitors progress. Data are collected continuously to measure the improvements in the process. Any changes in the process are documented, and further revisions are made as needed.

3. *Check.* The team analyzes the data collected during the *do* step to find out how closely the results correspond to the goals set in the *plan* step. If major shortcomings exist, the team reevaluates the plan or stops the project.

4. *Act.* If the results are successful, the team documents the revised process so that it becomes the standard procedure for all who may use it. The team may then instruct other employees in the use of the revised process.

Problem-solving projects often focus on those aspects of processes that do not add value to the service or product. Value is added in processes such as machining a part or serving a customer on a Web page. No value is added in activities such as inspecting parts for quality defects or routing requests for loan approvals to several different departments. The idea of continuous improvement is to reduce or eliminate activities that do not add value and, thus, are wasteful. For example, suppose that a firm has identified three non-value-added activities in the manufacture of its products: inspection of each part, repair of defects, and handling of materials between operations. The time that parts spend in each activity is not adding value to the product and, hence, is not generating revenue for the firm. Continuous improvement projects might focus on reducing materials handling time by rearranging machine locations to minimize the distances traveled by materials or improving the methods for producing the parts to reduce the need for inspection and rework.

> STATISTICAL PROCESS CONTROL <

Evaluating the performance of processes requires a variety of data gathering approaches. We already discussed checklists, histograms and bar charts, Pareto charts, scatter diagrams, cause-and-effect diagrams, and graphs (see Chapter 5, "Process Analysis").

Statistical process control (SPC) is the application of statistical techniques to determine whether a process is delivering what the customer wants. In SPC, tools called control charts are used primarily to detect defective services or products or to indicate that the process has changed and that services or products will deviate from their design specifications unless something is done to correct the situation. SPC can also be used to inform management of improved process changes. Examples of process changes that can be detected by SPC include the following:

- A decrease in the average number of complaints per day at a hotel
- A sudden increase in the proportion of defective gear boxes
- An increase in the time to process a mortgage application
- A decline in the number of scrapped units at a milling machine
- An increase in the number of claimants receiving late payment from an insurance company

Let us consider the last situation. Suppose that the manager of the accounts payable department of an insurance company notices that the proportion of claimants receiving late payments rose from an average of 0.01 to 0.03. The first question is whether the rise is a cause for alarm or just a random occurrence. Statistical process control can help the manager decide whether further action should be taken. If the rise in the proportion is large, the manager should not conclude that it was just a random occurrence and should seek other explanations of the poor performance. Perhaps the number of claims significantly increased, causing an overload on the employees in the department. The decision might be to hire more personnel. Or perhaps the procedures being used are ineffective or the training of employees is inadequate. SPC is an integral part of TQM. Managerial Practice 6.1 shows how TQM and SPC are used to produce chocolate products.

Another approach to quality management, **acceptance sampling** is the application of statistical techniques to determine whether a quantity of material should be accepted or rejected based on the inspection or test of a sample (see Supplement I, "Acceptance Sampling Plans" on the Student CD-ROM). In this section, we explore the techniques of statistical process control to understand better the role they play in decision making.

VARIATION OF OUTPUTS

No two services or products are exactly alike because the processes used to produce them contain many sources of variation, even if the processes are working as intended. Nonetheless, it is important to minimize the variation in outputs because frequently variation is what the customer sees and feels. Suppose a physicians' clinic submits claims on behalf of its patients to a particular insurance company. In this situation, the physicians' clinic is the customer of the insurance company's bill payment process. In some cases the clinic receives payment in 4 weeks, and in other cases 20 weeks. The time to process a request for payment varies because of the load on the insurance company's processes, the medical history of the patient, and the skills and attitudes of the employees. Meanwhile, the clinic must cover its expenses while it waits for payment. Similarly, in manufacturing, the diameter of two crankshafts may vary because of differences in tool wear, material hardness, operator skill, or temperature during the period in which they were produced. Whether the process is producing services or products, nothing can be done to eliminate variation in output completely; however, management should investigate the *causes* of the variation in order to minimize it.

Performance Measurements Performance can be evaluated in two ways. One way is to measure **variables**—that is, service or product characteristics, such as weight, length, volume, or time, that can be *measured*. For example, United Parcel Service (UPS) managers monitor the length of time drivers spend delivering packages. Similarly, inspectors at Harley-Davidson measure the diameter of a piston to determine whether the product adheres to the

statistical process control (SPC)
The application of statistical techniques to determine whether a process is delivering what the customer wants.

acceptance sampling
The application of statistical techniques to determine whether a quantity of material should be accepted or rejected based on the inspection or test of a sample.

variables
Service or product characteristics, such as weight, length, volume, or time, that can be measured.

MANAGERIAL **PRACTICE**	6.1	TQM AND SPC HELP ADM COCOA MAINTAIN A SWEET BUSINESS

ADM Cocoa produces chocolate drops and other chocolate products for a wide variety of customers in the confectionery, dairy, and baking industries. The production process for chocolate drops is a highly automated line process. Some 500,000 pounds of cocoa beans are unloaded, cleaned, and roasted each day. The roasted beans are ground into a liquid, called *liquor*, which is then blended with other ingredients according to a particular recipe for a given product to form a paste. The paste is heated to a specified temperature and then is pumped to a depositing machine that forms the paste into drops and controls their cooling. The drops then are packaged for delivery.

ADM utilizes TQM techniques with SPC to make sure the process produces what the customer wants. The characteristics of agricultural commodities used for raw materials in the production of chocolate differ. For example, the fat content of cocoa beans varies according to the conditions under which the beans were grown. Fat content is crucial to determining the proper amount of each additive for blending into a specific product. ADM samples each batch of liquor just before the blending operation to measure fat content. If the sample is unacceptable, the liquor is reprocessed until it has the proper fat content. Because the fat content is standardized, the blending operation also can be standardized from batch to batch.

ADM's customers count on receiving consistent quantities of chocolate drops. Customers have specifications such as 4,000 ± 200 drops per pound and gear their production processes accordingly. An essential step in production of the drops is the operation of ADM's depositing machine. Every hour, a random sample of 100 drops is taken from the production line, the total weight is recorded, and the average number of drops per pound is estimated. If the result is unacceptable, the operator of the machine explores the possible reasons for the problem (including the temperature of

Heated chocolate is poured from a holding tank into the depositing machine that forms the chocolate drops.

the paste and the setting of the aperture that forms the drops). Adjustments require 15 minutes to take effect because of the amount of time needed to clear the defective products. Operators must be well trained in both statistical process control techniques and machine operations because a mistake in the adjustment means that at least 30 minutes of production time will be lost.

Source: David Krajewski, Archer Daniels Midland Company, 2003, www.admworld.com.

attributes

Service or product characteristics that can be quickly counted for acceptable performance.

specifications (within the allowable tolerance) and they identify differences in the diameter over time. The advantage of using performance variables is that if a service or product misses its performance specifications, the inspector knows by how much. The disadvantage is that such measurements typically involve special equipment, employee skills, exacting procedures, and time and effort. Another way to evaluate performance is to measure **attributes**, or service or product characteristics that can be quickly *counted* for acceptable performance. This method allows inspectors to make a simple yes/no decision about whether a service or product meets the specifications. Attributes often are used when performance specifications are complex and measurement of variables is difficult or costly. Some examples of attributes that can be counted are the number of insurance forms containing errors that cause underpayments or overpayments, the proportion of radios inoperative at the final test, the proportion of airline flights arriving within 15 minutes of scheduled times, and the number of stovetop assemblies with spotted paint.

The advantage of counting attributes is that less effort and fewer resources are needed than for measuring variables. The disadvantage is that, even though attribute counts can reveal that process performance has changed, they do not indicate by how much. For example, a count may determine that the proportion of airline flights arriving within 15 minutes of their scheduled times declined, but the result does not show how much beyond the 15-minute allowance the flights are arriving. For that, the actual deviation from the scheduled arrival, a variable, would have to be measured. Managerial Practice 6.2 provides examples of quality measures used in the health care industry.

Robert Wood Johnson University Hospital Hamilton (RWJ Hamilton) is a $160 million private, not-for-profit, acute care community hospital serving more than 350,000 residents in Hamilton, New Jersey. Primary services include medical, surgical, obstetric, cardiology, orthopedic, and intensive care for adults and critically ill infants and children. RWJ Hamilton has 1,734 employees and more than 650 medical staff members. The residents of Hamilton are proud of this hospital because it is a 2004 recipient of the Malcolm Baldrige National Quality Award for Health Care. What are its secrets for success?

RWJ Hamilton relies on its leadership, its focus on service, finance, quality, people, and growth, as well as its strategic planning process and its measurement systems. You cannot manage what you cannot measure, so RWJ Hamilton uses its Organizational Performance Measurement System to track daily performance and operations. Key performance indicators are reviewed weekly by senior process leaders, monthly by managers, and quarterly by employees. Here are some examples of the measures that management considers important to the hospital.

- *Market share.* Customer satisfaction with the services offered by the hospital is often reflected in market share measures. RWJ Hamilton's market share in cardiology, surgery, and oncology significantly increased relative to its major competitor. This measure indicates that the hospital is growing.

- *Occupancy rates.* Continuous investment in technology, equipment, and facilities paid off for RWJ Hamilton. In 2003, its occupancy rate was 85 percent, while its best competitor had an occupancy rate of only 60 percent.

- *Delivery speed.* Patients in the emergency department are guaranteed that they will see a nurse within 15 minutes of arrival and a doctor within 30 minutes. Customer satisfaction has been shown to be related to delivery speed.

- *Customer satisfaction of services.* Customers are asked to fill out surveys regarding the services they received and how satisfied they were. For example, patient satisfaction with nursing efficiency and nursing courtesy increased from 70 percent in 1999 to 90 percent in 2004. These measures can be benchmarked against national norms.

- *Patient mortality rates.* All hospitals work to minimize this measure. A hospital's mortality rates can be benchmarked on a national basis for

A nurse at Robert Wood Johnson University Hospital in Hamilton, New Jersey, monitors the heart rate of a patient. The hospital uses a performance measurement system to track how well it accomplishes its daily operations—including customer satisfaction. The hospital's managers examine the data monthly, and employees, quarterly.

comparability. RWJ Hamilton's mortality rates showed a steady downward trend.

- *Percentage of patients receiving the wrong medication.* Scary as it sounds, the national median for receiving the wrong medication is 36 percent. At RWJ Hamilton, the rate is 7 percent.

- *Employee retention rates.* High retention rates mean that employees enjoy their work and feel that they are treated fairly. Retention rates at RWJ Hamilton are about 98 percent.

These measures can be tracked over time to assess changes in the hospital's processes and the need for managerial action. The analysis of the measures helps management to focus attention to those processes where improvements are required.

Source: The Robert Wood Johnson University Hospital Hamilton summary for the Malcolm Baldrige National Quality Award, 2004, available at www.nist.gov/public_affairs/releases/rwj_hamilton.htm; www.rwjhamilton.org/.

Sampling The most thorough approach to inspection is to inspect each service or product at each stage of the process for quality. This method, called *complete inspection,* is used when the costs of passing defects to an internal or external customer outweigh the inspection costs. Firms often use automated inspection equipment that can record, summarize, and display data. Many companies find that automated inspection equipment can pay for itself in a reasonably short time.

A well-conceived **sampling plan** can approach the same degree of protection as complete inspection. A sampling plan specifies a **sample size**, which is a quantity of randomly selected observations of process outputs; the time between successive samples; and decision rules that determine when action should be taken. Sampling is appropriate when

sampling plan

A plan that specifies a sample size, the time between successive samples, and decision rules that determine when action should be taken.

sample size

A quantity of randomly selected observations of process outputs.

inspection costs are high because of the special knowledge, skills, procedures, or expensive equipment required to perform the inspections.

Sampling Distributions Relative to a performance measure, a process will produce output that can be described by a *process distribution*, with a mean and variance that will be known only with a complete inspection with 100 percent accuracy. The purpose of sampling, however, is to estimate a variable or attribute measure for the output of the process without doing complete inspection. That measure is then used to assess the performance of the process itself. For example, the time required to process specimens at an intensive care unit lab in a hospital (a variable measure) will vary. If you measured the time to complete an analysis of a large number of patients and plotted the results, the data would tend to form a pattern that can be described as a process distribution. With sampling, we try to estimate the parameters of the process distribution using statistics such as the sample mean and the sample range or standard deviation.

1. The *sample mean* is the sum of the observations divided by the total number of observations:

$$\bar{x} = \frac{\sum_{i=1}^{n} x_i}{n}$$

where

x_i = observation of a quality characteristic (such as time)

n = total number of observations

$\bar{x}$ = mean

2. The *range* is the difference between the largest observation in a sample and the smallest. The *standard deviation* is the square root of the variance of a distribution. An estimate of the process standard deviation based on a sample is given by

$$\sigma = \sqrt{\frac{\Sigma(x_i - \bar{x})^2}{n-1}} \quad \text{or} \quad \sigma = \sqrt{\frac{\Sigma x_i^2 - \frac{(\Sigma x_i)^2}{n}}{n-1}}$$

where

σ = standard deviation of a sample

n = total number of observations in the sample

$\bar{x}$ = mean

x_i = observation of a quality characteristic

Relatively small values for the range or the standard deviation imply that the observations are clustered near the mean.

These sample statistics have their own distribution, which we call a *sampling distribution*. For example, in the lab analysis process, an important performance variable is the time it takes to get results to the critical care unit. Suppose that management wants results available in an average of 25 minutes. That is, it wants the process distribution to have a mean of 25 minutes. An inspector periodically taking a sample of five analyses and calculating the sample mean could use it to determine how well the process is doing. Suppose that the process is actually producing the analyses with a mean of 25 minutes. Plotting a large number of these means would show that they have their own sampling distribution with a mean centered on 25 minutes, as does the process distribution mean, but with much less variability. The reason is that the sample means offset the highs and lows of the individual times in each sample. Figure 6.3 shows the relationship between the sampling distribution for sample means and the process distribution for the analysis times.

Some sampling distributions (e.g., for means with sample sizes of 4 or more and proportions with sample sizes of 20 or more) can be approximated by the *normal* distribution, allowing the use of the normal tables (see the "Normal Distribution" Appendix 1). For example, suppose you wanted to determine the probability that a sample mean will be more than 2.0 standard deviations *greater* than the process mean. Go to the "Normal Distribution"

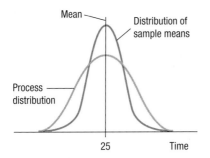

FIGURE **6.3**

Relationship Between the Distribution of Sample Means and the Process Distribution

appendix and note that the entry in the table for $z = 2.0$ standard deviations is 0.9772. Consequently, the probability is $1.0000 - 0.9772 = 0.0228$, or 2.28 percent. The probability that the sample mean will be more than 2.0 standard deviations lower than the process mean is also 2.28 percent because the normal distribution is symmetric to the mean. The ability to assign probabilities to sample results is important for the construction and use of control charts.

Common Causes The two basic categories of variation in output include common causes and assignable causes. **Common causes of variation** are the purely random, unidentifiable sources of variation that are unavoidable with the current process. A process distribution can be characterized by its *location, spread,* and *shape*. Location is measured by the *mean* of the distribution, while spread is measured by the *range* or *standard deviation*. The shape of process distributions can be characterized as either symmetric or skewed. A *symmetric* distribution has the same number of observations above and below the mean. A *skewed* distribution has a greater number of observations either above or below the mean. If process variability results solely from common causes of variation, a typical assumption is that the distribution is symmetric, with most observations near the center.

common causes of variation

The purely random, unidentifiable sources of variation that are unavoidable with the current process.

Assignable Causes The second category of variation, **assignable causes of variation**, also known as *special causes*, includes any variation-causing factors that can be identified and eliminated. Assignable causes of variation include an employee needing training or a machine needing repair. Let us return to the example of the lab analysis process. Figure 6.4 shows how assignable causes can change the distribution of output for the analysis process. The green curve is the process distribution when only common causes of variation are present. The purple lines depict a change in the distribution because of assignable causes. In Figure 6.4(a), the purple line indicates that the process took more time than planned in many of the cases, thereby increasing the average time of each analysis. In Figure 6.4(b), an increase in the variability of the time for each case affected the spread of the distribution. Finally, in Figure 6.4(c), the purple line indicates that the process produced a preponderance of the tests in less than average time. Such a distribution is skewed, or no longer symmetric to the average value. A process is said to be in statistical control when the location, spread, or shape of its distribution does not change over time. After the process is in statistical control, managers use SPC procedures to detect the onset of assignable causes so that they can be addressed.

assignable causes of variation

Any variation-causing factors that can be identified and eliminated.

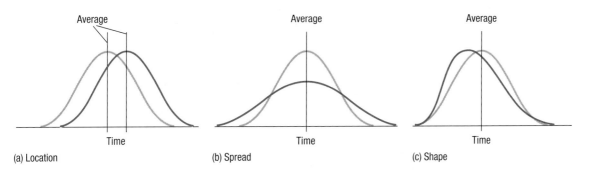

(a) Location   (b) Spread   (c) Shape

FIGURE 6.4 | Effects of Assignable Causes on the Process Distribution for the Lab Analysis Process

A doctor and his assistants measure immune responses in a medical lab. The time required to do lab work on patient samples can vary.

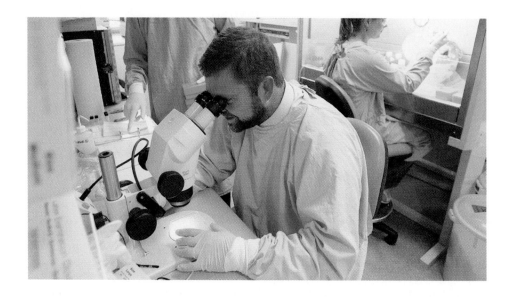

CONTROL CHARTS

control chart

A time-ordered diagram that is used to determine whether observed variations are abnormal.

To determine whether observed variations are abnormal, we can measure and plot the performance measure taken from the sample on a time-ordered diagram called a **control chart**. A control chart has a nominal value, or central line, which can be the process's historic average or a target managers would like the process to achieve, and two control limits based on the sampling distribution of the quality measure. The control limits are used to judge whether action is required. The larger value represents the *upper control limit* (UCL), and the smaller value represents the *lower control limit* (LCL). Figure 6.5 shows how the control limits relate to the sampling distribution. A sample statistic that falls between the UCL and the LCL indicates that the process is exhibiting common causes of variation; a statistic that falls outside the control limits indicates that the process is exhibiting assignable causes of variation.

Observations falling outside the control limits do not always mean poor quality. For example, in Figure 6.5 the assignable cause may be a new billing process introduced to reduce the number of incorrect bills sent to customers. If the proportion of incorrect bills, that is, the performance measure from a sample of bills, falls *below* the LCL of the control chart, the new procedure likely changed the billing process for the better, and a new control chart should be constructed.

Managers or employees responsible for evaluating a process can use control charts in the following ways:

1. Take a random sample from the process and calculate a variable or attribute performance measure.

FIGURE 6.5

How Control Limits Relate to the Sampling Distribution: Observations from Three Samples

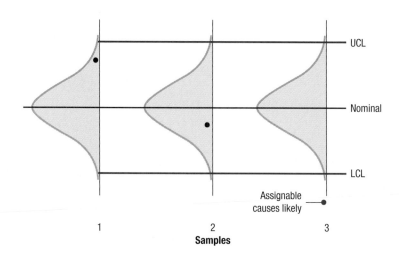

2. If the statistic falls outside the chart's control limits or exhibits unusual behavior, look for an assignable cause.

3. Eliminate the cause if it degrades performance; incorporate the cause if it improves performance. Reconstruct the control chart with new data.

4. Repeat the procedure periodically.

Sometimes problems with a process can be detected even though the control limits have not been exceeded. Figure 6.6 contains four examples of control charts. Chart (a) shows a process that is in statistical control. No action is needed. However, chart (b) shows a pattern called a *run*, or a sequence of observations with a certain characteristic. A typical rule is to take remedial action when five or more observations show a downward or upward trend, even if the points have not yet exceeded the control limits. Here, nine sequential observations are below the mean and show a downward trend. The probability is low that such a result could take place by chance.

Chart (c) shows that the process takes a sudden change from its normal pattern. The last four observations are unusual: the first drops close to the LCL and then the next two rise toward the UCL and the fourth remains above the nominal value. A manager should monitor processes with such sudden changes even though the control limits have not been exceeded. Finally, chart (d) indicates that the process went out of control twice because two sample results fell outside the control limits. The probability that the process distribution has changed is high. We discuss more implications of being out of statistical control when we discuss process capability later in this chapter.

Control charts are not perfect tools for detecting shifts in the process distribution because they are based on sampling distributions. Two types of error are possible with the use of control charts. A **type I error** occurs when the employee concludes that the process is out of control based on a sample result that falls outside the control limits, when in fact it was due to pure randomness. A **type II error** occurs when the employee concludes that the process is in control and only randomness is present, when actually the process is out of statistical control.

Management can control these errors by the choice of control limits. The choice would depend on the costs of looking for assignable causes when none exist versus the cost of not detecting a shift in the process. For example, setting control limits at three standard deviations from the mean reduces the type I error because chances are quite small that a sample result will fall outside of the control limits unless the process is out of statistical control. However, the type II error may be significant because more subtle shifts in the nature of the process distribution will go undetected because of the wide spread in the control limits. Alternatively, the spread in the control limits can be reduced to two standard deviations, thereby increasing the likelihood of sample results falling outside of the control limits. Now the type II error is smaller, but the type I error is larger because employees are likely to search for assignable causes when the sample result occurred solely by chance. As a general rule,

type I error

An error that occurs when the employee concludes that the process is out of control based on a sample result that falls outside the control limits, when in fact it was due to pure randomness.

type II error

An error that occurs when the employee concludes that the process is in control and only randomness is present, when actually the process is out of statistical control.

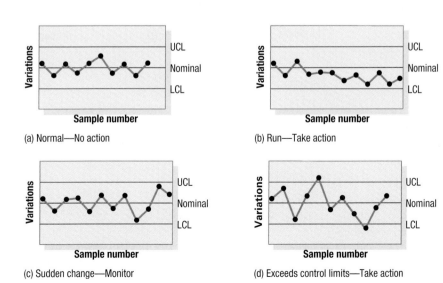

(a) Normal—No action

(b) Run—Take action

(c) Sudden change—Monitor

(d) Exceeds control limits—Take action

FIGURE 6.6

Control Chart Examples

managers will use wider limits when the cost for searching for assignable causes is large relative to the cost of not detecting a shift in the process distribution.

> STATISTICAL PROCESS CONTROL METHODS <

Statistical process control (SPC) methods are useful for both measuring the current process performance and detecting whether the process has changed in a way that will affect performance. In this section, we first discuss mean and range charts for variable measures of performance and then consider control charts for attributes measures.

CONTROL CHARTS FOR VARIABLES

R-chart

A chart used to monitor process variability.

Control charts for variables are used to monitor the mean and the variability of the process distribution.

R-Charts A range chart, or **R-chart**, is used to monitor process variability. To calculate the range of a set of sample data, the analyst subtracts the smallest from the largest measurement in each sample. If any of the data fall outside the control limits, the process variability is not in control.

The control limits for the R-chart are

$$\text{UCL}_R = D_4 \bar{R} \quad \text{and} \quad \text{LCL}_R = D_3 \bar{R}$$

where

$\bar{R}$ = average of several past R values and the central line of the control chart

D_3, D_4 = constants that provide three standard deviation (three-sigma) limits for a given sample size

x̄-chart

A chart used to see whether the process is generating output, on average, consistent with a target value set by management for the process or whether its current performance, with respect to the average of the performance measure, is consistent with past performance.

Notice that the values for D_3 and D_4 shown in Table 6.1 change as a function of the sample size. Notice, too, that the spread between the control limits narrows as the sample size increases. This change is a consequence of having more information on which to base an estimate for the process range.

x̄-Charts An **x̄-chart** (read "x-bar chart") is used to see whether the process is generating output, on average, consistent with a target value set by management for the process or whether its current performance, with respect to the average of the performance measure, is

TABLE 6.1	Factors for Calculating Three-Sigma Limits for the $\bar{x}$-chart and R-chart		
Size of Sample (*n*)	Factor for UCL and LCL for $\bar{x}$-Charts (A_2)	Factor for LCL for R-Charts (D_3)	Factor for UCL for R-Charts (D_4)
2	1.880	0	3.267
3	1.023	0	2.575
4	0.729	0	2.282
5	0.577	0	2.115
6	0.483	0	2.004
7	0.419	0.076	1.924
8	0.373	0.136	1.864
9	0.337	0.184	1.816
10	0.308	0.223	1.777

Source: 1950 *ASTM Manual on Quality Control of Materials,* copyright © American Society for Testing Materials. Reprinted with permission.

consistent with its past performance. A target value is useful when a process is completely redesigned and past performance is no longer relevant. When the assignable causes of process variability have been identified and the process variability is in statistical control, the analyst can then construct an $\bar{x}$-chart. The control limits for the $\bar{x}$-chart are

$$\text{UCL}_{\bar{x}} = \bar{\bar{x}} + A_2\bar{R} \quad \text{and} \quad \text{LCL}_{\bar{x}} = \bar{\bar{x}} - A_2\bar{R}$$

where

$\bar{\bar{x}}$ = central line of the chart, which can be either the average of past sample means or a target value set for the process

A_2 = constant to provide three-sigma limits for the sample mean

The values for A_2 are contained in Table 6.1. Note that the control limits use the value of $\bar{R}$; therefore, the $\bar{x}$-chart must be constructed *after* the process variability is in control.

To develop and use $\bar{x}$- and R-charts do the following:

Step 1. Collect data on the variable quality measurement (such as time, weight, or diameter) and organize the data by sample number. Preferably, at least 20 samples should be taken for use in constructing a control chart.

Step 2. Compute the range for each sample and the average range, $\bar{R}$, for the set of samples.

Step 3. Use Table 6.1 to determine the upper and lower control limits of the R-chart.

Step 4. Plot the sample ranges. If all are in control, proceed to step 5. Otherwise, find the assignable causes, correct them, and return to step 1.

Step 5. Calculate $\bar{x}$ for each sample and determine the central line of the chart, $\bar{\bar{x}}$.

Step 6. Use Table 6.1 to determine the parameters for $\text{UCL}_{\bar{x}}$ and $\text{LCL}_{\bar{x}}$ and construct the $\bar{x}$-chart.

Step 7. Plot the sample means. If all are in control, the process is in statistical control in terms of the process average and process variability. Continue to take samples and monitor the process. If any are out of control, find the assignable causes, correct them, and return to step 1. If no assignable causes are found after a diligent search, assume that the out-of-control points represent common causes of variation and continue to monitor the process.

Using $\bar{x}$- and R-Charts to Monitor a Process | EXAMPLE 6.1

The management of West Allis Industries is concerned about the production of a special metal screw used by several of the company's largest customers. The diameter of the screw is critical to the customer. Data from five samples appear in the accompanying table. The sample size is 4. Is the process in statistical control?

SOLUTION

Step 1: For simplicity, we use only 5 samples. In practice, more than 20 samples would be desirable. The data are shown in the following table.

Data for the $\bar{x}$- and R-Charts: Observations of Screw Diameter (in.)						
	Observation					
Sample Number	**1**	**2**	**3**	**4**	**R**	**$\bar{x}$**
1	0.5014	0.5022	0.5009	0.5027	0.0018	0.5018
2	0.5021	0.5041	0.5024	0.5020	0.0021	0.5027
3	0.5018	0.5026	0.5035	0.5023	0.0017	0.5026
4	0.5008	0.5034	0.5024	0.5015	0.0026	0.5020
5	0.5041	0.5056	0.5034	0.5047	0.0022	0.5045
				Average	0.0021	0.5027

ACTIVE MODEL 6.1

Active Model 6.1 on the Student CD-ROM provides additional insight on the *x*-bar and *R*-charts and their uses for the metal screw problem.

TUTOR 6.1

Tutor 6.1 on the Student CD-ROM provides a new example to practice the use of *x*-bar and *R*-charts.

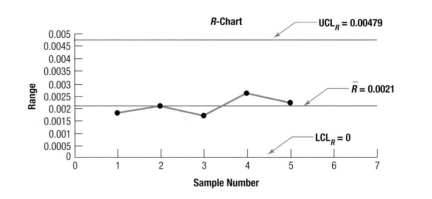

Step 2: Compute the range for each sample by subtracting the lowest value from the highest value. For example, in sample 1 the range is $0.5027 - 0.5009 = 0.0018$ in. Similarly, the ranges for samples 2, 3, 4, and 5 are 0.0021, 0.0017, 0.0026, and 0.0022 in., respectively. As shown in the table, $\bar{R} = 0.0021$.

Step 3: To construct the R-chart, select the appropriate constants from Table 6.1 for a sample size of 4. The control limits are

$$UCL_R = D_4\bar{R} = 2.282(0.0021) = 0.00479 \text{ in.}$$
$$LCL_R = D_3\bar{R} = 0(0.0021) = 0 \text{ in.}$$

Step 4: Plot the ranges on the R-chart, as shown in Figure 6.7. None of the sample ranges falls outside the control limits. Consequently, the process variability is in statistical control. If any of the sample ranges fall outside of the limits, or an unusual pattern appears (see Figure 6.6), we would search for the causes of the excessive variability, correct them, and repeat step 1.

Step 5: Compute the mean for each sample. For example, the mean for sample 1 is

$$\frac{0.5014 + 0.5022 + 0.5009 + 0.5027}{4} = 0.5018 \text{ in.}$$

Similarly, the means of samples 2, 3, 4, and 5 are 0.5027, 0.5026, 0.5020, and 0.5045 in., respectively. As shown in the table, $\bar{\bar{x}} = 0.5027$.

Step 6: Now construct the $\bar{x}$-chart for the process average. The average screw diameter is 0.5027 in., and the average range is 0.0021 in., so use $\bar{\bar{x}} = 0.5027$, $\bar{R} = 0.0021$, and A_2 from Table 6.1 for a sample size of 4 to construct the control limits:

$$UCL_{\bar{x}} = \bar{\bar{x}} + A_2\bar{R} = 0.5027 + 0.729(0.0021) = 0.5042 \text{ in.}$$
$$LCL_{\bar{x}} = \bar{\bar{x}} - A_2\bar{R} = 0.5027 - 0.729(0.0021) = 0.5012 \text{ in.}$$

Step 7: Plot the sample means on the control chart, as shown in Figure 6.8.

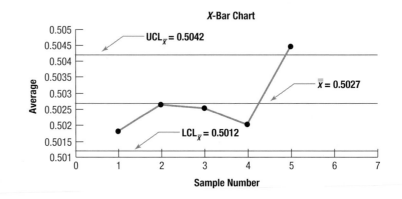

The mean of sample 5 falls above the UCL, indicating that the process average is out of control and that assignable causes must be explored, perhaps using a cause-and-effect diagram.

Decision Point A new employee operated the lathe machine that makes the screw on the day the sample was taken. To solve the problem, management initiated a training session for the employee. Subsequent samples showed that the process was back in statistical control.

If the standard deviation of the process distribution is known, another form of the $\bar{x}$-chart may be used:

$$\text{UCL}_{\bar{x}} = \bar{\bar{x}} + z\sigma_{\bar{x}} \quad \text{and} \quad \text{LCL}_{\bar{x}} = \bar{\bar{x}} - z\sigma_{\bar{x}}$$

where

$\sigma_{\bar{x}} = \sigma / \sqrt{n}$ = standard deviation of sample means

σ = standard deviation of the process distribution

n = sample size

$\bar{\bar{x}}$ = central line of the chart, which can be either the average of past sample means or a target value set for the process

z = normal deviate (number of standard deviations from the average)

The analyst can use an R-chart to be sure that the process variability is in control before constructing the $\bar{x}$-chart. The advantage of using this form of the $\bar{x}$-chart is that the analyst can adjust the spread of the control limits by changing the value of z. This approach can be useful for balancing the effects of type I and type II errors.

Designing an $\bar{x}$-Chart Using the Process Standard Deviation	EXAMPLE 6.2

The Sunny Dale Bank monitors the time required to serve customers at the drive-by window because it is an important quality factor in competing with other banks in the city. After analyzing the data gathered in an extensive study of the window operation, bank management determined that the mean time to process a customer at the peak demand period is 5 minutes, with a standard deviation of 1.5 minutes. Management wants to monitor the mean time to process a customer by periodically using a sample size of six customers. Assume that the process variability is in statistical control. Design an $\bar{x}$-chart that has a type I error of 5 percent. That is, set the control limits so that there is a 2.5 percent chance a sample result will fall below the LCL and a 2.5 percent chance that a sample result will fall above the UCL. After several weeks of sampling, two successive samples came in at 3.70 and 3.68 minutes, respectively. Is the customer service process in statistical control?

SOLUTION

$$\bar{\bar{x}} = 5.0 \text{ minutes}$$
$$\sigma = 1.5 \text{ minutes}$$
$$n = 6 \text{ customers}$$
$$z = 1.96$$

The process variability is in statistical control, so we proceed directly to the $\bar{x}$-chart. The control limits are

$$\text{UCL}_{\bar{x}} = \bar{\bar{x}} + z\sigma / \sqrt{n} = 5.0 + 1.96(1.5)/\sqrt{6} = 6.20 \text{ minutes}$$
$$\text{LCL}_{\bar{x}} = \bar{\bar{x}} - z\sigma / \sqrt{n} = 5.0 - 1.96(1.5)/\sqrt{6} = 3.80 \text{ minutes}$$

The value for z can be obtained in the following way. The normal distribution table (see the "Normal Distribution" appendix) gives the proportion of the total area under the normal curve from $-\infty$ to z. We want a type I error of 5 percent, or 2.5 percent of the curve above the UCL and 2.5 percent below the LCL. Consequently, we need to find the *z* value in the table that leaves only 2.5 percent in the upper portion of the normal curve (or 0.9750 in the table). The value is 1.96. The two new samples are below the LCL of the chart, implying that the average time to serve a customer has dropped. Assignable causes should be explored to see what caused the improvement.

Decision Point Management studied the time period over which the samples were taken and found that the supervisor of the process was experimenting with some new procedures. Management decided to make the new procedures a permanent part of the customer service process. After all employees were trained in the new procedures, new samples were taken and the control chart reconstructed.

CONTROL CHARTS FOR ATTRIBUTES

Two charts commonly used for performance measures based on attributes measures are the *p*- and *c*-chart. The *p*-chart is used for controlling the proportion of defects generated by the process. The *c*-chart is used for controlling the number of defects when more than one defect can be present in a service or product.

p-chart

A chart used for controlling the proportion of defective services or products generated by the process.

p-Charts The **p-chart** is a commonly used control chart for attributes. The performance characteristic is counted rather than measured, and the entire service or item can be declared good or defective. For example, in the banking industry, the attributes counted might be the number of nonendorsed deposits or the number of incorrect financial statements sent to customers. The method involves selecting a random sample, inspecting each item in it, and calculating the sample proportion defective, *p*, which is the number of defective units divided by the sample size.

Sampling for a *p*-chart involves a yes/no decision: The process output either is or is not defective. The underlying statistical distribution is based on the binomial distribution. However, for large sample sizes, the normal distribution provides a good approximation to it. The standard deviation of the distribution of proportion defectives, σ_p, is

$$\sigma_p = \sqrt{\bar{p}(1-\bar{p})/n}$$

where

n = sample size
$\bar{p}$ = central line on the chart, which can be either the historical average population proportion defective or a target value

We can use σ_p to arrive at the upper and lower control limits for a *p*-chart:

$$\mathrm{UCL}_p = \bar{p} + z\sigma_p \quad \text{and} \quad \mathrm{LCL}_p = \bar{p} - z\sigma_p$$

where

z = normal deviate (number of standard deviations from the average)

The chart is used in the following way. Periodically, a random sample of size *n* is taken, and the number of defective services or products is counted. The number of defectives is divided by the sample size to get a sample proportion defective, *p*, which is plotted on the chart. When a sample proportion defective falls outside the control limits, the analyst assumes that the proportion defective generated by the process has changed and searches for the assignable cause. Observations falling below the LCL_p indicate that the process may actually have improved. The analyst may find no assignable cause because it is always possible that an out-of-control proportion occurred randomly. However, if the analyst discovers assignable causes, those sample data should not be used to calculate the control limits for the chart.

Using a *p*-Chart to Monitor a Process	EXAMPLE 6.3

The operations manager of the booking services department of Hometown Bank is concerned about the number of wrong customer account numbers recorded by Hometown personnel. Each week a random sample of 2,500 deposits is taken, and the number of incorrect account numbers is recorded. The results for the past 12 weeks are shown in the following table. Is the booking process out of statistical control? Use three-sigma control limits.

ACTIVE MODEL 6.2

Active Model 6.2 on the Student CD-ROM provides additional insight on the *p*-chart and its uses for the booking services department.

TUTOR 6.2

Tutor 6.2 on the Student CD-ROM provides a new example to practice the use of the *p*-chart.

Sample Number	Wrong Account Numbers	Sample Number	Wrong Account Numbers
1	15	7	24
2	12	8	7
3	19	9	10
4	2	10	17
5	19	11	15
6	4	12	3
		Total	147

SOLUTION

Step 1: Using this sample data to calculate *p*-bar

$$\bar{p} = \frac{\text{Total defectives}}{\text{Total number of observations}} = \frac{147}{12(2,500)} = 0.0049$$

$$\sigma_p = \sqrt{\bar{p}(1-\bar{p})/n} = \sqrt{0.0049(1-0.0049)/2,500} = 0.0014$$

$$\text{UCL}_p = \bar{p} + z\sigma_p = 0.0049 + 3(0.0014) = 0.0091$$

$$\text{LCL}_p = \bar{p} - z\sigma_p = 0.0049 - 3(0.0014) = 0.0007$$

Step 2: Calculate the sample proportion defective. For sample 1, the proportion of defectives is 15/2,500 = 0.0060.

Step 3: Plot each sample proportion defective on the chart, as shown in Figure 6.9.

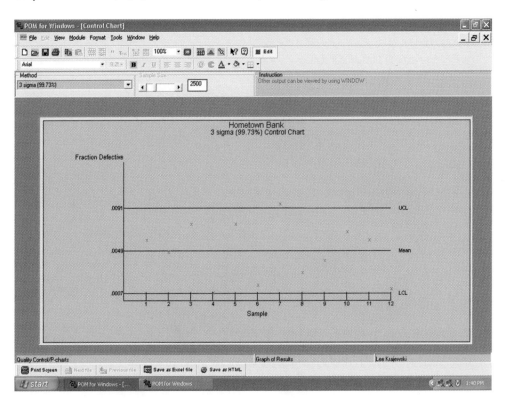

FIGURE 6.9

The *p*-Chart from POM for Windows for Wrong Account Numbers, Showing That Sample 7 Is out of Control

Sample 7 exceeds the UCL; thus, the process is out of control and the reasons for the poor performance that week should be determined.

Decision Point Management explored the circumstances when sample 7 was taken. The encoding machine used to print the account numbers on the checks was defective that week. The following week the machine was repaired; however, the recommended preventive maintenance on the machine was not performed for months prior to the failure. Management reviewed the performance of the maintenance department and instituted changes to the maintenance procedures for the encoding machine. After the problem was corrected, an analyst recalculated the control limits using the data without sample 7. Subsequent weeks were sampled, and the booking process was determined to be in statistical control. Consequently, the p-chart provides a tool to indicate when a process needs adjustment.

c-chart

A chart used for controlling the number of defects when more than one defect can be present in a service or product.

c-Charts Sometimes services or products have more than one defect. For example, a roll of carpeting may have several defects, such as tufted or discolored fibers or stains from the production process. Other situations in which more than one defect may occur include accidents at a particular intersection, bubbles in a television picture tube face panel, and complaints from a patron at a hotel. When management is interested in reducing the number of defects per unit or service encounter, another type of control chart, the **c-chart**, is useful.

The underlying sampling distribution for a c-chart is the Poisson distribution. The Poisson distribution is based on the assumption that defects occur over a continuous region on the surface of a product or a continuous time interval during the provision of a service. It further assumes that the probability of two or more defects at any one location on the surface or at any instant of time is negligible. The mean of the distribution is $\bar{c}$, and the standard deviation is $\sqrt{\bar{c}}$. A useful tactic is to use the normal approximation to the Poisson so that the central line of the chart is $\bar{c}$ and the control limits are

$$\text{UCL}_c = \bar{c} + z\sqrt{\bar{c}} \quad \text{and} \quad \text{LCL}_c = \bar{c} - z\sqrt{\bar{c}}$$

EXAMPLE 6.4	Using a c-Chart to Monitor Defects per Unit

TUTOR 6.3

Tutor 6.3 on the Student CD-ROM provides a new example to practice the use of the c-chart.

The Woodland Paper Company produces paper for the newspaper industry. As a final step in the process, the paper passes through a machine that measures various product quality characteristics. When the paper production process is in control, it averages 20 defects per roll.

a.   Set up a control chart for the number of defects per roll. For this example, use two-sigma control limits.

b.   Five rolls had the following number of defects: 16, 21, 17, 22, and 24, respectively. The sixth roll, using pulp from a different supplier, had 5 defects. Is the paper production process in control?

SOLUTION

a.   The average number of defects per roll is 20. Therefore

$$\text{UCL}_c = \bar{c} + z\sqrt{\bar{c}} = 20 + 2(\sqrt{20}) = 28.94$$

$$\text{LCL}_c = \bar{c} - z\sqrt{\bar{c}} = 20 - 2(\sqrt{20}) = 11.06$$

The control chart is shown in Figure 6.10.

b.   Because the first five rolls had defects that fell within the control limits, the process is still in control. Five defects, however, is less than the LCL, and therefore, the process is technically "out of control." The control chart indicates that something good has happened.

Decision Point The supplier for the first 5 samples has been used by Woodland Paper for many years. The supplier for the sixth sample is new to the company. Management decided to continue using the new supplier for a while, monitoring the number of defects to see whether it stays low. If the number remains below the LCL for 20 consecutive samples, management will make the switch permanent and recalculate the control chart parameters.

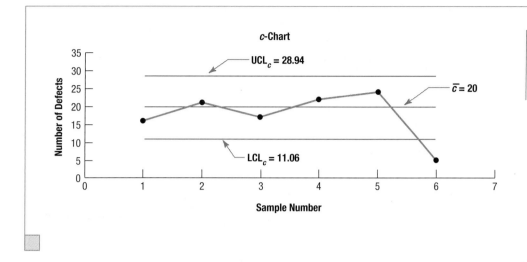

FIGURE **6.10**

The *c*-Chart from the OM Explorer
c-Chart Solver for Defects per Roll
of Paper

> PROCESS CAPABILITY <

Statistical process control techniques help managers achieve and maintain a process distribution that does not change in terms of its mean and variance. The control limits on the control charts signal when the mean or variability of the process changes. However, a process that is in statistical control may not be producing services or products according to their design specifications because the control limits are based on the mean and variability of the *sampling distribution*, not the design specifications. **Process capability** refers to the ability of the process to meet the design specifications for a service or product. Design specifications often are expressed as a **nominal value**, or target, and a **tolerance**, or allowance above or below the nominal value.

For example, the administrator of an intensive care unit lab might have a nominal value for the turnaround time of results to the attending physicians of 25 minutes and a tolerance of ±5 minutes because of the need for speed under life-threatening conditions. The tolerance gives an *upper specification* of 30 minutes and a *lower specification* of 20 minutes. The lab process must be capable of providing the results of analyses within these specifications, otherwise it will produce a certain proportion of "defects." The administrator is also interested in detecting occurrences of turnaround times of less than 20 minutes because something might be learned that can be built into the lab process in the future. For the present, the physicians are pleased with results that arrive within 20 to 30 minutes.

DEFINING PROCESS CAPABILITY

Figure 6.11 shows the relationship between a process distribution and the upper and lower specifications for the lab process turnaround time under two conditions. In Figure 6.11(a), the process is capable because the extremes of the process distribution fall within the upper and lower specifications. In Figure 6.11(b) the process is not capable because the lab process produces too many reports with long turnaround times.

Figure 6.11 shows clearly why managers are so concerned with reducing process variability. The less variability—represented by lower standard deviations—the less frequently bad output is produced. Figure 6.12 shows what reducing variability means for a process distribution that is a normal probability distribution. The firm with two-sigma quality (the tolerance limits equal the process distribution mean ±2 standard deviations) produces 4.56 percent defects, or 45,600 defects per million. The firm with four-sigma quality produces only 0.0063 percent defectives, or 63 defects per million. Finally, the firm with six-sigma quality produces only 0.0000002 percent defects, or 0.002 defects per million.[2]

How can a manager determine quantitatively whether a process is capable? Two measures commonly are used in practice to assess the capability of a process: the process capability ratio and the process capability index.

process capability

The ability of the process to meet the design specifications for a service or product.

nominal value

A target for design specifications.

tolerance

An allowance above or below the nominal value.

---

[2]Our discussion assumes that the process distribution has no assignable causes. Six Sigma programs, however, define defect performance with the assumption that the process average has moved 1.5 standard deviations. We discuss Six Sigma later in the chapter.

FIGURE **6.11**

The Relationship Between a Process
Distribution and Upper and Lower
Specifications

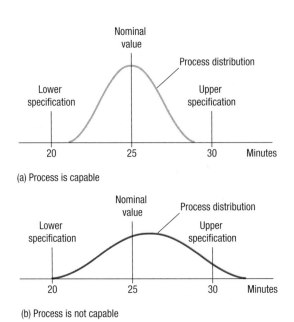

(a) Process is capable

(b) Process is not capable

Process Capability Ratio A process is *capable* if it has a process distribution whose extreme values fall within the upper and lower specifications for a service or product. As a general rule, most values of any process distribution fall within ±3 standard deviations of the mean. For example, if the process distribution is normal, 99.74 percent of the values fall within ±3 standard deviations. In other words, the range of values of the quality measure generated by a process is approximately 6 standard deviations of the process distribution. Hence, if a process is capable, the difference between the upper and lower specification, called the *tolerance width,* must be greater than 6 standard deviations. The **process capability ratio, C_p,** is defined as

process capability ratio, C_p

The tolerance width divided by
6 standard deviations (process variability).

$$C_p = \frac{\text{Upper specification} - \text{Lower specification}}{6\sigma}$$

where

σ = standard deviation of the process distribution

A C_p value of 1.0 implies that the firm is producing three-sigma quality (0.26 percent defects) and that the process is consistently producing outputs within specifications even though some defects are generated. C_p values greater than 1.0 imply higher levels of quality achievement. Firms striving to achieve greater than three-sigma quality use a critical value for the ratio that is greater than 1.0. For example, a firm targeting six-sigma quality will use

FIGURE **6.12**

Effects of Reducing Variability on
Process Capability

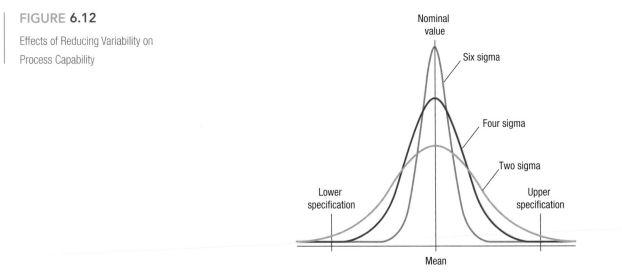

2.0, a firm targeting five-sigma quality will use 1.67, and a firm striving for four-sigma quality will use 1.33. Processes producing services or products with less than three-sigma quality will have C_p values less than 1.0.

Process Capability Index A process is capable only when the capability ratio is greater than the critical value and the process distribution is centered on the nominal value of the design specifications. For example, the lab process may have a process capability ratio greater than 1.33 for turnaround time. However, if the mean of the distribution of process output, $\bar{\bar{x}}$, is closer to the upper specification, lengthy turnaround times may still be generated. Likewise, if $\bar{\bar{x}}$ is closer to the lower specification, quick results may be generated. Thus, we need to compute a capability index that measures the potential for the output of the process to fall outside of either the upper or lower specifications.

The **process capability index, C_{pk}** is defined as

$$C_{pk} = \text{Minimum of} \left[\frac{\bar{\bar{x}} - \text{Lower specification}}{3\sigma}, \frac{\text{Upper specification} - \bar{\bar{x}}}{3\sigma} \right]$$

process capability index, C_{pk}
An index that measures the potential for a process to generate defective outputs relative to either upper or lower specifications.

We take the minimum of the two ratios because it gives the *worst-case* situation. If C_{pk} is greater than the critical value (say, 1.33 for four-sigma quality) and the process capability ratio is also greater than the critical value, we can finally say the process is capable. If C_{pk} is less than the critical value, either the process average is close to one of the tolerance limits and is generating defective output, or the process variability is too large.

The capability index will always be less than or equal to the capability ratio. Because of this, the capability index can be used as a first check for capability; if the capability index passes the test, the process can be declared capable. If it does not pass, the process capability ratio must be calculated to see if the process variability is a source of the problem. When C_{pk} equals C_p, the process is centered between the upper and lower specifications and, hence, the mean of the process distribution is centered on the nominal value of the design specifications.

USING CONTINUOUS IMPROVEMENT TO DETERMINE THE CAPABILITY OF A PROCESS

To determine the capability of a process to produce outputs within the tolerances, use the following steps.

Step 1. Collect data on the process output, and calculate the mean and the standard deviation of the process output distribution.

Step 2. Use the data from the process distribution to compute process control charts, such as an $\bar{x}$- or an R-chart.

Step 3. Take a series of random samples from the process and plot the results on the control charts. If at least 20 consecutive samples are within the control limits of the charts, the process is in statistical control. If the process is not in statistical control, look for assignable causes and eliminate them. Recalculate the mean and standard deviation of the process distribution and the control limits for the charts. Continue until the process is in statistical control.

Step 4. Calculate the process capability index and the process capability ratio, if necessary. If the results are acceptable, document any changes made to the process and continue to monitor the output by using the control charts. If the results are unacceptable, further explore assignable causes for reducing the variance in the output or centering the process distribution on the nominal value. As changes are made, recalculate the mean and standard deviation of the process distribution and the control limits for the charts and repeat step 3.

Assessing the Process Capability of the Intensive Care Unit Lab	**EXAMPLE 6.5**

The intensive care unit lab process has an average turnaround time of 26.2 minutes and a standard deviation of 1.35 minutes. The nominal value for this service is 25 minutes with an upper specification limit of 30 minutes and a lower specification limit of 20 minutes. The administrator of the lab wants to have four-sigma performance for her lab. Is the lab process capable of this level of performance?

ACTIVE MODEL 6.3

Active Model 6.3 on the Student CD-ROM provides additional insight on the process capability problem at the intensive care unit lab.

TUTOR 6.4

Tutor 6.4 on the Student CD-ROM provides a new example to practice the process capability measures.

SOLUTION

The administrator began by taking a quick check to see if the process is capable by applying the process capability index:

$$\text{Lower specification calculation} = \frac{26.2 - 20.0}{3(1.35)} = 1.53$$

$$\text{Upper specification calculation} = \frac{30.0 - 26.2}{3(1.35)} = 0.94$$

$$C_{pk} = \text{Minimum of}\,[1.53, 0.94] = 0.94$$

Since the target value for four-sigma performance is 1.33, the process capability index told her that the process was not capable. However, she did not know whether the problem was the variability of the process, the centering of the process, or both. The options available to improve the process depended on what is wrong.

She next checked the process variability with the process capability ratio:

$$C_p = \frac{30.0 - 20.0}{6(1.35)} = 1.23$$

The process variability did not meet the four-sigma target of 1.33. Consequently, she initiated a study to see where variability was introduced to the process. Two activities, report preparation and specimen slide preparation, were identified as having inconsistent procedures. These procedures were modified to provide consistent performance. New data were collected and the average turnaround was now 26.1 minutes with a standard deviation of 1.20 minutes. She now had the process variability at the four-sigma level of performance, as indicated by the process capability ratio:

$$C_p = \frac{30.0 - 20.0}{6(1.20)} = 1.39$$

However, the process capability index indicated additional problems to resolve:

$$C_{pk} = \text{Minimum of}\left[\frac{(26.1 - 20.0)}{3(1.20)}, \frac{(30.0 - 26.1)}{3(1.20)}\right] = 1.08$$

Decision Point The lab process was still not at the level of four-sigma performance on turnaround time. The lab administrator searched for the causes of the off-center turnaround time distribution. She discovered periodic backlogs at a key piece of testing equipment. Acquiring a second machine provided the capacity to reduce the turnaround times to four-sigma capability.

QUALITY ENGINEERING

quality engineering

An approach originated by Genichi Taguchi that invloves combining engineering and statistical methods to reduce costs and improve quality by optimizing product design and manufacturing processes.

quality loss function

The rationale that a service or product that barely conforms to the specifications is more like a defective service or product than a perfect one.

Originated by Genichi Taguchi, **quality engineering** is an approach that involves combining engineering and statistical methods to reduce costs and improve quality by optimizing product design and manufacturing processes. Taguchi believes that unwelcome costs are associated with *any* deviation from a quality characteristic's target value. Taguchi's view is that the **quality loss function** is zero when the quality characteristic of the service or product is exactly on the target value, and that the quality loss function value rises exponentially as the quality characteristic gets closer to the tolerance limits. The rationale is that a service or product that barely conforms to the specifications is more like a defective service or product than a perfect one. Figure 6.13 shows Taguchi's quality loss function schematically. Taguchi concluded that managers should continually search for ways to reduce *all* variability from the target value in the production process and not be content with merely adhering to specification limits.

> SIX SIGMA <

Six Sigma

A comprehensive and flexible system for achieving, sustaining, and maximizing business success by minimizing defects and variability in processes.

We have seen how TQM and SPC can improve process performance and quality. Nonetheless, another approach, relying heavily on the principles and tools of TQM, has gained in popularity. **Six Sigma** is a comprehensive and flexible system for achieving, sustaining, and maximizing business success by minimizing defects and variability in processes. Six Sigma is

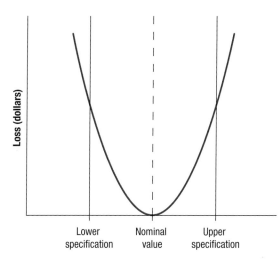

FIGURE **6.13**

Taguchi's Quality Loss Function

driven by a close understanding of customer needs; the disciplined use of facts, data, and statistical analysis; and diligent attention to managing, improving, and reinventing business processes. Although many of the principles and tools of Six Sigma are similar to those of TQM, the approach has more formality than TQM.

Motorola is credited with developing Six Sigma more than 20 years ago to improve its manufacturing capability in a world marketplace that was becoming increasingly competitive. Management noticed that some customers were complaining about the quality of Motorola's products and that competitor products were outperforming its products. Motorola initially responded by setting higher goals for each of its processes so as to reduce the number of defects to one-tenth the previous level of performance. To achieve such a goal required that they work smarter, not just harder.

Motorola began by soliciting new ideas from its employees and benchmarking its competitors. What followed were extensive changes to employee compensation and reward programs, training programs, and critical processes. The results were impressive. At one plant, after 10 months the defect rate improved 70 percent and the yield improved 55 percent.

The procedures for achieving those impressive results were documented and refined and became known as Six Sigma. Its name relates to the goal of achieving low rates of defective output even if the process's average shifts 1.5 standard deviations. The 1.5 standard deviation value is a fudge factor used to account for the shift and drift in the mean of a process's outputs due to assignable causes over the long term. Motorola found that this variation normally fell between 1.4 and 1.6 standard deviations. Under this assumption, a process achieving six-sigma quality would likely produce 3.4 defects per million opportunities over the long term. As we have discussed earlier, without a shift in the process average, a process generating six-sigma quality would have only 0.002 defects per million opportunities.[3]

General Electric views Six Sigma as a strategy, a discipline, and a set of tools. It is a strategy because it focuses on what the customer wants, whether the customer is internal or external, and it aims at total customer satisfaction. Consequently, Six Sigma leads to better business results as measured by market share, revenue, and profits. It is a discipline because it has a formal sequence of steps, called the Six Sigma Improvement Model, to accomplish the desired improvement in process performance. The goal is to simplify processes and close the gaps between a process's competitive priorities and its competitive capabilities. Finally, it is a set of tools because it makes use of powerful tools such as those discussed in this chapter and in Chapter 5, "Process Analysis." The tools help detect whether process performance has gone astray, and they provide a means to monitor performance on an ongoing basis.

Although Six Sigma was rooted in an effort to improve manufacturing processes, credit General Electric with popularizing the application of the approach to nonmanufacturing processes such as sales, human resources, customer service, and financial services. The concept of eliminating defects is the same, although the definition of "defect" depends on the process involved. For example, a human resource department's failure to meet a hiring target

---

[3]See www.isixsigma.com/library/content/sigma_table.asp for a complete table of Six Sigma conversions using the 1.5 standard deviation assumption. This site also explains the rationale behind the use of that assumption.

counts as a defect. Applying Six Sigma to service processes is more challenging than for manufacturing processes for the following reasons:

1. The "work product" is much more difficult to see because it often consists of information, requests, orders, proposals, presentations, meetings, invoices, designs, and ideas. Service processes are often involved with computers and networks, sometimes international, that make the process "virtual" and difficult to document. This virtual aspect makes it difficult for people working in diverse functional areas such as sales, marketing, and software development to understand that they are actually part of a process that needs analysis.

2. Service processes can be changed quickly. Responsibilities can be shifted, forms revised, and new steps added without capital investment. Service processes in many companies evolve, adapt, and grow almost continuously.

3. Hard facts on service process performance are often hard to come by. The data that do exist are often anecdotal or subjective. Big stacks of unprocessed documents are often easy to see; however, measuring backlogs, rework, delays, and the costs of working on them is difficult. For example, streamlining a loan closure process is complicated because the process may involve many different people, each only devoting a small slice of his or her workday.

Despite the challenges, Six Sigma has been successfully applied to a host of service processes, including financial services, human resource processes, marketing processes, and health care administrative processes. Managerial Practice 6.3 shows how Six Sigma was applied at a health care facility.

MANAGERIAL **PRACTICE**	6.3	APPLYING THE SIX-SIGMA PROCESS AT SCOTTSDALE HEALTHCARE'S OSBORN HOSPITAL

Dozens of leading companies, including General Electric, Seagate Technology, Bombardier, and AlliedSignal have adopted the Six-Sigma process pioneered by Motorola in the 1980s. The initial applications focused on manufacturing processes, but many recent applications focus on service processes. The health care industry is a case in point.

In Scottsdale, Arizona, thousands of snow birds, retirement-aged visitors from the north, flock to the city's sunny climate during the onset of the traditional flu season. Combined with Scottsdale's permanent residents, this population creates a huge demand for emergency services at hospitals such as Scottsdale Healthcare's Osborn Hospital. In one 6-month period, hospitals in the area reported more than 12,000 hours during which they closed their doors to new patients and diverted ambulance services to other hospitals. Osborn's emergency department (ED), one of the busiest of trauma centers, experienced an increase of 74 percent in its diversion rate and an alarming 272 percent increase in the number of patients who voluntarily left the ED before receiving any attention. Those who did remain long enough to be served gave the ED low satisfaction marks in exit surveys. The hospital estimated that it could lose $500,000 each quarter as a result.

Six Sigma consultants first mapped Osborn's ED process to identify potential problem areas. Three nested processes presented potential bottlenecks so significant that they could increase the probability of the need to divert patients to other hospitals. The process variables of concern were registration time, lab/radiology turnaround, and the time to transfer patients to inpatient beds when they require admission.

Hospital personnel at a trauma center rush a patient to the emergency room. Six Sigma can be used to improve service processes such as those in a trauma center.

Data were collected on these process variables for analysis. Improvements to the processes were identified and studied for feasibility. Some of the proposed improvements were implemented. For example, the analysis revealed that the average time to transfer a patient out of the ED was 80 minutes. However, for 40 of those minutes the inpatient bed was actually ready and waiting, which prompted the hospital to change its procedures for inpatient bed transfers. Having identified the key process variables with Six Sigma tools enabled hospital administrators to redesign their processes.

Source: Ian R. Lazarus and Keith Butler, "The Promise of Six Sigma," *Managed Healthcare Executive* (October 2001), pp. 22–26.

SIX SIGMA IMPROVEMENT MODEL

Figure 6.14 shows the Six Sigma Improvement Model, a five-step procedure that leads to improvements in process performance. The model can be applied to projects involving incremental improvements to processes or to projects requiring major changes, including a redesign of an existing process or the development of a new process.

- *Define.* Determine the characteristics of the process's output that are critical to customer satisfaction and identify any gaps between these characteristics and the process's capabilities. These gaps—whether a mismatch in the process's positioning in the customer-contact matrix (see Figure 4.3) or the product-process matrix (see Figure 4.5)—provide opportunities for improvement. Get a picture of the current process by documenting it using flowcharts and process charts. (See Chapter 5, "Process Analysis".)

- *Measure.* Quantify the work the process does that affects the gap. Select what to measure, identify data sources, and prepare a data collection plan.

- *Analyze.* Use the data on measures to perform process analysis, which may be focused on incremental process improvement or major process redesign. Use data analysis tools such as Pareto charts, scatter diagrams, and cause-and-effect diagrams and the statistical process control tools in this chapter to determine where improvements are necessary. Whether or not major redesign is necessary, establish procedures to make the desired outcome routine.

- *Improve.* Modify or redesign existing methods to meet the new performance objectives. Implement the changes.

- *Control.* Monitor the process to make sure that high performance levels are maintained. Once again, data analysis tools such as Pareto charts, bar charts, scatter diagrams, as well as the statistical process control tools can be used to control the process.

Successful users of Six Sigma have found that it is essential to rigorously follow the steps in the Six Sigma Improvement Model, which is sometimes referred to as the *DMAIC process* using the first letter of each step in the model.

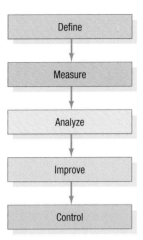

FIGURE 6.14

Six Sigma Improvement Model

IMPLEMENTATION

Implementing a successful Six Sigma program begins with an understanding that Six Sigma is not a product you can buy—it requires time and commitment. Here are some lessons that Motorola, General Electric, and other leaders in Six Sigma learned about implementing the program.

- *Top-Down Commitment.* Corporate leaders must show their commitment to the program and take a visible role in auditing processes and searching for ways to improve the business. They must set an example for everyone in the organization.

- *Measurement Systems to Track Progress.* Management must be committed to providing the means to track results and, along with employees, use those means to measure process performance.

- *Tough Goal Setting.* Establish the highest standards for the organization by regularly benchmarking "best-in-class" companies to assess the critical dimensions of customer satisfaction.

- *Education.* Employees must be trained in the "whys" and the "how-tos" of quality and what it means to customers, both internal and external. This learning is accomplished with "train-the-trainer" programs. Successful firms using Six Sigma develop a cadre of internal teachers who then are responsible for teaching and assisting teams involved in a process improvement project. These teachers have different titles depending on their experience and level of achievement. **Green Belts** devote part of their time to teaching and helping teams with their projects and the rest of their time to their normally assigned duties. **Black Belts** are full-time teachers and leaders of teams involved in Six Sigma projects. Finally, **Master Black Belts** are full-time teachers who review and mentor Black Belts. Selection criteria for Master Black Belts are quantitative skills and the ability to teach and mentor. According to the Six-Sigma Academy, a typical Black Belt can spearhead five to six projects a year, with average savings in the range of $175,000 per project.

Green Belt

An employee who achieved the first level of training in a Six Sigma program and spends part of his or her time teaching and helping teams with their projects.

Black Belt

An employee who reached the highest level of training in a Six Sigma program and spends all of his or her time teaching and leading teams involved in Six Sigma projects.

Master Black Belt

Full-time teachers and mentors to several Black Belts.

- *Communication.* Successes are as important to understand as failures. Communicating organizational successes is a critical step in ensuring that the firm can build upon them in the future.

- *Customer Priorities.* Never lose sight of the customer's priorities, which are translated into competitive priorities for the firm's processes. Identify where gaps exist.

Successful firms using Six Sigma are mindful of these lessons; however, they are never satisfied. Continuous improvement or redesign of existing processes must be on the minds of all employees. Continuous improvement is certainly the case at Starwood Hotels & Resorts, where more than 1,000 associates have been trained as Six Sigma Green Belts. Put yourself in the position of management trying to improve customer satisfaction at the Sheraton brand of Starwood. How would you address the issues described in the following Managerial Challenge?

> INTERNATIONAL QUALITY DOCUMENTATION STANDARDS <

Once a company has gone through the effort of making its processes capable, it must document its level of quality so as to better market its services or products. This documentation of quality is especially important in international trade. However, if each country had its own set of standards, companies selling in international markets would have difficulty complying with quality documentation standards in the countries where they did business. To overcome this problem, the International Organization for Standardization devised a set of standards called ISO 9000 for companies doing business in the European Union. Subsequently, a new set of documentation standards, ISO 14000, was devised for environmental management systems.

THE ISO 9000 DOCUMENTATION STANDARDS

ISO 9000

A set of standards governing documentation of a quality program.

ISO 9000 is a set of standards governing documentation of a quality program. Companies become certified by proving to a qualified external examiner that they comply with all the requirements. Once certified, companies are listed in a directory so that potential customers can see which companies are certified and to what level. Compliance with ISO 9000 standards says *nothing* about the actual quality of a product. Rather, it indicates to customers that companies can provide documentation to support whatever claims they make about quality.

ISO 9000 actually consists of five documents: ISO 9000–9004. ISO 9000 is an overview document, which provides guidelines for selection and use of the other standards. ISO 9001 is a standard that focuses on 20 aspects of a quality program for companies that design, produce, install, and service products. These aspects include management responsibility, quality system documentation, purchasing, product design, inspection, training, and corrective action. It is the most comprehensive and difficult standard to attain. ISO 9002 covers the same areas as ISO 9001 for companies that produce to the customer's designs or have their design and service activities at another location. ISO 9003 is the most limited in scope and addresses only the production process. ISO 9004 contains guidelines for interpreting the other standards.

ISO 14000: AN ENVIRONMENTAL MANAGEMENT SYSTEM

ISO 14000

Documentation standards that require participating companies to keep track of their raw materials use and their generation, treatment, and disposal of hazardous wastes.

The **ISO 14000** documentation standards require participating companies to keep track of their raw materials use and their generation, treatment, and disposal of hazardous wastes. Although not specifying what each company is allowed to emit, the standards require companies to prepare a plan for ongoing improvement in their environmental performance. ISO 14000 is a series of five standards that cover a number of areas, including the following:

- *Environmental Management System.* Requires a plan to improve performance in resource use and pollutant output.

- *Environmental Performance Evaluation.* Specifies guidelines for the certification of companies.

MANAGERIAL **CHALLENGE**   PROCESS PERFORMANCE AND QUALITY AT STARWOOD

DVD Starwood Hotels & Resorts is no stranger to quality measurement. In the most recent year, Starwood properties around the globe held 51 of approximately 700 spots on Conde Nast's Gold List of the world's best places to stay. Its spa and golf programs have consistently been ranked among the best in the world.

At Starwood, its processes and programs are driven by the work of its team of Six Sigma experts, called Black Belts. Developed by Motorola more than 20 years ago, Six Sigma is a comprehensive and flexible system for achieving, sustaining, and maximizing business success by driving out defects and variability in a process. Starwood uses the five-step DMAIC process: define, measure, analyze, improve, and control.

Clearly, understanding customer needs is paramount. To this end, Starwood collects data from customers on its Guest Satisfaction Index survey, called the "Voice of the Customer." The survey covers every department guests may have encountered during their stay, from the front desk and hotel room, to restaurants and concierge. Past surveys indicated that how well problems were resolved during the guest stay was a key driver in high guest satisfaction scores. To increase its scores for problem resolution, the Sheraton brand of Starwood launched the Sheraton Service Promise program in the United States and Canada. The program was designed to give guests a single point of contact for reporting any problems. It was intended to focus associate (employee) attention on taking care of service issues during the guest's stay within 15 minutes of first receiving notice.

However, although scores did increase, they didn't increase by enough. Consequently, Sheraton brought in its Six Sigma team to see what it could do. The team employed the basic Six Sigma model of define-measure-analyze-improve-control to guide their work. To define the problem, the Six Sigma team worked with data collected and analyzed by an independent survey organization, National Family Opinion. The study indicated that three key factors are needed in problem resolution: speed, empathy, and efficiency. All three must be met in order for the guests to be satisfied and the Sheraton Service Promise fulfilled. Then the team looked at the specific processes that affected performance: telephone operators' handling of requests, procedures for determining who to call, engineering workloads, and so on. The work identified in each area was measured. For example, call logs were established to track speed, empathy of associate handling the call, and efficiency of the staff charged with fixing the problem. The data collected were analyzed to determine why guests' problems weren't resolved within the 15-minute standard. Pareto charts and other techniques were used for the analysis.

The final step involved control and monitoring to be sure that the improved processes developed by the Six Sigma team became part of the property's culture, and that they weren't abandoned after the team's work is finished. Tracking continues for 12 to 18 months, with monthly feedback to the manager or department head responsible for the improvement of the

Personnel at a Sheraton Hotel track guest satisfaction scores as part of the chain's "Sheraton Service Promise." The program gives guests a single point of contact should they experience problems during their stay.

Sheraton Service Promise program. The improvement effort also receives visibility through the company's intranet so the rest of the organization sees the benefits—including service levels and financial performance—and can use the experience to improve their own operations.

Managerial Challenges for Improving Customer Satisfaction at Starwood

1. Implementing Six Sigma programs takes considerable time and commitment from an organization. In terms of top-down commitment, measurement systems to track progress, tough goal setting, education, communication, and customer priorities, evaluate the degree to which Starwood successfully addressed each with the redesign of the Sheraton Service Promise program.

2. How might the new Sheraton Service Promise process help Starwood avoid the four costs of poor process performance and quality (prevention, appraisal, internal failure, and external failure)?

3. Starwood is the first major hotel brand to commit to a dedicated Six Sigma program for improving quality. Why might an organization be reluctant to follow this type of formalized methodology? What other approaches could Starwood or its competitors use?

- ■ *Environmental Labeling.* Defines terms such as *recyclable, energy efficient,* and *safe for the ozone layer.*
- ■ *Life-Cycle Assessment.* Evaluates the lifetime environmental impact from the manufacture, use, and disposal of a product.

To maintain their certification, companies must be inspected by outside, private auditors on a regular basis.

BENEFITS OF ISO CERTIFICATION

Completing the certification process can take as long as 18 months and involve many hours of management and employee time. The cost of certification can exceed $1 million for large companies. Despite the expense and commitment involved in ISO certification, it bestows significant external and internal benefits. The external benefits come from the potential sales advantage that companies in compliance have. Companies looking for a supplier will more likely select a company that has demonstrated compliance with ISO documentation standards, all other factors being equal. Consequently, more and more firms are seeking certification to gain a competitive advantage. Hundreds of thousands of manufacturing sites worldwide are ISO 9000 certified.

Internal benefits can be substantial. Registered companies report an average of 48 percent increased profitability and 76 percent improvement in marketing. The British Standards Institute, a leading third-party auditor, estimates that most ISO 9000-registered companies experience a 10 percent reduction in the cost of producing a product because of the quality improvements they make while striving to meet the documentation requirements. Certification in ISO 9000 requires a company to analyze and document its procedures, which is necessary in any event for implementing continuous improvement, employee involvement, and similar programs. The guidelines and requirements of the ISO documentation standards provide companies with a jump start in pursuing TQM programs.

> MALCOLM BALDRIGE NATIONAL QUALITY AWARD <

Malcolm Baldrige National Quality Award

An award named for the late secretary of commerce, who was a strong proponent of enhancing quality as a means of reducing the trade deficit; the award promotes, recognizes, and publicizes quality strategies and achievements.

Regardless of where a company does business, it is clear that all organizations have to produce high-quality products and services if they are to be competitive. To emphasize that point, in August 1987, the United States Congress signed into law the Malcolm Baldrige National Quality Improvement Act, creating the **Malcolm Baldrige National Quality Award** (www.quality. nist.gov). Named for the late secretary of commerce, who was a strong proponent of enhancing quality as a means of reducing the trade deficit, the award promotes, recognizes, and publicizes quality strategies and achievements.

The application and review process for the Baldrige award is rigorous. However, the act of preparing the application itself is often a major benefit to organizations because it helps firms define what *quality* means for them. According to the U.S. Commerce Department's National Institute of Standards and Technology (NIST), investing in quality principles and performance excellence pays off in increased productivity, satisfied employees and customers, and improved profitability, both for customers and investors. The seven major criteria for the award are the following:[4]

1. *Leadership.* Examines how senior executives guide the organization and how the organization addresses its responsibilities to the public and practices good citizenship.
2. *Strategic Planning.* Examines how the organization sets strategic directions and how it determines key action plans.
3. *Customer and Market Focus.* Examines how the organization determines requirements and expectations of customers and markets; builds relationships with customers; and acquires, satisfies and retains customers.
4. *Measurement, Analysis, and Knowledge Management.* Examines the management, effective use, analysis, and improvement of data and information to support key organizational processes and the organization's performance management system.
5. *Human Resource Focus.* Examines how the organization enables its workforce to develop its full potential and how the workforce is aligned with the organization's objectives.
6. *Process Management.* Examines aspects of how key production/delivery and support processes are designed, managed, and improved.
7. *Business Results.* Examines the organization's performance and improvement in its key business goals: including customer satisfaction, financial and marketplace performance, human resources, supplier and partner performance, operational performance, and governance and social responsibility. The category also examines how the organization performs relative to competitors.

Customer satisfaction underpins these seven criteria. Criterion 7, business results, is given the most weight in selecting winners.

---

[4]Details on the Malcolm Baldrige National Quality program can be found at www.quality.nist.gov.

> STUDENT CD-ROM AND INTERNET RESOURCES <

The Student CD-ROM and the Companion Website at **www.prenhall.com/krajewski** contain many tools, activities, and resources designed for this chapter.

> KEY EQUATIONS <

1. Mean: $\bar{x} = \dfrac{\sum\limits_{i=1}^{n} x_i}{n}$

2. Standard deviation of a sample:

$$\sigma = \sqrt{\frac{\Sigma(x_i - \bar{x})^2}{n-1}} \quad \text{or} \quad \sigma = \sqrt{\frac{\Sigma x^2 - \dfrac{(\Sigma x_i)^2}{n}}{n-1}}$$

3. Control limits for variable process control charts

   a. R-chart, range of sample:

   Upper control limit $= \text{UCL}_R = D_4 \bar{R}$
   Lower control limit $= \text{LCL}_R = D_3 \bar{R}$

   b. $\bar{x}$-chart, sample mean:

   Upper control limit $= \text{UCL}_{\bar{x}} = \bar{\bar{x}} + A_2 \bar{R}$
   Lower control limit $= \text{LCL}_{\bar{x}} = \bar{\bar{x}} - A_2 \bar{R}$

   c. When the standard deviation of the process distribution, σ, is known:

   Upper control limit $= \text{UCL}_{\bar{x}} = \bar{\bar{x}} + z\sigma_{\bar{x}}$
   Lower control limit $= \text{LCL}_{\bar{x}} = \bar{\bar{x}} - z\sigma_{\bar{x}}$

where

$$\sigma_{\bar{x}} = \frac{\sigma}{\sqrt{n}}$$

4. Control limits for attribute process control charts

   a. p-chart, proportion defective:

   Upper control limit $= \text{UCL}_p = \bar{p} + z\sigma_p$
   Lower control limit $= \text{LCL}_p = \bar{p} - z\sigma_p$

   where

   $$\sigma_p = \sqrt{\bar{p}(1-\bar{p})/n}$$

   b. c-chart, number of defects:

   Upper control limit $= \text{UCL}_c = \bar{c} + z\sqrt{\bar{c}}$
   Lower control limit $= \text{LCL}_c = \bar{c} - z\sqrt{\bar{c}}$

5. Process capability ratio:

$$C_p = \frac{\text{Upper specification} - \text{Lower specification}}{6\sigma}$$

6. Process capability index:

$$C_{pk} = \text{Minimum of}$$
$$\left[\frac{\bar{\bar{x}} - \text{Lower specification}}{3\sigma}, \frac{\text{Upper specification} - \bar{\bar{x}}}{3\sigma} \right]$$

> KEY TERMS <

> SOLVED PROBLEM 1 <

The Watson Electric Company produces incandescent light-bulbs. The following data on the number of lumens for 40-watt lightbulbs were collected when the process was in control.

	Observation			
Sample	**1**	**2**	**3**	**4**
1	604	612	588	600
2	597	601	607	603
3	581	570	585	592
4	620	605	595	588
5	590	614	608	604

a. Calculate control limits for an R-chart and an $\bar{x}$-chart.

b. Since these data were collected, some new employees were hired. A new sample obtained the following readings: 570, 603, 623, and 583. Is the process still in control?

SOLUTION

a. To calculate $\bar{x}$, compute the mean for each sample. To calculate R, subtract the lowest value in the sample from the highest value in the sample. For example, for sample 1,

$$\bar{x} = \frac{604+612+588+600}{4} = 601$$

$$R = 612 - 588 = 24$$

Sample	$\bar{x}$	R
1	601	24
2	602	10
3	582	22
4	602	32
5	604	24
Total	2,991	112
Average	$\bar{\bar{x}} = 598.2$	$\bar{R} = 22.4$

The R-chart control limits are

$$\text{UCL}_R = D_4\bar{R} = 2.282(22.4) = 51.12$$
$$\text{LCL}_R = D_3\bar{R} = 0(22.4) = 0$$

The $\bar{x}$-chart control limits are

$$\text{UCL}_{\bar{x}} = \bar{\bar{x}} + A_2\bar{R} = 598.2 + 0.729(22.4) = 614.53$$
$$\text{LCL}_{\bar{x}} = \bar{\bar{x}} - A_2\bar{R} = 598.2 - 0.729(22.4) = 581.87$$

b. First check to see whether the variability is still in control based on the new data. The range is 53 (or 623 − 570), which is outside the UCL for the R-chart. Even though the sample mean, 594.75, is within the control limits for the process average, process variability is not in control. A search for assignable causes must be conducted.

> SOLVED PROBLEM 2 <

The data processing department of the Arizona Bank has five data entry clerks. Each day their supervisor verifies the accuracy of a random sample of 250 records. A record containing one or more errors is considered defective and must be redone. The results of the last 30 samples are shown in the table. All were checked to make sure that none were out of control.

Sample	Number of Defective Records	Sample	Number of Defective Records	Sample	Number of Defective Records	Sample	Number of Defective Records
1	7	9	6	17	12	24	7
2	5	10	13	18	4	25	13
3	19	11	18	19	6	26	10
4	10	12	5	20	11	27	14
5	11	13	16	21	17	28	6
6	8	14	4	22	12	29	11
7	12	15	11	23	6	30	9
8	9	16	8				
						Total	300

a. Based on these historical data, set up a *p*-chart using $z = 3$.

b. Samples for the next four days showed the following:

Sample	Number of Defective Records
31	17
32	15
33	22
34	21

What is the supervisor's assessment of the data-entry process likely to be?

SOLUTION

a. From the table, the supervisor knows that the total number of defective records is 300 out of a total sample of 7,500 [or 30(250)]. Therefore, the central line of the chart is

$$\bar{p} = \frac{300}{7,500} = 0.04$$

The control limits are

$$UCL_p = \bar{p} + z\sqrt{\frac{\bar{p}(1-\bar{p})}{n}} = 0.04 + 3\sqrt{\frac{0.04(0.96)}{250}} = 0.077$$

$$LCL_p = \bar{p} - z\sqrt{\frac{\bar{p}(1-\bar{p})}{n}} = 0.04 - 3\sqrt{\frac{0.04(0.96)}{250}} = 0.003$$

b. Samples for the next four days showed the following:

Sample	Number of Defective Records	Proportion
31	17	0.068
32	15	0.060
33	22	0.088
34	21	0.084

Samples 33 and 34 are out of control. The supervisor should look for the problem and, upon identifying it, take corrective action.

> SOLVED PROBLEM 3 <

The Minnow County Highway Safety Department monitors accidents at the intersection of Routes 123 and 14. Accidents at the intersection have averaged three per month.

a. Which type of control chart should be used? Construct a control chart with three-sigma control limits.

b. Last month, seven accidents occurred at the intersection. Is this sufficient evidence to justify a claim that something has changed at the intersection?

SOLUTION

a. The safety department cannot determine the number of accidents that did *not* occur, so it has no way to compute a proportion defective at the intersection. Therefore, the administrators must use a *c*-chart for which

$$UCL_c = \bar{c} + z\sqrt{\bar{c}} = 3 + 3\sqrt{3} = 8.20$$
$$LCL_c = \bar{c} - z\sqrt{\bar{c}} = 3 - 3\sqrt{3} = -2.196$$

There cannot be a negative number of accidents, so the LCL in this case is adjusted to zero.

b. The number of accidents last month falls within the UCL and LCL of the chart. We conclude that no assignable causes are present and that the increase in accidents was due to chance.

> SOLVED PROBLEM 4 <

Pioneer Chicken advertises "lite" chicken with 30 percent fewer calories. (The pieces are 33 percent smaller.) The process average distribution for "lite" chicken breasts is 420 calories, with a standard deviation of the population of 25 calories. Pioneer randomly takes samples of six chicken breasts to measure calorie content.

a. Design an $\bar{x}$-chart, using the process standard deviation.

b. The product design calls for the average chicken breast to contain 400 ± 100 calories. Calculate the process capability index (target = 1.33) and the process capability ratio. Interpret the results.

SOLUTION

a. For the process standard deviation of 25 calories, the standard deviation of the sample mean is

$$\sigma_{\bar{x}} = \frac{\sigma}{\sqrt{n}} = \frac{25}{\sqrt{6}} = 10.2 \text{ calories}$$

$$\text{UCL}_{\bar{x}} = \bar{\bar{x}} + z\sigma_{\bar{x}} = 420 + 3(10.2) = 450.6 \text{ calories}$$

$$\text{LCL}_{\bar{x}} = \bar{\bar{x}} - z\sigma_{\bar{x}} = 420 - 3(10.2) = 389.4 \text{ calories}$$

b. The process capability index is

$$C_{pk} = \text{Minimum of} \left[\frac{\bar{\bar{x}} - \text{Lower specification}}{3\sigma}, \frac{\text{Upper specification} - \bar{\bar{x}}}{3\sigma} \right]$$

$$= \text{Minimum of} \left[\frac{420 - 300}{3(25)} = 1.60, \frac{500 - 420}{3(25)} = 1.07 \right] = 1.07$$

The process capability ratio is

$$C_p = \frac{\text{Upper specification} - \text{Lower specification}}{6\sigma} = \frac{500 \text{ calories} - 300 \text{ calories}}{6(25)} = 1.33$$

Because the process capability ratio is 1.33, the process should be able to produce the product reliably within specifications. However, the process capability index is 1.07, so the current process is not centered properly for four-sigma performance. The mean of the process distribution is too close to the upper specification.

> DISCUSSION QUESTIONS <

1. Considerable success has been achieved by companies practicing TQM. What are the major hurdles to continuing quality improvements that manufacturers and service providers face?

2. Recently, the Polish General Corporation, well-known for manufacturing appliances and automobile parts, initiated a $13 billion project to produce automobiles. A great deal of learning on the part of management and employees was required. Even though pressure was mounting to get a new product to market in early 2007, the production manager of the newly formed automobile division insisted on almost a year of trial runs before sales started because workers have to do their jobs 60 to 100 times before they can memorize the right sequence. The launch date was set for early 2008. What are the consequences of using this approach to entering the market with a new product?

3. Form a group and choose a service provider or manufacturer and a functional area, such as accounting, finance, or marketing. Define a process important to that functional area and then identify a key performance measure for that process. How can SPC be used to manage that process?

> PROBLEMS <

Software, such as OM Explorer, Active Models, and POM for Windows, is packaged with every new copy of the textbook. Check with your instructor on how best to use it. In many cases, the instructor wants you to understand how to do the calculations by hand. At most, the software provides a check on your calculations. When calculations are particularly complex and the goal is interpreting the results in making decisions, the software replaces entirely the manual calculations. The software also can be a valuable resource well after your course is completed.

1. At Quickie Car Wash, the wash process is advertised to take less than 7 minutes. Consequently, management has set a target average of 390 seconds for the wash process. Suppose the average range for a sample of nine cars is 10 seconds. Use Table 6.1 to establish control limits for sample means and ranges for the car wash process.

2. At Isogen Pharmaceuticals, the filling process for its asthma inhaler is set to dispense 150 milliliters (ml) of steroid solution per container. The average range for a sample of 4 containers is 3 ml. Use Table 6.1 to establish control limits for sample means and ranges for the filling process.

3. Garcia's Garage desires to create some colorful charts and graphs to illustrate how reliably its mechanics "get under the hood and fix the problem." The historic average for

the proportion of customers that return for the same repair within the 30-day warranty period is 0.10. Each month, Garcia tracks 100 customers to see whether they return for warranty repairs. The results are plotted as a proportion to report progress toward the goal. If the control limits are to be set at two standard deviations on either side of the goal, determine the control limits for this chart. In March, 8 of the 100 customers in the sample group returned for warranty repairs. Is the repair process in control?

4. The Canine Gourmet Company produces delicious dog treats for canines with discriminating tastes. Management wants the box-filling line to be set so that the process average weight per packet is 45 grams. To make sure that the process is in control, an inspector at the end of the filling line periodically selects a random box of 10 packets and weighs each packet. When the process is in control, the range in the weight of each sample has averaged 6 grams.

   a. Design an R- and an $\bar{x}$-chart for this process.

   b. The results from the last five samples of 10 packets are

Sample	$\bar{x}$	R
1	44	9
2	40	2
3	46	5
4	39	8
5	48	3

   Is the process in control? Explain.

5. The Marlin Company produces plastic bottles to customer order. The quality inspector randomly selects four

bottles from the bottle machine and measures the outside diameter of the bottle neck, a critical quality dimension that determines whether the bottle cap will fit properly. The dimensions (in.) from the last six samples are

	Bottle			
Sample	1	2	3	4
1	0.604	0.612	0.588	0.600
2	0.597	0.601	0.607	0.603
3	0.581	0.570	0.585	0.592
4	0.620	0.605	0.595	0.588
5	0.590	0.614	0.608	0.604
6	0.585	0.583	0.617	0.579

   a. Assume that only these six samples are sufficient, and use the data to determine control limits for an R- and an $\bar{x}$-chart.

   b. Suppose that the specification for the bottle neck diameter is 0.600 ± 0.050 in. If the population standard deviation is 0.012 in., and the firm is seeking four-sigma quality, is the process capable of producing the bottle?

6. In an attempt to judge and monitor the quality of instruction, the administration of Mega-Byte Academy devised an examination to test students on the basic concepts that all should have learned. Each year, a random sample of 10 graduating students is selected for the test. The average score is used to track the quality of the educational process. Test results for the past 10 years are shown in Table 6.2.

TABLE 6.2 | Test Scores on Exit Exam

	Student										
Year	1	2	3	4	5	6	7	8	9	10	Average
1	63	57	92	87	70	61	75	58	63	71	69.7
2	90	77	59	88	48	83	63	94	72	70	74.4
3	67	81	93	55	71	71	86	98	60	90	77.2
4	62	67	78	61	89	93	71	59	93	84	75.7
5	85	88	77	69	58	90	97	72	64	60	76.0
6	60	57	79	83	64	94	86	64	92	74	75.3
7	94	85	56	77	89	72	71	61	92	97	79.4
8	97	86	83	88	65	87	76	84	81	71	81.8
9	94	90	76	88	65	93	86	87	94	63	83.6
10	88	91	71	89	97	79	93	87	69	85	84.9

Use these data to estimate the center and standard deviation for this distribution. Then calculate the two-sigma control limits for the process average. What comments would you make to the administration of the Mega-Byte Academy?

7. As a hospital administrator of a large hospital, you are concerned with the absenteeism among nurses' aides. The issue has been raised by registered nurses, who feel they often have to perform work normally done by their aides. To get the facts, absenteeism data were gathered for the last two weeks, which is considered a representative period for future conditions. After taking random samples of 64 personnel files each day, the following data were produced:

Day	Aides Absent	Day	Aides Absent
1	4	9	7
2	3	10	2
3	2	11	3
4	4	12	2
5	2	13	1
6	5	14	3
7	3	15	4
8	4		

Because your assessment of absenteeism is likely to come under careful scrutiny, you would like a type I error of only 1 percent. You want to be sure to identify any instances of unusual absences. If some are present, you will have to explore them on behalf of the registered nurses.

a. Design a p-chart.

b. Based on your p-chart and the data from the last 2 weeks, what can you conclude about the absenteeism of nurses' aides?

8. A textile manufacturer wants to set up a control chart for irregularities (e.g., oil stains, shop soil, loose threads, and tears) per 100 square yards of carpet. The following data were collected from a sample of twenty 100-square-yard pieces of carpet.

Sample	1	2	3	4	5	6	7	8	9	10
Irregularities	11	8	9	12	4	16	5	8	17	10
Sample	11	12	13	14	15	16	17	18	19	20
Irregularities	11	5	7	12	13	8	19	11	9	10

a. Using these data, set up a c-chart with $z = 3$.

b. Suppose that the next five samples had 15, 18, 12, 22, and 21 irregularities. What do you conclude?

9. The IRS is concerned with improving the accuracy of tax information given by its representatives over the telephone. Previous studies involved asking a set of 25 questions of a large number of IRS telephone representatives to determine the proportion of correct responses. Historically, the average proportion of correct responses has been 70 percent. Recently, IRS representatives have been receiving more training. On April 1, the set of 25 tax questions were again asked of 20 randomly selected IRS telephone representatives. The proportions of correct answers were 0.88, 0.76, 0.64, 1.00, 0.76, 0.76, 0.72, 0.88, 0.50, 0.50, 0.40, 1.00, 0.88, 1.00, 0.64, 0.76, 0.76, 0.88, 0.40, and 0.76. Interpret the results of that study.

10. A travel agency is concerned with the accuracy and appearance of itineraries prepared for its clients. Defects can include errors in times, airlines, flight numbers, prices, car rental information, lodging, charge card numbers, and reservation numbers, as well as typographical errors. As the possible number of errors is nearly infinite, the agency measures the number of errors that do occur. The current process results in an average of three errors per itinerary.

a. What are the two-sigma control limits for these defects?

b. A client scheduled a trip to Dallas. Her itinerary contained six errors. Interpret this information.

11. Jim's Outfitters, Inc., makes custom fancy shirts for cowboys. The shirts could be flawed in various ways, including flaws in the weave or color of the fabric, loose buttons or decorations, wrong dimensions, and uneven stitches. Jim randomly examined 10 shirts, with the following results:

Shirt	Defects
1	8
2	0
3	7
4	12
5	5
6	10
7	2
8	4
9	6
10	6

a. Assuming that 10 observations are adequate for these purposes, determine the three-sigma control limits for defects per shirt.

b. Suppose that the next shirt has 13 flaws. What can you say about the process now?

12. The Big Black Bird Company produces fiberglass camper tops. The process for producing the tops must be con-

trolled so as to keep the number of dimples low. When the process was in control, the following defects were found in randomly selected sheets over an extended period of time.

Top	Dimples
1	7
2	9
3	14
4	11
5	3
6	12
7	8
8	4
9	7
10	6

a. Assuming 10 observations are adequate for these purposes, determine the three-sigma control limits for dimples per camper top.

b. Suppose that the next camper top has 15 dimples. What can you say about the process now?

13. The production manager at Sunny Soda, Inc., is interested in tracking the quality of the company's 12-ounce bottle filling line. The bottles must be filled within the tolerances set for this product because the dietary information on the label shows 12 ounces as the serving size. The design standard for the product calls for a fill level of 12.00 ± 0.10 ounces. The manager collected the following sample data (in fluid ounces per bottle) on the production process:

	Observation			
Sample	1	2	3	4
1	12.00	11.97	12.10	12.08
2	11.91	11.94	12.10	11.96
3	11.89	12.02	11.97	11.99
4	12.10	12.09	12.05	11.95
5	12.08	11.92	12.12	12.05
6	11.94	11.98	12.06	12.08
7	12.09	12.00	12.00	12.03
8	12.01	12.04	11.99	11.95
9	12.00	11.96	11.97	12.03
10	11.92	11.94	12.09	12.00
11	11.91	11.99	12.05	12.10
12	12.01	12.00	12.06	11.97
13	11.98	11.99	12.06	12.03
14	12.02	12.00	12.05	11.95
15	12.00	12.05	12.01	11.97

a. Are the process average and range in statistical control?

b. Is the process capable of meeting the design standard at four-sigma quality? Explain.

14. The Money Pit Mortgage Company is interested in monitoring the performance of the mortgage process. Fifteen samples of five completed mortgage transactions each were taken during a period when the process was believed to be in control. The times to complete the transactions were measured. The means and ranges of the mortgage process transaction times, measured in days, are as follows.

Sample	1	2	3	4	5	6	7	8	9	10	11	12	13	14	15
Mean	17	14	8	17	12	13	15	16	13	14	16	9	11	9	12
Range	6	11	4	8	9	14	12	15	10	10	11	6	9	11	13

Subsequently, samples of size 5 were taken from the process every week for the next 10 weeks. The times were measured and the following results obtained.

Sample	16	17	18	19	20	21	22	23	24	25
Mean	11	14	9	15	17	19	13	22	20	18
Range	7	11	6	4	12	14	11	10	8	6

a. Construct the control charts for the mean and the range, using the original 15 samples. Were these samples sufficient for developing the control chart? Explain your answer.

b. On the control charts, plot the sample values subsequently obtained and comment on whether the process is in control.

c. In part (b), if you concluded that the process was out of control, would you attribute it to a drift in the mean, or an increase in the variability, or both? Explain your answer.

15. The Money Pit Mortgage Company of Problem 14 made some changes to the process and undertook a process capability study. The following data were obtained for 15 samples of size 5. Based on the individual observations, management estimated the process standard deviation to be 4.21 (days) for use in the process capability analysis. The lower and upper specification limits (in days) for the mortgage process times were 5 and 25.

Sample	1	2	3	4	5	6	7	8	9	10	11	12	13	14	15
Mean	11	12	8	16	13	12	17	16	13	14	17	9	15	14	9
Range	9	13	4	11	10	9	8	15	14	11	6	6	12	10	11

a. Calculate the process capability ratio and the process capability index values.

b. Suppose management would be happy with three-sigma performance. What conclusions is management likely to draw from the capability analysis? Can valid conclusions about the process be drawn from the analysis?

c. What remedial actions, if any, do you suggest that management take?

16. Webster Chemical Company produces mastics and caulking for the construction industry. The product is blended in large mixers and then pumped into tubes and capped. Management is concerned about whether the filling process for tubes of caulking is in statistical control. The process should be centered on 8 ounces per tube. Several samples of eight tubes were taken, each tube was weighed, and the weights in Table 6.3 were obtained.

a. Assume that only six samples are sufficient and develop the control charts for the mean and the range.

b. Plot the observations on the control chart and comment on your findings.

17. Management at Webster, in Problem 16, is now concerned as to whether caulking tubes are being properly capped. If a significant proportion of the tubes are not being sealed, Webster is placing its customers in a messy situation. Tubes are packaged in large boxes of 144. Several boxes are inspected, and the following numbers of leaking tubes are found:

Sample	Tubes	Sample	Tubes	Sample	Tubes
1	3	8	6	15	5
2	5	9	4	16	0
3	3	10	9	17	2
4	4	11	2	18	6
5	2	12	6	19	2
6	4	13	5	20	1
7	2	14	1	Total	72

Calculate p-chart three-sigma control limits to assess whether the capping process is in statistical control.

18. At Webster Chemical Company, lumps in the caulking compound could cause difficulties in dispensing a smooth bead from the tube. Even when the process is in control, an average of four lumps per tube of caulk will remain. Testing for the presence of lumps destroys the product, so an analyst takes random samples. The following results are obtained.

Tube No.	Lumps	Tube No.	Lumps	Tube No.	Lumps
1	6	5	6	9	5
2	5	6	4	10	0
3	0	7	1	11	9
4	4	8	6	12	2

Determine the c-chart two-sigma upper and lower control limits for this process.

19. A critical dimension of a certain service is its time. Periodically, random samples of three service instances are measured for time. The results of the last four samples are in the following table.

Sample	Time (sec)		
1	495	501	498
2	512	508	504
3	505	497	501
4	496	503	492

a. Assuming that management is willing to use three-sigma limits, and using only the historical information contained in the four samples, show that the process producing the service is in statistical control.

TABLE 6.3 | Ounces of Caulking per Tube

	Tube Number							
Sample	1	2	3	4	5	6	7	8
1	7.98	8.34	8.02	7.94	8.44	7.68	7.81	8.11
2	8.33	8.22	8.08	8.51	8.41	8.28	8.09	8.16
3	7.89	7.77	7.91	8.04	8.00	7.89	7.93	8.09
4	8.24	8.18	7.83	8.05	7.90	8.16	7.97	8.07
5	7.87	8.13	7.92	7.99	8.10	7.81	8.14	7.88
6	8.13	8.14	8.11	8.13	8.14	8.12	8.13	8.14

b. Suppose that the standard deviation of the process distribution is 5.77. If the specifications for the time of the service are 500 ± 18 sec, is the process capable? Why or why not? Assume three-sigma quality.

20. An automatic lathe produces rollers for roller bearings, and the process is monitored by statistical process control charts. The central line of the chart for the sample means is set at 8.50 and for the mean range at 0.31 mm. The process is in control, as established by samples of size 5. The upper and lower specifications for the diameter of the rollers are (8.50 + 0.25) and (8.50 − 0.25) mm, respectively.

   a. Calculate the control limits for the mean and range charts.

   b. If the standard deviation of the process distribution is estimated to be 0.13 mm, is the process capable of meeting specifications? Assume four-sigma quality.

   c. If the process is not capable, what percent of the output will fall outside the specification limits? (*Hint:* Use the normal distribution.)

ADVANCED PROBLEMS

21. Canine Gourmet Super Breath dog treats are sold in boxes labeled with a net weight of 12 ounces (340 grams) per box. Each box contains eight individual 1.5-ounce packets. To reduce the chances of shorting the customer, product design specifications call for the packet-filling process average to be set at 43.5 grams so that the average net weight per box will be 348 grams. Tolerances are set for the box to weigh 348 ± 12 grams. The standard deviation for the *packet-filling* process is 1.01 grams. The target process capability ratio is 1.33. One day, the packet-filling process average weight drifts down to 43.0 grams. Is the packaging process capable? Is an adjustment needed?

22. The Precision Machining Company makes hand-held tools on an assembly line that produces one product every minute. On one of the products, the critical quality dimension is the diameter (measured in thousandths of an inch) of a hole bored in one of the assemblies. Management wants to detect any shift in the process average diameter from 0.015 in. Management considers the variance in the process to be in control. Historically, the average range has been 0.002 in., regardless of the process average. Design an $\bar{x}$-chart to control this process, with a center line at 0.015 in. and the control limits set at three sigmas from the center line.

   Management provided the results of 80 minutes of output from the production line, as shown in Table 6.4. During this 80 minutes, the process average changed once. All measurements are in thousandths of an inch.

   a. Set up an $\bar{x}$-chart with $n = 4$. The frequency should be sample four, then skip four. Thus, your first sample would be for minutes 1–4, the second would be for minutes 9–12, and so on. When would you stop the process to check for a change in the process average?

   b. Set up an $\bar{x}$-chart with $n = 8$. The frequency should be sample eight, then skip four. When would you stop the process now? What can you say about the desirability of large samples on a frequent sampling interval?

23. Using the data from Problem 22, continue your analysis of sample size and frequency by trying the following plans.

   a. Using the $\bar{x}$-chart for $n = 4$, try the frequency sample four, then skip eight. When would you stop the process in this case?

   b. Using the $\bar{x}$-chart for $n = 8$, try the frequency sample eight, then skip eight. When would you consider the process to be out of control?

   c. Using your results from parts (a) and (b), determine what trade-offs you would consider in choosing between them.

24. The manager of the customer service department of Omega Credit Card Service Company is concerned about the number of defects produced by the billing

TABLE 6.4	Sample Data for Precision Machining Company

Minutes	Diameter											
1–12	15	16	18	14	16	17	15	14	14	13	16	17
13–24	15	16	17	16	14	14	13	14	15	16	15	17
25–36	14	13	15	17	18	15	16	15	14	15	16	17
37–48	18	16	15	16	16	14	17	18	19	15	16	15
49–60	12	17	16	14	15	17	14	16	15	17	18	14
61–72	15	16	17	18	13	15	14	14	16	15	17	18
73–80	16	16	17	18	16	15	14	17				

TABLE 6.5	Sample Data for Omega Credit Card Service								
Samples	**Number of Errors in Sample of 250**								
1–10	4	9	6	12	8	2	13	10	1	9
11–20	4	6	8	10	12	4	3	10	14	5
21–30	13	11	7	3	2	8	11	6	9	5

process. Every day a random sample of 250 statements was inspected for errors regarding incorrect entries involving account numbers, transactions on the customer's account, interest charges, and penalty charges. Any statement with one or more of these errors was considered a defect. The study lasted 30 days and yielded the data in Table 6.5. Based on the data, what can you tell the manager about the performance of the billing process? Do you see any nonrandom behavior in the billing process? If so, what might cause this behavior?

25. Red Baron Airlines serves hundreds of cities each day, but competition is increasing from smaller companies affiliated with major carriers. One of the key competitive priorities is on-time arrivals and departures. Red Baron defines *on time* as any arrival or departure that takes place within 15 minutes of the scheduled time. To stay on top of the market, management set the high standard of 98 percent on-time performance. The operations department was put in charge of monitoring the performance of the airline. Each week, a random sample of 300 flight arrivals and departures was checked for schedule performance. Table 6.6 contains the numbers of arrivals and departures over the last 30 weeks that did not meet Red Baron's definition of on-time service. What can you tell management about the quality of service? Can you identify any nonran-

dom behavior in the process? If so, what might cause the behavior?

26. Beaver Brothers, Inc., is conducting a study to assess the capability of its 150-gram bar soap production line. A critical quality measure is the weight of the soap bars after stamping. The upper and lower specification limits are 162 and 170 grams, respectively. As a part of an initial capability study, 25 samples of size 5 were collected by the quality assurance group and the observations in Table 6.7 were recorded.

After analyzing the data by using statistical control charts, the quality assurance group calculated the process capability ratio, C_p, and the process capability index, C_{pk}. It then decided to improve the stamping process, especially the feeder mechanism. After making all the changes that were deemed necessary, 18 additional samples were collected. The summary data for these samples are

$$\bar{\bar{x}} = 163 \text{ grams}$$
$$\bar{R} = 2.326 \text{ grams}$$
$$\sigma = 1 \text{ gram}$$

All sample observations were within the control chart limits. With the new data, the quality assurance group recalculated the process capability measures. It was pleased with the improved C_p but felt that the process

TABLE 6.6	Sample Data for Red Baron Airlines								
Samples	**Number of Late Planes in Sample of 300 Arrivals and Departures**								
1–10	3	8	5	11	7	2	12	9	1	8
11–20	3	5	7	9	12	5	4	9	13	4
21–30	12	10	6	2	1	8	4	5	8	2

TABLE 6.7	Sample Data for Beaver Brothers, Inc.				
Sample	**OBS.1**	**OBS.2**	**OBS.3**	**OBS.4**	**OBS.5**
1	167.0	159.6	161.6	164.0	165.3
2	156.2	159.5	161.7	164.0	165.3
3	167.0	162.9	162.9	164.0	165.4
4	167.0	159.6	163.7	164.1	165.4
5	156.3	160.0	162.9	164.1	165.5
6	164.0	164.2	163.0	164.2	163.9
7	161.3	163.0	164.2	157.0	160.6
8	163.1	164.2	156.9	160.1	163.1
9	164.3	157.0	161.2	163.2	164.4
10	156.9	161.0	163.2	164.3	157.3
11	161.0	163.3	164.4	157.6	160.6
12	163.3	164.5	158.4	160.1	163.3
13	158.2	161.3	163.5	164.6	158.7
14	161.5	163.5	164.7	158.6	162.5
15	163.6	164.8	158.0	162.4	163.6
16	164.5	158.5	160.3	163.4	164.6
17	164.9	157.9	162.3	163.7	165.1
18	155.0	162.2	163.7	164.8	159.6
19	162.1	163.9	165.1	159.3	162.0
20	165.2	159.1	161.6	163.9	165.2
21	164.9	165.1	159.9	162.0	163.7
22	167.6	165.6	165.6	156.7	165.7
23	167.7	165.8	165.9	156.9	165.9
24	166.0	166.0	165.6	165.6	165.5
25	163.7	163.7	165.6	165.6	166.2

should be centered at 166 grams to ensure that everything was in order. Its decision concluded the study.

a. Draw the control charts for the data obtained in the initial study and verify that the process was in statistical control.

b. What were the values obtained by the group for C_p and C_{pk} for the initial capability study? Comment on your

findings and explain why further improvements were necessary.

c. What are the C_p and C_{pk} after the improvements? Comment on your findings, indicating why the group decided to change the centering of the process.

d. What are the C_p and C_{pk} if the process were centered at 166? Comment on your findings.

> ACTIVE MODEL EXERCISE <

This Active Model appears on the Student CD-ROM. It allows you to see the effects of sample size and *z*-values on control charts.

ACTIVE MODEL 6.2

p-Chart Using Data from Example 6.3

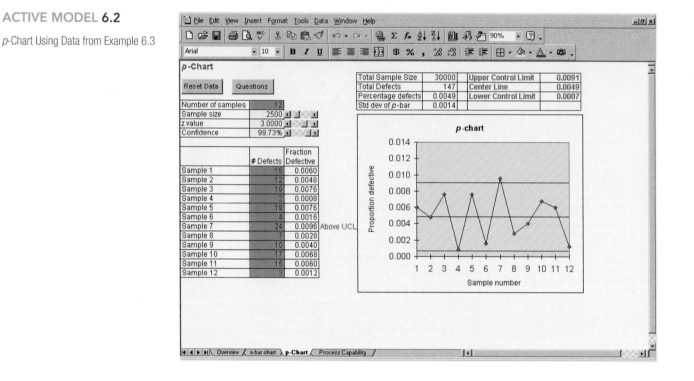

> QUESTIONS <

1. Has the booking process been in statistical control?

2. Suppose we use a 95 percent *p*-chart. How do the upper and lower control limits change? What are your conclusions about the booking process?

3. Suppose that the sample size is reduced to 2,000 instead of 2,500. How does this affect the chart?

4. What happens to the chart as we reduce the *z*-value?

5. What happens to the chart as we reduce the confidence level?

<table>
<tr><td>EXPERIENTIAL LEARNING</td><td>Statistical Process Control with a Coin Catapult</td></tr>
</table>

Exercise A: Control Charts for Variables

Materials

1 ruler

1 pen or pencil

1 coin (a quarter will do nicely)

1 yardstick

An exercise worksheet

Access to a calculator

Tasks

Divide into teams of two to four. If four people are on a team,

one person holds the yardstick and observes the action,

one person adjusts the catapult and launches the coin,

one person observes the maximum height for each trial, and

one person records the results.

If teams of fewer than four are formed, provide a support for the yardstick and combine the other tasks as appropriate.

Practice

To catapult the coin, put a pen or pencil under the 6-in. mark of the ruler. Put the coin over the 11-in. mark. Press both ends of the ruler down as far as they will go. Let the end that holds the coin snap up, catapulting the coin into the air. The person holding the yardstick should place the stick so that it is adjacent to, but does not interfere with, the trajectory of the coin. To observe the maximum height reached by the coin, the observer should stand back with his or her eye at about the same level as the top of the coin's trajectory. Practice until each person is comfortable with his or her role. The person operating the catapult should be sure that the pen or pencil fulcrum has not moved between shots and that the launch is done as consistently as possible.

Step 1: *Gather data.* Take four samples of five observations (launches) each. Record the maximum height reached by the coin in the first data table on the worksheet. When you have finished, determine the mean and range for each sample, and compute the mean of the means $\bar{\bar{x}}$ and the mean of the ranges $\bar{R}$.

Step 2: *Develop an R-chart.* Using the data gathered and the appropriate D_3 and D_4 values, compute the upper and lower three-sigma control limits for the range. Enter these values and plot the range for each of the four samples on the range chart on the worksheet. Be sure to indicate an appropriate scale for range on the y axis.

Step 3: *Develop an $\bar{x}$-chart.* Now, using the data gathered and the appropriate value for A_2, compute the upper and lower three-sigma control limits for the sample means. Enter these values and plot the mean for each of the four samples on the $\bar{x}$-chart on the worksheet. Again, indicate an appropriate scale for the y axis.

Step 4: *Observe the process.* Once a control chart has been established for a process, it is used to monitor the process and to identify when it isn't running "normally." Collect two more samples of five trials each, as you did to collect the first set of data. Plot the range and the sample mean on the charts you constructed on the worksheet each time you collect a sample. What have you observed that affects the process? Does the chart indicate that the process is operating the way it did when you first collected data?

Step 5: *Observe a changed process.* Now change something (for instance, move the pencil out to the 8-in. mark). Collect data for samples 7 and 8. Plot the range and the sample mean on the charts you constructed on the worksheet as you complete each sample. Can you detect a change in the process from your control chart? If the process has changed, how sure are you that this change is real and not just due to the particular sample you chose?

Exercise B: Control Charts for Attributes

Materials

1 ruler

1 pen or pencil

1 coin (a quarter will do nicely)

1 paper or plastic cup (with a 4-in. mouth)

An exercise worksheet

Access to a calculator

Tasks

Divide into teams of two or three. If three people are on a team,

one person adjusts the catapult and launches the coin,

one person observes the results and fetches the coin, and

one person records the results.

If teams of two are formed, combine the tasks as appropriate.

Practice

The object is to flip a coin into a cup using a ruler. To catapult the coin, put a pen or pencil under the 6-in. mark of the ruler.

Put a coin over the 11-in. mark and let its weight hold that end of the ruler on the tabletop. Strike the raised end of the ruler with your hand to flip the coin into the air. Position a cup at the place where the coin lands so that on the next flip, the coin will land inside. You will have to practice several times until you find out how hard to hit the ruler and the best position for the cup. Be sure that the pen or pencil fulcrum has not moved between shots and that the launch is done as consistently as possible.

Step 1: *Gather data.* Try to catapult the coin into the cup 10 times for each sample. Record each trial in the data table on the worksheet as a hit (H) when the coin lands inside or a miss (M) when it does not. The proportion of misses will be the number of misses divided by the sample size, n, in this case 10. A miss is a "defect," so the proportion of misses is the proportion defective, p.

Step 2: *Develop a p-chart.* Compute the upper and lower three-sigma control limits for the average fraction defective. Plot these values and the mean for each of the four samples on the p-chart on the worksheet.

Step 3: *Observe the process.* Once a chart has been established for a process, it is used to monitor the process and to identify abnormal behavior. Exchange tasks so that someone else is catapulting the coin. After several practice launches, take four more samples of 10. Plot the proportion defective for this person's output. Is the process still in control? If it is not, how sure are you that it is out of control? Can you determine the control limits for a 95 percent confidence level? With these limits, was your revised process still in control?

Source: The basis for Exercise A was written by J. Christopher Sandvig, Western Washington University, as a variation of the "Catapulting Coins" exercise from *Games and Exercises for Operations Management* by Janelle Heinke and Larry Meile (Prentice Hall, 1995). Given these foundations, Larry Meile of Boston College wrote Exercise A. He also wrote Exercise B as a new extension.

> SELECTED REFERENCES <

Besterfield, Dale. *Quality Control*, 6th ed. Upper Saddle River, NJ: Prentice Hall, 2001.

Brady, Diane. "Will Jeff Immelt's New Push Pay Off for GE?" *Business Week* (October 13, 2003), pp. 94–98.

Brown, Ed. "The Best Business Hotels." *Fortune* (March 17, 1997), pp. 204–205.

Collier, David A. *The Service Quality Solution.* New York: Irwin Professional Publishing; Milwaukee: ASQC Quality Press, 1994.

Crosby, Philip B. *Quality Is Free: The Art of Making Quality Certain.* New York: McGraw-Hill, 1979.

Deming, W. Edwards. *Out of the Crisis.* Cambridge, MA: Massachusetts Institute of Technology Center for Advanced Engineering Study, 1986.

Denton, D. Keith. "Lessons on Competitiveness: Motorola's Approach." *Production and Inventory Management Journal* (Third Quarter 1991), pp. 22–25.

Duncan, Acheson J. *Quality Control and Industrial Statistics*, 5th ed. Homewood, IL: Irwin, 1986.

Feigenbaum, A.V. *Total Quality Control: Engineering and Management*, 3d ed. New York: McGraw-Hill, 1983.

Hartvigsen, David. *SimQuick: Process Simulation with Excel*, 2d ed. Upper Saddle River, NJ: Prentice Hall, 2004.

Juran, J. M., and Frank Gryna, Jr. *Quality Planning and Analysis*, 2d ed. New York: McGraw-Hill, 1980.

Kalinosky, Ian S. "The Total Quality System—Going Beyond ISO 9000." *Quality Progress* (June 1990), pp. 50–53.

Katzenbach, Jon R., and Douglas K. Smith. "The Discipline of Teams." *Harvard Business Review* (March–April 1993), pp. 111–120.

Kerwin, Kathleen. "When Flawless Isn't Enough." *Business Week* (December 8, 2003), pp. 80–82.

Lazarus, Ian R., and Keith Butler. "The Promise of Six Sigma." *Managed Healthcare Executive* (October 2001), pp. 22–26.

Lucier, Gregory T., and Sridhar Seshadri. "GE Takes Six Sigma Beyond the Bottom Line." *Strategic Finance* (May 2001), pp. 41–46.

Miller, Bill. "ISO 9000 and the Small Company: Can I Afford It?" *APICS—The Performance Advantage* (September 1994), pp. 45–46.

Mitra, Amitava. *Fundamentals of Quality Control and Improvement*, 2d ed. Upper Saddle River, NJ: Prentice Hall, 1998.

Nakhai, Benham, and Joao S. Neves. "The Deming, Baldrige, and European Quality Awards." *Quality Progress* (April 1994), pp. 33–37.

Neves, Joao S., and Benham Nakhai. "The Evolution of the Baldrige Award." *Quality Progress* (June 1994), pp. 65–70.

Pande, Peter S., Robert P. Neuman, and Roland R. Cavanagh. *The Six Sigma Way*. New York: McGraw-Hill, 2000.

Rabbitt, John T., and Peter A. Bergh. *The ISO 9000 Book*. White Plains, NY: Quality Resources, 1993.

Roth, Daniel. "Motorola Lives!" *Fortune* (September 27, 1999). pp. 305–306.

Rust, Roland T., Timothy Keiningham, Stephen Clemens, and Anthony Zahorik. "Return on Quality at Chase Manhattan Bank." *Interfaces*, vol. 29, no. 2 (March–April 1999), pp. 62–72.

Sanders, Lisa. "Going Green with Less Red Tape." *Business Week* (September 23, 1996), pp. 75–76.

Schwarz, Anne. "Listening to the Voice of the Customer Is the Key to QVC's Success." *Journal of Organizational Excellence* (Winter 2004), pp. 3–11.

Sester, Dennis. "Motorola: A Tradition of Quality." *Quality* (October 2001), pp. 30–34.

Sullivan, Lawrence P. "The Power of Taguchi Methods." *Quality Progress*, vol. 20, no. 6 (1987), pp. 76–79.

7

LEARNING GOALS

*After reading this chapter,
you should be able to:*

1. Understand the theory of constraints.
2. Define capacity and utilization and their relationship to financial performance measures.
3. Identify bottlenecks.
4. Apply theory of constraints to product mix decisions.
5. Describe economies and diseconomies of scale.
6. Identify a systematic approach to capacity planning.
7. Describe how waiting-line models, simulation, and decision trees assist capacity decisions.

After mortgage rates dropped dramatically, Eastern Financial Florida Credit Union found itself overwhelmed with applications from people looking to refinance their home loans. Company managers solved the bottleneck by implementing theory-of-constraint principles!

EASTERN FINANCIAL FLORIDA CREDIT UNION

Eastern Financial Florida Credit Union (EFFCU) is the largest credit union in South Florida and the third largest in Florida with $1.8 billion in assets. It has 21 branches in South Florida and the Tampa Bay region, serves more than 900 member companies, and provides financial services to more than 197,000 individual members, or customers. The past three years have been the most intensive for refinancing mortgages, with rates dipping to their lowest in 40 years. During this time, 92 percent of mortgage holders had economic reasons to refinance. Because of these historic rates, EFFCU's mortgage department was faced with the problem of having more loan applicants (purchase and refinance) than they were able to process in a timely manner. As a result, EFFCU was unable to commit to a closing date until late in the process, lead times were too long, priorities were constantly being shuffled, and too much expediting was necessary. These conditions created a stressful work environment where it became difficult to respond to urgent member requests. EFFCU needed help.

In December 2002, the company decided to implement theory of constraints (TOC) and related principles to create an environment in which commitments to members could be met without disrupting work flow. The company subsequently found that the bottleneck in work flow was forming in its underwriting department. In order to manage this constraint, it took measures to ensure that the underwriting department was never

>

short of work, had files to work on at all times, and provided cross-training and backup to help the department when needed. By making all other decisions around the needs of the underwriting department, EFFCU's capacity to process loans and close them on time vastly improved.

EFFCU's implementation of TOC began in March 2003. All employees involved in the First Mortgage process received training, and their incentive systems were aligned with how well they adhered to the improvement plan. When three months later mortgage rates fell to their lowest point in 40 years, EFFCU was able to meet the high demand for loans, while many

other institutions were not. Mortgage closing dates were met at a rate of better than 99 percent, and member complaints fell dramatically, even at the peak of the refinance wave. In addition, with the improved work flow, the need for employee overtime decreased.

Not surprisingly, EFFCU's profits rose. The company is now thinking about implementing similar initiatives in its Home Equity Lending Area. It has committed to an on-going plan to manage work flows even better, shorten lead times further, and make its members even more satisfied.

Source: "Eastern Financial Florida Credit Union: Gaining a Competitive Advantage for Mortgage Lending", www.goldratt.com/effcu.htm; and www.effcu.org, June 2005.

S uppose one of a firm's processes were recently reengineered, and yet results were disappointing. Costs were still high or customer satisfaction still low. What could be wrong? The answer might be constraints that remain in one or more steps in the firm's processes. A **constraint** is any factor that limits the performance of a system and restricts its output, while **capacity** is the maximum rate of output of a process or a system. When constraints exist at any step, as they did at Eastern Financial Florida Credit Union, capacity can become imbalanced—too high in some departments and too low in others. As a result, the overall output of the system suffers.

Constraints can occur up or down the supply chain, with either the firm's suppliers or customers, or within one of the firm's processes like service/product development or order fulfillment. Srikanth and Umble (1997) identify three kinds of constraints: physical (usually machine, labor, or workstation capacity or material shortages, but could be space or quality), market (demand is less than capacity), or managerial (policy, metrics, or mind-sets that create constraints that impede work flow). **Bottleneck** is a special type of a constraint that relates to capacity shortage of a process, and hence is also referred to under certain conditions as a *capacity constraint resource* (CCR). It is specifically defined as any resource whose available capacity limits the organization's ability to meet the product volume, product mix, or demand fluctuation required by the marketplace. A business system or a process would have at least one constraint or a bottleneck; otherwise its output would be unlimited.

Managers are responsible for ensuring that the firm has the capacity to meet current and future demand. Otherwise, the organization will miss out on opportunities for growth and profits. Making adjustments to overcome constraints is therefore an important part of the job. The experience of Eastern Financial Florida Credit Union and other organizations in the health care, banking, and manufacturing industries demonstrates how important managing constraints and capacity plans can be to an organization's future.

constraint

Any factor that limits the performance of a system and restricts its output.

capacity

The maximum rate of output of a process or a system.

bottleneck

A capacity constraint resource (CCR) whose available capacity limits the organizations's ability to meet the product volume, product mix, or demand fluctuation required by the marketplace.

> MANAGING CONSTRAINTS ACROSS THE ORGANIZATION <

Constraint and capacity decisions related to a process need to be made in light of the role the process plays within the organization and the value chain as a whole, because increasing or decreasing the capacity of a process will have an impact on other processes in the chain. For example, to expand its capacity, in 1989, FedEx purchased Flying Tigers, an Asia-Pacific air freight business. Due to China's surge in economic activity, the decision has proven to be a good one. However, increasing aircraft capacity by itself was not what made the decision successful. FedEx also evaluated its customer relationship process to see whether enough customer volume would make the move worthwhile. The company also examined its ground delivery process to see whether it could handle the increased loads. The entire value chain, from order entry to delivery, had to be designed for effectiveness.

The FedEx and Flying Tigers example shows that firms must manage their constraints and make capacity choices at the individual-process level, as well as at the organization level. Detailed decisions and choices made within each of these levels affect where resource constraints or bottlenecks show up, both within and across departmental lines. Relieving a bottleneck in one part of an organization might not have the desired effect unless a bottleneck in another part of the organization is also addressed. Managers everywhere must understand how to identify and manage bottlenecks, how to relate the capacity and performance measures of one process to another, and how to use that information to determine the firm's best product mix. In addition, these decisions must be made in light of several long-term issues such as the firm's economies and diseconomies of scale, capacity cushions, timing and sizing strategies, and trade-offs between customer service and capacity utilization. This chapter, organized according to the type of constraint management decisions made for different time horizons, explains how managers can best make these decisions. The first part of the chapter focuses on how best to utilize available capacity in the short term, while the second part is about revising the capacity levels and determining when to add or reduce capacity for the longer term. Both short-term as well as long-term issues associated with managing constraints and capacity are important, and must be understood in conjunction with one another.

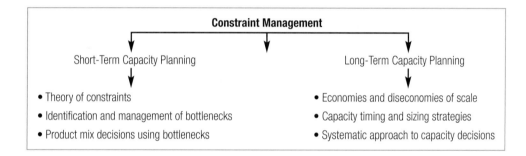

USING OPERATIONS TO COMPETE

Operations As a Competitive Weapon
Operations Strategy
Project Management

MANAGING PROCESSES

Process Strategy
Process Analysis
Process Performance and Quality
Constraint Management
Process Layout
Lean Systems

MANAGING VALUE CHAINS

Supply Chain Strategy
Location
Inventory Management
Forecasting
Sales and Operations Planning
Resource Planning
Scheduling

> THE THEORY OF CONSTRAINTS <

The **theory of constraints (TOC)** is a systematic management approach that focuses on actively managing those constraints that impede a firm's progress toward its goal of maximizing total value-added funds or sales less discounts and variable costs. The theory was developed nearly three decades ago by Eli Goldratt, a well-known business systems analyst. It outlines a deliberate process for identifying and overcoming constraints. The process focuses not just on the efficiency of individual processes, but also on the bottlenecks that constrain the system as a whole. EFFCU in the opening vignette followed this theory to improve its operations.

TOC methods increase the firm's profits more effectively than traditional cost accounting methods because they are more sensitive to the marketplace. Most cost accounting methods focus on maximizing the output of individual processes in the short run, rather than focusing on making material flow rapidly through the entire system. However, this approach will not increase systemwide profits if bottlenecks are the result. To increase profits, firms must look at the big picture—how its processes can be improved to increase the firm's overall work flows or reduce its inventory and workforce levels.

theory of constraints (TOC)
A systematic management approach that focuses on actively managing those constraints that impede a firm's progress toward its goal.

MEASURING CAPACITY, UTILIZATION, AND PERFORMANCE IN TOC

Clearly, a manager needs to be able to measure a process's capacity in order to manage short-term constraints and apply TOC. No single capacity measure is best for all situations. A retailer measures capacity as annual sales dollars generated per square foot, whereas an airline measures capacity as available seat-miles (ASMs) per month. A theater measures capacity as number of seats; a job shop measures capacity as number of machine hours. In general, capacity can be expressed in one of two ways: in terms of output measures or input measures.

Output Measures of Capacity *Output measures* of capacity are best utilized when applied to individual processes within the firm, or when the firm provides a relatively small number of standardized services and products. High-volume processes, such as those in a car manufacturing plant, are a good example. In this case, capacity would be measured in terms of the number of cars produced per day. However, many processes produce more than one service or product. As the amount of customization and variety in the product mix increases, output-based capacity measures become less useful. Then input measures of capacity become the usual choice for measuring capacity.

Input Measures of Capacity *Input measures* are generally used for low-volume, flexible processes, such as those associated with a custom furniture maker. In this case, the furniture maker might measure capacity in terms of inputs such as number of workstations or number of workers. The problem with input measures is that demand is invariably expressed as an output rate. If the furniture maker wants to keep up with demand, he or she must convert the business's annual demand for furniture into labor hours and number of employees required to fulfill those hours. We will explain precisely how this input–ouput conversion is done later in the chapter.

Utilization **Utilization** is the degree to which equipment, space, or the workforce is currently being used, and is measured as the ratio of average output rate to maximum capacity (expressed as a percent):

$$\text{Utilization} = \frac{\text{Average output rate}}{\text{Maximum capacity}} \times 100\%$$

The average output rate and the capacity must be measured in the same terms—that is, time, customers, units, or dollars. The utilization rate indicates the need for adding extra capacity or eliminating unneeded capacity. The greatest difficulty in calculating utilization lies in defining *maximum capacity*, the denominator in the ratio. A number, such as servicing 40 customers per day, does not indicate how long that rate can be sustained. Being able to handle 40 customers for a one-week peak is quite different from sustaining it for six months. Here we refer to maximum capacity as the greatest level of output that a process can reasonably sustain for a longer period, using realistic employee work schedules and the equipment currently in place. In some processes, this capacity level implies a one-shift operation; in others, it implies a three-shift operation. A process can be operated above its capacity level using marginal methods of production, such as overtime, extra shifts, temporarily reduced maintenance activities, overstaffing, and subcontracting. Although they help with temporary peaks, these options cannot be sustained for long. Employees do not want to work excessive overtime for extended periods, so quality drops. In addition, the costs associated with overtime drive up the firm's costs.

Operating processes close to (or even temporarily above) their capacity can result in low customer satisfaction, minimal profits, and even losing money despite high sales levels. Such was the case with U.S. aircraft manufacturers in the late 1980s, which culminated in Boeing acquiring McDonnell Douglas in 1997 in order to shore up skyrocketing costs and plummeting profits.

Performance Measures in TOC In order to fully comprehend the impact of utilization on performance, it is important to understand the relevant performance and capacity measures at the operational level, as well as their relationship to the more broadly understood financial measures at the firm level. These measures and relationships are critical in successfully applying the principles of TOC, and are defined in Table 7.1.

According to the TOC view, every capital investment in the system, including machines and work in process materials, represents inventory because they could all potentially be sold to make money. Producing a product or a service that does not lead to a sale will not increase a firm's throughput, but will increase its inventory and operating expenses. It is always best to manage the system so that utilization at the bottleneck resource is maximized in order to maximize throughout.

KEY PRINCIPLES OF TOC

The chief concept behind the TOC is that the bottlenecks should be scheduled to maximize their throughput of services or products while adhering to promised completion dates. For example, manufacturing a garden rake involves attaching a bow to the rake's head. Rake heads must be processed on the blanking press, welded to the bow, cleaned, and attached to the hand to make the rake, which is packaged and finally shipped to Sears, Home Depot, or Wal-Mart, according to a specific delivery schedule. Suppose that the delivery commitments for all styles of rakes for the next month indicate that the welder is loaded at 105 percent of its capacity but

utilization

The degree to which equipment, space, or the workforce is currently being used, and is measured as the ratio of average output rate to maximum capacity.

TABLE 7.1	How the Firm's Operational Measures Relate to Its Financial Measures	
Operational Measures	**TOC View**	**Relationship to Financial Measures**
Inventory (I)	All the money invested in a system in purchasing things that it intends to sell	A decrease in I leads to an increase in net profit, ROI, and cash flow.
Throughput (T)	Rate at which a system generates money through sales	An increase in T leads to an increase in net profit, ROI, and cash flows.
Operating Expense (OE)	All the money a system spends to turn inventory into throughput	A decrease in OE leads to an increase in net profit, ROI, and cash flows.
Utilization (U)	The degree to which equipment, space, or labor is currently being used, and is measured as the ratio of average output rate to maximum capacity, expressed as a percentage	An increase in U at the bottleneck leads to an increase in net profit, ROI, and cash flows.

that the other processes will be used at only 75 percent of their capacities. According to TOC, the welder is the bottleneck resource, whereas the blanking, cleaning, handle attaching, packaging, and shipping processes are nonbottleneck resources. Any idle time on the welder must be eliminated to maximize throughput. Managers should therefore focus on the welding schedule.

Seven key principles of TOC that revolve around the efficient use and scheduling of bottlenecks, and improving flow and throughput, are summarized in Table 7.2.

Practical application of TOC involves the implementation of following steps.

1. *Identify the System Bottleneck(s).* For the rake example, the bottleneck is the welder because it is restricting the firm's ability to meet the shipping schedule and, hence, total value-added funds. Other ways of identifying the bottleneck will be looked at in more detail a little later in this chapter.

2. *Exploit the Bottleneck(s).* Create schedules that maximize the throughput of the bottleneck(s). For the rake example, schedule the welder to maximize its utilization while meeting the shipping commitments to the extent possible. Also make sure that only good quality parts are passed on to the bottleneck.

3. *Subordinate All Other Decisions to Step 2.* Nonbottleneck resources should be scheduled to support the schedule of the bottleneck and not produce more than it can handle. That is, the blanking press should not produce more than the welder can handle, and the activities of the cleaning and subsequent operations should be based on the output rate of the welder.

4. *Elevate the Bottleneck(s).* After the scheduling improvements in steps 1–3 have been exhausted and the bottleneck is still a constraint to throughput, management should consider increasing the capacity of the bottleneck. For example, if welding is still a constraint after exhausting schedule improvements, consider increasing its capacity by

TABLE 7.2	Seven Key Principles of the Theory of Constraints

1. The focus should be on balancing flow, not on balancing capacity.

2. Maximizing the output and efficiency of every resource will not maximize the throughput of the entire system.

3. An hour lost at a bottleneck or a constrained resource is an hour lost for the whole system. In contrast, an hour saved at a nonbottleneck resource is a mirage because it does not make the whole system more productive.

4. Inventory is needed only in front of the bottlenecks in order to prevent them from sitting idle, and in front of assembly and shipping points in order to protect customer schedules. Building inventories elsewhere should be avoided.

5. Work, which can be materials, information to be processed, documents, or customers, should be released into the system only as frequently as the bottlenecks need it. Bottleneck flows should be equal to the market demand. Pacing everything to the slowest resource minimizes inventory and operating expenses.

6. Activating a nonbottleneck resource (using it for improved efficiency that does not increase throughput) is not the same as utilizing a bottleneck resource (that does lead to increased throughput). Activation of nonbottleneck resources cannot increase throughput, nor promote better performance on financial measures outlined in Table 7.1.

7. Every capital investment must be viewed from the perspective of its global impact on overall throughput (T), inventory (I), and operating expense (OE).

adding another shift or another welding machine. Other mechanisms are also available for increasing bottleneck capacity, and we address them a little later.

5. *Do Not Let Inertia Set In.* Actions taken in steps 3 and 4 will improve the welder throughput and may alter the loads on other processes. Consequently, the system constraint(s) may shift. Then the whole process must be repeated in order to identify and manage the new set of constraints.

Details on the scheduling method used in TOC can be found in Simons and Simpson (1997). Because of its potential for improving performance dramatically, many manufacturers have applied the principles of the theory of constraints, including National Semiconductor, Dresser Industries, Allied-Signal, Bethlehem Steel, Johnson Controls, and Rockwell Automotive. All manufacturers implementing TOC principles can also dramatically change the mind-set of employees and managers. Instead of focusing solely on their own functions, they can see the "big picture" and where other improvements in the system might lie. This benefit is evidenced by the experience of Bal Seal Engineering (see Managerial Practice 7.1).

MANAGERIAL **PRACTICE**   7.1   USING TOC PRINCIPLES PROFITS BAL SEAL ENGINEERING

Bal Seal Engineering designs and produces seals and springs for aerospace, automotive, medical and dental equipment, transportation, and electronics industries. Bal Seal has locations in both the United States and Europe. Its engineers specialize in unique sealing solutions and provide considerable product variety. Its manufacturing processes are best characterized as batch processes.

Before TOC practices were implemented at Bal Seal, improvement measures only focused on the efficiency of individual departments. As a result, Bal Seal was experiencing troublesome difficulties with excessive inventory, long lead times, and an entire production crew that was routinely working 55 to 58 hours per week. Despite operating well above capacity, the on-time shipment rate hovered just in the 80 to 85 percent range.

What was wrong? Bal Seal put together a team and learned about TOC and the critical thinking processes associated with it. The results were dramatic and highly visible. Almost immediately, bloated inventories began to dry up. Some production workers were concerned, because having inventory all over the place provided them with a sense of security. They also were worried about efficiency ratings and reduced pay. One member of the design team met with each direct production worker and explained that it was okay to have nothing to do. Under this new way of utilizing capacity and managing production rates, only the constraint must be kept productive all the time. The other work centers were tied to that constraint, and it was their job to be available and ready when work came their way.

Under TOC, extra capacity surfaced everywhere except at the constraint. Whereas the company had been able to produce a maximum of 65,000 parts per week, after TOC, total production was up to 100,000 per week. Even at this higher throughput rate, nonconstraint work centers were operating well below capacity most of the time. Other almost immediate effects were reduced customer response times (from six weeks to eight days) and improved on-time shipments up to 97 percent. Customer satisfaction increased, although initially customers questioned whether Bal Seal's performance was just a temporary condition. Time proved the permanence of the improvements.

TOC improvements did not come without other changes in the firm, though. Workers were used to continuous overtime pay of 15–18 hours per week. As Bal Seal's plant performance improved and throughput in-

Rotary Seals   BalShield EMI Gasketing   Reciprocating PTFE Seals

creased, workers feared the loss of pay. To ease their fears, management paid workers the same amount they were previously receiving, despite the shortened workweek. It was a win-win situation: management got higher throughput, and workers got more time off with the same take-home pay.

The improvements in operational and financial performance measures (see Table 7.1) with the application of TOC at Bal Seal Engineering were dramatic. Net profit doubled, operating expenses decreased, and the shortened lead times and improved customer service provided a true competitive edge. Now that the order fulfillment process is shipshape, the next challenge is to address the customer relationship process because Bal Seal's salespeople previously acted as order-takers. The goal is for salespeople to become more proactive, increase their customer contact, and seek out additional business to take advantage of the plant's higher production rate. The lessons of TOC can be applied there as well.

> IDENTIFICATION AND MANAGEMENT
OF BOTTLENECKS <

Bottlenecks can both be internal or external to the firm, and typically represent a process or a step with the lowest capacity and longest **throughput time**, which is the total time taken from the start to the finish of a process. Where a bottleneck lies in a given service or manufacturing process can be identified in several different ways. The bottleneck could be occurring at the workstation with the highest total time per unit processed, or the workstation with the highest average utilization and total workload, or the workstation where even a single minute reduction in its processing time would reduce the average throughput time for the entire process. Example 7.1 illustrates how a bottleneck step or activity can be identified for a loan approval process at a bank.

throughput time

Total time taken from the start to the finish of a process.

Identifying the Bottleneck in a Service Process	EXAMPLE 7.1

Managers at the First Community Bank are attempting to shorten the times it takes customers for getting credit loan applications approved and completed. The flowchart for this process, consisting of several different activities, each performed by a different bank employee, is shown in Figure 7.1. Loan applications first arrive at activity or step 1, where they are checked for completeness and put in order. At step 2, the loans are categorized into different classes according to the loan amount and whether they are being requested for personal or commercial reasons. While credit checking commences at step 3, loan application data are entered in parallel into the information system for record keeping purposes at step 4. These data are retained by the bank even if a loan is eventually rejected. The loan approval or rejection decision is made at step 5. If approved, all paperwork for setting up the new loan account is finished at step 6. The time taken in minutes is given in parenthesis.

Assuming that no wait time occurs at any of the steps, which single step is the bottleneck? The management is also interested in knowing the maximum possible number of loan accounts that the bank can complete processing in a 5-hour day.

SOLUTION

We define the step where a single-minute reduction in its time reduces the average throughput time as the bottleneck step. Using this definition, we can see that step 2 is the bottleneck in the loan approval process, because reducing its work content will reduce the total throughput time.

It takes $10 + 20 + \max(15, 12) + 5 + 10 = 60$ minutes to complete an approved loan application. Although we assume no waiting time in front of any step, in practice such a smooth process flow is not always the case. So the actual time taken for completing an approved loan will be longer than 60 minutes due to nonuniform arrival of applications, variations in actual processing times, and the related factors.

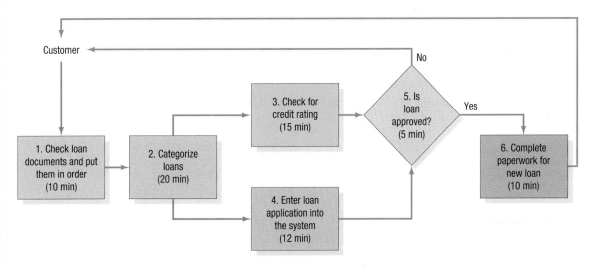

FIGURE 7.1 | Processing Credit Loan Applications at First Community Bank

The capacity for loan completions is derived by translating the "minutes per customer" at the bottleneck step to "customer per hour". At First Community Bank, it is 3 customers per hour because the bottleneck step 2 can process only one customer every 20 minutes (60/3).

Decision Point Step 2 is the bottleneck constraint. If all the loans are approved, the bank will be able to complete a maximum of only 3 loan accounts per hour, or 15 new loan accounts in a five-hour day.

A front-office process with high customer contact and divergence does not enjoy the simple line flows shown in Example 7.1. Its operations may service many different customer types, and the demands on any one operation could vary considerably from one day to the next. However, bottlenecks can still be identified by computing the average utilization of each operation. However, the variability in workload also creates *floating bottlenecks*. One week the mix of work may make operation 1 a bottleneck, and the next week it may make operation 3 the bottleneck. This type of variability increases the complexity of day-to-day scheduling. In this situation, management prefers lower utilization rates, which allow greater slack to absorb unexpected surges in demand.

If multiple services or products are involved, extra time usually is needed to change over from one service or product to the next, which in turn increases the overload at the workstation being changed over. **Setup time** is the time required to change or readjust a process or an operation from making one service or product to making another. Example 7.2 illustrates how a bottleneck can be identified in a manufacturing setting when setup times are negligible and the workstation with the highest total workload serves as the bottleneck.

setup time

The time required to change a process or an operation from making one service or product to making another.

EXAMPLE 7.2	Identifying the Bottleneck in a Manufacturing Process

Diablo Electronics manufactures four unique products (A, B, C, and D) that are fabricated and assembled in five different workstations (V, W, X, Y, and Z) using a small batch process. Each workstation is staffed by a worker who is dedicated to work a single shift per day on his or her assigned workstation. Batch setup times are negligible. A flowchart denotes the path each product follows through the manufacturing process as shown in Figure 7.2, where each product's price, demand per week, and processing times per unit are indicated as well. Inverted triangles represent purchased parts and raw materials consumed per unit at different workstations. Diablo can make and sell up to the limit of its demand per week, and no penalties are incurred for not being able to meet all the demand.

Which of the five workstations V, W, X, Y, or Z has the highest total workload, and thus serves as the bottleneck for Diablo Electronics?

SOLUTION

Using utilization to determine the bottleneck is not necessary, because the denominator in the utilization ratio is the same for every workstation, with one worker per machine at each step in the process. So we identify the bottleneck by computing aggregate workloads at each workstation.

The firm wants to satisfy as much of the product demand in a week as it can. Each week consists of 2,400 minutes of available production time. Multiplying the processing time at each station for a given product with the number of units demanded per week yields the capacity load. These loads are summed across all products going through that workstation and then compared with the existing capacity of 2,400 minutes.

Workstation	Load from Product A	Load from Product B	Load from Product C	Load from Product D	Total Load (min)
V	60 × 30 = 1,800	0	0	0	1,800
W	0	0	80 × 5 = 400	100 × 15 = 1,500	1,900
X	60 × 10 = 600	80 × 20 = 1,600	80 × 5 = 400	0	2,600
Y	60 × 10 = 600	80 × 10 = 800	80 × 5 = 400	100 × 5 = 500	2,300
Z	0	0	80 × 5 = 400	100 × 10 = 1,000	1,400

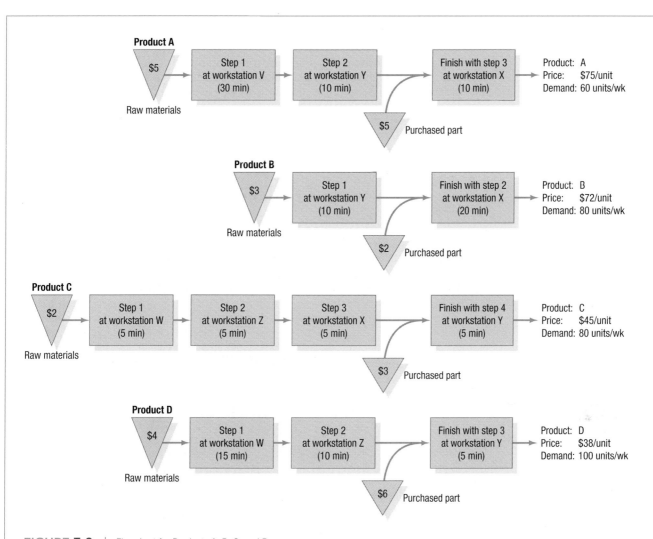

FIGURE 7.2 | Flowchart for Products A, B, C, and D

Decision Point Workstation X is the bottleneck for Diablo Electronics because the aggregate workload at X exceeds the aggregate workloads of workstations V, W, Y, and Z and the maximum available capacity of 2,400 minutes per week.

Identifying the bottlenecks becomes considerably harder when setup times are long and the degree of divergence in the process is greater than that shown in Example 7.2. Variability in the workloads will again likely create floating bottlenecks, especially if most processes involve multiple operations, and often their capacities are not identical. In practice, these bottlenecks can also be determined by asking workers and supervisors in the plant where the bottlenecks might lie and looking for piled up material in front of different workstations.

The key to preserving bottleneck capacity is to carefully monitor short-term schedules and keep bottlenecked resources as busy as practical. Managers should minimize idle time at the bottlenecks, caused by delays elsewhere in the system and make sure that the bottleneck has all the resources it needs to stay busy. When a changeover in the setup is made at a bottleneck, the number of units or customers processed before the next changeover should be large compared to the number processed at less critical operations. Maximizing the number of units processed per setup means fewer setups per year and, thus, less total time lost to setups. The number of setups also depends on the required product variety; more variety necessitates more frequent changeovers.

The long-term capacity of bottleneck operations can be expanded in various ways. Investments can be made in new equipment and in brick-and-mortar facility expansions. The bottleneck's capacity also can be expanded by operating it more hours per week, such as by hiring more employees and going from a one-shift operation to multiple shifts, or by hiring more employees and operating the plant six or seven days per week versus five days per week. Managers also might relieve the bottleneck by redesigning the process, either through *process reengineering* or *process improvement,* or by purchasing additional machines or machines that can handle more capacity.

TOC principles outlined here are fairly broad based and widely applicable. They can be useful for evaluating individual processes as well as large systems for manufacturers as well as service providers. Service organizations, such as Delta Airlines, United Airlines, and the U.S. Air Force, use TOC to their advantage. Managerial Practice 7.2 shows how TOC principles improved flows within the U.S. Airforce's health care system as well as at hospitals across the United States.

MANAGERIAL **PRACTICE**	7.2	CONSTRAINT MANAGEMENT IN HEALTH CARE

With U.S. population growing and baby boomers aging, the health care capacity of the United States is now stretched thin. Hospitals across the country are short of beds, emergency department (ED) space, and staff. Part of the problem is that expanding a hospital's facilities—putting up new buildings, and so forth—can take from two to five years and come with a hefty price tag. This situation leaves hospital administrators with few options except to try to maximize short-term capacity.

A 2005 survey of 487 CEOs of hospitals revealed that more than 75 percent of the respondents tried to cope with the problem by identifying bottlenecks or inefficiencies. Two-thirds of respondents said they attempted to do so by reducing the overall length of a patient's stay and speeding patients through the system, which can free up a hospital's capacity by 15 to 25 percent. The Institute of Healthcare Improvement conducted a study of 60 hospitals in the United States and the United Kingdom. It showed initiatives that included smoothing the flow of patients needing elective surgery (scheduling them at off-peak times), reducing the wait times for patients admitted to emergency departments, transferring patients from the intensive care to medical or surgical units in a timely fashion, and moving patients to "inpatient" status or to long-term care facilities more quickly.

The U.S. Air Force Health Care System uses these strategies as well. With 120 medical facilities and a patient base of about 3 million people, it continually strives to improve its performance. A team was put together to redesign its health care delivery process. Team members came from all levels of the Air Force, including the Air Force's headquarters, its command levels, and individual hospitals.

The team identified bottlenecks in the operating rooms, the highest-cost and highest revenue-generating portion of all of its processes. Using TOC principles, the team improved the system's performance by developing plans that subordinated all other resources to this key process. In another instance,

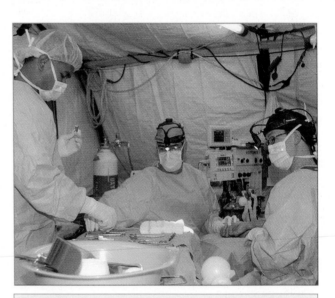

An operating room scrub technician, orthopedic surgeon, and general surgeon prepare for surgery on a patient at a forward-deployed location in support of Operation Enduring Freedom. The U.S. Air Force understands that surgeons are the key to the optimal operation of its health care processes.

the 366th Medical Group of the U.S. Air Force applied TOC principles to reduce the waiting time for routine primary care appointments from an average of 17 days to 4.5 days. Better yet, the group was able to accomplish the improvement without the medical group incurring any additional costs.

Sources: "Maximizing Hospital Capacity," *Healthcare Executive* (January–February 2003), pp. 58–59; C. Haraden and R. Resar, "Patient Flow in Hospitals: Understanding and Controlling it Better," Haraden and Resar, *Frontiers of Health Services Management,* vol. 20, no. 1, pp. 3–15; "Goldratt's Thinking Process Applied to Medical Claims Processing," *Hospital Topics: Research and Perspectives on Healthcare,* vol. 80, no. 4 (Fall 2002), pp. 13–21; "Confronting Capacity Shortages," *Healthcare Executive* (January–February 2005), p. 61.

PRODUCT MIX DECISIONS USING BOTTLENECKS

Managers might be tempted to produce the products with the highest profit margins or unit sales. The problem with this approach is that the firm's actual throughput and overall profitability depend more upon the profit margin generated at the bottleneck than by the profit margin of each individual product produced. Example 7.3 illustrates this concept.

Determining the Product Mix Using Bottlenecks	EXAMPLE 7.3

The senior management at Diablo Electronics wants to improve profitability by accepting the right set of orders, and collected some additional financial data. Each worker is paid $18 per hour. Variable overhead costs are $8,500 per week. The plant operates one 8-hour shift per day, or 40 hours each week. Currently, decisions are made to accept as much of the highest profit margin product as possible (up to the limit of its demand), followed by the next highest profit margin product, and so on until no more capacity is available. Because the firm cannot satisfy all the demand, the product mix must be chosen carefully. Pedro Rodriguez, the newly hired production supervisor, is knowledgeable about the theory of constraints and bottleneck-based scheduling. He believes that profitability can indeed be improved if bottleneck resources were exploited to determine the product mix. What is the change in profits if, instead of the traditional method used by Diablo Electronics, a bottleneck-based approach advocated by Pedro is used to select the product mix?

SOLUTION

Decision Rule 1: Select the best product mix according to the highest overall profit margin of each product.

Step 1: Calculate the profit margin per unit of each product as shown here.

	A	B	C	D
Price	$75.00	$72.00	$45.00	$38.00
Raw material and purchased parts	−10.00	−5.00	−5.00	−10.00
Labor	−15.00	−9.00	−6.00	−9.00
= Profit margin	$50.00	$58.00	$34.00	$19.00

When ordered from highest to lowest, the profit margin per unit sequence of these products is B, A, C, D.

Step 2: Allocate resources V, W, X, Y, and Z to the products in the order decided in step 1. Satisfy each demand until the bottleneck resource (workstation X) is encountered. Subtract minutes away from 2,400 minutes available for each week at each stage.

Work Center	Minutes at the Start	Minutes Left After Making 80 B	Minutes Left After Making 60 A	Can Only Make 40 C	Can Still Make 100 D
V	2,400	2,400	600	600	600
W	2,400	2,400	2,400	2,200	700
X	2,400	800	200	0	0
Y	2,400	1,600	1,000	800	300
Z	2,400	2,400	2,400	2,200	1,200

The best product mix according to this traditional approach is then 60 A, 80 B, 40 C, and 100 D.

Step 3: Compute profitability for the selected product mix.

	Profits
Revenue	$(60 \times \$75) + (80 \times \$72) + (40 \times \$45) + (100 \times \$38) =$ $15,860
Materials	$(60 \times \$10) + (80 \times \$5) + (40 \times \$5) + (100 \times \$10) = -$ $2,200
Labor	(5 workers) $\times$ (8 hours/day) $\times$ (5 days/week) $\times$ ($18/hour) $= -$ $3,600
Overhead	$= -$ $8,500
Profit	$1,560

Notice that in the absence of overtime, the labor cost is fixed at $3,600 per week regardless of the product mix selected. Manufacturing the product mix of 60 A, 80 B, 40 C, and 100 D will yield a profit of $1,560 per week.

Decision Rule 2: Select the best product mix according to the dollar profit margin per minute of processing time at the bottleneck workstation X. This rule would take advantage of the principles outlined in the theory of constraints and get the most dollar benefit from the bottleneck.

Step 1: Calculate the profit margin/minute of processing time at bottleneck workstation X:

	Product A	Product B	Product C	Product D
Profit margin	$50.00	$58.00	$34.00	$19.00
Time at bottleneck	10 minutes	20 minutes	5 minutes	0 minutes
Profit margin per minute	$5.00	$2.90	$6.80	Not defined

When ordered from highest to lowest profit margin/minute at the bottleneck, the manufacturing sequence of these products is D, C, A, B, which is reverse of the earlier order. Product D is scheduled first because it does not consume any resources at the bottleneck.

Step 2: Allocate resources V, W, X, Y, and Z to the products in the order decided in step 1. Satisfy each demand until the bottleneck resource (workstation X) is encountered. Subtract minutes away from 2,400 minutes available for each week at each stage.

Work Center	Minutes at the Start	Minutes Left After Making 100 D	Minutes Left After Making 80 C	Minutes Left After Making 60 A	Can Only Make 70 B
V	2,400	2,400	2,400	600	600
W	2,400	900	500	500	500
X	2,400	2,400	2,000	1,400	0
Y	2,400	1,900	1,500	900	200
Z	2,400	1,400	1,000	1,000	1,000

The best product mix according to this bottleneck based approach is then 60 A, 70 B, 80 C, and 100 D.

Step 3: Compute profitability for the selected product mix.

	Profits
Revenue	$(60 \times \$75) + (70 \times \$72) + (80 \times \$45) + (100 \times \$38) =$ $16,940
Materials	$(60 \times \$10) + (70 \times \$5) + (80 \times \$5) + (100 \times \$10) = -$2,350
Labor	(5 workers) $\times$ (8 hours/day) $\times$ (5 days/week) $\times$ ($18/hour) $= -$3,600
Overhead	$= -$8,500
Profit	$2,490

Manufacturing the product mix of 60 A, 70 B, 80 C, and 100 D will yield a profit of $2,490 per week.

Decision Point By focusing on the bottleneck resources in accepting customer orders and determining the product mix, the sequence in which products are selected for production is reversed from **B, A, C, D** to **D, C, A, B**. Consequently, the product mix is changed from 60 A, 80 B, 40 C, and 100 D to 60 A, 70 B, 80 C, and 100 D. The increase in profits by using the bottleneck-based scheduling method is $930 ($2,490 − $1,560), or almost 60 percent over the traditional approach.

Linear programming (see Supplement E) could also be used to find the best product mix in Example 7.3. It must be noted however that the problem in Example 7.3 did not involve significant setup times. Otherwise, they must be taken into consideration for not only identifying the bottleneck, but also in determining the product mix. The experiential learning exercise of Min-Yo Garment Company at the end of this chapter provides an interesting illustration of how the product mix can be determined when setup times are significant. In this way, the principles behind the theory of constraints can be exploited for making better decisions about a firm's most profitable product mix.

> CAPACITY PLANNING OVER LONGER TIME HORIZONS <

Capacity plans are made at two levels as shown in constraint management framework, and are closely intertwined with each other. So far, we dealt with managing constraints and capacity existing currently in the system; however, short-term capacity plans can also focus on workforce size, overtime budgets, inventories, and other types of decisions we explore more fully in later chapters on operating value chains. In contrast, long-term capacity plans deal with investments in new facilities and equipment at the organizational level, and require top management participation and approval because they are not easily reversed. These plans cover at least two years into the future, but construction lead times can sometimes be longer and result in longer planning time horizons.

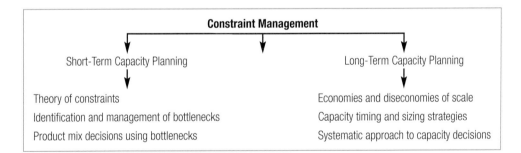

Long-term capacity planning is central to the success of an organization. Too much capacity can be as agonizing as too little. Often entire industries can fluctuate over time between too much and too little capacity, as evidenced in the airline and cruise ship industry over the past 20 years. When choosing a capacity strategy, managers must consider questions such as the following: How much of a cushion is needed to handle variable, or uncertain, demand? Should we expand capacity ahead of demand, or wait until demand is more certain? A systematic approach is needed to answer these and similar questions and to develop a capacity strategy appropriate for each situation.

ECONOMIES OF SCALE

A concept known as **economies of scale** states that the average unit cost of a service or good can be reduced by increasing its output rate. Managerial Practice 7.3 illustrates the importance of economies of scale for the airlines industry in China and South America, with very different results achieved by the airlines in these two world regions. Four principal reasons

economies of scale

A concept that states that the average unit cost of a service or good can be reduced by increasing its output rate.

| MANAGERIAL **PRACTICE** | 7.3 | ECONOMIES OF SCALE AT WORK |

China Southern Airlines

In light of the fierce battle for market share in China's aviation market, China Southern Airlines has a powerful objective: to be the strongest airline in China. The key to attaining this objective, according to company president Wang Changshun, is to embrace economies of scale. After instituting trade reforms and opening its doors to commerce in the early 1980s, China's civil aviation industry took off. The industry was dominated by a number of small airlines that were saddled with high operational costs due to their small sizes. Despite increasing passenger traffic, profitability was low, and service deteriorated. Yet one airline, China Southern Airlines (CSA), pursued a strategy to increase its economies of scale. In 1998, CSA purchased Guizhou Airlines and converted it into an aviation base in Southwest China. In 2000, a merger with Zhong Yuan Airlines resulted in a jump in CSA's market share in Zhengzhou to more than 64 percent. In that same year, CSA began turning a profit. Furthermore, its total assets doubled and the number of passengers carried increased by 26 percent. In 2003, CSA acquired China Northern Airlines and China Xinjiang Airlines. It also signed a "memorandum of understanding" on August 8, 2004, with a global alliance of airline companies around the world, called SKY. Partners in SKY include Delta Air Lines, Dragonair, KLM, Japan Air System, and Vietnam Airlines.

The restructuring and acquisitions helped CSA lower its operational costs and concentrate its marketing efforts on major routes. As a result, the company serviced 40 million passengers in 2004, becoming one of the top 10 passenger carriers in the world. CSA now operates 540 routes, including flights to some 435 domestic destinations. The company's international routes primarily cover Southeast Asia, but the airline also flies to Los Angeles, Amsterdam, and Osaka. Among all Chinese airlines, it boasts the largest fleet with the most bases, most extensive domestic networks, and highest flight frequencies. Renowned for its excellent passenger services, the airline won a Five-Star Diamond Award for flight services and has been honored as China's best airline by *TTG Asia* magazine.

South American Airlines

In the mid-1990s, many of the airlines in the Latin America region expanded their capacity, expecting demand to rise. Instead, it shrank in the wake of Brazil's devaluation crisis in early 1999. At the same time the airlines were facing ever more competition from U.S. airlines, which enjoy bigger economies of scale. Brazil's domestic flights in the first quarter of 2000 showed only 58 percent of seats booked—much below the 65 percent believed necessary to break even. Without enough volume over which to spread fixed costs, the results were inevitable.

One of those airlines, Aerolineas Argentinas, dramatically cut back on the number of domestic and international flights it offered. After restructuring its operations, Aerolineas Argentinas decided in mid-2002 to once again fly some of the international routes it had dropped. Meanwhile, Vasp,

A China Southern Airlines (CSA) jetliner taking off at the Guangzhou Baiyun International Airport, China. The Boeing 777-2000 plane, along with the others waiting to take off, are part of an expanding CSA fleet. The capacity expansion helped CSA gain economies of scale as well as garner a greater share of China's domestic market.

another one of Brazil's big four airlines, announced it was suspending flights to North America and Europe after Boeing demanded some of its airplanes back because Vasp was not keeping up with the lease payments on the planes.

TAM and Transbrasil, two of Brazil's other big airlines, were discussing an "operational partnership" to cut the overlap between their flights—a step many people thought would lead to an eventual merger, cuts, and cost savings for the two companies. Unfortunately for Transbrasil, an agreement was not reached and the carrier ceased operations in December 2001. It declared bankruptcy two years later. Although TAM has been profitable, it has remained a domestic airline, unable to successfully partner with another company to increase its economies of scale. In 2005, TAM's plan to merge with Varig airlines (with which TAM had previously shared 60 percent of its flights) collapsed. The president of the Brazilian Development Bank suggested that the market might have room for only one large local airline in Brazil, pointing to Canada and Mexico, where in each case, two big local airlines merged. With the weakening of the South American region's economy, a consolidation of the industry would benefit the remaining airlines due to the higher volumes associated with strong economies of scale.

Sources: "China Southern Airlines President Addresses IATA Confab," *Business Wire* (June 7, 2002); http://en.wikipedia.org/wiki/China_Southern_Airlines, June 2005; www.hoovers.com, June 2005; "Rival Operations," *Wall Street Journal* (June 6, 1990); "South American Airlines," *The Economist* (May 6, 2000); "Transbrasil Will Probably Lose Operating Certificate," *Aviation Daily* (October 12, 2002); www.tamairlines.com, June 2005.

explain why economies of scale can drive costs down when output increases: (1) Fixed costs are spread over more units; (2) construction costs are reduced; (3) costs of purchased materials are cut; and (4) process advantages are found.

Spreading Fixed Costs In the short term, certain costs do not vary with changes in the output rate. These fixed costs include heating costs, debt service, and managers' salaries. The depreciation of plant and equipment already owned is also a fixed cost in the accounting sense. When the output rate—and, therefore, the facility's utilization rate—increases, the average unit cost drops because fixed costs are spread over more units.

Reducing Construction Costs Certain activities and expenses are required to build small and large facilities alike: building permits, architects' fees, rental of building equipment. Doubling the size of the facility usually does not double construction costs.

Cutting Costs of Purchased Materials Higher volumes can reduce the costs of purchased materials and services. They give the purchaser a better bargaining position and the opportunity to take advantage of quantity discounts. Retailers such as Wal-Mart and Toys "R" Us reap significant economies of scale because their national and international stores buy and sell huge volumes of each item.

Finding Process Advantages High-volume production provides many opportunities for cost reduction. At a higher output rate, the process shifts toward a line process, with resources dedicated to individual products. Firms may be able to justify the expense of more efficient technology or more specialized equipment. The benefits from dedicating resources to individual services or products may include speeding up the learning effect, lowering inventory, improving process and job designs, and reducing the number of changeovers.

DISECONOMIES OF SCALE

At some point, a facility can become so large that **diseconomies of scale** set in; that is, the average cost per unit increases as the facility's size increases. The reason is that excessive size can bring complexity, loss of focus, and inefficiencies that raise the average unit cost of a service or product. Too many layers of employees and bureaucracy can cause management to lose touch with employees and customers. A less agile organization loses the flexibility needed to respond to changing demand. Many large companies become so involved in analysis and planning that they innovate less and avoid risks. The result is that small companies outperform corporate giants in numerous industries.

Figure 7.3 illustrates the transition from economies of scale to diseconomies of scale. The 500-bed hospital shows economies of scale because the average unit cost at its *best operating level*, represented by the blue dot, is less than that of the 250-bed hospital. However, further expansion to a 750-bed hospital leads to higher average unit costs and diseconomies of scale. One reason the 500-bed hospital enjoys greater economies of scale than the 250-bed hospital is that the cost of building and equipping it is less than twice the cost for the smaller hospital. The 750-bed facility would enjoy similar savings. Its higher average unit costs can be explained only by diseconomies of scale, which outweigh the savings realized in construction costs.

Figure 7.3 does not mean that the optimal size for all hospitals is 500 beds. Optimal size depends on the number of patients per week to be served. On the one hand, a hospital serving a small community would have lower costs by choosing a 250-bed capacity rather than the 500-bed capacity. On the other hand, assuming the same cost structure, a large community will be served more efficiently by two 500-bed hospitals than by one 1,000-bed facility.

diseconomies of scale

Occurs when the average cost per unit increases as the facility's size increases.

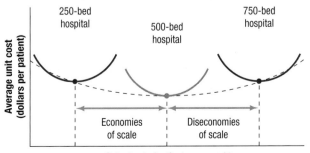

FIGURE 7.3

Economies and Diseconomies of Scale

> CAPACITY TIMING AND SIZING STRATEGIES <

Operations managers must examine three dimensions of capacity strategy before making capacity decisions: (1) sizing capacity cushions, (2) timing and sizing expansion, and (3) linking process capacity and other operating decisions.

SIZING CAPACITY CUSHIONS

Average utilization rates for any resource should not get too close to 100 percent over the long term, though it may occur for bottleneck processes from time to time in the short run. In those instances, the goal of TOC is to maximize the utilization of the bottleneck. If the demand keeps increasing over time, then long-term capacity must be increased at the bottleneck as well to provide some buffer against uncertainties. When average utilization rates approach 100 percent, it is usually a signal to increase capacity or decrease order acceptance to avoid declining productivity. The **capacity cushion** is the amount of reserve capacity a process uses to handle sudden increases in demand or temporary losses of production capacity; it measures the amount by which the average utilization (in terms of total capacity) falls below 100 percent. Specifically,

capacity cushion

The amount of reserve capacity a process uses to handle sudden increases in demand or temporary losses of production capacity; it measures the amount by which the average utilization (in terms of total capacity) falls below 100 percent.

$$\text{Capacity cushion} = 100\% - \text{Utilization rate (\%)}$$

The appropriate size of the cushion varies by industry. In the capital-intensive paper industry, where machines can cost hundreds of millions of dollars each, cushions well under 10 percent are preferred. The less capital-intensive hotel industry breaks even with a 60 to 70 percent utilization (40 to 30 percent cushion), and begins to suffer customer-service problems when the cushion drops to 20 percent. The more capital-intensive cruise ship industry, such as Carnival Cruise Line, prefers cushions as small as 5 percent. Large cushions are particularly vital for front-office processes where customers expect fast delivery times.

Businesses find large cushions appropriate when demand varies. In certain service industries (the grocery industry, for example), demand on some days of the week is predictably higher than on other days, and even hour-to-hour changes are typical. Long customer waiting times are not acceptable because customers grow impatient if they have to wait in a supermarket checkout line for more than a few minutes. Prompt customer service requires supermarkets to maintain a capacity cushion large enough to handle peak demand. Large cushions also are necessary when future demand is uncertain, particularly if resource flexibility is low. Simulation and waiting-line analysis (see Supplement B, "Simulation," and Supplement C, "Waiting Lines") can help managers anticipate better the relationship between capacity cushion and customer service.

Another type of demand uncertainty occurs with a changing product mix. Though total demand might remain stable, the load can shift unpredictably from one work center to another as the mix changes. Supply uncertainty also makes large capacity cushions helpful. Capacity often comes in large increments because a complete machine has to be purchased even if only a fraction of its available capacity is needed, which in turn creates a large cushion. Firms also need to build in excess capacity to allow for employee absenteeism, vacations, holidays, and any other delays. If a firm is experiencing high overtime costs and frequently needs to rely on subcontractors, it perhaps needs to increase its capacity cushions.

The argument in favor of small cushions is simple: Unused capacity costs money. For capital-intensive firms, minimizing the capacity cushion is vital. Studies indicate that businesses with high capital intensity achieve a low return on investment when the capacity cushion is high. This strong correlation does not exist for labor-intensive firms, however. Their return on investment is about the same because the lower investment in equipment makes high utilization less critical. Small cushions have other advantages. By implementing a small cushion, a company can sometimes uncover inefficiencies that were difficult to detect when cushions were larger. These inefficiencies might include employee absenteeism or unreliable suppliers. Once managers and workers identify such problems, they often can find ways to correct them.

TIMING AND SIZING EXPANSION

The second issue of capacity strategy concerns when to expand and by how much. Figure 7.4 illustrates two extreme strategies: the *expansionist strategy*, which involves large,

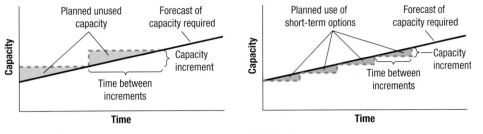

FIGURE **7.4**

Two Capacity Strategies

(a) Expansionist strategy

(b) Wait-and-see strategy

infrequent jumps in capacity, and the *wait-and-see strategy*, which involves smaller, more frequent jumps.

The timing and sizing of expansion are related; that is, if demand is increasing and the time between increments increases, the size of the increments must also increase. The expansionist strategy, which stays ahead of demand, minimizes the chance of sales lost to insufficient capacity. The wait-and-see strategy lags behind demand. To meet any shortfalls, it relies on short-term options, such as use of overtime, temporary workers, subcontractors, stockouts, and the postponement of preventive maintenance on equipment.

Several factors favor the expansionist strategy. Expansion can result in economies of scale and a faster rate of learning, thus helping a firm reduce its costs and compete on price. This strategy might increase the firm's market share or act as a form of preemptive marketing. By making a large capacity expansion or announcing that one is imminent, the firm can preempt the expansion of other firms. These other firms must sacrifice some of their market share or risk burdening the industry with overcapacity. To be successful, however, the preempting firm must have the credibility to convince the competition that it will carry out its plans—and must signal its plans before the competition can act.

The conservative wait-and-see strategy is to expand in smaller increments, such as by renovating existing facilities rather than building new ones. Because the wait-and-see strategy follows demand, it reduces the risks of overexpansion based on overly optimistic demand forecasts, obsolete technology, or inaccurate assumptions regarding the competition.

However, this strategy has its own risks, such as being preempted by a competitor or being unable to respond if demand is unexpectedly high. Critics claim the wait-and-see strategy is a short-term strategy typical of some U.S. management styles. Managers on the fast track to corporate advancement tend to take fewer risks. They earn promotions by avoiding the big mistakes and maximizing short-term profits and return on investment. The wait-and-see strategy fits this short-term outlook but can erode market share over the long run.

Management may choose one of these two strategies or one of the many between these extremes. With strategies in the more moderate middle, firms can expand more frequently (on a smaller scale) than they can with the expansionist strategy without lagging behind demand as with the wait-and-see strategy. An intermediate strategy could be to *follow the leader*, expanding when others do. If others are right, so are you, and nobody gains a competitive advantage. If others make a mistake and overexpand, so have you, but everyone shares in the agony of overcapacity.

LINKING PROCESS CAPACITY AND OTHER DECISIONS

Capacity decisions should be closely linked to processes and value chains throughout the organization. When managers make decisions about designing processes, determining degree of resource flexibility and inventory, and locating facilities, they must consider its impact on capacity cushions. Capacity cushions in the long run buffer the organization against uncertainty, as do resource flexibility, inventory, and longer customer lead times. If a change is made in any one decision area, then the capacity cushion may also need to be changed to compensate. For example, capacity cushions for a process can be lowered if less emphasis is placed on fast deliveries (*competitive priorities*), yield losses (*quality*) drop, or if investment in capital-intensive equipment increases or worker flexibility increases (*process design*). Capacity cushions can also be lowered if sales and operations planning is used more to smooth the output rate—for example, if the company is willing to raise prices when inventory is low and decrease prices when it is high.

> A SYSTEMATIC APPROACH TO LONG-TERM CAPACITY DECISIONS <

TOC looks at how best to manage existing capacity at the process level, but long-term decisions still must be made to plan for capacity of each process. Such planning would typically include how many machines should be bought for a given department, or how many workers staffed for a given process. Once ordered, it can take up to a year, or longer in some instances, for machines to be delivered. Hence a systematic approach is needed to plan for long-term capacity decisions, while the firm invokes TOC principles to manage day-to-day operations on an ongoing basis.

Although each situation is somewhat different, a four-step procedure generally can help managers make sound capacity decisions. (In describing this procedure, we assume that management already performed the preliminary steps of determining the process's existing capacity and assessing whether its current capacity cushion is appropriate.)

1. Estimate future capacity requirements.
2. Identify gaps by comparing requirements with available capacity.
3. Develop alternative plans for filling the gaps.
4. Evaluate each alternative, both qualitatively and quantitatively, and make a final choice.

STEP 1: ESTIMATE CAPACITY REQUIREMENTS

capacity requirement

What a process's capacity should be for some future time period to meet the demand of customers (external or internal), given the firm's desired capacity cushion.

planning horizon

The set of consecutive time periods considered for planning purposes.

A process's **capacity requirement** is what its capacity should be for some future time period to meet the demand of the firm's customers (external or internal), given the firm's desired capacity cushion. Larger requirements are practical for processes or workstations that could potentially be bottlenecks in the future, and management may even plan for larger cushions than normal.

Capacity requirements can be expressed in one of two ways: with an output measure or with an input measure. Either way, the foundation for the estimate is forecasts of demand, productivity, competition, and technological change. These forecasts normally need to be made for several time periods in a **planning horizon**, which is the set of consecutive time periods considered for planning purposes. Long-term capacity plans need to consider more of the future (perhaps a whole decade) than do short-term plans. Unfortunately, the farther ahead you look, the more chance you have of making an inaccurate forecast.

Using Output Measures   The simplest way to express capacity requirements is as an output rate. As discussed earlier, output measures are appropriate for high-volume processes with little product variety or process divergence. Here, demand forecasts for future years are used as a basis for extrapolating capacity requirements into the future. If demand is expected to double in the next five years (and the current capacity cushion is appropriate), then the capacity requirements also double. For example, if a process's current capacity requirement is 50 customers per day, then the requirement in five years would be 100 customers per day. If the desired capacity cushion is 20%, management should then plan for enough capacity to serve, $[100/(1 - 0.2)] = 125$ customers in five years.

Using Input Measures   Output measures may be insufficient in the following situations:

■ Product variety and process divergence is high.
■ The product or service mix is changing.
■ Productivity rates are expected to change.
■ Significant learning effects are expected.

In such cases, it is more appropriate to calculate capacity requirements using an input measure, such as the number of employees, machines, computers, or trucks. Using an input measure for the capacity requirement brings together demand forecasts, process time estimates, and the desired capacity cushion. When just one service or product is processed at an operation and the time period is a particular year, the capacity requirement, M, is

$$\text{Capacity requirement} = \frac{\text{Processing hours required for year's demand}}{\substack{\text{Hours available from a single capacity unit (such as an employee} \\ \text{or machine) per year, after deducting desired cushion}}}$$

$$M = \frac{Dp}{N[1 - (C/100)]}$$

where

D = demand forecast for the year (number of customers serviced or units of product)

p = processing time (in hours per customer served or unit produced)

N = total number of hours per year during which the process operates

C = desired capacity cushion (expressed as a percent)

M is the number of input units required and should be calculated for each year in the time horizon. The processing time, p, depends on the process and methods selected to do the work. The denominator is the total number of hours, N, available for the year from one unit of capacity (an employee or machine), multiplied by a proportion that accounts for the desired capacity cushion, C. The proportion is simply $1.0 - C$, where C is converted from a percent to a proportion by dividing by 100. For example, a 20 percent capacity cushion means that $1.0 - C$ equals 0.80.

Setups will be involved if multiple products are being manufactured. The total setup time is found by dividing the number of units forecast per year, D, by the number of units made in each lot (number of units processed between setups), which gives the number of setups per year, and then multiplying by the time per setup. For example, if the annual demand is 1,200 units and the average lot size is 100, there are $1,200/100 = 12$ setups per year. Accounting for both processing and setup times for multiple services (products), we get

$$\text{Capacity requirement} = \frac{\begin{array}{c}\text{Processing } and \text{ setup hours required for} \\ \text{year's demand, summed over all services or products}\end{array}}{\begin{array}{c}\text{Hours available from a single capacity unit per year,} \\ \text{after deducting desired cushion}\end{array}}$$

$$M = \frac{[Dp+(D/Q)s]_{\text{product 1}} + [Dp+(D/Q)s]_{\text{product 2}} + \cdots + [Dp+(D/Q)s]_{\text{product } n}}{N[1-(C/100)]}$$

where

Q = number of units in each lot

s = setup time (in hours) per lot

What to do when M is not an integer depends on the situation. For example, it is impossible to buy a fractional machine. In this case, round up the fractional part, unless it is cost efficient to use short-term options, such as overtime or stockouts to cover any shortfalls. If, instead, the capacity unit is the number of employees at a process, a value of 23.6 may be achieved using just 23 employees and a modest use of overtime (equivalent to having 60% of another full-time person). Here, the fractional value should be retained as useful information.

Estimating Capacity Requirements When Using Input Measures | **EXAMPLE 7.4**

A copy center in an office building prepares bound reports for two clients. The center makes multiple copies (the lot size) of each report. The processing time to run, collate, and bind each copy depends on, among other factors, the number of pages. The center operates 250 days per year, with one 8-hour shift. Management believes that a capacity cushion of 15 percent (beyond the allowance built into time standards) is best. It currently has three copy machines. Based on the following table of information, determine how many machines are needed at the copy center.

Item	Client X	Client Y
Annual demand forecast (copies)	2,000	6,000
Standard processing time (hour/copy)	0.5	0.7
Average lot size (copies per report)	20	30
Standard setup time (hours)	0.25	0.40

TUTOR 7.1

Tutor 7.1 on the Student CD-ROM provides a new example to practice calculating capacity requirements when using input measures.

SOLUTION

$$M = \frac{[Dp+(D/Q)s]_{\text{product }1}+[Dp+(D/Q)s]_{\text{product }2}+\cdots+[Dp+(D/Q)s]_{\text{product }n}}{N[1-(C/100)]}$$

$$= \frac{[2{,}000(0.5)+(2{,}000/20)(0.25)]_{\text{client X}}+[6{,}000(0.7)+(6{,}000/30)(0.40)]_{\text{client Y}}}{[(250 \text{ day/year})(1 \text{ shift/day})(8 \text{ hours/shift})][1.0-(15/100)]}$$

$$= \frac{5{,}305}{1{,}700} = 3.12$$

Rounding up to the next integer gives a requirement of four machines.

Decision Point The copy center's capacity is being stretched and no longer has the desired 15 percent capacity cushion. Not wanting customer service to suffer, management decided to use overtime as a short-term solution to handle past-due orders. If demand continues at the current level or grows, it will acquire a fourth machine.

STEP 2: IDENTIFY GAPS

capacity gap

Positive or negative difference between projected demand and current capacity.

A **capacity gap** is any difference (positive or negative) between projected demand and current capacity. Identifying gaps requires use of the correct capacity measure. Complications arise when multiple operations and several resource inputs are involved. Expanding the capacity of some operations may increase overall capacity. However, if one operation is a bottleneck, capacity can be expanded only if the capacity of the bottleneck operation is expanded.

STEP 3: DEVELOP ALTERNATIVES

base case

The act of doing nothing and losing orders from any demand that exceeds current capacity.

The next step is to develop alternative plans to cope with projected gaps. One alternative, called the **base case**, is to do nothing and simply lose orders from any demand that exceeds current capacity. Other alternatives are various timing and sizing options for adding new capacity, including the expansionist and wait-and-see strategies illustrated in Figure 7.4. Additional possibilities include expanding at a different location and using short-term options, such as overtime, temporary workers, and subcontracting.

STEP 4: EVALUATE THE ALTERNATIVES

In this final step, the manager evaluates each alternative, both qualitatively and quantitatively.

Qualitative Concerns Qualitatively, the manager looks at how each alternative fits the overall capacity strategy and other aspects of the business not covered by the financial analysis. Of particular concern might be uncertainties about demand, competitive reaction, technological change, and cost estimates. Some of these factors cannot be quantified and must be assessed on the basis of judgment and experience. Others can be quantified, and the manager can analyze each alternative by using different assumptions about the future. One set of assumptions could represent a worst case, in which demand is less, competition is greater, and construction costs are higher than expected. Another set of assumptions could represent the most optimistic view of the future. This type of "what-if" analysis allows the manager to get an idea of each alternative's implications before making a final choice.

cash flow

The difference between the flows of funds into and out of an organization over a period of time, including revenues, costs, and changes in assets and liabilities.

Quantitative Concerns Quantitatively, the manager estimates the change in cash flows for each alternative over the forecast time horizon compared to the base case. **Cash flow** is the difference between the flows of funds into and out of an organization over a period of time, including revenues, costs, and changes in assets and liabilities. The manager is concerned here only with calculating the cash flows attributable to the project.

EXAMPLE 7.5	Evaluating the Alternatives

Grandmother's Chicken Restaurant is experiencing a boom in business. The owner expects to serve 80,000 meals this year. Although the kitchen is operating at 100 percent capacity, the dining room can handle 105,000 diners per year. Forecasted demand for the next five years is 90,000 meals for next year, followed by a 10,000-meal increase in each of the succeeding years. One alternative is to expand both the kitchen and the dining room now, bringing their capacities up to 130,000 meals per year. The initial investment would be $200,000, made at the end of this year (year 0). The average meal is priced at $10, and the before-tax profit margin is 20 percent. The 20 percent figure was arrived at by determining that, for each $10 meal, $6 covers variable costs and $2 goes toward fixed costs (other than depreciation). The remaining $2 goes to pretax profit.

What are the pretax cash flows from this project for the next five years compared to those of the base case of doing nothing?

SOLUTION

Recall that the base case of doing nothing results in losing all potential sales beyond 80,000 meals. With the new capacity, the cash flow would equal the extra meals served by having a 130,000-meal capacity, multiplied by a profit of $2 per meal. In year 0, the only cash flow is $-$200,000 for the initial investment. In year 1, the 90,000-meal demand will be completely satisfied by the expanded capacity, so the incremental cash flow is $(90,000 - 80,000)(\$2) = \$20,000$. For subsequent years, the figures are as follows:

Year 2: Demand = 100,000; Cash flow = $(100,000 - 80,000)\$2 = \$40,000$

Year 3: Demand = 110,000; Cash flow = $(110,000 - 80,000)\$2 = \$60,000$

Year 4: Demand = 120,000; Cash flow = $(120,000 - 80,000)\$2 = \$80,000$

Year 5: Demand = 130,000; Cash flow = $(130,000 - 80,000)\$2 = \$100,000$

If the new capacity were smaller than the expected demand in any year, we would subtract the base case capacity from the new capacity (rather than the demand). The owner should account for the time value of money, applying such techniques as the net present value or internal rate of return methods (see Supplement J, "Financial Analysis," on the Student CD-ROM). For instance, the NPV of this project at a discount rate of 10 percent is calculated here, and equals $13,051.76.

$$\text{NPV} = -200,000 + [(20,000/1.1)] + [40,000/(1.1)^2] + [60,000/(1.1)^3] + [80,000/(1.1)^4] + [100,000/(1.1)^5]$$

$$= -\$200,000 + \$18,181.82 + \$33,057.85 + \$45,078.89 + \$54,641.07 + \$62,092.13$$

$$= \$13,051.76$$

Decision Point Before deciding on this capacity alternative, the owner should also examine the qualitative concerns, such as future location of competitors. In addition, the homey atmosphere of the restaurant may be lost with expansion. Furthermore, other alternatives should be considered (see Solved Problem 3).

TUTOR 7.2

Tutor 7.2 on the Student CD-ROM provides a new example to practice projecting cash flows for capacity decisions.

> TOOLS FOR CAPACITY PLANNING <

Capacity planning requires demand forecasts for an extended period of time. Unfortunately, forecast accuracy declines as the forecasting horizon lengthens. In addition, anticipating what competitors will do increases the uncertainty of demand forecasts. Finally, demand during any period of time is not evenly distributed; peaks and valleys of demand may (and often do) occur within the time period. These realities necessitate the use of capacity cushions. In this section, we introduce three tools that deal more formally with demand uncertainty and variability: (1) waiting-line models, (2) simulation, and (3) decision trees. Waiting-line models and simulation account for the random, independent behavior of many customers, in terms of both their time of arrival and their processing needs. Decision trees allow anticipation of events, such as competitors' actions.

WAITING-LINE MODELS

Waiting-line models often are useful in capacity planning, such as selecting an appropriate capacity cushion for a high customer-contact process. Waiting lines tend to develop in front of a work center, such as an airport ticket counter, a machine center, or a central computer. The reason is that the arrival time between jobs or customers varies, and the processing time may vary from one customer to the next. Waiting-line models use probability distributions to provide estimates of average customer delay time, average length of waiting lines, and utilization of the work center. Managers can use this information to choose the most cost-effective capacity, balancing customer service and the cost of adding capacity.

Supplement C, "Waiting Lines," follows this chapter and provides a fuller treatment of these models. It introduces formulas for estimating important characteristics of a waiting line, such as average customer waiting time and average facility utilization for different facility designs. For example, a facility might be designed to have one or multiple lines at each operation and to route customers through one or multiple operations. Given the estimating capability of these formulas and cost estimates for waiting and idle time, managers can select cost-effective designs and capacity levels that also provide the desired level of customer service.

Figure 7.5 shows output from POMS for Windows for waiting lines. A professor meeting students during office hours has an arrival rate of three students per hour and a service rate of six students per hour. The output shows that the capacity cushion is 50 percent (1 – average server utilization of 0.50). This result is expected because the processing rate is double the arrival rate. What might not be expected is that a typical student spends 0.33 hours either in line or talking with the professor, and the probability of having two or more students at the office is 0.125. These numbers might be surprisingly high, given such a large capacity cushion.

SIMULATION

More complex waiting-line problems must be analyzed with simulation (see Supplement B, "Simulation"). It can identify the process's bottlenecks and appropriate capacity cushions, even for complex processes with random demand patterns and predictable surges in demand during a typical day. The SimQuick simulation package, provided on the Student CD-ROM, allows you to build dynamic models and systems. Other simulation packages can be found with Extend, Simprocess, ProModel, and Witness.

DECISION TREES

A decision tree can be particularly valuable for evaluating different capacity expansion alternatives when demand is uncertain and sequential decisions are involved (see Supplement A, "Decision Making"). For example, the owner of Grandmother's Chicken Restaurant (see Example 7.5) may expand the restaurant now, only to discover in year 4 that demand growth is much higher than forecasted. In that case, she needs to decide whether to expand further. In terms of construction costs and downtime, expanding twice is likely to be much more expensive than building a larger facility from the outset. However, making a large expansion now, when demand growth is low, means poor facility utilization. Much depends on the demand.

FIGURE 7.5

POM for Windows Output for Waiting Line During Office Hours

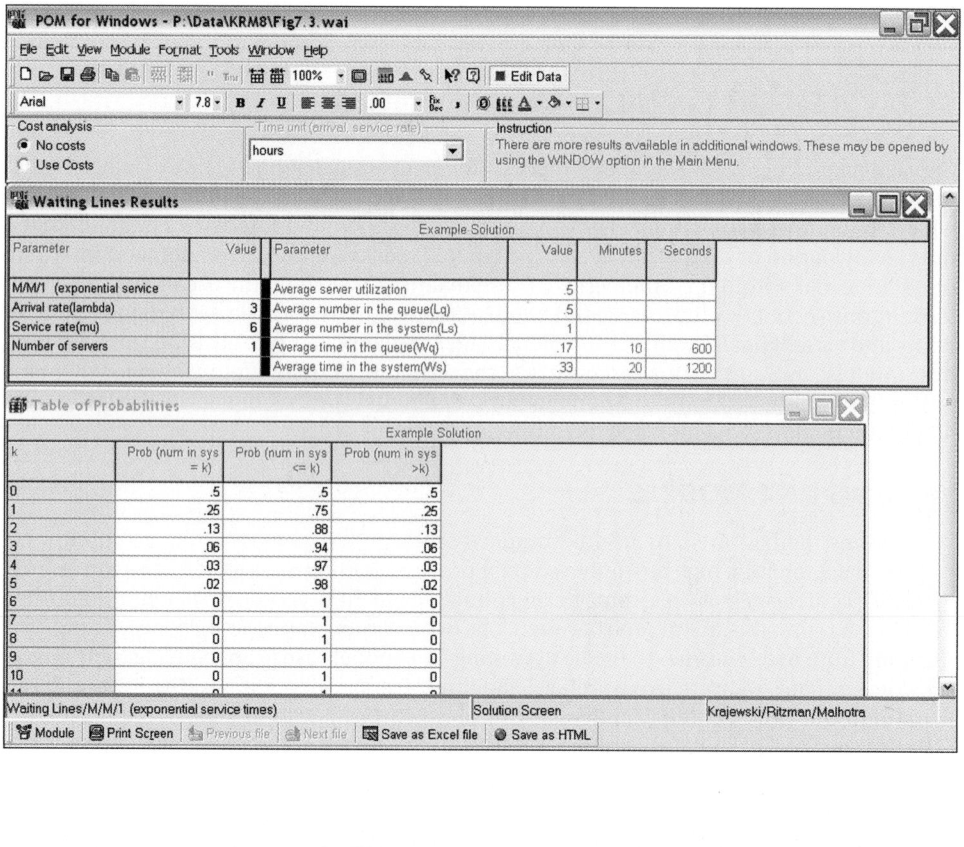

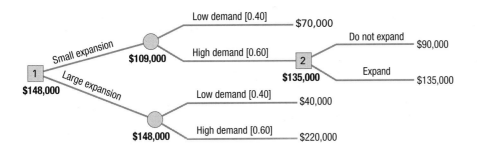

FIGURE **7.6**

A Decision Tree for Capacity Expansion

Figure 7.6 shows a decision tree for this view of the problem, with new information provided. Demand growth can be either low or high, with probabilities of 0.40 and 0.60, respectively. The initial expansion in year 1 (square node 1) can either be small or large. The second decision node (square node 2), whether to expand at a later date, is reached only if the initial expansion is small and demand turns out to be high. If demand is high and if the initial expansion was small, a decision must be made about a second expansion in year 4. Payoffs for each branch of the tree are estimated. For example, if the initial expansion is large, the financial benefit is either $40,000 or $220,000, depending on whether demand is low or high. Weighting these payoffs by the probabilities yields an expected value of $148,000. This expected payoff is higher than the $109,000 payoff for the small initial expansion, so the better choice is to make a large expansion in year 1.

For software support for decision tree analysis, see SmartDraw, Precision Tree decision analysis, and Decision Programming Language.

> STUDENT CD-ROM AND INTERNET RESOURCES <

The Student CD-ROM and the Companion Website at **www.prenhall.com/krajewski** contain many tools, activities, and resources designed for this chapter.

> KEY EQUATIONS <

1. Utilization, expressed as a percent:

$$\text{Utilization} = \frac{\text{Average output rate}}{\text{Maximum capacity}} \times 100\%$$

2. Capacity cushion, C, expressed as a percent:

$$C = 100\% - \text{Utilization rate (\%)}$$

3. **a.** Capacity requirement for one service or product:

$$M = \frac{Dp}{N[1-(C/100)]}$$

b. Capacity requirement for multiple services or products:

$$M = \frac{[Dp+(D/Q)s]_{\text{product 1}} + [Dp+(D/Q)s]_{\text{product 2}} + \cdots + [Dp+(D/Q)s]_{\text{product } n}}{N[1-(C/100)]}$$

> KEY TERMS <

base case 272
bottleneck 254
capacity 254
capacity cushion 268
capacity gap 272

capacity requirement 270
cash flow 272
constraint 254
diseconomies of scale 267
economies of scale 265

planning horizon 270
setup time 260
theory of constraints (TOC) 255
throughput time 259
utilization 256

> SOLVED PROBLEM 1 <

Bill's Car Wash offers two types of washes, Standard and Deluxe. The process flow for both types of customers is shown in the following chart. Both wash types are first processed through steps A1 and A2. The Standard wash then goes through steps A3 and A4 while the Deluxe is processed through steps A5, A6, and A7. Both offerings finish at the drying station (A8). The numbers in parentheses indicate the minutes it takes for that activity to process a customer.

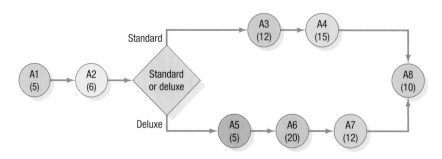

a. Which step is the bottleneck for Standard and Deluxe car wash process?

b. What is the capacity (measured as customers served per hour) of Bill's Car Wash to process Standard and Deluxe customers? Assume that no customers are waiting at step A1, A2, or step A8.

c. If 60 percent of the customers are Standard and 40 percent are Deluxe, what is the average capacity of the car wash in customers per hour?

d. Where would you expect Standard wash customers to experience waiting lines, assuming that new customers are always entering the shop and that no Deluxe customers are in the shop? Where would the Deluxe customers have to wait, assuming no Standard customers?

SOLUTION

a. Step A4 is the bottleneck for Standard car wash process, and Step A6 is the bottleneck for the Deluxe car wash process, because these steps take the longest time in the flow.

b. The capacity for Standard washes is 4 customers per hour because the bottleneck step A4 can process one customer every 15 minutes (60/15). The capacity for Deluxe car washes is 3 customers per hour (60/20). These capacities are derived by translating the "minutes per customer" of each bottleneck activity to "customers per hour."

c. The average capacity of the car wash is $[(0.60 \times 4) + (0.40 \times 3)] = 3.6$ customers per hour.

d. Standard wash customers would wait before steps A1, A2, A3, and A4 because the activities that immediately precede them have a higher rate of output (i.e., smaller processing times). Deluxe wash customers would experience a wait in front of steps A1, A2, and A6 for the same reasons. A1 is included for both types of washes because the arrival rate of customers could always exceed the capacity of A1.

> **SOLVED PROBLEM 2** <

You have been asked to put together a capacity plan for a critical bottleneck operation at the Surefoot Sandal Company. Your capacity measure is number of machines. Three products (men's, women's, and children's sandals) are manufactured. The time standards (processing and setup), lot sizes, and demand forecasts are given in the following table. The firm operates two 8-hour shifts, 5 days per week, 50 weeks per year. Experience shows that a capacity cushion of 5 percent is sufficient.

	Time Standards			
Product	**Processing (hr/pair)**	**Setup (hr/pair)**	**Lot Size (pairs/lot)**	**Demand Forecast (pairs/yr)**
Men's sandals	0.05	0.5	240	80,000
Women's sandals	0.10	2.2	180	60,000
Children's sandals	0.02	3.8	360	120,000

a. How many machines are needed?

b. If the operation currently has two machines, what is the capacity gap?

SOLUTION

a. The number of hours of operation per year, N, is

$N = (2 \text{ shifts/day})(8 \text{ hours/shifts})(250 \text{ days/machine-year})$

$\quad = 4{,}000 \text{ hours/machine-year}$

The number of machines required, M, is the sum of machine-hour requirements for all three products divided by the number of productive hours available for one machine:

$$M = \frac{[Dp+(D/Q)s]_{\text{men}} +[Dp+(D/Q)s]_{\text{women}} +[Dp+(D/Q)s]_{\text{children}}}{N[1-(C/100)]}$$

$$= \frac{\begin{array}{c}[80{,}000(0.05)+(80{,}000/240)0.5]+[60{,}000(0.10)+(60{,}000/180)2.2]\\ +[120{,}000(0.02)+(120{,}000/360)3.8]\end{array}}{4{,}000[1-(5/100)]}$$

$$= \frac{14{,}567 \text{ hours/year}}{3{,}800 \text{ hours/machine-year}} = 3.83 \quad \text{or} \quad 4 \text{ machines}$$

b. The capacity gap is 1.83 machines $(3.83 - 2)$. Two more machines should be purchased, unless management decides to use short-term options to fill the gap.

The Capacity Requirements Solver in OM Explorer confirms these calculations, as Figure 7.7 shows, using only the "Expected" scenario for the demand forecasts.

Shifts/Day	2		Components	3
Hours/Shift	8			
Days/Week	5		▲ More Components	
Weeks/Year	50		▼ Fewer Components	
Cushion (as %)	5%			
Current capacity	2			

Components	Processing (hr/unit)	Setup (hr/lot)	Lot Size (units/lot)	Demand Forecasts Pessimistic	Expected	Optimistic
Men's sandals	0.05	0.5	240		80,000	
Women's sandals	0.10	2.2	180		60,000	
Children's sandals	0.02	3.8	360		120,000	

Productive hours from
one capacity unit for a year   3,800

	Pessimistic Process	Setup	Expected Process	Setup	Optimistic Process	Setup
Men's sandals	0	0.0	4,000	166.7	0	0.0
Women's sandals	0	0.0	6,000	733.3	0	0.0
Children's sandals	0	0.0	2,400	1,266.7	0	0.0
	0	0.0	12,400	2,166.7	0	0.0
Total hours required		0.0		14,566.7		0.0

Total capacity requirements (M)	0.00	3.83	0.00
Rounded	0	4	0
Scenarios that can be met with current system/capacity:		Pessimistic, Optimistic	

If capacity increased by	0%	
Expanded current capacity	3,800	

Total capacity requirements (M)	0.00	3.83	0.00
Rounded	0	4	0
Scenarios that can be met with expanded current capacity:		Pessimistic, Optimistic	

FIGURE 7.7

Using the Capacity Requirements Solver for Solved Problem 2

> SOLVED PROBLEM 3 <

The base case for Grandmother's Chicken Restaurant (see Example 7.5) is to do nothing. The capacity of the kitchen in the base case is 80,000 meals per year. A capacity alternative for Grandmother's Chicken Restaurant is a two-stage expansion. This alternative expands the kitchen at the end of year 0, raising its capacity from 80,000 meals per year to that of the dining area (105,000 meals per year). If sales in year 1 and 2 live up to expectations, the capacities of both the kitchen and the dining room will be expanded at the *end* of year 3 to 130,000 meals per year. This upgraded capacity level should suffice up through year 5. The initial investment would be $80,000 at the end of year 0 and an additional investment of $170,000 at the end of year 3. The pretax profit is $2 per meal. What are the pretax cash flows for this alternative through year 5, compared with the base case?

SOLUTION

Table 7.3 shows the cash inflows and outflows. The year 3 cash flow is unusual in two respects. First, the cash inflow from sales is $50,000 rather than $60,000. The increase in sales over the base is 25,000 meals (105,000 − 80,000) instead of 30,000 meals (110,000 − 80,000) because the restaurant's capacity falls somewhat short of demand. Second, a cash outflow of $170,000 occurs at the end of year 3, when the second-stage expansion occurs. The net cash flow for year 3 is $50,000 − $170,000 = −$120,000.

For comparison purposes, the NPV of this project at a discount rate of 10 percent is calculated as follows, and equals negative $2,184.90.

$$NPV = -80,000 + (20,000/1.1) + [40,000/(1.1)^2] - [120,000/(1.1)^3] + [80,000/(1.1)^4]$$
$$+ [100,000/(1.1)^5]$$

$$= -\$80,000 + \$18,181.82 + \$33,057.85 - \$90,157.77 + \$54,641.07 + \$62,092.13$$

$$= -\$2,184.90$$

On a purely monetary basis, a single-stage expansion seems to be a better alternative than this two-stage expansion. However, other qualitative factors as mentioned earlier must be considered as well.

TABLE 7.3	Cash Flows for Two-Stage Expansion at Grandmother's Chicken Restaurant			

Year	Projected Demand (meals/yr)	Projected Capacity (meals/yr)	Calculation of Incremental Cash Flow Compared to Base Case (80,000 meals/yr)	Cash Inflow (outflow)
0	80,000	80,000	Increase kitchen capacity to 105,000 meals =	($80,000)
1	90,000	105,000	90,000 − 80,000 = (10,000 meals)($2/meal) =	$20,000
2	100,000	105,000	100,000 − 80,000 = (20,000 meals)($2/meal) =	$40,000
3	110,000	105,000	105,000 − 80,000 = (25,000 meals)($2/meal) =	$50,000
			Increase total capacity to 130,000 meals =	($170,000)
				($120,000)
4	120,000	130,000	120,000 − 80,000 = (40,000 meals)($2/meal) =	$80,000
5	130,000	130,000	130,000 − 80,000 = (50,000 meals)($2/meal) =	$100,000

> DISCUSSION QUESTIONS <

1. Identify a process that you encounter on a daily basis, such as the lunch cafeteria or the journey from your home to school/work. What are the bottlenecks that limit the throughput of this process, and how could its efficiency be improved?

2. What are the economies of scale in class size? As class size increases, what symptoms of diseconomies of scale appear? How are these symptoms related to customer contact?

3. A young boy sets up a lemonade stand on the corner of College Street and Air Park Boulevard. Temperatures in the area climb to 100° during the summer. The intersection is near a major university and a large construc-tion site. Explain to this young entrepreneur how his business might benefit from economies of scale. Explain also some conditions that might lead to diseconomies of scale.

> PROBLEMS <

Software, such as OM Explorer, Active Models, and POM for Windows, is packaged with every new copy of the textbook. Check with your instructor on how best to use it. In many cases, the instructor wants you to understand how to do the calculations by hand. At most, the software provides a check on your calculations. When calculations are particularly complex and the goal is interpreting the results in making decisions, the software replaces entirely the manual calculations. The software also can be a valuable resource well after your course is completed.

1. Bill's barbershop offers different types of cut and hair perm styling for women. The process flow in Figure 7.8 shows that all customers go through steps B1 and B2, and then can be served at either of the two workstations at step B3. They then proceed through step B4 or steps B5 and B6, then fin-ish with step B7. The numbers in parentheses indicate the minutes it takes that activity to process a customer.

   a. How long does it take for a customer to get through the entire service process if she was processed at steps B3-a, B4, and B7? At steps B3-b, B5, B6, and B7?

   b. What single activity is the bottleneck for the entire process?

   c. Assuming that the business operates on an 8-hour schedule and half the customers go through steps B3-a, B4, and B7, and the other half through steps B3-b, B5, B6, and B7, how many customers can be served?

2. Figure 7.9 details the process flow for two types of cus-tomers who enter Barbara's Boutique shop for cus-tomized dress alterations. After step T1, Type A customers proceed to step T2 and then to any of the three work-stations at T3, followed by step T4, and then step T7. After step T1, Type B customers proceed to step T5 and then steps T6 and T7. The numbers in parentheses are the min-utes it takes to process a customer.

   a. What is the capacity of Barbara's shop in terms of the numbers of Type A customers who can be served in an hour? Assume no customers are wait-ing at steps T1 or T7.

   b. If 30 percent of the customers are Type A customers and 70 percent are Type B customers, what is the aver-age capacity of Barbara's shop in customers per hour?

   c. When would you expect Type A customers to experi-ence waiting lines, assuming no Type B customers in the shop? Where would the Type B customers have to wait, assuming no Type A customers?

3. Canine Kernels Company (CKC) manufactures two differ-ent types of dog chew toys (A and B, sold in 1,000 count boxes) that are manufactured and assembled on three dif-ferent workstations (W, X, and Y) using a small-batch process (see Figure 7.10). Batch setup times are negligible. The flowchart denotes the path each product follows

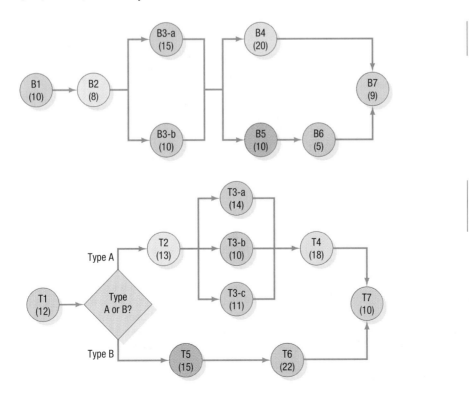

FIGURE 7.8

Process Flow for Bill's Barbershop

FIGURE 7.9

Process Flow for Barbara's Boutique Customers

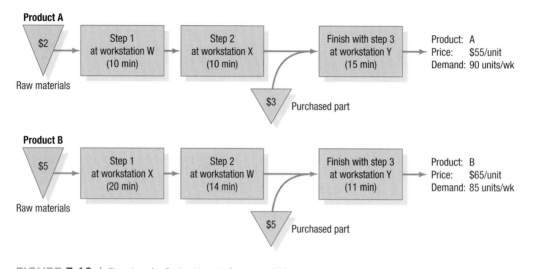

FIGURE 7.10 | Flowchart for Canine Kernels Company (CKC)

through the manufacturing process, and each product's price, demand per week, and processing times per unit are indicated as well. Purchased parts and raw materials consumed during production are represented by inverted triangles. CKC can make and sell up to the limit of its demand per week; no penalties are incurred for not being able to meet all the demand. Each workstation is staffed by a worker dedicated to work on that workstation alone, and is paid $6 per hour. Variable overhead costs are $3,500/week. The plant operates one 8-hour shift per day, or 40 hours/week. Which of the three workstations, W, X, or Y, has the highest aggregate workload, and thus serves as the bottleneck for CKC?

4. The senior management at Canine Kernels Company (CKC) is concerned with the existing capacity limitation, so they want to accept the mix of orders that maximizes the company's profits. Traditionally, CKC utilized a highest contribution margin method, whereby decisions are made to produce as much of the product with the highest profit margin as possible (up to the limit of its demand), followed by the next highest profit margin product, and so on until no more capacity is available. Because capacity is limited, choosing the proper product mix is crucial. Troy Hendrix, the newly hired production supervisor, is an avid follower of the theory of constraints philosophy and bottleneck-based scheduling. He believes that profitability can indeed be approved if bottleneck resources are exploited to determine the product mix.

   a. What is the profit if the traditional profit margin method is used for determining CKC's product mix?

   b. What is the profit if the bottleneck-based approach advocated by Troy is used for selecting the product mix?

   c. Calculate the profit gain, both in absolute dollars as well as in terms of percentage gains, by using TOC principles for determining product mix.

5. The Dahlia Medical Center has 30 labor rooms, 15 combination labor and delivery rooms, 3 delivery rooms, and 1 special delivery room reserved for complicated births. All of these facilities operate around the clock. Time spent in labor rooms varies from hours to days, with an average of about a day. The average uncomplicated delivery requires about one hour in a delivery room.

   During an exceptionally busy three-day period, 115 healthy babies were born at or received by Dahlia Medical Center. Sixty babies were born in separate labor and delivery rooms, 45 were born in combined labor and delivery rooms, 6 were born en route to the hospital, and only 4 babies required a labor room and the complicated-delivery room. Which of the facilities (labor rooms, labor and delivery rooms, or delivery rooms) had the greatest utilization rate?

6. A process currently services an average of 50 customers per day. Observations in recent weeks show that its utilization is about 90 percent, allowing for just a 10 percent capacity cushion. If demand is expected to be 75 percent of the current level in five years and management wants to have a capacity cushion of just 5 percent, what capacity requirement should be planned?

7. An airline company must plan its fleet capacity and its long-term schedule of aircraft usage. For one flight segment, the average number of customers per day is 70, which represents a 65 percent utilization rate of the equipment assigned to the flight segment. If demand is expected to increase to 84 customers for this flight segment in three years, what capacity requirement should be planned? Assume that management deems that a capacity cushion of 25 percent is appropriate.

8. An automobile brake supplier operates on two 8-hour shifts, 5 days per week, 52 weeks per year. Table 7.4 shows the time standards, lot sizes, and demand forecasts for three components. Because of demand uncertainties, the operations manager obtained three demand forecasts (pessimistic, expected, and optimistic). The manager believes that a 20 percent capacity cushion is best.

TABLE 7.4	Capacity Information for Automotive Brake Supplier					
	Time Standard			**Demand Forecast**		
Component	**Processing (hr/wait)**	**Setup (hr/lot)**	**Lot Size (units/lot)**	**Pessimistic**	**Expected**	**Optimistic**
A	0.05	1.0	60	15,000	18,000	25,000
B	0.20	4.5	80	10,000	13,000	17,000
C	0.05	8.2	120	17,000	25,000	40,000

a. What is the minimum number of machines needed? The expected number? The maximum number?

b. If the operation currently has three machines and the manager is willing to expand capacity by 20 percent through short-term options in the event that the optimistic demand occurs, what is the capacity gap?

9. Up, Up, and Away is a producer of kites and wind socks. Relevant data on a bottleneck operation in the shop for the upcoming fiscal year are given in the following table:

Item	Kites	Wind Socks
Demand forecast	30,000 units/year	12,000 units/year
Lot size	20 units	70 units
Standard processing time	0.3 hour/unit	1.0 hour/unit
Standard setup time	3.0 hours/lot	4.0 hours/lot

The shop works two shifts per day, 8 hours per shift, 200 days per year. Currently, the company operates four machines, and desires a 25 percent capacity cushion. How many machines should be purchased to meet the upcoming year's demand without resorting to any short-term capacity solutions?

10. Tuff-Rider, Inc., manufactures touring bikes and mountain bikes in a variety of frame sizes, colors, and component combinations. Identical bicycles are produced in lots of 100. The projected demand, lot size, and time standards are shown in the following table:

Item	Touring	Mountain
Demand forecast	5,000 units/year	10,000 units/year
Lot size	100 units	100 units
Standard processing time	.25 hour/unit	.50 hour/unit
Standard setup time	2 hours/lot	3 hours/lot

The shop currently works 8 hours a day, 5 days a week, 50 weeks a year. It operates five workstations, each producing one bicycle in the time shown in the table. The shop maintains a 15 percent capacity cushion. How many workstations will be required next year to meet expected demand without using overtime and without decreasing the firm's current capacity cushion?

11. Arabelle is considering expanding the floor area of her high-fashion import clothing store, The French Prints of Arabelle, by increasing her leased space in the upscale Cherry Creek Mall from 2,000 square feet to 3,000 square feet. The Cherry Creek Mall boasts one of the country's highest ratios of sales value per square foot. Rents (including utilities, security, and similar costs) are $110 per square foot per year. Salary increases related to French Prints' expansion are shown in the following table, along with projections of sales per square foot. The purchase cost of goods sold averages 70 percent of the sales price. Sales are seasonal, with an important peak during the year-end holiday season.

Year	Quarter	Sales (per sq ft)	Incremental Salaries
1	1	$ 90	$12,000
	2	60	8,000
	3	110	12,000
	4	240	24,000
2	1	99	12,000
	2	66	8,000
	3	121	12,000
	4	264	24,000

a. If Arabelle expands French Prints at the end of year 0, what will her quarterly pretax cash flows be through year 2?

b. Project the quarterly pretax cash flows assuming that the sales pattern (10% annually compounded increase) continues through year 3.

12. The Astro World amusement park has the opportunity to expand its size now (the end of year 0) by purchasing adjacent property for $250,000 and adding attractions at a cost of $550,000. This expansion is expected to increase attendance by 30 percent over projected attendance

without expansion. The price of admission is $30, with a $5 increase planned for the beginning of year 3. Additional operating costs are expected to be $100,000 per year. Estimated attendance for the next five years, *without expansion*, is as follows:

Year	1	2	3	4	5
Attendance	30,000	34,000	36,250	38,500	41,000

   a. What are the pretax combined cash flows for years 0 through 5 that are attributable to the park's expansion?

   b. Ignoring tax, depreciation, and the time value of money, determine how long it will take to recover (pay back) the investment.

13. Kim Epson operates a full-service car wash, which operates from 8 A.M. to 8 P.M. seven days a week. The car wash has two stations: an automatic washing and drying station and a manual interior cleaning station. The automatic washing and drying station can handle 30 cars per hour. The interior cleaning station can handle 200 cars per day. Based on a recent year-end review of operations, Kim estimates that future demand for the interior cleaning station for the seven days of the week, expressed in average number of cars per day, would be as follows:

Day	Mon.	Tues.	Wed.	Thurs.	Fri.	Sat.	Sun.
Cars	160	180	150	140	280	300	250

By installing additional equipment (at a cost of $50,000) Kim can increase the capacity of the interior cleaning station to 300 cars per day. Each car wash generates a pretax contribution of $4.00. Should Kim install the additional equipment if she expects a pretax payback period of three years or less?

14. Roche Brothers is considering a capacity expansion of its supermarket. The landowner will build the addition to suit in return for $200,000 upon completion and a five-year lease. The increase in rent for the addition is $10,000 per month. The annual sales projected through year 5 follow. The current effective capacity is equivalent to 500,000 customers per year. Assume a 2 percent pretax profit on sales.

Year	1	2	3	4	5
Customers	560,000	600,000	685,000	700,000	715,000
Average Sales per Customer	$50.00	$53.00	$56.00	$60.00	$64.00

   a. If Roche expands its capacity to serve 700,000 customers per year now (end of year 0), what are the projected annual incremental pretax cash flows attributable to this expansion?

   b. If Roche expands its capacity to serve 700,000 customers per year at the end of year 2, the landowner will build the same addition for $240,000 and a 3-year lease at $12,000 per month. What are the projected annual incremental pretax cash flows attributable to this expansion alternative?

ADVANCED PROBLEMS

Problems 17, 20, and 21 require reading of Supplement A, "Decision Making." Problems 18 and 20 require reading of Supplement J, "Financial Analysis," on the Student CD-ROM.

15. Yost-Perry Industries (YPI) manufactures a mix of affordable guitars (A, B, C) that are fabricated and assembled at four different processing stations (W, X, Y, Z). The operation is a batch process with small setup times that can be considered negligible. The product information (price, weekly demand, and processing times) and process sequences are shown in Figure 7.11. Raw materials and purchased parts (shown as a per-unit consumption rate) are represented by inverted triangles. YPI is able to make and sell up to the limit of its demand per week with no penalties incurred for not meeting the full demand. Each workstation is staffed by one highly skilled worker dedicated to work on that workstation alone and is paid $15 per hour. The plant operates one 8-hour shift per day and operates on a 5-day work week (i.e., 40 hours of production per person per week). Variable overhead costs are $9,000/week. Which of the four workstations, W, X, Y, or Z, has the highest aggregate workload, and thus serves as the bottleneck for Yost-Perry Industries?

16. Yost-Perry Industries' (YPI) senior management team wants to improve the profitability of the firm by accepting the right set of orders. Currently, decisions are made to accept as much of the highest profit margin product as possible (up to the limit of its demand), followed by the next highest profit margin product, and so on until all available capacity is utilized. Because the firm cannot satisfy all the demand, the product mix must be chosen carefully. Jay Perry, the newly promoted production supervisor, is knowledgeable about the theory of constraints and bottleneck-based scheduling. He believes that profitability can indeed be approved if bottleneck resources are exploited to determine the product mix. What is the change in profits if, instead of the traditional method that YPI has used thus far, a bottleneck-based approach advocated by Jay is used for selecting the product mix?

17. A manager is trying to decide whether to buy one machine or two. If only one machine is purchased and demand proves to be excessive, the second machine can be purchased later. Some sales would be lost, however, because the lead time for delivery of this type of machine is six months. In addition, the cost per machine will be lower if both machines are purchased at the same time. The probability of low demand is estimated to be 0.30 and that of high demand to be 0.70. The after-tax net present value (NPV) of the benefits from purchasing two machines together is $90,000 if demand is low and $170,000 if demand is high.

   If one machine is purchased and demand is low, the NPV is $120,000. If demand is high, the manager has three options. Doing nothing, which has an NPV of $120,000; subcontracting, with an NPV of $140,000; and buying the second machine, with an NPV of $130,000.

   a. Draw a decision tree for this problem.

   b. What is the best decision and what is its expected payoff?

18. Several years ago, River City built a water purification plant to remove toxins and filter the city's drinking water. Because of population growth, the demand for water next

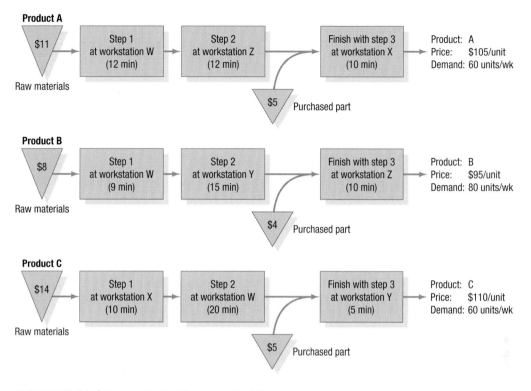

FIGURE 7.11 | Flowchart for Yost Perry Industries (YPI)

year will be more than the plant's capacity of 120 million gallons per year. Therefore, the city must expand the facility. The estimated demand over the next 20 years is given in Table 7.5.

The city planning commission is considering three alternatives.

- *Alternative 1:* Expand enough at the end of year 0 to last 20 years, which means an 80 million gallon increase (200 − 120).

- *Alternative 2:* Expand at the end of year 0 and at the end of year 10.

- *Alternative 3:* Expand at the end of years 0, 5, 10, and 15.

Each alternative would provide the needed 200 million gallons per year at the end of 20 years, when the value of

the plant would be the same regardless of the alternative chosen. Significant economies of scale can be achieved in construction costs: A 20 million gallon expansion would cost $18 million; a 40 million gallon expansion, $30 million; and an 80 million gallon expansion, only $50 million. The level of future interest rates is uncertain, leading to uncertainty about the hurdle rate. The city believes that it could be as low as 12 percent and as high as 16 percent (see Supplement A, "Decision Making").

a. Compute the cash flows for each alternative, compared to a base case of doing nothing. (*Note:* As a municipal utility, the operation pays no taxes.)

b. Which alternative minimizes the present value of construction costs over the next 20 years if the discount rate is 12 percent? 16 percent?

TABLE 7.5		Water Demand			
Year	**Demand**	**Year**	**Demand**	**Year**	**Demand**
0	120	7	148	14	176
1	124	8	152	15	180
2	128	9	156	16	184
3	132	10	160	17	188
4	136	11	164	18	192
5	140	12	168	19	196
6	144	13	172	20	200

c. Because the decision involves public policy and compromise, what political considerations does the planning commission face?

19. Two new alternatives have come up for expanding Grandmother's Chicken Restaurant (see Solved Problem 3). They involve more automation in the kitchen and feature a special cooking process that retains the original-recipe taste of the chicken. Although the process is more capital-intensive, it would drive down labor costs, so the pretax profit for *all* sales (not just the sales from the capacity added) would go up from 20 to 22 percent. This gain would increase the pretax profit by 2 percent of each sales dollar through $800,000 (80,000 meals × $10) and by 22 percent of each sales dollar between $800,000 and the new capacity limit. Otherwise, the new alternatives are much the same as those in Example 7.5 and Solved Problem 3.

■ *Alternative 1*: Expand both the kitchen and the dining area now (at the end of year 0), raising the capacity to 130,000 meals per year. The cost of construction, including the new automation, would be $336,000 (rather than the earlier $200,000).

■ *Alternative 2*: Expand only the kitchen now, raising its capacity to 105,000 meals per year. At the end of year 3, expand both the kitchen and the dining area to the 130,000 meals-per-year volume. Construction and equipment costs would be $424,000, with $220,000 at the end of year 0 and the remainder at the end of year 3. As with alternative 1, the contribution margin would go up to 22 percent.

With both new alternatives, the salvage value would be negligible. Compare the cash flows of all alternatives. Should Grandmother's Chicken Restaurant expand with the new or the old technology? Should it expand now or later?

20. Acme Steel Fabricators experienced booming business for the past five years. The company fabricates a wide range of steel products, such as railings, ladders, and light structural steel framing. The current manual method of materials handling is causing excessive inventories and congestion. Acme is considering the purchase of an overhead rail-mounted hoist system or a forklift truck to increase capacity and improve manufacturing efficiency.

The annual pretax payoff from the system depends on future demand. If demand stays at the current level, the probability of which is 0.50, annual savings from the overhead hoist will be $10,000. If demand rises, the hoist will save $25,000 annually because of operating efficiencies in addition to new sales. Finally, if demand falls, the hoist will result in an estimated annual loss of $65,000. The probability is estimated to be 0.30 for higher demand and 0.20 for lower demand.

If the forklift is purchased, annual payoffs will be $5,000 if demand is unchanged, $10,000 if demand rises, and –$25,000 if demand falls.

a. Draw a decision tree for this problem and compute the expected value of the payoff for each alternative.

b. Which is the best alternative, based on the expected values?

21. The vice president of operations at Dintell Corporation, a major supplier of passenger-side automotive air bags, is considering a $50 million expansion at the firm's Fort Worth production complex. The most recent economic projections indicate a 0.60 probability that the overall market will be $400 million per year over the next 5 years and a 0.40 probability that the market will be only $200 million per year during the same period. The marketing department estimates that Dintell has a 0.50 probability of capturing 40 percent of the market and an equal probability of obtaining only 30 percent of the market. The cost of goods sold is estimated to be 70 percent of sales. For planning purposes, the company currently uses a 12 percent discount rate, a 40 percent tax rate, and the MACRS depreciation schedule. The criteria for investment decisions at Dintell are (1) the net expected present value must be greater than zero; (2) there must be at least a 70 percent chance that the net present value will be positive; and (3) there must be no more than a 10 percent chance that the firm will lose more than 20 percent of the initial value.

a. Based on the stated criteria, determine whether Dintell should fund the project.

b. What effect will a probability of 0.70 of capturing 40 percent of the market have on the decision?

c. What effect will an increase in the discount rate to 15 percent have on the decision? A decrease to 10 percent?

d. What effect will the need for another $10 million in the third year have on the decision?

The Min-Yo Garment Company is a small firm in Taiwan that produces sportswear for sale in the wholesale and retail markets. Min-Yo's garments are unique because they offer fine embroidery and fabrics with a variety of striped and solid patterns. Over the 20 years of its existence, the Min-Yo Garment Company has become known as a quality producer of sports shirts with dependable deliveries. However, during that same period, the nature of the apparel industry was undergoing change. In the past, firms could be successful producing standardized shirts in high volumes with few pattern or color choices and long production lead times. Currently, with the advent of regionalized merchandising and intense competition at the retail level, buyers of the shirts are looking for shorter lead times and much more variety in patterns and colors. Consequently, many more business opportunities are available today than ever before to a respected company such as Min-Yo.

Even though the opportunity for business success seemed bright, the management meeting last week was gloomy. Min-Yo Lee, president and owner of Min-Yo Garment, expressed concerns over the performance of the company: "We are facing strong competition for our products. Large apparel firms are driving prices down on high-volume licensed brands. Each day more firms enter the customized shirt business. Our profits are lower than expected, and delivery performance is deteriorating. We must reexamine our capabilities and decide what we can do best."

Products

Min-Yo has divided its product line into three categories: licensed brands, subcontracted brands, and special garments.

Licensed Brands

Licensed brands are brands that are owned by one company but, through a licensing agreement, are produced by another firm that also markets the brand in a specific geographic region. The licenser may have licensees all over the world. The licensee pays the licenser a fee for the privilege of marketing the brand in its region, and the licenser agrees to provide some advertising for the product, typically through media outlets that have international exposure. A key aspect of the licensing agreement is that the licensee must agree to provide sufficient quantities of product at the retail level. Running out of stock hurts the image of the brand name.

Presently, only one licensed brand is manufactured by Min-Yo. The brand, called the Muscle Shirt, is owned by a large "virtual corporation" in Italy that has no manufacturing facilities of its own. Min-Yo has been licensed to manufacture Muscle Shirts and sell them to large retail chains in Taiwan. The retail chains require prompt shipments at the end of each week. Because of competitive pressures from other licensed brands, low prices are important. Min-Yo sells each Muscle Shirt to retail chains for $6.

The demand for Muscle Shirts averages 900 shirts per week. The following demand for Muscle Shirts has been forecasted for the next 12 weeks.

Week	Demand	Week	Demand
1*	700	7	1,100
2	800	8	1,100
3	900	9	900
4	900	10	900
5	1,000	11	800
6	1,100	12	700

*In other words, the company expects to sell 700 Muscle Shirts at the end of week 1.

Min-Yo's forecasts of Muscle Shirts are typically accurate to within ±200 shirts per week. If demand exceeds supply in any week, the excess demand is lost. No backorders are taken, and Min-Yo incurs no cost penalty for lost sales.

Subcontracted Brands

Manufacturers in the apparel industry often face uncertain demand. To maintain level production at their plants, many manufacturers seek subcontractors to produce their brands. Min-Yo is often considered as a subcontractor because of its reputation in the industry. Although price is a consideration, the owners of subcontracted brands emphasize dependable delivery and the ability of the subcontractor to adjust order quantities on short notice.

Currently, Min-Yo manufactures only one subcontracted brand, called the Thunder Shirt because of its bright colors. Thunder Shirts are manufactured to order for a company in Singapore. Min-Yo's price to this company is $7 per shirt. When orders are placed, usually twice a month, the customer specifies the delivery of certain quantities in each of the next two weeks. The last order the customer placed is overdue, forcing Min-Yo to pay a penalty charge. To avoid another penalty, 200 shirts must be shipped in week 1. The Singapore company is expected to specify the quantities it requires for weeks 2 and 3 at the beginning of week 1. The delivery schedule containing the orders for weeks 4 and 5 is expected to arrive at the beginning of week 3, and so on. The customer has estimated its average weekly needs for the year to be 200 shirts per week, although its estimates are frequently inaccurate.

Because of the importance of this large customer to Min-Yo and the lengthy negotiations of the sales department to get the business, management always tries to satisfy its needs. Management believes that, if Min-Yo Garment ever refuses to accept an order from this company, Min-Yo will lose the Thunder Shirt business. Under the terms of the sales contract, Min-Yo agreed to pay this customer $1 for every shirt not shipped on time for each week the shipment of the shirt is delinquent. Delinquent shipments must be made up.

Special Garments

Special garments are made only to customer order because of their low volume and specialized nature. Customers come to Min-Yo Garment to manufacture shirts for special promotions or special company occasions. Min-Yo's special garments are known as Dragon Shirts because of the elaborate embroidery and oriental flair of the designs. Because each shirt is made to a particular customer's specifications and requires a separate setup, special garments cannot be produced in advance of a firm customer order.

Although price is not a major concern for the customers of special garments, Min-Yo sells Dragon Shirts for $8 a shirt to ward off other companies seeking to enter the custom shirt market. Its customers come to Min-Yo because the company can produce almost any design with high quality and deliver an entire order on time. When placing an order for a Dragon Shirt, a customer specifies the design of the shirt (or chooses from Min-Yo's catalog), supplies specific designs for logos, and specifies the quantity of the order and the delivery date. In the past, management checked to see whether such an order would fit into the schedule, and then either accepted or rejected it on that basis. If Min-Yo accepts an order for delivery at the *end* of a certain week and fails to meet this commitment, it pays a penalty of $2 per shirt for each week delivery is delayed. This penalty is incurred weekly until the delinquent order is delivered. The company tried to forecast demand for specific designs of Dragon Shirts but has given up. Last week Min-Yo had four Dragon Shirt opportunities of 50, 75, 200, and 60 units but chose not to accept any of the orders. Dragon Shirt orders in the past ranged from 50 units to 300 units with varying lead times.

Figure 7.12, Min-Yo's current open-order file, shows that in some prior week Min-Yo accepted an order of 400 Thunder Shirts for delivery last week. The open-order file is important because it contains the commitment management made to customers. Commitments are for a certain quantity and a date of delivery. As customer orders are accepted, management enters the quantity in the green cell representing the week that they are due. Because Dragon Shirts are unique unto themselves, they each have their own order number for future use. No Dragon Shirt orders appear in the open-order file because Min-Yo has not committed to any in the past several weeks.

Manufacturing

Process

Min-Yo Garment has the latest process technology in the industry—a machine, called a garment maker, which is run

FIGURE 7.12

Min-Yo's Open Order File

Note: All orders are to be delivered at the end of the week indictated, after production for the week has been completed and before next week's production is started.

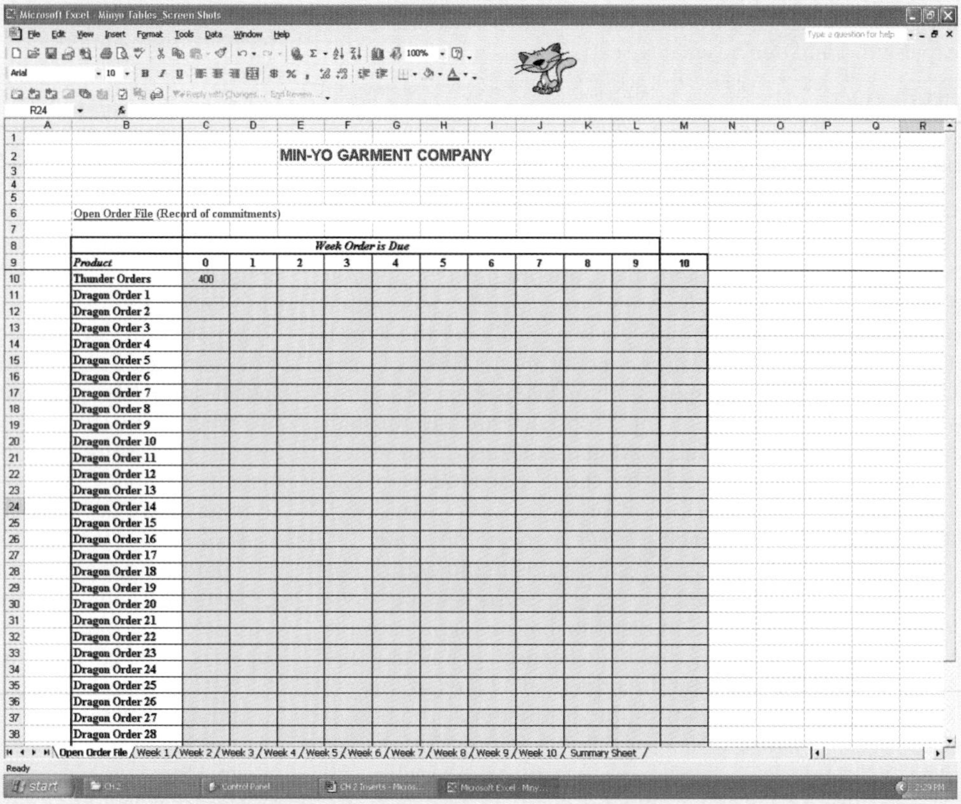
MIN-YO GARMENT COMPANY

Open Order File (Record of commitments)

	Week Order is Due										
Product	0	1	2	3	4	5	6	7	8	9	10
Thunder Orders	400										
Dragon Order 1											
Dragon Order 2											
Dragon Order 3											
Dragon Order 4											
Dragon Order 5											
Dragon Order 6											
Dragon Order 7											
Dragon Order 8											
Dragon Order 9											
Dragon Order 10											
Dragon Order 11											
Dragon Order 12											
Dragon Order 13											
Dragon Order 14											
Dragon Order 15											
Dragon Order 16											
Dragon Order 17											
Dragon Order 18											
Dragon Order 19											
Dragon Order 20											
Dragon Order 21											
Dragon Order 22											
Dragon Order 23											
Dragon Order 24											
Dragon Order 25											
Dragon Order 26											
Dragon Order 27											
Dragon Order 28											

by one operator on each of three shifts. This single machine process can make every garment Min-Yo produces; however, the changeover times consume a substantial amount of capacity. Company policy is to run the machine three shifts a day, five days a week. If business is insufficient to keep the machine busy, the workers are idle because Min-Yo is committed to never fire or lay off a worker. By the same token, the firm has a policy of never working on weekends. Thus, the capacity of the process is 5 days × 24 hours = 120 hours per week. The hourly wage is $10 per hour, so the firm is committed to a fixed labor cost of $10 × 120 = $1,200 per week. Once the machine has been set up to make a particular type of garment, it can produce them at the rate of 10 garments per hour, regardless of type. The cost of the material in each garment, regardless of type, is $4. Raw materials are never a problem and can be obtained overnight.

Scheduling the Garment Maker

Scheduling at Min-Yo Garment is done once each week, after production for the week has been completed and shipped, after new orders from customers have arrived, and before production for the next week has started. Scheduling results in two documents.

The first is a production schedule, shown in Figure 7.13. The schedule shows what management wants the garment maker process to produce in a given week. Two spreadsheet entries are required for each product that is to be produced in a given week. They are in the green shaded cells. The first is the

production quantity. In Figure 7.13, the schedule shows that Min-Yo produced quantities of 800 units for Muscle and 200 units for Thunder last week. The second input is a "1" if the machine is to be set up for a given product or a "blank" if no changeover is required. Figure 7.13 shows that last week changeovers were required for the Muscle and Thunder production runs. The changeover information is important because, at the end of a week, the garment maker process will be set up for the last product produced. If the same product is to be produced first the following week, no new changeover will be required. Management must keep track of the sequence of production each week to take advantage of this savings. The only exception to this rule is Dragon Shirts, which are unique orders that always require a changeover. In week 0, Min-Yo did not produce any Dragon Shirts. Finally, the spreadsheet calculates the hours required for the proposed schedule. Changeover times for Muscle, Thunder, and Dragon Shirts are 8, 10, and 25 hours respectively. Because the garment maker process produces 10 garments per hour regardless of type, the production hours required for Muscle Shirts is 8 + 800/10 = 88 hours, and the production hours for Thunder Shirts is 10 + 200/10 = 30 hours, as shown in Figure 7.13. The total time spent on the garment maker process on all products in a week cannot exceed 120 hours. The spreadsheet will not allow you to proceed if this constraint is violated.

The second document is a weekly profit and loss (P&L) statement that factors in sales and production costs, including penalty charges and inventory carrying costs, as shown

FIGURE 7.13 | Min-Yo's Production Schedule

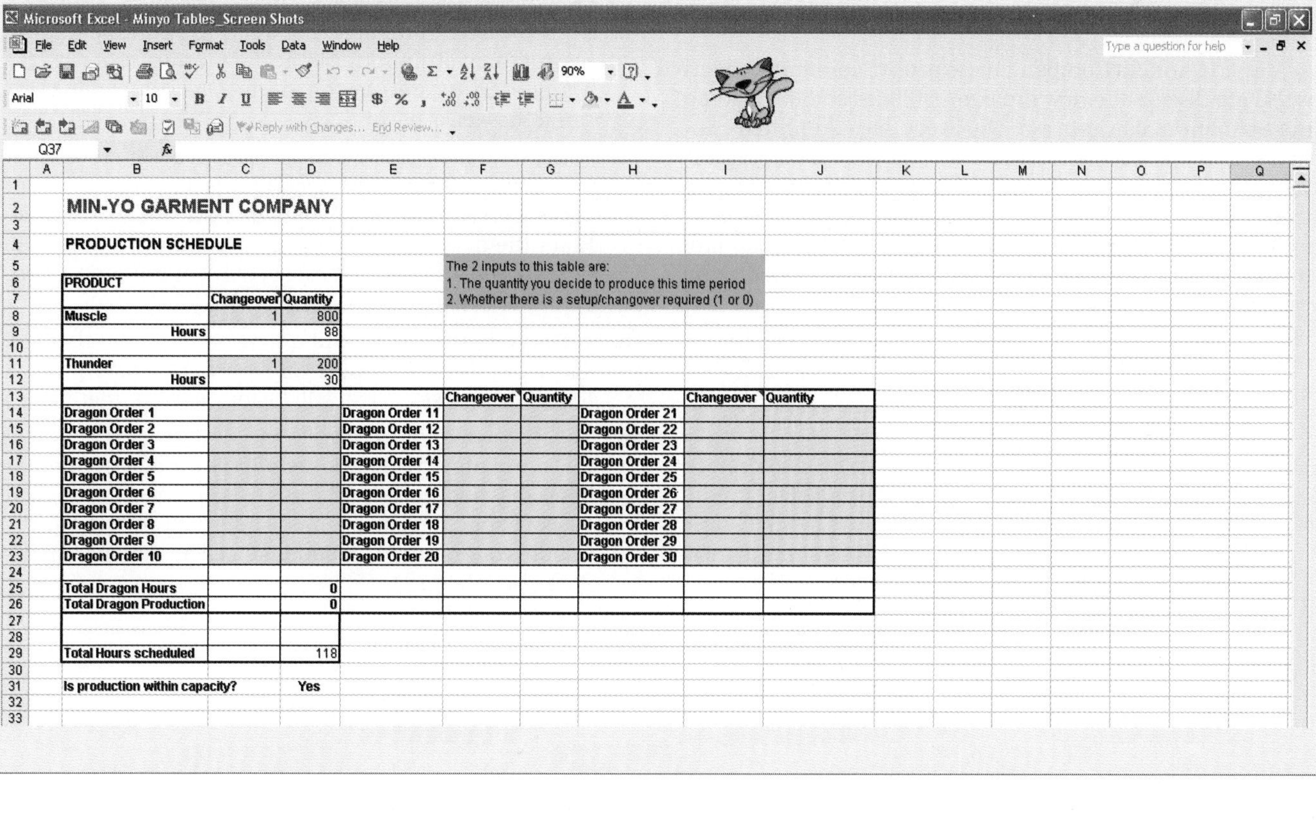

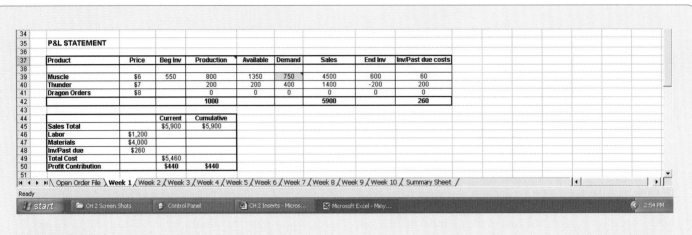

	P&L STATEMENT								
Product		Price	Beg Inv	Production	Available	Demand	Sales	End Inv	Inv/Past due costs
Muscle		$6	550	800	1350	750	4500	600	60
Thunder		$7		200	200	400	1400	-200	200
Dragon Orders		$8		0	0	0	0	0	0
				1000			5900		260
			Current	Cumulative					
Sales Total			$5,900	$5,900					
Labor		$1,200							
Materials		$4,000							
Inv/Past due		$260							
Total Cost			$5,460						
Profit Contribution			$440	$440					

FIGURE 7.14 | Min-Yo's P&L Schedule

Notes:

- The past due quantity of shirts are those shirts not shipped as promised, and appear as a negative number in the "End Inv" column.

- Available = Beginning inventory + Production

- Sales = Demand × Price when demand < available; Available × Price, otherwise

- Inventory cost = $0.10 times number of shirts in inventory. Past due cost equals past due quantity times the penalty ($1 for Thunder Shirts; $2 for Dragon Shirts). These two costs are combined in the "Inv/Past Due Costs" column.

in Figure 7.14. The inventory carrying cost for *any type of product* is $0.10 per shirt per week left in inventory after shipments for the week have been made. The spreadsheet automatically calculates the P&L statement, which links to the open-order file and the production schedule, after the actual demand for Muscle Shirts is known. Figure 7.14 shows that the actual demand for Muscle Shirts last week was 750 shirts.

The Simulation

At Min-Yo Garment Company, the executive committee meets weekly to discuss the new order possibilities and the load on the garment maker process. The executive committee consists of top management representatives from finance, marketing, and operations. You will be asked to participate on a team and play the role of a member of the executive committee in class. During this exercise, you must decide how far into the future to plan. Some decisions, such as the markets you want to exploit, are long-term in nature. Before class, you may want to think about the markets and their implications for manufacturing. Other decisions are short-term and have an impact on the firm's ability to meet its commitments. In class, the simulation will proceed as follows.

1. Use the Min-Yo Tables spreadsheet in OM Explorer on your Student CD-ROM. It is found in the Solver menu, under Operations Strategy. You will start by specifying the production schedule for week 1, based on the forecasts for week 1 in the case narrative for Muscle Shirts

and additional information on new and existing orders for the customized shirts from your instructor. This decision is to be made in collaboration with your executive committee colleagues in class.

2. When all the teams have finalized their production plans for week 1, the instructor will supply the actual demands for Muscle Shirts in week 1. Enter that quantity in the P&L statement in the spreadsheet for week 1.

3. After the P&L statement for week 1 is completed, the instructor will announce the new order requests for Thunder Shirts and Dragon Shirts to be shipped in week 2 and the weeks beyond.

4. You should look at your order requests, accept those that you want, and reject the rest. Add those that you accept for delivery in future periods to your open-order file. Enter the quantity in the cell representing the week the order is due. You are then irrevocably committed to them and their consequences.

5. You should then make out a new production schedule, specifying what you want your garment maker process to do in the next week (it will be for week 2 at that time).

6. The instructor will impose a time limit for each period of the simulation. When the time limit for one period has been reached, the simulation will proceed to the next week. Each week the spreadsheet will automatically update your production and financial information in the Summary Sheet.

CASE | Fitness Plus, Part A

Fitness Plus, Part B, explores alternatives to expanding a new downtown facility and is included in the Instructor's Manual. If you are interested in this topic, ask your instructor for a preview.

Fitness Plus is a full-service health and sports club in Greensboro, North Carolina. The club provides a range of facilities and services to support three primary activities: fitness, recreation, and relaxation. Fitness activities generally take place in four areas of the club: the aerobics room, which can accommodate 35 people per class; a room equipped with free weights; a workout room with 24 pieces of Nautilus equipment; and a large workout room containing 29 pieces of cardiovascular equipment. This equipment includes nine stairsteppers, six treadmills, six life-cycle bikes, three airdyne bikes, two cross-aerobics machines, two rowing machines, and one climber. Recreational facilities comprise eight racquetball courts, six tennis courts, and a large outdoor pool. Fitness Plus also sponsors softball, volleyball, and swim teams in city recreation leagues. Relaxation is accomplished through yoga classes held twice a week in the aerobics room, whirlpool tubs located in each locker room, and a trained massage therapist.

Situated in a large suburban office park, Fitness Plus opened its doors in 1995. During the first two years, membership was small and use of the facilities was light. By 1997, membership had grown as fitness began to play a large role in more and more people's lives. Along with this growth came increased use of club facilities. Records indicate that, in 2000, an average of 15 members per hour checked into the club during a typical day. Of course, the actual number of members per hour varied by both day and time. On some days during a slow period, only 6 to 8 members would check in per hour. At a peak time, such as Mondays from 4:00 P.M. to 7:00 P.M., the number would be as high as 40 per hour.

The club was open from 6:30 A.M. to 11:00 P.M. Monday through Thursday. On Friday and Saturday, the club closed at 8:00 P.M., and on Sunday the hours were 12:00 P.M. to 8:00 P.M.

As the popularity of health and fitness continued to grow, so did Fitness Plus. By May 2005, the average number of members arriving per hour during a typical day had increased to 25. The lowest period had a rate of 10 members per hour; during peak periods, 80 members per hour checked in to use the facilities. This growth brought complaints from members about overcrowding and unavailability of equipment. Most of these complaints centered on the Nautilus, cardiovascular, and aerobics fitness areas. The owners began to wonder whether the club was indeed too small for its membership. Past research indicated that individuals work out an average of 60 minutes per visit. Data collected from member surveys showed the following facilities usage pattern: 30 percent of the members do aerobics, 40 percent use the cardiovascular equipment, 25 percent use the Nautilus machines, 20 percent use the free weights, 15 percent use the racquetball courts, and 10 percent use the tennis courts. The owners wondered whether they could use this information to estimate how well existing capacity was being utilized.

If capacity levels were being stretched, now was the time to decide what to do. It was already May, and any expansion of the existing facility would take at least four months. The owners knew that January was always a peak membership enrollment month and that any new capacity needed to be ready by then. However, other factors had to be considered. The area was growing both in terms of population and geographically. The downtown area just received a major facelift, and many new offices and businesses were moving back to it, causing a resurgence in activity.

With this growth came increased competition. A new YMCA was offering a full range of services at a low cost. Two new health and fitness facilities had opened within the past year in locations 10 to 15 minutes from Fitness Plus. The first, called the Oasis, catered to the young adult crowd and restricted the access of children under 16 years old. The other facility, Gold's Gym, provided excellent weight and cardiovascular training only.

As the owners thought about the situation, they had many questions: Were the capacities of the existing facilities constrained, and if so, where? If capacity expansion was necessary, should the existing facility be expanded? Because of the limited amount of land at the present site, expansion of some services might require reducing the capacity of others. Finally, owing to increased competition and growth downtown, was now the time to open a facility to serve that market? A new facility would take six months to renovate, and the financial resources were not available to do both.

QUESTIONS

1. What method would you use to measure the capacity of Fitness Plus? Has Fitness Plus reached its capacity?

2. Which capacity strategy would be appropriate for Fitness Plus? Justify your answer.

3. How would you link the capacity decision being made by Fitness Plus to other types of operating decisions?

> SELECTED REFERENCES <

Bakke, Nils Arne, and Ronald Hellberg. "The Challenges of Capacity Planning." *International Journal of Production Economics*, vols. 31–30 (1993), pp. 243–264.

Bowman, Edward H. "Scale of Operations—An Empirical Study." *Operations Research* (June 1958), pp. 320–328.

Boyle, Matthew. "Why FedEx Is Flying High." *Fortune* (November 2004), pp. 145–150.

Goldratt, E. M., and J. Cox. *The Goal*, 2d rev. ed. New York: North River Press, 1992.

Hammesfahr, R., D. Jack, James A. Pope, and Alireza Ardalan. "Strategic Planning for Production Capacity." *International Journal of Operations and Production Management*, vol. 13, no. 5 (1993), pp. 41–53.

Hartvigsen, David. *SimQuick: Process Simulation with Excel*, 2d ed. Upper Saddle River, NJ: Prentice Hall, 2004.

"How Goliaths Can Act Like Davids." *Business Week/Enterprise* (1993), pp. 192–200.

"Intel's $10 Billion Gamble." *Fortune* (November 11, 2002), pp. 90–102.

Klassen, Kenneth J., and Thomas R. Rohleder. "Combining Operations and Marketing to Manage Capacity and Demand in Services." *The Service Industries Journal*, vol. 21, no. 2 (2001), pp. 1–30.

"Logan's Roadhouse." *Business Week* (May 27, 1996), p. 113.

Ritzman, Larry P., and M. Hossein Safizadeh. "Linking Process Choice with Plant-Level Decisions About Capital and Human Resources." *Production and Operations Management*, vol. 8, no. 4 (1999), pp. 374–392.

Simons, Jacob, Jr., and Wendell P. Simpson III. "An Exposition of Multiple Constraint Scheduling as Implemented in the Goal System (Formerly Disaster™)." *Production and Operations Management*, vol. 8, no. 1 (Spring 1997), pp. 3–22.

Srikanth, M. L., Cavallaro, H. E., and Cavallaro, H. E., Jr. *Regaining Competitiveness; Putting the Goal to Work*, 2d rev. ed. Guilford, CT: Spectrum Publishing Company, 1995.

Srikanth, Mokshagundam L., and Michael Umble. *Synchronous Management: Profit-Based Manufacturing for the 21st Century*, Vol. 1. Guilford, CT: Spectrum Publishing Company, 1997.

SUPPLEMENT
Waiting Lines

LEARNING GOALS

After reading this supplement, you should be able to:

1. Identify the elements of a waiting-line problem in a real situation.
2. Describe the single-server, multiple-server, and finite-source models.
3. Explain how to use waiting-line models to estimate the operating characteristics of a process.
4. Explain how waiting-lines can be used to make managerial decisions.

Anyone who ever waited at a stoplight, at McDonald's or at the registrar's office experienced the dynamics of waiting lines. Perhaps one of the best examples of effective management of waiting lines is that of Walt Disney World. One day the park may have only 25,000 customers, but on another day the numbers may top 90,000. Careful analysis of process flows, technology for people-mover (materials handling) equipment, capacity, and layout keeps the waiting times for attractions to acceptable levels.

The analysis of waiting lines is of concern to managers because it affects process design, capacity planning, process performance, and ultimately, value chain performance. In this supplement we discuss why waiting lines form, the uses of waiting-line models in operations management, and the structure of waiting-line models. We also discuss the decisions managers address with the models. Waiting lines can also be analyzed using computer simulation. Software such as SimQuick, a simulation package included in the Student CD-ROM, or Excel spreadsheets can be used to analyze the problems in this supplement.

> WHY WAITING LINES FORM <

A **waiting line** is one or more "customers" waiting for service. The customers can be people or inanimate objects, such as machines requiring maintenance, sales orders waiting for shipping, or inventory items waiting to be used. A waiting line forms because of a temporary imbalance between the demand for service and the capacity of the system to provide the service. In most real-life waiting-line problems, the demand rate varies; that is, customers arrive at unpredictable intervals. Most often, the rate of producing the service also varies, depending on customer needs. Suppose that bank customers arrive at an average rate of 15 per hour throughout the day and that the bank can process an average of 20 customers per hour. Why would a waiting line ever develop? The answers are that the customer arrival rate varies throughout the day and the time required to process a customer can vary. During the noon hour, 30 customers may arrive at the bank. Some of them may have complicated transactions, requiring above-average process times. The waiting line may grow to 15 customers for a period of time before it eventually disappears. Even though the bank manager provided for more than enough capacity on average, waiting lines can still develop.

Waiting lines can develop even if the time to process a customer is constant. For example, a subway train is computer controlled to arrive at stations along its route. Each train is programmed to arrive at a station, say, every 15 minutes. Even with the constant service time, waiting lines develop while riders wait for the next train or cannot get on a train because of the size of the crowd at a busy time of the day. Consequently, variability in the rate of demand determines the sizes of the waiting lines in this case. In general, if no variability in the demand occurs or service rates and enough capacity are provided, no waiting lines form.

> USES OF WAITING-LINE THEORY <

Waiting-line theory applies to service as well as manufacturing firms, relating customer arrival and service-system processing characteristics to service-system output characteristics. In our discussion, we use the term *service* broadly—the act of doing work for a customer. The service system might be hair cutting at a hair salon, satisfying customer complaints, or processing a production order of parts on a certain machine. Other examples of customers and services include lines of theatergoers waiting to purchase tickets, trucks waiting to be unloaded at a warehouse, machines waiting to be repaired by a maintenance crew, and patients waiting to be examined by a physician. Regardless of the situation, waiting-line problems have several common elements.

> STRUCTURE OF WAITING-LINE PROBLEMS <

Analyzing waiting-line problems begins with a description of the situation's basic elements. Each specific situation will have different characteristics, but four elements are common to all situations:

1. An input, or **customer population**, that generates potential customers
2. A waiting line of customers
3. The **service facility**, consisting of a person (or crew), a machine (or group of machines), or both necessary to perform the service for the customer
4. A **priority rule**, which selects the next customer to be served by the service facility.

Figure C.1 shows these basic elements. The triangles, circles, and squares are intended to show a diversity of customers with different needs. The **service system** describes the number of lines and the arrangement of the facilities. After the service has been performed, the served customers leave the system.

CUSTOMER POPULATION

A customer population is the source of input to the service system. If the potential number of new customers for the service system is appreciably affected by the number of customers

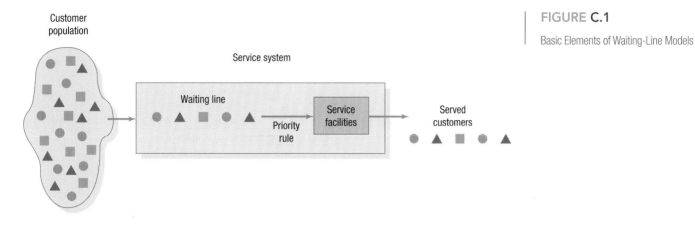

FIGURE **C.1**

Basic Elements of Waiting-Line Models

already in the system, the input source is said to be *finite*. For example, suppose that a maintenance crew is assigned responsibility for the repair of 10 machines. The customer population for the maintenance crew is 10 machines in working order. The population generates customers for the maintenance crew as a function of the failure rates for the machines. As more machines fail and enter the service system, either waiting for service or being repaired, the customer population becomes smaller and the rate at which it can generate another customer falls. Consequently, the customer population is said to be finite.

Alternatively, an *infinite* customer population is one in which the number of customers in the system does not affect the rate at which the population generates new customers. For example, consider a mail-order operation for which the customer population consists of shoppers who have received a catalog of products sold by the company. Because the customer population is so large and only a small fraction of the shoppers place orders at any one time, the number of new orders it generates is not appreciably affected by the number of orders waiting for service or being processed by the service system. In this case, the customer population is said to be infinite.

Customers in waiting lines may be *patient* or *impatient*, which has nothing to do with the colorful language a customer may use while waiting in line for a long time on a hot day. In the context of waiting-line problems, a patient customer is one who enters the system and remains there until being served; an impatient customer is one who either decides not to enter the system (balks) or leaves the system before being served (reneges). For the methods used in this supplement, we make the simplifying assumption that all customers are patient.

THE SERVICE SYSTEM

The service system may be described by the number of lines and the arrangement of facilities.

Number of Lines Waiting lines may be designed to be a *single line* or *multiple lines*. Figure C.2 shows an example of each arrangement. Generally, single lines are utilized at airline counters, inside banks, and at some fast-food restaurants; whereas multiple lines are utilized in grocery stores, at drive-in bank operations, and in discount stores. When multiple servers are available and each one can handle general transactions, the single-line arrangement keeps servers uniformly busy and gives customers a sense of fairness. Customers believe that they are being served on the basis of when they arrived, and not on how well they guessed their waiting time when selecting a particular line. The multiple-line design is best when some of the servers provide a limited set of services. In this arrangement, customers select the services they need and wait in the line where that service is provided, such as at a grocery store that provides special lines for customers paying with cash or having fewer than 10 items.

Sometimes, queues are not organized neatly into "lines." Machines that need repair on the production floor of a factory may be left in place, and the maintenance crew comes to them. Nonetheless, we can think of such machines as forming a single line or multiple lines, depending on the number of repair crews and their specialties. Likewise, passengers who telephone for a taxi also form a line even though they may wait at different locations.

FIGURE C.2

Waiting-Line Arrangements

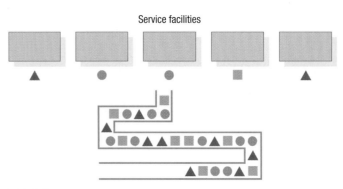

(a) Single line

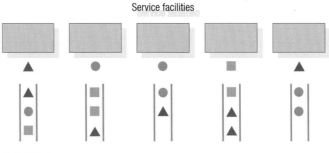

(b) Multiple lines

channel

One or more facilities required to perform a given service.

phase

A single step in providing a service.

Arrangement of Service Facilities Service facilities consist of the personnel and equipment necessary to perform the service for the customer. Service facility arrangement is described by the number of channels and phases. A **channel** is one or more facilities required to perform a given service. A **phase** is a single step in providing the service. Some services require a single phase, while others require a sequence of phases. Consequently, a service facility uses some combination of channels and phases. Managers should choose an arrangement based on customer volume and the nature of services provided. Figure C.3 shows

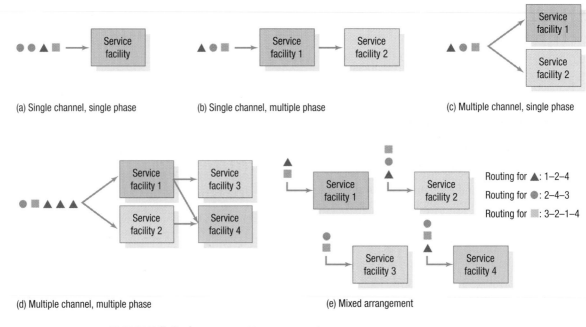

FIGURE C.3 | Examples of Service Facility Arrangements

examples of the five basic types of service facility arrangements.

In the *single-channel, single-phase* system, all services demanded by a customer can be performed by a single-server facility. Customers form a single line and go through the service facility one at a time. Examples are a drive-through car wash and a machine that must process several batches of parts.

The *single-channel, multiple-phase* arrangement is used when the services are best performed in sequence by more than one facility, yet customer volume or other constraints limit the design to one channel. Customers form a single line and proceed sequentially from one service facility to the next. An example of this arrangement is a McDonald's drive-through, where the first facility takes the order, the second takes the money, and the third provides the food.

Commuters wait in line to purchase tickets at Grand Central Station in New York City. This is an example of a multiple-channel, single-phase service design.

The *multiple-channel, single-phase* arrangement is used when demand is large enough to warrant providing the same service at more than one facility or when the services offered by the facilities are different. Customers form one or more lines, depending on the design. In the single-line design, customers are served by the first available server, as in the lobby of a bank. If each channel has its own waiting line, customers wait until the server for their line can serve them, as at a bank's drive-through facilities.

The *multiple-channel, multiple-phase* arrangement occurs when customers can be served by one of the first-phase facilities but then require service from a second-phase facility, and so on. In some cases, customers cannot switch channels after service has begun; in others they can. An example of this arrangement is a laundromat. Washing machines are the first-phase facilities, and dryers are the second-phase facilities. Some of the washing machines and dryers may be designed for extra-large loads, thereby providing the customer a choice of channels.

The most complex waiting-line problem involves customers who have unique sequences of required services; consequently, service cannot be described neatly in phases. A *mixed* arrangement is used in such a case. In the mixed arrangement, waiting lines can develop in front of each facility, as in a job shop, where each customized job may require the use of various machines and different routings.

PRIORITY RULE

The priority rule determines which customer to serve next. Most service systems that you encounter use the first-come, first-served (FCFS) rule. The customer at the head of the waiting line has the highest priority, and the customer who arrived last has the lowest priority. Other priority disciplines might take the customer with the earliest promised due date (EDD) or the customer with the shortest expected processing time (SPT).[1]

A **preemptive discipline** is a rule that allows a customer of higher priority to interrupt the service of another customer. For example, in a hospital emergency room, patients with the most life-threatening injuries receive treatment first, regardless of their order of arrival. Modeling of systems having complex priority disciplines is usually done using computer simulation.

preemptive discipline

A rule that allows a customer of higher priority to interrupt the service of another customer.

> PROBABILITY DISTRIBUTIONS <

The sources of variation in waiting-line problems come from the random arrivals of customers and the variations in service times. Each of these sources can be described with a probability distribution.

---

[1]We focus on FCFS in this supplement and discuss EDD and SPT in Chapter 16, "Scheduling."

ARRIVAL DISTRIBUTION

Customers arrive at service facilities randomly. The variability of customer arrivals often can be described by a Poisson distribution, which specifies the probability that n customers will arrive in T time periods:

$$P_n = \frac{(\lambda T)^n}{n!} e^{-\lambda T} \text{ for } n = 0,1,2,\ldots$$

where

P_n = probability of n arrivals in T time periods

λ = average number of customer arrivals per period

e = 2.7183

The mean of the Poisson distribution is λT, and the variance also is λT. The Poisson distribution is a discrete distribution; that is, the probabilities are for a specific number of arrivals per unit of time.

EXAMPLE C.1	Calculating the Probability of Customer Arrivals

Management is redesigning the customer service process in a large department store. Accommodating four customers is important. Customers arrive at the desk at the rate of two customers per hour. What is the probability that four customers will arrive during any hour?

SOLUTION

In this case $\lambda = 2$ customers per hour, $T = 1$ hour, and $n = 4$ customers. The probability that four customers will arrive in any hour is

$$P_4 = \frac{[2(1)]^4}{4!} e^{-2(1)} = \frac{16}{24} e^{-2} = 0.090$$

Decision Point The manager of the customer service desk can use this information to determine the space requirements for the desk and waiting area. There is a relatively small probability that four customers will arrive in any hour. Consequently, seating capacity for two or three customers should be more than adequate unless the time to service each customer is lengthy. Further analysis on service times is warranted.

interarrival times

The time between customer arrivals.

Another way to specify the arrival distribution is to do it in terms of customer **interarrival times**—that is, the time between customer arrivals. If the customer population generates customers according to a Poisson distribution, the *exponential distribution* describes the probability that the next customer will arrive in the next T time periods. As the exponential distribution also describes service times, we discuss the details of this distribution in the next section.

SERVICE TIME DISTRIBUTION

The exponential distribution describes the probability that the service time of the customer at a particular facility will be no more than T time periods. The probability can be calculated by using the formula

$$P(t \leq T) = 1 - e^{-\mu T}$$

where

μ = average number of customers completing service per period

t = service time of the customer

T = target service time

The mean of the service time distribution is $1/\mu$, and the variance is $(1/\mu)^2$. As T increases, the probability that the customer's service time will be less than T approaches 1.0.

For simplicity, let us look at a single-channel, single-phase arrangement.

Calculating the Service Time Probability	EXAMPLE C.2

The management of the large department store in Example C.1 must determine whether more training is needed for the customer service clerk. The clerk at the customer service desk can serve an average of three customers per hour. What is the probability that a customer will require less than 10 minutes of service?

SOLUTION

We must have all the data in the same time units. Because $\mu = 3$ customers per *hour*, we convert minutes of time to hours, or $T = 10$ minutes $= 10/60$ hour $= 0.167$ hour. Then

$$P(t \leq T) = 1 - e^{-\mu T}$$
$$P(t \leq 0.167 \text{ hour}) = 1 - e^{-3(0.167)} = 1 - 0.61 = 0.39$$

Decision Point The probability that the clerk will require only 10 minutes or less is not high, which leaves the possibility that customers may experience lengthy delays. Management should consider additional training for the clerk so as to reduce the time it takes to process a customer request.

Some characteristics of the exponential distribution do not always conform to an actual situation. The exponential distribution model is based on the assumption that each service time is independent of those that preceded it. In real life, however, productivity may improve as human servers learn about the work. Another assumption underlying the model is that very small, as well as very large, service times are possible. However, real-life situations often require a fixed-length start-up time, some cutoff on total service time, or nearly constant service time.

> USING WAITING-LINE MODELS TO ANALYZE OPERATIONS <

Operations managers can use waiting-line models to balance the gains that might be made by increasing the efficiency of the service system against the costs of doing so. In addition, managers should consider the costs of *not* making improvements to the system: long waiting lines or long waiting times may cause customers to balk or renege. Managers should therefore be concerned about the following operating characteristics of the system.

1. *Line Length*. The number of customers in the waiting line reflects one of two conditions. Short lines could mean either good customer service or too much capacity. Similarly, long lines could indicate either low server efficiency or the need to increase capacity.

2. *Number of Customers in System*. The number of customers in line and being served also relates to service efficiency and capacity. A large number of customers in the system causes congestion and may result in customer dissatisfaction, unless more capacity is added.

3. *Waiting Time in Line*. Long lines do not always mean long waiting times. If the service rate is fast, a long line can be served efficiently. However, when waiting time seems long, customers perceive the quality of service to be poor. Managers may try to change the arrival rate of customers or design the system to make long wait times seem shorter than they really are. For example, at Walt Disney World, customers in line for an attraction are entertained by videos and also are informed about expected waiting times, which seems to help them endure the wait.

4. *Total Time in System*. The total elapsed time from entry into the system until exit from the system may indicate problems with customers, server efficiency, or capacity. If some customers are spending too much time in the service system, it may be necessary to change the priority discipline, increase productivity, or adjust capacity in some way.

5. *Service Facility Utilization*. The collective utilization of service facilities reflects the percentage of time that they are busy. Management's goal is to maintain high utilization and profitability without adversely affecting the other operating characteristics.

The best method for analyzing a waiting-line problem is to relate the five operating characteristics and their alternatives to dollars. However, placing a dollar figure on certain characteristics (such as the waiting time of a shopper in a grocery store) is difficult. In such cases, an analyst must weigh the cost of implementing the alternative under consideration against a subjective assessment of the cost of *not* making the change.

We now present three models and some examples showing how waiting-line models can help operations managers make decisions. We analyze problems requiring the single-server, multiple-server, and finite-source models, all of which are single phase. References to more advanced models are cited at the end of this supplement.

SINGLE-SERVER MODEL

The simplest waiting-line model involves a single server and a single line of customers. To further specify the model, we make the following assumptions:

1. The customer population is infinite and all customers are patient.
2. The customers arrive according to a Poisson distribution, with a mean arrival rate of λ.
3. The service distribution is exponential, with a mean service rate of μ.
4. The mean service rate exceeds the mean arrival rate.
5. Customers are served on a first-come, first-served basis.
6. The length of the waiting line is unlimited.

With these assumptions, we can apply various formulas to describe the operating characteristics of the system:

$$\rho = \text{Average utilization of the system}$$
$$= \frac{\lambda}{\mu}$$
$$P_n = \text{Probability that } n \text{ customers are in the system}$$
$$= (1-\rho)\rho^n$$
$$L = \text{Average number of customers in the service system}$$
$$= \frac{\lambda}{\mu - \lambda}$$
$$L_q = \text{Average number of customers in the waiting line}$$
$$= \rho L$$
$$W = \text{Average time spent in the system, including service}$$
$$= \frac{1}{\mu - \lambda}$$
$$W_q = \text{Average waiting time in line}$$
$$= \rho W$$

EXAMPLE C.3	Calculating the Operating Characteristics of a Single-Channel, Single-Phase System

ACTIVE MODEL C.1

Active Model C.1 on the Student CD-ROM provides additional insight on the single-server model and its uses for this problem.

The manager of a grocery store in the retirement community of Sunnyville is interested in providing good service to the senior citizens who shop in her store. Currently, the store has a separate checkout counter for senior citizens. On average, 30 senior citizens per hour arrive at the counter, according to a Poisson distribution, and are served at an average rate of 3.5 customers per hour, with exponential service times. Find the following operating characteristics:

a.   Probability of zero customers in the system

b.   Average utilization of the checkout clerk

c.   Average number of customers in the system

d.   Average number of customers in line

e.   Average time spent in the system

f.   Average waiting time in line

SOLUTION

The checkout counter can be modeled as a single-channel, single-phase system. Figure C.4 shows the results from the Waiting-Lines Solver from OM Explorer. Manual calculations of the equations for the *single-server model* are demonstrated in Solved Problem 1 at the end of the supplement.

Servers		(Number of servers *s* assumed to be 1 in single-serve model)
Arrival Rate (λ)	30	
Service Rate (μ)	35	

Probability of zero customers in the system (P_0)	0.1429
Probability of exactly ▼ 0 customers in the system	0.1429
Average utilization of the server (ρ)	0.8571
Average number of customers in the system (L)	6.0000
Average number of customers in line (L_q)	5.1429
Average waiting/service time in the system (W)	0.2000
Average waiting time in line (W_q)	0.1714

FIGURE C.4

Waiting-Lines Solver for Single-Channel, Single-Phase System

Both the average waiting time in the system (*W*) and the average time spent waiting in line (W_q) are expressed in hours. To convert the results to minutes, simply multiply by 60 minutes/hour. For example, $W = 0.20(60) = 12.00$ minutes, and $W_q = 0.1714(60) = 10.28$ minutes.

Analyzing Service Rates with the Single-Server Model	EXAMPLE C.4

The manager of the Sunnyville grocery in Example C.3 wants answers to the following questions:

a. What service rate would be required so that customers averaged only eight minutes in the system?

b. For that service rate, what is the probability of having more than four customers in the system?

c. What service rate would be required to have only a 10 percent chance of exceeding four customers in the system?

TUTOR C.1

Tutor C.1 on the Student CD-ROM provides a new example to practice the single-server model.

SOLUTION

The Waiting-Lines Solver from OM Explorer could be used iteratively to answer the questions. Here we show how to solve the problem manually.

a. We use the equation for the average time in the system and solve for μ.

$$W = \frac{1}{\mu - \lambda}$$

$$8 \text{ minutes} = 0.133 \text{ hour} = \frac{1}{\mu - 30}$$

$$0.133\mu - 0.133(30) = 1$$

$$\mu = 37.52 \text{ customers/hour}$$

b. The probability of more than four customers in the system equals 1 minus the probability of four or fewer customers in the system.

$$P = 1 - \sum_{n=0}^{4} P_n$$

$$= 1 - \sum_{n=0}^{4} (1-\rho)\rho^n$$

and

$$\rho = \frac{30}{37.52} = 0.8\iota$$

Then,

$$P = 1 - 0.2(1 + 0.8 + 0.8^2 + 0.8^3 + 0.8^4)$$

$$= 1 - 0.672 = 0.328$$

Therefore, there is a nearly 33 percent chance that more than four customers will be in the system.

c. We use the same logic as in part (b), except that μ is now a decision variable. The easiest way to proceed is to find the correct average utilization first, and then solve for the service rate.

$$P = 1 - (1 - \rho)(1 + \rho + \rho^2 + \rho^3 + \rho^4)$$
$$= 1 - (1 + \rho + \rho^2 + \rho^3 + \rho^4) + \rho(1 + \rho + \rho^2 + \rho^3 + \rho^4)$$
$$= 1 - 1 - \rho - \rho^2 - \rho^3 - \rho^4 + \rho + \rho^2 + \rho^3 + \rho^4 + \rho^5$$
$$= \rho^5$$

or

$$\rho = P^{1/5}$$

If $P = 0.10$,

$$\rho = (0.10)^{1/5} = 0.63$$

Therefore, for a utilization rate of 63 percent, the probability of more than four customers in the system is 10 percent. For $\lambda = 30$, the mean service rate must be

$$\frac{30}{\mu} = 0.63$$

$$\mu = 47.62 \text{ customers/hour}$$

Decision Point The service rate would only have to increase modestly to achieve the eight-minute target. However, the probability of having more than four customers in the system is too high. The manager must now find a way to increase the service rate from 35 per hour to approximately 48 per hour. She can increase the service rate in several different ways, ranging from employing a high school student to help bag the groceries to installing electronic point-of-sale equipment that reads the prices from bar-coded information on each item.

MULTIPLE-SERVER MODEL

With the multiple-server model, customers form a single line and choose one of s servers when one is available. The service system has only one phase. We make the following assumptions in addition to those for the single-server model: There are s identical servers, and the service distribution for each server is exponential, with a mean service time of $1/\mu$. It should always be the case that $s\mu$ exceeds λ.

With these assumptions, we can apply several formulas to describe the operating characteristics of the service system:

$$\rho = \text{Average utilization of the system}$$
$$= \frac{\lambda}{s\mu}$$

$$P_0 = \text{Probability that zero customers are in the system}$$
$$= \left[\sum_{n=0}^{s-1} \frac{(\lambda/\mu)^n}{n!} + \frac{(\lambda/\mu)^s}{s!}\left(\frac{1}{1-\rho}\right) \right]^{-1}$$

$$P_n = \text{Probability that } n \text{ customers are in the system}$$
$$= \begin{cases} \dfrac{(\lambda/\mu)^n}{n!} P_0 & 0 < n < s \\[2ex] \dfrac{(\lambda/\mu)^n}{s!s^{n-s}} P_0 & n \geq s \end{cases}$$

$$L_q = \text{Average number of customers in the waiting line}$$
$$= \frac{P_0(\lambda/\mu)^s \rho}{s!(1-\rho)^2}$$

$$W_q = \text{Average waiting time of customers in line}$$
$$= \frac{L_q}{\lambda}$$

$$W = \text{Average time spent in the system, including service}$$
$$= W_q + \frac{1}{\mu}$$

$$L = \text{Average number of customers in the service system}$$
$$= \lambda W$$

Estimating Idle Time and Hourly Operating Costs with the Multiple-Server Model	EXAMPLE C.5

The management of the American Parcel Service terminal in Verona, Wisconsin, is concerned about the amount of time the company's trucks are idle, waiting to be unloaded. The terminal operates with four unloading bays. Each bay requires a crew of two employees, and each crew costs $30 per hour. The estimated cost of an idle truck is $50 per hour. Trucks arrive at an average rate of three per hour, according to a Poisson distribution. On average, a crew can unload a semitrailer rig in one hour, with exponential service times. What is the total hourly cost of operating the system?

SOLUTION

The *multiple-server model* is appropriate. To find the total cost of labor and idle trucks, we must calculate the average number of trucks in the system.

Figure C.5 shows the results for the American Parcel Service problem using the Waiting-Lines Solver from OM Explorer. Manual calculations using the equations for the *multiple-server model* are demonstrated in Solved Problem 2 at the end of this supplement. The results show that the four-bay design will be utilized 75 percent of the time and that the average number of trucks either being serviced or waiting in line is 4.53 trucks. We can now calculate the hourly costs of labor and idle trucks:

Labor cost:	$30(s) = $30(4)$	= $120.00
Idle truck cost:	$50(L) = $50(4.53) =$	226.50
	Total hourly cost	= $346.50

Servers	4
Arrival Rate (λ)	3
Service Rate (μ)	1

Probability of zero customers in the system (P_0)	0.0377
Probability of exactly ▼ 0 customers in the system	0.0377
Average utilization of the servers (p)	0.7500
Average number of customers in the system (L)	4.5283
Average number of customers in line (L_q)	1.5283
Average waiting/service time in the system (W)	1.5094
Average waiting time in line (W_q)	0.5094

Decision Point Management must now assess whether $346.50 per day for this operation is acceptable. Attempting to reduce costs by eliminating crews will only increase the waiting time of the trucks, which is more expensive per hour than the crews. However, the service rate can be increased through better work methods; for example, L can be reduced and daily operating costs will be less.

FIGURE C.5

Waiting-Lines Solver for Multiple-Server Model

LITTLE'S LAW

One of the most practical and fundamental laws in waiting-line theory is **Little's law**, which relates the number of customers in a waiting-line system to the waiting time of customers. Using the same notation we used for the single-server and multiple-server models, Little's law can be expressed as $L = \lambda W$ or $L_q = \lambda W_q$. This relationship holds for a wide variety of arrival processes, service-time distributions, and numbers of servers. The practical advantage of Little's law is that you only need to know two of the parameters to estimate the third. For example, consider the manager of a motor vehicle licensing facility who receives many complaints about the time people must spend either having their licenses renewed or getting new license plates. It would be difficult to obtain data on the times individual customers spend at the facility. However, the manager can have an assistant monitor the number of people who arrive at the facility each hour and compute the average (λ). The manager also could periodically count the number of people in the sitting area and at the stations being served and compute that average (L). Using Little's law, the manager can then estimate W, the average time each customer spent in the facility. If the time a customer spends at the

Little's law

A fundamental law that relates the number of customers in a waiting-line system to the waiting time of customers.

Customers of the motor vehicle administration in Beltsville, Maryland, wait for their number to be called. Little's law can be used to estimate the average time each customer spends in the facility.

facility is unreasonable, the manager can focus on either adding capacity or improving the work methods to reduce the time spent serving the customers.

Likewise, Little's law can be used for manufacturing processes. Suppose that a production manager knows the average lead time of a unit of product through a manufacturing process (W) and the average number of units per hour that arrive at the process (λ). The production manager can then estimate the average work-in-process (L) using Little's law. Knowing the relationship between the arrival rate, the lead time, and the work-in-process, the manager has a basis for measuring the effects of process improvements on the work-in-process at the facility. For example, adding some capacity to a bottleneck in the process can reduce the lead time of the product, thereby reducing the work-in-process inventory.

Even though Little's law is applicable in many situations in both service and manufacturing environments, it is not applicable in situations where the customer population is finite, which we address next.

FINITE-SOURCE MODEL

We now consider a situation in which all but one of the assumptions of the single-server model are appropriate. In this case, the customer population is finite, having only N potential customers. If N is greater than 30 customers, the single-server model with the assumption of an infinite customer population is adequate. Otherwise, the finite-source model is the one to use. The formulas used to calculate the operating characteristics of this service system include the following:

$$P_0 = \text{Probability that zero customers are in the system}$$

$$= \left[\sum_{n=0}^{N} \frac{N!}{(N-n)!} \left(\frac{\lambda}{\mu} \right)^n \right]^{-1}$$

$$\rho = \text{Average utilization of the server}$$

$$= 1 - P_0$$

$$L_q = \text{Average number of customers in the waiting line}$$

$$= N - \frac{\lambda + \mu}{\lambda}(1 - P_0)$$

$$L = \text{Average number of customers in the service system}$$

$$= N - \frac{\mu}{\lambda}(1 - P_0)$$

$$W_q = \text{Average waiting time in line}$$

$$= L_q[(N-L)\lambda]^{-1}$$

$$W = \text{Average time spent in the system, including service}$$

$$= L[(N-L)\lambda]^{-1}$$

Analyzing Maintenance Costs with the Finite-Source Model	EXAMPLE C.6

The Worthington Gear Company installed a bank of 10 robots about three years ago. The robots greatly increased the firm's labor productivity, but recently, attention has focused on maintenance. The firm does no preventive maintenance on the robots because of the variability in the breakdown distribution. Each machine has an exponential breakdown (or interarrival) distribution with an average time between failures of 200 hours. Each machine hour lost to downtime costs $30, which means that the firm has to react quickly to machine failure. The firm employs one maintenance person, who needs 10 hours on average to fix a robot. Actual maintenance times are exponentially distributed. The wage rate is $10 per hour for the maintenance person, who can be put to work productively elsewhere when not fixing robots. Determine the daily cost of labor and robot downtime.

ACTIVE MODEL C.3

Active Model C.3 on the Student CD-ROM provides additional insight on the finite-source model and its uses for this problem.

TUTOR C.3

Tutor C.3 on the Student CD-ROM provides a new example to practice the finite-source model.

SOLUTION

The *finite-source model* is appropriate for this analysis because the customer population consists of only 10 machines and the other assumptions are satisfied. Here, $\lambda = 1/200$, or 0.005 break-down per hour, and $\mu = 1/10 = 0.10$ robot per hour. To calculate the cost of labor and robot downtime, we need to estimate the average utilization of the maintenance person and L, the average number of robots in the maintenance system. Figure C.6 shows the results for the Worthington Gear Problem using the Waiting-Lines Solver from OM Explorer. Manual computations using the equations for the *finite-source model* are demonstrated in Solved Problem 3 at the end of this supplement. The results show that the maintenance person is utilized only 46.2 percent of the time, and the average number of robots waiting in line or being repaired is 0.76 robot. However, a failed robot will spend an average of 16.43 hours in the repair system, of which 6.43 hours of that time is spent waiting for service.

The daily cost of labor and robot downtime is

Labor cost:	($10/hour)(8 hours/day)(0.462 utilization) =	$ 36.96
Idle robot cost:	(0.76 robot)($30/robot hour)(8 hours/day) =	182.40
	Total daily cost =	$219.36

FIGURE C.6

Waiting-Lines Solver for Finite-Source Model

Customers	10
Arrival Rate (λ)	0.005
Service Rate (μ)	0.1

Probability of zero customers in the system (P₀)	0.5380
Probability of fewer than ▼ 0 customers in the system	#N/A
Average utilization of the server (ρ)	0.4620
Average number of customers in the system (L)	0.7593
Average number of customers in line (L_q)	0.2972
Average waiting/service time in the system (W)	16.4330
Average waiting time in line (W_q)	6.4330

Decision Point The labor cost for robot repair is only 20 percent of the idle cost of the robots. Management might consider having a second repair person on call in the event two or more robots are waiting for repair at the same time.

> DECISION AREAS FOR MANAGEMENT <

After analyzing a waiting-line problem, management can improve the service system by making changes in one or more of the following areas.

1. *Arrival Rates.* Management often can affect the rate of customer arrivals, λ, through advertising, special promotions, or differential pricing. For example, a telephone

company uses differential pricing to shift residential long-distance calls from daytime hours to evening hours.

2. *Number of Service Facilities.* By increasing the number of service facilities, such as tool cribs, toll booths, or bank tellers; or by dedicating some facilities in a phase to a unique set of services, management can increase system capacity.

3. *Number of Phases.* Managers can decide to allocate service tasks to sequential phases if they determine that two sequential service facilities may be more efficient than one. For instance, in assembly lines a decision concerns the number of phases or workers needed along the assembly line. Determining the number of workers needed on the line also involves assigning a certain set of work elements to each one. Changing the facility arrangement can increase the service rate, μ, of each facility and the capacity of the system.

4. *Number of Servers per Facility.* Managers can influence the service rate by assigning more than one person to a service facility.

5. *Server Efficiency.* By adjusting the capital-to-labor ratio, devising improved work methods, or instituting incentive programs, management can increase the efficiency of servers assigned to a service facility. Such changes are reflected in μ.

6. *Priority Rule.* Managers set the priority rule to be used, decide whether to have a different priority rule for each service facility, and decide whether to allow preemption (and, if so, under what conditions). Such decisions affect the waiting times of the customers and the utilization of the servers.

7. *Line Arrangement.* Managers can influence customer waiting times and server utilization by deciding whether to have a single line or a line for each facility in a given phase of service.

Obviously, these factors are interrelated. An adjustment in the customer arrival rate, λ, might have to be accompanied by an increase in the service rate, μ, in some way. Decisions about the number of facilities, the number of phases, and waiting-line arrangements also are related.

For each of the problems we analyzed with the waiting-line models, the arrivals had a Poisson distribution (or exponential interarrival times), the service times had an exponential distribution, the service facilities had a simple arrangement, and the priority discipline was first-come, first-served. Waiting-line theory has been used to develop other models in which these criteria are not met, but these models are complex. Many times, the nature of the customer population, the constraints on the line, the priority rule, the service-time distribution, and the arrangement of the facilities are such that waiting-line theory is no longer useful. In these cases, simulation often is used.

> STUDENT CD-ROM AND INTERNET RESOURCES <

The Student CD-ROM and the Companion Website at **www.prenhall.com/krajewski** contain many tools, activities, and resources designed for this supplement.

> KEY EQUATIONS <

1. Customer arrival Poisson distribution: $P_n = \dfrac{(\lambda T)^n}{n!} e^{-\lambda T}$

2. Service-time exponential distribution: $P[t \le T] = 1 - e^{-\mu T}$

	Single-Server Model	Multiple-Server Model	Finite-Source Model
Average utilization of the system	$\rho = \dfrac{\lambda}{\mu}$	$\rho = \dfrac{\lambda}{s\mu}$	$\rho = 1 - P_0$
Probability that n customers are in the system	$P_n = (1 - \rho)\rho^n$	$P_n = \begin{cases} \dfrac{(\lambda/\mu)^n}{n!}P_0 & 0 < n < s \\[2ex] \dfrac{(\lambda/\mu)^n}{s!\, s^{n-s}}P_0 & n \geq s \end{cases}$	
Probability that zero customers are in the system	$P_0 = 1 - \rho$	$P_0 = \left[\displaystyle\sum_{n=0}^{s-1} \dfrac{(\lambda/\mu)^n}{n!} + \dfrac{(\lambda/\mu)^s}{s!}\left(\dfrac{1}{1-\rho}\right) \right]^{-1}$	$P_0 = \left[\displaystyle\sum_{n=0}^{N} \dfrac{N!}{(N-n)!}\left(\dfrac{\lambda}{\mu}\right)^n \right]^{-1}$
Average number of customers in the service system	$L = \dfrac{\lambda}{\mu - \lambda}$	$L = \lambda W$	$L = N - \dfrac{\mu}{\lambda}(1 - P_0)$
Average number of customers in the waiting line	$L_q = \rho L$	$L_q = \dfrac{P_0(\lambda/\mu)^s \rho}{s!(1-\rho)^2}$	$L_q = N - \dfrac{\lambda + \mu}{\lambda}(1 - P_0)$
Average time spent in the system, including service	$W = \dfrac{1}{\mu - \lambda}$	$W = W_q + \dfrac{1}{\mu}$	$W = L[(N - L)\lambda]^{-1}$
Average waiting time in line	$W_q = \rho W$	$W_q = \dfrac{L_q}{\lambda}$	$W_q = L_q[(N - L)\lambda]^{-1}$

> KEY TERMS <

channel 294
customer population 292
interarrival times 296
Little's law 301

phase 294
preemptive discipline 295
priority rule 292

service facility 292
service system 292
waiting line 292

> SOLVED PROBLEM 1 <

A photographer takes passport pictures at an average rate of 20 pictures per hour. The photographer must wait until the customer blinks or scowls, so the time to take a picture is exponentially distributed. Customers arrive at a Poisson-distributed average rate of 19 customers per hour.

a. What is the utilization of the photographer?

b. How much time will the average customer spend with the photographer?

SOLUTION

a. The assumptions in the problem statement are consistent with a single-server model. Utilization is

$$\rho = \frac{\lambda}{\mu} = \frac{19}{20} = 0.95$$

b. The average customer time spent with the photographer is

$$W = \frac{1}{\mu - \lambda} = \frac{1}{20 - 19} = 1 \text{ hour}$$

> SOLVED PROBLEM 2 <

The Mega Multiplex Movie Theater has three concession clerks serving customers on a first-come, first-served basis. The service time per customer is exponentially distributed with an average of 2 minutes per customer. Concession customers wait in a single line in a large lobby, and arrivals are Poisson distributed with an average of 81 customers per hour. Previews run for 10 minutes before the start of each show. If the average time in the concession area exceeds 10 minutes, customers become dissatisfied.

   a. What is the average utilization of the concession clerks?
   b. What is the average time spent in the concession area?

SOLUTION

a. The problem statement is consistent with the multiple-server model, and the average utilization rate is

$$\rho = \frac{\lambda}{s\mu} = \frac{81 \text{ customers/hour}}{(3 \text{ servers})\left(\dfrac{60 \text{ minutes/server hour}}{2 \text{ minutes/customer}}\right)} = 0.90$$

The concession clerks are busy 90 percent of the time.

b. The average time spent in the system, W, is

$$W = W_q + \frac{1}{\mu}$$

Here,

$$W_q = \frac{L_q}{\lambda} \quad L_q = \frac{P_0(\lambda/\mu)^s \rho}{s!(1-\rho)^2} \quad \text{and} \quad P_0 = \left[\sum_{n=0}^{s-1}\frac{(\lambda/\mu)^n}{n!} + \frac{(\lambda/\mu)^s}{s!}\left(\frac{1}{1-\rho}\right)\right]^{-1}$$

We must solve for P_0, L_q, and W_q, in that order, before we can solve for W:

$$P_0 = \left[\sum_{n=0}^{s-1}\frac{(\lambda/\mu)^n}{n!} + \frac{(\lambda/\mu)^s}{s!}\left(\frac{1}{1-\rho}\right)\right]^{-1}$$

$$= \frac{1}{1 + \dfrac{(81/30)}{1} + \dfrac{(2.7)^2}{2} + \left[\dfrac{(2.7)^3}{6}\left(\dfrac{1}{1-0.9}\right)\right]}$$

$$= \frac{1}{1+2.7+3.645+32.805} = \frac{1}{40.15} = 0.0249$$

$$L_q = \frac{P_0(\lambda/\mu)^s \rho}{s!(1-\rho)^2} = \frac{0.0249(81/30)^3(0.9)}{3!(1-0.9)^2} = \frac{0.4411}{6(0.01)} = 7.352 \text{ customers}$$

$$W_q = \frac{L_q}{\lambda} = \frac{7.352 \text{ customers}}{81 \text{ customers/hour}} = 0.0908 \text{ hour}$$

$$W = W_q + \frac{1}{\mu} = 0.0908 \text{ hour} + \frac{1}{30}\text{hour} = (0.1241 \text{ hour})\left(\frac{60 \text{ minutes}}{\text{hour}}\right)$$

$$= 7.45 \text{ minutes}$$

With three concession clerks, customers will spend an average of 7.45 minutes in the concession area.

> SOLVED PROBLEM 3 <

The Severance Coal Mine serves six trains having exponentially distributed interarrival times averaging 30 hours. The time required to fill a train with coal varies with the number of cars, weather-related delays, and equipment breakdowns. The time to fill a train can be approximated by an exponential distribution with a mean of 6 hours 40 minutes. The railroad requires the coal mine to pay large demurrage charges in the event that a train spends more than 24 hours at the mine. What is the average time a train will spend at the mine?

SOLUTION

The problem statement describes a finite-source model, with $N = 6$. The average time spent at the mine is $W = L\,[(N - L)\lambda]^{-1}$, with $1/\lambda = 30$ hours/train, $\lambda = 0.8$ train/day, and $\mu = 3.6$ trains/day. In this case,

$$P_0 = \left[\sum_{n=0}^{N} \frac{N!}{(N-n)!}\left(\frac{\lambda}{\mu}\right)^n\right]^{-1} = \frac{1}{\displaystyle\sum_{n=0}^{6} \frac{6!}{(6-n)!}\left(\frac{0.8}{3.6}\right)^n}$$

$$= \frac{1}{\left[\dfrac{6!}{6!}\left(\dfrac{0.8}{3.6}\right)^0\right] + \left[\dfrac{6!}{5!}\left(\dfrac{0.8}{3.6}\right)^1\right] + \left[\dfrac{6!}{4!}\left(\dfrac{0.8}{3.6}\right)^2\right] + \left[\dfrac{6!}{3!}\left(\dfrac{0.8}{3.6}\right)^3\right] + \left[\dfrac{6!}{2!}\left(\dfrac{0.8}{3.6}\right)^4\right] + \left[\dfrac{6!}{1!}\left(\dfrac{0.8}{3.6}\right)^5\right] + \left[\dfrac{6!}{0!}\left(\dfrac{0.8}{3.6}\right)^6\right]}$$

$$= \frac{1}{1+1.33+1.48+1.32+0.88+0.39+0.09} = \frac{1}{6.49} = 0.1541$$

$$L = N - \frac{\mu}{\lambda}(1-P_0) = 6 - \left[\frac{3.6}{0.8}(1-0.1541)\right] = 2.193 \text{ trains}$$

$$W = L[(N-L)\lambda]^{-1} = \frac{2.193}{(3.807)0.8} = 0.72 \text{ day}$$

Arriving trains will spend an average of 0.72 day at the coal mine.

> PROBLEMS <

Software, such as OM Explorer, Active Models, and POM for Windows, is packaged with every new copy of the textbook. Check with your instructor on how best to use it. In many cases, the instructor wants you to understand how to do the calculations by hand. At most, the software provides a check on your calculations. When calculations are particularly complex and the goal is interpreting the results in making decisions, the software replaces entirely the manual calculations. The software also can be a valuable resource well after your course is completed.

1. The Solomon, Smith, and Samson law firm produces many legal documents that must be word processed for clients and the firm. Requests average 8 pages of documents per hour, and they arrive according to a Poisson distribution. The secretary can word process 10 pages per hour on average according to an exponential distribution.

   a. What is the average utilization rate of the secretary?

   b. What is the probability that more than 4 pages are waiting or being word processed?

   c. What is the average number of pages waiting to be word processed?

2. Benny's Arcade has six video game machines. The average time between machine failures is 50 hours. Jimmy, the maintenance engineer, can repair a machine in 15 hours on the average. The machines have an exponential failure distribution, and Jimmy has an exponential service-time distribution.

   a. What is Jimmy's utilization?

   b. What is the average number of machines out of service, that is, waiting to be repaired or being repaired?

   c. What is the average time a machine is out of service?

3. Moore, Aiken, and Payne is a dental clinic serving the needs of the general public on a first-come, first-served basis. The clinic has three dental chairs, each staffed by a dentist. Patients arrive at the rate of five per hour, according to a Poisson distribution, and do not balk or renege. The average time required for a dental checkup is 30 minutes, according to an exponential distribution.

   a. What is the probability that no patients are in the clinic?

   b. What is the probability that six or more patients are in the clinic?

   c. What is the average number of patients waiting?

   d. What is the average total time that a patient spends in the clinic?

4. Fantastic Styling Salon is run by two stylists, Jenny Perez and Jill Sloan, each capable of serving five customers per hour, on average. Eight customers, on average, arrive at the salon each hour.

   a. If all arriving customers wait in a common line for the next available stylist, how long would a customer wait in line, on average, before being served?

   b. Suppose that 50 percent of the arriving customers want to be served only by Perez and that the other 50 percent want only Sloan. How long would a customer wait in line, on average, before being served by Perez? By Sloan? What is the average customer waiting time in the line?

   c. Do you observe a difference in the answers to parts (a) and (b)? If so, why? Explain.

5. You are the manager of a local bank where three tellers provide services to customers. On average, each teller takes three minutes to serve a customer. Customers arrive, on average, at a rate of 50 per hour. Having recently received complaints from some customers that they waited a long time before being served, your boss asks you to evaluate the service system. Specifically, you must provide answers to the following questions:

   a. What is the average utilization of the three-teller service system?

   b. What is the probability that no customers are being served by a teller or are waiting in line?

   c. What is the average number of customers waiting in line?

   d. On average, how long does a customer wait in line before being served?

   e. On average, how many customers would be at a teller's station and in line?

6. Jake Tweet hosts a psychology talk show on KRAN radio. Jake's advice averages 10 minutes per caller but varies according to an exponential distribution. The average time between calls is 25 minutes, exponentially distributed. Generating calls in this local market is difficult, so Jake does not want to lose any calls to busy signals. The radio station has only three telephone lines. What is the probability that a caller receives a busy signal?

7. The supervisor at the Precision Machine Shop wants to determine the staffing policy that minimizes total operating costs. The average arrival rate at the tool crib, where tools are dispensed to the workers, is 8 machinists per hour. Each machinist's pay is $20 per hour. The supervisor can staff the crib either with a junior attendant who is paid $5 per hour and can process 10 arrivals per hour or with a senior attendant who is paid $12 per hour and can process 16 arrivals per hour. Which attendant should be selected, and what would be the total estimated hourly cost?

8. The daughter of the owner of a local hamburger restaurant is preparing to open a new fast-food restaurant called Hasty Burgers. Based on the arrival rates at her father's outlets, she expects customers to arrive at the drive-up window according to a Poison distribution, with a mean of 20 customers per hour. The service rate is flexible; however, the service times are expected to follow an exponential distribution. The drive-in window is a single-server operation.

   a. What service rate is needed to keep the average number of customers in the service system (waiting line and being served) to 4?

   b. For the service rate in part (a), what is the probability that more than 4 customers are in line and being served?

   c. For the service rate in part (a), what is the average waiting time in line for each customer? Does this average seem satisfactory for a fast-food business?

ADVANCED PROBLEMS

9. Three employees in the maintenance department are responsible for repairing the video games at Pinball Wizard, a video arcade. A maintenance worker can fix one video game machine every 8 hours on average, with an exponential distribution. An average of one video game machine fails every 3 hours, according to a Poisson distribution. Each down machine costs the Wizard $10 per hour in lost income. A new maintenance worker would cost $8 per hour.

   Should the manager hire any new personnel? If so, how many? What would you recommend to the manager, based on your analysis?

10. The College of Business and Public Administration at Benton University has a copy machine on each floor for faculty use. Heavy use of the five copy machines causes frequent failures. Maintenance records show that a machine fails every 2.5 days (or $\lambda = 0.40$ failure/day). The college has a maintenance contract with the authorized dealer of the copy machines. Because the copy machines fail so frequently, the dealer has assigned one person to the college to repair them. This person can repair an average of 2.5 machines per day. Using the finite-source model, answer the following questions:

   a. What is the average utilization of the maintenance person?

   b. On average, how many copy machines are being repaired or waiting to be repaired?

   c. What is the average time spent by a copy machine in the repair system (waiting and being repaired)?

11. You are in charge of a quarry that supplies sand and stone aggregates to your company's construction sites. Empty trucks from construction sites arrive at the quarry's huge piles of sand and stone aggregates and wait in line to enter the station, which can load either sand or aggregate. At the station, they are filled with material, weighed, checked out, and proceed to a construction site. Currently, nine empty trucks arrive per hour, on average. Once a truck has entered a loading station, it takes 6 minutes for it to be filled, weighed, and checked out. Concerned that trucks are spending too much time waiting and being filled, you are evaluating two alternatives to reduce the average time the trucks spend in the system. The first alternative is to add side boards to the trucks (so that more material could be loaded) and to add a helper at the loading station (so that filling time could be reduced) at a total cost of $50,000. The arrival rate of trucks would change to six per hour, and the filling time would be reduced to 4 minutes. The second alternative is to add another loading station at a cost of $80,000. The trucks would wait in a common line and the truck at the front of the line would move to the next available station.

   Which alternative would you recommend if you want to reduce the current average waiting time in the system?

> SELECTED REFERENCES <

Cooper, Robert B. *Introduction to Queuing Theory*, 2d ed. New York: Elsevier-North Holland, 1980.

Hartvigsen, David. *SimQuick: Process Simulation with Excel*, 2d ed. Upper Saddle River, NJ: Prentice Hall, 2004.

Hillier, F. S., and G. S. Lieberman. *Introduction to Operations Research*, 2d ed. San Francisco: Holden-Day, 1975.

Little, J. D. C. "A Proof for the Queuing Formula: $L = \lambda W$." *Operations Research*, vol. 9, (1961), pp. 383–387.

Moore, P. M. *Queues, Inventories and Maintenance.* New York: John Wiley & Sons, 1958.

Saaty, T. L. *Elements of Queuing Theory with Applications.* New York: McGraw-Hill, 1961.

8

The Internet has revolutionized the way traditional businesses design their processes, even to the point of layout design. RiverTown Crossings Mall has clustered company stores to improve comparison shopping, a convenience that Web retailing already offers online customers.

CHAPTER 8

Process Layout

RIVERTOWN CROSSINGS

A 35-year-old mother does not know it, but the Internet has made her trips to the mall a little easier. In 2000, RiverTown Crossings opened its doors in Grandville, Michigan. Since then, she rarely ventures beyond just one section of the mall—the one with Abercrombie Kids, Gap Kids, Gymboree, and other kids' clothing stores. She can shop in that wing and find almost everything she needs. In an effort to compete with the allure of online shopping, the mall owner, General Growth Properties, Inc., selected a layout that runs counter to decades of retailing wisdom: It clustered competing stores together. Shoppers were asking for such clusters long before Web retailing took off, and General Growth began experimenting with the idea three years ago. Now, all of its new malls will have clusters.

Worried about a future when shoppers point and click instead of park and walk and wait in line, developers are finally trying to make it more convenient to shop in malls. Some owners are revising their existing layouts by removing large fixtures, such as planters and fountains, to clear sight lines to storefronts. Others are adding directories that are easier to understand than current mall maps. A few malls in the design stages are opting to put anchor department stores closer together—a layout that cuts down on walking. A few malls are trying to offer shoppers elements of the Web using high-tech directories. At the Dayton Mall in Ohio, sleek electronic kiosks give shoppers e-mail access and let them search for names of stores carrying types of merchandise, such as "sweaters." The

For additional chapter resources check the Student CD-ROM or the Companion Website at **www.prenhall.com/krajewski**

kiosks also have printers that can spit out a map with a store's location highlighted.

Beneath the new layout designs is an old retailing secret: The traditional mall was designed to be difficult. This planned inconvenience made customers who wanted to comparison-shop walk from one end of the mall to the other, so that they had every chance to make impulse purchases in between. Many developers left little to chance in directing the traffic flow to their advantage, using plants, carpeting, and other fixtures to set winding routes past stores.

Revising the layout of existing malls to make them more convenient is costly. Most of them are jungles of escalators, fountains, and play areas—and those are the

easy obstacles. The tougher problem is figuring out how to rearrange similar stores that are probably operating on long leases. After all, a mall developer cannot simply order four shoe store tenants to pick up and move. And many retailers still prefer to keep their distance from competitors. RiverTown's Hallmark Gold Crown store is located on the first level on the north end of the mall, while an American Greetings store is on the second level on the south end. Hallmark Cards' location strategy calls for space between its stores and competitors.

layout planning

Planning that involves decisions about the physical arrangement of economic activity centers needed by a facility's various processes.

economic activity center

Anything that consumes space; for example, a person or a group of people, a customer reception area, a teller window, a machine, a workstation, a department, an aisle, or a storage room.

Revising layouts is another way of improving processes. Layouts put other decisions on processes in tangible, physical form, converting process structures, flowcharts, and capacity plans into brick and mortar. The new layout of RiverTown Crossings demonstrates the impact of layout on customer attitudes and satisfaction. In this chapter, we focus on **layout planning**, which involves decisions about the physical arrangement of economic activity centers needed by a facility's various processes. An **economic activity center** can be anything that consumes space: a person or group of people, a customer reception area, a teller window, a machine, a workstation, a department, an aisle, a storage room, and so on. The goal of layout planning is to allow customers, workers, and equipment to operate most effectively.

We begin by defining four basic layout types and associated performance measures. After examining hybrid layouts, we consider a variety of techniques and settings for flexible-flow layouts. Warehouse and office layouts are given special attention, due to their prevalence. We conclude with the design of line-flow layouts.

Layouts affect not just the flow of work between processes at a facility; they also affect processes elsewhere in a value chain. Consider a manufacturer enjoying higher volumes, which modified its layout to allow more line flows. The new layout has several production lines, each with its own unloading dock for purchased parts and raw materials. With the new layout, suppliers can deliver their items right to the production line rather that to a central receiving area for storage. Suppliers now deliver smaller quantities, more frequently, and to a specific production schedule. The new layout also enables more consistent production flows, which results in more predictable capacity needs for the delivery process. Thus process layout decisions should be made in light of their effects on the entire value chain.

> MANAGING PROCESS LAYOUT ACROSS THE ORGANIZATION <

Layouts are found in every area of a business because every facility has a layout. Good layouts can improve coordination across departmental lines and functional area boundaries. Each process in a facility has a layout that should be carefully designed. The layouts of retail operations, such as the mall at RiverTown Crossings or one of the stores at The Limited, can affect customer attitudes and therefore sales. How a manufacturing or warehousing process is laid out affects materials handling costs, throughput times, and worker productivity. Redesigning layouts can require significant capital investments, which need to be analyzed from an accounting and financial perspective. Layouts also affect employee attitudes, whether on a production line or in an office.

> LAYOUT PLANNING <

Layout plans translate the broader decisions about the competitive priorities, process strategy, quality, and capacity of its processes into actual physical arrangements of people, equipment, and space. Before a manager can make decisions regarding physical arrangement, four questions must be addressed.

1. *What Centers Should the Layout Include?* Centers should reflect process decisions and maximize productivity. For example, a customer information desk near the entrance of a bank or hotel can better guide customers to the desired services.

2. *How Much Space and Capacity Does Each Center Need?* Inadequate space can reduce productivity, deprive employees of privacy, and even create safety hazards. However, excessive space is wasteful, can reduce productivity, and can isolate employees unnecessarily.

3. *How Should Each Center's Space Be Configured?* The amount of space, its shape, and the elements in a center are interrelated. For example, placement of a desk and chair relative to the other furniture is determined by the size and shape of the office, as well as the activities performed there. Providing a pleasing atmosphere also should be considered as part of the layout configuration decisions, especially in retail outlets and offices.

4. *Where Should Each Center Be Located?* Location can significantly affect productivity. For example, employees who must frequently interact with one another face to face should be placed in a central location rather than in separate, remote locations to reduce time lost traveling back and forth.

The location of a center has two dimensions: (1) *relative location*, or the placement of a center relative to other centers and (2) *absolute location*, or the particular space that the center occupies within the facility. Both affect a center's performance. Look at the grocery store layout in Figure 8.1(a). It shows the location of five departments, with the dry groceries department allocated twice the space of each of the others. The location of frozen foods relative to bread is the same as the location of meats relative to vegetables, so the distance between the first pair of departments equals the distance between the second pair of departments. Relative location is normally the crucial issue when travel time, materials handling cost, and communication effectiveness are important.

Now look at the plan in Figure 8.1(b). Although the relative locations are the same, the absolute locations have changed. This modified layout might prove unworkable. For example, the cost of moving the meats to the upper-left corner could be excessive; or customers might react negatively to the placement of vegetables in the bottom-left corner, preferring them to be near the entrance.

> STRATEGIC ISSUES <

Layout choices can help immensely in communicating an organization's product plans and competitive priorities. As Managerial Practice 8.1 illustrates, if a retailer plans to upgrade the quality of its merchandise, the store layout should convey more exclusiveness and luxury.

Layout has many practical and strategic implications. Altering a layout can affect an organization and how well it meets its competitive priorities in the following ways:

- Increasing customer satisfaction and sales at a retail store
- Facilitating the flow of materials and information
- Increasing the efficient utilization of labor and equipment
- Reducing hazards to workers
- Improving employee morale
- Improving communication

USING OPERATIONS TO COMPETE

Operations As a Competitive Weapon
Operations Strategy
Project Management

MANAGING PROCESSES

Process Strategy
Process Analysis
Process Performance and Quality
Constraint Management
Process Layout
Lean Systems

MANAGING VALUE CHAINS

Supply Chain Strategy
Location
Inventory Management
Forecasting
Sales and Operations Planning
Resource Planning
Scheduling

(a) Original layout

(b) Revised layout

FIGURE 8.1

Identical Relative Locations
and Different Absolute Locations

The Limited

The Limited, Inc., the specialty clothing retailer with more than 4,500 stores across North America, uses the look of its stores to match its strategy. Once a small outlet geared to teenagers, the store has quadrupled in size and changed its look to that of a European boutique in order to attract older customers. From the grainy wood floors to the black lacquered display cases, the store serves as a stage for trendy sportswear for women. The Limited spent millions on a fresh look. The look is intended to entice customers to spend more time in its stores and pay more for merchandise.

In 1999, The Limited spun off Limited Too, a rapidly growing retailer that sells apparel, swimwear, underwear, lifestyle, and personal care products for active fashion-aware girls between 7 and 14 years. The layout of these stores is quite different. They are colorful and fun with a high-energy atmosphere. The lighting, which includes handmade globe lights with broken glass color mosaics, enhances the excitement. Limited Too added a new high-tech element in select stores: full spectrum digital lighting. It uses a light-emitting diode (LED)-based system. This system generates colors and colored-lighting effects via microprocessor-controlled red, green, and blue LEDs. Limited Too is using the digital lighting to highlight its signature and most eye-catching layout element: a 3-D banner soffit curved-wall projection that is 5 feet high and about 50 feet long. The color-changing digital lights bring the banner soffit to life and reflect the playful, youthful spirit of the store.

Color Kinetics lighting brings Limited Too's cool, colorful graphics to life through C-Series fixtures, which illuminate the store's soffit.

Wal-Mart

Wal-Mart, the discount giant and largest U.S. retailer, appeals to customers who are as concerned about service as about low prices. With wide aisles, less-cramped racks, sitting areas for customers, and attractive displays, the store looks more like an upscale department store than a discount store. As in department stores, the displays organize related products—such as shower curtains, towels, and ceramic bathroom accessories—into visual "vignettes" that encourage sales of "multiples" of related products. Unlike department stores, however, the store has the same bargain-basement prices and wide selection offered in all its outlets. Many retailing executives consider Wal-Mart the leader in attention to the layout details that help shape shoppers' attitudes. The chain is particularly adept at striking the delicate balance needed to convince customers that its prices are low without making people feel that its stores are cheap.

Wal-Mart's Web site (www.walmart.com) provides a virtual storefront that is quite consistent with the shopping experience at its brick-and-mortar physical store. Behind the Amazon.com-like site architecture is the floor plan of your local superstore: products organized by department in aisles, with checkout registers and customer service at the door. While the Web site might be exactly right for its target customers, some critics believe the site reflects a legacy mind-set in its efforts in the virtual world.

Sources: "Lighting Goes High-Tech," *Chain Store Age* (January 1, 2000); "The Business Logic of Site Architecture," *The Industry Standard* (April 17, 2000).

The type of operation determines layout requirements. For example, in warehouses, materials flows and stockpicking costs are dominant considerations. In retail stores, customer convenience and sales may dominate, whereas communication effectiveness and team building may be crucial in an office.

LAYOUT TYPES

The choice of layout type depends largely on process structure—the position of the processes on the customer-contact matrix for service providers and on the product-process matrix for manufacturing processes. The four basic types of layout include (1) flexible flow, (2) line flow, (3) hybrid, and (4) fixed position.

Flexible-Flow Layouts Front-office and job processes with highly divergent work flows have low volume and high customization. For such processes, the manager should choose a **flexible-flow layout**, which organizes resources (employees and equipment) by function rather than by service or product. For example, in the metal-working job processes shown in

flexible-flow layout

A layout that organizes resources (employees and equipment) by function rather than by service or product.

FIGURE **8.2**

Two Layout Types

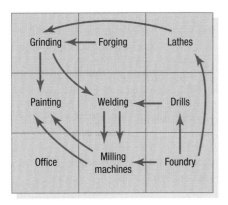

(a) Layout of a job shop

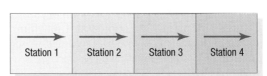

(b) Layout of a production line

Figure 8.2(a), all drills are located in one area of the machine shop and all milling machines are located in another area. The flexible-flow layout is most common when the operation must intermittently serve many different customer types or manufacture many different products or parts. Demand levels are too low or unpredictable for management to set aside human and capital resources exclusively for a particular type of customer or product line. Advantages of the flexible-flow layout over the line-flow layout, illustrated by Figure 8.2(b), where centers are arranged in a linear path, include general-purpose and less capital-intensive resources, more flexibility to handle changes in product mix, more specialized employee supervision when job content requires a good deal of technical knowledge, and higher equipment utilization. When volumes are low, dedicating resources to each service or product (as done with a line-flow layout) would require more equipment than would pooling the requirements for all products.[1] A major challenge in designing a flexible-flow layout is to locate centers so that they bring some order to the apparent chaos of divergent processes with flexible work flows.

Line-Flow Layouts Back offices and line processes typically have linear work flows and repetitive tasks. For such processes, the manager should dedicate resources to individual services, products, or tasks. This strategy is achieved by a **line-flow layout**, illustrated by Figure 8.2(b), in which workstations or departments are arranged in a linear path. As in an automated car wash, the customer or product moves along in a smooth, continuous flow. Resources are arranged around the customer's or product's route, rather than shared across many of them. Although line-flow layouts often follow a straight line, a straight line is not always best, and layouts may take an L, O, S, or U shape. The layout often is called a *production line* or an *assembly line*. The difference between the two is that an assembly line is limited to assembly processes, whereas a production line can be used to perform other processes, such as machining.

Such layouts often rely heavily on specialized, capital-intensive resources. When volumes are high, the advantages of line-flow layouts over flexible-flow layouts include faster processing rates, lower inventories, and less unproductive time lost to changeovers and materials handling. Less need to decouple one operation from the next allows management to cut inventories. The Japanese refer to a line process as *overlapped operations*, whereby materials move directly from one operation to the next without waiting in queues.

For line-flow layouts, deciding where to locate centers is easy because operations must occur in a prescribed order. Centers can simply be placed to follow the work flow, which ensures that all interacting pairs of centers are as close together as possible or have a common boundary. The challenge of line-flow layout is to group activities into workstations and achieve the desired output rate with the least resources. The composition and number of workstations are crucial decisions, which we explore later in the chapter.

Hybrid Layouts More often than not, the layout combines elements of both divergent and line-flow processes. This intermediate strategy calls for a **hybrid layout**, in which some portions of the facility are arranged in a flexible-flow layout and others are arranged in a line-flow layout. Hybrid layouts are used in facilities that have both fabrication and assembly

line-flow layout

A layout in which workstations or departments are arranged in a linear path.

hybrid layout

An arrangement in which some portions of the facility have a flexible-flow layout and others have a line-flow layout.

[1]However, management would not allow utilization to get too high. A larger capacity cushion for divergent processes absorbs the more unpredictable demands of customized services and products.

operations, as would be the case if both types of layout shown in Figure 8.2 were in the same building. Fabrication operations—in which components are made from raw materials—have a jumbled flow, whereas assembly operations—in which components are assembled into finished products—have a line flow. Operations managers also create hybrid layouts when introducing cells and flexible automation, such as a flexible manufacturing system (FMS). A *cell* is two or more dissimilar workstations located close together through which a limited number of parts or models are processed with line flows. We cover two special types of cells—group technology (GT) cells and one-worker, multiple-machines (OWMM) cells—later in this chapter. An *FMS* is a group of computer-controlled workstations at which materials are automatically handled and machine loaded. These technologies help achieve repeatability, even when product volumes are too low to justify dedicating a single line to one product, by bringing together all resources needed to make a family of parts in one center.

fixed-position layout

An arrangement in which the service or manufacturing site is fixed in place; employees, along with their equipment, come to the site to do their work.

Fixed-Position Layout The fourth basic type of layout is the **fixed-position layout**. In this arrangement, the service or manufacturing site is fixed in place; employees, along with their equipment, come to the site to do their work. Many projects have this arrangement. This type of layout makes sense when the product is particularly massive or difficult to move, as in building a new office complex, shipbuilding, assembling locomotives, making huge pressure vessels, building dams, or repairing home furnaces. A fixed-position layout minimizes the number of times that the product must be moved and often is the only feasible solution.

PERFORMANCE CRITERIA

Other fundamental choices facing the layout planner concern *performance criteria*, which may include one or more of the following factors:

- Customer satisfaction
- Level of capital investment
- Requirements for materials handling
- Ease of stockpicking
- Work environment and "atmosphere"
- Ease of equipment maintenance
- Employee and internal customer attitudes
- Amount of flexibility needed
- Customer convenience and level of sales

Managers must decide early in the process which factors to emphasize in order to come up with a good layout solution. In most cases, multiple criteria are used. For example, a warehouse manager may emphasize ease in stockpicking, flexibility, and amount of space needed (capital investment).

Customer Satisfaction When customer contact (either external or internal) is high and the customer is present and actively involved when a service is being provided, customer satisfaction is a key performance measure. The layout uses "spatial language" to communicate the competitive priorities associated with the service. Customer loyalty, emotional connection, customer convenience, and level of sales can all be influenced by the layout. For example, a retail store manager may emphasize atmosphere, customer satisfaction, flexibility, and sales as the top performance criteria. Sales are particularly important to the layout of retail facilities, where managers place items with high-profitability per cubic foot of shelf space in the most prominent display areas and impulse-buy items near the entrance of the checkout counter. A good layout depends on how the various measures of customer satisfaction are met and how well it communicates the competitive priorities that the

A financial consultant discusses options with a young couple at their home. This process has a fixed-position layout because the consultant goes to customer sites to provide his or her services.

owner wants the customers to experience. Of course, capital expenditure and flexibility considerations also enter the equation.

Capital Investment Floor space, equipment needs, and inventory levels are assets that the firm buys or leases. These expenditures are an important criterion in all settings. If an office layout is to have partitions to increase privacy, the cost rises. Even increasing space for filing cabinets can add up. A four-drawer lateral file occupies about nine square feet, including the space needed to open it. At $25 per square foot, that translates into a floor space "rental" of $225 a year.

Materials Handling Relative locations of centers should restrict large flows to short distances. Centers between which frequent trips or interactions are required should be placed close to one another. In a manufacturing plant, this approach minimizes materials handling costs. In a warehouse, stockpicking costs are reduced by storing items typically needed for the same order next to one another. In a retail store, customer convenience improves if items are grouped predictably to minimize customer search and travel time. In an office, communication and cooperation often improve when people or departments that must interact frequently are located near one another, because telephone calls and memos can be poor substitutes for face-to-face communication. Spatial separation is one big reason why cross-functional coordination between departments can be challenging.

The modular furniture and partitions in this office facility allow considerable flexibility. The components used to build the workstations can be put together like a tinker toy set, configuring the space as desired. Such flexibility allows entirely new arrangements to be created as business needs change.

Flexibility A flexible layout allows a firm to adapt quickly to changing customer needs and preferences and is best for many situations. **Layout flexibility** means either that the facility remains desirable after significant changes occur or that it can be easily and inexpensively adapted in response to changes. The changes can be in the mix of customers served by a store, goods made at a plant, space requirements in a warehouse, or organizational structure in an office. Using modular furniture and partitions, rather than permanent load-bearing walls, is one way to minimize the cost of office layout changes. So can having wide bays (fewer columns), heavy-duty floors, and extra electrical connections in a plant.

layout flexibility

The property of a facility to remain desirable after significant changes occur or to be easily and inexpensively adapted in response to changes.

For retailers, the height of flexibility is the kiosks that display a variety of novelty and specialty items on sale in the center aisles of malls. They have an ever-changing array of merchandise that transform once-utilitarian passageways into retailing hot spots. The kiosks are right where the customers have to walk and create a stream of impulse purchases.

Other Criteria Other criteria that may be important include labor productivity, machine maintenance, work environment, and organizational structure. Labor productivity can be affected if certain workstations can be operated by common personnel in some layouts but not in others. Downtime spent waiting for materials can be caused by materials handling difficulties resulting from poor layout.

> CREATING HYBRID LAYOUTS <

When volumes are not high enough to justify dedicating a single line of multiple workers to a single customer type or product, managers still may be able to derive the benefits of line-flow layout—simpler materials handling, low setups, and reduced labor costs—by creating line-flow layouts in some portions of the facility. Two techniques for creating hybrid layouts are one-worker, multiple-machines (OWMM) cells and group technology (GT) cells.

ONE WORKER, MULTIPLE MACHINES

If volumes are not sufficient to keep several workers busy on one production line, the manager might set up a line small enough to keep one worker busy. A one-person cell is the theory behind the **one-worker, multiple-machines (OWMM) cell**, in which a worker operates several different machines simultaneously to achieve a line flow. Having one worker operate several identical machines is not unusual. However, with an OWMM cell, several different machines are in the line.

one-worker, multiple-machines (OWMM) cell

A one-person cell in which a worker operates several different machines simultaneously to achieve a line flow.

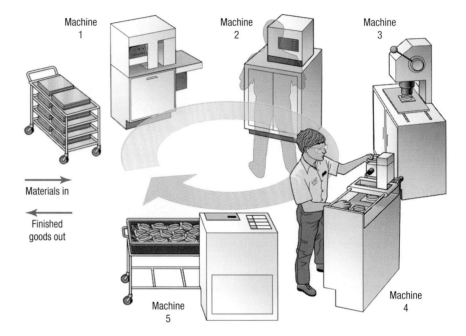

Figure 8.3 illustrates a five-machine OWMM cell that is being used to produce a flanged metal part, with the machines encircling one operator in the center. (A U shape also is common.) The operator moves around the circle, performing tasks (typically loading and unloading) that have not been automated. Different products or parts can be produced in an OWMM cell by changing the machine setups. If the setup on one machine is especially time-consuming for one part, management can add a duplicate machine to the cell for use whenever that part is being produced.

An OWMM arrangement reduces both inventory and labor requirements. Inventory is cut because, rather than piling up in queues, materials move directly into the next operation. Labor is cut because more work is automated. The addition of several low-cost automated devices can maximize the number of machines included in an OWMM arrangement: automatic tool changers, loaders and unloaders, start and stop devices, and fail-safe devices that detect defective parts or products. Japanese manufacturers are applying the OWMM concept widely because of their desire to achieve low inventories.

GROUP TECHNOLOGY

group technology (GT)

An option for achieving line-flow layouts with low-volume processes; this technique creates cells not limited to just one worker and has a unique way of selecting work to be done by the cell.

A second option for achieving line-flow layouts with low volume processes is **group technology (GT)**. This manufacturing technique creates cells not limited to just one worker and has a unique way of selecting work to be done by the cell. The GT method groups parts or products with similar characteristics into *families* and sets aside groups of machines for their production. Families may be based on size, shape, manufacturing or routing requirements, or demand. The goal is to identify a set of products with similar processing requirements and minimize machine changeover or setup. For example, all bolts might be assigned to the same family because they all require the same basic processing steps regardless of size or shape.

Once parts have been grouped into families, the next step is to organize the machine tools needed to perform the basic processes on these parts into separate cells. The machines in each cell require only minor adjustments to accommodate product changeovers from one part to the next in the same family. By simplifying product routings, GT cells reduce the time a job is in the shop. Queues of materials waiting to be worked on are shortened or eliminated. Frequently, materials handling is automated so that, after loading raw materials into the cell, a worker does not handle machined parts until the job has been completed.

Figure 8.4 compares process flows before and after creation of GT cells. Figure 8.4(a) shows a shop floor where machines are grouped according to function: lathing, milling, drilling, grinding, and assembly. After lathing, a part is moved to one of the milling machines, where it waits in line until it has a higher priority than any other job competing for the machine's capacity. When the milling operation on the part has been finished, the part is

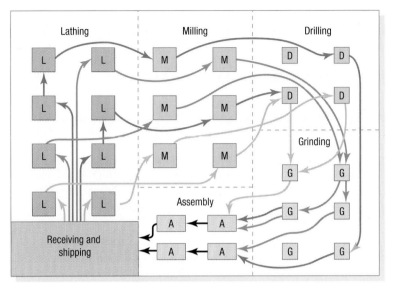

(a) Jumbled flows in a job shop without GT cells

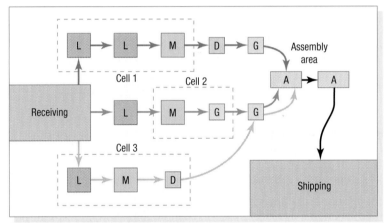

(b) Line flows in a job shop with three GT cells

FIGURE 8.4

Process Flows Before and After

the Use of GT Cells

Source: Mikell P. Groover. *Automation, Production Systems, and Computer-Aided Manufacturing.* 1st Edition, © 1980. Reprinted by permission of Pearson Education, Inc., Upper Saddle River, NJ.

moved to a drilling machine, and so on. The queues can be long, creating significant time delays. Flows of materials are jumbled because the parts being processed in any one area of the shop have so many different routings.

By contrast, the manager of the shop shown in Figure 8.4(b) identified three product families that account for a majority of the firm's production. One family always requires two lathing operations followed by one operation at the milling machines. The second family always requires a milling operation followed by a grinding operation. The third family requires the use of a lathe, a milling machine, and a drill press. For simplicity, only the flows of parts assigned to these three families are shown. The remaining parts are produced at machines outside the cells and still have jumbled routings. Some equipment might have to be duplicated, as when a machine is required for one or more cells and for operations outside the cells. However, by creating three GT cells, the manager has definitely created more line flows and simplified routings.

> DESIGNING FLEXIBLE-FLOW LAYOUTS <

The approach to designing a layout depends on whether a flexible-flow layout or a line-flow layout has been chosen. A fixed-position format basically eliminates the layout problem, whereas the design of the hybrid layout partially uses flexible-flow layout principles and partially uses line-flow layout principles.

Flexible-flow layout involves three basic steps, whether the design is for a new layout or for revising an existing layout: (1) gather information, (2) develop a block plan, and (3) design a detailed layout.

STEP 1: GATHER INFORMATION

The Office of Budget Management (OBM), which is a major division in a large state government, consists of 120 employees assigned to six different departments. It is one of several divisions occupying a relatively new office tower. Workloads have expanded to the extent that 30 new employees must be hired and somehow housed in the space allocated to OBM. While changing the layout, it also makes sense to review the layout to make sure that it is arranged as effectively as possible. The goal is to improve communication among people who must interact and to create a good work environment. Three types of information are needed to begin designing the revised layout for OBM: (1) space requirements by center, (2) available space, and (3) closeness factors.

Space Requirements by Center OBM has grouped its processes into six different departments: administration, social services, institutions, accounting, education, and internal audit. The exact space requirements of each department, in square feet, are as follows.

Department	Area Needed (ft²)
1. Administration	3,500
2. Social services	2,600
3. Institutions	2,400
4. Accounting	1,600
5. Education	1,500
6. Internal audit	3,400
Total	15,000

The layout designer must tie space requirements to capacity and staffing plans; calculate the specific equipment and space needs for each center; and allow circulation space, such as aisles and the like. At OBM, a way must be found to include all 150 employees in its assigned area. Consulting with the managers and employees involved can help avoid excessive resistance to change and make the transition smooth.

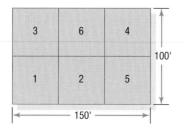

FIGURE 8.5

Current Block Plan for the Office of Budget Management

block plan

A plan that allocates space and indicates placement of each department.

closeness matrix

A table that gives a measure of the relative importance of each pair of centers being located close together.

Available Space A **block plan** allocates space and indicates placement of each department. To describe a new facility layout, the plan need only provide the facility's dimensions and space allocations. When an existing facility layout is being modified, the current block plan also is needed. OBM's available space is 150 feet by 100 feet, or 15,000 square feet. The designer could begin the design by dividing the total amount of space into six equal blocks (2,500 square feet each). The equal-space approximation shown in Figure 8.5 is sufficient until the detailed layout stage, when larger departments (such as administration) are assigned more space than smaller departments.

Closeness Factors The layout designer must also know which centers need to be located close to one another. The following table shows OBM's **closeness matrix**, which gives a measure of the relative importance of each pair of centers being located close together. The metric used depends on the type of processes involved and the organizational setting. It can be a qualitative judgment on a scale from 0 to 10 that the manager uses to account for multiple performance criteria, as in the OBM's case. Only the right-hand portion of the matrix is used. The closeness factors are indicators of the need for proximity based on an analysis of information flows and the need for face-to-face meetings. They give clues as to which departments should be located close together. For example, the most important interaction is between the administration and internal audit departments for OBM, with a score of 10. This closeness factor is given in the first row and last column. Thus, the designer should locate departments 1 and 6 close together, which is not the arrangement in the current layout. Entries in both the columns and rows result in five factor scores for each department.

	Closeness Factors					
Department	**1**	**2**	**3**	**4**	**5**	**6**
1. Administration	—	3	6	5	6	10
2. Social services		—	8	1	1	
3. Institutions			—	3	9	
4. Accounting				—	2	
5. Education					—	1
6. Internal audit						—

At a manufacturing plant, the closeness factor could be the number of trips (or some other measure of materials movement) between each pair of centers per day. This information can be gleaned by conducting a statistical sampling, polling supervisors and materials handlers, or using the routings and ordering frequencies for typical items made at the plant.

Other Considerations Finally, the information gathered for OBM includes performance criteria that depend on the *absolute* location of a department. OBM has two criteria based on absolute location.

1. Education (department 5) should remain where it is because it is next to the office library.
2. Administration (department 1) should remain where it is because that location has the largest conference room, which administration uses often. Relocating the conference room would be costly.

Noise levels and management preference are other potential sources of performance criteria that depend on absolute location. The closeness matrix cannot reflect these criteria because it reflects only *relative* location considerations. The layout designer must list these criteria separately.

STEP 2: DEVELOP A BLOCK PLAN

The second step in layout design is to develop a block plan that best satisfies performance criteria and area requirements. The most elementary way to do so is by trial and error. Because success depends on the designer's ability to spot patterns in the data, this approach does not guarantee the selection of the best or even a nearly best solution. When supplemented by the use of a computer to evaluate solutions, however, research shows that such an approach compares quite favorably with more sophisticated computerized techniques.

Developing a Block Plan	**EXAMPLE 8.1**

Develop an acceptable block plan for the Office of Budget Management, using trial and error. The goal is to locate the departments that have the greatest interaction between them (largest closeness factor) as close to each other as possible.

SOLUTION

A good place to start is with the largest closeness ratings (say, 8 and above). Beginning with the largest factor scores and working down the list, you might plan to locate departments as follows:

a. Departments 1 and 6 close together,

b. Departments 3 and 5 close together,

c. Departments 2 and 3 close together.

Departments 1 and 5 should remain at their current locations because of the "other considerations."

If after several attempts you cannot meet all three requirements, drop one or more and try again. If you can meet all three easily, add more (such as for interactions below 8).

The block plan in Figure 8.6 shows a trial-and-error solution that satisfies all three requirements. We started by keeping departments 1 and 5 in their original locations. As the first requirement is to locate departments 1 and

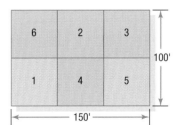

FIGURE 8.6

Proposed Block Plan

6 close to each other, we put 6 in the upper-left corner of the layout. The second requirement is to have departments 3 and 5 close to each other, so we placed 3 in the space just above the 5, and so on.

Decision Point This solution fell into place easily for this particular problem, but it might not be the best layout. Management wants to consider several alternative layouts before making a final choice and needs some measure of effectiveness with which to compare the alternative layouts.

APPLYING THE WEIGHTED-DISTANCE METHOD

weighted-distance method

A mathematical model used to evaluate flexible-flow layouts based on proximity factors.

When *relative* locations are a primary concern, such as for effective information flow, communication, material handling, and stockpicking, the weighted-distance method can be used to compare alternative block plans. The **weighted-distance method** is a mathematical model used to evaluate flexible-flow layouts based on proximity factors. A similar approach, sometimes called the *load-distance method,* can be used to evaluate facility locations. The objective is to select a layout (or facility location) that minimizes the total weighted distances. The distance between two points is expressed by assigning the points to grid coordinates on a block diagram or map. An alternative approach is to use time rather than distance.

Euclidean distance

The straight-line distance, or shortest possible path, between two points.

Distance Measures For a rough calculation, which is all that is needed for the weighted-distance method, either a Euclidean or rectilinear distance measure may be used. **Euclidean distance** is the straight-line distance, or shortest possible path, between two points. To calculate this distance, we create a graph. The distance between two points, say, points A and B, is

$$d_{AB} = \sqrt{(x_A - x_B)^2 + (y_A - y_B)^2}$$

where

$$d_{AB} = \text{distance between points } A \text{ and } B$$
$$x_A = x\text{-coordinate of point } A$$
$$y_A = y\text{-coordinate of point } A$$
$$x_B = x\text{-coordinate of point } B$$
$$x_B = y\text{-coordinate of point } B$$

rectilinear distance

The distance between two points with a series of 90 degree turns, as along city blocks.

Rectilinear distance measures distance between two points with a series of 90-degree turns, as along city blocks. The distance traveled in the x-direction is the absolute value of the difference in x-coordinates. Adding this result to the absolute value of the difference in the y-coordinates gives

$$d_{AB} = |x_A - x_B| + |y_A - y_B|$$

For assistance in calculating distances using either measure, see Tutor 8.1 in OM Explorer.

TUTOR 8.1

Tutor 8.1 on the Student CD-ROM provides an example to calculate both Euclidean and rectilinear distance measures.

Calculating a Weighted-Distance Score The designer seeks to minimize the weighted-distance (wd) score by locating centers that have high-closeness ratings close together.

To calculate a layout's wd score, we use either of the distance measures and simply multiply the proximity scores by the distances between centers. The sum of those products becomes the layout's final wd score—the lower the better. The location of a center is defined by its x-coordinate and y-coordinate.

EXAMPLE 8.2	Calculating the Weighted-Distance Score

How much better, in terms of the wd score, is the proposed block plan that was shown in Figure 8.6 than the current plan that was shown in Figure 8.5? Use the rectilinear distance measure.

SOLUTION

The accompanying table lists each pair of departments that has a nonzero closeness factor in the closeness matrix. For the third column, calculate the rectilinear distances between the departments in the current layout. For example, departments 3 and 5 in the current plan are in the upper-left corner and bottom-right corner of the building, respectively. The distance between the centers of these blocks is three units (two horizontally and one vertically). For the fourth column, we multiply the weights (closeness factors) by the distances, and then add the results for a total *wd* score of 112 for the current plan. Similar calculations for the proposed plan produce a *wd* score of only 82. For example, between departments 3 and 5 is just one unit of distance (one vertically and zero horizontally).

Department Pair	Closeness Factor (*w*)	Current Plan Distance (*d*)	Current Plan Weighted-Distance Score (*wd*)	Proposed Plan Distance (*d*)	Proposed Plan Weighted-Distance Score (*wd*)
1, 2	3	1	3	2	6
1, 3	6	1	6	3	18
1, 4	5	3	15	1	5
1, 5	6	2	12	2	12
1, 6	10	2	20	1	10
2, 3	8	2	16	1	8
2, 4	1	2	2	1	1
2, 5	1	1	1	2	2
3, 4	3	2	6	2	6
3, 5	9	3	27	1	9
4, 5	2	1	2	1	2
5, 6	1	2	2	3	3
		Total	112	Total	82

Current Plan

| 3 | 6 | 4 |
| 1 | 2 | 5 |

Proposed Plan

| 6 | 2 | 3 |
| 1 | 4 | 5 |

To be exact, we could multiply the two *wd* total scores by 50 because each unit of distance represents 50 feet. However, the relative difference between the two totals remains unchanged.

Decision Point The *wd* score for the proposed layout makes a sizeable drop from 112 to 82, but management is not sure the improvement outweighs the cost of relocating four of the six departments (i.e., all departments but 1 and 5).

Although the *wd* score for the proposed layout in Example 8.2 represents an almost 27 percent improvement, the designer may be able to do better. Furthermore, the designer must determine whether the revised layout is worth the cost of relocating four of the six departments. If relocation costs are too high, a less-expensive proposal must be found.

OM Explorer can help identify some even more attractive proposals. For example, one option is to modify the proposed plan by switching the locations of departments 3 and 4. The output in Figure 8.7 shows that the *wd* score for this second revision not only drops to 80, but requires that only three departments must be relocated compared with the original layout in Figure 8.5. Perhaps this second proposed plan is the best solution.

STEP 3: DESIGN A DETAILED LAYOUT

After finding a satisfactory block plan, the layout designer translates it into a detailed representation, showing the exact size and shape of each center; the arrangement of elements (e.g., desks, machines, and storage areas); and the location of aisles, stairways, and other service space. These visual representations can be two-dimensional drawings, three-dimensional models, or computer-aided graphics. This step helps decision makers discuss the proposal and problems that might otherwise be overlooked. Such visual representations can be particularly important when evaluating high customer-contact processes.

FIGURE **8.7**

Second Proposed Block Plan
(Analyzed with Flexible-Flow
Layout Solver)

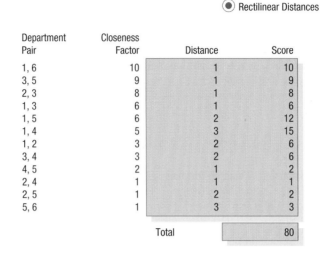

Department Pair	Closeness Factor	Distance	Score
1, 6	10	1	10
3, 5	9	1	9
2, 3	8	1	8
1, 3	6	1	6
1, 5	6	2	12
1, 4	5	3	15
1, 2	3	2	6
3, 4	3	2	6
4, 5	2	1	2
2, 4	1	1	1
2, 5	1	2	2
5, 6	1	3	3
Total			80

automated layout design program (ALDEP)

A computer software package that constructs a good layout from scratch, adding one department at a time.

computerized relative allocation of facilities technique (CRAFT)

A heuristic method that begins with the closeness matrix and an initial block layout, and makes a series of paired exchanges of departments to find a better block plan.

OTHER DECISION SUPPORT TOOLS

Several more advanced software packages are now available for designing more complex flexible-flow layouts. The **automated layout design program (ALDEP)** is a computer software package that constructs a good layout from scratch, adding one department at a time. Being a heuristic method, it generally provides good—but not necessarily the best—solutions.

Another powerful computer software package, the **computerized relative allocation of facilities technique (CRAFT)**, is a heuristic method that begins with the closeness matrix and an initial block layout. Working from an initial block plan (or starting solution), CRAFT evaluates all possible paired exchanges of departments. The exchange that causes the greatest reduction in the total *wd* score is incorporated into a new starting solution. This process continues until no other exchanges can be found to reduce the *wd* score.

WAREHOUSE LAYOUTS

Warehouses are one of the invisible nerve centers of e-commerce. Warehouses are similar to manufacturing plants in that materials are moved between activity centers. Much of the preceding discussion on flexible-flow layouts applies to warehouses. However, warehouses are a special case because a warehouse's central process is one of storage. Basically, a warehouse receives items at the dock and moves them to a storage area. Later, stockpickers withdraw inventory to fill individual customer orders.

Various options are available for warehouse layouts. First, various ways of utilizing space offer additional layout options. For example, an 82,000-square-foot, 32-foot-high racked warehouse can handle the same volume as a 107,000-square-foot, low-ceilinged warehouse, with the higher stockpicking productivity of the high-ceilinged warehouse offsetting the added rack and equipment costs. Another space-saving design assigns all incoming materials to the nearest available space, rather than to a predetermined area where all like items are clustered. A computer system tracks the location of each item. When it is time to retrieve an item, the system prints its location on the shipping bill and identifies the shortest route for the stockpicker.

Second, different layout patterns offer still more layout options. The most basic layout pattern is the *out-and-back pattern*, as illustrated in Figure 8.8. Items are picked one at a time, with the stockpicker traveling back and forth from the dock to the storage area. In Figure 8.8, storage area 1 could be where toasters are stored, storage area 2 could be for air conditioners, and so forth. Some items require more space than others, depending on their size and inventory requirements. In general, the high-volume items are stored closest to the dock with this layout pattern. In a *route collection system*, the stockpicker selects a variety of items to be shipped to a customer. In a *batch-picking system*, the stockpicker gathers the quantity of an item required to satisfy a group of customer orders to be shipped in the same truck or rail car. Finally, in the *zone system*, the stockpicker gathers all needed items in her assigned zone and places them on a powered conveyor line. Figure 8.9 illustrates the zone system for a warehouse. The conveyor line consists of five feeder lines and one trunk line.

FIGURE **8.8**

Out-and-Back Warehouse Layout

FIGURE **8.9**

Zone System for a Warehouse

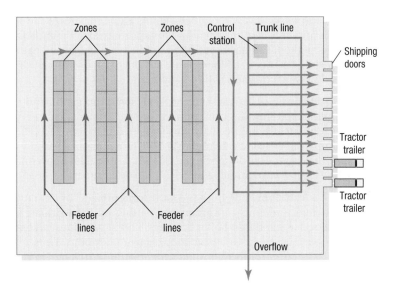

When the merchandise arrives at the control station, an operator directs it to the correct tractor trailer for outbound shipment. The advantage of the zone system is that pickers need not travel throughout the warehouse to fill orders. They are responsible only for their own zones.

OFFICE LAYOUTS

More than 40 percent of the U.S. workforce is employed in offices, and office layout can affect both productivity and the quality of work life. In a recent survey, three-fourths of 1,400 employees polled said that productivity could be raised by improvements in their work environments.

Proximity Accessibility to coworkers and supervisors can enhance communication and develop mutual interest. Conversations tend to become more formal as individuals are placed farther apart. The famous Hawthorne study in 1939 showed that the physical work setting influences group formation. In the study, management used spatial language to tell workers in the experimental group that they were important. More recent studies confirm that proximity to others can help clarify what is expected of an employee on the job and in other ways.

Two Views of the Layout at a Modern Warehouse That Holds About 16 Million Books in Inventory and Processes Between 2,000 and 5,000 Orders per Day

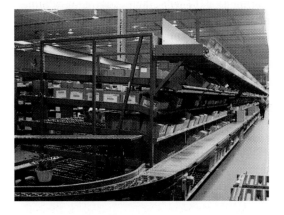

Cases of the fastest-selling titles are stacked outside the flow racks in the "golden zone," where the 80 fastest-selling titles are stored. These titles comprise about 50 percent of all shipments. Whole cases are picked here in response to specific orders.

A floor-level conveyor transports boxes of books to the packaging area. There, the boxes pass over a computerized weight-in-motion scale, which compares the total weight of the package to the sum of weights of individual titles.

Most formal procedures for designing office layouts try to maximize the proximity of workers whose jobs require frequent interaction. This approach can be implemented with the weighted-distance method. Certain procedures can be used to identify natural clusters of workers to be treated as a center in a block plan. The goal of such approaches is to design layouts around work flows and communication patterns.

Privacy Another key factor in office design—and one that is somewhat culturally dependent—is privacy. Outside disruptions and crowding can hurt a worker's performance. At Sperry Rand's and McDonald's world headquarters, employee reactions to open offices were favorable. However, when a newspaper company tried to increase worker proximity by going from private work spaces to an open-plan office, the results were disappointing. Studies at several state government departments revealed a strong link between privacy and satisfaction with the supervisor and the job.

Options in Office Layout Providing both proximity and privacy for employees poses a dilemma for management. Proximity is gained by opening up the work area. Privacy is gained by more liberal space standards, baffled ceilings, doors, partitions, and thick carpeting that absorbs noise—expensive features that reduce layout flexibility. Thus, management must generally arrive at a compromise between proximity and privacy. No single type of space fits all workers. For example, Microsoft in Redmond, Washington, found that software developers do their best work in a private, quiet space. But its sales and marketing people work in a mixture of private and open spaces; the emphasis is on facilitating interactions among sales and marketing personnel and providing good spaces for meetings with customers. Its product support offices are about 90 percent open space.

Four different approaches are available: traditional layouts, office landscaping, activity settings, and electronic cottages. The choice requires an understanding of work requirements, the workforce itself, and top management's philosophy of work.

Traditional layouts call for closed offices for management and those employees whose work requires privacy and open areas (or bullpens) for all others. The resulting layout may be characterized by long hallways lined with closed doors, producing considerable isolation, and by open areas filled uniformly with rows of desks. In traditional layouts, each person has a designated place. With these layouts, location, size, and furnishings signify the person's status in the organization.

An approach developed in Germany during the late 1950s puts everyone (including top management) in an open area. The idea is to achieve closer cooperation among employees at *all* levels. An extension of this concept is called *office landscaping:* Attractive plants, screens, and portable partitions increase privacy and cluster or separate groups. Movable workstations and accessories help maintain flexibility. Because the workstations (or cubicles) are only semiprivate, employees might have trouble concentrating or might feel uncomfortable trying to hold sensitive discussions. Construction costs are as much as 40 percent less than for traditional layouts, and rearrangement costs are less still.

Activity settings represent a relatively new concept for achieving both proximity and privacy. The full range of work needs is covered by multiple workplaces, including a library, teleconferencing facility, reception area, conference room, special graphics area, and shared terminals. Employees move from one activity setting to the next as their work requires during the day. Each person also gets a small, personal office as a home base. Managerial Practice 8.2 describes one recent transition to the activity settings concept.

More and more employees work at home or in neighborhood offices connected to the main office by computer. Called *telecommuting* or *electronic cottages*, this approach represents a modern-day version of the cottage industries that existed prior to the Industrial Revolution. Besides saving on commuting time, it offers flexibility in work schedules. Many working men and women with children, for example, prefer such flexibility. More than 9 million Americans already have a taste of this arrangement, working at least part of the week at home. However, telecommuting can have drawbacks, such as lack of equipment, too many family disruptions, and too few opportunities for interaction.

> DESIGNING LINE-FLOW LAYOUTS <

Line-flow layouts raise management issues entirely different from those of flexible-flow layouts. Often called a production or assembly line, a line-flow layout arranges workstations in sequence. The product moves from one station to the next until its completion at the end of the

ABB, a global leader in power and automation technologies, has approximately 100,000 employees located close to customers in nearly 100 countries. ABB USA alone has more than 100 locations. One of them is a new office building in Westerville, Ohio, which focuses on automation and process control equipment. It is home for more than 200 engineers, scientists, technicians, marketers, human resource specialists, and supply chain managers. They provide services to employees and customers worldwide, such as developing software for new equipment, diagnosing equipment problems, training customers and employees on new installations, and repairing parts of customer equipment already in the field. Almost all employees previously had private offices with doors and floor-to-ceiling partitions in their prior office space. They now have smaller offices spaces, ranging from the smallest of 7′ by 9′ to largest of 10′ by 12′. Partition walls are as low as 4,′ and as high as 7′ for manager stations. The workstations are built with modular partitions and furniture, and so can be rearranged as future needs dictate. Workstations basically provide desk surface, a telephone, a computer, and limited filing area. Little space is available for extra chairs. Although their new workstations are much smaller and less private, almost all employees actually prefer their new office space for several reasons.

Employees made inputs on their office needs before moving in. A "floor captain" assigned to each floor consulted the employees as to their space and equipment needs, and proximity requirements. Being involved in the facility design gave people a sense of "buy in" and ownership. Everybody has access to common areas, including conference rooms, classrooms for customers and employees alike, special facilities for lab work, coffee bars, copy machines, central files, phone booths for private conversations, and mobile easels with flip charts and whiteboards. The previous engineering library is no longer needed, because everything now can be obtained online. Many conference rooms are intimate, with just three or four chairs. The America's Room, often called the "boardroom," is the largest and can easily accommodate 40 people. Presentations can be shown on either a projection screen at one end of the room, or a plasma screen at the other end. The room can be divided into two rooms with ease, if two smaller meeting rooms are needed for the moment.

Employees now communicate more easily with their colleagues. The facility is wireless, so people can take their laptops out of their workstations to another sitting area for a change of scenery. The space is pleasantly furnished with art pieces and plants. Window space is ample, with light streaming in from many directions. White noise is piped into the areas and can be regulated to muffle particularly noisy areas. Common spaces seem homey and comfortable.

Even the conference rooms are named to increase the sense of home. Conference rooms on the first floor are named after trees, because

Although workstations are small and semiprivate, "outposts" are available. This common area has easy chairs fitted with arms that provide a surface for writing or laptops. People meet comfortably for face-to-face talks, rather than communicating by e-mail.

the pulp and paper industry (such as for paper mills) is a big ABB customer. The second floor houses marketing and engineering; conference rooms are named after scientists, physicists, and mathematicians. The third floor is for corporate management, with rooms named after international destinations. ABB also is equipped worldwide with *Sametime*, an IBM Lotus Instant Messaging and Web Conferencing platform for real-time collaboration with employees, teams, suppliers, and customers who are geographically dispersed. The supply chain manager at the Westerville facility, for example, can converse virtually through the exchange of text-, audio-, or video-based information in real time. She does Web conferencing to share information, an application, or engage in team white boarding. Many engineers in the facility use such capabilities to communicate with their European counterparts, making the best use of everybody's time. Such virtual conferences broaden communications choice beyond the telephone, e-mail, and in-person meetings. They also improve customer-specific response times.

Using activity settings, the new 111,000-square-foot facility not only provides effective workspace for its employees, but saves investment dollars because it is much smaller than would be needed using a traditional office design.

Source: Conversation with Charles Rowland at ABB; ww.abb.com.

line. Typically, one worker operates each station, performing repetitive tasks. Little inventory is built up between stations, so stations cannot operate independently. Thus, the line is only as fast as its slowest workstation. In other words, if the slowest station takes five minutes per customer or unit, the line's fastest possible output is one customer or unit every five minutes.

LINE BALANCING

Line balancing is the assignment of work to stations in a line so as to achieve the desired output rate with the smallest number of workstations. Normally, one worker is assigned to a station. Thus, the line that produces at the desired pace with the fewest workers is the most efficient one. Achieving this goal is much like the theory of constraints, because both approaches are concerned about bottlenecks. Line balancing differs in how it addresses bottlenecks. Rather than (1) taking on new customer orders to best use bottleneck capacity or (2) scheduling so that bottleneck resources are conserved, line balancing takes a third approach. It creates workstations with workloads as evenly balanced as possible. It seeks to create workstations so that the capacity utilization for the bottleneck is not much higher than for the other workstations in the line. Another difference is that line balancing applies only to line processes that do assembly work, or to work that can be bundled in many ways to create the jobs for each workstation in the line.

Line balancing must be performed when a line is set up initially, when a line is rebalanced to change its hourly output rate, or when product or process changes. The goal is to obtain workstations with well-balanced workloads (e.g., every station takes roughly 5 minutes per customer or unit processed).

The analyst begins by separating the work into **work elements**, which are the smallest units of work that can be performed independently. The analyst then obtains the time standard for each element and identifies the work elements, called **immediate predecessors**, that must be done before the next element can begin.

Precedence Diagram Most lines must satisfy some technological precedence requirements; that is, certain work elements must be done before the next can begin. However, most lines also allow for some latitude and more than one sequence of operations. To help you visualize immediate predecessors better, let us run through the construction of a **precedence diagram**.[2] We denote the work elements by circles, with the time required to perform the work shown below each circle. Arrows lead from immediate predecessors to the next work element. Example 8.3 illustrates a manufacturing process, but a back office with a line-flow process can be approached in a similar way.

line balancing
The assignment of work to stations in a line so as to achieve the desired output rate with the smallest number of workstations.

work elements
The smallest units of work that can be performed independently.

immediate predecessors
Work elements that must be done before the next element can begin.

precedence diagram
A diagram that allows one to visualize immediate predecessors better; work elements are denoted by circles, with the time required to perform the work shown below each circle.

EXAMPLE 8.3	Constructing a Precedence Diagram

Green Grass, Inc., a manufacturer of lawn and garden equipment, is designing an assembly line to produce a new fertilizer spreader, the Big Broadcaster. Using the following information on the production process, construct a precedence diagram for the Big Broadcaster.

Work Element	Description	Time (sec)	Immediate Predecessor(s)
A	Bolt leg frame to hopper	40	None
B	Insert impeller shaft	30	A
C	Attach axle	50	A
D	Attach agitator	40	B
E	Attach drive wheel	6	B
F	Attach free wheel	25	C
G	Mount lower post	15	C
H	Attach controls	20	D, E
I	Mount nameplate	18	F, G
	Total	244	

[2]Precedence relationships and precedence diagrams are important in the entirely different context of project management.

SOLUTION

Figure 8.10 shows the complete diagram. We begin with work element A, which has no immediate predecessors. Next, we add elements B and C, for which element A is the only immediate predecessor. After entering time standards and arrows showing precedence, we add elements D and E, and so on. The diagram simplifies interpretation. Work element F, for example, can be done anywhere on the line after element C is completed. However, element I must await completion of elements F and G.

Decision Point Management now has enough information to develop a line-flow layout that clusters work elements to form workstations, with a goal being to balance the workloads and, in the process, minimize the number of workstations required.

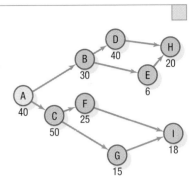

FIGURE **8.10**

Precedence Diagram for Assembling the Big Broadcaster

Desired Output Rate The goal of line balancing is to match the output rate to the staffing or production plan. For example, if the plan calls for 4,000 units (customers or products) per week and the line operates 80 hours per week, the desired output rate ideally would be 50 units (4,000/80) per hour. Matching output to demand ensures on-time delivery and prevents buildup of unwanted inventory or customer delays. However, managers should avoid rebalancing a line too frequently because each time a line is rebalanced many workers' jobs on the line must be redesigned, temporarily hurting productivity and sometimes even requiring a new detailed layout for some stations.

Cycle Time After determining the desired output rate for a line, the analyst can calculate the line's cycle time. A line's **cycle time** is the maximum time allowed for work on a unit at each station.[3] If the time required for work elements at a station exceeds the line's cycle time, the station will be a bottleneck, preventing the line from reaching its desired output rate. The target cycle time is the reciprocal of the desired hourly output rate:

cycle time

The maximum time allowed for work on a unit at each station.

$$c = \frac{1}{r}$$

where

c = cycle time in hours per unit

r = desired output rate in units per hour

For example, if the line's desired output rate is 60 units per hour, the cycle time is $c = 1/60$ hour per unit, or 1 minute.

Theoretical Minimum To achieve the desired output rate, managers use line balancing to assign every work element to a station, making sure to satisfy all precedence requirements and to minimize the number of stations, n, formed. If each station is operated by a different worker, minimizing n also maximizes worker productivity. Perfect balance is achieved when the sum of the work-element times at each station equals the cycle time, c, and no station has any idle time. For example, if the sum of each station's work-element times is 1 minute, which is also the cycle time, the line achieves perfect balance. Although perfect balance usually is unachievable in practice, owing to the unevenness of work-element times and the inflexibility of precedence requirements, it sets a benchmark, or goal, for the smallest number of stations possible. The **theoretical minimum (TM)** for the number of stations is

theoretical minimum (TM)

A benchmark or goal for the smallest number of stations possible, where the total time required to assemble each unit (the sum of all work-element standard times) is divided by the cycle time.

$$TM = \frac{\Sigma t}{c}$$

where

Σt = total time required to assemble each unit (the sum of all work-element standard times)

c = cycle time

[3]Except in the context of line balancing, *cycle time* has a different meaning. It is the elapsed time between starting and completing a job. Some researchers and practitioners prefer the term *lead time*.

For example, if the sum of the work-element times is 15 minutes and the cycle time is 1 minute, TM = 15/1, or 15 stations. Any fractional values obtained for TM are rounded up because fractional stations are impossible.

Idle Time, Efficiency, and Balance Delay Minimizing n automatically ensures (1) minimal idle time, (2) maximal efficiency, and (3) minimal balance delay. Idle time is the total unproductive time for all stations in the assembly of each unit:

$$\text{Idle time} = nc - \Sigma t$$

where

$$n = \text{number of stations}$$

$$c = \text{cycle time}$$

$$\Sigma t = \text{total standard time required to assemble each unit}$$

Efficiency is the ratio of productive time to total time, expressed as a percent:

$$\text{Efficiency (\%)} = \frac{\Sigma t}{nc}(100)$$

balance delay

The amount by which efficiency falls short of 100 percent.

Balance delay is the amount by which efficiency falls short of 100 percent:

$$\text{Balance delay(\%)} = 100 - \text{Efficiency}$$

As long as c is fixed, we can optimize all three goals by minimizing n.

EXAMPLE 8.4	Calculating the Cycle Time, Theoretical Minimum, and Efficiency

TUTOR 8.2

Tutor 8.2 on the Student CD-ROM provides another example to calculate these line-balancing measures.

Green Grass's plant manager just received marketing's latest forecasts of Big Broadcaster sales for the next year. She wants its production line to be designed to make 2,400 spreaders per week for at least the next 3 months. The plant will operate 40 hours per week.

a. What should be the line's cycle time?

b. What is the smallest number of workstations that she could hope for in designing the line for this cycle time?

c. Suppose that she finds a solution that requires only five stations. What would be the line's efficiency?

SOLUTION

a. First convert the desired output rate (2,400 units per week) to an hourly rate by dividing the weekly output rate by 40 hours per week to get $r = 60$ units per hour. Then the cycle time is

$$c = \frac{1}{r} = \frac{1}{60} \text{hour/unit} = 1 \text{ minute/unit}$$

b. Now calculate the theoretical minimum for the number of stations by dividing the total time, Σt, by the cycle time, $c = 1$ minute = 60 seconds. Assuming perfect balance, we have

$$\text{TM} = \frac{\Sigma t}{c} = \frac{244 \text{ seconds}}{60 \text{ seconds}} = 4.067 \text{ or } 5 \text{ stations}$$

c. Now calculate the efficiency of a five-station solution, assuming for now that one can be found:

$$\text{Efficiency (\%)} = \frac{\Sigma t}{nc}(100) = \frac{244}{5(60)}(100) = 81.3\%$$

Decision Point Thus, if the manager finds a solution with five stations, that is the minimum number of stations possible. However, the efficiency (sometimes called the *theoretical maximum efficiency*) will be only 81.3 percent. Perhaps the line should be operated less than 40 hours per week and the employees transferred to other kinds of work when the line does not operate.

Finding a Solution Often, many assembly-line solutions are possible, even for such simple problems as Green Grass's. The goal is to cluster the work elements into workstations so that (1) the number of workstations required is minimized, and (2) the precedence and cycle-time requirements are not violated. Here we use the trial-and-error method to find a solution, although commercial software packages are also available. Figure 8.11 shows a good solution that creates just five workstations. We know that five is the minimum possible, because five is the theoretical minimum found in Example 8.4. All of the precedence and cycle-time requirements are also satisfied. For example, workstation S5 consists of work elements E, H, and I, which one worker will perform on each unit that comes along the assembly line. The processing time per unit is 44 seconds (6 + 20 + 18), which does not exceed the cycle time of 60 seconds (see Example 8.4). Furthermore, the immediate predecessors of these three work elements are assigned to this workstation or upstream workstations, so their precedence requirements are satisfied. For example, the worker at workstation S5 can do element I at any time but will not start element H until element E is finished.

OTHER CONSIDERATIONS

In addition to balancing a line for a given cycle time, managers must also consider four other options: (1) pacing, (2) behavioral factors, (3) number of models produced, and (4) cycle times.

Pacing The movement of product from one station to the next as soon as the cycle time has elapsed is called **pacing**. Pacing manufacturing processes allows materials handling to be automated and requires less inventory storage area. However, it is less flexible in handling unexpected delays that require either slowing down the entire line or pulling the unfinished work off the line to be completed later.

pacing

The movement of product from one station to the next as soon as the cycle time has elapsed.

Behavioral Factors The most controversial aspect of line-flow layouts is behavioral response. Studies show that installing production lines increases absenteeism, turnover, and grievances. Paced production and high specialization (say, cycle times of less than two minutes) lower job satisfaction. Workers generally favor inventory buffers as a means of avoiding mechanical pacing. One study even showed that productivity increased on unpaced lines.

Number of Models Produced A **mixed-model line** produces several items belonging to the same family. In contrast, a single-model line produces one model with no variations. Mixed-model production enables a plant to achieve both high-volume production *and* product variety. However, it complicates scheduling and increases the need for good communication about the specific parts to be produced at each station.

mixed-model line

A production line that produces several items belonging to the same family.

Cycle Times A line's cycle time depends on the desired output rate (or sometimes on the maximum number of workstations allowed). In turn, the maximum line efficiency varies considerably with the cycle time selected. Thus, exploring a range of cycle times makes sense. A manager might go with a particularly efficient solution even if it does not match the output rate. The manager can compensate for the mismatch by varying the number of hours the line operates through overtime, extending shifts, or adding shifts. Multiple lines might even be the answer.

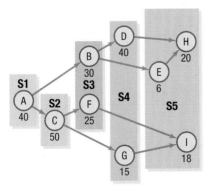

FIGURE 8.11

Big Broadcaster Precedence Diagram Solution

> STUDENT CD-ROM AND INTERNET RESOURCES <

The Student CD-ROM and the Companion Website at **www.prenhall.com/krajewski** contain many tools, activities, and resources designed for this chapter.

> KEY EQUATIONS <

1. Euclidean distance: $d_{AB} = \sqrt{(x_A - x_B)^2 + (y_A - y_B)^2}$

2. Rectilinear distance: $d_{AB} = |x_A - x_B| + |y_A - y_B|$

3. Cycle time: $c = \dfrac{1}{r}$

4. Theoretical minimum number of workstations: $TM = \dfrac{\Sigma t}{c}$

5. Idle time (in seconds): $nc - \Sigma t$

6. Efficiency (%): $\dfrac{\Sigma t}{nc}(100)$

7. Balance delay (%): $100 - $ Efficiency

> KEY TERMS <

automated layout design program (ALDEP) 324
balance delay 330
block plan 320
closeness matrix 320
computerized relative allocation of facilities technique (CRAFT) 324
cycle time 329
economic activity center 312
Euclidean distance 322

fixed-position layout 316
flexible-flow layout 314
group technology (GT) 318
hybrid layout 315
immediate predecessors 328
layout flexibility 317
layout planning 312
line balancing 328
line-flow layout 315
mixed-model line 331

one-worker, multiple-machines (OWMM) cell 317
pacing 331
precedence diagram 328
rectilinear distance 322
theoretical minimum (TM) 329
weighted-distance method 322
work elements 328

> SOLVED PROBLEM I <

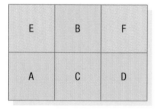

FIGURE 8.12

Current Layout

A defense contractor is evaluating its machine shop's current flexible-flow layout. Figure 8.12 shows the current layout, and the table shows the closeness matrix for the facility measured as the number of trips per day between department pairs. Safety and health regulations require departments E and F to remain at their current locations.

	Trips Between Departments					
Department	A	B	C	D	E	F
A	—	8	3		9	5
B		—		3		
C			—		8	9
D				—		3
E					—	3
F						—

a. Use trial and error to find a better layout.

b. How much better is your layout than the current layout in terms of the *wd* score? Use rectilinear distance.

SOLUTION

a. In addition to keeping departments E and F at their current locations, a good plan would locate the following department pairs close to each other: A and E, C and F, A and B, and C and E. Figure 8.13 was worked out by trial and error and satisfies all these requirements. Start by placing E and F at their current locations. Then, because C must be as close as possible to both E and F, put C between them. Place A below E, and B next to A. All of the heavy traffic concerns have now been accommodated. Department D, located in the remaining space, does not need to be relocated.

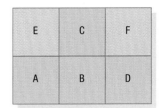

FIGURE 8.13

Proposed Layout

		Current Plan		Proposed Plan	
Department Pair	Number of Trips (1)	Distance (2)	*wd* Score (1) × (2)	Distance (3)	*wd* Score (1) × (3)
A, B	8	2	16	1	8
A, C	3	1	3	2	6
A, E	9	1	9	1	9
A, F	5	3	15	3	15
B, D	3	2	6	1	3
C, E	8	2	16	1	8
C, F	9	2	18	1	9
D, F	3	1	3	1	3
E, F	3	2	6	2	6
			wd = 92		*wd* = 67

b. The table reveals that the *wd* score drops from 92 for the current plan to 67 for the revised plan, a 27 percent reduction.

> SOLVED PROBLEM 2 <

A company is setting up an assembly line to produce 192 units per 8-hour shift. The following table identifies the work elements, times, and immediate predecessors.

Work Element	Time (sec)	Immediate Predecessor(s)
A	40	None
B	80	A
C	30	D, E, F
D	25	B
E	20	B
F	15	B
G	120	A
H	145	G
I	130	H
J	115	C, I
Total	720	

a. What is the desired cycle time (in seconds)?

b. What is the theoretical minimum number of stations?

c. Use trial and error to work out a solution, and show your solution on a precedence diagram.

d. What are the efficiency and balance delay of the solution found?

SOLUTION

a. Substituting in the cycle-time formula, we get

$$c = \frac{1}{r} = \frac{8 \text{ hours}}{192 \text{ units}}(3{,}600 \text{ seconds/hour}) = 150 \text{ seconds/unit}$$

b. The sum of the work-element times is 720 seconds, so

$$TM = \frac{\Sigma t}{c} = \frac{720 \text{ seconds/unit}}{150 \text{ seconds/unit-station}} = 4.8 \quad \text{or} \quad 5 \text{ stations}$$

which may not be achievable.

c. The precedence diagram is shown in Figure 8.14. Each row in the following table shows work elements assigned to each of the five workstations in the proposed solution.

Station	Candidate(s)	Choice	Work-Element Time (sec)	Cumulative Time (sec)	Idle Time (c = 150 sec)
S1	A	A	40	40	110
	B	B	80	120	30
	D, E, F	D	25	145	5
S2	E, F, G	G	120	120	30
	E, F	E	20	140	10
S3	F, H	H	145	145	5
S4	F, I	I	130	130	20
	F	F	15	145	5
S5	C	C	30	30	120
	J	J	115	145	5

d. Calculating the efficiency, we get

$$\text{Efficiency} = \frac{\Sigma t}{nc}(100) = \frac{720 \text{ seconds/unit}}{5[150 \text{ seconds/unit}]}(100)$$

$$= 96\%$$

Thus, the balance delay is only 4 percent (100 − 96).

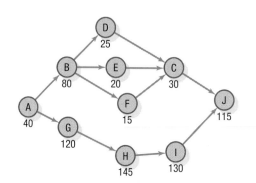

FIGURE 8.14 | Precedence Diagram

> DISCUSSION QUESTIONS <

1. Identify the types of layout performance criteria that might be most important in the following settings.

    a. Airport

    b. Bank

    c. Classroom

    d. Office of product designers

    e. Law firm

    f. Fabrication of sheet-metal components

    g. Parking lot

    h. Human resources department

2. Describe two processes with which you are familiar, one with a flexible-flow layout and one with a line-flow layout. How do these layout designs relate to process structure? Explain.

> PROBLEMS <

Software, such as OM Explorer, Active Models, and POM for Windows is packaged with every new copy of the textbook. Check with your instructor on how best to use it. In many cases, the instructor wants you to understand how to do the calculations by hand. At most, the software provides a check on your calculations. When calculations are particularly complex and the goal is interpreting the results in making decisions, the software replaces entirely the manual calculations. The software also can be a valuable resource well after your course is completed.

1. Baker Machine Company is a job shop that specializes in precision parts for firms in the aerospace industry. Figure 8.15 shows the current block plan for the key manufacturing centers of the 75,000-square-foot facility. Refer to the closeness matrix below and use rectilinear distance (the current distance from inspection to shipping and receiving is three units) to calculate the change in the weighted distance, *wd*, score if Baker exchanges the locations of the tool crib and inspection.

2. Use trial and error to find a particularly good block plan for Baker Machine (see Problem 1). Because of excessive relocation costs, shipping and receiving (department 3) must remain at its current location. Compare *wd* scores to evaluate your new layout, again assuming rectilinear distance.

3. The head of the information systems group at Conway Consulting must assign six new analysts to offices. The following closeness matrix shows the expected frequency of contact between analysts. The block plan in Figure 8.16 shows the available office locations (1–6) for the six analysts (A–F). Assume equal-sized offices and rectilinear distance. Owing to their tasks, analyst A must be assigned to location 4 and analyst D to location 3. What are the best locations for the other four analysts? What is the *wd* score for your layout?

Closeness Matrix					
Trips Between Departments					
Department	1	2	3	4	5	6
1. Burr and grind	—	8	3		9	5
2. NC equipment		—	3			
3. Shipping and receiving			—		8	9
4. Lathes and drills				—		3
5. Tool crib					—	3
6. Inspection						—

Closeness Matrix						
Contacts Between Analysts						
Analyst	A	B	C	D	E	F
Analyst A	—		6			
Analyst B		—		12		
Analyst C			—	2	7	
Analyst D				—		4
Analyst E					—	
Analyst F						—

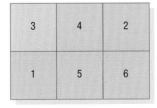

FIGURE **8.15** | Current Layout

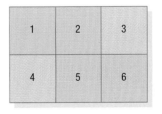

FIGURE **8.16** | Conway Consulting's Block Plan

4. Richard Garber is the head designer for Matthews and Novak Design Company. Garber has been called in to design the layout for a newly constructed office building. From statistical samplings over the past 3 months, Garber developed the closeness matrix shown for daily trips between the department's offices.

Closeness Matrix						
Trips Between Departments						
Department	**A**	**B**	**C**	**D**	**E**	**F**
A	—	25	90			185
B		—			105	
C			—		125	125
D				—	25	
E					—	105
F						—

a. If other factors are equal, which two offices should be located closest together?

b. Figure 8.17 shows an alternative layout for the department. What is the total weighted-distance score for this plan based on rectilinear distance and assuming that offices A and B are three units of distance apart?

c. Swapping which two departments will most improve the total weighted-distance score?

5. A firm with four departments has the following closeness matrix and the current block plan shown in Figure 8.18.

a. What is the weighted-distance score for the current layout (assuming rectilinear distance)?

Closeness Matrix				
Trips Between Departments				
Department	**A**	**B**	**C**	**D**
A	—	12	10	8
B		—	20	6
C			—	0
D				—

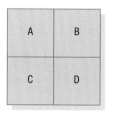

FIGURE 8.18 | Current Block Plan

b. Develop a better layout. What is its total weighted-distance score?

6. The department of engineering at a university in New Jersey must assign six faculty members to their new offices. The closeness matrix shown indicates the expected number of contacts per day between professors. The available office spaces (1–6) for the six faculty members are shown in Figure 8.19. Assume equal-sized offices. The distance between offices 1 and 2 (and between offices 1 and 3) is 1 unit.

Closeness Matrix						
Contacts Between Professors						
Professor	**A**	**B**	**C**	**D**	**E**	**F**
A	—		4			
B		—		12		10
C			—	2	7	
D				—		4
E					—	
F						—

a. Because of their academic positions, professor A must be assigned to office 1, professor C must be assigned to office 2, and professor D must be assigned to office 6. Which faculty members should be assigned to offices 3, 4, and 5, respectively, to minimize the total weighted-distance score (assuming rectilinear distance)?

b. What is the weighted-distance score of your solution?

FIGURE 8.17 | Alternative Layout

Alternative Layout block plan:

C	F	A
B	E	D

FIGURE 8.17 | Alternative Layout

Available Space block plan:

1	2
3	4
5	6

FIGURE 8.19 | Available Space

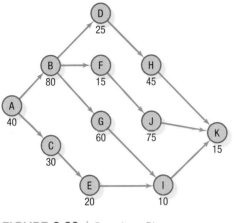

Work Element	Time (sec)	Immediate Predecessor(s)
A	40	None
B	30	A
C	50	A
D	40	B
E	6	B
F	25	C
G	15	C
H	20	D, E
I	18	F, G
J	30	H, I
	Total 274	

FIGURE 8.20 | Precedence Diagram

7. Use trial and error to balance the assembly line described in the following table and Figure 8.20 so that it will produce 40 units per hour.

   a. What is the cycle time?

   b. What is the theoretical minimum number of workstations?

   c. Which work elements are assigned to each workstation?

   d. What are the resulting efficiency and balance delay percentages?

Work Element	Time (sec)	Immediate Predecessor(s)
A	40	None
B	80	A
C	30	A
D	25	B
E	20	C
F	15	B
G	60	B
H	45	D
I	10	E, G
J	75	F
K	15	H, I, J
	Total 415	

8. Johnson Cogs wants to set up a line to serve 60 customers per hour. The work elements and their precedence relationships are shown in the following table.

   a. What is the theoretical minimum number of stations?

   b. How many stations are required using trial and error to find a solution?

   c. Suppose that a solution requiring five stations is obtained. What is its efficiency?

9. The *trim line* at PW is a small subassembly line that, along with other such lines, feeds into the final chassis line. The entire assembly line, which consists of more than 900 workstations, is to make PW's new E cars. The trim line itself involves only 13 work elements and must handle 20 cars per hour. In addition to the usual precedence constraints, there are two *zoning constraints*. First, work elements K and L should be assigned to the same station; both use a common component, and assigning them to the same station conserves storage space. Second, work elements H and J cannot be performed at the same station. Work-element data are as follows:

Work Element	Time (sec)	Immediate Predecessor(s)
A	1.8	None
B	0.4	None
C	1.6	None
D	1.5	A
E	0.7	A
F	0.5	E
G	0.8	B
H	1.4	C
I	1.4	D
J	1.4	F, G
K	0.5	H
L	1.0	J
M	0.8	I, K, L

   a. Draw a precedence diagram.

   b. What cycle time (in minutes) results in the desired output rate?

   c. What is the theoretical minimum number of stations?

   d. Using trial and error, balance the line as best you can.

   e. What is the efficiency of your solution?

ADVANCED PROBLEMS

10. CCI Electronics makes various products for the communications industry. One of its manufacturing plants makes a device for sensing when telephone calls are placed. A closeness matrix (giving flows in both directions) is shown in Table 8.1; the current layout appears in Figure 8.21. Management is reasonably satisfied with the current layout, although it has heard some complaints about the placement of departments D, G, K, and L. Use information in the from–to matrix to create a closeness matrix, and then find a revised block plan for moving only the four departments about which complaints have been made. Show that the weighted-distance score is improved. Assume rectilinear distance.

11. A paced assembly line has been devised to manufacture calculators, as the following data show:

Station	Work Element Assigned	Work Element Time (min)
S1	A	2.7
S2	D, E	0.6, 0.9
S3	C	3.0
S4	B, F, G	0.7, 0.7, 0.9
S5	H, I, J	0.7, 0.3, 1.2
S6	K	2.4

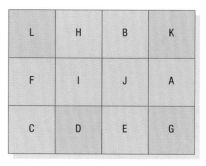

FIGURE 8.21 | Current Block Plan

a. What is the maximum hourly output rate from this line? (*Hint:* The line can go only as fast as its slowest workstation.)

b. What cycle time corresponds to this maximum output rate?

c. If a worker is at each station and the line operates at this maximum output rate, how much idle time is lost during each 10-hour shift?

d. What is the line's efficiency?

12. The manager of Sugar Hams wants to organize the tasks involved in the preparation and delivery of hams. The manager plans to produce 60 hams per 10-hour workday. The table at the top of the next page presents work-element times and precedence relationships.

TABLE 8.1 | From–To Matrix

Department	A	B	C	D	E	F	G	H	I	J	K	L
A. Network lead forming	—											80
B. Wire forming and subassembly		—							50	70		
C. Final assembly			—			120						
D. Inventory storage				—	40							
E. Presoldering				80	—						90	
F. Final testing						—	120					
G. Inventory storage		30					—	40	50			
H. Coil winding								—	80			
I. Coil assembly			70		40				—		60	
J. Network preparation	90									—		
K. Soldering			80								—	
L. Network insertion			60									—

Work Element	Time (min)	Immediate Predecessor(s)
A	3	None
B	5	A
C	2	B
D	7	B
E	7	C, D
F	6	E
G	2	D, E
H	3	F
I	8	G
J	6	H
K	3	I, J
L	8	K

TABLE 8.2	Closeness Matrix							
Trips Between Departments								
Department	**1**	**2**	**3**	**4**	**5**	**6**	**7**	**8**
1. Reception	—	25	35	5	10	15		20
2. Business office		—	5	10	15			15
3. Examining room			—	20	30	20		10
4. X-ray				—	25	15		25
5. Laboratory					—	20		25
6. Surgery						—	40	
7. Postsurgery							—	15
8. Doctor's office								—

a. Construct a precedence diagram for this process.

b. What cycle time corresponds to the desired output rate?

c. Try to identify the best possible line-balancing solution. What work elements are assigned to each station?

d. What is the impact on your solution if the time for work element D increases by 3 minutes? Decreases by three minutes?

13. The associate administrator at Getwell Hospital wants to evaluate the layout of the outpatient clinic. Table 8.2 shows the interdepartmental flows (patients/day) between departments; Figure 8.22 shows the current layout.

a. Determine the effectiveness of the current layout, as measured by the total *wd* score, using rectilinear distances.

FIGURE 8.22 | Current Layout

b. Try to find the best possible layout based on the same effectiveness measure.

c. What is the impact on your new solution if it must be revised to keep department 1 at its present location?

d. How should the layout developed in part (c) be revised if the interdepartmental flow between the examining room and the X-ray department is increased by 50 percent? Decreased by 50 percent?

> ## ACTIVE MODEL EXERCISE < ─────────────────────────

This Active Model for Example 8.1 appears on the Student CD-ROM. It allows you to see the effects of performing paired swaps of departments.

ACTIVE MODEL 8.1

Flexible Flow Layout Using Data from Example 8.1

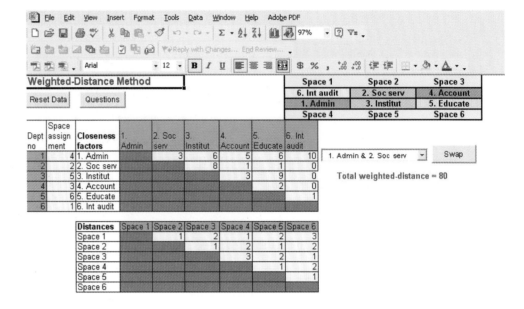

QUESTIONS

1. What is the current total weighted-distance score?

2. Use the swap button one swap at a time. If the swap helps, move to the next pair. If the swap does not help, hit the swap button once again to put the departments back.

What is the minimum weighted-distance score after all swaps have been tried?

3. Look at the two data tables, and use the yellow-shaded column to put departments in spaces. What space assignments lead to the minimum cost? What is this cost?

CASE 1 Hightec, Inc.

"It's hard to believe," thought Glenn Moore as he walked into the employee lunch area, "that it has been only 6 years since I founded Hightec." He was not interested in lunch because it was only 9:30 A.M. His purpose was to inspect the new microcomputer, which had just been purchased to improve management of the company's inventory and accounting functions. The computer had to be housed at the rear of the employee lunch area, right next to the coffee, hot soup, and hot chocolate vending machines. There was absolutely no room for the computer elsewhere.

Hightec is a manufacturer of transducers, which convert gas or liquid pressure into an electrical signal. Another form of the device converts weight or force into an electrical signal. A typical customer order is for only 3 to 10 units. The firm currently rents a 12,000-square-foot, L-shaped building, housing four basic sections: the office area, an engineering area, a machine shop, and an assembly area. The 80 employees comprise machinists, engineers, assemblers, secretaries, and salespeople.

Although Moore concentrated on finance and marketing during the first two years of Hightec's existence, his activities now are more concerned with production costs, inventory, and capacity. Sales have been increasing about 30 percent per year, and this growth is expected to continue. Specific symptoms of Hightec's problems include the following.

- Space limitations delayed the purchase of a numerical control machine and a more efficient testing machine. Both promise greater capacity and higher productivity, and their costs are easily justified.

- The machine shop is so crowded that equipment not in constant use had to be moved into the inventory storage area.

- More machines are being operated on second and third shifts than would normally be justified. Productivity is falling, and quality is slipping.

- Approximately 10 percent of the workforce's time is spent moving materials to and from the inventory storage area, where inventory at all stages of production is kept. The chaotic supply room makes finding wanted parts difficult, and considerable time is lost searching.

- Approximately 1,000 square feet of storage space must be rented outside the plant.

- Lack of capacity has forced Moore to forgo bidding on several attractive jobs. One salesperson is particularly disgruntled because she lost a potentially large commission.

- Several office workers have complained about the cramped quarters and lack of privacy. The quality of employee space also leaves an unfavorable impression on prospective customers who visit the plant.

- Additional help was just hired for the office. To make room for their desks, Moore had to discard his favorite tropical plant, which started as a cutting when Hightec was formed and had sentimental value.

The Options

Glenn Moore identified three options for increasing capacity at Hightec. The first is to renew the rental contract on the current facility for another 5 years and rent portable units to ease the cramped conditions. He discarded this option as being inadequate for a growing problem. The second option is to purchase land and build a new 19,000-square-foot facility. The most attractive site would cost $100,000 for land, and the construction cost is estimated at $40 per square foot. His cost of capital is about 15 percent.

The third option is to renew the rental contract on the current building for another 5 years and rent an adjacent 7,000-square-foot building only 30 feet from the current one. The rental cost of both buildings would be $2,800 per month. Moore's choice of this third option would necessitate building a $15,000 corridor connecting the buildings. However, Moore estimates the relocation costs (such as for moving and installing the machines and the loss of regular-time capacity) to be $20,000 less than with the second alternative.

The Layout

Regardless of which option Moore chooses, he must improve on the existing layout. It suffers in terms of materials handling costs and departmental coordination. When Moore initially designed the existing layout, he located the office first and then fit the other departments around it as best he could. The main consideration for the other departments was not to have the machine shop next to the cleaning room. Moore put together the information needed for planning the new layout, as shown in Table 8.3 and Figure 8.23. The projected area requirements should be sufficient for the next 5 years. Both layouts provide for 19,000 square feet. The closeness matrix emphasizes materials handling and communication patterns.

Glenn Moore walked back to the office with a fresh cup of coffee in his hand. He hated hot chocolate, and it was too early for soup. He wondered what he should do next. Whatever the choice, he wanted a more attractive work environment for the engineering and supply chain management staffs, currently located in a cramped, open-office setting. Attracting creative people in these areas had been difficult. He made a mental note that the adjacent building also is quite drab.

TABLE 8.3 | Closeness Matrix

																Area Needed
Closeness Rating Between Departments																
Department	**1**	**2**	**3**	**4**	**5**	**6**	**7**	**8**	**9**	**10**	**11**	**12**	**13**	**14**	**15**	**(blocks*)**
1. Administrative office	—	1	6	5		6	5	3	3	3	3	4	5	3		3
2. Conference room		—														1
3. Engineering & supply chain mgt.			—	4			3	6	5	5	4	5	5		3	2
4. Production manager				—		6	6	6	6	6	4	4	5	3	6	1
5. Lunch room					—											2
6. Computer						—	6					3	4			1
7. Inventory storage							—	6	3	3	3	3				2
8. Machine shop								—	6		4	3			4	6
9. Assembly area									—	6	6	4		4	6	7
10. Cleaning										—	3	3				1
11. Welding											—	3				1
12. Electronic												—	5			1
13. Sales and accounting													—	3		2
14. Shipping and receiving														—		1
15. Load test															—	1

*Each block represents approximately 585 square feet.

FIGURE 8.23

Available Space for Option 2
and Option 3

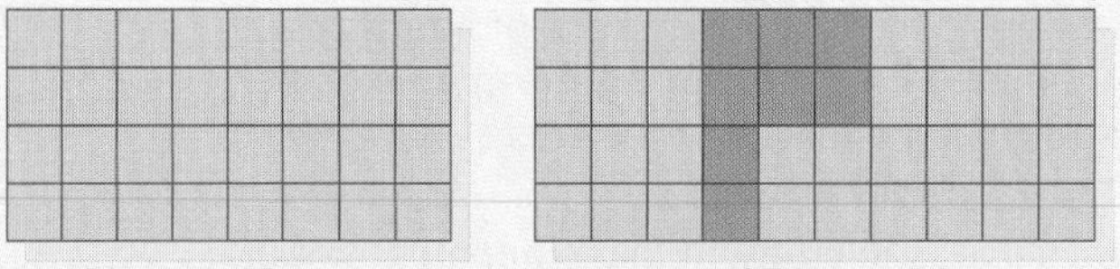

(a) Available space for new
plan (Option 2)

(b) Available space for renting
buildings (Option 3)

QUESTIONS

1. Which expansion option would you recommend to Glenn
   Moore? Justify your position.
2. Design an effective block plan and evaluate it. Cite any
   qualitative considerations that you believe make your
   design attractive.

| CASE 2 | The Pizza Connection |

Dave Collier owns and operates The Pizza Connection in Worthington, Ohio. The restaurant is a franchise of a large, national chain of pizza restaurants; its product and operations are typical of the industry. As Figure 8.24 shows, the facility is divided into two areas: customer contact and pizza production. Customers enter the facility and wait to be seated by a hostess. In the case of a carry-out order, the customer goes directly to the cashier at the front of the facility to place an order or to pick up a previously phoned-in order. Dine-in customers are served by waiters and waitresses; upon completion of their meal and receipt of the check from the server, they proceed to the cashier to pay their bill and leave. During peak hours at lunch and dinner, the cashier's area becomes quite crowded with customers waiting for carry-out orders and dine-in customers trying to pay their bills.

The pizza production area is somewhat of a hybrid layout. Major operations that comprise the pizza production process, such as the preparation tasks, baking, and the cut and box tasks, are grouped together. These individual work centers are arranged in a flexible-flow pattern around the production area.

Historically, Collier's operation has been successful, benefiting from the rise in popularity of pizza that swept across the country during the past few years. To help take advantage of this trend, the franchiser's home office provided coordinated national and regional marketing and advertising support. It also provided strong product development support, resulting in a new line of specialty pizzas designed to expand pizza's market appeal.

Recently, however, Collier noticed a decline in sales. Over the past few months the number of customers declined steadily. After doing some research, he came to the following conclusions, which he felt explained the decline in sales.

To begin with, customer demand had changed. Providing high-quality pizza at a reasonable price no longer was enough. The customers now demanded speed, convenience, and alternative dining options. If they were dine-in patrons, they wanted to be able to get in, eat, and get out quickly. Phoned-in, carry-out customers wanted their orders ready when they arrived. Also, restaurant "parties" were a growing trend. Little league baseball teams, youth soccer teams, and birthdays all had been part of a growing demand for "party

| FIGURE **8.24**

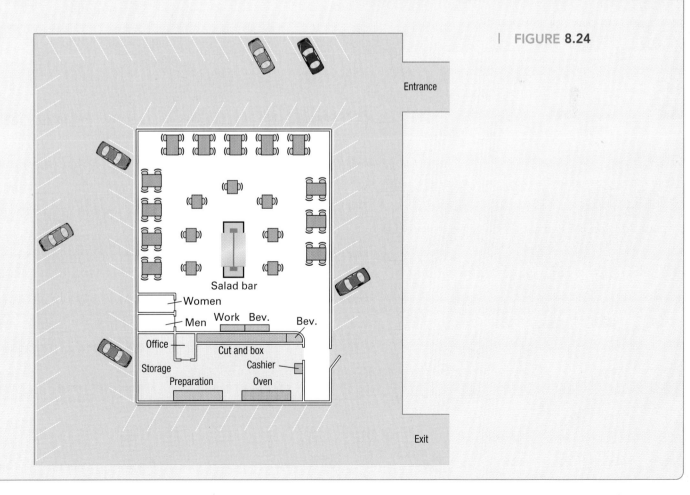

space" in restaurants. The busy, fast-paced lifestyle of today's families was contributing to moving celebrations out of the home and into restaurants and activity centers such as Putt-Putt or the Discovery Zone.

Besides these changing market demands, competition for the consumer's dining dollar increased significantly in the geographic area Collier's restaurant served. The number of dining establishments in the area more than tripled during the last two years. They ranged from drive-through to dine-in options and covered the entire spectrum from Mexican to Chinese and chicken to burgers.

Collier wondered how he should respond to what he had learned about his market. He thought that a reconfiguration of the restaurant's layout would enable him to address some of these changing customer demands. He hoped that a change in facilities would also help with labor turnover problems. Collier was having difficulty keeping trained servers, which he knew was driving up labor costs and causing a deterioration in service to his customers.

QUESTIONS

1. Reconfigure the layout shown in Figure 8.24 to respond to customers' demands for speed and convenience.

2. Explain how your new layout addresses the issues that Dave Collier identified.

3. How can the effectiveness of this new layout be measured?

Source: This case was prepared by Dr. Brooke Saladin, Wake Forest University, as a basis for classroom discussion.

> SELECTED REFERENCES <

Barry, Curt. "One Warehouse or Two?" *Catalog Age* (March 1, 2002).

Berry, L., L. Carbone, and S. Haeckel. "Managing the Total Customer Experience." *MIT Sloan Management Review*, vol. 43, no. 3 (Spring 2002), pp. 85–89.

Bitner, Mary Jo. "Evaluating Service Encounters: The Effects of Physical Surroundings and Employee Response." *Journal of Marketing*, vol. 54 (April 1990), pp. 69–82.

Bitner, Mary Jo. "Servicescapes: The Impact of Physical Surroundings on Customers and Employees." *Journal of Marketing*, vol. 56 (April 1992), pp. 57–71.

"Bloomie's Tries Losing the Attitude." *Business Week* (November 13, 1995), p. 52.

Bozer, Y. A., and R. D. Meller. "A Reexamination of the Distance-Based Layout Problem." *IIE Transactions*, vol. 29, no. 7 (1997), pp. 549–580.

Carbone, L., and S. Haeckel. "Engineering Customer Experience." *Marketing Management*, vol. 3, no. 3 (Winter 1994), pp. 8–19.

"Cool Offices." *Fortune* (December 9, 1996), pp. 204–210.

"Cummins Engine Flexes Its Factory." *Harvard Business Review* (March–April 1990), pp. 120–127.

"Deck the Malls with Kiosks." *Business Week* (December 13, 1999), p. 86.

Faaland, B. H., T. D. Klastorin, T. G. Schmitt, and A. Shtub. "Assembly Line Balancing with Resource Dependent Task Times." *Decision Sciences*, vol. 23, no. 2 (1992), pp. 343–363.

Francis, Richard L., Leon F. McGinnis, Jr., and John A. White. *Facility Layout and Location: An Analytical Approach*, 2d ed. Englewood Cliffs, NJ: Prentice Hall, 1992.

Frazier, G. V., and M. T. Spriggs, "Achieving Competitive Advantage Through Group Technology." *Business Horizons*, vol. 39, no. 3 (1996), pp. 83–90.

Gupta, S., and M. Vajic. "The Contextual and Dialectical Nature of Experiences," p. 33–51 in Fitzsimmons and Fitzsimmons (eds.), *New Service Development*. Thousand Oaks, CA: Sage Publications Inc., 1999.

Heragu, Sunderesh. *Facilities Design*. Boston, MA: PWS Publishing Company, 1997.

"How Nokia Thrives by Breaking the Rules." *Wall Street Journal* (January 3, 2003).

Hyer, N. L., and K. H. Brown. "The Discipline of Real Cells." *Journal of Operations Management*, vol. 17, no. 5 (1999), pp. 557–574.

"Making Malls (Gasp!) Convenient." *Wall Street Journal* (February 8, 2000).

Oldham, G. R., and D. J. Brass. "Employee Reactions to an Open-Plan Office: A Naturally Occurring Quasi-Experiment." *Administrative Science Quarterly*, vol. 24 (1979), pp. 267–294.

Pesch, Michael J., Larry Jarvis, and Loren Troyer. "Turning Around the Rust Belt Factory: The $1.98 Solution." *Production and Inventory Management Journal* (Second Quarter 1993).

Pine, B., and J. Gilmore. *The Experience Economy*. Boston, MA: Harvard Business School Press, 1999.

Pinto, Peter D., David Dannenbring, and Basheer Khumawala. "Assembly Line Balancing with Processing Alternatives." *Management Science*, vol. 29, no. 7 (1983), pp. 817–830.

Pullman, Madeleine E., and Michael A. Gross. "Making the Connection: An Exploration of the Relationship Between Customer Loyalty and Experience Design Elements." Working Paper, Colorado State University, February 2003.

"Retailing: Confronting the Challenges That Face Bricks-and-Mortar Stores." *Harvard Business Review* (July–August 1999), p. 159.

Schuler, Randall S., Larry P. Ritzman, and Vicki L. Davis. "Merging Prescriptive and Behavioral Approaches for Office Layout." *Journal of Operations Management*, vol. 1, no. 3 (1981), pp. 131–142.

Stone, Phillip J., and Robert Luchetti. "Your Office Is Where You Are." *Harvard Business Review* (March–April 1985), pp. 102–117.

Sule, D. R. *Manufacturing Facilities: Location, Planning, and Design*. Boston, MA: PWS Publishing Company, 1994.

Suresh, N. C., and J. M. Kay, eds. *Group Technology and Cellular Manufacturing: A State-of-the-Art Synthesis of Research and Practice*. Boston, MA: Kluwer Academic Publishers, 1997.

"The Most Devastating Retailer in the World." *The New Yorker* (September 2000).

"Tools of the Remote Trade." *Business Week* (March 27, 2000), p. F20.

Wakefield, K., and G. Blodgett. "The Effect of the Servicescape on Customers' Behavioral Intentions in Leisure Service Settings." *Journal of Services Marketing*, vol. 10, no. 6 (1996), pp. 45–61.

Wasserman, V., Rafaeli, A., and A. Kluger. "Aesthetic Symbols as Emotional Cues," pp. 140–165 in Fineman, S. (ed.), *Emotion in Organizations*. London: Sage Publications, 2000.

"Will This Open Space Work?" *Harvard Business Review* (May–June 1999), p. 28.

Winarchick, C., and R. D. Caldwell. "Physical Interactive Simulation: A Hands-On Approach to Facilities Improvements." *IIE Solutions*, vol. 29, no. 5 (1997), pp. 34–42.

Wolf, M. J. *The Entertainment Economy: How Mega-Media Forces Are Transforming Our Lives*. New York: Times Books, Random House, 1999.

9

An employee helps assemble a vehicle in Toyota City in central Japan. Toyota's production system is among the most-admired lean manufacturing systems in the world.

TOYOTA PRODUCTION SYSTEM

If you were to select one company that is exemplary of excellence in automobile manufacturing, it would probably be Toyota. Worldwide in its presence, in 2004 Toyota had a total investment of $16.6 billion in 12 manufacturing plants that employed 37,351 associates producing 1.44 million vehicles in North America alone. Toyota was at the forefront of firms developing lean systems for manufacturing. Today the Toyota Production System (TPS) is one of the most admired lean manufacturing systems in existence. Replicating the system, however, is fraught with difficulties. What makes the system tick, and why has Toyota been able to use the system so successfully in many different plants whereas other automakers have not?

Most outsiders see the TPS as a set of tools and procedures that are readily visible during a plant tour. Even though they are important for the success of the TPS, they are not the key. What most people overlook is that through the process of continuous improvement, Toyota built a learning organization over the course of 50 years. Lean systems require constant improvements to increase efficiency and reduce waste. Toyota created a system that stimulates employees to experiment to find better ways to do their jobs. In fact, Toyota sets up all of its operations as "experiments" and teaches employees at all levels how to use the scientific method of problem solving.

Four principles form the basis of the TPS. First, all work must be completely specified as to content, sequence, timing, and outcome. Detail is important, otherwise a foundation for improvements is missing. Second, every customer–supplier

>

connection must be direct, unambiguously specifying the people involved, the form and quantity of the services or goods to be provided, the way the requests are made by each customer, and the expected time in which the requests will be met. Customer–supplier connections can be internal (employee to employee) or external (company to company).

Third, the pathway for every service and product must be simple and direct. That is, services and goods do not flow to the next available person or machine, but to a specific person or machine. With this principle, employees can determine, for example, whether a capacity problem exists at a particular workstation and then analyze ways to solve it.

The first three principles define the system in detail by specifying how employees do work, interact with each other, and how the work flows are designed. However, these specifications actually are "hypotheses" about the way the system should work. For example, if something goes wrong at a workstation enough times, the hypothesis about the methods the employee uses to do work is rejected. The fourth principle, then, is that any improvement to the system must be made in accordance with the scientific method, under the guidance of a teacher, at the lowest possible organizational level. The scientific method involves clearly stating a verifiable hypothesis of the form, "If we make the following specific changes, we expect to achieve this specific outcome." The hypothesis must then be tested under a variety of conditions. Working with a teacher, who is often the employees' supervisor, is a key to becoming a learning organization. Employees learn the scientific method and eventually become teachers of others. Finally, making improvements at the lowest level of the organization means that the employees who are actually doing the work are actively involved in making the improvements. Managers are advised to coach employees only—not to fix their problems for them.

These four principles are deceptively simple. However, they are difficult but not impossible to replicate. Those organizations that successfully implement them enjoy the benefits of a lean system that adapts to change. For Toyota, their lean system made them an innovative leader in the auto industry and served as an important cornerstone of their success.

Source: Steven Spear and H. Kent Bowen, "Decoding the DNA of the Toyota Production System," *Harvard Business Review* (September–October 1999), pp. 97–106; Steven J. Spear, "Learning to Lead at Toyota," *Harvard Business Review* (May 2004), pp 78–86; www.toyota.com, August 2005.

lean systems

Operations systems that maximize the value added by each of a company's activities by paring unnecessary resources and delays from them.

The Toyota Production System (TPS) is an excellent example of an approach for designing value chains known as **lean systems**. Lean systems are operations systems that maximize the value added by each of a company's activities by paring unnecessary resources and delays from them. Lean systems encompass the company's operations strategy, process design, quality management, constraint management, layout design, supply chain design, and technology and inventory management and can be used by both service and manufacturing firms. Like a manufacturer, each service business takes an order from a customer; then it delivers a service and collects revenue. Each service business purchases services or items, receives and pays for them, and hires and pays employees. Each of these activities bears considerable similarity to those in manufacturing firms. They also typically contain huge amounts of waste. In the first part of the text, we discussed many ways to improve processes, regardless of whether they are manufacturing or nonmanufacturing processes. These same principles can be applied to make service processes lean, whether they are front-office, hybrid-office, or back-office designs. We conclude the first part of the text by continuing that discussion of managing processes in this chapter.

just-in-time (JIT) philosophy

The belief that waste can be eliminated by cutting unnecessary capacity or inventory and removing non-value-added activities in operations.

One of the most popular systems that incorporate the generic elements of lean systems is the just-in-time (JIT) system. The **just-in-time (JIT) philosophy** is simple but powerful—

eliminate waste by cutting excess capacity or inventory and removing non-value-added activities. The goals are to produce services and products as needed and to continuously improve the value-added benefits of operations. A **JIT system** organizes the resources, information flows, and decision rules that enable a firm to realize the benefits of JIT principles. We begin by identifying the characteristics of lean systems for service and manufacturing processes. We then discuss how lean systems can be used to continuously improve operations. We also address some of the implementation issues that companies face.

> LEAN SYSTEMS ACROSS THE ORGANIZATION <

Lean systems affect a firm's internal linkages between its core and supporting processes and its external linkages with its customers and suppliers. The design of value chains using the lean systems approach is important to various departments and functional areas across the organization. Marketing relies on lean systems to deliver high-quality services or products on time and at reasonable prices. Human resources must put in place the right incentive systems that reward teamwork. This department must also recruit, train, and evaluate the employees needed to create a flexible workforce that can successfully operate a lean system. Engineering must design products that use more common parts, so that fewer setups are required and focused factories can be used. Operations is responsible for maintaining close ties with suppliers and using the lean system in the production of services or goods. Accounting must adjust its billing and cost accounting practices to take advantage of lean systems. Finally, top management must embrace the lean philosophy and make it a part of organizational culture and learning, as was done by Toyota in our opening vignette.

> CHARACTERISTICS OF LEAN SYSTEMS FOR SERVICES AND MANUFACTURING <

In this section, we discuss the following characteristics of lean systems: pull method of work flow, consistent quality at the source, small lot sizes, uniform workstation loads, standardized components and work methods, close supplier ties, flexible workforce, line flows, automation, Five S (5S) practices, and preventive maintenance.

PULL METHOD OF WORK FLOW

Lean systems utilize the pull method of work flow. However, another popular method is the push method of work flow. To differentiate between these two methods, let us use a service example that involves a favorite pastime, eating. Consider a cafeteria on a busy downtown corner. During the busy periods around 12 P.M. and 5 P.M. lines develop, with hungry patrons eager to eat and then move on to other activities. The cafeteria offers choices of chicken (roasted or deep fried), roast beef, pork chops, hamburgers, hot dogs, salad, soup (chicken, pea, and clam chowder), bread (three types), beverages, and desserts (pies, ice cream, and cookies). Close coordination is required between the cafeteria's "front office," where its employees interface with customers; and its "back office," the kitchen, where the food is prepared and then placed along the cafeteria's buffet line. Because it takes substantial time to cook some of the food items, the cafeteria uses a **push method**, which involves preparing the food sold to customers prior to their ordering it. The food items prepared in the cafeteria are actually an "inventory of food," and the push method is geared to make sure that an adequate inventory is available. After all, shortages in food could cause riotous conditions (recall that customers are hungry), whereas preparing an excess amount of food will be wasteful because it will go uneaten. To make sure that neither of these conditions occurs the cafeteria must accurately forecast the number of customers it expects to serve.

Now consider a five-star restaurant in which you are seated at a table and offered a menu of exquisite dishes, appetizers, soups, salads, and desserts. You can choose from filet mignon, porterhouse steak, yellowfin tuna, grouper, and lamb chops. Your choice of several salads is prepared at your table. Although some appetizers, soups, and desserts can be prepared in advance and brought to temperature just before serving, the main course and salads cannot. Your order for the salad and the main course signals the chef to begin preparing your specific requests. For these items, the restaurant is using the **pull method**. When the pull method is

JIT system

A system that organizes the resources, information flows, and decision rules that enable a firm to realize the benefits of JIT principles.

USING OPERATIONS TO COMPETE

Operations As a Competitive Weapon
Operations Strategy
Project Management

MANAGING PROCESSES

Process Strategy
Process Analysis
Process Performance and Quality
Constraint Management
Process Layout
Lean Systems

MANAGING VALUE CHAINS

Supply Chain Strategy
Location
Inventory Management
Forecasting
Sales and Operations Planning
Resource Planning
Scheduling

push method

A method in which production of the item begins in advance of customer needs.

pull method

A method in which customer demand activates production of the service or item.

Diners fill their plates at a restaurant buffet. Because the food items must be prepared in advance, the restaurant uses a push method of work flow.

used, customer demand activates the production of a good or service. Firms using the pull method must be able to fulfill the customer's demands within an acceptable amount of time. The cafeteria would have a difficult time using the pull method because it could not wait until an item was nearly gone before asking the kitchen to begin processing another batch.

The choice between the push and pull methods is often situational. Firms with highly repetitive processes and well-defined work flows of standardized items often use the pull method because it allows closer control of inventory and output at the workstations. The five-star restaurant uses the pull method to control inventory costs (and the freshness and taste of the meal). Firms with processes that involve long lead times and reasonably accurate forecasts of demand, a variety of products that require common processes, and customers who will not wait long for the product, tend to produce using a push method. These factors are often the case with the cafeteria and many manufacturing firms. Firms using an assemble-to-order strategy sometimes use both methods: the push method to produce the standardized components and the pull method to fulfill the customer's request for a particular combination of the components.

QUALITY AT THE SOURCE

Consistently meeting the customer's expectations is an important characteristic of lean systems. One way to achieve this goal is by adhering to a practice called *quality at the source,* which is an organization-wide effort to improve the quality of a firm's products by having employees act as their own quality inspectors. The goal for workers is to never pass on defective units to the next process. For example, a soldering operation at the Texas Instruments antenna department had a defect rate that varied from zero to 50 percent on a daily basis, averaging about 20 percent. To compensate, production planners increased the lot sizes, which only increased inventory levels and did nothing to reduce the number of defective items. The company's engineers then discovered through experimentation that gas temperature was a critical variable in producing defect-free items. They subsequently devised statistical control charts for the firm's equipment operators to use to monitor the temperature and adjust it themselves. Process yields immediately improved and stabilized at 95 percent, and Texas Instruments was eventually able to implement a lean system.

poka-yoke

Mistake-proofing methods aimed at designing fail-safe systems that minimize human error.

One approach for implementing quality at the source is to use **poka-yoke**, or mistake-proofing methods aimed at designing fail-safe systems that attack and minimize human error. Consider for instance a company that makes modular products. The company could use the poka-yoke method by making different parts of the modular product in such a way that allows them to be assembled in only one way—the correct way. Similarly, a company's shipping boxes could be designed to be packed only in a certain way to minimize damage and eliminate all chances of mistakes. Poka-yoke systems work well in practice. Another approach for implementing quality at the source is a practice the Japanese call *jidoka,* and *andon,* which gives machines and machine operators the ability to detect the occurrence of any abnormal condition. Employees are then authorized to signal for help or stop the production line if needed. Stopping a production line can, however, cost a company thousands of dollars each minute production is halted. Needless to say, management must realize the enormous responsibility this method puts on employees and must prepare them properly.

SMALL LOT SIZES

lot

A quantity of items that are processed together.

Lean systems use lot sizes that are as small as possible. A **lot** is a quantity of items that are processed together. Small lots have the advantage of reducing the average level of inventory relative to large lots. Small lots pass through the system faster than large lots. In addition, if any defective items are discovered, large lots cause longer delays because the entire lot must be examined to find all the items that need rework. Finally, small lots help achieve a uniform workload on the system. Large lots consume large chunks of capacity at workstations and, therefore, complicate scheduling. Small lots can be juggled more effectively, enabling schedulers to efficiently utilize capacities.

Although small lots are beneficial to operations, they have the disadvantage of increased setup frequency. A **setup** is the group of activities needed to change or readjust a process between successive lots of items, sometimes referred to as a *changeover*. Typically, a setup takes the same time regardless of the lot size. Consequently, many small lots, in lieu of several large lots, may result in waste in the form of idle employees and equipment. Setup times must be brief to realize the benefits of small-lot production.

Achieving brief setup times often requires close cooperation among engineering, management, and labor. For example, changing dies on large presses to form automobile parts from sheet metal can take three to four hours. At Honda's Marysville, Ohio, plant—where four stamping lines stamp all the exterior and major interior body panels for Accord production—teams worked on ways to reduce the changeover time for the massive dies. As a result, a complete change of dies for a giant 2,400-ton press now takes less than 8 minutes. The goal of **single-digit setup** means having setup times of less than 10 minutes. Some techniques used to reduce setup times at the Marysville plant include using conveyors for die storage, moving large dies with cranes, simplifying dies, enacting machine controls, using microcomputers to automatically feed and position work, and preparing for changeovers while a job presently in production is still being processed.

setup

The group of activities needed to change or readjust a process between successive lots of items.

single-digit setup

The goal of having a setup time of less than 10 minutes.

UNIFORM WORKSTATION LOADS

A lean system works best if the daily load on individual workstations is relatively uniform. Service processes can achieve uniform workstation loads by using reservation systems. For example, hospitals schedule surgeries in advance of the actual service so that the facilities and facilitating goods can be ready when the time comes. The load on the surgery rooms and surgeons can be evened out to make the best use of these resources. Another approach is to use differential pricing of the service to manage the demand for it. Uniform loads is the rationale behind airlines promoting weekend travel or red-eye flights that begin late in the day and end in the early morning. Efficiencies can be realized when the load on the firm's resources can be managed.

For manufacturing processes, uniform loads can be achieved by assembling the same type and number of units each day, thus creating a uniform daily demand at all workstations. Capacity planning, which recognizes capacity constraints at critical workstations, and line balancing are used to develop the master production schedule. For example, at Toyota, the production plan may call for 4,500 vehicles per week for the next month. That requires two full shifts, five days per week, producing 900 vehicles each day, or 450 per shift. Three models are produced: Camry (C), Avalon (A), and Sienna (S). Suppose that Toyota needs 200 Camrys, 150 Avalons, and 100 Siennas per shift to satisfy market demand. To produce 450 units in one shift of 480 minutes, the line must roll out a vehicle every 480/450 = 1.067 minutes.

Three ways of devising a master production schedule for the vehicles are of interest here. First, with big-lot production, all daily requirements of a model are produced in one batch before another model is started. The sequence of 200 Cs, 150 As, and 100 Ss would be repeated once per shift. Not only would these big lots increase the average cycle inventory level, but they also would cause lumpy requirements on all the workstations feeding the assembly line.

The second option uses **mixed-model assembly**, producing a mix of models in smaller lots. Note that the production requirements are in the ratio of 4 Cs to 3 As to 2 Ss, found by dividing the model's production requirements by the greatest common divisor, or 50. Thus, the Toyota planner could develop a production cycle consisting of 9 units: 4 Cs, 3 As, and 2 Ss. The cycle would repeat in 9(1.067) = 9.60 minutes, for a total of 50 times per shift (480 min/9.60 min = 50).

mixed-model assembly

A type of assembly that produces a mix of models in smaller lots.

A sequence of C–S–C–A–C–A–C–S–A, repeated 50 times per shift, would achieve the same total output as the other options. This third option is feasible only if the setup times are brief. The sequence generates a steady rate of component requirements for the various models and allows the use of small lot sizes at the feeder workstations. Consequently, the capacity requirements at those stations are greatly smoothed. These requirements can be compared to actual capacities during the planning phase, and modifications to the production cycle, production requirements, or capacities can be made as necessary.

STANDARDIZED COMPONENTS AND WORK METHODS

In highly repetitive service operations, great efficiencies can be gained by analyzing work methods and documenting the improvements for all employees to use. For example, UPS consistently monitors its work methods and revises them as necessary to improve service. In manufacturing, the standardization of components, called *part commonality* or *modularity*, increases repeatability. For example, a firm producing 10 products from 1,000 different components could redesign its products so that they consist of only 100 different components with larger daily requirements. Because the requirements per component increase, so does repeatability; that is, each worker performs a standardized task or work method more often each day. Productivity tends to increase because, with increased repetition, workers learn to do their tasks more efficiently. Standardizing components and work methods helps a firm achieve the high-productivity, low-inventory objectives of a lean system.

CLOSE SUPPLIER TIES

Because lean systems operate with low levels of capacity slack or inventory, firms that use them need to have a close relationships with their suppliers. Supplies must be shipped frequently, have short lead times, arrive on schedule, and be of high quality. A contract might even require a supplier to deliver goods to a facility as often as several times per day. Purchasing managers have three ways to tighten up a company's ties with its suppliers: reduce the number of its suppliers, use local suppliers, and improve supplier relations.

Typically, one of the first actions undertaken when a lean system is implemented is to pare down the number of suppliers. Xerox, for example, reduced the number of its suppliers from 5,000 to just 300. This approach puts a lot of pressure on these suppliers to deliver high-quality components on time. To compensate, lean system users extend their contracts with these suppliers and give them firm advance-order information. In addition, they include their suppliers in the early phases of product design to avoid problems after production begins. They also work with their suppliers' vendors, trying to achieve synchronized inventory flows throughout the entire supply chain.

Manufacturers using lean systems generally utilize local suppliers. For instance, when GM located its Saturn complex in Tennessee, many suppliers clustered nearby. Harley-Davidson reduced the number of its suppliers and gave preference to those close to its plants: Three-fourths of the suppliers for its Milwaukee engine plant are located within a 175-mile radius, for example. Geographic proximity means that the company can reduce the need for safety stocks. Companies that have no suppliers close by must rely on a finely tuned supplier delivery system. For example, New United Motor Manufacturing, Incorporated (NUMMI), the joint venture between GM and Toyota in California, has suppliers in Indiana, Ohio, and Michigan. Through a carefully coordinated system involving trains and piggyback truck trailers, suppliers deliver enough parts for exactly one day's production each day.

Users of lean systems also find that a cooperative orientation with suppliers is essential. The lean system philosophy is to look for ways to improve efficiency and reduce inventories throughout the supply chain. Close cooperation between companies and their suppliers can be a win–win situation for everyone. Better communication of component requirements, for example, enables more efficient inventory planning and delivery scheduling by suppliers, thereby improving supplier profit margins. Customers can then negotiate lower component prices. Close supplier relations cannot be established and maintained if companies view their suppliers as adversaries whenever contracts are negotiated. Rather, they should consider suppliers to be partners in a venture, wherein both parties have an interest in maintaining a long-term, profitable relationship.

FLEXIBLE WORKFORCE

Workers in flexible workforces can be trained to perform more than one job. A benefit of flexibility is the ability to shift workers among workstations to help relieve bottlenecks as they arise without the need for inventory buffers—an important aspect of the uniform flow of lean systems. Also, workers can step in and do the job for those who are on vacation or who are out sick. Although assigning workers to tasks they do not usually perform can temporarily reduce their efficiency, some job rotation tends to relieve boredom and refreshes workers.

The more customized the service or product is, the greater the firm's need for a multiskilled workforce. For example, stereo repair shops require broadly trained personnel who can identify a wide variety of component problems when the customer brings the defective unit into the shop and who then can repair the unit. Alternatively, back-office designs, such as the mail-processing operations at a large post office, have employees with more narrowly defined jobs because of the repetitive nature of the tasks they must perform. These employees do not have to acquire as many alternative skills. In situations such as at the Texas Instruments antenna department, shifting workers to other jobs may require them to undergo extensive, costly training.

LINE FLOWS

Managers of hybrid-office and back-office service processes can organize their employees and equipment to provide uniform work flows through the process and, thereby, eliminate wasted employee time. Banks use this strategy in their check-processing operations, as does UPS in its parcel-sorting process. Line flows can reduce the frequency of setups. If volumes of specific products are large enough, groups of machines and workers can be organized into a line-flow layout to eliminate setups entirely. If volume is insufficient to keep a production line of similar products busy, *group technology* can be used to design small production lines that manufacture, in volume, families of components with common attributes. Changeovers from a component in one product family to the next component in the same family are minimal.

Another tactic used to reduce or eliminate setups is the one-worker, multiple-machines (OWMM) approach, which essentially is a one-person line. One worker operates several machines, with each machine advancing the process a step at a time. Because the same product is made repeatedly, setups are eliminated.

AUTOMATION

Automation plays a big role in lean systems and is a key to low-cost operations. Money freed up because of inventory reductions or other efficiencies can be invested in automation to reduce costs. The benefits, of course, are greater profits, greater market share (because prices can be cut), or both. Automation can play a big role when it comes to providing lean services. For example, banks offer ATMs that provide various bank services on demand 24 hours a day. Automation should be planned carefully, however. Many managers believe that if some automation is good, more is better, which is not always the case. When GM initiated Buick City, for example, it installed 250 robots, some with vision systems for mounting wind-shields. Unfortunately, the robots skipped black cars because they could not "see" them. New software eventually solved the problem. Nonetheless, 30 robots were replaced with humans because GM found that humans do some jobs better.

FIVE S

Five S (5S) is a methodology for organizing, cleaning, developing, and sustaining a produc-tive work environment. It represents five related terms, each beginning with an *S,* that describe workplace practices conducive to visual controls and lean production. These five practices of sorting, straightening, shining, standardizing, and sustaining are done systemat-ically to achieve lean systems. They are not something that can be done as a stand-alone pro-gram. As such, they represent an essential foundation of lean systems. Table 9.1 shows the terms[1] that represent the 5S and what they imply.

It is commonly accepted that 5S forms an important cornerstone of waste reduction and removal of unneeded tasks, activities, and materials. Implementation of 5S practices can lead to lowered costs, improved on-time delivery and productivity, higher product quality, and a safe working environment.

five S (5S)

A methodology consisting of five workplace practices—sorting, straightening, shining, standardizing, and sustaining—that are conducive to visual controls and lean production.

TABLE 9.1	5S Defined

5S Term	Definition
1. Sort	Separate needed from unneeded items (including tools, parts, materials, and paperwork), and discard the unneeded.
2. Straighten	Neatly arrange what is left, with a place for everything and everything in its place. Organize the work area so that it is easy to find what is needed.
3. Shine	Clean and wash the work area and make it shine.
4. Standardize	Establish schedules and methods of performing the cleaning and sorting. Formalize the cleanliness that results from regularly doing the first three S practices so that perpetual cleanliness and a state of readiness is maintained.
5. Sustain	Create discipline to perform the first four S practices, whereby everyone understands, obeys, and practices the rules when in the plant. Implement mechanisms to sustain the gains by involving people and recognizing them via a performance measurement system.

[1]The Japanese words for these 5S terms are *seiri, seiton, seiso, seiketsu,* and *shitsuke,* respectively.

Employees of United Parcel Service work on a small automated package line in the $1 billion air hub in Louisville, Kentucky. The packages (in the center of the photo) are automatically deposited in the bin dedicated to their destination.

PREVENTIVE MAINTENANCE

Because lean systems emphasize finely tuned flows of work and little capacity slack or buffer inventory between workstations, unplanned machine downtime can be disruptive. Preventive maintenance can reduce the frequency and duration of machine downtime. After performing their routine maintenance activities, technicians can test other machine parts that might need to be replaced. Replacing parts during regularly scheduled maintenance periods is easier and quicker than dealing with machine failures during production. Maintenance is done on a schedule that balances the cost of the preventive maintenance program against the risks and costs of machine failure. Routine preventive maintenance is important for service businesses that rely heavily on machinery. For example, the rides at Walt Disney World need routine preventive maintenance to keep them from breaking down and customers from being hurt.

A monorail heads toward Cinderella's Castle and Space Mountain in Florida's Disney World. Preventive maintenance ensures reliable service to customers.

Another tactic is to make workers responsible for routinely maintaining their own equipment and develop employee pride in keeping their machines in top condition. This tactic, however, typically is limited to general housekeeping chores, minor lubrication, and adjustments. Maintaining high-tech machines requires trained specialists. Nonetheless, performing even simple maintenance tasks goes a long way toward improving the performance of machines.

Managerial Practice 9.1 shows how the principles of lean systems have been used by New Balance Athletic Shoe Company to create a different type of manufacturing firm in the shoe industry.

> CONTINUOUS IMPROVEMENT USING
A LEAN SYSTEMS APPROACH <

By spotlighting areas that need improvement, lean systems lead to continuous improvement in quality and productivity. The Japanese term for this approach to process improvement is *kaizen*. The key to kaizen is the understanding that excess capacity or inventory hides underlying problems with the processes that produce a service or product. Lean systems provide the mechanism for management to reveal the problems by systematically lowering capacities or inventories until the problems are exposed. For example, Figure 9.1 characterizes the philosophy behind continuous improvement with lean systems. In services, the water sur-

MANAGERIAL **PRACTICE**	**9.1** LEAN SYSTEMS AT NEW BALANCE ATHLETIC SHOE COMPANY

New Balance (NB), headquartered in Boston, makes and markets a full line of performance footwear and apparel for men, women, and children in 120 countries with global sales of $1.3 billion in 2003. Founded in 1906 to make arch supports, Chairman and CEO Jim Davis bought New Balance on the day of the 1972 Boston Marathon. NB remains the only athletic shoe company offering multiple widths across its entire shoe line, and also the only company in that industry that retains about 25 percent of its global production in the United States. Despite such a broad product line and labor cost differences between the United States and China, how then does New Balance maintain its profitability and growth? New Balance follows the principles of lean manufacturing and ships directly to retailers and customers without the intervening intermediaries who may discount their products.

NB's largest and oldest plant in the United States is in Lawrence, Massachusetts. The company's research and development group is located there, too, so the company's design and manufacturing operations are tightly integrated. The Lawrence plant makes all the styles exclusive to the North American market. Most new designs are first made at Lawrence and then transferred out to other NB American plants, all of which follow the same production methods. During the past few years, NB migrated away from the shoe industry's traditional batch and queue method towards small-lot, cellular flow production. Some production steps remain manual, although NB automates processes wherever it can.

Shoe production begins in the cutting room, where 60 upper parts per shoe pair are cut from flat stock. Downstream, shoes are assembled in lot sizes of 12 of the same style and size. Until recently, about 50 percent of a day's worth of shoes had to be produced in the cutting room before a lot could be moved to the next operation in the process. After a lean system was implemented, however, the lot sizes were cut dramatically. The parts are next assembled in uppers in the first stage of automated stitching, with parts that cannot be automated being processed in a manual stitching cell. Then the nearly complete uppers are stretched on a form (a shoemaker's "last"), which usually determines the shoe's width. Care is important here for proper fit. Cross-trained operators never pass on a defective unit, and they always check the prior operator's work as well as their own. Finally, the uppers are joined to the soles with an adhesive, which is quickly cured using heat.

When deciding how many shoes of each style to schedule, NB thinks of "sales orders" and not "production orders." Instead of pushing shoes to

A worker moves a stack of partially assembled athletic shoes from her stitching station at the New Balance factory in Skowhegan, Maine. She and five other members of her team have worked out a plan so that each person is cross-trained in another's skills. Similar ideas for improving proficiency, which are discussed during biweekly meetings with workers and supervisors, have led to improved performance at New Balance.

the market, NB uses more of a pull strategy. In other words, its production schedules are driven by market demand. By using lean concepts and techniques, NB reduced lot sizes by a factor of 8, and manufacturing cycle times by a factor of 4. Even though these reduction levels vary somewhat because the company manufactures many different products, NB's work flow is still uniform. Along with fostering teamwork and a culture of continuous improvement, NB's lean manufacturing journey allowed the company to grow from the small specialty producer it was in 1972 to the global company it is today. Along with Reebok, it holds the number two spot in the sports shoe industry, with Nike leading the pack.

Source: Robert W. Hall, "New Balance Athletic Shoe Company," *Target*, vol. 20, no. 5 (2004), pp. 5–10. Reprinted/Excerpted from Target with permission of the Association for Manufacturing Excellence (AME), www.ame.org.

face represents service system capacity, such as staff levels. In manufacturing, the water surface represents product and component inventory levels. The rocks represent problems encountered in the fulfillment of services or products. When the water surface is high enough, the boat passes over the rocks because the high level of capacity or inventory covers up problems. As capacity or inventory shrinks, rocks are exposed. Ultimately, the boat will hit a rock if the water surface falls far enough. Through lean systems, workers, supervisors, engineers, and analysts apply methods for continuous improvement to demolish the exposed rock. The coordination required for the pull system of material flows in lean systems identifies problems in time for corrective action to be taken.

Maintaining low inventories, periodically stressing the system to identify problems, and focusing on the elements of the lean system lie at the heart of continuous improvement. For example, a Kawasaki plant in Nebraska periodically cuts its safety stocks almost to zero. The

FIGURE 9.1

Continuous Improvement
with Lean Systems

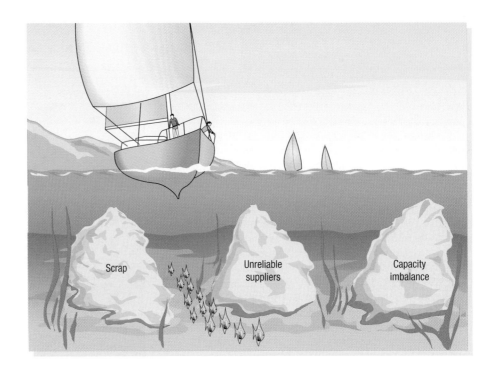

problems at the plant are exposed, recorded, and later assigned to employees as improvement projects. After improvements are made, inventories are permanently cut to the new level. Many firms use this trial-and-error process to develop more efficient manufacturing operations. Service processes, such as scheduling, billing, order taking, accounting, and financial planning can be improved with lean systems, too. In service operations, a common approach used by managers is to place stress on the system by reducing the number of employees doing a particular activity or series of activities until the process begins to slow or come to a halt. The problems can be identified, and ways for overcoming them explored. Other kaizen tactics can be used as well. Eliminating the problem of too much scrap might require improving the firm's work processes, providing employees with additional training, or finding higher-quality suppliers. Eliminating capacity imbalances might involve revising the firm's master production schedule and improving the flexibility of its workforce.

> THE KANBAN SYSTEM <

kanban

A Japanese word meaning "card" or "visible record" that refers to cards used to control the flow of production through a factory.

One of the most publicized aspects of lean systems, and the TPS in particular, is the kanban system developed by Toyota. **Kanban**, meaning "card" or "visible record" in Japanese, refers to cards used to control the flow of production through a factory. In the most basic kanban system, a card is attached to each container of items produced. The container holds a given percent of the daily production requirements for an item. When the user of the parts empties a container, the card is removed from the container and put on a receiving post. The empty container is then taken to the storage area, and the card signals the need to produce another container of the part. When the container has been refilled, the card is put back on the container, which is then returned to a storage area. The cycle begins again when the user of the parts retrieves the container with the card attached.

Figure 9.2 shows how a single-card kanban system works when a fabrication cell feeds two assembly lines. As an assembly line needs more parts, the kanban card for those parts is taken to the receiving post, and a full container of parts is removed from the storage area. The receiving post accumulates cards for assembly lines and a scheduler sequences the production of replenishment parts. In this example, the fabrication cell will produce product 2 (red) before it produces product 1 (green). The cell consists of three different operations, but operation 2 has two workstations. Once production has been initiated in the cell, the product begins on operation 1, but could be routed to either of the workstations performing operation 2, depending on the workload at the time. Finally, the product is processed on operation 3 before being taken to the storage area.

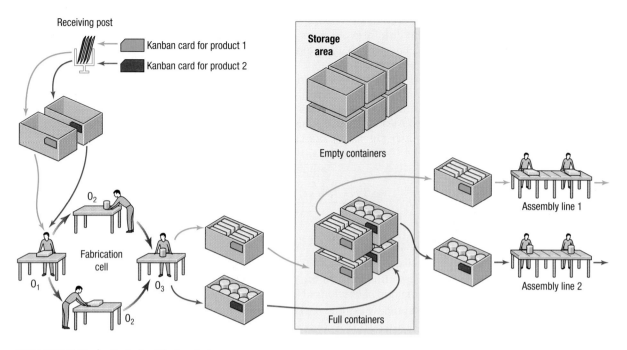

FIGURE 9.2 | Single-Card Kanban System

GENERAL OPERATING RULES

The operating rules for the single-card system are simple and are designed to facilitate the flow of materials while maintaining control of inventory levels.

1. Each container must have a card.

2. The assembly line always withdraws materials from the fabrication cell. The fabrication cell never pushes parts to the assembly line because, sooner or later, parts will be supplied that are not yet needed for production.

3. Containers of parts must never be removed from a storage area without a kanban first being posted on the receiving post.

4. The containers should always contain the same number of good parts. The use of nonstandard containers or irregularly filled containers disrupts the production flow of the assembly line.

5. Only nondefective parts should be passed along to the assembly line to make the best use of materials and worker's time. This rule reinforces the notion of building quality at the source, which is an important characteristics of lean systems.

6. Total production should not exceed the total amount authorized on the kanbans in the system.

Toyota uses a two-card system, based on a withdrawal card and a production-order card, to control withdrawal quantities more closely. The withdrawal card specifies the item and the quantity the user of the item should withdraw from the producer of the item, as well as the stocking locations for both the user and the producer. The production-order card specifies the item and the quantity to be produced, the materials required and where to find them, and where to store the finished item. Materials cannot be withdrawn without a withdrawal card, and production cannot begin without a production-order card. The cards are attached to containers when production commences.

DETERMINING THE NUMBER OF CONTAINERS

The number of authorized containers in the TPS determines the amount of authorized inventory. Management must make two determinations: (1) the number of units to be held by each container, and (2) the number of containers flowing back and forth between the supplier station and the user station. The first decision amounts to determining the lot size, which requires balancing the cost of setup with the cost of holding inventory in stock, among other considerations.

The number of containers flowing back and forth between two stations directly affects the quantities of work-in-process inventory and safety stock. The containers spend some time in production, in a line waiting, in a storage location, or in transit. The key to determining the number of containers required is to estimate the average lead time needed to produce a container of parts. The lead time is a function of the processing time per container at the supplier station, the waiting time during the production process, and the time required for materials handling. The number of containers needed to support the user station equals the average demand during the lead time, plus some safety stock to account for unexpected circumstances, divided by the number of units in one container. Therefore, the number of containers is

$$\kappa = \frac{\text{Average demand during lead time} + \text{Safety stock}}{\text{Number of units per container}}$$

$$= \frac{d(\bar{\omega} + \bar{\rho})(1 + \alpha)}{c}$$

where

κ = number of containers for a part

d = expected daily demand for the part, in units

$\bar{\omega}$ = average waiting time during the production process plus materials handling time per container, in fractions of a day

$\bar{\rho}$ = average processing time per container, in fractions of a day

c = quantity in a standard container of the part

α = a policy variable that adds safety stock to cover for unexpected circumstances (Toyota uses a value of no more than 10 percent.)

The number of containers must, of course, be an integer. Rounding up κ provides more inventory than desired, whereas rounding down κ provides less.

The container quantity, c, and the efficiency factor, α, are variables that management can use to control inventory. Adjusting c changes the lot sizes, and adjusting α changes the amount of safety stock. The kanban system allows management to fine-tune the flow of materials in the system in a straightforward way. For example, removing cards from the system reduces the number of authorized containers of the part, thus reducing the inventory of the part. Thus a major benefit is the simplicity of the system, whereby product mix or volume changes can easily be accomplished by adjusting the number of kanbans in the system.

TUTOR 9.1

Tutor 9.1 on the Student CD-ROM provides a new example of using the model to determine the number of containers.

EXAMPLE 9.1	Determining the Appropriate Number of Containers

The Westerville Auto Parts Company produces rocker-arm assemblies for use in the steering and suspension systems of four-wheel-drive trucks. A typical container of parts spends 0.02 day in processing and 0.08 day in materials handling and waiting during its manufacturing cycle. The daily demand for the part is 2,000 units. Management believes that demand for the rocker-arm assembly is uncertain enough to warrant a safety stock equivalent of 10 percent of its authorized inventory.

a. If each container contains 22 parts, how many containers should be authorized?

b. Suppose that a proposal to revise the plant layout would cut materials handling and waiting time per container to 0.06 day. How many containers would be needed?

SOLUTION

a. If d = 2,000 units/day, $\bar{\rho}$ = 0.02 day, α = 0.10, $\bar{\omega}$ = 0.08 day, and c = 22 units,

$$\kappa = \frac{2{,}000(0.08 + 0.02)(1.10)}{22} = \frac{220}{22} = 10 \text{ containers}$$

b. Figure 9.3 from OM Explorer shows that the number of containers drops to 8.

Decision Point The average lead time per container is $\bar{\omega} + \bar{\rho}$. With a lead time of 0.10 day, 10 containers are needed. However, if the improved facility layout reduces the materials handling time and waiting time, $\bar{\omega}$, to 0.06 day, only 8 containers are needed. The maximum authorized inventory of the rocker-arm assembly is κc units. Thus, in part (a), the maximum authorized inventory is 220 units, but in part (b), it is only 176 units. Reducing $\bar{\omega} + \bar{\rho}$ by 20 percent reduces the inventory of the part by 20 percent. Management must balance the cost of the relayout (a one-time charge) against the long-term benefits of inventory reduction.

Solver-Number of Containers

Enter data in yellow-shaded area.

Daily Expected Demand	2000
Quantity in Standard Container	22
Container Waiting Time (days)	0.06
Processing Time (days)	0.02
Policy Variable	10%
Containers Required	8

FIGURE 9.3

OM Explorer Solver for Number of Containers

Managerial Practice 9.2 illustrates how the University of Pittsburgh Medical Center Shadyside used principles of kanban systems, 5S methodology, cellular layouts, and continuous flow processes to significantly improve performance in their pathology department.

OTHER KANBAN SIGNALS

Cards are not the only way to signal the need for more production of a part. Other, less formal methods are possible, including container and containerless systems.

Container System Sometimes, the container itself can be used as a signal device: An empty container signals the need to fill it. Unisys took this approach for low-value items. The amount of inventory of the part is adjusted by adding or removing containers. This system works well when the container is specially designed for a particular part and no other parts could accidentally be put in the container. Such is the case when the container is actually a pallet or fixture used to position the part during precision processing.

Containerless System Systems requiring no containers have been devised. In assembly-line operations, operators use their own workbench areas to put completed units on painted

---

| MANAGERIAL **PRACTICE** | 9.2 | LEAN SYSTEMS AT UNIVERSITY OF PITTSBURGH MEDICAL CENTER SHADYSIDE |

The University of Pittsburgh Medical Center (UPMC) at Shadyside is a 486-bed advanced-care hospital with a medical staff of more than 600 primary care physicians and specialists. Always seeking to improve, UPMC first applied principles of the Toyota Production System in 2001 in a 40-bed surgical unit and then systematized the concepts into a lean approach called the Clinical Design Initiative (CDI). This approach focuses on determining the root cause of a problem through direct observation, and then eliminating it by designing solutions that are visual, simple, and unambiguous. These solutions are then tested in a small area and improved until the desired clinical and cost outcomes, along with enhanced patient and staff satisfaction, are achieved. Once perfected, the improved process is rolled out to other areas of the hospital.

UPMC used the CDI methodology recently to speed up turnaround time in the pathology lab. The layout and workflows of the lab were based on a batch-and-queue push system that led to long lead times, complexity in tracking and moving large lots, delays in discovering quality problems, and high storage costs. Before making the transition to the lean system, UPMC ran a workshop on lean concepts for the staff members of the lab and followed it with a 5S exercise to better organize the department. Counter spaces were cleared so that the lab's equipment could be rearranged. Unneeded items were identified with red tags and removed. Visual controls were used to arrange the remaining items in a neat and easy-to-use manner.

The 5S exercise of cleaning house boosted staff morale. Kanban cards with reordering information were then attached to most items. When a reorder point is reached, the card is removed and hung on a board. Reordering supplies now takes only a few minutes a day. Stockouts and expensive rush orders have been eliminated and the overall inventory level of supplies reduced by 50 percent to 60 percent.

To move away from the batch and queue system to one based on line flows, equipment was moved around in the lab to create a cellular layout. The new arrangement allows tissue samples being processed to move through the lab cell from embedding, to cutting, to the oven, and slide staining. The samples move more quickly, and few or no samples

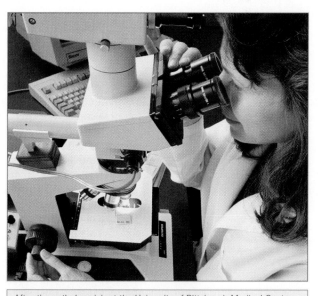

After the pathology lab at the University of Pittsburgh Medical Center adopted a lean operations approach based on a line system versus a batch-and-queue system, the time it took to process samples dropped from days to just hours. Diagnoses were made more quickly as a result, and patients' stays at the hospital were shortened.

end up waiting between steps. As a result, the overall time needed to prepare and analyze tissue samples fell from one or two days to less than a day. The reduction in turnaround time means doctors get pathology results quicker, which in turn speeds up diagnosis and leads to shorter stays for patients. Moreover, the lab does the same amount of work with 28 percent fewer people, and fewer errors because quality mistakes are discovered immediately.

Source: "The Anatomy of Innovation," *Lean Enterprise Institute,* www.lean.org.

squares, one unit per square. Each painted square represents a container, and the number of painted squares on each operator's bench is calculated to balance the line flow. When the subsequent user removes a unit from one of the producer's squares, the empty square signals the need to produce another unit.

McDonald's uses a containerless system. Information entered by the order taker at the cash register is transmitted to the cooks and assemblers, who produce the sandwiches requested by the customer.

> VALUE STREAM MAPPING <

value stream mapping (VSM)

A qualitative lean tool for eliminating waste or *muda* that involves a current state drawing, a future state drawing, and an implementation plan.

Value stream mapping (VSM) is a widely used qualitative lean tool aimed at eliminating waste or *muda*. Waste in many processes can be as high as 60 percent. Value stream mapping is helpful because it creates a visual "map" of every process involved in the flow of materials and information in a product's value chain. These maps consist of a *current state drawing*, a *future state drawing*, and an implementation plan. Value stream mapping spans the entire value chain, from the firm's receipt of raw materials to the delivery of the finished good to the customer. Thus, it tends to be broader in scope, displaying far more information than a typical process map or a flowchart used with Six Sigma process improvement efforts. Creating such a big picture representation helps managers identify the source of wasteful non-value-added activities.

Value stream mapping follows the steps shown in Figure 9.4. The first step is to focus on one product family for which mapping can be done. It is then followed by drawing a current state map of the existing production situation: Analysts start from the customer end and work upstream to draw the map by hand and record actual process times rather than rely on information not obtained by firsthand observation. Information for drawing the material and information flows can be gathered from the shop floor, including the data related to each process: cycle time (C/T), setup or changeover time (C/O), uptime (on-demand available machine time expressed as a percentage), production batch sizes, number of people required to operate the process, number of product variations, pack size (for moving the product to the next stage), working time (minus breaks), and scrap rate. Value stream mapping uses a standard set of icons for material flow, information flow, and general information (to denote operators, safety stock buffers, and so on). Even though the complete glossary is extensive, a representative set of these icons is shown in Figure 9.5. These icons provide a common language for describing in detail how a facility should operate to create a better flow.

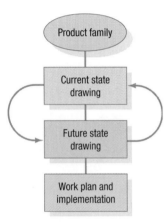

FIGURE 9.4

Value Stream Mapping Steps

Source: Mike Rother and John Shook, *Learning to See* (Brookline, MA: The Lean Enterprise Institute, 2003), p. 9.

We use the VSM icons to illustrate in Figure 9.6 what a current state map could look like for a hypothetical bearing manufacturing company, which receives raw material sheets from Kline Steel Company every Monday for a product family of retainers (casings in which ball bearings are held), and then ships its finished product on a daily basis to a second-tier automative manufacturing customer named GNK Enterprises. The product family of the bearing manufacturing company under consideration consists of two types of retainers—large (L) and small (S)—that are packaged for shipping in returnable trays with 60 retainers in each tray. The manufacturing process consists of a pressing operation, a piercing and forming cell, and a finish grind operation, after which the two types of retainers are staged for shipping. The process characteristics and inventory buffers in front of each process are shown in the current state map of Figure 9.6. One worker occupies each station. Although the total processing time for each retainer is only 1 minute, it takes 16 days for the cumulative production lead time. Clearly opportunities exist for reconfiguring the existing processes and eliminating inventories.

The process flows shown at the bottom of Figure 9.6 are similar to the flowcharts discussed in Chapter 5 "Process Analysis," except that more detailed information is presented here for each process. However, what really sets the value stream maps apart from flowcharts is the inclusion of information flows at the top of Figure 9.6, which plan and coordinate all the process activities. The value stream maps are more comprehensive than process flowcharts, and meld together planning and control systems (discussed in detail in Chapter 15) with detailed flowcharts (discussed in Chapter 5) to create a comprehensive supply chain view that includes both information and material flows between the firm and its suppliers and customers.

Once the current state map is done, the analysts can then use principles of lean systems such as load leveling, pull scheduling, kanban cards, and such to create a future state map with more streamlined product flows. The future state drawing highlights sources of waste and how to eliminate them. The arrows between the current and future state in Figure 9.4 go both ways, indicating that development of the current and future states are overlapping

Material Flow Icons

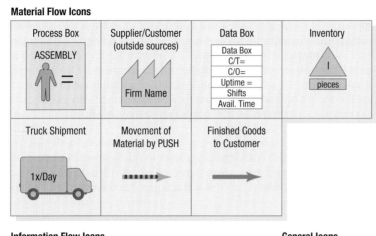

Information Flow Icons

General Icons

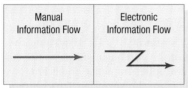

FIGURE 9.5

Selected Set of Value Stream
Mapping Icons

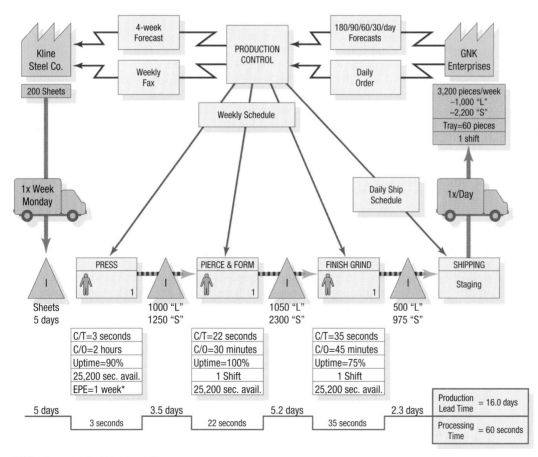

* EPE = 1 means every part every week.

FIGURE 9.6 | A Representative Current State Map for a Family of Retainers at a Bearings Manufacturing Company

efforts. Finally, the last step is aimed at preparing and actively using an implementation plan to achieve the future state. It may take only a couple of days from the creation of a future state map to the point where implementation can begin for a single product family. At this stage, the future state map essentially becomes a blueprint for implementing a lean system, and is fine-tuned as implementation progresses. As the future state becomes reality, a new future state map is drawn, thus denoting continuous improvement at the value stream level.

Unlike the Theory of Constraints (see Chapter 7), which accepts the existing system bottlenecks and then strives to maximize the throughput given that set of constraint(s), value stream mapping endeavors to understand through current state and future state maps how existing processes can be altered to eliminate bottlenecks and other wasteful activities. The goal is to bring the production rate of the entire process closer to the customer's desired demand rate. The benefits of applying this tool to the waste-removal process include reduced lead times and work-in-process inventories, reduced rework and scrap rates, and lower indirect labor costs.

> JIT II <

The JIT II concept was conceived and implemented by the Bose Corporation, a producer of high-quality professional sound and speaker systems. In a JIT II system, the supplier is brought into the plant to be an active member of the purchasing office of the customer. The *in-plant representative* is on site full-time at the supplier's expense and is empowered to plan and schedule the replenishment of materials from the supplier. This arrangement is an example of vendor-managed inventories. Typically, the representative's duties include issuing purchase orders to his or her own firm on behalf of the buyer, working on design ideas to help reduce costs and improve manufacturing processes, and managing production schedules for suppliers, materials contractors, and other subcontractors. The in-plant representative replaces the buyer, the salesperson, and sometimes the materials planner in a typical JIT arrangement. Thus, JIT II fosters extremely close interaction with suppliers. The qualifications for a supplier to be included in the program are stringent.

In general, JIT II can offer benefits to both buyers and suppliers because it provides the organizational structure needed to improve supplier coordination by integrating the logistics, production, and purchasing processes together. Several large corporations have implemented JIT II in their supply chains, including IBM, Intel, Honeywell, Roadway Express, Ingersoll-Rand, and Westinghouse, among others.

> OPERATIONAL BENEFITS AND IMPLEMENTATION ISSUES <

When an organization needs to make dramatic improvements, a lean system can be the solution. Lean systems can be an integral part of a corporate strategy based on speed because they cut cycle times, improve inventory turnover and increase labor productivity. Recent studies also show that practices representing different components of lean systems such as JIT, TQM, total preventive maintenance (TPM), and human resource management (HRM), individually as well as cumulatively, improve the performance of manufacturing plants. Lean systems also involve a considerable amount of employee participation through small-group interaction sessions, which have resulted in improvements in many aspects of operations, not the least of which is service or product quality.

Even though the benefits of lean systems can be outstanding, problems can still arise after a lean system has long been operational. Even the Japanese, who pioneered JIT practices in the automobile industry, are not immune to problems: Tokyo is experiencing monumental traffic jams owing in large measure to truck deliveries to JIT manufacturers. In addition, as Managerial Practice 9.3 shows, implementing a lean system can take a long time. We consequently address in this section some of the issues managers should be aware of when implementing a lean system.

ORGANIZATIONAL CONSIDERATIONS

Implementing a lean system requires management to consider issues of worker stress, cooperation and trust among workers and management, and reward systems and labor classifications.

Cessna Aircraft is a leading manufacturer of business jets; utility planes; and single-engine, piston-powered personal aircraft. Cessna has produced over 184,000 aircraft to date. More than half of the general aviation aircraft flying today, in fact, were made by Cessna. The planes range in price from $150,000 for a single-engine, piston-powered aircraft to more than $17 million for a business jet. However, in 1986, the company decided to abandon the production of single-engine, piston-powered planes because the cost of liability insurance was so expensive. Whenever a Cessna plane crashed, the company found itself being sued—even when the crash was unrelated to the performance of the plane (for example, was due to pilot error, weather, and so forth). After federal legislation in 1994 limited the liability of aircraft manufacturers, Cessna decided to get back into the game, and built a new plant in Independence, Kansas. It was an opportunity to incorporate a new, lean manufacturing system to a product line that hadn't changed much over the years, with the exception of the avionics in the cockpit and a new, efficient engine, which was outsourced. To do so, however, Cessna had to learn how to go from a craftwork mentality, which is what it had when it last produced small aircraft, to a modern manufacturing mentality, which involved a whole new way of doing things.

Cessna adopted three lean manufacturing practices in its new plant. First, management committed to the team concept. Teamwork fosters workforce flexibility because members of a team learn one another's duties and can shift across assembly lines as needed. However, because of a shortage of technically qualified employees in the industry, Cessna had to hire employees who were short on sheet metal skills. Productivity initially suffered, but retired assembly-line workers were recalled to serve as mentors to teach the new employees the skills and confidence they needed to do their jobs. It took four years to bring the teams to the point where they were proficient at conflict resolution, problem solving, and flexibility.

Second, Cessna arranged for several of its suppliers to manage its inventories. For example, two Honeywell field engineers who also help with problems after installation maintain a 30-day avionics inventory worth $30 million on-site. In addition, a warehouse nearby was opened to house the inventories of several suppliers. The warehouse operations are being integrated with the plant schedule so that inventory will be delivered daily to the production line. Suppliers who initially balked at the idea eventually saw its advantages.

Finally, Cessna incorporated manufacturing cells and group technology in its manufacturing process and moved away from a batch process approach that supported a make-to-stock strategy. In the past, Cessna maintained a network of dealers who took what was sent to them. It required large inventories to support the dealers' demands. If it overesti-

Single-engine Cessna airplanes roll off the assembly line at Independence, Kansas. Three versions of single-engine planes are built at the southeast Kansas plant, using the concepts of lean manufacturing systems.

mated demand and produced too many planes, the company then had to offer the dealers purchasing incentives to get rid of the excess inventory. Today, Cessna assembles to order. This change in manufacturing strategy required a change in the manufacturing process as well as a change in the way Cessna does business with its dealers.

Cessna made the transition from craftwork to modern manufacturing, but not without hard work. Although its investment in inventory showed improvement, it still takes Cessna twice as many hours to build a model 172 than it did in the 1980s. The theoretical capacity of the plant is 2,000 planes a year, but the annual target four years after the start of operations was only 975 planes a year. Much of the slow start-up was due to a brand-new workforce. This experience at Cessna shows that switching to lean manufacturing is a long-term commitment. Cessna continues to build on that commitment, and in 2004 broke ground on a new $20.4 million expansion to its Independence facility. When the expansion is completed, it will support the production and delivery of Cessna's single-engine aircraft product line and its new entry-level business jet, the Citation Mustang.

Source: Phillip Siekman, "Cessna Tackles Lean Manufacturing," *Fortune* (May 1, 2000), pp. 1222 B–1222 Z; www.cessna.com, August 2005.

The Human Costs of Lean Systems Lean systems can be coupled with statistical process control (SPC) to reduce variations in output. However, this combination requires a high degree of regimentation and sometimes stresses the workforce. For example, in the Toyota Production System, workers must meet specified cycle times, and, with SPC, they must follow prescribed problem-solving methods. Such systems might make workers feel pushed and stressed, causing productivity losses or quality reductions. In addition, workers might feel a loss of some autonomy because of the close linkages in work flows between stations with little or no excess capacity or safety stocks. Managers can mitigate some of these effects by allowing for some slack in the system—either safety stock inventories or capacity slack—and by emphasizing work flows instead of worker pace. Managers also can promote the use of work teams and allow them to determine their task assignments within their domains of responsibility.

Cooperation and Trust In a lean system, workers and first-line supervisors must take on responsibilities formerly assigned to middle managers and support staff. Activities such as scheduling, expediting, and improving productivity become part of the duties of lower-level personnel. Consequently, the work relationships in the organization must be reoriented in a way that fosters cooperation and mutual trust between the workforce and management. However, this environment can be difficult to achieve, particularly in light of the historical adversarial relationship between the two groups.

Reward Systems and Labor Classifications In some instances, the reward system must be revamped when a lean system is implemented. At General Motors, for example, a plan to reduce stock at one plant ran into trouble because the production superintendent refused to cut back on the number of unneeded parts being made. Why? Because his salary was based on the plant's production volume.

The realignment of reward systems is not the only hurdle. Labor contracts traditionally crippled a company's ability to reassign workers to other tasks as the need arises. For example, a typical automobile plant in the United States has several unions and dozens of labor classifications. Generally, the people in each classification are allowed to do only a limited range of tasks. In some cases, companies have managed to give these employees more flexibility by agreeing to other types of union concessions and benefits. In other cases, however, companies relocated their plants to take advantage of nonunion or foreign labor.

PROCESS CONSIDERATIONS

Firms using lean systems typically have some dominant work flows. To take advantage of lean practices, firms might have to change their existing layouts. Certain workstations might have to be moved closer together, and cells of machines devoted to particular component families may have to be established. A survey of 68 firms using lean systems indicated that the single most important factor in successful implementation is changing product flows and layout to a cellular design. However, rearranging a plant to conform to lean practices can be costly. For example, many plants currently receive raw materials and purchased parts by rail, but to facilitate smaller and more frequent shipments, truck deliveries would be preferable. Loading docks might have to be reconstructed or expanded and certain operations relocated to accommodate the change in transportation mode and quantities of arriving materials.

INVENTORY AND SCHEDULING

Manufacturing firms need to have stable master production schedules, short setups, and frequent, reliable supplies of materials and components to achieve the full potential of the lean systems concept.

Schedule Stability Daily production schedules in high-volume, make-to-stock environments must be stable for extended periods. At Toyota, the master production schedule is stated in fractions of days over a three-month period and is revised only once a month. The first month of the schedule is frozen to avoid disruptive changes in the daily production schedule for each workstation; that is, the workstations execute the same work schedule each day of the month. At the beginning of each month, kanbans are reissued for the new daily production rate. Stable schedules are needed so that production lines can be balanced and new assignments found for employees who otherwise would be underutilized. Lean systems used in high-volume, make-to-stock environments cannot respond quickly to scheduling changes because little slack inventory or capacity is available to absorb these changes.

Setups If the inventory advantages of a lean system are to be realized, small lot sizes must be used. However, because small lots require a large number of setups, companies must significantly reduce setup times. Some companies have not been able to achieve short setup times and, therefore, have to use large-lot production, negating some of the advantages of lean practices. Also, lean systems are vulnerable to lengthy changeovers to new products because the low levels of finished goods inventory will be insufficient to cover demand while the system is down. If changeover times cannot be reduced, large finished goods inventories of the old product must be accumulated to compensate. In the automobile industry, every week that a plant is shut down for new-model changeover costs between $16 million and $20 million in pretax profits.

Purchasing and Logistics If frequent, small shipments of purchased items cannot be arranged with suppliers, large inventory savings for these items cannot be realized. For example, in the United States, such arrangements may prove difficult because of the geographic dispersion of suppliers.

The shipments of raw materials and components must be reliable because of the low inventory levels in lean systems. A plant can be shut down because of a lack of materials. For example, a strike at the GM plant in Lordstown, Ohio, caused the Saturn plant in Spring Hill, Tennessee, to shut down, resulting in the loss of production of 1,000 cars per day. Lordstown supplies parts to Saturn, which does not stockpile the parts because of lean practices. Similarly, recovery becomes more prolonged and difficult in a lean system after supply chains are disrupted, which is what happened immediately after 9/11.

> STUDENT CD-ROM AND INTERNET RESOURCES <

The Student CD-ROM and the Companion Website at **www.prenhall.com/krajewski** contain many tools, activities, and resources designed for this chapter.

> KEY EQUATION <

Number of containers:

$$\kappa = \frac{\text{Average demand during lead time} + \text{Safety stock}}{\text{Number of units per container}}$$

$$= \frac{d(\bar{\omega} + \bar{p})(1 + \alpha)}{c}$$

> KEY TERMS <

five S (5S) 353	lot 350	setup 351
JIT system 349	mixed-model assembly 351	single-digit setup 351
just-in-time (JIT) philosophy 348	poka-yoke 350	value stream mapping (VSM) 359
kanban 356	pull method 349	
lean systems 348	push method 349	

> SOLVED PROBLEM <

A company using a kanban system has an inefficient machine group. For example, the daily demand for part L105A is 3,000 units. The average waiting time for a container of parts is 0.8 day. The processing time for a container of L105A is 0.2 day, and a container holds 270 units. Currently, 20 containers are used for this item.

a. What is the value of the policy variable, α?

b. What is the total planned inventory (work-in-process and finished goods) for item L105A?

c. Suppose that the policy variable, α, were 0. How many containers would be needed now? What is the effect of the policy variable in this example?

SOLUTION

a. We use the equation for the number of containers and then solve for α:

$$\kappa = \frac{d(\bar{\omega} + \bar{\rho})(1 + \alpha)}{c}$$

$$= \frac{3{,}000(0.8 + 0.2)(1 + \alpha)}{270} = 20$$

and

$$(1 + \alpha) = \frac{20(270)}{3{,}000(0.8 + 0.2)} = 1.8$$

$$\alpha = 1.8 - 1 = 0.8$$

b. With 20 containers in the system and each container holding 270 units, the total planned inventory is 20(270) = 5,400 units.

c. If $\alpha = 0$

$$\kappa = \frac{3{,}000(0.8 + 0.2)(1 + 0)}{270} = 11.11 \text{ or } 12 \text{ containers}$$

The policy variable adjusts the number of containers. In this case, the difference is quite dramatic because $\bar{\omega} + \bar{\rho}$ is fairly large and the number of units per container is small relative to daily demand.

> DISCUSSION QUESTIONS <

1. Compare and contrast the following two situations:
   a. A company's lean system stresses teamwork. Employees feel more involved and, therefore productivity and quality increase at the company. The problem is that workers also experienced a loss of individual autonomy.
   b. A humanities professor believes that all students want to learn. To encourage students to work together and learn from each other—thereby increasing the involvement, productivity, and the quality of the learning experience—the professor announces that all students in the class will receive the same grade and that it will be based on the performance of the group.

2. Which elements of lean systems would be most troublesome for manufacturers to implement? Why?

3. Identify a service or a manufacturing process that you are familiar with, and draw a current state value stream map to depict its existing information and material flows.

> PROBLEMS <

Software, such as OM Explorer, Active Models, and POM for Windows, is packaged with every new copy of the textbook. Check with your instructor on how best to use it. In many cases, the instructor wants you to understand how to do the calculations by hand. At most, the software provides a check on your calculations. When calculations are particularly complex and the goal is interpreting the results in making decisions, the software replaces entirely the manual calculations. The software also can be a valuable resource well after your course is completed.

1. The Harvey motorcycle company produces three models: the Tiger, a sure-footed dirt bike; the LX2000, a nimble cafe racer; and the Golden, a large interstate tourer. This month's master production schedule calls for the production of 54 Goldens, 42 LX2000s, and 30 Tigers per 7-hour shift.
   a. What average cycle time is required for the assembly line to achieve the production quota in seven hours?

   b. If mixed-model scheduling is used, how many of each model will be produced before the production cycle is repeated?

   c. Determine a satisfactory production sequence for the ultimate in small-lot production: one unit.

   d. The design of a new model, the Cheetah, includes features from the Tiger, LX2000, and Golden models. The resulting blended design has an indecisive character and is expected to attract some sales from the other models. Determine a mixed-model schedule resulting in 52 Goldens, 39 LX2000s, 26 Tigers, and 13 Cheetahs per seven-hour shift. Although the total number of motorcycles produced per day will increase only slightly, what problem might be anticipated in implementing this change from the production schedule indicated in part (b)?

2. A fabrication cell at Spradley's Sprockets uses the pull method to supply gears to an assembly line. George Jitson is in charge of the assembly line, which requires 500 gears per day. Containers typically wait 0.20 day in the fabrication cell. Each container holds 20 gears, and one container requires 1.8 days in machine time. Setup times are negligible. If the policy variable for unforeseen contingencies is set at 5 percent, how many containers should Jitson authorize for the gear replenishment system?

3. You are asked to analyze the kanban system of LeWin, a French manufacturer of gaming devices. One of the workstations feeding the assembly line produces part M670N. The daily demand for M670N is 1,800 units. The average processing time per unit is 0.003 day. LeWin's records show that the average container spends 1.05 days waiting at the feeder workstation. The container for M670N can hold 300 units. Twelve containers are authorized for the part. Recall that $\bar\rho$ is the average processing time per container, not per individual part.

 a. Find the value of the policy variable, α, that expresses the amount of implied safety stock in this system.

 b. Use the implied value of α from part (a) to determine the required reduction in waiting time if one container was removed. Assume that all other parameters remain constant.

4. An assembly line requires two components: gadjits and widjits. Gadjits are produced by center 1 and widjits by center 2. Each unit of the end item, called a jit-together, requires 3 gadjits and 2 widjits, as shown in Figure 9.7. The daily production quota on the assembly line is 800 jit-togethers.

  The container for gadjits holds 80 units. The policy variable for center 1 is set at 0.09. The average waiting time for a container of gadjits is 0.09 day, and 0.06 day is needed to produce a container. The container for widjits holds 50 units, and the policy variable for center 2 is 0.08. The average waiting time per container of widgits is 0.14 day, and the time required to process a container is 0.20 day.

 a. How many containers are needed for gadjits?

 b. How many containers are needed for widjits?

5. Gestalt, Inc., uses a kanban system in its automobile production facility in Germany. This facility operates 8 hours

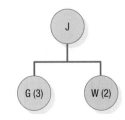

FIGURE 9.7 | Components for End Item J

per day to produce the Jitterbug, a replacement for the obsolete but immensely popular Jitney Beetle. Suppose that a certain part requires 150 seconds of processing at machine cell 33B and a container of parts average 1.6 hours of waiting time there. Management allows a 10 percent buffer for unexpected occurrences. Each container holds 30 parts, and 8 containers are authorized. How much daily demand can be satisfied with this system? (*Hint:* Recall that $\bar\rho$ is the average processing time per container, not per individual part.)

6. A U.S. Postal Service supervisor is looking for ways to reduce stress in the sorting department. With the existing arrangement, stamped letters are machine-canceled and loaded into tubs with 375 letters per tub. The tubs are then pushed to postal clerks, who read and key zip codes into an automated sorting machine at the rate of one tub per 375 seconds. To overcome the stress caused when the stamp canceling machine outpaces the sorting clerks, a pull system is proposed. When the clerks are ready to process another tub of mail, they will pull the tub from the canceling machine area. How many tubs should circulate between the sorting clerks and the canceling machine if 90,000 letters are to be sorted during an eight-hour shift, the safety stock policy variable, α, is 0.18, and the average waiting time plus materials handling time is 25 minutes per tub?

7. The production schedule at Mazda calls for 1,200 Mazdas to be produced during each of 22 production days in January and 900 Mazdas to be produced during each of 20 production days in February. Mazda uses a kanban system to communicate with Gesundheit, a nearby supplier of tires. Mazda purchases four tires per vehicle from Gesundheit. The safety stock policy variable, α, is 0.15. The container (a delivery truck) size is 200 tires. The average waiting time plus materials handling time is 0.16 day per container. Assembly lines are rebalanced at the beginning of each month. The average processing time per container in January is 0.10 day. February processing time will average 0.125 day per container. How many containers should be authorized for January? How many for February?

8. Jitsmart is a retailer of plastic action-figure toys. The action figures are purchased from Tacky Toys, Inc., and arrive in boxes of 48. Full boxes are stored on high shelves out of reach of customers. A small inventory is maintained on child-level shelves. Depletion of the lower-shelf inventory signals the need to take down a box of action figures to replenish the inventory. A reorder card is then removed from the box and sent to Tacky Toys to authorize replenishment of a container of action figures. The average demand rate for a popular action figure, Agent 99, is 36 units per day. The total lead time (waiting plus processing) is 11 days. Jitsmart's safety stocky policy variable, α is 0.25. What is the authorized stock level for Jistmart?

CASE | Copper Kettle Catering

Copper Kettle Catering (CKC) is a full-service catering company that provides services ranging from box lunches for picnics or luncheon meetings to large wedding, dinner, or office parties. Established as a lunch delivery service for offices in 1972 by Wayne and Janet Williams, CKC has grown to be one of the largest catering businesses in Raleigh, North Carolina. The Williamses divide customer demand into two categories: *deliver only* and *deliver and serve*.

The deliver-only side of the business delivers boxed meals consisting of a sandwich, salad, dessert, and fruit. The menu for this service is limited to six sandwich selections, three salads or potato chips, and a brownie or fruit bar. Grapes and an orange slice are included with every meal, and iced tea can be ordered to accompany the meals. The overall level of demand for this service throughout the year is fairly constant, although the mix of menu items delivered varies. The planning horizon for this segment of the business is short: Customers usually call no more than a day ahead of time. CKC requires customers to call deliver-only orders in by 10:00 A.M. to guarantee delivery the same day.

The deliver-and-serve side of the business focuses on catering large parties, dinners, and weddings. The extensive range of menu items includes a full selection of hors d'oeuvres, entrées, beverages, and special-request items. The demand for these services is much more seasonal, with heavier demands occurring in the late spring–early summer for weddings and the late fall–early winter for holiday parties. However, this segment also has a longer planning horizon. Customers book dates and choose menu items weeks or months ahead of time.

CKC's food preparation facilities support both operations. The physical facilities layout resembles that of a job shop. Five major work areas consist of a stove–oven area for hot food preparation, a cold area for salad preparation, an hors d'oeuvre preparation area, a sandwich preparation area, and an assembly area where deliver-only orders are boxed and deliver-and-serve orders are assembled and trayed. Three walk-in coolers store foods requiring refrigeration, and a large pantry houses nonperishable goods. Space limitations and the risk of spoilage limit the amount of raw materials and prepared food items that can be carried in inventory at any one time. CKC purchases desserts from outside vendors. Some deliver the desserts to CKC; others require CKC to send someone to pick up desserts at their facilities.

The scheduling of orders is a two-stage process. Each Monday, the Williamses develop the schedule of deliver-and-serve orders to be processed each day. CKC typically has multiple deliver-and-serve orders to fill each day of the week. This level of demand allows a certain efficiency in the preparation of multiple orders. The deliver-only orders are scheduled day to day, owing to the short-order lead times. CKC sometimes runs out of ingredients for deliver-only menu items because of the limited inventory space.

Wayne and Janet Williams have 10 full-time employees: 2 cooks and 8 food preparation workers, who also work as servers for the deliver-and-serve orders. In periods of high demand, the Williamses hire additional part-time servers. The position of cook is specialized and requires a high degree of training and skill. The rest of the employees are flexible and move between tasks as needed.

The business environment for catering is competitive. The competitive priorities are high-quality food, delivery reliability, flexibility, and cost—in that order. "The quality of the food and its preparation is paramount," states Wayne Williams. "Caterers with poor-quality food will not stay in business long." Quality is measured by both freshness and taste. Delivery reliability encompasses both on-time delivery and the time required to respond to customer orders (in effect, the order lead time). Flexibility focuses on both the range of catering requests that a company can satisfy and menu variety.

Recently, CKC began to notice that customers are demanding more menu flexibility and faster response times. Small specialty caterers who entered the market are targeting specific well-defined market segments. One example is a small caterer called Lunches-R-Us, which located a facility in the middle of a large office complex to serve the lunch trade and competes with CKC on cost.

Wayne and Janet Williams are impressed by the lean systems concept, especially the ideas related to increasing flexibility, reducing lead times, and lowering costs. They sound like what CKC needs to remain competitive. However, the Williamses wonder whether lean concepts and practices are transferable to a service business.

QUESTIONS

1. Are the operations of Copper Kettle Catering conducive to the application of lean concepts and practices? Explain.

2. What, if any, are the major barriers to implementing a lean system at Copper Kettle Catering?

3. What would you recommend that Wayne and Janet Williams do to take advantage of lean concepts in operating CKC?

Source: This case was prepared by Dr. Brooke Saladin, Wake Forest University, as a basis for classroom discussion.

> SELECTED REFERENCES <

Ansberry, Clare. "Hurry-Up Inventory Method Hurts Where It Once Helped." *Wall Street Journal Online* (June 25, 2002).

Beckett, W. K., and K. Dang. "Synchronous Manufacturing, New Methods, New Mind Set." *Journal of Business Strategy,* vol. 12 (1992), pp. 53–56.

Billesbach, Thomas J. "A Study of the Implementation of Just-in-Time in the United States." *Production and Inventory Management Journal* (Third Quarter 1991), pp. 1–4.

Dixon, Lance. "Tomorrow's Ideas Take Flight in Today's Leading Edge Corporations." *APICS—The Performance Advantage* (July 1996) p. 60.

Fuime, Orrest. "Lean Accounting and Finance." *Target,* vol. 18, no. 4 (Fourth Quarter 2002), pp. 6–14.

Golhar, D. Y., and C. L. Stam. "The Just-in-Time Philosophy: A Literature Review." *International Journal of Production Research,* vol. 29 (1991), pp. 657–676.

Greenblatt, Sherwin. "Continuous Improvement in Supply Chain Management." *Chief Executive* (June 1993), pp. 40–43.

Hall, Robert W. "New Balance Athletic Shoe Company." *Target,* vol. 20, no. 5(2004), pp. 5–10.

Klein, J. A. "The Human Costs of Manufacturing Reform." *Harvard Business Review* (March–April 1989), pp. 60–66.

Manufacturing Engineering Website, www.mfgeng.com/5S.htm.

Mascitelli, Ron. "Lean Thinking: It's About Efficient Value Creation." *Target,* vol. 16, no. 2 (Second Quarter 2000), pp. 22–26.

Millstein, Mitchell. "How to Make Your MRP System Flow." *APICS—The Performance Advantage* (July 2000), pp. 47–49.

Moody, Patricia E. "Bose Corporation: Hi-Fi Leader Stretches to Meet Growth Challenges." *Target* (Winter 1991), pp. 17–22.

Rother, Mike, and John Shook. *Learning to See.* Brookline, MA: The Lean Enterprise Institute, 2003.

Schaller, Jeff. "A 'Just Do It Now' Philosophy Rapidly Creates a Lean Culture, Produces Dramatic Results at Novametix Medical Systems." *Target,* vol. 18, no. 2 (Second Quarter 2002), pp. 48–54.

Shah, Rachna, and Peter T. Ward. "Lean Manufacturing: Context, Practice Bundles, and Performance." *Journal of Operations Management,* vol. 21 (2003), pp. 129–149.

Spear, Steven J. "Learning to Lead at Toyota." *Harvard Business Review* (May 2004), pp. 78–86.

Stewart, Douglas M., and John R. Grout. "The Human Side of Mistake Proofing." *Production and Operations Management,* vol. 10, no. 4 (Winter 2001), pp. 440–459.

Syberg, Keith. "Best Practices (BP) Program: Honda of America Manufacturing." *Target,* vol. 15, no. 2 (Second Quarter 1999), pp. 46–48.

Tonkin, Lea. "System Sensor's Lean Journey." *Target,* vol. 18, no. 2 (Second Quarter 2002), pp. 44–47.

PART 3

MANAGING VALUE CHAINS

LEARNING GOALS

After reading this chapter,
you should be able to:

1. Identify the nature of supply chains for service providers, as well as for manufacturers.

2. Define the key design issues associated with supply chain processes.

3. Define the critical supply chain measures.

4. Explain the strategic importance of supply chain design and give real examples of its application in service situations, as well as in manufacturing situations.

5. Describe how the Internet enables the development of virtual supply chains.

6. Explain how efficient supply chains differ from responsive supply chains and the environments best suited for each type of supply chain.

A custom computer makes its way through Dell's ultra-efficient, supply chain system.

DELL INC.

Dell Inc., a mass customizer of personal computers with annual revenues of $51.1 billion, is experiencing phenomenal growth and profitability in an industry with traditionally low profit margins. In 1996, Dell was selling laptops, desktops, and servers at the rate of $1 million a day. Today, Dell's Web site alone sells more than $50 million in products a day. This success defines Dell as a leader among PC makers. What is Dell's secret? In a single word: speed. A customer's order for a customized computer can be on a delivery truck in 36 hours. This capability allows Dell to keep parts costs and inventories low, enabling it to sell at prices 10 to 15 percent below those of competitors. Dell's focus is on how fast the inventory moves, not on how much is there.

A primary factor in filling customers' orders is Dell's manufacturing operations and the performance of its suppliers. Dell's manufacturing process is flexible enough to postpone the ordering of components and the assembly of computers until an order is booked. In addition, Dell's warehousing plan calls for the bulk of its components to be warehoused within 15 minutes of its Austin (Texas), Limerick (Ireland), and Penang (Malaysia) plants. Dell's top 33 suppliers, which supply 90 percent of its goods, use a Web site for data on how they measure up to Dell's standards, what orders they have shipped, and the best way to ship them. Dell links the supplier Web site to its order placement Web site so that as customers place orders, the suppliers know when to ship components such as motherboards or liquid-crystal displays.

At its Austin plant, Dell does not actually have to order the components because the suppliers restock the warehouse and manage their own

>

For additional chapter resources check the Student CD-ROM or the Companion Website at
www.prenhall.com/krajewski

inventories. Dell uses the components as needed and is not billed for them until they leave the warehouse. This system of suppliers and manufacturing operations provides a great advantage over competitors. For example, a software package called Factory Planner manages the factory schedule so that machines are built while the parts needed for the next 2 hours of orders are being shipped from suppliers' hubs. The hub has 15 minutes to confirm that it has the needed parts, and 1 hour and 15 minutes to get them to the plant.

Dell's efficient operations carry over to its service providers who also are used to lower costs and reduce lead time. For example, Dell might send an e-mail message to UPS requesting that a computer monitor from Sony be sent to a certain customer as part of a purchased computer system. UPS pulls a monitor from the monitor supplier's stocks and schedules it to arrive with the PC, saving Dell shipping and inventory costs.

By carefully managing its supply chain, Dell is able to operate more efficiently than any other computer company.

Sources: "The Power of Virtual Integration: An Interview with Dell Computer's Michael Dell," *Harvard Business Review* (March–April 1998), pp. 72–85; Daniel Roth, "Dell's Big New Act," *Fortune* (December 6, 1999), pp. 152–156; Stacy Perman, "Automate or Die," *Business Week* (July 2001); "Dell Welcomes Millions to Its Web Site," www.dell.com, 2004.

Dell Inc. is an excellent example of how a firm manages its value chain to gain a competitive advantage. Value chains involve internal linkages between a firm's core processes, its supporting processes, and its external linkages with the processes of its customers and suppliers. The firm's operations strategy and competitive priorities guide its value chain choices. So far in the text, we emphasized that the analysis of individual processes should be done within the context of their value chains. Then, the synergy of individual processes provides value to customers.

Because we already discussed the new service/product development process in Chapter 2, "Operations Strategy," in this chapter we focus on what is commonly referred to as the **supply chain**, which is the network of services, material, and information flows that link a firm's customer relationship, order fulfillment, and supplier relationship processes to those of its suppliers and customers.[1] It is important to note, however, that a firm may have multiple supply chains, depending on the mix of services or products it produces. A supplier in one supply chain may not be a supplier in another supply chain because the service or product may be different or the supplier may simply be unable to negotiate a successful contract.

Supply chain management consists of developing a strategy to organize, control, and motivate the resources involved in the flow of services and materials within the supply chain. A **supply chain strategy**, an essential aspect of supply chain management, seeks to design a firm's supply chain to meet the competitive priorities of the firm's operations strategy. To get a better understanding of the strategic issues facing supply chain managers, we begin with a comment on the organizational perspectives of supply chain strategy and its importance to service providers as well as manufacturers. Next, we provide an overview of the nature of supply chains for service providers and for manufacturers. We then discuss the operating and financial measures of supply chain performance and the dynamics in supply chains, followed by how developing integrated supply chains and designing effective customer relationship, order fulfillment, and supplier relationship processes can mitigate some of the negative effects of those dynamics. Finally, we discuss supply chain strategies that companies use for competitive advantage.

supply chain

The network of services, material, and information flows that link a firm's customer relationship, order fulfillment, and supplier relationship processes to those of its suppliers and customers.

supply chain management

Developing a strategy to organize, control, and motivate the resources involved in the flow of services and materials within the supply chain.

supply chain strategy

Designing a firm's supply chain to meet the competitive priorities of the firm's operations strategy.

> SUPPLY CHAIN STRATEGY ACROSS THE ORGANIZATION <

Supply chains permeate the entire organization. It is hard to envision a process in a firm that is not in some way affected by a supply chain. Supply chains must be managed to coordinate the inputs with the outputs in a firm to achieve the appropriate competitive priorities of the

[1]The terms *value chain* and *supply chain* are sometimes used interchangeably.

firm's enterprise processes. The Internet offers firms an alternative to traditional methods for managing the supply chain. However, the firm must be committed to reengineering its information flows throughout the organization, especially the customer relationship, order fulfillment, and supplier relationship processes. These processes intersect all of the traditional functional areas of the firm.

A supply chain strategy is essential for service as well as manufacturing firms. In fact, service providers are beginning to realize the potential benefits of reengineering their supply chain processes. For example, hospitals have notoriously held to old-fashioned approaches for purchasing and materials management. Even with the advent of group purchasing organizations and centralized buying groups, such as Premier, Inc., a typical hospital collects orders from throughout the hospital for medical supplies and equipment ranging from latex gloves to operating tables. Often, the merchandise is chosen from a stack of outdated catalogs. Prices must be checked and the orders sent by phone or fax to literally thousands of distributors and suppliers.

Can this process be improved? Columbia/HCA Health Care Corporation thinks so. It is funding separate ventures to create an electronic marketplace for placing orders online. The systems will link to the suppliers of several hundred thousand medical and surgical supplies. Of course, to take full advantage of the marketplace, hospitals will have to reengineer their supplier relationship processes to realize the benefits. Nonetheless, the potential benefits are considerable.

> SUPPLY CHAINS FOR SERVICES AND MANUFACTURING <

Every firm or organization is a member of some supply chain. In this section we show the similarities and differences regarding supply chains for services and manufacturing.

SERVICES

Supply chain design for a service provider is driven by the need to provide support for the essential elements of the various service packages it delivers. Recall that a *service package* consists of supporting facilities, facilitating goods, explicit services, and implicit services. To see the connection between supply chains and service packages, consider the example of Flowers-on-Demand, a florist with 27 retail stores in the greater Boston metropolitan area.[2] Customers can place orders for customized floral arrangements by visiting one of the stores, using a toll-free number, or going to the florist's Web page. The 1-800 number and the Web page are operated by a local Internet services company, which takes orders and relays them to the florist. The arrangements are produced at a distribution center, and deliveries are made using either local couriers, or FedEx, if the delivery is outside of the Boston area. Fresh flowers, flown in from all over the world, are used in the arrangements.

What differentiates Flowers-on-Demand from floral wire services, such as Teleflora or FTD, is that it assembles all the arrangements and can ship out-of-area orders for next-day delivery anywhere in the country. The elements of its service package include the following:

- *Supporting Facilities:* Retail stores, a delivery center, computers, point-of-sale equipment, and employees
- *Facilitating Goods:* Flowers that are sourced globally as are arrangement materials, such as pots, baskets, greeting cards, and packing materials
- *Explicit Services:* Arranging the flowers per the customer's order and delivering the arrangement as specified by the customer
- *Implicit Services:* Convenience, which is facilitated by the location of the retail outlets and the opportunity to place orders via the Internet or the toll-free number, and the psychological impressions derived from friendly, attentive, and helpful personnel

The supply chain must support the service package of Flowers-on-Demand. Figure 10.1 illustrates a simplified supply chain for the florist, showing how the suppliers support various elements of the service package. Each of the suppliers, of course, has its own supply

FIGURE 10.1

Supply Chain for a Florist

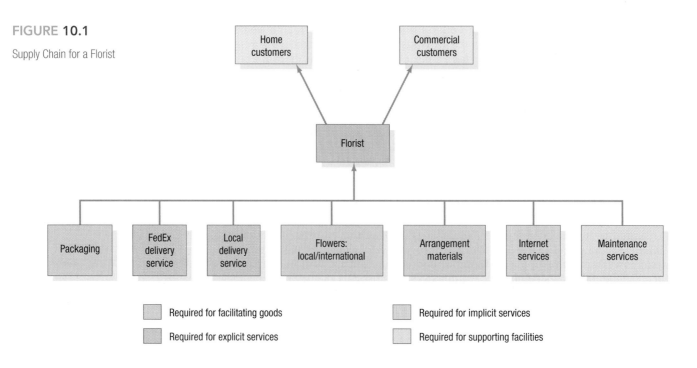

chain (not shown). For example, the supplier for the arrangement materials may get baskets from one supplier and pots from another. The suppliers in the florist's supply chain play an integral role in its ability to meet its competitive priorities for the service package, such as top quality, delivery speed, and customization.

Managerial Practice 10.1 shows how 7-Eleven Japan redesigned its supply chain to gain a competitive edge in a dynamic service environment.

MANUFACTURING

A fundamental purpose of supply chain design for manufacturers is to control inventory by managing the flow of materials. The typical manufacturer spends more than 60 percent of its total income from sales on purchased services and materials, whereas the typical service provider spends only 30 to 40 percent. Because materials comprise such a large component of the sales dollar, manufacturers can reap large profits with a small reduction in the cost of materials, which makes supply chain management a key competitive weapon.

Inventory is a stock of materials used to satisfy customer demand or to support the production of services or goods. Figure 10.2 shows how inventories are created through the

inventory

A stock of materials used to satisfy customer demand or to support the production of services or goods.

FIGURE 10.2

Creation of Inventory

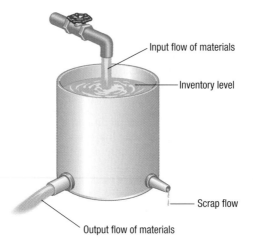

| MANAGERIAL **PRACTICE** | 10.1 | SUPPLY CHAIN EXCELLENCE AT 7-ELEVEN JAPAN |

Seven-Eleven Japan (SEJ) is a $21 billion convenience store chain with low stockout rates, low inventories, and a gross profit margin of 30 percent. SEJ is arguably at the top of its game even though it must service 9,000 retail stores with its supply chain every day. Since SEJ began in the early 1970s, founder Toshifumi Suzuki upgraded SEJ processes to better satisfy customers' demand for convenience, quality, and service. These upgrades involved redesigning the supply chain to respond to the quick changes in overall demand, not simply to focus on fast or cheap deliveries. Its real-time information systems detect changes in customer preferences and track data on sales and consumer demographics at every store. Orders can be electronically processed in less than seven minutes and sent to 230 distribution centers that work exclusively for SEJ. If a particular type of *bento* (take-out lunch box) sells out by midday, extra stock can be in the store by early afternoon. If it is raining and *bentos* will not be in high demand, deliveries are reduced. However, the information system reminds operators to put umbrellas on sale next to the cash register. This responsiveness to customer needs is made possible by a sophisticated point-of-sale data collection system and an electronic ordering system that link individual stores to a central distribution area.

Because customers place a high premium on freshness, the company makes multiple daily deliveries. Stores receive four batches of fresh inventory each day, and employees reconfigure the store shelves at least three times each day to cater to different customer segments and demands at different hours. SEJ schedules deliveries to each store within a 10-minute window. Truck drivers carry cards with bar codes that are scanned into store computers when they arrive with a delivery. If a truck is late by more than 30 minutes, the carrier pays a penalty equal to the gross margin of the products carried to the store. The information system keeps track of the performance of drivers. If a driver is chronically late, managers will review that particular route and possibly add another truck to lighten the load.

SEJ could not achieve this performance if it relied exclusively on trucks for logistics. Japan's city streets and highways are congested; trucks can be delayed in traffic jams. To deal with the problem, the kinds of vehicles used were expanded from trucks to motorcycles, boats, and even

Seven-Eleven Japan's finely tuned supply chain system utilizes point-of-sale data to detect changes in customers' preferences on a minute-by-minute basis at each of its thousands of stores. Multiple deliveries are made daily to stores in vehicles ranging from trucks, motorcycles, boats, and even helicopters—whatever it takes to cut through traffic on Japan's busy streets.

helicopters. These various modes of transportation provide an added level of agility to the supply chain. For example, less than 6 hours after the Kobe earthquake in 1995, when relief trucks were crawling at two miles per hour on the highways, SEJ sent seven helicopters and 125 motorcycles to deliver 64,000 rice balls to the city. Achieving the agility to respond to changes quickly has resulted in a supply chain that is the envy of SEJ's competitors.

Sources: "Seven-Eleven: Over the Counter E-Commerce," *The Economist* (May 27, 2001); "Demand Chain Excellence: A Tale of Two Retailers," *Supply Chain Management Review* (March 1, 2001), p. 40; Hau L. Lee, "The Triple-A Supply Chain," *Harvard Business Review* (October 2004), pp. 102–112.

analogy of a water tank. The flow of water into the tank raises the water level. The inward flow of water represents input materials, such as steel, component parts, office supplies, or a finished product. The water level represents the amount of inventory held at a plant, service facility, warehouse, or retail outlet. The flow of water from the tank lowers the water level in the tank. The outward flow of water represents the demand for materials in inventory, such as customer orders for a Huffy bicycle or requirements for supplies such as soap, food, or furnishings. Another possible outward flow is that of scrap, which also lowers the level of useable inventory. Together, the rates of input and output flows determine the level of inventory. Inventories rise when more material flows into the tank than flows out; they fall when more material flows out than flows in. Figure 10.2 also shows clearly why firms utilize Six Sigma and total quality management (TQM) to reduce defective materials: The larger the scrap flows, the larger will be the input flow of materials required for a given level of output.

FIGURE **10.3**

Inventory at Successive
Stocking Points

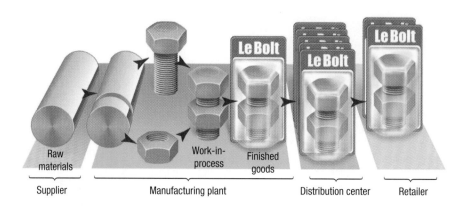

Inventory exists in three aggregate categories that are useful for accounting purposes. **Raw materials (RM)** are the inventories needed for the production of services or goods. They are considered to be inputs to the transformation processes of the firm. **Work-in-process (WIP)** consists of items, such as components or assemblies, needed to produce a final product in manufacturing. WIP is also present in some service operations, such as repair shops, restaurants, check-processing centers, and package delivery services. **Finished goods (FG)** in manufacturing plants, warehouses, and retail outlets are the items sold to the firm's customers. The finished goods of one firm may actually be the raw materials for another.

Figure 10.3 shows how inventory can be held in different forms and at various stocking points. In this example, raw materials—the finished goods of the supplier—are held both by the supplier and the manufacturer. Raw materials at the plant pass through one or more processes, which transform them into various levels of WIP inventory. Final processing of this inventory yields finished goods inventory. Finished goods can be held at the plant, the distribution center (which may be a warehouse owned by the manufacturer or the retailer), and retail locations.

The supply chain for a manufacturing firm can be complicated, as Figure 10.4 illustrates. However, the supply chain depicted is an oversimplification because many companies have hundreds, if not thousands, of suppliers. In this example, the firm owns its distribution and transportation services. However, companies that engineer products to customer specifications normally do not have distribution centers as part of their supply chains. Such companies often ship products directly to their customers. Suppliers are often identified by their position in the supply chain. Here, tier 1 suppliers provide materials or services that are used directly by the firm, tier 2 suppliers supply tier 1 suppliers, and so on.

The value of supply chain management becomes apparent when the complexity of the supply chain is recognized. As we showed earlier, the flow of materials determines inventory levels. The performance of numerous suppliers and the firm's supplier relationship process determines the inward flow of materials. The performance of the firm's order fulfillment and customer relationship processes determines the outward flow of products.

> MEASURES OF SUPPLY CHAIN PERFORMANCE <

In this section, we first define the typical inventory measures used to monitor supply chain performance. We then present some process measures. Finally, we relate some commonly used supply chain performance measures to several important financial measures.

INVENTORY MEASURES

All methods of measuring inventory begin with a physical count of units, volume, or weight. However, measures of inventories are reported in three basic ways: (1) average aggregate inventory value, (2) weeks of supply, and (3) inventory turnover.

The **average aggregate inventory value** is the total value of all items held in inventory by a firm. We express the dollar values in this inventory measure at cost because we can then sum the values of individual items in raw materials, work-in-process, and finished goods: Final sales dollars have meaning only for final services or products and cannot be used for all

raw materials (RM)

The inventories needed for the
production of services or goods.

work-in-process (WIP)

Items, such as components or
assemblies, needed to produce a final
product in manufacturing.

finished goods (FG)

The items in manufacturing plants,
warehouses, and retail outlets that are
sold to the firm's customers.

**average aggregate
inventory value**

The total value of all items held in
inventory for a firm.

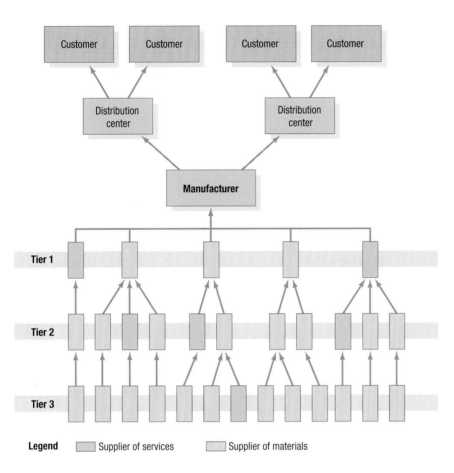

FIGURE **10.4**

Supply Chain for a Manufacturing Firm

inventory items. It is an average because it usually represents the inventory investment over some period of time. Suppose a retailer holds items A and B in stock. One unit of item A may be worth only a few dollars, whereas one unit of item B may be valued in the hundreds of dollars because of the labor, technology, and other value-added operations performed in manufacturing the product. This measure for an inventory consisting of only items A and B is

$$
\begin{aligned}
\text{Average aggregate} \atop \text{inventory value} = &\left(\text{Number of units of item A} \atop \text{typically on hand}\right)\left(\text{Value of each} \atop \text{unit of item A}\right) \\
&+\left(\text{Number of units of item B} \atop \text{typically on hand}\right)\left(\text{Value of each} \atop \text{unit of item B}\right)
\end{aligned}
$$

Summed over all items in an inventory, this total value tells managers how much of a firm's assets are tied up in inventory. Manufacturing firms typically have about 25 percent of their total assets in inventory, whereas wholesalers and retailers average about 75 percent.

To some extent, managers can decide whether the aggregate inventory value is too low or too high by historical or industry comparisons or by managerial judgment. However, a better performance measure would take demand into account because it would show how long the inventory resides in the firm. **Weeks of supply** is an inventory measure obtained by dividing the average aggregate inventory value by sales per week at cost. (In some low-inventory operations, days or even hours are a better unit of time for measuring inventory.) The formula (expressed in weeks) is

$$
\text{Weeks of supply} = \frac{\text{Average aggregate inventory value}}{\text{Weekly sales (at cost)}}
$$

Although the numerator includes the value of all items a firm holds in inventory (raw materials, WIP, and finished goods), the denominator represents only the finished goods sold—at cost rather than the sale price after markups or discounts. This cost is referred to as the *cost of goods sold*.

TUTOR 10.1

Tutor 10.1 on the Student CD-ROM provides a new example to practice the calculation of inventory measures.

weeks of supply

An inventory measure obtained by dividing the average aggregate inventory value by sales per week at cost.

inventory turnover

An inventory measure obtained by dividing annual sales at cost by the average aggregate inventory value maintained during the year.

Inventory turnover (or *turns*) is an inventory measure obtained by dividing annual sales at cost by the average aggregate inventory value maintained during the year, or

$$\text{Inventory turnover} = \frac{\text{Annual sales (at cost)}}{\text{Average aggregate inventory value}}$$

The "best" inventory level, even when expressed as turnover, cannot be determined easily. A good starting point is to benchmark the leading firms in an industry.

EXAMPLE 10.1	Calculating Inventory Measures

The Eagle Machine Company averaged $2 million in inventory last year, and the cost of goods sold was $10 million. Figure 10.5 shows the breakout of raw materials, work-in-process, and finished goods inventories. The best inventory turnover in the company's industry is six turns per year. If the company has 52 business weeks per year, how many weeks of supply were held in inventory? What was the inventory turnover? What should the company do?

FIGURE 10.5

Calculating Inventory Measures Using Inventory Estimator Solver

Cost of Goods Sold	$10,000,000
Weeks of Operation	52

	Item Number	Average Level	Unit Value	Total Value
Raw Materials	1	1,400	$50.00	$70,000
	2	1,000	$32.00	$32,000
	3	400	$60.00	$24,000
	4	2,400	$10.00	$24,000
	5	800	$15.00	$12,000
Work in Process	6	320	$700.00	$224,000
	7	160	$900.00	$144,000
	8	280	$750.00	$210,000
	9	240	$800.00	$192,000
	10	400	$1,000.00	$400,000
Finished Goods	11	60	$2,000.00	$120,000
	12	40	$3,500.00	$140,000
	13	50	$2,800.00	$140,000
	14	20	$5,000.00	$100,000
	15	40	$4,200.00	$168,000
Total				$2,000,000

Average Weekly Sales at Cost	$192,308
Weeks of Supply	10.4
Inventory Turnover	5.0

SOLUTION

The average aggregate inventory value of $2 million translates into 10.4 weeks of supply and five turns per year, calculated as follows:

$$\text{Weeks of supply} = \frac{\$2 \text{ million}}{(\$10 \text{ million})/(52 \text{ weeks})} = 10.4 \text{ weeks}$$

$$\text{Inventory turns} = \frac{\$10 \text{ million}}{\$2 \text{ million}} = 5 \text{ turns/year}$$

Decision Point The analysis indicates that management must improve the inventory turns by 20 percent. Management should improve its order fulfillment process to reduce finished goods inventory. Supply chain operations can also be improved to reduce the need to have so much raw materials and work-in-process inventory stock. It will take an inventory reduction of about 16 percent to achieve the target of six turns per year. However, inventories would not have to be reduced as much if sales increased. If the sales department targets an increase in sales of 8 percent ($10.8 million), inventories need only be reduced by 10 percent ($1.8 million) to get six turns a year. Management can now do sensitivity analyses to see what effect reductions in the inventory of specific items or increases in the annual sales have on weeks of supply or inventory turns.

PROCESS MEASURES

Three major processes related to supply chains are customer relationship, order fulfillment, and supplier relationship. It is important to monitor the performance of these internal processes as well as the entire supply chain itself. Supply chain managers monitor performance by measuring costs, time, and quality. Table 10.1 contains examples of operating measures for the three processes. Note that many of the measures for the internal processes also measure supply chain performance because the internal processes interface with suppliers and customers. For example, the time to fulfill an order or the percent of botched services and returned items reflects on the performance of the firm as well as its suppliers.

Managers periodically collect data on these measures and track them to note changes in level or direction. Statistical process control charts can be used to determine whether the changes are statistically significant.

LINKS TO FINANCIAL MEASURES

How the supply chain is managed has a huge financial impact on the firm. Inventory is an investment because it is needed for future use. However, inventory ties up funds that might be used more profitably in other operations.

Return on Assets Managing the supply chain so as to reduce the aggregate inventory investment will reduce the *total assets* portion of the firm's balance sheet. An important financial measure is *return on assets* (*ROA*), which is net income divided by total assets. Consequently, reducing aggregate inventory investment will increase ROA. Nonetheless, the objective should be to have the proper amount of inventory, not the least amount of inventory. ROA can also be increased by reducing the costs of operating the value chain, which will increase the net income. Techniques for reducing inventory, transportation, and operating costs related to resource usage and scheduling are discussed in the chapters to follow.

Working Capital Weeks of inventory and inventory turns are reflected in another financial measure, *working capital*, which is money used to finance ongoing operations. Decreasing weeks of supply or increasing inventory turns reduces the working capital

TABLE 10.1	Supply Chain Process Measures	
Customer Relationship	**Order Fulfillment**	**Supplier Relationship**
• Percent of orders taken accurately	• Percent of incomplete orders shipped	• Percent of suppliers' deliveries on time
• Time to complete the order placement process	• Percent of orders shipped on time	• Suppliers' lead times
• Customer satisfaction with the order placement process	• Time to fulfill the order	• Percent defects in services and purchased materials
	• Percent of botched services or returned items	• Cost of services and purchased materials
	• Cost to produce the service or item	• Inventory levels of supplies and purchased components
	• Customer satisfaction with the order fulfillment process	
	• Inventory levels of work-in-process and finished goods	

needed to finance inventories. Reductions in working capital can be accomplished by improving the customer relationship, order fulfillment, or supplier relationship processes. For example, reducing supplier lead times has the effect of reducing weeks of supply and increasing inventory turns: Matching the input and output flows of materials is easier because shorter-range, more reliable forecasts of demand can be used. Similarly, improvements in the other measures in Table 10.1 can be traced to improvements in working capital.

Cost of Goods Sold Being able to buy materials at a better price and process, or transform them more efficiently, will improve a firm's *cost of goods sold* measure and ultimately its *net income*. These improvements will also have an effect on *contribution margin*, which is the difference between price and the variable costs to produce a service or good. Reducing production, material, and poor quality costs increases the contribution margin, allowing for greater profits. Contribution margins are often used as inputs to decisions regarding the portfolio of services or products the firm offers.

Total Revenue Supply chain performance measures related to time also have financial implications. Many service providers and manufacturers measure the percent of on-time deliveries of their services or product to their customers, as well as services and materials from their suppliers. Increasing the percent of on-time deliveries to customers will increase *total revenue* because satisfied customers will buy more services and products from the firm. Increasing the percent of on-time deliveries from suppliers has the effect of reducing the costs of inventories, which has implications for the cost of goods sold and contribution margins.

Cash Flow The Internet brings another financial measure related to time to the forefront: *Cash-to-cash* is the time lag between paying for the services and materials needed to produce a service or product and receiving payment for it. The shorter the time lag, the better the *cash flow* position of the firm because it needs less working capital. The firm can then use the freed-up funds for other projects or investments. Reengineering the order placement process, so that payment for the service or product is made at the time the order is placed, can reduce the time lag. By contrast, billing the customer after the service is performed or the order is shipped increases the need for working capital. The ultimate is to have a negative cash-to-cash situation, which is possible when the customer pays for the service or product before the firm has to pay for the resources and materials needed to produce it. In such a case, the firm must have supplier inventories on consignment, which allows it to pay for materials as it uses them. Dell, discussed in the chapter opener, is a prime example of a firm with a negative cash-to-cash situation.

> SUPPLY CHAIN DYNAMICS <

Supply chain dynamics can wreak havoc on supply chain performance measures. Each firm in a supply chain depends on other firms for services, materials, or the information needed to supply its immediate external customer in the chain. Because firms are typically owned and managed independently, the actions of downstream supply chain members (positioned nearer the end user of the service or product) can affect the operations of upstream members. The reason is that upstream members of a supply chain must react to the demands placed on them by downstream members of the chain. These demands are a function of the policies these firms have for replenishing their inventories, the actual levels of those inventories, the demands of their customers, and the accuracy of the information they have to work with. As you examine the order patterns of firms in a supply chain, you will frequently see the variability in order quantities increase as you proceed upstream. This

The bullwhip effect can cause costly disruptions to upstream members of a supply chain as the variance in orders increases. Paperboard manufacturing processes, such as this one at a Weyerhauser Company facility, are vulnerable to the bullwhip effect.

increase in variability is referred to as the **bullwhip effect**, which gets its name from the action of a bullwhip—the handle of the whip initiates the action; however, the tip of the whip experiences the wildest action. The slightest change in customer demands can ripple through the entire chain, with each member receiving more variability in demands from the member immediately downstream.

Figure 10.6 shows the bullwhip effect in a supply chain for facial tissue. The retailer's orders to the manufacturer exhibit more variability than the actual demands from the consumers of the facial tissue. The manufacturer's orders to the package supplier have more variability than the retailer's orders. Finally, the package supplier's orders to the card-board supplier have the most variability. Because supply patterns do not match demand patterns, inventories accumulate in some firms and shortages occur in others. The firms with too much inventory stop ordering, and those that have shortages place expedite orders. The culprits are unexpected changes in demands or supplies that are based on a number of causes.

bullwhip effect

The phenomenon in supply chains whereby ordering patterns experience increasing variance as you proceed upstream in the chain.

EXTERNAL CAUSES

A firm has the least amount of control over its external customers and suppliers, who can periodically cause disruptions. Typical external disruptions include the following:

- *Volume Changes.* Customers may change the quantity of the service or product they had ordered for a specific date or unexpectedly demand more of a standard service or product. If the market demands short lead times, the firm needs a quick reaction from its suppliers. For example, an electric company experiencing an unusually warm day may require immediate power backup from another electric company to avoid a brownout.

- *Service and Product Mix Changes.* Customers may change the mix of items in an order and cause a ripple effect throughout the supply chain. For example, a major-appliance store chain may change the mix of washing machines in its orders from 60 percent Whirlpool brand and 40 percent Kitchen Aid brand to 40 percent Whirlpool and 60 percent Kitchen Aid. This decision changes the production schedule of the Whirlpool plant that makes both brands, causing imbalances in its inventories. In addition, the company that makes the face plates for the washing machines must change its schedules, thereby affecting *its* suppliers.

- *Late Deliveries.* Late deliveries of materials or delays in essential services can force a firm to switch its schedule from production of one product model to another. Firms that supply model-specific items may have their schedules disrupted. For example, the Whirlpool plant may find that a component supplier for its Model A washing machine

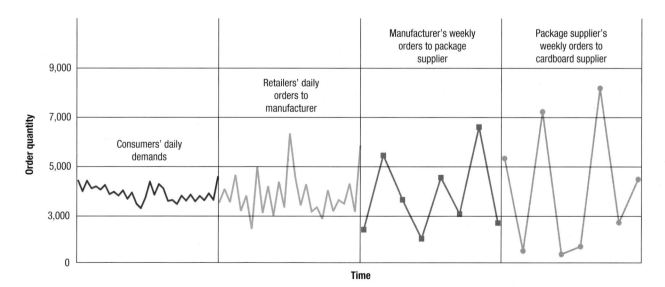

FIGURE **10.6** | Supply Chain Dynamics for Facial Tissue

could not supply the part on time. To avoid shutting down the assembly line, which is an expensive action, Whirlpool may decide to switch to Model B production. Suddenly, the demand on the suppliers of Model B-specific parts increases.

- *Underfilled Shipments.* Suppliers that send partial shipments do so because of disruptions at their own plants. The effects of underfilled shipments are similar to those of late shipments unless it contains enough to allow the firm to operate until the next shipment.

INTERNAL CAUSES

A famous line from a Pogo cartoon is "We have seen the enemy, and it is us!" Unfortunately, this statement is true for many firms when it comes to disruptions in the supply chain. A firm's own operations can be the culprit in what becomes the source of constant dynamics in the supply chain. Typical internal disruptions include the following:

- *Internally Generated Shortages.* A shortage of parts manufactured by a firm may occur because of machine breakdowns or inexperienced workers. This shortage can cause a change in the firm's production schedule affecting suppliers. A strike at a manufacturing plant will reduce the need for trucking services, for example. Labor shortages due to high turnover have a similar effect.

- *Engineering Changes.* Changes to the design of services or products can have a direct impact on suppliers. For example, changing cable TV feed lines to fiber-optic technology increases the benefits to the cable company's customers but affects the demand for cable. Similarly, reducing the complexity of a dashboard assembly may not be noticeable (functionally) to the buyers of an automobile, but it will change demand for the outsourced parts that go into the dashboard.

- *New Service or Product Introductions.* New services or products always affect the supply chain. A firm decides on the number of introductions, as well as their timing, and hence introduces a dynamic in the supply chain. New services or products may even require a new supply chain or the addition of new members to an existing supply chain. For example, the introduction of a new refrigerated trucking service will affect the suppliers of refrigerated trucks and the maintenance items for the new service.

- *Service or Product Promotions.* A common practice of firms producing standardized services or products is to use price discounts to promote sales. This practice creates a spike in demand that is felt throughout the supply chain. The Campbell Soup Company found out about spikes when its annual deep discount pricing program caused customers to buy large quantities of chicken soup, causing overtime production at its chicken-processing plant. The practice of buying in excess of immediate needs to take advantage of price discounts is called *forward buying.*

  Pricing programs, however, can induce efficiencies in the supply chain if they discourage activities that increase costs. For example, Campbell initiated a *strategic pricing program* that offered customers financial incentives for ordering more efficiently by engaging in electronic ordering, accepting direct plant deliveries or picking up orders themselves, and buying full truckloads and pallets of the product. Customer orders are assigned to pricing brackets based on the cost Campbell incurs to service them. Campbell shares the savings with their customers, thereby creating a win–win situation for everyone.

- *Information Errors.* Demand forecast errors can cause a firm to order too many, or too few, services and materials. Also, forecast errors can result in expedited orders that force suppliers to react more quickly to avoid shortages in the supply chain. In addition, errors in the physical count of items in stock can cause shortages (leading to panic purchases) or too much inventory (leading to a slowdown in purchases). Finally, communication links between buyers and suppliers can be faulty. For example, inaccurate order quantities and delays in information flows will affect supply chain dynamics.

  Many disruptions are simply caused by ineffective coordination in the supply chain because so many firms and separate operations are involved. It is therefore unrealistic to think that all disruptions can be eliminated. Nonetheless, the challenge for supply chain managers is to remove as many disruptions as possible and minimize the impact of those disruptions that cannot be eliminated.

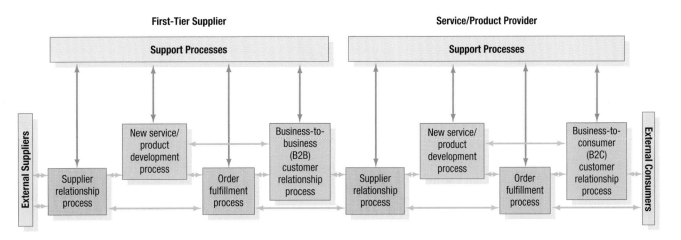

FIGURE 10.7 | External Value-Chain Linkages

INTEGRATED SUPPLY CHAINS

A starting point for minimizing supply chain disruptions is to develop a supply chain with a high degree of functional and organizational integration. Such integration does not happen overnight; it must include linkages between the firm and its suppliers and customers, as shown in Figure 10.7. The supplier relationship, which includes purchasing; order fulfillment, which includes production and distribution; and customer relationship processes, as well as their internal and external linkages, are integrated into the normal business routine. The firm takes on a customer orientation. However, rather than merely reacting to customer demand, the firm strives to work with its customers so that everyone benefits from improved flows of services and materials. Similarly, the firm must develop a better understanding of its suppliers' organizations, capacities, strengths, and weaknesses—and include its suppliers earlier into the design of new services or products.

The design of an integrated supply chain is complex. We already provided some key insights into the design decisions at the process level in Part 1 and Part 2 of the text. The customer relationship, order fulfillment, and supplier relationship processes need to be analyzed from the perspective of process structure, process improvement, layout, and capacity, for example. It is important to know that an integrated supply chain provides a framework for the operating decisions in a firm. We now turn to a discussion of some additional considerations related to the design and management of the processes in an integrated supply chain.

> THE CUSTOMER RELATIONSHIP PROCESS <

The customer relationship process addresses the interface between the firm and its customers downstream in the supply chain. The purpose of the customer relationship process is to identify, attract, and build relationships with customers and to facilitate the transmission and tracking of orders. Key nested processes include:

- *Marketing Process.* The marketing process focuses on such issues as determining the customers to target, how to target them, what services or products to offer and how to price them, and how to manage promotional campaigns.

- *Order Placement Process.* The order placement process involves the activities required to execute a sale, register the specifics of the order request, confirm the acceptance of the order, and track the progress of the order until it is completed. Often the firm has a salesforce that visits prospective and current customers to encourage a sale.

E-COMMERCE AND THE MARKETING PROCESS

Electronic commerce (e-commerce) has had a huge impact up and down the supply chain. In particular, it has dramatically changed the way companies design their customer relationship process and the nested marketing and order placement processes. In this section, we

electronic commerce (e-commerce)

The application of information and communication technology anywhere along the value chain of business processes.

focus on two e-commerce technologies that relate to the marketing process: business-to-consumer and business-to-business systems.

Business-to-Consumer Systems Business-to-consumer (B2C) systems, which allow customers to transact business over the Internet, are commonplace. B2C e-commerce offers a new distribution channel for businesses, and consumers can avoid crowded department stores with long checkout lines and parking-space shortages. Many of the advantages of e-commerce were first exploited by retail "e-businesses," such as Amazon.com, E*TRADE, and Auto-by-tel. These three companies created Internet versions of traditional bookstores, brokerage firms, and auto dealerships. The Internet is changing operations, processes, and cost structures for even traditional retailers, and the overall growth in its usage has been dramatic. Today, anyone with an Internet connection can open a store in cyberspace.

Many leading retailers and catalog companies have opened Web "stores" with thousands of virtual aisles and millions of items. This channel allows customers to do much more shopping in an hour than they could possibly do in person at a traditional retail outlet. E-commerce is particularly attractive for products that the consumer does not have to look at carefully or touch. The Internet offers an advantage with higher-value branded convenience goods over the in-store experience.

Business-to-Business Systems The biggest growth, however, has been in business-to-business (B2B) e-commerce systems, or commerce between firms. In fact, business-to-business e-commerce outpaces business-to-consumer transactions, with trade between businesses making up more than 70 percent of the regular economy.

Consider Fruit of the Loom, Inc., an apparel maker that depends on its wholesalers to ship products to various retailer customers. Fruit of the Loom put its wholesalers on the Web and gave each one a complete computer system that displays colorful catalogs, processes electronic orders around the clock, and manages inventories. If one of its distributors is out of stock, the company's central warehouse is notified to ship replacement stock directly to the customer. Building such an integrated e-commerce system took only a few months. The firm's retail customers need only an Internet connection and a Web browser.

E-COMMERCE AND THE ORDER PLACEMENT PROCESS

The Internet enables firms to reengineer their order placement process to benefit both the customer and the firm. For example, a traveler may arrive at The Ritz-Carlton on Maui and request a room without an advance reservation. An employee at the hotel will take the appropriate information regarding the order, including the dates of stay, suite or other type of room requested, double or single occupancy, king-size bed or double beds, smoking or nonsmoking, and then check to see which rooms (if any) are available. This approach is costly because of the time required of the employee, particularly at busy periods, not to mention the risk that the hotel will be unable to serve the customer. Alternatively, the traveler could use the hotel's Web site several weeks in advance, provide the same information, and get confirmation of the reservation. These two versions of the order placement process for the hotel involve different amounts of employee time and provide different levels of service to the customer. The Internet provides the following advantages for a firm's order placement process.

- *Cost Reduction.* Using the Internet can reduce the costs of processing orders because it allows for greater participation by the customer. Customers can select the services or products they want and place an order with the firm without actually talking to anyone. This approach reduces the need for call centers, which are labor intensive and often take longer to place orders.

- *Revenue Flow Increase.* A firm's Web page can allow customers to enter credit card information or purchase-order numbers as part of the order placement process. This approach reduces the time lags often associated with billing the customer or waiting for checks sent in the mail.

- *Global Access.* Another advantage the Internet provides to firms is the opportunity to accept orders 24 hours a day. Traditional brick-and-mortar firms only take orders during their normal business hours. Firms with Internet access can reduce the time it takes to satisfy customers, who can shop and purchase at any time. This access gives these firms a competitive advantage over brick-and-mortar firms.

- *Pricing Flexibility.* Firms with their services and products posted on the Web can easily change prices as the need arises, thereby avoiding the cost and delay of publishing new catalogs. Customers placing orders have current prices to consider when making their choices. From the perspective of supply chains, Dell Inc. uses this capability to control for component shortages. Because of its direct-sales approach and promotional pricing, Dell can steer customers to certain configurations of computers for which ample supplies exist.

> THE ORDER FULFILLMENT PROCESS <

The order fulfillment process is tightly linked to the customer relationship process. In fact, in many instances, they occur simultaneously. For example, a customer at a Barnes & Noble brick-and-mortar store has, in effect, ordered a book, and the store has delivered it when she checks out at the service desk. However, Barnes & Noble also has a Web page, where the order placement and the order fulfillment processes are separate but linked. Customers doing business on its Web page must accept a delay in receiving their books, a delay Barnes & Noble seeks to minimize in its supply chain.

At Dell, the order placement and order fulfillment processes are tightly linked. The eight steps in its order fulfillment process are shown in Figure 10.8.

1. Customers communicate and buy from Dell in one of three ways: Web site, voice-to-voice, and face-to-face. The latter two ways involve actual human contact. An experienced representative takes the customer's order, reviews the information, and enters it into the system.

2. Order information is transmitted to the inventory system. Materials are received from suppliers and placed in racks the manufacturing area. Dell receives only the materials it is immediately ready to use—those specified by the customer.

3. All of the customer's unique product configuration information is contained in the Traveler, which is a sheet that travels with the system the customer has ordered throughout its assembly and shipping.

4. When the Traveler is pulled, all internal parts and components required to make the system are picked and placed in a tote, or kit. This procedure is called *kitting.*

5. A team of workers uses the kit to assemble and initially test the entire system.

6. Systems are then extensively tested using Dell diagnostic procedures. Standard or custom hardware and software are factory installed and tested.

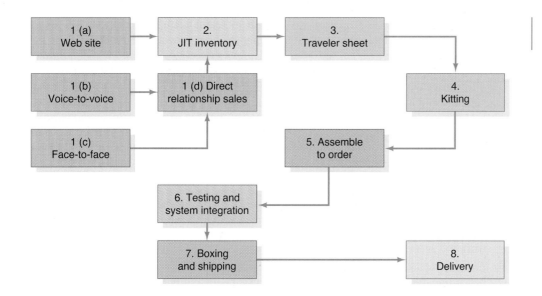

FIGURE 10.8

Dell's Order Fulfillment Process

7. Completed systems are placed in boxes along with documentation and manuals, then sealed and placed on trucks for shipping to the customer.

8. The system is delivered to the customer. The entire assemble-to-order cycle takes only a few hours.

Dell strives to drive out all non-value-added activities so as to increase the speed of manufacturing and delivering customer orders while maintaining high levels of quality and productivity. Sometimes this process requires a major overhaul of the order fulfillment process. For example, Dell installed robots and automatic equipment at its Nashville plant that receive direct online orders and build, test, and package the product for shipment.

Designing the order fulfillment process certainly can have competitive implications. We already discussed many of the order fulfillment activities associated with the production of a service or product in earlier chapters. In the remainder of this section we will discuss several tactics and tools that can help manage the order fulfillment processes involving material flows between the firm and its external customers.

INVENTORY PLACEMENT

centralized placement

Keeping all the inventory of a product at a single location such as a firm's manufacturing plant or a warehouse and shipping directly to each of its customers.

inventory pooling

A reduction in inventory and safety stock because of the merging of variable demands from customers.

forward placement

Locating stock closer to customers at a warehouse, DC, wholesaler, or retailer.

A fundamental supply chain decision that affects the performance of order fulfillment processes is where to locate an inventory of finished goods. Placing inventories can have strategic implications, as in the case of international companies locating *distribution centers* (DC) in foreign countries to preempt local competition by reducing customer delivery times. However, the issue for any firm producing standardized products is where to position the inventory in the supply chain. At one extreme, the firm could use **centralized placement**, which means keeping all the inventory of a product at a single location, such as a firm's manufacturing plant or a warehouse, and shipping directly to each of its customers. The advantage would come from what is referred to as **inventory pooling**, which is a reduction in inventory and safety stock because of the merging of uncertain and variable demands from the customers. A higher-than-expected demand from one customer can be offset by a lower-than-expected demand from another so that the total demand remains fairly stable. We discuss the methods for determining the amount of safety stock in Chapter 12, "Inventory Management." A disadvantage of placing inventory at a central location, however, is the added cost of shipping smaller, uneconomical quantities directly to customers over long distances.

Another approach is to use **forward placement**, which means locating stock closer to customers at a warehouse, DC, wholesaler, or retailer. Forward placement can have two advantages for the order fulfillment process—faster delivery times and reduced transportation costs—that can stimulate sales. As inventory is placed closer to the customer, such as at a DC, the pooling effect of the inventories is reduced because safety stocks for the item must increase to take care of uncertain demands at each DC, rather than just a single location. However, the time to get the product to the customer is reduced. Consequently, service to the customer is quicker, and the firm can take advantage of larger, less costly shipments to the DCs from the manufacturing plant, at the expense of larger overall inventories.

VENDOR-MANAGED INVENTORIES

vendor-managed inventories (VMI)

An extreme application of the forward placement tactic, which involves locating the inventories at the customer's facilities.

A tactic that employs an extreme case of forward placement is **vendor-managed inventories (VMI),** a system in which the supplier has access to the customer's inventory data and is responsible for maintaining the inventory level required by the customer. The inventory is on the customer's site, and often the supplier retains possession of the inventory until it is used by the customer. Companies such as Wal-Mart and Dell leverage their market position to mandate VMI. Vendor-managed inventories have several key elements.

■ *Collaborative Effort.* For VMI to succeed, the customers must be willing to allow the supplier access to their inventory. The implication is that the supplier assumes an important administrative role in the management of the inventory. Thus, an atmosphere of trust and accountability is required.

■ *Cost Savings.* Suppliers and customers eliminate the need for excess inventory through better operational planning. VMI reduces costs by removing administrative and inventory costs. Order placement costs are also reduced.

- *Customer Service.* The supplier is frequently on site and better understands the operations of the customer, improving response times and reducing stockouts.

- *Written Agreement.* It is important that both parties fully understand the responsibilities of each partner. Areas such as billing procedures, forecast methods, and replenishment schedules should be clearly specified. Further, the responsibility for obsolete inventory resulting from forecast revisions and changes in contract lengths should be included.

VMI can be used by service providers and manufacturers. AT&T, Roadway Express, Wal-Mart, Dell, Westinghouse, and Bose are among the companies that use it.

CONTINUOUS REPLENISHMENT PROGRAM

The execution of VMI requires a formal program to be effective. A number of such programs are available. Managerial Practice 10.2 explains a program used by Campbell Soup Company called **continuous replenishment program (CRP)**, where the supplier monitors the customer's inventory levels and replenishes the stock as needed. IBM, Heinz Pet Products, and Purina are among the many companies that utilize this approach to forward inventory placement. CRP helps reduce inventories and boost efficiencies in warehousing and transportation.

    The successes with CRP spurred the development of a program called *collaborative planning, forecasting, and replenishment (CPFR)*, which allows the supplier and the customer to develop replenishment quantities jointly. In an iterative process, the customer and the supplier fine-tune and coordinate their forecasts of demands for each individual item.

continuous replenishment program (CRP)
A VMI method in which the supplier monitors the customer's inventory levels and replenishes the stock as needed.

RADIO FREQUENCY IDENTIFICATION

An important requirement for the execution of order fulfillment processes is accurate information regarding the quantity and location of inventories. A new application of an old technology presents some tantalizing benefits. **Radio frequency identification (RFID)** is a method for identifying items through the use of radio signals from a tag attached to an item. The tag has information about the item and sends signals to a device that can read the information and even write new information on the tag. Data from the tags can be transmitted wirelessly from one place to another through electronic product code (EPC) networks and the Internet, making it theoretically possible to uniquely identify every item a company produces and track it until the tag is destroyed.

    Wal-Mart and Gillette, among a number of large retailers, manufacturers, government agencies, and suppliers, are in the process of implementing RFID in their supply chains. In Wal-Mart's case, RFID tags on cases and pallets will be read when inventory enters a stockroom and when those cases and pallets go to the retail floor. Wal-Mart will use the data to draw conclusions about when to bring additional stock to the floor and to figure out if too much of a product has been ordered by a store and is sitting in the stockroom or in the distribution center. The data could also help some 30,000 suppliers check inventory levels and sales. The use of RFID data can increase a supplier's service level to Wal-Mart. Pilferage reduction is another major advantage of the RFID technology. Gillette hopes to use RFID to reduce the amount of razor-blade theft, which amounts to as much as 30 percent.

    Whether RFID will be universally accepted is still unknown. Global data synchronization using industry standards is critical to ensure that accurate and consistent product information is exchanged between trading partners. Much work is still to be done. According to Wal-Mart managers, the best way to make RFID to happen is if retail stores are all into the project together.

radio frequency identification (RFID)
A method for identifying items through the use of radio signals from a tag attached to an item.

DISTRIBUTION PROCESSES

A key aspect of order fulfillment is the distribution process that brings the product or service to the customer. Three important decisions determine the design and implementation of distribution processes.

- *Ownership.* The firm has the most control over the distribution process if it owns and operates it, thereby becoming a *private carrier.* Although this approach may help to better achieve the firm's competitive priorities, the cost of equipment, labor, facilities, and maintenance could be high. The firm could instead leave the distribution to a *contract carrier*, negotiating with the carrier for specific services. Those services could involve taking over a major portion of the order fulfillment process. For example, UPS's Supply

MANAGERIAL **PRACTICE**   10.2   CONTINUOUS REPLENISHMENT AT THE CAMPBELL SOUP COMPANY

The Campbell Soup Company makes products that are price sensitive. An important competitive priority for the company is low-cost operations, which extends to the entire supply chain. Campbell operates in an environment with a high degree of certainty. Only 5 percent of its products are new each year; the rest have been on the market for years, making forecasting demand easy. Even though Campbell already had high levels of customer service—98 percent of the time Campbell's products were available in retailers' inventories—management believed that improvements in costs were possible. It scrutinized the entire supply chain to determine where performance could be improved.

The outcome was a program called the *continuous replenishment program (CRP)*, which reduced the inventories of retailers from an average of four to two weeks' supply. This reduction amounts to savings on the order of 1 percent of retail sales. When the average retailer's profits are only 2 percent of sales, the result was a 50 percent increase in the average retailer's profits from the sale of Campbell's products. Because of that increase in profitability, retailers purchased a broader line of Campbell products, thereby increasing Campbell's sales. The program works in the following way.

- Each morning Campbell uses Electronic Data Interchange to link with retailers.

- Retailers inform Campbell of demands for its products and the current inventory levels in their distribution centers.

- Campbell determines which products need replenishment based on upper and lower inventory limits established with each retailer.

- Campbell makes daily deliveries of needed products.

Campbell must avoid actions that would disrupt the supply chain. For example, retailers on the continuous replenishment program had to forgo forward buying, whereby retailers in the industry often buy excess stock at discounted prices so that they can offer price promotions. Forward buying causes ripples in the supply chain, increasing everyone's costs, which is what happened with chicken soup. Campbell would offer deep discounts once a year and retailers would take advantage of them, sometimes buying an entire year's supply. Because of the bulge in demand, the chicken-processing plant would have to go on overtime. When that happened, costs in the entire supply chain increased—Campbell's production costs increased, and retailers had to pay for warehousing large stocks of chicken soup. With the continuous replenishment system, those extra costs are eliminated, and everyone wins.

The success of CRP led Campbell to pursue additional ways to improve efficiency in the supply chain. One improvement is quicker order

Campbell Soup Company managed to wring out greater profits for its retailers by electronically monitoring each retailer's inventory and shipping soup to it as needed. However, "forward buying," whereby retailers could purchase large amounts of discounted soup, had to be discontinued. The practice led to surges in demand that wrought havoc with Campbell's system.

turnaround for those customers who participate in a new program, called *collaborative planning, forecasting, and replenishment (CPFR)*, which is a movement gaining ground in the grocery industry. The program allows Campbell to determine replenishment quantities in concert with the retailer and thereby remove redundant inventory and improve customer service.

To combat inefficient customer-ordering patterns, Campbell also initiated a "strategic pricing program" that rewards customers for ordering electronically and in quantities that fill trucks and pallets, rather than by the case. Customers get allowances or price breaks for picking up the goods themselves. Campbell observed a significant change in the ordering patterns of its customers because of the program, and about two-thirds of its customers now meet the criteria for the best pricing bracket. The strategic pricing program netted several million dollars in savings for Campbell and its trading partners.

Sources: Marshall L. Fisher, "What Is the Right Supply Chain for Your Product?" *Harvard Business Review* (March–April 1997), pp. 105–116; Leslie Hansen Harps, "Shopping for Supply Chain Excellence," inboundlogistics.com, 2002; Dan Gilmore, "Campbell Soup Solves Demand Planning Problem," *Supply Chain Digest* (February 2004), www.scdigest.com; www.campbellsoup.com, 2005.

Chain Solutions unit controls more than 1 million square feet of warehouse space to help manage inventories for clients near Shanghai and Guangzhou in China. The clients use UPS to ship items to the warehouse, and then UPS manages the deliveries to the specific sites in China.

■ *Mode Selection.* The five basic modes of transportation are truck, train, ship, pipeline, and airplane. The drivers for the selection should be the firm's competitive priorities. Trucks provide the greatest flexibility because they can go wherever roads go. Transit times are good, and rates are usually better than trains for small quantities and short distances. Rail transportation can move large quantities cheaply; however the transit times are long and often variable. Water transportation provides high capacity and low costs, and is necessary for overseas shipments of bulky items; however the transit times are slow and highway or rail transportation is often needed to get the product to its ultimate destination. Pipeline transportation is highly specialized and is used for liquids, gases, or solids in slurry form. Although it has limited geographical flexibility, transporting via pipeline requires no packaging, and the operating costs per mile are low. Finally, air transportation is the fastest and most costly mode per mile. Nonetheless, getting a product to the customer fast using air transportation may actually reduce total costs when the costs of inventory and warehouse handling are considered for alternative modes. The cost of the funds tied up in some in-transit inventories can be considerable.

■ *Cross-Docking.* Low-cost operations and delivery speed can be enhanced with a technique called **cross-docking**, which is the packing of products on incoming shipments so that they can be easily sorted at intermediate warehouses for outgoing shipments based on their final destinations; the items are carried from the incoming-vehicle docking point to the outgoing-vehicle docking point without being stored in inventory at the warehouse. For example, a truck from Nebraska carrying shipments to customers in Ohio, Pennsylvania, and Virginia arrives at a warehouse in Columbus, Ohio, where warehouse personnel unload its contents and reload them on trucks headed for destinations in Ohio, Pennsylvania, and Virginia. Inbound shipments must be tightly coordinated with outbound shipments for cross-docking to work. The warehouse becomes a short-term staging area for organizing efficient shipments to customers. The benefits of cross-docking include reductions in inventory investment, storage space requirements, handling costs, and lead times, as well as increased inventory turnover and accelerated cash flow.

cross-docking

The packing of products on incoming shipments so that they can be easily sorted at intermediate warehouses for outgoing shipments based on their final destinations; the items are carried from the incoming-vehicle docking point to the outgoing-vehicle docking point without being stored in inventory at the warehouse.

> SUPPLIER RELATIONSHIP PROCESS <

The supplier relationship process focuses on the interaction of the firm and upstream suppliers. The major nested processes include the following:

■ *Sourcing Process.* The sourcing process qualifies, selects, manages the contracts, and evaluates suppliers.

■ *Design Collaboration Process.* The design collaboration process focuses on jointly designing new services or products with key suppliers. This process seeks to eliminate costly delays and mistakes incurred when many suppliers concurrently, but independently, design service packages or manufactured components. Without sharing information between the suppliers, the end result can be far off the mark

■ *Negotiation Process.* The negotiation process focuses on obtaining an effective contract that meets the price, quality, and delivery requirements of the supplier relationship process's internal customers.

■ *Buying Process.* The buying process relates to the actual procurement of the service or material from the supplier. This process includes the creation, management, and approval of purchase orders.

■ *Information Exchange Process.* The information exchange process facilitates the exchange of pertinent operating information, such as forecasts, schedules, and inventory levels between the firm and its supplier.

In this section we focus on several important decision areas that affect the design of the supplier relationship process. We begin our discussion with the considerations firms make in selecting and certifying suppliers, an important activity in the sourcing process. Next, we discuss the nature of supplier relations, which reflects on the negotiation processes and design collaboration. The next decision area is electronic purchasing, which affects the buying and information exchange processes. We then discuss the implications of centralized versus localized buying, which affects the negotiation and buying processes. Finally, we discuss the technique of value analysis, which lies at the heart of the design collaboration process.

SUPPLIER SELECTION AND CERTIFICATION

purchasing

The activity that decides which suppliers to use, negotiates contracts, and determines whether to buy locally.

Purchasing is the activity that decides which suppliers to use, negotiates contracts, and determines whether to buy locally. Firms continuously seek better buys and new materials from suppliers. A firm's purchasing unit is responsible for selecting better suppliers and conducting certification programs. These two activities are important in the sourcing process.

Supplier Selection To make supplier selection decisions and to review the performance of current suppliers, management must review the market segments it wants to serve and relate their needs to the supply chain. Competitive priorities are a starting point in developing a list of performance criteria to be used. For example, if you were a manager of a food-service firm, you would likely use on-time delivery and quality as two top criteria for selecting suppliers. These criteria reflect the requirements that food service supply chains need to meet.

Three criteria often considered by firms selecting new suppliers are price, quality, and delivery. Because firms spend a large percentage of their total income on purchased items, finding suppliers that charge low *prices* is a key objective. However, the *quality* of a supplier's materials also is important. The hidden costs of poor quality can be high, particularly if defects are not detected until after considerable value has been added by subsequent operations. For a retailer, poor merchandise quality can mean loss of customer goodwill and future sales. Finally, shorter lead times and on-time *delivery* help the buying firm maintain acceptable customer service with less inventory. For example, Maimonides Medical Center, a 700-bed hospital in Brooklyn, buys many of its materials from one supplier. The supplier offers short lead times from a nearby warehouse, which allowed Maimonides to pare its inventory from about $1,200 to only $150 per bed.

A fourth criterion is becoming important in the selection of suppliers—environmental impact. Many firms are engaging in **green purchasing**, which involves identifying, assessing, and managing the flow of environmental waste and finding ways to reduce it and minimize its impact on the environment. Suppliers are being asked to be environmentally conscious when designing and manufacturing their products. Claims such as *green, biodegradable, natural*, and *recycled* must be substantiated when bidding on a contract. In the not-too-distant future, this criterion could be one of the most important in the selection of suppliers.

green purchasing

The process of identifying, assessing, and managing the flow of environmental waste and finding ways to reduce it and minimize its impact on the environment.

Supplier Certification Supplier certification programs verify that potential suppliers have the capability to provide the services or materials the buying firm requires. Certification typically involves site visits by a cross-functional team from the buying firm who do an in-depth evaluation of the supplier's capability to meet cost, quality, delivery, and flexibility targets from process and information system perspectives. The team may consist of members from operations, purchasing, engineering, information systems, and accounting. Every aspect of producing the services or materials is explored. The team observes the supplier's processes in action and reviews the documentation for completeness and accuracy. Once certified, the supplier can be used by purchasing without its having to make background checks. Performance is monitored and performance records are kept. After a certain period of time, or if performance declines, the supplier may have to be recertified.

SUPPLIER RELATIONS

The nature of relations maintained with suppliers can affect the quality, timeliness, and price of a firm's services and products. The firm's orientation toward supplier relations will affect the negotiation and design collaboration processes.

competitive orientation

A supplier relation that views negotiations between buyer and seller as a zero-sum game: Whatever one side loses, the other side gains, and short-term advantages are prized over long-term commitments.

Competitive Orientation The **competitive orientation** sees negotiations between buyer and seller as a zero-sum game: Whatever one side loses, the other side gains. Short-term advantages are prized over long-term commitments. The buyer may try to beat the supplier's price down to the lowest survival level or to push demand to high levels during boom times and order almost nothing during recessions. In contrast, the supplier presses for higher prices for specific levels of quality, customer service, and volume flexibility. Which party wins depends largely on who has the most clout.

Purchasing power determines the clout that a firm has. A firm has purchasing power when its purchasing volume represents a significant share of the supplier's sales or the purchased service or item is standardized and many substitutes are available. For example, Premier, Inc., a cooperative with 1,759 member hospitals, spends $10 billion a year on services and materials for its members. Suppliers are uneasy because they have to give Premier prices far lower than they do their other customers to keep its business. Premier will buy from the lowest bidder without much loyalty to any supplier. Analysts estimate that Premier helped reduce the cost of health care by $2 billion a year because of its efforts.

Cooperative Orientation The **cooperative orientation** emphasizes that buyer and seller are partners, each helping the other as much as possible. A cooperative orientation means long-term commitment, joint work on quality and service or product designs, and support by the buyer of the supplier's managerial, technological, and capacity development. A cooperative orientation favors fewer suppliers of a particular service or item, with just one or two suppliers being the ideal number. As order volumes increase, the supplier gains economies of scale, which lowers costs. When contracts are large and a long-term relationship is ensured, the supplier might even build a new facility and hire a new workforce, perhaps relocating close to the buyer's plant. Suppliers become almost an extension of the buyer.

A cooperative orientation means that the buyer shares more information with the supplier about its future buying intentions. This forward visibility allows suppliers to make better, more reliable forecasts of future demand. The buyer visits suppliers' plants and cultivates cooperative attitudes. The buyer may even suggest ways to improve the suppliers' operations. This close cooperation with suppliers could even mean that the buyer does not need to inspect incoming materials. It also could mean involving the supplier more in designing services or products, implementing cost-reduction ideas, and sharing in savings.

One advantage of reducing the number of suppliers in the supply chain is a reduction in the complexity of managing them. However, reducing the number of suppliers for a service or item may increase the risk of an interruption in supply. It also means less opportunity to drive a good bargain unless the buyer has a lot of clout. **Sole sourcing**, which is the awarding of a contract for a service or item to only one supplier, can amplify any problems with the supplier that may crop up.

Both the competitive and cooperative orientations have their advantages and disadvantages. The key is to use the approach that serves the firm's competitive priorities best. Some companies utilize a mixed strategy, applying a competitive approach for its commodity-like supplies and a cooperative approach for its complex, high-valued, or high-volume services and materials.

ELECTRONIC PURCHASING

Although not all purchasing opportunities involve the Internet, the emergence of the virtual marketplace has, indeed, provided firms with many opportunities to improve their buying and information exchange processes. In this section, we discuss four approaches to e-purchasing: (1) electronic data interchange, (2) catalog hubs, (3) exchanges, and (4) auctions.

Electronic Data Interchange The most used form of e-purchasing today is **electronic data interchange (EDI)**, a technology that enables the transmission of routine, standardized business documents from computer to computer over telephone or direct leased lines. Special communications software translates documents into and out of a generic form, allowing organizations to exchange information even if they have different hardware and software components. Invoices, purchase orders, and payments information are some of the routine documents that EDI can handle—it replaces the phone call or mailed document.

An e-purchasing system with EDI might work as follows. Buyers browse an electronic catalog and click on items to purchase from a supplier. A computer sends the order directly to the supplier. The supplier's computer checks the buyer's credit and determines that the items are available. The supplier's warehouse and shipping departments are notified electronically, and the items are readied for shipment. Finally, the supplier's accounting department bills the buyer electronically. Savings (ranging from $5 to $125 per document) are considerable in light of the hundreds to thousands of documents many firms typically handle daily.

cooperative orientation
A supplier relation in which the buyer and seller are partners, each helping the other as much as possible.

sole sourcing
The awarding of a contract for a service or item to only one supplier.

electronic data interchange (EDI)
A technology that enables the transmission of routine business documents having a standard format from computer to computer over telephone or direct leased lines.

catalog hubs

A system whereby suppliers post their catalog of items on the Internet and buyers select what they need and purchase them electronically.

exchange

An electronic marketplace where buying firms and selling firms come together to do business.

auction

A marketplace where firms place competitive bids to buy something.

Catalog Hubs **Catalog hubs** can be used to reduce the costs of placing orders to suppliers as well as the costs of the services or goods themselves. Suppliers post their catalog of items on the hub, and buyers select what they need and purchase them electronically. The hub connects the firm to potentially hundreds of suppliers through the Internet, saving the costs of EDI, which requires one-to-one connections to individual suppliers. Moreover, the buying firm can negotiate prices with individual suppliers for items such as office supplies, technical equipment, services, and so forth. The catalog that the buying firm's employees see consists only of the approved items and the prices the buyer has prenegotiated with its suppliers. Employees use their PCs to select the items they need, and the system generates the purchase orders, which are electronically dispatched to the suppliers.

Exchanges An **exchange** is an electronic marketplace where buying firms and selling firms come together to do business. The exchange maintains relationships with buyers and sellers, making it easy to do business without the aspect of contract negotiations or other types of long-term conditions. Exchanges are often used for "spot" purchases to satisfy an immediate need at the lowest possible cost. Commodity items such as oil, steel, or energy fit this category. However, exchanges can also be used for most any item. For example, Marriott International and Hyatt Corporation formed an exchange for purchasing hotel supplies. Hotels traditionally bought supplies from thousands of firms using faxes, telephones, and forms in quadruplicate. Placing orders was expensive, with little opportunity to do comparison shopping. The new exchange, which features thousands of supplies from many firms, makes for one-stop shopping for hotels using the service.

Auctions An extension of the exchange is the **auction**, where firms place competitive bids to buy something. For example, a site may be formed for a particular industry, and firms with excess capacity or materials can offer them for sale to the highest bidder. Bids can either be closed or open to the competition. Industries where auctions have value include steel, chemicals, and the home mortgage industry, where financial institutions can bid for mortgages. Analogies in the B2C world include eBay and Priceline.com.

An approach that has received considerable attention is the so-called *reverse auction*, where suppliers bid for contracts with buyers. One such site is FreeMarkets, an electronic marketplace where *Fortune* 500 companies offer supply contracts for open bidding. Each bid is posted, so suppliers can see how much lower their next bid must be to remain in the running for the contract. Each contract has an electronic prospectus that provides all the specifications, conditions, and other requirements that are nonnegotiable. The only thing left to determine is the cost to the buyer. Savings can be dramatic. For example, a company posted a contract for plastic parts with a benchmark starting price of $745,000, which was the most recent price for that contract. Twenty-five suppliers vied for the contract over a 20-minute bidding period. Within minutes of opening, the price was $738,000, then it plummeted to $612,000. With 30 seconds remaining in the auction, the price went to $585,000, then finally to $518,000 after 13 minutes of overtime bidding. In little more than a half-hour, the company saved about 31 percent. The concept of the reverse auction has grown in its application. Ford, GM, and DaimlerChrysler put together a reverse auction marketplace to procure parts from suppliers. Similar marketplaces are forming around the buying and selling of paper, plastic, steel, bandwidth, chemicals, and the like.

Our discussion of these electronic purchasing approaches should not leave you with the impression that cost is the only consideration firms make. Exchanges and auctions are more useful for commodities, near-commodities, or infrequently needed items that require only short-term relationships with suppliers. Nonetheless, suppliers should be thought of as partners when the needed supply is significant and steady over extended periods of time. Supplier involvement in service or product design and supply chain performance improvement requires long-term relationships not found with competitive pricing on the Internet.

CENTRALIZED VERSUS LOCALIZED BUYING

When an organization has several facilities (stores, hospitals, or plants, for example), management must decide whether to buy locally or centrally. This decision has implications for the control of supply chain flows and the negotiation and buying processes.

Centralized buying has the advantage of increasing purchasing clout. Savings can be significant, often on the order of 10 percent or more. Increased buying power can mean getting better service, ensuring long-term supply availability, or developing new supplier capability. Companies with overseas suppliers favor centralization because the specialized skills (for example, understanding of foreign languages and cultures) needed to buy from foreign sources can be centralized in one location. Buyers also need to understand international commercial and contract law regarding the transfer of services and goods. Another trend that favors centralization is the growth of computer-based information systems and the Internet, which give specialists at headquarters access to data previously available only at the local level.

Probably the biggest disadvantage of centralized buying is loss of control at the local level. Centralized buying is undesirable for items unique to a particular facility. These items should be purchased locally whenever possible. The same holds for purchases that must be closely meshed with production schedules. Localized buying is also an advantage when the firm has major facilities in foreign countries because the managers there, often foreign nationals, have a much better understanding of the local culture than staff members at the home office. Also, centralized buying often means longer lead times and another level in the firm's hierarchy.

Perhaps the best solution is a compromise strategy, whereby both local autonomy and centralized buying are possible. For example, the corporate purchasing group at IBM negotiates contracts on a centralized basis only at the request of local plants. Management at one of the plants then monitors the contract for all the participating plants.

VALUE ANALYSIS

A systematic effort to reduce the cost or improve the performance of services or products, either purchased or produced, is referred to as **value analysis**. It is an intensive examination of the services, materials, processes, information systems, and flows of material involved in the production of a service or an item. Benefits include reduced production, materials, and distribution costs; improved profit margins; and increased customer satisfaction. Because teams involving purchasing, production, and engineering personnel from both the firm and its major suppliers play a key role in value analysis, another potential benefit is increased employee morale.

Value analysis encourages employees of the firm and its suppliers to address questions such as the following: What is the function of the service or the item? Is the function necessary? Can a lower-cost standard part that serves the purpose be identified? Can the service or the item be simplified or its specifications relaxed to achieve a lower price? Can the service or the item be designed so that it can be produced more efficiently or more quickly? Can features that the customer values highly be added to the service or the item? Value analysis should be part of a continual effort to improve the performance of the supply chain and increase the value of the service or the item to the customer.

Value analysis can focus solely on internal processes with some success, but its true potential lies in applying it to the entire value chain as well. An approach that many firms are using in their design collaboration process is called **early supplier involvement**, which is a program that includes suppliers in the design phase of a service or product. Suppliers provide suggestions for design changes and materials choices that will result in more efficient operations and higher quality. In the automotive industry, an even higher level of early supplier involvement is known as **presourcing**, whereby suppliers are selected early in a product's concept development stage and are given significant, if not total, responsibility for the design of certain components or systems of the product. Presourced suppliers also take responsibility for the cost, quality, and on-time delivery of the items they produce.

Now that we have discussed the supplier relationship process, put yourself in the position of Starwood management in the following managerial challenge. How would you address the challenges of sourcing the bed linens and terrycloth?

value analysis

A systematic effort to reduce the cost or improve the performance of services or products, either purchased or produced.

early supplier involvement

A program that includes suppliers in the design phase of a service or product.

presourcing

A level of supplier involvement in which suppliers are selected early in a product's concept development stage and are given significant, if not total, responsibility for the design of certain components or systems of the product.

> SUPPLY CHAIN STRATEGIES <

In this section, we discuss several contemporary supply chain strategies and demonstrate how they can support the operations strategies of firms.

STRATEGIC FOCUS

A supply chain is, of course, a network of firms. Thus, each firm in the chain should build its own supply chains to support the competitive priorities of its services or products. Even though extensive technologies such as electronic data interchange (EDI), the Internet,

MANAGERIAL CHALLENGE

SUPPLY CHAIN STRATEGY AT STARWOOD

DVD Bath towels. Televisions. Fresh produce. Uniforms. On the surface, these items may not appear to have any relationship to each other. Sure, they exist in most households, even though they were probably bought independently of one another. Yet to the supply chain manager employed in the hospitality industry, they not only have a relationship, but their purchase can be critical to gaining a competitive advantage.

Just ask Paul Davis, vice president of Strategic Sourcing for Starwood's North American operations. With hundreds of hotels and resorts in the United States, Canada, and the Caribbean, Davis's goal is to create the hospitality industry's best supply chain organization. The items procured within his organization not only include replenishable goods such as fresh produce and food items but also extend to the sourcing of national contracts for nonperishable goods such as bath towels, electronics, staff apparel, energy, and contract services.

It's easy to confuse supply chain processes with the routine procurement of goods and services. Starwood's supply chain certainly does include contracting, but it is much more: It consists of the customer relationship, order fulfillment, and supplier relationship processes. Strong linkages exist among the company's upstream suppliers of services, materials, and information, and the customers of Starwood's hotels and resorts. If the upstream relationships are not carefully managed, downstream delivery of consistency, quality, and value to Starwood's guests may suffer. As a result, significant effort is placed on the nested processes within the supplier relationship process such as design collaboration, sourcing, negotiation, contracting, and information exchange.

Any number of events will trigger the involvement of Paul Davis's supply chain team:

Existing contracts expire.

Individual hotel brands seek new products.

Hotel property design teams generate ideas.

Suppliers bring new ideas to Starwood.

New categories of products emerge and need evaluation.

A particular hotel needs help with a local service contract.

When a product or service needs to be sourced, the specifications are driven by internal customers such as restaurant chefs, housekeeping, and maintenance. If the product or service doesn't already exist, domestic and international suppliers who might be able to create the item are researched, as are regional and local vendors. Sometimes, sourcing an existing item simply means renewing an agreement with a current supplier. Still other situations demand creating a new category that hasn't been sourced before or using a third party to help locate sources.

Due diligence is always performed by sending potential suppliers a "request for information" in either paper or electronic form. The responses returned by the supplier are entered into a database and help Starwood to prequalify them. A good match is sought, requiring the supplier to meet minimum requirements for financial viability, quality, scope of operations, references, and legal risk avoidance. With a suitable potential supplier candidate pool, Starwood then takes one of two paths. The first one is to conduct a reverse auction where preselected vendors bid against each other.

The Starwood hotel chain has turned strategic sourcing into art. Starwood purchases high-value and complex products from a select set of suppliers and commoditized items using more conventional methods like competitive bidding. The chain also works closely with its suppliers to help improve not only its own profit margins, but theirs as well.

This method is used with shorter-term contracts on commodity items that have low external customer visibility. Kitchen uniforms, hotel room door keys, and paint are sourced this way. The second option is to send out a request for proposal (RFP), which requires the vendor to put its best terms forward at the outset for consideration.

After review by the supply chain team, the vendor winning the auction or emerging from the RFP review activity as the best fit is engaged in negotiations. Throughout the supplier relationship building process, Starwood gets to know the vendors, but it becomes much more personal at this point as both parties move toward concluding their contract negotiations.

Starwood maintains a cooperative orientation toward its supplier relationships, building a partnership to maximize value for each party to ensure that each side is comfortable with the price, quality, and delivery requirements they've agreed upon in the contract negotiation process. When contract negotiations are complete, the different brands are notified and the buying and information exchange processes begin.

At this point, you might think the job of the supply chain team is done. Yet managing the existing supplier relationship after the contract ink dries is perhaps the most challenging task of all. The contract involving sourcing of bed linens and terrycloth items is a perfect example. Not long after the contract was finalized, an alternate supplier approached Starwood with an offer to supply comparable quality goods at a much lower cost. Supply chain managers had a choice to make: continue to work with the existing supplier or buy out the current supplier's contract and begin sourcing with the new one.

Managerial Challenges for Sourcing Materials and Services at Starwood

1. Should Starwood maintain a cooperative orientation or a competitive orientation with its suppliers for the kind of items described here?

2. What types of information should Starwood exchange with its bed linens and terrycloth supplier? What does Starwood risk by sharing too much information?

3. How would you approach the sourcing of bed linens and terrycloth items? That is, would you use a reverse auction or request for proposal? Under what circumstances would you change suppliers?

4. In addition to performing value analysis on the services its properties offer, Starwood evaluates the performance of its suppliers against contract metrics. Using the bed linens and terrycloth supplier as an example, describe some of the metrics Starwood should use.

computer-assisted design, flexible manufacturing, and automated warehousing have been applied to all stages of the supply chain, the performance of many supply chains remains dismal. A study of the U.S. food industry estimated that poor coordination among supply chain partners wastes $30 billion annually. One possible cause for failures is that managers do not understand the nature of the demand for their services or products and, therefore, cannot devise supply chain strategies to satisfy those demands. Two distinct designs used to competitive advantage are *efficient supply chains* and *responsive supply chains* (Fisher, 1997). Table 10.2 shows the environments that best suit each design.

Efficient Supply Chains The nature of demand for the firm's services or products is a key factor in the best choice of supply chain strategy. Efficient supply chains work best in environments where demand is highly predictable, such as demand for staple items purchased at grocery stores or demand for a package delivery service. The focus of the supply chain is on the efficient flows of services and materials and keeping inventories to a minimum. Because of the markets the firms serve, service or product designs last a long time, new introductions are infrequent, and variety is small. Such firms typically produce for markets in which price is crucial to winning an order. Contribution margins are low and efficiency is important. Consequently, the firm's competitive priorities are low-cost operations, consistent quality, and on-time delivery.

Responsive Supply Chains Responsive supply chains are designed to react quickly in order to hedge against uncertainties in demand. They work best when firms offer a great variety of services or products and demand predictability is low. To stay competitive, firms in such a supply chain frequently introduce new services or products. Nonetheless, because of the innovativeness of their services or products, they enjoy high contribution margins. Typical competitive priorities are development speed, fast delivery times, customization, variety, volume flexibility, and top quality. The firms may not even know what services or products they need to provide until customers place orders. In addition, demand may be short-lived, as in the case of fashion goods. The focus of responsive supply chains is reaction time, which helps avoid keeping costly inventories that ultimately must be sold at

TABLE 10.2	Environments Best Suited for Efficient and Responsive Supply Chains	
Factor	**Efficient Supply Chains**	**Responsive Supply Chains**
Demand	Predictable, low forecast errors	Unpredictable, high forecast errors
Competitive priorities	Low cost, consistent quality, on-time delivery	Development speed, fast delivery times, customization, volume flexibility, variety, top quality
New-service/product introduction	Infrequent	Frequent
Contribution margins	Low	High
Product variety	Low	High

Suppose you are shopping for the latest hip fashions in a men's knit vest or a black dress with red and beige accents at a quality level closer to Banana Republic than Gap, and at prices in line with Old Navy. You are in luck if you are shopping at Zara, a chain of 650 clothing retail stores in Europe, the Americas, and the Middle East that caters to the dressier European tastes. Zara is a part of Inditex, a $2.8 billion retail conglomerate, which has 1,315 stores in 50 countries. Zara contributes 70 percent of Inditex's sales, which grew at an annual rate of 31 percent in 2001, and continues to grow when competitors, such as Gap and Sweden's H&M, retrench. What is its secret?

In fashion retailing, nothing is as important as time to market—not advertising (Zara advertises only twice a year), sales promotions (Zara uses promotions sparingly), or labor costs. Rather than going to Third World countries to manufacture their items at low cost, Zara designed a supply chain that can react quickly to changes in customer preferences. The factories it chose had to be flexible and geared for quick response—something that would have been difficult to manage if the factories were located in South America or Asia.

It all begins at the new product development group, which is located at Zara's headquarters in La Coruna, Spain. There, some 200 designers and product managers decide what to create, given inputs from the 650 store managers worldwide. The group develops more than 10,000 new items each year, far more than the competition does. The designers draw up their ideas on computers and send them along to the factories, which are located across the highway from the headquarters. Within days, the cutting, dyeing, stitching, and pressing operations begin.

A key element of the supply chain is a four-story, 5-million-square-foot (the equivalent of 90 football fields) warehouse that is connected to 14 factories through a series of tunnels, each equipped with a rail and cable system. Coats, pants, dresses, and other products produced in the plants are put on racks and moved by cables through the tunnels to the warehouse, where the merchandise is selected, sorted, rerouted, resorted, and then taken to a special area where each Zara store has its own staging area. As soon as a store's order is complete, it is packed and shipped to its destination—by truck if it is a European destination or by plane if it is outside of Europe. The vast majority of the items are in the warehouse in only a few hours.

Zara's management believes that flexibility and speed are the two top competitive priorities for its supply chain. The elapsed time from developing a new garment to hanging it up in a store for sale is just three weeks. In contrast, it takes Gap nine months for the same cycle. Such performance, however, comes at a price. Zara's manufacturing costs run 15 to 20 percent higher than those of its rivals. The key point is that the business is still highly profitable. Zara maintains a profit margin of 10 percent, which is on par with the best in the industry.

Sources: Miguel Helft, "Fashion Fast Forward," *Business Week* (May 2002); Kasra Ferdows, Michael A. Lewis, and Jose A. D. Machuca, "Rapid Fire Fulfillment," *Harvard Business Review* (November 2004), pp. 104–110.

deep discounts. Managerial Practice 10.3 shows how a European clothing retailer used a responsive supply chain to gain a competitive advantage.

Combining Efficient and Responsive Supply Chains A firm may need to utilize both types of supply chains, especially when it focuses its operations on specific market segments or it can segment the supply chain to achieve two different requirements. For example, the supply chain for a standard product, such as an oil tanker, has different requirements than that for a customized product, such as a luxury liner, even though both are ocean-going vessels and both may be manufactured by the same company. You might also see elements of efficiency and responsiveness in the same supply chain. For example, Gillette uses an efficient supply chain to manufacture its products so that it can utilize a capital-intensive manufacturing process, and then it uses a responsive supply chain for the packaging and delivery processes to be responsive to retailers. The packaging operation involves customization in the form of printing in different languages. Just as processes can be broken into parts, with different process structures for each, supply chain processes can be segmented to achieve optimal performance.

The Design of Efficient and Responsive Supply Chains Table 10.3 contains the basic design features for efficient and responsive supply chains. The more downstream in an efficient supply chain that a firm is, the more likely it is to have a line-flow strategy that supports high volumes of standardized services or products. Consequently, suppliers in efficient supply chains should have low capacity cushions because high utilization keeps the cost per unit low. High inventory turns are desired because inventory investment must be kept low to achieve low costs. Firms should work with their suppliers to shorten lead

TABLE 10.3	Design Features for Efficient and Responsive Supply Chains

Factor	Efficient Supply Chains	Responsive Supply Chains
Operation strategy	Make-to-stock or standardized services or products; emphasize high volumes	Assemble-to-order, make-to-order, or customized services or products; emphasize variety
Capacity cushion	Low	High
Inventory investment	Low; enable high inventory turns	As needed to enable fast delivery time
Lead time	Shorten, but do not increase costs	Shorten aggressively
Supplier selection	Emphasize low prices, consistent quality, on-time delivery	Emphasize fast delivery time, customization, variety, volume flexibility, top quality

times, but care must be taken to use tactics that do not appreciably increase costs. For example, lead times for a supplier could be shortened by switching from rail to air transportation; however, the added cost may offset the savings obtained from the shorter lead times. Suppliers should be selected with emphasis on low prices, consistent quality, and on-time delivery. Because of low capacity cushions, disruptions in an efficient supply chain can be costly and must be avoided.

By contrast, firms in a responsive supply chain should be flexible and have high capacity cushions. WIP inventories should be positioned in the chain to support delivery speed, but inventories of expensive finished goods should be avoided. Firms should aggressively work with their suppliers to shorten lead times because it allows them to wait longer before committing to a customer order—it gives them greater flexibility, in other words. Firms should select suppliers to support the competitive priorities of the services or products provided, which in this case would include the ability to provide quick deliveries, customize services or components, adjust volumes quickly to match demand cycles, offer variety, and provide top quality. Our discussion of Dell Inc. at the beginning of this chapter is an example of the use of a responsive supply chain for competitive advantage.

Poor supply chain performance often is the result of using the wrong supply chain design for the services or products provided. A common mistake is to use an efficient supply chain in an environment that calls for a responsive supply chain. Over time, a firm may add options to its basic service or product, or introduce variations, so that the variety of its offerings increases dramatically and demand for any given service or product predictability drops. Yet, the firm continues to measure the performance of its supply chain as it always has, emphasizing efficiency, even when contribution margins would allow a responsive supply chain design. Clearly, aligning supply chain operations to the firm's competitive priorities has strategic implications.

MASS CUSTOMIZATION

A firm's operations strategy addresses certain competitive priorities that will win orders from customers. Often customers want more than a wide selection of standard services or products; they want a personalized service or product and they want it fast. For example, suppose you want to paint your living room a new color. You need to complement all of the existing furnishings, wall decorations, and carpet. You go to your local paint retail store and select a color from a stack of books that spans every color of the rainbow. The store can give you all the paint you need in your selected color while you wait. How can the store provide that service economically? Certainly the store cannot stock thousands of colors in sufficient quantities for any job. The store stocks the base colors and pigments separately and mixes them as needed, thereby supplying an unlimited variety of colors without maintaining the inventory required to match each customer's particular color needs. The paint retailer is practicing a strategy known as **mass customization**, whereby a firm's flexible processes generate a wide

mass customization

A strategy whereby a firm's flexible processes generate a wide variety of personalized services or products at reasonably low costs.

variety of personalized services or products at reasonably low costs. Essentially, the firm allows customers to select from a variety of standard options to create the service or product of their choice.

Competitive Advantages A mass customization strategy has three important competitive advantages.[3]

- *Managing Customer Relationships.* Mass customization requires detailed inputs from customers so that the ideal service or product can be produced. The firm can learn a lot about its customers from the data it receives. Once customers are in the database, the firm can keep track of them over time. For example, at My Twinn doll company's Web site, kids can create their own doll onscreen, selecting its hair style, skin, hair, and eye colors, facial features, and clothing. Artisans can even match the doll face to the child's face from a photo you supply. Once the customer receives the custom-assembled doll, My Twinn continues to market clothing and accessories as the "doll" grows up with its human twin. A significant competitive advantage is realized through these close customer relationships based on a strategy of mass customization.

- *Eliminate Finished Goods Inventory.* Producing to a customer's order is more efficient than producing to a forecast because forecasts are not perfect. The trick is to have everything you need to produce the order quickly. A technology some firms use for their order placement process is a software system called a *configurator*, which gives firms and customers easy access to data relevant to the options available for the service or product. Both Dell and Gateway use configurators that allow customers to design their own computer from a set of standard components that are in stock. Once the order is placed, the product is assembled and then delivered. Using sales promotions, the firm can exercise some control over the requirements for the inventory of components by steering customers away from options that are out of stock in favor of options that are in stock. This capability takes pressure off the supply chain while keeping the customer satisfied.

  Service providers also take advantage of mass customization to reduce the level of inventory. British Airways is trying to personalize the service of customers once they are on board. It has a software system that tracks the preferences of its most favored customers down to the magazines they read. This information allows the airline to more accurately plan what to pack on each flight. This information saves the airline a significant amount of money because it doesn't pack amenities passengers don't want.

- *Increase Perceived Value of Services or Products.* With mass customization, customers can have it their way. Take, for example, the ultralight two-seater Swatchmobile, the European product of a joint venture between DaimlerChrysler and the Swiss maker of Swatch watches. Customers can use a menu of mix-and-match components to design their own car. With only 13 suppliers that provide major modules, the car can be assembled in only 4.5 hours, far less than the 20 hours required for the assembly of most nonmodular cars. Mass customization avoids confusion and excessive delivery delays, thereby saving costs. In general, mass customization often has a higher value in the mind of the customer than it actually costs to produce. This perception allows firms to charge prices that provide a nice margin.

Supply Chain Design How does mass customization affect the design of supply chains? We address three major considerations. First, the underlying process design is an assemble-to-order strategy. This strategy involves two stages in the provision of the service or product. Initially, standardized components are produced or purchased and held in stock. This stage is important because it enables the firm to produce or purchase these standard items in large volumes to keep the costs low. In the second stage the firm assembles these standard components to a specific customer order. In mass customization, this

Employees at DaimlerChrysler's Smart division assemble a Smart Roadster car at the company's plant in Hambach, France. The company has a unique arrangement with its suppliers. The suppliers provide the equipment and staff for the plant so that they can respond quickly to changes in requirements, thereby supporting the mass customization of the Swatchmobile.

---

[3]Laurie J. Flynn, "Built to Order," *Knowledge Management* (December 11, 2000), www.destinationkm.com.

stage must flexible to handle a large number of potential combinations, and be capable of producing the order quickly and accurately. For example, for the My Twinn customized dolls, customers can choose from more than 325,000 different doll combinations. To ensure accuracy, the Web site steps the customer through the required choices and allows the customer to see the doll as the various options are chosen. Managerial Practice 10.4 shows how Lands' End implemented mass customization and how computer and process technology played a big role.

Second, the service or product must have a modular design that enables the "customization" the customer desires. This approach requires careful attention to service/product designs so that the assembly can be done economically and fast in response to a customer order. This concept is useful to service providers as well as manufacturers. For example, The Ritz-Carlton, an upscale chain of hotels, records the preferences expressed by customers during their stay and uses them to tailor the services the customers receive on their next visit. Requests for items such as hypoallergenic pillows, additional towels, or even chocolate chip cookies are recorded for future use. When the customer checks in, special services and facilitating goods are added to the customized service package.

Finally, successful mass customizers postpone the task of differentiating a service or product for a specific customer until the last possible moment. **Postponement** is an organizational concept whereby some of the final activities in the provision of a service or product are delayed until the orders are received. Doing so allows the greatest application of standard modules of the service package or product before specific customization is done. Postponement is a key decision because it specifies where in the process volume-oriented, standardized operations are separated from custom-oriented, assembly operations. Sometimes the final customization occurs in the last step. For example, Travelocity, an online travel agency, was built around the Sabre travel reservation system—a massive standardized database system for searching and booking travel itineraries. Using a slick customer interface system, Travelocity postpones the actual assembly of itineraries until the very last moment

postponement

An organizational concept whereby some of the final activities in the provision of a service or product are delayed until the orders are received.

MANAGERIAL PRACTICE | 10.4 | MASS CUSTOMIZATION AT LANDS' END

Have you ever felt that your jeans could use a little more room here, and little less room there, a little shorter or a little longer? Have you ever wondered what a pair of jeans made for your body would feel like? If so, Lands' End, a Dodgeville, Wisconsin, catalog and online retailer, is looking for you. Here's how you can get a customized pair of jeans. You complete a brief online profile by answering a few simple questions regarding things such as height, weight, shoe size, and several other body shape details and exercise habits—nothing requiring complicated measurements. Your information is used by a sophisticated program from Archetype Solutions, Inc., to create a mathematical model of your body. The reason that you do not have to give a lot of data about your body is that the system makes use of a massive database of more than 5 million detailed sets of body measurements to calculate all of the other measurements needed for your jeans. You also select pocket options, fit styles, and colors. Click "Submit" and in two to three weeks you can expect your jeans to be delivered to your home. One more thing—you need to pay. Expect to spend $20 to $30 *more* than the standard version of your jeans.

Your part in the process is quite simple. However, behind the scenes it is quite different. Lands' End decided to try to mass customize jeans and chino slacks just to garner publicity and increase the sales of its other products. What a surprise when management discovered that online sales of customized chinos well exceeded projections and that 25 percent of new customers purchased customized clothing. How does mass customization work at Lands' End? Each night Lands' End gathers orders posted on their Web site and electronically sends them to Archetype, where the software replicates the customer's body size and weight distribution, factors in individual fit preferences, and adjusts the basic fabric patterns accordingly. The files are then sent to a contract manufacturer in Mexico. The supplier transfers the individual patterns to numerically controlled cutting equipment that cuts one layer of fabric at a time. After the various pieces of the pants have been cut, they are bagged and moved to an eight-machine sewing process, where the pants flow through one at a time. The last station in the process checks five critical measurements on each pair of pants. If any are incorrect, the pants are scrapped and remade. The garments are bulk shipped to a distribution center to clear U.S. customs, and then sorted, packaged, and mailed directly to customers.

Success did not come without some headaches, however. Lands' End had to train its Mexican manufacturing partners, which had to switch to new machinery. The new manufacturing process is far different from producing mass quantities, which relied on batch processing. Nonetheless, the mass customization strategy is proving to be profitable. Lands' End is expanding the strategy to dress shirts and tailored pants with partners in the Dominican Republic and expanding jeans and chino capacity in the Far East.

Sources: David Drickhammer, "A Leg Up on Mass Customization," *Industry Week* (September 1, 2002); Anne D'Innocenzio, "Lands' End Adds More Size Options Online," *The Mercury News* (September 9, 2002); www.landsend.com.

when the customer actively participates in the choice of a final package. Travelocity uses its databases proactively to e-mail travel information to customers as well as to maintain customized travel pages for them.

The assemble-to-order strategy can be extended to supply chains. The costs of inventory and transportation often determine the extent that a manufacturer uses postponement in the supply chain. With postponement, manufacturers can avoid inventory buildup. Some firms take advantage of a process called **channel assembly**, whereby members of the distribution channel act as if they were assembly stations in the factory. Distribution centers or warehouses can perform the last-minute customizing operations after specific orders have been received. This approach is particularly useful when the required customizing has some geographical rationale, such language differences or technical requirements. Hewlett-Packard provides a good example. Hewlett-Packard postpones the assembly of its printers needing a country-specific power supply and a language-specific user's manual until the last step in the process, which is performed by the distributor in the region where the printer is being delivered. In general, beyond the inventory advantages, the advantage of postponement in the distribution channel is that the firm's plants can focus on the standardized aspects of the product, while the distributor can focus on customizing a product that may require additional components from local suppliers.

> **channel assembly**
>
> The process of using members of the distribution channel as if they were assembly stations in the factory.

LEAN SUPPLY CHAINS

As we discussed in Chapter 9, "Lean Systems," Toyota's production system has been touted as the premier example of a lean manufacturing system. The trick is to apply this "leanness" to the supply chain. A major difference, however, is that the firm must now deal with independent customers and suppliers rather than its own in-house processes. A starting point is to develop an integrated supply chain, which we already discussed, and to apply lean systems to all of its internal processes. Beyond that, three key activities are required to attain a lean supply chain.

- *Strategic Sourcing.* Regardless of whether the firm is a service provider or a manufacturer, an essential step is to identify items or services that are of high value or complexity and purchase them from a select set of suppliers with whom the firm establishes a close relationship. These strategic suppliers should offer high quality and delivery performance. Commodities with low value can be sourced using conventional approaches such as competitive bidding and reverse auctions.

- *Cost Management.* The traditional approach to driving costs out of the supply chain is to focus on price reductions through tough negotiations. By limiting the number of suppliers, the lean supply chain approach gives the firm more time to work with its strategic suppliers to reduce costs by changing the cost structure, not by negotiating prices. Realistically, reducing a supplier's profit margin is not an effective long-term strategy. Helping the supplier reduce its costs, while keeping its margins intact, allows it to remain profitable as well as reduce prices for the buyer. This method necessitates developing cost standards and then collaborating with the supplier to reduce costs. Such collaboration is difficult to obtain because it requires mutual trust, integrity, and confidentiality between the firm and the supplier. Nonetheless, an effective cost management program helps to identify areas where improvements can be made.

- *Supplier Development.* Developing a lean supply chain is a long-term effort because, in part, it requires a shift from price negotiation to cost management. Further, the firm may have to devote its own personnel to work with the supplier to achieve lean operations. These efforts, although initially costly, can result in dramatic improvements in process improvements, operational productivity, quality, and delivery performance. Obviously, such an effort should focus on the firm's strategic suppliers.

Delphi, a $28 billion world leader in mobile electronics and transportation components and systems technology, is experiencing the benefits of a lean supply chain.[4] The suppliers

---

[4]R. David Nelson, "How Delphi Went Lean," *Supply Chain Management Review* (November–December 2004), pp. 32–37.

involved in the process are realizing the same double-digit improvements as Delphi, which include reductions of 20 to 50 percent in labor costs, increases in productivity from 30 to 60 percent, and improved first-time quality from 10 to 45 percent.

OUTSOURCING AND OFFSHORING

All businesses buy at least some inputs to their processes (such as professional services, raw materials, or manufactured parts) from other producers. Most businesses also purchase services to get their products to their customers. How many of the processes that produce those purchased items and services should a firm own and operate instead? The answer to that question determines the extent of the firm's vertical integration. The more processes in the value chain that the organization performs itself, the more vertically integrated it is. If it does not perform some processes itself, it must rely on **outsourcing**, or paying suppliers and distributors to perform those processes and provide needed services and materials. When managers opt for more vertical integration, by definition less outsourcing occurs. These decisions are sometimes called **make-or-buy decisions**, with a *make* decision meaning more integration and a *buy* decision meaning more outsourcing. After deciding what to outsource and what to do in-house, management must find ways to coordinate and integrate the various processes and suppliers involved.

Vertical Integration Vertical integration can be in two directions. **Backward integration** represents a firm's movement upstream toward the sources of raw materials, parts, and services through acquisitions, such as a major grocery chain having its own plants to produce house brands of ice cream, frozen pizza dough, and peanut butter. **Forward integration** means that the firm acquires more channels of distribution, such as its own distribution centers (warehouses) and retail stores. It can also mean that the firm goes even further by acquiring its business customers. A firm chooses vertical integration when it has the skills, volume, and resources to hit the competitive priorities better than outsiders can. Doing the work within its organizational structure may mean better quality and more timely delivery, as well as taking better advantage of the firm's human resources, equipment, and space. Extensive vertical integration is generally attractive when input volumes are high because high volumes allow task specialization and greater efficiency. It is also attractive if the firm has the relevant skills and views the processes that it is integrating as particularly important to its future success.

Management must identify, cultivate, and exploit its core competencies to prevail in global competition. Recall that core competencies are the collective learning of the firm, especially its ability for coordinating diverse processes and integrating multiple technologies. They define the firm and provide its reason for existence. Management must be constantly attentive to bolstering core competencies, perhaps by looking upstream toward its suppliers and downstream toward its customers and acquiring those processes that support its core competencies—those that allow the firm to organize work and deliver value better than its competitors. To do otherwise poses a risk that the firm will lose control over critical areas of its business.

Outsourcing Notwithstanding the arguments in favor of increased vertical integration, many firms are outsourcing important processes. The NCNB bank in Charlotte, North Carolina, outsourced the processing of card transactions and saved $5 million per year. Merrill Lynch, Sears Roebuck, and Texaco outsource their mailroom and photocopying operations to Pitney Bowes Management Services. Many firms do the same with payroll, security, cleaning, and other types of services, rather than employ personnel to provide these services. One recent survey showed that 35 percent of more than 1,000 large corporations have increased the amount of outsourcing they do. Outsourcing is particularly attractive to those that have low volumes. For example, LoanCity.com, an online mortgage company, set up shop in August 1999. It started life with zero revenue but planned to serve more than a million customers in a few years. Any online operation of that size would require a sprawling computing center, which in turn would require a few million dollars of hardware, software licenses, and a staff of as many as 20 specialists. Instead, the company hired an application service provider (ASP) to set up and run the various business-software packages needed to handle its sales, accounting, and human resource processes. LoanCity's

outsourcing

Paying suppliers and distributors to perform processes and provide needed services and materials.

make-or-buy decision

A managerial choice between whether to outsource a process or do it in-house.

backward integration

A firm's movement upstream toward the sources of raw materials, parts, and services through acquisitions.

forward integration

Acquiring more channels of distribution, such as distribution centers (warehouses) and retail stores, or even business customers.

employees then use the Internet to connect to the applications they need housed on machines located at the ASP.

What prompted these firms to outsource rather than vertically integrate? These firms realized that another firm can perform the outsourced process more efficiently and with better quality than they can. They opted to add external suppliers to their supply chains rather than to keep internal suppliers. However, the outsourcing decision is a serious one because the firm can lose the skills and knowledge needed to conduct the process. All learning about process advancements is left to the outsourcing partner, which makes it difficult to ever bring that process back into the firm.

Offshoring The strategy of globalizing a firm adds a new dimension to the development of supply chains. **Offshoring** is a supply chain strategy that involves moving processes to another country. As such, offshoring is more encompassing than outsourcing because it also includes vertical integration by locating internal processes in other countries. Firms are motivated to initiate operations offshore by the market potential and the cost advantages it provides. The firm may be able to create new markets because of its presence in other countries and its ability to offer competitive prices due to its cost efficiencies. Competitive priorities other than low costs, such as delivery speed to distant customers, can drive the decision, too. As for costs, several factors drive the offshoring strategy.

> **offshoring**
>
> A supply chain strategy that involves moving processes to another country.

- *Comparative Labor Costs.* Some countries have a huge edge when it comes to labor costs. Two countries with a major advantage are India and China. In India, the salary for a computer programmer is about one-sixth that of a programmer in the United States with comparable skills. It is no wonder that firms move programming processes to India. In China, the average monthly wages are less than 4 percent of those in Japan. In general, firms can save from 30 to 50 percent on labor costs by relocating processes to low labor-cost countries.

- *Logistics Costs.* Even if labor costs are not favorable, it may still be less costly to offshore processes to other countries to reduce the logistical costs of delivering products to international customers. For example, Hewlett-Packard sourced the final assembly of a computer server to Singapore and Australia, two higher-cost locations, to get closer to targeted customers in Australia and Southeast Asia. The savings in logistical costs offset the higher labor costs in those countries.

- *Tariffs and Taxes.* Some countries offer tax incentives to firms that do business within their borders. Tariffs can also be a stumbling block for firms looking to do business in a country. Sometimes they are high enough that the firm decides to assemble the products in that country rather than export the products in. Hewlett-Packard decided to assemble a product in India with imported parts for sale to Indian customers for that reason.

- *Labor Laws and Unions.* Some countries have fewer unions or restrictions on the flexible use of labor. The ability to use workers to perform a number of different tasks without restrictions can be important to firms trying to achieve flexibility in operations. Nonetheless, firms must be cognizant of local labor laws and customs and strive to achieve a high level of ethical behavior when doing business in other countries.

- *Internet.* The Internet reduces the transaction costs of managing distant partners or operations.

Even though offshoring appears to offer some big advantages, it also has some pitfalls that firms should carefully explore before using this strategy.

- *Pulling the Plug Too Quickly.* A major mistake is to decide to offshore a process before making a good-faith effort to fix the existing one. We discussed many ways to improve processes in Parts 1 and 2 of this text; these methods should be explored first. It is not always the case that offshoring or outsourcing is the answer, even if local labor wages far exceed those of other countries. Canon, for example, decided to keep its manufacturing in Japan rather than shift it to lower-cost countries in Southeast Asia. The strategy is to compete on technology innovations via its line of high-end cameras. To achieve that strategy, Canon kept its new product development process and its manufacturing process close to each other to support speedy new product introductions and communication between engineers and manufacturing managers. Canon improved its manufacturing process by removing its assembly lines and replacing them with manufacturing cells, thereby improving teamwork, reducing its inventory and factory costs, and increasing its ability to make innovative products faster. The message: Make sure you really need to offshore in order to accomplish your operations strategy.

■ *Technology Transfer.* Often an offshoring strategy involves creating a *joint venture* with a company in another country. With a joint venture, two firms agree to jointly produce a service or product together. Typically a transfer of technology takes place to bring one partner up to speed regarding the service or product. The danger is that the firm with the technology advantage will essentially be setting up the other firm to be a future competitor. For example, GM set up a joint venture with the Shanghai Auto Industry Corporation (SAIC) to produce Buicks. SAIC got a license to use GM's technical know-how in the form of drawings, blueprints, math data, and computer files. As GM develops local engineering design capability, it transfers technical knowledge to the Chinese staff. Because SAIC is planning to develop and produce its own cars, it is possible that GM and other joint venture partners with SAIC are creating a new competitor in China.

■ *Process Integration.* Despite the power of the Internet, it is difficult to fully integrate offshore processes with the firm's other processes. Time, distance, and communication can be formidable hurdles. Managing offshore processes won't be the same as managing processes located next door. Often considerable managerial time must be expended to coordinate offshore processes.

VIRTUAL SUPPLY CHAINS

The advent of the Internet opened an entirely new set of opportunities for supply chain design. Many companies redesign their supply chains to outsource some part of their entire order fulfillment process with the help of sophisticated, Web-based information technology support packages. In effect, these companies manage the order fulfillment aspects of their business as if the process was actually in-house. Nike, for example, coordinates the manufacture and distribution of its sporting apparel and athletic shoes worldwide without owning the facilities responsible for these processes. This approach allows Nike to focus on its core processes of customer relationship and new product development. About 30 percent of all Internet retailers embrace the idea of virtual supply chains by using a technique called *drop shipping*, whereby a retailer passes customer orders directly to a wholesaler or manufacturer, which then ships the order directly to the customer with the retailer's label on it. These retailers outsource their warehouse operations to avoid the costs of holding their own inventories.

The benefits from using virtual supply chains include the following:

■ *Reduced Investment in Inventories and Order Fulfillment Infrastructure.* The investment in inventory, equipment, warehouses, and personnel to operate an order fulfillment process is significant. The firm must generate high volumes to make it pay off.

■ *Greater Service or Product Variety.* Without the overhead of one's own order fulfillment process, the firm can have the freedom to select from a wide variety of wholesalers, service providers, and manufacturers, thereby providing the firm the flexibility to match dynamic competitive priorities.

■ *Lower Costs Due to Economies of Scale.* The supplier typically handles more volume than does the firm doing the outsourcing because the supplier may have a number of customers for the same service or product. This added volume opens the possibility that the costs of the outsourcing firm will be much lower than if the order fulfillment process were done in-house.

■ *Lower Transportation Costs.* Retailers realize the advantage of lower transportation costs. Traditionally, retailers pay transportation costs to acquire the goods from a wholesaler and then pay to have the goods shipped to the customer. With drop shipping in a virtual supply chain, the only transportation cost is shipping the goods from the wholesaler to the customer.

Virtual supply chains are not a panacea for all the problems service providers or manufacturers face in the design of their supply chains. First, a lack of information transparency between a firm and its order fulfillment partner can cause customer service problems. For example, the firm needs to know whether the order fulfillment partner has the inventory to transact a sale or enough capacity to provide a critical service. Acquiring the appropriate software may be prohibitive. Second, outsourcing the order fulfillment process makes the outsourcing firm vulnerable to *order rationing* by the order fulfillment partner. Order rationing occurs when the order fulfillment partner does not have enough capacity or inventory to satisfy all the orders from its customers, and the order fulfillment partner then imposes some rationing process across all customers. Finally, increased information transparency between the firm and its order fulfillment partner poses the risk that the order fulfillment partner could use the information to bypass the firm completely and go directly to the customers.

Supply chain designers must choose between the traditional approach, which keeps the order fulfillment process in-house, and the virtual supply chain. The traditional approach is favored in these circumstances:

■ *Sales Volumes Are High.* The volumes are needed to offset the high infrastructure costs. It can also be a strategic move. If a firm wants to grow and dominate its industry, keeping the order fulfillment process in-house is important.

■ *Order Consolidation Is Important.* Virtual supply chains lose their appeal if many suppliers are needed to satisfy a single customer's order. Coordination is difficult and transportation costs increase because of inefficiencies in shipping. With the traditional approach, the firm has its own warehouses and can coordinate the supplies from a large group of suppliers. Nonetheless, the need for order consolidation in virtual supply chains opens the door of opportunity for *third-party logistics (3PL) providers.* For example, FedEx partnered with Cisco to coordinate the shipments of many independent suppliers to make sure that all components of major systems arrive at the customer within a small window of time.

■ *Small-Order Fulfillment Capability of Suppliers Is Important.* Retaining the order fulfillment process, particularly in warehouse operations, may be necessary if it is important for customers that deal with small quantities, and the suppliers do not have the capability to handle small orders. Although small-order fulfillment technology is becoming more common, manufacturers in many industries still do not have the capability. The durable goods industry is a good example.

The virtual supply chain approach is favored in these circumstances:

■ *Demand Is Highly Volatile.* Volatile demand presents risks for holding inventories, which can prove costly for a firm. A more cost-effective approach may be to find a supplier that is supplying the same stock item for other firms with similar demand uncertainties. The suppliers can smooth the random fluctuations in demands from multiple customers and provide the item at a cost-effective price, with less risk of stockouts.

■ *High Service or Product Variety Is Important.* Partnering with a supplier can broaden the provision of services or products dramatically. For example, a typical Circuit City store carries 500 to 3,000 movie titles. When designing the Internet presence for the company, management discovered that Internet shoppers expected to have about 55,000 titles to choose from. The solution was to partner with another company to provide the product variety. Shoppers using CircuitCity.com can now place orders for movie titles, which will be fulfilled through virtual inventories.

The trade-offs between a traditional approach to the order fulfillment process and virtual supply chains are important considerations for a firm. This choice involves two other implications: First, virtual supply chains relinquish direct control of the order fulfillment process to other firms. Consequently, it is important to have the appropriate contractual relationship with members of the virtual supply chain. Strategic alliances, partnerships, and long-term contracts provide much more control than do short-term contracts. The more important an activity is for the achievement of the firm's competitive priorities, the greater the degree of control the firm will want. Second, virtual supply chains provide the firm with more flexibility to change the design of its service packages or its products because it does not have the heavy overhead investment in the order fulfillment process.

The firm needs to balance the need for control against the need for flexibility in choosing its supply chain design.

The concept of virtual supply chains carries over to value chains, which include linkages to supporting processes. Managerial Practice 10.5 shows how one company found a niche by supplying services to major corporations, and thereby becoming an important supplier in its customers' value chains.

MANAGERIAL **PRACTICE**	10.5	HCL CORPORATION PROVIDES SERVICE PROCESSES IN VIRTUAL VALUE CHAINS

HCL Corporation is a $600 million transnational group with interests in computers, networking, office automation, systems integration, software services, consulting, and computer-based education. With major technology centers located in India, the company has joint ventures, partnerships, and strategic alliances with a host of international giants, including Hewlett-Packard, Perot Systems Corporation, Microsoft, Cisco, and Cigna Corporation. HCL works with its customers to design certain business processes and then operates them from remote locations around the world. With the help of advanced technology and high-speed Internet connections, the processes become part of the customer's virtual value chain. Processes that HCL manages for clients in virtual value chains include process support services and contact center services, among many others in sales and marketing and software development.

Process Support

HCL provides customers the opportunity to outsource process support services, such as human resource services, accounting, and transaction services.

- *Human Resource Services.* Country service representatives from HCL have knowledge about country-specific human resource policies, rules, and regulations, in addition to communication and language skills. The services HCL can provide include health and benefits administration, employee record management, visa filing and administration, resume management, and payroll. HCL can also provide a complete Web-enabled secretarial assistance service for customers. For example, a work task from a customer of a client of HCL, an online secretarial services company in the United Kingdom, goes to an HCL *back office* located in India, where it follows a defined process and is sent back to a team at the client's firm, and then finally goes back to the client's customer. These services are provided around the clock by using a center located in India; however, the center could have been located anywhere in the world.

- *Accounting Services.* Customers can completely outsource their accounting processes and have the services performed anywhere in the world. To accomplish this feat, HCL must be skilled at understanding the customer-specific regulatory and compliance requirements. Typical services include accounts payable, general accounting, customer invoicing, credit and collections, accounts receivables, fixed-asset accounting, and travel and expense accounting.

- *Transaction Services.* Speed and accuracy are important for these services. HCL needs to be responsive to the requests of the cus-

Many companies outsource their transaction services, which may be provided from locations anywhere in the world. Here, employees process health insurance data from a U.S. firm at an office in Accra, the capital of Ghana.

tomers of their customer. Typical services include customer database maintenance, customer e-mail responses, customer correspondence, application capture, claims processing, and underwriting.

Contact Center Services

Companies can outsource their customer contact services; however, it is a major decision because of the high level of personal interaction with customers. HCL and other companies in this business must have personnel with high levels of language, interaction, and accent-sensitive skills. A major advantage of Web-enabled contact center services is that the customer has 24/7 access, which nicely supports global businesses. Typical services include surveys, help desks, order capture, collection, verification, authorization calls, and customer inquiries.

HCL Corporation is but one example of a firm that found a niche making virtual value chains feasible for a number of leading companies.

Sources: www.perotsystems.com, 2001; HCL Perot Systems; www.hcltech.com, 2004.

> STUDENT CD-ROM AND INTERNET RESOURCES <

The Student CD-ROM and the Companion Website at **www.prenhall.com/krajewski** contain many tools, activities, and resources designed for this chapter.

> KEY EQUATIONS <

1. Weeks of supply $= \dfrac{\text{Average aggregate inventory value}}{\text{Weekly sales (at cost)}}$

2. Inventory turnover $= \dfrac{\text{Annual sales (at cost)}}{\text{Average aggregate inventory value}}$

> KEY TERMS <

auction 392
average aggregate inventory value 376
backward integration 401
bullwhip effect 381
catalog hubs 392
centralized placement 386
channel assembly 400
competitive orientation 390
continuous replenishment program
    (CRP) 387
cooperative orientation 391
cross-docking 389
early supplier involvement 393
electronic commerce (e-commerce) 383

electronic data interchange (EDI) 391
exchange 392
finished goods (FG) 376
forward integration 401
forward placement 386
green purchasing 390
inventory 374
inventory pooling 386
inventory turnover 378
make-or-buy decision 401
mass customization 397
offshoring 402
outsourcing 401
postponement 399

presourcing 393
purchasing 390
radio frequency identification
    (RFID) 387
raw materials (RM) 376
sole sourcing 391
supply chain 372
supply chain management 372
supply chain strategy 372
value analysis 393
vendor-managed inventories (VMI) 386
weeks of supply 377
work-in-process (WIP) 376

> SOLVED PROBLEM 1 <

A firm's cost of goods sold last year was $3,410,000, and the firm operates 52 weeks per year. It carries seven items in inventory: three raw materials, two work-in-process items, and two finished goods. The following table contains last year's average inventory level for each item, along with its value.

a. What is the average aggregate inventory value?

b. What is the weeks of supply the firm maintains?

c. What was the inventory turnover last year?

Category	Part Number	Average Level	Unit Value
Raw materials	1	15,000	$ 3.00
	2	2,500	5.00
	3	3,000	1.00
Work-in-process	4	5,000	14.00
	5	4,000	18.00
Finished goods	6	2,000	48.00
	7	1,000	62.00

SOLUTION

a.

Part Number	Average Level		Unit Value		Total Value
1	15,000	×	$3.00	=	$ 45,000
2	2,500	×	5.00	=	12,500
3	3,000	×	1.00	=	3,000
4	5,000	×	14.00	=	70,000
5	4,000	×	18.00	=	72,000
6	2,000	×	48.00	=	96,000
7	1,000	×	62.00	=	62,000
	Average aggregate inventory value			=	$360,500

b. Average weekly sales at cost = $3,410,000/52 weeks = $65,577/week

$$\text{Weeks of supply} = \frac{\text{Average aggregate inventory value}}{\text{Weekly sales (at cost)}} = \frac{\$360,500}{\$65,577} = 5.5 \text{ weeks}$$

c. $$\text{Inventory turnover} = \frac{\text{Annual sales (at cost)}}{\text{Average aggregate inventory value}} = \frac{\$3,410,000}{\$360,500} = 9.5 \text{ turns}$$

> DISCUSSION QUESTIONS <

1. Under the Defense Industry Initiative on Business Ethics and Conduct, 46 contractors agreed to establish internal codes of ethics, to conduct training sessions, and to report suspected abuses.

   a. Is this initiative an example of moving toward competitive or cooperative supplier relations?

   b. Suppose that you are a defense contracts manager. You have a friend in the military whom you have known for 20 years. As a gesture of friendship, she offers useful inside information about a competing contractor's bid. What would you do if your company were part of the industry's ethics project? What would you do if your company were not part of it?

   c. To build a win–win relationship with its suppliers, the armed forces made agreements calling for suppliers to be reimbursed for the costs of supplier training and employee morale-building programs. According to that agreement, your company decided to hold a private party for employees to "build morale." Because the expenses were to be reimbursed, the party planners were not especially careful in making the arrangements and got carried away. They rented the city auditorium and hired a nationally known music group to provide entertainment. Furthermore, the planners did not do a good job of contract negotiation and ended up paying five times the going rate for these services. The bill for the party now reaches your desk: $250,000! Under the terms of your agreement, your company is entitled to reimbursement of the entire amount. What should you do?

2. DaimlerChrysler and General Motors vigorously compete with each other in many automobile and truck markets. When Jose Ignacio Lopez was vice president of purchasing for GM, he made it clear that his buyers were not to accept luncheon invitations from suppliers. Thomas Stalcamp, head of purchasing for Chrysler before the merger with Daimler, instructed his buyers to take suppliers to lunch. Rationalize these two directives in light of supply chain design and management.

3. The Wal-Mart retail chain enjoys great purchasing clout with its suppliers. The Limited retail chain owns Mast Industries, which is responsible for producing many of the fashion items sold in The Limited stores. The Limited boasts that it can go from the concept for a new garment to the store shelf in 1,000 hours. Compare and contrast the implications for supply chain strategy for these two retail systems.

4. Canon, a Japanese manufacturer of photographic equipment, decided against offshoring and kept its manufacturing and new product development processes in Japan, which has relatively high labor costs. In contrast, GM, headquartered in the United States, has a joint venture with Shanghai Auto Industry Corporation to produce cars in China. Given our discussion of offshoring and supply chain strategies, explain why these two companies chose different approaches to their supply chains.

> PROBLEMS <

Software, such as OM Explorer, Active Models, and POM for Windows, is packaged with every new copy of the textbook. Check with your instructor on how best to use it. In many cases, the instructor wants you to understand how to do the calculations by hand. At most, the software provides a check on your calculations. When calculations are particularly complex and the goal is interpreting the results in making decisions, the software replaces entirely the manual calculations. The software also can be a valuable resource well after your course is completed.

1. Buzzrite, a retailer of casual clothes, ended the current year with annual sales (at cost) of $48 million. During the year, the inventory of apparel turned over six times. For the next year, Buzzrite plans to increase annual sales (at cost) by 25 percent.

   a. What is the increase in the average aggregate inventory value required if Buzzrite maintains the same inventory turnover during the next year?

   b. What change in inventory turns must Buzzrite achieve if, through better supply chain management, it wants to support next year's sales with no increase in the average aggregate inventory value?

2. Jack Jones, the materials manager at Precision Enterprises, is beginning to look for ways to reduce inventories. A recent accounting statement shows the following inventory investment by category: raw materials, $3,129,500; work-in-process, $6,237,000; and finished goods, $2,686,500. This year's cost of goods sold will be about $32.5 million. Assuming 52 business weeks per year, express total inventory as

   a. Weeks of supply

   b. Inventory turns

3. One product line has 10 turns per year and an annual sales volume (at cost) of $985,000. How much inventory is being held, on average?

4. The Bawl Corporation supplies alloy ball bearings to auto manufacturers in Detroit. Because of its specialized manufacturing process, considerable work-in-process and raw materials are needed. The current inventory levels are $2,470,000 and $1,566,000, respectively. In addition, finished goods inventory is $1,200,000 and sales (at cost) for the current year are expected to be about $48 million. Express total inventory as

   a. Weeks of supply

   b. Inventory turns

5. The following data were collected for a retailer:

Cost of goods sold	$3,500,000
Gross profit	$ 700,000
Operating costs	$ 500,000
Operating profit	$ 200,000
Total inventory	$1,200,000
Fixed assets	$ 750,000
Long-term debt	$ 300,000

   Assuming 52 business weeks per year, express total inventory as

   a. Weeks of supply

   b. Inventory turns

ADVANCED PROBLEMS

Problems 6 and 7 require prior reading of Supplement A, "Decision Making."

6. The Bennet Company purchases one of its essential raw materials from three suppliers. Bennet's current policy is to distribute purchases equally among the three. The owner's son, Benjamin Bennet, just graduated from business college. He proposes that these suppliers be rated (high numbers mean a good performance) on six performance criteria weighted as shown in Table 10.4. A total score hurdle of 0.60 is proposed to screen suppliers. Purchasing policy would be revised to order raw materials from suppliers with performance scores greater than the total score hurdle, in proportion to their performance rating scores.

		Rating		
Performance Criterion	**Weight**	**Supplier A**	**Supplier B**	**Supplier C**
1. Price	0.2	0.6	0.5	0.9
2. Quality	0.2	0.6	0.4	0.8
3. Delivery	0.3	0.6	0.3	0.8
4. Production facilities	0.1	0.5	0.9	0.6
5. Warranty and claims policy	0.1	0.7	0.8	0.6
6. Financial position	0.1	0.9	0.9	0.7

TABLE 10.4 | Bennet Supplier Performance Scores

TABLE 10.5 | Beagle Supplier Performance Scores

Criteria	Supplier A	Supplier B	Supplier C
Price	8	6	6
Quality	9	7	7
Delivery	7	9	6
Flexibility	5	8	9

a. Use a preference matrix to calculate the total weighted score for each supplier.

b. Which supplier(s) survived the total score hurdle? Under the younger Bennet's proposed policy, what proportion of orders would each supplier receive?

c. What advantages does the proposed policy have over the current policy?

7. Beagle Clothiers uses a weighted score for the evaluation and selection of its suppliers of trendy fashion garments. Each supplier is rated on a 10-point scale (10 = highest) for four different criteria: price, quality, delivery, and flexibility (to accommodate changes in quantity and timing). Because of the volatility of the business in which Beagle operates, flexibility is given twice the weight of each of the other three criteria, which are equally weighted. Table 10.5 shows the scores for three potential suppliers for the four performance criteria. Based on the highest weighted score, which supplier should be selected?

8. Sterling, Inc., operates 52 weeks per year, and its cost of goods sold last year was $6,500,000. The firm carries eight items in inventory: four raw materials, two work-in-process items, and two finished goods. Table 10.6 shows last year's average inventory levels for these items, along with their unit values.

a. What is the average aggregate inventory value?

b. How many weeks of supply does the firm have?

c. What was the inventory turnover last year?

TABLE 10.6 | Sterling Inventory Items

Category	Part Number	Average Inventory Units	Value per Unit
Raw materials	RM-1	20,000	$ 1
	RM-2	5,000	5
	RM-3	3,000	6
	RM-4	1,000	8
Work-in-process	WIP-1	6,000	10
	WIP-2	8,000	12
Finished goods	FG-1	1,000	65
	FG-2	500	88

Scenario

Sonic Distributors produces and sells music CDs. The CDs are pressed at a single facility (factory), issued through the company's distribution center, and sold to the public from various retail stores. The goal is to operate the distribution chain at the lowest total cost.

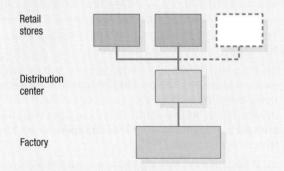

Materials (available from instructor)

Retail and distributor purchase order forms

Factory work order forms

Factory and distributor materials delivery forms

Inventory position worksheets

A means of generating random demand (typically a pair of dice)

Setup

Each team is in the business of manufacturing music CDs and distributing them to retail stores where they are sold. Two or more people play the role of retail outlet buyers. Their task is to determine the demand for the CDs and order replenishment stock from the distributor. The distributor carries forward-placed stock obtained from the factory. The factory produces in lot sizes either to customer order or to stock.

Tasks

Divide into teams of four or five.

Two or three people operate the retail stores.

One person operates the distribution center.

One person schedules production at the factory.

Every day, as play progresses, the participants at each level of the supply chain estimate demand, fill customer orders, record inventory levels, and decide how much to order or produce and when to place orders with their supplier.

Costs and Conditions

Unless your instructor indicates otherwise, the following costs and conditions hold.

Costs

Holding cost per unit per day	Retail outlets: $1.00/CD/day
	Distribution Center: $0.50/CD/day
	Factory: $0.25/CD/day
Pipeline inventory cost	Assume that pipeline cost can be ignored for this exercise (consider it zero).
Ordering cost (retailers and distributors)	$20/order
Factory setup cost (to run an order)	$50 (*Note:* Cost is per order, not per day, because even though successive orders from distributors are for the same item, the factory is busy fabricating other things between orders.)
Stockout (lost margin) cost	Retail Store: $8 per CD sale lost in a period
	$0 for backorders for shortages from the factory or shipping new orders
Shipping cost	Because other products are already being distributed through this chain and because CDs are light and take up little volume, consider the cost to be zero.

Conditions

Starting inventory	Retail stores each have 15 CDs
	Distribution center has 25 CDs
	Factory has 100 CDs
Lot-sizing restrictions	Retail outlets and distribution centers—no minimum order. Any amount may be stored. Factory production lot sizes and capacity—produce in minimum lots of 20. Maximum capacity: 200/day.
Outstanding orders	None

Delays

Ordering Delay. One day to send an order from a retail store to the distributor and from the distributor to the factory (that is, 1 day is lost between placing an order and acting on it).

No delay occurs in starting up production once an order has been received (but one day is needed for delivery of an order from the distributor to the factory).

Delivery Delay. One-day shipping time between the distributor and a retail store and between the factory and the distributor (that is, 1 day is lost between shipping an order and receiving it).

Run the Exercise

For simplicity sake, assume all transactions take place simultaneously at the middle of the day. For every simulated day, the sequence of play goes as follows.

Retailers

a. Each retailer receives any shipment due in from its distributor (one day after shipment) and places it in sales inventory (adds the quantity indicated on any incoming Material Delivery Form from the distributor—after its 1-day delay—to the previous day's ending inventory level on the Retailer's Inventory Position Worksheet). (*Note:* For the first day of the exercise, no order will come in.)

b. The retailers each determine the day's retail demand (the quantity of CDs requested) by rolling a pair of dice. The roll determines the number demanded.

c. Retailers fill demand from available stock, if possible. Demand is filled by subtracting it from the current inventory level to develop the ending inventory level, which is recorded. If demand exceeds supply, sales are lost. Record all lost sales on the worksheet.

d. Retailers determine whether an order should be placed. If an order is required, the desired quantity of CDs is written on a Retail Store Purchase Order, which is forwarded to the distributor (who receives it after a one-day delay). If an order is made, it should be noted on the worksheet. Retailers may also desire to keep track of outstanding orders separately.

Distributor

a. The distributor receives any shipment due in from the factory and places the CDs in available inventory (adds the quantity indicated on any incoming Material Delivery Form from the factory—after its one-day delay—to the previous day's ending inventory level on the distributor's inventory position worksheet).

b. All outstanding backorders are filled (the quantity is subtracted from the current inventory level indicated on the worksheet) and prepared for shipment. CDs are shipped by filling out a Distribution Center Material Delivery Form indicating the quantity of CDs to be delivered.

c. The distributor uses the purchase orders received from the retail stores (after the designated 1-day delay) to prepare shipments for delivery from available inventory.

Quantities shipped are subtracted from the current level to develop the ending inventory level, which is recorded. If insufficient supply exists, backorders are generated.

d. The distributor determines whether a replenishment order should be placed. If an order is required, the quantity of CDs is written on a Distribution Center Purchase Order, which is forwarded to the factory (after a 1-day delay). If an order is made, it should be noted on the worksheet. The distributor may also desire to keep track of outstanding orders separately.

Factory

a. The factory places any available new production into inventory (adds the items produced the previous day to the previous day's ending inventory level on the Factory Inventory Position Worksheet).

b. All outstanding backorders are filled (the quantity is subtracted from the current inventory level indicated on the worksheet) and prepared for shipment. CDs are shipped by filling out a Factory Material Delivery Form, indicating the quantity of CDs to be delivered.

c. The factory obtains the incoming distributor's purchase orders (after the designated one-day delay) and ships them from stock, if it can. These amounts are subtracted from the current values on the inventory worksheet. Any unfilled orders become backorders for the next day.

d. The factory decides whether to issue a work order to produce CDs either to stock or to order. If production is required, a Factory Work Order is issued, and the order is noted on the inventory worksheet. Remember that a setup cost applies to each *production* order. It is important to keep careful track of all production in process.

Remember, once an order has been placed, it cannot be changed and no partial shipments can be made. For each day, record your ending inventory position, backorder or lost sales amount, and whether an order was made (or a production run initiated). After everyone completes the transactions for the day, the sequence repeats, beginning at retailer step (a). Your instructor will tell you how many simulated days to run the exercise.

When the play is stopped, find the cumulative amount of inventory and other costs. You can do so by summing up the numbers in each column and then multiplying these totals by the costs previously listed. Use the total of these costs to assess how well your team operated the distribution chain.

Source: This exercise was developed by Larry Meile, Carroll School of Management, Boston College.

CASE 1   Wolf Motors

John Wolf, president of Wolf Motors, just returned to his office after visiting the company's newly acquired automotive dealership. It was the fourth Wolf Motors' dealership in a network that served a metropolitan area of 400,000 people. Beyond the metropolitan area, but within a 45-minute drive, were another 500,000 people. Each of the dealerships in the network marketed a different make of automobile and historically had operated autonomously.

Wolf was particularly excited about this new dealership because it was the first "auto supermarket" in the network. Auto supermarkets differ from traditional auto dealerships in that they sell multiple makes of automobiles at the same location. The new dealership sold a full line of Chevrolets, Nissans, and Volkswagens.

Starting 15 years ago with the purchase of a bankrupt Dodge dealership, Wolf Motors had grown steadily in size and in reputation. Wolf attributed this success to three highly interdependent factors. The first was volume. By maintaining a high volume of sales and turning over inventory rapidly, economies of scale could be achieved, which reduced costs and provided customers with a large selection. The second factor was a marketing approach called the "hassle-free buying experience." Listed on each automobile was the "one price–lowest price." Customers came in, browsed, and compared prices without being approached by pushy salespeople. If they had questions or were ready to buy, a walk to a customer service desk produced a knowledgeable salesperson to assist them. Finally, and Wolf thought perhaps most important, was the after-sale service. Wolf Motors established a solid reputation for servicing, diagnosing, and repairing vehicles correctly and in a timely manner—the first time.

High-quality service after the sale depended on three essential components. First was the presence of a highly qualified, well-trained staff of service technicians. Second was the use of the latest tools and technologies to support diagnosis and repair activities. Third was the availability of the full range of parts and materials necessary to complete the service and repairs without delay. Wolf invested in training and equipment to ensure that the trained personnel and technology were provided. What he worried about, as Wolf Motors grew, was the continued availability of the right parts and materials. This concern caused him to focus on the supplier relationship process and management of the service parts and materials flows in the supply chain.

Wolf thought back on the stories in the newspaper's business pages describing the failure of companies that had not planned appropriately for growth. These companies outgrew their existing policies, procedures, and control systems. Lacking a plan to update their systems, the companies experienced myriad problems that led to inefficiencies and an inability to compete effectively. He did not want that to happen to Wolf Motors.

Each of the four dealerships purchased its own service parts and materials. Purchases were based on forecasts derived from historical demand data, which accounted for factors such as seasonality. Batteries and alternators had a high failure rate in the winter, and air-conditioner parts were in great demand during the summer. Similarly, coolant was needed in the spring to service air conditioners for the summer months, whereas antifreeze was needed in the fall to winterize automobiles. Forecasts also were adjusted for special vehicle sales and service promotions, which increased the need for materials used to prep new cars and service other cars.

One thing that made the purchase of service parts and materials so difficult was the tremendous number of different parts that had to be kept on hand. Some of these parts would be used to service customer automobiles, and others would be sold over the counter. Some had to be purchased from the automobile manufacturers or their certified wholesalers, and to support, for example, the "guaranteed GM parts" promotion. Still, other parts and materials such as oils, lubricants, and fan belts could be purchased from any number of suppliers. The purchasing department had to remember that the success of the dealership depended on (1) lowering costs to support the hassle-free, one price–lowest price concept and (2) providing the right parts at the right time to support fast, reliable after-sale service.

As Wolf thought about the purchasing of parts and materials, two things kept going through his mind: the amount of space available for parts storage and the level of financial resources available to invest in parts and materials. The acquisition of the auto supermarket dealership put an increased strain on both finances and space, with the need to support three different automobile lines at the same facility. Investment dollars were becoming scarce, and space was at a premium. Wolf wondered what could be done in the purchasing area to address some of these concerns and alleviate some of the pressures.

QUESTIONS

1. What recommendations would you make to John Wolf with respect to structuring the supplier relationship process for the Wolf Motors dealership network?

2. How might purchasing policies and procedures differ as the dealerships purchase different types of service parts and materials (for example, lubricants versus genuine GM parts)?

3. How can supply chain strategy help John Wolf reduce investment and space requirements while maintaining adequate service levels?

Source: This case was prepared by Dr. Brooke Saladin, Wake Forest University, as a basis for classroom discussion.

<table>
<tr><td>CASE 2</td><td>Brunswick Distribution, Inc.</td></tr>
</table>

James Brunswick, CEO of Brunswick Distribution, Inc. (BDI), looked out his office window at another sweltering day and wondered what could have gone wrong at his company. He just finished reviewing his company's recent financial performance and noticed something that worried him. Brunswick Distribution, Inc., had experienced a period of robust growth over the last four years. "What could be going wrong?" he thought to himself. "Our sales have been growing at an average rate of 8 percent over the last four years but we still appear to be worse off than before." He sat back in his chair with a heavy sigh and continued reviewing the report on his desk.

Sales had risen consistently over the past four years but the future was uncertain. James Brunswick was aware that part of the past growth had largely been the result of a few competitors in the region going out of business, a situation that was unlikely to continue. Net earnings, however, had been declining for the last three years and were expected to decline next year.

Brunswick was determined to turn his company around within the next three years. He sat back from his desk and buzzed his personal assistant. "Carla, could you ask Lew and Frank to come up?"

Background

The distribution business, in its simplest form, involves the purchase of inventory from a variety of manufacturers and its resale to retailers. Over the last three to five years, demands on inventory changed considerably; neither manufacturers nor retailers want to handle inventory, leaving distributors to pick up the slack. In addition, an increased tendency of retailers to order directly from manufacturers placed further strain on the profitability of distributorships in general.

BDI was started as a simple distributor of products from local manufacturers, which resold them to small customers in and around the town of Moline, Illinois. James Brunswick had been the senior logistics officer at a large freight company based in Chicago that operated in seven midwestern states. After five years with the freight company, he left to open up his own distribution business in his hometown using his personal finances and a small line of credit from his local bank.

With the help of two of his old college buddies, Lew Jackson and Frank Pulaski, Brunswick Distribution, Inc., was founded as a small but profitable distribution company. In the first nine months, the trio operated from a shed behind Brunswick's grandmother's house. Brunswick had been able to convince the local bank to issue him a small-business loan, which he used to purchase two used vans.

As business increased, BDI relocated from the shed to larger premises in the outskirts of the town. The company moved to a 10,000 square-foot leased facility. In 1997, BDI

began distributing high-end appliance products. For example, to supplement its low-margin products, BDI entered into an agreement with KitchenHelper Corp., a large manufacturer of high-end kitchen appliances, located 35 miles from Moline, to distribute KitchenHelper appliances to customers in the region. Over the years BDI enjoyed steady growth and expanded its area of coverage. As of December 2007, Brunswick was covering an area with a radius of 200 miles from the company's main facility. Given the rapid growth, BDI purchased the leased facility and made additions to it to bring its capacity to 30,000 square feet.

The demise of several of its competitors resulted in the acquisition of new retailer customers and some new product lines. Traditional ordering in the retailer-distributor-manufacturer chain took place via fax or phone. Brunswick considered implementing an Internet-based ordering system but was unsure of the potential operational and marketing benefits that it could provide.

Concerns
Market

Direct competition from distributors increased over the past five years. As a result, the most successful distributors adopted a value-added strategy in order to remain competitive. Retailers want dependable delivery to support sales promotions and promises to customers. They also want the freedom to hold sales promotions at any time as competitive conditions dictate and with only short notice to distributors. They also want the opportunity to choose from a wide variety of appliances. Nonetheless, many orders are won on the basis of price and lost on the basis of delivery problems.

Financial

Manufacturers commonly demand payment in 30 to 45 days and provide no financing considerations. Retailers, on the other hand, pay in 50 to 60 days. This difference often leaves BDI in a cash-poor situation that puts an unnecessary strain on its current operating loan. The company's borrowing capacity has almost been exhausted. Any additional financing will have to be sought from alternative sources. Given BDI's financial situation, any additional financing will be issued at a higher charge than the company's existing debt.

Operations

Inventory turnover also presented a problem for the past 5 years. In the past two years, however, a significant downturn in turnover occurred. This trend seems likely to continue.

Orders from retailers come in as their customers near completion of construction or renovations. Even though historical information provided a good benchmark of future sales, the changing market lessened the reliability of the information. The changes also affect BDI's ordering. Manufacturers require projections 60, 90, and 120 days out in order to budget their production. Sometimes penalties are assessed when BDI changes an order after it is placed with a manufacturer.

Strategic Issues

As Lew and Frank walked into Brunswick's office, he was still pondering the report. "Grab a seat, gentlemen," he grunted. They knew they were going to have a long day. Brunswick quickly briefed the men on why he had summoned them, and they all immediately dived into a spirited discussion. Brunswick pointed out that BDI would need to be properly structured to deal with the recession and the reality of today's market. "We need to be well-positioned for growth as the market stabilizes," he said. In order to meet this challenge, BDI must evaluate a number of alternative options. Some of the possible options might include expanding current systems and, when necessary, developing new systems that interface with suppliers, customers, and commercial transportation resources to gain total asset visibility.

Before making any investment decision, Brunswick reminded them that BDI would have to evaluate any new capital requirements, as well as the expected contribution to the company's bottom line and market share, that any option might provide. Exhibit 1 shows financial statements covering the past four years, with projections for 2008.

Investing in New Infrastructure

Frank Pulaski, vice president of operations, said, "Since Associated Business Distribution Corp. ceased operations 4 years ago, we have been inundated with phone calls and e-mails from potential customers across the Midwest looking for an alternative to ABD's services. These requests come not only from former ABD customers but also from potential customers that have not dealt with either ABD or us in the past. We cannot adequately service this market from our current warehouse because the customers do not want to wait for lengthy deliveries. We are presently servicing some customers in that region; however, I do not think we can keep them much longer. In order to take advantage of this opportunity, we would have to construct a new storage facility to complement our already strained resources. We are challenged by an inadequate infrastructure far too small for our requirements. We only have the Moline warehouse at this time." The addition of new facilities would provide Brunswick Distribution, Inc., with an opportunity for increased penetration in key industrial markets in the upper Midwest where BDI has had a limited presence.

The financing resources for this option would be a challenge, given that BDI was approaching its credit limit with its principal bank. Additional financing from larger banks in Chicago, however, was not ruled out. It would be expensive (with current interest rates for long-term loans starting at 11 percent). According to Frank, this option would cost $2 million

for property and $10 million for plant and equipment. The additional facilities would be depreciated over 20 years. The 20-year loan would be repaid with a single balloon payment at the end of the loan. With the additional infrastructure, BDI would be able to increase its annual sales by $4,426,000. In addition, delivery lead times to customers in the region would be reduced from 5 days to 2 days, which would be very competitive. Because of the added warehouse capacity, BDI could also increase the number of brands and models of appliances to better serve the retailers' needs for more variety. However, certain operating costs would also increase. Total shipping costs, which include supplier deliveries to the warehouse as well as deliveries to the customer, would increase by $955,000. Materials costs (for the added inventories) and labor costs would each increase by 6 percent. Accounts receivable would increase by $1,500,000. As for the effect on current liabilities, "other liabilities" are expected to increase by the annual interest payments on the new loan.

Streamlining the Order Fulfillment System

Lew Jackson, the vice president of logistics, stated, "I believe there is an opportunity to capitalize on the void left by our fallen rivals by utilizing a cost-efficient distribution system. We do not need a new facility; we can continue to serve the customers in the Midwest as best as we can. However, what we do need is an efficient distribution system. We are holding a considerable amount of stock that has not moved simply because of our inefficient inventory systems. One of our top priorities is working diligently with the inventory control department to keep what we need and dispose of what we do not need. This approach will allow us to use the space recovered from the unneeded items for automated warehouse equipment that will enable us to become more efficient. Everything we do and every dollar we spend affects our customers. We need to keep our prices competitive. Our cost of operations is our customers' cost. Our goal is to enable customers to spend their resources on readiness and the tools of their trade, not logistics. This option will not help us much with product variety or delivery speed; however it will increase our on-time delivery performance and improve our flexibility to respond to changes in retailer orders to support their sales programs."

The option of having an integrated center, comprised of sophisticated automation systems, advanced materials handling equipment, and specially developed information technology, would provide BDI with both the versatility and capacity to offer improved products and services to Brunswick's customers. Two versions of the system were available, either of which could be installed in the present warehouse facilities. The "Basic" system would support real-time ordering, logistics planning and scheduling, and after-sales service. When an order is received through a call center at Brunswick's offices in Moline, it will be forwarded to a logistics center for processing. The customer is given a delivery date based on truck availability. Orders would be grouped by destination so that trucks could be efficiently loaded to maximize the truck capacity. The order would then be scheduled for delivery and the customer notified of the estimated

Brunswick Balance Sheet
(in thousands of dollars)

	2008	2007	2006	2005	2004
Assets					
Current Assets					
Inventory	6,789	6,398	4,945	3,491	2,610
Accounts Receivable	5,603	5,117	3,973	3,538	3,530
Other Current Assets	1,381	907	981	1,242	921
Cash	3,223	2,841	2,756	2,912	3,105
	16,996	15,263	12,655	11,183	10,166
Long-Term Assets					
Net PP&E	12,174	13,139	13,729	12,110	12,687
Long-Term Investments	1,000	1,000	1,000	1,000	750
	13,174	14,139	14,729	13,110	13,437
Total Assets	**30,170**	**29,402**	**27,384**	**24,293**	**23,603**
Liabilities					
Current Liabilities					
Accounts Payable	2,582	2,654	2,811	3,480	3,510
Notes Payable	1,099	894	964	1,263	1,522
Short-Term Debt	2,859	3,050	3,320	3,061	3,650
	6,540	6,598	7,095	7,804	8,682
Long-Term Liabilities					
Long-Term Loans	6,519	8,260	8,460	7,839	8,960
	13,059	14,858	15,555	15,643	17,642
Equity	17,111	14,544	11,829	8,650	5,961
Total Debt & Equity	**30,170**	**29,402**	**27,384**	**24,293**	**23,603**

Brunswick Income Statement
(in thousands of dollars)

	2008	2007	2006	2005	2004
Sales	33,074	31,109	29,255	27,030	23,694
Cost of Sales	21,620	19,532	17,040	15,700	14,668
Gross Profit	11,454	11,577	12,215	11,330	9,026
SG&A	4,873	4,630	4,510	4,426	4,256
Depreciation	1,794	1,794	1,794	1,794	1,794
Operating Incoming	4,787	5,153	5,911	5,110	2,976
Interest	838	976	1,020	973	1,130
Taxable Income	3,949	4,177	4,891	4,137	1,846
Taxes	1,382	1,462	1,712	1,448	646
Net Income	2,567	2,715	3,179	2,689	1,200

EXHIBIT 1

Company Financial Statements

arrival. This new information technology would improve BDI's reliability in delivering the products when promised. The capital costs of this system would be $4.7 million. The "Fully Integrated" system has everything the Basic system has but also includes an automatic storage and retrieval system (AS/RS). The AS/RS selects a customer order and moves it to a dock for loading on a truck headed for the customer's location. The capital costs for this system would be $7 million. Regardless of the system, these costs would be depreciated over a 10-year period. The operating costs including training would run at $0.5 million each year for either system. These costs would be considered fixed expenses by Brunswick. The improved system, however, would have tremendous cost savings. The Basic system would result in 10 percent savings in shipping and 10 percent savings in labor expenses while the Fully Integrated system would save up to 16 percent in each. BDI could finance this option using a 10-year loan at a 10 percent rate of interest. The loan would be repaid with a balloon payment at the end of the loan. BDI's current liabilities, specifically "other liabilities," would increase by the annual interest payments on the loan.

These savings would come from more efficient handling of customers' orders by the call center, better planning and scheduling of shipments, and improved communication with the warehouse and the customer, resulting in a dramatic reduction in the shipping costs in the supply chain. Additional savings would result from the reduction in personnel costs; fewer operators would be required, which would reduce short-term liabilities. Lew Jackson thought that BDI could maintain its present level of service with either of these options while becoming much more efficient.

The Decision

James Brunswick pondered the two options posed by Frank and Lew. Frank's option enabled the firm to increase its revenues by serving more customers. The capital outlay was sizable, however. Lew's option focused on serving the firm's existing customers more efficiently. The value of that option was its dramatic reduction in costs; however, it was uncertain whether BDI could hold onto its current upper Midwest customers. Brunswick realized that he could not undertake both options, given the company's current financial position. How will each option affect the firm's financial ratios and net worth, which investors watch closely? Which one would be better for the company?

The Financial Measures Analyzer, a program on the Student CD-ROM in OM Explorer (see the Supply Chain Strategy folder) contains spreadsheets for Brunswick's Profit and Loss, Balance Sheet, and Financial Ratios. They contain the 2008 data as a starting point. Changes, or "shocks," to the starting position resulting from an investment option can be entered in the center column. The program computes the effects of the shocks in the right-hand column.

> SELECTED REFERENCES <

Bowersox, D. J., and D. J. Closs. *Logistical Management: The Integrated Supply Chain Process*. New York: McGraw-Hill, 1996.

Champion, David. "Mastering the Value Chain." *Harvard Business Review* (June 2001), pp. 109–115.

Conner, Martin P. "The Supply Chain's Role in Leveraging Product Life Cycle Management." *Supply Chain Management Review* (March 2004), pp. 36–43.

Cook, Robert L., Brian Gibson, and Douglas MacCurdy. "A Lean Approach to Cross-Docking." *Supply Chain Management Review* (March 2005), pp. 54–59.

Duray, Rebecca, Peter. T. Ward, Glenn W. Milligan, and William L. Berry. "Approaches to Mass Customization: Configurations and Empirical Validation." *Journal of Operations Management*, vol. 18 (2000), pp. 605–625.

Duray, Rebecca. "Mass Customization Origins: Mass or Custom Manufacturing?" *International Journal of Operations and Production Management*, vol. 22, no. 3 (2002), pp. 314–328.

Ellram, Lisa M., and Baohong Liu. "The Financial Impact of Supply Management." *Supply Chain Management Review* (November–December 2002), pp. 30–37.

Farrell, Diana. "Beyond Offshoring: Assess Your Company's Global Potential." *Harvard Business Review* (December 2004), pp. 82–90.

Fisher, Marshall L. "What Is the Right Supply Chain for Your Product?" *Harvard Business Review* (March–April 1997), pp. 105–116.

Freund, Brian C., and June M. Freund. "Hands-On VMI." *APICS—The Performance Advantage* (March 2003), pp. 34–39.

Fugate, Brian S., and John T. Mentzer. "Dell's Supply Chain DNA." *Supply Chain Management Review* (October 2004), pp. 20–24.

Hammer, Michael. "The Superefficient Company." *Harvard Business Review* (September 2001), pp. 82–91.

Handfield, Robert, S. Walton, Robert Sroufe, and Steven Melnyk. "Applying Environmental Criteria to Supplier Assessment: A Study of the Application of the Analytical Hierarchy Process." *European Journal of Operational Research*, vol. 41, no. 1 (2002), pp. 70–87.

Hartvigsen, David. *SimQuick: Process Simulation with Excel*, 2d ed. Upper Saddle River, NJ: Prentice Hall, 2004.

Lee, Hau L. "The Triple-A Supply Chain." *Harvard Business Review* (October 2004), pp. 102–112.

Lee, Hau L., and Corey Billington. "Managing Supply Chain Inventory: Pitfalls and Opportunities." *Sloan Management Review* (Spring 1992), pp. 65–73.

Liker, Jeffrey K., and Thomas Y. Choi. "Building Deep Supplier Relationships." *Harvard Business Review* (December 2004), pp. 104–113.

Maloni, M., and W. C. Benton. "Power Influences in the Supply Chain." *Journal of Business Logistics*, vol. 21 (2000), pp. 49–73.

Melnyk, Steven, and Robert Handfield. "Green Speak." *Purchasing Today*, vol. 7, no. 7 (1996), pp. 32–36.

Melnyk, Steven, Robert Sroufe, and Roger Calantone. "Assessing the Impact of Environmental Management Systems on Corporate and Environmental Performance." *Journal of Operations Management*, vol. 21, no. 3 (2003).

Metersky, Jeff, and J. Michael Kilgore. "How to Improve Your Inventory Deployment." *Supply Chain Management Review* (October 2004), pp. 26–32.

Moeeni, Farhad. "Quality Decision Making, Input Technologies, and IT Education." *Decision Line* (May 2004), pp. 14–17.

Randall, Taylor, Serguei Netessine, and Nils Rudi. "Should You Take the Virtual Fulfillment Path?" *Supply Chain Management Review* (November–December 2002), pp. 54–58.

Siekman, Philip. "The Smart Car Is Looking More So." *Fortune* (April 15, 2002), pp. 310I–310P.

Steerman, Hank. "A Practical Look at CPFR: The Sears-Michelin Experience." *Supply Chain Management Review* (July–August 2003), pp. 46–53.

Sullivan, Laurie. "Wal-Mart's Way." *Informationweek.com* (September 27, 2004), pp. 37–50.

Trent, Robert J. "What Everyone Needs to Know About SCM." *Supply Chain Management Review* (March 2004), pp. 52–59.

Venkatesan, Ravi. "Strategic Sourcing: To Make or Not to Make." *Harvard Business Review* (November–December 1992), pp. 98–107.

11

LEARNING GOALS

After reading this chapter, you should be able to:

1. Explain how location decisions relate to the design of value chains.

2. Identify factors affecting location choices.

3. Understand the role of geographical information systems in making location decisions.

4. Understand single facility location techniques.

5. Explain how to apply the center of gravity, load-distance method, break-even analysis, transportation method, and other multiple facilities location methods.

Fluctuating exchange rates and other economic factors led Bavarian Motor Works (BMW) to consider manufacturing outside of Europe. The question was, where? After an extensive study and numerous government concessions, Spartanburg, South Carolina, became the exclusive manufacturer of the BMW Z4 Roadster and BMW X5 Sports Activity Vehicles.

CHAPTER 11
Location

BAVARIAN MOTOR WORKS (BMW)

Bavarian Motor Works (BMW), founded in 1917 and headquartered in Munich, Germany, is a manufacturer of select premium segment brands such as BMW, MINI, and Rolls-Royce Motor Cars in the international automobile market. When faced with fluctuating exchange rates and increasing production costs in late 1980s, BMW decided that it was time to consider operating a new production facility outside the European borders. A "blank page" approach was used to compile a list of 250 potential worldwide plant sites. Further analysis pared the list down to 10 viable options; a plant location in the United States was preferred due to its proximity to a large market segment for BMW's automobiles.

The selection of the plant site involved many factors that had to be analyzed prior to its con-struction. BMW considered the labor climate in each country, geographical requirements and constraints, and its relations with the governments of the countries in which the prospective sites were located. In terms of the labor climate, a technologically capable workforce was needed due to the complex nature of the automotive manufacturing process. Because the cost to train a single worker in the automotive industry is between $10,000 and $20,000, this factor was especially critical. Additionally, BMW decided that if the plant were located in the United States, it should be in a "right-to-work" state to satisfy American unions. Geographical factors had to be examined because thousands of automobile parts needed to be delivered from both domestic and foreign suppliers. In order to keep the supply chain costs down, it was decided

>

For additional chapter resources check the Student CD-ROM or the Companion Website at
www.prenhall.com/krajewski

that the new location should have ample highway/ interstate access and be reasonably close to a port from which both supplies and finished automobiles could be easily transported. Another consideration was easy access to an airport for BMW's executives traveling back and forth to its headquarters in Germany. The final location factor was government related. BMW wanted to move to a location that was "business friendly" in terms of making concessions on issues such as infrastructural improvements, tax abatements, and employee screening and education programs. The overall goal was to make the relationship between BMW and the local community as mutually beneficial as possible through a coordinated improvement effort.

After a three-and-half-year search process that stringently evaluated the 10 viable options across these location factors, BMW finally decided to build a new 2 million square-foot production facility in Spartanburg, South Carolina. The final decision was made based on a good match between the aforementioned selection criteria and the environment in Spartanburg. South Carolina lawmakers proved flexible and open as to how the state would address the needs set forth by BMW. For instance, they agreed to acquire the 500 acres necessary to build the plant (requiring a $25 million bond package be passed), improve the highway system around the facility (requiring $10 million), and lengthen the runway

and modernize the terminal at the Spartanburg airport ($40 million expenditure). The legislature also agreed to provide tax incentives, property tax relief, and establish an employee screening and training program to ensure the right mix of workers were available. (Processing the applications alone proved to be a daunting task because more than 50,000 applications were received.) South Carolina may not have scored the highest on each decision criteria, but taken as a whole, the Spartanburg location was best for BMW.

This location proved to be a good one. The plant, which opened in 1994, subsequently underwent a $200 million expansion in 1996, a $50 million expansion in 1999, and a $300 million expansion in 2000. It now employs approximately 4,700 workers who produce more than 500 vehicles a day. BMW Manufacturing Corporation in South Carolina today is part of BMW Group's global manufacturing network, and is the exclusive manufacturing plant for all Z4 Roadster and X5 Sports Activity Vehicles. South Carolina also reaped rewards in the form of business growth (BMW brought along 39 of its suppliers), employment (approximately 12,000 new jobs were created), and community improvements—a success story all around.

Sources: "Manager's Journal; Why BMW Cruised into Spartanburg," Wall Street Journal (July 6, 1992), p. A10; "BMW Announces Its Plans for a Plant in South Carolina," Wall Street Journal (June 24, 1992), p. B2; P. Galuszka, "The South Shall Rise Again," Chief Executive (November 2004), pp. 50–54; Southern Business & Development, www.sb-d.com (June 2005); www.bmwusfactory.com, June 2005.

facility location

The process of determing geographic sites for a firm's operations.

Facility location is the process of determining geographic sites for a firm's operations. Location choices can be critically important for firms, and have a profound impact on a firm's value chain. For example, they can affect the supplier relationship process: the expanding global economy gives firms greater access to suppliers around the world, many of whom can offer lower input costs or better-quality services and products. Nonetheless, when manufacturing facilities are off-shored, locating far from one's suppliers can lead to higher transportation costs and coordination difficulties. The customer relationship process can also be affected by the firm's location decisions. If the customer must be physically present at the process, it is unlikely that a location will be acceptable if the time or distance between the service provider and customer is great. If on the other hand, customer contact is more passive and impersonal, or if materials or information is processed rather than people, then location may be less of an issue. Information technology and the Internet can sometimes help overcome the disadvantages related to a company's location. Still, one thing is clear: The location of a business's facilities has a significant impact on the company's operating costs, the prices it charges for services and goods, and its ability to compete in the marketplace and penetrate new customer segments.

Analyzing location patterns to discover a firm's underlying strategy is fascinating. For example, why does White Castle often locate restaurants near manufacturing plants? Why do competing new-car sales showrooms cluster near one another? White Castle's strategy is to cater to blue-collar workers. As a result, it tends to locate near the target population and away from competitors, such as Wendy's and McDonald's. In contrast, managers of new-car showrooms deliberately locate near one another because customers prefer to do their comparison shopping in one area. In each case, the location decision reflects a particular strategy.

Recognizing the strategic impact location decisions have on implementing a firm's strategy and value chain design, we first consider the qualitative factors that influence location choices and their implications across the organization. Subsequently we examine an important trend in location patterns: the use of geographical information systems (GIS) to identify market segments and how serving each segment can profitably affect the firm's location decisions. We end by presenting some analytic and GIS-based techniques for making single- and multiple-facility location decisions.

> LOCATION DECISIONS ACROSS THE ORGANIZATION <

Location decisions affect processes and departments throughout the organization. When locating new retail facilities, such as Wendy's stores, marketing must carefully assess how the location will appeal to customers and possibly open up new markets. Relocating all or part of an organization can significantly affect the attitudes of the firm's workforce and the organization's ability to operate effectively across departmental lines. Location also has implications for a firm's human resources department, which must be attuned to the firm's hiring and training needs. Locating new facilities or relocating existing facilities is usually costly; therefore, these decisions must be carefully evaluated by the organization's accounting and finance departments. For instance, when BMW located its manufacturing plant in South Carolina, the economic environment of the state and the monetary incentives offered by its legislators played a role in the financial payoff associated with the proposed new plant. Finally, operations also has an important stake in location decisions because the location needs to be able to meet current customer demand and provide the right amount of customer contact (for both external and internal customers). International operations, like those of McDonald's, Ford, and Wal-Mart introduce a new set of challenges because setting up and managing facilities and employees in foreign countries can be extremely time consuming and difficult.

USING OPERATIONS TO COMPETE

Operations As a Competitive Weapon
Operations Strategy
Project Management

MANAGING PROCESSES

Process Strategy
Process Analysis
Process Performance and Quality
Constraint Management
Process Layout
Lean Systems

MANAGING VALUE CHAINS

Supply Chain Strategy
Location
Inventory Management
Forecasting
Sales and Operations Planning
Resource Planning
Scheduling

Wal-Mart Stores, the world's largest retailer, has gone global. Here, two customers leave a Wal-Mart store in Mexico City. Wal-Mart's trademark yellow smiley face, low prices, and focus on customer service was first introduced to larger U.S. cities and then abroad, to Canada, Puerto Rico, Brazil, the United Kingdom, Germany, South Korea, Japan, China, as well as Mexico.

> FACTORS AFFECTING LOCATION DECISIONS <

Managers of both service and manufacturing organizations must weigh many factors when assessing the desirability of particular locations, including their proximity to customers and suppliers, labor costs, and transportation costs. Managers generally can disregard factors that fail to meet at least one of the following two conditions.

1. *The Factor Must Be Sensitive to Location.* In other words, managers should not consider a factor not affected by the location decision. For example, if community attitudes are uniformly good at all the locations under consideration, community attitudes should not be considered as a factor.

2. *The Factor Must Have a High Impact on the Company's Ability to Meet Its Goals.* For example, although different facilities will be located at different distances from suppliers, if the shipments from them can take place overnight and the communication with them is done via fax or e-mail, the distance isn't likely to have a large impact on the firm's ability to meet its goals. It should therefore not be considered as a factor.

Managers can divide location factors into dominant and secondary factors. Dominant factors are derived from competitive priorities (cost, quality, time, and flexibility) and have a particularly strong impact on sales or costs. For example, a favorable labor climate and monetary incentives were dominant factors affecting the decision to locate the BMW plant in Spartanburg, South Carolina. Secondary factors also are important, but management may downplay or even ignore some of these secondary factors if other factors are more important. Thus, for GM's Saturn plant, which makes many of its parts onsite, inbound transportation costs were considered less important and therefore were a secondary factor.

DOMINANT FACTORS IN MANUFACTURING

The following six groups of factors dominate the decisions firms, including BMW, make about the location of new manufacturing plants.

1. Favorable labor climate
2. Proximity to markets
3. Quality of life
4. Proximity to suppliers and resources
5. Proximity to the parent company's facilities
6. Utilities, taxes, and real estate costs

Favorable Labor Climate A favorable labor climate may well be the most important factor for labor-intensive firms in industries such as textiles, furniture, and consumer electronics. Labor climate is a function of wage rates, training requirements, attitudes toward work, worker productivity, and union strength. Many executives perceive weak unions or a low probability of union organizing efforts as a distinct advantage. Having a favorable climate applies not only to the workforce already on site, but as illustrated by General Electric's Energy Division relocation in Managerial Practice 11.1, also to the employees that a firm hopes will transfer to or will be attracted to the new site.

Proximity to Markets After determining where the demand for services and goods is greatest, management must select a location for the facility that will supply that demand. Locating near markets is particularly important when the final goods are bulky or heavy and *outbound* transportation rates are high. For example, manufacturers of products, such as plastic pipe and heavy metals, all require proximity to their markets.

Quality of Life Good schools, recreational facilities, cultural events, and an attractive lifestyle contribute to **quality of life**. This factor can make the difference in location decisions. In the United States during the past two decades, more than 50 percent of new industrial jobs went to nonurban regions. A similar shift is taking place in Japan and Europe. Reasons for this movement include high costs of living, high crime rates, and general decline in the quality of life in many large cities.

Proximity to Suppliers and Resources Firms dependent on inputs of bulky, perishable, or heavy raw materials emphasize proximity to their suppliers and resources. In such cases,

quality of life

A factor that considers the availability of good schools, recreational facilities, cultural events, and an attractive lifestyle.

MANAGERIAL **PRACTICE**	11.1	RELOCATING GENERAL ELECTRIC'S ENERGY DIVISION

General Electric's Energy Division, with 4,700 employees, is one of the world's leading suppliers of power generation technology, energy services, and management systems, and is the largest single business unit within GE accounting for revenues of more than $15 billion. The decision in 2001 to relocate the Energy Division's corporate headquarters from Schenectady, New York, to Atlanta, Georgia, came as a surprise because GE had a 100-year history in New York dating back to the days of Thomas Edison. However, a move was needed because, among other reasons, GE's customer base had shifted geographically over time and the relocation would provide better access to its customers.

The decision to relocate was made based on more favorable living conditions and climate in Georgia, along with other factors such as the proximity of numerous electric utility companies (the primary buyers of GE's turbines), convenient access to Hartsfield Airport, and most importantly, an available pool of technologically oriented workers. In addition, GE was offered major incentives by government entities in Atlanta to relocate there. The selection process took nearly six years to complete with so much at stake. A concern of President and CEO John Rice was that many current employees would not be willing to relocate to the Atlanta area. However, Rice noted, "The quality of life—cheap housing, good recreation, good cultural events, and climate— were such big draws that not many workers turned us down when they were offered transfers." As a result, the workforce in New York was downsized considerably, even though the plant there was still functional as a manufacturing unit. The move was successful for both Atlanta and GE. Atlanta area saw an increase in the number of jobs, while GE experienced sustained business growth. The situation truly has Rice happily whistling *Dixie*.

A GE Energy Division employee works at the company's remote diagnostics center located inside its new division headquarters building in Atlanta, Georgia. Despite a 100-year history in Schenectady, New York, the division relocated to Atlanta in 2001. Among the factors that led to the move: GE's customers are concentrated in and around Atlanta, and the city has a deep talent base of technologically oriented workers.

Sources: "Power System's Relocation to Atlanta Is Official," *The Business Review* (February 9, 2001); www.bizjournals.com/albany; P. Galuszka, "The South Shall Rise Again," *Chief Executive* (November 2004), pp. 50–54.

inbound transportation costs become a dominant factor, encouraging such firms to locate facilities near suppliers. For example, locating paper mills near forests and food-processing facilities near farms is practical. Another advantage of locating near suppliers is the ability to maintain lower inventories.

Proximity to the Parent Company's Facilities In many companies, plants supply parts to other facilities or rely on other facilities for management and staff support. These ties require frequent coordination and communication, which can become more difficult as distance increases.

Utilities, Taxes, and Real Estate Costs Other location decision factors include utility costs (telephone, energy, and water), local and state taxes, financing incentives offered by local or state governments, relocation costs, and land costs. For example, the location of the Daimler Chrysler plant in Alabama for manufacturing its "M series" vehicles, the BMW plant in South Carolina in the opening vignette, and a Toyota plant in Georgetown, Kentucky, were all attractive to these companies in part due to the incentives from local governments.

Other Factors Still other factors may need to be considered, including room for expansion, construction costs, accessibility to multiple modes of transportation, the cost of shuffling people and materials between plants, insurance costs, competition from other firms for the workforce, local ordinances (such as pollution or noise control regulations), community attitudes, and many others. For global operations, firms need a good local infrastructure and local employees who are educated and have good skills. Many firms are concluding that large, centralized manufacturing facilities in low-cost countries with poorly trained workers are not sustainable. Smaller, flexible facilities located in the countries that the firm serves allow it to avoid problems related to trade barriers like tariffs and quotas and the risk that changing exchange rates will adversely affect its sales and profits.

DOMINANT FACTORS IN SERVICES

The factors mentioned for manufacturers also apply to service providers with one important addition: the impact of location on sales and customer satisfaction. Customers usually care about how close a service facility is, particularly if the process requires considerable customer contact.

Proximity to Customers Location is a key factor in determining how conveniently customers can carry on business with a firm. For example, few people will patronize a remotely located dry cleaner or supermarket if another is more convenient. Thus, the influence of location on revenues tends to be the dominant factor. In addition, customer proximity by itself is not enough—the key is proximity to customers who will patronize the facility and seek its services. For instance, Mirage opened the opulent Beau Rivage casino in Biloxi, Mississippi, in 1999. Its revenues turned out lower than expectations because the new casino did not cater as well to the needs of local customers, who came there to view and admire it but gambled elsewhere. Revenues picked up only after the cuisine at Beau Rivage was tailored to local tastes, costs were slashed, valet parking capacity was increased, and other changes were made. Being close to customers who match a firm's target market and service offerings is thus important for profitability.

Transportation Costs and Proximity to Markets For warehousing and distribution operations, transportation costs and proximity to markets are extremely important. With a warehouse nearby, many firms can hold inventory closer to the customer, thus reducing delivery time and promoting sales. For example, Invacare Corporation of Elyria, Ohio, gained a competitive edge in the distribution of home health care products by decentralizing inventory into 32 warehouses across the country. Invacare sells wheelchairs, hospital beds, and other patient aids—some of which it produces and some of which it buys from other firms—to small dealers who sell to consumers. Previously the dealers, often small mom-and-pop operations, had to wait three weeks for deliveries, which meant their cash was tied up in excess inventory. With Invacare's new distribution network, the dealers get daily deliveries of products from one source. Invacare's location strategy shows how timely delivery can be a competitive advantage.

Location of Competitors One complication related to estimating the sales potential of different locations is the impact of competitors. Management must not only consider the current location of competitors but also try to anticipate their reaction to the firm's new location. Avoiding areas where competitors are already well established often pays off. However, in some industries, such as new-car sales showrooms and fast-food chains, locating near competitors is actually advantageous. The strategy is to create a **critical mass**, whereby several competing firms clustered in one location attract more customers than the total number who would shop at the same stores at scattered locations. Recognizing this effect, some firms use a follow-the-leader strategy when selecting new sites.

Site-Specific Factors Retailers also must consider the level of retail activity, residential density, traffic flow, and site visibility. Retail activity in the area is important because shoppers often decide on impulse to go shopping or to eat in a restaurant. Traffic flows and visibility are important because businesses' customers arrive in cars. Management considers possible traffic tie-ups, traffic volume and direction by time of day, traffic signals, intersections, and the position of traffic medians. Visibility involves distance from the street and the size of nearby buildings and signs. A high residential density increases nighttime and weekend business if the population in the area fits the firm's competitive priorities and target market segment.

> ## GEOGRAPHICAL INFORMATION SYSTEMS
AND LOCATION DECISIONS <

A **geographical information system (GIS)** is a system of computer software, hardware, and data that the firm's personnel can use to manipulate, analyze, and present information relevant to a location decision. A GIS can also integrate different systems to create a visual representation of a firm's location choices. Among other things, it can be used to (1) store data-

---

critical mass

A situation whereby several competing firms clustered in one location attract more customers than the total number who would shop at the same stores at scattered locations.

geographical information system (GIS)

A system of computer software, hardware, and data that the firm's personnel can use to manipulate, analyze, and present information relevant to a location decision.

bases, (2) display maps, and (3) create models that can take information from existing datasets, apply analytic functions, and write results into new derived datasets. Together, these three functionalities of data storage, map displays, and modeling are critical parts of an intelligent GIS, and used to a varying extent in all GIS applications. Managerial Practice 11.2 illustrates how fast-food chains use GIS to select their sites.

A GIS system can be a really useful decision-making tool because many of the decisions made by businesses today have a geographical aspect. A GIS stores information in several databases that can be naturally linked to places, such as customer sales and locations, or a census tract, or the percentage of residents in the tract that make a certain amount of money a year. The

MANAGERIAL **PRACTICE**   11.2   HOW FAST-FOOD CHAINS USE GIS TO SELECT THEIR SITES

Until recently, fast-food chains used consultants to analyze geodemographic data (description of different characteristics about people based upon the location where they live or work) for strategic planning, and making franchise location and marketing decisions. Now with the availability of easy-to-use GIS systems that cost less than $5,000 and can be operated on a regular PC, small and large fast-food chains are doing it on their own. For instance, Marco's Franchising, headquartered in Toledo, Ohio, currently has 127 Marco's Pizza restaurants primarily in Ohio, Indiana, Michigan, and Nevada. Marco's Franchising uses MapInfo's GIS solutions to identify new markets where the customer and competitor landscape are best for new sites. MapInfo's Smart Site Solutions and AnySite Online technologies supply interactive mapping and reporting functionality to examine market level deployment strategies and individual site opportunities. These programs can estimate the total dollars up for grabs in a market by analyzing local age and income data from the U.S. Census Bureau as well as sales data from stores in an area—numbers that are commonly available through third-party vendors. The programs can also tell the optimal number and locations of stores in a market, and how much in sales a store can expect. Analyses can be run for any U.S. market and can rank markets in order of viability. A list of realistic sites with high sales potential can be put together at times in less than one minute. Other small fast-food chains in the United States like Cousins Subs, and 99 Restaurants and Pubs, are using in-house GIS and getting a handsome return on their investments. For instance, 99 Restaurants and Pubs found that they were able to recoup their GIS-related investment in a single week.

Bigger nationwide fast-food chains such as Domino's Pizza use GIS software to screen alternative sites for new franchises, determine how moving a store a few blocks away can affect sales, and decide when they should relocate or remodel existing stores. They can also use GIS to identify overlapping delivery zones and zones that aren't being covered. AFC Enterprises, which owns and franchises Popeye's and Church's chain of restaurants, uses GIS to help it sell franchises. The level of detailed information that they can provide to prospective franchisees can make all the difference when it comes to closing the deal. The company developed a GIS-based system called AFC Online, which allows franchisees to perform their own geographical analysis.

Arby's and Burger King use GIS to analyze where their customers come from and how they get to their stores. This information allows them to determine the effect of the encroachment of other fast-food restaurants, as well as the cannibalization of their own outlets. Generally, consumers

Customers wait in the drive-through line at a Burger King restaurant in Park Ridge, Illinois. Burger King uses GIS to see if other fast-food restaurants—or other Burger King stores—are adversely affecting the sales of one of its restaurants.

will only drive five miles to go to a fast-food restaurant. However, Arby's found that their customers who bought roast beef sandwiches tended to be 20 percent further away than those customers that bought their chicken entrées. Thus, Arby's is more of a destination restaurant for their roast beef offerings than for their chicken offerings.

Because of its ability to provide these insights, GIS provides a useful tool for expanding fast-food chains that need to quickly master the demographic details of competitive terrains in thousands of locations across the country. "Years ago, guys like myself did this on gut feelings," says John Dawson, chief development officer for Dunkin' Brands, the Canton, Massachusetts, parent of Dunkin' Donuts, Baskin-Robbins, and Togo's. "We would have to knock on doors and stand on street corners with hand counters and use our best judgment. The process took a long time, it was very arduous, and we made a lot of mistakes." Then, in 1998, Dunkin' Brands, a unit of U.K.-based Allied Domecq PLC, started using iSITE software from geoVue Inc. At the time, Dunkin' Brands was opening about 300 stores a year. Today, it has more than 12,000 locations worldwide, and it expects to add about 800 a year for the next several years. "Our goal is to get to over 1,000 per year," Dawson says. "And we couldn't do it without these tools."

Sources: www.gis.com/whatisgis/index.html; Ed Rubinstein, "Chains Chart Their Course of Actions with Geographic Information Systems," *Nation's Restaurant News*, vol. 32, no. 6 (1998), p. 49; "MapInfo Delivers Location Intelligence for Marco's Pizza," *Directions Magazine* (December 14, 2004), www.directionsmag.com/press.releases/?duty=Show&id=10790; Ryan Chittum, "Location, Location, and Technology: Where to Put That New Store? Site-Selection Software May Be Able to Help," *Wall Street Journal* (July 18, 2005), p. R7.

demographics of an area include the number of people in the metropolitan statistical area, city, or ZIP code; average income; number of families with children; and so forth. These demographics may all be important variables in the decision of how best to reach the target market. Similarly, the road system, including bridges and highways; location of nearby airports and seaports; and the terrain (mountains, forests, lakes, and so forth) play an important role in facility location decisions. As such, a GIS can have a diverse set of location-related applications in different industries such as the retail, real estate, government, transportation, and logistics.

As also highlighted in Managerial Practice 11.2, governmental data can provide a statistical motherlode of information used to make better GIS-based location decisions. For example, the U.S. Census Bureau has a minutely detailed computerized map of the entire United States—the so-called Tiger file. Its formal name is the Topologically Integrated Geographic Encoding and Reference file. It lists in digital form every highway, street, bridge, and tunnel in the 50 states. When combined with a database, such as the results of the census or a company's own customer files, Tiger provides GIS-type of functionalities and gives desktop computer users the ability to ask various "what-if" questions about different location alternatives. Internet sites on Yahoo!, Mapquest, and Expedia, among others, allow people to pull up maps, distances and travel times, and routes between locations, such as between Toronto, Ontario, and San Diego, California. In addition, search engines such as Google can be integrated with population demographics to create information of interest in social and business domains. Web sites are using Google maps to display crime sites, the location of cheap gas, and apartments for rent.

Many different types of GIS packages are available, such as ArcInfo (from ESRI), MapInfo (from MapInfo), SAS/GIS (from SAS Institute, Inc.), and SiteAmerica (from Tactician). Many of these systems are tailored to a specific application such as locating retail stores, redistricting legislative districts, analyzing logistics and marketing data, environmental management, and so forth. However, in this chapter, we explore the use of a particular GIS, Microsoft's MapPoint 2004. One of the nice features of MapPoint is that the maps and much of the census data come with the software itself, while in many other systems, the maps and the data are purchased separately from the GIS software vendor. MapPoint is an easy-to-use and fairly inexpensive GIS that mainly focuses on everyday business use by nontechnical analysts. Its ability to display information on maps can be a powerful decision-making tool.

USING GIS TO IDENTIFY LOCATIONS AND DEMOGRAPHIC CUSTOMER SEGMENTS

GIS can be useful for identifying locations that relate well to a firm's target market based on customer demographics. When coupled with other location models, sales forecasting models, and geodemographic systems, it can give a firm a formidable array of decision-making tools for its location decisions, as illustrated by Managerial Practice 11.3, about how Starbucks makes one of its most important strategic decisions: the location of its stores.

Starbucks video on the Student CD-ROM shows how to do such a geodemographic analaysis using MapPoint 2004

To get more practical insights into the application of GIS and demographics for understanding location choices made by Starbucks, let us examine further the Hamilton, Ontario, area showcased in the trade area map in Managerial Practice 11.3. The Starbucks store addresses within 20 miles of Hamilton were obtained from the Starbucks Web site and imported into MapPoint. These store locations are denoted by yellow dots around a coffee cup pushpin on Figure 11.1(a). Then, demographics that come with MapPoint were overlaid on the map. The map thus obtained shows the population density per square kilometer for each census subdivision. Hamilton (the darkest area) has a population density of 2,730 per square kilometer, while Oakville has a population density of 1,024 per square kilometer. Yet Oakville has more stores than Hamilton. It suggests that store location is not being driven by population density alone. The most densely population area around Hamilton has only one Starbucks store; further investigation reveals that it is on a road leading to the airport. In contrast, Ancaster, in the bottom left corner of the map has a Starbucks, even though its population density is only 141 per square kilometer.

We then look to see whether per capita income could explain the locations of the Starbucks store. The second map in Figure 11.1(b) shows the demographics by average per capita household income. Applying these data to the map, we see that Oakville and Ancaster (the darkest cities in map 2) have a per capita income of Canadian $96,545 and $98,422, respectively. Burlington has a moderate population density and moderate per capita income. Oakville has five stores while Burlington has three stores, all of them located on well-trafficked roads. So, at least in this one particular case, it appears that Starbucks predominantly locates its stores in more affluent areas, and future expansion of stores in the area are likely to occur in and around Ancaster if population grows there further.

An important aspect of the Starbucks service strategy is the location of its stores. In 2004 alone the chain opened approximately 1,300 stores, bringing the total to more than 9,400 stores. This phenomenal growth is aided by new site selection technology. Starbucks relies on location analysis to evaluate where to place new stores.

In Starbucks' early days, a relatively small number of people participated in new store decisions, which was more of an experiential than a systematic process. As Starbucks grew, however, more planners became involved in the process and used a more standard, formal analysis. If a site's potential is not within a certain set of parameters, its planners do not waste their time giving it additional consideration.

Starbucks' original strategy was to expand in major urban areas, clustering in prime locations and placing outlets across from one another, sometimes even in the same block. This approach maximized the company's market share in areas with the highest volume potential—usually urban, affluent areas. Then rural areas began demanding Starbucks be located there too. Over the past few years, Starbucks' domestic expansion strategy definitely evolved. Smaller city markets, and new store types, like those located in retail and airport locations are being utilized. Another change to the original strategy is the implementation of a geodemographic GIS system as a productivity and process tool. This GIS system determines the impact over the course of a year of opening an additional store one day sooner or one day later. Starbucks' site-acquisition process includes a number of elements that use spatial models, geodemographics, as well as the sales-forecasting models based upon them. To identify potential locations, maps, such as the trade area map shown here, are used by the company to show walk-time trade areas that pinpoint hotspots for gourmet coffee consumption.

In addition to growing domestically, Starbucks also expanded internationally, opening stores in Asia, the Middle East, Europe, and South America. When seeking potentially viable sites abroad, Starbucks encounters additional challenges, such as the lack of available and accurate data. Internationally, there is not a countrywide collection of information. In addition, the systems available to use those data vary. There is no central place to get information about data availability in certain countries, which translates into comparability issues and increases the risks of erring in expansion analyses.

Although Starbucks continues to grow rapidly, it has already taken the premium locations in many markets. The company is now forced to look for lower-volume locations that will still provide a good return. More than ever before, the use of location analysis limits Starbucks' risk, and has become paramount to the firm.

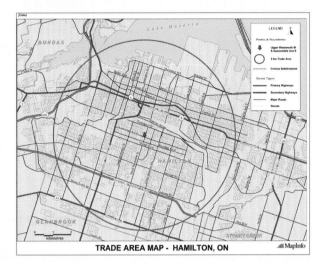

TRADE AREA MAP - HAMILTON, ON

Sources: "Location Analysis Tools Help Starbucks Brew Up New Ideas," *Business Geographics,* www.geoplace.com; Vijay Vishwanath and David Hardling, "The Starbucks Effect," *Harvard Business Review* (March–April 2000), pp. 17–18; Starbucks Corporate Information page, www.starbucks.com (June 2005).

> CHOOSING BETWEEN AN ONSITE EXPANSION, NEW LOCATION, OR RELOCATION <

Managers must first decide whether to expand onsite, build another facility, or relocate to another site. Onsite expansion has the advantage of keeping people together, reducing construction time and costs, and avoiding splitting up operations. However, as a firm expands a facility, at some point diseconomies of scale set in. Poor materials handling, increasingly complex production control, and simple lack of space are reasons for building a new plant or relocating the existing plant.

The advantages of building a new plant or moving to a new retail or office space are that the firm does not have to rely on the production from a single plant. A new plant allows it to hire more employees, install newer, more-productive machinery and better technology, and reduce transportation costs. Most firms that choose to relocate are small (comprised of fewer than 10 employees). They tend to be single-location companies cramped for space and needing to redesign their production processes and layouts. More than 80 percent of all

FIGURE 11.1(a)

Population Map of Hamilton, Ontario

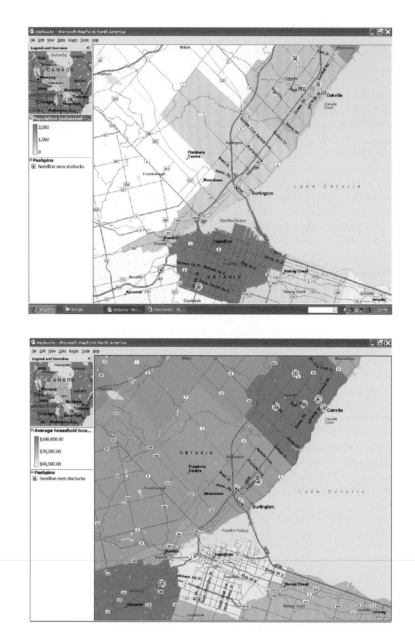

FIGURE 11.1(b)

Per Capita Household Income Map of
Hamilton, Ontario

relocations are made within 20 miles of companies' original locations, which enables the firms to retain their current employees.

It is less costly to relocate a service-oriented business than a manufacturing business. Because proximity to customers is important, the location of service facilities must constantly be reevaluated in the context of shifting populations and their changing needs. At times, a combination of all three options—staying at the same location, relocating, and opening a new facility—might simultaneously be considered, as illustrated in Example 11.1 for locating Emergency Medical Services (EMS) in Tyler, Texas.

EXAMPLE 11.1	Tyler Emergency Medical Services (EMS) Location

Tyler, Texas, has two Emergency Medical Service (EMS) facilities to serve its population's medical needs. The locations of Tyler's two existing EMS facilities are shown on the map in Figure 11.2. Each is designated by a pushpin in the shape of a circled cross. The population density for each of the city's tracts is also shown. The darker red areas have up to 5,000 people per square mile. The southeast part of Tyler, census tract 18.03, experienced rapid growth, with its population almost doubling in the last 12 years. The residents of this tract have complained that it takes too long for the EMS vehicles to reach them.

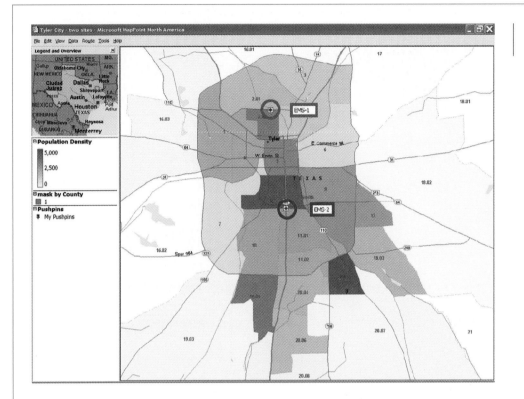

FIGURE **11.2**

Population Density for Tyler, Texas

A general guideline for locating EMS facilities in urban areas is that an EMS vehicle should be able to answer 95 percent of its calls within 10 minutes. This guideline was adopted by Tyler's city council after evaluating these complaints. The council commissioned a study to investigate whether this goal was being met in tracts that have a population density of 1,000 people per square mile. The council also decided that census tract 7, on the west side of the city with a population density of 967 people per square mile, should be included in the study as well. Thus, the census tracts that are as dark as or darker than census tract 7 should be within a 10-minute drive time zone of an EMS facility. The council is willing to redeploy Tyler's existing facilities, as well as fund one new location, giving it a total of three EMS facilities.

Where should EMS locate the three facilities so as to meet its coverage goals for Tyler? Assume that each EMS facility will have enough capacity to meet the needs of residents assigned to its coverage area.

SOLUTION

With MapPoint, it is easy to calculate a drive time zone by just selecting the pushpin and going under "Tools" on the menu bar to select drive time zone in terms of the number of minutes of drive time. The results are shown in Figure 11.3. The blue line shows the drive time zone for the EMS-1 facility, and the red line shows the drive time zone for the EMS-2 facility. This simple mapping confirms the complaints of the residents of census tract 18.03, most of whom cannot be reached in 10 minutes from EMS-2. In fact, running the drive time function again, it is determined that it takes 16 minutes to cover all of tract 18.03, which is clearly not acceptable. Furthermore, a small portion of census tract 1 and 20.06 are also within a ten minute drive time zone of EMS-2. In contrast, EMS-1 is located fairly centrally and is just about able to cover most of the northern census tracts in the city. So EMS-1 can be left where it is, but the relocation for EMS-2 and the location for new EMS-3 must be examined further.

Several sets of EMS locations were chosen through a trial-and-error approach and evaluated using MapPoint. The trial solutions were evaluated on the area left uncovered by the drive time zone and the population density of the uncovered area, which is judged by looking at the street map. The video on the Student CD-ROM better explores these alternatives. The greater the degree of coverage achieved, the better the solution. The best three-EMS facility solution that could be found is illustrated with the map in Figure 11.4 that shows different color shaded drive time zones for each of the three facilities. Unfortunately, a small region of census tract 20.06 (at the bottom of the map) is still not within a 10-minute drive time zone.

However, the entire census tract can be covered in a 12-minute drive time zone. The population of that census tract is less than 5 percent of the area under investigation, and the uncovered portion is a small percentage of the census tract. Clearly, more than 95 percent of the population of the city area will be within 10 minutes of an EMS facility with the recommended configuration.

Tyler EMS video on the Student CD-ROM shows how to do such a relocation analysis using MapPoint 2004

FIGURE **11.3**

EMS Response Drive Times
for Tyler, Texas

FIGURE **11.3**

EMS Response Drive Times
for Tyler, Texas

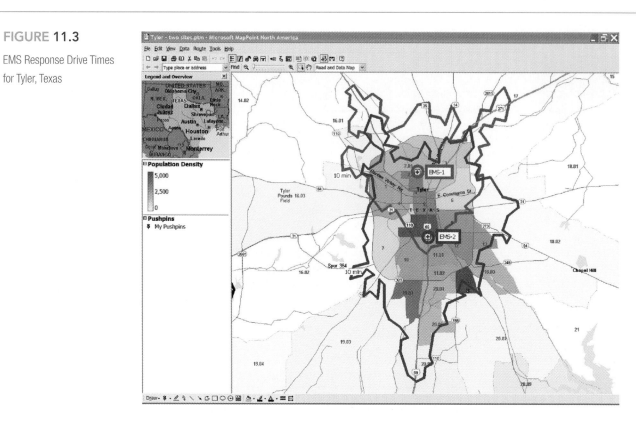

FIGURE **11.4**

Recommended Three-EMS
Solution for Tyler, Texas

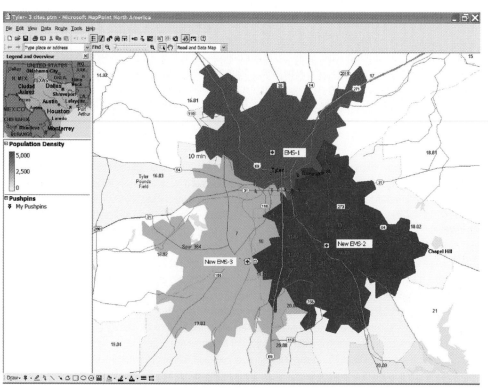

Decision Point Keep EMS-1 at its current location, and locate EMS-2 at the edge of census tract 18.03 in the southeast part of Tyler. Create a third EMS facility near the intersection of census tract 7, 10, and 19.01.

> LOCATING A SINGLE FACILITY <

Having examined trends and important factors in location, we now consider more specifically how a firm can make location decisions. In this section, we consider the case of locating only one new facility. When the facility is part of a firm's larger network of facilities, we assume that it is not interdependent; that is, a decision to open a restaurant in Tampa, Florida, is independent of whether the chain has a restaurant in Austin, Texas. Let us begin by considering how to decide whether a new location is needed, and then examine a systematic selection process aided by what's known as the *load–distance method* to deal with proximity.

COMPARING SEVERAL SITES

A systematic selection process begins after a perception or evidence indicates that opening a retail outlet, warehouse, office, or plant in a new location will improve performance. A team may be responsible for the selection decision in a large corporation, or an individual may make the decision in a small company. The process of selecting a new facility location involves a series of steps.

1. Identify the important location factors and categorize them as dominant or secondary.
2. Consider alternative regions; then narrow the choices to alternative communities and finally to specific sites.
3. Collect data on the alternatives from location consultants, state development agencies, city and county planning departments, chambers of commerce, land developers, electric power companies, banks, and onsite visits. Some of these data and information may also be contained inside the GIS.
4. Analyze the data collected, beginning with the *quantitative* factors—factors that can be measured in dollars, such as annual transportation costs or taxes. The quantitative factors can also be measured in terms other than dollars such as driving time and miles. These dollar values may be broken into separate cost categories (for example, inbound and outbound transportation, labor, construction, and utilities) and separate revenue sources (say sales, stock or bond issues, and interest income). These financial factors can then be converted to a single measure of financial merit such as total costs, return on investment (ROI), or net present value (NPV), and used to compare two or more sites, especially if capital costs for the new facility are also considered.
5. Bring the qualitative factors pertaining to each site into the evaluation. A *qualitative* factor is one that cannot be evaluated in dollar terms, such as community attitudes or quality of life. To merge quantitative and qualitative factors, some managers review the expected performance of each factor, while others assign each factor a weight of relative importance and calculate a weighted score for each site, using a preference matrix. What is important in one situation may be unimportant or less important in another. The site with the highest weighted score is best.

After thoroughly evaluating all potential sites, those making the study prepare a final report containing site recommendations, along with a summary of the data and analyses on which they are based. An audiovisual presentation of the key findings usually is delivered to top management in large firms.

Calculating Weighted Scores in a Preference Matrix	EXAMPLE 11.2

A new medical facility, Health-Watch, is to be located in Erie, Pennsylvania. The following table shows the location factors, weights, and scores (1 = poor, 5 = excellent) for one potential site. The weights in this case add up to 100 percent. A weighted score (*WS*) will be calculated for each site. What is the *WS* for this site?

Location Factor	Weight	Score
Total patient miles per month	25	4
Facility utilization	20	3
Average time per emergency trip	20	3
Expressway accessibility	15	4
Land and construction costs	10	1
Employee preferences	10	5

SOLUTION

The *WS* for this particular site is calculated by multiplying each factor's weight by its score and adding the results:

$$WS = (25 \times 4) + (20 \times 3) + (20 \times 3) + (15 \times 4) + (10 \times 1) + (10 \times 5)$$
$$= 100 + 60 + 60 + 60 + 10 + 50$$
$$= 340$$

The total *WS* of 340 can be compared with the total weighted scores for other sites being evaluated.

APPLYING THE LOAD–DISTANCE METHOD

load–distance method

A mathematical model used to evaluate locations based on proximity factors.

In the systematic selection process, the analyst must identify attractive candidate locations and compare them on the basis of quantitative factors. The load–distance method is one way to facilitate this step. It works much like the weighted-distance method does for designing flexible flow layouts. Several location factors relate directly to distance: proximity to markets, average distance to target customers, proximity to suppliers and resources, and proximity to other company facilities. The **load–distance method** is a mathematical model used to evaluate locations based on proximity factors. The objective is to select a location that minimizes the sum of the loads times the distance the load travels. Time may be used instead of distance if so desired.

Calculating a Load–Distance Score Suppose that a firm planning a new location wants to select a site that minimizes the distances that loads, particularly the larger ones, must travel to and from the site. Depending on the industry, a *load* may be shipments from suppliers, shipments between plants or to customers, or it may be customers or employees traveling to and from the facility. The firm seeks to minimize its load–distance (*ld*) score, generally by choosing a location, so that loads go short distances.

To calculate *ld* score for any potential location, we use the actual distance between any two points using a GIS system, and simply multiply the loads flowing to and from the facility by the distances traveled. Alternately, rectilinear or Euclidean distance as calculated in Chapter 8, "Process Layout," can also be used as an approximation for distance using the *x* coordinate and *y* coordinate. Travel time, actual miles, or rectilinear distances when using a grid approach, are all appropriate measures for distance. The formula for the *ld* score is

$$ld = \sum_{i} l_i d_i$$

These loads may be expressed as the number of potential customers needing physical presence for a service facility; loads may be tons or number of trips per week for a manufacturing facility. The score is the sum of these load–distance products. By selecting a new location based on *ld* scores, customer service is improved or transportation costs reduced.

The goal is to find one acceptable facility location that minimizes the score, where the location is defined by its *x* coordinate and *y* coordinate or the longitude and the latitude. Practical considerations rarely allow managers to select the exact location with the lowest possible score. For example, land might not be available there at a reasonable price, or other location factors may make the site undesirable.

Center of Gravity Testing different locations with the load–distance model is relatively simple if some systematic search process is followed. **Center of gravity** is a good starting point to evaluate locations in the target area using the load–distance method. The first step is to determine the *x* and *y* coordinates of different locations either in the form of the longitude and latitude of the locations, or by creating an (*x*, *y*) grid as was used in constructing flexible flow layouts in Chapter 8. The center of gravity's *x* coordinate, denoted *x**, is found by multiplying each point's *x* coordinate (either the longitude of the location or the *x* coordinate on a grid), by its load (l_i), summing these products ($\Sigma\, l_i x_i$), and then dividing by the sum of the loads ($\Sigma\, l_i$). The center of gravity's *y* coordinate (either the latitude or the *y* coordinate on a grid), denoted *y**, is found the same way. The formulas are as follows:

$$x^* = \frac{\sum_i l_i x_i}{\sum_i l_i} \quad \text{and} \quad y^* = \frac{\sum_i l_i y_i}{\sum_i l_i}$$

This location generally is not the optimal one for the distance measures, but it still is an excellent starting point. The load–distance scores for locations in its vicinity can be calculated until the solution is near optimal.

center of gravity

A good starting point to evaluate locations in the target area using the load–distance model.

| Finding the Center of Gravity for Health-Watch | EXAMPLE 11.3 |

The new Health-Watch facility is targeted to serve seven census tracts in Erie, Pennsylvania. Customers will travel from the seven census-tract centers to the new facility when they need health care. What is the target area's center of gravity for the Health-Watch medical facility?

SOLUTION

We use MapPoint in this solution, with coordinates represented in the form of latitude and longitude rather than an (*x*, *y*) grid to calculate the center of gravity. First the target area is displayed on the map of Erie, Pennsylvania, using MapPoint. In Figure 11.5 a pushpin is placed in the approximate geographical center of the census tracts. The location sensor is then turned on. By moving the cursor over the pushpin, the location sensor will register the

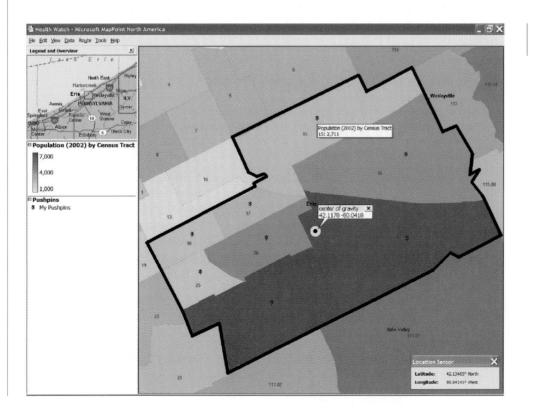

FIGURE **11.5**

Center of Gravity for Health-Watch

longitude and latitude for the pushpin. The population of each census tract is added to the map using MapPoint's built-in demographic data. Thus, we obtain the following table in which latitudes and longitudes for each of the seven census-tracts are given, along with their actual populations, in thousands.

ACTIVE MODEL 11.1

Active Model 11.1 on the Student CD-ROM explores the *ld* scores of locations in the vicinity of the center of gravity.

TUTOR 11.2

Tutor 11.2 on the Student CD-ROM provides another example on how to calculate the center of gravity.

Census Tract	Population	Latitude	Longitude	Population × Latitude	Population × Longitude
15	2,711	42.134	−80.041	114,225.27	−216,991.15
16	4,161	42.129	−80.023	175,298.77	−332,975.70
17	2,988	42.122	−80.055	125,860.54	−239,204.34
25	2,512	42.112	−80.066	105,785.34	−201,125.79
26	4,342	42.117	−80.052	182,872.01	−347,585.78
27	6,687	42.116	−80.023	281,629.69	−535,113.80
28	6,789	42.107	−80.051	285,864.42	−543,466.24
Total	**30,190**			**1,271,536.04**	**−2,416,462.80**

Next we solve for the center of gravity x^* and y^*. Because the coordinates are given as longitude and latitude, x^* is the longitude and y^* is the latitude for the center of gravity.

$$x^* = \frac{1,271,536.05}{30,190} = 42.1178$$

$$y^* = \frac{-2,416,462.81}{30,190} = -80.0418$$

Active Model 11.1 on the Student CD-ROM confirms these calculations for center of gravity, and allows us to explore other alternative locations as well.

Decision Point The center of gravity is (42.12 North, 80.04 West), and is shown on the map to be fairly central to the target area. Solved Problem 3 at the end of this chapter illustrates an example of using grid coordinates rather than latitude and longitude for center of gravity and load–distance problems.

USING BREAK-EVEN ANALYSIS

Break-even analysis can help a manager compare location alternatives on the basis of quantitative factors that can be expressed in terms of total cost. It is particularly useful when the manager wants to define the ranges over which each alternative is best. The basic steps for graphic and algebraic solutions are as follows.

1. Determine the variable costs and fixed costs for each site. Recall that *variable costs* are the portion of the total cost that varies directly with the volume of output. Recall that *fixed costs* are the portion of the total cost that remains constant regardless of output levels.

2. Plot the total cost lines—the sum of variable and fixed costs—for all the sites on a single graph (for assistance, see Tutors A.1 and A.2 in OM Explorer).

3. Identify the approximate ranges for which each location has the lowest cost.

4. Solve algebraically for the break-even points over the relevant ranges.

EXAMPLE 11.4	Break-Even Analysis for Location

An operations manager narrowed the search for a new facility location to four communities. The annual fixed costs (land, property taxes, insurance, equipment, and buildings) and the variable costs (labor, materials, transportation, and variable overhead) are as follows:

Community	Fixed Costs per Year	Variable Costs per Unit
A	$150,000	$62
B	$300,000	$38
C	$500,000	$24
D	$600,000	$30

Step 1. Plot the total cost curves for all the communities on a single graph. Identify on the graph the approximate range over which each community provides the lowest cost.

Step 2. Using break-even analysis, calculate the break-even quantities over the relevant ranges. If the expected demand is 15,000 units per year, what is the best location?

SOLUTION

Step 1. To plot a community's total cost line, let us first compute the total cost for two output levels: $Q = 0$ and $Q = 20,000$ units per year. For the $Q = 0$ level, the total cost is simply the fixed costs. For the $Q = 20,000$ level, the total cost (fixed plus variable costs) is as follows:

Community	Fixed Costs	Variable Costs (Cost per Unit) (No. of Units)	Total Cost (Fixed + Variable)
A	$150,000	$62(20,000) = $1,240,000	$1,390,000
B	$300,000	$38(20,000) = $ 760,000	$1,060,000
C	$500,000	$24(20,000) = $ 480,000	$ 980,000
D	$600,000	$30(20,000) = $ 600,000	$1,200,000

Figure 11.6 shows the graph of the total cost lines. The line for community A goes from (0, 150) to (20, 1,390). The graph indicates that community A is best for low volumes, B for intermediate volumes, and C for high volumes. We should no longer consider community D, because both its fixed *and* its variable costs are higher than community C's.

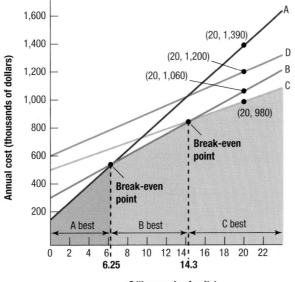

ACTIVE MODEL 11.2

Active Model 11.2 on the Student CD-ROM provides insight on defining the three relevant ranges for this example.

TUTOR 11.3

Tutor 11.3 on the Student CD-ROM provides another example to practice break-even analysis for location decisions.

FIGURE 11.6

Break-Even Analysis of Four Candidate Locations

Step 2. The break-even quantity between A and B lies at the end of the first range, where A is best, and the beginning of the second range, where B is best. We find it by setting their total cost equations equal to each other and solving:

$$\underset{(A)}{\$150,000 + \$62Q} = \underset{(B)}{\$300,000 + \$38Q}$$

$$Q = 6,250 \text{ units}$$

The break-even quantity between B and C lies at the end of the range over which B is best and the beginning of the final range where C is best. It is

$$\underset{(B)}{\$300,000 + \$38Q} = \underset{(C)}{\$500,000 + \$24Q}$$

$$Q = 14,286 \text{ units}$$

No other break-even quantities are needed. The break-even point between A and C lies above the shaded area, which does not mark either the start or the end of one of the three relevant ranges.

Decision Point   Management located the new facility at Community C, because the 15,000 units-per-year demand forecast lies in the high-volume range.

> LOCATING A FACILITY WITHIN A NETWORK OF FACILITIES <

When a firm with a network of existing facilities plans a new facility, one of two conditions exists: Either the facilities operate independently (examples include a chain of restaurants, health clinics, banks, or retail establishments) or the facilities interact (examples include component manufacturing plants, assembly plants, and warehouses). Independently operating units can be located by treating each as a separate single facility, as described in the preceding section. Locating interacting facilities introduces new issues, such as how to allocate work between the facilities and how to determine the best capacity for each. Changing the work allocations in turn affects the size (or capacity utilization) of the various facilities. Thus, the multiple-facility location problem has three dimensions—location, allocation, and capacity—that must be solved simultaneously. In many cases, the analyst can identify a workable solution merely by looking for patterns in the cost, demand, and capacity data and using trial-and-error calculations. In other cases, more formal approaches are needed.

THE GIS METHOD FOR LOCATING MULTIPLE FACILITIES

The use of GIS tools often simplifies the search for solution. Visualizing customer locations and data, as well as the transportation structure of roads and interstate highways, allows the analyst to quickly arrive at a reasonable solution to the multiple facility location problems. Load–distance score and center of gravity data can be merged with customer databases in Excel to arrive at trial locations for facilities, which can then be evaluated for annual driving time or distance using a GIS such as MapPoint and a Visual Basic Macro in Excel. A five-step framework that captures the use of GIS for locating multiple facilities is outlined here.

1. Map the data for existing customers and facilities in the GIS.
2. Visually split the entire operating area into the number of parts or subregions that equal the number of facilities to be located.
3. Assign a facility location for each region based on the visual density of customer concentration or other factors. Alternately, determine the center of gravity for each part or subregion identified in step 2 as the starting location point for the facility in that subregion.

4. Search for alternate sites around the center of gravity to pick a feasible location that meets the firm's managerial criteria such as proximity to major metropolitan areas or highways.

5. Compute total load–distance scores and perform capacity checks before finalizing the locations for each region.

Such an approach can have many applications, including the design of supply chain distribution networks as illustrated in Example 11.5 and the accompanying video on the Student CD-ROM.

Locating Multiple Facilities for Witherspoon Automotive	EXAMPLE 11.5

Witherspoon Automotive, a remanufacturer of automotive components and subassemblies, delivers full truckloads of parts to its customers, and returns with a shipment of used automotive parts for disassembly and remanufacturing. The company presently operates out of two locations in the Southeast: Spartanburg, South Carolina, and Orlando, Florida. Each of these locations has a remanufacturing facility, along with an attached warehouse that serves as a distribution center (DC). The Spartanburg facility covers a total of 362 customers in Georgia, North Carolina, South Carolina, and parts of Alabama, Tennessee, and Virginia. The Orlando facility covers a total of 66 customers mostly in Florida, and a small portion of Alabama and Georgia. The Spartanburg DC and Orlando DC shipped 17,219 and 4,629 full truckloads, respectively, to their customers last year. The operating regions and the specific customer locations (in the form of pushpins) covered by both these facilities are shown in Figure 11.7.

The senior management at Witherspoon Automotive decided to close the Spartanburg facility because of its age and obsolescence, and instead split the Spartanburg region into two new regions, each with its own manufacturing and distribution center. In addition, the following five important location factors affect their final decision:

1. In order to promote a better quality of life for its workers, the new facilities should be located in a major metropolitan area.

2. Distribution costs are a major determinant of profits, and so the total load–distance score should be minimized in order to minimize the distribution costs.

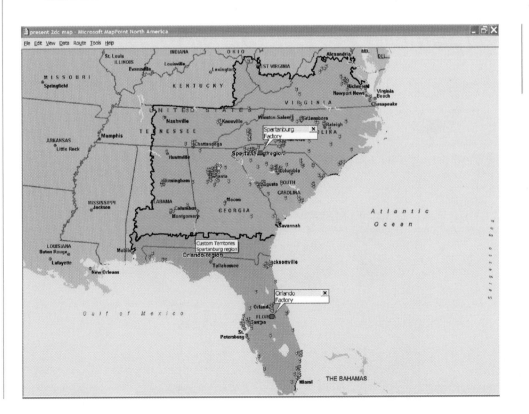

FIGURE **11.7**

Operating Regions and Customer Location for Witherspoon Automotive

3. Because of the diseconomies of scale previously experienced with the Spartanburg plant, the size of the two new facilities should not exceed a maximum of 9,500 truckloads of output per year.

4. The customer truckloads allocated between the two facilities should be fairly balanced given the previous year's demand data.

5. Marketing indicated that they are going to develop the northern Alabama market. Consequently, the new distribution network should be able to accommodate up to an additional 1,000 full truckload shipments per year from the Alabama market.

Where should the two new facilities be opened, assuming that the Orlando DC will stay where it is, and that fixed cost differences in opening a new facility are comparable across most potential sites in the region?

SOLUTION

Using the data in their system and MapPoint, the managers at Witherspoon automotive overlaid the locations and the number of full truckload shipments delivered last year for each customer in the Spartanburg region onto a map. A video on the Student CD-ROM shows how to perform this analysis using MapPoint. The map was arbitrarily coded such that customers that received 52 to 80 shipments last year were shown in blue or white, while customers with 10 to 37 shipments were coded in black or red. To achieve a greater degree of aggregation in customer base and to also give due consideration to the quality of life location factor, the map was changed from displaying data for each street address (customer) to an aggregate view that displays data for each Metropolitan Statistical Area (MSA). (It is simple to change the representation of the data on the map in MapPoint.) The darker the shade, the greater is the number of truckloads in the MSA. It was visually clear that Atlanta and Charlotte were the major markets, with Columbia, South Carolina; Greenville, South Carolina; and Richmond, Virginia, also having a heavy concentration of customers. From this map in Figure 11.8, it was easy to see that the dark green shaded area in Atlanta has a heavy customer-trips concentration. It represents 4,475 full truckloads, which would easily support half a facility. Because one of the major objectives was to minimize the total load–distance score, it seems reasonable for the management to locate one of the two new facilities near Atlanta. This decision will also achieve two other management objectives, in that the facility is near a major metropolitan area and is also well placed to serve the proposed expansion of the northern Alabama market. Management stated that if it decides to locate a facility near the Atlanta area, it would be in Buford, Georgia.

Witherspoon Automotive video on the Student CD-ROM shows how to locate multiple facilities using MapPoint 2004

FIGURE 11.8

Truckload Concentration for Witherspoon

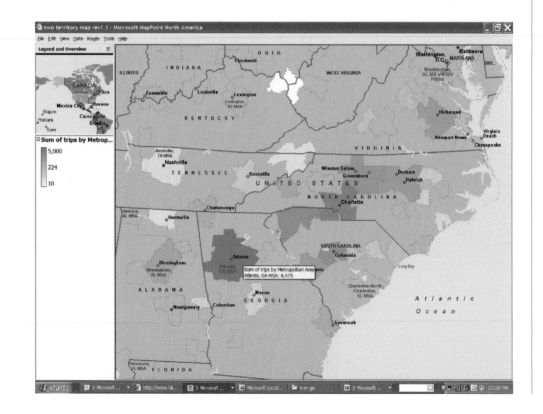

FIGURE **11.9**

Witherspoon's Facilities Areas

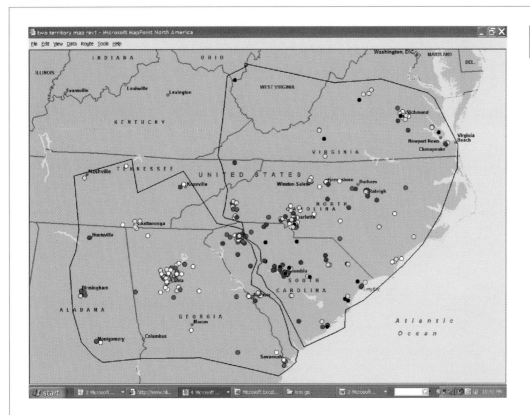

The next step was to partition the customers into two regions, each with a total demand of less than 9,500 truckloads. Because it seemed clear that the Atlanta area would have a facility, one region was circled around Atlanta as shown in Figure 11.9. Furthermore, if the northern Alabama market develops as hoped, it would handle an additional 1,000 truckloads. Because of this potential, the Atlanta region can only handle 8,500 truckloads for current customers. After a careful look at the map data, it was decided that Georgia, Tennessee, Alabama, and the parts of South Carolina that were within 2.5 hours of the Atlanta facility would be assigned to the Atlanta region. The Augusta/Aiken MSA that straddles the Georgia/South Carolina border was also added to this region to balance the two regions. This scenario results in the Atlanta region being assigned 8,397 truckloads and the second region having 8,822 trips, and achieves a 48.8 percent to 51.2 percent split while still allowing capacity in the Atlanta region for the proposed expansion of the northern Alabama market.

In order to identify a good location for the second facility, the center of gravity for the second region was determined to find a good starting point. This calculation was done by Witherspoon Automotive managers by selecting the proposed boundaries for the second region and importing the customer data to Excel. Then management used a Visual Basic for Applications (VBA) macro that accessed the data in MapPoint to determine the center of gravity. An OM Explorer Solver file titled "Center of Gravity Using MS MapPoint 2004-Example 11.5" is included on the Student CD-ROM to perform this function.

Looking at the map in Figure 11.9, it appears that the center of the second region is around Durham, North Carolina. The center of gravity, however, is considerably south and west of Durham. The center of gravity for the second region is close to a National Forest in Randolph County, North Carolina—not too far from Charlotte (see Figure 11.10). Such an outcome is to be expected because the Charlotte and to a lesser extent Columbia, South Carolina, markets have such a large percentage of the truckload volume for this region. However, the center of gravity does not appear to be a promising site because it is only near one customer (see the center of gravity location on the map in Figure 11.10).

Given this dilemma, the management of Witherspoon Automotive decided to pick a site next to the center of gravity as well as several sites in the general area of the center of gravity that are near Interstate I-85 (because almost every trip would require the truck driver to first drive to or go near Interstate I-85.) Load–distance scores were computed using driving mileage and driving time based on last year's demand for each of the possible locations. This computation was performed using a VBA macro in Excel, and which is available on the Student CD-ROM as an OM Explorer Solver file titled "Multiple Facilities Location-Driving Time and Distance Calculator Using MS MapPoint 2004-Example 11.5." More sophisticated GIS systems have this capability, and inexpensive

FIGURE **11.10**

Potential Sites for Witherspoon's Second Facility

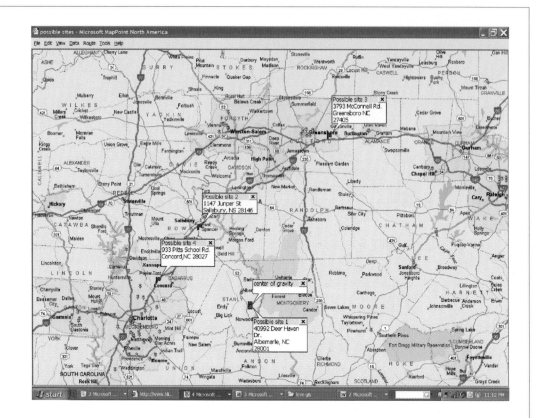

add-ins to MapPoint that can perform this calculation, are available as well. The following results were obtained for load–distance calculations based on one-way trips.

Site	City	Load–Distance Using One-Way Mileage	Load–Distance Using One-Way Travel Hours
1	Albemarle	1,331,608	22,194
2	Salisbury	1,075,839	18,541
3	Greensboro	1,222,675	20,378
4	Concord	1,037,424	17,938

As the Witherspoon Automotive managers reviewed the results, they noted that Concord and Salisbury locations would provide the minimum mileage and drive time. The Albemarle site, which is near the center of gravity, is the worst of the four possibilities. Concord has the additional advantage of being near Charlotte—fulfilling the managerial objective of being located near a major city. If the company located the Atlanta region facility at Buford, Georgia, and the Charlotte region facility at Concord, North Carolina, it could reduce its one-way miles by 1,770,461 miles and reduce one-way travel time by 28,473 hours over the present arrangement with a location in Spartanburg, South Carolina.

Another attractive feature of this solution is that the Greenville, South Carolina, and the Augusta, Georgia, markets are almost as close to the Concord facility as they are to the Buford facility. Management can reassign customers in these markets to the Charlotte region at little additional cost if the northern Alabama market grows faster than expected.

Decision Point The Witherspoon Automotive management decided to locate the first facility in Buford, and the second one in Concord along the I-85 corridor. These locations are within the MSA of Atlanta and Charlotte, respectively, and reflect the wishes of management to be near a major metropolitan area. Creating two distribution centers in what is presently the Spartanburg region will reduce total mileage for Witherspoon Automotive by more than 3.5 million miles, and reduce annual drive time by almost 57,000 hours. These logistical savings are substantial, and meet all the location criteria that had been specified at the beginning of the decision-making process.

THE TRANSPORTATION METHOD

The **transportation method** is a quantitative approach that can help solve multiple-facility location problems. We use it here to determine the allocation pattern that minimizes the cost of shipping products from two or more plants, or *sources of supply,* to two or more warehouses, or *destinations.*[1] We focus on the setup and interpretation of the problem, leaving the rest of the solution process to a software package on a computer. The transportation method is based on linear programming. More efficient algorithms for solving this problem can be found in textbooks covering quantitative methods and management science.

The transportation method does not solve *all* facets of the multiple-facility location problem. If only finds the *best* shipping pattern between plants and warehouses for a particular set of plant locations, each with a given capacity. The analyst must try a variety of location–capacity combinations and use the transportation method to find the optimal distribution for each one. Distribution costs (variable shipping and possibly variable production costs) are but one important input in evaluating a particular location–allocation combination. Investment costs and other fixed costs also must be considered, along with various qualitative factors. This complete analysis must be made for each reasonable location–capacity combination. Because of the importance of making a good decision, this extra effort is well worth its cost.

Setting up the Initial Tableau The first step in solving a transportation problem is to format it in a standard matrix, sometimes called a *tableau.* The basic steps in setting up an initial tableau are as follows:

1. Create a row for each plant (existing or new) being considered and a column for each warehouse.

2. Add a column for plant capacities and a row for warehouse demands and insert their specific numerical values.

3. Each cell not in the requirements row or capacity column represents a shipping route from a plant to a warehouse. Insert the unit costs in the upper right-hand corner of each of these cells.

The Sunbelt Pool Company is considering building a new 500-unit plant because business is booming. One possible location is Atlanta. Figure 11.11 shows a tableau with its plant capacity, warehouse requirements, and shipping costs. The tableau shows, for example, that shipping one unit from the existing Phoenix plant to warehouse 1 in San Antonio, Texas, costs $5.00. Costs are assumed to increase linearly with the size of the shipment; that is, the cost is the same *per unit* regardless of the size of the total shipment.

In the transportation method, the sum of the shipments in a row must equal the corresponding plant's capacity. For example, in Figure 11.11, the total shipments from the Atlanta plant to warehouses 1, 2, and 3 located in San Antonio, Texas; Hot Springs, Arkansas; and Sioux Falls, South Dakota, respectively, must add up to 500. Similarly, the sum of shipments to a column must equal the corresponding warehouse's demand requirements. Thus, shipments to warehouse 1 in San Antonio, Texas, from Phoenix and Atlanta must total 200 units.

Dummy Plants or Warehouses The transportation method also requires that the sum of capacities equal the sum of demands, which happens to be the case at 900 units (see

transportation method

A quantitative approach that can help solve multiple-facility location problems.

FIGURE 11.11

Initial Tableau

Plant	Warehouse			Capacity
	San Antonio, TX (1)	Hot Springs, AR (2)	Sioux Falls, SD (3)	
Phoenix	5.00	6.00	5.40	400
Atlanta	7.00	4.60	6.60	500
Requirements	200	400	300	900 / 900

[1]It can also be used to determine an optimal sales and operations plan (see Chapter 14, "Sales and Operations Planning") or an optimal allocation of service accounts to service centers.

Figure 11.11). In many real problems, total capacity may exceed requirements, or vice versa. If capacity exceeds requirements by r units, we add an extra column (a *dummy warehouse*) with a demand of r units and make the shipping costs in the newly created cells $0. Shipments are not actually made, so they represent unused plant capacity. Similarly, if requirements exceed capacity by r units, we add an extra row (a *dummy plant*) with a capacity of r units. We assign shipping costs equal to the stockout costs of the new cells. If stockout costs are unknown or are the same for all warehouses, we simply assign shipping costs of $0 per unit to each cell in the dummy row. The optimal solution will not be affected because the shortage of r units is required in all cases. Adding a dummy warehouse or dummy plant ensures that the sum of capacities equals the sum of demands. Some software packages automatically add them when we make the data inputs.

Finding a Solution After the initial tableau has been set up, the goal is to find the least-cost allocation pattern that satisfies all demands and exhausts all capacities. This pattern can be found by using the transportation method, which guarantees the optimal solution. The initial tableau is filled in with a feasible solution that satisfies all warehouse demands and exhausts all plant capacities. Then a new tableau is created, defining a new solution that has a lower total cost. This iterative process continues until no improvements can be made in the current solution, signaling that the optimal solution has been found. When using a computer package, all that you have to input is the information for the initial tableau.

Another procedure is the simplex method (see Supplement E, "Linear Programming"), although more inputs are required. The transportation problem is actually a special case of linear programming, which can be modeled with a decision variable for each cell in the tableau, a constraint for each row in the tableau (requiring that each plant's capacity be fully utilized), and a constraint for each column in the tableau (requiring that each warehouse's demand be satisfied).

Whichever method is used, the number of nonzero shipments in the optimal solution will never exceed the sum of the numbers of plants and warehouses minus 1. The Sunbelt Pool Company has 2 plants and 3 warehouses, so not more than 4 (or $3 + 2 - 1$) shipments are needed in the optimal solution.

EXAMPLE 11.6	Interpreting the Optimal Solution

The optimal solution for the Sunbelt Pool Company is shown in Figure 11.12. Tutor 11.4 can also be used to solve such problems, and is set up to handle up to three sources and four destinations (for larger problems, use the Transportation Method Solver). With only two sources, we make the third row a "dummy" with a capacity of 0, and the fourth warehouse a "dummy" with a demand of 0. The bold numbers show the optimal shipments. Verify that each plant's capacity is exhausted and that each warehouse's demand is filled. Also confirm that the total transportation cost of the solution is $4,580.

FIGURE 11.12

Optimal Tableau for Sunbelt Pool Company

Sources	Destinations				Capacity
	San Antonio, TX	Hot Springs, AR	Sioux Falls, SD	Dummy	
Phoenix	5.00 / **200**	6.00	5.40 / **200**	0.00	400
Atlanta	7.00	4.60 / **400**	6.60 / **100**	0.00	500
Dummy	0.00	0.00	0.00	0.00	0
Requirements	200	400	300	0.00 / 900	900

	San Antonio, TX	Hot Springs, AR	Sioux Falls, SD	Dummy	
Costs	$1,000	$1,840	$1,740	$0	
Total Cost					$4,580

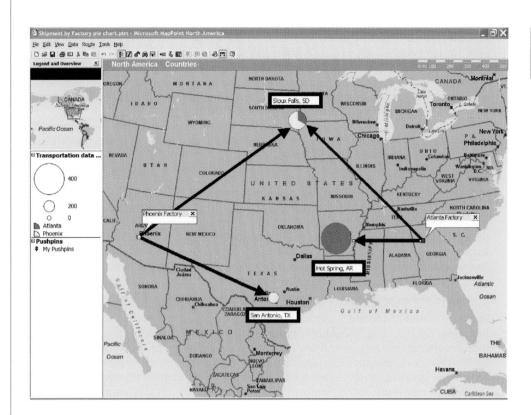

FIGURE 11.13

Optimal Transportation Solution
for Sunbelt Pool Company

SOLUTION

The existing network of plants and how they supply the three warehouses are shown on the map in Figure 11.13, with Phoenix plant and its shipments represented in yellow and Atlanta plant and its shipments represented in red. The size of the circles for the three warehouses represents their capacities and how much of that capacity is being supplied from which plant. Phoenix ships 200 units to warehouse 1 in San Antonia, Texas, and 200 units to warehouse 3 in Sioux Falls, South Dakota, exhausting its 400-unit capacity. Atlanta ships 400 units of its 500-unit capacity to warehouse 2 in Hot Springs, Arkansas, and the remaining 100 units to warehouse 3 in Sioux Falls, South Dakota. All warehouse demand is satisfied: warehouse 1 in San Antonio, Texas, is fully supplied by Phoenix and warehouse 2 in Hot Springs, Arkansas, by Atlanta. Warehouse 3 in Sioux Falls, South Dakota, receives 200 units from Phoenix and 100 units from Atlanta, satisfying its 300-unit demand. The total transportation cost is 200($5.00) + 200($5.40) + 400($4.60) + 100($6.60) = $4,580.

Decision Point Management must evaluate other plant locations before deciding on the best one. The optimal solution does not necessarily mean that the best choice is to open an Atlanta plant. It just means that the best allocation pattern for the current choices on the other two dimensions of this multiple-facility location problem (that is, a capacity of 400 units at Phoenix and the new plant's location at Atlanta) results in total transportation costs of $4,580.

TUTOR 11.4

Tutor 11.4 on the Student CD-ROM provides another example of how to apply the transportation method to location decisions.

The Larger Solution Process Other costs and various qualitative factors also must be considered as additional parts of a complete evaluation. For example, the annual profits earned from the expansion must be balanced against the land and construction costs of a new plant in Atlanta. Thus, management might use the preference matrix approach (see Example 11.1) to account for the full set of location factors.

The analyst should also evaluate other capacity and location combinations. For example, one possibility is to expand in Phoenix and build a smaller plant at Atlanta. Alternatively, a new plant could be built at another location, or several new plants could be built. The analyst must repeat the analysis for each such likely location strategy.

OTHER METHODS OF LOCATION ANALYSIS

Many location analysis problems are even more complex than those discussed so far. Consider the complexity that a medium-sized manufacturer faces when distributing products through warehouses, or *distribution centers,* to various demand centers. The problem is to determine the number, size, allocation pattern, and location of the warehouses. The situation may involve thousands of demand centers, hundreds of potential warehouse locations, several plants, and multiple product lines. Transportation rates depend on the direction of shipment, product, quantity, rate breaks, and geographic area.

Such complexity requires the use of a computer for a comprehensive evaluation. Three basic types of computer models have been developed for this purpose: (1) heuristics, (2) simulation, and (3) optimization.

heuristics

Solution guidelines, or rules of thumb, that find feasible—but not necessarily the best—solutions to problems.

Heuristics Solution guidelines, or rules of thumb, that find feasible—but not necessarily the best—solutions to problems are called **heuristics**. Their advantages include efficiency and an ability to handle general views of a problem. The systematic search procedure utilizing a target area's center of gravity, described earlier for single-facility location problems, is a typical heuristic procedure. One of the first heuristics to be computerized for location problems was proposed four decades ago to handle several hundred potential warehouse sites and several thousand demand centers (Kuehn and Hamburger, 1963). Many other heuristic models are available today for analyzing a variety of situations.

simulation

A modeling technique that reproduces the behavior of a system.

Simulation A modeling technique that reproduces the behavior of a system is called **simulation**. Simulation allows certain variables to be manipulated and shows what effect they have on select operating measures. Simulation models allow the analyst to evaluate different location alternatives by trial and error. It is up to the analyst to propose the most reasonable alternatives. A simulation model can handle more realistic views of a problem and involves the analyst in the solution process itself. For each run, the analyst, inputs the facilities to be opened, and the simulator typically makes the allocation decisions based on some reasonable assumptions that have been written into the computer program.

The Ralston-Purina Company used simulation to assist the company in locating warehouses to serve 137 demand centers, five field warehouses, and four plants. Random demand at each demand center by product type was simulated over a period of time. Demand was met by the closest warehouse that had available inventory. Data were produced by simulating inventory levels, transportation costs, warehouse operating costs, and backorders. Ralston-Purina implemented the result of the simulation, which showed that the least-cost alternative would be to consolidate the five field warehouse into only three.

optimization

A procedure used to determine the "best" solution; generally utilizes simplified and less realistic views of a problem.

Optimization The transportation method was one of the first optimization procedures for solving one part (the allocation pattern) of multiple-facility location problems. In contrast to heuristics and simulation, **optimization** involves procedures to determine the *best* solution. Even though this approach might appear to be preferable, it has a limitation: Optimization procedures generally utilize simplified and less realistic views of a problem. However, the payoffs can be substantial.

> STUDENT CD-ROM AND INTERNET RESOURCES <

The Student CD-ROM and the Companion Website at **www.prenhall.com/krajewski** contain many tools, activities, and resources designed for this chapter.

> KEY EQUATIONS <

1. Load–distance score: $ld = \sum_i l_i d_i$

2. Center of gravity: $x^* = \dfrac{\sum_i l_i x_i}{\sum_i l_i}$ and $y^* = \dfrac{\sum_i l_i y_i}{\sum_i l_i}$

> KEY TERMS <

center of gravity 433
critical mass 424
facility location 420
geographical information
    system (GIS) 424

heuristics 444
load–distance method 432
optimization 444

quality of life 422
simulation 444
transportation method 441

> SOLVED PROBLEM 1 <

An electronics manufacturer must expand by building a second facility. The search is narrowed to four locations, all of which are acceptable to management in terms of dominant factors. Assessment of these sites in terms of seven location factors is shown in Table 11.1. For example, location A has a factor score of 5 (excellent) for labor climate; the weight for this factor (20) is the highest of any.

    Calculate the weighted score for each location. Which location should be recommended?

SOLUTION

Based on the weighted scores shown in Table 11.2, location C is the preferred site, although location B is a close second.

TABLE 11.1 | Factor Information for Electronics Manufacturer

		Factor Score for Each Location			
Location Factor	**Factor Weight**	**A**	**B**	**C**	**D**
1. Labor climate	20	5	4	4	5
2. Quality of life	16	2	3	4	1
3. Transportation system	16	3	4	3	2
4. Proximity to markets	14	5	3	4	4
5. Proximity to materials	12	2	3	3	4
6. Taxes	12	2	5	5	4
7. Utilities	10	5	4	3	3

TABLE 11.2 | Calculating Weighted Scores for Electronics Manufacturer

		Weighted Score for Each Location			
Location Factor	**Factor Weight**	**A**	**B**	**C**	**D**
1. Labor climate	20	100	80	80	100
2. Quality of life	16	32	48	64	16
3. Transportation system	16	48	64	48	32
4. Proximity to markets	14	70	42	56	56
5. Proximity to materials	12	24	36	36	48
6. Taxes	12	24	60	60	48
7. Utilities	10	50	40	30	30
Totals	100	348	370	374	330

> SOLVED PROBLEM 2 <————————————————————————————————————

The operations manager for Mile-High Beer narrowed the search for a new facility location to seven communities. Annual fixed costs (land, property taxes, insurance, equipment, and buildings) and variable costs (labor, materials, transportation, and variable overhead) are shown in Table 11.3.

a. Which of the communities can be eliminated from further consideration because they are dominated (both variable and fixed costs are higher) by another community?

b. Plot the total cost curves for all remaining communities on a single graph. Identify on the graph the approximate range over which each community provides the lowest cost.

c. Using break-even analysis, calculate the break-even quantities to determine the range over which each community provides the lowest cost.

SOLUTION

a. Aurora and Colorado Springs are dominated by Fort Collins, because both fixed and variable costs are higher for those communities than for Fort Collins. Englewood is dominated by Golden.

b. Figure 11.14 shows that Fort Collins is best for low volumes, Boulder for intermediate volumes, and Denver for high volumes. Although Golden is not dominated by any community, it is the second or third choice over the entire range. Golden does not become the lowest-cost choice at any volume.

c. The break-even point between Fort Collins and Boulder is

$$\$1,200,000 + \$15Q = \$2,000,000 + \$12Q$$
$$Q = 266,667 \text{ barrels per year}$$

TABLE 11.3	Fixed and Variable Costs for Mile-High Beer	
Community	**Fixed Costs per Year**	**Variable Costs per Barrel**
Aurora	$1,600,000	$17.00
Boulder	$2,000,000	$12.00
Colorado Springs	$1,500,000	$16.00
Denver	$3,000,000	$10.00
Englewood	$1,800,000	$15.00
Fort Collins	$1,200,000	$15.00
Golden	$1,700,000	$14.00

FIGURE **11.14**

Break-Even Analysis of Four
Candidate Locations

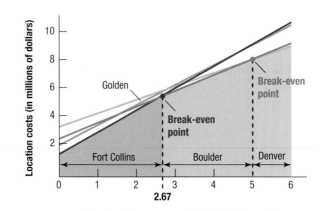

The break-even point between Denver and Boulder is

$$\$3,000,000 + \$10Q = \$2,000,000 + \$12Q$$
$$Q = 500,000 \text{ barrels per year}$$

> **SOLVED PROBLEM 3** <

A supplier to the electric utility industry has a heavy product, and the transportation costs are high. One market area includes the lower part of the Great Lakes region and the upper portion of the southeastern region. More than 600,000 tons are to be shipped to eight major customer locations as shown in Table 11.4.

a. Calculate the center of gravity, rounding coordinates to the nearest tenth.
b. Calculate the load–distance score for this location, using rectilinear distance.

SOLUTION

a. The center of gravity is (12.4, 9.2).

$$\sum_i l_i = 5+92+70+35+9+227+16+153 = 607$$

$$\sum_i l_i x_i = 5(7)+92(8)+70(11)+35(11)+9(12)+227(13)+16(14)+153(15)$$
$$= 7,504$$

$$x^* = \frac{\sum_i l_i y_i}{\sum_i l_i} = \frac{7,504}{607} = 12.4$$

$$\sum_i l_i y_i = 5(13)+92(12)+70(10)+35(7)+9(4)+227(11)+16(10)+153(5) = 5,572$$

$$y^* = \frac{\sum_i l_i y_i}{\sum_i l_i} = \frac{5,572}{607} = 9.2$$

b. The load–distance score is

$$ld = \sum_i l_i d_i = 5(5.4+3.8)+92(4.4+2.8)+70(1.4+0.8)+35(1.4+2.2)$$
$$+9(0.4+5.2)+227(0.6+1.8)+16(1.6+0.8)+153(2.6+4.2)$$
$$= 2,662.4$$

where

$$d_i = |x_i - x^*| + |y_i - y^*|$$

TABLE 11.4	Markets for Electric Utilities Supplier	
Customer Location	**Tons Shipped**	**x, y Coordinates**
Three Rivers, MI	5,000	(7, 13)
Fort Wayne, IN	92,000	(8, 12)
Columbus, OH	70,000	(11, 10)
Ashland, KY	35,000	(11, 7)
Kingsport, TN	9,000	(12, 4)
Akron, OH	227,000	(13, 11)
Wheeling, WV	16,000	(14, 10)
Roanoke, VA	153,000	(15, 5)

> SOLVED PROBLEM 4 <

The Arid Company makes canoe paddles to serve distribution centers in Worchester, Rochester, and Dorchester from existing plants in Battle Creek and Cherry Creek. Annual demand is expected to increase as projected in the bottom row of the tableau shown in Figure 11.15. Arid is considering locating a plant near the headwaters of Dee Creek. Annual capacity for each plant is shown in the right-hand column of the tableau. Transportation costs per paddle are shown in the tableau in the small boxes. For example, the cost to ship one paddle from Battle Creak to Worchester in $4.37. The optimal allocations are also shown. For example, Battle Creek ships 12,000 units to Rochester. What are the estimated transportation costs associated with this allocation pattern?

FIGURE 11.15

Optimal Solution for Arid Company

Source	Destination			Capacity
	Worchester	Rochester	Dorchester	
Battle Creek	$4.37	$4.25 **12,000**	$4.89	12,000
Cherry Creek	$4.00 **6,000**	$5.00 **4,000**	$5.27	10,000
Dee Creek	$4.13	$4.50 **6,000**	$3.75 **12,000**	18,000
Demand	6,000	22,000	12,000	40,000

SOLUTION

The total cost is $167,000.

Ship 12,000 units from Battle Creek to Rochester @ $4.25.	Cost = $ 51,000
Ship 6,000 units from Cherry Creek to Worchester @ $4.00.	Cost = $ 24,000
Ship 4,000 units from Cherry Creek to Rochester @ $5.00.	Cost = $ 20,000
Ship 6,000 units from Dee Creek to Rochester @ $4.50.	Cost = $ 27,000
Ship 12,000 units from Dee Creek to Dorchester @ $3.75.	Cost = $ 45,000
	Total $167,000

> DISCUSSION QUESTIONS <

1. Break into teams. Select two organizations, one in services and one in manufacturing, which are known to some of your team members. What are the key factors that each organization would consider in locating a new facility? What data would you want to collect before evaluating the location options, and how would you collect the data? Explain.

2. The owner of a major league baseball team is considering moving his team from its current city in the upper Midwest to a city in the Southeast that offers a larger television market and a new stadium and holds the potential for greater fan support. What other factors should the owner consider before actually making the decision to relocate?

> PROBLEMS <

Software, such as OM Explorer, Active Models, and POM for Windows, is packaged with every new copy of the textbook. Check with your instructor on how best to use it. In many cases, the instructor wants you to understand how to do the calculations by hand. At most, the software provides a check on your calculations. When calculations are particularly complex and the goal is interpreting the results in making decisions, the software replaces entirely the manual calculations.

The software also can be a valuable resource well after your course is completed.

1. Calculate the weighted score for each location (A, B, C, and D) shown in Table 11.5. Which location would you recommend?

2. John and Jane Darling are newlyweds trying to decide among several available rentals. Alternatives were scored on a scale of 1 to 5 (5 = best) against weighted performance criteria, as shown in Table 11.6. The criteria included rent, proximity to work and recreational opportunities, security, and other neighborhood characteristics associated with the couple's values and lifestyle. Alternative A is an apartment, B is a bungalow, C is a condo, and D is a downstairs apartment in Jane's parents' home.

   Which location is indicated by the preference matrix? What qualitative factors might cause this preference to change?

3. Two alternative locations are under consideration for a new plant: Jackson, Mississippi, and Dayton, Ohio. The Jackson location is superior in terms of costs. However, management believes that sales volume would decline if this location were chosen because it is farther from the market, and the firm's customers prefer local suppliers. The selling price of the product is $250 per unit in either case. Use the following information to determine which location yields the higher total profit contribution per year.

Location	Annual Fixed Cost	Variable Cost per Unit	Forecast Demand per Year
Jackson	$1,500,000	$50	30,000 units
Dayton	$2,800,000	$85	40,000 units

4. Fall-Line, Inc., is a Great Falls, Montana, manufacturer of a variety of downhill skis. Fall-Line is considering four locations for a new plant: Aspen, Colorado; Medicine Lodge, Kansas; Broken Bow, Nebraska; and Wounded Knee, South Dakota. Annual fixed costs and variable costs per pair of skis are shown in the table at the top of the next page.

TABLE 11.5	Factors for Locations A–D

		Factor Score for Each Location			
Location Factor	**Factor Weight**	**A**	**B**	**C**	**D**
1. Labor climate	5	5	4	3	5
2. Quality of life	30	2	3	5	1
3. Transportation system	5	3	4	3	5
4. Proximity to markets	25	5	3	4	4
5. Proximity to materials	5	3	2	3	5
6. Taxes	15	2	5	5	4
7. Utilities	15	5	4	2	1
Total	100				

TABLE 11.6	Factors for Newlyweds

		Factor Score for Each Location			
Location Factor	**Factor Weight**	**A**	**B**	**C**	**D**
1. Rent	25	3	1	2	5
2. Quality of life	20	2	5	5	4
3. Schools	5	3	5	3	1
4. Proximity to work	10	5	3	4	3
5. Proximity to recreation	15	4	4	5	2
6. Neighborhood security	15	2	4	4	4
7. Utilities	10	4	2	3	5
Total	100				

Location	Annual Fixed Costs	Variable Cost per Pair
Aspen	$8,000,000	$250
Medicine Lodge	$2,400,000	$130
Broken Bow	$3,400,000	$ 90
Wounded Knee	$4,500,000	$ 65

a. Plot the total cost curves for all the communities on a single graph (see Solved Problem 2). Identify on the graph the range in volume over which each location would be best.

b. What break-even quantity defines each range?

Although Aspen's fixed and variable costs are dominated by those of the other communities, Fall-Line believes that both the demand and the price would be higher for skis made in Aspen than for skis made in the other locations. The following table shows those projections.

Location	Price per Pair	Forecast Demand per Year
Aspen	$500	60,000 pairs
Medicine Lodge	$350	45,000 pairs
Broken Bow	$350	43,000 pairs
Wounded Knee	$350	40,000 pairs

c. Determine which location yields the highest total profit contribution per year.

d. Is this location decision sensitive to forecast accuracy? At what minimum sales volume does Aspen become the location of choice?

5. Wiebe Trucking, Inc., is planning a new warehouse to serve the west. Denver, Santa Fe, and Salt Lake City are under consideration. For each location, annual fixed costs (rent, equipment, and insurance) and average variable costs per shipment (labor, transportation, and utilities) are listed in the following table. Sales projections range from 550,000 to 600,000 shipments per year.

Location	Annual Fixed Costs	Variable Costs per Shipment
Denver	$5,000,000	$4.65
Santa Fe	$4,200,000	$6.25
Salt Lake City	$3,500,000	$7.25

a. Plot the total cost curves for all the locations on a single graph.

b. Which city provides the lowest overall costs?

6. Sam Hutchins is planning to operate a specialty bagel sandwich kiosk but is undecided about whether to locate in the downtown shopping plaza or in a suburban shop-

ping mall. Based on the following data, which location would you recommend?

Location	Downtown	Suburban
Annual rent, including utilities	$12,000	$8,000
Expected annual demand (sandwiches)	30,000	25,000
Average variable costs per sandwich	$1.50	$1.00
Average selling price per sandwich	$3.25	$2.85

7. The following three points are the locations of important facilities in a transportation network: (20, 20), (50, 10), and (50, 60). The coordinates are in miles.

a. Calculate the Euclidean distances (in miles) between each of the three pairs of facilities.

b. Calculate these distances using rectilinear distances.

8. Centura High School is to be located at the population center of gravity of three communities: Boelus, population 228; Cairo, population 737; and Dannebrog, population 356. The Boelus community is located at 106.72°E, 46.31°N; Cairo is located at 106.68°E, 46.37°N; and Dannebrog is located at 106.77°E, 46.34°N. Where should Centura High School be located?

QUESTIONS 9, 10, AND 16 REQUIRE THE MS MAPPOINT 2004 SOFTWARE.

9. Snappy Pizza decided to locate a pizza and take-out delivery restaurant in Fargo, North Dakota. They want to locate close to the densely populated areas of the town. Snappy management created a map of the population density of the various census tracts in Fargo. The map can be found in the file "Snappy.ptm" on your Student CD-ROM. Choose a site that has as many people as possible within a 5-minute drive time zone. Print the map with your 5-minute drive time zone. You may wish to watch the Tyler EMS video on your Student CD-ROM before starting this problem.

10. Office Warehouse has decided to locate their new facility in Red Bluff, California. A map of its customers can be found in the "Office Warehouse.ptm" file on your Student CD-ROM. The loads delivered annually to each customer (expressed in tons of material) are:

Customer Name	Address	Tons of Material Delivered Annually
Standard Products	2808 Live Oak Road Red Bluff, CA 96080	4,000
National Products	1437 Warren Ave Red Bluff, CA 96080	3,000
Golf Cart, Inc.	630 Nicklaus Avenue Red Bluff, CA 96080	7,000
Acme Corp.	277 Gurnsey Dr. Red Bluff, CA 96080	2,000
Speedy Electronics	1371 Trinity Avenue Red Bluff, CA 96080	1,000

Determine the center of gravity for Office Warehouse's customers in Red Bluff. Use the location sensor in MapPoint to determine the longitude and latitude for each of their customers and then use Active Model 11.1.

11. Val's Pizza is looking for a single central location to make pizza for delivery only. This college town is arranged on a grid with arterial streets, as shown in Figure 11.16. The main campus (A), located at 14th and R, is the source of 4,000 pizza orders per week. Three smaller campuses (B, C, and D) are located at 52nd and V, at 67th and Z, and at 70th and South. Orders from the smaller campuses average 1,000 pizzas a week. In addition, the State Patrol headquarters (E) at 10th and A orders 500 pizzas per week.

a. At about what intersection should Val start looking for a suitable site? (Estimate coordinates for the major demands accurate to the nearest one-quarter mile, and then find the center of gravity.)

b. What is the rectilinear weekly load–distance score for this location?

c. If the delivery person can travel 1 mile in 2 minutes on arterial streets and $\frac{1}{4}$ mile per minute on residential streets, going from the center of gravity location to the farthest demand location will take how long?

12. A larger and more modern main post office is to be constructed at a new location in Davis, California. Growing suburbs caused a shift in the population density from where it was 40 years ago, when the current facility was built. Annette Werk, the postmaster, asked her assistants to draw a grid map of the seven points where mail is picked up and delivered in bulk. The coordinates and trips per day to and from the seven mail source points and the current main post office, M, are shown in the following table. M will continue to act as a mail source point after relocation.

Mail Source Point	Round Trips per Day	x, y Coordinates (miles)
1	6	(2, 8)
2	3	(6, 1)
3	3	(8, 5)
4	3	(13, 3)
5	2	(15, 10)
6	7	(6, 14)
7	5	(18, 1)
M	3	(10, 3)

a. Calculate the center of gravity as a possible location for the new facility (round to the nearest whole number).

b. Compare the load–distance scores for the location in part (a) and the current location, using rectilinear distance.

13. Paramount Manufacturing is investigating which location would best position its new plant relative to two suppliers (located in cities A and B) and one market area (represented by city C). Management limited the search for this plant to those three locations and compiled the following information.

Location	Coordinates (miles)	Tons per Year	Freight Rate ($/ton-mile)
A	(100, 200)	4,000	$3.00
B	(400, 100)	3,000	$1.00
C	(100, 100)	4,000	$3.00

a. Which of the three locations gives the lowest total cost, based on Euclidean distances? [*Hint:* The annual cost of inbound shipments from supplier A to the new plant is $12,000 per mile (4,000 tons per year × $3.00 per ton-mile).]

b. Which location is best, based on rectilinear distances?

c. What are the coordinates of the center of gravity?

14. A personal computer manufacturer plans to locate its assembly plant in Taiwan and to ship its computers back to the United States through either Los Angeles or San Francisco. It has distribution centers in Atlanta, New York, and Chicago and will ship to them from whichever city is chosen as the port of entry on the West Coast. Overall transportation cost is the only criterion for choosing the port. Use the load–distance model and the information in Table 11.7 to select the more cost-effective city.

ADVANCED PROBLEMS

15. Fire Brand makes picante sauce in El Paso and New York City. Distribution centers are located in Atlanta, Omaha, and Seattle. For the capacities, locations, and shipment

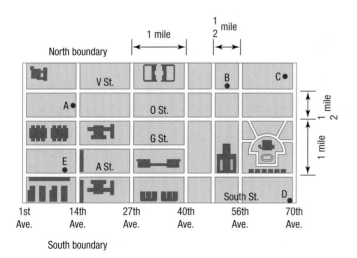

FIGURE 11.16 | Map of Campus Area

TABLE 11.7	Distances and Costs for PC Manufacturer			
		Distribution Center (units/year)		
		Chicago (10,000)	**Atlanta (7,500)**	**New York (12,500)**
PORT OF ENTRY	*Los Angeles*			
	Distance (miles)	1,800	2,600	3,200
	Shipping cost ($/unit)	0.0017/mile	0.0017/mile	0.0017/mile
	San Francisco			
	Distance (miles)	1,700	2,800	3,000
	Shipping cost ($/unit)	0.0020/mile	0.0020/mile	0.0020/mile

costs per case shown in Figure 11.17, determine the shipping pattern that will minimize transportation costs. What are the estimated transportation costs associated with this optimal allocation pattern?

16. Metro Supply decided to relocate its warehouse. Determine a good location for its new warehouse based on minimizing the number of miles traveled. The addresses and number of trips made to each of its customers last year can be found in the "Metro Supply.xls" file and displayed in a "Metro Supply.ptm" file (a MapPoint map) on the Student CD-ROM. For your convenience, the center of gravity is displayed on the map. Enter the street address of your proposed warehouse location on the "Distribution Centers" worksheet in the "Metro Supply.xls" file and run the macro by selecting the button on the "Customers" worksheet to determine the total one-way mileage (which is essentially the load–distance score). You may wish to watch the Witherspoon Automotive video on your Student CD-ROM before starting this problem.

17. The Pelican Company has four distribution centers (A, B, C, and D) that require 40,000, 60,000, 30,000, and 50,000 gallons of diesel fuel, respectively, per month for their long-haul trucks. Three fuel wholesalers (1, 2, and 3) indicated their willingness to supply as many as 50,000, 70,000, and 60,000 gallons of fuel, respectively. The total cost (shipping plus price) of delivering 1,000 gallons of fuel from each wholesaler to each distribution center is shown in the following table.

	Distribution Center			
Wholesaler	**A**	**B**	**C**	**D**
1	$1.30	$1.40	$1.80	$1.60
2	$1.30	$1.50	$1.80	$1.60
3	$1.60	$1.40	$1.70	$1.50

a. Determine the optimal solution. Show that all capacities have been exhausted and that all demands can be met with this solution.

b. What is the total cost of the solution?

18. The Acme Company operates four factories that ship products to five warehouses. The shipping costs, requirements capacities, and optimal allocations are shown in Figure 11.18. What is the total cost of the optimal solution?

19. The Giant Farmer Company processes food for sale in discount food stores. It has two plants: one in Chicago and one in Houston. The company also operates warehouses in Miami, Denver, Lincoln, Nebraska, and Jackson, Mississippi. Forecasts indicate that demand soon will exceed supply and that a new plant with a capacity of 8,000 cases per week is needed. The question is where to locate the new plant. Two potential sites are Buffalo, New York, and Atlanta. The following data on capacities, forecasted demand, and shipping costs have been gathered.

Source	Destination			Capacity
	Atlanta	Omaha	Seattle	
El Paso	$4	$5	$6	12,000
New York City	$3	$7	$9	10,000
Demand	8,000	10,000	4,000	22,000

FIGURE 11.17 | Transportation Tableau for Fire Brand

Factory	Shipping Cost per Case to Warehouse					Capacity
	W1	W2	W3	W4	W5	
F1	$1 / 60,000	$3 / 20,000	$4	$5	$6	80,000
F2	$2	$2	$1 / 50,000	$4 / 10,000	$5	60,000
F3	$1	$5	$1	$3 / 20,000	$1 / 40,000	60,000
F4	$5	$2 / 50,000	$4	$5	$4	50,000
Demand	60,000	70,000	50,000	30,000	40,000	250,000

FIGURE 11.18

Optimal Solution for Acme Company

Plant	Capacity (cases per week)	Warehouse	Demand (cases per week)
Chicago	10,000	Miami	7,000
Houston	7,500	Denver	9,000
New plant	8,000	Lincoln	4,500
Total	25,500	Jackson	5,000
		Total	25,500

	Shipping Cost to Warehouse (per case)			
Plant	Miami	Denver	Lincoln	Jackson
Chicago	$7.00	$ 2.00	$4.00	$5.00
Houston	$3.00	$ 1.00	$5.00	$2.00
Buffalo (alternative 1)	$6.00	$ 9.00	$7.00	$4.00
Atlanta (alternative 2)	$2.00	$10.00	$8.00	$3.00

For each alternative new plant location, determine the shipping pattern that will minimize total transportation costs. Where should the new plant be located?

20. The Ajax International Company operates four factories that ship products to five warehouses. The shipping costs, requirements, and capacities are shown in Figure 11.19. Use the transportation method to find the shipping schedule that minimizes shipping cost.

21. Consider further the Ajax International Company situation described in Problem 20. Ajax decides to close F3 because of high operating costs. In addition, the com-

pany decides to add 50,000 units of capacity to F4. The logistics manager is worried about the effect of this move on transportation costs. Currently, F3 is shipping 30,000 units to W4 and 50,000 units to W5 at a cost of $140,000 [or 30,000(3) + 50,000(1)]. If these warehouses were to be served by F4, the cost would increase to $350,000 [or 30,000(5) + 50,000(4)]. As a result, the Ajax logistics manager requests a budget increase of $210,000 (or $350,000 − $140,000).

a. Should the logistics manager get the budget increase?

b. If not, how much would you budget for the increase in shipping costs?

22. Consider the facility location problem at the Giant Farmer Company described in Problem 19. Management is considering a third site, at Memphis. The shipping costs per case from Memphis are $3 to Miami, $11 to Denver, $6 to Lincoln, and $5 to Jackson. Find the minimum cost plan for an alternative plant in Memphis. Would this result change the decision in Problem 19?

23. The Chambers Corporation produces and markets an automotive theft-deterrent product, which it stocks in various warehouses throughout the country. Recently, its market research group compiled a forecast indicating that a significant increase in demand will occur in the near future, after which demand will level off for the foreseeable future. The company decides to satisfy this demand by constructing new plant capacity. Chambers already has plants in Baltimore and Milwaukee and has no desire to relocate those facilities. Each plant is capable of producing 600,000 units per year.

After a thorough search, the company developed three site and capacity alternatives. Alternative 1 is to build a 600,000-unit plant in Portland. Alternative 2 is to build a 600,000-unit plant in San Antonio. Alternative 3 is to build a 300,000-unit plant in Portland and a 300,000-unit plant in San Antonio. The company's four warehouses distribute

FIGURE **11.19**

Transportation Tableau for Ajax
International

Factory	Shipping Cost per Case to Warehouse						Capacity
	W1	W2	W3	W4	W5	Dummy	
F1	$1	$3	$3	$5	$6	$0	50,000
F2	$2	$2	$1	$4	$5	$0	80,000
F3	$1	$5	$1	$3	$1	$0	80,000
F4	$5	$2	$4	$5	$4	$0	40,000
Demand	45,000	30,000	30,000	35,000	50,000	60,000	250,000

the product to retailers. The market research study provided the following data.

Warehouse	Expected Annual Demand
Atlanta (AT)	500,000
Columbus (CO)	300,000
Los Angeles (LA)	600,000
Seattle (SE)	400,000

The logistics department compiled the following cost table specifying the cost per unit to ship the product from each plant to each warehouse in the most economical manner, subject to the reliability of the various carriers involved.

Plant	Warehouse			
	AT	CO	LA	SE
Baltimore	$0.35	$0.20	$0.85	$0.75
Milwaukee	$0.55	$0.15	$0.70	$0.65
Portland	$0.85	$0.60	$0.30	$0.10
San Antonio	$0.55	$0.40	$0.40	$0.55

As one part of the location decision, management wants an estimate of the total distribution cost for each alternative. Use the transportation method to calculate these estimates.

> ACTIVE MODEL EXERCISE <

Active Model 11.1 appears on the Student CD-ROM. It allows you to find the location that minimizes the total load–distance score.

QUESTIONS

1. What is the total load–distance score to the new Health-Watch medical facility if it is located at the center of gravity?

2. Fix the y coordinate, and use the scroll bar to modify the x coordinate. Can you reduce the total load–distance score?

3. Fix the x coordinate, and use the scroll bar to modify the y coordinate. Can you reduce the total load–distance score?

4. The center of gravity does not necessarily find the site with the minimum total load–distance score. Use both scroll bars to move the trial location, and see whether you can improve (lower) the total load–distance score.

| CASE 1 | Industrial Repair, Inc. |

For 25 years, Industrial Repair (IR) operated its industrial machine repair business out of its main office located at 26 Arbor Street, Hartford, Connecticut. Initially, almost all of its customers were based in Hartford only. However, its good reputation for timely service allowed IR to grow, and as a result it presently serves "customers" throughout the state of Connecticut. When its customers' heavy industrial machines break down, IR is called in to fix them. Upon receiving a service request, IR sends a crew of two technicians and a truck to the customer site as quickly as possible. Because downtime on machines is expensive for IR's customers, it is important that IR responds quickly to customers' calls.

IR noticed a number of changes in the industrial repair market over the past couple of years. Several other companies entered the market and increased the level of competition. Also, as customers become more just-in-time oriented, they are less tolerant of long delays in the arrival of repair crews. IR's management believes that it will be increasingly difficult to keep or attract customers that are more than a 30-minute drive away from its facility. Because so many of its customers are farther than a 30-minute drive, IR's managers realize that they will have to look more closely at IR's location choices. Ideally, management would like to simply relocate the present facility. However, it may be necessary to operate two facilities to cover the entire customer base and also provide for future expansion. If IR operates two facilities, IR will keep its present facility and open a new one elsewhere. To help with their analysis, managers gathered for each customer the address and the number of repairs performed last year.

IR's accountants determined that the technicians cost the company approximately $75 per hour including pay, fringe benefits, and frequent training workshops. Since technicians always work in teams of two, one hour of driving time costs IR $150. Additionally, after taking into account all fixed and variable costs associated with their trucks, IR figures that the trucks cost $2 per mile to operate

If IR opens a facility, it will cost them $100,000 in initial expenses (which they must depreciate over 10 years using straight-line depreciation). If they decide to operate two facilities, it will cost them an extra $70,000 per year in operating expenses. IR uses a 12 percent discount rate in their investment decisions. Their tax rate is 40 percent.

IR management assigned Andrew Morgan, the facility manager, to the task of investigating and making recommendations on the best locations if IR uses a single facility or two facilities. As mentioned earlier, IR decided that for the two facilities option, they would retain their present facility and open up one new facility. Management also requested that Morgan's recommendations consider both the transportation costs and the percent of customers within a 30-minute drive time zone of IR's facilities.

(The addresses and the number of repairs for each customer last year have already been entered in the OM Explorer Solver for "Center of Gravity Using MS MapPoint 2004-IR Case" and OM Explorer Solver for "Multiple Facilities Location-Driving Time and Distance Calculator Using MS MapPoint 2004-IR Case." Note that the latter OM Explorer Solver displays the travel time for each customer to the nearest facility. For the case where you use the present facility in conjunction with a new facility, you can enter both locations into the OM Explorer Solver to determine the travel time to the closest facility).

QUESTIONS

1. Determine the best location if IR decides to use only one facility. Be sure to report on the net present value (NPV) using a 10-year horizon for this relocation and the percentage of repairs that are within 30 minutes of the chosen location.

2. Determine the best location for the new site if IR decides to use two facilities (retaining the existing site for the first one). Be sure to report on the NPV using a 10-year horizon for this relocation and the percentage of repairs that are within 30 minutes of the chosen locations.

3. What should Andrew recommend? Provide an explanation for supporting the recommendation.

Source: This case was prepared by Dr. Patrick R. Philipoom, University of South Carolina, as a basis for classroom discussion.

CASE 2	R.U. Reddie for Location

The R.U. Reddie Corporation, located in Chicago, manufactures clothing specially designed for stuffed cartoon animals such as Snoopy and Wile E. Coyote. Among the popular products are a wedding tuxedo for Snoopy and a flak jacket for Wile E. Coyote. The latter is capable of stopping an Acme Rocket at close range . . . sometimes.

For many sales, the company relies upon the help of spoiled children who refuse to leave the toy store until their parents purchase a wardrobe for their stuffed toys. Rhonda Ulysses Reddie, owner of the company, is concerned over the market projections that indicate demand for the product is substantially greater than current plant capacity. The "most likely" projections indicate that the company will be short by 400,000 units next year, and thereafter 700,000 units annually. As such, Rhonda is considering opening a new plant to produce additional units.

Background

The R.U. Reddie Corporation currently has three plants located in Boston, Cleveland, and Chicago, respectively. The company's first plant was the Chicago plant, but as sales grew in the Midwest and Northeast, the Cleveland and Boston plants were built in short order. As the demand for wardrobes for stuffed animals moved west, warehouse centers were opened in St. Louis and Denver. The capacities of the three plants were increased to accommodate the demand. Each plant has its own warehouse to satisfy demands in its own area. Extra capacity was used to ship the product to St. Louis or Denver.

The new long-term forecasts provided by the sales department were both good news and bad news. The added revenues would certainly help Rhonda's profitability, but the company would have to buy another plant to realize the added profits. Space is not available at the existing plants, and the benefits of the new technology for manufacturing stuffed animal wardrobes are tantalizing. These factors motivated the search for the best location for a new plant. Rhonda identified Denver and St. Louis as possible locations for the new plant.

Rhonda's Concerns

A plant addition is a big decision. Rhonda started to think about the accuracy of the data she was able to obtain. She had market, financial, and operations concerns.

Market

The projected demands for years 2 through 10 show an annual increase of 700,000 units to a total of 2,000,000 units for each year. She had two concerns here. First, what if the projections for each city were off plus or minus 10 percent equally across the board? That is, total annual demands could be as low as 1,800,000 or as high as 2,200,000, with each city

being affected the same as the others. Second, the marketing manager expressed a concern over a possible market shift from the Midwest and Northeast to the West. Under this scenario, additional demand would reach 50,000 units in St. Louis and 150,000 units in Denver, with the other cities staying at the "most likely" demand projections.

Financial

Rhonda realized that the net present value (NPV) of each alternative is an important input to the final decision. However, the accuracy of the estimates for the various costs is critical to determining good estimates of cash flows. She wondered whether her decision would change if the COGS (variable production plus transportation costs) for each option was off by ±10 percent. That is, what if the variable production costs and transportation costs of St. Louis are 10 percent higher than estimated while the variable production costs and transportation costs for Denver are 10 percent lower than estimated? Or vice versa? Furthermore, what if the estimate for fixed costs are off by ±10 percent? For example, suppose St. Louis is 10 percent higher while Denver is 10 percent lower, or vice versa. Would the recommendation change under any of these situations?

Operations

The ultimate location of the new plant will determine the distribution assignments and the level of utilization of each plant in the network. Cutting back production in any of the plants will change the distribution assignments of all plants. Because the "most likely" demand projections with a new plant will mean excess capacity in the system, the capacity of the Cleveland plant could be cut in year 2 and beyond. Suppose Cleveland cuts back production by 50(000) units a year from year 2 and beyond. Will this action affect the choice between Denver and St. Louis? What is the impact on the distribution assignments of the plant? Some nonquantifiable concerns also need consideration. First, the availability of a good workforce is much better in Denver than St. Louis because of the recent shutdown of a Beanie Baby factory. The labor market is much tighter in St. Louis and the prognosis is for continued short supply in the foreseeable future. Second, Denver metropolitan area just instituted strict environmental regulations. Rhonda's new plant would adhere to existing laws, but the area is highly environmentally conscious and more regulations may be coming in the future. It is costly to modify a plant once operations begin. Finally, Denver has a number of good suppliers with the capability to assist in production design (new wardrobe fashions). St. Louis also has suppliers, but they cannot help with product development. Proximity to suppliers with product development capability is a "plus" for this industry.

Data

The following data have been gathered for Rhonda:

1. The per-unit shipping cost based on the average ton-mile rates for the most efficient carriers is $0.0005 per mile. The average revenue per outfit is $8.00.

2. The company currently has the following capacity constraints:

Capacity	
(i) Boston	400
(ii) Cleveland	400
(iii) Chicago	500

3. Data concerning the various locations are found in Table 11.8.

4. New plant information:

Alternative	Building and Equipment[1]	Annual Fixed Costs (SGA)[1,3]	Variable Production Costs/ Unit	Land[1]
Denver	$12,100	$550	$3.15	$1,200
St. Louis	10,800	750	3.05	800

[1]Figures are given in thousands.

[2]Net book value of plant and equipment with remaining depreciable life of 10 years.

[3]Annual fixed costs do not include depreciation on plant and equipment.

5. The road mileage between the cities is:

	Boston	Cleveland	Chicago	St. Louis	Denver
Boston	—	650	1,000	1,200	2,000
Cleveland		—	350	600	1,400
Chicago			—	300	1,000
St. Louis				—	850
Denver					—

6. Basic assumptions you should follow:
   - Terminal value (in 10 years) of the new investment is 50 percent of plant, equipment, and land cost.
   - Tax rate is 40 percent.
   - Straight-line depreciation is used for all assets over a 10-year life.
   - R. U. Reddie is a 100 percent equity company with all equity financing and a weighted average cost of capital (WACC) of 11 percent.
   - Capacity of the new plant production for the first year will be 500 (000) units.
   - Capacity of the new plant production thereafter will be 900 (000) units.
   - Cost of goods sold (COGS) equals variable costs of production plus total transportation costs.
   - Costs to ship from a plant to its own warehouse are zero; however, production costs are applicable.

7. R. U. Reddie operations and logistics managers determined the shipping plan and cost of goods sold for the option of

TABLE 11.8	Location Data for R.U. Reddie

City	Most Likely Demand First Year[1]	Most Likely Demand After Years 2–10[1]	Current Costs, Building and Equipment[1,2]	Annual Fixed Costs (SGA)[1,3]	Variable Production Costs/Unit	Land[1]
Boston	80	140	$9,500	$600	$3.80	$500
Cleveland	200	260	7,700	300	3.00	400
Chicago	370	430	8,600	400	3.25	600
St. Louis	440	500				
Denver	610	670				

[1]Figures are given in thousands.

[2]Net book value of plant and equipment with remaining depreciable life of 10 years.

[3]Annual fixed costs do not include depreciation on plant and equipment.

not building a new plant and simply using the existing capacities to their fullest extent (status quo solution):

Year 1	COGS = $4,692,000
Boston to Boston	80
Boston to St. Louis	320
Cleveland to Chicago	80
Cleveland to Cleveland	200
Cleveland to St. Louis	120
Chicago to Chicago	290
Chicago to Denver	210

Years 2–10	COGS = $4,554,000
Boston to Boston	140
Boston to St. Louis	260
Cleveland to Cleveland	260
Cleveland to St. Louis	140
Chicago to Chicago	430
Chicago to St. Louis	70

QUESTIONS

Your team has been asked to determine whether R.U. Reddie should build a new plant and, if so, where it should be located. Your report should consist of six parts.

1. A memo from your team to R. U. Reddie indicating your recommendation and a brief overview of the supporting evidence.

2. Model the location decision as a linear model. The objective function should be to minimize the total variable costs (production plus transportation costs). The variables should be the quantity to ship from each of the plants (including one of the alternative new plants) to each of the warehouses. You should have 20 variables (four plants and five warehouses). You should also have nine constraints (four plant capacity constraints and five warehouse demand constraints). See the addendum for hints. You will need two models—one for Denver and one for St. Louis.

3. Use the Linear Programming Solver or the Transportation Method Solver in OM Explorer, or a similar capability in POM for Windows, to solve for the optimal distribution plan for each alternative (i.e., Denver and St. Louis).

4. Compute the NPV of each alternative. Use the results from the linear models for the COGS for each alternative. (*Hint:* Your analysis will be simplified if you think in terms of incremental cash flows.) Create an easy-to-read spreadsheet for each alternative.

5. Do a sensitivity analysis of the quantitative factors mentioned in the case: Forecast errors (across the board and market shift), errors in COGS estimate, and errors in fixed cost estimates. Do each factor independent of the others and use the "most likely" projections as the base case. Summarize the results in one table.

6. Use the analysis in Question 5 to identify the key quantitative variables that determine the superiority of one alternative over another. Rationalize your final recommendation in light of all the considerations R. U. Reddie must make.

Addendum

Here are some hints for your model.

1. The capacity constraint for Boston would look like this:

$$1B\text{-}B + 1B\text{-}CL + 1B\text{-}CH + 1B\text{-}D + 1B\text{-}SL \leq 400$$

The variable B-CH means Boston to Chicago in this example. You will need a total of four capacity constraints, one for each of the existing sites and one for the alternative site you are evaluating. Remember that the new site will have a capacity limit of 500 in the first year, and 900 in the second year.

2. The demand constraint for Boston would look like this:

$$1B\text{-}B + 1CL\text{-}B + 1CH\text{-}B + 1D\text{-}B = 140$$

The Denver location alternative is depicted in this example (D-B represents the number of units produced in Denver and shipped to Boston). You will need a total of five demand constraints, one for each warehouse location. Notice that the demand constraints have equal signs to indicate that exactly that quantity must be received at each warehouse.

3. Define your variables to be "thousands of units shipped," and omit the three zeros after each demand and capacity value. Then remember to multiply your final decisions and total variable costs by a thousand after you get your solution from the model.

4. Because the capacity and demand changes from year 1 to year 2, you need to run your model twice for each location to get the necessary data. You will also run the model and spreadsheets multiple times for question 5 of the report.

> SELECTED REFERENCES <

Andel, T. "Site Selection Tools Dig Data." *Transportation & Distribution,* vol. 37, no. 6 (1996), pp. 77–81.

Bartness, A. D. "The Plant Location Puzzle." *Harvard Business Review* (March–April 1994), pp. 20–30.

"BMW Announces Its Plans for a Plant in South Carolina." *Wall Street Journal* (June 24, 1992), p. B2.

Chittum, Ryan. "Location, Location, and Technology: Where to Put That New Store? Site-Selection Software May Be Able to Help." *Wall Street Journal* (July 18, 2005), p. R7.

Cook, David P., Chon-Huat Goh, and Chen H. Chung. "Service Typologies: A State of the Art Survey." *Production and Operations Management,* vol. 8, no. 3 (1999), pp. 318–338.

Cook, Thomas M., and Robert A. Russell. *Introduction to Management Sciences.* Englewood Cliffs, NJ: Prentice Hall, 1993.

DeForest, M. E. "Thinking of a Plant in Mexico?" *The Academy of Management Executive,* vol. 8, no. 1 (1994), pp. 33–40.

"Doing Well by Doing Good." *The Economist* (April 22, 2000), pp. 65–67.

Drezner, Z. *Facility Location: A Survey of Applications and Methods.* Secaucus, NJ: Springer-Verlag, 1995.

Ferdows, Kasra, "Making the Most of Foreign Factories." *Fortune* (March–April 1997), pp. 73–88.

Galuszka, P. "The South Shall Rise Again." *Chief Executive,* November 2004, pp. 50–54.

"How Legend Lives Up to Its Name." *Business Week* (February 15, 1999), pp. 75–78.

Kuehn, Alfred A., and Michael J. Hamburger. "A Heuristic Program for Locating Warehouses." *Management Science,* vol. 9, no. 4 (1963), pp. 643–666.

"Location Analysis Tools Help Starbucks Brew Up New Ideas." *Business Geographics,* www.geoplace.com.

Love, Robert F., James G. Morris, and George O. Weslowsky. *Facilities Location: Models and Methods.* New York: North-Holland, 1988.

Lovelock, Christopher H., and George S, Yip. "Developing Global Strategies for Service Businesses." *California Management Review,* vol. 38, no. 2 (1996), pp. 64–86.

"Manager's Journal: Why BMW Cruised into Spartanburg." *Wall Street Journal* (July 6, 1992), p. A10.

"MapInfo Delivers Location Intelligence for Marco's Pizza." *Directions Magazine* (December 14, 2004), www.directions mag.com/press.releases/?duty=Show&id=10790.

Porter, Michael E. "The Competitive Advantage of Nations." *Harvard Business Review* (March–April 1990), pp. 73–93.

"Power System's Relocation to Atlanta Is Official." *The Business Review* (February 9, 2001).

Roth, Aleda. "The Second Generation of Quality: Global Supply-Chain Integration in Japan and the United States." *The Quality Yearbook: 1998 Edition,* J. W. Cortada and J. A. Woods (eds.). New York: McGraw-Hill, 1998.

Rubinstein, Ed. "Chain Chart Their Course of Actions with Geographic Information Systems." *Nation's Restaurant News,* vol. 32, no. 6 (1998), p. 49.

Schmenner, Roger W. *Making Business Location Decisions.* Englewood Cliffs, NJ: Prentice Hall, 1982.

"The Science of Site Selection." *National Real Estate Investor* (October 11, 2002).

Vishwanath, Vijay, and David Hardling. "The Starbucks Effect." *Harvard Business Review* (March–April 2000), pp. 17–18.

12

State-of-the-art technology, including new radio frequency identification (RFID) tags, help move merchandise efficiently through Wal-Mart's distribution centers.

INVENTORY MANAGEMENT AT WAL-MART

In the market for shaver blade replacements? A printer? First-aid supplies? Dog food? Hair spray? If so, you expect that the store you shop at will have what you want. However, making sure that the shelves are stocked with tens of thousands of products is no simple matter for inventory managers at Wal-Mart, which has 1,276 Wal-Mart stores, 1,838 Supercenters, 556 SAM'S CLUBs, and 92 Neighborhood Markets in the United States, and an additional 1,617 stores in nine other countries. You can imagine in an operation this large that some things can get lost. Linda Dillman, CIO at Wal-Mart, recounts the story of the missing hair spray at one of the stores. The shelf needed to be restocked with a specific hair spray; however, it took three days to find the case in the backroom. Most customers will not swap hair sprays, so Wal-Mart lost three days of sales on that product.

Knowing what is in stock, in what quantity, and where it is being held is critical to effective inventory management. Without accurate inventory information, companies can make major mistakes by ordering too much, not enough, or shipping products to the wrong location. Companies can have large inventories and still have stockouts of product because they have too much inventory of some products and not enough of others. Wal-Mart, with inventories in excess of $29 billion, is certainly aware of the potential benefits from improved inventory management and is constantly experimenting with ways to reduce inventory investment. For example, Wal-Mart realizes that effective inventory management must include >

For additional chapter resources check the Student CD-ROM or the Companion Website at
www.prenhall.com/krajewski

461

the entire supply chain. The firm is implementing radio frequency identification (RFID) technology in its supply chain. RFID chips with small antennae are attached to cases or pallets of a product. When passed near a "reader," the chip activates, and its unique product identifier code is transmitted to an inventory control system. Readers used by Wal-Mart have an average range of 15 feet. RFID readers installed at dock doors will automatically let Wal-Mart's operations teams as well as its suppliers know when a shipment arrives inside a building, whether it is a distribution center or a store. Wal-Mart uses the data to decide when to bring additional stock to the store shelf and to figure out whether a store ordered too much of a product (by monitoring how long a case of the product sits in the stockroom before its contents are emptied) or whether too much stock sits in the supply chain (if the case does not get shipped out of a distribution center for days). Better merchandise availability provides a major consumer benefit.

The potential for this technology is awesome, however it is still in its infancy stage for application to inventory management in the supply chain. Much technological development is needed before the benefits become truly evident. Nonetheless, it appears that Wal-Mart may have solved the problem of the missing hair spray. One handheld RFID reader could have found the missing case in a few minutes.

Sources: Laurie Sullivan, "Wal-Mart's Way," Informationweek.com (September 27, 2004), pp. 36–50; Gus Whitcomb and Christi Gallagher, "Wal-Mart Begins Roll-Out of Electronic Product Codes in Dallas/Fort Worth Area," www.walmartstores.com (April, 30, 2004), and Investor Information, 2005 Financial Reports.

inventory management

The planning and controlling of inventories in order to meet the competitive priorities of the organization.

Inventory management, the planning and controlling of inventories in order to meet the competitive priorities of the organization, is an important concern for managers in all types of businesses. Effective inventory management is essential for realizing the full potential of any value chain. For companies that operate on relatively low profit margins, poor inventory management can seriously undermine the business. The challenge is not to pare inventories to the bone to reduce costs or to have plenty around to satisfy all demands, but to have the right amount to achieve the competitive priorities of the business most efficiently. This type of efficiency can only happen if the right amount of inventory is flowing through the value chain—through suppliers, the firm, warehouses or distribution centers, and customers. These decisions were so important for Wal-Mart that it decided to use technology to improve the information flows in the supply chain.

Managing inventories is a process that requires information about expected demands, amounts of inventory on hand and on order for every item stocked by the firm at all of its locations, and the appropriate timing and size of the reorder quantities. The inventory management process can be analyzed and its capabilities measured relative to the firm's competitive priorities, such as achieving low-cost operations (How much of the inventory management process should be automated?) or maintaining consistent quality (How can errors related to on-hand quantities and demand forecasts be minimized?). In this chapter we focus on the decision-making aspects of the process. We begin with an overview of the impact inventory management has on the organization and then discuss the basic concepts of inventory management for all types of businesses. A major segment of the chapter is devoted to retail and distribution inventory control systems.

> INVENTORY MANAGEMENT ACROSS THE ORGANIZATION <

Inventories are important to all types of organizations and their employees. Inventories profoundly affect everyday operations because they must be counted, paid for, used in operations, used to satisfy customers, and managed. Inventories require an investment of funds, as does the purchase of a new machine. Monies invested in inventory are not available for investment in other things; thus, they represent a drain on the cash flows of an organization. Nonetheless, companies realize that the availability of products is a key selling point in many markets and downright critical in many more.

So, is inventory a boon or a bane? Certainly, too much inventory on hand reduces profitability, and too little inventory on hand damages customer confidence. Inventory management therefore involves trade-offs. Let's discover how companies can effectively manage inventories across the organization.

> INVENTORY BASICS <

Inventory is created when the receipt of materials, parts, or finished goods exceeds their disbursement; it is depleted when their disbursement exceeds their receipt. In this section, we identify the pressures associated with maintaining low and high inventories and we define the different types of inventory. We then discuss tactics that can be used to reduce inventories when appropriate, identify the trade-offs involved in making inventory placement decisions, and discuss how to identify the inventory items that need the most attention.

PRESSURES FOR LOW INVENTORIES

An inventory manager's job is to balance the advantages and disadvantages of both low and high inventories and find a happy medium between the two levels. The primary reason for keeping inventories low is that inventory represents a temporary monetary investment. As such, the firm incurs an opportunity cost, which we call the cost of capital, arising from the money tied up in inventory that could be used for other purposes. The **inventory holding cost** (or carrying cost) is the sum of the cost of capital plus the variable costs of keeping items on hand, such as storage and handling costs and taxes, insurance, and shrinkage costs. When these components change with inventory levels, so does the holding cost.

Companies usually state an item's holding cost per period of time as a percent of its value. The annual cost to maintain one unit in inventory typically ranges from 15 to 35 percent of its value.[1] Suppose that a firm's holding cost is 20 percent. If the average value of total inventory is 20 percent of sales, the average annual cost to hold inventory is 4 percent [0.20(0.20)] of total sales. This cost is sizable in terms of gross profit margins, which often are less than 10 percent. Thus, the components of holding cost create pressures for low inventories.

Cost of Capital The cost of capital is the opportunity cost of investing in an asset relative to the expected return on assets of similar risk. Inventory is an asset; consequently we should use a cost measure that adequately reflects the firm's approach to financing assets. Most firms use the *weighted average cost of capital (WACC)*, which is the average of the required return on a firm's stock equity and the interest rate on its debt, weighted by the proportion of equity and debt in its portfolio. The cost of capital usually is the largest component of holding cost, as high as 15 percent, depending on the particular capitalization portfolio of the firm. Firms typically update the WACC on an annual basis because it is used to make many financial decisions.

Storage and Handling Costs Inventory takes up space and must be moved into and out of storage. Storage and handling costs may be incurred when a firm rents space on either a long- or short-term basis. A cost is incurred when a firm could use storage space productively in some other way.

Taxes, Insurance, and Shrinkage More taxes are paid if end-of-year inventories are high, and the cost of insuring the inventories increases, too. Shrinkage takes three forms. The first, *pilferage*, or theft of inventory by customers or employees, is a significant percentage of sales for some businesses. The second form of shrinkage, called *obsolescence*, occurs when inventory cannot be used or sold at full value, owing to model changes, engineering modifications, or unexpectedly low demand. Obsolescence is a big expense in the retail clothing industry.

---

[1]Stephen G. Timme and Christine Williams-Timme, "The Real Cost of Holding Inventory," *Supply Chain Management Review* (July–August 2003), pp. 30–37. This article provides a detailed discussion of the calculation of the weighted cost of capital and the implications of underestimating the inventory holding cost.

USING OPERATIONS TO COMPETE

Operations As a Competitive Weapon
Operations Strategy
Project Management

MANAGING PROCESSES

Process Strategy
Process Analysis
Process Performance and Quality
Constraint Management
Process Layout
Lean Systems

MANAGING VALUE CHAINS

Supply Chain Strategy
Location
Inventory Management
Forecasting
Sales and Operations Planning
Resource Planning
Scheduling

inventory holding cost

The sum of the cost of capital and the variable costs of keeping items on hand, such as storage and handling, taxes, insurance, and shrinkage.

Drastic discounts on seasonal clothing frequently must be offered on many of these products at the end of a season. Finally, *deterioration* through physical spoilage or damage results in lost value. Food and beverages, for example, lose value and might even have to be discarded when their shelf life is reached. When the rate of deterioration is high, building large inventories may be unwise.

PRESSURES FOR HIGH INVENTORIES

Given the costs of holding inventory, why not eliminate it altogether? Let us look briefly at the pressures related to maintaining inventories.

Customer Service Creating inventory can speed delivery and improve the firm's on-time delivery of goods. High inventory levels reduce the potential for stockouts and backorders, which are key concerns of wholesalers and retailers. A stockout occurs when an item that is typically stocked is not available to satisfy a demand the moment it occurs, resulting in loss of the sale. A backorder is a customer order that cannot be filled when promised or demanded but is filled later. Customers don't like waiting for backorders to be filled. Many of them will take their business elsewhere. Sometimes, customers are given discounts for the inconvenience of waiting.

ordering cost

The cost of preparing a purchase order for a supplier or a production order for the shop.

Ordering Cost Each time a firm places a new order, it incurs an **ordering cost**, or the cost of preparing a purchase order for a supplier or a production order for the shop. For the same item, the ordering cost is the same, regardless of the order size: The purchasing agent must take the time to decide how much to order and, perhaps, select a supplier and negotiate terms. Time also is spent on paperwork, follow-up, and receiving the item(s). In the case of a production order for a manufactured item, a blueprint and routing instructions often must accompany the shop order. The Internet streamlines the order process and reduces the costs of placing orders, however.

setup cost

The cost involved in changing over a machine to produce a different item.

Setup Cost The cost involved in changing over a machine to produce a different item is the **setup cost**. It includes labor and time to make the changeover, cleaning, and sometimes new tools or equipment. Scrap or rework costs are also higher at the start of the production run. Setup cost also is independent of order size, which creates pressure to make or order a large supply of the items and hold them in inventory rather than smaller batches.

Labor and Equipment Utilization By creating more inventory, management can increase workforce productivity and facility utilization in three ways. First, placing larger, less frequent production orders reduces the number of unproductive setups, which add no value to a service or product. Second, holding inventory reduces the chance of the costly rescheduling of production orders because the components needed to make the product are not in inventory. Third, building inventories improves resource utilization by stabilizing the output rate when demand is cyclical or seasonal. The firm uses inventory built during slack periods to handle extra demand in peak seasons. This approach minimizes the need for extra shifts, hiring, layoffs, overtime, and additional equipment.

Transportation Cost Sometimes, outbound transportation cost can be reduced by increasing inventory levels. Having inventory on hand allows more carload shipments to be made and minimizes the need to expedite shipments by more expensive modes of transportation. The *forward placement* of inventory can also reduce outbound transportation costs, even though the *inventory pooling* effect is lessened and more inventory is necessary. Inbound transportation costs can also be reduced by creating more inventory. Sometimes, several items are ordered from the same supplier. Placing these orders at the same time may lead to rate discounts, thereby decreasing the costs of transportation and raw materials.

quantity discount

A drop in the price per unit when an order is sufficiently large.

Payments to Suppliers A firm often can reduce total payments to suppliers if it can tolerate higher inventory levels. Suppose that a firm learns that a key supplier is about to increase its prices. In this case, it might be cheaper for the firm to order a larger quantity than usual—in effect delaying the price increase—even though inventory will increase temporarily. A firm can also take advantage of quantity discounts this way. A **quantity discount**, whereby the price per unit drops when the order is sufficiently large, is an incentive to order larger quantities. Supplement D, "Special Inventory Models," shows how to determine order quantities in such a situation.

TYPES OF INVENTORY

Another perspective on inventory is to classify it by how it is created. In this context, inventory takes four forms: (1) cycle, (2) safety stock, (3) anticipation, and (4) pipeline. They cannot be identified physically, that is, an inventory manager cannot look at a pile of widgets and identify which ones are cycle inventory and which ones are pipeline inventory. However, conceptually, each of the four types comes into being in an entirely different way. Once you understand these differences, you can prescribe different ways to reduce inventory, which we discuss in the next section.

Cycle Inventory The portion of total inventory that varies directly with lot size is called **cycle inventory**. Determining how frequently to order, and in what quantity, is called **lot sizing**. Two principles apply.

1. The lot size, Q, varies directly with the elapsed time (or cycle) between orders. If a lot is ordered every 5 weeks, the average lot size must equal five weeks' demand.

2. The longer the time between orders for a given item, the greater the cycle inventory must be.

At the beginning of the interval, the cycle inventory is at its maximum, or Q. At the end of the interval, just before a new lot arrives, cycle inventory drops to its minimum, or 0. The average cycle inventory is the average of these two extremes:

$$\text{Average cycle inventory} = \frac{Q+0}{2} = \frac{Q}{2}$$

This formula is exact only when the demand rate is constant and uniform. However, it does provide a reasonably good estimate even when demand rates are not constant. Factors other than the demand rate (e.g., scrap losses) also may cause estimating errors when this simple formula is used.

Safety Stock Inventory To avoid customer service problems and the hidden costs of unavailable components, companies hold safety stock. **Safety stock inventory** is surplus inventory that protects against uncertainties in demand, lead time, and supply changes. Safety stocks are desirable when suppliers fail to deliver either the desired quantity on the specified date or items of acceptable quality, or when manufactured items require significant amounts of scrap or rework. Safety stock inventory ensures that operations are not disrupted when such problems occur, allowing subsequent operations to continue.

To create safety stock, a firm places an order for delivery earlier than when the item is typically needed.[2] The replenishment order therefore arrives ahead of time, giving a cushion against uncertainty. For example, suppose that the average lead time from a supplier is three weeks but a firm orders five weeks in advance just to be safe. This policy creates a safety stock equal to a two weeks' supply (5−3).

Anticipation Inventory Inventory used to absorb uneven rates of demand or supply, which businesses often face, is referred to as *anticipation inventory*. Predictable, seasonal demand patterns lend themselves to the use of anticipation inventory. Uneven demand can motivate a manufacturer to stockpile anticipation inventory during periods of low demand so that output levels do not have to be increased much when demand peaks. Anticipation inventory also can help when suppliers are threatened with a strike or have severe capacity limitations.

Pipeline Inventory Inventory moving from point to point in the materials flow system is called **pipeline inventory**. Materials move from suppliers to a plant, from one operation to

Inventory management begins with knowing how much inventory you have on hand. Here a grocer uses a handheld scanner to check inventory on supermarket shelves.

cycle inventory

The portion of total inventory that varies directly with lot size.

lot sizing

The determination of how frequently and in what quantity to order inventory.

safety stock inventory

Surplus inventory that a company holds to protect against uncertainties in demand, lead time, and supply changes.

pipeline inventory

Inventory moving from point to point in the materials flow system.

[2]When orders are placed at fixed intervals, a second way to create safety stock is used. Each new order placed is larger than the quantity typically needed through the next delivery date.

the next in the plant, from the plant to a distribution center or customer, and from the distribution center to a retailer. Pipeline inventory consists of orders that have been placed but not yet received. For example, NUMMI, the joint venture between General Motors and Toyota in California, uses parts produced in the Midwest. Shipments arrive daily at the plant, but the transportation lead time required a pipeline inventory of parts in rail cars enroute from the Midwest at all times. Pipeline inventory between two points, for either transportation or production, can be measured as the average demand during lead time, $\bar{D}_L$, which is the average demand for the item per period (d) times the number of periods in the item's lead time (L) to move between the two points, or

$$\text{Pipeline inventory} = \bar{D}_L = dL$$

Note that the lot size does not directly affect the average level of the pipeline inventory. Increasing Q inflates the size of each order, so if an order has been placed but not received, there is more pipeline inventory for that lead time. However, that increase is canceled by a proportionate decrease in the number of orders placed per year. The lot size can *indirectly* affect pipeline inventory, however, if increasing Q causes the lead time to increase. Here $\bar{D}_L$, and therefore pipeline inventory, will increase.

Managerial Practice 12.1 shows how Amazon.com designed an inventory system to improve customer service.

EXAMPLE 12.1	**Estimating Inventory Levels**

TUTOR 12.1

Tutor 12.1 on the Student CD-ROM provides a new example to practice the estimation of Inventory levels.

A plant makes monthly shipments of electric drills to a wholesaler in average lot sizes of 280 drills. The wholesaler's average demand is 70 drills a week, and the lead time from the plant is three weeks. The wholesaler must pay for the inventory from the moment the plant makes a shipment. If the wholesaler is willing to increase its purchase quantity to 350 units, the plant will guarantee a lead time of two weeks. What is the effect on cycle and pipeline inventories?

SOLUTION

The current cycle and pipeline inventories are

$$\text{Cycle inventory} = \frac{Q}{2} = \frac{280}{2} = 140 \text{ drills}$$

$$\text{Pipeline inventory} = \bar{D}_L = dL = (70 \text{ drills/week})(3 \text{ weeks}) = 210 \text{ drills}$$

Figure 12.1 shows the cycle and pipeline inventories if the wholesaler accepts the new proposal.

FIGURE 12.1

Estimating Inventory Levels
for Cycle and Pipeline
Inventories Using Tutor 12.1

1. Enter the average lot size, average demand during a period, and the number of periods of lead time:

Average lot size	350
Average demand	70
Lead time	2

2. To compute cycle inventory, simply divide average lot size by 2. To compute pipeline inventory, multiply average demand by lead time:

Cycle inventory	175
Pipeline inventory	140

Decision Point The effect of the new proposal on cycle inventories is to increase them by 35 units, or 25 percent. The reduction in pipeline inventories, however, is 70 units, or 33 percent. The proposal would reduce the total investment in cycle and pipeline inventories. Also, it is advantageous to have shorter lead times because the wholesaler only has to commit to purchases two weeks in advance, rather than three.

INVENTORY REDUCTION TACTICS

Managers always are eager to find cost-effective ways to reduce inventory. Later in this chapter, we examine various ways for finding optimal lot sizes. Here, we discuss something more

Amazon.com had a rough holiday season in 1999, owing primarily to mismanaged inventories and chaotic warehouse operations that resulted in a large amount of unsold goods. Most of Amazon's customers were happy, but the company bought far too much inventory, including a 50-week supply of Kermit the Frog telephones! Since then Amazon has changed its ways. For example, it previously housed items such as DVDs and DVD players in different states, which complicated collecting orders for a single customer. Now the items are grouped together in its shipping facilities. Also, Amazon now forecasts demands by areas of the country. Palm handheld computers are forecasted by ZIP code and the proper inventories are sent to the warehouse serving that area. This approach reduces the time it takes to get a product to the customer.

Jeffrey Wilke, vice president and general manager of operations at Amazon, identified four ways in which Amazon improved customer service by managing inventory better.

- It increased its warehouse capacity quickly. Three million square feet of warehouse capacity were added in less than a year, which enabled Amazon to develop the appropriate amount of cycle, safety stock, and anticipation inventories to service its customers.

- It introduced state-of-the-art automation and mechanization. Amazon's warehouses are now efficient and flexible enough to move items in container sizes, pallet sizes, or lot sizes of 1, thereby reducing handling costs.

- It linked order information to a customer archive using information technology. When a customer places an order for a particular basket of goods, the system captures the data and adds them to a database of past purchases from that customer. This process enables Amazon to forecast future purchases and tailor the shopping experience the customer receives.

- It replicated the system across its distribution centers where possible. Linking capacity, automation, and information technology will now allow Amazon to expand its product breadth via new partnerships and alliances. Through system replication, Amazon can expand in modular fashion as new warehouses are added.

Amazon also changed its strategy on inventory management: It now uses a combination of in-house and outsourced warehouse operations. For example, Amazon outsourced the distribution of cell phones, computers, and books, excluding those on the bestseller lists. Cell phones require spe-

Amazon.com has improved its inventory systems dramatically over the past decade by increasing its warehouse capacity and introducing state-of-the art-mechanization to ship products and track customers' needs. Although Amazon warehouses many of the items it sells, it now outsources other items to independent warehouses.

cialized, extensive customer service and computers take up huge amounts of warehouse space. Other bulky and awkward items, such as vacuum cleaners, food processors, and table saws, are also potential candidates for outsourcing. This move allows Amazon to focus on what it does best. Nonetheless, it may prove risky because it puts Amazon's hard-earned reputation in the hands of others. However, by cutting costs and boosting its profit margins through better inventory management, Amazon hopes to pass along some of the savings to its customers, increase its number of shoppers, and minimize any of the disadvantages the new inventory system may have.

Sources: Nick Wingsfield, "Amazon Vows to Avoid Mess of 1999 Christmas Rush: Too Many Kermit Phones," *Wall Street Journal* (September 25, 2000), p. B1; "Q&A with Jeffrey Wilke," *Business Week* (November 1, 1999), www.ebiz.businessweek.com; Greg Sandoval, "How Lean Can Amazon Get?" *CNET News.com* (April 19, 2002).

fundamental—the basic tactics (which we call *levers*) for reducing inventory. A primary lever is one that must be activated if inventory is to be reduced. A secondary lever reduces the penalty cost of applying the primary lever and the need for having inventory in the first place.

Cycle Inventory   The primary lever to reduce cycle inventory is simply to reduce the lot size. However, making such reductions in Q without making any other changes can be devastating. For example, setup costs can skyrocket. If these changes occur, two secondary levers can be used:

1. Streamline the methods for placing orders and making setups, in order to reduce ordering and setup costs and allow Q to be reduced.

2. Increase repeatability to eliminate the need for changeovers. **Repeatability** is the degree to which the same work can be done again. Repeatability can be increased through high product demand; the use of specialization; the devotion of resources exclusively to a product; the use of the same part in many different products; through *flexible automation*; the use of the *one-worker, multiple-machines* concept; or through *group technology*. Increased repeatability may justify new setup methods, reduce transportation costs, and allow quantity discounts from suppliers.

Safety Stock Inventory   The primary lever to reduce safety stock inventory is to place orders closer to the time when they must be received. However, this approach can lead to unacceptable customer service unless demand, supply, and delivery uncertainties can be minimized. Four secondary levers can be used in this case:

1. Improve demand forecasts so that fewer surprises come from customers. Perhaps customers can even be encouraged to order items before they need them.

2. Cut the lead times of purchased or produced items to reduce demand uncertainty. For example, local suppliers with short lead times could be selected whenever possible.

3. Reduce supply uncertainties. Suppliers are likely to be more reliable if production plans are shared with them. Surprises from unexpected scrap or rework can be reduced by improving manufacturing processes. Preventive maintenance can minimize unexpected downtime caused by equipment failure.

4. Rely more on equipment and labor buffers, such as capacity cushions and cross-trained workers. These buffers are important to businesses in the service sector because they generally cannot inventory their services.

Anticipation Inventory   The primary lever to reduce anticipation inventory is simply to match demand rate with production rate. Secondary levers can be used to even out customer demand in one of the following ways:

1. Add new products with different demand cycles so that a peak in the demand for one product compensates for the seasonal low for another.

2. Provide off-season promotional campaigns.

3. Offer seasonal pricing plans.

Pipeline Inventory   An operations manager has direct control over lead times but not demand rates. Because pipeline inventory is a function of demand during the lead time, the primary lever is to reduce the lead time. Two secondary levers can help managers cut lead times:

1. Find more responsive suppliers and select new carriers for shipments between stocking locations or improve materials handling within the plant. Introducing a computer system could overcome information delays between a distribution center and retailer.

2. Decrease Q, at least in those cases where the lead time depends on the lot size. Smaller jobs generally require less time to complete.

PLACEMENT OF INVENTORIES

The positioning of a firm's inventories supports its competitive priorities. Inventories can be held at the raw materials, work-in-process, and finished goods levels. Managers make inventory placement decisions by designating an item as either a special or a standard. A **special** is an item made to order or, if purchased, it is bought to order. Just enough are ordered to cover

repeatability

The degree to which the same work can be done again.

special

An item made to order; if purchased, it is bought to order.

the latest customer request. A **standard** is an item that is made to stock, or ordered to stock, and normally the item is available upon request. For example, retailers typically deal with standard items and hold them in stock on the store's shelves to satisfy customer demand. Such is the case at Wal-Mart or Marshall Field's, although occasionally you can order items not normally in stock. Expect to wait a while for delivery if the item is a specialty item. Buffet-style cafeterias display standard food items from which customers can choose to make a meal. Alternatively, a tailor deals with special items because the tailor would not know a customer's exact measurements or cloth preferences until the customer arrived at the store. Dealing with special items is also the case at a fine restaurant, where a specific meal cannot be prepared until the diner discusses it with the server. The ingredients for the meal are available, but the meal itself is considered a special item.

Holding a high level of inventory of finished goods will allow the firm to deliver products quickly to customers, but it also requires a higher dollar investment in inventory. The inventory placement at Shamrock Chemicals, a Newark, New Jersey, manufacturer of materials used in printing inks, illustrates this trade-off. Shamrock can ship a product the same day a customer orders it. However, because finished goods are treated as standards rather than specials, Shamrock is forced to maintain a large inventory of finished goods. Holding inventory at the raw materials level would reduce the cost of carrying inventory, but at the expense of the quick customer response time that gives Shamrock its competitive advantage. R.R. Donnelley, a large manufacturer of books and other printed materials, chooses an opposite strategy by positioning its inventory back at the raw materials level (e.g., in rolled paper stock and ink). The reason is that the products Donnelley produces (like this textbook) are made to order and, therefore, considered specials. Each print job produces a unique product. Placing inventories closer to the raw materials level gives Donnelley great flexibility to meet a variety of customer demands.

IDENTIFYING CRITICAL INVENTORY ITEMS WITH ABC ANALYSIS

Thousands of items are held in inventory by a typical organization, but only a small percentage of them deserves management's closest attention and tightest control. **ABC analysis** is the process of dividing items into three classes, according to their dollar usage, so that managers can focus on items that have the highest dollar value. This method is the equivalent of creating a *Pareto chart* except that it is applied to inventory rather than to process errors. As Figure 12.2 shows, class A items typically represent only about 20 percent of the items but account for 80 percent of the dollar usage. Class B items account for another 30 percent of the items but only 15 percent of the dollar usage. Finally, 50 percent of the items fall in class C, representing a mere 5 percent of the dollar usage. The goal of ABC analysis is to identify the inventory levels of class A items so management can control them tightly by using the levers just discussed.

The analysis begins by multiplying the annual demand rate for one item by the dollar value (cost) of one unit to determine its dollar usage. After ranking the items on the basis of dollar

FIGURE 12.2

Typical Chart Using ABC Analysis

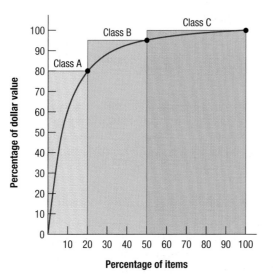

usage and creating the Pareto chart, the analyst looks for "natural" changes in slope. The dividing lines in Figure 12.2 between classes are inexact. Class A items could be somewhat higher or lower than 20 percent of all items but normally account for the bulk of the dollar usage.

A manager ensures that class A items are reviewed frequently to reduce the average lot size and keep inventory records current. By contrast, class B items require an intermediate level of control. For class C items, much looser control is appropriate. A stockout of a class C item can be as crucial as for a class A item, but the inventory holding cost of class C items tends to be low. These features suggest that higher inventory levels can be tolerated and that more safety stock, larger lot sizes, and perhaps even a visual system, which we discuss later, may suffice for class C items. See Solved Problem 2 for a detailed example of ABC analysis.

> ECONOMIC ORDER QUANTITY <

economic order quantity (EOQ)

The lot size that minimizes total annual inventory holding and ordering costs.

Recall that managers face conflicting pressures to keep inventories low enough to avoid excess inventory holding costs but high enough to reduce ordering and setup costs. A good starting point for balancing these conflicting pressures and determining the best cycle-inventory level for an item is finding the **economic order quantity (EOQ)**, which is the lot size that minimizes total annual cycle-inventory holding and ordering costs. The approach to determining the EOQ is based on the following assumptions:

1. The demand rate for the item is constant (for example, always 10 units per day) and known with certainty.

2. No constraints are placed (such as truck capacity or materials handling limitations) on the size of each lot.

3. The only two relevant costs are the inventory holding cost and the fixed cost per lot for ordering or setup.

4. Decisions for one item can be made independently of decisions for other items. In other words, no advantage is gained in combining several orders going to the same supplier.

5. The lead time is constant (e.g., always 14 days) and known with certainty. The amount received is exactly what was ordered and it arrives all at once rather than piecemeal.

The economic order quantity will be optimal when all five assumptions are satisfied. In reality, few situations are so simple. Nonetheless, the EOQ is often a reasonable approximation of the appropriate lot size, even when several of the assumptions do not quite apply. Here are some guidelines on when to use or modify the EOQ.[3]

- **Don't use the EOQ**
  - If you use the "make-to-order" strategy and your customer specifies the entire order be delivered in one shipment
  - If the order size is constrained by capacity limitations such as the size of the firm's ovens, amount of testing equipment, or number of delivery trucks

- **Modify the EOQ**
  - If significant quantity discounts are given for ordering larger lots
  - If replenishment of the inventory is not instantaneous, which can happen if the items must be used or sold as soon as they are finished without waiting until the entire lot has been completed (see Supplement D, "Special Inventory Models," for several useful modifications to the EOQ)

- **Use the EOQ**
  - If you follow a "make-to-stock" strategy and the item has relatively stable demand.
  - If your carrying costs and setup or ordering costs are known and relatively stable

[3]See Alan R. Cannon and Richard E. Crandall, "The Way Things Never Were," *APICS—The Performance Advantage* (January 2004), pp. 32–35, for a more detailed discussion of the EOQ, its relevance to JIT, and when to use the EOQ.

FIGURE **12.3**

Cycle-Inventory Levels

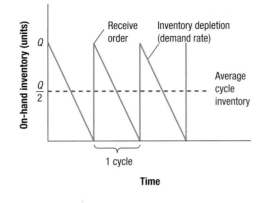

The EOQ was never intended to be an optimizing tool. Nonetheless, if you need to determine a reasonable lot size, it can be helpful in many situations.

CALCULATING THE EOQ

We begin by formulating the total cost for any lot size Q. Next, we derive the EOQ, which is the Q that minimizes total annual cycle-inventory cost. Finally, we describe how to convert the EOQ into a companion measure, the elapsed time between orders.

When the EOQ assumptions are satisfied, cycle inventory behaves as shown in Figure 12.3. A cycle begins with Q units held in inventory, which happens when a new order is received. During the cycle, on-hand inventory is used at a constant rate and, because demand is known with certainty and the lead time is a constant, a new lot can be ordered so that inventory falls to 0 precisely when the new lot is received. Because inventory varies uniformly between Q and 0, the average cycle inventory equals half the lot size, Q.

The annual holding cost for this amount of inventory, which increases linearly with Q, as Figure 12.4(a) shows, is

Annual holding cost = (Average cycle inventory)(Unit holding cost)

The annual ordering cost is

Annual ordering cost = (Number of orders/Year)(Ordering or setup cost)

The average number of orders per year equals annual demand divided by Q. For example, if 1,200 units must be ordered each year and the average lot size is 100 units, then 12 orders will be placed during the year. The annual ordering or setup cost decreases nonlinearly as Q increases, as shown in Figure 12.4(b), because fewer orders are placed.

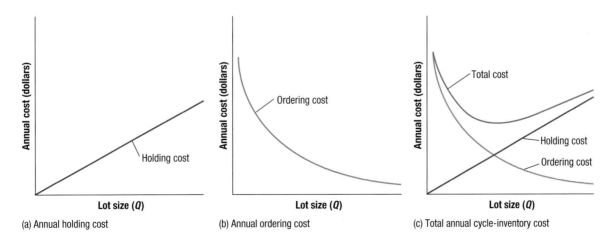

(a) Annual holding cost   (b) Annual ordering cost   (c) Total annual cycle-inventory cost

FIGURE **12.4** | Graphs of Annual Holding, Ordering, and Total Costs

The total annual cycle-inventory cost,[4] as graphed in Figure 12.4(c), is the sum of the two cost components:

Total cost = Annual holding cost + Annual ordering or setup cost[5]

$$C = \frac{Q}{2}(H) + \frac{D}{Q}(S)$$

where

C = total annual cycle-inventory cost

Q = lot size, in units

H = cost of holding one unit in inventory for a year, often expressed as a percentage of the item's value

D = annual demand, in units per year

S = cost of ordering or setting up one lot, in dollars per lot

EXAMPLE 12.2	Costing Out a Lot-Sizing Policy

A museum of natural history opened a gift shop two years ago. Managing inventories has become a problem. Low inventory turnover is squeezing profit margins and causing cash-flow problems.

One of the top-selling items in the container group at the museum's gift shop is a bird feeder. Sales are 18 units per week, and the supplier charges $60 per unit. The cost of placing an order with the supplier is $45. Annual holding cost is 25 percent of a feeder's value, and the museum operates 52 weeks per year. Management chose a 390-unit lot size so that new orders could be placed less frequently. What is the annual cycle-inventory cost of the current policy of using a 390-unit lot size? Would a lot size of 468 be better?

SOLUTION

We begin by computing the annual demand and holding cost as

$$D = (18 \text{ units/week})(52 \text{ weeks/year}) = 936 \text{ units}$$
$$H = 0.25(\$60/\text{unit}) = \$15$$

The total annual cycle-inventory cost for the current policy is

$$C = \frac{Q}{2}(H) + \frac{D}{Q}(S)$$

$$= \frac{390}{2}(\$15) + \frac{936}{390}(\$45) = \$2{,}925 + \$108 = \$3{,}033$$

The total annual cycle-inventory cost for the alternative lot size is

$$C = \frac{468}{2}(\$15) + \frac{936}{468}(\$45) = \$3{,}510 + \$90 = \$3{,}600$$

Decision Point The lot size of 468 units, which is a half-year supply, would be a more expensive option than the current policy. The savings in order costs are more than offset by the increase in holding costs. Management should use the total annual cycle-inventory cost function to explore other lot-size alternatives.

Figure 12.5 displays the impact of using several Q values for the bird feeder in Example 12.2. Eight different lot sizes were evaluated in addition to the current one. Both holding and ordering costs were plotted, but their sum—the total annual cycle-inventory

---

[4]Expressing the total cost on an annual basis usually is convenient (although not necessary). Any time horizon can be selected, as long as D and H cover the same time period. If the total cost is calculated on a monthly basis, D must be monthly demand and H must be the cost of holding a unit for 1 month.
[5]The number of orders actually placed in any year is always a whole number, although the formula allows the use of fractional values. However, rounding is not needed because what is being calculated is an average for multiple years. Such averages often are nonintegers.

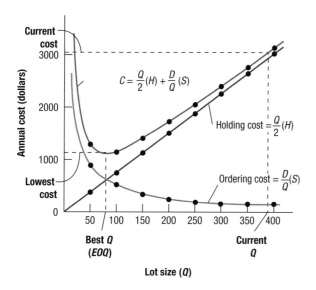

FIGURE **12.5**

Total Annual Cycle-Inventory Cost
Function for Bird Feeder

cost curve—is the important feature. The graph shows that the best lot size, or EOQ, is the lowest point on the total annual cost curve, or between 50 and 100 units. Obviously, reducing the current lot-size policy ($Q = 390$) can result in significant savings.

A more efficient approach is to use the EOQ formula:

$$\text{EOQ} = \sqrt{\frac{2DS}{H}}$$

We use calculus to obtain the EOQ formula from the total annual cycle-inventory cost function. We take the first derivative of the total annual cycle-inventory cost function with respect to Q, set it equal to 0, and solve for Q. As Figure 12.5 indicates, the EOQ is the order quantity for which annual holding cost equals annual ordering cost. Using this insight, we can also obtain the EOQ formula by equating the formulas for annual ordering cost and annual holding cost and solving for Q. The graph in Figure 12.5 also reveals that when the annual holding cost for any Q exceeds the annual ordering cost, as with the 390-unit order, we can immediately conclude that Q is too big. A smaller Q reduces holding cost and increases ordering cost, bringing them into balance. Similarly, if the annual ordering cost exceeds the annual holding cost, Q should be increased.

Sometimes, inventory policies are based on the time between replenishment orders, rather than on the number of units in the lot size. The **time between orders (TBO)** for a particular lot size is the average elapsed time between receiving (or placing) replenishment orders of Q units. Expressed as a fraction of a year, the TBO is simply Q divided by annual demand. When we use the EOQ and express time in terms of months, the TBO is

$$\text{TBO}_{\text{EOQ}} = \frac{\text{EOQ}}{D}(12 \text{ months/year})$$

In Example 12.3, we show how to calculate TBO for years, months, weeks, and days.

time between orders (TBO)

The average elapsed time between receiving (or placing) replenishment orders of Q units for a particular lot size.

Finding the EOQ, Total Cost, and TBO	EXAMPLE **12.3**

For the bird feeders in Example 12.2, calculate the EOQ and its total annual cycle-inventory cost. How frequently will orders be placed if the EOQ is used?

SOLUTION

Using the formulas for EOQ and annual cost, we get

$$\text{EOQ} = \sqrt{\frac{2DS}{H}} = \sqrt{\frac{2(936)(45)}{15}} = 74.94 \quad \text{or} \quad 75 \text{ units}$$

Figure 12.6 shows that the total annual cost is much less than the $3,033 cost of the current policy of placing 390-unit orders.

TUTOR 12.3

Tutor 12.3 on the Student CD-ROM provides a new example to practice the application of the EOQ model.

FIGURE 12.6

Total Annual Cycle-Inventory Costs
Based on EOQ Using Tutor 12.3

Parameters

Current Lot Size (Q)	390	Economic Order Quantity	75
Demand (D)	936		
Order Cost (S)	$45		
Unit Holding Cost (H)	$15		

Annual Costs

Orders per Year	2.4
Annual Ordering Cost	$108.00
Annual Holding Cost	$2,925.00
Annual Inventory Cost	$3,033.00

Annual Costs based on EOQ

Orders per Year	12.48
Annual Ordering Cost	$561.60
Annual Holding Cost	$562.50
Annual Inventory Cost	$1,124.10

ACTIVE MODEL 12.1

Active Model 12.1 on the Student CD-ROM provides additional insight on the EOQ model and its uses.

When the EOQ is used, the time between orders (TBO) can be expressed in various ways for the same time period.

$$TBO_{EOQ} = \frac{EOQ}{D} = \frac{75}{936} = 0.080 \text{ year}$$

$$TBO_{EOQ} = \frac{EOQ}{D}(12 \text{ months/year}) = \frac{75}{936}(12) = 0.96 \text{ month}$$

$$TBO_{EOQ} = \frac{EOQ}{D}(52 \text{ weeks/year}) = \frac{75}{936}(52) = 4.17 \text{ weeks}$$

$$TBO_{EOQ} = \frac{EOQ}{D}(365 \text{ days/year}) = \frac{75}{936}(365) = 29.25 \text{ days}$$

Decision Point Using the EOQ, about 12 orders per year will be required. Using the current policy of 390 units per order, an average of 2.4 orders will be needed each year (every five months). The current policy saves on ordering costs but incurs a much larger cost for carrying the cycle inventory. Although it is easy to see which option is best on the basis of total ordering and holding costs, other factors may affect the final decision. For example, if the supplier would reduce the price per unit for large orders, it may be better to order the larger quantity.

UNDERSTANDING THE EFFECT OF CHANGES

Subjecting the EOQ formula to *sensitivity analysis* can yield valuable insights into the management of inventories. Sensitivity analysis is a technique for systematically changing crucial parameters to determine the effects of a change. Let us consider the effects on the EOQ when we substitute different values into the numerator or denominator of the formula.

A Change in the Demand Rate Because D is in the numerator, the EOQ (and, therefore, the best cycle-inventory level) increases in proportion to the square root of the annual demand. Therefore, when demand rises, the lot size also should rise, but more slowly than actual demand.

A Change in the Setup Costs Because S is in the numerator, increasing S increases the EOQ and, consequently, the average cycle inventory. Conversely, reducing S reduces the EOQ, allowing smaller lot sizes to be produced economically. This relationship explains why manufacturers are so concerned about reducing setup time and costs. When weeks of supply decline, inventory turns increase. When setup cost and setup time become trivial, a major impediment to small-lot production is removed.

A Change in the Holding Costs Because H is in the denominator, the EOQ declines when H increases. Conversely, when H declines, the EOQ increases. Larger lot sizes are justified by lower holding costs.

Errors in Estimating D, H, and S Total cost is fairly insensitive to errors, even when the estimates are wrong by a large margin. The reasons are that errors tend to cancel each other out and that the square root reduces the effect of the error. Suppose that we incorrectly estimate the holding cost to be double its true value; that is, we calculate EOQ using $2H$, instead of H. For Example 12.3, this 100 percent error increases total cycle-inventory cost by only 6 percent, from \$1,124 to \$1,192. Thus, the EOQ lies in a fairly large zone of acceptable lot sizes, allowing managers to deviate somewhat from the EOQ to accommodate supplier contracts or storage constraints.

EOQ AND LEAN SYSTEMS

On the surface it may seem that the EOQ is diametrically opposed to the principles of *lean systems*, which rely on small lot sizes and low inventory levels. However, the same process improvements that lead to a lean system create an environment that approaches the rather restrictive assumptions of the EOQ: For example, yearly, monthly, daily, or hourly demand rates are known with reasonable certainty in lean systems, and the rate of demand is relatively uniform. Lean systems can also have few process constraints if the firm practices *constraint management*. In addition, lean systems strive for constant delivery lead times and dependable delivery quantities from suppliers, both of which are assumptions of the EOQ. Consequently, the EOQ as a lot sizing tool is quite compatible with the principles of lean systems.

> INVENTORY CONTROL SYSTEMS <

The EOQ and other lot-sizing methods answer the important question: How much should we order? Another important question that needs an answer is: When should we place the order? An inventory control system responds to both questions. In selecting an inventory control system for a particular application, the nature of the demands imposed on the inventory items is crucial. An important distinction between types of inventory is whether an item is subject to dependent or independent demand. Retailers, such as JCPenney, and distributors must manage **independent demand items**—that is, items for which demand is influenced by market conditions and is not related to the inventory decisions for any other item held in stock. Independent demand inventory includes

independent demand items
Items for which demand is influenced by market conditions and is not related to the inventory decisions for any other item held in stock.

- Wholesale and retail merchandise
- Service support inventory, such as stamps and mailing labels for post offices, office supplies for law firms, and laboratory supplies for research universities
- Product and replacement-part distribution inventories
- Maintenance, repair, and operating (MRO) supplies—that is, items that do not become part of the final service or product, such as employee uniforms, fuel, paint, and machine repair parts

Managing independent demand inventory can be tricky because demand is influenced by external factors. For example, the owner of a bookstore may not be sure how many copies of the latest best-seller novel customers will purchase during the coming month. As a result, the manager may decide to stock extra copies as a safeguard. Independent demand, such as the demand for various book titles, must be forecasted.

In this chapter, we focus on inventory control systems for independent demand items, which is the type of demand the bookstore owner, other retailers, service providers, and distributors face. Even though demand from any one customer is difficult to predict, low demand from some customers often is offset by high demand from others. Thus, total demand for any independent demand item may follow a relatively smooth pattern, with some random fluctuations. *Dependent demand items* are those required as components or inputs to a service or product. Dependent demand exhibits a pattern very different from that of independent demand and must be managed with different techniques (see Chapter 15, "Resource Planning").

In this section, we discuss and compare two inventory control systems: (1) the continuous review system, called a *Q* system, and (2) the periodic review system, called a *P* system. We close with a look at hybrid systems, which incorporate features of both the *P* and *Q* systems.

continuous review (Q) system
A system designed to track the remaining inventory of an item each time a withdrawal is made to determine whether it is time to reorder.

CONTINUOUS REVIEW SYSTEM

A **continuous review (*Q*) system**, sometimes called a **reorder point (ROP) system** or fixed order-quantity system, tracks the remaining inventory of an item each time a withdrawal is made to determine whether it is time to reorder. In practice, these reviews are done frequently

reorder point (ROP) system
See **continuous review (*Q*) system.**

inventory position (IP)

The measurement of an item's ability to satisfy future demand.

scheduled receipts (SR)

Orders that have been placed but have not yet been received.

open orders

See **scheduled receipts (SR)**.

reorder point (R)

The predetermined minimum level that an inventory position must reach before a fixed quantity Q of the item is ordered.

(e.g., daily) and often continuously (after each withdrawal). The advent of computers and electronic cash registers linked to inventory records has made continuous reviews easy. At each review, a decision is made about an item's inventory position. If it is judged to be too low, the system triggers a new order. The **inventory position (IP)** measures the item's ability to satisfy future demand. It includes **scheduled receipts (SR)**, which are orders that have been placed but have not yet been received, plus on-hand inventory (OH) minus backorders (BO). Sometimes, scheduled receipts are called **open orders**. More specifically,

$$\text{Inventory position} = \text{On-hand inventory} + \text{Scheduled receipts} - \text{Backorders}$$

$$\text{IP} = \text{OH} + \text{SR} - \text{BO}$$

When the inventory position reaches a predetermined minimum level, called the **reorder point (R)**, a fixed quantity Q of the item is ordered. In a continuous review system, although the order quantity Q is fixed, the time between orders can vary. Hence, Q can be based on the EOQ, a price break quantity (the minimum lot size that qualifies for a quantity discount), a container size (such as a truckload), or some other quantity selected by management.

Selecting the Reorder Point When Demand Is Certain To demonstrate the concept of a reorder point, suppose that the demand for feeders at the museum gift shop in Example 12.3 is always 18 per week, the lead time is a constant two weeks, and the supplier always ships the exact number ordered on time. With both demand and lead time certain, the museum's buyer can wait until the inventory position drops to 36 units, or (18 units/week) (2 weeks), to place a new order. Thus, in this case, the reorder point, R, equals the *demand during lead time*, with no added allowance for safety stock.

Figure 12.7 shows how the system operates when demand and lead time are constant. The downward-sloping line represents the on-hand inventory, which is being depleted at a constant rate. When it reaches reorder point R (the horizontal line), a new order for Q units is placed. The on-hand inventory continues to drop throughout lead time L until the order is received. At that time, which marks the end of the lead time, on-hand inventory jumps by Q units. A new order arrives just when inventory drops to 0. The time between orders (TBO) is the same for each cycle.

The inventory position, IP, shown in Figure 12.7 corresponds to the on-hand inventory, except during the lead time. Just after a new order is placed, at the start of the lead time, IP increases by Q, as shown by the dashed line. The IP exceeds OH by this same margin throughout the lead time.[6] At the end of the lead time, when the scheduled receipts convert to on-hand inventory, IP = OH once again. The key point here is to compare IP, not OH, with R in deciding whether to reorder. A common error is to ignore scheduled receipts or backorders.

EXAMPLE 12.4	Determining Whether to Place an Order

Demand for chicken soup at a supermarket is always 25 cases a day and the lead time is always 4 days. The shelves were just restocked with chicken soup, leaving an on-hand inventory of only 10 cases. No backorders currently exist, but there is one open order for 200 cases. What is the inventory position? Should a new order be placed?

SOLUTION

$$R = \text{Average demand during lead time} = (25)(4) = 100 \text{ cases}$$
$$\text{IP} = \text{OH} + \text{SR} - \text{BO}$$
$$= 10 + 200 - 0 = 210 \text{ cases}$$

Decision Point Because IP exceeds R (210 versus 100), do not reorder. Inventory is almost depleted, but a new order need not be placed because the scheduled receipt is on the way.

---

[6]A possible exception is the unlikely situation when more than one scheduled receipt is open at the same time because of long lead times.

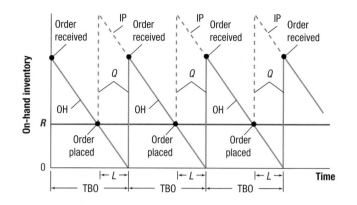

FIGURE 12.7

Q System When Demand and Lead Time Are Constant and Certain

Selecting the Reorder Point When Demand Is Uncertain In reality, demand and lead times are not always predictable. For instance, the museum's buyer knows that *average* demand is 18 feeders per week and that the *average* lead time is two weeks. That is, a variable number of feeders may be purchased during the lead time, with an average demand during lead time of 36 feeders (assuming that each week's demand is identically distributed). This situation gives rise to the need for safety stocks. Suppose that the museum's buyer sets *R* at 46 units, thereby placing orders before they typically are needed. This approach will create a safety stock, or stock held in excess of expected demand, of 10 units (46 − 36) to buffer against uncertain demand. In general,

$$\text{Reorder point} = \text{Average demand during lead time} + \text{Safety stock}$$

Figure 12.8 shows how the *Q* system operates when demand is variable and uncertain. We assume that the variability in lead times is negligible and, therefore, can be treated as a constant, as we did in the development of the EOQ model. The wavy downward-sloping line indicates that demand varies from day to day. Its slope is steeper in the second cycle, which means that the demand rate is higher during this time period. The changing demand rate means that the time between orders changes, so $\text{TBO}_1 \neq \text{TBO}_2 \neq \text{TBO}_3$. Because of uncertain demand, sales during lead time are unpredictable, and safety stock is added to hedge against lost sales. This addition is why *R* is higher in Figure 12.8 than in Figure 12.7. It also explains why the on-hand inventory usually does not drop to 0 by the time a replenishment order arrives. The greater the safety stock, and thus the higher reorder point *R*, the less likely a stockout.

Because the average demand during lead time is variable and uncertain, the real decision to be made when selecting *R* concerns the safety stock level. Deciding on a small or large safety stock is a trade-off between customer service and inventory holding costs. Cost minimization models can be used to find the best safety stock, but they require estimates of stockout and backorder costs, which are usually difficult to make with any precision. The usual approach for determining *R* is for management—based on judgment—to set a

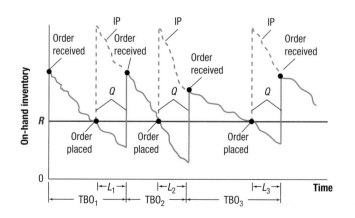

FIGURE 12.8

Q System When Demand Is Uncertain

reasonable service-level policy for the inventory and then determine the safety stock level that satisfies this policy.

Choosing an Appropriate Service-Level Policy   Managers must weigh the benefits of holding safety stock against the cost of holding it. One way to determine the safety stock is to set a **service level**, or **cycle-service level**—the desired probability of not running out of stock in any one ordering cycle, which begins at the time an order is placed and ends when it arrives in stock. In a bookstore, the manager may select a 90 percent cycle-service level for a book. In other words, the probability is 90 percent that demand will not exceed the supply during the lead time. For the Q system, the lead time is also the **protection interval**, or the period over which safety stock must protect the user from running out of stock. The probability of running short *during the protection interval*, creating a stockout or backorder, is only 10 percent (100 − 90). This stockout risk, which occurs only during the lead time in the Q system, is greater than the overall risk of a stockout because the risk is nonexistent outside the ordering cycle.

To translate this policy into a specific safety stock level, we must know how demand during the lead time is distributed. If demand varies little around its average, the safety stock can be small. Conversely, if demand during the lead time varies greatly from one order cycle to the next, the safety stock must be large. Variability is measured with probability distributions, which are specified by a mean and a variance.

Finding the Safety Stock   When selecting the safety stock, the inventory planner often assumes that demand during lead time is normally distributed, as shown in Figure 12.9. The average demand during the lead time is the centerline of the graph, with 50 percent of the area under the curve to the left and 50 percent to the right. Thus, if a cycle-service level of 50 percent were chosen, the reorder point R would be the quantity represented by this centerline. Because R equals the average demand during the lead time plus the safety stock, the safety stock is 0 when R equals this average demand. Demand is less than average 50 percent of the time and, thus, having no safety stock will be sufficient only 50 percent of the time.

To provide a service level above 50 percent, the reorder point must be greater than the average demand during the lead time. In Figure 12.9 that requires moving the reorder point to the right of the centerline so that more than 50 percent of the area under the curve is to the left of R. An 85 percent cycle-service level is achieved in Figure 12.9 with 85 percent of the area under the curve to the left of R (in blue) and only 15 percent to the right (in pink). We compute the safety stock by multiplying the number of standard deviations from the mean needed to multiply the cycle-service level, z, by the standard deviation of demand during lead time probability distribution,[7] σ_L:

$$\text{Safety stock} = z\sigma_L$$

The higher the value of z, the higher the safety stock and the cycle-service level should be. If $z = 0$, there is no safety stock, and stockouts will occur during 50 percent of the order cycles.

FIGURE 12.9

Finding Safety Stock with a Normal Probability Distribution for an 85 Percent Cycle-Service Level

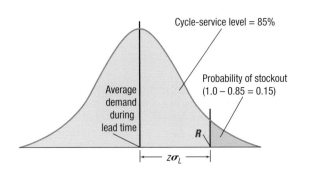

[7]Some inventory planners who use manual systems prefer to work with the mean absolute deviation (MAD) rather than the standard deviation because it is easier to calculate. The MAD is simply the average of the absolute deviations between actual demands and their average. To approximate the standard deviation you simply multiply the MAD by 1.25. Then, proceed to calculate the safety stock.

service level

The desired probability of not running out of stock in any one ordering cycle, which begins at the time an order is placed and ends when it arrives in stock.

cycle-service level

See **service level.**

protection interval

The period over which safety stock must protect the user from running out of stock.

Finding the Safety Stock and *R*	EXAMPLE **12.5**

Records show that the demand for dishwasher detergent during the lead time is normally distributed, with an average of 250 boxes and $\sigma_L = 22$. What safety stock should be carried for a 99 percent cycle-service level? What is *R*?

SOLUTION

The first step is to find *z*, the number of standard deviations to the right of average demand during the lead time that places 99 percent of the area under the curve to the left of that point (0.9900 in the body of the table in the Normal Distribution appendix). The closest number in the table is 0.9901, which corresponds to 2.3 in the row heading and 0.03 in the column heading. Adding these values gives a *z* of 2.33. With this information, you can calculate the safety stock and reorder point:

$$\text{Safety stock} = z\sigma_L = 2.33\ (22) = 51.3 \quad \text{or} \quad 51 \text{ boxes}$$
$$\text{Reorder point} = \text{Average demand during lead time} + \text{Safety stock}$$
$$= 250 + 51 = 301 \text{ boxes}$$

We rounded the safety stock to the nearest whole number. In this case, the theoretical cycle-service level will be less than 99 percent. Raising the safety stock to 52 boxes will yield a cycle-service level greater than 99 percent.

Decision Point Management can control the quantity of safety stock by choosing a service level. Another approach to reducing safety stock is to reduce the standard deviation of demand during the lead time, which can be accomplished by closer coordination with major customers through information technology.

Finding the appropriate reorder point and safety stock in practice requires estimating the distribution for the demand during the lead time. Sometimes average demand during the lead time and the standard deviation of demand during the lead time, σ_L, are not directly available and must be calculated by combining information on the demand rate with information on the lead time. This additional calculation is based on the following two reasons:

1. It may be easier to estimate demand first and then estimate the lead time. Demand information comes from the customer, whereas lead times come from the supplier.
2. Records are not likely to be collected for a time interval that is exactly the same as the lead time. The same inventory control system may be used to manage thousands of different items, each with a different lead time. For example, if demand is reported *weekly*, these records can be used directly to compute the average and the standard deviation of demand during the lead time if the lead time is exactly one week. However, if the lead time is three weeks, the computation is more difficult.

We can get at the more difficult case by making some reasonable assumptions. Suppose that the average demand, *d*, is known along with the standard deviation of demand, σ_t, over some time interval *t* (say, days or weeks), where *t* does not equal the lead time. Also, suppose that the probability distributions of demand for each time interval *t* are identical and independent of each other. For example, if the time interval is a week, the probability distributions of demand are the same each week (identical *d* and σ_t), and the total demand in one week does not affect the total demand in another week. Let *L* be the constant lead time, expressed as a multiple (or fraction) of *t*. If *t* represents a week and the lead time is three weeks, $L = 3$. Under these assumptions, average demand during the lead time will be the sum of the averages for each of the *L* identical and independent distributions of demand, or $d + d + d + \cdots = dL$. In addition, the variance of the demand distribution for the lead time will be the sum of the variances of the *L* identical and independent distributions of demand, or $\sigma_t^2 + \sigma_t^2 + \sigma_t^2 + \cdots = \sigma_t^2 L$. Finally, the standard deviation of the sum of two or more identically distributed independent random variables is the square root of the sum of their variances, or

$$\sigma_L = \sqrt{\sigma_t^2 L} = \sigma_t \sqrt{L}$$

FIGURE 12.10

Development of Demand Distribution for the Lead Time

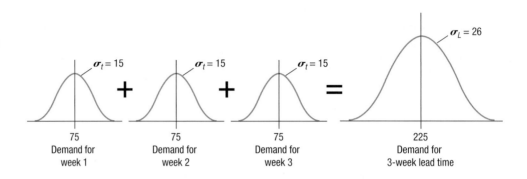

Figure 12.10 shows how the demand distribution of the lead time is developed from the individual distributions of weekly demands, where $d = 75$, $\sigma_t = 15$, and $L = 3$ weeks. In this case, average demand during the lead time is $(75)(3) = 225$ units and $\sigma_L = 15\sqrt{3} = 25.98$, or 26.

Calculating Total Q System Costs   Total costs for the continuous review (Q) system is the sum of three cost components:

Total cost = Annual cycle inventory holding cost + Annual ordering cost
+ Annual safety stock holding cost

$$C = \frac{Q}{2}(H) + \frac{D}{Q}(S) + Hz\sigma_L$$

The annual cycle-inventory holding cost and annual ordering cost are the same equations we used for computing the total annual cycle-inventory cost in Examples 12.2 and 12.3. The annual cost of holding the safety stock is computed under the assumption that the safety stock is on hand all the time. Referring to Figure 12.8 in each order cycle, we will sometimes experience a demand greater than the average demand during lead time, and sometimes we will experience less. On average over the year, we can assume the safety stock will be on hand.

EXAMPLE 12.6	**Finding the Safety Stock and R When the Demand Distribution for the Lead Time Must Be Developed**

TUTOR 12.4

Tutor 12.4 on the Student CD-ROM provides a new example to determine the safety stock and the reorder point for a Q system.

Let us return to the bird feeder example. Suppose that the average demand is 18 units per week with a standard deviation of 5 units. The lead time is constant at two weeks. Determine the safety stock and reorder point if management wants a 90 percent cycle-service level. What is the total cost of the Q system?

SOLUTION

In this case, $t = 1$ week, $\sigma_t = 5$, $d = 18$ units, and $L = 2$ weeks, so

$$\sigma_L = \sigma_t \sqrt{L} = 5\sqrt{2} = 7.1$$

Consult the body of the table in the Normal Distribution appendix for 0.9000, which corresponds to a 90 percent cycle-service level. The closest number is 0.8997, which corresponds to a z value of 1.28. With this information, we calculate the safety stock and reorder point as follows:

Safety stock = $z\sigma_L$ = 1.28(7.1) = 9.1   or   9 units

Reorder point = dL + Safety stock

= 2(18) + 9 = 45 units

Hence, the Q system for the bird feeder operates as follows: Whenever the inventory position reaches 45 units, order the EOC of 75 units. The total Q system cost for the bird feeder is

$$C = \frac{75}{2}(\$15) + \frac{936}{75}(\$45) + 9(\$15) = \$562.50 + \$561.60 + \$135.00 = \$1,259.10$$

Decision Point Various order quantities and safety stock levels can be used in the Q system. For example, management could specify a different order quantity (because of shipping constraints) or a different safety stock (because of storage limitations). The total costs of such systems can be calculated, and the trade-off between costs and service levels could be assessed.

Selecting the Reorder Point When Demand and Lead Time Are Uncertain In practice, it is often the case that both the demand and the lead time are uncertain. The key to determining the reorder point is to develop the demand during the protection interval probability distribution under these more complicated conditions. However, once the distribution is known and a desired cycle-service level is specified, we can select the reorder point as we did before for the case where the lead time was constant. If the theoretical distributions for demand per unit of time and the lead time are known, the joint probability distribution of demand during lead time can be analytically derived with a lot of work. A more practical approach is to use computer simulation. A lead time is randomly drawn from the lead time distribution, and then demands for each period of the lead time are randomly drawn from the demand distribution. The total demand for that lead time is recorded, and the procedure is repeated a large number of times to arrive at a demand during the lead time distribution.

We will demonstrate this approach using discrete probability distributions for the demand and lead time distributions. Discrete probability distributions can be used to approximate theoretical probability distributions, and they can be used in situations where actual demands or lead times do not follow any of the known theoretical distributions. A discrete probability distribution for lead time lists each possible lead time in time intervals t (say, days or weeks) and its probability. A discrete probability distribution for demand lists each possible demand that could occur during a time interval of length t and its probability. Consider the following information, which is based on the bird feeder data from Example 12.6. Suppose that the lead time has the probability distribution shown in Table 12.1. The average lead time is 2 weeks, as it is in Example 12.6. However, now there is considerable variability in the actual lead times that could be experienced.

Now consider the following distribution for demand as shown in Table 12.2. The average demand per week is 18 units, and the standard deviation is 5 units (rounded to the nearest whole number), as in Example 12.6. The demand during the protection interval probability distribution can be estimated using an Excel spreadsheet, as shown in Figure 12.11.

With a normal distribution, the safety stock is computed first and then is added to the average demand during the lead time to get the reorder point; whereas with a discrete distribution, the sequence is reversed. We assume that the demand levels listed in Figure 12.11 are the only demand levels that can occur (nothing in between). We then select R from the list of demand levels in the distribution. The cumulative probability of demands at or less than the chosen value for R must equal or exceed the desired cycle-service level, and R is the smallest such quantity. This conservative approach ensures we will meet or exceed our inventory service goals. For example, if the desired cycle-service level for the bird feeder is 90 percent, we would set R equal to 64 units in Figure 12.11, which actually will give us a cycle-service level of 93 percent. To calculate the level of safety stock, subtract the average demand during the lead time in the simulation from R. In our example, the safety stock is $64 - 36 = 28$ units.

TABLE 12.1	Probability Distribution of Lead Time	
Lead Time (weeks)	**Probability of Lead Time**
1	0.35
2	0.45
3	0.10
4	0.05
5	0.05

TABLE 12.2 | Probability Distribution for Demand

Demand (units per week)	Probability of Demand
10	0.10
13	0.20
18	0.40
23	0.20
26	0.10

Left side (columns A–D)

1 Demand Probability Distribution
2 (Units Per Period)

	A	B	C	D
3	Probabilty of Demand	Lower Range Probability	Demand (Units)	
4	0.10	0.00	10	
5	0.20	0.10	13	
6	0.40	0.30	18	
7	0.20	0.70	23	
8	0.10	0.90	26	

10 Lead Time Probability Distribution

	A	B	C
12–13	Probability of Lead Time	Lower Range	Protection Interval
14	0.35	0.00	1
15	0.45	0.35	2
16	0.10	0.80	3
17	0.05	0.90	4
18	0.05	0.95	5

20 Demand During Protection Interval Distribution

	BINS	Demand	Frequency	Cumulative Percentage
23	10	10	24	0.05
24	22	16	84	0.22
25	34	28	141	0.50
26	46	40	145	0.79
27	58	52	49	0.89
28	70	64	23	0.93
29	82	76	17	0.97
30	94	88	10	0.99
31	106	100	5	1.00
32	118	112	2	1.00
33	130	More	0	1.00
35		Total	500	

	A	B
37	Lower Bound	10
38	Upper Bound	130
40	Range	120
42	Bins	10
44	Bin Range	12

Right side — Random Numbers (row 2: Demand Per Period in Protection Interval)

Row	Lead Time (F)	Period 1 (G)	Period 2 (H)	Period 3 (I)	Period 4 (J)	Period 5 (K)	Period 6 (L)	Period 7 (M)	Period 8 (N)	Period 9 (O)	Period 10 (P)
4	0.1637	0.0833	0.5102	0.2518	0.5184	0.2025	0.7836	0.1628	0.5987	0.3116	0.4781
5	0.6769	0.8404	0.6872	0.0135	0.1993	0.6971	0.3746	0.4923	0.4031	0.1828	0.5277
6	0.6847	0.7367	0.9619	0.9626	0.5671	0.5760	0.6335	0.1021	0.6465	0.1341	0.3566
7	0.2129	0.6666	0.7249	0.4595	0.2043	0.6652	0.6160	0.9479	0.7499	0.5985	0.0808
8	0.2541	0.0365	0.4230	0.2839	0.7738	0.3001	0.8734	0.0667	0.8477	0.7052	0.0513
9	0.5016	0.6766	0.6239	0.3281	0.6489	0.4644	0.6653	0.5601	0.9461	0.5983	0.6157
10					0.7195	0.0047	0.6908	0.5194	0.4332	0.1357	0.9932
11					0.3818	0.7743	0.9017	0.2498	0.8027	0.1885	0.7843
12					0.2327	0.6862	0.2880	0.2900	0.1826	0.0995	0.1947
13					0.9474	0.1487	0.0656	0.8645	0.4554	0.1548	0.6615
14					0.6635	0.1279	0.5530	0.1295	0.0743	0.8928	0.2884
15					0.7150	0.6383	0.4391	0.5368	0.7860	0.0648	0.5368
16	0.7255	0.8283	0.0944	0.8689	0.2304	0.4721	0.5777	0.0694	0.0299	0.4083	0.1546
17	0.0536	0.3992	0.1281	0.8438	0.1844	0.7781	0.6994	0.8040	0.5647	0.2609	0.2157
18	0.7607	0.6912	0.8048	0.3671	0.8267	0.8732	0.2523	0.0433	0.2588	0.4854	0.2447
19	0.2107	0.7238	0.9769	0.4767	0.4132	0.0630	0.7979	0.6091	0.5206	0.8320	0.5991
20	0.2335	0.4533	0.6874	0.9631	0.6808	0.8151	0.3555	0.5553	0.7274	0.4522	0.3312
21	0.0386	0.3003	0.4065	0.3505	0.9062	0.5987	0.4494	0.8158	0.4851	0.2432	0.2846
22	0.5019	0.9661	0.2541	0.6851	0.2483	0.0343	0.4933	0.2734	0.1725	0.7055	0.5887
23	0.4108	0.8023	0.0978	0.0657	0.9296	0.6807	0.9976	0.2785	0.5228	0.2677	0.6724
24	0.3744	0.5385	0.7282	0.7645	0.8855	0.0943	0.6941	0.2202	0.0919	0.0393	0.0131
25	0.2122	0.7615	0.7820	0.0261	0.1679	0.0716	0.2459	0.2291	0.6456	0.6446	0.5195
26	0.0925	0.8525	0.2320	0.0427	0.7376	0.6809	0.4502	0.7044	0.5545	0.8276	0.4048
27	0.8343	0.6395	0.7648	0.8997	0.3425	0.3840	0.6041	0.8482	0.3168	0.8569	0.2660
28							0.9964	0.9124	0.9332	0.0995	0.1204
29							0.2084	0.4818	0.2383	0.0342	0.9235
30							0.2432	0.6588	0.2063	0.1991	0.6926
31							0.5117	0.1409	0.9094	0.3037	0.1828
32							0.1725	0.3838	0.6962	0.9058	0.6118
33	0.6475	0.7993	0.6954	0.2517	0.8252	0.0122	0.2091	0.0821	0.2956	0.7970	0.6666
34	0.2870	0.2413	0.1980	0.9134	0.7304	0.5016	0.5433	0.5863	0.9347	0.7322	0.9262
35	0.1155	0.4369	0.6033	0.6577	0.9506	0.6063	0.8189	0.2593	0.5367	0.7205	0.6265
36	0.8156	0.0910	0.8654	0.3667	0.7712	0.5901	0.1183	0.2655	0.1137	0.7680	0.2330
37	…23			0.5130	0.9228	0.5766	0.9350	0.9113	0.5257	0.7750	0.9551
38	…92			0.0563	0.4335	0.2733	0.4960	0.8591	0.6733	0.7491	0.8072
39	…46			0.0315	0.7549	0.6415	0.0524	0.6159	0.9905	0.7097	0.1597
40	…84			0.0015	0.4733	0.8386	0.3708	0.7001	0.1249	0.6756	0.9454
41	…26			0.3777	0.0219	0.9943	0.2587	0.8397	0.3581	0.4197	0.1695
42	…97			0.0735	0.4363	0.7587	0.3205	0.4638	0.7741	0.4405	0.2971
43	…36			0.1646	0.4396	0.0534	0.1325	0.2512	0.5349	0.0922	0.6232
44	…01			0.2910	0.4212	0.0393	0.0922	0.7903	0.9088	0.2052	0.2047
45	…752			0.8870	0.1202	0.7112	0.6327	0.7573	0.9966	0.0188	0.2281
46	0.3492	0.9502	0.0280	0.7639	0.8914	0.5056	0.3405	0.4324	0.1394	0.1070	0.0724
47	0.5814	0.5982	0.5455	0.7837	0.4116	0.5398	0.8612	0.8702	0.3948	0.6403	0.1019
48	0.3771	0.2760	0.9884	0.8313	0.5897	0.6728	0.4663	0.5004	0.2913	0.9015	0.6352

Callout notes:

Random numbers are generated by using the Random Number generator function RAND (). These numbers are frozen by copying the numbers and pasting them as values from cell F4 to P503.

Frequencies are calculated by using the FREQUENCY ARRAY function: **=FREQUENCY(AD4:AD503,A23:A33)** Cells AD4:AD503 are the data array inputs and cells A23:A33 are the bin array input of the function.

"Bins" are the upper bounds of the intervals that we need to group the total demand during the protection interval.

They are obtained by subtracting the lower bound from the upper bound and dividing the difference by 10. This will be the range of each bin, thus allowing 10 bins of the same size. Simply start with the lower bound and add to it the Bin Range (cell B44, which is cell B40 divided by cell B42, in this case).

FIGURE 12.11 | Excel Spreadsheet Showing How to Simulate Demand During the Protection Interval for a *Q* System (continued on p. 483)

We can now specify the complete continuous review (*Q*) system. The order quantity is determined as before; here, as in Example 12.6, we use an EOQ of 75 units. The reorder point is 64 units, and the safety stock is 28 units. The total cost, *C*, of this system is

$$C = \frac{75}{2}(\$15) + \frac{936}{75}(\$45) + 28(\$15) = \$562.50 + \$561.60 + \$420.00 = \$1,544.10$$

OM Explorer has two spreadsheet solvers that can be used to analyze *Q* systems when both the demand and the lead time are uncertain. The Demand During the Protection Interval Simulator can be used to develop the probability distribution for the protection interval from which you can choose an appropriate value of *R* for a given cycle-service level. Once the reorder point and the order quantity have been specified, the *Q* system can be simulated using the *Q* System Simulator. (Solved Problem 8 shows an application of this solver.)

Q	R	S	T	U	V	W	X	Y	Z	AA	AB	AC	AD
	Simulation												
						Demand Per Period in Protection Interval							
	Inventory Cycle	Lead Time (# Periods)	Period 1	Period 2	Period 3	Period 4	Period 5	Period 6	Period 7	Period 8	Period 9	Period 10	Total during Protection Interval
	1	1	10	0	0	0	0	0	0	0	0	0	10
	2	2	23	18	0	0	0	0	0	0	0	0	41
	3	2	23	26	0	0	0	0	0	0	0	0	49
	4	1	18									0	18
	5	1	10									0	10
	6	2	18									0	36
	7	1	10									0	10
	8	1	10									0	10
	9	1	18									0	18
	10	2	13									0	36
	11	1	13									0	13
	12	3	23									0	54
	13	2	10	0	0	0	0	0	0	0		33
	14	1	18	0	0	0	0	0	0	0	0	18
	15	2	18	23	0	0	0	0	0	0	0	41
	16	1	23	0	0	0	0	0	0	0	0	23
	17	1	18	0	0	0	0	0	0	0	0	18
	18	1	18	0	0						0	18
	19	2	26	13	0						0	39
	20	2	23	10	0						0	33
	21	2	18	23	0						0	41
	22	1	23	0	0						0	23
	23	1	23	0	0						0	23
	24	3	18	23	23	0	0	0	0	0	0	64
	25	2	18	18	0	0	0	0	0	0	0	36
	26	1	13	0	0	0	0	0	0	0	0	13
	27	3	18	26	18	0	0	0	0	0	0	62
	28	3	18	18	18	0	0	0	0	0	0	54
	29	1	18	0	0	0	0	0	0	0	0	18
	30	2	23	18	0	0	0	0	0	0	0	41
	31	1	13	0	0	0	0	0	0	0	0	13
	32	1	18	0	0	0	0	0	0	0	0	18
	33	3	10	23	18	0	0	0	0	0	0	51
	34	3	13	18	18	0	0	0	0	0	0	49
	35	2	26	18	0	0	0	0	0	0	0	44
	36	1	23	0	0	0	0	0	0	0	0	23
	37	2	13	23	0	0	0	0	0	0	0	36
	38	2	18	18	0	0	0	0	0	0	0	36
	39	4	18	13	10	18	0	0	0	0	0	59
	40	2	23	26	0	0	0	0	0	0	0	49
	41	2	13	18	0	0	0	0	0	0	0	31
	42	2	18	10	0	0	0	0	0	0	0	28
	43	1	26	0	0	0	0	0	0	0	0	26
	44	2	18	18	0	0	0	0	0	0	0	36
	45	2	13	26	0	0	0	0	0	0	0	39

> To obtain the demand per period, it is necessary to use the **value look up function**. With this function the corresponding demand value will be based on the random number and the match up of that number with the probability distribution of demand. Enter the formula: **IF($S4>=1,VLOOKUP(G4,$B$4:$C$8,2),0)** into cell T4. This formula will look up the value in Lower Range Probability and the units of Demand assigned to each probability. The units demanded will be assigned based on the value of the Random Number in the specific period. Copy this relationship in cells T4:AC503. The entry in cell U4 should be: **IF($S4>=2,VLOOKUP(H4,$B$4:$C$8,2),0)**.

> The total demand is simply the summation of the demand at every individual period, which can be obtained by using the summation function: **=SUM(T4:AC4)** Copy it and paste it as a formula through cells AD4:AD503.

FIGURE **12.11** (cont.)

visual system

A system that allows employees to place orders when inventory visibly reaches a certain marker.

two-bin system

A visual system version of the Q system in which an item's inventory is stored at two different locations.

Two-Bin System The concept of a Q system can be incorporated in a **visual system,** that is, a system that allows employees to place orders when inventory visibly reaches a certain marker. Visual systems are easy to administer because records are not kept on the current inventory position. The historical usage rate can simply be reconstructed from past purchase orders. Visual systems are intended for use with low-value items that have a steady demand, such as nuts and bolts or office supplies. Overstocking is common, but the extra inventory holding cost is minimal because the items have relatively little value.

A visual system version of the Q system is the **two-bin system** in which an item's inventory is stored at two different locations. Inventory is first withdrawn from one bin. If the first bin is empty, the second bin provides backup to cover demand until a replenishment order arrives. An empty first bin signals the need to place a new order. Premade order forms placed near the bins let workers send one to purchasing or even directly to the supplier. When the new order arrives, the second bin is restored to its normal level and the rest is put in the first bin. The two-bin system operates like a Q system, with the normal level in the second bin being the reorder point R. The system also may be implemented with just one bin by marking the bin at the reorder point level.

PERIODIC REVIEW SYSTEM

periodic review (P) sytem

A system in which an item's inventory position is reviewed periodically rather than continuously.

An alternative inventory control system is the **periodic review (P) system**, sometimes called a *fixed interval reorder system* or *periodic reorder system*, in which an item's inventory position is reviewed periodically rather than continuously. Such a system can simplify delivery scheduling because it establishes a routine. A new order is always placed at the end of each review, and the time between orders (TBO) is fixed at P. Demand is a random variable, so total demand between reviews varies. In a P system, the lot size, Q, may change from one order to the next, but the time between orders is fixed. An example of a periodic review system is that of a soft-drink supplier making weekly rounds of grocery stores. Each week, the supplier reviews the store's inventory of soft drinks and restocks the store with enough items to meet demand and safety stock requirements until the next week.

Under a P system, four of the original EOQ assumptions are maintained: (1) no constraints are placed on the size of the lot; (2) the relevant costs are holding and ordering costs; (3) decisions for one item are independent of decisions for other items; and (4) lead times are certain and supply is known. However, demand uncertainty is again allowed for. We will allow for lead time uncertainty later. Figure 12.12 shows the periodic review system under these assumptions. The downward-sloping line again represents on-hand inventory. When the predetermined time, P, has elapsed since the last review, an order is placed to bring the inventory position, represented by the dashed line, up to the target inventory level, T. The lot size for the first review is Q_1, or the difference between inventory position IP_1 and T. As with the continuous review system, IP and OH differ only during the lead time. When the order arrives, at the end of the lead time, OH and IP again are identical. Figure 12.12 shows that lot sizes vary from one order cycle to the next. Because the inventory position is lower at the second review, a greater quantity is needed to achieve an inventory level of T.

FIGURE 12.12

P System When Demand Is Uncertain

Determining How Much to Reorder in a *P* System	EXAMPLE 12.7

A distribution center has a backorder for five 36-inch color TV sets. No inventory is currently on hand, and now is the time to review. How many should be reordered if $T = 400$ and no receipts are scheduled?

SOLUTION

$$IP = OH + SR - BO$$
$$= 0 + 0 - 5 = -5 \text{ sets}$$
$$T - IP = 400 - (-5) = 405 \text{ sets}$$

That is, 405 sets must be ordered to bring the inventory position up to *T* sets.

Selecting the Time Between Reviews To run a *P* system, managers must make two decisions: the length of time between reviews, *P*, and the target inventory level, *T*. Let us first consider the time between reviews, *P*. It can be any convenient interval, such as each Friday or every other Friday. Another option is to base *P* on the cost trade-offs of the EOQ. In other words, *P* can be set equal to the average time between orders for the economic order quantity, or TBO_{EOQ}. Because demand is variable, some orders will be larger than the EOQ and some will be smaller. However, over an extended period of time, the average lot size should be close to the EOQ. If other models are used to determine the lot size (e.g., those described in Supplement D, "Special Inventory Models"), we divide the lot size chosen by the annual demand, *D*, and use this ratio as *P*. It will be expressed as the fraction of a year between orders, which can be converted into months, weeks, or days as needed.

Selecting the Target Inventory Level When Demand Is Uncertain Now let's calculate the target inventory level, *T*, when demand is uncertain but the lead time is constant. Figure 12.12 reveals that an order must be large enough to make the inventory position, IP, last beyond the next review, which is *P* time periods away. The checker must wait *P* periods to revise, correct, and reestablish the inventory position. Then, a new order is placed, but it does not arrive until after the lead time, *L*. Therefore, as Figure 12.12 shows, a protection interval of *P* + *L* periods is needed. A fundamental difference between the *Q* and *P* systems is the length of time needed for stockout protection. A *Q* system needs stockout protection only during the lead time because orders can be placed as soon as they are needed and will be received *L* periods later. A *P* system, however, needs stockout protection for the longer *P* + *L* protection interval because orders are placed only at fixed intervals, and the inventory is not checked until the next designated review time.

As with the *Q* system, we need to develop the appropriate distribution of demand during the protection interval to specify the system fully. In a *P* system, we must develop the distribution of demand for *P* + *L* time periods. The target inventory level *T* must equal the expected demand during the protection interval of *P* + *L* periods, plus enough safety stock to protect against demand uncertainty over this same protection interval. We use the same statistical assumptions that we made for the *Q* system. Thus, the average demand during the protection interval is $d(P + L)$, or

$$T = d(P + L) + \text{Safety stock for the protection interval}$$

We compute safety stock for a *P* system much as we did for the *Q* system. However, the safety stock must cover demand uncertainty for a longer period of time. When using a normal probability distribution, we multiply the desired standard deviations to implement the cycle-service level, *z*, by the standard deviation of demand during the protection interval, σ_{P+L}. The value of *z* is the same as for a *Q* system with the same cycle-service level. Thus,

$$\text{Safety stock} = z\sigma_{P+L}$$

Based on our earlier logic for calculating σ_L, we know that the standard deviation of the distribution of demand during the protection interval is

$$\sigma_{P+L} = \sigma_t \sqrt{P + L}$$

<table>
<tr><td>MANAGERIAL **PRACTICE**</td><td>**12.2**</td><td>IMPLEMENTING A PERIODIC REVIEW INVENTORY
SYSTEM AT HEWLETT-PACKARD</td></tr>
</table>

Hewlett-Packard manufactures computers, accessories, and a wide variety of instrumentation devices in more than 100 separate business units. Each unit is responsible for its own product design, marketing, and manufacturing as well as maintaining the required inventory to service its customers. At most HP businesses, inventory-driven costs (which include inventory devaluation, obsolescence, price protection, and financing) are now the biggest control lever that the manufacturing organization has on business performance, measured in terms of return on assets or economic value added. Inventory is a major cost driver and the most variable element on the balance sheet.

Most of HP's business units were inefficient, carrying more inventory than needed in order to achieve a desired level of product delivery performance. The units often used simplified approaches, such as ABC analysis, to determine their safety stocks for independent demand items, ignoring supply or demand uncertainty, part commonality, desired part availability, or cost.

The solution was to develop a periodic review system that used part availability targets and included as many uncertainties as possible. The system, although in principle similar to the *P* system discussed in this chapter, uses complex equations to determine the review interval and target inventory parameters. The complexity arises from considering uncertainties in supply as well as demand in the determination of the safety stocks.

Even though the system could reduce inventories and improve customer service, no benefits could be realized until the planning and procurement staff actually used it. Because each business unit had some unique characteristics, the results had to be easily understandable and credible, and the system had to be easily configurable to each situation. Consequently, HP developed a software wizard that allows the user to enter product data and costs in a friendly environment, develops the equations for the periodic review system, and then translates the results to the user's format requirements. The wizard is programmed in Excel, which allows users access to all of Excel's functions for conducting their own analyses.

The periodic review system and the software wizard proved successful. At HP's integrated Circuit Manufacturing Division, for example, planners cut inventories by $1.6 million while simultaneously improving on-time delivery performance from 93 percent to 97 percent. Other benefits included less expediting, fewer disagreements about operating policy, and more control of the production system. The system is used across a wide variety of product lines and geographies worldwide. HP believes that the system has clearly led to more efficient operations at the divisions.

Sources: Brian Cargille, Steve Kakouros, and Robert Hall, "Part Tool, Part Process: Inventory Optimization at Hewlett-Packard Co," *OR/MS/TODAY* (October 1999), pp. 18–24; Gianpaolo Callioni, Xavier de Montgros, Regine Slagmulder, Luk N. Van Wassenhove, and Linda Wright, "Inventory-Driven Costs," *Harvard Business Review* (March 2005), pp. 135–141.

Because a *P* system requires safety stock to cover demand uncertainty over a longer time period than a *Q* system, a *P* system requires more safety stock; that is, σ_{P+L} exceeds σ_L. Hence, to gain the convenience of a *P* system requires that overall inventory levels be somewhat higher than those for a *Q* system.

Calculating Total *P* System Costs   The total costs for the *P* system are the sum of the same three cost elements as for the *Q* system. The differences are in the calculation of the order quantity and the safety stock. As shown in Figure 12.12, the average order quantity will be the average consumption of inventory during the *P* periods between orders. Consequently, $Q = dP$. Total costs for the *P* system are

$$C = \frac{dP}{2}(H) + \frac{D}{dP}(S) + Hz\sigma_{P+L}$$

Managerial Practice 12.2 shows how Hewlett-Packard implemented a periodic review inventory system for many of its business units.

<table>
<tr><td>EXAMPLE **12.8**</td><td>**Calculating *P* and *T***</td></tr>
</table>

Again, let us return to the bird feeder example. Recall that demand for the bird feeder is normally distributed with a mean of 18 units per week and a standard deviation in weekly demand of 5 units. The lead time is 2 weeks, and the business operates 52 weeks per year. The *Q* system developed in Example 12.6 called for an EOQ of 75 units and a safety stock of 9 units for a cycle-service level of 90 percent. What is the equivalent *P* system? What is the total cost? Answers are to be rounded to the nearest integer.

SOLUTION

We first define D and then P. Here, P is the time between reviews, expressed as a multiple (or fraction) of time interval t ($t = 1$ week because the data are expressed as demand *per week*):

$$D = (18 \text{ units/week})(52 \text{ weeks/year}) = 936 \text{ units}$$

$$P = \frac{EOQ}{D}(52) = \frac{75}{936}(52) = 4.2 \text{ or } 4 \text{ weeks}$$

With $d = 18$ units per week, we can also calculate P by dividing the EOQ by d to get $75/18 = 4.2$ or 4 weeks. Hence, we would review the bird feeder inventory every 4 weeks. We now find the standard deviation of demand over the protection interval ($P + L = 6$):

$$\sigma_{P+L} = \sigma_t \sqrt{P+L} = 5\sqrt{6} = 12 \text{ units}$$

Before calculating T, we also need a z value. For a 90 percent cycle-service level, $z = 1.28$ (see the Normal Distribution appendix). We now solve for T:

$T = $ Average demand during the protection interval + Safety stock

$\quad = d(P + L) + z\sigma_{P+L}$

$\quad = (18 \text{ units/week})(6 \text{ weeks}) + 1.28(12 \text{ units}) = 123 \text{ units}$

Every 4 weeks we would order the number of units needed to bring inventory position IP (counting the new order) up to the target inventory level of 123 units. The safety stock for this P system is $1.28(12) = 15$ units.

The total P system cost for the bird feeder is

$$C = \frac{4(18)}{2}(\$15) + \frac{936}{4(18)}(\$45) + 15(\$15) = \$540 + \$585 + \$225 = \$1,350$$

Decision Point The P system requires 15 units in safety stock, while the Q system only needs 9 units. If cost were the only criterion, the Q system would be the choice for the bird feeder. As we discuss later, other factors may sway the decision in favor of the P system.

TUTOR 12.5

Tutor 12.5 on the Student CD-ROM provides a new example to determine the review interval and the target inventory for a P system.

Selecting the Target Inventory Level When Demand and Lead Times Are Uncertain

The procedure for selecting the target inventory level when both demand and lead times are uncertain is similar to the approach we used for the continuous review system. The difference is that now we must consider the demand over the protection interval, $P + L$. Using a computer simulation is a practical approach, given the probability distributions for demand and lead times. The review period, P, is considered a constant. The simulation proceeds by randomly drawing a lead time L and adding it to P to arrive at a protection interval. Next, demands are randomly drawn from the demand distribution for each period in the protection interval. The total demand is recorded, and the procedure is repeated.

Consider the bird feeder data that we used previously. Example 12.8 showed that the best review interval, P, is four weeks. Figure 12.13 shows the distribution of the demand during the protection interval for the bird feeder data using the Demand During the Protection Interval Simulator in OM Explorer. We select T from the list of demand levels in the distribution. The cumulative probability of demands at or less than the selected T must equal or exceed the desired cycle-service level. In this example, the desired cycle-service level is 90 percent; therefore, the best choice is $T = 136$. The amount of safety stock required for that level of service is found by subtracting the average demand during the protection level from T. Here, the safety stock is $136 - 108 = 28$ units.[8]

The total cost for the P system when both demands and lead times are uncertain is

$$C = \frac{4(18)}{2}(\$15) + \frac{936}{4(18)}(\$45) + 28(\$15) = \$540.00 + \$585.00 + \$420.00 = \$1,545.00$$

[8]Recall that our development of the Q system using the Demand During the Protection Interval Simulator resulted in the same safety stock quantity. Simulations of this sort should be run multiple times before drawing conclusions. Typically, the safety stock required for a P system exceeds that the Q system.

FIGURE 12.13

Demand During the Protection
Interval Probability Distribution
for a *P* System

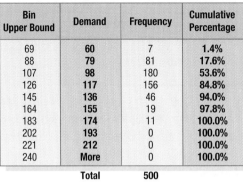

Demand During Protection Interval Distribution

Bin Upper Bound	Demand	Frequency	Cumulative Percentage
69	60	7	1.4%
88	79	81	17.6%
107	98	180	53.6%
126	117	156	84.8%
145	136	46	94.0%
164	155	19	97.8%
183	174	11	100.0%
202	193	0	100.0%
221	212	0	100.0%
240	More	0	100.0%
	Total	**500**	

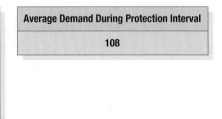

Average Demand During Protection Interval
108

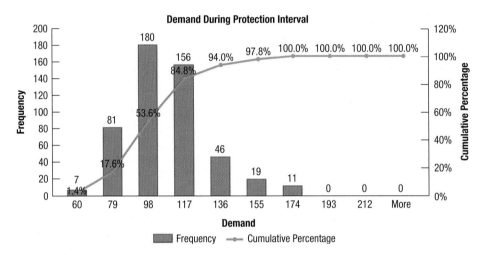

The Demand During the Protection Interval Simulator in OM Explorer can be used to develop the demand distribution for periodic review systems when both demand and lead times are uncertain.

Single-Bin System   The concept of a *P* system can be translated into a simple visual system of inventory control. In the **single-bin system**, a maximum level is marked on the storage shelf or bin on a measuring rod, and the inventory is brought up to the mark periodically—say, once a week. The single bin may be, for example, a gasoline storage tank at a service station or a storage bin for small parts at a manufacturing plant.

COMPARATIVE ADVANTAGES OF THE Q AND P SYSTEMS

Neither the *Q* nor the *P* system is best for all situations. Three *P*-system advantages must be balanced against three *Q*-system advantages. The advantages of one system are implicitly disadvantages of the other system.

The primary advantages of *P* systems are the following:

1. The system is convenient because replenishments are made at fixed intervals. Employees can regularly set aside a day or part of a day to concentrate on this particular task. Fixed replenishment intervals also allow for standardized pickup and delivery times.

2. Orders for multiple items from the same supplier can be combined into a single purchase order. This approach reduces ordering and transportation costs and can result in a price break from the supplier.

3. The inventory position, IP, needs to be known only when a review is made (not continuously, as in a *Q* system). However, this advantage is moot for firms using computerized record-keeping systems, in which a transaction is reported upon each receipt or withdrawal. When inventory records are always current, the system is called a **perpetual inventory system**.

single-bin system

A system of inventory control in which a maximum level is marked on the storage shelf or bin on a measuring rod, and the inventory is brought up to the mark periodically.

perpetual inventory system

A system of inventory control in which the inventory records are always current.

The primary advantages of Q systems are the following:

1. The review frequency of each item may be individualized. Tailoring the review frequency to the item can reduce total ordering and holding costs.

2. Fixed lot sizes, if large enough, can result in quantity discounts. The firm's physical limitations, such as its truckload capacities, materials handling methods, and shelf space might also necessitate a fixed lot size.

3. Lower safety stocks result in savings.

In conclusion, the choice between Q and P systems is not clear cut. Which system is better depends on the relative importance of its advantages in various situations.

HYBRID SYSTEMS

Various hybrid inventory control systems merge some but not all the features of the P and Q systems. We briefly examine two such systems: (1) optional replenishment and (2) base stock.

Optional Replenishment System Sometimes called the optional review, min–max, or (s, S) system, the **optional replenishment system** is much like the P system. It is used to review the inventory position at fixed time intervals and, if the position has dropped to (or below) a predetermined level, to place a variable-sized order to cover expected needs. The new order is large enough to bring the inventory position up to a target inventory, similar to T for the P system. However, orders are not placed after a review unless the inventory position has dropped to the predetermined minimum level. The minimum level acts as the reorder point R does in a Q system. If the target is 100 and the minimum level is 60, the minimum order size is 40 (or 100 − 60). Because continuous reviews need not be made, this system is particularly attractive when both review and ordering costs are high.

optional replenishment system

A system used to review the inventory position at fixed time intervals and, if the position has dropped to (or below) a predetermined level, to place a variable-sized order to cover expected needs.

Base-Stock System In its simplest form, the **base-stock system** issues a replenishment order, Q, each time a withdrawal is made, for the same amount as the withdrawal. This one-for-one replacement policy maintains the inventory position at a base-stock level equal to expected demand during the lead time plus safety stock. The base-stock level, therefore, is equivalent to the reorder point in a Q system. However, order quantities now vary to keep the inventory position at R at all times. Because this position is the lowest IP possible that will maintain a specified service level, the base-stock system may be used to minimize cycle inventory. More orders are placed, but each order is smaller. This system is appropriate for expensive items, such as replacement engines for jet airplanes. No more inventory is held than the maximum demand expected until a replacement order can be received.

base-stock system

An inventory control system that issues a replenishment order, Q each time a withdrawal is made, for the same amount of the withdrawal.

INVENTORY RECORD ACCURACY

Regardless of the inventory system in use, record accuracy is crucial to its success. One way of achieving accuracy is to assign responsibility to specific employees for issuing and receiving materials and accurately reporting each transaction. A second method is to secure inventory behind locked doors or gates to prevent unauthorized or unreported withdrawals. This method also guards against accidentally storing newly received inventory in the wrong locations, where it can be lost for months. **Cycle counting** is a third method, whereby storeroom personnel physically count a small percentage of the total number of items each day, correcting errors that they find. Class A items are counted most frequently. A final method, for computerized systems, is to make logic error checks on each transaction reported and fully investigate any discrepancies. The discrepancies can include: (1) actual receipts when no receipts are scheduled, (2) disbursements that exceed the current on-hand inventory balance, and (3) receipts with an inaccurate (nonexistent) part number.

cycle counting

An inventory control method, whereby storeroom personnel physically count a small percentage of the total number of items each day, correcting errors that they find.

These methods can keep inventory records accurate within acceptable bounds. A side benefit is that auditors may not require end-of-year inventory counts if the records prove to be sufficiently accurate.

> STUDENT CD-ROM AND INTERNET RESOURCES <

The Student CD-ROM and the Companion Website at **www.prenhall.com/krajewski** contain many tools, activities, and resources designed for this chapter.

> KEY EQUATIONS <

1. Cycle inventory $= \dfrac{Q}{2}$

2. Pipeline inventory $= dL$

3. Total annual cycle-inventory cost = Annual holding cost + Annual ordering or setup cost

$$C = \frac{Q}{2}(H) + \frac{D}{Q}(S)$$

4. Economic order quantity: $\text{EOQ} = \sqrt{\dfrac{2DS}{H}}$

5. Time between orders, expressed in weeks:

$$\text{TBO}_{\text{EOQ}} = \frac{\text{EOQ}}{D}(52 \text{ weeks/year})$$

6. Inventory position = On-hand inventory + Scheduled receipts − Backorders

$$\text{IP} = \text{OH} + \text{SR} - \text{BO}$$

7. Continuous review system:

Reorder point(R) = Average demand during the protection interval + Safety stock

$$= dL + z\sigma_L$$

Protection interval = Lead time(L)

Standard deviation of demand during the lead time $= \sigma_L$

$$= \sigma_t \sqrt{L}$$

Order quantity = EOQ

Replenishment rule: Order EOQ units when IP $\leq R$

Total Q system cost: $C = \dfrac{Q}{2}(H) + \dfrac{D}{Q}(S) + Hz\sigma_L$

8. Periodic review system:

Target inventory level (T) = Average demand during the protection interval + Safety stock

$$= d(P+L) + z\sigma_{P+L}$$

Protection interval = Time between orders + Lead time

$$= P + L$$

Review interval = Time between orders $= P$

Standard deviation of demand during the protection interval $= \sigma_{P+L} = \sigma_t \sqrt{P+L}$

Order quantity = Target inventory level – Inventory position $= T - IP$

Replenishment rule: Every P time periods, order $T - IP$ units

Total P system cost: $C = \dfrac{dP}{2}(H) + \dfrac{D}{dP}(S) + Hz\sigma_{P+L}$

> KEY TERMS <

ABC analysis 469
base-stock system 489
continuous review (Q) system 475
cycle counting 489
cycle inventory 465
cycle-service level 478
economic order quantity (EOQ) 470
independent demand items 475
inventory holding cost 463
inventory management 462
inventory position (IP) 476

lot sizing 465
open orders 476
optional replenishment system 489
ordering cost 464
periodic review (P) system 484
perpetual inventory system 488
pipeline inventory 465
protection interval 478
quantity discount 464
reorder point (R) 476
reorder point (ROP) system 475

repeatability 468
safety stock inventory 465
scheduled receipts (SR) 476
service level 478
setup cost 464
single-bin system 488
special 468
standard 469
time between orders (TBO) 473
two-bin system 484
visual system 484

> SOLVED PROBLEM 1 <

A distribution center experiences an average weekly demand of 50 units for one of its items. The product is valued at $650 per unit. Average inbound shipments from the factory warehouse average 350 units. Average lead time (including ordering delays and transit time) is 2 weeks. The distribution center operates 52 weeks per year; it carries a 1-week supply of inventory as safety stock and no anticipation inventory. What is the average aggregate inventory being held by the distribution center?

SOLUTION

Type of Inventory	Calculation of Average Inventory Quantity	
Cycle	$\dfrac{Q}{2} = \dfrac{350}{2} =$	175 units
Safety stock	1-week supply =	50 units
Anticipation	None	
Pipeline	dL = (50 units/week)(2 weeks)	= 100 units
	Average aggregate inventory	= 325 units

> SOLVED PROBLEM 2 <

Booker's Book Bindery divides inventory items into three classes, according to their dollar usage. Calculate the usage values of the following inventory items and determine which is most likely to be classified as an A item.

Part Number	Description	Quantity Used per Year	Unit Value ($)
1	Boxes	500	3.00
2	Cardboard (square feet)	18,000	0.02
3	Cover stock	10,000	0.75
4	Glue (gallons)	75	40.00
5	Inside covers	20,000	0.05
6	Reinforcing tape (meters)	3,000	0.15
7	Signatures	150,000	0.45

SOLUTION

Part Number	Description	Quantity Used per Year		Unit Value($)		Annual Dollar Usage($)
1	Boxes	500	×	3.00	=	1,500
2	Cardboard (square feet)	18,000	×	0.02	=	360
3	Cover stock	10,000	×	0.75	=	7,500
4	Glue (gallons)	75	×	40.00	=	3,000
5	Inside covers	20,000	×	0.05	=	1,000
6	Reinforcing tape (meters)	3,000	×	0.15	=	450
7	Signatures	150,000	×	0.45	=	67,500
					Total	81,310

The annual dollar usage for each item is determined by multiplying the annual usage quantity by the value per unit. As shown in Figure 12.14, the items are then sorted by annual dollar usage, in declining order. Finally, A–B and B–C class lines are drawn roughly, according to the guidelines presented in the text. Here, class A includes only one item (signatures), which represents only 1/7, or 14 percent, of the items but accounts for 83 percent of annual dollar usage. Class B includes the next two items, which taken together represent 28 percent of the items and account for 13 percent of annual dollar usage. The final four items, class C, represent over half the number of items but only 4 percent of total annual dollar usage.

FIGURE 12.14

Annual Dollar Usage for Class A, B, and C Items Using Tutor 12.2

Part #	Description	Qty Used/Year	Value	Dollar Usage	Pct of Total	Cumulative % of Dollar Value	Cumulative % of Item	Class
7	Signatures	150,000	$0.45	$67,500	83.0%	83.0%	14.3%	A
3	Cover stock	10,000	$0.75	$7,500	9.2%	92.2%	28.6%	B
4	Glue	75	$40.00	$3,000	3.7%	95.9%	42.9%	B
1	Boxes	500	$3.00	$1,500	1.8%	97.8%	57.1%	C
5	Inside covers	20,000	$0.05	$1,000	1.2%	99.0%	71.4%	C
6	Reinforcing tape	3,000	$0.15	$450	0.6%	99.6%	85.7%	C
2	Cardboard	18,000	$0.02	$360	0.4%	100.0%	100.0%	C

Total $81,310

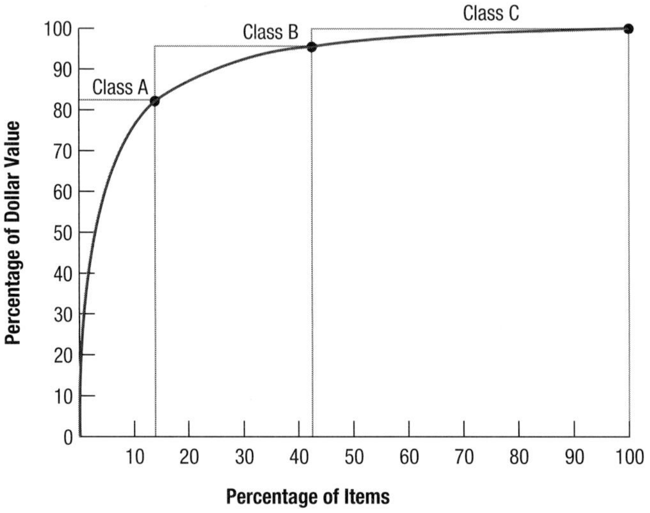

> **SOLVED PROBLEM 3** <

In Example 12.3, the economic order quantity, EOQ, is 75 units when annual demand, D, is 936 units/year, setup cost, S, is $45, and holding cost, H, is $15/unit/year. Suppose that we mistakenly estimate inventory holding cost to be $30/unit/year.

a. What is the new order quantity, Q, if $D = 936$ units/year, $S = $45, and $H = $30/unit/year?

b. What is the change in order quantity, expressed as a percentage of the economic order quantity (75 units)?

SOLUTION

a. The new order quantity is

$$EOQ = \sqrt{\frac{2DS}{H}} = \sqrt{\frac{2(936)($45)}{$30}} = \sqrt{2,808} = 52.99 \quad \text{or} \quad 53 \text{ units}$$

b. The change in percentage is

$$\left(\frac{53-75}{75}\right)(100) = -29.33 \text{ percent}$$

The new order quantity (53) is about 29 percent smaller than the correct order quantity (75).

> **SOLVED PROBLEM 4** <

In Example 12.3, the total annual cost, C, is $1,124.

a. What is the annual total cost when $D = 936$ units/year, $S = $45, $H = $15/unit/year, and Q is the result from Solved Problem 3(a)?

b. What is the change in total cost, expressed as a percentage of the total cost ($1,124)?

SOLUTION

a. With 53 as the order quantity, the total annual cycle-inventory cost is

$$C = \frac{Q}{2}(H) + \frac{D}{Q}(S) = \frac{53}{2}(\$15) + \frac{936}{53}(\$45) = \$397.50 + \$794.72$$

$$= \$1,192.22 \quad \text{or} \quad \text{about } \$1,192$$

b. The change expressed as a percentage is

$$\left(\frac{\$1,192 - \$1,124}{\$1,124} \right)(100) = 6.05\% \text{ or about } 6\%$$

A 100 percent error in estimating the holding cost caused the order quantity to be 29 percent too small, and that in turn increased annual costs by about 6 percent.

> SOLVED PROBLEM 5 <

A regional warehouse purchases hand tools from various suppliers and then distributes them on demand to retailers in the region. The warehouse operates 5 days per week, 52 weeks per year. Only when it is open can orders be received. The following data are estimated for 3/8-inch hand drills with double insulation and variable speeds:

Average daily demand = 100 drills

Standard deviation of daily demand (σ_t) = 30 drills

Lead time (L) = 3 days

Holding cost (H) = \$9.40/unit/year

Ordering cost (S) = \$35/order

Cycle-service level = 92 percent

The warehouse uses a continuous review (Q) system.

a. What order quantity Q, and reorder point, R, should be used?

b. If on-hand inventory is 40 units, one open order for 440 drills is pending, and no backorders exist, should a new order be placed?

SOLUTION

a. Annual demand is

$$D = (5 \text{ days/week})(52 \text{ weeks/year})(100 \text{ drills/day}) = 26,000 \text{ drills/year}$$

The order quantity is

$$EOQ = \sqrt{\frac{2DS}{H}} = \sqrt{\frac{2(26,000)(\$35)}{\$9.40}} = \sqrt{193,167} = 440.02 \quad \text{or} \quad 440 \text{ drills}$$

and the standard deviation is

$$\sigma_L = \sigma_t \sqrt{L} = (30 \text{ drills})\sqrt{3} = 51.96 \quad \text{or} \quad 52 \text{ drills}$$

A 92 percent cycle-service level corresponds to $z = 1.41$ (see the Normal Distribution appendix). Therefore,

Safety stock = $z\sigma_L$ = 1.41(52 drills) = 73.38 or 73 drills

Average demand during the lead time = 100(3) = 300 drills

Reorder point = Average demand during the lead time + Safety stock

= 300 drills + 73 drills = 373 drills

With a continuous review system, $Q = 440$ and $R = 373$.

b. Inventory position = On-hand inventory + Scheduled receipts − Backorders

$$IP = OH + SR - BO = 40 + 440 - 0 = 480 \text{ drills}$$

Because IP(480) exceeds R(373), do not place a new order.

> SOLVED PROBLEM 6 <

Suppose that a periodic review (P) system is used at the warehouse, but otherwise the data are the same as in Solved Problem 5.

a. Calculate the P (in workdays, rounded to the nearest day) that gives approximately the same number of orders per year as the EOQ.

b. What is the value of the target inventory level, T? Compare the P system to the Q system in Solved Problem 5.

c. It is time to review the item. On-hand inventory is 40 drills; receipt of 440 drills is scheduled, and no backorders exist. How much should be reordered?

SOLUTION

a. The time between orders is

$$P = \frac{\text{EOQ}}{D}(260 \text{ days/year}) = \frac{440}{26,000}(260) = 4.4 \text{ or } 4 \text{ days}$$

b. Figure 12.15 shows that $T = 812$. The corresponding Q system for the hand drill requires less safety stock.

c. Inventory position is the amount on hand plus scheduled receipts minus backorders, or

$$\text{IP} = \text{OH} + \text{SR} - \text{BO} = 40 + 440 - 0 = 480 \text{ drills}$$

The order quantity is the target inventory level minus the inventory position, or

$$Q = T - \text{IP} = 812 \text{ drills} - 480 \text{ drills} = 332 \text{ drills}$$

In a periodic review system, the order quantity for this review period is 332 drills.

FIGURE 12.15

OM Explorer Solver for
Inventory Systems

Continuous Review (Q) System		Periodic Review (P) System	
z	1.41	Time Between Reviews (P)	4.00 Days
Safety Stock	73		☑ Enter manually
Reorder Point	373	Standard Deviation of Demand During Protection Interval	79.37
Annual Cost	$4,822.38	Safety Stock	112
		Average Demand During Protection Interval	700
		Target Inventory Level (T)	812
		Annual Cost	$5,207.80

> SOLVED PROBLEM 7 <

Zeke's Hardware Store sells furnace filters. The cost to place an order to the distributor is $25 and the annual cost to hold a filter in stock is $2. The average demand per week for the filters is 32 units, and the store operates 50 weeks per year. The weekly demand for filters has the following probability distribution:

Demand	Probability
24	0.15
28	0.20
32	0.30
36	0.20
40	0.15

The delivery lead time from the distributor is uncertain and has the following probability distribution:

Lead Time (wks)	Probability
1	0.05
2	0.25
3	0.40
4	0.25
5	0.05

Suppose Zeke wants to use a P system with $P = 6$ weeks and a cycle-service level of 90 percent. What is the appropriate value for T and the associated annual cost of the system?

SOLUTION

Figure 12.16 contains output from the Demand During the Protection Interval Simulator from OM Explorer.

Given the desired cycle-service level of 90 percent, the appropriate T value is 322 units. The simulation estimated the average demand during the protection interval to be 289 units, consequently the safety stock is $322 - 289 = 33$ units.

The annual cost of this P system is

$$C = \frac{6(32)}{2}(\$2) + \frac{50(32)}{6(32)}(\$25) + 33(\$2) = \$192.00 + \$208.33 + \$66.00 = \$466.3$$

Demand During Protection Interval Distribution

Bin Upper Bound	Demand	Frequency	Cumulative Percentage
196	182	0	0.0%
224	210	17	3.4%
252	138	66	16.6%
280	266	135	43.6%
308	294	140	71.6%
336	322	109	93.4%
364	350	30	99.4%
392	378	3	100.0%
420	406	0	100.0%
448	More	0	100.0%
Total		500	

Average Demand During Protection Interval
289

FIGURE **12.16**

OM Explorer Solver for Demand During the Protection Interval

> SOLVED PROBLEM 8 <

Consider Zeke's inventory in Solved Problem 7. Suppose that he wants to use a continuous review (Q) system for the filters, with an order quantity of 200 and a reorder point of 140. Initial inventory is 170 units. If the stockout cost is $5 per unit, and all of the other data in Solved Problem 7 are the same, what is the expected cost per week of using the Q system?

SOLUTION

Figure 12.17 shows output from the Q System Simulator in OM Explorer. Only weeks 1 through 13 and weeks 41 through 50 are shown in the figure. The average total cost per week is $305.62. Notice that no stockouts occurred in this simulation. These results are dependent on Zeke's choices for the reorder point and lot size. It is possible that stockouts would occur if the simulation were run for more than 50 weeks.

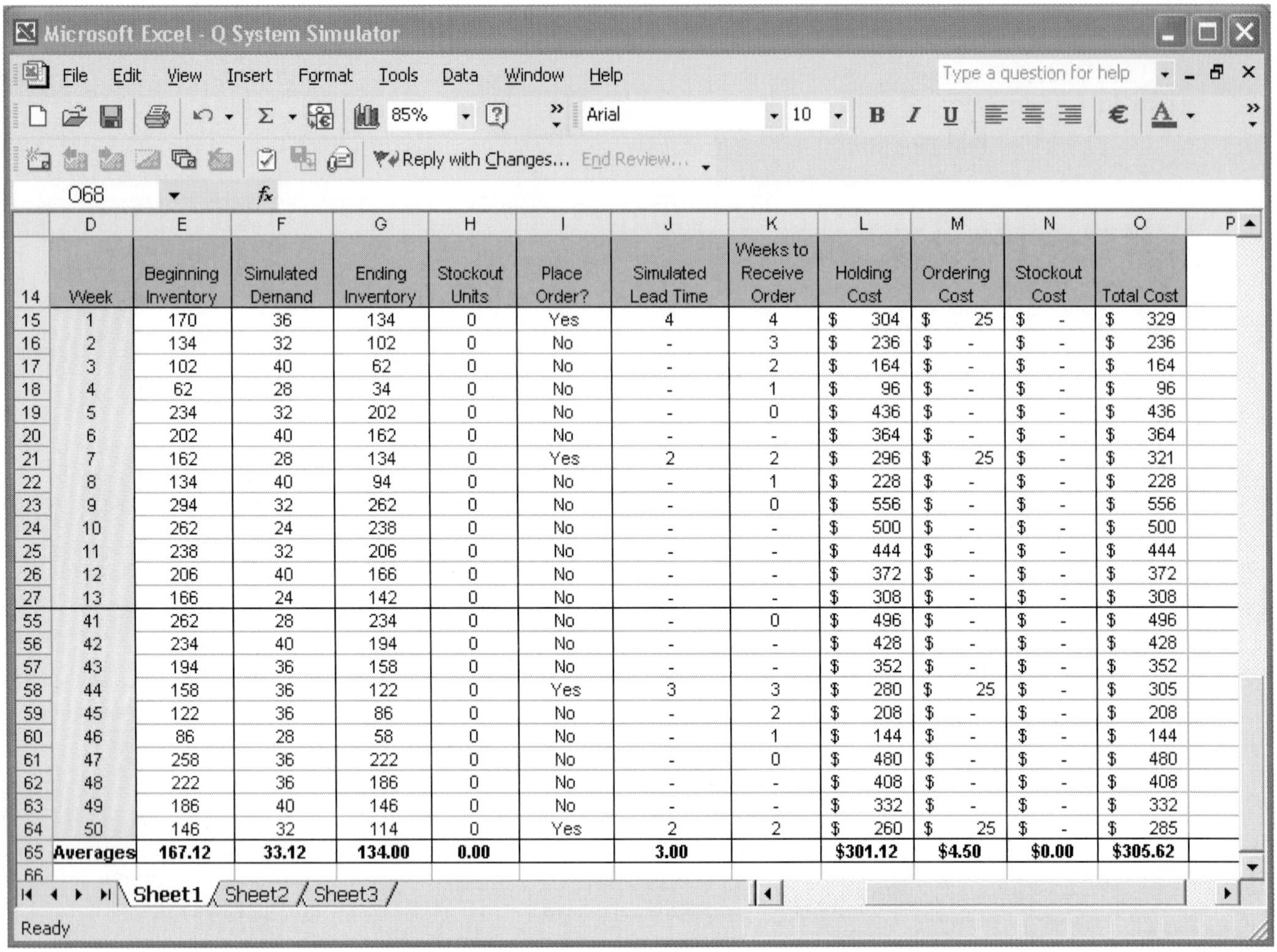

14 Week	Beginning Inventory	Simulated Demand	Ending Inventory	Stockout Units	Place Order?	Simulated Lead Time	Weeks to Receive Order	Holding Cost	Ordering Cost	Stockout Cost	Total Cost
15 1	170	36	134	0	Yes	4	4	$ 304	$ 25	$ -	$ 329
16 2	134	32	102	0	No	-	3	$ 236	$ -	$ -	$ 236
17 3	102	40	62	0	No	-	2	$ 164	$ -	$ -	$ 164
18 4	62	28	34	0	No	-	1	$ 96	$ -	$ -	$ 96
19 5	234	32	202	0	No	-	0	$ 436	$ -	$ -	$ 436
20 6	202	40	162	0	No	-	-	$ 364	$ -	$ -	$ 364
21 7	162	28	134	0	Yes	2	2	$ 296	$ 25	$ -	$ 321
22 8	134	40	94	0	No	-	1	$ 228	$ -	$ -	$ 228
23 9	294	32	262	0	No	-	0	$ 556	$ -	$ -	$ 556
24 10	262	24	238	0	No	-	-	$ 500	$ -	$ -	$ 500
25 11	238	32	206	0	No	-	-	$ 444	$ -	$ -	$ 444
26 12	206	40	166	0	No	-	-	$ 372	$ -	$ -	$ 372
27 13	166	24	142	0	No	-	-	$ 308	$ -	$ -	$ 308
55 41	262	28	234	0	No	-	0	$ 496	$ -	$ -	$ 496
56 42	234	40	194	0	No	-	-	$ 428	$ -	$ -	$ 428
57 43	194	36	158	0	No	-	-	$ 352	$ -	$ -	$ 352
58 44	158	36	122	0	Yes	3	3	$ 280	$ 25	$ -	$ 305
59 45	122	36	86	0	No	-	2	$ 208	$ -	$ -	$ 208
60 46	86	28	58	0	No	-	1	$ 144	$ -	$ -	$ 144
61 47	258	36	222	0	No	-	0	$ 480	$ -	$ -	$ 480
62 48	222	36	186	0	No	-	-	$ 408	$ -	$ -	$ 408
63 49	186	40	146	0	No	-	-	$ 332	$ -	$ -	$ 332
64 50	146	32	114	0	Yes	2	2	$ 260	$ 25	$ -	$ 285
65 Averages	167.12	33.12	134.00	0.00		3.00		$301.12	$4.50	$0.00	$305.62

FIGURE 12.17 | OM Explorer *Q* System Simulator

> DISCUSSION QUESTIONS <

1. What is the relationship between inventory and the nine competitive priorities? Suppose that two competing manufacturers, Company H and Company L, are similar except that Company H has much higher investments in raw materials, work-in-process, and finished goods inventory than Company L. In which of the nine competitive priorities will Company H have an advantage?

2. Form a discussion group in which each member represents a different functional area of a retailer. Suppose that cycle inventories are to be reduced. Discuss the implications of that decision for each functional area.

3. Will organizations ever get to the point where they will no longer need inventories? Why or why not?

> PROBLEMS <

Software, such as OM Explorer, Active Models, and POM for Windows, is packaged with every new copy of the textbook. Check with your instructor on how best to use it. In many cases, the instructor wants you to understand how to do the calculations by hand. At most, the software provides a check on your calculations. When calculations are particularly complex and the goal is interpreting the results in making decisions, the software replaces entirely the manual calculations. The software also can be a valuable resource well after your course is completed.

1. A part is produced in lots of 1,000 units. It is assembled from two components worth $50 total. The value added in production (for labor and variable overhead) is $60 per unit, bringing total costs per completed unit to $110. The average lead time for the part is 6 weeks and annual demand is 3,800 units, based on 50 business weeks per year.

   a. How many units of the part are held, on average, in cycle inventory? What is the dollar value of this inventory?

b. How many units of the part are held, on average, in pipeline inventory? What is the dollar value of this inventory? (*Hint.* Assume that the typical part in pipeline inventory is 50 percent completed. Thus, half the labor and variable overhead costs has been added, bringing the unit cost to $80, or $50 + $60/2.)

2. Prince Electronics, a manufacturer of consumer electronic goods, has five distribution centers in different regions of the country. For one of its products, a high-speed modem priced at $350 per unit, the average weekly demand at *each* distribution center is 75 units. Average shipment size to each distribution center is 400 units, and average lead time for delivery is two weeks. Each distribution center carries two weeks' supply as safety stock but holds no anticipation inventory.

a. On a average, how many dollars of pipeline inventory will be in transit to each distribution center?

b. How much total inventory (cycle, safety, and pipeline) does Prince hold for all five distribution centers?

3. Lockwood Industries is considering the use of ABC analysis to focus on the most critical items in its inventory. For a random sample of eight items, the following table shows the annual dollar usage. Rank the items, and assign them to the A, B, or C class.

Item	Dollar Value	Annual Usage
1	$0.01	1,200
2	$0.03	120,000
3	$0.45	100
4	$1.00	44,000
5	$4.50	900
6	$0.90	350
7	$0.30	70,000
8	$1.50	200

4. Terminator, Inc., manufactures a motorcycle part in lots of 250 units. The raw materials cost for the part is $150, and the value added in manufacturing one unit from its components is $300, for a total cost per completed unit of $450. The lead time to make the part is 3 weeks; and the annual demand is 4,000 units. Assume 50 working weeks per year.

a. How many units of the part are held, on average, as cycle inventory? What is its value?

b. How many units of the part are held, on average, as pipeline inventory? What is its value?

5. Stock-Rite, Inc., is considering the use of ABC analysis to focus on the most critical items in its inventory. For a random sample of eight items, the following table shows the item's unit value and annual demand. Categorize these items as A, B, and C classes.

Item Code	Unit Value	Demand (units)
A104	$40.25	80
D205	80.75	120
X104	10.00	150
U404	40.50	150
L205	60.70	50
S104	80.20	20
X205	80.15	20
L104	20.05	100

6. Yellow Press, Inc., buys slick paper in 1,500-pound rolls for textbook printing. Annual demand is 2,500 rolls. The cost per roll is $800, and the annual holding cost is 15 percent of the cost. Each order costs $50.

a. How many rolls should Yellow Press order at a time?

b. What is the time between orders?

7. Babble, Inc., buys 400 blank cassette tapes per month for use in producing foreign language courseware. The ordering cost is $12.50. Holding cost is $0.12 per cassette per year.

a. How many tapes should Babble order at a time?

b. What is the time between orders?

8. At Dot Com, a large retailer of popular books, demand is constant at 32,000 books per year. The cost of placing an order to replenish stock is $10, and the annual cost of holding is $4 per book. Stock is received 5 working days after an order has been placed. No backordering is allowed. Assume 300 working days a year.

a. What is Dot Com's optimal order quantity?

b. What is the optimal number of orders per year?

c. What is the optimal interval (in working days) between orders?

d. What is demand during the lead time?

e. What is the reorder point?

f. What is the inventory position immediately after an order has been placed?

9. Leaky Pipe, a local retailer of plumbing supplies, faces demand for one of its inventoried items at a constant rate of 30,000 units per year. It costs Leaky Pipe $10 to process an order to replenish stock and $1 per unit per year to carry the item in stock. Stock is received 4 working days after an order is placed. No backordering is allowed. Assume 300 working days a year.

a. What is Leaky Pipe's optimal order quantity?

b. What is the optimal number of orders per year?

c. What is the optimal interval (in working days) between orders?

d. What is the demand during the lead time?

e. What is the reorder point?

f. What is the inventory position immediately after an order has been placed?

10. Sam's Cat Hotel operates 52 weeks per year, 6 days per week, and uses a continuous review inventory system. It purchases kitty litter for $11.70 per bag. The following information is available about these bags.

Demand = 90 bags/week

Order cost = $54/order

Annual holding cost = 27% of cost

Desired cycle-service level = 80%

Lead time = 3 weeks (18 working days)

Standard deviation of weekly demand = 15 bags

Current on-hand inventory is 320 bags, with no open orders or backorders.

  a. What is the EOQ? What would be the average time between orders (in weeks)?

  b. What should R be?

  c. An inventory withdrawal of 10 bags was just made. Is it time to reorder?

  d. The store currently uses a lot size of 500 bags (i.e., $Q = 500$). What is the annual holding cost of this policy? Annual ordering cost? Without calculating the EOQ, how can you conclude from these two calculations that the current lot size is too large?

  e. What would be the annual cost saved by shifting from the 500-bag lot size to the EOQ?

11. Consider again the kitty litter ordering policy for Sam's Cat Hotel in Problem 10.

  a. Suppose that the weekly demand forecast of 90 bags is incorrect and actual demand averages only 60 bags per week. How much higher will total costs be, owing to the distorted EOQ caused by this forecast error?

  b. Suppose that actual demand is 60 bags but that ordering costs are cut to only $6 by using the Internet to automate order placing. However, the buyer does not tell anyone, and the EOQ is not adjusted to reflect this reduction in S. How much higher will total costs be, compared to what they could be if the EOQ were adjusted?

12. In a Q system, the demand rate for gizmos is normally distributed, with an average of 300 units *per week*. The lead time is 9 weeks. The standard deviation of *weekly* demand is 15 units.

  a. What is the standard deviation of demand during the 9-week lead time?

  b. What is the average demand during the 9-week lead time?

  c. What reorder point results in a cycle-service level of 99 percent?

13. Petromax Enterprises uses a continuous review inventory control system for one of its inventory items. The following information is available on the item. The firm operates 50 weeks in a year.

Demand = 50,000 units/year

Ordering cost = $35/order

Holding cost = $2/unit/year

Average lead time = 3 weeks

Standard deviation of weekly demand = 125 units

  a. What is the economic order quantity for this item?

  b. If Petromax wants to provide a 90 percent cycle-service level, what should be the safety stock and the reorder point?

14. In a perpetual inventory system, the lead time for dohickeys is five weeks. The standard deviation of demand during the lead time is 85 units. The desired cycle-service level is 99 percent. The supplier of dohickeys streamlined its operations and now quotes a one-week lead time. How much can safety stock be reduced without reducing the 99 percent cycle-service level?

15. In a two-bin inventory system, the demand for whatchamacallits during the two-week lead time is normally distributed, with an average of 53 units per week. The standard deviation of weekly demand is 5 units. What cycle-service level is provided when the normal level in the second bin is set at 120 units?

16. Nationwide Auto Parts uses a periodic review inventory control system for one of its stock items. The review interval is six weeks, and the lead time for receiving the materials ordered from its wholesaler is three weeks. Weekly demand is normally distributed, with a mean of 100 units and a standard deviation of 20 units.

  a. What is the average and the standard deviation of demand during the protection interval?

  b. What should be the target inventory level if the firm desires 97.5 percent stockout protection?

  c. If 350 units were in stock at the time of a certain periodic review, how many units should be ordered?

17. In a P system, the lead time for gadgets is two weeks and the review period is one week. Demand during the protection interval averages 218 units, with a standard deviation of 40 units. What is the cycle-service level when the target inventory level is set at 300 units?

18. You are in charge of inventory control of a highly successful product retailed by your firm. Weekly demand for this item varies, with an average of 200 units and a standard deviation of 16 units. It is purchased from a wholesaler at a cost of $12.50 per unit. The supply lead time is 4 weeks. Placing an order costs $50, and the inventory carrying rate per year is 20 percent of the item's cost. Your firm operates 5 days per week, 50 weeks per year.

  a. What is the optimal ordering quantity for this item?

  b. How many units of the item should be maintained as safety stock for 99 percent protection against stockouts during an order cycle?

  c. If supply lead time can be reduced to 2 weeks, what is the percent reduction in the number of units maintained as safety stock for the same 99 percent stockout protection?

  d. If through appropriate sales promotions, the demand variability is reduced so that the standard deviation of weekly demand is 8 units instead of 16, what is the percent reduction [compared to that in part (b)] in the number of units maintained as safety stock for the same 99 percent stockout protection?

19. Suppose that Sam's Cat Hotel in Problem 10 uses a *P* system instead of a *Q* system. The average daily demand is 15 bags (90/6), and the standard deviation of *daily* demand is 6.124 bags $(15/\sqrt{6})$.

    a. What *P* (in working days) and *T* should be used to approximate the cost trade-offs of the EOQ?

    b. How much more safety stock is needed than with a *Q* system?

    c. It is time for the periodic review. How much kitty litter should be ordered?

20. Your firm uses a continuous review system and operates 52 weeks per year. One of the items handled has the following characteristics.

Demand (D) = 20,000 units/year

Ordering cost (S) = \$40/order

Holding cost (H) = \$2/unit/year

Lead time (L) = 2 weeks

Cycle-service level = 95%

Demand is normally distributed, with a standard deviation of *weekly* demand of 100 units.
    Current on-hand inventory is 1,040 units, with no scheduled receipts and no backorders.

    a. Calculate the item's EOQ. What is the average time, in weeks, between orders?

    b. Find the safety stock and reorder point that provide a 95 percent cycle-service level.

    c. For these policies, what are the annual costs of (i) holding the cycle inventory and (ii) placing orders?

    d. A withdrawal of 15 units just occurred. Is it time to reorder? If so, how much should be ordered?

21. Suppose that your firm uses a periodic review system, but otherwise the data are the same as in Problem 20.

    a. Calculate the *P* that gives approximately the same number of orders per year as the EOQ. Round your answer to the nearest week.

    b. Find the safety stock and the target inventory level that provide a 95 percent cycle-service level.

    c. How much larger is the safety stock than with a *Q* system?

22. A company begins a review of ordering policies for its continuous review system by checking the current policies for a sample of items. Following are the characteristics of one item.

Demand (D) = 64 units/week (Assume 52 weeks per year)

Ordering and setup cost (S) = \$50/order

Holding cost (H) = \$13/unit/year

Lead time (L) = 2 weeks

Standard deviation of *weekly* demand = 12 units

Cycle-service level = 88 percent

    a. What is the EOQ for this item?

    b. What is the desired safety stock?

    c. What is the reorder point?

    d. What are the cost implications if the current policy for this item is Q = 200 and R = 180?

23. Using the same information as in Problem 22, develop the best policies for a periodic review system.

    a. What value of *P* gives the same approximate number of orders per year as the EOQ? Round to the nearest week.

    b. What safety stock and target inventory level provide an 88 percent cycle-service level?

24. Wood County Hospital consumes 1,000 boxes of bandages per week. The price of bandages is \$35 per box, and the hospital operates 52 weeks per year. The cost of processing an order is \$15, and the cost of holding one box for a year is 15 percent of the value of the material.

    a. The hospital orders bandages in lot sizes of 900 boxes. What *extra* cost does the hospital incur, which it could save by using the EOQ method?

    b. Demand is normally distributed, with a standard deviation of weekly demand of 100 boxes. The lead time is 2 weeks. What safety stock is necessary if the hospital uses a continuous review system and a 97 percent cycle-service level is desired? What should be the reorder point?

    c. If the hospital uses a periodic review system, with *P* = 2 weeks, what should be the target inventory level, *T*?

25. A golf specialty wholesaler operates 50 weeks per year. Management is trying to determine an inventory policy for its 1-irons, which have the following characteristics:

Demand (D) = 2,000 units/year

Demand is normally distributed

Standard deviation of *weekly* demand = 3 units

Ordering cost = \$40/order

Annual holding cost (H) = \$5/units

Desired cycle-service level = 90%

Lead time (L) = 4 weeks

    a. If the company uses a periodic review system, what should *P* and *T* be? Round *P* to the nearest week.

    b. If the company uses a continuous review system, what should *R* be?

ADVANCED PROBLEMS

It may be helpful to review Supplement B, "Simulation," before working Problems 26–29.

26. The Office Supply Shop estimates that the monthly demand for ballpoint pens has the following distribution:

Demand (thousands)	Probability
5	0.1
10	0.3
15	0.4
20	0.1
25	0.1

Furthermore, the lead time for the ballpoint pens from the distributor has the following distribution:

Lead Time (weeks)	Probability
1	0.2
2	0.4
3	0.2
4	0.1
5	0.1

a. If management wants to have a cycle-service level of 95 percent for their continuous review system, what should the reorder point be?

b. What quantity of safety stock must be held?

27. The manager of a grocery store orders health care items from a regional distributor every 3 weeks. One item, Happy Breath Toothpaste, has the following weekly demand distribution:

Demand	Probability
10	0.08
15	0.12
20	0.35
25	0.25
30	0.20

The service the manager gets from the distributor has not been consistent. The lead time for a resupply of Happy Breath has the following distribution:

Lead Time (weeks)	Probability
1	0.10
2	0.25
3	0.30
4	0.25
5	0.10

a. If the manager wants to maintain a cycle-service level of 85 percent on Happy Breath Toothpaste, what target level (T) would she have to use?

b. Suppose the manager could redesign her order placement process and work more closely with the distributor so that the lead time was a constant 3 weeks. That is, in the table for lead time, the probability for a 3-week lead time would be 1.0, and for all other options it would be zero. What would the cycle-service level be for the same target inventory level you found for part (a)?

28. The manager of a floral shop sells 2,550 flower baskets per year. The baskets provide a nice souvenir to the recipients

of the floral arrangements. The floral shop is open 50 weeks a year. The baskets must be ordered from a supplier whose lead times have been erratic in the past. The cost to place an order to the supplier is $30, and the cost to hold a basket in inventory for a year is $1. The manager has estimated that the cost to the floral shop is $10 for each basket not in stock when a customer demands one.

The probability distribution for weekly demand is as follows:

Demand	Probability
40	0.40
50	0.30
60	0.15
70	0.10
80	0.05

The distribution for lead times is

Lead Time (weeks)	Probability
1	0.3
2	0.4
3	0.2
4	0.1
5	0.0

a. Specify the order quantity and reorder point for a continuous review system that will provide at least a 90 percent cycle-service level. Use the Demand During the Protection Interval Simulator in OM Explorer.

b. Use the Q System Simulator in OM Explorer to estimate the average cost per day of using the Q system you developed. Assume the beginning inventory is 300 baskets.

29. The Georgia Lighting Center stocks more than 3,000 lighting fixtures, including chandeliers, swags, wall lamps, and track lights. The store sells at retail, operates 6 days per week, and advertises itself as the "brightest spot in town." One expensive fixture is selling at an average rate of 5 units per day. The reorder policy is $Q = 40$ and $R = 15$. A new order is placed on the day the reorder point is reached. The lead time is 3 business days. For example, an order placed on Monday will be delivered on Thursday. Simulate the performance of this Q system for the next 3 weeks (18 workdays). Any stockouts result in lost sales (rather than backorders). The beginning inventory is 19 units, and no receipts are scheduled. Table 12.3 simulates the first week of operation. Extend Table 12.3 to simulate operations for the next 2 weeks if demand for the next 12 business days is 7, 4, 2, 7, 3, 6, 10, 0, 5, 10, 4, and 7.

a. What is the average daily ending inventory over the 18 days?

b. How many stockouts occurred?

	Beginning	Orders	Daily	Ending	Inventory	Order
Workday	Inventory	Received	Demand	Inventory	Position	Quantity
1. Monday	19	—	5	14	14	40
2. Tuesday	14	—	3	11	51	—
3. Wednesday	11	—	4	7	47	—
4. Thursday	7	40	1	46	46	—
5. Friday	46	—	10	36	36	—
6. Saturday	36	—	9	27	27	—

TABLE 12.3 First Week of Operation

> ACTIVE MODEL EXERCISE <

This Active Model appears on the Student CD-ROM. It allows you to evaluate the sensitivity of the EOQ and associated costs to changes in the demand and cost parameters.

QUESTIONS

1. What is the EOQ and what is the lowest total cost?

2. What is the annual cost of holding inventory at the EOQ and the annual cost of ordering inventory at the EOQ?

3. From the graph, what can you conclude about the relationship between the lowest total cost and the costs of ordering and holding inventory?

4. How much does the total cost increase if the store manager orders twice as many bird feeders as the EOQ? How much does the total cost increase if the store manager orders half as many bird feeders as the EOQ?

5. What happens to the EOQ and the total cost when demand is doubled? What happens to the EOQ and the total cost when unit price is doubled?

6. Scroll through the lower order cost values and describe the changes to the graph. What happens to the EOQ?

7. Comment on the sensitivity of the EOQ model to errors in demand or cost estimates.

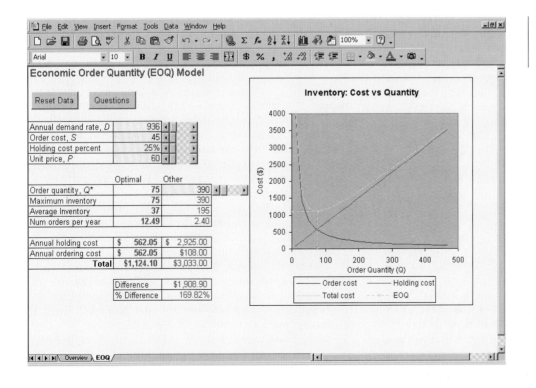

ACTIVE MODEL 12.1

The Economic Order Quantity Model Using Data from Example 12.3

EXPERIENTIAL LEARNING

Swift Electronic Supply, Inc.

It was a typical fall afternoon in Southern California, with thousands of tourists headed to the beaches to have fun. About 40 miles away, however, Steven Holland, the CEO of the Swift Electronic Supply, Inc., faced a severe problem with Swift's inventory management.

An Intel veteran, Steven Holland worked in the electronic components distribution industry for more than 20 years. Seven years ago, he founded the Swift Electronic Supply, Inc., an electronic distributor. After a couple of successful years, the company is now troubled with eroding profit margins. Recent economic downturns worsened the situation further. Factors such as the growth of B2B e-commerce, the globalization of markets, the increased popularity of value-added services, and ongoing consolidations among electronic distributors affect the future of Swift.

To reverse these influences, Holland talked to a prestigious local university. After consultation, Holland found the most effective way to increase profitability is to cut inventory costs. As a starting point, he studied in detail a representative product, dynamic random access memory (DRAM), as the basis for his plan.

Industry and Company Preview

Owing to a boom in the telecommunications industry and the information technology revolution, electronics distributors experienced double-digit annual growth over the last decade. To cut the cost of direct purchasing forces, large component manufacturers such as Intel, Cisco, and Texas Instruments decided to outsource their procurement so that they could focus on product development and manufacturing. Therefore, independent electronic distributors like Swift started offering procurement services to these companies.

Swift serves component manufacturers in California and Arizona. Working as the intermediary between its customers and overseas original equipment manufacturers (OEMs), Swift's business model is quite simple. Forecasting customer demand, Swift places orders to a number of OEMs, stocks those products, breaks the quantities down, and delivers the products to its end customers.

Recently, due to more intense competition and declines in demand, Swift offered more flexible delivery schedules and was willing to accommodate small order quantities. However, customers can always shift to Swift's competitors should Swift not fulfill their orders. Steven Holland was in a dilemma: The intangible costs of losing customers can be enormous; however, maintaining high levels of inventory can also be costly.

DRAM

Holland turned his attention to DRAM as a representative product. Previously, the company ordered a big amount every time it felt it was necessary. Holland's assistant developed a table (Table 12.4), which has two months of demand history. From Holland's experience, the demand for DRAM is relatively

TABLE 12.4			Historical Demand Data for the DRAM (units)		
Day	Demand	Day	Demand	Day	Demand
1	869	21	663	41	959
2	902	22	1,146	42	703
3	1,109	23	1,016	43	823
4	947	24	1,166	44	862
5	968	25	829	45	966
6	917	26	723	46	1,042
7	1,069	27	749	47	889
8	1,086	28	766	48	1,002
9	1,066	29	996	49	763
10	929	30	1,122	50	932
11	1,022	31	962	51	1,052
12	959	32	829	52	1,062
13	756	33	862	53	989
14	882	34	793	54	1,029
15	829	35	1,039	55	823
16	726	36	1,009	56	942
17	666	37	979	57	986
18	879	38	976	58	736
19	1,086	39	856	59	1,009
20	992	40	1,036	60	852

stable in the company's product line and it had no sales seasonality. The sales staff agrees that conditions in the current year will not be different from those of past years, and historical demand will be a good indicator of what to expect in the future.

The primary manufacturers of DRAM are those in Southeast Asia. Currently, Swift can purchase one unit of 64M DRAM for $10. After negotiation with a reputable supplier, Holland managed to sign a long-term agreement, which kept the price at $10 and allowed Swift to place orders at any time. The supplier also supplies other items in Swift's inventory. In addition, it takes the supplier of the DRAM two days to deliver the goods to Swift's warehouse using air carriers.

When Swift does not have enough inventory to fill a customer's order, the sales are lost; that is, Swift was not able to backorder the shortage because its customers fill their requirements through competitors. The customers will accept partial shipments, however.

It costs Swift $200 to place an order with the suppliers. This amount covers the corresponding internal ordering costs and the costs of delivering the products to the company.

Holland estimates that the cost of lost sales amounts to $2 per unit of DRAM. This rough estimate includes the loss of profits, as well as the intangible damage to customer goodwill.

To simplify its inventory management system, Swift has a policy of maintaining a cycle-service level of 95 percent. The holding cost per day per unit is estimated to be 0.5 percent of the cost of goods, regardless of the product. Inventory holding costs are calculated on the basis of the ending inventory each day. The present balance is 1,700 units of DRAM in stock.

The daily purchasing routine is as follows. Orders are placed at the *beginning* of the day, before Swift is open for customer business. The orders arrive at the beginning of the day, two days later, and can be used for sales that day. For example, an order placed at the beginning of day 1 will arrive at Swift before Swift is open for business on day 3. The actual daily demand is always recorded at the *end* of the day, after Swift has closed for customer business. All cost computations are done at the end of the day after the total demand has been recorded.

Simulation

Holland believes that simulation is a useful approach to assess various inventory control alternatives. The historical data from Table 12.4 could be used to develop attractive inventory policies. The table was developed to record various costs and evaluate different alternatives. An example showing some recent DRAM inventory decisions is shown in Table 12.5.

1. Design a new inventory system for Swift Electronic Supply, Inc., using the data provided.
2. Provide the rationale for your system, which should include the decision rules you would follow to determine how much to order and when.
3. Simulate the use of your inventory system and record the costs using Table 12.6. You may need to bring several copies of Table 12.6 to class so that all the periods of the simulation will be covered. Your instructor will provide actual demands on a day-to-day basis during the simulation.

TABLE 12.5 | Example Simulation

Day	1	2	3	4	5	6	7	8	9	10
Beginning inventory position	1,700	831	1,500	391	3,000	3,232	2,315			
Number ordered	1,500		3,000	1,200			1,900			
Daily demand	869	902	1,109	947	968	917	1,069			
Day-ending inventory	831	−71	391	−556	2,032	2,315	1,246			
Ordering costs ($200 per order)	200		200	200			200			
Holding costs ($0.05 per piece per day)	41.55	0.00	19.55	0.00	101.60	115.75	62.30			
Shortage costs ($2 per piece)	0	142	0	1112	0	0	0			
Total cost for day	241.55	142.00	219.55	1,312.00	101.60	115.75	262.30			
Cumulative cost from last day	0.00	241.55	383.55	603.10	1,915.10	2,016.70	2,132.45			
Cumulative costs to date	241.55	383.55	603.10	1,915.10	2,016.70	2,132.45	2,394.75			

TABLE 12.6 | Simulation Evaluation Sheet

Day	1	2	3	4	5	6	7	8	9	10
Beginning inventory position										
Number ordered										
Daily demand										
Day-ending inventory										
Ordering costs ($200 per order)										
Holding costs ($0.05 per piece per day)										
Shortage costs ($2 per piece)										
Total cost for day										
Cumulative cost from last day										
Cumulative costs to date										

Parts Emporium, Inc., was formed in 1973 as a wholesale distributor of automobile parts by two disenchanted auto mechanics, Dan Block and Ed Spriggs. Originally located in Block's garage, the firm showed slow but steady growth until 1976, when it relocated to an old, abandoned meat-packing warehouse on Chicago's South Side. With increased space for inventory storage, the company was able to begin offering an expanded line of auto parts. This increased selection, combined with the trend toward longer car ownership, led to an explosive growth of the business. By 1998, Parts Emporium was the largest independent distributor of auto parts in the north central region.

Recently, Parts Emporium relocated in a sparkling new office and warehouse complex off Interstate 55 in suburban Chicago. The warehouse space alone occupied more than 100,000 square feet. Although only a handful of new products have been added since the warehouse was constructed, its utilization increased from 65 percent to more than 90 percent of capacity. During this same period, however, sales growth stagnated. These conditions motivated Block and Spriggs to hire the first manager from outside the company in the firm's history.

It is June 6, Sue McCaskey's first day in the newly created position of materials manager for Parts Emporium. A recent graduate of a prominent business school, McCaskey is eagerly awaiting her first real-world problem. At approximately 8:30 A.M., it arrives in the form of status reports on inventory and orders shipped. At the top of an extensive computer printout is a handwritten note from Joe Donnell, the purchasing manager: "Attached you will find the inventory and customer service performance data. Rest assured that the individual inventory levels are accurate because we took a complete physical inventory count at the end of last week. Unfortunately, we do not keep compiled records in some of the areas as you requested. However, you are welcome to do so yourself. Welcome aboard!"

A little upset that aggregate information is not available, McCaskey decides to randomly select a small sample of approximately 100 items and compile inventory and customer service characteristics to get a feel for the "total picture." The results of this experiment reveal to her why Parts Emporium decided to create the position she now fills. It seems that the inventory is in all the wrong places. Although an *average* of approximately 60 days of inventory is on hand, the firm's customer service is inadequate. Parts Emporium tries to backorder the customer orders not immediately filled from stock, but some 10 percent of demand is being lost to competing distributorships. Because stockouts are costly, relative to inventory holding costs, McCaskey believes that a cycle-service level of at least 95 percent should be achieved.

McCaskey knows that although her influence to initiate changes will be limited, she must produce positive results immediately. Thus, she decides to concentrate on two products from the extensive product line: the EG151 exhaust gasket and the DB032 drive belt. If she can demonstrate significant gains from proper inventory management for just two products, perhaps Block and Spriggs will give her the backing needed to change the total inventory management system.

The EG151 exhaust gasket is purchased from an overseas supplier, Haipei, Inc. Actual demand for the first 21 weeks of this year is shown in the following table:

Week	Actual Demand	Week	Actual Demand
1	104	12	97
2	103	13	99
3	107	14	102
4	105	15	99
5	102	16	103
6	102	17	101
7	101	18	101
8	104	19	104
9	100	20	108
10	100	21	97
11	103		

A quick review of past orders, shown in another document, indicates that a lot size of 150 units is being used and that the lead time from Haipei is fairly constant at two weeks. Currently, at the end of week 21, no inventory is on hand; 11 units are backordered, and the company is awaiting a scheduled receipt of 150 units.

The DB032 drive belt is purchased from the Bendox Corporation of Grand Rapids, Michigan. Actual demand so far this year is shown in the following table:

Week	Actual Demand	Week	Actual Demand
11	18	17	50
12	33	18	53
13	53	19	54
14	54	20	49
15	51	21	52
16	53		

Because this product is new, data are available only since its introduction in week 11. Currently, 324 units are on hand, with no backorders and no scheduled receipts. A lot size of 1,000 units is being used, with the lead time fairly constant at three weeks.

The wholesale prices that Parts Emporium charges its customers are $12.99 for the EG151 exhaust gasket and $8.89 for the DB032 drive belt. Because no quantity discounts are offered on these two highly profitable items, gross margins based on current purchasing practices are 32 percent of the wholesale price for the exhaust gasket and 48 percent of the wholesale price for the drive belt.

Parts Emporium estimates its cost to hold inventory at 21 percent of its inventory investment. This percentage recognizes the opportunity cost of tying money up in inventory and the variable costs of taxes, insurance, and shrinkage. The annual report notes other warehousing expenditures for utilities and maintenance and debt service on the 100,000-square-foot warehouse, which was built for $1.5 million. However, McCaskey reasons that these warehousing costs can be ignored because they will not change for the range of inventory policies that she is considering.

Out-of-pocket costs for Parts Emporium to place an order with suppliers are estimated to be $20 per order for exhaust gaskets and $10 per order for drive belts. On the outbound side, the company can charge a delivery fee. Although most customers pick up their parts at Parts Emporium, some orders are delivered to customers. To provide this service, Parts Emporium contracts with a local company for a flat fee of $21.40 per order, which is added to the customer's bill. McCaskey is unsure whether to increase the ordering costs for Parts Emporium to include delivery charges.

QUESTIONS

1. Put yourself in Sue McCaskey's position and prepare a detailed report to Dan Block and Ed Spriggs on managing the inventory of the EG151 exhaust gasket and the DB032 drive belt. Be sure to present a proper inventory system and recognize all relevant costs.

2. By how much do your recommendations for these two items reduce annual cycle inventory, stockout, and ordering costs?

> SELECTED REFERENCES <

Bastow, B. J. "Metrics in the Material World." *APICS—The Performance Advantage* (May 2005), pp. 49–52.

Berlin, Bob. "Solving the OEM Puzzle at Valleylab." *APICS—The Performance Advantage* (March 1997), pp. 58–63.

Callioni, Gianpaolo, Xavier de Montgros, Regine Slagmulder, Luk N. Van Wassenhove, and Linda Wright. "Inventory-Driven Costs." *Harvard Business Review* (March 2005), pp. 135–141.

Cannon, Alan R., and Richard E. Crandall. "The Way Things Never Were." *APICS—The Performance Advantage* (January 2004), pp. 32–35.

Chikan, A., A. Milne, and L. G. Sprague. "Reflections on Firm and National Inventories." Budapest: International Society for Inventory Research, 1996.

Greene, James H. *Production and Inventory Control Handbook*, 3d ed. New York: McGraw-Hill, 1997.

Hartvigsen, David. *SimQuick: Process Simulation with Excel*, 2d ed. Upper Saddle River, NJ: Prentice Hall, 2004.

Inventory Management Reprints. Falls Church, VA: American Production and Inventory Control Society, 1993.

Krupp, James A. G. "Are ABC Codes an Obsolete Technology?" *APICS—The Performance Advantage* (April 1994), pp. 34–35.

Silver, Edward A. "Changing the Givens in Modeling Inventory Problems: The Example of Just-in-Time Systems." *International Journal of Production Economics*, vol. 26 (1996), pp. 347–351.

Silver, Edward A., D. E. Pyke, and Rein Peterson. *Inventory Management, Production Planning, and Scheduling*, 3d ed. New York: John Wiley & Sons, 1998.

Tersine, Richard J. *Principles of Inventory and Materials Management*, 4th ed. Upper Saddle River, NJ: Prentice Hall, 1994.

Timme, Stephen G., and Christine Williams-Timme. "The Real Cost of Holding." *Supply Chain Management Review* (July–August 2003), pp. 30–37.

SUPPLEMENT

Special Inventory Models

LEARNING GOALS

After reading this supplement, you should be able to:

1. Define the relevant costs that should be considered to determine the order quantity when discounts are available.

2. Identify the situations where the economic lot size should be used rather than the economic order quantity.

3. Calculate the optimal lot size when replenishment is not instantaneous.

4. Determine the optimal order quantity when materials are subject to quantity discounts.

5. Calculate the order quantity that maximizes the expected profits for a one-period inventory decision.

Many real world problems require relaxation of certain assumptions on which the EOQ model is based. This supplement addresses three realistic situations that require going beyond the simple EOQ formulation.

1. Noninstantaneous Replenishment. *Particularly in situations in which manufacturers use a continuous process to make a primary material, such as a liquid, gas, or powder, production is not instantaneous. Thus, inventory is replenished gradually, rather than in lots.*

2. Quantity Discounts. *Three annual costs are: the inventory holding cost, the fixed cost for ordering and setup, and the cost of materials. For service providers and for manufacturers alike, the unit cost of purchased materials sometimes depends on the order quantity.*

3. One-Period Decisions. *Retailers and manufacturers of fashion goods often face a situation in which demand is uncertain and occurs during just one period or season.*

This supplement assumes you have read Chapter 12, "Inventory Management" and Supplement A, "Decision Making."

> NONINSTANTANEOUS REPLENISHMENT <

If an item is being produced internally rather than purchased, finished units may be used or sold as soon as they are completed, without waiting until a full lot is completed. For example, a restaurant that bakes its own dinner rolls begins to use some of the rolls from the first pan even before the baker finishes a five-pan batch. The inventory of rolls never reaches the full five-pan level, the way it would if the rolls all arrived at once on a truck sent by a supplier.

Figure D.1 depicts the usual case, in which the production rate, p, exceeds the demand rate, d.[1] Cycle inventory accumulates faster than demand occurs; that is, a buildup of $p - d$ units occurs per time period. For example, if the production rate is 100 units per day and the demand is 5 units per day, the buildup is 95 (or $100 - 5$) units each day. This buildup continues until the lot size, Q, has been produced, after which the inventory depletes at a rate of 5 units per day. Just as the inventory reaches 0, the next production interval begins. To be consistent, both p and d must be expressed in units of the same time period, such as units per day or units per week. Here, we assume that they are expressed in units per day.

The $p - d$ buildup continues for Q/p days because Q is the lot size and p units are produced each day. In our example, if the lot size is 300 units, the production interval is 3 days (300/100). For the given rate of buildup over the production interval, the maximum cycle inventory, I_{max}, is

$$I_{max} = \frac{Q}{p}(p-d) = Q\left(\frac{p-d}{p}\right)$$

Cycle inventory is no longer $Q/2$, as it was with the basic EOQ method; instead, it is $I_{max}/2$. Setting up the total annual cost equation for this production situation, where D is annual demand, as before, and d is daily demand, we get

Total annual cost = Annual holding cost + Annual ordering or setup cost

$$C = \frac{I_{max}}{2}(H) + \frac{D}{Q}(S) = \frac{Q}{2}\left(\frac{p-d}{p}\right)(H) + \frac{D}{Q}(S)$$

economic production lot size (ELS)

The optimal lot size in a situation in which replenishment is not instantaneous.

Based on this cost function, the optimal lot size, often called the **economic production lot size (ELS)**, is

$$ELS = \sqrt{\frac{2DS}{H}}\sqrt{\frac{p}{p-d}}$$

FIGURE D.1

Lot Sizing with Noninstantaneous Replenishment

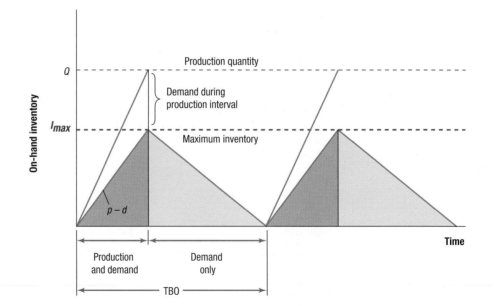

[1]If demand and production were equal, production would be continuous with no buildup of cycle inventory. If the production rate is lower than the demand rate, sales opportunities are being missed on an ongoing basis. We assume that $p > d$ in this supplement.

Because the second term is a ratio greater than 1, the ELS results in a larger lot size than the EOQ.

| **Finding the Economic Production Lot Size** | **EXAMPLE D.1** |

A plant manager of a chemical plant must determine the lot size for a particular chemical that has a steady demand of 30 barrels per day. The production rate is 190 barrels per day, annual demand is 10,500 barrels, setup cost is $200, annual holding cost is $0.21 per barrel, and the plant operates 350 days per year.

a. Determine the economic production lot size (ELS).

b. Determine the total annual setup and inventory holding cost for this item.

c. Determine the TBO, or cycle length, for the ELS.

d. Determine the production time per lot.

What are the advantages of reducing the setup time by 10 percent?

SOLUTION

a. Solving first for the ELS, we get

$$\text{ELS} = \sqrt{\frac{2DS}{H}}\sqrt{\frac{p}{p-d}} = \sqrt{\frac{2(10,500)(\$200)}{\$0.21}}\sqrt{\frac{190}{190-30}}$$

$$= 4,873.4 \text{ barrels}$$

b. The total annual cost with the ELS is

$$C = \frac{Q}{2}\left(\frac{p-d}{p}\right)(H) + \frac{D}{Q}(S)$$

$$= \frac{4,873.4}{2}\left(\frac{190-30}{190}\right)(\$0.21) + \frac{10,500}{4,873.4}(\$200)$$

$$= \$430.91 + \$430.91 = \$861.82$$

c. Applying the TBO formula to the ELS, we get

$$\text{TBO}_{\text{ELS}} = \frac{\text{ELS}}{D}(350 \text{ days/year}) = \frac{4,873.4}{10,500}(350)$$

$$= 162.4 \quad \text{or} \quad 162 \text{ days}$$

d. The production time during each cycle is the lot size divided by the production rate:

$$\frac{\text{ELS}}{p} = \frac{4,873.4}{190} = 25.6 \quad \text{or} \quad 26 \text{ days}$$

Decision Point As OM Explorer shows in Figure D.2, the net effect of reducing the setup cost by 10 percent is to reduce the lot size, the time between orders, and the production cycle time. Consequently, total annual costs are also reduced. This adds flexibility to the manufacturing process because items can be made quicker with less expense. Management must decide whether the added cost of improving the setup process is worth the added flexibility and inventory cost reductions.

TUTOR D.1

Tutor D.1 on the Student CD-ROM provides a new example to determine the ELS.

ACTIVE MODEL D.1

Active Model D.1 on the Student CD-ROM provides additional insight on the ELS model and its uses.

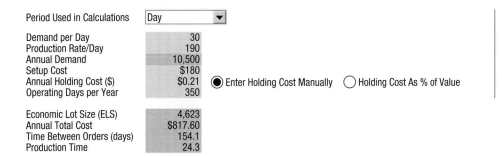

Period Used in Calculations	Day ▼
Demand per Day	30
Production Rate/Day	190
Annual Demand	10,500
Setup Cost	$180
Annual Holding Cost ($)	$0.21 ● Enter Holding Cost Manually ○ Holding Cost As % of Value
Operating Days per Year	350
Economic Lot Size (ELS)	4,623
Annual Total Cost	$817.60
Time Between Orders (days)	154.1
Production Time	24.3

FIGURE D.2

OM Explorer Solver for the Economic Production Lot Size Showing the Effect of a 10 Percent Reduction in Setup Cost

> QUANTITY DISCOUNTS <

Quantity discounts, which are price incentives to purchase large quantities, create pressure to maintain a large inventory. For example, a supplier may offer a price of $4.00 per unit for orders between 1 and 99 units, a price of $3.50 per unit for orders between 100 and 199 units, and a price of $3.00 per unit for orders of 200 or more units. The item's price is no longer fixed, as assumed in the EOQ derivation; instead, if the order quantity is increased enough, the price is discounted. Hence, a new approach is needed to find the best lot size—one that balances the advantages of lower prices for purchased materials and fewer orders (which are benefits of large order quantities) against the disadvantage of the increased cost of holding more inventory.

The total annual cost now includes not only the holding cost, $(Q/2)(H)$ and the ordering cost, $(D/Q)(S)$, but also the cost of purchased materials. For any per-unit price level, P, the total cost is

$$\text{Total annual cost} = \text{Annual holding cost} + \text{Annual ordering or setup cost} + \text{Annual cost of materials}$$

$$C = \frac{Q}{2}(H) + \frac{D}{Q}(S) + PD$$

The unit holding cost, H, usually is expressed as a percent of the unit price because the more valuable the item held in inventory, the higher the holding cost is. Thus, the lower the unit price, P, is, the lower H is. Conversely, the higher P is, the higher H is.

The total cost equation yields U-shaped total cost curves. Adding the annual cost of materials to the total cost equation raises each total cost curve by a fixed amount, as shown in Figure D.3(a). The three cost curves illustrate each of the price levels. The top curve applies when no discounts are received; the lower curves reflect the discounted price levels. No single curve is relevant to all purchase quantities. The relevant, or *feasible*, total cost begins with the top curve, then drops down, curve by curve, at the price breaks. A *price break* is the minimum quantity needed to get a discount. In Figure D.3, two price breaks occur at $Q = 100$ and $Q = 200$. The result is a total cost curve, with steps at the price breaks.

Figure D.3(b) also shows three additional points—the minimum point on each curve, obtained with the EOQ formula at each price level. These EOQs do not necessarily produce the best lot size for two reasons.

1. The EOQ at a particular price level may not be feasible: The lot size may not lie in the range corresponding to its per-unit price. Figure D.3(b) illustrates two instances of an infeasible EOQ. First, the minimum point for the $3.00 curve appears to be less than 200 units. However, the supplier's quantity discount schedule does not allow purchases of that small a quantity at the $3.00 unit price. Similarly, the EOQ for the $4.00 price level is greater than the first price break, so the price charged would be only $3.50.

2. The EOQ at a particular price level may be feasible but may not be the best lot size: The feasible EOQ may have a *higher* cost than is achieved by the EOQ or price break quantity on a *lower* price curve. In Figure D.3(b), for example, the 200-unit price break quantity for the $3.00 price level has a lower total cost than the feasible EOQ for the $3.50 price level. A feasible EOQ always is better than any feasible point on cost curves with higher price levels, but not necessarily those with lower levels. Thus, the only time we can immediately conclude, without comparing total costs, that a feasible EOQ is the best order quantity is when it is on the curve for the *lowest* price level. This conclusion is not possible in Figure D.3(b) because the only feasible EOQ is at the middle price level, $P = \$3.50$.

We must therefore pay attention only to feasible price–quantity combinations, shown as solid lines in Figure D.3(b), as we search for the best lot size. The following two-step procedure may be used to find the best lot size.[2]

Step 1. Beginning with the *lowest* price, calculate the EOQ for each price level until a feasible EOQ is found. It is feasible if it lies in the range corresponding to its price. Each subsequent

[2]Another approach that often reduces the number of iterations can be found in S. K. Goyal, "A Simple Procedure for Price Break Models," *Production Planning and Control*, vol. 6, no. 6 (1995), pp. 584–585.

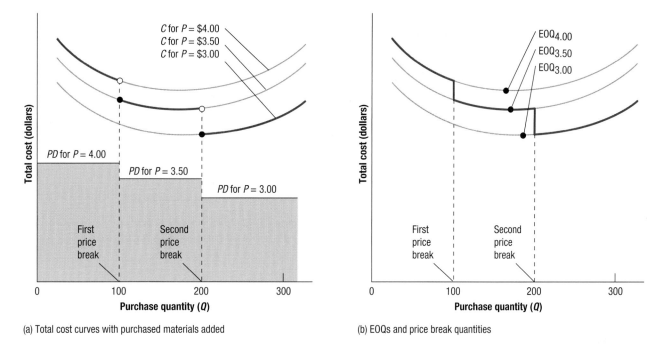

(a) Total cost curves with purchased materials added

(b) EOQs and price break quantities

FIGURE D.3 | Total Cost Curves with Quantity Discounts

EOQ is smaller than the previous one because P, and thus H, gets larger and because the larger H is in the denominator of the EOQ formula.

    Step 2. If the first feasible EOQ found is for the *lowest* price level, this quantity is the best lot size. Otherwise, calculate the total cost for the first feasible EOQ and for the larger price break quantity at each *lower* price level. The quantity with the lowest total cost is optimal.

Finding Q with Quantity Discounts at St. LeRoy Hospital	EXAMPLE D.2

A supplier for St. LeRoy Hospital has introduced quantity discounts to encourage larger order quantities of a special catheter. The price schedule is

Order Quantity	Price per Unit
0 to 299	$60.00
300 to 499	$58.80
500 or more	$57.00

The hospital estimates that its annual demand for this item is 936 units, its ordering cost is $45.00 per order, and its annual holding cost is 25 percent of the catheter's unit price. What quantity of this catheter should the hospital order to minimize total costs? Suppose the price for quantities between 300 and 499 is reduced to $58.00. Should the order quantity change?

SOLUTION

Step 1: Find the first feasible EOQ, starting with the lowest price level:

$$EOQ_{57.00} = \sqrt{\frac{2DS}{H}} = \sqrt{\frac{2(936)(\$45.00)}{0.25(\$57.00)}} = 77 \text{ units}$$

TUTOR D.2

Tutor D.2 on the Student CD-ROM provides a new example for choosing the best order quantity when discounts are available.

ACTIVE MODEL D.2

Active Model D.2 on the Student CD-ROM provides additional insight on the quantity discount model and its uses.

A 77-unit order actually costs $60.00 per unit, instead of the $57.00 per unit used in the EOQ calculation, so this EOQ is infeasible. Now try the $58.80 level:

$$EOQ_{58.80} = \sqrt{\frac{2DS}{H}} = \sqrt{\frac{2(936)(\$45.00)}{0.25(\$58.80)}} = 76 \text{ units}$$

This quantity also is infeasible because a 76-unit order is too small to qualify for the $58.80 price. Try the highest price level:

$$EOQ_{60.00} = \sqrt{\frac{2DS}{H}} = \sqrt{\frac{2(936)(\$45.00)}{0.25(\$60.00)}} = 75 \text{ units}$$

This quantity is feasible, because it lies in the range corresponding to its price, $P = \$60.00$.

Step 2: The first feasible EOQ of 75 does not correspond to the lowest price level. Hence, we must compare its total cost with the price break quantities (300 and 500 units) at the *lower* price levels ($58.80 and $57.00):

$$C = \frac{Q}{2}(H) + \frac{D}{Q}(S) + PD$$

$$C_{75} = \frac{75}{2}[(0.25)(\$60.00)] + \frac{936}{75}(\$45.00) + \$60.00(936) = \$57,284$$

$$C_{300} = \frac{300}{2}[(0.25)(\$58.80)] + \frac{936}{300}(\$45.00) + \$58.80(936) = \$57,382$$

$$C_{500} = \frac{500}{2}[(0.25)(\$57.00)] + \frac{936}{500}(\$45.00) + \$57.00(936) = \$56,999$$

The best purchase quantity is 500 units, which qualifies for the deepest discount.

Decision Point If the price per unit for the range of 300 to 499 units is reduced to $58.00, the best decision is to order 300 catheters, as shown by OM Explorer in Figure D.4. This result shows that the decision is sensitive to the price schedule. A reduction of slightly more than 1 percent is enough to make the difference in this example. In general, however, it is not always the case that you should order more than the economic order quantity when given price discounts. When discounts are small, holding cost H is large, and demand D is small, small lot sizes are better even though price discounts are forgone.

FIGURE D.4

OM Explorer Solver for Quantity Discounts Showing the Best Order Quantity

	More	Fewer	
Min. Amount Req'd for Price Point	Lot Sizes	Price/Unit	
...	0–299	$60.00	
300	300–499	$58.00	
500	500 or more	$57.00	

Annual Demand	936
Order Cost	$45
Holding Cost (% or price)	25%

Best Order Quantity	300

	Price Point	EOQ or Req'd Order for Price Point	Inventory Cost	Order Cost	Purchase Cost	Total Cost
	$60.00	75	$562.50	$561.60	$56,160	$57,284
>>	$58.00	300	$2,175	$140.40	$54,288	$56,603 <<
	$57.00	500	$3,563	$84.24	$53,352	$56,999

> ONE-PERIOD DECISIONS <

One of the dilemmas facing many retailers is how to handle seasonal goods, such as winter coats. Often, they cannot be sold at full markup next year because of changes in styles. Furthermore, the lead time can be longer than the selling season, allowing no second chance to rush through another order to cover unexpectedly high demand. A similar problem exists for manufacturers of fashion goods.

This type of situation is often called the *newsboy problem.* If the newspaper seller does not buy enough newspapers to resell on the street corner, sales opportunities are lost. If the seller buys too many newspapers, the overage cannot be sold because nobody wants yesterday's newspaper.

The following process is a straightforward way to analyze such problems and decide on the best order quantity.

1. List the different levels of demand that are possible, along with the estimated probability of each.

2. Develop a *payoff table* that shows the profit for each purchase quantity, Q, at each assumed demand level, D. Each row in the table represents a different order quantity, and each column represents a different demand level. The payoff for a given quantity–demand combination depends on whether all units are sold at the regular profit margin during the regular season, which results in two possible cases.

   a. If demand is high enough ($Q \le D$), then all units are sold at the full profit margin, p, during the regular season,

   $$\text{Payoff} = (\text{Profit per unit})(\text{Purchase quantity}) = pQ$$

   b. If the purchase quantity exceeds the eventual demand ($Q > D$), only D units are sold at the full profit margin, and the remaining units purchased must be disposed of at a loss, l, after the season. In this case,

   $$\text{Payoff} = \left(\begin{array}{c}\text{Profit per unit sold} \\ \text{during season}\end{array}\right)(\text{Demand}) - \left(\begin{array}{c}\text{Loss per} \\ \text{unit}\end{array}\right)\left(\begin{array}{c}\text{Amount disposed of} \\ \text{after season}\end{array}\right)$$

   $$= pD - l(Q - D)$$

3. Calculate the expected payoff for each Q (or row in the payoff table) by using the *expected value* decision rule. For a specific Q, first multiply each payoff in the row by the demand probability associated with the payoff, and then add these products.

4. Choose the order quantity Q with the highest expected payoff.

Using this decision process for all such items over many selling seasons will maximize profits. However, it is not foolproof, and it can result in an occasional bad outcome.

| **Finding Q for One-Period Inventory Decisions** | **EXAMPLE D.3** |

One of many items sold at a museum of natural history is a Christmas ornament carved from wood. The gift shop makes a $10 profit per unit sold during the season, but it takes a $5 loss per unit after the season is over. The following discrete probability distribution for the season's demand has been identified:

Demand	10	20	30	40	50
Demand Probability	0.2	0.3	0.3	0.1	0.1

How many ornaments should the museum's buyer order?

SOLUTION

Each demand level is a candidate for best order quantity, so the payoff table should have five rows. For the first row, where $Q = 10$, demand is at least as great as the purchase quantity. Thus, all five payoffs in this row are

$$\text{Payoff} = pQ = (\$10)(10) = \$100$$

This formula can be used in other rows but only for those quantity-demand combinations where all units are sold during the season. These combinations lie in the upper-right portion of the payoff table, where $Q \le D$. For example, the payoff when $Q = 40$ and $D = 50$ is

$$\text{Payoff} = pQ = (\$10)(40) = \$400$$

The payoffs in the lower-left portion of the table represent quantity-demand combinations where some units must be disposed of after the season ($Q > D$). For this case, the payoff must be calculated with the second formula. For example, when $Q = 40$ and $D = 30$,

$$\text{Payoff} = pD - l(Q - D) = (\$10)(30) - (\$5)(40 - 30) = \$250$$

TUTOR D.3

Tutor D.3 on the Student CD-ROM provides a new example to practice the one-period Inventory decision.

ACTIVE MODEL D.3

Active Model D.3 on the Student CD-ROM provides additional Insight on the one-period Inventory decision model and its uses.

Using OM Explorer, we obtain the payoff table in Figure D.5.

FIGURE D.5

OM Explorer Solver for One-Period
Inventory Decisions Showing
the Payoff Table

Profit	$10.00	(if sold during preferred period)
Loss	$5.00	(if sold after preferred period)

Enter the possible demands along with the probability of each occuring. Use the buttons to increase or decrease the number of allowable demand forecasts. NOTE: Be sure to enter demand forecasts and probablities in all tinted cells, and be sure probabilities add up to 1.

	<	>			
Demand	10	20	30	40	50
Profitability	0.2	0.3	0.3	0.1	0.1

Payoff Table

Demand

Quantity	10	20	30	40	50
10	100	100	100	100	100
20	50	200	200	200	200
30	0	150	300	300	300
40	−50	100	250	400	400
50	−100	50	200	350	500

Now we calculate the expected payoff for each Q by multiplying the payoff for each demand quantity by the probability of that demand and then adding the results. For example, for $Q = 30$,

$$\text{Payoff} = 0.2(\$0) + 0.3(\$150) + 0.3(\$300) + 0.1(\$300) + 0.1(\$300) = \$195$$

Using OM Explorer, Figure D.6 shows the expected payoffs.

FIGURE D.6

OM Explorer Solver Showing the
Expected Payoffs

Weighted Payoffs

Order Quantity	Expected Payoff		
10	100	Greatest Expected Payoff	195
20	170		
30	195	Associated with Order Quantity	30
40	175		
50	140		

Decision Point Because $Q = 30$ has the highest payoff at $195, it is the best order quantity. Management can use OM Explorer to do sensitivity analysis on the demands and their probabilities to see how confident they are with that decision.

The need for one-time inventory decisions also can arise in manufacturing plants when (1) customized items (specials) are made (or purchased) to a single order, *and* (2) scrap quantities are high.[3] A special item produced for a single order is never intentionally held in stock because the demand for it is too unpredictable. In fact, it may never be ordered again so the manufacturer would like to make just the amount requested by the customer—no more, no less. The manufacturer also would like to satisfy an order in just one run to avoid an extra setup and a delay in delivering goods ordered. These two goals may conflict if the likelihood of some units being scrapped is high. Suppose that a customer places an order for 20 units. If the manager orders 20 units from the shop or from the supplier, one or two units may have to be scrapped. This shortage will force the manager to place a second (or even third) order to replace the defective units. Replacement can be costly if setup time is high and can also delay shipment to the customer. To avoid such problems, the manager could order more than 20 units the first time. If some units are left over, the customer might be willing to buy the extras or the manager might find an internal use for them. For example, some manufacturing companies set up a special account for obsolete materials. These materials can be "bought" by departments within the company at less than their normal cost, as an incentive to use them.

[3]One goal of TQM is to eliminate scrap. Achievement of that TQM goal makes this discussion moot.

> STUDENT CD-ROM AND INTERNET RESOURCES <

The Student CD-ROM and the Companion Website at **www.prenhall.com/krajewski**
contain many tools, activities, and resources designed for this supplement.

> KEY EQUATIONS <

1. Noninstantaneous replenishment:

    Maximum inventory: $I_{max} = Q\left(\dfrac{p-d}{p}\right)$

    Total annual cost = Annual holding cost + Annual ordering or setup cost

    $$C = \frac{Q}{2}\left(\frac{p-d}{p}\right)(H) + \frac{D}{Q}(S)$$

    Economic production lot size: $\text{ELS} = \sqrt{\dfrac{2DS}{H}}\sqrt{\dfrac{p}{p-d}}$

    Time between orders, expressed in years: $\text{TBO}_{\text{ELS}} = \dfrac{\text{ELS}}{D}$

2. Quantity discounts:

    Total annual cost = Annual holding cost + Annual ordering or setup cost + Annual cost of material

    $$C = \frac{Q}{2}(H) + \frac{D}{Q}(S) + PD$$

3. One-period decisions:

    Payoff matrix: $\text{Payoff} = \begin{cases} pQ & \text{if } Q \le D \\ pD - l(Q-D) & \text{if } Q > D \end{cases}$

> KEY TERM <

economic production lot size (ELS) 508

> SOLVED PROBLEM 1 <

Peachy Keen, Inc., makes mohair sweaters, blouses with Peter Pan collars, pedal pushers, poodle skirts, and other popular clothing styles of the 1950s. The average demand for mohair sweaters is 100 per week. Peachy's production facility has the capacity to sew 400 sweaters per week. Setup cost is $351. The value of finished goods inventory is $40 per sweater. The annual per-unit inventory holding cost is 20 percent of the item's value.

a. What is the economic production lot size (ELS)?

b. What is the average time between orders (TBO)?

c. What is the total of the annual holding cost and setup cost?

SOLUTION

a. The production lot size that minimizes total cost is

$$\text{ELS} = \sqrt{\frac{2DS}{H}}\sqrt{\frac{p}{p-d}} = \sqrt{\frac{2(100 \times 52)(\$351)}{0.20(\$40)}}\sqrt{\frac{400}{(400-100)}}$$

$$= \sqrt{456,300}\sqrt{\frac{4}{3}} = 780 \text{ sweaters}$$

b. The average time between orders is

$$\text{TBO}_{\text{ELS}} = \frac{\text{ELS}}{D} = \frac{780}{5,200} = 0.15 \text{ year}$$

Converting to weeks, we get

$$\text{TBO}_{\text{ELS}} = (0.15 \text{ year})(52 \text{ weeks/year}) = 7.8 \text{ weeks}$$

c. The minimum total of ordering and holding costs is

$$C = \frac{Q}{2}\left(\frac{p-d}{p}\right)(H) + \frac{D}{Q}(S) = \frac{780}{2}\left(\frac{400-100}{400}\right)(0.20 \times \$40) + \frac{5,200}{780}(\$351)$$

$$= \$2,340/\text{year} + \$2,340/\text{year} = \$4,680/\text{year}$$

> SOLVED PROBLEM 2 <

A hospital buys disposable surgical packages from Pfisher, Inc. Pfisher's price schedule is $50.25 per package on orders of 1 to 199 packages and $49.00 per package on orders of 200 or more packages. Ordering cost is $64 per order, and annual holding cost is 20 percent of the per-unit purchase price. Annual demand is 490 packages. What is the best purchase quantity?

SOLUTION

We first calculate the EOQ at the *lowest* price:

$$\text{EOQ}_{49.00} = \sqrt{\frac{2DS}{H}} = \sqrt{\frac{2(490)(\$64.00)}{0.20(\$49.00)}} = \sqrt{6,400} = 80 \text{ packages}$$

This solution is infeasible because, according to the price schedule, we cannot purchase 80 packages at a price of $49.00 each. Therefore, we calculate the EOQ at the next lowest price ($50.25):

$$\text{EOQ}_{50.25} = \sqrt{\frac{2DS}{H}} = \sqrt{\frac{2(490)(\$64.00)}{0.20(\$50.25)}} = \sqrt{6,241} = 79 \text{ packages}$$

This EOQ is feasible, but $50.25 per package is not the lowest price. Hence, we have to determine whether total costs can be reduced by purchasing 200 units and thereby obtaining a quantity discount.

$$C = \frac{Q}{2}(H) + \frac{D}{Q}(S) + PD$$

$$C_{79} = \frac{79}{2}(0.20 \times \$50.25) + \frac{490}{79}(\$64.00) + \$50.25(490)$$

$$= \$396.98/\text{year} + \$396.98/\text{year} + \$24,622.50/\text{year} = \$25,416.44/\text{year}$$

$$C_{200} = \frac{200}{2}(0.20 \times \$49.00) + \frac{490}{200}(\$64.00) + \$49.00(490)$$

$$= \$980.00/\text{year} + \$156.80/\text{year} + \$24,010.00/\text{year} = \$25,146.80/\text{year}$$

Purchasing 200 units per order will save $269.64/year, compared to buying 79 units at a time.

> SOLVED PROBLEM 3 <

Swell Productions is sponsoring an outdoor conclave for owners of collectible and classic Fords. The concession stand in the T-Bird area will sell T-shirts, poodle skirts, and other souvenirs of the 1950s. Poodle skirts are purchased from Peachy Keen, Inc., for $40 each and are sold during the event for $75 each. If any skirts are left over, they can be returned to Peachy for a refund of $30 each. Poodle skirt sales depend on the weather, attendance, and other variables. The following table shows the probability of various sales quantities. How many poodle skirts should Swell Productions order from Peachy Keen for this one-time event?

Sales Quantity	Probability	Sales Quantity	Probability
100	0.05	400	0.34
200	0.11	500	0.11
300	0.34	600	0.05

TABLE D.1	Payoffs						
	Demand, D						
Q	**100**	**200**	**300**	**400**	**500**	**600**	**Expected Payoff**
100	$3,500	$3,500	$ 3,500	$ 3,500	$ 3,500	$ 3,500	$ 3,500
200	$2,500	$7,000	$ 7,000	$ 7,000	$ 7,000	$ 7,000	$ 6,775
300	$1,500	$6,000	$10,500	$10,500	$10,500	$10,500	$ 9,555
400	$ 500	$5,000	$ 9,500	$14,000	$14,000	$14,000	$10,805
500	($ 500)	$4,000	$ 8,500	$13,000	$17,500	$17,500	$10,525
600	($1,500)	$3,000	$ 7,500	$12,000	$16,500	$21,000	$ 9,750

SOLUTION

Table D.1 is the payoff table that describes this one-period inventory decision. The upper-right portion of the table shows the payoffs when the demand, D, is greater than or equal to the order quantity, Q. The payoff is equal to the per-unit profit (the difference between price and cost) multiplied by the order quantity. For example, when the order quantity is 100 and the demand is 200,

$$\text{Payoff} = (p - c)\, Q = (\$75 - \$40)100 = \$3,500$$

The lower-left portion of the payoff table shows the payoffs when the order quantity exceeds the demand. Here the payoff is the profit from sales, pD, minus the loss associated with returning overstock, $l(Q - D)$, where l is the difference between the cost and the amount refunded for each poodle skirt returned and $Q - D$ is the number of skirts returned. For example, when the order quantity is 500 and the demand is 200,

$$\text{Payoff} = pD - l(Q - D) = (\$75 - \$40)200 - (\$40 - \$30)(500 - 200) = \$4,000$$

The highest expected payoff occurs when 400 poodle skirts are ordered:

$$\begin{aligned}\text{Expected payoff}_{400} = &\ (\$500 \times 0.05) + (\$5,000 \times 0.11) + (\$9,500 \times 0.34) \\ &+ (\$14,000 \times 0.34) + (\$14,000 \times 0.11) + (\$14,000 \times 0.05) \\ = &\ \$10,805\end{aligned}$$

> PROBLEMS <

Software, such as OM Explorer, Active Models, and POM for Windows, is packaged with every new copy of the textbook. Check with your instructor on how best to use it. In many cases, the instructor wants you to understand how to do the calculations by hand. At most, the software provides a check on your calculations. When calculations are particularly complex and the goal is interpreting the results in making decisions, the software replaces entirely the manual calculations. The software also can be a valuable resource well after your course is completed.

1. Bold Vision, Inc., makes laser printer and photocopier toner cartridges. The demand rate is 625 EP cartridges per week. The production rate is 1,736 EP cartridges per week, and the setup cost is $100. The value of inventory is $130 per unit, and the holding cost is 20 percent of the inventory value. What is the economic production lot size?

2. Sharpe Cutter is a small company that produces specialty knives for paper cutting machinery. The annual demand for a particular type of knife is 100,000 units. The demand is uniform over the 250 working days in a year. Sharpe Cutter produces this type of knife in lots and, on average, can produce 450 knives a day. The cost to set up a production lot is $300, and the annual holding cost is $1.20 per knife.

   a. Determine the economic production lot size (ELS).
   b. Determine the total annual setup and inventory holding cost for this item.
   c. Determine the TBO, or cycle length, for the ELS.
   d. Determine the production time per lot.

3. Suds's Bottling Company does bottling, labeling, and distribution work for several local microbreweries. The

demand rate for Wortman's beer is 600 cases (24 bottles each) per week. Suds's bottling production rate is 2,400 cases per week, and the setup cost is $800. The value of inventory is $12.50 per case, and the annual holding cost is 30 percent of the inventory value. What is the economic production lot size?

4. The Bucks Grande major league baseball team breaks an average of four bats per week. The team orders baseball bats from Corky's, a bat manufacturer noted for its access to the finest hardwood. The order cost is $70, and the annual holding cost per bat per year is 38 percent of the purchase price. Corky's price structure is

Order Quantity	Price per Unit
0 to 11	$54.00
12 to 143	$51.00
144 or more	$48.50

   a. How many bats should the team buy per order?

   b. What are the total annual costs associated with the best order quantity?

   c. Corky discovers that, owing to special manufacturing processes required for the Bucks' bats, it has underestimated setup costs. Rather than raise prices, Corky adds another category to the price structure to provide an incentive for larger orders and reduce the number of setups required. If the Bucks buy 180 bats or more, the price will drop to $45.00 each. Should the Bucks revise the order quantity to 180 bats?

5. To boost sales, Pfisher (refer to Solved Problem 2) announces a new price structure for disposable surgical packages. Although the price break no longer is available at 200 units, Pfisher now offers an even greater discount if larger quantities are purchased. On orders of 1 to 499 packages, the price is $50.25 per package. For orders of 500 or more, the price per unit is $47.80. Ordering costs, annual holding costs, and annual demand remain at $64 per order, 20 percent of the per-unit cost, and 490 packages per year, respectively. What is the new lot size?

6. The University Bookstore at a prestigious private university buys mechanical pencils from a wholesaler. The wholesaler offers discounts for large orders according to the following price schedule:

Order Quantity	Price per Unit
0 to 200	$4.00
201 to 2,000	$3.50
2,001 or more	$3.25

The bookstore expects an annual demand of 2,500 units. It costs $10 to place an order, and the annual cost of holding a unit in stock is 30 percent of the unit's price. Determine the best order quantity.

7. Mac-in-the-Box, Inc., sells computer equipment by mail and telephone order. Mac sells 1,200 flat-bed scanners per year. Ordering cost is $300, and annual holding cost is 16 percent of the item's price. The scanner manufacturer offers the following price structure to Mac-in-the-Box:

Order Quantity	Price per Unit
0 to 11	$520
12 to 143	$500
144 or more	$400

What order quantity minimizes total annual costs?

8. As inventory manager, you must decide on the order quantity for an item that has an annual demand of 2,000 units. Placing an order costs you $20 each time. Your annual holding cost, expressed as a percentage of average inventory value, is 20 percent. Your supplier has provided the following price schedule:

Minimum Order Quantity	Price per Unit
1	$2.50
200	$2.40
300	$2.25
1,000	$2.00

What ordering policy do you recommend?

9. National Printing Company must decide how many wall calendars it should produce for sale during the upcoming sale season. Each calendar sells for $8.50 and costs $2.50 to produce. The local school district has agreed to buy all unsold calendars at a unit price of $1.50. National estimates the following probability distribution for the season's demand:

Demand	Probability
2,000	0.05
3,000	0.20
4,000	0.25
5,000	0.40
6,000	0.10

How many calendars should National produce to maximize its expected profit?

10. Dorothy's pastries are freshly baked and sold at several specialty shops throughout Perth. When they are a day old, they must be sold at reduced prices. Daily demand is distributed as follows:

Demand	Probability
50	0.25
150	0.50
200	0.25

Each pastry sells for $1.00 and costs $0.60 to make. Each one not sold at the end of the day can be sold the next day for $0.30 as day-old merchandise. How many pastries should be baked each day?

11. The Aggies will host Tech in this year's homecoming football game. Based on advance ticket sales, the athletic department has forecast hot dog sales as shown in the following table. The school buys premium hot dogs for $1.50 and sells them during the game at $3.00 each. Hot dogs left over after the game will be sold for $0.50 each to the Aggie student cafeteria to be used in making beanie weenie casserole.

Sales Quantity	Probability
2,000	0.10
3,000	0.30
4,000	0.30
5,000	0.20
6,000	0.10

Use a payoff matrix to determine the number of hot dogs to buy for the game.

> SELECTED REFERENCES <

"Factors That Make or Break Season Sales." *Wall Street Journal* (December 9, 1991).

Greene, James H. *Production and Inventory Control Handbook,* 3d ed. New York: McGraw-Hill, 1997.

Inventory Management Reprints. Falls Church, VA: American Production and Inventory Control Society, 1993.

Silver, Edward A., D. F. Pyke, and Rein Peterson. *Inventory Management, Production Planning, and Scheduling,* 3d ed. New York: John Wiley & Sons, 1998.

Sipper, Daniel, and Robert L. Bulfin, Jr. *Production Planning, Control, and Integration.* New York: McGraw-Hill, 1997.

Tersine, Richard J. *Principles of Inventory and Materials Management,* 4th ed. Upper Saddle River, NJ: Prentice Hall, 1994.

13

LEARNING GOALS

After reading this chapter, you should be able to:

1. Explain collaborative planning, forecasting, and replenishment (CPFR).

2. Describe the various judgmental forecasting approaches.

3. Explain the use of regression to make forecasts.

4. Show how to compute forecasts using the most common approaches for time-series analysis.

5. Describe the various measures of forecast errors.

6. Explain how forecast errors are used to monitor and control forecast performance.

Lipton tea is one of the many Unilever products, and its demand must be forecast for around the world. For centuries, globalism's story traveled with merchants who shepherded spices along Eurasian trade routes. Now it travels over wires and radio waves, satellites, airplanes, and gigabytes.

CHAPTER 13

Forecasting

UNILEVER

One of the critical drivers in managing value chains is effective customer demand planning (CDP), which begins with accurate forecasts. CDP is a business-planning process that enables sales teams (and customers) to develop demand forecasts as input to service-planning processes, production and inventory planning, and revenue planning. **Forecasting** is generally seen as the process of developing the most probable view of what future demand will be, given a set of assumptions about technology, competitors, pricing, marketing, expenditures, and sales effort. Planning, on the other hand, is the process of making management decisions on how to deploy resources to best respond to the demand forecasts.

Forecasts must generally precede plans: It is not possible to make decisions on staffing levels, purchasing commitments, and inventory levels until forecasts are developed that give reasonably accurate views of demand over the forecasting time horizon.

Unilever, the fast-moving consumer products supplier, has a state-of-the-art CDP system. Using software from Manugistics, the system blends historical shipment data with promotional data, allowing information sharing and collaboration with important customers. The system begins with shipment history and current order information, the foundation upon which Unilever's system is built. This baseline forecast depends solely on past and present information, so reliable data is a critical requirement. However, because data frequently are collected from disparate legacy systems, they may contain errors and may not necessarily lead to the best forecast. Moreover, statistical information is not

For additional chapter resources check the Student CD-ROM or the Companion Website at **www.prenhall.com/krajewski**

useful in forecasting the outcomes of certain events, promotions, rollouts, and special packages, which are common in the industry. To overcome this problem, planners at Unilever must adjust the statistical forecasts with planned promotion predictions conducted by special sales teams. For each promotion, the sales-planning system predicts the "lift," or projected increase in sales, and routes it to the demand-planning system, which applies it to appropriate stock-keeping units (SKUs) and distribution centers each week. In turn, these forecasts are reviewed and adjusted if needed.

Unilever also conducts external market research and internal sales projections that are analyzed, combined with the retail customer promotions, and fed into the demand-planning system. To further improve the accuracy of its forecasts and reduce inventory lead times, Unilever—the purveyor of Dove, Lipton, Hellmann's, and hundreds of other brands—compares point-of-sale (POS) data with its own forecasts. Unfortunately, not all customers provide POS data. Moreover, integrating the data is not easy because they *come in different formats, which forces the company to build interfaces in order to manage it. Because creating these interfaces is expensive and time consuming, most companies, including Unilever, only collect POS data from their largest customers. Ultimately, planners at Unilever negotiate the final numbers each week and feed these forecasts into the demand-planning system.*

*Overall, the current CDP system has been a success. Unilever has reduced its inventory and improved its customer service. However, if collaboration and the usage of POS data were to increase, Unilever would likely reap even larger benefits. The next step for Unilever is to collaborate with its customers and suppliers, a process by which forecasts, promotion plans, and other data are shared among these firms to determine the final forecast. This process is known as **collaborative planning, forecasting, and replenishment (CPFR)**.*

Sources: Robert L. Mitchell, "Case Study: Unilever Crosses the Data Streams," *Computerworld* (December 17, 2001); Robert L. Mitchell, "Tech Check: Getting Demand Planning Right," *Computerworld* (December 17, 2001); Chana R. Schoenberger, "The Weakest Link," *Forbes* (October 1, 2001); www.forbes.com/global/2001/1001/044_print.html.

forecast

A prediction of future events used for planning purposes.

Unilever's success to date demonstrates the value of forecasting. A **forecast** is a prediction of future events used for planning purposes. At Unilever, management needed accurate forecasts to ensure value-chain success. Changing business conditions resulting from global competition, rapid technological change, and increasing environmental concerns exert pressure on a firm's capability to generate accurate forecasts.

Forecasting methods may be based on mathematical models that use available historical data or on qualitative methods that draw on managerial experience and customer judgments, or they may be based on a combination of both. Unilever's CDP system combines these methods and CPFR promises to deliver even more improvements to the forecasting process.

In this chapter, our focus is on demand forecasts. We begin with different types of demand patterns and designing the forecasting system. We examine forecasting methods in three basic categories: judgment, causal, and time-series methods. Forecast errors are defined, providing important clues for making better forecasts. We conclude with multiple techniques, which bring together insights from several sources.

Forecasts are useful for both managing processes and managing value chains. At the value chain level, a firm needs forecasts to coordinate with its customers and suppliers. At the process level, output forecasts are needed to design the various processes throughout the organization, including identifying and dealing with in-house bottlenecks. For example, Hewlett-Packard produces network cards that turn dedicated HP printers into network, shared printers. However, HP's market forecasters consistently overestimated the actual sales of the network cards because the forecasts were heavily influenced by sales quotas and revenue expectations. The result was that HP's production planning team, a part of the order fulfillment process, generated too much inventory. Giving the responsibility for the forecasting process to the production planning team resulted in a 20 to 30 percent reduction in inventory levels while maintaining high levels of product availability. Recognizing the important role of the forecasting process resulted in better overall performance of the value chain.

> FORECASTING ACROSS THE ORGANIZATION <

As the Hewlett-Packard example shows, the organization-wide forecasting process cuts across functional areas. Forecasting overall demand typically originates with marketing, but internal customers throughout the organization depend on forecasts to formulate and execute their plans as well. Forecasts are critical inputs to business plans, annual plans, and budgets. Finance needs forecasts to project cash flows and capital requirements. Human resources needs forecasts to anticipate hiring and training needs. Marketing is a primary source for sales forecast information because it is closest to external customers. Operations needs forecasts to plan output levels, purchases of services and materials, workforce and output schedules, inventories, and long-term capacities.

Managers throughout the organization make forecasts on many variables other than future demand, such as competitor strategies, regulatory changes, technological changes, processing times, supplier lead times, and quality losses. Tools for making these forecasts are basically the same tools covered here for demand: judgment, opinions of knowledgeable people, averages of experience, regression, and time-series techniques. Using these tools, forecasting can be improved. Still, forecasts are rarely perfect. As Samuel Clemens (Mark Twain) said in *Following the Equator*, "Prophesy is a good line of business, but it is full of risks." Smart managers recognize this reality and find ways to update their plans when the inevitable forecast error or unexpected event occurs.

> DEMAND PATTERNS <

At the root of most business decisions is the challenge of forecasting customer demand. It is a difficult task because the demand for services and goods can vary greatly. For example, demand for lawn fertilizer predictably increases in the spring and summer months; however, the particular weekends when demand is heaviest may depend on uncontrollable factors such as the weather. Sometimes patterns are more predictable. Thus, the peak hours of the day for a large bank's call center is from 9:00 A.M. to 12:00 P.M., and the peak day of the week is Monday. For its statement-rendering processes, the peak months are January, April, July, and October, which is when the quarterly statements are sent out. Forecasting demand in such situations requires uncovering the underlying patterns from available information. In this section, we discuss the basic patterns of demand.

The repeated observations of demand for a service or product in their order of occurrence form a pattern known as a **time series**. There are five basic patterns of most demand time series.

1. *Horizontal.* The fluctuation of data around a constant mean.
2. *Trend.* The systematic increase or decrease in the mean of the series over time.
3. *Seasonal.* A repeatable pattern of increases or decreases in demand, depending on the time of day, week, month, or season.
4. *Cyclical.* The less predictable gradual increases or decreases in demand over longer periods of time (years or decades).
5. *Random.* The unforecastable variation in demand.

Cyclical patterns arise from two influences. The first is the business cycle, which includes factors that cause the economy to go from recession to expansion over a number of years. The other influence is the service or product life cycle, which reflects the stages of demand from development through decline. Business cycle movement is difficult to predict because it is affected by national or international events, such as presidential elections or political turmoil in other countries. Predicting the rate of demand buildup or decline in the life cycle also is difficult. Sometimes firms estimate demand for a new product by starting with the demand history for the product it is replacing.

USING OPERATIONS TO COMPETE

Operations As a Competitive Weapon
Operations Strategy
Project Management

MANAGING PROCESSES

Process Strategy
Process Analysis
Process Performance and Quality
Constraint Management
Process Layout
Lean Systems

MANAGING VALUE CHAINS

Supply Chain Strategy
Location
Inventory Management
Forecasting
Sales and Operations Planning
Resource Planning
Scheduling

---

time series

The repeated observations of demand for a service or product in their order of occurrence.

Four of the patterns of demand—horizontal, trend, seasonal, and cyclical—combine in varying degrees to define the underlying time pattern of demand for a service or product. The fifth pattern, random variation, results from chance causes and thus cannot be predicted. Random variation is an aspect of demand that makes every forecast wrong. Figure 13.1 shows the first four patterns of a demand time series, all of which contain random variation. A time series may comprise any combination of these patterns.

> DESIGNING THE FORECASTING SYSTEM <

Before using forecasting techniques to analyze operations management problems, a manager must make three decisions: (1) what to forecast, (2) what type of forecasting technique to use, and (3) what type of computer software to use.

DECIDING WHAT TO FORECAST

Although some sort of demand estimate is needed for the individual services or goods produced by a company, forecasting total demand for groups or clusters and then deriving individual service or product forecasts may be easiest. Also, selecting the correct unit of measurement (e.g., service or product units or machine hours) for forecasting may be as important as choosing the best method.

Level of Aggregation Few companies err by more than 5 percent when forecasting total demand for all their services or products. However, errors in forecasts for individual items may be much higher. By clustering several similar services or products in a process called **aggregation**, companies can obtain more accurate forecasts. Many companies use a two-tier forecasting system. They first make forecasts for families of services or goods that have similar demand requirements and common processing, labor, and materials requirements, and then they derive forecasts for individual items, which are sometimes called stock-keeping units. A **stock-keeping unit (SKU)** is an individual item or product that has an identifying code and is held in inventory somewhere along the value chain, such as a distribution center. This two-tier approach maintains consistency between planning for the final stages of manufacturing (which requires the unit forecasts) and longer-term planning for sales, profit, and capacity (which requires the product family forecasts).

aggregation

The act of clustering several similar services or products so that companies can obtain more accurate forecasts.

stock-keeping unit (SKU)

An individual item or product that has an identifying code and is held in inventory somewhere along the value chain.

FIGURE **13.1**

Patterns of Demand

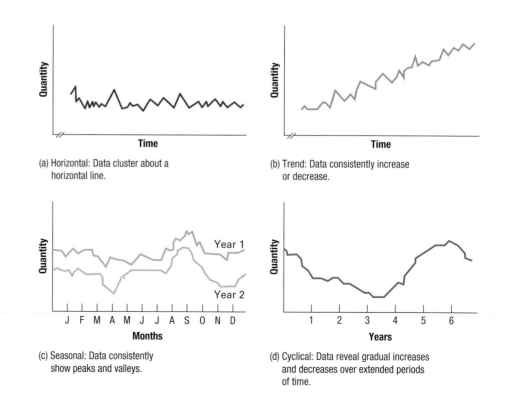

(a) Horizontal: Data cluster about a horizontal line.

(b) Trend: Data consistently increase or decrease.

(c) Seasonal: Data consistently show peaks and valleys.

(d) Cyclical: Data reveal gradual increases and decreases over extended periods of time.

Units of Measurement Rather than using dollars as the initial unit of measurement, the most useful forecasts for planning and analyzing operations problems begin with service or product units, such as SKUs, express packages to deliver, or customers needing maintenance service or repairs for their cars, for example. Forecasts of sales revenue are not as helpful because prices often fluctuate. Forecasting the number of units of demand—and then translating these estimates to sales revenue estimates by multiplying them by the price—often is the better method. If accurately forecasting the number of units of demand for a service or product is not possible, forecasting the standard labor or machine *hours* required of each of the critical resources, based on historical patterns, often is better. For companies that produce services or goods to customer order, estimates of labor or machine hours are important to scheduling and capacity planning.

CHOOSING THE TYPE OF FORECASTING TECHNIQUE

The forecaster's objective is to develop a useful forecast from the information at hand with the technique that is appropriate for the different patterns of demand. Two general types of forecasting techniques are used for demand forecasting: qualitative methods and quantitative methods. Unilever's CDP process uses a combination of both methods. Qualitative methods include **judgment methods**, which translate the opinions of managers, expert opinions, consumer surveys, and salesforce estimates into quantitative estimates. Quantitative methods include causal methods and time-series analysis. **Causal methods** use historical data on independent variables, such as promotional campaigns, economic conditions, and competitors' actions, to predict demand. **Time-series analysis** is a statistical approach that relies heavily on historical demand data to project the future size of demand and recognizes trends and seasonal patterns.

A key factor in choosing the proper forecasting approach is the time horizon for the decision requiring forecasts. Forecasts can be made for the short term, medium term, and long term. Table 13.1 contains examples of demand-forecasting applications and the typical planning horizon for each. In addition, this choice sometimes involves a trade-off between forecast accuracy and costs, such as software costs, the time required to develop a forecast, and personnel training.

FORECASTING WITH COMPUTERS

In many short-term forecasting applications, computers are a necessity. Often companies must prepare forecasts for hundreds or even thousands of services or products repeatedly. For example, a large network of health care facilities must calculate demand forecasts for each of its services for every department. This undertaking involves voluminous data that must be manipulated frequently. Analysts must examine the time series for each service or

judgment methods

A type of qualitative method that translates the opinions of managers, expert opinions, consumer surveys, and salesforce estimates into quantitative estimates.

causal methods

A type of quantitative method that uses historical data on independent variables, such as promotional campaigns, economic conditions, and competitors' actions, to predict demand.

time-series analysis

A statistical approach that relies heavily on historical demand data to project the future size of demand and recognizes trends and seasonal patterns.

TABLE 13.1	Demand Forecast Applications		
	Time Horizon		
Application	**Short Term** (0 to 3 months)	**Medium Term** (3 months to 2 years)	**Long Term** (more than 2 years)
Forecast quantity	Individual services or products	Total sales Groups or families of services or products	Total sales
Decision area	Inventory management Final assembly scheduling Workforce scheduling Master production scheduling	Staff planning Production planning Master production scheduling Purchasing Distribution	Facility location Capacity planning Process management
Forecasting technique	Time series Causal Judgment	Causal Judgment	Causal Judgment

product and arrive at a forecast. However, new software can ease the burden of making these forecasts and coordinating the forecasts between retailers and suppliers.

Many forecasting software packages are available for all sizes of computers and offer a wide variety of forecasting capabilities and report formats, including Manugistics, Forecast Pro, and SAS. A more comprehensive list, including a recent survey of available software, can be found at www.lionhrtpub.com/orms/surveys/FSS/fss-fr.html and www.morris.wharton.upenn.edu/forecast/software.html. Software packages for forecasting typically can read data inputs from spreadsheet files, plot graphs of the data and the forecasts, and save forecast files for spreadsheet display of results. The prices of these programs range from $150 to more than $10,000, depending on the data analysis functions they provide. The design of these programs for personal computers and their relatively low price place these packages within the reach of any business.

An important development in forecasting is the general approach taken by Unilever, which uses software to share information and collaborate with its customers. Managerial Practice 13.1 describes a formal approach to doing so and Wal-Mart's experience with this new process. **Collaborative planning, forecasting, and replenishment (CPFR)** is a nine-step process for value-chain management, in which forecasting plays a pivotal role, that allows a manufacturer and its customers to collaborate on making the forecast by using the Internet. Companies are giving this approach careful attention, with promising pilot studies reported. However, factors such as legacy systems, mutual trust, and geography have caused uneven adoption of CPFR to date.

> JUDGMENT METHODS <

Forecasts from quantitative methods are possible only when there is adequate historical data, often called the *history file* by various commercial software packages. However, the history file may be nonexistent when a new product is introduced or when technology is expected to change. The history file might exist but be less useful when certain events (such as rollouts or special packages) are reflected in the past data, or when certain events are expected to occur in the future. The experience of Unilever is a good example. In some cases, judgment methods are the only practical way to make a forecast. In other cases, judgment methods can also be used to modify forecasts that are generated by quantitative methods to anticipate upcoming special events that otherwise would not be reflected in the forecast. Finally, judgment methods can be used to adjust the history file that will be analyzed with quantitative methods to discount the impact of special one-time events that occurred in the past. If judgment methods are not used, the quantitative methods would give unreliable forecasts. In this section, we discuss four of the more successful judgment methods currently in use: (1) salesforce estimates, (2) executive opinion, (3) market research, and (4) the Delphi method.

SALESFORCE ESTIMATES

Sometimes the best information about future demand comes from the people closest to the external customer. **Salesforce estimates** are forecasts compiled from estimates made periodically by members of a company's salesforce. This approach has several advantages.

- The salesforce is the group most likely to know which services or products customers will be buying in the near future and in what quantities.
- Sales territories often are divided by district or region. Information broken down in this manner can be useful for inventory management, distribution, and salesforce staffing purposes.
- The forecasts of individual salesforce members can be combined easily to get regional or national sales.

It also has several disadvantages.

- Individual biases of the salespeople may taint the forecast; moreover, some people are naturally optimistic, whereas others are more cautious.
- Salespeople may not always be able to detect the difference between what a customer "wants" (a wish list) and what a customer "needs" (a necessary purchase).
- If the firm uses individual sales as a performance measure, salespeople may underestimate their forecasts so that their performance will look good when they exceed their projections, or they may work hard only until they reach their required minimum sales.

collaborative planning, forecasting, and replenishment (CPFR)

A nine-step process for value-chain management that allows a manufacturer and its customers to collaborate on making the forecast by using the Internet.

salesforce estimates

The forecasts that are compiled from estimates of future demands made periodically by members of a company's salesforce.

MANAGERIAL **PRACTICE** | 13.1 | WAL-MART USES CPFR AND THE INTERNET TO IMPROVE FORECAST PERFORMANCE

Wal-Mart has long been known for its careful analysis of cash register receipts and for working with suppliers to reduce inventories. In the past, like many other retailers, Wal-Mart did not share its forecasts with its suppliers. The result was forecast errors as much as 60 percent of actual demand. Retailers ordered more than they needed, and suppliers produced more than they could sell.

To combat the ill effects of forecast errors on inventories, Benchmarking Partners, Inc., was funded in the mid-1990s by Wal-Mart, IBM, SAP, and Manugistics to develop a software package called CFAR (pronounced "SEE far"), which stands for collaborative forecasting and replenishment. A key benefit of the package was the capability of providing more reliable medium-term forecasts. The system allowed manufacturers and merchants to work together on forecasts by using the Internet rather than fax or phone, which would have been a heavy burden with the thousands of items stocked at each store requiring weekly forecasts.

Wal-Mart initiated CFAR with Warner-Lambert's Listerine product. The system worked in the following way. Wal-Mart and Warner-Lambert independently calculated the demand they expected for Listerine six months into the future, taking into consideration factors such as past sales trends and promotion plans. They then exchanged their forecasts over the Internet. If the forecasts differed by more than a predetermined percentage, the retailer and the manufacturer used the Internet to exchange written comments and supporting data. The parties went through as many cycles as needed to converge on an acceptable forecast. After the pilot ended, the benefits to Wal-Mart included an improvement in in-stock position from 85 percent to 98 percent as well as significant increases in sales and reductions in inventory costs. Likewise, Warner-Lambert benefited by having a smoother production plan and lower average costs.

The project was overseen by the Voluntary Interindustry Commerce Standards association (VICS), which later generalized CFAR into a model dubbed CPFR, which stands for collaborative planning, forecasting, and replenishment. CPFR is a nine-step process for supply management, and, as in CFAR, forecasting plays a major role. The goal of CPFR is to create significantly more accurate information that can drive the value chain to greater sales and profits. In other words, CPFR can remove costs from the value chain and improve profitability. Much like CFAR, the more general CPFR model calls for the comparison of two forecasts (one for each partner). However, it should be noted that the process is still valuable when one forecast is compared to actual sales or when the current forecast is compared to the previous forecast. Either way, collaboration improves forecast accuracy.

Following the pilot with Warner-Lambert, Wal-Mart had a CPFR pilot with Sara Lee in which the firms exchanged information such as forecasts and replenishment data. In return, Wal-Mart benefited by ensuring that it had the right item at the right time and at the right place, thus increasing customer satisfaction and profitability.

Listerine was the "test case" for a new forecasting standard called CPFR, which stands for "collaborate planning, forecasting, and replenishment." Using the Internet, retailers like Wal-Mart and manufacturers like Warner-Lambert exchange their forecasts for products such as Listerine and are much better able to match supply with demand.

In addition to Wal-Mart, several other leading companies have already engaged in pilot plans to test CPFR. Examples include Kimberly-Clark, Kmart, Walgreens, Schering-Plough, Nabisco, and Wegmans Food Markets among others. In general, companies that participated in pilots contend that the investment committed to CPFR was relatively small because the Internet and communications standards already existed and human resources implications were few. In return, companies adopting CPFR can reduce working capital, so that the funds can be invested in more productive uses, such as new product development and marketing, the reduction of fixed capital and infrastructure expenses, the reduction of operating expenses, and the growth of sales each year.

Despite promising pilots, CPFR's adoption rate has been slower than predicted. First, many companies still have legacy systems that delay implementation. Second, information sharing, which is critical to the success of CPFR, requires that partners trust that they are working in each other's best interests. Without this trust, complete information sharing will not materialize, and CPFR will not be successful. Lastly, implementation of CPFR differs in terms of geography. For instance, in Europe CPFR has encountered different barriers than in the United States, leading some practitioners to consider regional models of CPFR rather than one general approach.

Sources: VICS (2002), "Collaborative Planning, Forecasting, and Replenishment," Version 2.0, www.cpfr.org; Robert J. Bowman, "Access to Data in Real Time: Seeing Isn't Everything," *Global Logistics and Supply-Chain Strategies* (May 2002); Noah Schachtman, "Trading Partners Collaborate to Increase Sales," *Information Week.com* (October 9, 2000).

EXECUTIVE OPINION

executive opinion

A forecasting method in which the opinions, experience, and technical knowledge of one or more managers are summarized to arrive at a single forecast.

When a new service or product is contemplated, the salesforce may not be able to make accurate demand estimates. **Executive opinion** is a forecasting method in which the opinions, experience, and technical knowledge of one or more managers are summarized to arrive at a single forecast. As we discuss later, executive opinion can be used to modify an existing sales forecast to account for unusual circumstances, such as a new sales promotion or unexpected international events. Executive opinion can also be used for **technological forecasting**. The quick pace of technological change makes keeping abreast of the latest advances difficult. The key to effective use of executive opinion is to ensure that the forecast reflects not a series of independent modifications but consensus among executives on a single forecast.

technological forecasting

An application of executive opinion to keep abreast of the latest advances in technology.

MARKET RESEARCH

market research

A systematic approach to determine external consumer interest in a service or product by creating and testing hypotheses through data-gathering surveys.

Market research is a systematic approach to determine external consumer interest in a service or product by creating and testing hypotheses through data-gathering surveys. Conducting a market research study includes designing a questionnaire, deciding how to administer it, selecting a representative sample, and analyzing the information using judgment and statistical tools to interpret the responses. Although market research yields important information, it typically includes numerous qualifications and hedges in the findings.

DELPHI METHOD

Delphi method

A process of gaining consensus from a group of experts while maintaining their anonymity.

The **Delphi method** is a process of gaining consensus from a group of experts while maintaining their anonymity. This form of forecasting is useful when no historical data are available from which to develop statistical models and when managers inside the firm have no experience on which to base informed projections. A coordinator sends questions to each member of the group of outside experts, who may not even know who else is participating. The coordinator prepares a statistical summary of the responses along with a summary of arguments for particular responses. The report is sent to the same group for another round, and the participants may choose to modify their previous responses. These rounds continue until consensus is obtained.

The Delphi method can be used to develop long-range forecasts of product demand and new-product sales projections. It can also be used for technological forecasting.

GUIDELINES FOR USING JUDGMENT FORECASTS

Judgment forecasting is clearly needed when no quantitative data are available to use quantitative forecasting approaches. However, judgment approaches can be used in concert with quantitative approaches to improve forecast quality. Guidelines for the use of judgment to adjust quantitative forecasts are as follows:

- *Adjust quantitative forecasts when they tend to be inaccurate and the decision maker has important contextual knowledge.* Contextual knowledge is knowledge that practitioners gain through experience, such as cause-and-effect relationships, environmental cues, and organizational information that may have an effect on the variable being forecast. Often, these factors cannot be incorporated into quantitative forecasting approaches.

- *Make adjustments to quantitative forecasts to compensate for specific events.* Specific events, such as advertising campaigns, the actions of competitors, or international developments often are not recognized in quantitative forecasting and should be acknowledged when a final forecast is being made.

In the remainder of this chapter, we focus on the commonly used quantitative forecasting approaches.

> CAUSAL METHODS: LINEAR REGRESSION <

Causal methods are used when historical data are available and the relationship between the factor to be forecasted and other external or internal factors (e.g., government actions or advertising promotions) can be identified. These relationships are expressed in mathematical terms and can be complex. Causal methods provide the most sophisticated forecasting tools and are good for predicting turning points in demand and for preparing long-range forecasts. Although many causal methods are available, we focus here on linear regression, one of the best known and most commonly used causal methods.

In **linear regression**, one variable, called a dependent variable, is related to one or more independent variables by a linear equation. The **dependent variable** (such as demand for doorknobs) is the one the manager wants to forecast. The **independent variables** (such as advertising expenditures and new housing starts) are assumed to affect the dependent variable and thereby "cause" the results observed in the past. Figure 13.2 shows how a linear regression line relates to the data. In technical terms, the regression line minimizes the squared deviations from the actual data.

In the simplest linear regression models, the dependent variable is a function of only one independent variable and, therefore, the theoretical relationship is a straight line:

$$Y = a + bX$$

where

Y = dependent variable

X = independent variable

a = Y-intercept of the line

b = slope of the line

The objective of linear regression analysis is to find values of a and b that minimize the sum of the squared deviations of the actual data points from the graphed line. Computer programs are used for this purpose. For any set of matched observations for Y and X, the program computes the values of a and b and provides measures of forecast accuracy. Three measures commonly reported are the sample correlation coefficient, the sample coefficient of determination, and the standard error of the estimate.

The *sample correlation coefficient, r,* measures the direction and strength of the relationship between the independent variable and the dependent variable. The value of r can range from -1.00 to $+1.00$. A correlation coefficient of $+1.00$ implies that period-by-period changes in direction (increases or decreases) of the independent variable are always accompanied by changes in the same direction by the dependent variable. An r of -1.00 means that decreases in the independent variable are always accompanied by increases in the dependent variable, and vice versa. A zero value of r means no linear relationship exists between the variables. The closer the value of r is to ± 1.00, the better the regression line fits the points.

The *sample coefficient of determination* measures the amount of variation in the dependent variable about its mean that is explained by the regression line. The coefficient of determination is the square of the correlation coefficient, or r^2. The value of r^2 ranges from 0.00 to 1.00. Regression equations with a value of r^2 close to 1.00 are desirable because the variations in the dependent variable and the forecast generated by the regression equation are closely related.

linear regression

A causal method in which one variable (the dependent variable) is related to one or more independent variables by a linear equation.

dependent variable

The variable that one wants to forecast.

independent variables

Variables that are assumed to affect the dependent variable and thereby "cause" the results observed in the past.

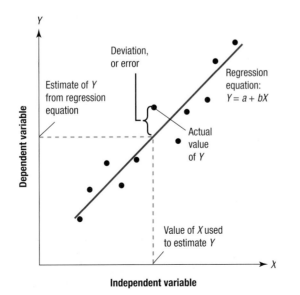

FIGURE 13.2

Linear Regression Line Relative to Actual Data

The *standard error of the estimate, s_{yx},* measures how closely the data on the dependent variable cluster around the regression line. Although it is similar to the sample standard deviation, it measures the error from the dependent variable, Y, to the regression line, rather than to the mean. Thus, it is the standard deviation of the difference between the actual demand and the estimate provided by the regression equation. When determining which independent variable to include in the regression equation, you should choose the one with the smallest standard error of the estimate.

EXAMPLE 13.1	Using Linear Regression to Forecast Product Demand

ACTIVE MODEL 13.1

Active Model 13.1 on the Student CD-ROM provides insight on varying the intercept and slope of the model.

The person in charge of production scheduling for a company must prepare forecasts of product demand in order to plan for appropriate production quantities. During a luncheon meeting, the marketing manager gives her information about the advertising budget for a brass door hinge. The following are sales and advertising data for the past 5 months:

Month	Sales (thousands of units)	Advertising (thousands of $)
1	264	2.5
2	116	1.3
3	165	1.4
4	101	1.0
5	209	2.0

The marketing manager says that next month the company will spend $1,750 on advertising for the product. Use linear regression to develop an equation and a forecast for this product.

SOLUTION

We assume that sales are linearly related to advertising expenditures. In other words, sales are the dependent variable, Y, and advertising expenditures are the independent variable, X. Using the paired monthly observations of sales and advertising expenditures supplied by the marketing manager, we use the computer to determine the best values of a, b, the correlation coefficient, the coefficient of determination, and the standard error of the estimate.

$$a = -8.135$$
$$b = 109.229X$$
$$r = 0.980$$
$$r^2 = 0.960$$
$$s_{yx} = 15.603$$

The regression equation is

$$Y = -8.135 + 109.229X$$

and the regression line is shown in Figure 13.3.

Are advertising expenditures a good choice to use in forecasting sales? Note that the sample correlation coefficient, r, is 0.98. Because the value of r is very close to 1.00, we conclude that a strong positive relationship exists between sales and advertising expenditures and that the choice was a good one.

Next, we examine the sample coefficient of determination, r^2, or 0.96. This value of r^2 implies that 96 percent of the variation in sales is explained by advertising expenditures. Most relationships between advertising and sales in practice are not this strong because other variables, such as general economic conditions and the strategies of competitors, often combine to affect sales.

As the advertising expenditure will be $1,750, the forecast for month 6 is

$$Y = -8.135 + 109.229(1.75)$$
$$= 183.016 \quad \text{or} \quad 183,016 \text{ units}$$

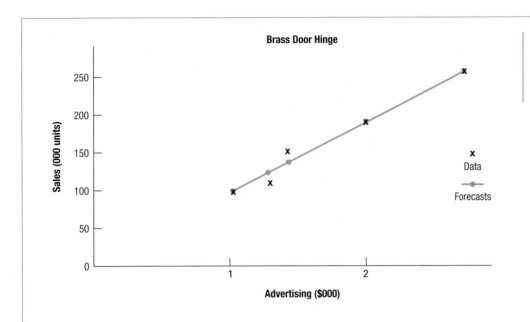

FIGURE **13.3**

Linear Regression Line for the Sales and Advertising Data Using POM for Windows

Decision Point The production scheduler can use this forecast to determine the quantity of brass door hinges needed for month 6. Suppose that she has 62,500 units in stock. The requirement to be filled from production is $183,016 - 62,500 = 120,516$ units, assuming that she does not want to lose any sales.

Often several independent variables may affect the dependent variable. For example, advertising expenditures, new corporation start-ups, and residential building contracts all may be important for estimating the demand for door hinges. In such cases, *multiple regression analysis* is helpful in determining a forecasting equation for the dependent variable as a function of several independent variables. Such models can be analyzed with POM for Windows or OM Explorer and can be quite useful for predicting turning points and solving many planning problems.

> TIME-SERIES METHODS <

Rather than using independent variables for the forecast as regression models do, time-series methods use historical information regarding only the dependent variable. These methods are based on the assumption that the dependent variable's past pattern will continue in the future. Time-series analysis identifies the underlying patterns of demand that combine to produce an observed historical pattern of the dependent variable and then develops a model to replicate it. In this section, we focus on time-series methods that address the horizontal, trend, and seasonal patterns of demand. Before we discuss statistical methods, let us take a look at the simplest time-series method for addressing all patterns of demand—the naive forecast.

NAIVE FORECAST

A method often used in practice is the **naive forecast**, whereby the forecast for the next period equals the demand for the current period (D_t). So, if the actual demand for Wednesday is 35 customers, the forecasted demand for Thursday is 35 customers. If the actual demand on Thursday is 42 customers, the forecasted demand for Friday is 42 customers. The naive forecast method may be adapted to take into account a demand trend. The increase (or decrease) in demand observed between the last two periods is used to adjust the current demand to arrive at a forecast. Suppose that last week the demand was 120 units and the week before it was 108 units. Demand increased 12 units in one week, so the forecast for next week would be $120 + 12 = 132$ units. If the actual demand next week turned out to be 127 units, the next forecast would be $127 + 7 = 134$ units. The naive forecast method also may

naive forecast

A time-series method whereby the forecast for the next period equals the demand for the current period, or Forecast $= D_t$.

be used to account for seasonal patterns. If the demand last July was 50,000 units, the forecast for this July would be 50,000 units. Similarly, forecasts of demand for each month of the coming year may simply reflect actual demand in the same month last year.

The advantages of the naive forecast method are its simplicity and low cost. The method works best when the horizontal, trend, or seasonal patterns are stable and random variation is small. If random variation is large, using last period's demand to estimate next period's demand can result in highly variable forecasts that are not useful for planning purposes. Nonetheless, if its level of accuracy is acceptable, the naive forecast is an attractive approach for time-series forecasting.

ESTIMATING THE AVERAGE

Every demand time series has at least two of the five patterns of demand: horizontal and random. It *may* have trend, seasonal, or cyclical patterns. We begin our discussion of statistical methods of time-series forecasting with demand that has no trend, seasonal, or cyclical patterns. The horizontal pattern in a time series is based on the mean of the demands, so we focus on forecasting methods that estimate the average of a time series of data. Consequently, for all the methods of forecasting we discuss in this section, the forecast of demand for *any* period in the future is the average of the time series computed in the current period. For example, if the average of past demand calculated on Tuesday is 65 customers, the forecasts for Wednesday, Thursday, and Friday are 65 customers each day.

Consider Figure 13.4, which shows patient arrivals at a medical clinic over the past 28 weeks. Assume that the demand pattern for patient arrivals has no trend, seasonal, or cyclical pattern. The time series has only a horizontal and random pattern. Because no one can predict random error, we focus on estimating the average. The statistical techniques useful for forecasting such a time series are (1) simple moving averages, (2) weighted moving averages, and (3) exponential smoothing.

simple moving average method

A time-series method used to estimate the average of a demand time series by averaging the demand for the *n* most recent time periods.

Simple Moving Averages The **simple moving average method** is used to estimate the average of a demand time series and thereby remove the effects of random fluctuation. It is most useful when demand has no pronounced trend or seasonal influences. Applying a moving average model simply involves calculating the average demand for the *n* most recent time periods and using it as the forecast for the next time period. For the next period, after the demand is known, the oldest demand from the previous average is replaced with the most recent demand and the average is recalculated. In this way, the *n* most recent demands are used, and the average "moves" from period to period.

Specifically, the forecast for period $t + 1$, can be calculated as

$$F_{t+1} = \frac{\text{Sum of last } n \text{ demands}}{n} = \frac{D_t + D_{t-1} + D_{t-2} + \cdots + D_{t-n+1}}{n}$$

where

D_t = actual demand in period t

n = total number of periods in the average

F_{t+1} = forecast for period $t + 1$

FIGURE **13.4**

Weekly Patient Arrivals at a Medical Clinic

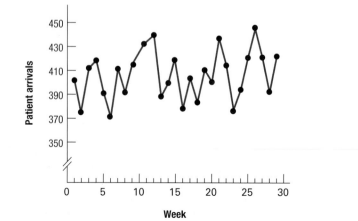

With the moving average method, the forecast of next period's demand equals the average calculated at the end of this period.

For any forecasting method, it is important to measure the accuracy of its forecasts. **Forecast error** is simply the difference found by subtracting the forecast from actual demand for a given period, or

$$E_t = D_t - F_t$$

where

E_t = forecast error for period t

D_t = actual demand for period t

F_t = forecast for period t

forecast error

The difference found by subtracting the forecast from actual demand for a given period.

| **Using the Moving Average Method to Estimate Average Demand** | EXAMPLE 13.2 |

a. Compute a *three-week* moving average forecast for the arrival of medical clinic patients in week 4. The numbers of arrivals for the past 3 weeks were

Week	Patient Arrivals
1	400
2	380
3	411

b. If the actual number of patient arrivals in week 4 is 415, what is the forecast for week 4?

c. What is the forecast for week 5?

SOLUTION

a. The moving average forecast at the end of week 3 is

$$F_4 = \frac{411 + 380 + 400}{3} = 397.0$$

b. The forecast error for week 4 is

$$E_4 = D_4 - F_4 = 415 - 397 = 18$$

c. The forecast for week 5 requires the actual arrivals from weeks 2 through 4, the three most recent weeks of data.

$$F_5 = \frac{415 + 411 + 380}{3} = 402.0$$

Decision Point Thus, the forecast at the end of week 3 would have been 397 patients for week 4, which fell short of actual demand by 18 patients. The forecast for week 5, made at the end of week 4, would be 402 patients. In addition, at the end of week 4, the forecast for week 6 and beyond is also 402 patients.

ACTIVE MODEL 13.2

Active Model 13.2 on the Student CD-ROM provides insight on the impact of varying n, using the example in Figures 13.4 and 13.10.

TUTOR 13.1

Tutor 13.1 on the Student CD-ROM provides another example to practice making forecasts with the moving average method.

The moving average method may involve the use of as many periods of past demand as desired. The stability of the demand series generally determines how many periods to include (i.e., the value of n). Stable demand series are those for which the average (to be estimated by the forecasting method) only infrequently experiences changes. Large values of n should be used for demand series that are stable, and small values of n should be used for those that are susceptible to changes in the underlying average.

Consider Figure 13.5, which compares actual patient arrivals to a 3-week and a 6-week moving average forecast for the medical clinic data. Note that the 3-week moving average forecast varies more and reacts more quickly to large swings in demand. Conversely, the 6-week moving average forecast is more stable because large swings in demand tend to cancel each other. We defer discussion of which of the two forecast methods is better for this problem until we discuss the criteria for choosing time-series methods later in the chapter.

Including more historical data in the average by increasing the number of periods results in a forecast that is less susceptible to random variations. If the underlying average in the series is changing, however, the forecasts will tend to lag behind the changes for a longer time interval because of the additional time required to remove the old data from the forecast. We address other considerations in the choice of *n* when we discuss choosing a time-series method.

Weighted Moving Averages In the simple moving average method, each demand has the same weight in the average—namely, $1/n$. In the **weighted moving average method**, each historical demand in the average can have its own weight. The sum of the weights equals 1.0. For example, in a *three-period* weighted moving average model, the most recent period might be assigned a weight of 0.50, the second most recent might be weighted 0.30, and the third most recent might be weighted 0.20. The average is obtained by multiplying the weight of each period by the value for that period and adding the products together:

$$F_{t+1} = 0.50D_t + 0.30D_{t-1} + 0.20D_{t-2}$$

For a numerical example of using the weighted moving average method to estimate average demand, see Solved Problem 2 and Tutor 13.2 in the OM Explorer.

The advantage of a weighted moving average method is that it allows you to emphasize recent demand over earlier demand. (It can even handle seasonal effects by putting higher weights on prior periods in the same season.) The forecast will be more responsive to changes in the underlying average of the demand series than the simple moving average forecast. Nonetheless, the weighted moving average forecast will still lag behind demand because it merely averages *past* demands. This lag is especially noticeable with a trend because the average of the time series is systematically increasing or decreasing.

The weighted moving average method has the same shortcomings as the simple moving average method: Data must be retained for *n* periods of demand to allow calculation of the average for each period. Keeping this amount of data is not a great burden in simple situations, such as the preceding three- and six-week examples.

Exponential Smoothing The **exponential smoothing method** is a sophisticated weighted moving average method that calculates the average of a time series by giving recent demands more weight than earlier demands. It is the most frequently used formal forecasting method because of its simplicity and the small amount of data needed to support it. Unlike the weighted moving average method, which requires *n* periods of past demand and *n* weights, exponential smoothing requires only three items of data: the last period's forecast; the demand for this period; and a smoothing parameter, alpha (α), which has a value between 0 and 1.0. To obtain an exponentially smoothed forecast, we simply calculate a weighted average of the most recent demand and the forecast calculated last period. The equation for the forecast is

$$F_{t+1} = \alpha(\text{Demand this period}) + (1 - \alpha)(\text{Forecast calculated last period})$$
$$= \alpha D_t + (1 - \alpha)F_t$$

weighted moving average method

A time-series method in which each historical demand in the average can have its own weight; the sum of the weights equals 1.0.

TUTOR 13.2

Tutor 13.2 on the Student CD-ROM provides a new practice example for making forecasts with the weighted moving average method.

exponential smoothing method

A weighted moving average method that calculates the average of a time series by giving recent demands more weight than earlier demands.

FIGURE 13.5

Comparison of 3- and 6-Week Moving Average Forecasts

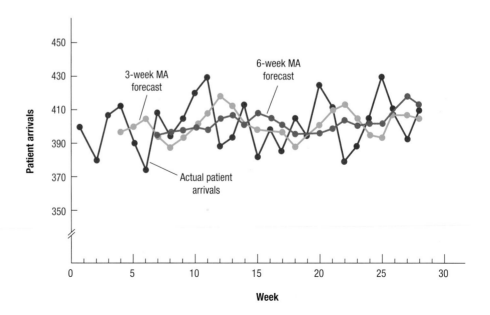

An equivalent equation is

$$F_{t+1} = F_t + \alpha(D_t - F_t)$$

This form of the equation shows that the forecast for the next period equals the forecast for the current period plus a proportion of the forecast error for the current period.

The emphasis given to the most recent demand levels can be adjusted by changing the smoothing parameter. Larger α values emphasize recent levels of demand and result in forecasts more responsive to changes in the underlying average. Smaller α values treat past demand more uniformly and result in more stable forecasts. This approach is analogous to adjusting the value of n in the moving average methods except there, smaller values of n emphasize recent demand and larger values give greater weight to past demand. In practice, various values of α are tried and the one producing the best forecasts is chosen.

Exponential smoothing requires an initial forecast to get started. There are two ways to get this initial forecast: Either use last period's demand or, if some historical data are available, calculate the average of several recent periods of demand. The effect of the initial estimate of the average on successive estimates of the average diminishes over time because, with exponential smoothing, the weights given to successive historical demands used to calculate the average decay exponentially. We can illustrate this effect with an example. If we let $\alpha = 0.20$, the forecast for period $t + 1$ is

$$F_{t+1} = 0.20D_t + 0.80F_t$$

Using the equation for F_t, we expand the equation for F_{t+1}:

$$F_{t+1} = 0.20D_t + 0.80(0.20D_{t-1} + 0.80F_{t-1}) = 0.20D_t + 0.16D_{t-1} + 0.64F_{t-1}$$

Continuing to expand, we get

$$F_{t+1} = 0.20D_t + 0.16D_{t-1} + 0.128D_{t-2} + 0.1024D_{t-3} + \cdots$$

Eventually, the weights of demands many periods ago approach zero. As with the weighted moving average method, the sum of the weights must equal 1.0, which is implicit in the exponential smoothing equation.

Using Exponential Smoothing to Estimate Average Demand	EXAMPLE 13.3

a. Reconsider the patient arrival data in Example 13.2. It is now the end of week 3. Using $\alpha = 0.10$, calculate the exponential smoothing forecast for week 4.

b. What was the forecast error for week 4 if the actual demand turned out to be 415?

c. What is the forecast for week 5?

SOLUTION

a. The exponential smoothing method requires an initial forecast. Suppose that we take the demand data for the first two weeks and average them, obtaining $(400 + 380)/2 = 390$ as an initial forecast. To obtain the forecast for week 4, using exponential smoothing with $\alpha = 0.10$, we calculate the average at the end of week 3 as

$$F_4 = 0.10(411) + 0.90(390) = 392.1$$

Thus, the forecast for week 4 would be 392 patients.

b. The forecast error for week 4 is

$$E_4 = 415 - 392 = 23$$

c. The new forecast for week 5 would be

$$F_5 = 0.10(415) + 0.90(392.1) = 394.4$$

or 394 patients. Note that we used F_4, not the integer-value forecast for week 4, in the computation for F_5. In general, we round off (when it is appropriate) only the final result to maintain as much accuracy as possible in the calculations.

ACTIVE MODEL 13.3

Active Model 13.3 on the Student CD-ROM provides insight on the impact of varying α, using the example in Figures 13.4 and 13.10.

TUTOR 13.3

Tutor 13.3 on the Student CD-ROM provides a new practice example of how to make forecasts with the exponential smoothing method.

Decision Point Using this exponential smoothing model, the analyst's forecasts would have been 392 patients for week 4 and then 394 patients for week 5 and beyond. As soon as the actual demand for week 5 is known, then the forecast for week 6 will be updated.

Because exponential smoothing is simple and requires minimal data, it is inexpensive and attractive to firms that make thousands of forecasts for each time period. However, its simplicity also is a disadvantage when the underlying average is changing, as in the case of a demand series with a trend. Like any method geared solely to the assumption of a stable average, exponential smoothing results will lag behind changes in the underlying average of demand. Higher α values may help reduce forecast errors when there is a change in the average; however, the lags will still occur if the average is changing systematically. Typically, if large α values (e.g., > 0.50) are required for an exponential smoothing application, chances are good that a more sophisticated model is needed because of a significant trend or seasonal influence in the demand series.

INCLUDING A TREND

Let us now consider a demand time series that has a trend. A *trend* in a time series is a systematic increase or decrease in the average of the series over time. Where a significant trend is present, exponential smoothing approaches must be modified; otherwise, the forecasts tend to be below or above the actual demand.

To improve the forecast, we need to calculate an estimate of the trend. We start by calculating the *current* estimate of the trend, which is the difference between the average of the series computed in the current period and the average computed last period. To obtain an estimate of the long-term trend, you can average the current estimates. The method for estimating a trend is similar to that used for estimating the demand average with exponential smoothing.

The method for incorporating a trend in an exponentially smoothed forecast is called the **trend-adjusted exponential smoothing method**. With this approach, the estimates for both the average and the trend are smoothed, requiring two smoothing constants. For each period, we calculate the average and the trend:

$$A_t = \alpha(\text{Demand this period}) + (1 - \alpha)(\text{Average} + \text{Trend estimate last period})$$
$$= \alpha D_t + (1 - \alpha)(A_{t-1} + T_{t-1})$$
$$T_t = \beta(\text{Average this period} - \text{Average last period})$$
$$+ (1 - \beta)(\text{Trend estimate last period})$$
$$= \beta(A_t - A_{t-1}) + (1 - \beta)T_{t-1}$$
$$F_{t+1} = A_t + T_t$$

where

A_t = exponentially smoothed average of the series in period t

T_t = exponentially smoothed average of the trend in period t

α = smoothing parameter for the average, with a value between 0 and 1

β = smoothing parameter for the trend, with a value between 0 and 1

F_{t+1} = forecast for period $t + 1$

To make forecasts for periods beyond the next period, we multiply the trend estimate (T_t) by the number of additional periods that we want in the forecast, and add the results to the current average (A_t). Thus, trend-adjusted exponential smoothing differs from the previous methods covered. For those methods, the forecast for all future periods is the same as the forecast for the next period.

Estimates for last period's average and trend needed for the first forecast can be derived from past data or they can be based on an educated guess if no historical data exist. To find values for α and β, often an analyst systematically adjusts α and β until the forecast errors are lowest. This process can be carried out in an experimental setting with the model used to forecast historical demands.

| Using Trend-Adjusted Exponential Smoothing to Forecast a Demand Series with a Trend | EXAMPLE 13.4 |

Medanalysis, Inc., provides medical laboratory services to patients of Health Providers, a group of 10 family-practice doctors associated with a new health maintenance program. Managers are interested in forecasting the number of blood analysis requests per week. Supplies must be purchased and a decision made regarding the number of blood samples to be sent to another laboratory because of capacity limitations at the main laboratory. Recent publicity about the damaging effects of cholesterol on the heart has caused a national increase in requests for standard blood tests. Medanalysis ran an average of 28 blood tests per week during the past four weeks. The trend over that period was 3 additional patients per week. This week's demand was for 27 blood tests. We use $\alpha = 0.20$ and $\beta = 0.20$ to calculate the forecast for next week.

SOLUTION

$$A_0 = 28 \text{ patients} \quad \text{and} \quad T_0 = 3 \text{ patients}$$

The forecast for week 2 (next week) is

$$A_1 = 0.20(27) + 0.80(28 + 3) = 30.2$$
$$T_1 = 0.20(30.2 - 28) + 0.80(3) = 2.8$$
$$F_2 = 30.2 + 2.8 = 33 \text{ blood tests}$$

If the actual number of blood tests requested in week 2 proved to be 44, the updated forecast for week 3 would be

$$A_2 = 0.20(44) + 0.80(30.2 + 2.8) = 35.2$$
$$T_2 = 0.2(35.2 - 30.2) + 0.80(2.8) = 3.2$$
$$F_3 = 35.2 + 3.2 = 38.4 \quad \text{or} \quad 38 \text{ blood tests}$$

Decision Point Using this trend-adjusted exponential smoothing model, the forecast for week 2 was 33 blood tests, and then 38 blood tests for week 3. If the analyst makes forecasts at the end of week 2 for periods beyond week 3, the forecast would be even greater because of the upward trend estimated to be 3.2 blood tests per week.

ACTIVE MODEL 13.4

Active Model 13.4 on the Student CD-ROM provides insight on varying α and β, using the example in Figure 13.6.

TUTOR 13.4

Tutor 13.4 on the Student CD-ROM provides another practice example and explanation of how to make forecasts with the trend-adjusted exponential smoothing method.

Figure 13.6 shows the trend-adjusted forecast (the blue line) for Medanalysis for a period of 15 weeks. We set α at 0.20, β at 0.20, the initial demand at 28, and the initial estimate of trend at 3. At the end of each week, we calculated a forecast for the next week, using the number of blood tests for the current week. Note that the forecasts (shown in Table 13.2) vary less than actual demand because of the smoothing effect of the procedure for calculating the estimates for the average and the trend. By adjusting α and β, we may be able to come up with a better forecast.

To make forecasts for periods beyond the next period, we multiply the trend estimate by the number of additional periods that we want in the forecast and add the result to the

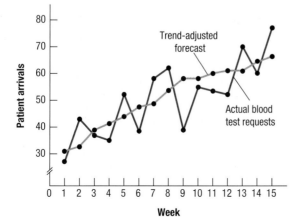

FIGURE 13.6

Trend-Adjusted Forecast for Medanalysis

		Smoothed	Trend		Forecast
Week	Arrivals	Average	Average	Forecast	Error
0	28	28	3		
1	27	30.20	2.84	31	−4
2	44	35.23	3.28	33.04	10.96
3	37	38.21	3.22	38.51	−1.51
4	35	40.14	2.96	41.43	−6.43
5	53	45.08	3.36	43.10	9.90
6	38	46.35	2.94	48.44	−10.44
7	57	50.83	3.25	49.29	7.71
8	61	55.46	3.52	54.08	6.92
9	39	54.99	2.72	58.99	−19.99
10	55	57.17	2.62	57.72	−2.72
11	54	58.63	2.38	59.79	−5.79
12	52	59.21	2.02	61.02	−9.02
13	60	60.99	1.97	61.24	−1.24
14	60	62.37	1.86	62.96	−2.96
15	75	66.38	2.29	64.23	10.78

TABLE 13.2 | Forecasts for Medanalysis Using the Trend-Adjusted Exponential Smoothing Model

current average. For example, if we were at the end of week 2 and wanted to estimate the demand for blood tests in week 6 (i.e., 4 weeks ahead), the forecast would be 35.23 + 4(3.28) = 48 tests.

Once we reach week 15 and learn that the actual number of arrivals was 75 patients, we update the smoothed average to be 66.38 and trend average to be 2.29. Then we can make forecasts for several weeks into the future. For example, the forecasts for the next 3 weeks would be:

$$\text{Forecast for week } 16 = 66.38 + (1)(2.29) = 68.67$$

$$\text{Forecast for week } 17 = 66.38 + (2)(2.29) = 70.96$$

$$\text{Forecast for week } 18 = 66.38 + (3)(2.29) = 73.25$$

The trend-adjusted exponential smoothing method has the advantage of being able to adjust the forecast to *changes* in the trend. Nonetheless, when the trend is changing, the farther ahead we project the trend estimate, the more tenuous the forecast becomes. Thus, the use of time-series methods should be restricted to short-term forecasting.

SEASONAL PATTERNS

Many organizations experience seasonal demand for their services or goods. Seasonal patterns are regularly repeating upward or downward movements in demand measured in periods of less than one year (hours, days, weeks, months, or quarters). In this context, the time periods are called *seasons*. For example, customer arrivals at a fast-food shop on any day may peak between 11 A.M. and 1 P.M. and again from 5 P.M. to 7 P.M. Here, the seasonal pattern lasts a day, and each hour of the day is a season. Similarly, the demand for haircuts may peak on Saturday, week to week. In this case, the seasonal pattern lasts a week, and the seasons are the days of the week. Seasonal patterns may last a month, as in the weekly applications for driver's license renewals, or a year, as in the monthly volumes of mail processed and the monthly demand for automobile tires.

An easy way to account for seasonal effects is to use one of the techniques already described but to limit the data in the time series to those time periods in the same season. For example, for a day-of-the-week seasonal effect, one time series would be for Mondays, one for Tuesdays, and so on. If the naive forecast is used, then the forecast for this Tuesday is the actual demand 7 days ago (last Tuesday), rather than the actual demand one day ago (Monday). If the weighted moving average method is used, high weights are placed on prior periods belonging to the same season. These approaches account for seasonal effects but have the disadvantage of discarding considerable information on past demand.

Other methods are available that analyze all past data, using one model to forecast demand for all of the seasons. We describe only the **multiplicative seasonal method**, whereby seasonal factors are multiplied by an estimate of average demand to arrive at a seasonal forecast. The four-step procedure presented here involves the use of simple averages of past demand, although more sophisticated methods for calculating averages, such as a moving average or exponential smoothing approach, could be used. The following description is based on a seasonal pattern lasting one year and seasons of one month, although the procedure can be used for any seasonal pattern and season of any length.

> **multiplicative seasonal method**
>
> A method whereby seasonal factors are multiplied by an estimate of average demand to arrive at a seasonal forecast.

1. For each year, calculate the average demand per season by dividing annual demand by the number of seasons per year. For example, if the total demand for a year is 6,000 units and each month is a season, the average demand per season is 6,000/12 = 500 units.

2. For each year, divide the actual demand for a season by the average demand per season. The result is a *seasonal index* for each season in the year, which indicates the level of demand relative to the average demand. For example, suppose that the demand for March was 400 units. The seasonal index for March then is 400/500 = 0.80, which indicates that March's demand is 20 percent below the average demand per month. Similarly, a seasonal index of 1.14 for April implies that April's demand is 14 percent greater than the average demand per month.

3. Calculate the average seasonal index for each season, using the results from step 2. Add the seasonal indices for a season and divide by the number of years of data. For example, suppose that we have calculated three seasonal indices for April: 1.14, 1.18, and 1.04. The average seasonal index for April is (1.14 + 1.18 + 1.04)/3 = 1.12. We will use this index for forecasting April's demand.

4. Calculate each season's forecast for next year. Begin by estimating the average demand per season for next year. Use the naive method, moving averages, exponential smoothing, trend-adjusted exponential smoothing, or linear regression to forecast annual demand. Divide annual demand by the number of seasons per year. Then obtain the seasonal forecast by multiplying the seasonal index by the average demand per season.

At the end of each year, the average seasonal factor for each season can be updated. We calculate the average of all historical factors for the season or, if we want some control over the relevance of past demand patterns, we calculate a moving average or single exponential smoothed average.

Using the Muliplicative Seasonal Method to Forecast the Number of Customers	EXAMPLE 13.5

The manager of the Stanley Steemer carpet cleaning company needs a quarterly forecast of the number of customers expected next year. The carpet cleaning business is seasonal, with a peak in the third quarter and a trough in the first quarter. Following are the quarterly demand data from the past 4 years:

Quarter	Year 1	Year 2	Year 3	Year 4
1	45	70	100	100
2	335	370	585	725
3	520	590	830	1,160
4	100	170	285	215
Total	1,000	1,200	1,800	2,200

The manager wants to forecast customer demand for each quarter of year 5, based on an estimate of total year 5 demand of 2,600 customers.

SOLUTION

Figure 13.7 shows the solution using the Seasonal Forecasting Solver in OM Explorer. (For a numerical example calculated manually, see Solved Problem 5 at the end of this chapter.) For the Inputs sheet, a forecast for the total demand in year 5 is needed. The annual demand has been increasing by an average of 400 customers each year (from 1,000 in year 1 to 2,200 in year 4, or 1,200/3 = 400). The computed forecast demand is found by extending that trend, and projecting an annual demand in year 5 of 2,200 + 400 = 2,600 customers. The option of a user-supplied forecast is also available if the manager wishes to make a judgmental forecast based on additional information.

The Results sheet shows quarterly forecasts by multiplying the seasonal factors by the average demand per quarter. For example, the average demand forecast in year 5 is 650 customers (or 2,600/4 = 650). Multiplying that by the seasonal index computed for the first quarter gives a forecast of 133 customers (or 650 × 0.2043 = 132.795).

FIGURE 13.7

Demand Forecasts Using the Seasonal Forecast Solver of OM Explorer

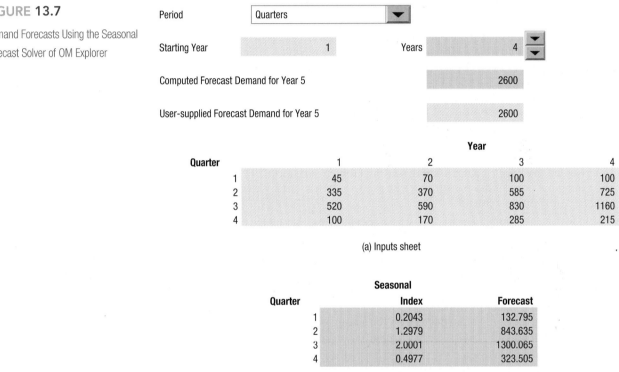

(a) Inputs sheet

Quarter	Seasonal Index	Forecast
1	0.2043	132.795
2	1.2979	843.635
3	2.0001	1300.065
4	0.4977	323.505

(b) Results

Decision Point Using this seasonal method, the analyst makes a demand forecast as low as 133 customers in the first quarter and as high as 1,300 customers in the third quarter. The season of the year clearly makes a difference.

additive seasonal method

A method in which seasonal forecasts are generated by adding a constant to the estimate of average demand per season.

The multiplicative seasonal method gets its name from the way seasonal factors are calculated and used. Multiplying the seasonal factor by an estimate of the average period demand implies that the seasonal pattern depends on the level of demand. The peaks and valleys are more extreme when average demand is high, a situation faced most often by firms that produce services and goods having a seasonal demand. Figure 13.8(a) shows a time series with a multiplicative seasonal pattern. Note how the amplitude of the seasons increases, reflecting an upward trend in demand. The reverse occurs with a downward trend in demand. An alternative to the multiplicative seasonal method is the **additive seasonal method**, whereby seasonal forecasts are generated by adding a constant (say, 50 units) to the estimate of average demand per season. This approach is based on the assumption that the seasonal pattern is constant, regardless of average demand. Figure 13.8(b) shows a time series with an additive seasonal pattern. Here, the amplitude of the seasons remains the same regardless of the level of demand.

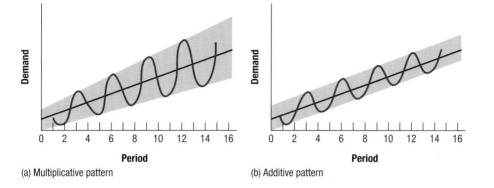

FIGURE **13.8**

Comparison of Seasonal Patterns

(a) Multiplicative pattern   (b) Additive pattern

> CHOOSING A TIME-SERIES METHOD <

We now turn to factors that managers must consider in selecting a method for time-series forecasting. One important consideration is forecast performance, as determined by forecast errors. Managers need to know how to measure forecast errors and how to detect when something is going wrong with the forecasting system. After examining forecast errors and their detection, we discuss criteria that managers can use to choose an appropriate time-series forecasting method.

FORECAST ERROR

Forecasts almost always contain errors. Forecast errors can be classified as either *bias errors* or *random errors*. Bias errors are the result of consistent mistakes—the forecast is always too high or too low. These errors often are the result of neglecting or not accurately estimating patterns of demand, such as a trend, seasonal, or cyclical pattern.

The other type of forecast error, random error, results from unpredictable factors that cause the forecast to deviate from the actual demand. Forecasting analysts try to minimize the effects of bias and random errors by selecting appropriate forecasting models, but eliminating all forms of errors is impossible.

Measures of Forecast Error Our earlier definition of forecast error for a given time period ($E_t = D_t - F_t$) is the starting point for creating several measures of forecast error that cover a relatively long period of time.

The **cumulative sum of forecast errors (CFE)** measures the total forecast error:

$$CFE = \Sigma E_t$$

cumulative sum of forecast errors (CFE)

A measurement of the total forecast error that assesses the bias in a forecast.

Large positive errors tend to be offset by large negative errors in the CFE measure. Nonetheless, CFE is useful in assessing *bias* in a forecast. For example, if a forecast is always lower than actual demand, the value of CFE will gradually get larger and larger. This increasingly large error indicates some systematic deficiency in the forecasting approach. Perhaps the analyst omitted a trend element or a cyclical pattern, or perhaps seasonal influences changed from their historical pattern. Note that the average forecast error, sometimes called the *mean bias*, is simply

$$\bar{E} = \frac{CFE}{n}$$

The **mean squared error (MSE)**, **standard deviation (σ)**, and **mean absolute deviation (MAD)** measure the dispersion of forecast errors:

$$MSE = \frac{\Sigma E_t^2}{n}$$

$$\sigma = \sqrt{\frac{\Sigma(E_t - \bar{E})^2}{n-1}}$$

$$MAD = \frac{\Sigma |E_t|}{n}$$

mean squared error (MSE)

A measurement of the dispersion of forecast errors.

standard deviation (σ)

A measurement of the dispersion of forecast errors.

mean absolute deviation (MAD)

A measurement of the dispersion of forecast errors.

The mathematical symbol | | is used to indicate the absolute value—that is, it tells you to disregard positive or negative signs. If MSE, σ, or MAD is small, the forecast is typically close to actual demand; by contrast, a large value indicates the possibility of large forecast errors. The two measures differ in the way they emphasize errors. Large errors get far more weight in MSE and σ because the errors are squared. MAD is a widely used measure of forecast error because managers can easily understand it; it is merely the mean of the forecast errors over a series of time periods, without regard to whether the error was an overestimate or an underestimate. MAD also is used in tracking signals and inventory control. Later, we discuss how MAD or σ can be used to determine safety stocks for inventory items.

mean absolute percent error (MAPE)

A measurement that relates the forecast error to the level of demand and is useful for putting forecast performance in the proper perspective.

The **mean absolute percent error (MAPE)** relates the forecast error to the level of demand and is useful for putting forecast performance in the proper perspective:

$$MAPE = \frac{(\Sigma |E_t| / D_t)(100)}{n} \text{ (expressed as a percentage)}$$

For example, an absolute forecast error of 100 results in a larger percentage error when the demand is 200 units than when the demand is 10,000 units. MAPE is the best error measure to use when making comparisons between time series for different SKUs.

EXAMPLE 13.6	Calculating Forecast Error Measures

The following table shows the actual sales of upholstered chairs for a furniture manufacturer and the forecasts made for each of the last eight months. Calculate CFE, MSE, σ, MAD, and MAPE for this product.

Month, t	Demand, D_t	Forecast, F_t	Error, E_t	Error Squared, E_t^2	Absolute Error, $|E_t|$	Absolute Percent Error, $(|E_t|/D_t)(100)$
1	200	225	−25	625	25	12.5%
2	240	220	20	400	20	8.3
3	300	285	15	225	15	5.0
4	270	290	−20	400	20	7.4
5	230	250	−20	400	20	8.7
6	260	240	20	400	20	7.7
7	210	250	−40	1,600	40	19.0
8	275	240	35	1,225	35	12.7
		Total	−15	5,275	195	81.3%

SOLUTION

Using the formulas for the measures, we get

Cumulative forecast error (bias): CFE $= -15$

Average forecast error (mean bias): $\bar{E} = \dfrac{CFE}{8} = -1.875$

Mean squared error: $MSE = \dfrac{\Sigma E_t^2}{n} = \dfrac{5,275}{8} = 659.4$

Standard deviation: $\sigma = \sqrt{\dfrac{\Sigma [E_t - (-1.875)]^2}{7}} = 27.4$

Mean absolute deviation: $MAD = \dfrac{\Sigma |E_t|}{n} = \dfrac{195}{8} = 24.4$

Mean absolute percent error: $\qquad \text{MAPE} = \dfrac{[\Sigma |E_t| / D_t] \, 100}{n} = \dfrac{81.3\%}{8} = 10.2\%$

A CFE of -15 indicates that the forecast has a slight bias to overestimate demand. The MSE, σ, and MAD statistics provide measures of forecast error variability. A MAD of 24.4 means that the average forecast error was 24.4 units in absolute value. The value of σ, 27.4, indicates that the sample distribution of forecast errors has a standard deviation of 27.4 units. A MAPE of 10.2 percent implies that, on average, the forecast error was about 10 percent of actual demand. These measures become more reliable as the number of periods of data increases.

Decision Point Although reasonably satisfied with these forecast performance results, the analyst decided to test out a few more forecasting methods before reaching a final forecasting method to use for the future.

Tracking Signals A **tracking signal** is a measure that indicates whether a method of forecasting is accurately predicting actual changes in demand. The tracking signal measures the number of MADs represented by the cumulative sum of forecast errors, the CFE. The CFE tends to be 0 when a correct forecasting system is being used. At any time, however, random errors can cause the CFE to be a nonzero number. The tracking signal formula is

tracking signal
A measure that indicates whether a method of forecasting is accurately predicting actual changes in demand.

$$\text{Tracking signal} = \dfrac{\text{CFE}}{\text{MAD}}$$

Each period, the CFE and MAD are updated to reflect current error, and the tracking signal is compared to some predetermined limits. The MAD can be calculated in one of two ways: (1) as the simple average of all absolute errors (as demonstrated in Example 13.6) or (2) as a weighted average determined by the exponential smoothing method:

$$\text{MAD}_t = \alpha |E_t| + (1-\alpha)\text{MAD}_{t-1}$$

If forecast errors are normally distributed with a mean of 0, the relationship between σ and MAD is simple:

$$\sigma = (\sqrt{\pi/2})(\text{MAD}) \cong 1.25(\text{MAD})$$
$$\text{MAD} = 0.7978\sigma \cong 0.8\sigma$$

where

$$\pi = 3.1416$$

This relationship allows use of the normal probability tables to specify limits for the tracking signal. If the tracking signal falls outside those limits, the forecasting model no longer is tracking demand adequately. A tracking system is useful when forecasting systems are computerized because it alerts analysts when forecasts are getting far from desirable limits. Table 13.3 shows the area of the normal probability distribution within the control limits of 1 to 4 MAD.

Figure 13.9 shows tracking signal results for 23 periods plotted on a *control chart*. The control chart is useful for determining whether any action needs to be taken to improve the forecasting model. In the example, the first 20 points cluster around 0, as we would expect if the forecasts are not biased. The CFE will tend toward 0. When the underlying characteristics of demand change but the forecasting model does not, the tracking signal eventually goes out of control. The steady increase after the 20th point in Figure 13.9 indicates that the process is going out of control. The 21st and 22nd points are acceptable, but the 23rd point is not.

Forecast Error Ranges Calculating MAD can also provide additional information. Forecasts that are stated as a single value, such as 1,200 units or 26 customers, can be less useful because they do not indicate the range of likely errors that the forecast typically generates. A better approach can be to provide the manager with a forecasted value and an error range. For example, suppose that the forecasted value for a product is 1,000 units, with a MAD of 20 units. Table 13.3 shows a 95 percent chance that actual demand will fall within ±2.5 MAD of the forecast; that is, for a forecast of 1,000 units, we can say with a 95 percent confidence level that actual demand will fall in the range of 950 to 1,050 units.

TABLE 13.3	Percentage of the Area of the Normal Probability Distribution Within the Control Limits of the Tracking Signal

Control Limit Spread (number of MAD)	Equivalent Number of σ*	Percentage of Area Within Control Limits†
±1.0	±0.80	57.62
±1.5	±1.20	76.98
±2.0	±1.60	89.04
±2.5	±2.00	95.44
±3.0	±2.40	98.36
±3.5	±2.80	99.48
±4.0	±3.20	99.86

*The equivalent number of standard deviations is found by using the approximation of MAD = 0.8σ.

†The area of the normal curve included within the control limits is found in Appendix I. For example, the cumulative area from $-\infty$ to 0.80σ is 0.7881. The area between 0 and $+0.80\sigma$ is $0.7881 - 0.5000 = 0.2881$. Because the normal curve is symmetric, the area between -0.80σ and 0 is also 0.2881. Therefore, the area between $\pm0.80\sigma$ is $0.2881 + 0.2881 = 0.5762$.

Computer Support Computer support, such as from *OM Explorer*, makes error calculations easy when evaluating how well forecasting models fit with past data (i.e., the *history file*). Figure 13.10 shows the output from the Time-Series Forecasting Solver, when applied to the medical clinic patient arrivals (see the original plot in Figure 13.4). Four different models are evaluated: naive forecasts (obtained with moving averages when $n = 1$), weighted moving averages ($n = 3$), exponential smoothing ($\alpha = 0.10$), and trend-adjusted exponential smoothing ($\alpha = 0.10$, $\beta = 0.10$). Figure 13.10(a) is a worksheet that allows you to select the methods to be evaluated and then calculates the resulting errors for each method on a period-by-period basis. Initial forecasts must be selected for the exponential smoothing method and the trend-adjusted exponential smoothing method. Here we simply equate them to the actual demand for the week of January 2, 2006. Other reasonable starting points would not affect the results in a significant way.

Figure 13.10(b) shows the various error measures across the entire history file for each method evaluated. For the medical clinic, the exponential smoothing model provides the best fit with past data in terms of MAPE (3.54 percent), MSE (293.39), and MAD (14.42). It is worse than the weighted moving average on CFE or bias (75.26 versus 14.10). Other versions of these models could be evaluated by testing other reasonable values for n, α, and β.

FIGURE **13.9**

Tracking Signal

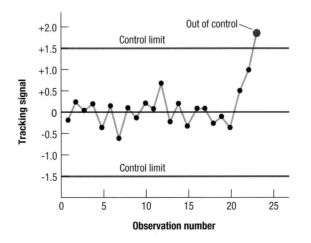

1 - Period Moving Average	3 - Period Weighted Moving Average **Enter weights**		Exponential Smoothing		Trend-Adj. Esp. Smoothing	
	Most recent	0.70	α	0.10	α	0.10
	2nd most recent	0.20	Initial Forecast	400	β	0.10
	3rd most recent	0.10			Initial Average	400
			Initial Forecast = av. Of 1st 3 pds.		Initial Trend	0

Actual Data		1-Period Moving Average			3-Period Weighted Moving Average			Exponential Smoothing			Trend-Adj. Esp. Smoothing		
		Forecast	Error	CFE	Forecast	Error	CFE	Forecast	Error	CFE	Forecast	Error	CFE
1/2/2006	400							400.00	0.00	0.00	400.00	0.00	0.00
1/9/2006	380	400.00	−20.00	−20.00				400.00	−20.00	−20.00	400.00	−20.00	−20.00
1/16/2006	411	380.00	31.00	11.00				398.00	13.00	−7.00	397.80	13.20	−6.80
1/23/2006	415	411.00	4.00	15.00	403.70	11.30	11.30	399.30	15.70	8.70	399.05	15.95	9.15
1/30/2006	393	415.00	−22.00	−7.00	410.70	−17.70	−6.40	400.87	−7.87	0.83	400.74	−7.74	1.41
2/6/2006	375	393.00	−18.00	−25.00	399.20	−24.20	−30.60	400.08	−25.08	−24.25	399.98	−24.98	−23.57
2/13/2006	410	375.00	35.00	10.00	382.60	27.40	−3.20	397.57	12.43	−11.83	397.25	15.75	−10.81
2/20/2006	395	410.00	−15.00	−5.00	401.30	−6.30	−9.50	398.82	−3.82	−15.64	398.41	−3.41	−14.23
2/27/2006	406	395.00	11.00	6.00	396.00	10.00	0.50	398.44	7.56	−8.08	397.93	8.07	−6.16
3/6/2006	424	406.00	18.00	24.00	404.20	19.80	20.30	399.19	24.81	16.73	398.67	25.33	19.17
3/13/2006	433	424.00	9.00	33.00	417.50	15.50	35.80	401.67	31.33	48.05	401.40	31.60	50.77
3/20/2006	391	433.00	−42.00	−9.00	428.50	−37.50	−1.70	404.81	−13.81	34.25	405.07	−14.07	36.71
3/27/2006	396	391.00	−5.00	−4.00	402.70	−6.70	−8.40	403.42	−7.42	26.82	404.03	−8.03	28.68
4/3/2006	417	396.00	21.00	17.00	398.70	18.30	9.90	402.68	14.32	41.14	403.51	13.49	42.17
4/10/2006	383	417.00	−34.00	−17.00	410.20	−27.20	−17.30	404.11	−21.11	20.03	405.28	−22.28	19.89
4/17/2006	402	383.00	19.00	2.00	391.10	10.90	−6.40	402.00	0.00	20.03	403.25	−1.25	18.63
4/24/2006	387	402.00	−15.00	−13.00	399.70	−12.70	−19.10	402.00	−15.00	5.02	403.31	−16.31	2.32
5/1/2006	410	387.00	23.00	10.00	389.60	20.40	1.30	400.50	9.50	14.52	401.71	8.29	10.61
5/8/2006	398	410.00	−12.00	−2.00	404.60	−6.60	−5.30	401.45	−3.45	11.07	402.64	−4.64	5.97
5/15/2006	433	398.00	35.00	33.00	399.30	33.70	28.40	401.11	31.89	42.96	402.24	30.73	36.74
5/22/2006	415	433.00	−18.00	15.00	423.70	−8.70	19.70	404.30	10.70	53.67	405.68	9.32	46.06
5/29/2006	380	415.00	−35.00	−20.00	416.90	−36.90	−17.20	405.37	−25.37	28.30	407.07	−27.07	18.98
6/5/2006	394	380.00	14.00	−6.00	392.30	1.70	−15.50	402.83	−8.83	19.47	404.56	−10.56	8.43
6/12/2006	412	394.00	18.00	12.00	393.30	18.70	3.20	401.95	10.05	29.52	403.58	8.42	16.84
6/19/2006	439	412.00	27.00	39.00	405.20	33.80	37.00	402.95	36.05	65.57	404.59	34.41	51.25
6/26/2006	416	439.00	−23.00	16.00	429.10	−13.10	23.90	406.56	9.44	75.01	408.55	7.45	58.70
7/3/2006	395	416.00	−21.00	−5.00	420.20	−25.20	−1.30	407.50	−12.50	62.51	409.88	−14.88	43.82
7/10/2006	419	395.00	24.00	19.00	403.60	15.40	14.10	406.25	12.75	75.26	408.83	10.17	53.99

FIGURE 13.10(a) | Output from Time-Series Forecasting Solver for Medical Clinic Patient Arrivals Worksheet

Figure 13.10(b) also makes forecasts for the next period. Forecasts for all future periods made at this point of time (the end of the history file) would be identical to next period's forecasts. The only exception is for the trend-adjusted exponential smoothing method, which provides forecasts for several periods in the future that account for the latest trend estimate (0.54 per week). If the exponential smoothing method is selected to make next period's forecast (because of its good performance to date), the expectation would be for 408 patients (calculated as 407.53). The forecast would be 414 patients (calculated as 413.90) using the weighted moving average method. Averaging these two numbers (see *combination forecasts* in the next section) would give a forecast of 411 patients.

CRITERIA FOR SELECTING TIME-SERIES METHODS

Forecast error measures provide important information for choosing the best forecasting method for a service or product. They also guide managers in selecting the best values for the parameters needed for the method: n for the moving average method, the weights for the weighted moving average method, and α for the exponential smoothing method. The criteria to use in making forecast method and parameter choices include (1) minimizing bias; (2) minimizing MAPE, MAD, or MSE; (3) meeting managerial expectations of changes in the components of demand; and (4) minimizing the forecast error last period. The first two criteria relate to statistical measures based on historical performance, the third reflects expectations of the future that may not be rooted in the past, and the fourth is a way to use whatever method seems to be working best at the time a forecast must be made.

Method 1 - Moving Average:

1 -Period Moving Average

Forecast for 7/17/06	419.00
CFE	19.00
MAD	21.07
MSE	532.41
MAPE	5.22%

Method 2 - Weighted Moving Average:

3 -Period Weighted Moving Average

Forecast for 7/17/06	413.90
CFE	14.10
MAD	18.39
MSE	437.07
MAPE	4.54%

Method 3 - Exponential Smoothing:

α	0.10
Initial Forecast	400.00
Forecast for 7/17/06	407.53
CFE	75.26
MAD	14.42
MSE	293.39
MAPE	3.54%

Method 4 - Trend-Adjusted Exponential Smoothing:

α	0.10
β	0.10
Initial Average	400.00
Initial Trend	0.00
Average for last period	409.85
Trend for last period	0.54
Forecast for 7/17/06	410.39
Forecast for 7/24/06	410.93
Forecast for 7/31/06	411.47
Forecast for 8/7/06	412.01
Forecast for 8/14/06	412.55
Forecast for 8/21/06	413.03
CFE	53.99
MAD	14.44
MSE	303.82
MAPE	3.69%

Using Statistical Criteria Statistical performance measures can be used in the selection of a forecasting method. The following guidelines will help when searching for the best time-series models.

1. For projections of more stable demand patterns, use lower α and β values or larger n values to emphasize historical experience.

2. For projections of more dynamic demand patterns, using the models covered in this chapter, try higher α and β values or smaller n values. When historical demand patterns are changing, recent history should be emphasized.

Often, the forecaster must make trade-offs between bias (CFE) and the measures of forecast error dispersion (MAPE, MAD, and MSE). Managers also must recognize that the best technique in explaining the past data is not necessarily the best technique to predict the future, and that "overfitting" past data can be deceptive. A forecasting method may have small errors, relative to the history file, but may generate high errors for future time periods. For this reason, some analysts prefer to use a **holdout set** as a final test. To do so, they set aside some of the more recent periods from the time series and use only the earlier time periods to develop and test different models. Once the final models have been selected in the first phase, then they are tested again with the holdout set. Performance measures, such as MAPE and CFE, would still be used but they would be applied to the holdout sample. Whether this idea is used or not, managers should monitor future forecast errors, perhaps with tracking signals, and modify their forecasting approaches as needed. Maintaining data on forecast performance is the ultimate test of forecasting power—rather than how well a model fits past data or holdout samples.

holdout set

Actual demands from the more recent time periods in the time series, which are set aside to test different models developed from the earlier time periods.

> USING MULTIPLE TECHNIQUES <

We described several individual forecasting methods and showed how to assess their forecast performance. However, we need not rely on a single forecasting method. For example, Unilever and Wal-Mart combine several different forecasts to arrive at a final forecast. Initial statistical forecasts using several time-series methods and regression are distributed to knowledgeable individuals, such as marketing directors and sales teams, for their adjustments. They can account for current market and customer conditions that are not necessarily reflected in past data. Multiple forecasts may come from different sales teams, and some teams may have a better record on forecast errors than others. Finally, the collaborative process of CPFR introduces forecasts from suppliers and even customers. Two approaches to take when using several forecasting techniques in unison include (1) combination forecasts and (2) focus forecasting.

COMBINATION FORECASTS

Research during the last two decades suggests that combining forecasts from multiple sources often produces more accurate forecasts. **Combination forecasts** are forecasts that are produced by averaging independent forecasts based on different methods or different data or both. It is intriguing that combination forecasts often perform better over time than does even the *best* single forecasting procedure. For example, suppose that the forecast for the next period is 100 units from technique 1 and 120 units from technique 2 and that technique 1 has provided more accurate forecasts to date. The combination forecast for next period, giving equal weight to each technique, is 110 units (or $0.5 \times 100 + 0.5 \times 120$). When this averaging technique is used consistently into the future, its combination forecasts often will be much more accurate than those of any single best forecasting technique (in this example, technique 1). Combining is most effective when the individual forecasts bring different kinds of information into the forecasting process. Forecasters have achieved excellent results by weighting forecasts equally, and this is a good starting point. However, unequal weights may provide better results under some conditions.

OM Explorer and POM for Windows allow you to evaluate several forecasting models, and then create combination forecasts from them. The models can be the ones evaluated separately in Figure 13.10, but they can also include forecasts from the regression, judgment, or naive method. To evaluate the judgment method, the forecaster should be given actual demand just one period at a time, preferably as the actual events are happening, and then commit to a forecast for the next period. To be informed, the forecaster should also be aware of how well the other forecasting methods have been performing, particularly in the recent past.

combination forecasts

Forecasts that are produced by averaging independent forecasts based on different methods or different data or both.

FOCUS FORECASTING

Another way to take advantage of multiple techniques is **focus forecasting**, which selects the best forecast from a group of forecasts generated by individual techniques. Every period, all techniques are used to make forecasts for each item. The forecasts are made with a computer because there can be 100,000 SKUs at a company, each needing to be forecast. Using the history file as the starting point for each method, the computer generates forecasts for the current period. The forecasts are compared to actual demand, and the method that produces the forecast with the least error is used to make the forecast for the next period. The method used for each item may change from period to period.

focus forecasting

A method of forecasting that selects the best forecast from a group of forecasts generated by individual techniques.

> PUTTING IT ALL TOGETHER:
FORECASTING AS A PROCESS <

A TYPICAL FORECASTING PROCESS

Many *inputs* to the forecasting process are informational, beginning with the *history file* on past demand. The history file is kept up-to-date with the actual demands. Clarifying notes and adjustments are made to the database to explain unusual demand behavior, such as the impact of special promotions and closeouts. Often the database is separated into two parts: *base* data and *nonbase* data. The second category reflects irregular demands. Final forecasts just made at the end of the prior cycle are entered in the history file, so as to track forecast errors. Other information sources are from salesforce estimates, outstanding bids on new orders, booked orders, market research studies, competitor behavior, economic outlook, new product introductions, pricing, and promotions. If CPFR is used, considerable information sharing will take place with customers and suppliers. For new products, a history database is fabricated based on the firm's experience with prior products and the judgment of personnel.

Outputs of the process are forecasts for multiple time periods into the future. Typically they are on a monthly basis and are projected out from six months to two years. Most software packages have the ability to "roll up" or "aggregate" forecasts for individual stock-keeping units (SKUs) into forecasts for whole product families. Forecasts can also be "blown down" or "disaggregated" into smaller pieces. In a make-to-stock environment, forecasts tend to be more detailed and can get down to specific individual products. In a make-to-order environment, the forecasts tend to be for groups of products. Similarly, if the lead times to buy raw materials and manufacture a product or provide a service are long, the forecasts go further out into the future.

The forecast process itself, typically done on a monthly basis, consists of structured steps. They often are facilitated by someone who might be called a demand manager, forecast analyst, or demand/supply planner. However, many other people are typically involved before the plan for the month is authorized.

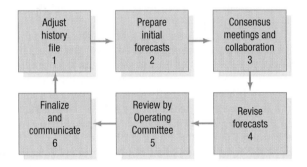

Step 1. The cycle begins mid-month just after the forecasts have been finalized and communicated to the stakeholders. Now is the time to update the history file and review forecast accuracy. At the end of the month, enter actual demand and review forecast accuracy.

Step 2. Prepare initial forecasts using some forecasting software package and judgment. Adjust the parameters of the software to find models that fit the past demand well and yet reflect the demand manager's judgment on irregular events and information about future sales pulled from various sources and business units.

Step 3. Hold consensus meetings with the stakeholders, such as marketing, sales, supply chain planners, and finance. Make it easy for business unit and field sales personnel to make inputs. Use the Internet to get collaborative information from key customers and suppliers. The goal is to arrive at consensus forecasts from all of the important players.

Step 4. Revise the forecasts using judgment, considering the inputs from the consensus meetings and collaborative sources.

Step 5. Present the forecasts to the operating committee for review and to reach a final set of forecasts. It is important to have a set of forecasts that everybody agrees upon and will work to support.

Step 6. Finalize the forecasts based on the decisions of the operating committee and communicate them to the important stakeholders. Supply chain planners are usually the biggest users.

As with all work activity, forecasting is a process and should be continually reviewed for improvements. A better process will foster better relationships between departments such as marketing, sales, and operations. It will also produce better forecasts. This principle is the first one in Table 13.4 to guide process improvements.

FORECASTING AS A NESTED PROCESS

Forecasting is not a stand-alone activity, but instead part of a larger process that encompasses the remaining chapters. After all, demand is only half of the equation—the other half is supply. Future plans must be developed to supply the resources needed to meet the forecasted demand. Resources include the workforce, materials, inventories, dollars, and equipment capacity. Making sure that demand and supply plans are in balance begins in the next chapter, "Sales and Operations Planning" (Chapter 14) and continues through Chapter 15, "Resource Planning," and Chapter 16, "Scheduling."

TABLE 13.4	Some Principles for the Forecasting Process

- Better processes yield better forecasts.
- Demand forecasting is being done in virtually every company, either formally or informally. The challenge is to do it well—better than the competition.
- Better forecasts result in better customer service and lower costs, as well as better relationships with suppliers and customers.
- The forecast can and must make sense based on the big picture, economic outlook, market share, and so on.
- The best way to improve forecast accuracy is to focus on reducing forecast error.
- Bias is the worst kind of forecast error; strive for zero bias.
- Whenever possible, forecast at higher, aggregate levels. Forecast in detail only where necessary.
- Far more can be gained by people collaborating and communicating well than by using the most advanced forecasting technique or model.

Source: Adapted from Thomas F. Wallace and Robert A. Stahl, *Sales Forecasting: A New Approach* (Cincinnati, OH: T. E. Wallace & Company, 2002), p. 112.

> STUDENT CD-ROM AND INTERNET RESOURCES <

The Student CD-ROM and the Companion Website at **www.prenhall.com/krajewski** contain many tools, activities, and resources designed for this chapter.

> KEY EQUATIONS <

1. Linear regression: $Y = a + bX$

2. Naive forecasting: Forecast $= D_t$

3. Simple moving average:

$$F_{t+1} = \frac{D_t + D_{t-1} + D_{t-2} + \cdots + D_{t-n+1}}{n}$$

4. Weighted moving average:

$$F_{t+1} = \text{Weight}_1(D_t) + \text{Weight}_2(D_{t-1}) + \text{Weight}_3(D_{t-2}) + \cdots + \text{Weight}_n(D_{t-n+1})$$

5. Exponential smoothing:
$$F_{t+1} = \alpha D_t + (1 - \alpha)F_t$$
$$F_{t+1} = F_t + \alpha(D_t - F_t)$$

6. Trend-adjusted exponential smoothing:

$$A_t = \alpha D_t + (1 - \alpha)(A_{t-1} + T_{t-1})$$
$$T_t = \beta(A_t - A_{t-1}) + (1 - \beta)T_{t-1}$$
$$F_{t+1} = A_t + T_t$$

7. Forecast error:

$$E_t = D_t - F_t$$
$$\text{CFE} = \Sigma E_t$$
$$\bar{E} = \frac{\text{CFE}}{n}$$
$$\text{MSE} = \frac{\Sigma E_t^2}{n}$$
$$\sigma = \sqrt{\frac{\Sigma(E_t - \bar{E})^2}{n-1}}$$
$$\text{MAD} = \frac{\Sigma|E_t|}{n}$$
$$\text{MAPE} = \frac{(\Sigma|E_t|/D_t)(100\%)}{n}$$

8. Tracking signal: $\dfrac{\text{CFE}}{\text{MAD}}$ or $\dfrac{\text{CFE}}{\text{MAD}_t}$

9. Exponentially smoothed error:

$$\text{MAD}_t = \alpha|E_t| + (1-\alpha)\text{MAD}_{t-1}$$

> KEY TERMS <

> SOLVED PROBLEM 1 <

Chicken Palace periodically offers carryout five-piece chicken dinners at special prices. Let Y be the number of dinners sold and X be the price. Based on the historical observations and calculations in the following table, determine the regression equation, correlation coefficient, and coefficient of determination. How many dinners can Chicken Palace expect to sell at $3.00 each?

Observation	Price (X)	Dinners Sold (Y)
1	$ 2.70	760
2	$ 3.50	510
3	$ 2.00	980
4	$ 4.20	250
5	$ 3.10	320
6	$ 4.05	480
Total	$19.55	3,300
Average	$ 3.258	550

SOLUTION

We use the computer to calculate the best values of a, b, the correlation coefficient, and the coefficient of determination.

$$a = 1,454.60$$
$$b = -277.63$$
$$r = -0.84$$
$$r^2 = 0.71$$

The regression line is

$$Y = a + bX = 1,454.60 - 277.63$$

The correlation coefficient ($r = -0.84$) shows a negative correlation between the variables. The coefficient of determination ($r^2 = 0.71$) is relatively small, which suggests that other variables (in addition to price) might appreciably affect sales.

   If the regression equation is satisfactory to the manager, estimated sales at a price of $3.00 per dinner may be calculated as follows:

$$Y = a + bX = 1,454.60 - 277.63(3.00)$$
$$= 621.71 \quad \text{or} \quad 622 \text{ dinners}$$

> SOLVED PROBLEM 2 <

The Polish General's Pizza Parlor is a small restaurant catering to patrons with a taste for European pizza. One of its specialties is Polish Prize pizza. The manager must forecast weekly demand for these special pizzas so that he can order pizza shells weekly. Recently, demand has been as follows:

Week	Pizzas	Week	Pizzas
June 2	50	June 23	56
June 9	65	June 30	55
June 16	52	July 7	60

a. Forecast the demand for pizza for June 23 to July 14 by using the simple moving average method with $n = 3$. Then repeat the forecast by using the weighted moving average method with $n = 3$ and weights of 0.50, 0.30, and 0.20, with 0.50 applying to the most recent demand.

b. Calculate the MAD for each method.

SOLUTION

a. The simple moving average method and the weighted moving average method give the following results.

Current Week	Simple Moving Average Forecast for Next Week	Weighted Moving Average Forecast for Next Week
June 16	$\dfrac{52+65+50}{3} = 55.7$ or 56	$[(0.5 \times 52) + (0.3 \times 65) + (0.2 \times 50)] = 55.5$ or 56
June 23	$\dfrac{56+52+65}{3} = 57.7$ or 58	$[(0.5 \times 56) + (0.3 \times 52) + (0.2 \times 65)] = 56.6$ or 57
June 30	$\dfrac{55+56+52}{3} = 54.3$ or 54	$[(0.5 \times 55) + (0.3 \times 56) + (0.2 \times 52)] = 54.7$ or 55
July 7	$\dfrac{60+55+56}{3} = 57.0$ or 57	$[(0.5 \times 60) + (0.3 \times 55) + (0.2 \times 56)] = 57.7$ or 58

b. The mean absolute deviation is calculated as follows:

Week	Actual Demand	Simple Moving Average Forecast	Absolute Errors $|E_t|$	Weighted Moving Average Forecast	Absolute Errors $|E_t|$
June 23	56	56	$|56 - 56| = 0$	56	$|56 - 56| = 0$
June 30	55	58	$|55 - 58| = 3$	57	$|55 - 57| = 2$
July 7	60	54	$|60 - 54| = 6$	55	$|60 - 55| = 5$
			$\text{MAD} = \dfrac{0+3+6}{3} = 3$		$\text{MAD} = \dfrac{0+2+5}{3} = 2.3$

For this limited set of data, the weighted moving average method resulted in a slightly lower mean absolute deviation. However, final conclusions can be made only after analyzing much more data.

> SOLVED PROBLEM 3 < ————————————————————————

The monthly demand for units manufactured by the Acme Rocket Company has been as follows:

Month	Units	Month	Units
May	100	September	105
June	80	October	110
July	110	November	125
August	115	December	120

a. Use the exponential smoothing method to forecast the number of units for June to January. The initial forecast for May was 105 units; $\alpha = 0.2$.

b. Calculate the absolute percentage error for each month from June through December and the MAD and MAPE of forecast error as of the end of December.

c. Calculate the tracking signal as of the end of December. What can you say about the performance of your forecasting method?

SOLUTION

a.

Current Month, t	$F_{t+1} = \alpha D_t + (1 - \alpha) F_t$			Forecast for Month $t + 1$
May	$0.2(100) + 0.8(105)$	$= 104.0$	or 104	June
June	$0.2(80) + 0.8(104.0) =$	99.2	or 99	July
July	$0.2(110) + 0.8(99.2)$	$= 101.4$	or 101	August
August	$0.2(115) + 0.8(101.4) = 104.1$		or 104	September
September	$0.2(105) + 0.8(104.1) = 104.3$		or 104	October
October	$0.2(110) + 0.8(104.3) = 105.4$		or 105	November
November	$0.2(125) + 0.8(105.4) = 109.3$		or 109	December
December	$0.2(120) + 0.8(109.3) = 111.4$		or 111	January

b.

Month, t	Actual Demand, D_t	Forecast, F_t	Error, $E_t = D_t - F_t$	Absolute Error, $|E_t|$	Absolute Percentage Error, $(|E_t|/D_t)$ (100%)
June	80	104	-24	24	30.0%
July	110	99	11	11	10.0
August	115	101	14	14	12.2
September	105	104	1	1	0.9
October	110	104	6	6	5.4
November	125	105	20	20	16.0
December	120	109	11	11	9.2
Total	765		39	87	83.7%

$$\text{MAD} = \frac{\Sigma |E_t|}{n} = \frac{87}{7} = 12.4 \quad \text{and} \quad \text{MAPE} = \frac{(\Sigma |E_t|/D_t)(100)}{n} = \frac{83.7\%}{7} = 11.96$$

c. As of the end of December, the cumulative sum of forecast errors (CFE) is 39. Using the mean absolute deviation calculated in part (b), we calculate the tracking signal:

$$\text{Tracking signal} = \frac{\text{CFE}}{\text{MAD}} = \frac{39}{12.4} = 3.14$$

The probability that a tracking signal value of 3.14 could be generated completely by chance is small. Consequently, we should revise our approach. The long string of forecasts lower than actual demand suggests use of a trend method.

> ## SOLVED PROBLEM 4 <

The demand for Krispee Crunchies, a favorite breakfast cereal of people born in the 1940s, is experiencing a decline. The company wants to monitor demand for this product closely as it nears the end of its life cycle. The trend-adjusted exponential smoothing method is used with $\alpha = 0.1$ and $\beta = 0.2$. At the end of December, the updated estimate for the average number of cases sold per month, A_t, was 900,000 and the updated trend, T_t, was −50,000 per month. The following table shows the actual sales history for January, February, and March. Generate forecasts for February, March, and April.

Month	Sales
January	890,000
February	800,000
March	825,000

SOLUTION

We know the initial condition at the end of December and actual demand for January, February, and March. We must now update the forecast method and prepare a forecast for April. Our equations for use with trend-adjusted exponential smoothing are

$$A_t = \alpha D_t + (1 - \alpha)(A_{t-1} + T_{t-1})$$
$$T_t = \beta(A_t - A_{t-1}) + (1 - \beta)T_{t-1}$$
$$F_{t+1} = A_t + T_t$$

For January, we have

$$A_{\text{Jan}} = 0.1(890,000) + 0.9(900,000 - 50,000)$$
$$= 854,000 \text{ cases}$$
$$T_{\text{Jan}} = 0.2(854,000 - 900,000) + 0.8(-50,000)$$
$$= -49,200 \text{ cases}$$
$$F_{\text{Feb}} = A_{\text{Jan}} + T_{\text{Jan}} = 854,000 - 49,200 = 804,800 \text{ cases}$$

For February, we have

$$A_{\text{Feb}} = 0.1(800,000) + 0.9(854,000 - 49,200)$$
$$= 804,320 \text{ cases}$$
$$T_{\text{Feb}} = 0.2(804,320 - 854,000) + 0.8(-49,200)$$
$$= -49,296 \text{ cases}$$
$$F_{\text{Mar}} = A_{\text{Feb}} + T_{\text{Feb}} = 804,320 - 49,296 = 755,024 \text{ cases}$$

For March, we have

$$A_{Mar} = 0.1(825,000) + 0.9(804,320 - 49,296)$$
$$= 762,021.6 \quad \text{or} \quad 762,022 \text{ cases}$$

$$T_{Mar} = 0.2(762,022 - 804,320) + 0.8(-49,296)$$
$$= -47,896.4 \quad \text{or} \quad -47,897 \text{ cases}$$

$$F_{Apr} = A_{Mar} + T_{Mar} = 762,022 - 47,897 = 714,125 \text{ cases}$$

> SOLVED PROBLEM 5 <

The Northville Post Office experiences a seasonal pattern of daily mail volume every week. The following data for two representative weeks are expressed in thousands of pieces of mail:

Day	Week 1	Week 2
Sunday	5	8
Monday	20	15
Tuesday	30	32
Wednesday	35	30
Thursday	49	45
Friday	70	70
Saturday	15	10
Total	224	210

a. Calculate a seasonal factor for each day of the week.

b. If the postmaster estimates 230,000 pieces of mail to be sorted next week, forecast the volume for each day of the week.

SOLUTION

a. Calculate the average daily mail volume for each week. Then for each day of the week divide the mail volume by the week's average to get the seasonal factor. Finally, for each day, add the two seasonal factors and divide by 2 to obtain the average seasonal factor to use in the forecast (see part (b)).

	Week 1		Week 2		
Day	Mail Volume	Seasonal Factor (1)	Mail Volume	Seasonal Factor (2)	Average Seasonal Factor [(1) + (2)]/2
Sunday	5	5/32 = 0.15625	8	8/30 = 0.26667	0.21146
Monday	20	20/32 = 0.62500	15	15/30 = 0.50000	0.56250
Tuesday	30	30/32 = 0.93750	32	32/30 = 1.06667	1.00209
Wednesday	35	35/32 = 1.09375	30	30/30 = 1.00000	1.04688
Thursday	49	49/32 = 1.53125	45	45/30 = 1.50000	1.51563
Friday	70	70/32 = 2.18750	70	70/30 = 2.33333	2.26042
Saturday	15	15/32 = 0.46875	10	10/30 = 0.33333	0.40104
Total	224		210		
Average	224/7 = 32		210/7 = 30		

b. The average daily mail volume is expected to be $230,000/7 = 32,857$ pieces of mail. Using the average seasonal factors calculated in part (a), we obtain the following forecasts:

Day	Calculation	Forecast
Sunday	$0.21146(32,857) =$	6,948
Monday	$0.56250(32,857) =$	18,482
Tuesday	$1.00209(32,857) =$	32,926
Wednesday	$1.04688(32,857) =$	34,397
Thursday	$1.51563(32,857) =$	49,799
Friday	$2.26042(32,857) =$	74,271
Saturday	$0.40104(32,857) =$	13,177
	Total	230,000

> DISCUSSION QUESTIONS <

1. Figure 13.11 shows summer air visibility measurements for Denver. The acceptable visibility standard is 100, with readings above 100 indicating clean air and good visibility, and readings below 100 indicating temperature inversions caused by forest fires, volcanic eruptions, or collisions with comets.

   a. Is a trend evident in the data? Which time-series techniques might be appropriate for estimating the average of these data?

   b. A medical center for asthma and respiratory diseases located in Denver has great demand for its services when air quality is poor. If you were in charge of developing a short-term (say, 3-day) forecast of visibility, which causal factor(s) would you analyze? In other words, which external factors hold the potential to significantly affect visibility in the *short term?*

   c. Tourism, an important factor in Denver's economy, is affected by the city's image. Air quality, as measured by visibility, affects the city's image. If you were responsible for development of tourism, which causal factor(s) would you analyze to forecast visibility for the *medium term* (say, the next two summers)?

   d. The federal government threatens to withhold several hundred million dollars in Department of Transportation funds unless Denver meets visibility standards within eight years. How would you proceed to generate a *long-term* judgment forecast of technologies that will be available to improve visibility in the next 10 years?

2. Kay and Michael Passe publish *What's Happening?*—a biweekly newspaper to publicize local events. *What's Happening?* has few subscribers; it typically is sold at checkout stands. Much of the revenue comes from advertisers of garage sales and supermarket specials. In an effort to reduce costs associated with printing too many papers or delivering them to the wrong location, Michael implemented a computerized system to collect sales data. Sales-counter scanners accurately record sales data for each location. Since the system was implemented, total sales volume has steadily declined. Selling advertising space and maintaining shelf space at supermarkets are getting more difficult.

   Reduced revenue makes controlling costs all the more important. For each issue, Michael carefully makes a forecast based on sales data collected at each location. Then he orders papers to be printed and distributed in quantities matching the forecast. Michael's forecast reflects a downward trend, which *is* present in the sales data. Now only a few papers are left over at only a few locations. Although the sales forecast accurately predicts the actual sales at most locations, *What's Happening?* is spiraling toward oblivion. Kay suspects that Michael is doing something wrong in preparing the forecast but can find no mathematical errors. Tell her what is happening.

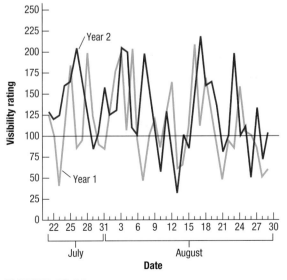

FIGURE 13.11

> PROBLEMS <

Software, such as OM Explorer, Active Models, and POM for Windows, is packaged with every new copy of the textbook. Check with your instructor on how best to use it. In many cases, the instructor wants you to understand how to do the calculations by hand. At most, the software provides a check on your calculations. When calculations are particularly complex and the goal is interpreting the results in making decisions, the software replaces entirely the manual calculations. The software also can be a valuable resource well after your course is completed.

Problem 7(vi) and Problems 12 through 14 involve considerable computations. The use of regression software or a spreadsheet is recommended.

1. The owner of a computer store rents printers to some of her preferred customers. She is interested in arriving at a forecast of rentals so that she can order the correct quantities of supplies that go with the printers. Data for the last 10 weeks are shown here.

Week	Rentals	Week	Rentals
1	23	6	28
2	24	7	32
3	32	8	35
4	26	9	26
5	31	10	24

   a. Prepare a forecast for weeks 6 through 10 by using a five-week moving average. What is the forecast for week 11?

   b. Calculate the mean absolute deviation as of the end of week 10.

2. Sales for the past 12 months at Dalworth Company are given here.

Month	Sales ($ millions)	Month	Sales ($ millions)
January	20	July	53
February	24	August	62
March	27	September	54
April	31	October	36
May	37	November	32
June	47	December	29

   a. Use a 3-month moving average to forecast the sales for the months April through December.

   b. Use a 4-month moving average to forecast the sales for the months May through December.

   c. Compare the performance of the two methods by using the mean absolute deviation as the performance criterion. Which method would you recommend?

   d. Compare the performance of the two methods by using the mean absolute percent error as the performance criterion. Which method would you recommend?

   e. Compare the performance of the two methods by using the mean squared error as the performance criterion. Which method would you recommend?

3. Karl's Copiers sells and repairs photocopy machines. The manager needs weekly forecasts of service calls so that he can schedule service personnel. The forecast for the week of July 3 was 24 calls. The manager uses exponential smoothing with $\alpha = 0.20$. Forecast the number of calls for the week of August 7, which is next week.

Week	Actual Service Calls
July 3	24
July 10	32
July 17	36
July 24	23
July 31	25

4. Consider the sales data for Dalworth Company given in Problem 2. For parts (c) through (e), use only the data from April through December.

   a. Use a three-month weighted moving average to forecast the sales for the months April through December. Use weights of (3/6), (2/6), and (1/6), giving more weight to more recent data.

   b. Use exponential smoothing with $\alpha = 0.6$ to forecast the sales for the months April through December. Assume that the initial forecast for January was $22 million.

   c. Compare the performance of the two methods by using the mean absolute deviation as the performance criterion. Which method would you recommend?

   d. Compare the performance of the two methods by using the mean absolute percent error as the performance criterion. Which method would you recommend?

   e. Compare the performance of the two methods by using the mean squared error as the performance criterion. Which method would you recommend?

5. A convenience store recently started to carry a new brand of soft drink in its territory. Management is interested in estimating future sales volume to determine whether it should continue to carry the new brand or replace it with another brand. At the end of April, the average monthly sales volume of the new soft drink was 700 cans and the trend was +50 cans per month. The actual sales volume figures for May, June, and July are 760, 800, and 820, respectively. Use trend-adjusted exponential smoothing with $\alpha = 0.2$ and $\beta = 0.1$ to forecast usage for June, July, and August.

6. Community Federal Bank in Dothan, Alabama, recently installed a new automatic teller machine to perform the standard banking services and handle loan applications

and investment transactions. The new machine is a bit complicated to use, so management is interested in tracking its past use and projecting its future use. Additional machines may be needed if projected use is high enough.

At the end of April, the average monthly use was 600 customers and the trend was +60 customers per month. The actual use figures for May, June, and July are 680, 710, and 790, respectively. Use trend-adjusted exponential smoothing with $\alpha = 0.3$ and $\beta = 0.2$ to forecast usage for June, July, and August.

7. The number of heart surgeries performed at Heartville General Hospital has increased steadily over the past several years. The hospital's administration is seeking the best method to forecast the demand for such surgeries in year 6. The data for the past 5 years are shown. Six years ago, the forecast for year 1 was 41 surgeries, and the estimated trend was an increase of 2 per year.

Year	Demand
1	45
2	50
3	52
4	56
5	58

The hospital's administration is considering the following forecasting methods.

(i) Exponential smoothing, with $\alpha = 0.6$
(ii) Exponential smoothing, with $\alpha = 0.9$
(iii) Trend-adjusted exponential smoothing, with $\alpha = 0.6$ and $\beta = 0.1$
(iv) Three-year moving average
(v) Three-year weighted moving average, using weights (3/6), (2/6), and (1/6), with more recent data given more weight
(vi) Regression model, $Y = 42.6 + 3.2X$, where Y is the number of surgeries and X is the index for the year (e.g., $X = 1$ for year 1, $X = 2$ for year 2, etc.)

a. If MAD is the performance criterion chosen by the administration, which forecasting method should it choose?
b. If MSE is the performance criterion chosen by the administration, which forecasting method should it choose?
c. If MAPE is the performance criterion chosen by the administration, which forecasting method should it choose?

8. The following data are for calculator sales in units at an electronics store over the past 5 weeks:

Week	Sales
1	46
2	49
3	43
4	50
5	53

Use trend-adjusted exponential smoothing with $\alpha = 0.2$ and $\beta = 0.2$ to forecast sales for weeks 3 through 6. Assume that the average of the time series was 45 units and that the average trend was +2 units per week just before week 1.

9. Forrest and Dan make boxes of chocolates for which the demand is uncertain. Forrest says, "That's life." On the other hand, Dan believes that some demand patterns exist that could be useful for planning the purchase of sugar, chocolate, and shrimp. Forrest insists on placing a surprise chocolate-covered shrimp in some boxes so that "You never know what you'll get." Quarterly demand (in boxes of chocolates) for the last three years follows:

Quarter	Year 1	Year 2	Year 3
1	3,000	3,300	3,502
2	1,700	2,100	2,448
3	900	1,500	1,768
4	4,400	5,100	5,882
Total	10,000	12,000	13,600

a. Use intuition and judgment to estimate quarterly demand for the fourth year.
b. If the expected sales for chocolates are 14,800 cases for year 4, use the multiplicative seasonal method to prepare a forecast for each quarter of the year. Are any of the quarterly forecasts different from what you thought you would get in part (a)?

10. The manager of Snyder's Garden Center must make her annual purchasing plans for rakes, gloves, and other gardening items. One of the items she stocks is Fast-Grow, a liquid fertilizer. The sales of this item are seasonal, with peaks in the spring, summer, and fall months. Quarterly demand (in cases) for the past 2 years follows:

Quarter	Year 1	Year 2
1	40	60
2	350	440
3	290	320
4	210	280
Total	890	1,100

If the expected sales for Fast-Grow are 1,150 cases for year 3, use the multiplicative seasonal method to prepare a forecast for each quarter of the year.

11. The manager of a utility company in the Texas panhandle wants to develop quarterly forecasts of power loads for the next year. The power loads are seasonal, and the data

on the quarterly loads in megawatts (MW) for the last four years are as follows:

Quarter	Year 1	Year 2	Year 3	Year 4
1	103.5	94.7	118.6	109.3
2	126.1	116.0	141.2	131.6
3	144.5	137.1	159.0	149.5
4	166.1	152.5	178.2	169.0

The manager estimates the total demand for the next year at 600 MW. Use the multiplicative seasonal method to develop the forecast for each quarter.

12. Demand for oil changes at Garcia's Garage has been as follows:

Month	Number of Oil Changes
January	41
February	46
March	57
April	52
May	59
June	51
July	60
August	62

a. Use simple linear regression analysis to develop a forecasting model for monthly demand. In this application, the dependent variable, Y, is monthly demand and the independent variable, X, is the month. For January, let $X = 1$; for February, let $X = 2$; and so on.

b. Use the model to forecast demand for September, October, and November. Here, $X = 9$, 10, and 11, respectively.

13. At a hydrocarbon processing factory, process control involves periodic analysis of samples for a certain process quality parameter. The analytic procedure currently used is costly and time consuming. A faster and more economical alternative procedure has been proposed. However, the numbers for the quality parameter given by the alternative procedure are somewhat different from those given by the current procedure, not because of any inherent errors but because of changes in the nature of the chemical analysis.

Management believes that, if the numbers from the new procedure can be used to forecast reliably the corresponding numbers from the current procedure, switching to the new procedure would be reasonable and cost effective. The following data were obtained for the quality parameter by analyzing samples using both procedures:

Current (Y)	Proposed (X)	Current (Y)	Proposed (X)
3.0	3.1	3.1	3.1
3.1	3.9	2.7	2.9
3.0	3.4	3.3	3.6
3.6	4.0	3.2	4.1
3.8	3.6	2.1	2.6
2.7	3.6	3.0	3.1
2.7	3.6	2.6	2.8

a. Use linear regression to find a relation to forecast Y, which is the quality parameter from the current procedure, using the values from the proposed procedure, X.

b. Is there a strong relationship between Y and X? Explain.

14. Ohio Swiss Milk Products manufactures and distributes ice cream in Ohio, Kentucky, and West Virginia. The company wants to expand operations by locating another plant in northern Ohio. The size of the new plant will be a function of the expected demand for ice cream within the area served by the plant. A market survey is currently under way to determine that demand.

Ohio Swiss wants to estimate the relationship between the manufacturing cost per gallon and the number of gallons sold in a year to determine the demand for ice cream and, thus, the size of the new plant. The following data have been collected:

Plant	Cost per Thousand Gallons (Y)	Thousands of Gallons Sold (X)
1	$ 1,015	416.9
2	973	472.5
3	1,046	250.0
4	1,006	372.1
5	1,058	238.1
6	1,068	258.6
7	967	597.0
8	997	414.0
9	1,044	263.2
10	1,008	372.0
Total	$10,182	3,654.4

a. Develop a regression equation to forecast the cost per gallon as a function of the number of gallons produced.

b. What are the correlation coefficient and the coefficient of determination? Comment on your regression equation in light of these measures.

c. Suppose that the market survey indicates a demand of 325,000 gallons in the Bucyrus, Ohio, area. Estimate the manufacturing cost per gallon for a plant producing 325,000 gallons per year.

ADVANCED PROBLEMS

15. The director of a large public library must schedule employees to reshelve books and periodicals checked out of the library. The number of items checked out will determine the labor requirements. The following data reflect the numbers of items checked out of the library for the past 3 years:

Month	Year 1	Year 2	Year 3
January	1,847	2,045	1,986
February	2,669	2,321	2,564
March	2,467	2,419	2,635
April	2,432	2,088	2,150
May	2,464	2,667	2,201
June	2,378	2,122	2,663
July	2,217	2,206	2,055
August	2,445	1,869	1,678
September	1,894	2,441	1,845
October	1,922	2,291	2,065
November	2,431	2,364	2,147
December	2,274	2,189	2,451

The director needs a time-series method for forecasting the number of items to be checked out during the next month. Find the best simple moving average forecast you can. Decide what is meant by "best" and justify your decision.

16. Using the data in Problem 15, find the best exponential smoothing solution you can. Justify your choice.

17. Using the data in Problem 15, find the best trend-adjusted exponential smoothing solution you can. Compare the performance of this method with those of the best moving average method and the exponential smoothing method. Which of the three methods would you choose?

18. Cannister, Inc., specializes in the manufacture of plastic containers. The data on the monthly sales of 10-ounce shampoo bottles for the past 5 years are as follows:

Year	1	2	3	4	5
January	742	741	896	951	1,030
February	697	700	793	861	1,032
March	776	774	885	938	1,126
April	898	932	1,055	1,109	1,285
May	1,030	1,099	1,204	1,274	1,468
June	1,107	1,223	1,326	1,422	1,637
July	1,165	1,290	1,303	1,486	1,611
August	1,216	1,349	1,436	1,555	1,608
September	1,208	1,341	1,473	1,604	1,528
October	1,131	1,296	1,453	1,600	1,420
November	971	1,066	1,170	1,403	1,119
December	783	901	1,023	1,209	1,013

a. Using the multiplicative seasonal method, calculate the monthly seasonal indices.

b. Develop a simple linear regression equation to forecast annual sales. For this regression, the dependent variable, Y, is the demand in each year and the independent variable, X, is the index for the year (i.e., $X = 1$ for year 1, $X = 2$ for year 2, and so on until $X = 5$ for year 5).

c. Forecast the annual sales for year 6 by using the regression model you developed in part (b).

d. Prepare the seasonal forecast for each month by using the monthly seasonal indices calculated in part (a).

19. The Midwest Computer Company serves a large number of businesses in the Great Lakes region. The company sells supplies and replacements and performs service on all computers sold through seven sales offices. Many items are stocked, so close inventory control is necessary to assure customers of efficient service. Recently, business has been increasing, and management is concerned about stockouts. A forecasting method is needed to estimate requirements several months in advance so that adequate replenishment quantities can be purchased. An example of the sales growth experienced during the last 50 months is the growth in demand for item EP-37, a laser printer cartridge, shown in Table 13.5.

| TABLE 13.5 | | EP-37 Sales and Lease Data | | | |

Month	EP-37 Sales	Leases	Month	EP-37 Sales	Leases
1	80	32	26	1,296	281
2	132	29	27	1,199	298
3	143	32	28	1,267	314
4	180	54	29	1,300	323
5	200	53	30	1,370	309
6	168	89	31	1,489	343
7	212	74	32	1,499	357
8	254	93	33	1,669	353
9	397	120	34	1,716	360
10	385	113	35	1,603	370
11	472	147	36	1,812	386
12	397	126	37	1,817	389
13	476	138	38	1,798	399
14	699	145	39	1,873	409
15	545	160	40	1,923	410
16	837	196	41	2,028	413
17	743	180	42	2,049	439
18	722	197	43	2,084	454
19	735	203	44	2,083	441
20	838	223	45	2,121	470
21	1,057	247	46	2,072	469
22	930	242	47	2,262	490
23	1,085	234	48	2,371	496
24	1,090	254	49	2,309	509
25	1,218	271	50	2,422	522

a. Develop a trend-adjusted exponential smoothing solution for forecasting demand. Find the "best" parameters and justify your choices. Forecast demand for months 51 through 53.

b. A consultant to Midwest's management suggested that new office building leases would be a good leading indicator for company sales. He quoted a recent university study finding that new office building leases precede office equipment and supply sales by 3 months. According to the study findings, leases in month 1 would affect sales in month 4; leases in month 2 would affect sales in month 5; and so on. Use linear regression to develop a forecasting model for sales, with leases as the independent variable. Forecast sales for months 51 through 53.

c. Which of the two models provides better forecasts? Explain.

20. A certain food item at P&Q Supermarkets has the demand pattern shown in the following table. Find the "best" forecast you can for month 25 and justify your methodology. You may use some of the data to find the best parameter value(s) for your method and the rest to test the forecast model. Your justification should include both quantitative and qualitative considerations.

Month	Demand	Month	Demand
1	33	13	37
2	37	14	43
3	31	15	56
4	39	16	41
5	54	17	36
6	38	18	39
7	42	19	41
8	40	20	58
9	41	21	42
10	54	22	45
11	43	23	41
12	39	24	38

21. The data for the visibility chart in Discussion Question 1 are shown in Table 13.6. The visibility standard is set at 100. Readings below 100 indicate that air pollution has reduced visibility, and readings above 100 indicate that the air is clearer.

a. Use several methods to generate a visibility forecast for August 31 of the second year. Which method seems to produce the best forecast?

b. Use several methods to forecast the visibility index for the summer of the third year. Which method seems to produce the best forecast? Support your choice.

22. Tom Glass forecasts electrical demand for the Flatlands Public Power District (FPPD). The FPPD wants to take its Comstock power plant out of service for maintenance when demand is expected to be low. After shutdown, per-

forming maintenance and getting the plant back on line takes 2 weeks. The utility has enough other generating capacity to satisfy 1,550 megawatts (MW) of demand while Comstock is out of service. Table 13.7 shows weekly peak demands (in MW) for the past several autumns. When next fall should the Comstock plant be scheduled for maintenance?

23. A manufacturing firm has developed a skills test, the scores from which can be used to predict workers' production rating factors. Data on the test scores of various workers and their subsequent production ratings are shown.

Worker	Test Score	Production Rating	Worker	Test Score	Production Rating
A	53	45	K	54	59
B	36	43	L	73	77
C	88	89	M	65	56
D	84	79	N	29	28
E	86	84	O	52	51
F	64	66	P	22	27
G	45	49	Q	76	76
H	48	48	R	32	34
I	39	43	S	51	60
J	67	76	T	37	32

a. Using linear regression, develop a relationship to forecast production ratings from test scores.

b. If a worker's test score was 80, what would be your forecast of the worker's production rating?

c. Comment on the strength of the relationship between the test scores and production ratings.

24. The materials handling manager of a manufacturing company is trying to forecast the cost of maintenance for the company's fleet of over-the-road tractors. He believes that the cost of maintaining the tractors increases with their age. He collected the following data:

Age (years)	Yearly Maintenance Cost ($)	Age (years)	Yearly Maintenance Cost ($)
4.5	619	5.0	1,194
4.5	1,049	0.5	163
4.5	1,033	0.5	182
4.0	495	6.0	764
4.0	723	6.0	1,373
4.0	681	1.0	978
5.0	890	1.0	466
5.0	1,522	1.0	549
5.5	987		

a. Use linear regression to develop a relationship to forecast the yearly maintenance cost based on the age of a tractor.

b. If a section has 20 three-year-old tractors, what is the forecast for the annual maintenance cost?

TABLE 13.6 | Visibility Data

Date	Year 1	Year 2	Date	Year 1	Year 2	Date	Year 1	Year 2
July 22	125	130	Aug. 5	105	200	Aug. 19	170	160
23	100	120	6	205	110	20	125	165
24	40	125	7	90	100	21	85	135
25	100	160	8	45	200	22	45	80
26	185	165	9	100	160	23	95	100
27	85	205	10	120	100	24	85	200
28	95	165	11	85	55	25	160	100
29	200	125	12	125	130	26	105	110
30	125	85	13	165	75	27	100	50
31	90	105	14	60	30	28	95	135
Aug. 1	85	160	15	65	100	29	50	70
2	135	125	16	110	85	30	60	105
3	175	130	17	210	150			
4	200	205	18	110	220			

TABLE 13.7 | Weekly Peak Power Demands

	August		September				October					November	
Year	1	2	3	4	5	6	7	8	9	10	11	12	13
1	2,050	1,925	1,825	1,525	1,050	1,300	1,200	1,175	1,350	1,525	1,725	1,575	1,925
2	2,000	2,075	2,225	1,800	1,175	1,050	1,250	1,025	1,300	1,425	1,625	1,950	1,950
3	1,950	1,800	2,150	1,725	1,575	1,275	1,325	1,100	1,500	1,550	1,375	1,825	2,000
4	2,100	2,400	1,975	1,675	1,350	1,525	1,500	1,150	1,350	1,225	1,225	1,475	1,850
5	2,275	2,300	2,150	1,525	1,350	1,475	1,475	1,175	1,375	1,400	1,425	1,550	1,900

> ACTIVE MODEL EXERCISE <

This Active Model appears on the Student CD-ROM. It allows you to see the effects of the intercept (*a*) and slope (*b*) of a linear regression line on the standard error of estimate and on MAD.

QUESTIONS

1. How many units are sold for each dollar spent in advertising, according to the regression model?

2. Use the scroll bar to lower the intercept. What happens to the standard error? What happens to the MAD?

3. Use the scroll bar to lower the slope. What happens to the standard error? What happens to the MAD?

4. Use the scroll bars for the slope and intercept to determine the values that minimize the MAD. Are they the same values that regression yields?

ACTIVE MODEL 13.1

Linear Regression Using Data from Example 13.1

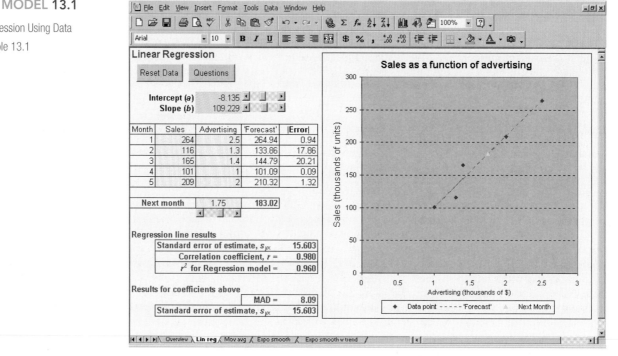

CASE	Yankee Fork and Hoe Company

The Yankee Fork and Hoe Company is a leading producer of garden tools ranging from wheelbarrows, mortar pans, and hand trucks to shovels, rakes, and trowels. The tools are sold in four different product lines ranging from the top-of-the-line Hercules products, which are rugged tools for the toughest jobs, to the Garden Helper products, which are economy tools for the occasional user. The market for garden tools is extremely competitive because of the simple design of the products and the large number of competing producers. In addition, more people are using power tools, such as lawn edgers, hedge trimmers, and thatchers, reducing demand for their manual counterparts. These factors compel Yankee to maintain low prices while retaining high quality and dependable delivery.

Garden tools represent a mature industry. Unless new manual products can be developed or a sudden resurgence occurs in home gardening, the prospects for large increases in sales are not bright. Keeping ahead of the competition is a constant battle. No one knows this better than Alan Roberts, president of Yankee.

The types of tools sold today are, by and large, the same ones sold 30 years ago. The only way to generate new sales and retain old customers is to provide superior customer service and produce a product with high customer value. This approach puts pressure on the manufacturing system, which has been having difficulties lately. Recently, Roberts has been receiving calls from long-time customers, such as Sears and Tru-Value Hardware Stores, complaining about late shipments. These customers advertise promotions for garden tools and require on-time delivery.

Roberts knows that losing customers like Sears and Tru-Value would be disastrous. He decides to ask consultant Sharon Place to look into the matter and report to him in one week. Roberts suggests that she focus on the bow rake as a case in point because it is a high-volume product and has been a major source of customer complaints of late.

Planning Bow Rake Production

A bow rake consists of a head with 12 teeth spaced 1 inch apart, a hardwood handle, a bow that attaches the head to the handle, and a metal ferrule that reinforces the area where the bow inserts into the handle. The bow is a metal strip that is welded to the ends of the rake head and bent in the middle to form a flat tab for insertion into the handle. The rake is about 64 inches long.

Place decides to find out how Yankee plans bow rake production. She goes straight to Phil Stanton, who gives the following account:

Planning is informal around here. To begin, marketing determines the forecast for bow rakes by month for the next year. Then they pass it along to me. Quite frankly,

the forecasts are usually inflated—must be their big egos over there. I have to be careful because we enter into long-term purchasing agreements for steel, and having it just sitting around is expensive. So, I usually reduce the forecast by 10 percent or so. I use the modified forecast to generate a monthly final-assembly schedule, which determines what I need to have from the forging and woodworking areas. The system works well if the forecasts are good. But when marketing comes to me and says they are behind on customer orders, as they often do near the end of the year, it wreaks havoc with the schedules. Forging gets hit the hardest. For example, the presses that stamp the rake heads from blanks of steel can handle only 7,000 heads per day, and the bow rolling machine can do only 5,000 per day. Both operations are also required for many other products.

Because the marketing department provides crucial information to Stanton, Place decides to see the marketing manager, Ron Adams. Adams explains how he arrives at the bow rake forecasts.

Things don't change much from year to year. Sure, sometimes we put on a sales promotion of some kind, but we try to give Phil enough warning before the demand kicks in—usually a month or so. I meet with several managers from the various sales regions to go over shipping data from last year and discuss anticipated promotions, changes in the economy, and shortages we experienced last year. Based on these meetings, I generate a monthly forecast for the next year. Even though we take a lot of time getting the forecast, it never seems to help us avoid customer problems.

The Problem

Place ponders the comments from Stanton and Adams. She understands Stanton's concerns about costs and keeping inventory low and Adams's concern about having enough rakes on hand to make timely shipments. Both are also somewhat concerned about capacity. Yet she decides to check actual customer demand for the bow rake over the past four years (in Table 13.8) before making her final report to Roberts.

QUESTIONS

1. Comment on the forecasting system being used by Yankee. Suggest changes or improvements that you believe are justified.

2. Develop your own forecast for bow rakes for each month of the next year (year 5). Justify your forecast and the method you used.

TABLE 13.8	Four-Year Demand History for the Bow Rake			
	Demand			
Month	**Year 1**	**Year 2**	**Year 3**	**Year 4**
1	55,220	39,875	32,180	62,377
2	57,350	64,128	38,600	66,501
3	15,445	47,653	25,020	31,404
4	27,776	43,050	51,300	36,504
5	21,408	39,359	31,790	16,888
6	17,118	10,317	32,100	18,909
7	18,028	45,194	59,832	35,500
8	19,883	46,530	30,740	51,250
9	15,796	22,105	47,800	34,443
10	53,665	41,350	73,890	68,088
11	83,269	46,024	60,202	68,175
12	72,991	41,856	55,200	61,100

Note: The demand figures shown in the table are the number of units promised for delivery each month. Actual delivery quantities differed because of capacity or shortages of materials.

> SELECTED REFERENCES <

Armstrong, J. S. *Long-Range Forecasting: From Crystal Ball to Computer.* New York: John Wiley & Sons, 1995.

Armstrong, J. Scott, and F. Collopy. "Integration of Statistical Methods and Judgment for Time Series Forecasting: Principles from Empirical Research," in G. Wright and P. Goodwin (eds.), *Forecasting with Judgement,* New York: John Wiley and Sons, 1998.

Blattberg, R. C., and S. J. Hoch. "Database Models and Managerial Intuition: 50% Model + 50% Manager." *Management Science,* vol. 36 (1990), pp. 887–899.

Bowerman, Bruce L., and Richard T. O'Connell. *Forecasting and Time Series: An Applied Approach,* 3d ed., Belmont, CA: Duxbury Press, 1993.

Bowman, Robert J. "Access to Data in Real Time: Seeing Isn't Everything." *Global Logistics and Supply-Chain Strategies* (May 2002).

Chambers, John C., Satinder K. Mullick, and Donald D. Smith. "How to Choose the Right Forecasting Technique." *Harvard Business Review* (July–August 1971), pp. 45–74.

"Clearing the Cobwebs from the Stockroom." *Business Week* (October 21, 1996), p. 140.

Clemen, R. T. "Combining Forecasts: A Review and Annotated Bibliography." *International Journal of Forecasting,* vol. 5 (1989), pp. 559–583.

Hudson, William J. *Executive Economics: Forecasting and Planning for the Real World of Business.* New York: John Wiley & Sons, 1993.

Jenkins, Carolyn. "Accurate Forecasting Reduces Inventory and Increases Output at Henredon." *APIC—The Performance Advantage* (September 1992), pp. 37–39.

Kakouros, Steve, Dorothea Kuettner, and Brian Cargille. "Measure, Then Manage." *APICS—The Performance Advantage* (October 2002), pp. 25–29.

Kimes, Sheryl E., and James A. Fitzsimmons. "Selecting Profitable Hotel Sites at La Quinta Motor Inns." *Interfaces,* vol. 20, no. 2 (1990), pp. 12–20.

Li, X. "An Intelligent Business Forecaster for Strategic Business Planning." *Journal of Forecasting,* vol. 18, no. 3 (1999), pp. 181–205.

Lim, J. S., and M. O'Connor. "Judgmental Forecasting with Time Series and Causal Information." *International Journal of Forecasting,* vol. 12 (1996), pp. 139–153.

Melnyk, Steven. "1997 Forecasting Software Product Listing." *APICS—The Performance Advantage* (April 1997), pp. 62–65.

Mitchell, Robert L. "Case Study: Unilever Crosses the Data Streams." *Computerworld* (December 17, 2001).

Moon, Mark A., John T. Mentzer, and Dwight E. Thomas Jr. "Customer Demand Planning at Lucent Technologies: A Case Study in Continuous Improvement Through Sales Forecast Auditing." *Industrial Marketing Management,* vol. 29, no. 1 (2000).

Principles of Forecasting: A Handbook for Researchers and Practitioners. J. Scott Armstrong (ed.). Norwell, MA: Kluwer Academic Publishers, 2001. Also visit www-marketing.wharton.upenn.edu/forecast for valuable information on forecasting, including frequently asked questions, forecasting methodology tree, and dictionary.

Raghunathan, Srinivasan. "Interorganizational Collaborative Forecasting and Replenishment Systems and Supply-Chain Implications." *Decision Sciences,* vol. 30, no. 5 (1999), pp. 1053–1067.

Sanders, Nada R., and L. P. Ritzman. "Bringing Judgment into Combination Forecasts." *Journal of Operations Management,* vol. 13 (1995), pp. 311–321.

Sanders, Nada R., and Karl B. Manrodt. "Forecasting in Practice: Use, Satisfaction, and Performance." *Interfaces,* vol. 33, no. 5 (2003), pp. 90–93.

Sanders, Nada R., and Larry P. Ritzman. "The Need for Contextual and Technical Knowledge in Judgmental Forecasting." *Journal of Behavioral Decision Making,* vol. 5, no. 1 (1992), pp. 39–52.

Schachtman, Noah. "Trading Partners Collaborate to Increase Sales." *Information Week.com* (October 9, 2000), www.informationweek.com/807/cpfr.htm.

Schoenberger, Chana R. "The Weakest Link." *Forbes* (October 1, 2001). www.forbes.com/forbes/2001/1001/114.print.html.

Seifert, Dirk. *Collaborative Planning, Forecasting, and Replenishment: How to Create a Supply-Chain Advantage.* Bonn, Germany: Galileo Press, 2002.

Smith, Bernard. *Focus Forecasting: Computer Techniques for Inventory Control.* Boston: CBI Publishing, 1984.

VICS (2002) "Collaborative Planning, Forecasting, and Replenishment," Version 2.0, www.cpfr.org.

Wallace, Thomas F., and Robert A. Stahl. *Sales Forecasting: A New Approach.* Cincinnati, OH: T. E. Wallace & Company, 2002.

Yurkiewicz, Jack. "Forecasting 2000." *OR/MS Today,* vol. 27, no. 1 (2000), pp. 58–65.

Yurkiewicz, Jack. "2003 Forecasting Software Survey." *OR/MS Today* (February 2003).

LEARNING GOALS

After reading this chapter, you should be able to:

1. Define sales and operations planning.

2. Explain why aggregation helps the planning process.

3. Explain how sales and operations plans relate to other plans.

4. Identify the pros and cons of each reactive and aggressive alternative.

5. Describe the planning process.

6. Explain how spreadsheets and the transportation method can be used.

An employee stocks a Whirlpool air conditioner at a Lowe's store in Westborough, Massachusetts. The demand for window-unit air conditioners not only fluctuates by season but by year—some years are hotter or colder than others. Instead of ramping up or ramping down production based on a particular year, Whirlpool bases its sales and operations plans on the *average* year.

CHAPTER 14

Sales and Operations Planning

WHIRLPOOL CORPORATION

Whirlpool Corporation, with annual sales of more than $12 billion, 68,000 employees, and nearly 50 manufacturing and technology research centers around the globe, manufactures and markets major home appliances. It is also a leading producer of room air conditioners. The demand for window units is highly seasonal and also depends on variations in the weather. Typically, Whirlpool begins production of room air conditioners in the fall and holds them as inventory until they are shipped in the spring. Building inventory in the slack season allows the company to even out production rates over much of the year and still satisfy demand in the peak periods (spring and summer) when retailers are placing most of their orders. However, when summers are hotter than usual, demand increases dramatically and stockouts can occur. If Whirlpool increases its output and the summer is hot, it stands to increase its sales and market share. But if the summer is cool, the company is stuck with expensive inventories of unsold machines.

Whirlpool prefers to make its production plans based on the average year, taking into account industry forecasts for total sales and traditional seasonalities. Whirlpool's increasingly global operations help smooth out the company's overall variations in demand. For example, strong demand in North America and Europe might more than offset weak economic and business conditions in Latin America and Asia, and so on.

Source: www.whirlpoolcorp.com/about/default.asp, May 2005.

For additional chapter resources check the Student CD-ROM or the Companion Website at
www.prenhall.com/krajewski

sales and operations planning (S&OP)

The process of planning future aggregate resource levels so that supply is in balance with demand.

staffing plan

A sales and operations plan of a service firm, which centers on staffing and other human resource–related factors.

production plan

A sales and operations plan of a manufacturing firm, which centers on production rates and inventory holdings.

D emand often is uneven over time, as we saw with Whirlpool, which experiences seasonal shifts in demand for its products. However, managing value chains effectively requires more than just good demand forecasts. Demand is the first half of the equation, but the other half is supply. The firm must develop plans to supply the resources needed to meet the forecasted demand. These resources include the workforce, materials, inventories, dollars, and equipment capacity.

Making sure that demand and supply plans are in balance begins with **sales and operations planning (S&OP)**, which is the process of planning future aggregate resource levels so that supply is in balance with demand. Sometimes called an *aggregate plan*, it is a statement of a company's or department's production rates, workforce levels, and inventory holdings that are consistent with demand forecasts and capacity constraints. The sales and operations plan is time-phased, meaning that it is projected for several time periods (such as months) into the future.

A sales and operations plan for a service firm, often called a **staffing plan**, centers on staffing and on other human resource–related factors. A sales and operations plan of a manufacturing firm, often called a **production plan**, generally focuses on production rates and inventory holdings. For both service and manufacturing types of firms, the plan must balance supply with demand in a way that achieves the best compromise between sometimes conflicting performance measures such as customer service, workforce stability, cost, and profit. It must satisfy the overall operations strategy and competitive priorities of the firm.

In this chapter, we focus on the sales and operations plan. We begin with its purpose and the role of aggregation. We examine how it relates with other plans and functional areas within the firm. We describe a typical planning process, and various strategies to cope with uneven demand. We conclude with two tools finding good solutions for further consideration: spreadsheets and the transportation method.

USING OPERATIONS TO COMPETE

↓

Operations As a Competitive Weapon
Operations Strategy
Project Management

MANAGING PROCESSES

↓

Process Strategy
Process Analysis
Process Performance and Quality
Constraint Management
Process Layout
Lean Systems

MANAGING VALUE CHAINS

↓

Supply Chain Strategy
Location
Inventory Management
Forecasting
Sales and Operations Planning
Resource Planning
Scheduling

> SALES AND OPERATIONS PLANNING ACROSS THE ORGANIZATION <

Sales and operations planning is meaningful for each organization along the value chain. First, it requires managerial inputs from all of the firm's functions. Marketing provides inputs on demand and customer requirements, and accounting provides important cost data and a firm's financial condition. One of finance's objectives might be to cut inventory, whereas operations might argue for a more stable workforce and for less reliance on overtime. Second, each function is affected by the plan. A sales and operations plan that calls for expanding or reducing the workforce has a direct impact on the hiring and training requirements for the human resources function. As the plan is implemented, it creates revenue and cost streams that finance must deal with as it manages the firm's cash flows. Third, each department and group in a firm has its own workforce. Managers of these departments must make choices on hiring, overtime, and vacations. Sales and operations planning is an activity for the whole organization, involves senior management, and must often achieve consensus among conflicting objectives of different functional areas.

> THE PURPOSE OF SALES AND OPERATIONS PLANS <

In this section, we explain why companies need sales and operations plans and how they use them to take a macro, or big picture, view of their business. We also discuss how the sales and operations plan relates to a company's long- and short-term plans.

AGGREGATION

The sales and operations plan is useful because it focuses on a general course of action, consistent with the company's strategic goals and objectives, without getting bogged down in details. For example, the sales and operations plan allows Whirlpool's managers to determine whether they can satisfy budgetary goals without having to schedule each of the company's thousands of products and employees individually. Even if a planner could prepare such a detailed plan, the time and effort required to update the plan would make it uneconomical.

For this reason, production and staffing plans are prepared by grouping, or *aggregating,* similar services, products, units of labor, or units of time. For instance, a manufacturer of bicycles that produces 12 different models of bikes might divide them into two groups, mountain bikes and road bikes, for the purpose of preparing the sales and operations plan. The manufacturer might also consider its workforce needs in terms of units of labor needed per month. In general, companies perform aggregation along three dimensions: services or products, labor, and time.

Product Families A group of customers, services, or products that have similar demand requirements and common process, labor, and materials requirements is called a **product family**. Sometimes, product families relate to market groupings or to specific processes. A firm can aggregate its services or products into a set of relatively broad families, avoiding too much detail at this stage of the planning process. The bicycle manufacturer that has aggregated all products into two families—mountain bikes and road bikes—is a good example. Common and relevant measurements, such as number of customers, dollars, standard hours, gallons, or units, should be used to develop sales and operations plans for each product family.

Labor A company can aggregate its workforce in various ways as well, depending on its flexibility. For example, if workers at the bicycle manufacturer are trained to work on either mountain bikes or road bikes, for planning purposes management can consider its workforce to be a single aggregate group, even though the skills of individual workers may differ.

Alternatively, management can aggregate employees along product family lines by splitting the workforce into subgroups and assigning a different group to the production of each product family. In service operations, such as a city government, workers are aggregated by the type of service they provide: firefighters, police officers, sanitation workers, and administrators.

Time The planning horizon covered by a sales and operations plan typically is one year, although it can differ in various situations. To avoid the expense and disruptive effect of frequent changes in output rates and the workforce, adjustments usually are made monthly or quarterly. In other words, the company looks at time in the aggregate—months, quarters, or seasons—rather than in days or hours.

Some companies use monthly planning periods for the near portion of the planning horizon and quarterly periods for the later portion. In practice, planning periods reflect a balance between the needs for (1) a limited number of decision points to reduce planning complexity, and (2) flexibility to adjust output rates and workforce levels when demand forecasts exhibit seasonal variations. The bicycle manufacturer, for example, may choose monthly planning periods so that timely adjustments to inventory levels can be made without excessively disruptive changes to the workforce.

THE RELATIONSHIP OF SALES AND OPERATIONS PLANS TO OTHER PLANS

A financial assessment of the organization's near future—that is, for 1 or 2 years ahead—is called either a business plan (in for-profit firms) or an annual plan (in nonprofit services). A **business plan** is a projected statement of income, costs, and profits. It usually is accompanied by budgets, a projected (pro forma) balance sheet, and a projected cash flow statement, showing sources and allocations of funds. The business plan unifies the plans and expectations of a firm's operations, finance, sales, and marketing managers. In particular, it reflects plans for market penetration, new product introduction, and capital investment. Manufacturing firms and for-profit service organizations, such as a retail store, a firm of attorneys, or a hospital, prepare such plans. A nonprofit service organization, such as the United Way or a municipal government, prepares a different type of plan for financial assessment, called an **annual plan or financial plan**.

Figure 14.1 illustrates the relationships among the business or annual plan, sales and operations plan, and detailed plans and schedules derived from it. For service providers in the value chain, top management sets the organization's direction and objectives in the business plan (in a for-profit organization) or annual plan (in a not-for-profit organization). This plan then provides the framework for developing the sales and operations plan, which typically focuses on staffing and other human resource–related factors at a more aggregate level.

product family

A group of customers, services, or products that have similar demand requirements and common process, labor, and materials requirements.

business plan

A projected statement of income, costs, and profits.

annual plan or financial plan

A plan for financial assessment used by a nonprofit service organization.

FIGURE **14.1**

The Relationship of Sales and
Operations Plan to Other Plans

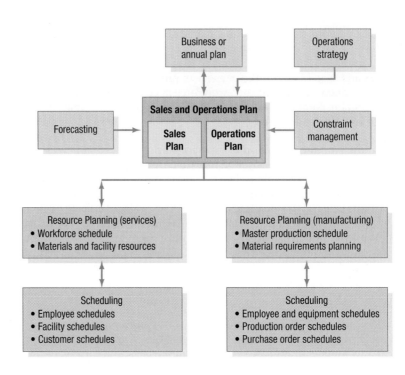

It presents the number and types of employees needed to meet the objectives of the business or annual plan.

Based on the sales and operations plan for a service provider, the next planning level is *resource planning* to determine the firm's workforce schedules and other resource requirements, such as materials and facilities, on a more detailed level. The *workforce schedule* details the specific work schedule for each category of employee. For example, a sales and operations plan might allocate 10 police officers for the day shift in a particular district; the workforce schedule might assign 5 of them to work Monday through Friday and the other 5 to work Wednesday through Sunday to meet the varying daily needs for police protection in that district. The lowest planning level is *scheduling*, which puts together day-to-day schedules for individual employees and customers.

For manufacturing firms in the value chain, top management sets the company's strategic objectives for at least the next year in the business plan. It provides the overall framework, along with inputs coming from operations strategy, forecasting, and capacity constraint management. The sales and operations plan specifies product family production rates, inventory levels, and workforce levels. The next planning level beneath the sales and operations plan is resource planning, which gets specific as to individual products within each product family, purchased materials, and resources on a detailed level. The *master production schedule* specifies the timing and size of production quantities for each product in the product families. The *material requirements planning* process then derives plans for components, purchased materials, and workstations. As with service providers, the lowest and most detailed planning level is scheduling. It puts together day-to-day schedules or priorities for employees, equipment, and production or purchase orders. Thus, the sales and operations plan plays a key role in translating the strategies of the business plan into an operational plan for the manufacturing process.

As the arrows in Figure 14.1 indicate, information flows in two directions: from the top down (broad to detailed) and from the bottom up (detailed to broad). If a sales and operations plan cannot be developed to satisfy the objectives of the business or annual plan with the existing resources, the business or annual plan might need some adjustment. Similarly, if a feasible master production schedule or workforce schedule cannot be developed, the sales and operations plan might need some adjustment. The planning process is dynamic, with periodic plan revisions or adjustments based on two-way information flows, typically on a monthly basis.

> THE DECISION CONTEXT <

Developing sales and operations plans means making decisions. In this section, we concentrate on the information inputs, objectives, alternatives, and strategies that go into these decisions.

INFORMATION INPUTS

Just as it is needed to forecast the demand side, consensus is needed among the firm's departments when decisions for the supply side are made. Information inputs are sought to create a plan that works for all. Figure 14.1 shows the key inputs: the business or annual plan, operations strategy, capacity constraints, and the demand forecast. Figure 14.2 goes further by listing inputs from each functional area. They must be accounted for to make sure that the plan is a good one and also doable. Such coordination helps synchronize the flow of services, materials, and information through the value chain to best balance supply with customer demand.

TYPICAL OBJECTIVES

The many functional areas in an organization that give input to the sales and operations plan typically have different objectives for the use of the organization's resources. Six objectives usually are considered during development of a plan:

1. *Minimize Costs/Maximize Profits.* If customer demand is not affected by the plan, minimizing costs will also maximize profits.
2. *Maximize Customer Service.* Improving delivery time and on-time delivery may require additional workforce, machine capacity, or inventory resources.
3. *Minimize Inventory Investment.* Inventory accumulations are expensive because the money could be used for more productive investments.
4. *Minimize Changes in Production Rates.* Frequent changes in production rates can cause difficulties in coordinating the supply of materials and require production line rebalancing.
5. *Minimize Changes in Workforce Levels.* Fluctuating workforce levels may cause lower productivity because new employees typically need time to become fully productive.
6. *Maximize Utilization of Plant and Equipment.* Capital-intensive line processes require uniformly high utilization of plant and equipment.

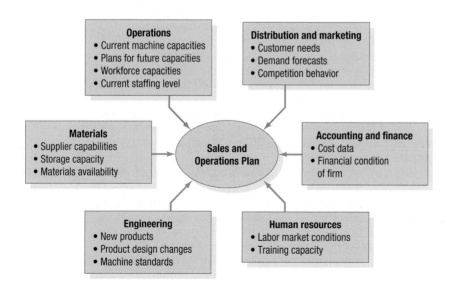

FIGURE 14.2

Managerial Inputs from Functional Areas to Sales and Operations Plans

Balancing these various objectives to arrive at an acceptable sales and operations plan involves consideration of various alternatives. The two basic types of alternatives are (1) reactive and (2) aggressive. Reactive alternatives are actions that respond to given demand patterns, whereas aggressive alternatives are actions that attempt to modify demand patterns and, consequently, resource requirements.

REACTIVE ALTERNATIVES

reactive alternatives

Actions that can be taken to cope with demand requirements.

Reactive alternatives are actions that can be taken to cope with demand requirements. Typically, an operations manager controls reactive alternatives. That is, the operations manager accepts forecasted demand as a given and modifies workforce levels, overtime, vacation schedules, inventory levels, subcontracting, and planned backlogs to meet that demand.

anticipation inventory

Inventory that can be used to absorb uneven rates of demand or supply.

Anticipation Inventory **Anticipation inventory** can be used to absorb uneven rates of demand or supply. For example, a plant facing seasonal demand can stock anticipation inventory during light demand periods and use it during heavy demand periods. Manufacturers of air conditioners, such as Whirlpool, can experience 90 percent of their annual demand during just three months of a year. Smoothing output rates with inventory can increase productivity because workforce adjustments can be costly. Extra, or *anticipation inventory*, also can help when supply, rather than demand, is uneven. For example, a company can stock up on a certain purchased item if the company's suppliers expect severe capacity limitations. Despite its advantages, anticipation inventory can be costly to hold, particularly if stocked in its finished state. Moreover, when services or products are customized, anticipation inventory is not usually an option. A product cannot be produced to inventory if its specifications are unknown or if customers are unlikely to want what has been produced in advance because it does not meet their exact requirements.

Service providers in the value chain generally cannot use anticipation inventory because services cannot be stocked. In some instances, however, services can be performed prior to actual need. For example, telephone company workers usually lay cables for service to a new subdivision before housing construction begins. They can do this work during a period when the workload for scheduled services is low.

Workforce Adjustment Management can adjust workforce levels by hiring or laying off employees. The use of this alternative can be attractive if the workforce is largely unskilled or semiskilled and the labor pool is large. These conditions are more likely found in some countries than in others. However, for a particular company, the size of the qualified labor pool may limit the number of new employees that can be hired at any one time. Also, new employees must be trained, and the capacity of the training facilities themselves might limit the number of new hires at any one time. In some industries, laying off employees is difficult or unusual for contractual reasons (unions); in other industries, such as tourism and agriculture, seasonal layoffs and hirings are the norm.

overtime

The time that employees work that is longer than the regular workday or workweek, for which they receive additional pay.

Workforce Utilization An alternative to a workforce adjustment is a change in workforce utilization involving overtime and undertime. **Overtime** means that employees work longer than the regular workday or workweek and receive additional pay for the extra hours. It can be used to satisfy output requirements that cannot be completed on regular time. However, overtime is expensive (typically 150 percent of the regular-time pay rate). Moreover, workers often do not want to work a lot of overtime for an extended period of time, and excessive overtime may result in declining quality and productivity.

undertime

The situation that occurs when employees do not have enough work for the regular-time workday or workweek.

Undertime means that employees do not have enough work for the regular-time workday or workweek. For example, they cannot be fully utilized for eight hours per day or for five days per week. Undertime occurs when labor capacity exceeds demand requirements (net of anticipation inventory), and this excess capacity cannot or should not be used productively to build up inventory or to satisfy customer orders earlier than the delivery dates already promised.

Undertime can either be paid or unpaid. An example of *unpaid undertime* is when part-time employees are paid only for the hours or days worked. Perhaps they only work during the peak times of the day or peak days of the week. Sometimes, part-time arrangements provide predictable work schedules, such as the same hours each day for five consecutive days each week. At other times, such as with stockpickers at some warehouse operations, worker schedules are unpredictable and depend on customer shipments expected for the next day. If the workload is light, some workers are not called in to work. Such arrangements are more common in low-skill positions or when the supply of workers seeking such an arrangement is sufficient. Although unpaid undertime may minimize costs, the firm must balance cost considerations against the ethical issues of being a good employer.

An example of *paid undertime* is when employees are kept on the payroll rather than being laid off. In this scenario, employees work a full day and receive their full salary but are not as busy because of the light workload. Some companies use paid undertime (though they do not call it that) during slack periods, particularly with highly skilled, hard-to-replace employees or when there are obstacles to laying off workers. The disadvantages of paid undertime include the cost of paying for work not performed and lowered productivity.

Vacation Schedules A manufacturer can shut down during an annual lull in sales, leaving a skeleton crew to cover operations and perform maintenance. Hospital employees might be encouraged to take all or part of their allowed vacation time during slack periods. The use of this alternative depends on whether the employer can mandate the vacation schedules of its employees. In any case, employees may be strongly discouraged from taking vacations during peak periods or encouraged to take vacations during slack periods.

Subcontractors Subcontractors can be used to overcome short-term capacity shortages, such as during peaks of the season or business cycle. Subcontractors can supply services, make components and subassemblies, or even assemble an entire product. If the subcontractor can supply components or services of equal or better quality less expensively than the company can produce them itself, these arrangements may become permanent.

Backlogs, Backorders, and Stockouts Firms in the value chain that maintain a backlog of orders as a normal business practice can allow the backlog to grow during periods of high demand and then reduce it during periods of low demand. A **backlog** is an accumulation of customer orders that have been promised for delivery at some future date. Firms that use backlogs do not promise instantaneous delivery, as do wholesalers or retailers farther forward in the value chain. Instead, they impose a lead time between when the order is placed and when it is delivered. Firms that are most likely to use backlogs—and increase the size of them during periods of heavy demand—make customized products and provide customized services. They tend to have a make-to-order or customized services strategy. Examples include aircraft manufacturers (such as Boeing and Airbus), dental offices, TV repair shops, and automobile repair shops. Backlogs reduce the uncertainty of future production requirements and also can be used to level these requirements. However, they become a competitive disadvantage if they get too big. Delivery speed often is an important competitive priority, but large backlogs mean long delivery times.

Service providers that offer standardized services with little customer contact and manufacturers with a make-to-stock strategy are expected to provide immediate delivery. For them, poor customer service during peak demand periods takes the form of backorders and stockouts rather than large backlogs. A **backorder** is a customer order that cannot be filled immediately but is filled as soon as possible. Although the customer is not pleased with the delay, the customer order is not lost and it is filled at a later date. For example, a customer may go to a store expecting to buy a certain type of watch that is temporarily out of stock. The retailer promises to place a replenishment order as soon as possible, and to call the customer as soon as it arrives.

A **stockout** is much the same, except that the order is lost and the customer goes elsewhere. A backorder adds to the next period's requirement, whereas a stockout does not increase future requirements. Backorders and stockouts can lead dissatisfied customers to do their future business with another firm. Generally, backorders and stockouts are to be avoided.

In conclusion, decisions about the use of each alternative for each period of the planning horizon specify the output rate for each period. In other words, the output rate is a function of the choices among these alternatives.

AGGRESSIVE ALTERNATIVES

Coping with seasonal or volatile demand by using reactive alternatives can be costly. Another approach is to attempt to change demand patterns to achieve efficiency and reduce costs. **Aggressive alternatives** are actions that attempt to modify demand and, consequently, resource requirements. Typically, marketing managers are responsible for specifying these actions in the marketing plan.

Complementary Products One way a company can even out the load on resources is to produce **complementary products** or services that have similar resource requirements but

backlog
An accumulation of customer orders that have been promised for delivery at some future date.

backorder
A customer order that cannot be filled immediately but is filled as soon as possible.

stockout
An order that is lost and causes the customer to go elsewhere.

aggressive alternatives
Actions that attempt to modify demand and, consequently, resource requirements.

complementary products
Services or products that have similar resource requirements but different demand cycles.

different demand cycles. For example, manufacturers of matzoh balls for the Jewish Passover holiday are in a seasonal business. The B. Manischewitz Company, a kosher foods manufacturer in Jersey City, previously experienced 40 percent of its annual sales for the 8-day Passover alone. It expanded toward markets with year-round appeal such as low-carb, low-fat foods, including canned soups and crackers, borscht, cake mixes, dressing and spreads, juices, and condiments. For service providers, a city parks and recreation department can counterbalance seasonal staffing requirements for summer activities by offering ice skating, tobogganing, or indoor activities during the winter months. The key is to find services and products that can be produced with the existing resources and can level off the need for resources over the year.

Creative Pricing Promotional campaigns are designed to increase sales with creative pricing. Examples include automobile rebate programs, price reductions for winter clothing in the late summer months, reduced prices on airline tickets for travel during off-peak periods, and "two for the price of one" automobile tire sales.

PLANNING STRATEGIES

Managers can combine reactive and aggressive alternatives in various ways. For the remainder of this chapter, let us assume that the expected results of the aggressive alternatives are already incorporated into the demand forecasts. Here we focus on reactive alternatives that define output rates and workforce levels. Three different strategies are useful starting points in searching for the best plan.

chase strategy

A strategy that involves hiring and laying off employees to match the demand forecast.

1. *Chase Strategy.* The **chase strategy** involves hiring and laying off employees to match the demand forecast over the planning horizon. Varying the workforce's regular-time capacity to equate supply to demand requires no inventory investment, overtime, or undertime. The drawbacks are the expense of continually adjusting workforce levels, the potential alienation of the workforce, and the loss of productivity and quality because of constant changes in the workforce.

level-utilization strategy

A strategy that keeps the workforce constant, but varies its utilization to match the demand forecast.

2. *Level-Utilization Strategy.* The **level-utilization strategy** involves keeping the workforce constant (except possibly at the beginning of the planning horizon) but varying its utilization to match the demand forecast via overtime, undertime (paid or unpaid), and vacation planning (i.e., paid vacations when demand is low). A constant workforce can be sized at many levels: managers can choose to maintain a large workforce so as to minimize the planned use of overtime during peak periods (which, unfortunately, also maximizes the need for undertime during slack periods). Alternately, they can choose to maintain a smaller workforce and rely heavily on overtime during the peak periods (which places a strain on the workforce and endangers quality).

level-inventory strategy

A strategy that relies on anticipation inventories, backorders, and stockouts to keep both the output rate and the workforce constant.

3. *Level-Inventory Strategy.* A **level-inventory strategy** keeps both the output rate and the workforce constant (except possibly at the beginning of the planning horizon). Demand variability is handled with anticipation inventory, backorders, and stockouts. Anticipation inventories are built up in the slack periods to cover peak demand. If inventories do not suffice, the shortfall is covered with backorders and stockouts. Once again, the constant workforce can be sized at many levels.

mixed strategy

A strategy that considers and implements a fuller range of reactive alternatives than any one "pure" strategy.

A sole strategy used alone is unlikely to produce the best acceptable sales and operations plan. Neither the workforce nor the output rate can be kept exactly level, and supply will not exactly match forecasted demand on a period-by-period basis. Anticipation inventories can be built up, but not to the fullest extent. The best strategy, therefore, usually is a **mixed strategy** that considers and implements a fuller range of reactive alternatives than any one "pure" strategy. For example, some effective plans make use of subcontracting, including temporary help during the peak season. Managerial Practice 14.1 describes using still another option—Hallmark keeps its workforce stable while using worker flexibility to avoid undertime.

RELEVANT CONSTRAINTS AND COSTS

An acceptable sales and operations plan must recognize relevant constraints or costs. Constraints can be either physical limitations or related to managerial policies. Examples of physical constraints might include training facilities capable of handling only so many new hires at a time, machine capacities that limit maximum output, or inadequate inventory storage space. Policy constraints might include limitations on the number of backorders or

Hallmark

Hallmark, with annual revenues of $4.4 billion and 18,000 full-time employees in 2004, spends considerable resources to effectively produce and distribute more than 40,000 different products such as greeting cards, flowers, gifts, and keepsake ornaments through 43,000 retail outlets in the United States alone. It made significant gains in efficiency—all without imposing layoffs. Hallmark has never used layoffs to adjust production rates of greeting cards, even though the business is highly competitive, exhibits little growth, and is seasonal. For instance, more people celebrate birthdays during the third quarter months of July, August, and September than any other time of year. Employee flexibility is the key to this strategy. The company's four plants produce millions of cards each day, along with gift wrapping paper and other party goods. Even though technology in the industry makes production processes increasingly more labor efficient, Hallmark follows a philosophy of retraining its employees continually to make them more flexible. For example, a cutting machine operator might also be a custom card imprinter, a painter, or a modular office assembler as needed. To keep workers busy, Hallmark shifts production from its Kansas City plant to branch plants in Topeka, Leavenworth, and Lawrence, Kansas, to keep those plants fully utilized. It uses the Kansas City plant as its "swing facility." When demand is down, Kansas City employees may take jobs in clerical positions, all at factory pay rates. They might also be in classrooms learning new skills.

According to former CEO Irvine O. Hockaday, Hallmark must protect its employees from cyclical markets and other unexpected happenings beyond their control. The added job security, however, carries the expectation that employees' performance will be commensurate with their compensation package. This philosophy pays off. For example, reducing setup times to support short production runs is crucial to keeping inventories and costs low. Employees suggest ways to significantly cut setup times. A stable workforce policy is a major factor in allowing Hallmark to become the market leader and capture some 57 percent of the $8 billion domestic card market.

Lincoln Electric

Lincoln Electric, a welding equipment manufacturer founded in Cleveland, Ohio, in 1895, offered guaranteed employment to those with three or more years of service since the 1950s. Lincoln cross-trains employees so that they can be moved to different positions and areas as needed. Although a

Even though Hallmark's business is seasonal, the company has never laid off employees. Instead the company's employees are trained to do different jobs at different times, and at different plants, if need be. Because they know they have greater job security, they work hard to keep setup times short and Hallmark's costs low.

no-layoff policy seems to be the exception rather than the rule in corporate America, executives at no-layoff companies, such as Hallmark and Southwest Airlines, argue that maintaining their ranks even in terrible times breeds fierce loyalty, higher productivity, and the innovation needed to enable their companies to snap back once the economy recovers. In addition, companies that avoid downsizing also tend to have a recruiting edge over companies that routinely lay off employees, and they provide a higher rate of return to their shareholders over time. On the other hand, when companies choose to implement massive layoffs, the results can backfire. When severance and rehiring costs, potential lawsuits from aggrieved workers, lack of staffers when the economy rebounds, and distrust in management are all taken into account, the benefits of downsizing seem to disappear.

Sources: "Loyal to a Fault," *Forbes* (March 14, 1994), pp. 58–60; Stephanie Armour, "Some Companies Choose No-Layoff Policy," *USA Today* (December 17, 2001), p. 1B; Michelle Conlin, "Where Layoffs Are a Last Resort," *Business Week* (October 8, 2001), p. 42; Elizabeth Smith Barnes, "No Layoff Policy," *Workforce* (July 2003), pp. 96–99; www.hallmark.com, July 2005.

the use of subcontractors or overtime, as well as the minimum inventory levels needed to achieve desired safety stocks.

Typically, many plans can contain a number of constraints. The planner usually considers several types of costs when preparing sales and operations plans:

1. *Regular-Time Costs.* These costs include regular-time wages paid to employees plus contributions to benefits, such as health insurance, dental care, Social Security, retirement funds, and pay for vacations, holidays, and certain other types of absences.

Overtime and subcontracting (using part-time employees) are two reactive alternatives used extensively in the health industry to keep costs in check. However, excessive use of these alternatives is opposed by nurses. Here, registered nurses hold a poster during a news conference at the state house in Boston, where a survey was released saying nurse-staffing levels in hospitals across the state is threatening proper patient care. Similar protests have occurred recently in other states, such as California, Hawaii, Minnesota, Ohio, and Pennsylvania.

2. *Overtime Costs.* Overtime wages typically are 150 percent of regular-time wages, exclusive of fringe benefits. Some companies offer a 200 percent rate for working overtime on Sundays and holidays.

3. *Hiring and Layoff Costs.* Hiring costs include the costs of advertising jobs, interviews, training programs for new employees, scrap caused by the inexperience of new employees, loss of productivity, and initial paperwork. Layoff costs include the costs of exit interviews, severance pay, retraining remaining workers and managers, and lost productivity.

4. *Inventory Holding Costs.* Inventory holding costs include costs that vary with the *level* of inventory investment: the costs of capital tied up in inventory, variable storage and warehousing costs, pilferage and obsolescence costs, insurance costs, and taxes.

5. *Backorder and Stockout Costs.* As discussed earlier, the use of backorders and stockouts can lead to additional costs to expedite past-due orders, the costs of lost sales, and the potential cost of losing a customer to a competitor (sometimes called loss of goodwill).

> SALES AND OPERATIONS PLANNING AS A PROCESS <

Sales and operations planning is a decision-making process, involving both planners and management. It is dynamic and continuing, as aspects of the plan are updated periodically when new information becomes available and new opportunities emerge. It is a cross-functional process that seeks a set of plans that all of a firm's functions can support. For each product family, decisions are made based on cost trade-offs, recent history, recommendations by planners and middle management, and the executive team's judgment.

Figure 14.3 shows a typical plan for a manufacturer. The plan is for one of the manufacturer's make-to-stock product families expressed in aggregate units. This simple spreadsheet shows the interplay between demand and supply. The history on the left for January through March shows how forecasts are tracking actual sales, and how well actual production conforms to the plan. The inventory projections are of particular interest to finance because they significantly affect the manufacturer's cash requirements. The last two columns on the top right show how current fiscal year sales projections match up with the current business plan.

This particular plan is projected out for 18 months, beginning with April. The forecast, operations, and inventory sections for the first six months are shown on a month-by-month basis. They then are shown on a quarterly basis for the second six months. Finally the totals for the last six months in the time horizon are given in just one column. This display gives more precision to the short term and yet gives coverage well into the future—all with a limited number of columns.

Artic Air Company—April 2006 Sales and Operations Plan

FIGURE **14.3**

Sales and Operations Plan
for Make-to-Stock Product Family

Source: Thomas F. Wallace, *Sales &
Operations Planning: The How-To
Handbook*, 2d ed. (Cincinnati, OH: T. E.
Wallace & Company, 2004).

Family: Medium window units (make-to-stock)   *Unit of measure:* 100 units

SALES	HISTORY J	F	M	A*	M	J	J	A	S	3rd 3 Mos**	4th 3 Mos	Mos 13–18	Fiscal Year Projection ($000)	Business Plan ($000)
New forecast	45	55	60	70	85	95	130	110	70	150	176	275	$8,700	$8,560
Actual sales	52	40	63											
Diff for month	7	–15	3											
Cum		–8	–5											
OPERATIONS														
New Plan	75	75	75	75	75	85	85	85	75	177	225			
Actual	75	78	76											
Diff for month	0	3	1											
Cum		3	4											
INVENTORY														
Plan	85	105	120	125	115	105	60	35	40	198	321			
Actual	92	130	143											

DEMAND ISSUES AND ASSUMPTIONS
1. New product design to be launched in January 2007.

SUPPLY ISSUES
1. Vacations primarily in November and December.
2. Overtime in July–August.

* April is the first month of the planning horizon for this current plan. When next month's plan is developed, its first month in the planning
horizon will be May, and the most recent month of the history will be April (with January no longer shown in the history).

** This column provides the sales, operations, and inventory totals for October through December. For example, the forecast of 150 units
translates into an average of 50 units per month (or 150/3 = 50).

This particular make-to-stock family experiences highly seasonal demand. The operations plan is to build up seasonal inventory in the slack season, schedule vacations as much as possible in November and December, and use overtime in the peak season of June, July, and August. Plan spreadsheets use different formats depending on production and inventory strategy. For an assemble-to-order strategy, the inventory does not consist of finished goods. Instead, it is inventory of standardized components and subassemblies built for the finishing and assembly operations. For the make-to-order strategy, the inventory section in the plan of Figure 14.3 is replaced by a section showing the planned and actual order backlog quantities.

Plans for service providers are quite different. For one thing, their plan does not contain an inventory section, but focuses instead on the demand and supply of human resources. Forecasts are typically expressed in terms of employees required, with separate rows for regular time, overtime, vacations, part-time workers, and so on. Different departments or worker classifications replace product families.

The process itself, typically done on a monthly basis, consists of six basic steps. They are much like the steps we discussed in Chapter 13, "Forecasting."

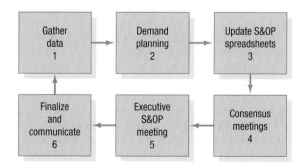

Step 1: Begin to "roll forward" the plan for the new planning horizon. Start preliminary work right after the month's end. Update files with actual sales, production, inventory, costs, and constraints.

Step 2: Participate in the forecasting and demand planning to create the authorized demand forecasts. For service providers, the forecasts are staff requirements for each workforce group. For example, a director of nursing in a hospital can develop a workload index for a nursing staff and translate a projection of the month-to-month patient load into an equivalent total amount of nursing care time—and thus the number of nurses—required for each month of the year.

Step 3: Update the sales and operations planning spreadsheet for each family, recognizing relevant constraints and costs including availability of materials from suppliers, training facilities capable of handling only so many new hires at a time, machine capacities, or limited storage space. Policy constraints might include limitations on the number of backorders, or the use of subcontractors or overtime, as well as the minimum inventory levels needed to achieve desired safety stocks. Typically, many plans can satisfy a specific set of constraints. The planner searches for a plan that best balances costs, customer service, workforce stability, and the like. This process may necessitate revising the plan several times.

Step 4: Have one or more consensus meetings with the stakeholders on how best to balance supply with demand. Participants could include the supply chain manager, plant manager, controller, purchasing manager, production control manager, or logistics manager. The goal is one set of recommendations to present at the firm's executive sales and operations planning (S&OP) meeting. Where agreement cannot be reached, prepare scenarios of alternative plans. Also prepare an updated financial view of business by rolling up the plans for all product families into a spreadsheet expressed in total dollars.

Step 5: Present recommendations by product family at the executive S&OP meeting, which typically includes the firm's president and the vice presidents of functional areas. The plan is reviewed relative to the business plan, new product issues, special projects, and other relevant factors. The executives may ask for final changes to the plan, such as to balance conflicting objectives better. Acceptance of this authorized plan does not necessarily mean that everyone is in total agreement, but it does imply that everyone will work to achieve the plan.

Step 6: Update the spreadsheets to reflect the authorized plan, and communicate the plans to the important stakeholders for implementation. Important recipients include those who do resource planning, covered in the next chapter.

> DECISION SUPPORT TOOLS <

The sales and operations plan in Figure 14.3 does not show much on the reactive alternatives used in the operations plan or their cost implications. Here we discuss two decision support tools that do just that: spreadsheets and the transportation method. Both techniques could be used on the side as a planner develops prospective plans in step 3 of the planning process.

SPREADSHEETS

Various spreadsheets can be used, including ones that you develop on your own. Here we work with the *Sales and Operations Planning with Spreadsheets* solver in OM Explorer. Figure 14.4 shows a plan for a manufacturer, which uses all reactive alternatives except overtime.

Spreadsheets for a Manufacturer The top part of the spreadsheet (in yellow) shows the *input values* that give the forecasted demand requirements and the reactive alternative choices period by period. Vary these "levers" as you search for better plans.

The next part of the spreadsheet (in green) shows the *derived values* that must follow from the input values. The first row of derived values is called *utilized time,* which is that portion of the workforce's regular time that is paid for and productively used. In any period, the utilized time equals the workforce level minus undertime and vacation time. For example, in period 1 the utilized time is 94 (or 120 − 6 − 20). The hires and layoffs rows can be derived from the workforce levels. In this example, the workforce is increased for period 2 from its initial size of 120 employees to 158, which means that 38 employees are hired. Because the workforce size remains constant throughout the planning horizon, no other hirings or layoffs happen. Sometimes overtime and undertime can be derived directly from the first two rows of input values. When a period's workforce level exceeds the forecasted demand, overtime is zero and undertime equals the difference. When a period's workforce level is less than the forecasted demand, undertime is zero, and overtime equals the difference. For the general case, when additional alternatives such as vacations, inventory, and backorders are all

MANAGERIAL CHALLENGE

SALES AND OPERATIONS PLANNING AT STARWOOD

DVD Business travel often means staying overnight in a hotel. Upon arrival, you may be greeted by a doorman or valet to assist you with your luggage. Front desk staff awaits your check-in. Behind the scenes, housekeeping, maintenance, and culinary staff prepare for your stay. Making a reservation gives the hotel notice of your plan to stay, but even before your trip is ever conceived, the hotel is staffed and ready. How? Through a process called *sales and operations planning.*

Sales and operations planning is a process every organization performs to some degree. Called a staffing plan (or service resource plan if more detailed) in service organizations, the plan must strike the right level of customer service while maintaining workforce stability and cost control so as to achieve the organization's profit expectations. So where do companies begin? Let's take a look at Starwood Hotels and Resorts to see how it's done.

Starwood operates more than 750 locations around the globe. At the highest levels, Starwood engages in sales and operations planning on an annual basis, with adjustments made as needed each month by region and by property. Budgeted revenues and other projections come from headquarters; the regions and individual properties then break down the forecasts to meet their expected occupancies. Typically, the director of human resources determines the staffing mix needed across divisions such as food and beverage service, rooms (including housekeeping, spa, guest services), engineering, Six Sigma, revenue management, and accounting.

At the property level, general managers and their staff must provide input into next year's plan while implementing and monitoring activity in the current year. For most properties, payroll is close to 40 percent of budgeted revenues, and represents the largest single expense the hotel incurs. It is also the most controllable. Many of the hotels and most resorts experience patterns of seasonality that affect demand for rooms and services. This seasonality, in turn, significantly affects the organization's staffing plan.

To determine the staffing levels, the company uses a proprietary software program that models occupancy demand based on historical data. The key drivers of staffing are occupied rooms and restaurant meals, called "covers." Starwood knows on a *per room* and *per cover* basis how many staff are required to function properly. When occupancy and covers are entered into the software program, the output models a recommended staffing level for each division. This recommendation is then reviewed by division managers and adjusted, as needed, to be sure staffing is in line with budgeted financial plans. Job fairs to recruit nonmanagement staff are held several times a year so a qualified candidate pool of both part-time and full-time staff is ready when needed. Most hotels maintain a pool of part-time workers who can contract or expand the hours worked if property guest levels require it. Vacations for management are scheduled for low season. Overtime will be worked as needed, but is less desirable than scheduling the appropriate level of staff in each division.

The program also takes into account both the complexity and positioning of the property within Starwood. For example, a 400-room city hotel that is essentially a high-rise building is not as complex as a 400-room sprawling resort with golf, spa, convention, and other services the city hotel doesn't offer. Positioning also is important. A five-star resort hotel's customer service expectations are much greater than a three-star airport hotel location and will require much higher ratios of staff to guests. Finally, if the

A software program that models occupancy based on historical data helps Starwood maintain proper staffing levels at its hotels. Managers know on a per-room, or "per cover," basis how many hotel employees should be scheduled so customers get good service.

hotel is a brand new property, historical data from similar properties will be used to model staffing for the first year or two of operation.

Starwood attempts to modify demand and smooth out the peaks and valleys of its demand patterns. Many of the company's hotels experience three seasons: high, mid (called "shoulder"), and low season. Starwood, like its competitors, offers special rates, family packages, and weekend specials to attract different segments of the market during slower business periods. Staff will be cross-trained to work in multiple areas, such as front reception and the concierge desk, so additional staff does not have to be added across seasons. Employees may also be temporarily redeployed among Starwood's properties to help out during peak periods. For example, when occupancy is forecast to be high in one region of the country, staff from areas entering their low season will be assigned to cover the demand.

Questions

1. At what points in the planning process would you expect accounting/finance, marketing, information systems, and operations to play a role? What inputs should these areas provide, and why?

2. Does Starwood employ a chase, level-utilization, level-inventory, or mixed strategy? Why is this approach the best choice for the company?

3. How would staffing for the opening of a new hotel or resort differ from that of an existing property? What data might Starwood rely upon to make sure the new property is not over- or understaffed in its first year of operation?

FIGURE 14.4

Manufacturer's Plan Using a
Spreadsheet and Mixed Strategy

	1	2	3	4	5	6	Total
Inputs							
Forecasted demand	24	142	220	180	136	168	870
Workforce level	120	158	158	158	158	158	910
Undertime	6	0	0	0	0	0	6
Overtime	0	0	0	0	0	0	0
Vacation time	20	6	0	0	4	10	40
Subcontracting time	0	0	0	0	0	6	6
Backorders	0	0	0	4	0	0	4
Derived							
Utilized time	94	152	158	158	154	148	864
Inventory	70	80	18	0	14	0	182
Hires	0	38	0	0	0	0	38
Layoffs	0	0	0	0	0	0	0
Calculated							
Utilized time cost	$376,000	$608,000	$632,000	$632,000	$616,000	$592,000	$3,456,000
Undertime cost	$24,000	$0	$0	$0	$0	$0	$24,000
Overtime cost	$0	$0	$0	$0	$0	$0	$0
Vacation time cost	$80,000	$24,000	$0	$0	$16,000	$40,000	$160,000
Inventory cost	$2,800	$3,200	$720	$0	$560	$0	$7,280
Backorders cost	$0	$0	$0	$4,000	$0	$0	$4,000
Hiring cost	$0	$91,200	$0	$0	$0	$0	$91,200
Layoff cost	$0	$0	$0	$0	$0	$0	$0
Subcontracting cost	$0	$0	$0	$0	$0	$43,200	$43,200
Total cost	$482,800	726,400	632,720	636,000	632,560	675,200	$3,785,680

possible, the overtime and undertime cannot be derived just from information on forecasted demand and workforce levels. Thus, undertime and overtime are shown as input values (rather than derived values) in the spreadsheet, and the user must be careful to specify consistent input values.

The final part of the spreadsheet, the *calculated values* of the plan, shows the plan's cost consequences. Along with qualitative considerations, the cost of each plan determines whether the plan is satisfactory or whether a revised plan should be considered. When seeking clues about how to improve a plan already evaluated, we identify its highest cost elements. Revisions that would reduce these specific costs might produce a new plan with lower overall costs. Spreadsheet programs make analyzing these plans easy, and they present a whole new set of possibilities for developing sound sales and operations plans.

The plan in Figure 14.4 definitely is for a manufacturer because it uses inventory to its advantage, particularly in the first two periods. Clearly it is a mixed strategy. The workforce level changes in period 2, but it does not exactly match the forecasted demand as with a chase strategy. It has some elements of the level-utilization strategy, because undertime and vacation time are part of the plan, but it does not rely exclusively on this strategy. Finally, it has some elements of the level-inventory strategy in that inventory and backorders are used, but the workforce is not level. Finally, some use of subcontracting also puts the plan in the category of a mixed strategy.

Care must be taken to recognize differences in how inputs are measured. The workforce level might be expressed as the number of employees, but the forecasted demand and inventory are expressed as units of the product. The OM Explorer spreadsheets require a common unit of measure, so we must translate some of the data prior to entering the input values. Perhaps the easiest approach is to express the forecasted demand and reactive alternatives as *employee-period equivalents*. If demand forecasts are given as units of product, we can convert them to employee-period equivalents by dividing them by the productivity of a worker. For example, if the demand is for 1,500 units of product and the average employee produces 100 units in one period, the demand requirement is 15 employee-period equivalents.

Spreadsheets for a Service Provider The same spreadsheets can be used by service providers, except anticipation inventory is not an option. Whereas Figure 14.4 shows a good plan found after several revisions, here we illustrate with Example 14.1 how to find a good plan for a service provider beginning with two pure strategies: the chase and level-utilization strategies. These approaches can provide insights that lead to even better mixed strategy plans.

		EXAMPLE 14.1
Using the Chase and Level-Utilization Strategies as Starting Points		

The manager of a large distribution center must determine how many part-time stockpickers to maintain on the payroll. She wants to develop a staffing plan that minimizes total costs, and wants to begin with the chase strategy and level-utilization strategy. For the level-utilization strategy, she wants to first try the workforce level that meets demand with the minimum use of undertime.

First, the manager divides the next year into six time periods, each one two months long. Each part-time employee can work a maximum of 20 hours per week on regular time, but the actual number can be less. Instead of paying undertime, each worker's day is shortened during slack periods. Once on the payroll, each worker is used each day, but they may work only a few hours. Overtime can be used during peak periods.

The distribution center's forecasted demand is shown as the number of part-time employees required for each time period at the maximum regular time of 20 hours per week. For example, in period 3, an estimated 18 part-time employees working 20 hours per week on regular time will be needed.

ACTIVE MODEL 14.1

Active Model 14.1 on the Student CD-ROM shows the impact of changing the workforce level, the cost structure, and overtime capacity.

	Time Period						
	1	**2**	**3**	**4**	**5**	**6**	**Total**
Forecasted demand*	6	12	18	15	13	14	78

*Number of part-time employees.

Currently, 10 part-time clerks are employed. They have not been subtracted from the forecasted demand shown. Constraints and cost information are as follows:

a. The size of training facilities limits the number of new hires in any period to no more than 10.

b. No backorders are permitted; demand must be met each period.

c. Overtime cannot exceed 20 percent of the regular-time capacity (that is, 4 hours) in any period. Therefore, the most that any part-time employee can work is 1.20(20) = 24 hours per week.

d. The following costs can be assigned:

Regular-time wage rate	$2,000 per time period at 20 hours per week
Overtime wages	150 percent of the regular-time rate
Hires	$1,000 per person
Layoffs	$500 per person

Framed by thousands of ski poles, a part-time worker sorts and inventories new products in the receiving department of REI's Distribution Center in Sumner, Washington. REI employs a high percentage of part-time workers, many of whom are college students. They tend to be young people who participate in outdoor sports and are familiar with the equipment that REI sells.

FIGURE **14.5**

Spreadsheet for Chase Strategy

	1	2	3	4	5	6	Total
Inputs							
Forecasted demand	6	12	18	15	13	14	78
Workforce level	6	12	18	15	13	14	78
Undertime	0	0	0	0	0	0	0
Overtime	0	0	0	0	0	0	0
Derived							
Utilized time	6	12	18	15	13	14	78
Hires	0	6	6	0	0	1	13
Layoffs	4	0	0	3	2	0	9
Calculated							
Utilized time cost	$12,000	$24,000	$36,000	$30,000	$26,000	$28,000	$156,000
Undertime cost	$0	$0	$0	$0	$0	$0	$0
Hiring cost	$0	$6,000	$6,000	$0	$0	$1,000	$13,000
Layoff cost	$2,000	$0	$0	$1,500	$1,000	$0	$4,500
Total cost	$14,000	30,000	42,000	31,500	27,000	29,000	$173,500

TUTOR **14.1**

Tutor 14.1 on the Student CD-ROM provides a new example to plan using the chase strategy with hiring and layoffs.

TUTOR **14.2**

Tutor 14.2 on the Student CD-ROM provides a new example for planning using the level-utilization strategy with overtime and undertime.

SOLUTION

a. Chase Strategy

This strategy simply involves adjusting the workforce as needed to meet demand, as shown in Figure 14.5. Rows in the spreadsheet which do not apply (such as inventory and vacations) are hidden. The workforce level row is identical to the forecasted demand row. A large number of hirings and layoffs begin with laying off 4 part-time employees immediately because the current staff is 10 and the staff level required in period 1 is only 6. However, many employees, such as college students, prefer part-time work. The total cost is $173,500, and most of the cost increase comes from frequent hiring and layoffs, which add $17,500 to the cost of utilized regular-time costs.

b. Level-Utilization Strategy

In order to minimize undertime, the maximum use of overtime possible must occur in the peak period. For this particular level-utilization strategy, the most overtime that she can use is 20 percent of the regular-time capacity, w, so

$$1.20w = 18 \text{ employees required in peak period (period 3)}$$

$$w = \frac{18}{1.20} = 15 \text{ employees}$$

A 15-employee staff size minimizes the amount of undertime for this level strategy. Because the staff already includes 10 part-time employees, the manager should immediately hire 5 more. The complete plan is shown in Figure 14.6. The total cost is $164,000, which seems reasonable because the minimum con-

FIGURE **14.6**

Spreadsheet for Level-Utilization Strategy with Overtime and Minimum Undertime

	1	2	3	4	5	6	Total
Inputs							
Forecasted demand	6	12	18	15	13	14	78
Workforce level	15	15	15	15	15	15	90
Undertime	9	3	0	0	2	1	15
Overtime	0	0	3	0	0	0	3
Derived							
Utilized time	6	12	15	15	13	14	75
Hires	5	0	0	0	0	0	5
Layoffs	0	0	0	0	0	0	0
Calculated							
Utilized time cost	$12,000	$24,000	$30,000	$30,000	$26,000	$28,000	$150,000
Undertime cost	$0	$0	$0	$0	$0	$0	$0
Overtime cost	$0	$0	$9,000	$0	$0	$0	$9,000
Hiring cost	$5,000	$0	$0	$0	$0	$0	$5,000
Layoff cost	$0	$0	$0	$0	$0	$0	$0
Total cost	$17,000	24,000	39,000	30,000	26,000	28,000	$164,000

ceivable cost is only $156,000 (78 periods × $2,000/period). This cost could be achieved only if the manager found a way to cover the forecasted demand for all 78 periods with regular time. The plan seems reasonable primarily because it involves the use of large amounts of undertime (15 periods), which in this example are unpaid.

Decision Point The manager, now having a point of reference with which to compare other plans, decided to evaluate some other plans before making a final choice, beginning with the chase strategy. The only way to reduce costs is somehow to reduce the premium for 3 overtime employee periods (3 periods × $3,000/period) or to reduce the hiring cost of 5 employees (5 hires × $1,000/person). Nonetheless, better solutions may be possible. For example, undertime can be reduced by delaying the hiring until period 2 because the current workforce is sufficient until then. This delay would decrease the amount of unpaid undertime, which is a qualitative improvement. See Active Model 14.1 for additional insights.

THE TRANSPORTATION METHOD

The major advantage of the spreadsheet approach is its simplicity. However, the planner still must make many choices for each period of the planning horizon in an effort to develop the best possible plan. The cost consequences of the plan chosen are significant, and so considerable thought should go into the analysis. Several mathematical methods can help with this search process. Linear programming is particularly powerful because it can include all reactive alternatives, including hiring and layoff decision variables. To learn more about its use, see the tutorial on the Student CD-ROM.

Here we present and demonstrate the **transportation method of production planning**, a special case of linear programming. Earlier, we applied it to locating a facility within a network of facilities. The transportation method, when applied to sales and operations planning, is particularly helpful in determining anticipation inventories. Thus, it relates more to manufacturers' production plans than to service providers' staffing plans. In fact, the workforce levels for each period are inputs to the transportation method rather than outputs from it. Different workforce adjustment plans should be evaluated. Thus, several transportation method solutions may be obtained before a final plan is selected.

transportation method of production planning

The use of the transportation method to solve production planning problems, assuming that a demand forecast is available for each period, along with a possible workforce adjustment plan.

Using the transportation method for production planning is based on the assumption that a demand forecast is available for each period, along with a possible workforce adjustment plan. Capacity limits on overtime and the use of subcontractors also are needed for each period. Another assumption is that all costs are linearly related to the amount of goods produced; that is, a change in the amount of goods produced creates a proportionate change in costs.

To develop a sales and operations plan for a manufacturer, we do the following:

1. Obtain the demand forecasts for each period to be covered by the sales and operations plan and identify the initial inventory level currently available that can be used to meet future demand.

2. Select a candidate workforce adjustment plan, using a chase strategy, level-utilization strategy, level-inventory strategy, or a mixed strategy. Specify the capacity limits of each production alternative (regular time, overtime, and subcontracting) for each period covered by the plan.

3. Estimate the cost of holding inventory, and the cost of possible production alternatives (regular time production, overtime production, and subcontracting).

4. Input the information gathered in steps 1–3 into a computer routine that solves the transportation problem. After getting the solution, calculate the anticipation inventory levels and identify high-cost elements of the plan.

5. Repeat the process with other plans for regular-time, overtime, and subcontracting capacities until you find the solution that best balances cost and qualitative considerations. Even though this process involves trial and error, the transportation method yields the best mix of regular time, overtime, and subcontracting for each capacity plan.

Example 14.3 demonstrates this approach using POMS for Windows package. You may instead want to use OM Explorer's Transportation Method of Production Planning solver.

| EXAMPLE 14.2 | Preparing a Production Plan with the Transportation Method |

TUTOR OPT.2

Tutor OPT.2 on the Student CD-ROM provides another example of production planning with the transportation method.

The Tru-Rainbow Company produces a variety of paint products for both commercial and private use. The demand for paint is highly seasonal, peaking in the third quarter. Current inventory is 250,000 gallons, and ending inventory should be 300,000 gallons.

Tru-Rainbow's manufacturing manager wants to determine the best production plan, using the following demand requirements and capacity plan. Demands and capacities here are expressed in thousands of gallons (rather than employee-period equivalents). The manager knows that the regular-time cost is $1.00 per unit, overtime cost is $1.50 per unit, subcontracting cost is $1.90 per unit, and inventory holding cost is $0.30 per gallon per quarter.

	Quarter				
	1	2	3	4	Total
Demand Capacities	300	850	1,500	350	3,000
Regular time	450	450	750	450	2,100
Overtime	90	90	150	90	420
Subcontracting	200	200	200	200	800

The following constraints apply:

a. The maximum allowable overtime in any quarter is 20 percent of the regular-time capacity in that quarter.

b. The subcontractor can supply a maximum of 200,000 gallons in any quarter. Production can be subcontracted in one period and the excess held in inventory for a future period to avoid a stockout.

c. No backorders or stockouts are permitted.

SOLUTION

Figure 14.7 shows the POMS for Windows screen that displays the basic input data. It looks much like the table shown above, but with one exception. The demand for quarter 4 is shown to be 650,000 gallons rather than the demand forecast of only 350,000. The larger number reflects the desire of the manager to have an ending inventory in quarter 4 of 300,000 gallons.

Figure 14.8 shows a second screen on how the input data gets translated into a table, called a transportation tableau. It is similar to Figure 11.11 in Chapter 11, "Location," except now it is used for sales and operations planning rather than location planning.

Some points to note include the following:

1. A row for each supply alternative (instead of the "sources" or plants in Figure 11.12), on a quarter-by-quarter basis, indicates the maximum amount that can be used to meet demand. The first row is the initial inventory available, and the rows that follow are for regular-time, overtime, and subcontracting production in each of the four quarters. The initial inventory can be used to satisfy demand in any of the four quarters. The sec-

FIGURE 14.7

Input Data for Prospective
Tru-Rainbow Company
Production Plan

Period	Demand	Regular tm Capacity	Overtime Capacity	Subcontract Capacity	Unit cost	Value
Quarter 1	300	450	90	200	Regular time	1
Quarter 2	850	450	90	200	Overtime	1.5
Quarter 3	1500	750	150	200	Subcontracting	1.9
Quarter 4	650	450	90	200	Holding cost	.3
					Shortage cost	Not allowed
					Initial Inventory	250

	Quarter 1	Quarter 2	Quarter 3	Quarter 4	Capacity
Init Inventory	0	.3	.6	.9	250
Quarter 1 RegTime	1	1.3	1.6	1.9	450
Quarter 1 Overtime	1.5	1.8	2.1	2.4	90
Quarter 1 Subcntract	1.9	2.2	2.5	2.8	200
Quarter 2 RegTime	9999	1	1.3	1.6	450
Quarter 2 Overtime	9999	1.5	1.8	2.1	90
Quarter 2 Subcntract	9999	1.9	2.2	2.5	200
Quarter 3 RegTime	9999	9999	1	1.3	750
Quarter 3 Overtime	9999	9999	1.5	1.8	150
Quarter 3 Subcntract	9999	9999	1.9	2.2	200
Quarter 4 RegTime	9999	9999	9999	1	450
Quarter 4 Overtime	9999	9999	9999	1.5	90
Quarter 4 Subcntract	9999	9999	9999	1.9	200
Demand	300	850	1500	650	270

FIGURE 14.8

Transportation Tableau for
Tru-Rainbow Company

ond row (regular-time production in period 1) can also be used to satisfy demand in any of the four periods the plan will cover, and so on. The numbers in the last column give the maximum capacity made available for the supply alternatives. For example, the regular-time capacity for quarter 3 increases from the usual 450,000 gallons to 750,000 gallons, to help with the peak demand forecasted to be 1,500,000 gallons.

2. A column indicates each future quarter of demand (instead of "destinations" or warehouses in Figure 11.12). For example, the demand for the fourth quarter is 650 units, which includes the desired amount of ending inventory. The number in the last row of this capacity column (270 units) has a special meaning. It is the amount by which total capacity exceeds total demand.

3. The numbers in the other cells (excluding the cells in the last row or last column) show the cost of producing a unit in one period and, in some cases, carrying the unit in inventory for sale in a future period. These numbers correspond to the costs in the upper right corners of the cells in Figure 11.12. For example, the cost per unit of regular-time production in quarter 1 is $1.00 per gallon if it is used to meet the demand in quarter 1. This cost is found in row 2 and column 1 of the tableau. However, if it produced to meet demand in quarter 2, the cost increases to $1.30 (or $1.00 + $0.30) because we must hold the unit in inventory for one quarter. Satisfying a unit of demand in quarter 3 by producing in quarter 1 on regular time and carrying the unit for two quarters costs $1.60, or [$1.00 + (2 × $0.30)], and so on. A similar approach is used for the costs of overtime and subcontracting.

4. The cells in the bottom left portion of the tableau with a cost of $9,999 are associated with backorders (or producing in a period to satisfy in a past period). Here we disallow backorders by making the backorder cost an arbitrarily large number, in this case $9,999 per unit. If backorder costs are so large, the transportation method will try to avoid backorders because it seeks a solution that minimizes total cost. If that is not possible, we increase the staffing plan and the overtime and subcontracting capacities.

5. The least expensive alternatives are those in which the output is produced and sold in the same period. For example, the cost for quarter 2 overtime production is only $1.50 per gallon if it is designated to meet demand in quarter 2 (row 6, column 2). The cost increases to $2.10 if it is designated for quarter 4 demand. However, we may not always be able to avoid alternatives that create inventory because of capacity restrictions.

6. Finally, the per-unit holding cost for the beginning inventory in period 1 is 0 because it is a function of previous production-planning decisions.

Figure 14.9 shows the POMS for Windows screen that displays an optimal solution (this problem has more than one optimal solution) for this particular workforce adjustment plan. It is similar to Figure 11.12 in Chapter 11, "Location." For example, the first row shows that 230 units of the initial inventory are used to help satisfy the demand in quarter 1. The remaining 20 units in the first row are earmarked for helping supply the demand in quarter 3. The sum of the allocations across row 1 (230 + 0 + 20 + 0) does not exceed the maximum capacity of 250, given in the right column. With the transportation method, this result must occur with each row. Any shortfalls are unused capacity.

Similarly, the sum of the allocations down each column must equal the total demand for the quarter. For example, the demand for quarter 1 is supplied from 230 units of the initial inventory, 50 units of quarter 1 regular-time

FIGURE 14.9

Solution Screen for Prospective Tru-Rainbow Company Production Plan

Optimal cost = $4,010	Quarter 1	Quarter 2	Quarter 3	Quarter 4	Capacity
Init Inventory	230		20		250
Quarter 1 RegTime	50	400			450
Quarter 1 Overtime			90		90
Quarter 1 Subcntract	20				200
Quarter 2 RegTime		450			450
Quarter 2 Overtime			90		90
Quarter 2 Subcntract			200		200
Quarter 3 RegTime			750		750
Quarter 3 Overtime			150		150
Quarter 3 Subcntract			200		200
Quarter 4 RegTime				450	450
Quarter 4 Overtime				90	90
Quarter 4 Subcntract				110	200
Demand	300	850	1500	650	270

production, and 20 units of quarter 1 subcontracting production. Summed together, they equal the forecasted demand of 300 units.

To further interpret the solution, we can convert Figure 14.9 into the following table. For example, the total regular-time production in quarter 1 is 450,000 gallons (50,000 gallons to meet demand in quarter 1 and 400,000 gallons to help satisfy demand in quarter 2).

The anticipation inventory held at the end of each quarter is obtained in the last column. For any quarter, it is the quarter's beginning inventory plus total production (regular-time and overtime production, plus subcontracting) minus demand. For example, for quarter 1 the beginning inventory (250,000) plus the total from production and subcontracting (560,000) minus quarter 1 demand (300,000) results in an ending inventory of 510,000, which also is the beginning inventory for quarter 2.

Quarter	Regular-Time Production	Overtime Production	Subcontracting	Total Supply	Anticipation Inventory
1	450	90	20	560	250 + 560 − 300 = 510
2	450	90	200	740	510 + 740 − 850 = 400
3	750	150	200	1,100	400 + 1,100 − 1,500 = 0
4	450	90	110	650	0 + 650 − 350 = 300
Totals	2,100	420	530	3,050	

Note: Anticipation inventory is the amount at the end of each quarter, where Beginning inventory + Total production − Actual Demand = Ending inventory.

The breakdown of costs can be found by multiplying the allocation in each cell of Figure 14.9 by the cost per unit in that cell in Figure 14.8. Computing the cost column by column (it can also be down on a row-by-row basis) yields a total cost of $4,010,000, or $4,010 × 1,000.

Cost Calculations by Column		
Quarter 1	230($0) + 50($1.00) + 20($1.90)	= $ 88
Quarter 2	400($1.30) + 450($1.00)	= 970
Quarter 3	20($0.60) + 90($2.10) + 90($1.80) + 200($2.20) + 750($1.00) + 150($1.50) + 200($1.90)	= 2,158
Quarter 4	450($1.00) + 90($1.50) + 110($1.90)	= 794
		Total = $4,010

> **Decision Point** This plan requires too much overtime and subcontracting, and the anticipation inventory cost is substantial. The manager decided to search for a better capacity plan—with increases in the workforce to boost regular-time production capacity—that could lower production costs, perhaps even low enough to offset the added capacity costs.

> MANAGERIAL CONSIDERATIONS <

Mathematical models and analytical techniques can be useful in developing and evaluating sound sales and operations plans, but they are only aids to the planning process. Managers—not techniques—make the decisions. After arriving at an acceptable production plan, management must, of course, implement the plan. However, because the sales and operations plan is stated in aggregate terms, the first step in implementation, therefore, is to disaggregate the plan; that is, break the plan down into specific products, work centers, and dates. We address these processes in the next two chapters on resource planning and scheduling.

> STUDENT CD-ROM AND INTERNET RESOURCES <

The Student CD-ROM and the Companion Website at **www.prenhall.com/krajewski** contain many tools, activities, and resources designed for this chapter.

> KEY TERMS <

aggressive alternatives 573
annual plan or financial plan 569
anticipation inventory 572
backlog 573
backorder 573
business plan 569
chase strategy 574
complementary products 573

level-inventory strategy 574
level-utilization strategy 574
mixed strategy 574
overtime 572
product family 569
production plan 568
reactive alternatives 572

sales and operations planning
   (S&OP) 568
staffing plan 568
stockout 573
transportation method of production
   planning 583
undertime 572

> SOLVED PROBLEM 1 <

The Cranston Telephone Company employs workers who lay telephone cables and perform various other construction tasks. The company prides itself on good service and strives to complete all service orders within the planning period in which they are received.

Each worker puts in 600 hours of regular time per planning period and can work as much as an additional 100 hours overtime. The operations department has estimated the following workforce requirements for such services over the next four planning periods:

Planning Period	1	2	3	4
Demand (hours)	21,000	18,000	30,000	12,000

Cranston pays regular-time wages of $6,000 per employee per period for any time worked up to 600 hours (including undertime). The overtime pay rate is $15 per hour over 600 hours. Hiring, training, and outfitting a new employee costs $8,000. Layoff costs are $2,000 per employee. Currently, 40 employees work for Cranston in this capacity. No delays in service, or backorders, are allowed. Use the spreadsheet approach to answer the following questions:

a. Prepare a chase strategy using only hiring and layoffs. What are the total numbers of employees hired and laid off?

TUTOR 14.3

Tutor 14.3 on the Student CD-ROM provides another example for practicing sales and operations planning using a variety of strategies.

FIGURE 14.10

Spreadsheet for Chase Strategy

	1	2	3	4	Total
Inputs					
Forecasted demand	35	30	50	20	135
Workforce level	35	30	50	20	135
Undertime	0	0	0	0	0
Overtime	0	0	0	0	0
Derived					
Utilized time	35	30	50	20	135
Hires	0	0	20	0	20
Layoffs	5	5	0	30	40
Calculated					
Utilized time cost	$210,000	$180,000	$300,000	$120,000	$810,000
Undertime cost	$0	$0	$0	$0	$0
Overtime cost	$0	$0	$0	$0	$0
Hiring cost	$0	$0	$160,000	$0	$160,000
Layoff cost	$10,000	$10,000	$0	$60,000	$80,000
Total cost	$220,000	190,000	460,000	180,000	$1,050,000

b. Develop a workforce plan that uses the level-utilization strategy. Maximize the use of overtime during the peak period so as to minimize the workforce level and amount of undertime.

c. Propose an effective mixed-strategy plan.

d. Compare the total costs of the three plans.

SOLUTION

a. The chase strategy workforce is calculated by dividing the demand for each period by 600 hours, or the amount or regular-time work for one employee during one period. This strategy calls for a total of 20 workers to be hired and 40 to be laid off during the four-period plan. Figure 14.10 shows the "chase strategy" solution that OM Explorer's Sales and Operations Planning with Spreadsheets solver produces. We simply hide any unneeded columns and rows in this general-purpose solver.

b. The peak demand is 30,000 hours in period 3. As each employee can work 700 hours per period (600 on regular time and 100 on overtime), the level workforce of the level-utilization strategy that minimizes undertime is 30,000/700 = 42.86, or 43 employees. The level-utilization strategy calls for three employees to be hired in the first quarter and for none to be laid off. To convert the demand requirements into employee-period equivalents, divide the demand in hours by 600. For example, the demand of 21,000 hours in period 1 translates into 35 employee-period equivalents (21,000/600) and demand in the third period translates into 50 employee-period equivalents (30,000/600). Figure 14.11 shows OM Explorer's spreadsheet for this level-utilization strategy that minimizes undertime.

FIGURE 14.11

Spreadsheet for Level-Utilization Strategy

	1	2	3	4	Total
Inputs					
Forecasted demand	35	30	50	20	135
Workforce level	43	43	43	43	172
Undertime	8	13	0	13	34
Overtime	0	0	7	0	7
Derived					
Utilized time	35	30	43	30	138
Hires	3	0	0	0	3
Layoffs	0	0	0	0	0
Calculated					
Utilized time cost	$210,000	$180,000	$258,000	$180,000	$828,000
Undertime cost	$48,000	$78,000	$0	$78,000	$204,000
Overtime cost	$0	$0	$63,000	$0	$63,000
Hiring cost	$24,000	$0	$0	$0	$24,000
Layoff cost	$0	$0	$0	$0	$0
Total cost	$282,000	258,000	321,000	258,000	$1,119,000

	1	2	3	4	Total
Inputs					
Forecasted demand	35	30	50	20	135
Workforce level	35	35	43	30	143
Undertime	0	5	0	10	15
Overtime	0	0	7	0	7
Derived					
Utilized time	35	30	43	20	128
Hires	0	0	8	0	8
Layoffs	5	0	0	13	18
Calculated					
Utilized time cost	$210,000	$180,000	$258,000	$120,000	$768,000
Undertime cost	$0	$30,000	$0	$60,000	$90,000
Overtime cost	$0	$0	$63,000	$0	$63,000
Hiring cost	$0	$0	$64,000	$0	$64,000
Layoff cost	$10,000	$0	$0	$26,000	$36,000
Total cost	$220.000	210,000	385,000	206,000	$1,021,000

FIGURE 14.12

Spreadsheet for Mixed Strategy

c. The mixed-strategy plan that we propose uses a combination of hires, layoffs, and over-time to reduce total costs. The workforce is reduced by 5 at the beginning of the first period, increased by 8 in the third period, and reduced by 13 in the fourth period. Figure 14.12 shows the results.

d. The total cost of the chase strategy is $1,050,000. The level-utilization strategy results in a total cost of $1,119,000. The mixed-strategy plan was developed by trial and error and results in a total cost of $1,021,000. Further improvements to the mixed strategy are possible.

> SOLVED PROBLEM 2 <

The Arctic Air Company produces residential air conditioners. The manufacturing manager wants to develop a sales and operations plan for the next year based on the following demand and capacity data (in hundreds of product units):

	Period					
	Jan–Feb (1)	Mar–Apr (2)	May–Jun (3)	Jul–Aug (4)	Sep–Oct (5)	Nov–Dec (6)
Demand	50	60	90	120	70	40
Capacities						
Regular time	65	65	65	80	80	65
Overtime	13	13	13	16	16	13
Subcontractor	10	10	10	10	10	10

Undertime is unpaid, and no cost is associated with unused overtime or subcontractor capacity. Producing one air conditioning unit on regular time costs $1,000, including $300 for labor. Producing a unit on overtime costs $1,150. A subcontractor can produce a unit to Arctic Air specifications for $1,250. Holding an air conditioner in stock costs $60 for each 2-month period, and 200 air conditioners are currently in stock. The plan calls for 400 units to be in stock at the end of period 6. No backorders are allowed. Use the transportation method to develop a plan that minimizes costs.

Alternatives		Time Period 1	2	3	4	5	6	Unused Capacity	Total Capacity
Period	Initial Inventory	0	60	120	180 **2**	240	300	0	2
1	Regular time	1,000 **50**	1,060 **15**	1,120	1,180	1,240	1,300	0	65
1	Overtime	1,150	1,210	1,270	1,330	1,390	1,450	13	13
1	Subcontract	1,250	1,310	1,370	1,430	1,490	1,550	10	10
2	Regular time	99,999	1,000 **41**	1,060 **12**	1,120 **12**	1,180	1,240	0	65
2	Overtime	99,999	1,150 **4**	1,210	1,270	1,330	1,390	9	13
2	Subcontract	99,999	1,250	1,310	1,370	1,430	1,490	10	10
3	Regular time	99,999	99,999	1,000 **65**	1,060	1,120	1,180	0	65
3	Overtime	99,999	99,999	1,150 **13**	1,210	1,270	1,330	0	13
3	Subcontract	99,999	99,999	1,250	1,310	1,370	1,430	10	10
4	Regular time	99,999	99,999	99,999	1,000 **80**	1,060	1,120	0	80
4	Overtime	99,999	99,999	99,999	1,150 **16**	1,210	1,270	0	16
4	Subcontract	99,999	99,999	99,999	1,250 **10**	1,310	1,370	0	10
5	Regular time	99,999	99,999	99,999	99,999	1,000 **70**	1,060	10	80
5	Overtime	99,999	99,999	99,999	99,999	1,150	1,210	16	16
5	Subcontract	99,999	99,999	99,999	99,999	1,250	1,310	10	10
6	Regular time	99,999	99,999	99,999	99,999	99,999	1,000 **44**	21	65
6	Overtime	99,999	99,999	99,999	99,999	99,999	1,150	13	13
6	Subcontract	99,999	99,999	99,999	99,999	99,999	1,250	10	10
	Demand	50	60	90	120	70	44	132	566

FIGURE 14.13 | Tableau for Optimal Production and Inventory Plans

SOLUTION

The following tables identify the optimal production and inventory plans. Figure 14.13 shows the tableau that corresponds to this solution. An arbitrarily large cost ($99,999 per period) was used for backorders, which effectively ruled them out. Again, all production quantities are in hundreds of units. Note that demand in period 6 is 4,400. That amount is the period 6 demand plus the desired ending inventory of 400. The anticipation inventory is measured as the amount at the end of each period. Cost calculations are based on the assumption that workers are not paid for undertime or are productively put to work elsewhere in the organization whenever they are not needed for this work.

One initially puzzling aspect of this solution is that it allocates the initial inventory of 200 units to meet demand in period 4 rather than in period 1. The explanation is that multiple optimal solutions exist and this solution is only one of them. However, all solutions result in the same production and anticipation inventory plans derived on the next page.

Production Plan				
Period	Regular-Time Production	Overtime Production	Subcontracting	Total
1	6,500	—	—	6,500
2	6,500	400	—	6,900
3	6,500	1,300	—	7,800
4	8,000	1,600	1,000	10,600
5	7,000	—	—	7,000
6	4,400	—	—	4,400

Anticipation Inventory		
Period	Beginning Inventory Plus Total Production Minus Demand	Anticipation (Ending) Inventory
1	200 + 6,500 − 5,000	1,700
2	1,700 + 6,900 − 6,000	2,600
3	2,600 + 7,800 − 9,000	1,400
4	1,400 + 10,600 − 12,000	0
5	0 + 7,000 − 7,000	0
6	0 + 4,400 − 4,000	400

> DISCUSSION QUESTIONS <

1. Quantitative methods can help managers evaluate alternative sales and operations plans on the basis of cost. These methods require cost estimates for each of the controllable variables, such as overtime, subcontracting, hiring, firing, and inventory investment. Say that the existing workforce is made up of 10,000 direct-labor employees, each having skills valued at $40,000 per year. The plan calls for "creating alternative career opportunities"—in other words, laying off 500 employees. List the types of costs incurred when employees are laid off, and make a rough estimate of the length of time required for payroll savings to recover restructuring costs. If business is expected to improve in one year, are layoffs financially justified? What costs are incurred in a layoff that are difficult to estimate in monetary terms?

2. In your community, some employers maintain stable workforces at all costs, and others furlough and recall workers seemingly at the drop of a hat. What are the differences in markets, management, products, financial position, skills, costs, and competition that could explain these two extremes in personnel policy?

3. As the fortunes of the Big Three domestic automakers improved in the mid-1990s, workers at one GM plant went on strike. The striking workers produced transmissions used in other GM plants. Almost immediately, many other GM plants shut down for lack of transmissions. Facing lost production during a hot market, GM management quickly acceded to labor's demands to recall more furloughed workers and schedule less overtime. What production-planning decisions regarding the controllable variables (listed in Discussion Question 1) are apparent in this situation?

> PROBLEMS <

Software, such as OM Explorer, Active Models, and POM for Windows, is packaged with every new copy of the textbook. Check with your instructor on how best to use it. In many cases, the instructor wants you to understand how to do the calculations by hand. At most, the software provides a check on your calculations. When calculations are particularly complex and the goal is interpreting the results in making decisions, the software replaces entirely the manual calculations. The software also can be a valuable resource well after your course is completed.

1. The Barberton Municipal Division of Road Maintenance is charged with road repair in the city of Barberton and the surrounding area. Cindy Kramer, road maintenance director, must submit a staffing plan for the next year based on a set schedule for repairs and on the city budget. Kramer estimates that the labor hours required for the next four quarters are 6,000, 12,000, 19,000, and 9,000, respectively. Each of the 11 workers on the workforce can contribute 500 hours per quarter. Payroll costs are $6,000 in wages per worker for regular time worked up to 500 hours, with an overtime pay rate of $18 for each overtime hour. Overtime is limited to 20 percent of the regular-time capacity in any quarter. Although unused overtime capacity has no cost, unused regular time is paid at $12 per hour. The cost of hiring a worker is $3,000, and the cost of laying off a worker is $2,000. Subcontracting is not permitted.

   a. Find a level-utilization workforce plan that allows no delay in road repair and minimizes undertime. Overtime can be used to its limits in any quarter. What is the total cost of the plan and how many undertime hours does it call for?

   b. Use a chase strategy that varies the workforce level without using overtime or undertime. What is the total cost of this plan?

   c. Propose a plan of your own. Compare your plan with those in part (a) and part (b) and discuss its comparative merits.

2. Bob Carlton's golf camp estimates the following workforce requirements for its services over the next two years.

Quarter	1	2	3	4
Demand (hours)	4,200	6,400	3,000	4,800

Quarter	5	6	7	8
Demand (hours)	4,400	6,240	3,600	4,800

   Each certified instructor puts in 480 hours per quarter regular time and can work an additional 120 hours overtime. Regular-time wages and benefits cost Carlton $7,200 per employee per quarter for regular time worked up to 480 hours, with an overtime cost of $20 per hour. Unused regular time for certified instructors is paid at $15 per hour. There is no cost for unused overtime capacity. The cost of hiring, training, and certifying a new employee is $10,000. Layoff costs are $4,000 per employee. Currently, eight employees work in this capacity.

   a. Find a workforce plan using the level-utilization strategy that allows for no delay in service and minimizes undertime. What is the total cost of this plan?

   b. Use a chase strategy that varies the workforce level without using overtime or undertime. What is the total cost of this plan?

   c. Propose a low-cost, mixed-strategy plan and calculate its total cost.

3. Continuing Problem 2, now assume that Carlton is permitted to employ some uncertified, part-time instructors, provided they represent no more than 15 percent of the total workforce hours in any quarter. Each part-time instructor can work up to 240 hours per quarter, with no overtime or undertime cost. Labor costs for part-time instructors are $12 per hour. Hiring and training costs are $2,000 per uncertified instructor, and there are no layoff costs.

   a. Propose a low-cost, mixed-strategy plan and calculate its total cost.

   b. What are the primary advantages and disadvantages of having a workforce consisting of both regular and temporary employees?

4. The Donald Fertilizer Company produces industrial chemical fertilizers. The projected manufacturing requirements (in thousands of gallons) for the next four quarters are 80, 50, 80, and 130, respectively. Stockouts and backorders are to be avoided. A level-inventory production strategy is desired.

   a. Determine the quarterly production rate required to meet total demand for the year, without resorting to backorders or stockouts. Use the level-inventory strategy that minimizes the anticipation inventory that would be left over at the end of the year. Beginning inventory is zero.

   b. Specify the anticipation inventories that will be produced.

   c. Suppose that the requirements for the next four quarters are revised to 80, 130, 50, and 80, respectively. If total demand is the same, what level of production rate is needed now, using the same strategy as part (a)?

5. Management at the Davis Corporation has determined the following demand schedule (in units).

Month	1	2	3	4
Demand	500	800	1,000	1,400

Month	5	6	7	8
Demand	2,000	1,600	1,400	1,200

Month	9	10	11	12
Demand	1,000	2,400	3,000	1,000

   An employee can produce an average of 10 units per month. Each worker on the payroll costs $2,000 in regular-time wages per month. Undertime is paid at the same rate as regular time. In accordance with the labor contract in force, Davis Corporation does not work overtime or use subcontracting. Davis can hire and train a new employee for $2,000 and lay off one for $500. Inventory costs $32 per unit on hand at the end of each month. At present, 140 employees are on the payroll and anticipation inventory is zero.

   a. Prepare a production plan with the level-inventory strategy that only uses hires and anticipation inventory as possible alternatives, and minimizes the inventory left over at the end of the year. Layoffs, undertime, vacations, subcontracting, backorders, and stockouts are not options. The plan may call for a one-time adjustment of the workforce before month 1.

b. Prepare a production plan with the chase strategy, relying only on hires and layoffs.

c. Compare and contrast these two plans on the basis of annual costs and other factors that you believe to be important.

d. Propose a mixed-strategy plan that is better than these two plans. Explain why you believe that your plan is better.

6. The Flying Frisbee Company has forecasted the following staffing requirements for full-time employees. Demand is seasonal, and management wants three alternative staffing plans to be developed.

Month	1	2	3	4
Requirement	2	2	4	6

Month	5	6	7	8
Requirement	18	20	12	18

Month	9	10	11	12
Requirement	7	3	2	1

The company currently has 10 employees. No more than 10 new hires can be accommodated in any month because of limited training facilities. No backorders are allowed, and overtime cannot exceed 25 percent of regular-time capacity in any month. There is no cost for unused overtime capacity. Regular-time wages are $1,500 per month, and overtime wages are 150 percent of regular-time wages. Undertime is paid at the same rate as regular time. The hiring cost is $2,500 per person, and the layoff cost is $2,000 per person.

a. Prepare a staffing plan utilizing a level-utilization workforce strategy. The plan may call for a one-time adjustment of the workforce before month 1.

b. Using a chase strategy, prepare a plan that is consistent with the constraint on hiring and minimizes use of overtime.

c. Prepare a low-cost, mixed-strategy plan.

d. Which strategy is most cost-effective? What are the advantages and disadvantages of each plan?

7. The Twilight Clothing Company makes jeans for children. Management prepared a forecast of sales (in pairs of jeans) for next year and now must prepare a production plan. The company has traditionally maintained a level-utilization workforce strategy. Currently, all eight workers have been with the company for a number of years. Each employee can produce 2,000 pairs of jeans during a 2-month planning period. Every year management authorizes overtime in periods 1, 5, and 6, up to a maximum of 20 percent of regular-time capacity. Management wants to avoid stockouts and backorders and will not accept any plan that calls for such shortages. At present, finished goods inventory holds 12,000 pairs of jeans. The demand forecast is as follows:

Period	1	2	3
Sales	25,000	6,500	15,000

Period	4	5	6
Sales	19,000	32,000	29,000

a. Is it feasible to hold the workforce constant, assuming that overtime is used only in periods 1, 5, and 6? Explain.

b. Find two alternative plans that would satisfy management's concern over stockouts and backorders, disregarding costs. What trade-offs between these two plans must be considered?

ADVANCED PROBLEMS

Linear programming approaches, including the transportation method, are recommended for solving Advanced Problems 8 through 10. Additional applications of these production-planning problems may be found in Supplement E, "Linear Programming," for Problems 16, 17, and 20.

8. The Bull Grin Company makes a supplement for the animal feed produced by a number of companies. Sales are seasonal, but Bull Grin's customers refuse to stockpile the supplement during slack sales periods. In other words, the customers want to minimize their inventory investments, insist on shipments according to their schedules, and will not accept backorders.

Bull Grin employs manual, unskilled laborers who require little or no training. Producing 1,000 pounds of supplement costs $830 on regular time and $910 on overtime. No additional cost is incurred for unused regular time, overtime, or subcontractor capacity. These figures include materials, which account for 80 percent of the cost. Overtime is limited to production of a total of 20,000 pounds per quarter. In addition, subcontractors can be hired at $1,000 per thousand pounds, but only 30,000 pounds per quarter can be produced this way.

The current level of inventory is 40,000 pounds, and management wants to end the year at that level. Holding 1,000 pounds of feed supplement in inventory per quarter costs $100. The latest annual forecast is shown in Table 14.1.

Use the transportation method of production planning to find the optimal production plan and calculate its cost, or use the spreadsheet approach to find a good production plan and calculate its cost.

9. The Cut Rite Company is a major producer of industrial lawn mowers. The cost to Cut Rite for hiring a semiskilled worker for its assembly plant is $3,000, and the cost for laying off one is $2,000. The plant averages an output of 36,000 mowers per quarter, with its current workforce of 720 employees. Regular-time capacity is directly proportional to the number of employees. Overtime is limited to a maximum of 3,000 mowers per quarter, and subcontracting is limited to 1,000 mowers per quarter. The costs to produce one mower are $2,430 on regular time (including materials), $2,700 on overtime, and $3,300 via subcontracting. Unused regular-time capacity costs $270 per mower. No additional cost is incurred for unused overtime or subcontractor capacity. The current level of inventory is 4,000 mowers, and management wants to end the year at that level. Customers do not tolerate backorders, and holding a mower in inventory per quarter costs $300. The demand for mowers this coming year is

Quarter	1	2	3	4
Demand	10,000	41,000	77,000	44,000

TABLE 14.1	Forecasts and Capacities				
	Period				
	Quarter 1	**Quarter 2**	**Quarter 3**	**Quarter 4**	**Total**
Demand (pounds)	130,000	400,000	800,000	470,000	1,800,000
Capacities (pounds)					
Regular time	390,000	400,000	460,000	380,000	1,630,000
Overtime	20,000	20,000	20,000	20,000	80,000
Subcontract	30,000	30,000	30,000	30,000	30,000

Two workforce plans have been proposed, and management is uncertain as to which one to use. The following table shows the number of employees per quarter under each plan.

Quarter	1	2	3	4
Plan 1	720	780	920	720
Plan 2	860	860	860	860

a. Which plan would you recommend to management? Explain, supporting your recommendation with an analysis using the transportation method of production planning.

b. If management used creative pricing to get customers to buy mowers in nontraditional time periods, the following demand schedule would result:

Quarter	1	2	3	4
Demand	20,000	54,000	54,000	44,000

Which workforce plan would you recommend now?

10. Gretchen's Kitchen is a fast-food restaurant located in an ideal spot near the local high school. Gretchen Lowe must prepare an annual staffing plan. The only menu items are hamburgers, chili, soft drinks, shakes, and french fries. A sample of 1,000 customers taken at random revealed that they purchased 2,100 hamburgers, 200 pints of chili, 1,000 soft drinks and shakes, and 1,000 bags of french fries. Thus, for purposes of estimating staffing requirements, Lowe assumes that each customer purchases 2.1 hamburgers, 0.2 pint of chili, 1 soft drink or shake, and 1 bag of french fries. Each hamburger requires 4 minutes of labor, a pint of chili requires 3 minutes, and a soft drink or shake and a bag of fries each take 2 minutes of labor.

The restaurant currently has 10 part-time employees who work 80 hours a month on staggered shifts. Wages are $400 per month for regular time and $7.50 per hour for overtime. Hiring and training costs are $2.50 per new employee, and layoff costs are $50 per employee.

Lowe realizes that building up seasonal inventories of hamburgers (or any of the products) would not be wise because of shelf-life considerations. Also, any demand not satisfied is a lost sale and must be avoided. Three strategies come to mind.

■ Use a level-utilization workforce strategy with up to 20 percent of regular-time capacity on overtime.

■ Maintain a base of 10 employees, hiring and laying off as needed to avoid any overtime.

■ Utilize a chase strategy, hiring and firing employees as demand changes to avoid overtime.

When performing her calculations, Lowe always rounds to the next highest integer for the number of employees. She also follows a policy of not using an employee more than 80 hours per month, except when overtime is needed. The projected demand by month (number of customers) for next year is as follows:

Jan.	3,200	July	4,800
Feb.	2,600	Aug.	4,200
Mar.	3,300	Sept.	3,800
Apr.	3,900	Oct.	3,600
May	3,600	Nov.	3,500
June	4,200	Dec.	3,000

a. Develop the schedule of service requirements for the next year.

b. Which of the strategies is most effective?

c. Suppose that an arrangement with the high school enables the manager to identify good prospective employees without having to advertise in the local newspaper. This source reduces the hiring cost to $50, which is mainly the cost of charred hamburgers during training. If cost is her only concern, will this method of hiring change Gretchen Lowe's strategy? Considering other objectives that may be appropriate, do you think she should change strategies?

11. The Holloway Calendar Company produces a variety of printed calendars for both commercial and private use. The demand for calendars is highly seasonal, peaking in the third quarter. Current inventory is 165,000 calendars, and ending inventory should be 200,000 calendars.

Ann Ritter, Holloway's manufacturing manager, wants to determine the best production plan for the demand requirements and capacity plan shown in the following table. (Here, demand and capacities are expressed as thousands of calendars rather than as employee-period equivalents.) Ritter knows that the regular-time cost is $0.50 per unit, overtime cost is $0.75 per unit, subcontracting cost is $0.90 per unit, and inventory holding cost is $0.10 per calendar per quarter.

	Quarter				
	1	**2**	**3**	**4**	**Total**
Demand	250	515	1,200	325	2,290
Capacities					
Regular time	300	300	600	300	1,500
Overtime	75	75	150	75	375
Subcontracting	150	150	150	150	600

a. Recommend a production plan to Ritter, using the transportation method of production planning. (Do not allow any stockouts or backorders to occur.)

b. Interpret and explain your recommendation.

c. Calculate the total cost of your recommended production plan.

> ACTIVE MODEL EXERCISE <

This Active Model appears on the Student CD-ROM. It allows you to evaluate the effects of modifying the size of a constant workforce.

QUESTIONS

1. If we use the same number of workers in each period, what happens as the number of workers increases from 15?

2. If we use the same number of workers in each period, what happens as the number of workers decreases from 15?

3. Suppose the hiring cost is $1,100, what happens as the number of workers increases?

4. Suppose the overtime cost is $3,300, what happens as the number of workers increases?

5. Suppose the undertime cost is the same as the regular-time cost (i.e., paid undertime). What is the best number of worker to have in each month and still meet the demand?

6. If the overtime capacity increases to 30 percent, what is the minimum number of workers that meets the demand in every month?

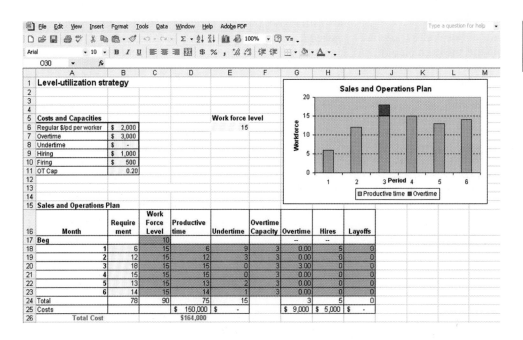

ACTIVE MODEL 14.1

Sales and Operations Planning Using Data from Example 14.1

Memorial Hospital

Memorial Hospital is a 265-bed regional health care facility located in the mountains of western North Carolina. The mission of the hospital is to provide quality health care to the people of Ashe County and the six surrounding counties. To accomplish this mission, Memorial Hospital's CEO has outlined three objectives: (1) maximize customer service to increase customer satisfaction, (2) minimize costs to remain competitive, and (3) minimize fluctuations in workforce levels to help stabilize area employment.

The hospital's operations are segmented into eight major wards for the purposes of planning and scheduling the nursing staff. These wards are listed in Table 14.2, along with the number of beds, targeted patient-to-nurse ratios, and average patient census for each ward. The overall demand for hospital services remained relatively constant over the past few years even though the population of the seven counties served increased. This stable demand can be attributed to increased competition from other hospitals in the area and the rise in alternative health care delivery systems, such as health maintenance organizations (HMOs). However, demand for Memorial Hospital's services does vary considerably by type of ward and time of year. Table 14.3 provides a historical monthly breakdown of the average daily patient census per ward.

The director of nursing for Memorial Hospital is Darlene Fry. Each fall she confronts one of the most challenging aspects of her job: planning the nurse-staffing levels for the next calendar year. Although the average demand for nurses has remained relatively stable over the past couple of years, the staffing plan usually changes because of changing work policies, changing pay structures, and temporary nurse availability and cost. With fall quickly approaching, Fry is collecting information to plan next year's staffing levels.

The nurses at Memorial Hospital work a regular schedule of four 10-hour days per week. The average regular-time pay across all nursing grades is $12.00 per hour. Overtime may be scheduled when necessary. However, because of the intensity of the demands placed on nurses, only a limited amount of overtime is permitted per week. Nurses may be scheduled for as many as 12 hours per day, for a maximum of 5 days per week. Overtime is compensated at a rate of $18.00 per hour. In periods of extremely high demand, temporary part-time nurses may be hired for a limited period of time. Temporary nurses are paid $15.00 per hour. Memorial Hospital's policy limits the proportion of temporary nurses to 15 percent of the total nursing staff.

Finding, hiring, and retaining qualified nurses is an ongoing problem for hospitals. One reason is that various forms of private practice lure many nurses away from hospitals with higher pay and greater flexibility. This situation has caused Memorial to guarantee its full-time staff nurses pay for a minimum of 30 hours per week, regardless of the demand

TABLE 14.2	Ward Capacity Data		
Ward	**Number of Beds**	**Patients per Nurse**	**Patient Census***
Intensive care	20	2	10
Cardiac	25	4	15
Maternity	30	4	10
Pediatric	40	4	22
Surgery	5	†	†
Post-Op	15	5	8 (T–F daily equivalent)‡
Emergency	10	3	5 (daily equivalent)‡
General	120	8	98

* Yearly average per day.

† The hospital employs 20 surgical nurses. Routine surgery is scheduled on Tuesdays and Fridays; five surgeries can be scheduled per day per operating room (bed) on these days. Emergency surgery is scheduled as needed.

‡ Daily equivalents are used to schedule nurses because patients flow through these wards in relatively short periods of time. A daily equivalent of 5 indicates that throughout a typical day, an average of five patients are treated in the ward.

| TABLE 14.3 | Average Daily Patient Census per Month |

Ward	Month											
	J	F	M	A	M	J	J	A	S	O	N	D
Intensive care	13	10	8	7	7	6	11	13	9	10	12	14
Cardiac	18	16	15	13	14	12	13	12	13	15	18	20
Maternity	8	8	12	13	10	8	13	13	14	10	8	7
Pediatric	22	23	24	24	25	21	22	20	18	20	21	19
Surgery*	20	18	18	17	16	16	22	21	17	18	20	22
Post-Op†	10	8	7	7	6	6	10	10	7	8	9	10
Emergency†	6	4	4	7	8	5	5	4	4	3	4	6
General	110	108	100	98	95	90	88	92	98	102	107	94

*Average surgeries per day.

†Daily equivalents.

placed on nursing services. In addition, each nurse receives four weeks of paid vacation each year. However, vacation scheduling may be somewhat restricted by the projected demand for nurses during particular times of the year.

At present, the hospital employs 130 nurses, including 20 surgical nurses. The other 110 nurses are assigned to the remaining seven major areas of the hospital. The personnel department informed Fry that the average cost to the hospital for hiring a new full-time nurse is $400 and for laying off or firing a nurse is $150. Although layoffs are an option, Fry is aware of the hospital's objective of maintaining a level workforce.

After looking over the information that she collected, Darlene Fry wants to consider staffing changes in all areas except the surgery ward, which is already correctly staffed.

QUESTIONS

1. Explain the alternatives available to Darlene Fry as she develops a nurse-staffing plan for Memorial Hospital. How does each meet the objective stated by the CEO?

2. Based on the data presented, develop a nurse staffing plan for Memorial Hospital. Explain your rationale for this plan.

Source: This case was prepared by Dr. Brooke Saladin, Wake Forest University, as a basis for classroom discussion.

> SELECTED REFERENCES <

Armacost, R. L., R. L. Penlesky, and S. C. Ross. "Avoiding Problems Inherent in Spreadsheet-Based Simulation Models—An Aggregate Planning Application." *Production and Inventory Management*, vol. 31 (1990), pp. 62–68.

Brandimarte, P., and A. Villa (eds.). *Modeling Manufacturing Systems: From Aggregate Planning to Real-Time Control.* New York: Springer, 1999.

Buxey, G. "Production Planning and Scheduling for Seasonal Demand." *International Journal of Operations and Production Management*, vol. 13, no. 7 (1993), pp. 4–21.

"Cycle Management—Cycle Proficiency." *Post Magazine* (July 1, 2004), p. 22.

Fisher, M. L., J. H. Hammond, W. R. Obermeyer, and A. Raman. "Making Supply Meet Demand in an Uncertain World." *Harvard Business Review*, vol. 72, no. 3 (1994), pp. 83–93.

Fogarty, Donald W., John H. Blackstone Jr., and Thomas R. Hoffman. *Production and Inventory Management.* Cincinnati: South-Western Publishing, 1991.

Heskett, J., W. E. Sasser, and C. Hart. *Service Breakthroughs: Changing the Rules of the Game.* New York: The Free Press, 1990.

Hopp, Wallace J., and Mark L. Spearman. *Factory Physics,* 2d ed. New York: Irwin/McGraw-Hill, 2001.

Lee, S. M., and L. J. Moore. "A Practical Approach to Production Scheduling." *Production and Inventory Management* (First Quarter 1974), pp. 79–92.

Lee, W. B., and B. M. Khumawala. "Simulation Testing of Aggregate Production Planning Models in an Implementation Methodology." *Management Science,* vol. 20, no. 6 (1974), pp. 903–911.

Narasimhan, S., D. W. McLeavey, and P. J. Billington. *Production Planning and Inventory Control.* Englewood Cliffs, NJ: Prentice Hall, 1995.

Ryan, D. M. "Optimization Earns Its Wings." *OR/MS Today*, vol. 27, no. 2 (2000), pp. 26–30.

Silver, E. A., F. F. Pyke, and R. Peterson. *Inventory Management and Production Planning and Scheduling.* New York: Wiley, 1998.

Sipper, D., and R. Bulfin. *Production: Planning, Control, and Integration.* New York: McGraw-Hill, 1997.

Smith-Daniels, V., S. Scheweikhar, and D. Smith-Daniels. "Capacity Management in Health Care Services: Review and Future Research Directions." *Decision Sciences,* vol. 91 (1988), pp. 889–919.

Vollmann, T. E., W. L. Berry, D. C. Whybark, and F. R. Jacobs. *Manufacturing Planning and Control for Supply Chain Management*, 5th ed. New York: Irwin/McGraw-Hill, 2004.

Wallace, Thomas F. *Sales & Operations Planning: The How-To Handbook*, 2d ed. Cincinnati, OH: T. E. Wallace & Company, 2004.

Wallace, Thomas F., and Robert A. Stahl. *Sales Forecasting: A New Approach.* Cincinnati, OH: T. E. Wallace & Company, 2002.

SUPPLEMENT

Linear Programming

In many business situations, resources are limited and demand for them is great. For example, a limited number of vehicles may have to be scheduled to make multiple trips to customers, or a staffing plan may have to be developed to cover expected variable demand with the fewest employees. In this supplement, we describe a technique called **linear programming,** which is useful for allocating scarce resources among competing demands. The resources may be time, money, or materials, and the limitations are known as constraints. Linear programming can help managers find the best allocation solution and provide information about the value of additional resources.

LEARNING GOALS

After reading this supplement, you should be able to:

1. Identify the characteristics and assumptions of linear programming models.
2. Describe formulating models for various problems.
3. Demonstrate graphic analysis and solutions for two-variable problems.
4. Define slack and surplus variables.
5. Explain sensitivity analysis.
6. Describe computer output of a linear programming solution.

> BASIC CONCEPTS <

linear programming

A technique that is useful for allocating scarce resources among competing demands.

objective function

An expression in linear programming models that states mathematically what is being maximized (e.g., profit or present value) or minimized (e.g., cost or scrap).

decision variables

The variables that represent choices the decision maker can control.

constraints

The limitations that restrict the permissible choices for the decision variables.

feasible region

A region that represents all permissible combinations of the decision variables in a linear programming model.

parameter

A value that the decision maker cannot control and that does not change when the solution is implemented.

certainty

The word that is used to describe that a fact is known without doubt.

linearity

A characteristic of linear programming models that implies proportionality and additivity—there can be no products or powers of decision variables.

nonnegativity

An assumption that the decision variables must be positive or zero.

Before we can demonstrate how to solve problems in operations management with linear programming, we must first explain several characteristics of all linear programming models and mathematical assumptions that apply to them: (1) objective function, (2) decision variables, (3) constraints, (4) feasible region, (5) parameters, (6) linearity, and (7) nonnegativity.

Linear programming is an *optimization* process. A single **objective function** states mathematically what is being maximized (e.g., profit or present value) or minimized (e.g., cost or scrap). The objective function provides the scorecard on which the attractiveness of different solutions is judged.

Decision variables represent choices that the decision maker can control. Solving the problem yields their optimal values. For example, a decision variable could be the number of units of a product to make next month or the number of units of inventory to hold next month. Linear programming is based on the assumption that decision variables are *continuous;* they can be fractional quantities and need not be whole numbers. Often, this assumption is realistic, as when the decision variable is expressed in dollars, hours, or some other continuous measure. Even when the decision variables represent nondivisible units, such as workers, tables, or trucks, we sometimes can simply round the linear programming solution up or down to get a reasonable solution that does not violate any constraints, or we can use a more advanced technique, called *integer programming.*

Constraints are limitations that restrict the permissible choices for the decision variables. Each limitation can be expressed mathematically in one of three ways: a less-than-or-equal-to ($\leq$), an equal-to ($=$), or a greater-than-or-equal-to ($\geq$) constraint. A $\leq$ constraint puts an upper limit on some function of decision variables and most often is used with maximization problems. For example, a $\leq$ constraint may specify the maximum number of customers who can be served or the capacity limit of a machine. An $=$ constraint means that the function must equal some value. For example, 100 (not 99 or 101) units of one product must be made. An $=$ constraint often is used for certain mandatory relationships, such as the fact that ending inventory always equals beginning inventory plus production minus sales. A $\geq$ constraint puts a lower limit on some function of decision variables. For example, a $\geq$ constraint may specify that production of a product must exceed or equal demand.

Every linear programming problem must have one or more constraints. Taken together, the constraints define a **feasible region**, which represents all permissible combinations of the decision variables. In some unusual situations, the problem is so tightly constrained that there is only one possible solution—or perhaps none. However, in the usual case, the feasibility region contains infinitely many possible solutions, assuming that the feasible combinations of the decision variables can be fractional values. The goal of the decision maker is to find the best possible solution.

The objective function and constraints are functions of decision variables and parameters. A **parameter**, also known as a *coefficient* or *given constant*, is a value that the decision maker cannot control and that does not change when the solution is implemented. Each parameter is assumed to be known with **certainty**. For example, a computer programmer may know that running a software program will take three hours—no more, no less.

The objective function and constraint equations are assumed to be linear. **Linearity** implies proportionality and additivity—there can be no products (e.g., $10x_1x_2$) or powers (e.g., x_1^3) of decision variables. Suppose that the profit gained by producing two types of products (represented by decision variables x_1 and x_2) is $2x + 3x_2$. Proportionality implies that one unit of x_1 contributes $2 to profits and two units contribute $4, regardless of how much of x_2 is produced. Similarly, each unit of x_2 contributes $3, whether it is the first or the tenth unit produced. Additivity means that the total objective function value equals the profits from x_1 plus the profits from x_2.

Finally, we make an assumption of **nonnegativity**, which means that the decision variables must be positive or zero. A firm that makes spaghetti sauce, for example, cannot produce a negative number of jars. To be formally correct, a linear programming formulation should show a ≥ 0 constraint for each decision variable.

Although the assumptions of linearity, certainly, and continuous variables are restrictive, linear programming can help managers analyze many complex resource allocation problems. The process of building the model forces managers to identify the important decision variables and constraints, which is a useful step in its own right. Identifying the nature and scope of the problem represents a major step toward solving it. In a later section, we show how sensitivity analysis can help the manager deal with uncertainties in the parameters and answer "what-if" questions.

FORMULATING A PROBLEM

Linear programming applications begin with the formulation of a *model* of the problem with the general characteristics just described. We illustrate the modeling process here with the **product-mix problem**, which is a one-period type of planning problem, the solution of which yields optimal output quantities (or product mix) of a group of services or products subject to resource capacity and market demand constraints. Formulating a model to represent each unique problem, using the following three-step sequence, is the most creative and perhaps the most difficult part of linear programming.

product-mix problem

A one-period type of planning problem, the solution of which yields optimal output quantities (or product mix) of a group of services or products subject to resource capacity and market demand constraints.

Step 1. Define the Decision Variables. What must be decided? Define each decision variable specifically, remembering that the definitions used in the objective function must be equally useful in the constraints. The definitions should be as specific as possible. Consider the following two alternative definitions:

x_1 = product 1

x_1 = number of units of product 1 to be produced and sold next month

The second definition is much more specific than the first, making the remaining steps easier.

Step 2. Write Out the Objective Function. What is to be maximized or minimized? If it is next month's profits, write out an objective function that makes next month's profits a linear function of the decision variables. Identify parameters to go with each decision variable. For example, if each unit of x_1 sold yields a profit of \$7, the total profit from product $x_1 = 7x_1$. If a variable has no impact on the objective function, its objective function coefficient is 0. The objective function often is set equal to Z, and the goal is to maximize or minimize Z.

Step 3. Write Out the Constraints. What limits the values of the decision variables? Identify the constraints and the parameters for each decision variable in them. As with the objective function, the parameter for a variable that has no impact in a constraint is 0. To be formally correct, also write out the nonnegativity constraints.

As a consistency check, make sure that the same unit of measure is being used on both sides of each constraint and in the objective function. For example, suppose that the right-hand side of a constraint is hours of capacity per month. Then, if a decision variable on the left-hand side of the constraint measures the number of units produced per month, the dimensions of the parameter that is multiplied by the decision variable must be hours per unit because

$$\left(\frac{\text{Hours}}{\text{Unit}}\right)\left(\frac{\text{Units}}{\text{Month}}\right)=\left(\frac{\text{Hours}}{\text{Month}}\right)$$

Of course, you can also skip around from one step to another, depending on the part of the problem that has your attention. If you cannot get past step 1, try a new set of definitions for the decision variables. Often the problem can be modeled correctly in more than one way.

Formulating a Linear Programming Model	EXAMPLE E.1

The Stratton Company produces two basic types of plastic pipe. Three resources are crucial to the output of pipe: extrusion hours, packaging hours, and a special additive to the plastic raw material. The following data represent next week's situation. All data are expressed in units of 100 feet of pipe.

	Product		
Resource	**Type 1**	**Type 2**	**Resource Availability**
Extrusion	4 hr	6 hr	48 hr
Packaging	2 hr	2 hr	18 hr
Additive mix	2 lb	1 lb	16 lb

The contribution to profits and overhead per 100 feet of pipe is $34 for type 1 and $40 for type 2. Formulate a linear programming model to determine how much of each type of pipe should be produced to maximize contribution to profits and to overhead.

SOLUTION

Step 1: To define the decision variables that determine product mix, we let

x_1 = amount of type 1 pipe to be produced and sold next week, measured in 100-foot increments (e.g., $x_1 = 2$ means 200 feet of type 1 pipe)

and

x_2 = amount of type 2 pipe to be produced and sold next week, measured in 100-foot increments.

Step 2:   Next, we define the objective function. The goal is to maximize the total contribution that the two products make to profits and overhead. Each unit of x_1 yields $34, and each unit of x_2 yields $40. For specific values of x_1 and x_2, we find the total profit by multiplying the number of units of each product produced by the profit per unit and adding them. Thus, our objective function becomes

$$\text{Maximize: } \$34x_1 + \$40x_2 = Z$$

Step 3:   The final step is to formulate the constraints. Each unit of x_1 and x_2 produced consumes some of the critical resources. In the extrusion department, a unit of x_1 requires 4 hours and a unit of x_2 requires 6 hours. The total must not exceed the 48 hours of capacity available, so we use the $\leq$ sign. Thus, the first constraint is

$$4x_1 + 6x_2 \leq 48 \text{ (extrusion)}$$

Similarly, we can formulate constraints for packaging and raw materials:

$$2x_1 + 2x_2 \leq 18 \text{ (packaging)}$$
$$2x_1 + x_2 \leq 16 \text{ (additive mix)}$$

These three constraints restrict our choice of values for the decision variable because the values we choose for x_1 and x_2 must satisfy all of the constraints. Negative values for x_1 and x_2 do not make sense, so we add nonnegativity restrictions to the model:

$$x_1 \geq 0 \quad \text{and} \quad x_2 \geq 0 \text{ (nonnegativity restrictions)}$$

We can now state the entire model, made complete with the definitions of variables.

$$\text{Maximize: } \$34x_1 + \$40x_2 = Z$$
$$\text{Subject to: } 4x_1 + 6x_2 \leq 48$$
$$2x_1 + 2x_2 \leq 18$$
$$2x_1 + x_2 \leq 16$$
$$x_1 \geq 0 \quad \text{and} \quad x_2 \geq 0$$

where

x_1 = amount of type 1 pipe to be produced and sold next week, measured in 100-foot increments
x_2 = amount of type 2 pipe to be produced and sold next week, measured in 100-foot increments

graphic method of linear programming

A type of graphic analysis that involves the following five steps: plotting the constraints, identifying the feasible region, plotting an objective function line, finding a visual solution, and finding the algebraic solution.

> GRAPHIC ANALYSIS <

With the model formulated, we now seek the optimal solution. In practice, most linear programming problems are solved with a computer. However, insight into the meaning of the computer output—and linear programming concepts in general—can be gained by analyzing a simple two-variable problem with the **graphic method of linear programming**. Hence, we begin with the graphic method, even though it is not a practical technique for solving problems that have three or more decision variables. The five basic steps are (1) *plot the con-*

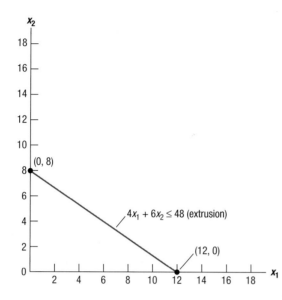

FIGURE **E.1**

Graph of the Extrusion Constraint

straints, (2) *identify the feasible region*, (3) *plot an objective function line*, (4) *find the visual solution*, and (5) *find the algebraic solution*.

PLOT THE CONSTRAINTS

We begin by plotting the constraint equations, disregarding the inequality portion of the constraints (< or >). Making each constraint an equality (=) transforms it into the equation for a straight line. The line can be drawn as soon as we identify two points on it. Any two points reasonably spread out may be chosen; the easiest ones to find are the *axis intercepts*, where the line intersects each axis. To find the x_1 axis intercept, set x_2 equal to 0 and solve the equation for x_1. For the Stratton Company in Example E.1, the equation of the line for the extrusion process is

$$4x_1 + 6x_2 = 48$$

For the x_1 axis intercept, $x_2 = 0$, so

$$4x_1 + 6(0) = 48$$
$$x_1 = 12$$

To find the x_2 axis intercept, set $x_1 = 0$ and solve for x_2:

$$4(0) + 6x_2 = 48$$
$$x_2 = 8$$

We connect points (0, 8) and (12, 0) with a straight line, as shown in Figure E.1.

Plotting the Constraints	EXAMPLE **E.2**

For the Stratton Company problem, plot the other constraints: one constraint for packaging and one constraint for the additive mix.

SOLUTION

The equation for the packaging process's line is $2x_1 + 2x_2 = 18$. To find the x_1 intercept, set $x_2 = 0$:

$$2x_1 + 2(0) = 18$$
$$x_1 = 9$$

To find the x_2 axis intercept, set $x_1 = 0$:

$$2(0) + 2x_2 = 18$$
$$x_2 = 9$$

ACTIVE MODEL E.1

Active Model E.1 on the Student CD-ROM offers many insights on graphic analysis and sensitivity analysis. Use it when studying Examples E.2 through E.5.

TUTOR E.1

Tutor E.1 on the Student CD-ROM provides a new practice example for plotting the constraints.

The equation for the additive mix's line is $2x_1 + x_2 = 16$. To find the x_1 intercept, set $x_2 = 0$:

$$2x_1 + 0 = 16$$
$$x_1 = 8$$

To find the x_2 axis intercept, set $x_1 = 0$:

$$2(0) + x_2 = 16$$
$$x_2 = 16$$

With a straight line, we connect points $(0, 9)$ and $(9, 0)$ for the packaging constraint and points $(0, 16)$ and $(8, 0)$ for the additive mix constraint. Figure E.2 shows the graph with all three constraints plotted.

FIGURE E.2

Graph of the Three Constraints

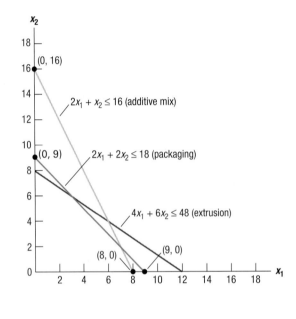

IDENTIFY THE FEASIBLE REGION

The feasible region is the area on the graph that contains the solutions that satisfy all the constraints simultaneously, including the nonnegativity restrictions. To find the feasible region, first locate the feasible points for each constraint and then the area that satisfies all constraints. Generally, the following three rules identify the feasible points for a given constraint:

1. For the = constraint, only the points on the line are feasible solutions.
2. For the ≤ constraint, the points on the line and the points below or to the left of the line are feasible solutions.
3. For the ≥ constraint, the points on the line and the points above or to the right of the line are feasible solutions.

Exceptions to these rules occur when one or more of the parameters on the left-hand side of a constraint is negative. In such cases, we draw the constraint line and test a point on one side of it. If the point does not satisfy the constraint, it is in the infeasible part of the graph. Suppose that a linear programming model has the following five constraints plus the nonnegativity constraints:

$$2x_1 + x_2 \geq 10$$
$$2x_1 + 3x_2 \geq 18$$
$$x_1 \leq 7$$
$$x_2 \leq 5$$
$$-6x_1 + 5x_2 \leq 5$$
$$x_1, x_2 \geq 0$$

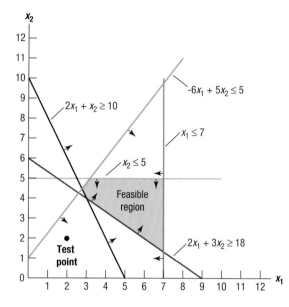

The feasible region is the shaded portion of Figure E.3. The arrows shown on each constraint identify which side of each line is feasible. The rules work for all but the fifth constraint, which has a negative parameter, -6, for x_1. We arbitrarily select $(2, 2)$ as the test point, which Figure E.3 shows is below the line and to the right. At this point, we find $-6(2) + 5(2) = -2$. Because -2 does not exceed 5, the portion of the figure containing $(2, 2)$ is feasible, at least for this fifth constraint.

Identifying the Feasible Region	EXAMPLE **E.3**

Identify the feasible region for the Stratton Company problem.

SOLUTION

Because the problem contains only $\leq$ constraints, and the parameters on the left-hand side of each constraint are not negative, the feasible portions are to the left of and below each constraint. The feasible region, shaded in Figure E.4, satisfies all three constraints simultaneously.

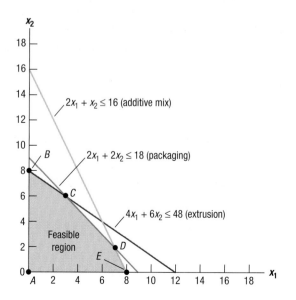

PLOT AN OBJECTIVE FUNCTION LINE

corner point

A point that lies at the intersection of two (or possibly more) constraint lines on the boundary of the feasible region.

Now we want to find the solution that optimizes the objective function. Even though all the points in the feasible region represent possible solutions, we can limit our search to the corner points. A **corner point** lies at the intersection of two (or possibly more) constraint lines on the boundary of the feasible region. No interior points in the feasible region need be considered because at least one corner point is better than any interior point. Similarly, other points on the boundary of the feasible region can be ignored because a corner point is at least as good as any of them.

In Figure E.4 the five corner points are marked *A, B, C, D,* and *E*. Point *A* is the origin (0, 0) and can be ignored because any other feasible point is a better solution. We could try each of the other corner points in the objective function and select the one that maximizes *Z*. For example, corner point *B* lies at (0, 8). If we substitute these values into the objective function, the resulting *Z* value is 320:

$$34x_1 + 40x_2 = Z$$
$$34(0) + 40(8) = 320$$

However, we may not be able to read accurately the values of x_1 and x_2 for some of the points (e.g., *C* or *D*) on the graph. Algebraically solving two linear equations for each corner point also is inefficient when there are many constraints and, thus, many corner points.

The best approach is to plot the objective function on the graph of the feasible region for some arbitrary *Z* values. From these objective function lines, we can spot the best solution visually. If the objective function is profits, each line is called an *iso-profit line* and every point on that line will yield the same profit. If *Z* measures cost, the line is called an *iso-cost line* and every point on it represents the same cost. We can simplify the search by plotting the first line in the feasible region—somewhere near the optimal solution, we hope. For the Stratton Company example, let us pass a line through point *E* (8, 0). This point is a corner point. It might even be the optimal solution because it is far from the origin. To draw the line, we first identify its *Z* value as 34(8) + 40(0) = 272. Therefore, the equation for the objective function line passing through *E* is

$$34x_1 + 40x_2 = 272$$

Every point on the line defined by this equation has an objective function *Z* value of 272. To draw the line, we need to identify a second point on it, and then connect the two points. Let us use the x_2 intercept, where $x_1 = 0$:

$$34(0) + 40x_2 = 272$$
$$x_2 = 6.8$$

Figure E.5 shows the iso-profit line that connects points (8, 0) and (0, 6.8). A series of other dashed lines could be drawn parallel to this first line. Each would have its own *Z* value. Lines above the first line we drew would have higher *Z* values. Lines below it would have lower *Z* values.

FIND THE VISUAL SOLUTION

We now eliminate corner points *A* and *E* from consideration as the optimal solution because better points lie above and to the right of the *Z* = 272 iso-profit line. Our goal is to maximize profits, so the best solution is a point on the iso-profit line *farthest* from the origin but still touching the feasible region. (For minimization problems, it is a point in the feasible region on the iso-cost line *closest* to the origin.) To identify which of the remaining corner points is optimal (*B, C,* or *D*), we draw, parallel to the first line, one or more iso-profit lines that give better *Z* values (higher for maximization and lower for minimization). The line that just touches the feasible region identifies the optimal solution. For the Stratton Company problem, Figure E.6 shows the second iso-profit line. The optimal solution is the last point touching the feasible region: point *C*. It appears to be in the vicinity of (3, 6), but the visual solution is not exact.

A linear programming problem can have more than one optimal solution. This situation occurs when the objective function is parallel to one of the faces of the feasible region. Such would be the case if our objective function in the Stratton Company problem were $\$38x_1 + \$38x_2$. Points (3, 6) and (7, 2) would be optimal, as would any other point on the line connecting these two corner points. In such a case, management probably would base a final

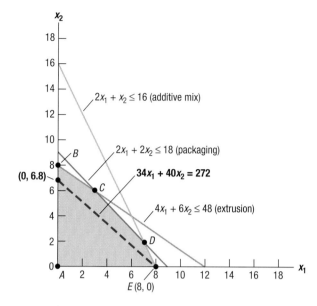

decision on nonquantifiable factors. It is important to understand, however, that we need to consider only the corner points of the feasible region when optimizing an objective function.

FIND THE ALGEBRAIC SOLUTION

To find an exact solution, we must use algebra. We begin by identifying the pair of constraints that define the corner point at their intersection. We then list the constraints as equations and solve them simultaneously to find the coordinates (x_1, x_2) of the corner point. Simultaneous equations can be solved several ways. For small problems, the easiest way is as follows:

Step 1. Develop an equation with just one unknown. Start by multiplying both sides of one equation by a constant so that the coefficient for one of the two decision variables is *identical* in both equations. Then subtract one equation from the other and solve the resulting equation for its single unknown variable.

Step 2. Insert this decision variable's value into either one of the original constraints and solve for the other decision variable.

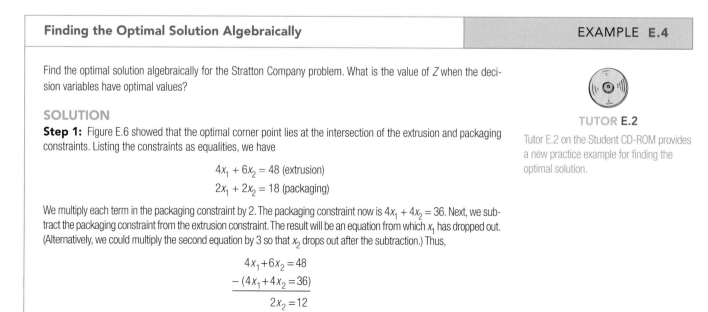

| **Finding the Optimal Solution Algebraically** | EXAMPLE **E.4** |

Find the optimal solution algebraically for the Stratton Company problem. What is the value of Z when the decision variables have optimal values?

SOLUTION
Step 1: Figure E.6 showed that the optimal corner point lies at the intersection of the extrusion and packaging constraints. Listing the constraints as equalities, we have

$$4x_1 + 6x_2 = 48 \text{ (extrusion)}$$
$$2x_1 + 2x_2 = 18 \text{ (packaging)}$$

We multiply each term in the packaging constraint by 2. The packaging constraint now is $4x_1 + 4x_2 = 36$. Next, we subtract the packaging constraint from the extrusion constraint. The result will be an equation from which x_1 has dropped out. (Alternatively, we could multiply the second equation by 3 so that x_2 drops out after the subtraction.) Thus,

$$
\begin{array}{r}
4x_1 + 6x_2 = 48 \\
- (4x_1 + 4x_2 = 36) \\
\hline
2x_2 = 12 \\
x_2 = 6
\end{array}
$$

TUTOR E.2

Tutor E.2 on the Student CD-ROM provides a new practice example for finding the optimal solution.

FIGURE **E.6**

Drawing the Second Iso-Profit Line

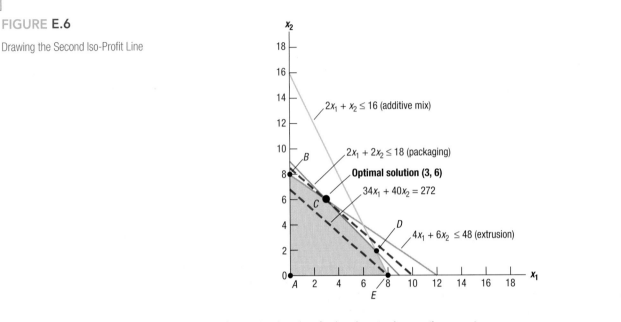

Step 2: Substituting the value of x_2 into the extrusion equation, we get

$$4x_1 + 6(6) = 48$$
$$4x_1 = 12$$
$$x_1 = 3$$

Thus, the optimal point is (3, 6). This solution gives a total profit of $34(3) + 40(6) = \$342$.

Decision Point Management at the Stratton Company decided to produce 300 feet of type 1 pipe and 600 feet of type 2 pipe for the next week.

SLACK AND SURPLUS VARIABLES

Figure E.6 showed that the optimal product mix will exhaust all the extrusion and packaging resources because at the optimal corner point (3, 6) the two constraints are equalities. Substituting the values of x_1 and x_2 into these constraints shows that the left-hand sides equal the right-hand sides:

$$4(3) + 6(6) = 48 \text{ (extrusion)}$$
$$2(3) + 2(6) = 18 \text{ (packaging)}$$

binding constraint

A constraint that helps form the optimal corner point; it limits the ability to improve the objective function.

A constraint (such as the one for extrusion) that helps form the optimal corner point is called a **binding constraint** because it limits the ability to improve the objective function. If a binding constraint is *relaxed*, or made less restrictive, a better solution is possible. Relaxing a constraint means increasing the right-hand-side parameter for a ≤ constraint or decreasing it for a ≥ constraint. No improvement is possible from relaxing a constraint that is not binding, such as the additive mix constraint in Figure E.6. If the right-hand side were increased from 16 to 17 and the problem solved again, the optimal solution would not change. In other words, there is already more additive mix than needed.

slack

The amount by which the left-hand side falls short of the right-hand side.

surplus

The amount by which the left-hand side exceeds the right-hand side.

For nonbinding inequality constraints, knowing how much the left and right sides differ is helpful. Such information tells us how close the constraint is to becoming binding. For a ≤ constraint, the amount by which the left-hand side falls short of the right-hand side is called **slack**. For a ≥ constraint, the amount by which the left-hand side exceeds the right-hand side is called **surplus**. To find the slack for a ≤ constraint algebraically, we *add* a slack variable to the constraint and convert it to an equality. Then we substitute in the values of the decision variables and solve for the slack. For example, the additive mix constraint in Figure E.6, $2x_1 + x_2 \leq 16$, can be rewritten by adding slack variable s_1:

$$2x_1 + x_2 + s_1 = 16$$

We then find the slack at the optimal solution (3, 6):

$$2(3) + 6 + s_1 = 16$$
$$s_1 = 4$$

The procedure is much the same to find the surplus for a $\geq$ constraint, except that we *subtract* a surplus variable from the left-hand side. Suppose that $x_1 + x_2 \geq 6$ was another constraint in the Stratton Company problem, representing a lower bound on the number of units produced. We would then rewrite the constraint by subtracting a surplus variable s_2:

$$x_1 + x_2 - s_2 = 6$$

The slack at the optimal solution (3, 6) would be

$$3 + 6 - s_2 = 6$$
$$s_2 = 3$$

TUTOR E.3

Tutor E.3 on the Student CD-ROM provides another practice example for finding slack.

> SENSITIVITY ANALYSIS <

Rarely are the parameters in the objective function and constraints known with certainty. Often, they are just estimates of actual values. For example, the available packaging and extrusion hours for the Stratton Company are estimates that do not reflect the uncertainties associated with absenteeism or personnel transfers, and the required hours per unit to package and extrude may be work standards that essentially are averages. Likewise, profit contributions used for the objective function coefficients do not reflect uncertainties in selling prices and such variable costs as wages, raw materials, and shipping.

Despite such uncertainties, initial estimates are needed to solve the problem. Accounting, marketing, and work-standard information systems often provide these initial estimates. After solving the problem using these estimated values, the analyst can determine how much the optimal values of the decision variables and the objective function value Z would be affected if certain parameters had different values. This type of postsolution analysis for answering "what-if" questions is called *sensitivity analysis*.

One way of conducting sensitivity analysis for linear programming problems is the brute-force approach of changing one or more parameter values and re-solving the entire problem. This approach may be acceptable for small problems, but it is inefficient if the problem involves many parameters. For example, brute-force sensitivity analysis using 3 separate values for each of 20 objective function coefficients requires 3^{20}, or 3,486,784,401, separate solutions! Fortunately, efficient methods are available for getting sensitivity information without re-solving the entire problem, and they are routinely used in most linear programming computer software packages.

Table E.1 describes the four basic types of sensitivity analysis information provided by linear programming. See the Student CD-ROM for a fuller description of sensitivity analysis, by continuing with the graphical analysis of the Stratton Company.

TABLE E.1	Sensitivity Analysis Information Provided by Linear Programming
Term	**Definition**
coefficient sensitivity	The measurement of how much the objective function coefficient of a decision variable must improve (increase for maximization or decrease for minimization) before the optimal solution changes and the decision variable becomes some positive number.
range of feasibility	The interval over which the right-hand-side parameter can vary while its shadow price remains valid.
range of optimality	The lower and upper limits over which the optimal values of the decision variables remain unchanged.
shadow price	The marginal improvement in Z (increase for maximization and decrease for minimization) caused by relaxing the constraint by one unit.

> COMPUTER SOLUTION <

Most real-world linear programming problems are solved on a computer, so we concentrate here on understanding the use of linear programming and the logic on which it is based. The solution procedure in computer codes is some form of the **simplex method**, which is an iterative algebraic procedure for solving linear programming problems.

simplex method

An iterative algebraic procedure for solving linear programming problems.

SIMPLEX METHOD

The graphic analysis gives insight into the logic of the simplex method, beginning with the focus on corner points. One corner point will always be the optimum, even when multiple optimal solutions are available. Thus, the simplex method starts with an initial corner point and then systematically evaluates other corner points in such a way that the objective function improves (or, at worst, stays the same) at each iteration. In the Stratton Company problem, an improvement would be an increase in profits. When no more improvements are possible, the optimal solution has been found.[1] The simplex method also helps generate the sensitivity analysis information that we developed graphically.

Each corner point has no more than m variables that are greater than 0, where m is the number of constraints (not counting the nonnegativity constraints). The m variables include slack and surplus variables, not just the original decision variables. Because of this property, we can find a corner point by simultaneously solving m constraints, where all but m variables are set equal to 0. For example, point B in Figure E.6 has three nonzero variables: x_2, the slack variable for packaging, and the slack variable for the additive mix. Their values can be found by solving simultaneously the three constraints, with x_1 and the slack variable for extrusion equal to 0. After finding this corner point, the simplex method applies information similar to the coefficient sensitivity to decide which new corner point to find next that gives an even better Z value. It continues in this way until no better corner point is possible. The final corner point evaluated is the optimal one.

COMPUTER OUTPUT

Computer programs dramatically reduce the amount of time required to solve linear programming problems. Special-purpose programs can be developed for applications that must be repeated frequently. Such programs simplify data input and generate the objective function and constraints for the problem. In addition, they can prepare customized managerial reports.

The capabilities and displays of software packages are not uniform. For example, OM Explorer and POM for Windows can handle small- to medium-sized linear programming problems. OM Explorer relies on Microsoft's *Excel Solver* to find the optimal solutions, and, thus, Excel's "Solver Add-In" must be installed so that it is compatible with OM Explorer's linear programming spreadsheet. Solving linear programming problems with these packages, rather than using Excel's Solver directly, is more convenient. The inputs are easily made and nonnegativity constraints need not be entered. For other software for linear programming, see the ILOG Optimization Suite (www.ilog.com/products/optimization), Lindo Systems (www.lindo.com), IBM's Optimization Subroutine Library (www.research.ibm.com/osl), FrontLine's Premium Solver Products for Microsoft Excel (www.frontsys.com/xlprod.htm), and Lionheart's latest linear programming software survey (lionhrtpub.com/orms/surveys/LP/LP-survey.html).

Here we show output from OM Explorer, although you might find POM for Windows more convenient to use. OM Explorer has three worksheets of output, which we illustrate for the Stratton Company. The output from the first two worksheets is shown in Figure E.7.

The *Inputs Worksheet* asks for the number of decision variables and constraints, and also whether it is a maximization or minimization problem. After making these inputs and clicking the Setup Problem button, the *Work Area Worksheet* is opened. The user may choose to enter labels for the decision variables, right-hand-side values, objective function, and constraints. Here, the first decision variable is labeled as "X1," the right-hand-side values as "RHV," the objective function as "Max-Z," and the extrusion constraint as "Extrusion." For convenience in specifying the type of constraint ($\leq$, $=$, or $\geq$), just enter "<" for a $\leq$ constraint

---

[1]For more information on how to perform the simplex method manually, see Render, Stair, and Hanna (2003) or any other current textbook on management science.

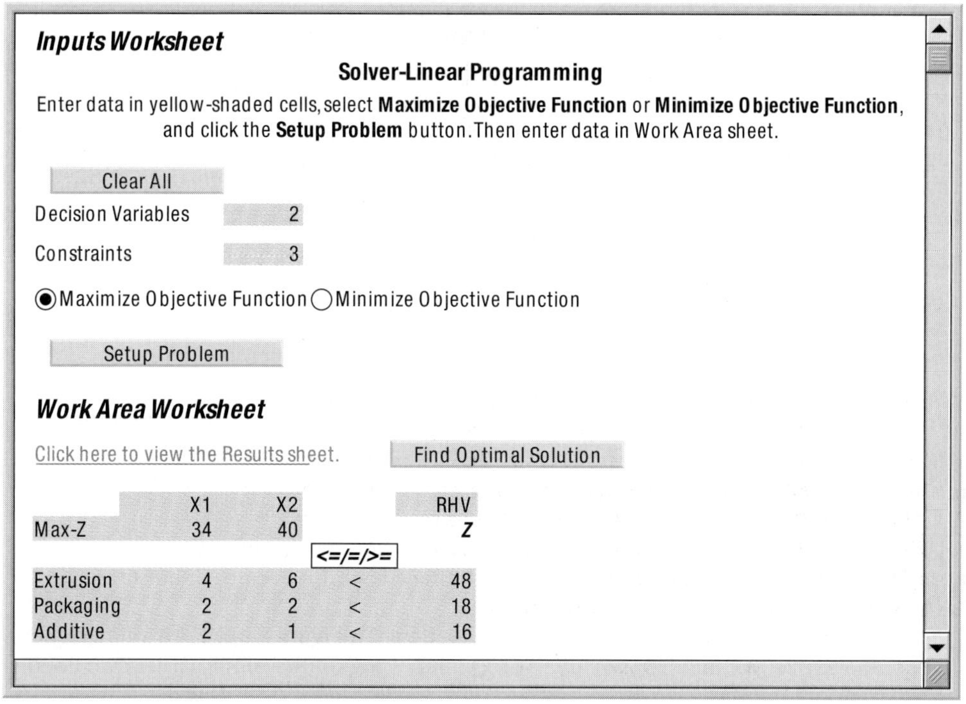

Inputs Worksheet

Solver-Linear Programming

Enter data in yellow-shaded cells, select **Maximize Objective Function** or **Minimize Objective Function**, and click the **Setup Problem** button. Then enter data in Work Area sheet.

Clear All

Decision Variables   2

Constraints   3

◉ Maximize Objective Function ◯ Minimize Objective Function

Setup Problem

Work Area Worksheet

Click here to view the Results sheet.   Find Optimal Solution

	X1	X2		RHV
Max-Z	34	40		Z
			<=/=/>=	
Extrusion	4	6	<	48
Packaging	2	2	<	18
Additive	2	1	<	16

FIGURE **E.7**

Inputs Worksheet

and ">" for a ≥ constraint. Slack and surplus variables will be added automatically as needed. When all of the inputs are made, click the "Find Optimal Solution" button.

The *Results Worksheet*, shown in Figure E.8, gives the optimal solution for the Stratton Company problem. OM Explorer begins by showing the optimal values of the decision variables (X1 = 3.0000 and X2 = 6.0000), their objective function coefficients, and their coefficient sensitivities. It also indicates a coefficient sensitivity number for each decision variable's objective function coefficient. Two tips on interpreting its value are

1. The sensitivity number is relevant only for a decision variable that is 0 in the optimal solution. If the decision variable is greater than 0, ignore the coefficient sensitivity number.

2. OM Explorer reports the absolute value of the coefficient sensitivity number, ignoring any minus sign. Thus, the value always tells how much the objective function coefficient must *improve* (increase for maximization problems or decrease for minimization problems) before the optimal solution would change. At that point, the decision variable associated with the coefficient enters the optimal solution at some positive level. To learn the new solution, apply OM Explorer again with a coefficient improved by slightly more than the coefficient sensitivity number.

Solution			
Variable Label	Variable Value	Original Coefficient	Coefficient Sensitivity
X1	3.0000	34.0000	0
X2	6.0000	40.0000	0
Constraint Label	Original RHV	Slack or Surplus	Shadow Price
Extrusion	48	0	3.0000
Packaging	18	0	11.0000
Additive	16	4	0
Objective Function Value:			342

Sensitivity Analysis and Ranges			
Objective Function Coefficients			
Variable Label	Lower Limit	Original Coefficient	Upper Limit
X1	26.66666667	34	40
X2	34	40	51
Right-Hand-Side Values			
Constraint Label	Lower Limit	Original Value	Upper Limit
Extrusion	40	48	54
Packaging	16	18	20
Additive	12	16	No Limit

FIGURE **E.8**

Results Worksheet

Thus, for the Stratton Company problem, the coefficient sensitivities provide no new insight because they are always 0 when decision variables have positive values in the optimal solution. Look instead at the lower and upper limits on the objective function coefficients, given in a following output section.

For the constraints, Figure E.8 shows the original right-hand-side values, the slack or surplus variables, and the shadow prices. A shadow price is given for each right-hand-side value or, more specifically, the constraint's slack or surplus variable. Two tips on interpreting its value follow:

1. The number is relevant only for a binding constraint, where the slack or surplus variable is 0 in the optimal solution. For a nonbinding constraint, the shadow price is 0.

2. OM Explorer reports the absolute value of the shadow price numbers, ignoring any minus sign. Thus, the value always tells how much the objective function's Z value *improves* (increases for maximization problems or decreases for minimization problems) by "relaxing" the constraint by one unit. Relaxing means increasing the right-hand-side value for a $\leq$ constraint or decreasing it for a $\geq$ constraint. The shadow price can also be interpreted as the marginal loss (or penalty) in Z caused by making the constraint more restrictive by one unit.

Thus, the Stratton Company problem has 4 pounds of the additive mix slack, so the shadow price is 0. Packaging, on the other hand, is a binding constraint because it has no slack. The shadow price of one more packaging hour is $11.

Finally, at the end of the Solution output (as shown in Figure E.8), OM Explorer reports the optimal objective function Z value as $342. All output confirms our earlier calculations and the graphic analysis.

The Sensitivity Analysis and Ranges portion of the *Results Worksheet*, shown in Figure E.8, begins with the range over which the objective function coefficients can vary without changing the optimal values of the decision variables. Note that c_1, which currently has a value of $34, has a range of optimality from $26.67 to $40. The objection function's Z value would change with coefficient changes over this range, but the optimal values of the decision variables remain the same. Finally, OM Explorer reports the range of feasibility, over which the right-hand-side parameters can range without changing the shadow prices. For example, the $11 shadow price for packaging is valid over the range from 16 to 20 hours. Again, these findings are identical to the sensitivity analysis done graphically. The difference is that OM Explorer can handle more than two decision variables (up to 99) and can be solved much more quickly.

The number of variables in the optimal solution (counting the decision variables, slack variables, and surplus variables) that are greater than 0 never exceeds the number of constraints. Such is the case for the Stratton Company problem, with its three constraints (not counting the implicit nonnegativity constraints) and three nonzero variables in the optimal solution (X1, X2, and the additive mix slack variable). On some rare occasions, the number of nonzero variables in the optimal solution can be less than the number of constraints—a condition called **degeneracy**. When degeneracy occurs, the sensitivity analysis information is suspect. Ignore the sensitivity analysis portion of the OM Explorer's output that is suspect. If you want more "what-if" information, simply run OM Explorer again using the new parameter values that you want to investigate.

degeneracy

A condition that occurs when the number of nonzero variables in the optimal solution is less than the number of constraints.

EXAMPLE E.5	**Using Shadow Prices for Decision Making**

The Stratton Company needs answers to three important questions: Would increasing capacities in the extrusion or packaging area pay if it cost an extra $8 per hour over and above the normal costs already reflected in the objective function coefficients? Would increasing packaging capacity pay if it cost an additional $6 per hour? Would buying more raw materials pay?

SOLUTION

Expanding extrusion capacity would cost a premium of $8 per hour, but the shadow price for that capacity is only $3 per hour. However, expanding packaging hours would cost only $6 per hour more than the price reflected in the objective function, and the shadow price is $11 per hour. Finally, buying more raw materials would not pay because a surplus of 4 pounds already exists; the shadow price is 0 for that resource.

Decision Point Management decided to increase its packaging hours capacity but not to expand extrusion capacity or buy more raw materials.

> APPLICATIONS <

Many problems in operations management, and in other functional areas, have been modeled as linear programming problems. Knowing how to formulate a problem generally, the decision maker can then adapt it to the situation at hand.

The following list identifies some problems that can be solved with linear programming. The review problems at the end of this supplement and at the end of other chapters illustrate many of these types of problems.

- **Constraint Management**

  Product Mix. Find the best mix of products to produce, given capacity and demand constraints.

- **Distribution**

  Shipping. Find the optimal shipping assignments from factories to distribution centers or from warehouses to retailers.

- **Inventory**

  Stock Control. Determine the optimal mix of products to hold in inventory in a warehouse.

  Supplier Selection. Find the optimal combination of suppliers to minimize the amount of unwanted inventory.

- **Location**

  Plants or Warehouses. Determine the optimal location of a plant or warehouse, with respect to total transportation costs between various alternative locations and existing supply and demand sources.

- **Process Management**

  Stock Cutting. Given the dimensions of a roll or sheet of raw material, find the cutting pattern that minimizes the amount of scrap material.

- **Sales and Operations Planning**

  Production. Find the minimum-cost production schedule, taking into account hiring and layoffs, inventory carrying, overtime, and subcontracting costs, subject to various capacity and policy constraints.

  Staffing. Find the optimal staffing levels for various categories of workers, subject to various demand and policy constraints.

  Blends. Find the optimal proportions of various ingredients used to make products, such as gasoline, paints, and food, subject to certain minimal requirements.

- **Scheduling**

  Shifts. Determine the minimum-cost assignment of workers to shifts, subject to varying demand.

  Vehicles. Assign vehicles to products or customers and determine the number of trips to make, subject to vehicle size, vehicle availability, and demand constraints.

  Routing. Find the optimal routing of a service or product through several sequential processes, with each having its own capacity and other characteristics.

> STUDENT CD-ROM AND INTERNET RESOURCES <

The Student CD-ROM and the Companion Website at **www.prenhall.com/krajewski** contain many tools, activities, and resources designed for this supplement.

> KEY TERMS <

> SOLVED PROBLEM 1 <

TUTOR E.4

Tutor E.4 on the Student CD-ROM provides a practice example for finding the graphic and algebraic solution.

O'Connel Airlines is considering air service from its hub of operations in Cicely, Alaska, to Rome, Wisconsin, and Seattle, Washington. O'Connel has one gate at the Cicely Airport, which operates 12 hours per day. Each flight requires 1 hour of gate time. Each flight to Rome consumes 15 hours of pilot crew time and is expected to produce a profit of $2,500. Serving Seattle uses 10 hours of pilot crew time per flight and will result in a profit of $2,000 per flight. Pilot crew labor is limited to 150 hours per day. The market for service to Rome is limited to nine flights per day.

a. Use the graphic method of linear programming to maximize profits for O'Connel Airlines.

b. Identify slack and surplus constraints, if any.

SOLUTION

a. The objective function is to maximize profits, Z:

$$\text{Maximize: } \$2,500x_1 + \$2,000x_2 = Z$$

where

$$x_1 = \text{number of flights per day to Rome, Wisconsin}$$
$$x_2 = \text{number of flights per day to Seattle, Washington}$$

The constraints are

$$x_1 + x_2 \le 12 \text{ (gate capacity)}$$
$$15x_1 + 10x_2 \le 150 \text{ (labor)}$$
$$x_1 \le 9 \text{ (market)}$$
$$x_1 \ge 0 \quad \text{and} \quad x_1 \ge 0$$

A careful drawing of iso-profit lines parallel to the one shown in Figure E.9 will indicate that point D is the optimal solution. It is at the intersection of the labor and gate capacity constraints. Solving algebraically, we get

$$
\begin{array}{rl}
15x_1 + 10x_2 = & 150 \text{ (labor)} \\
\underline{-10x_1 - 10x_2} = & \underline{-120} \text{ (gate} \times -10) \\
5x_1 + 0x_2 = & 30 \\
x_1 = & 6 \\
6 + x_2 = & 12 \text{ (gate)} \\
x_2 = & 6
\end{array}
$$

The maximum profit results from making six flights to Rome and six flights to Seattle:

$$\$2,500(6) + \$2,000(6) = \$27,000$$

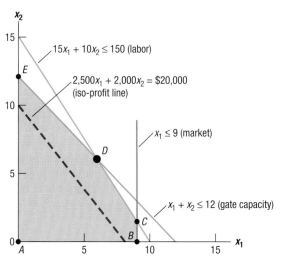

FIGURE **E.9**

Graphic Solution for O'Connel Airlines

b. The market constraint has three units of slack, so the demand for flights to Rome is not fully met:

$$x_1 \leq 9$$
$$x_1 + s_3 = 9$$
$$6 + s_3 = 9$$
$$s_3 = 3$$

> DISCUSSION QUESTION <

A particular linear programming maximization problem has the following less-than-or-equal-to constraints: (1) raw materials, (2) labor hours, and (3) storage space. The optimal solution occurs at the intersection of the raw materials and labor hours constraints, so those constraints are binding. Management is considering whether to authorize overtime. What use-ful information could the linear programming solution provide to management in making this decision? Suppose a warehouse becomes available for rent at bargain rates. What would management need to know in order to decide whether to rent the warehouse? How could the linear programming model be helpful?

> PROBLEMS <

Software, such as OM Explorer, Active Models, and POM for Windows, is packaged with every new copy of the textbook. Check with your instructor on how best to use it. In many cases, the instructor wants you to understand how to do the calculations by hand. At most, the software provides a check on your calculations. When calculations are particularly complex and the goal is interpreting the results in making decisions, the software replaces entirely the manual calculations. The software also can be a valuable resource well after your course is completed.

1. The Really Big Shoe is a manufacturer of basketball and football shoes. Ed Sullivan, the manager of marketing, must decide the best way to spend advertising resources. Each football team sponsored requires 120 pairs of shoes. Each basketball team requires 32 pairs of shoes. Football coaches receive $300,000 for shoe sponsorship, and basketball coaches receive $1,000,000. Sullivan's promotional budget is $30,000,000. The Really Big Shoe has a limited supply (4 liters or 4000 cubic centimeters) of flubber, a rare and costly compound used in promotional athletic shoes. Each pair of basketball shoes requires 3 cc of flubber, and each pair of football shoes requires 1 cc. Sullivan wants to sponsor as many basketball and football teams as resources allow.

   a. Create a set of linear equations to describe the objective function and the constraints.

   b. Use graphic analysis to find the visual solution.

   c. What is the maximum number of each type of team The Really Big Shoe can sponsor?

2. A business student at Nowledge College must complete a total of 65 courses to graduate. The number of business courses must be greater than or equal to 23. The number of nonbusiness courses must be greater than or equal to 20. The average business course requires a textbook costing $60 and 120 hours of study. Nonbusiness courses

require a textbook costing $24 and 200 hours of study. The student has $3,000 to spend on books.

   a. Create a set of linear equations to describe the objective function and the constraints.

   b. Use graphic analysis to find the visual solution.

   c. What combination of business and nonbusiness courses minimizes total hours of study?

   d. Identify the slack or surplus variables.

3. In Problem 2, suppose that the objective is to minimize the cost of books and that the student's total study time is limited to 12,600 hours.

   a. Use graphic analysis to determine the combination of courses that minimizes the total cost of books.

   b. Identify the slack or surplus variables.

4. Mile-High Microbrewery makes a light beer and a dark beer. Mile-High has a limited supply of barley, limited bottling capacity, and a limited market for light beer. Profits are $0.20 per bottle of light beer and $0.50 per bottle of dark beer.

   a. The following table shows resource availability of products at the Mile-High Microbrewery. Use the graphic method of linear programming to maximize profits. How many bottles of each product should be produced per month?

Product			
Resource	Light Beer (x_1)	Dark Beer (x_2)	Resource Availability (per month)
Barley	0.1 gram	0.6 gram	2,000 grams
Bottling	1 bottle	1 bottle	6,000 bottles
Market	1 bottle	—	4,000 bottles

   b. Identify any constraints with slack or surplus.

5. The plant manager of a plastic pipe manufacturer has the opportunity to use two different routings for a particular type of plastic pipe. Routing 1 uses extruder A, and routing 2 uses extruder B. Both routings require the same melting process. The following table shows the time requirements and capacities of these processes:

Time Requirements (hr/100 ft)			
Process	Routing 1	Routing 2	Capacity (hr)
Melting	1	1	45
Extruder A	3	0	90
Extruder B	0	1	160

Each 100 feet of pipe processed on routing 1 uses 5 pounds of raw material, whereas each 100 feet of pipe processed on routing 2 used only 4 pounds. This difference results from differing scrap rates of the extruding

machines. Consequently, the profit per 100 feet of pipe processed on routing 1 is $60 and on routing 2 is $80. A total of 200 pounds of raw material is available.

   a. Create a set of linear equations to describe the objective function and the constraints.

   b. Use graphic analysis to find the visual solution.

   c. What is the maximum profit?

6. A manufacturer of textile dyes can use two different processing routings for a particular type of dye. Routing 1 uses drying press A, and routing 2 uses drying press B. Both routings require the same mixing vat to blend chemicals for the dye before drying. The following table shows the time requirements and capacities of these processes:

Time Requirements (hr/kg)			
Process	Routing 1	Routing 2	Capacity (hr)
Mixing	2	2	54
Dryer A	6	0	120
Dryer B	0	8	180

Each kilogram of dye processed on routing 1 uses 20 liters of chemicals, whereas each kilogram of dye processed on routing 2 uses only 15 liters. The difference results from differing yield rates of the drying presses. Consequently, the profit per kilogram processed on routing 1 is $50 and on routing 2 is $65. A total of 450 liters of input chemicals is available.

   a. Write the constraints and objective function to maximize profits.

   b. Use the graphic method of linear programming to find the optimal solution.

   c. Identify any constraints with slack or surplus.

7. The Trim-Look Company makes several lines of skirts, dresses, and sport coats. Recently, a consultant suggested that the company reevaluate its South Islander line and allocate its resources to products that would maximize contribution to profits and to overhead. Each product requires the same polyester fabric and must pass through the cutting and sewing departments. The following data were collected for the study:

Processing Time (hr)			
Product	Cutting	Sewing	Material (yd)
Skirt	1	1	1
Dress	3	4	1
Sport coat	4	6	4

The cutting department has 100 hours of capacity, sewing has 180 hours of capacity, and 60 yards of material are available. Each skirt contributes $5 to profits and overhead; each dress, $17; and each sport coat, $30.

a. Specify the objective function and constraints for this problem.

b. Use a computer package to solve the problem.

8. Consider Problem 7 further.

a. How much would you be willing to pay for an extra hour of cutting time? For an extra hour of sewing time? For an extra yard of material? Explain your response to each question.

b. Determine the range of right-hand-side values over which the shadow price would be valid for the cutting constraint and for the material constraint.

9. Polly Astaire makes fine clothing for big and tall men. A few years ago Astaire entered the sportswear market with the Sunset line of shorts, pants, and shirts. Management wants to make the amount of each product that will maximize profits. Each type of clothing is routed through two departments, A and B. The relevant data for each product are as follows:

Processing Time (hr)			
Product	Department A	Department B	Material (yd)
Shirts	2	1	2
Shorts	2	3	1
Pants	3	4	4

Department A has 120 hours of capacity, department B has 160 hours of capacity, and 90 yards of material are available. Each shirt contributes $10 to profits and overhead; each pair of shorts, $10; and each pair of pants, $23.

a. Specify the objective function and constraints for this problem.

b. Use a computer package to solve the problem.

c. How much should Astaire be willing to pay for an extra hour of department A capacity? How much for an extra hour of department B capacity? For what range of right-hand values are these shadow prices valid?

10. The Butterfield Company makes a variety of hunting knives. Each knife is processed on four machines. The processing times required are as follows. Machine capacities (in hours) are 1,500 for machine 1; 1,400 for machine 2; 1,600 for machine 3; and 1,500 for machine 4.

Processing Time (hr)				
Knife	Machine 1	Machine 2	Machine 3	Machine 4
A	0.05	0.10	0.15	0.05
B	0.15	0.10	0.05	0.05
C	0.20	0.05	0.10	0.20
D	0.15	0.10	0.10	0.10
E	0.05	0.10	0.10	0.05

Each product contains a different amount of two basic raw materials. Raw material 1 costs $0.50 per ounce, and raw material 2 costs $1.50 per ounce. There are 75,000 ounces of raw material 1 and 100,000 ounces of raw material 2 available.

Requirements (oz/unit)			
Knife	Raw Material 1	Raw Material 2	Selling Price ($/unit)
A	4	2	15.00
B	6	8	25.50
C	1	3	14.00
D	2	5	19.50
E	6	10	27.00

a. If the objective is to maximize profit, specify the objective function and constraints for the problem. Assume that labor costs are negligible.

b. Solve the problem with a computer package.

11. The Nutmeg Corporation produces five different nut and mixed nut products: almond pack, walnut pack, gourmet pack, fancy pack, and thrifty pack. Each product (individual or mix) comes in a one-pound can. The firm can purchase almonds at $0.80 per pound, walnuts at $0.60 per pound, and peanuts at $0.35 per pound. Peanuts are used to complete each mix, and the company has an unlimited supply of them. The supply of almonds and walnuts is limited. The company can buy up to 3,000 pounds of almonds and 2,000 pounds of walnuts. The resource requirements and forecasted demand for the products follow. Use a computer package to solve this problem.

Minimum Requirements (%)			
Product	Almonds	Walnuts	Demand (cans)
Almonds	100	—	1,250
Walnuts	—	100	750
Gourmet	45	45	1,000
Fancy	30	30	500
Thrifty	20	20	1,500

a. What mix minimizes the cost of meeting the demand for all five products?

b. What is the impact on the product mix if only 2,000 pounds of peanuts are available?

c. What is the impact on the product mix if the gourmet pack requires 50 percent almonds and 50 percent walnuts?

d. What is the impact on the product mix if demand for the fancy pack doubles?

12. A problem often of concern to managers in processing industries is blending. Consider the task facing Lisa Rankin, procurement manager of a company that manufactures special additives. She must determine the proper amount of each raw material to purchase for the production of a certain product. Each gallon of the finished product must have a combustion point of at least 220°F. In addition, the product's gamma content (which causes hydrocarbon pollution) cannot exceed 6 percent of volume, and the product's zeta content (which cleans the internal moving parts of engines) must be at least 12 percent by volume. Three raw materials are available. Each raw material has a different rating on these characteristics.

	Raw Material		
Characteristic	**A**	**B**	**C**
Combustion point (°F)	200	180	280
Gamma content (%)	4	3	10
Zeta content (%)	20	10	8

Raw material A costs $0.60 per gallon; raw materials B and C cost $0.40 and $0.50 per gallon, respectively. The procurement manager wants to minimize the cost of raw materials per gallon of product. Use linear programming to find the optimal proportion of each raw material for a gallon of finished product. (*Hint:* Express the decision variables in terms of fractions of a gallon; the sum of the fractions must equal 1.00.)

13. A small fabrication firm makes three basic types of components for use by other companies. Each component is processed on three machines. The processing times follow. Total capacities (in hours) are 1,600 for machine 1; 1,400 for machine 2; and 1,500 for machine 3.

	Processing Time (hr)		
Component	**Machine 1**	**Machine 2**	**Machine 3**
A	0.25	0.10	0.05
B	0.20	0.15	0.10
C	0.10	0.05	0.15

Each component contains a different amount of two basic raw materials. Raw material 1 costs $0.20 per ounce, and raw material 2 costs $0.35 per ounce. At present, 200,000 ounces of raw material 1 and 85,000 ounces of raw material 2 are available.

	Requirement (oz/unit)		
Component	**Raw Material 1**	**Raw Material 2**	**Selling Price ($/unit)**
A	32	12	40
B	26	16	28
C	19	9	24

a. Assume that the company must make at least 1,200 units of component B, that labor costs are negligible, and that the objective is to maximize profits. Specify the objective function and constraints for the problem.

b. Use a computer package to solve the problem.

14. The following is a linear programming model for analyzing the product mix of Maxine's Hat Company, which produces three hat styles:

Maximize: $\$7x_1 + \$5x_2 + \$2x_3 = Z$

Subject to:
$$3x_1 + 5x_2 + x_3 \leq 150 \text{ (machine A time)}$$
$$5x_1 + 3x_2 + 2x_3 \leq 100 \text{ (machine B time)}$$
$$x_1 + 2x_2 + x_3 \leq 160 \text{ (machine C time)}$$
$$x_1 \geq 0, x_2 \geq 0, \text{ and } x_3 \geq 0$$

The OM Explorer printout in Figure E.10 shows the optimal solution to the problem. Consider each of the following statements independently, and state whether it is true or false. Explain each answer.

a. If the price of hat 3 were increased to $2.50, it would be part of the optimal product mix.

b. The capacity of machine C can be reduced to 65 hours without affecting profits.

c. If machine A had a capacity of 170 hours, the production output would remain unchanged.

15. The Washington Chemical Company produces chemicals and solvents for the glue industry. The production process is divided into several "focused factories," each producing a specific set of products. The time has come to prepare the production plan for one of the focused factories. This particular factory produces five products, which must pass through both the reactor and the separator. Each product also requires a certain combination of raw materials. Production data are shown in Table E.2.

The Washington Chemical Company has a long-term contract with a major glue manufacturer that requires annual production of 3,000 pounds of both products 3 and 4. More of these products could be produced because demand currently exceeds production capacity.

a. Determine the annual production quantity of each product that maximizes contribution to profits. Assume the company can sell all it can produce.

b. Specify the lot size for each product.

Solution

Variable Label	Variable Value	Original Coefficient	Coefficient Sensitivity
X1	3.1250	7.0000	0
X2	28.1250	5.0000	0
X3	0.0000	2.0000	0.7500

Constraint Label	Original RHV	Slack or Surplus	Shadow Price
Machine A	150	0	0.2500
Machine B	100	0	1.2500
Machine C	160	100.6250	0

Objective Function Value:		162.5

Sensitivity Analysis and Ranges

Objective Function Coefficients

Variable Label	Lower Limit	Original Coefficient	Upper Limit
X1	5.2857	7	8.3333
X2	4.2000	5	11.6667
X3	No Limit	2	2.75

Right-Hand-Side Values

Constraint Label	Lower Limit	Original Value	Upper Limit
Extrusion	60	150	166.6667
Packaging	90	100	250
Additive	59.3750	160	No Limit

FIGURE E.10 | OM Explorer Solver Output for Maxine's Hat Company

16. The Warwick Manufacturing Company produces shovels for industrial and home use. Sales of the shovels are seasonal, and Warwick's customers refuse to stockpile them during slack periods. In other words, the customers want to minimize inventory, insist on shipments according to their schedules, and will not accept backorders.

Warwick employs manual, unskilled laborers who require only basic training. Producing 1,000 shovels costs $3,500 on regular time and $3,700 on overtime. These amounts include materials, which account for more than 85 percent of the cost. Overtime is limited to production of 15,000 shovels per quarter. In addition, subcontractors can be hired at $4,200 per thousand shovels, but Warwick's labor contract restricts this type of production to 5,000 shovels per quarter.

The current level of inventory is 30,000 shovels, and management wants to end the year at that level. Holding 1,000 shovels in inventory costs $280 per quarter. The latest annual demand forecast is

Quarter	Demand
1	70,000
2	150,000
3	320,000
4	100,000
Totals	640,000

Build a linear programming model to determine the *best* regular-time capacity plan. Assume the following:

■ The firm has 30 workers now, and management wants to have the same number in quarter 4.

TABLE E.2 | Production Data for Washington Chemical

	Product					Total Resources
Resource	1	2	3	4	5	Available
Reactor (hr/lb)	0.05	0.10	0.80	0.57	0.15	7,500 hr*
Separator (hr/lb)	0.20	0.02	0.20	0.09	0.30	7,500 hr*
Raw material 1 (lb)	0.20	0.50	0.10	0.40	0.18	10,000 lb
Raw material 2 (lb)	—	0.70	—	0.50	—	6,000 lb
Raw material 3 (lb)	0.10	0.20	0.40	—	—	7,000 lb
Profit contribution ($/lb)	4.00	7.00	3.50	4.00	5.70	

*The total time available has been adjusted to account for setups. The five products have a prescribed sequence owing to the cost of changeovers between products. The company has a 35-day cycle (or 10 changeovers per year per product). Consequently, the time for these changeovers has been deducted from the total time available for these machines.

- Each worker can produce 4,000 shovels per quarter.
- Hiring a worker costs $1,000, and laying off a worker costs $600.

17. The management of Warwick Manufacturing Company is willing to give price breaks to its customers as an incentive to purchase shovels in advance of the traditional seasons. Warwick's sales and marketing staff estimates that the demand for shovels resulting from the price breaks would be

Quarter	Demand	Original Demand
1	120,000	70,000
2	180,000	150,000
3	180,000	320,000
4	160,000	100,000
Totals	640,000	640,000

Calculate the optimal production plan (including the workforce staffing plan) under the new demand schedule. Compare it to the optimal production plan under the original demand schedule. Evaluate the potential effects of demand management.

18. The Bull Grin Company produces a feed supplement for animal foods produced by a number of companies. Sales are seasonal, and Bull Grin's customers refuse to stockpile the supplement during slack sales periods. In other words, the customers want to minimize inventory, insist on shipments according to their schedules, and will not accept backorders.

   Bull Grin employs manual, unskilled laborers who require little or no training. Producing 1,000 pounds of supplement costs $810 on regular time and $900 on overtime. These amounts include materials, which account for more than 80 percent of the cost. Overtime is limited to production of 30,000 pounds per quarter. In addition, subcontractors can be hired at $1,100 per thousand pounds, but only 10,000 pounds per quarter can be produced this way.

   The current level of inventory is 40,000 pounds, and management wants to end the year at that level. Holding 1,000 pounds of feed supplement in inventory costs $110 per quarter. The latest annual forecast follows:

Quarter	Demand (lb)
1	100,000
2	410,000
3	770,000
4	440,000
Total	1,720,000

The firm currently has 180 workers, a number that management wants to keep in quarter 4. Each worker can produce 2,000 pounds per quarter, so regular-time production costs $1,620 per worker. Idle workers must be paid at that same rate. Hiring one worker costs $1,000, and laying off a worker costs $600.

Write the objective function and constraints describing this production planning problem after fully defining the decision variables.

19. Insight Traders, Inc., invests in various types of securities. The firm has $5 million for immediate investment and wants to maximize the interest earned over the next year. Four investment possibilities are presented in the following table. To further structure the portfolio, the board of directors has specified that at least 40 percent of the investment must be in corporate bonds and common stock. Furthermore, no more than 20 percent of the investment may be in real estate.

Investment	Expected Interest Earned (%)
Corporate bonds	8.5
Common stock	9.0
Gold certificates	10.0
Real estate	13.0

Write the objective function and constraints for this portfolio investment problem after fully defining the decision variables.

20. JPMorgan Chase has a scheduling problem. Operators work eight-hour shifts and can begin work at midnight, 4 A.M., 8 A.M., noon, 4 P.M., or 8 P.M. Operators are needed to satisfy the following demand pattern. Formulate a linear programming model to cover the demand requirements with the minimum number of operators.

Time Period	Operators Needed
Midnight to 4 A.M.	4
4 A.M. to 8 A.M.	6
8 A.M. to noon	90
Noon to 4 P.M.	85
4 P.M. to 8 P.M.	55
8 P.M. to 12 midnight	20

> SELECTED REFERENCES <

Asim, R., E. De Falomir, and L. Lasdon. "An Optimization-Based Decision Support System for a Product-Mix Problem." *Interfaces*, vol. 12, no. 2 (1982), pp. 26–33.

Bonini, Charles P., Warren H. Hausman, and Harold Bierman, Jr. *Quantitative Analysis for Management*, 9th ed. Chicago: Irwin, 1997.

Cook, Thomas M., and Robert A. Russell. *Introduction to Management Sciences*. Englewood Cliffs, NJ: Prentice Hall, 1993.

Eppen, G. D., F. J. Gould, C. P. Schmidt, Jeffrey H. Moore, and Larry R. Weatherford. *Introductory Management Science: Decision Modeling with Spreadsheets*, 5th ed. Upper Saddle River, NJ: Prentice Hall, 1998.

Fourer, Robert. "Software Survey: Linear Programming." *OR/MS Today* (April 1997), pp. 54–63.

Greenberg, H. J. "How to Analyze the Results of Linear Programs—Part 2: Price Interpretation." *Interfaces*, vol. 23, no. 5 (1993), pp. 97–114.

Hess, Rick. *Managerial Spreadsheet Modeling and Analysis*. Chicago: Irwin, 1997.

Jayaraman, V., R. Srivastava, and W. C. Benton. "Supplier Selection and Order Quantity Allocation." *Journal of Supply Chain Management*, vol. 35, no. 2 (1999), pp. 50–58.

Krajewski, L. J., and H. E. Thompson. *Management Science: Quantitative Methods in Context*. New York: John Wiley & Sons, 1981.

Markland, Robert E., and James R. Sweigart. *Quantitative Methods: Applications to Managerial Decision Making*. New York: John Wiley & Sons, 1987.

Perry, C., and K. C. Crellin. "The Precise Management Meaning of a Shadow Price." *Interfaces*, vol. 12, no. 2 (1982), pp. 61–63.

Ragsdale, Cliff T., and Rick Hess. *Spreadsheet Modeling and Decision Analysis; A Practical Introduction to Management Science*, 2d ed. Cincinnati, OH: South-Western, 1998.

Render, B., R.M. Stair, and Michael Hanna. *Quantitative Analysis for Management*, 8th ed. Upper Saddle River, NJ: Prentice Hall, 2003.

Taylor, Bernard W., III. *Introduction to Management Science*. Needham Heights, MA: Allyn & Bacon, 1990.

Verma, Rohit. "My Operations Management Students Love Linear Programming." *Decision Line* (July 1997), pp. 9–12.

Winston, Wayne L., S. Christian Albright, and Mark Broadie. *Practical Management Science: Spreadsheet Modeling and Applications*. Pacific Grove, CA: Duxbury, 1996.

15

LEARNING GOALS

*After reading this chapter,
you should be able to:*

1. Explain how ERP systems can foster better resource planning.

2. Explain how the concept of dependent demand is fundamental to resource planning.

3. Describe a master production schedule (MPS) and the information it provides.

4. Create an MPS and compute available-to-promise quantities.

5. Discuss the logic of a material requirements planning (MRP) system.

6. Identify production and purchase orders needed for dependent demand items.

7. Describe how Drum-Buffer-Rope systems implement Theory of Constraints (TOC) principles for resource planning.

8. Apply MRP principles to the provision of services and distribution inventories.

A concierge for the Hotel Gritti Palace greets a rowing team competing in the Volgalonga. Boaters must row from the Piazza San Marco to Buranoa and back, a total distance of 20 miles. The Hotel Gritti Palace is one of many properties of Starwood Hotels and Resorts Worldwide that faces complex resource planning issues.

STARWOOD

Resource planning at a company such as Starwood Hotels and Resorts Worldwide is complex, not only because of the size of the business, but also because of the wide variety of its different facilities. Starwood manages the employees, equipment, and supplies at its 750 hotels around the world to ensure that the needs and expectations of each and every customer are met. To help forecast these needs, Starwood now uses an enterprise resource planning (ERP) system developed by Oracle, a software company headquartered in California. Included in the Oracle system is an electronic reservation system that profiles the preferences of guests, which allows the staff to better serve them each time they stay at a Starwood hotel: preference for feather or foam pillows, certain types of newspapers, suites or regular rooms,

rooms on lower floors versus upper floors, and even handicapped accommodations or special physical requirements. The profile is used at the time a reservation is made to estimate the various types of rooms and locations, newspapers, pillows, and any other resources each Starwood facility needs. The guest profiling system also allows Starwood to provide a "customized" experience for each guest.

Starwood's reservation system is also linked to a property management system for each hotel. The property management system schedules the hotel's staff members, for example, and projects the amount of food and beverages needed for the hotel's food-service department. Starwood knows on a per-room basis what level of resources (staff members, food, towels, and the like) it needs at any point in

>

For additional chapter resources check the Student CD-ROM or the Companion Website at
www.prenhall.com/krajewski

time. Detailed projections of these quantities are made, and managers then adjust these projections to line them up with the company's financial plans. Because the managers of each hotel have access to occupancy rates weeks in advance, they are better able to plan for these needs.

Starwood's ERP system also features a centralized database with accounting data, including payroll, accounts payable information, the company's general ledger and balance sheet, as well as income statements for its various properties. Because the Oracle-based system is so extensive and involves so many of Starwood's functional activities, the company integrated it gradually over time with its older information systems.

Source: David Baum, "Setting the Standard for Service," Profit Magazine (1999); www.oracle.com (updated 2003); www.starwood.com (2005).

Starwood demonstrates that companies can gain a competitive edge by using an effective information system to help with their resource planning. Companies must ensure that all of the resources they need to produce finished services or products are available at the right time. If they aren't, a firm risks losing business. For a manufacturer, this task can mean keeping track of thousands of subassemblies, components, and raw materials as well as key equipment capacities. For a service provider, this task can mean keeping track of numerous supplies and carefully scheduling the time and capacity requirements of different employees and types of equipment.

We begin this chapter by describing enterprise resource planning (ERP) systems, which have become a valuable tool for, among other things, resource planning. We then examine various approaches to resource planning, including material requirements planning (MRP), Drum-Buffer-Rope (DBR), and lean systems (JIT). Because lean systems were already covered in Chapter 9, we then move on to demonstrate how service providers such as Starwood go about resource planning. The entire concluding section of the chapter illustrates how service providers manage their supplies, human resources, equipment, and financial resources.

> RESOURCE PLANNING ACROSS THE ORGANIZATION <

resource planning

A process that takes sales and operations plans; processes information in the way of time standards, routings, and other information on how the firm produces its services or products; and then plans the input requirements.

Resource planning lies at the heart of any organization, cutting across all of its different functional areas. It takes sales and operations plans; processes information in the way of time standards, routings, and other information on how services or products are produced; and then plans the input requirements. It also can create reports for managers of the firm's major functional areas, such as human resources, purchasing, sales and marketing, and finance and accounting. In essence, resource planning is a process in and of itself that can be analyzed relative to the firm's competitive priorities.

> ENTERPRISE RESOURCE PLANNING <

enterprise process

A companywide process that cuts across functional areas, business units, geographical regions, and product lines.

An **enterprise process** is a companywide process that cuts across functional areas, business units, geographic regions, and product lines. **Enterprise resource planning (ERP) systems** are large, integrated information systems that support many enterprise processes and data storage needs. Today, ERP systems are being used by traditional brick-and-mortar organizations such as manufacturers, restaurants, airlines, hospitals, and hotels, as well as by Internet companies that rely extensively on Web connectivity to link their customers and suppliers.

enterprise resource planning (ERP) systems

Large, integrated information systems that support many enterprise processes and data storage needs.

WHAT AN ERP SYSTEM DOES

By integrating the firm's functional areas, ERP systems allow an organization to view its operations as a whole rather than having to try to put together the different information pieces produced by its various functions and divisions. For example, suppose that a U.S. manufacturer of telecommunications products has an ERP system and that an Athens-based sales representative wants to prepare a customer quote. When the salesperson enters information about the customer's needs into a laptop computer, the ERP system automatically generates a formal contract, in Greek, listing the product's specifications, delivery date, and price. After the customer accepts the quote and agrees to purchase the product, the salesperson makes an entry, and the ERP system verifies the customer's credit limit and records the order. The system then schedules the shipment of the product using the best routing. Working backwards from the delivery date, it reserves the necessary materials in inventory and determines when to release a purchase order to its suppliers followed by a production order to its factory floor. The system then updates the company's sales and production forecasts with the new order, and credits the sales representative's payroll account with the appropriate commission from the sale. Simultaneously the system's accounting application calculates the product's cost to make and its profitability and reflects the transaction in the firm's accounts payable and accounts receivable ledgers. Divisional and corporate balance sheets are updated, as are the firm's cash levels. In short, the system supports all of the firm's enterprise processes prior to and following the sale.

HOW ERP SYSTEMS ARE DESIGNED

ERP revolves around a single comprehensive database that can be made available across the entire organization (or enterprise). Passwords are generally issued to allow certain personnel to access certain areas of the system. Having a single database for all of the firm's information makes it much easier for managers to monitor all of the company's products, at all locations, and at all times. The database collects data and feeds them into the various modular applications (or suites) of the software system. As new information is entered as a *transaction* in one application, related information is automatically updated in the other applications, including the firm's financial and accounting databases, its human resource and payroll databases, sales and customer databases, and so forth. In this way, the ERP system streamlines the data flows throughout the organization and provides employees with direct access to a wealth of real-time operating information. This process eliminates many of the cross-functional coordination problems older nonintegrated systems suffered from. Figure 15.1 shows some of the typical applications, with a few subprocesses nested within each one. Some of the applications are for back-office operations such as manufacturing and payroll, while others are for front-office operations such as customer service.

USING OPERATIONS TO COMPETE

Operations As a Competitive Weapon
Operations Strategy
Project Management

MANAGING PROCESSES

Process Strategy
Process Analysis
Process Performance and Quality
Constraint Management
Process Layout
Lean Systems

MANAGING VALUE CHAINS

Supply Chain Strategy
Location
Inventory Management
Forecasting
Sales and Operations Planning
Resource Planning
Scheduling

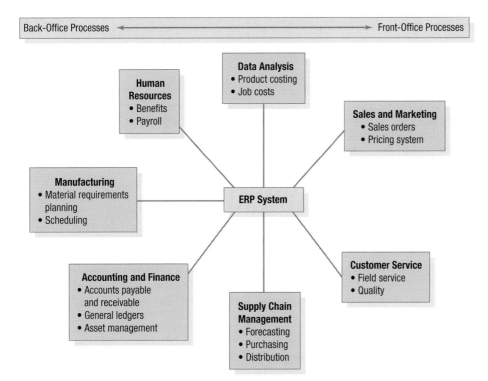

Back-Office Processes ⟷ Front-Office Processes

Human Resources
• Benefits
• Payroll

Data Analysis
• Product costing
• Job costs

Sales and Marketing
• Sales orders
• Pricing system

Manufacturing
• Material requirements planning
• Scheduling

ERP System

Accounting and Finance
• Accounts payable and receivable
• General ledgers
• Asset management

Supply Chain Management
• Forecasting
• Purchasing
• Distribution

Customer Service
• Field service
• Quality

FIGURE 15.1

ERP Application Modules

Source: Reprinted by permission of Harvard Business School Press. From *Enterprise Resource Planning (ERP)* by Scalle and Cotteleer. Boston, MA, 1999, No. 9-699-020. Copyright © 1999 by the Harvard Business School Publishing Corporation; all rights reserved.

Amazon.com is one company that uses an ERP system. The supply chain application of Amazon's system is particularly important because it allows Amazon.com to link customer orders to warehouse shipments and, ultimately, to supplier replenishment orders. Other applications are more important in other businesses. For example, universities put particular emphasis on the human resources and accounting and finance applications, and manufacturers have an interest in almost every application suite. Not all applications in Figure 15.1 need to be integrated into an ERP system, but those left out will not share their information with the ERP system. Sometimes, however, ERP systems are designed to interface with a firm's existing, older information systems (called "legacy systems"). Starwood used this approach, as discussed in the opening case.

Designing an ERP system requires that a company carefully analyze its major processes so that appropriate decisions about the coordination of legacy systems and new software can be made. Sometimes, a company's processes must be completely reengineered before the firm can enjoy the benefits of an integrated information system. However, a recent study showed that companies reap the greatest rewards when they keep their ERP implementations simple, work with a small number of vendors, and use standardized systems rather than customizing them extensively. Firms can otherwise end up spending excessive amounts of money on ERP systems that are complex to use and costly to manage.

Most ERP systems today use a graphical user interface, although the older keyboard-driven, text-based systems are still popular because of their dependability and technical simplicity. Users navigate through various screens and menus. Training, such as during ERP implementation, focuses on these screens and how users can utilize them to get their jobs done. The biggest supplier of these off-the-shelf commercial ERP packages is SAP AG, a German company, followed by Oracle, J. D. Edwards, and Baan.

ERP systems underwent significant changes over the past several years. One direction relates to their **interoperability**—the ability of one piece of software to interact with others. Electronic data interchange, a system that allows data to be transferred between companies on a batch basis, had been a major workhorse over the years. However, interest in the new economy of e-commerce is increasing. For example, XML (Extensible Markup Language) lets companies structure and exchange information without rewriting their existing software or having to purchase new software or hardware. XML has the potential to reduce costs and allow information to be automated and shared in real time like never before because it increases the interoperability of systems. IBM's WebSphere MQ, and Microsoft's MSMQ are two XML-based systems. The goal of all such methods is to automate, in almost real time, the sharing of information across enterprise boundaries.

interoperability

The ability of one piece of software to interact with others.

> PLANNING AND CONTROL SYSTEMS FOR MANUFACTURERS <

The Manufacturing and Supply Chain Management modules in Figure 15.1 deal with resource planning. Understanding resource planning begins with the concept of *dependent demand,* which sets it apart from the techniques covered in Chapter 12, "Inventory Management." In this section, we discuss the nature of dependent demand and then identify three basic planning and control systems that deal with it.

DEPENDENT DEMAND

To illustrate the concept of dependent demand, let's consider a Huffy bicycle produced for retail outlets. Demand for a final product, such as a bicycle, is called *independent demand* because it is influenced only by market conditions and not by the production plan of any other type of bicycle Huffy holds in its inventory. Huffy must *forecast* this demand using techniques such as those discussed in Chapter 13, "Forecasting." However, Huffy also keeps many other items in inventory—handlebars, pedals, frames, and wheel rims—used to make completed bicycles. Each of these items has a **dependent demand** because the quantity required varies with the production plans for other items held in the firm's inventory—finished bikes, in this case. For example, the demand for frames, pedals, and wheel rims is *dependent* on the production of completed bicycles. Operations can *calculate* the demand for dependent demand items once the bicycle production levels are laid out in the sales and opera-

dependent demand

The demand for an item that occurs because the quantity required varies with the production plans for other items held in the firm's inventory.

MANAGERIAL **PRACTICE**	15.1	ERP AT VF CORPORATION

What do Wrangler, Rustler, and Lee jeans, Timber Creek khakis, Vanity Fair underwear, Healthtex clothes for kids, Red Kap and Bulwark industrial work clothes, The North Face outdoor gear and apparel, Jantzen bathing suits, Nautica sportswear, and JanSport backpacks have in common? Each of these brands is manufactured by VF Corporation. VF Corporation is a 102-year-old, $6 billion-a-year company, with more than 53,000 workers. It is also the world's largest apparel producer.

In recent years, VF Corporation's earnings have seen solid growth. In 1999, however, the company's sales were flat. At the time, VF's 14 divisions operated as independent entities, each with its own purchasing, production, marketing, and computer systems. VF's managers subsequently decided to restructure the company into five integrated "coalitions": jeanswear, intimates, playwear, knitwear, and international operations and marketing. The coalitions need to work together to take advantage of their common resources. However, resource planning across such a complex organization posed major challenges.

To establish the critical information links needed between the coalitions, VF decided to install a modified version of SAP's R/3 ERP system. This version is specifically designed for apparel and footwear manufacturers. However, VF also decided to implement a *best-of-breed* software strategy. This strategy allowed VF to use the best individual applications modules for the system produced by any vendor as well as retain some of the modules from its legacy systems. For example, the heart of the system has only four R/3 modules: order management, production planning, materials management, and finance. However, each coalition had its favorite applications from other vendors that had to be included. Intimates uses WebPDM from Gerber to cut down on its product design costs and Rhythm from i2 to optimize its materials utilization and assembly-line space. Information from Rhythm is then fed back into the R/3 production planning module. Jeanswear uses software from Logility to forecast customer demand. These forecasts are then fed back into the production planning and financial modules in R/3. VF's own customized software tracks production in the firm's plants using information from the R/3 production planning, order management, and materials management modules, which is then fed back to the R/3 system so managers can fine-tune the company's production plans. VF also has developed a "micromarketing" system that is so sophisticated it can, for example, forecast the demand for a specific size and color of Wrangler jeans sold at the beginning of summer at a particular Wal-Mart store.

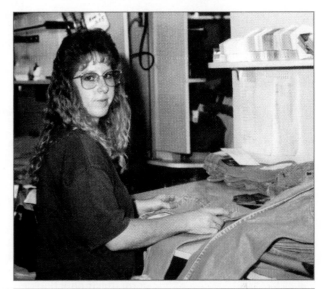

Data on quality are important inputs for VF's ERP system. Here an employee inspects jeans to assure they conform to VF's quality standards and meet customer expectations.

The two key modules related to resource planning, however, are the material requirements and capacity planning modules of the system. The material requirements planning system is contained in the production planning module and uses forecasts from the Logility sales and demand planning module to determine the purchase quantities and delivery dates for supplies and materials, such as leather, fabric, or linings; the production of finished goods, such as jeans, backpacks, or shirts; and the manufacture of assemblies, such as shoe soles or bootlegs. This information is useful for production planning as well as financial planning. For example, the timing of planned purchase quantities can be translated into the need for funds to pay for them. The output can also be used by the capacity planning module, which can ensure that VF's five coalitions have the skilled employees and equipment they need to support their production plans.

Sources: Eryn Brown, "VF Corp. Changes Its Underware," *Fortune* (December 7, 1998), pp. 115–118; VFC Press Release, "VF Corporation Launches First Large Scale Apparel Industry-Specific SAP Solution" (May 31, 2000); www.hoover.com, August 2005; www.vfc.com, August 2005.

tions plan. For example, every bicycle needs two wheel rims, so 1,000 completed bicycles need 1,000(2) = 2,000 rims. Forecasting techniques are not needed for these items.

The bicycle, or any other product that is manufactured from one or more components, is called a **parent**. The wheel rim is an example of a **component**—an item that goes through one or more operations to be transformed into or become part of one or more parents. A wheel rim, for example, will have several different parents if the rim is used to make more than one style of bicycle. This parent–component relationship can cause erratic dependent demand patterns for components. Suppose that every time inventory falls to 500 units (a reorder point), an order for 1,000 more bicycles is placed, as shown in Figure 15.2(a). The assembly supervisor then authorizes the withdrawal of 2,000 rims from inventory, along with

parent

Any product that is manufactured from one or more components.

component

An item that goes through one or more operations to be transformed into or become part of one or more parents.

FIGURE 15.2

Lumpy Dependent Demand Resulting from Continuous Independent Demand

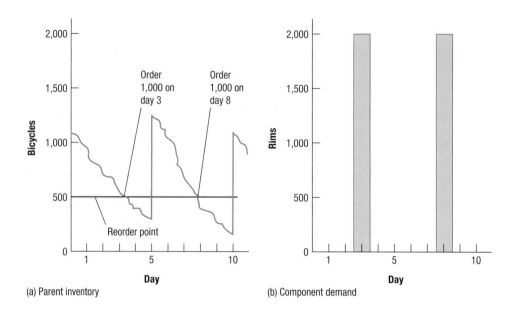

(a) Parent inventory

(b) Component demand

other components for the finished product. The demand for the rim is shown in Figure 15.2(b). So, even though customer demand for the finished bicycle is continuous and reasonably uniform, the production demand for wheel rims is "lumpy"; that is, it occurs sporadically, usually in relatively large quantities. Thus, the production decisions for the assembly of bicycles, which account for the costs of assembling the bicycles and the projected assembly capacities at the time the decisions are made, determine the demand for wheel rims.

POSSIBLE PLANNING AND CONTROL SYSTEMS

For years, many companies tried to manage production and their dependent demand inventories using independent demand systems, but the outcome was seldom satisfactory. However, several systems are now available that recognize and help firms deal with dependent demand. The most prominent systems now in use are the material requirements planning (MRP) system, the Drum-Buffer-Rope (DBR) system, and lean systems. Figure 15.3 shows the distinctive characteristics of each system.

These different systems help businesses reduce their inventory levels, utilize their labor and facilities better, and improve their customer service. The advantages of using them are as follows:

1. Lumpy component demand often results in large forecasting errors. However, compensating for these errors by increasing the firm's safety stock of components is costly, with no guarantee that stockouts can be avoided. When the dependent demand of components can be calculated from the production schedules of their parents, better plans can be made. The small-lot production strategy of lean systems takes a different approach because it smoothes out component demand, essentially eliminating lumpy demand.

FIGURE 15.3

Distinctive Characteristics of MRP, DBR, and Lean Systems

MRP	DBR	Lean Systems
• Products with many levels of components, and more customization • Lumpy demand, often with larger batch sizes	• Capacity is leveraged to control bottlenecks and entire system flow • Simpler product structures and more standardized products	• Using system as catalyst for continuous improvement • Small lot sizes, consistent quality, reliable suppliers, and flexible workforce
• Make-to-order, assemble-to-order, and make-to-stock strategies • Lower and intermediate volumes, with flexible flows	• Assemble-to-order or make-to-stock strategy • Relatively higher volumes, with flexible flows transitioning to line flows	• Assemble-to-order or make-to-stock strategy • High volumes and well-balanced line flows

2. The systems provide managers with information useful for capacity and financial planning. For example, the information can be used to forecast when components might be unavailable because of capacity shortages, supplier delivery delays, and the like. In terms of financial planning, production schedules and materials purchases can be translated into capacity requirements and the dollar amounts projected in the time periods in which they will appear.

3. The systems automatically update the dependent demand and inventory replenishment schedules for components when the production schedules of parent items change, and alert employees whenever action is needed on a component.

Each system has its own merits and is more effective in some situations than in others. MRP has been around the longest, and explicitly deals with dependent demand. It excels when the dependent demand is "lumpier," meaning that it occurs sporadically and production is in larger batch sizes. Even though it can be used in a broad spectrum of environments, MRP is best used when the product is complex. Product complexity means that a product has many components, which in turn have many components of their own, and these components also have their own components, and so on. MRP can also be made to work well in customized or make-to-order environments.

DBR excels when capacity is a particularly important issue, bottlenecks are identifiable and costly, and TOC concepts can be applied to advantage. DBR is more suited for an assemble-to-order or make-to-stock operation in which volumes are higher and products more standardized. It is a way of scheduling production to implement TOC concepts more effectively than can be done with MRP.

Lean systems, as we already noted in Chapter 9, work well with high volumes, line flows, and either a make-to-stock or assemble-to-order strategy. The manufacturing environment can be made more predictable. For example, quality can be made more consistent, lot sizes smaller, and the firm's workforce more flexible. In such an environment, lean systems can become a catalyst for continued improvement and potentially far outperform MRP and DBR.

Of course, manufacturers can meld together the principles of several systems. For example, lean systems can still be used in conjunction with MRP to identify the average demand rates for various components (an input to determining the number of kanban containers). MRP systems can benefit from DBR when it comes to setting lot sizes and break points in the routing of production process, and scheduling the release of materials onto the shop floor.

Having already devoted a full chapter to lean systems in Chapter 9, the two planning and control systems that we examine more fully here are MRP and then DBR.

> MATERIAL REQUIREMENTS PLANNING <

Material requirements planning (MRP) is a computerized information system developed specifically to help manufacturers manage dependent demand inventory and schedule replenishment orders. The key inputs of an MRP system are a bill of materials database, a master production schedule, and an inventory record database, as shown in Figure 15.4. Using this information, the MRP system identifies the actions planners must take to stay on schedule, such as releasing new production orders, adjusting order quantities, and expediting late orders.

An MRP system translates the master production schedule and other sources of demand, such as independent demand for replacement parts and maintenance items, into the requirements for all subassemblies, components, and raw materials needed to produce the required parent items. This process is called an **MRP explosion** because it converts the requirements of various final products into a *material requirements plan* that specifies the replenishment schedules of all the subassemblies, components, and raw materials needed by the final products.

BILL OF MATERIALS

The replenishment schedule for a component is determined from the production schedules of its parents. Hence, the system needs accurate information on parent–component relationships. A **bill of materials (BOM)** is a record of all the components of an item, the parent–component relationships, and the usage quantities derived from engineering and process

material requirements planning (MRP)

A computerized information system developed specifically to help manufacturers manage dependent demand inventory and schedule replenishment orders.

MRP explosion

A process that converts the requirements of various final products into a *material requirements plan* that specifies the replenishment schedules of all the subassemblies, components, and raw materials needed to produce final products.

bill of materials (BOM)

A record of all the components of an item, the parent–component relationships, and the usage quantities derived from engineering and process designs.

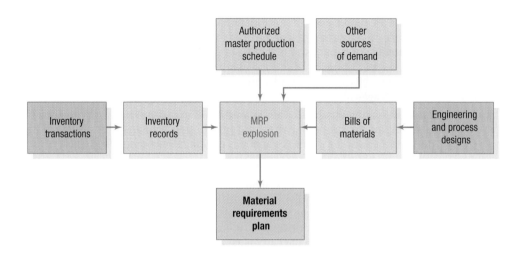

designs. In Figure 15.5, the BOM of a simple ladder-back chair shows that the chair is made from a ladder-back subassembly, a seat subassembly, front legs, and leg supports. In turn, the ladder-back subassembly is made from back legs and back slats, and the seat subassembly is made from a seat frame and a seat cushion. Finally, the seat frame is made from seat-frame boards. For convenience, we refer to these items by the letters shown in Figure 15.5.

All items except item A are components because they are needed to make a parent. Items A, B, C, and H are parents because they all have at least one component. The BOM also specifies the **usage quantity**, or the number of units of a component that are needed to make one unit of its immediate parent. Figure 15.5 shows usage quantities for each parent–component relationship in parentheses. Note that one chair (item A) is made from one ladder-back subassembly (item B), one seat subassembly (item C), two front legs (item D), and four leg supports (item E). In addition, item B is made from two back legs (item F) and four back slats (item G). Item C needs one seat frame (item H) and one seat cushion (item I). Finally, item H needs four seat-frame boards (item J).

Four terms frequently used to describe inventory items are *end items, intermediate items, subassemblies,* and *purchased items.* An **end item** typically is the final product sold to the customer; it is a parent but not a component. Item A in Figure 15.5, the completed ladder-back chair, is an end item. Accounting statements classify inventory of end items as either work-in-process (WIP), if work remains to be done, or finished goods. An **intermediate item** is one such as item B, C, or H that has at least one parent and at least one component. Some products have several levels of intermediate items; the parent of one intermediate item also is an intermediate item. Inventory of intermediate items—whether completed or still on the shop floor—is classified as WIP. A **subassembly** is an intermediate item that is *assembled* (as opposed to being transformed by other means) from *more* than one component. Items B and C are subassemblies. A **purchased item** has no components because it comes from a supplier, but it has one or more parents. Examples are items D, E, F, G, I, and J in Figure 15.5. Inventory of purchased items is treated as raw materials in accounting statements.

A component may have more than one parent. **Part commonality**, sometimes called *standardization of parts* or *modularity,* is the degree to which a component has more than one immediate parent. As a result of commonality, the same item may appear in several places in the bill of materials for a product, or it may appear in the bills of materials for several different products. For example, the seat subassembly in Figure 15.5 is a component of the ladder-back chair and of a kitchen chair that is part of the same family of products. The usage quantity specified in the bill of materials relates to a specific parent–component relationship. The usage quantity for any component can therefore change, depending on the parent item. Part commonality, or using the same part in many parents, increases its volume and repeatability, which provides several process advantages and helps minimize inventory costs.

MASTER PRODUCTION SCHEDULING

The second input into a material requirements plan is the **master production schedule (MPS)**, which details how many end items will be produced within specified periods of time. It breaks the sales and operations plan into specific product schedules. Figure 15.6 shows

---

usage quantity

The number of units of a component that are needed to make one unit of its immediate parent.

end item

The final product sold to a customer.

intermediate item

An item that has at least one parent and at least one component.

subassembly

An intermediate item that is *assembled* (as opposed to being transformed by other means) from *more* than one component.

purchased item

An item that has one or more parents but no components because it comes from a supplier.

part commonality

The degree to which a component has more than one immediate parent.

master production schedule (MPS)

A part of the material requirements plan that details how many end items will be produced within specified periods of time.

FIGURE **15.5**

BOM for a Ladder-Back Chair

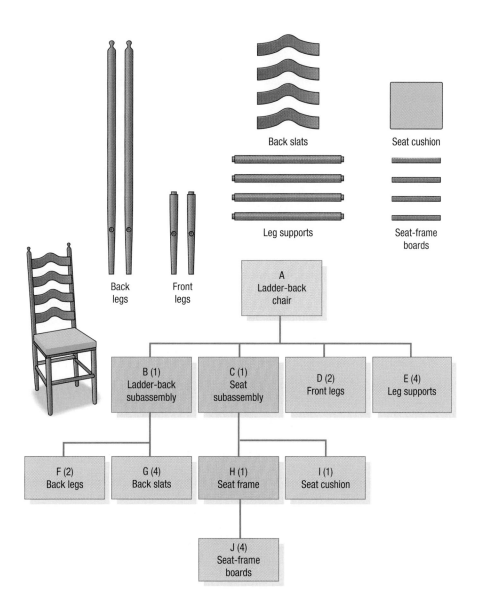

how a sales and operations plan for a family of chairs breaks down into the weekly MPS for each specific chair type (the time period can be hours, days, weeks, or months). The chair example demonstrates the following aspects of master scheduling:

1. The sums of the quantities in the MPS must equal those in the sales and operations plan. This consistency between the plans is desirable because of the economic analysis done to arrive at the sales and operations plan.

2. The production quantities must be allocated efficiently over time. The specific mix of chair types—the number of each type as a percent of the total family's quantity—is based on historic demand and on marketing and promotional considerations. The planner must select lot sizes for each chair type, taking into consideration economic factors, such as production setup costs and inventory carrying costs.

3. Capacity limitations, such as machine or labor capacity, storage space, or working capital, may determine the timing and size of MPS quantities. The planner must acknowledge these limitations by recognizing that some chair styles require more resources than others and setting the timing and size of the production quantities accordingly.

Figure 15.7 shows the master production scheduling process. Operations must first create a prospective MPS to test whether it meets the schedule with the resources (e.g., machine capacities, labor, overtime, and subcontractors) provided for in the sales and operations plan. Operations then revises the MPS until a schedule that satisfies all of the resource

FIGURE **15.6**

MPS for a Family of Chairs

	April				May			
	1	2	3	4	5	6	7	8
Ladder-back chair	150					150		
Kitchen chair				120			120	
Desk chair		200	200		200			200
Sales and operations plan for chair family			670				670	

limitations is developed or until it is determined that no feasible schedule can be developed. In the latter event, the production plan must be revised to adjust production requirements or increase authorized resources. Once a feasible prospective MPS has been accepted by the firm's managers, operations uses the authorized MPS as input to material requirements planning. Operations can then determine specific schedules for component production and assembly. Actual performance data such as inventory levels and shortages are inputs to preparing the prospective MPS for the next period, and so the master production scheduling process is repeated from one period to the next.

Developing a Master Production Schedule The process of developing a master production schedule includes (1) calculating the projected on-hand inventory and (2) determining the timing and size of the production quantities of specific products. We use the manufacturer of the ladder-back chair to illustrate the process. For simplicity, we assume that the firm does not utilize safety stocks for end items, even though many firms do. In addition, we use weeks as our planning periods, even though hours, days, or months could be used.

Step 1. *Calculate Projected On-Hand Inventories.* The first step is to calculate the projected on-hand inventory, which is an estimate of the amount of inventory available each week after demand has been satisfied:

$$\begin{pmatrix} \text{Projected on-hand} \\ \text{inventory at end} \\ \text{of this week} \end{pmatrix} = \begin{pmatrix} \text{On-hand} \\ \text{inventory at} \\ \text{end of last week} \end{pmatrix} + \begin{pmatrix} \text{MPS quantity} \\ \text{due at start} \\ \text{of this week} \end{pmatrix} - \begin{pmatrix} \text{Projected} \\ \text{requirements} \\ \text{this week} \end{pmatrix}$$

In some weeks, no MPS quantity for a product may be needed because sufficient inventory already exists. For the projected requirements for this week, the scheduler uses whichever is larger—the forecast or the customer orders booked—recognizing that the forecast is subject to error. If actual booked orders exceed the forecast, the projection will be more accurate if the scheduler uses the booked orders because booked orders are a known quantity. Conversely, if the forecast exceeds booked orders for a week, the forecast will provide a better estimate of the requirements needed for that week because some orders are yet to come in.

FIGURE **15.7**

Master Production Scheduling Process

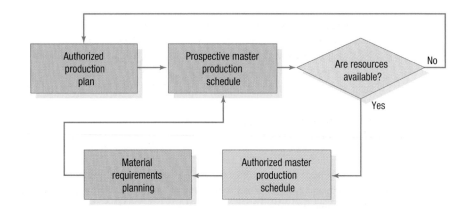

FIGURE **15.8**

Master Production Schedule
for Weeks 1 and 2

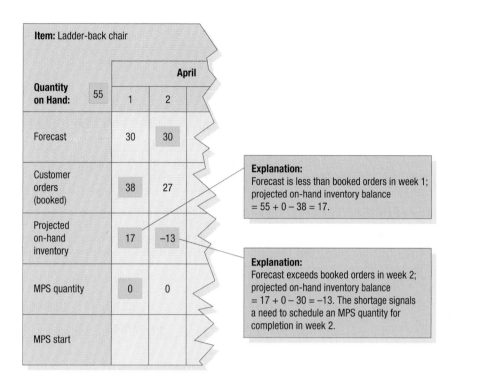

The manufacturer of the ladder-back chair produces the chair to stock and needs to develop an MPS for it. Marketing has forecasted a demand of 30 chairs for the first week of April, but actual customer orders booked are for 38 chairs. The current on-hand inventory is 55 chairs. No MPS quantity is due in week 1. Figure 15.8 shows an MPS record with these quantities listed. Because actual orders for week 1 are greater than the forecast, the scheduler uses that figure for actual orders to calculate the projected inventory balance at the end of week 1:

$$\text{Inventory} = \begin{pmatrix} 55 \text{ chairs} \\ \text{currently} \\ \text{in stock} \end{pmatrix} + \begin{pmatrix} \text{MPS quantity} \\ (0 \text{ for week 1}) \end{pmatrix} - \begin{pmatrix} 38 \text{ chairs already} \\ \text{promised for} \\ \text{delivery in week 1} \end{pmatrix} = 17 \text{ chairs}$$

In week 2, the forecasted quantity exceeds actual orders booked, so the projected on-hand inventory for the end of week 2 is $17 + 0 - 30 = -13$. The shortage signals the need for more chairs to be produced and available for week 2.

Step 2. *Determine the Timing and Size of MPS Quantities.* The goal of determining the timing and size of MPS quantities is to maintain a nonnegative projected on-hand inventory balance. As shortages in inventory are detected, MPS quantities should be scheduled to cover them. The first MPS quantity should be scheduled for the week when the projected on-hand inventory reflects a shortage, such as week 2 in Figure 15.8.[1] The scheduler adds the MPS quantity to the projected on-hand inventory and searches for the next period when a shortage occurs. This shortage signals a need for a second MPS quantity, and so on.

Figure 15.9 shows a master production schedule for the ladder-back chair for the next 8 weeks. The order policy requires production lot sizes of 150 units. A shortage of 13 chairs in week 2 will occur unless the scheduler provides for an MPS quantity for that period.

Once the MPS quantity is scheduled, the updated projected inventory balance for week 2 is

$$\text{Inventory} = \begin{pmatrix} 17 \text{ chairs in} \\ \text{inventory at the} \\ \text{end of week 1} \end{pmatrix} + \begin{pmatrix} \text{MPS quantity} \\ \text{of 150 chairs} \end{pmatrix} - \begin{pmatrix} \text{Forecast of} \\ 30 \text{ chairs} \end{pmatrix} = 137 \text{ chairs}$$

[1]In some cases, new orders will be planned before a shortage is encountered. Two such instances occur when safety stocks and anticipation inventories are built up.

FIGURE **15.9**

Master Production Schedule
for Weeks 1–8

Item: Ladder-back chair   **Order Policy:** 150 units   **Lead Time:** 1 week

Quantity on Hand: **55**		April				May			
		1	2	3	4	5	6	7	8
Forecast		30	30	30	30	35	35	35	35
Customer orders (booked)		38	27	24	8	0	0	0	0
Projected on-hand inventory		17	137	107	77	42	7	122	87
MPS quantity		0	150	0	0	0	0	150	0
MPS start		150	0	0	0	0	150	0	0

Explanation:
The time needed to assemble 150 chairs
is 1 week. The assembly department must
start assembling chairs in week 1
to have them ready by week 2.

Explanation:
On-hand inventory balance
= 17 + 150 − 30 = 137. The MPS quantity
is needed to avoid a shortage of
30 − 17 = 13 chairs in week 2.

The scheduler proceeds column by column through the MPS record until reaching the end, filling in the MPS quantities as needed to avoid shortages. The 137 units will satisfy forecasted demands until week 7, when the inventory shortage in the absence of an MPS quantity is $7 + 0 − 35 = −28$. This shortage signals the need for another MPS quantity of 150 units. The updated inventory balance is $7 + 150 − 35 = 122$ chairs for week 7.

The last row in Figure 15.9 indicates the periods in which production of the MPS quantities must *begin* so that they will be available when indicated in the MPS quantity row. In the upper-right portion of the MPS record, a lead time of one week is indicated for the ladder-back chair; that is, one week is needed to assemble 150 ladder-back chairs, assuming that items B, C, D, and E are available. For each MPS quantity, the scheduler works backward through the lead time to determine when the assembly department must start producing chairs. Consequently, a lot of 150 units must be started in week 1 and another in week 6.

Available-to-Promise Quantities In addition to providing manufacturing with the timing and size of production quantities, the MPS provides marketing with information useful for negotiating delivery dates with customers. The quantity of end items that marketing can promise to deliver on specified dates is called **available-to-promise (ATP) inventory**. It is the difference between the customer orders already booked and the quantity that operations is planning to produce. As new customer orders are accepted, the ATP inventory is reduced to reflect the commitment of the firm to ship those quantities, but the actual inventory stays unchanged until the order is removed from inventory and shipped to the customer. An available-to-promise inventory is associated with each MPS quantity because the MPS quantity specifies the timing and size of new stock that can be earmarked to meet future bookings.

Figure 15.10 shows an MPS record with an additional row for the available-to-promise quantities. The ATP in week 2 is the MPS quantity minus booked customer orders until the next MPS quantity, or $150 − (27 + 24 + 8 + 0 + 0) = 91$ units. The ATP indicates to marketing that, of the 150 units scheduled for completion in week 2, 91 units are uncommitted, and total new orders up to that quantity can be promised for delivery as early as week 2. In week 7, the ATP is 150 units because there are no booked orders in week 7 and beyond.

available-to-promise (ATP) inventory

The quantity of end items that marketing can promise to deliver on specified dates.

TUTOR **15.1**

Tutor 15.1 on the Student CD-ROM
provides a new example to practice
completing a master production schedule.

Item: Ladder-back chair					Order Policy: 150 units Lead Time: 1 week			
Quantity on Hand: 55	**April**				**May**			
	1	2	3	4	5	6	7	8
Forecast	30	30	30	30	35	35	35	35
Customer orders (booked)	38	27	24	8	0	0	0	0
Projected on-hand inventory	17	137	107	77	42	7	122	87
MPS quantity	0	150	0	0	0	0	150	0
MPS start	150	0	0	0	0	150	0	0
Available-to-promise (ATP) inventory	17	91					150	

FIGURE 15.10

MPS Record with an ATP Row

Explanation:
The total of customer orders booked until the next MPS receipt is 38 units. The ATP = 55 (on-hand) + 0 (MPS quantity) − 38 = 17.

Explanation:
The total of customer orders booked until the next MPS receipt is 27 + 24 + 8 = 59 units. The ATP = 150 (MPS quantity) − 59 = 91 units.

The procedure for calculating available-to-promise information is slightly different for the first (current) week of the schedule than for other weeks because it accounts for the inventory currently in stock. The ATP inventory for the first week equals *current on-hand inventory* plus the MPS quantity for the first week, minus the cumulative total of booked orders up to (but not including) the week in which the next MPS quantity arrives. So, in Figure 15.10, the ATP for the first week is 55 + 0 − 38 = 17. This information indicates to the sales department that it can promise as many as 17 units this week, 91 more units sometime in weeks 2 through 6, and 150 more units in week 7 or 8. If customer order requests exceed ATP quantities in those time periods, the MPS must be changed before the customer orders can be booked or the customers must be given a later delivery date—when the next MPS quantity arrives. See Solved Problem 2 at the end of this chapter for an example of decision making using the ATP quantities.

Freezing the MPS The master production schedule is the basis of all end item, sub-assembly, component, and materials schedules. For this reason, changes to the MPS can be costly, particularly if they are made to MPS quantities soon to be completed. Increases in an MPS quantity can result in material shortages, delayed shipments to customers, and excessive expediting costs. Decreases in MPS quantities can result in unused materials or components (at least until another need for them arises) and valuable capacity being used to create products not needed. Similar costs occur when forecasted need dates for MPS quantities are changed. For these reasons, many firms, particularly those with a make-to-stock strategy and a focus on low-cost operations, *freeze,* or disallow changes to, the near-term portion of the MPS.

Reconciling the MPS with Sales and Operations Plans Because the master production schedule is based on both forecasts as well as actual orders received, it can differ from the sales and operations plan when summed across different periods in a month. For instance, in Figure 15.6, if the sum total MPS quantities of the three models of chairs in the month of April was 725 instead of 670, then either the management must revise the sales and operations plan upwards by authorizing additional resources to match supply with demand, or reduce the quantities of MPS in the month of April to match the sales and operations plan. Master production schedules drive plant and supplier activity, so they must be synchronized with the sales and operations plans to ensure that the firm's planning decisions are actually being implemented on an ongoing basis.

INVENTORY RECORD

Inventory records are a third major input to MRP, and inventory transactions are the basic building blocks of up-to-date records (see Figure 15.4). These transactions include releasing new orders, receiving scheduled receipts, adjusting due dates for scheduled receipts, withdrawing inventory, canceling orders, correcting inventory errors, rejecting shipments, and verifying scrap losses and stock returns. Recording the transactions accurately is essential if the firm's on-hand inventory balances are to be correct and its MRP system is to operate effectively.

inventory record

A record that shows an item's lot-size policy, lead time, and various time-phased data.

The **inventory record** divides the future into time periods called *time buckets*. In our discussion, we use weekly time buckets for consistency with our MPS example, although other time periods could as easily be used. The inventory record shows an item's lot-size policy, lead time, and various time-phased data. The purpose of the inventory record is to keep track of inventory levels and component replenishment needs. The time-phased information contained in the inventory record consists of (1) *gross requirements*, (2) *scheduled receipts*, (3) *projected on-hand inventory*, (4) *planned receipts*, and (5) *planned order releases*.

We illustrate the discussion of inventory records with the seat subassembly, item C, that was shown in Figure 15.5. It is used in two products: a ladder-back chair and a kitchen chair.

gross requirements

The total demand derived from *all* parent production plans.

Gross Requirements The **gross requirements** are the total demand derived from *all* parent production plans. They also include demand not otherwise accounted for, such as demand for replacement parts for units already sold. Figure 15.11 shows an inventory record for item C, the seat subassembly. Item C is produced in lots of 230 units and has a lead time of two weeks. The inventory record also shows item C's gross requirements for the next eight weeks, which come from the master production schedule for the ladder-back and kitchen chairs (see Figure 15.6). The MPS start quantities for each parent are added to arrive at each week's gross requirements. The seat subassembly's gross requirements exhibit lumpy demand: Operations will withdraw seat subassemblies from inventory in only four of the eight weeks.

The MRP system works with release dates to schedule production and delivery for components and subassemblies. Its program logic anticipates the removal of all materials required by a parent's production order from inventory at the *beginning* of the parent item's lead time—when the scheduler first releases the order to the shop.

Scheduled Receipts Recall that *scheduled receipts* (sometimes called *open orders*) are orders that have been placed but not yet completed. For a purchased item, the scheduled receipt could be in one of several stages: being processed by a supplier, being transported to the purchaser, or being inspected by the purchaser's receiving department. If the firm is making the item in-house, the order could be on the shop floor being processed, waiting for components, waiting for a machine to become available, or waiting to be moved to its next operation. According to Figure 15.11 one 230-unit order of item C is due in week 1. Given the two-week lead time, the inventory planner probably released the order two weeks ago.

projected on-hand inventory

An estimate of the amount of inventory available each week after gross requirements have been satisfied.

Projected On-Hand Inventory The **projected on-hand inventory** is an estimate of the amount of inventory available each week after gross requirements have been satisfied. The beginning inventory, shown as the first entry (37) in Figure 15.11, indicates the on-hand inventory available at the time the record was computed. As with scheduled receipts, entries are made for each actual withdrawal and receipt to update the MRP database. Then, when the MRP system produces the revised record, the correct inventory will appear.

Other entries in the row show inventory expected in future weeks. Projected on-hand inventory is calculated as

$$\begin{pmatrix} \text{Projected on-hand} \\ \text{inventory balance} \\ \text{at end of week } t \end{pmatrix} = \begin{pmatrix} \text{Inventory on} \\ \text{hand at end of} \\ \text{week } t-1 \end{pmatrix} + \begin{pmatrix} \text{Scheduled} \\ \text{or planned} \\ \text{receipts in} \\ \text{week } t \end{pmatrix} - \begin{pmatrix} \text{Gross} \\ \text{requirements} \\ \text{in week } t \end{pmatrix}$$

FIGURE **15.11**

MRP Record for the Seat Subassembly

Item: C Description: Seat subassembly						Lot Size: 230 units Lead Time: 2 weeks			
		Week							
		1	2	3	4	5	6	7	8
Gross requirements		150	0	0	120	0	150	120	0
Scheduled receipts		230	0	0	0	0	0	0	0
Projected on-hand inventory	37	117	117	117	−3	−3	−153	−273	−273
Planned receipts									
Planned order releases									

Explanation:
Gross requirements are the total demand for the two chairs. Projected on-hand inventory in week 1 is 37 + 230 − 150 = 117 units.

The projected on-hand calculation includes the consideration of **planned receipts**, which are orders not yet released to the shop or the supplier. Planned receipts should not be confused with scheduled receipts. Planned receipts are still at the planning stage and can still change from one week to the next, whereas scheduled receipts are actual orders that are being acted upon by the shop or supplier. In Figure 15.11, the planned receipts are all zero. The on-hand inventory calculations for each week are as follows:

planned receipts

Orders that are not yet released to the shop or the supplier.

$$
\begin{aligned}
\text{Week 1:} && 37 + 230 - 150 &= 117 \\
\text{Weeks 2 and 3:} && 117 + 0 - 0 &= 117 \\
\text{Week 4:} && 117 + 0 - 120 &= -3 \\
\text{Week 5:} && -3 + 0 - 0 &= -3 \\
\text{Week 6:} && -3 + 0 - 150 &= -153 \\
\text{Week 7:} && -153 + 0 - 120 &= -273 \\
\text{Week 8:} && -273 + 0 - 0 &= -273
\end{aligned}
$$

In week 4, the balance drops to −3 units, which indicates that a shortage of 3 units will occur unless more seat subassemblies are built. This condition signals the need for a planned receipt to arrive in week 4. In addition, unless more stock is received, the shortage will grow to 273 units in weeks 7 and 8.

Planned Receipts Planning for receipt of new orders will keep the projected on-hand balance from dropping below zero. The planned receipt row is developed as follows:

1. Weekly on-hand inventory is projected until a shortage appears. Completion of the initial planned receipt is scheduled for the week in which the shortage is projected. The addition of the newly planned receipt should increase the projected on-hand balance so that it equals or exceeds zero. It will exceed zero when the lot size exceeds requirements in the week it is planned to arrive.

2. The projection of on-hand inventory continues until the next shortage occurs. This shortage signals the need for the second planned receipt.

This process is repeated until the end of the planning horizon by proceeding column by column through the MRP record—filling in planned receipts as needed and completing the projected on-hand inventory row. Figure 15.12 shows the planned receipts for the seat subassembly. In week 4, the projected on-hand inventory will drop below zero, so a planned receipt of 230 units is scheduled for week 4. The updated inventory on-hand balance is 117 (inventory at end of week 3) + 230 (planned receipts) − 120 (gross requirements) = 227 units. The projected on-hand inventory remains at 227 for week 5 because no scheduled receipts or gross requirements are anticipated. In week 6, the projected on-hand inventory is 227 (inventory at end of week 5) − 150 (gross requirements) = 77 units. This quantity is greater than zero, so no new planned receipt is needed. In week 7, however, a shortage will occur unless more seat subassemblies are received. With a planned receipt in week 7, the updated inventory balance is 77 (inventory at end of week 6) + 230 (planned receipts) − 120 (gross requirements) = 187 units.

planned order release

An indication of when an order for a specified quantity of an item is to be issued.

Planned Order Releases A **planned order release** indicates when an order for a specified quantity of an item is to be issued. We must place the planned order release quantity in the proper time bucket. To do so, we must assume that all inventory flows—scheduled receipts, planned receipts, and gross requirements—occur at the same point of time in a time period. Some firms assume that all flows occur at the beginning of a time period; other firms assume that they occur at the end of a time period or at the middle of the time period. Regardless of when the flows are assumed to occur, we find the release date by subtracting the lead time from the receipt date. For example, the release date for the first planned order release in Figure 15.12 is: 4 (planned receipt date) − 2 (lead time) = 2 (planned order release date). Figure 15.12 shows the planned order releases for the seat subassembly. If all goes according

FIGURE 15.12

Completed Inventory Record for the Seat Subassembly

Item: C Description: Seat subassembly							Lot Size: 230 units Lead Time: 2 weeks		
		Week							
		1	2	3	4	5	6	7	8
Gross requirements		150	0	0	120	0	150	120	0
Scheduled receipts		230	0	0	0	0	0	0	0
Projected on-hand inventory	37	117	117	117	227	227	77	187	187
Planned receipts					230			230	
Planned order releases			230			230			

Explanation:
Without a planned receipt in week 4, a shortage of 3 units will occur: 117 + 0 + 0 − 120 = −3 units. Adding the planned receipt brings the balance to 117 + 0 + **230** − 120 = 227 units. Offsetting for a 2-week lead time puts the corresponding planned order release back to week 2.

Explanation:
The first planned receipt lasts until week 7, when projected inventory would drop to 77 + 0 + 0 − 120 = −43 units. Adding the second planned receipt brings the balance to 77 + 0 + **230** − 120 = 187 units. The corresponding planned order release is for week 5 (or week 7 minus 2 weeks).

to the plan, we will release an order for 230 seat assemblies next week (in week 2). This order release sets off a series of updates to the inventory record. First, the planned order release for the order is removed. Next, the planned receipt for 230 units in week 4 is also removed. Finally, a new scheduled receipt for 230 units will appear in the scheduled receipt row for week 4.

PLANNING FACTORS

The planning factors in a MRP inventory record play an important role in the overall performance of the MRP system. By manipulating these factors, managers can fine-tune inventory operations. In this section, we discuss planning lead time, lot-sizing rules, and safety stock.

Planning Lead Time Planning lead time is an estimate of the time between placing an order for an item and receiving the item in inventory. Accuracy is important in planning lead time. If an item arrives in inventory sooner than needed, inventory holding costs increase. If an item arrives too late, stockouts, excessive expediting costs, or both may occur.

For purchased items, the planning lead time is the time allowed for receiving a shipment from the supplier after the order has been sent, including the normal time to place the order. Often, the purchasing contract stipulates the delivery date. For items manufactured in-house, the planning lead time consists of estimates for the following factors:

- Setup time
- Processing time
- Materials handling time between operations
- Waiting time

Each of these times must be estimated for every operation along the item's route. Estimating setup, processing, and materials handling times can be relatively easy, but estimating the waiting time for materials handling equipment or for a machine to perform a particular operation can be more difficult. In a facility that uses a make-to-order strategy, such as a machine shop, the load on the shop varies considerably over time, causing actual waiting times for a particular order to fluctuate widely. Therefore, being able to accurately estimate the waiting time is especially important when it comes to estimating the planning lead time. However, in a facility that uses a make-to-stock strategy, such as an assembly plant, product routings are more standard and waiting time is more predictable; hence, waiting time generally is a less-troublesome part of planning lead times.

Lot-Sizing Rules A lot-sizing rule determines the timing and size of order quantities. A lot-sizing rule must be assigned to each item before planned receipts and planned order releases can be computed. The choice of lot-sizing rules is important because they determine the number of setups required and the inventory holding costs for each item. We present three lot-sizing rules: (1) fixed order quantity, (2) periodic order quantity, and (3) lot-for-lot.

Fixed Order Quantity The **fixed order quantity (FOQ)** rule maintains the same order quantity each time an order is issued. For example, the lot size might be the size dictated by equipment capacity limits, such as when a full lot must be loaded into a furnace at one time. For purchased items, the FOQ could be determined by the quantity discount level, truckload capacity, or minimum purchase quantity. Alternatively, the lot size could be determined by the economic order quantity (EOQ) formula. Figure 15.12 illustrates the FOQ rule. However, if an item's gross requirement within a week is particularly large, the FOQ might be insufficient to avoid a shortage. In such unusual cases, the inventory planner must increase the lot size beyond the FOQ, typically to a size large enough to avoid a shortage. Another option is to make the order quantity an integer multiple of the FOQ. This option is appropriate when capacity constraints limit production to FOQ sizes (at most) and setup costs are high.

Periodic Order Quantity The **periodic order quantity (POQ)** rule allows a different order quantity for each order issued but tends to issue the order at predetermined time intervals, such as every two weeks. The order quantity equals the amount of the item needed

fixed order quantity (FOQ)

A rule that maintains the same order quantity each time an order is issued.

periodic order quantity (POQ)

A rule that allows a different order quantity for each order issued but tends to issue the order at predetermined time intervals.

during the predetermined time between orders and must be large enough to prevent shortages. Specifically, the POQ is

$$
\begin{pmatrix} \text{POQ lot size} \\ \text{to arrive in} \\ \text{week } t \end{pmatrix} = \begin{pmatrix} \text{Total gross requirements} \\ \text{for } P \text{ weeks, including} \\ \text{week } t \end{pmatrix} - \begin{pmatrix} \text{Projected on-hand} \\ \text{inventory balance at} \\ \text{end of week } t-1 \end{pmatrix}
$$

This amount exactly covers P weeks' worth of gross requirements. That is, the projected on-hand inventory should equal zero at the end of the Pth week.

Suppose that we want to switch from the FOQ rule used in Figure 15.12 to the POQ rule. Figure 15.13 shows the application of the POQ rule, with $P = 3$ weeks, to the seat subassembly inventory. The first order is required in week 4 because it is the first week that projected inventory balance will fall below zero. The first order using $P = 3$ weeks is

$$
\begin{pmatrix} \text{POQ lot size} \end{pmatrix} = \begin{pmatrix} \text{Gross requirements} \\ \text{for weeks} \\ 4, 5, \text{and } 6 \end{pmatrix} - \begin{pmatrix} \text{Inventory at} \\ \text{end of week } 3 \end{pmatrix}
$$

$$
= (120 + 0 + 150) - 117 = 153 \text{ units}
$$

The second order must arrive in week 7, with a lot size of $(120 + 0) - 0 = 120$ units. This second order reflects only two weeks' worth of gross requirements—to the end of the planning horizon.

The POQ rule does *not* mean that operations must issue a new order every P weeks. Rather, when an order *is* planned, its lot size must be enough to cover P successive weeks. One way to select a P value is to divide the average lot size desired, such as the EOQ, or some other applicable lot size, by the average weekly demand. That is, express the target lot size as the desired weeks of supply (P) and round to the nearest integer.

Lot for Lot A special case of the POQ rule is the **lot-for-lot (L4L) rule**, under which the lot size ordered covers the gross requirements of a single week. Thus, $P = 1$, and the goal is to minimize inventory levels. This rule ensures that the planned order is just large enough to prevent a shortage in the single week it covers. The L4L lot size is

$$
\begin{pmatrix} \text{L4L lot size} \\ \text{to arrive in} \\ \text{week } t \end{pmatrix} = \begin{pmatrix} \text{Gross requirements} \\ \text{for week } t \end{pmatrix} - \begin{pmatrix} \text{Projected on-hand} \\ \text{inventory balance at} \\ \text{end of week } t-1 \end{pmatrix}
$$

The projected on-hand inventory combined with the new order will equal zero at the end of week t. Following the first planned order, an additional planned order will be used to match each subsequent gross requirement.

This time we want to switch from the FOQ rule to the L4L rule. Figure 15.14 shows the application of the L4L rule to the seat subassembly inventory. As before, the first order is needed in week 4:

$$
\begin{pmatrix} \text{L4L lot size} \end{pmatrix} = \begin{pmatrix} \text{Gross requirements} \\ \text{in week } 4 \end{pmatrix} - \begin{pmatrix} \text{Inventory balance} \\ \text{at end of week } 3 \end{pmatrix}
$$

$$
= 120 - 117 = 3
$$

The stockroom must receive additional orders in weeks 6 and 7 to satisfy each of the subsequent gross requirements. The planned receipt for week 6 is 150 and for week 7 is 120.

TUTOR 15.2

Tutor 15.2 on the Student CD-ROM provides a new example to practice lot-sizing decisions using the FOQ, POQ, and L4L rules.

lot-for-lot (L4L) rule

A rule under which the lot size ordered covers the gross requirements of a single week.

FIGURE 15.13

The POQ ($P = 3$) Rule for the Seat Subassembly

Periods		8								
Item		Seat Assembly		Period (P) for POQ		3	Lot Size (FOQ)			
Description							Lead Time			2
POQ Rule	▼									
		1	2	3	4	5	6	7	8	
Gross requirements		150			120		150	120		
Scheduled receipts		230								
Projected on-hand Inventory	37	117	117	117	150	150				
Planned receipts					153			120		
Planned order releases			153			120				

Comparing Lot-Sizing Rules Choosing a lot-sizing rule can have important implications for inventory management. Lot-sizing rules affect inventory costs and setup and ordering costs. The FOQ, POQ, and L4L rules differ from one another in one or both respects. In our example, each rule took effect in week 4, when the first order was placed. Let's compare the projected on-hand inventory averaged over weeks 4 through 8 of the planning horizon. The data are shown in Figures 15.12, 15.13, and 15.14, respectively.

$$\text{FOQ:} \quad \frac{227+227+77+187+187}{5} = 181 \text{ units}$$

$$\text{POQ:} \quad \frac{150+150+0+0+0}{5} = 60 \text{ units}$$

$$\text{L4L:} \quad \frac{0+0+0+0+0}{5} = 0 \text{ units}$$

The performance of the L4L rule with respect to average inventory levels comes at the expense of an additional planned order and its accompanying setup time and cost. We can draw three conclusions from this comparison.

1. The FOQ rule generates a high level of average inventory because it creates inventory *remnants*. A remnant is inventory carried into a week, but it is too small to prevent a shortage. Remnants occur because the FOQ does not match requirements exactly. For example, according to Figure 15.12, the stockroom must receive a planned order in week 7, even though 77 units are on hand at the beginning of that week. The remnant is the 77 units that the stockroom will carry for three weeks, beginning with receipt of the first planned order in week 4. Although they increase average inventory levels, inventory remnants introduce stability into the production process by buffering unexpected scrap losses, capacity bottlenecks, inaccurate inventory records, or unstable gross requirements.

2. The POQ rule reduces the amount of average on-hand inventory because it does a better job of matching order quantity to requirements. It adjusts lot sizes as requirements increase or decrease. Figure 15.13 shows that in week 7, when the POQ rule has fully taken effect, the projected on-hand inventory is zero—no remnants.

3. The L4L rule minimizes inventory investment, but it also maximizes the number of orders placed. This rule is most applicable to expensive items or items with small ordering or setup costs. It is the only rule that can be used for a low-volume item made to order. It can also approximate the small-lot production of a lean system.

By avoiding remnants, both the POQ and the L4L rule may introduce instability by tying the lot-sizing decision so closely to requirements. If any requirement changes, so must the lot size, which can disrupt component schedules. Last-minute increases in parent orders may be hindered by missing components.

Safety Stock An important managerial decision is the quantity of safety stock to carry. It is more complex for dependent demand items than for independent demand items. Safety stock for dependent demand items with lumpy demand (gross requirements) is helpful only when future gross requirements, the timing or size of scheduled receipts, and the amount of scrap that will be produced are uncertain. As these uncertainties are resolved, safety stock should be reduced and ultimately eliminated. The usual policy is to use safety stock for end

Periods		8								
Item	Seat Assembly			Period (P) for POQ			Lot Size (FOQ)			
Description							Lead Time			2
L4L Rule		1	2	3	4	5	6	7	8
Gross requirements		150			120		150	120	
Scheduled receipts		230							
Projected on-hand inventory	37	117	117	117					
Planned receipts					3		150	120	
Planned order releases			3		150	120			

FIGURE **15.14**

The L4L Rule for the Seat Subassembly

FIGURE **15.15**

Inventory Record for the Seat
Subassembly Showing the
Application of a Safety Stock

FOQ Rule							Lot Size		230
							Lead Time		2
							Safety Stock		80
		1	2	3	4	5	6	7	8
Gross requirements		150	0	0	120	0	150	120	0
Scheduled receipts		230	0	0	0	0	0	0	0
Projected on-hand inventory	37	117	117	117	227	227	307	187	187
Planned receipts		0	0	0	230	0	230	0	0
Planned order releases		0	230	0	230	0	0	0	0

items and purchased items to protect against fluctuating customer orders and unreliable suppliers of components but to avoid using it as much as possible for intermediate items. Safety stocks can be incorporated in the MRP logic by using the following rule: Schedule a planned receipt whenever the projected on-hand inventory balance drops below the desired safety stock level (rather than zero, as before). The objective is to keep a minimum level of planned inventories equal to the safety stock quantity. Figure 15.15 shows what happens when the requirement is set at 80 units of safety stock for the seat assembly using an FOQ of 230 units. Compare these results to Figure 15.12. The net effect is to move the second planned order release from week 5 to week 4 to avoid dropping below 80 units in week 6.

OUTPUTS FROM MRP

MRP systems provide many reports, schedules, and notices to help managers control dependent demand inventories, as indicated in Figure 15.16. In this section, we discuss the MRP explosion process, notices that alert planners to items needing attention, resource requirement reports, and performance reports.

MRP Explosion MRP translates, or *explodes*, the MPS and other sources of demand into the requirements needed for all of the subassemblies, components, and raw materials the firm needs to produce parent items. This process generates the material requirements plan for each component item.

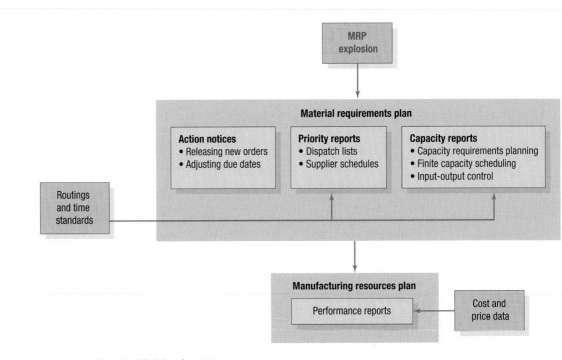

FIGURE **15.16** | MRP Outputs

An item's gross requirements are derived from three sources:

1. The MPS for immediate parents that are end items
2. The planned order releases for parents below the MPS level
3. Any other requirements not originating in the MPS, such as the demand for replacement parts

Consider the seat subassembly and its inventory record shown in Figure 15.12. The seat subassembly requires a seat cushion and a seat frame, which in turn needs four seat-frame boards. Its BOM is shown in Figure 15.17 (see also Figure 15.5, which shows how the seat subassembly BOM relates to the product as a whole). How many seat cushions should we order from the supplier? How many seat frames should we produce to support the seat subassembly schedule? How many seat-frame boards do we need to make? The answers to these questions depend on the existing inventories of these items and the replenishment orders already in progress. MRP can help answer these questions through the explosion process.

Figure 15.18 shows the MRP records for the seat subassembly and its components. We already showed how to develop the MRP record for the seat subassembly. We now concentrate on the MRP records of its components. The lot-size rules are an FOQ of 300 units for the seat frame, L4L for the seat cushion, and an FOQ of 1,500 for the seat-frame boards. All three components have a one-week lead time. The key to the explosion process is to determine the proper timing and size of the gross requirements for each component. After we make those determinations, we can derive the planned order release schedule for each component by using the logic already demonstrated.

In our example, the components have no independent demand for replacement parts. Consequently, in Figure 15.18, the gross requirements of a component come from the planned order releases of its parents. The seat frame and the seat cushion get their gross requirements from the planned order release schedule of the seat subassembly. Both components have gross requirements of 230 units in weeks 2 and 5, the same weeks in which we will be releasing orders to make more seat subassemblies. In week 2, for example, the materials handler for the assembly department will withdraw 230 seat frames and 230 seat cushions from inventory so that the assembly department can produce the seat subassemblies in time to avoid a stockout in week 4. The materials plans for the seat frame and the seat cushion must allow for that.

Using the gross requirements in weeks 2 and 5, we can develop the MRP records for the seat frame and the seat cushion, as shown in Figure 15.18. For a scheduled receipt of 300 seat frames in week 2, an on-hand quantity of 40 units, and a lead time of one week, we need to release an order of 300 seat frames in week 4 to cover the assembly schedule for the seat subassembly. The seat cushion has no scheduled receipts and no inventory on hand; consequently, we must place orders for 230 units in weeks 1 and 4, using the L4L logic with a lead time of one week.

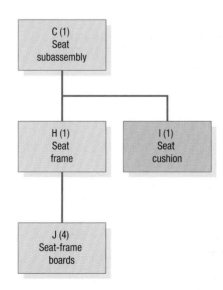

FIGURE 15.17

BOM for the Seat Subassembly

Item: Seat subassembly
Lot size: 230 units

Lead time: 2 weeks	Week							
	1	2	3	4	5	6	7	8
Gross requirements	150	0	0	120	0	150	120	0
Scheduled receipts	230	0	0	0	0	0	0	0
Projected inventory 37	117	117	117	227	227	77	187	187
Planned receipts				230			230	
Planned order releases		230			230			

Usage quantity: 1   Usage quantity: 1

Item: Seat frames
Lot size: 300 units

Lead time: 1 week	Week							
	1	2	3	4	5	6	7	8
Gross requirements	0	230	0	0	230	0	0	0
Scheduled receipts	0	300	0	0	0	0	0	0
Projected inventory 40	40	110	110	110	180	180	180	180
Planned receipts					300			
Planned order releases				300				

Item: Seat cushion
Lot size: L4L

Lead time: 1 week	Week							
	1	2	3	4	5	6	7	8
Gross requirements	0	230	0	0	230	0	0	0
Scheduled receipts	0	0	0	0	0	0	0	0
Projected inventory 0	0	0	0	0	0	0	0	0
Planned receipts		230			230			
Planned order releases	230			230				

Usage quantity: 4

Item: Seat-frame boards
Lot size: 1,500 units

Lead time: 1 week	Week							
	1	2	3	4	5	6	7	8
Gross requirements	0	0	0	1,200	0	0	0	0
Scheduled receipts	0	0	0	0	0	0	0	0
Projected inventory 200	200	200	200	500	500	500	500	500
Planned receipts				1,500				
Planned order releases			1,500					

FIGURE 15.18 | MRP Explosion of Seat Assembly Components

After determining the replenishment schedule for the seat frame, we can calculate the gross requirements for the seat-frame boards. We plan to begin producing 300 seat frames in week 4. Each frame requires 4 boards, so we need to have 300(4) = 1,200 boards available in week 4. Consequently, the gross requirement for seat-frame boards is 1,200 in week 4. Given no scheduled receipts, 200 boards in stock, a lead time of one week, and an FOQ of 1,500 units, we need a planned order release of 1,500 in week 3.

The questions posed earlier can now be answered. We should plan to release the following orders: 300 seat frames in week 4, 230 seat cushions in each of weeks 1 and 4, and 1,500 seat-frame boards in week 3. If MRP plans are updated weekly, only the planned order for week 1 should be released now. Releasing it creates a scheduled receipt of 230 seat cushions that will appear in the updated inventory record. The other orders remain in the planning stage, and even might be revised by the MRP explosion done next week.

Other Important Reports Once computed, inventory records for any item appearing in the BOM can be printed in hard copy or displayed on a computer video screen. Inventory planners use a computer-generated memo called an **action notice** to make decisions about releasing new orders and adjusting the due dates of scheduled receipts. These notices are generated every time the system is updated, such as once per week. The action notice alerts planners to only the items that need their attention, such as those items that have a planned order release in the current period or a scheduled receipt that needs its due date revised. Planners can then view the full records for those items and take the necessary actions. An action notice can simply be a list of part numbers for items that need attention; or it can be the full record for such items, with a note at the bottom identifying the action needed.

By itself, the MRP system does not recognize capacity limitations when computing planned orders; that is, it may call for a planned order release that exceeds the amount that can be physically produced. An essential role of planners is to monitor the capacity requirements of material requirements plans, adjusting a plan when it cannot be met. To facilitate this process, various types of capacity reports can be provided. For example, **capacity requirements planning (CRP)** reports project time-phased capacity requirements for workstations. They calculate workload according to the work required to complete the scheduled receipts already in the shop and to complete the planned order releases not yet released. Bottlenecks are those workstations at which the projected loads exceed station capacities.

Other types of outputs are also possible, such as priority reports on orders already placed to the shop or with suppliers. Priority reports begin with the due dates assigned to scheduled receipts, which planners keep up to date so that they continue to reflect when receipt is really needed. On a broader scale, the information in an MRP system is useful to functional areas other than operations. MRP evolved into **manufacturing resource planning (MRP II)**, a system that ties the basic MRP system to the company's financial system and to other core and supporting processes. For example, management can project the dollar value of shipments, product costs, overhead allocations, inventories, backlogs, and profits by using the MRP plan along with prices and product and activity costs from the accounting system. Also, information from the MPS, scheduled receipts, and planned orders can be converted into cash flow projections, which are broken down by product families. Similar computations are possible for other performance measures of interest to management. In fact, MRP II ultimately evolved into enterprise resource planning (ERP), which was introduced at the beginning of this chapter.

MRP AND THE ENVIRONMENT

Consumer and governmental concern about the deterioration of the natural environment has driven manufacturers to reengineer their processes to become more environmentally friendly. The recycling of base materials is becoming more commonplace, and products are being designed in such a way that they can be remanufactured after their useful lives. Nonetheless, manufacturing processes often produce a number of waste materials that need to be properly disposed of. Wastes come in many forms:

- Effluents, such as carbon monoxide, sulfur dioxide, and hazardous chemicals associated with the processes used to manufacture the product
- Materials, such as metal shavings, oils, and chemicals associated with specific operations

action notice
A computer-generated memo alerting planners about releasing new orders and adjusting the due dates of scheduled receipts.

capacity requirements planning (CRP)
A technique used for projecting time-phased capacity requirements for workstations; its purpose is to match the material requirements plan with the capacity of key processes.

manufacturing resource planning (MRP II)
A system that ties the basic MRP system to the company's financial system and to other core and supporting processes.

■ Packaging materials, such as unusable cardboard and plastics associated with certain products or purchased items

■ Scrap associated with unusable products or component defects generated by the manufacturing process

Companies can modify their MRP systems to help them track these wastes and plan for their disposal. The type and amount of waste associated with each item can be entered into its BOM by treating the waste much like you would a component of the item. When the MPS is developed for a product, reports can be generated that project the amount of waste expected during the production process and when it will occur. Although this approach can require that a firm's BOM be modified substantially, the benefits are also substantial. Firms can identify their waste problems in advance to eliminate them in some cases and plan for their proper disposal in others. It also gives the firm a way to generate any formal documentation required by the government to verify that it has complied with environmental laws and policies.

> DRUM-BUFFER-ROPE SYSTEM <

Drum-Buffer-Rope (DBR)

A planning and control system that regulates the flow of work-in-process materials at the bottleneck or the capacity constrained resource (CCR) in a productive system.

Drum-Buffer-Rope (DBR) is a planning and control system that regulates the flow of work-in-process materials at the bottleneck or the capacity constrained resource (CCR) in a productive system. The process with the least capacity is called a bottleneck if its output is less than the market demand, or called a CCR if it is the least capable resource in the system but still has higher capacity than the market demand. The DBR system is based on the theory of constraints (TOC), which we discussed at length in Chapter 7, "Constraint Management."

The CCR schedule is the *drum* because it sets the beat or the production rate for the entire plant and is linked to the market demand. The *buffer* is a time buffer that plans early flows to the CCR and thus protects it from disruption. It also ensures that the bottleneck is never starved for work. A finished-goods inventory buffer can also be placed in front of the shipping point in order to protect customer shipping schedules. Finally, the *rope* represents the tying of material release to the drum beat, which is the rate at which the bottleneck or the CCR controls the throughput of the entire plant. It is a communication device to ensure that raw material is not introduced into the system at a rate faster than what the CCR can handle. Completing the loop, *buffer management* constantly monitors the execution of incoming CCR work. Working together, the drum, the buffer, and the rope can help managers create a production schedule that reduces lead times and inventories while simultaneously increasing throughput and on-time delivery.

To better understand the drum-buffer-rope system, consider the schematic layout shown in Figure 15.19. Process B, with a capacity of only 500 units per week, is the CCR because the upstream Process A and downstream Process C have capacities of 800 units per week and 700 units per week respectively, and the market demand is 650 units per week, on

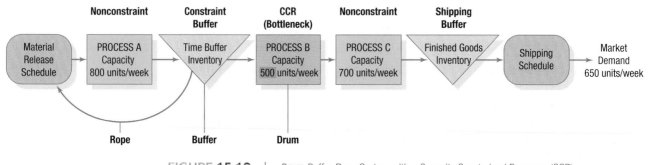

FIGURE 15.19 | Drum-Buffer-Rope System with a Capacity Constrained Resource (CCR)

average. In this case, because the capacity at process B is less than the market demand, the CCR can also be called a bottleneck. A constraint time buffer, which can be in the form of materials arriving earlier than needed, is placed right in front of the CCR (Process B). A shipping buffer, in the form of finished goods inventory, can also be placed prior to the shipping schedule in order to protect customer orders that are firm. Finally, a rope ties the material release schedule to match the schedule, or drum beat, at the CCR. The material flow is pulled forward by the drum beat prior to the CCR, while it is pushed downstream toward the customer subsequent to the CCR. For this reason, DBR is a combination of a pull-push system.

Unlike an MRP system, the master production scheduling and component scheduling processes take place simultaneously in a DBR system. Even though MRP is not focused on any one resource, DBR specifically strives to improve throughput by better utilizing the bottleneck resource and protecting it from disruption through the time buffer and protective buffer capacity elsewhere. So while the process batch at the DBR is any size that minimizes setups and improves utilization at the CCR, it is a lot-for-lot elsewhere at nonconstrained resources. The material can consequently be released in small batches known as *transfer batches* at the release point, which then combine at the constraint buffer to make a full process batch at the CCR. Transfer batches can be as small as one unit each, to allow a downstream workstation to start work on a batch before it is completely finished at the prior process. Using transfer batches typically facilitates a reduction in overall lead time.

DBR can be an effective system to use when the product the firm produces is relatively simple, with only a few levels in the bill of materials, and the production process has more line flows. Planning is greatly simplified in this case and primarily revolves around scheduling the constrained resource and triggering other points to meet that CCR's schedule. Effectively implementing a DBR system requires an understanding of the TOC principles highlighted in Chapter 7, "Constraint Management." However such a system can be utilized in many different kinds of manufacturing and service organizations, either by itself or in conjunction with other planning and control systems such as MRP. Managerial Practice 15.2 illustrates how the use of a DBR system within a MRP II-based system improved the performance of the Marine Corps Maintenance Center in Albany, Georgia.

> RESOURCE PLANNING FOR SERVICE PROVIDERS <

We have seen how manufacturing companies can disaggregate an MPS of finished products, which in turn must be translated into the needs for resources, such as staff, equipment, components, and financial assets. The driver for these resource requirements is a material requirements plan. Service providers, of course, must plan their resources just as manufacturers do. However, unlike finished goods, services cannot be inventoried. They must be provided on demand. In terms of resource planning then, service organizations must focus on maintaining the *capacity* to serve their customers. In this section, we will discuss how service providers use the concept of dependent demand and a bill of resources in managing capacity.

DEPENDENT DEMAND FOR SERVICES

When we discussed planning and control systems for manufacturers earlier in this chapter, we introduced the concept of *dependent demand,* which is demand for an item that is a function of the production plans for some other item the company produces. For service resource planning, it is useful to define the concept of dependent demand to include demands for resources that are driven by forecasts of customer requests for services or by plans for various activities in support of the services the company provides. Here are some other examples of dependent demands for service providers.

Restaurants Every time you order from the menu at a restaurant, you initiate the restaurant's need for certain types of goods (uncooked food items, plates, and napkins), staff (chef, servers, and dishwashers), and equipment (stoves, ovens, and cooking utensils). Using a forecast of the demand for each type of meal, the manager of the restaurant can estimate the need for these resources. Many restaurants, for example, feature "specials" on certain days,

MANAGERIAL **PRACTICE** | 15.2 | THE DRUM-BUFFER-ROPE SYSTEM AT A U.S. MARINE CORPS MAINTENANCE CENTER

The U.S. Marine Corps Maintenance Center in Albany, Georgia, overhauls and repairs vehicles used by the Corps, such as fuel tankers, trucks, earth-moving equipment, amphibious vehicles, and light armored vehicles. The overhaul process starts with the disassembly of each vehicle to determine the amount and nature of work that needs to be performed. The type and duration of the repair work can vary tremendously for even the same type of vehicle. Faced with such uncertainty, the center was struggling until four years ago to complete its equipment repairs on time, and it had an increasing backlog to boot. For instance, the center was able to repair only about 5 MK-48s (heavy-duty haulers) per month, when twice as many MK-48s—10 per month—typically needed repair. Different units of the Corps were threatening to divert their orders to the private-sector repair companies.

The scheduling at the center was based on an MRP II push system, and TOC principles were used to identify the bottlenecks on the shop floor. After the center's operations were studied in depth, however, contrary to everyone's expectations, it was discovered that more than enough capacity was available to repair and overhaul 10 MK-48s per month. The problem wasn't capacity; it was the center's scheduling system. Products were being pushed out onto the shop floor without regard for the status of the resources on the floor. Thus, what the center had was a policy constraint related to the scheduling process, not an actual physical resource constraint.

In order to improve the center's performance, its managers implemented a simplified form of a drum-buffer-rope system as shown in Figure 15.19. Since the Marine Corp Maintenance Center was not constrained by any internal resource, the drum in such a simplified system was based on firm orders. As orders came in, a quick check was done to measure the total load the center's least-capable resource was handling. If the resource was not too heavily loaded, the order was accepted and released into the shop floor for processing. The rope tied the shipping schedule directly to the material release schedule instead of the CCR schedule, and the only buffer maintained was the shipping buffer. Such a simplified DBR system did not require any specialized software. It focused simply on the market demand for repairs. The MRP II system that was used for scheduling was simply facilitated by the DBR schedules.

Repairs to equipment like this amphibious assault vehicle can vary tremendously at the U.S. Marine Corps Maintenance Center in Albany, Georgia. The center struggled to keep up with its repairs until managers implemented the simplified form of a drum-buffer-rope system shown in Figure 15.19. The result? Repair times fell from 167 days to just 58 days, on average.

The center's results following the change were impressive. Repair cycle times were reduced from an average of 167 days to 58 days, work-in-process levels were reduced from 550 percent of demand to 140 percent, and the cost to repair products went down by 25 to 30 percent due to an increased throughput. The center's ability to repair MK-48s became much more flexible, too. In fact, it can now repair as many as 23 MK-48s per month. Carrying out these simple improvements made the Albany Maintenance Center a world-class overhaul and repair operation.

Source: M. Srinivasan, Darren Jones, and Alex Miller, "Corps Capabilities," *APICS Magazine* (March 2005), pp. 46–50.

---

say, fish on Fridays or prime rib on Saturdays. Specials improve the accuracy of the forecasts managers need to make for different types of meals (and the food products that are required to make them) and typically signal the need for above-average staffing levels. How much of these resources will be needed, however, depends on the number of meals the restaurant ultimately expects to serve. As such, these items—food products and staff members—are dependent demands.

Airlines Whenever an airline schedules a flight, certain supporting goods are needed (beverages, snacks, and fuel), labor (pilots, flight attendants, and airport services), and equipment (a plane and airport gate). The number of flights and passengers the airline forecasts it will serve determines the amount of these resources needed. Just like a manufacturer, the airline can explode its master schedule of flights to make this determination.

Hospitals With the exception of the emergency room services, hospitals can use their admission appointments to create a master schedule. The master schedule can be exploded to determine the resources the hospital will need during a certain period. For example, when you schedule a surgical procedure, you generate a need for facilitating goods such as medicines, surgical gowns, linens, staff (a surgeon, nurses, and anesthesiologist), and equipment (an operating room, surgical tools, and recovery bed). As they build their master schedules, hospitals must ensure that certain equipment and personnel do not become over-committed—that capacity is maintained, in other words. For example, an appointment for a key operation might have to be scheduled in advance at a time a surgeon is available to do it, even though the hospital's other resources—operating room, nurses, and so forth—might be available.

A couple enjoys eating at a fine restaurant. Each meal initiates the need for facilitating goods, staff, and equipment.

Hotels A traveler who makes a reservation at a hotel generates demand for facilitating goods (soap and towels), staff (front desk, housekeeping, and concierge), and equipment (fax, television, and exercise bicycle). To determine its dependent resource needs, a hotel adds the number of reservations already booked to the number of "walk-in" customers it forecasts it will have. This figure is used to create the hotel's master schedule. One resource a hotel cannot easily adjust, however, is the number of rooms it has. If the hotel is over-booked, for instance, it cannot simply add more rooms. If it has too few guests, it cannot "downsize" its number of rooms. Given the high capital costs needed for this resource, hotels try to maintain as high a utilization rate as possible by offering group rates or special promotions at certain times of the year. In other words, they try to drive up dependent demand for this particular resource.

BILL OF RESOURCES

The service analogy to the bill of materials in a manufacturing company is the **bill of resources (BOR)**, which is a record of a service firm's parent–component relationships and all of the materials, equipment time, staff, and other resources associated with them, including usage quantities. Once the service firm has completed its master schedule, the BOR can be used to determine what resources the firm will need, how much of them it will need, and when. A BOR for a service provider can be as complex as a BOM for a manufacturer. Consider a hospital that just scheduled treatment of a patient with an aneurysm. As shown in Figure 15.20, the BOR for treatment of an aneurysm has seven levels, starting at the top (end item): (1) discharge; (2) intermediate care; (3) postoperative care (step down); (4) postoperative care (intensive); (5) surgery; (6) preoperative care (angiogram); and (7) preoperative care (testing). Each level of the BOR has a set of material and resource requirements and an associated lead time. For example, at level 6, shown in Figure 15.20(b), the patient needs 6 hours of nurses' time, 1 hour of the primary MD's time, 1 hour of the respiratory therapist's time, 24 hours of bed time, 3 different lab tests, 1 meal, and 10 different medicines from the pharmacy. The lead time for this level is 1 day. The lead time for the entire stay for treatment of the aneurysm is 12.2 days. A master schedule of patient admissions and the BORs for each illness enable the hospital to manage its critical resources. Reports analogous to the MRP II reports we discussed earlier in the chapter can be generated for the people who manage the various functional areas of the hospital.

One resource every service provider needs, however, is cash. Service organizations have to forecast the number of customers they expect to serve so that they have enough cash on hand to purchase materials that support the services—labor and other products. Purchasing these items increases the firm's accounts payable. As services are actually completed for customers, the firm's accounts receivable increases. The firm's master schedule and its accounts receivable and payable help a company predict the amount and timing of its cash flows.

bill of resources (BOR)

A record of a service firm's parent–component relationships and all of the materials, equipment time, staff, and other resources associated with them, including usage quantities.

FIGURE **15.20**

BOR for Treating an Aneurysm

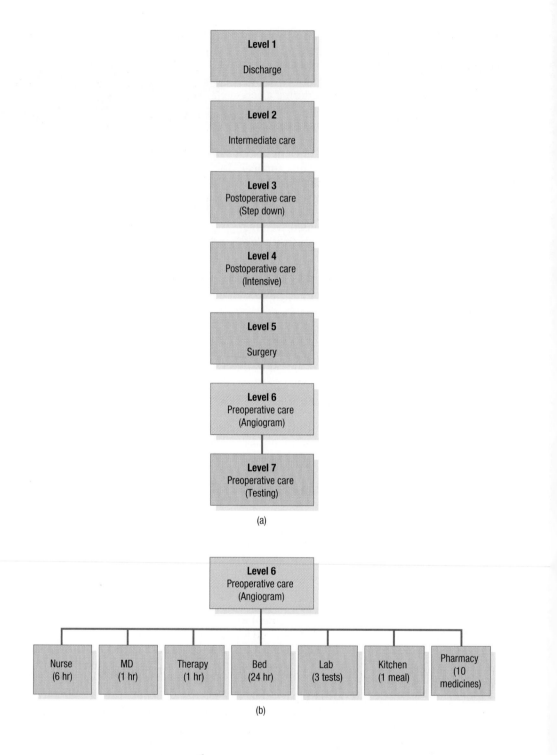

> ## STUDENT CD-ROM AND INTERNET RESOURCES <

The Student CD-ROM and the Companion Website at **www.prenhall.com/krajewski** contain many tools, activities, and resources designed for this chapter.

> ## KEY TERMS <

action notice 645
available-to-promise (ATP) inventory 634

bill of materials (BOM) 629
bill of resources (BOR) 649

capacity requirements planning
(CRP) 645

> SOLVED PROBLEM 1 <

Refer to the bill of materials for product A shown in Figure 15.21.

If there is no existing inventory, how many units of items G, E, and D must be purchased to produce five units of end item A?

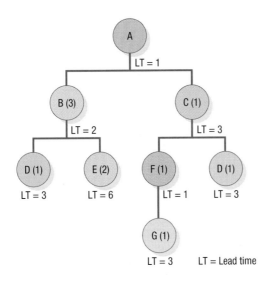

FIGURE **15.21**

BOM for Product A

SOLUTION

Five units of item G, 30 units of item E, and 20 units of item D must be purchased to make 5 units of A. The usage quantities shown in Figure 15.21 indicate that 2 units of E are needed to make 1 unit of B and that 3 units of B are needed to make 1 unit of A; therefore, 5 units of A require 30 units of E $(2 \times 3 \times 5 = 30)$. One unit of D is consumed to make 1 unit of B, and 3 units of B per unit of A result in 15 units of D $(1 \times 3 \times 5 = 15)$; plus 1 unit of D in each unit of C and 1 unit of C per unit of A result in another 5 units of D $(1 \times 1 \times 5 = 5)$. The total requirements to make 5 units of A are 20 units of D $(15 + 5)$. The calculation of requirements for G is simply $1 \times 1 \times 1 \times 5 = 5$ units.

> SOLVED PROBLEM 2 <

The order policy is to produce end item A in lots of 50 units. Using the data shown in Figure 15.22 and the FOQ lot-sizing rule, complete the projected on-hand inventory and MPS quantity rows. Then complete the MPS start row by offsetting the MPS quantities for the final assembly lead time. Finally, compute the available-to-promise inventory for item A. If in week 1, a

FIGURE 15.22

MPS Record for End Item A

Item: A									Order Policy: 50 units Lead Time: 1 week		
						Week					
Quantity on Hand:	5	1	2	3	4	5	6	7	8	9	10
Forecast		20	10	40	10	0	0	30	20	40	20
Customer orders (booked)		30	20	5	8	0	2	0	0	0	0
Projected on-hand inventory		25									
MPS quantity		50									
MPS start											
Available-to- promise (ATP) inventory											

customer requests a new order for 30 units of item A, when is the earliest date the entire order could be shipped?

SOLUTION

The projected on-hand inventory for the second week is

$$\begin{pmatrix} \text{Projected on-hand} \\ \text{inventory at end} \\ \text{of week 2} \end{pmatrix} = \begin{pmatrix} \text{On-hand} \\ \text{inventory in} \\ \text{week 1} \end{pmatrix} + \begin{pmatrix} \text{MPS quantity} \\ \text{due in week 2} \end{pmatrix} - \begin{pmatrix} \text{Requirements} \\ \text{in week 2} \end{pmatrix}$$

$$= 25 + 0 - 20 = 5 \text{ units}$$

where requirements are the larger of the forecast or actual customer orders booked for shipment during this period. No MPS quantity is required.

Without an MPS quantity in the third period, a shortage of item A will occur: $5 + 0 - 40 = -35$. Therefore, an MPS quantity equal to the lot size of 50 must be scheduled for completion in the third period. Then the projected on-hand inventory for the third week will be $5 + 50 - 40 = 15$.

Figure 15.23 shows the projected on-hand inventories and MPS quantities that would result from completing the MPS calculations. The MPS start row is completed by simply shifting a copy of the MPS quantity row to the left by one column to account for the one-week final assembly lead time. Also shown are the available-to-promise quantities. In week 1, the ATP is

$$\begin{pmatrix} \text{Available-to-} \\ \text{promise in} \\ \text{week 1} \end{pmatrix} = \begin{pmatrix} \text{On-hand} \\ \text{quantity in} \\ \text{week 1} \end{pmatrix} + \begin{pmatrix} \text{MPS quantity} \\ \text{in week 1} \end{pmatrix} - \begin{pmatrix} \text{Orders booked up} \\ \text{to week 3 when the} \\ \text{next MPS arrives} \end{pmatrix}$$

$$= 5 + 50 - (30 + 20) = 5 \text{ units}$$

Lot Size 50 Lead Time 1		1	2	3	4	5	6	7	8	9	10	11	12	13	14	15
Quantity on Hand	5															
Forecast		20	10	40	10			30	20	40	20					
Customer Orders (Booked)		30	20	5	8		2									
Projected On-Hand Inventory		25	5	15	5	5	3	23	3	13	43					
MPS Quantity		50		50				50		50	50					
MPS start			50				50		50	50						
Available-to-Promise Inv (ATP)		5		35				50		50	50					

FIGURE **15.23**

Completed MPS Record for End Item A

The ATP for the MPS quantity in week 3 is

$$\begin{pmatrix} \text{Available-to-} \\ \text{promise in} \\ \text{week 3} \end{pmatrix} = \begin{pmatrix} \text{MPS quantity} \\ \text{in week 3} \end{pmatrix} - \begin{pmatrix} \text{Orders booked up} \\ \text{to week 7 when the} \\ \text{next MPS arrives} \end{pmatrix}$$

$$= 50 - (5 + 8 + 0 + 2) = 35 \text{ units}$$

The other ATPs equal their respective MPS quantities because no orders are booked for those weeks. As for the new order for 30 units in week 1, the earliest it can be shipped is week 3 because the ATP for week 1 is insufficient. If the customer accepts the delivery date of week 3, the ATP for week 1 will stay at 5 units and the ATP for week 3 will be reduced to 5 units. This acceptance allows the firm the flexibility to immediately satisfy an order for 5 units or less, if one comes in. The customer orders booked for week 3 would be increased to 35 to reflect the new order's shipping date.

> SOLVED PROBLEM 3 <

The MPS for product A calls for the assembly department to begin final assembly according to the following schedule: 100 units in week 2; 200 units in week 4; 120 units in week 6; 180 units in week 7; and 60 units in week 8. Develop a material requirements plan for the next eight weeks for items B, C, and D. The BOM for A is shown in Figure 15.24, and data from the inventory records are shown in Table 15.1.

SOLUTION

We begin with items B and C and develop their inventory records, as shown in Figure 15.25. The MPS for product A must be multiplied by 2 to derive the gross requirements for item C because of the usage quantity. Once the planned order releases for item C are found, the gross requirements for item D can be calculated.

ACTIVE MODEL 15.1

Active Model 15.1 on the Student CD-ROM provides additional insight on lot-sizing decisions for MRP.

FIGURE 15.24

BOM for Product A

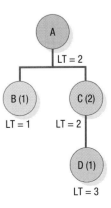

TABLE 15.1	Inventory Record Data			
		Item		
Data Category	**B**	**C**	**D**	
Lot-sizing rule	POQ ($P = 3$)	L4L	FOQ = 500 units	
Lead time (LT)	1 week	2 weeks	3 weeks	
Scheduled receipts	None	200 (week 1)	None	
Beginning (on-hand) inventory	20	0	425	

FIGURE 15.25

Inventory Records for Items B, C, and D

Item: B
Description:

Lot Size: POQ (P = 3)
Lead Time: 1 week

		Week									
		1	2	3	4	5	6	7	8	9	10
Gross requirements			100		200		120	180	60		
Scheduled receipts											
Projected on-hand inventory	20	20	200	200	0	0	240	60	0	0	0
Planned receipts			280				360				
Planned order releases		280				360					

Item: C
Description:

Lot Size: L4L
Lead Time: 2 weeks

		Week									
		1	2	3	4	5	6	7	8	9	10
Gross requirements			200		400		240	360	120		
Scheduled receipts		200									
Projected on-hand inventory	0	200	0	0	0	0	0	0	0	0	0
Planned receipts					400		240	360	120		
Planned order releases			400		240	360	120				

Item: D
Description:

Lot Size: FOQ = 500 units
Lead Time: 3 weeks

		Week									
		1	2	3	4	5	6	7	8	9	10
Gross requirements			400		240	360	120				
Scheduled receipts											
Projected on-hand inventory	425	425	25	25	285	425	305	305	305	305	305
Planned receipts					500	500					
Planned order releases		500	500								

> DISCUSSION QUESTIONS <

1. For an organization of your choice, such as where you previously worked, discuss how an ERP system could be used and whether it would increase effectiveness.

2. Form a group in which each member represents a different functional area of a firm. Provide a priority list of the information that could be generated from an MPS, from the most important to the least important, for each functional area. Rationalize the differences in the lists.

3. Consider the master flight schedule of a major airline, such as Air New Zealand. Discuss the ways in which it is analogous to a master production schedule for a manufacturer.

4. Consider a service provider that is in the delivery business, such as UPS or FedEx. How can the principles of MRP be useful to such a company?

> PROBLEMS <

Software, such as OM Explorer, Active Models, and POM for Windows, is packaged with every new copy of the textbook. Check with your instructor on how best to use it. In many cases, the instructor wants you to understand how to do the calculations by hand. At most, the software provides a check on your calculations. When calculations are particularly complex and the goal is interpreting the results in making decisions, the software replaces entirely the manual calculations. The software also can be a valuable resource well after your course is completed.

1. Consider the bill of materials (BOM) in Figure 15.26.

    a. How many immediate parents (one level above) does item I have? How many immediate parents does item E have?

    b. How many unique components does product A have at all levels?

    c. Which of the components are purchased items?

    d. How many intermediate items does product A have at all levels?

    e. Given the lead times (LT) noted on Figure 15.26, how far in advance of shipment must a purchase commitment be for any of the purchased items identified in part (c)?

2. Product A is made from components B, C, and D. Item B is a subassembly that requires 2 units of C and 1 unit of E. Item D also is an intermediate item, made from F. All other usage quantities are 2. Draw the BOM for product A.

3. What is the lead time (in weeks) to respond to a customer order for product A, based on the BOM shown in Figure 15.27, assuming no existing inventories or scheduled receipts?

4. Product A is made from components B and C. Item B, in turn, is made from D and E. Item C also is an intermediate item, made from F and H. Finally, intermediate item E is made from H and G. Note that item H has two parents. The following are item lead times:

Item	A	B	C	D	E	F	G	H
Lead Time (weeks)	1	2	2	6	5	6	4	3

    a. What lead time (in weeks) is needed to respond to a customer order for product A, assuming no existing inventories or scheduled receipts?

    b. What is the customer response time if all purchased items (i.e., D, F, G, and H) are in inventory?

    c. If you are allowed to keep just one purchased item in stock, which one would you choose?

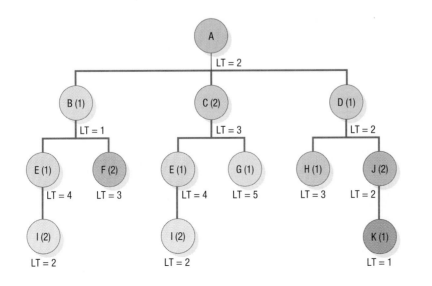

FIGURE **15.26**

BOM for Product A

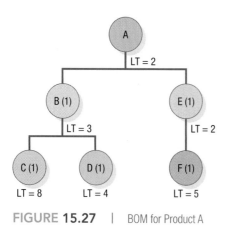

FIGURE 15.27 | BOM for Product A

9. Figure 15.30 shows a partially completed MPS record for ball bearings.

   a. Develop the MPS for ball bearings.

   b. Four customer orders arrived in the following sequence:

Order	Quantity	Week Desired
1	500	4
2	400	5
3	300	1
4	300	7

Assume that you must commit to the orders in the sequence of arrival and cannot change the desired shipping dates or your MPS. Which orders should you accept?

5. Refer to Figure 15.21 and Solved Problem 1. If inventory consists of 2 units of B, 1 unit of F, and 3 units of G, how many units of G, E, and D must be purchased to produce 5 units of product A?

6. Complete the MPS record in Figure 15.28 for a single item.

7. Complete the MPS record shown in Figure 15.29 for a single item.

8. An end item's demand forecasts for the next 10 weeks are 30, 20, 35, 50, 25, 25, 0, 40, 0, and 50 units. The current on-hand inventory is 80 units. The order policy is to produce in lots of 100. The booked customer orders for the item, starting with week 1, are 22, 30, 15, 9, 0, 0, 5, 3, 7, and 0 units. At present, no MPS quantities are on-hand for this item. The lead time is two weeks. Develop an MPS for this end item.

10. Morrison Electronics forecasted the following demand for one of its products for the next eight weeks: 70, 70, 65, 60, 55, 85, 75, and 85. The booked customer orders for this product, starting in week 1, are 50, 60, 55, 40, 35, 0, 0, and 0 units. The current on-hand inventory is 100 units, the order quantity is 150 units, and the lead time is one week.

   a. Develop an MPS for this product.

   b. The marketing department at Morrison revised its forecasts. Starting with week 1, the new forecasts are 70, 70, 75, 70, 70, 100, 100, and 110 units. Assuming that the prospective MPS you developed in part (a) does not change, prepare a revised MPS record. Comment on the situation that Morrison now faces.

FIGURE 15.28

MPS Record for Single Item

Item: A									Order Policy: 60 units Lead Time: 1 week	
		Week								
Quantity on Hand: 35	1	2	3	4	5	6	7	8		
Forecast	20	18	28	28	23	30	33	38		
Customer orders (booked)	15	17	9	14	9	0	7	0		
Projected on-hand inventory										
MPS quantity										
MPS start										

Item: A						Order Policy: 100 units		
						Lead Time: 1 week		
Quantity on Hand: 75		January				February		
	1	2	3	4	5	6	7	8
Forecast	65	65	65	45	50	50	50	50
Customer orders (booked)	40	10	85	0	35	70	0	0
Projected on-hand inventory								
MPS quantity								
MPS start								

FIGURE 15.29

MPS Record for Single Item

Item: Ball bearings								Order Policy: 500 units		
								Lead Time: 1 week		
Quantity on Hand: 400					Week					
	1	2	3	4	5	6	7	8	9	10
Forecast	550	300	400	450	300	350	200	300	450	400
Customer orders (booked)	300	350	250	250	200	150	100	100	100	100
Projected on-hand inventory										
MPS quantity	500									
MPS start										
Available-to-promise (ATP) inventory										

FIGURE 15.30

MPS Record for Ball Bearings

11. Figure 15.31 shows a partially completed MPS record for 2″ pneumatic control valves. Suppose that you receive the following orders for the valves (shown in the order of their arrival). As they arrive, you must decide whether to accept or reject them. Which orders would you accept for shipment?

Order	Amount (units)	Week Requested
1	15	2
2	30	5
3	25	3
4	75	7

12. The forecasted requirements for an electric hand drill for the next six weeks are 15, 40, 10, 20, 50, and 30 units. The marketing department has booked orders totaling 20, 25, 10, and 20 units for delivery in the first (current), second, third, and fourth weeks. Currently, 30 hand drills are in stock. The policy is to order in lots of 60 units. Lead time is one week.

   a. Develop the MPS record for the hand drills.

   b. A distributor of the hand drills places an order for 15 units. What is the appropriate shipping date for the entire order?

13. A forecast of 240 units in January, 320 units in February, and 240 units in March has been approved for the seismic-sensory product family manufactured at the

Rockport facility of Maryland Automated, Inc. Three products, A, B, and C, comprise this family. The product mix ratio for products A, B, and C for the past 2 years has been 35 percent, 40 percent, and 25 percent, respectively. Management believes that the monthly forecast requirements are evenly spread over the 4 weeks of each month. Currently, 10 units of product C are on hand. The company produces product C in lots of 40, and the lead time is 2 weeks. A production quantity of 40 units from the previous period is scheduled to arrive in week 1. The company has accepted orders of 25, 12, 8, 10, 2, and 3 units of product C in weeks 1 through 6, respectively. Prepare a prospective MPS for product C and calculate the available-to-promise inventory quantities.

14. The partially completed inventory record for the tabletop subassembly in Figure 15.32 shows gross requirements, scheduled receipts, lead time, and current on-hand inventory.

   a. Complete the last three rows of the record for an FOQ of 110 units.

   b. Complete the last three rows of the record by using the L4L lot-sizing rule.

   c. Complete the last three rows of the record by using the POQ lot-sizing rule, with $P = 2$.

15. The partially completed inventory record for the rotor subassembly in Figure 15.33 shows gross requirements, scheduled receipts, lead time, and current on-hand inventory.

   a. Complete the last three rows of the record for an FOQ of 150 units.

FIGURE 15.31

MPS Record for 2″ Pneumatic Control Valve

Item: 2″ Pneumatic control valve									Order Policy: 75 units Lead Time: 1 week	
		Week								
Quantity on Hand: 10		1	2	3	4	5	6	7	8	
Forecast		40	40	40	40	30	30	50	50	
Customer orders (booked)		60	45	30	35	10	5	5	0	
Projected on-hand inventory										
MPS quantity		75	75							
MPS start		75								
Available-to-promise (ATP) inventory										

Item: M405—X Description: Tabletop subassembly								Lot Size: Lead Time: 2 weeks		
	Week									
	1	2	3	4	5	6	7	8	9	10
Gross requirements	90		85		80		45	90		
Scheduled receipts	110									
Projected on-hand inventory 40										
Planned receipts										
Planned order releases										

FIGURE 15.32

Inventory Record for the Tabletop Subassembly

b. Complete the last three rows of the record by using the L4L lot-sizing rule.

c. Complete the last three rows of the record by using the POQ lot-sizing rule, with $P = 2$.

16. The partially completed inventory record for the driveshaft subassembly in Figure 15.34 shows gross requirements, scheduled receipts, lead time, and current on-hand inventory.

   a. Complete the last three rows of the record for an FOQ of 50 units.

   b. Complete the last three rows of the record by using the L4L lot-sizing rule.

   c. Complete the last three rows of the record by using the POQ lot-sizing rule, with $P = 4$.

17. Figure 15.35 shows a partially completed inventory record for the rear wheel subassembly. Gross requirements, scheduled receipts, lead time, and current on-hand inventory are shown.

   a. Complete the last three rows of the record for an FOQ of 300 units.

   b. Complete the last three rows of the record by using the L4L rule.

   c. Complete the last three rows of the record by using the POQ rule, with $P = 4$.

18. A partially completed inventory record for the motor subassembly is shown in Figure 15.36.

   a. Complete the last three rows of the record for an FOQ of 60 units.

Item: Rotor subassembly								Lot Size: Lead Time: 2 weeks	
	Week								
	1	2	3	4	5	6	7	8	
Gross requirements	65	15	45	40	80	80	80	80	
Scheduled receipts	150								
Projected on-hand inventory 20									
Planned receipts									
Planned order releases									

FIGURE 15.33

Inventory Record for the Rotor Subassembly

FIGURE **15.34**

Inventory Record for the
Driveshaft Subassembly

Item: Driveshaft subassembly   **Lot Size:**
Lead Time: 3 weeks

		Week							
		1	2	3	4	5	6	7	8
Gross requirements		35	25	15	20	40	40	50	50
Scheduled receipts		80							
Projected on-hand inventory	10								
Planned receipts									
Planned order releases									

FIGURE **15.35**

Inventory Record for the Rear
Wheel Subassembly

Item: MQ—09   **Lot Size:**
Description: Rear wheel subassembly   **Lead Time:** 1 week

		Week									
		1	2	3	4	5	6	7	8	9	10
Gross requirements		205		130	85		70	60	95		
Scheduled receipts		300									
Projected on-hand inventory	100										
Planned receipts											
Planned order releases											

Item: GF—4   **Lot Size:**
Description: Motor subassembly   **Lead Time:** 3 weeks

		Week											
		1	2	3	4	5	6	7	8	9	10	11	12
Gross requirements			50		35		55		30		10		25
Scheduled receipts			60										
Projected on-hand inventory	40												
Planned receipts													
Planned order releases													

FIGURE **15.36** | Inventory Record for the Motor Subassembly

b. Revise the planned order release row by using the L4L rule.

c. Revise the planned order release row by using the POQ rule. Find the value of P that should (in the long run) yield an average lot size of 60 units. Assume that the average weekly demand for the foreseeable future is 15 units.

ADVANCED PROBLEMS

19. The BOM for product A is shown in Figure 15.37, and data from the inventory records are shown in Table 15.2. In the master production schedule for product A, the MPS start row has 500 units in week 6. The lead time for production of A is two weeks. Develop the material requirements plan for the next six weeks for items B, C, and D. (*Hint:* You cannot derive an item's gross requirements unless you know the planned order releases of all its parents.)

20. The BOMs for products A and B are shown in Figure 15.38. Data from inventory records are shown in Table 15.3. The MPS calls for 85 units of product A to be started in week 3 and 100 units in week 6. The MPS for product B calls for 180 units to be started in week 5. Develop the material requirements plan for the next six weeks for items C, D, E, and F.

21. Figure 15.39 illustrates the BOM for product A. The MPS start row in the master production schedule for product A calls for 50 units in week 2, 65 units in week 5, and 80 units in week 8. Item C is produced to make A and to meet the forecasted demand for replacement parts. Past replacement part demand has been 20 units per week (add 20 units to C's gross requirements). The lead times for items F and C are one week, and for the other items the lead time is two weeks. No safety stock is required for items B, C, D, E, and F. The L4L lot-sizing rule is used for items B and F; the POQ lot-sizing rule ($P = 3$) is used for C. Item E has an FOQ of 600 units, and D has an FOQ of 250 units. On-hand inventories are 50 units of B, 50 units of C, 120 units of D, 70 units of E, and 250 units of F. Item B has a scheduled receipt of 50 units in week 2.

Develop a material requirements plan for the next eight weeks for items B, C, D, E, and F.

22. The following information is available for three MPS items.

Product A	An 80-unit order is to be started in week 3.
	A 55-unit order is to be started in week 6.
Product B	A 125-unit order is to be started in week 5.
Product C	A 60-unit order is to be started in week 4.

Develop the material requirements plan for the next 6 weeks for items D, E, and F. The BOMs are shown in Figure 15.40, and data from the inventory records are shown in Table 15.4. (*Warning:* A safety stock requirement

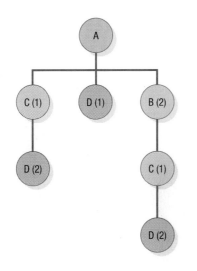

FIGURE 15.37 | BOM for Product A

TABLE 15.2	Inventory Record Data		
	Item		
Data Category	**B**	**C**	**D**
Lot-sizing rule	L4L	L4L	FOQ = 2,000
Lead time	3 weeks	1 week	1 week
Scheduled receipts	None	None	2,000 (week 1)
Beginning inventory	0	0	200

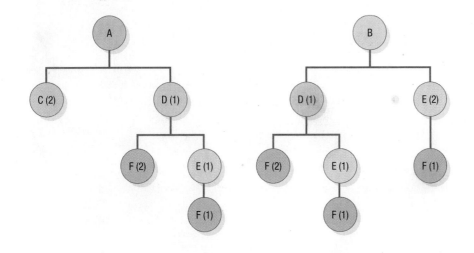

FIGURE 15.38

BOMs for Product A and Product B

TABLE 15.3	Inventory Record Data			
	Item			
Data Category	C	D	E	F
Lot-sizing rule	FOQ = 220	L4L	FOQ = 300	POQ ($P = 2$)
Lead time	3 weeks	2 weeks	3 weeks	2 weeks
Scheduled receipts	280 (week 1)	None	300 (week 3)	None
Beginning inventory	25	0	150	600

FIGURE **15.39**

BOM for Product A

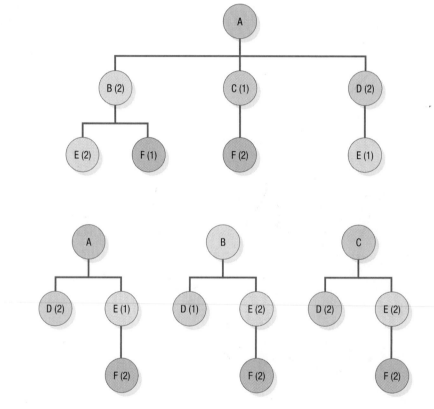

FIGURE **15.40**

BOMs for Products A, B, and C

TABLE 15.4	Inventory Record Data		
	Item		
Data Category	D	E	F
Lot-sizing rule	FOQ = 150	L4L	POQ ($P = 2$)
Lead time	3 weeks	1 week	2 weeks
Safety stock	0	0	30
Scheduled receipts	150 (week 3)	120 (week 2)	None
Beginning inventory	150	0	100

applies to item F. Be sure to plan a receipt for any week in which the projected on-hand inventory becomes less than the safety stock.)

23. Figure 15.41 shows the BOMs for two products, A and B. Table 15.5 shows the MPS quantity start date for each one. Table 15.6 contains data from inventory records for items C, D, and E. There are no safety stock requirements for any of the items. Determine the material requirements plan for items C, D, and E for the next eight weeks.

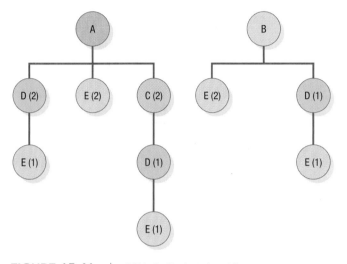

FIGURE 15.41 | BOMs for Products A and B

TABLE 15.6	Inventory Record Data		
	Item		
Data Category	**C**	**D**	**E**
Lot-sizing rule	L4L	POQ ($P = 3$)	FOQ = 800
Lead time	3 weeks	2 weeks	1 week
Scheduled receipts	200 (week 2)	None	800 (week 1)
Beginning inventory	85	625	350

24. The BOM for product A is shown in Figure 15.42. The MPS for product A calls for 120 units to be started in weeks 2, 4, 5, and 8. Table 15.7 shows data from the inventory records. Develop the material requirements plan for the next eight weeks for each item.

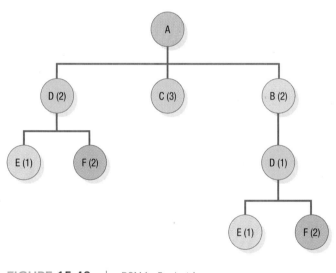

FIGURE 15.42 | BOM for Product A

TABLE 15.5	MPS Quantity Start Dates							
	Date							
Product	**1**	**2**	**3**	**4**	**5**	**6**	**7**	**8**
A		125		95		150		130
B			80			70		

TABLE 15.7	Inventory Record Data				
	Item				
Data Category	**B**	**C**	**D**	**E**	**F**
Lot-sizing rule	L4L	FOQ = 700	FOQ = 700	L4L	L4L
Lead time	3 weeks	3 weeks	4 weeks	2 weeks	1 week
Safety stock	0	0	0	50	0
Scheduled receipts	150 (week 2)	450 (week 2)	700 (week 1)	None	1,400 (week 1)
Beginning inventory	125	0	235	750	0

25. Develop the material requirements plan for all components and intermediate items associated with product A for the next ten weeks. Refer to Solved Problem 1 (Figure 15.21) for the bill of materials and Table 15.8 for component inventory record information. The MPS for product A calls for 50 units to be started in weeks 2, 6, 8, and 9. (*Warning:* Safety stock requirements apply to items B and C.)

TABLE 15.8	Inventory Record Data

			Item			
Data Category	**B**	**C**	**D**	**E**	**F**	**G**
Lot-sizing rule	L4L	L4L	POQ ($P = 2$)	L4L	L4L	FOQ = 100
Lead time	2 weeks	3 weeks	3 weeks	6 weeks	1 week	3 weeks
Safety stock	30	10	0	0	0	0
Scheduled receipts	150 (week 2)	50 (week 2)	None	400 (week 6)	40 (week 3)	None
Beginning inventory	30	20	60	400	0	0

> ACTIVE MODEL EXERCISE <

This Active Model appears on the Student CD-ROM. It allows you to evaluate the relationship between the inventory record data and the planned order releases.

QUESTIONS

1. Suppose that the POQ for item B is changed from 3 weeks to 2 weeks. How does this change affect the order releases for items B, C, and D?

2. As the on-hand inventory for item C increases from 0 to 200, what happens to the order releases for items B, C, and D?

3. As the fixed order quantity (FOQ) for item D increases from 500 to 750, what happens to the order releases for items B, C, and D?

4. As the lead time for item C changes, what happens to the order releases for items B, C, and D?

ACTIVE MODEL 15.1

Material Requirements Planning Using Data from Solved Problem 3 and Table 15.1

Flashy Flashers, Inc.

Jack Jacobs, the production and inventory manager of Flashy Flashers Inc., stopped for a moment to adjust his tie knot and run his fingers through his hair before entering the office of Ollie Prout, the vice president of operations. From the tone of Prout's voice over the telephone, Jacobs knew that he was not being called for a social visit.

Company Background

Flashy Flashers is a medium-sized firm employing 500 persons and 75 managerial and administrative personnel. The firm produces a line of automotive electrical components. It supplies about 75 auto parts stores and "Moonbird Silverstreak" car dealers in its region.

Johnny Bennett, who serves as the president, founded the company. Bennett is a great entrepreneur who started producing cable assemblies in his garage. By working hard, delivering consistent product quality, and by providing good customer service, he expanded his business to produce a variety of electrical components. Bennett's commitment to customer service is so strong that his company motto, "Love Thy Customers As Thyself," is etched on a big cast-iron plaque under his giant oil portrait in the building's front lobby.

The company's two most profitable products are the automotive front sidelamp and the headlamp. With the recent boom in the auto industry and the rising popularity of Eurosport sedans, such as the Moonbird Silverstreak, Flashy Flashers has enjoyed substantial demand for these two lamp items.

Last year, on Prout's recommendation—and for better management of the inventory system—Bennett approved the installation of a new MRP system. Prout worked closely with the task force that was created to bring MRP online. He frequently attended the training sessions for selected employees, emphasizing how MRP should help Flashy Flashers secure a better competitive edge. On the day the system "went up," everyone felt an aura of tranquility and goodwill. The days of the informal system of firefighting were over!

A year later, Prout's mood is quite different. Inventory and overtime levels failed to drop as much as expected, customer service continues to get worse, and complaints about late shipments are still prevalent. Convinced that these issues should not happen with MRP, Prout is attempting to find out what is going wrong.

The Problems

Jacobs took barely two steps inside Prout's office when his voice cut across the room. "Jack, what's going on out there? I've just received another call from a customer complaining that we've fallen behind on our lamp shipments to them again! This is the umpteenth time I've received complaints about late shipments. Johnny has been on my back about this. Why isn't our system working as it is supposed to, and what do we have to do to hold onto valuable customers and stay in business?"

Jacobs gulped and took a moment to regain his composure before answering Prout. "We're trying our best to maintain the inventory records and BOM files. With our system, there's a new explosion each week. It gives us an updated material requirements plan and action notices for launching new orders. Some of the employees in my group think we should extend our outputs to get priority and capacity reports. As you know, we decided to get the order-launching capability well established first. However, we don't seem to have a formal system of priority planning, which is creating scheduling problems on the shop floor.

"I think our purchasing and marketing departments also are at fault. We seem to experience too many stockouts of purchased parts even though we've worked closely with Jayne Spring's group to get realistic lead-time estimates. And marketing keeps taking last-minute orders from favorite customers. These orders wreak havoc with our master production schedule."

"Well, I'm really getting fed up with this," Prout cut in. "Talk with the people concerned and find out what exactly is going wrong. I'll expect a complete report from you in two weeks, giving me all the details and recommendations for improvement."

Jacobs decided to get to the bottom of things, as he walked out of Prout's office. He first called on Sam McKenzie, the shop superintendent.

Production

Jacobs's conversation with McKenzie suggested that the pre-MRP informal system is still alive and well. "I'm starting to wonder about this MRP system, even though it looks great on paper," McKenzie commented. "Last week we hardly had any work, and I was forced to overproduce on several orders just to keep everyone busy. This week is just the opposite—so many new orders were released with short fuses that almost everyone will need to work overtime. It's either feast or famine! Our priority planners don't seem to update the due dates assigned to each order, but things change pretty quickly around here.

"Another thing is the inventory records. When I get an order, I first check the inventory record for that item to find out the current stock situation. More often than not, the actual number of units is less than what the records indicate, then I have to produce more than planned, which wreaks havoc with our capacity plans. We can't stick to our lead times when things are so fluid around here!"

Purchasing

Jacobs's next conversation was with Jayne Spring, the purchasing manager. It was equally disconcerting. "Our buyers are really getting frustrated with this new system. There's no time for creative buying. Almost all of their time is spent following up on late orders because of constant expediting action notices. For example, the other day the system told us to bring in 200 units of part HL222P in just two weeks. We tried all possible vendors, but they said that a delivery in two weeks was impossible. What are the planners doing? The perplexing thing is that the planned lead time in the inventory record for this part is correctly stated as four weeks. Doesn't MRP offset for lead time? Some problems with unreliable vendor lead times also mean that we have to carry more safety stock for some items than is necessary."

Jacobs tried to assimilate all this information. He then proceeded to collect all the required information about the sidelamps and headlamps (shown in Table 15.9 through Table 15.13 and in Figure 15.43) and decided to gain further insight into the problem by working out the MRP explosion manually for the next six weeks.

TABLE 15.9	Part Numbers and Descriptions

Part Number	Description
C206P	Screws
C310P	Back rubber gasket
HL200E	Headlamp
HL211A	Head frame subassembly
HL212P	Head lens
HL222P	Headlamp module
HL223F	Head frame
SL100E	Sidelamp
SL111P	Side lens
SL112A	Side frame subassembly
SL113P	Side lens rubber gasket
SL121F	Side frame
SL122A	Side bulb subassembly
SL123A	Flasher bulb subassembly
SL131F	Side cable grommet and receptacle
SL132P	Side bulb
SL133F	Flasher cable grommet and receptacle
SL134P	Flasher bulb

TABLE 15.10	Master Production Schedule

Item Description and Part Number	Quantity	MPS Start Date
Headlamp (HL200E)	120	Week 14
	90	Week 15
	75	Week 16
Sidelamp (SL100E)	100	Week 13
	80	Week 15
	110	Week 16

TABLE 15.11 | Replacement Part Demand

Item Description and Part Number	Quantity	Date
Side lens (SL111P)	40	Week 13
	35	Week 16

TABLE 15.12 | Selected Data from Inventory Records

Part Number	Lead Time (weeks)	Safety Stock (units)	Lot-Sizing Rule	On-Hand (units)	Scheduled Receipt (units and due dates)
C206P	1	30	FOQ = 2,500	150	—
C310P	1	20	FOQ = 180	30	180 (week 12)
HL211A	2	0	L4L	10	50 (week 12)
HL212P	2	15	FOQ = 350	15	—
HL222P	4	10	POQ (P = 4 weeks)	50	110 (week 14)
HL223F	1	0	L4L	70	—
SL111P	2	0	FOQ = 350	15	—
SL112A	3	0	L4L	20	100 (week 13)
SL113P	1	20	FOQ = 100	20	—
SL121F	3	0	L4L	0	70 (week 13)
SL122A	1	0	L4L	10	50 (week 12)
SL123A	1	0	L4L	0	—
SL131F	2	0	POQ (P = 2 weeks)	0	—
SL132P	1	25	FOQ = 100	35	100 (week 12)
SL133F	2	0	POQ (P = 2 weeks)	0	180 (week 12)
SL134P	1	25	FOQ = 100	20	100 (week 11)

Your Assignment

Put yourself in Jacobs's place and write the report to your boss, Ollie Prout. Specifically, you are required to do a manual MRP explosion for the sidelamps and headlamps for the next 6 weeks (beginning with the current week). Assume that it is now the start of week 11. Fill in the planned order releases form provided in Table 15.13. It should show the planned order releases for all items for the next six weeks. Include it in your report.

Your report should identify the good and bad points of MRP implementation at Flashy Flashers. Supplement your report with worksheets on the manual MRP explosion, indicating where adjustments must be made for order releases and scheduled receipts. Conclude by making suggestions for change.

Source: This case was prepared by Professor Soumen Ghosh, Georgia Institute of Technology, for the purpose of classroom discussion only.

TABLE 15.13 | Planned Order Release Form

Fill in the planned order releases for all components.

Item Description and Part Number	Week					
	11	12	13	14	15	16
Side lens (SL111P)						
Side lens rubber gasket (SL113P)						
Side frame subassembly (SL112A)						
Side frame (SL121F)						
Side bulb subassembly (SL122A)						
Flasher bulb subassembly (SL123A)						
Side cable grommet and receptacle (SL131F)						
Flasher cable grommet and receptacle (SL133F)						
Side bulb (SL132P)						
Flasher bulb (SL134P)						
Head frame subassembly (HL211A)						
Head lens (HL212P)						
Headlamp module (HL222P)						
Head frame (HL223F)						
Back rubber gasket (C310P)						
Screws (C206P)						

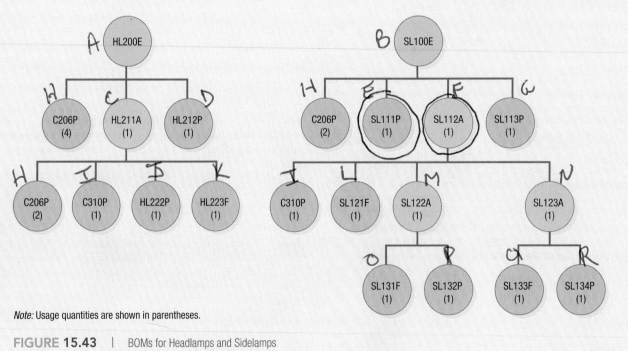

Note: Usage quantities are shown in parentheses.

FIGURE 15.43 | BOMs for Headlamps and Sidelamps

> SELECTED REFERENCES <

Blackstone, J. H. *Capacity Management.* Cincinnati: South-Western, 1989.

Bruggeman, J. J., and S. Haythornthwaite. "The Master Schedule." *APICS—The Performance Advantage* (October 1991), pp. 44–46.

Conway, Richard W. "Linking MRP II and FCS." *APICS—The Performance Advantage* (June 1996), pp. 40–44.

Cotten, Jim. "Starting from Scratch." *APICS—The Performance Advantage* (November 1996), pp. 34–37.

Davenport, Thomas H. "Putting the Enterprise into the Enterprise System." *Harvard Business Review* (July–August 1998), pp. 121–131.

Dollries, Joseph. "Don't Pick a Package—Match One." *APICS—The Performance Advantage* (May 1996), pp. 50–52.

Goddard, Walter, and James Correll. "MRP II in the Year 2000." *APICS—The Performance Advantage* (March 1994), pp. 38–42.

Goldratt, E. M. *Theory of Constraints.* Great Barrington, MA: North River Press, 1990.

Haddock, Jorge, and Donald E. Hubicki. "Which Lot-Sizing Techniques Are Used in Material Requirements Planning?" *Production and Inventory Management Journal,* vol. 30, no. 3 (1989), pp. 53–56.

Hoy, Paul A. "The Changing Role of MRP II." *APICS—The Performance Advantage* (June 1996), pp. 50–53.

Jacobs, F. Robert, and D. Clay Whybark. *Why ERP?* New York: Irwin McGraw-Hill, 2000.

Jemigan, Jeff. "Comprehensiveness, Cost-Effectiveness Sweep Aside Operations Challenges." *APICS—The Performance Advantage* (March 1993), pp. 44–45.

Lunn, Terry, and Susan Neff. *MRP: Integrating Material Requirements Planning and Modern Business.* Homewood, IL: Irwin Professional Publishing, 1992.

Melnyk, Steven A., Robert Sroufe, Frank Montabon, Roger Calantone, R. Lal Tummala, and Timothy J. Hinds. "Integrating Environmental Issues into Material Planning: 'Green' MRP." *Production and Inventory Management Journal* (Third Quarter 1999), pp. 36–45.

Ormsby, Joseph G., Susan Y. Ormsby, and Carl R. Ruthstrom. "MRP II Implementation: A Case Study." *Production and Inventory Management,* vol. 31, no. 4 (1990), pp. 77–82.

Prouty, Dave. "Shiva Finite Capacity Scheduling System." *APICS—The Performance Advantage* (April 1997), pp. 58–61.

Ptak, Carol. *MRP and Beyond.* Homewood, IL: Irwin Professional Publishing, 1996.

Roth, Aleda V., and Roland Van Dierdonck. "Hospital Resource Planning: Concepts, Feasibility, and Framework." *Production and Operations Management,* vol. 4, no. 1 (1995), pp. 2–29.

Scalle, Cedric X., and Mark J. Cotteleer. *Enterprise Resource Planning (ERP).* Boston, MA: Harvard Business School Publishing, 1999, No. 9-699-020.

Srinivasan, Mandyam, Darren Jones, and Alex Miller. "Corps Capabilities." *APICS Magazine* (March 2005), pp. 46–50.

Steele, Daniel C., Patrick R. Philipoom, Manoj K. Malhotra, and Timothy D. Fry. "Comparisons Between Drum-Buffer-Rope and Material Requirements Planning: A Case Study." *International Journal of Production Research,* vol. 43, no. 15 (2005), pp. 3181–3208.

Turbide, David A. "This Is Not Your Father's MRP!" *APICS—The Performance Advantage* (March 1994), pp. 28–37.

Umble, M. M., and M. L. Srikanth. *Synchronous Management-Profit Based Manufacturing for the 21st Century,* Vol. 2. Wallingford, CT: Spectrum Publishing Company, 1997.

Vollmann, T. E., W. L. Berry, D. C. Whybark, and F. R. Jacobs. *Manufacturing Planning and Control for Supply Chain Management,* 5th ed. New York: Irwin/McGraw-Hill, 2004.

Wallace, Thomas F. *Sales & Operations Planning: The How-To Handbook,* 2d ed. Cincinnati, OH: T. E. Wallace & Company, 2004.

Wallace, Thomas F., and Robert A. Stahl. *Master Scheduling in the 21st Century.* Cincinnati, OH: T. E. Wallace & Company, 2003.

ZDWire Plus. "Customization, Complexity Still Dog ERP Efforts." Thompson Dialogue, July 19, 2005.

16

LEARNING GOALS

*After reading this chapter,
you should be able to:*

1. Define the key performance
   measures to consider when
   selecting a schedule.
2. Identify the situations in which
   demands can be scheduled by
   appointments, reservations, or
   backlogs.
3. Describe the components of
   advanced planning systems that
   link operations schedules to the
   supply chain.
4. Explain the importance of
   scheduling to the performance
   of the firm.
5. Determine a schedule of
   employees that allows for two
   consecutive days off per
   employee.
6. Determine schedules for single
   and multiple workstations.

Scheduling at an airline like Air New
Zealand is a sophisticated task. By law,
flight crews are only allowed to be on
duty a certain number of hours per day,
which can cause complications should
weather or repair delays occur.

CHAPTER 16
Scheduling

AIR NEW ZEALAND

How important is scheduling to an airline company? Certainly, customer satisfaction regarding on-time schedule performance is critical in a highly competitive industry such as air transportation. In addition, airlines lose a lot of money when expensive equipment, such as an aircraft, is idle. Flight and crew scheduling, however, is a complex process. For example, Air New Zealand has 9,000 employees and operates more than 85 domestic and 50 international flights daily. Scheduling begins with a five-year market plan that identifies the new and existing flight segments that are needed to remain competitive in the industry. This general plan is further refined to a three-year plan, and then is put into an annual budget in which flight segments have specific departure and arrival times.

Next, crew availability must be matched to the flight schedules. The two types of crews—pilots and attendants—each comes with its own set of constraints. Pilots, for example, cannot be scheduled for more than 35 hours in a 7-day week and no more than 100 hours in a 28-day cycle. They also must have a 36-hour break every 7 days and 30 days off in an 84-day cycle. Sophisticated optimization models are used to design generic minimum-cost schedules that cover every flight and recognize all the constraints. Each pilot's tour of duty begins and ends at a crew base and consists of an alternating sequence of duty periods and rest periods, with duty periods including one or more flights. The tours of duty are posted, and crew members bid on them within a specified period of time. Actual crew rosters are then constructed from the bids received. The roster must ensure that each flight has a qualified crew and that each crew member has a feasible schedule *over the roster period. From the crew's point of view, it is also important to satisfy as many crew requests and preferences as possible.*

Scheduling does not end with the finalization of the flights and crew rosters, however. Daily disruptions, such as severe weather conditions or mechanical failures, can cause schedule changes that affect attendants, pilots, and even planes. Customers expect these

problems to be resolved quickly, and the company needs to find the least-cost solution. In the airline industry, the scheduling process can determine a company's long-term competitive strength.

Sources: David M. Ryan, "Optimization Earns Its Wings," *OR/MS Today* (April 2000), pp. 26–30; "Service Scheduling at Air New Zealand," *Operations Management 8e Video Library* (Upper Saddle River, NJ: Prentice Hall, 2007).

scheduling

The allocation of resources over time to accomplish specific tasks.

As the crew scheduling example at Air New Zealand demonstrates, effective scheduling is essential to successful operations. **Scheduling** allocates resources over time to accomplish specific tasks. Up to this point in the text, we discussed the design of processes, how they are linked to form value chains, and the key planning techniques for effectively operating them. Scheduling is the activity that brings all of these design and planning activities to fruition. For example, police protection services must have consistent quality, fast delivery, variety and volume flexibility, and be low-cost. Decisions must be made about the location of police stations and the quantity of patrol cars at each station. The information technology must be chosen, and forecasting methods selected for estimating police services on an hourly, daily, weekly, monthly, and annual basis. A staffing plan must then be determined for each station.

All of these design and planning activities, however, will not achieve the competitive priorities of the police service unless effective work schedules can be devised for the police officers. Scheduling is a critical link between the planning and execution phases of operations. Without effective scheduling, value chains will not meet their potential. For this reason, supply chain management software and enterprise resource planning systems that include scheduling applications are becoming more common.

Although it is an important aspect of value chain management, scheduling is itself a process. It requires gathering data from sources such as demand forecasts or specific customer orders, resource availability from the sales and operations plan, and specific constraints to be reckoned with from employees and customers. It then involves generating a work schedule for employees or a production schedule for a manufacturing process. The schedule has to be coordinated with the employees and suppliers to make sure that all constraints are satisfied. As with any process, this process can be measured against the firm's competitive priorities that may include low-cost operations (How much does it cost to create a schedule?), delivery speed (How fast can schedules be generated?), consistent quality (How often must schedules be revised after they are initiated?), and variety flexibility (How many different employee, service, or product groups can it handle?).

In this chapter, we begin with a discussion of scheduling for service and manufacturing processes, focusing on useful performance measures and the application of Gantt charts. We then discuss **demand scheduling**, which involves assigning customers to a definite time for order fulfillment. Next, we discuss a technique for **workforce scheduling**, which involves determining when employees work. Finally, we explore several techniques for **operations scheduling**, which involves assigning jobs to workstations or employees to jobs for specified time periods. Effectively solving these three scheduling problems will help managers achieve the full potential of their value chains.

demand scheduling

A type of scheduling whereby customers are assigned to a definite time for order fulfillment.

workforce scheduling

A type of scheduling that determines when employees work.

operations scheduling

A type of scheduling in which jobs are assigned to workstations or employees are assigned to jobs for specified time periods.

> SCHEDULING ACROSS THE ORGANIZATION <

Scheduling is important for service as well as manufacturing processes. Whether the business is an airline, hotel, computer manufacturer, or university, schedules are a part of everyday life. Schedules involve an enormous amount of detail and affect every process in a firm. For example, service, product and employee schedules determine specific cash flow requirements, trigger the firm's billing process, and initiate requirements for the employee training process. The order fulfillment process depends on good performance in terms of due dates for promised services or products, which is the result of a good scheduling process. In addition, when customers place orders using a Web-based order-entry process, the scheduling process determines when they can expect to receive their order. Certainly, regardless of the discipline, schedules affect everyone in a firm.

Given the development of computer hardware and software and the availability of the Internet, firms have transformed the scheduling process into a competitive weapon. In this chapter we shall see how firms use the scheduling process to lower their costs and improve their supply chain responsiveness by finding a way to produce complex schedules quickly. These schedules can affect operations up and down the supply chain worldwide.

> SCHEDULING SERVICE AND MANUFACTURING PROCESSES <

The scheduling techniques we discuss in this chapter cut across the various process types found in services and manufacturing. Many service firms are characterized by a *front-office process* with high customer contact, flexible work flows, customization and, consequently, a complex scheduling environment. Inventories cannot be used to buffer demand uncertainties, which puts a premium on scheduling employees to handle the varied needs of customers. Demand scheduling and workforce scheduling are two useful techniques in service industries. At the other extreme in the service industry, a *back-office process* has low customer involvement, uses more line work flows, and provides standardized services. Inanimate objects are processed; these processes take on the appearance of manufacturing processes. In this case, workforce schedules are important as are operations schedules.

Manufacturing processes also benefit from demand scheduling, workforce scheduling, and operations scheduling techniques. Our discussion of the operations scheduling techniques in this chapter has application for job, batch, and line processes in services as well as in manufacturing. Schedules for continuous processes can be developed with *linear programming*. Although the scheduling techniques in this chapter provide some structure to the selection of good schedules, many alternatives typically need to be evaluated. Before we explore the techniques for generating job and employee schedules, let us look at the performance measures managers use to select good schedules.

PERFORMANCE MEASURES

From the manager's perspective, identifying the performance measures to be used in selecting a schedule is important. If the competitive priorities of a process are to be achieved, the schedules should reflect managerially acceptable performance measures consistent with those competitive priorities. The following performance measures are commonly used for scheduling both services and manufacturing processes. In this regard, a *job* is the object receiving service or being manufactured. For example, a job may be a customer waiting for service at a state licensing bureau or it may be a batch of pistons waiting for a manufacturing process.

- *Job Flow Time.* The amount of time a job spends in the service or manufacturing system is called **job flow time**. It is the sum of the waiting time for servers or machines; the process time, including setups; the time spent moving between operations; and delays resulting from machine breakdowns, unavailability of facilitating goods or components, and the like. Minimizing job flow times supports the competitive priorities of cost (lower inventory) and time (delivery speed).

  Job flow time = Time of completion − Time job was available for first processing operation

  Note that the starting time is the time the job was available for its first processing operation, not necessarily when the job began its first operation. Job flow time is sometimes referred to as *throughout time* or *time spent in the system, including service.*

- *Makespan.* The total amount of time required to complete a *group* of jobs is called **makespan**. Minimizing makespan supports the competitive priorities of cost (lower inventory) and time (delivery speed).

  Makespan = Time of completion of last job − Starting time of first job

---

USING OPERATIONS TO COMPETE

Operations As a Competitive Weapon
Operations Strategy
Project Management

MANAGING PROCESSES

Process Strategy
Process Analysis
Process Performance and Quality
Constraint Management
Process Layout
Lean Systems

MANAGING VALUE CHAINS

Supply Chain Strategy
Location
Inventory Management
Forecasting
Sales and Operations Planning
Resource Planning
Scheduling

---

job flow time

The amount of time a job spends in the service or manufacturing system.

makespan

The total amount of time required to complete a *group* of jobs.

past due

The amount of time by which a job missed its due date or the percentage of total jobs processed over some period of time that missed their due dates.

tardiness

See **past due**.

work-in-process (WIP) inventory

Any job that is waiting in line, moving from one operation to the next, being delayed for some reason, being processed, or residing in a semifinished state.

total inventory

The sum of scheduled receipts and on-hand inventories.

- *Past Due.* The measure **past due** can be expressed as the amount of time by which a job missed its due date (also referred to as **tardiness**) or as the percentage of total jobs processed over some period of time that missed their due dates. Minimizing the past due measure supports the competitive priorities of cost (penalties for missing due dates), quality (perceptions of poor service), and time (on-time delivery).

- *Work-in-Process Inventory.* Any job that is waiting in line, moving from one operation to the next, being delayed for some reason, being processed, or residing in a semifinished state is considered to be **work-in-process (WIP) inventory**. WIP is also referred to as *pipeline inventory* or as *the number of customers in the service system.* Minimizing the WIP inventory supports the competitive priority of cost (inventory holding costs).

- *Total Inventory.* This performance measure is used to measure how effective schedules for manufacturing processes are. The sum of *scheduled receipts* and *on-hand inventories* is the **total inventory**.

  Total inventory = Scheduled receipts for all items + On-hand inventories of all items

  Minimizing total inventory supports the competitive priority of cost (inventory holding costs). Essentially, total inventory is the sum of WIP and finished goods inventories.

- *Utilization.* The percentage of work time that is productively spent by an employee or a machine is called *utilization.* Maximizing the utilization of a process supports the competitive priority of cost (slack capacity).

These performance measures often are interrelated. For example, minimizing the average job flow time tends to reduce WIP inventory and increase utilization. Minimizing the makespan for a group of jobs tends to increase utilization. Understanding how job flow time, makespan, past due, WIP inventory, total inventory, and utilization interact can make the selection of good schedules easier.

GANTT CHARTS

The *Gantt chart* can be used as a tool to monitor the progress of work and to view the load on workstations. The chart takes two basic forms: (1) the job or activity progress chart, and (2) the workstation chart. The Gantt *progress chart* graphically displays the current status of each job or activity relative to its scheduled completion date. For example, suppose that an automobile parts manufacturer has three jobs under way, one each for Ford, Nissan, and Pontiac. The actual status of these orders is shown by the colored bars in Figure 16.1; the red lines indicate the desired schedule for the start and finish of each job. For the current date, April 21, this Gantt chart shows that the Ford order is behind schedule because operations has completed only the work scheduled through April 18. The Nissan order is exactly on schedule, and the Pontiac order is ahead of schedule.

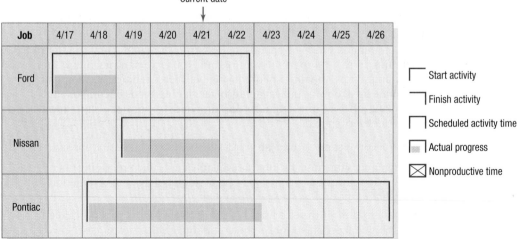

FIGURE **16.1** | Gantt Progress Chart for an Auto Parts Company

Figure 16.2 shows a Gantt *workstation chart* of the operating rooms at a hospital for a particular day. Using the same notation as in Figure 16.1, the chart shows the load on the operating rooms and the nonproductive time. The time slots assigned to each doctor include the time needed to clean the room prior to the next surgery. The chart can be used to identify time slots for unscheduled emergency surgeries. It can also be used to accommodate requests to change the time of surgeries. For example, Dr. Flowers may be able to change the start of her surgery to 2 P.M. by swapping time slots with Dr. Gillespie in operating room C or by asking Dr. Brothers to start her surgery one hour earlier in operating room A and asking Dr. Bright to schedule her surgery for the morning in operating room C. In any event, the hospital administrator would have to get involved in rescheduling the surgeries.

Gantt charts can be used to generate schedules for employees or workstations; however, the approach only works on a trial-and-error basis. We now turn to some techniques that can be used to arrive systematically at good schedules.

> SCHEDULING CUSTOMER DEMAND <

Capacity, which can be in the form of employees or equipment, is crucial for service providers and manufacturers. One way to manage capacity with a scheduling system is to schedule customers for definite periods of order fulfillment. With this approach, capacity is assumed to be fixed and demand is leveled to provide timely order fulfillment and a desired capacity utilization. Three methods are commonly used to schedule customer demand: (1) appointments, (2) reservations, and (3) backlogs.

APPOINTMENTS

An appointment system assigns specific times for service to customers. The advantages of this method are timely customer service and the high utilization of service personnel. Doctors, dentists, lawyers, and automobile repair shops are examples of service providers that use appointment systems. Doctors can use the system to schedule parts of their day to visit hospital patients, and lawyers can set aside time to prepare cases. If timely service is to be provided, however, care must be taken to tailor the length of appointments to individual customer needs rather than merely scheduling customers at equal time intervals.

RESERVATIONS

Reservation systems, although quite similar to appointment systems, are used when the customer actually occupies or uses facilities associated with the service. For example, customers reserve hotel rooms, automobiles, airline seats, and concert seats. The major advantage of reservation systems is the lead time they give service managers to plan the efficient use of facilities. Often, reservations require some form of down payment to reduce the problem of no-shows.

Time

Workstation	7 A.M.	8 A.M.	9 A.M.	10 A.M.	11 A.M.	12 P.M.	1 P.M.	2 P.M.	3 P.M.	4 P.M.	5 P.M.	6 P.M.
Operating Room A	Dr. Jon Adams		✕		Dr. Aubrey Brothers				✕	Dr. Alaina Bright		
Operating Room B	✕	Dr. Gary Case			✕	Dr. Jeff Dow		✕	Dr. Madeline Easton			
Operating Room C	Dr. Jordanne Flowers				✕	Dr. Dan Gillespie						

FIGURE 16.2 | Gantt Workstation Chart for Operating Rooms at a Hospital

BACKLOGS

Backlogs take one of two forms. In the first form, the customer is given a *due date* for the fulfillment a product order. For example, the repair department of a car dealership may agree with an automotive parts manufacturer to receive delivery of a batch of 100 door latches for a particular car model next Tuesday. The parts manufacturer uses that due date to plan its production of door latches within its capacity limits. The equivalent of the due date for services is the use of appointments or reservations.

The second form of backlog is to simply allow a backlog to develop as customers arrive at the system. In this case, customers may never know exactly when their orders will be fulfilled. An order request is presented to an order taker, who adds the customer's new order request to the waiting line of orders already in the system. Television repair shops, restaurants, banks, grocery stores, or any waiting line situation are examples of the use of this system of demand scheduling.

> SCHEDULING EMPLOYEES <

Another way to manage capacity with a scheduling system is to specify the on-duty and off-duty periods for each employee over a certain time period, as in assigning postal clerks, nurses, pilots, attendants, or police officers to specific workdays and shifts. This approach is used when customers demand quick response and total demand can be forecasted with reasonable accuracy. In these instances, capacity is adjusted to meet the expected loads on the service system.

Workforce schedules translate the staffing plan into specific schedules of work for each employee. Determining the workdays for each employee in itself does not make the staffing plan operational. Daily workforce requirements, stated in aggregate terms in the staffing plan, must be satisfied. The workforce capacity available each day must meet or exceed daily workforce requirements. If it does not, the scheduler must try to rearrange days off until the requirements are met. If no such schedule can be found, management might have to change the staffing plan and hire more employees, authorize overtime hours, or allow for larger backlogs.

CONSTRAINTS

The technical constraints imposed on the workforce schedule are the resources provided by the staffing plan and the requirements placed on the operating system. However, other constraints, including legal and behavioral considerations, also can be imposed. For example, Air New Zealand is required to have at least a minimum number of flight attendants on duty at all times. Similarly, a minimum number of fire and safety personnel must be on duty at a fire station at all times. Such constraints limit management's flexibility in developing workforce schedules.

When it comes to services like firefighting, schedulers can't manage the customer demand. Fires will occur whenever they occur, of course. The workforce capacity available each day at a firehouse must therefore always meet or exceed daily requirements.

The constraints imposed by the psychological needs of workers complicate scheduling even more. Some of these constraints are written into labor agreements. For example, an employer might agree to give employees a certain number of consecutive days off per week or to limit employees' consecutive workdays to a certain maximum. Other provisions might govern the allocation of vacations, days off for holidays, or rotating shift assignments. In addition, the preferences of the employees themselves need to be considered.

One way that managers deal with certain undesirable aspects of scheduling is to use a **rotating schedule**, which rotates employees through a series of workdays or hours. Thus, over a period of time, each person has the same opportunity to have weekends and holidays off and to work days, as well as evenings and nights. A rotating schedule gives each employee the next employee's schedule the following week. In contrast, a **fixed schedule** calls for each employee to work the same days and hours each week.

rotating schedule

A schedule that rotates employees through a series of workdays or hours.

fixed schedule

A schedule that calls for each employee to work the same days and hours each week.

DEVELOPING A WORKFORCE SCHEDULE

Suppose that we are interested in developing a workforce schedule for a company that operates 7 days a week and provides each employee with 2 consecutive days off. In this section, we demonstrate a method that recognizes this constraint.[1] The objective is to identify the 2 consecutive days off for each employee that will minimize the amount of total slack capacity, thereby maximizing the utilization of the workforce. The work schedule for each employee, then, is the 5 days that remain after the 2 days off have been determined. The procedure involves the following steps.

Step 1. From the schedule of net requirements for the week, find all the pairs of consecutive days that exclude the maximum daily requirements. Select the unique pair that has the lowest total requirements for the 2 days. In some unusual situations, all pairs may contain a day with the maximum requirements. If so, select the pair with the lowest total requirements. Suppose that the numbers of employees required are

Monday: 8   Thursday: 12   Saturday: 4
Tuesday: 9   Friday: 7   Sunday: 2
Wednesday: 2

The maximum capacity requirement is 12 employees, on Thursday. The consecutive pair with the lowest total requirements is Saturday and Sunday, with $4 + 2 = 6$.

Step 2. If a tie occurs, choose one of the tied pairs, consistent with the provisions written into the labor agreement, if any. Alternatively, the tie could be broken by asking the employee being scheduled to make the choice. As a last resort, the tie could be broken arbitrarily. For example, preference could be given to Saturday–Sunday pairs.

Step 3. Assign the employee the selected pair of days off. Subtract the requirements satisfied by the employee from the net requirements for each day the employee is to work. In this example, the employee is assigned Saturday and Sunday off. After requirements are subtracted, Monday's requirement is 7, Tuesday's is 8, Wednesday's is 1, Thursday's is 11, and Friday's is 6. Saturday's and Sunday's requirements do not change because no employee is yet scheduled to work those days.

Step 4. Repeat steps 1 through 3 until all the requirements have been satisfied or a certain number of employees have been scheduled.

This method reduces the amount of slack capacity assigned to days with low requirements and forces the days with high requirements to be scheduled first. It also recognizes some of the behavioral and contractual aspects of workforce scheduling in the tie-breaking rules. However, the schedules produced might *not* minimize total slack capacity. Different rules for finding the days-off pair and breaking ties are needed to ensure minimal total slack capacity.

Developing a Workforce Schedule	EXAMPLE 16.1

The Amalgamated Parcel Service is open 7 days a week. The schedule of requirements is

Day	M	T	W	Th	F	S	Su
Required number of employees	6	4	8	9	10	3	2

[1]See Tibrewala, Philippe, and Browne (1972) for an optimizing approach.

TUTOR 16.1

Tutor 16.1 on the Student CD-ROM provides a new example to practice workforce scheduling.

The manager needs a workforce schedule that provides two consecutive days off and minimizes the amount of total slack capacity. To break ties in the selection of off days, the scheduler gives preference to Saturday and Sunday if it is one of the tied pairs. If not, she selects one of the tied pairs arbitrarily.

SOLUTION

Friday contains the maximum requirements, and the pair S–Su has the lowest total requirements. Therefore, employee 1 is scheduled to work Monday through Friday.

Note that Friday still has the maximum requirements and that the requirements for the S–Su pair are carried forward because these are employee 1's days off. These updated requirements are the ones the scheduler uses for the next employee.

The day-off assignments for the employees are shown in the following table.

							Scheduling Days Off	
M	T	W	Th	F	S	Su	Employee	Comments
6	4	8	9	10	3	2	1	The S–Su pair has the lowest total requirements. Assign employee 1 to a Monday through Friday schedule and update the requirements.
5	3	7	8	9	3	2	2	The S–Su pair has the lowest total requirements. Assign employee 2 to a Monday through Friday schedule and update the requirements.
4	2	6	7	8	3	2	3	The S–Su pair has the lowest total requirements. Assign employee 3 to a Monday through Friday schedule and update the requirements.
3	1	5	6	7	3	2	4	The M–T pair has the lowest total requirements. Assign employee 4 to a Wednesday through Sunday schedule and update the requirements.
3	1	4	5	6	2	1	5	The S–Su pair has the lowest total requirements. Assign employee 5 to a Monday through Friday schedule and update the requirements.
2	0	3	4	5	2	1	6	The M–T pair has the lowest total requirements. Assign employee 6 to a Wednesday through Sunday schedule and update the requirements.
2	0	2	3	4	1	0	7	The S–Su pair has the lowest total requirements. Assign employee 7 to a Monday through Friday schedule and update the requirements.
1	0	1	2	3	1	0	8	Four pairs have the minimum requirement and the lowest total: S–Su, Su–M, M–T, and T–W. Choose the S–Su pair according to the tie-breaking rule. Assign employee 8 to a Monday through Friday schedule and update the requirements.
0	0	0	1	2	1	0	9	Arbitrarily choose the Su–M pair to break ties because the S–Su pair does not have the lowest total requirements. Assign employee 9 to a Tuesday through Saturday schedule and update the requirements.
0	0	0	0	1	0	0	10	Choose the S–Su pair according to the tie-breaking rule. Assign employee 10 to a Monday through Friday schedule.

In this example, Friday always has the maximum requirements and should be avoided as a day off. The final schedule for the employees is shown in the following table.

			Final Schedule					
Employee	**M**	**T**	**W**	**Th**	**F**	**S**	**Su**	**Total**
1	X	X	X	X	X	off	off	
2	X	X	X	X	X	off	off	
3	X	X	X	X	X	off	off	
4	off	off	X	X	X	X	X	
5	X	X	X	X	X	off	off	
6	off	off	X	X	X	X	X	
7	X	X	X	X	X	off	off	
8	X	X	X	X	X	off	off	
9	off	X	X	X	X	X	off	
10	X	X	X	X	X	off	off	
Capacity, C	7	8	10	10	10	3	2	50
Requirements, R	6	4	8	9	10	3	2	42
Slack, $C - R$	1	4	2	1	0	0	0	8

Decision Point With its substantial amount of slack capacity, the schedule is not unique. Employee 9, for example, could have Sunday and Monday, Monday and Tuesday, or Tuesday and Wednesday off without causing a capacity shortage. Indeed, the company might be able to get by with one fewer employee because of the total of eight slack days of capacity. However, all 10 employees are needed on Fridays. If the manager were willing to get by with only 9 employees on Fridays or if someone could work one day of overtime on a rotating basis, he would not need employee 10. As indicated in the table, the net requirement left for employee 10 to satisfy amounts to only one day, Friday. Thus, employee 10 can be used to fill in for vacationing or sick employees.

COMPUTERIZED WORKFORCE SCHEDULING SYSTEMS

Workforce scheduling often entails myriad constraints and concerns. In some types of firms, such as telephone companies, mail-order catalog houses, or emergency hotline agencies, employees must be on duty 24 hours a day, seven days a week. Sometimes a portion of the staff is part-time, which allows management a great deal of flexibility but adds considerable complexity to the scheduling requirements. The flexibility comes from the opportunity to match anticipated loads closely through the use of overlapping shifts or odd shift lengths; the complexity comes from the need to evaluate the numerous possible alternatives. Management also must consider the timing of lunch breaks and rest periods, the number and starting times of shift schedules, and the days off for each employee. An additional typical concern is that the number of employees on duty at any particular time be sufficient to answer calls within a reasonable amount of time.

Computerized scheduling systems are available to cope with the complexity of workforce scheduling. The programs select the schedule that minimizes the sum of expected costs of over- and understaffing. Managerial Practice 16.1 describes the complexity of workforce scheduling at call centers and how computerized scheduling systems can help.

> OPERATIONS SCHEDULING <

Operations schedules are short-term plans designed to implement the master production schedule. Operations scheduling focuses on how best to use existing capacity, taking into account technical production constraints. Often, several jobs must be processed at one or more workstations. Typically, a variety of tasks can be performed at each workstation. If schedules are not carefully planned to avoid bottlenecks, waiting lines may develop. For

MANAGERIAL PRACTICE   16.1   SCHEDULING EMPLOYEES AT CALL CENTERS

It is late at night and your printer suddenly starts to skip several letters in the middle of each line. The printer manual sheds no light on the problem, and shaking the machine does nothing more than vent some of your frustration. So you turn to the 24/7 service "help" line. While you wait for your call to be answered, you do not care where in the world the person you will talk to lives; you only care that the wait is short, you get the right solution, and the person speaks in your language. Welcome to the world of call centers.

As a consumer with a problem, you might not think it's rocket science for a manufacturer to have someone available to solve your problems any time you need help. Actually, managing a call center is no easy task. Good workforce schedules are critical to the success of call centers. Scheduling too few agents drives away customers. Scheduling too many agents is costly for the company. Managers try to staff their call centers so that they meet certain performance measures. One such measure is the percentage of calls answered (PCA) within a specified time interval, termed the service objective (SO). Typically in a call center, the PCA is in the range of 80 to 90 percent, and the SO is 15 to 30 seconds. Obviously, the more agents on the staff at a certain time, the better the PCA will be. The problem is that the requirements for agents change over time. For example, a call center may handle 4,500 calls on a Monday morning in July, but if New Year's Day happens to fall on a Monday, the volume might drop by 60 percent. The total daily hours of contact time isn't constant either. Also, the callers are likely to speak different languages. For example, customers speak English, Spanish, or German, but the call center may have groups of agents who speak English and German, Spanish and German, or English and Spanish.

Determining how many of each group of agents to have on hand at all times is not easy.

Fortunately, workforce management software is available to help managers cope with this complexity. Sophisticated forecasting models can estimate call volumes taking into consideration customers who receive busy signals (and therefore wanted service but did not get it when they wanted it), customers who hang up before an agent answers, and call-volume patterns that are dependent on special events. The forecasting models also project language skill requirements in order to provide a better picture of multiskilled agents the call center needs for each shift. In addition, agents can stipulate preferred start and end times or preferred days off, and employees can be rotated through less desirable shifts. Agents can use the Internet to request changes to their schedules and even swap schedules or shifts with other agents, making the workforce management system an interactive environment. New developments also include the ability to forecast and schedule agents for e-mail or Web chat work. Many companies are seeing a significant increase in customer communication via these modes, but agents generally need training before they can effectively help these customers.

How much impact does efficient workforce scheduling have on a call center? One prominent *Fortune* 500 company estimates that they were scheduling 2,500 agents at 80 percent efficiency before it improved its scheduling system. Thereafter, efficiency improved to 94 percent, for a savings in the neighborhood of $7 to $8 million annually. Although the results for smaller companies will be less dramatic, the percentage changes indicate that the impact will be significant, nonetheless.

Sources: Dennis Cox, "Darwinian Call Centers," *Call Center Technology Solutions,* www.tmcnet.com/articles/ccsmag/0999/0999pipkins.htm (September 1999); Jim Hogan, "Workforce Management Software: A Mission-Critical Call Center Component," *Call Center CRM Solutions,* www.tmcnet.com/articles (July 2000); "Skill Set Scheduling," www.pipkins.com/articles, 2005.

---

example, Figure 16.3 depicts the complexity of scheduling a manufacturing process. When a job order is received for a part, the raw materials are collected and the batch is moved to its first operation. The colored arrows show that jobs follow different routes through the manufacturing process, depending on the product being made. At each workstation, someone must determine the next job to process because the arrival rate of jobs at a workstation often differs from the processing rate of the jobs at a workstation, thereby creating a waiting line. In addition, new jobs can enter the process at any time, thereby creating a dynamic environment. Such complexity puts pressure on managers to develop scheduling procedures that will handle the workload efficiently.

In this section, we focus on scheduling approaches used in two environments: (1) job shops and (2) flow shops. A **job shop** is a firm that specializes in low- to medium-volume production and utilizes *job* or *batch* processes. Tasks in this type of flexible flow environment are difficult to schedule because of the variability in job routings and the continual introduction of new jobs to be processed. Figure 16.3 depicts a job shop environment. A **flow shop** specializes in medium- to high-volume production and utilizes *line* or *continuous* processes. Tasks are easier to schedule because the jobs in a line flow facility have a common flow pattern through the system. Nonetheless, scheduling mistakes can be costly in either situation.

job shop

A firm that specializes in low- to medium-volume production and utilizes job or batch processes.

flow shop

A firm that specializes in medium- to high-volume production and utilizes line or continuous processes.

JOB SHOP DISPATCHING

Just as many schedules are feasible for a specific group of jobs at a particular set of workstations, numerous ways can be used to generate schedules. They range from straightforward

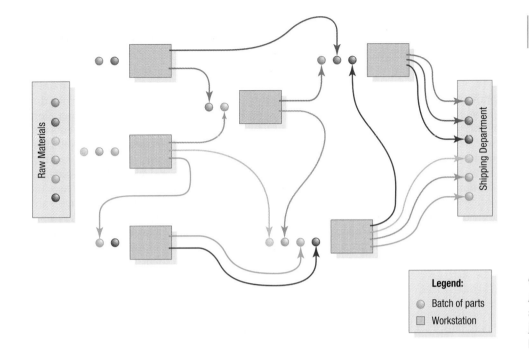

Legend:
- Batch of parts
- Workstation

manual methods, such as manipulating Gantt charts, to sophisticated computer models for developing optimal schedules. One way to generate schedules in job shops is with **dispatching**, which allows the schedule for a workstation to evolve over a period of time. The decision about which job to process next is made with simple priority rules whenever the workstation becomes available for further processing. One advantage of this method is that last-minute information on operating conditions can be incorporated into the schedule as it evolves.

Dispatching determines the job to process next with the help of **priority sequencing rules**. When several jobs are waiting in line at a workstation, priority rules specify the job processing sequence. These rules can be applied by a worker or incorporated into a computerized scheduling system that generates a dispatch list of jobs and priorities for each workstation. The following priority sequencing rules are commonly used in practice.

- *Critical Ratio.* The **critical ratio (CR)** is calculated by dividing the time remaining until a job's due date by the total shop time remaining for the job, which is defined as the setup, processing, move, and expected waiting times of all remaining operations, including the operation being scheduled. The formula is

$$CR = \frac{\text{Due date} - \text{Today's date}}{\text{Total shop time remaining}}$$

The difference between the due date and today's date must be in the same time units as the total shop time remaining. A ratio less than 1.0 implies that the job is behind schedule, and a ratio greater than 1.0 implies that the job is ahead of schedule. The job with the lowest CR is scheduled next.

- *Earliest Due Date.* The job with the **earliest due date (EDD)** is the next job to be processed.
- *First-Come, First-Served.* The job arriving at the workstation first has the highest priority under a **first-come, first-served (FCFS)** rule.
- *Shortest Processing Time.* The job requiring the **shortest processing time (SPT)** at the workstation is processed next.
- *Slack per Remaining Operations.* Slack is the difference between the time remaining until a job's due date and the total shop time remaining, including that of the operation being scheduled. A job's priority is determined by dividing the slack by the number of operations that remain, including the one being scheduled, to arrive at the **slack per remaining operations (S/RO)**.

$$S/RO = \frac{(\text{Due date} - \text{Today's date}) - \text{Total shop time remaining}}{\text{Number of operations remaining}}$$

The job with the lowest S/RO is scheduled next. Ties are broken in a variety of ways if two or more jobs have the same priority. One way is to arbitrarily choose one of the tied jobs for processing next.

Although the priority sequencing rules seem simple, the actual task of scheduling hundreds of jobs through hundreds of workstations requires intensive data gathering and manipulation. The scheduler needs information on each job's processing requirements: the job's due date; its routing; the standard setup, processing, and expected waiting times at each operation; whether alternative workstations could be used at each operation; and the components and raw materials needed at each operation. In addition, the scheduler needs to know the job's current status: its location (waiting in line for a workstation or being processed at a workstation), how much of the operation has been completed, the actual arrival and departure times at each operation or waiting line, and the actual processing and setup times. The scheduler uses the priority sequencing rules to determine the processing sequence of jobs at a workstation and the remaining information for estimating job arrival times at the next workstation, determining whether an alternative workstation should be used when the primary one is busy, and predicting the need for materials-handling equipment. Because this information may change throughout the day, computers are needed to track the data and to maintain valid priorities.

SCHEDULING JOBS FOR ONE WORKSTATION

Any priority sequencing rule can be used to schedule any number of workstations with the dispatching procedure. For the purpose of illustrating the rules, however, we focus on scheduling several jobs on a single machine. We divide the rules into two categories: (1) single-dimension rules and (2) multiple-dimension rules.

single-dimension rules

A set of rules that bases the priority of a job on a single aspect of the job, such as arrival time at the workstation, the due date, or the processing time.

Single-Dimension Rules   Some priority sequencing rules (e.g., FCFS, EDD, and SPT) base a job's priority assignment only on information on the jobs waiting for processing at the individual workstation. We call these rules **single-dimension rules** because they determine priority based on a single aspect of the job, such as arrival time at the workstation, the due date, or the processing time. We begin with an example of single-dimension rules.

EXAMPLE 16.2	Comparing the EDD and SPT Rules

TUTOR 16.2

Tutor 16.2 on the Student CD-ROM provides a new example to practice EDD and SPT rules.

ACTIVE MODEL 16.1

Active Model 16.1 on the Student CD-ROM provides additional Insight on the use of single-dimension rules.

The Taylor Machine Shop rebores engine blocks. Currently, five engine blocks are waiting for processing. At any time, the company has only one engine expert on duty who can do this type of work. The engine problems have been diagnosed, and the processing times for the jobs have been estimated. Expected completion times have been agreed upon with the shop's customers. The accompanying table shows the situation as of Monday morning. Because the Taylor Machine Shop is open from 8 A.M. until 5 P.M. each weekday, plus weekend hours as needed, the customer pickup times are measured in business hours from Monday morning. Determine the schedule for the engine expert by using (a) the EDD rule and (b) the SPT rule. For each rule, calculate the average hours early, hours past due, WIP inventory, and total inventory. If low job flow times and WIP inventories are critical, which rule should be chosen?

Engine Block	Processing Time, Including Setup (hours)	Scheduled Customer Pickup Time (business hours from now)
Ranger	8	10
Explorer	6	12
Bronco	15	20
Econoline 150	3	18
Thunderbird	12	22

SOLUTION

a.   The EDD rule states that the first engine block in the sequence is the one with the closest due date. Consequently, the Ranger engine block is processed first. The Thunderbird engine block, with its due date furthest in the future, is processed last. The sequence is shown in the following table, along with the job flow times, the hours early, and the hours past due.

Engine Block Sequence	Begin Work	Processing Time (hr)			Job Flow Time (hr)	Scheduled Customer Pickup Time	Actual Customer Pickup Time	Hours Early	Hours Past Due
Ranger	0	+	8	=	8	10	10	2	—
Explorer	8	+	6	=	14	12	14	—	2
Econoline 150	14	+	3	=	17	18	18	1	—
Bronco	17	+	15	=	32	20	32	—	12
Thunderbird	32	+	12	=	44	22	44	—	22

The flow time for each job equals the waiting time plus the processing time. For example, the Explorer engine block had to wait 8 hours before the engine expert started to work on it. The process time for the job is 6 hours, so its flow time is 14 hours. The average flow time and the other performance measures for the EDD schedule for the five engine blocks are

$$\text{Average job flow time} = \frac{8+14+17+32+44}{5} = 23 \text{ hours}$$

$$\text{Average hours early} = \frac{2+0+1+0+0}{5} = 0.6 \text{ hours}$$

$$\text{Average hours past due} = \frac{0+2+0+12+22}{5} = 7.2 \text{ hours}$$

$$\text{Average WIP inventory} = \frac{\text{Sum of flow times}}{\text{Makespan}} = \frac{8+14+17+32+44}{44}$$

$$= 2.61 \text{ engine blocks}$$

You might think of the sum of flow times as the total *job hours* spent by the engine blocks waiting for the engine expert and being processed. (This example contains no component or subassembly inventories, so WIP inventory consists only of those engine blocks waiting or being processed.) Dividing this sum by the makespan, or the total elapsed time required to complete work on all the engine blocks, provides the average WIP inventory.

Finally,

$$\text{Average total inventory} = \frac{\text{Sum of time in system}}{\text{Makespan}} = \frac{10+14+18+32+44}{44}$$

$$= 2.68 \text{ engine blocks}$$

Total inventory is the sum of the WIP inventory and the completed jobs waiting to be picked up by customers. The average total inventory equals the sum of the times each job spent in the shop—in this example, the total job hours spent waiting for the engine expert, being processed, and waiting for pickup—divided by the makespan. For example, the first job to be picked up is the Ranger engine block, which spent 10 hours in the system. Then the Explorer engine block is picked up, after spending 14 job hours in the system. The time spent by any job in the system equals its actual customer pickup time because all jobs were available for processing at time zero.

b. Under the SPT rule, the sequence starts with the engine block that has the shortest processing time, the Econoline 150, and it ends with the engine block that has the longest processing time, the Bronco. The sequence, along with the job flow times, early hours, and past due hours, is contained in the following table.

Engine Block Sequence	Begin Work	Processing Time (hr)			Job Flow Time (hr)	Scheduled Customer Pickup Time	Actual Customer Pickup Time	Hours Early	Hours Past Due
Econoline 150	0	+	3	=	3	18	18	15	—
Explorer	3	+	6	=	9	12	12	3	—
Ranger	9	+	8	=	17	10	17	—	7
Thunderbird	17	+	12	=	29	22	29	—	7
Bronco	29	+	15	=	44	20	44	—	24

The performance measures are

$$\text{Average job flow time} = \frac{3+9+17+29+44}{5} = 20.4 \text{ hours}$$

$$\text{Average hours early} = \frac{15+3+0+0+0}{5} = 3.6 \text{ hours}$$

$$\text{Average past due hours} = \frac{0+0+7+7+24}{5} = 7.6 \text{ hours}$$

$$\text{Average WIP inventory} = \frac{3+9+17+29+44}{44} = 2.32 \text{ engine blocks}$$

$$\text{Average total inventory} = \frac{18+12+17+29+44}{44} = 2.73 \text{ engine blocks}$$

Decision Point The SPT rule is clearly superior to the EDD rule with respect to average job flow time and average WIP inventory. If these criteria outweigh all others, management should use SPT.

As the solution of Example 16.2 shows, the SPT schedule provided a lower average job flow time and lower WIP inventory. The EDD schedule, however, gave better customer service, as measured by the average hours past due, and a lower maximum hours past due (22 versus 24). It also provided a lower total inventory because fewer job hours were spent waiting for customers to pick up their engine blocks after they had been completed. The SPT priority rule will push jobs through the system to completion more quickly than will the other rules. Speed can be an advantage—but only if jobs can be delivered sooner than promised and revenue collected earlier. If they cannot, the completed job must stay in finished inventory, canceling the advantage of minimizing the average WIP inventory. Consequently, the priority rule chosen can help or hinder the firm in meeting its competitive priorities.

In Example 16.2, SPT and EDD provided schedules that resulted in different values for the performance criteria; however, both schedules have the same makespan of 44 hours. This result always will occur in single-operation scheduling for a *fixed number* of jobs available for processing—regardless of the priority rule used—because no idle workstation times occur between any two jobs.

Researchers have studied the implications of the single-dimension rules for various performance measures. In most of these studies, all jobs were considered to be independent, and the assumption was made that sufficient capacity generally was available. These studies found that the EDD rule performs well with respect to the percentage of jobs past due and the variance of hours past due. For any set of jobs to be processed at a single workstation, it minimizes the maximum of the past due hours of any job in the set. The EDD rule is popular with firms that are sensitive to due date changes, although it does not perform well with respect to flow time, WIP inventory, or utilization.

Often referred to as the *world champion,* the SPT rule tends to minimize the mean flow time, the WIP inventory, and the percentage of jobs past due and it tends to maximize shop utilization. For the single-workstation case, the SPT rule always will provide the lowest mean flow time. However, it could increase total inventory because it tends to push all work to the finished state. In addition, it tends to produce a large variance in past due hours because the larger jobs might have to wait a long time for processing. Also, it provides no opportunity to adjust schedules when due dates change. The advantage of this rule over others diminishes as the load on the shop increases.

Finally, though the FCFS rule is considered fair to the jobs (or customers), it performs poorly with respect to all performance measures. This result is to be expected because FCFS does not acknowledge any job (or customer) characteristics.

Multiple-Dimension Rules Priority rules, such as CR and S/RO, incorporate information about the remaining workstations at which the job must be processed, in addition to the processing time at the present workstation or the due date considered by single-dimension rules. We call these rules **multiple-dimension rules** because they apply to more than one aspect of the job. Example 16.3 demonstrates their use for sequencing jobs.

multiple-dimension rules

A set of rules that apply to more than one aspect of a job.

| Sequencing with the CR and S/RO Rules | EXAMPLE 16.3 |

The first five columns of the following table contain information about a set of four jobs currently waiting at an engine lathe. Several operations, including the one at the engine lathe, remain to be done on each job. Determine the schedule by using (a) the CR rule and (b) the S/RO rule. Compare these schedules to those generated by FCFS, SPT, and EDD.

TUTOR 16.3

Tutor 16.3 on the Student CD-ROM provides a new example to practice the CR and S/RO rules.

Job	Operation Time at Engine Lathe (hr)	Time Remaining Until Due Date (days)	Number of Operations Remaining	Shop Time Remaining (days)	CR	S/RO
1	2.3	15	10	6.1	2.46	0.89
2	10.5	10	2	7.8	1.28	1.10
3	6.2	20	12	14.5	1.38	0.46
4	15.6	8	5	10.2	0.78	−0.44

SOLUTION

a. Using CR to schedule the machine, we divide the time remaining until the due date by the shop time remaining to get the priority index for each job. For job 1,

$$CR = \frac{\text{Time remaining until the due date}}{\text{Shop time remaining}} = \frac{15}{6.1} = 2.46$$

By arranging the jobs in sequence with the lowest critical ratio first, we determine that the sequence of jobs to be processed by the engine lathe is 4, 2, 3, and finally 1, assuming that no other jobs arrive in the meantime.

b. Using S/RO, we divide the difference between the time remaining until the due date and the shop time remaining by the number of remaining operations. For job 1,

$$S/RO = \frac{\text{Time remaining until the due date} - \text{Shop time remaining}}{\text{Number of operations remaining}} = \frac{15 - 6.1}{10} = 0.89$$

Arranging the jobs by starting with the lowest S/RO yields a 4, 3, 1, 2 sequence of jobs.

Decision Point Note that the application of the two priority rules gives two different schedules. Moreover, the SPT sequence, based on operation times (measured in hours) at the engine lathe only, is 1, 3, 2, and 4. No preference is given to job 4 in the SPT schedule, even though it may not be finished by its due date. The FCFS sequence is 1, 2, 3, and 4; and the EDD sequence is 4, 2, 1, and 3. The following table shows the comparative performance of the five dispatching rules at the engine lathe.

Priority Rule Summary					
	FCFS	**SPT**	**EDD**	**CR**	**S/RO**
Average flow time	17.175	16.100	26.175	27.150	24.025
Average early time	3.425	6.050	0	0	0
Average past due	7.350	8.900	12.925	13.900	10.775
Average WIP	1.986	1.861	3.026	3.139	2.777
Average total inventory	2.382	2.561	3.026	3.139	2.777

The S/RO rule is better than the EDD rule and the CR rule but it is much worse than the SPT rule and the FCFS rule for this example. However, the S/RO has the advantage of allowing schedule changes when due dates change. These results cannot be generalized to other situations because only four jobs are being processed.

Research studies have shown that S/RO is better than EDD with respect to the percentage of jobs past due but worse than SPT and EDD with respect to average job flow times. These studies also indicate that CR results in longer job flow times than SPT, but CR also results in less variance in the distribution of past due hours. Consequently, even though the use of the multiple-dimension rules requires more information, no choice is clearly best. Each rule should be tested in the environment for which it is intended.

SCHEDULING JOBS FOR MULTIPLE WORKSTATIONS

Priority sequencing rules can be used to schedule more than one operation with the dispatching procedure. Each operation is treated independently. When a workstation becomes idle, the priority rule is applied to the jobs waiting for that operation, and the job with the highest priority is selected. When that operation is finished, the job is moved to the next operation in its routing, where it waits until it again has the highest priority. At any workstation, the jobs in the waiting line change over a period of time, so the choice of a priority rule can make quite a difference in the processing sequence. Schedules can be evaluated with the performance measures already discussed.

Identifying the best priority rule to use at a particular operation in a process is a complex problem because the output from one operation becomes the input to another. The priority rule at a workstation determines the sequence of work the workstation will perform, which in turn determines the arrival of work at the next workstation downstream. Computer *simulation* models are effective tools to determine which priority rules work best in a given situation. Once the current process is modeled, the analyst can make changes to the priority rules at various operations and measure the impact on performance measures, such as past due, work-in-progress, job flow time, and utilization. Example 16.4 demonstrates simulation using Extend, a sophisticated simulation software package. SimQuick, included on the Student CD-ROM that is packaged with each new textbook, is also useful.

EXAMPLE 16.4	Simulation of Precision AutoBody Operations

Precision AutoBody has an excellent reputation in the local market for doing high-quality autobody repair work. Repair of a vehicle body consists of two general steps: body repair and finishing. For body repair, vehicles are classified as having either minor or major damage. Those with minor damage require, on average, one 8-hour day to complete. Two-thirds of the vehicles serviced by Precision fell into this category. In contrast, vehicles with major damage require more extensive repairs that extend beyond the surface sheet metal, and damages often include hidden problems that are not evident when first inspected. As a result, this repair work averages 2 days. Of those vehicles with major damage, about half need to have the underlying frame of the vehicle straightened on special hydraulic equipment in a dedicated area adjacent to the repair bays. This extra operation tends to add an average of one additional day to the completion time.

After body repair, the vehicle is moved to the finishing area. A small percentage of vehicles, 25 percent of those with minor damage, move directly to the finishing area. Here, an apprentice prepares the vehicle by doing final sanding and masking off areas that are not to be painted. Next, the vehicle is moved to one of several paint booths, where the painter mixes the paint color to match the vehicle, taking into account any fading that has occurred. Virtually all vehicles require two coats—a colored base coat followed by a clear coat applied the next day. After completion, the vehicle's exterior and interior are thoroughly cleaned to give that "just new" impression to the customer when the vehicle is delivered. The times to complete each operation are summarized in the following table.

	Precision Autobody Process Times	
	Time to Perform	
Operation	**Average (hr)**	**Standard Deviation**
1. Frame straightening*	8	2
2a. Body repair, major damage*	16	4
2b. Body repair, minor damage*	8	2
3. Paint preparation	1 1/4	1/3
4. Paint application (two coats)	1 1/2	1/2
5. Clean up	3	1/2
*Not necessary for all vehicles.		

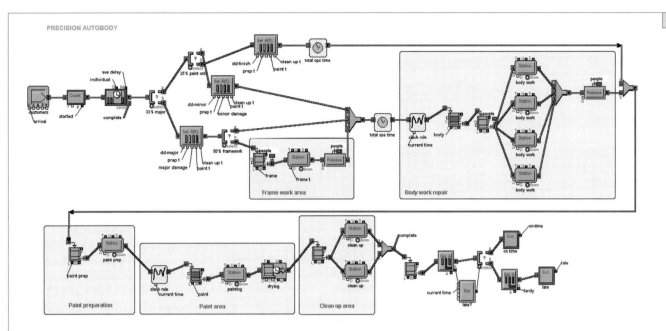

FIGURE 16.4 | Precision AutoBody Operations Using Extend Software

Bill Curtis, manager at Precision, schedules each vehicle at the body repair and paint operations on a first-come, first-served basis with a quoted delivery time of about 1 week (that is, 5 business days), plus any lead time needed for delivery of the parts. A review of the last month's data indicated that 18.17 percent of the jobs were delivered late, and the average throughput time (flow time) per auto was 30.49 hours. In addition, the average number of vehicles in the system (work-in-process) was 9.6 autos. Curtis wanted to know whether the application of the SPT rule to the body repair and paint operations would improve delivery performance and reduce flow times and work-in-process.

SOLUTION

The Extend software is used to model and simulate the Precision AutoBody operations. Figure 16.4 shows the simulation model. The five operations are boxed in the diagram. As the simulation proceeds, vehicles arrive and require major repair with a 33 percent chance. If major repair is needed, there is a 50 percent chance that the vehicle will need the frame work operation before the body repair operation. If minor repair is needed, there is a 25 percent chance that the vehicle will go straight to the paint preparation operation. After body repair, all vehicles go through paint preparation, painting, and cleanup. The activities after cleanup are needed to gather the statistics for each vehicle before it exits the simulation. The SPT priority rule for each operation was selected in the Controls box (not shown).

The results of the simulation using the SPT rule for the body repair operation and the finishing operations (paint preparation, paint, and cleanup) are shown in Figure 16.5. Notice that the percentage of late deliveries, the average number of vehicles in the system, and the average throughput time have been improved with the use of SPT. The average tardiness statistic, shown in Figure 16.5, is another form of the past-due measure of performance. It is the average number of hours past the due date for those vehicles that were delivered late.

Decision Point The results show that SPT is superior to the FCFS priority rule for Precision AutoBody. Curtis should consider changing the priority rule. Further improvements in the percentage of late deliveries might be achieved by increasing the lead time in setting the due dates or by changing the priority rules. The simulation model can help determine the best solution.

Source: This case and simulation experience was provided by Professor Robert Klassen, University of Western Ontario.

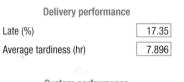

Delivery performance	
Late (%)	17.35
Average tardiness (hr)	7.896

System performance	
Average number of vehicles in system	9.422
Overall throughput time (hr)	
average	29.67
standard deviation	10.92

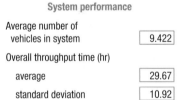

Operation utilization	
Body repair	0.8338
Paint operation	0.7687

FIGURE 16.5

Results of the SPT Rule for the Body Repair and Finishing Operations of Precision AutoBody

SCHEDULING JOBS FOR A TWO-STATION FLOW SHOP

Suppose that a flow shop has several jobs ready for processing at two workstations and that the routings of all jobs are identical. Whereas in single-workstation scheduling the makespan is the same regardless of the priority rule chosen, in the scheduling of two or more workstations in a flow shop, the makespan varies according to the sequence chosen. Determining a production sequence for a group of jobs to minimize the makespan has two advantages.

1. The group of jobs is completed in minimum time.

2. The utilization of the two-station flow shop is maximized. Utilizing the first workstation continuously until it processes the last job minimizes the idle time on the *second* workstation.

Johnson's rule is a procedure that minimizes makespan when scheduling a group of jobs on two workstations. S. M. Johnson showed that the sequence of jobs at the two stations should be identical and that the priority assigned to a job should therefore be the same at both. The procedure is based on the assumption of a known set of jobs, each with a known processing time and available to begin processing on the first workstation. The procedure is as follows.

Step 1. Scan the processing times at each workstation and find the shortest processing time among the jobs not yet scheduled. If two or more jobs are tied, choose one job arbitrarily.

Step 2. If the shortest processing time is on workstation 1, schedule the corresponding job as early as possible. If the shortest processing time is on workstation 2, schedule the corresponding job as late as possible.

Step 3. Eliminate the last job scheduled from further consideration. Repeat steps 1 and 2 until all jobs have been scheduled.

Johnson's rule

A procedure that minimizes makespan when scheduling a group of jobs on two workstations.

EXAMPLE 16.5	Scheduling a Group of Jobs on Two Workstations

TUTOR 16.4

Tutor 16.4 on the student CD-ROM provides a new example to practice Johnson's rule.

The Morris Machine Company just received an order to refurbish five motors for materials handling equipment that were damaged in a fire. The motors will be repaired at two workstations in the following manner.

Workstation 1   Dismantle the motor and clean the parts.

Workstation 2   Replace the parts as necessary, test the motor, and make adjustments.

The customer's shop will be inoperable until all the motors have been repaired, so the plant manager is interested in developing a schedule that minimizes the makespan and has authorized around-the-clock operations until the motors have been repaired. The estimated time to repair each motor is shown in the following table.

	Time (hr)	
Motor	**Workstation 1**	**Workstation 2**
M1	12	22
M2	4	5
M3	5	3
M4	15	16
M5	10	8

SOLUTION

The logic for the optimal sequence is shown in the following table.

Establishing a Job Sequence		
Iteration	**Job Sequence**	**Comments**
1	M3	The shortest processing time is 3 hours for M3 at workstation 2. Therefore, M3 is scheduled as late as possible.

(continued)

Iteration	Job Sequence				Comments
2	M2			M3	Eliminate M3's time from the table of estimated times. The next shortest processing time is 4 hours for M2 at workstation 1. M2 is therefore scheduled first.
3	M2		M5	M3	Eliminate M2 from the table. The next shortest processing time is 8 hours for M5 at workstation 2. Therefore, M5 is scheduled as late as possible.
4	M2	M1	M5	M3	Eliminate M5 from the table. The next shortest processing time is 12 hours for M1 at workstation 1. M1 is scheduled as early as possible.
5	M2	M1	M4 M5	M3	The last motor to be scheduled is M4. It is placed in the last remaining position, in the middle of the schedule.

Decision Point No other sequence of jobs will produce a lower makespan. To determine the makespan, we have to draw a Gantt chart, as shown in Figure 16.6. In this case, refurbishing and reinstalling all five motors will take 65 hours. This schedule minimizes the idle time of workstation 2 and gives the fastest repair time for all five motors. Note that the schedule recognizes that a job cannot begin at workstation 2 until it has been completed at workstation 1.

Workstation

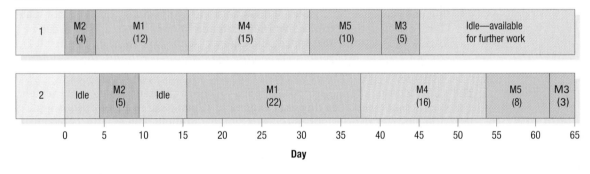

FIGURE 16.6 | Gantt Chart for the Morris Machine Company Repair Schedule

LABOR-LIMITED ENVIRONMENTS

Thus far, we have assumed that a job never has to wait for lack of a worker. The limiting resource has been the number of machines or workstations available. More typical, however, is a **labor-limited environment** in which the resource constraint is the amount of labor available, not the number of machines or workstations. In this case, workers are trained to work on a variety of machines or tasks to increase the flexibility of operations.

In a labor-limited environment, the scheduler not only must decide which job to process next at a particular workstation but also must assign workers to their next workstations. The scheduler can use priority rules to make these decisions, as we used them to schedule engine blocks in Example 16.2. In labor-limited environments, the labor-assignment policies, as well as the dispatching priority rules, affect performance. The following examples provide some labor-assignment rules.

■ Assign personnel to the workstation with the job that has been in the system longest.
■ Assign personnel to the workstation with the most jobs waiting for processing.
■ Assign personnel to the workstation with the largest standard work content.
■ Assign personnel to the workstation with the job that has the earliest due date.

labor-limited environment

An environment in which the resource constraint is the amount of labor available, not the number of machines or workstations.

LINKING OPERATIONS SCHEDULING TO THE SUPPLY CHAIN

advanced planning and scheduling (APS) systems

Systems that seek to optimize resources across the supply chain and align daily operations with strategic goals.

In Chapter 10, "Supply Chain Strategy," we discussed how firms design and manage the linkages between customers and suppliers with the concept of an integrated supply chain. True integration requires the manipulation of large amounts of complex data in real time because the customer order work flow must be synchronized with the required material, manufacturing, and distribution activity. Attempting to accomplish this integration with piecemeal systems can be resource-intensive and ultimately less than satisfactory. The Internet, new computer software, and improved data storage and manipulation methods have given rise to **advanced planning and scheduling (APS) systems**, which seek to optimize resources across the supply chain and align daily operations with strategic goals. These systems typically have four major components.

1. *Demand Planning.* This capability enables companies in a supply chain to share demand forecasts, thereby providing more visibility of future requirements. A broad range of forecasting techniques is provided.

2. *Supply Network Planning.* Optimization models based on linear programming can be used to make long-term decisions, such as the number and location of plants and distribution centers the firm should have, the suppliers it should use, and the amount of inventory it should have on hand and where it should be located.

3. *Available-to-Promise.* Firms can use this capability to promise delivery to customers by checking the availability of components and materials at its suppliers, who may be located anywhere in the world (see Chapter 15, "Resource Planning"). Variants of this capability include *capable-to-promise*—for suppliers who produce to customer order and have reserve capacity—and *capable-to-deliver*—for suppliers of transportation services.

4. *Manufacturing Scheduling.* This module attempts to determine an optimal grouping and sequencing of manufacturing orders based on detailed product attributes, production line capacities, and material flows. In some applications, schedules for material, labor, and equipment can be determined minute-by-minute. Gantt charts can be used to view the schedule and make adjustments (see Figure 16.1 and Figure 16.2). The schedules are "constraint-based" and use the *theory of constraints* to schedule around bottlenecks in the manufacturing process.

The manufacturing scheduling process is a key element of an integrated supply chain. APS systems attempt to link the scheduling process to demand data and forecasts, supply chain facility and inventory decisions, and the capability of suppliers so that the entire chain can operate as efficiently as possible. A firm's ability to change its schedules quickly and still keep the supply chain flowing smoothly provides a competitive edge. Managerial Practice 16.2 demonstrates the complexity of scheduling an automobile assembly plant.

> STUDENT CD-ROM AND INTERNET RESOURCES <

The Student CD-ROM and the Companion Website at **www.prenhall.com/krajewski** contain many tools, activities, and resources designed for this chapter.

> KEY EQUATIONS <

1. Performance measures:

$$\text{Job flow time} = \text{Time of completion} - \text{Time job was available for first processing operation}$$

$$\text{Makespan} = \text{Time of completion of last job} - \text{Starting time of first job}$$

$$\text{Average WIP inventory} = \frac{\text{Sum of flow times}}{\text{Makespan}}$$

$$\text{Average total inventory} = \frac{\text{Sum of time in system}}{\text{Makespan}}$$

MANAGERIAL **PRACTICE**	**16.2**	CAR SEQUENCING AT NISSAN'S SUNDERLAND PLANT

The typical way to manufacture a new car model is to either build a new plant or add another assembly line to an existing plant. However, when Nissan decided to introduce the Almera to the European market, its approach was anything but typical. Manufacturing new models in an existing facility in the market where they are to be sold reduces transportation and new plant construction costs for starters. It is no wonder, then, that Nissan decided to build the Almera at its Sunderland plant, located in the British countryside near Newcastle. Sunderland has long been recognized as Europe's most productive auto manufacturing facility. It boasts a ratio of 94 cars manufactured per assembly line worker per year, a remarkable productivity rate. Why not use the Sunderland plant for the Almera?

Management had two options: The first option would be to construct a dedicated assembly line for the Almera, which would take a year and cost several hundred million dollars. The construction would threaten the productivity of the plant to produce the Micra and Primera models already being manufactured at the plant. The second option was to produce the Almera on the existing assembly lines in the plant. That option raised scheduling concerns. Sunderland produced the Micra and Primera on two dedicated assembly lines. A typical assembly line consisted of three shops: the body shop where the initial chassis is assembled; the paint shop, consisting of two spray bays; and the trim shop where all trim is added to the painted chassis. Between the shops is a buffer area where cars wait for the next step. Scheduling an automobile assembly plant is complex because of the many constraints involved. For example, the paint bays are time consuming and pose environmental constraints related to the need for grouping cars of the same color. Also, special model requirements such as sunroofs cannot be scheduled back-to-back because that would delay the entire line at the point of the sunroof installation. Adding a new model to one of the existing lines would threaten the efficiency of the plant.

Nissan management decided to take the second option. To accomplish this feat, the scheduling approach would have to be changed. Before the introduction of Almera, the lines were scheduled on the basis of the constraints posed by each shop on a given day; management would iron out the conflicts in a control room where an ad hoc solution would be devised. To include Almera in the mix, the scheduling approach was changed to schedule all three shops of each line in a single coordinated

Even at the most-efficient automobile assembly plants like Nissan's Sunderland plant in the United Kingdom, scheduling is complex because of the many constraints involved. The painting portion of the job is particularly time consuming, but it only one of thousands of tasks the plant must efficiently schedule.

flow. A sophisticated software package called ILOG Solver, from ILOG, Inc., was used to recognize the more than 2,500 possible constraints. The new manufacturing system assigned Almera and Primera to their own lines and Micra (the simplest car to manufacture) to both lines with multiple crossover points during the assembly process. The new scheduling approach was successful. Capacity increased by 30 percent with little additional capital investment.

The Sunderland plant continues to be Nissan's shining star in Europe. The plant will produce Nissan's new crossover vehicle (part people carrier, part hatchback) in addition to its current models, increasing the plant's total volume to about 400,000 cars per year. Even though this new model will pose its challenges, given Sunderland's track record with multiple-vehicle scheduling, who would doubt that it will be successful once again?

Sources: Denis Sennechael, and Iain MacLean, "Car-Sequencing Challenge at a Nissan Plant Calls for Complex Scheduling," *APICS—The Performance Challenge* (March 2001), pp. 39–40; "Nissan in Europe," *Automotive Intelligence News,* www.autointell.com/asian_companies/nissan/nissan_europe.htm 2000; "Nissan Announces New Model for Sunderland Plant," *Automotive Intelligence News,* www.autointell-news.com/News-2005/Feb-2005/Feb-2005-1/Feb-02-05-p3.htm (February 2, 2005).

$$\text{Total inventory} = \text{Scheduled receipts for all items} + \text{On-hand inventories of all items}$$

2. Critical ratio: $CR = \dfrac{\text{Due date} - \text{Today's date}}{\text{Total shop time remaining}}$

3. Slack per remaining operations:

$$S/RO = \dfrac{(\text{Due date} - \text{Today's date}) - \text{Total shop time remaining}}{\text{Number of operations remaining}}$$

> KEY TERMS <

advanced planning and scheduling
    (APS) systems 690
critical ratio (CR) 681
demand scheduling 672
dispatching 681
earliest due date (EDD) 681
first-come, first-served (FCFS) 681
fixed schedule 677
flow shop 680
job flow time 673

job shop 680
Johnson's rule 688
labor-limited environment 689
makespan 673
multiple-dimension rules 684
operations scheduling 672
past due 674
priority sequencing rules 681
rotating schedule 677

scheduling 672
shortest processing time (SPT) 681
single-dimension rules 682
slack per remaining operations
    (S/RO) 681
tardiness 674
total inventory 674
workforce scheduling 672
work-in-process (WIP) inventory 674

> SOLVED PROBLEM 1 <

The Food Bin grocery store operates 24 hours per day, 7 days per week. Fred Bulger, the store manager, has been analyzing the efficiency and productivity of store operations recently. Bulger decided to observe the need for checkout clerks on the first shift for a 1-month period. At the end of the month, he calculated the average number of checkout registers that should be open during the first shift each day. His results showed peak needs on Saturdays and Sundays.

Day	M	T	W	Th	F	S	Su
Number of Clerks Required	3	4	5	5	4	7	8

Bulger now has to come up with a workforce schedule that guarantees each checkout clerk two consecutive days off but still covers all requirements.

a. Develop a workforce schedule that covers all requirements while giving two consecutive days off to each clerk. How many clerks are needed? Assume that the clerks have no preference regarding which days they have off.

b. Plans can be made to use the clerks for other duties if slack or idle time resulting from this schedule can be determined. How much idle time will result from this schedule, and on what days?

SOLUTION

a. We use the method demonstrated in Example 16.1 to determine the number of clerks needed.

	Day						
	M	T	W	Th	F	S	Su
Requirements	3	4	5	5	4	7	8*
Clerk 1	off	off	X	X	X	X	X
Requirements	3	4	4	4	3	6	7*
Clerk 2	off	off	X	X	X	X	X
Requirements	3	4	3	3	2	5	6*
Clerk 3	X	X	X	off	off	X	X
Requirements	2	3	2	3	2	4	5*
Clerk 4	X	X	X	off	off	X	X
Requirements	1	2	1	3	2	3	4*
Clerk 5	X	off	off	X	X	X	X

(continued)

	Day						
	M	**T**	**W**	**Th**	**F**	**S**	**Su**
Requirements	0	2	1	2	1	2	3*
Clerk 6	off	off	X	X	X	X	X
Requirements	0	2*	0	1	0	1	2*
Clerk 7	X	X	off	off	X	X	X
Requirements	0	1*	0	1*	0	0	1*
Clerk 8	X	X	X	X	off	off	X
Requirements	0	0	0	0	0	0	0

* Maximum requirements.

The minimum number of clerks is eight.

b. Based on the results in part (a), the number of clerks on duty minus the requirements is the number of idle clerks available for other duties:

	Day						
	M	**T**	**W**	**Th**	**F**	**S**	**Su**
Number on duty	5	4	6	5	5	7	8
Requirements	3	4	5	5	4	7	8
Idle clerks	2	0	1	0	1	0	0

The slack in this schedule would indicate to Bulger the number of employees he might ask to work part-time (fewer than 5 days per week). For example, clerk 7 might work Tuesday, Saturday, and Sunday and clerk 8 might work Tuesday, Thursday, and Sunday. That would eliminate slack from the schedule.

> **SOLVED PROBLEM 2** <

The Neptune's Den Machine Shop specializes in overhauling outboard marine engines. Some engines require replacement of broken parts, whereas others need a complete overhaul. Currently, five engines with varying problems are awaiting service. The best estimates for the labor times involved and the promise dates (in number of days from today) are shown in the following table. Customers usually do not pick up their engines early.

Engine	Estimated Labor Time (days)	Promise Date (days from now)
50-hp Evinrude	5	8
7-hp Johnson	4	15
100-hp Mercury	10	12
4-hp Sportsman	1	20
75-hp Nautique	3	10

a. Develop separate schedules by using the SPT and EDD rules. Compare the two schedules on the basis of average job flow time, percentage of past due jobs, and maximum past due days for any engine.

b. For each schedule, calculate average WIP inventory (in engines) and average total inventory (in engines).

SOLUTION

a. Using the SPT rule, we obtain the following schedule:

Repair Sequence	Processing Time	Job Flow Time	Promise Date	Actual Pickup Date	Days Early	Days Past Due
4-hp Sportsman	1	1	20	20	19	—
75-hp Nautique	3	4	10	10	6	—
7-hp Johnson	4	8	15	15	7	—
50-hp Evinrude	5	13	8	13	—	5
100-hp Mercury	10	23	12	23	—	11
		Total 49		81		

Using the EDD we obtain this schedule:

Repair Sequence	Processing Time	Job Flow Time	Promise Date	Actual Pickup Date	Days Early	Days Past Due
50-hp Evinrude	5	5	8	8	3	—
75-hp Nautique	3	8	10	10	2	—
100-hp Mercury	10	18	12	18	—	6
7-hp Johnson	4	22	15	22	—	7
4-hp Sportsman	1	23	20	23	—	3
		Total 76		81		

Average job flow time is 9.8 (or 49/5) days for SPT and 15.2 (or 76/5) days for EDD. The percentage of past due jobs is 40 percent (2/5) for SPT and 60 percent (3/5) for EDD. The EDD schedule minimizes the maximum days past due but has a greater flow time and causes more jobs to be past due.

b. For SPT, inventory averages are as follows:

$$\text{Average WIP inventory} = \frac{\text{Sum of flow times}}{\text{Makespan}} = \frac{49}{23} = 2.13 \text{ engines}$$

$$\text{Average total inventory} = \frac{\text{Sum of time in system}}{\text{Makespan}} = \frac{81}{23} = 3.52 \text{ engines}$$

For EDD, they are

$$\text{Average WIP inventory} = \frac{76}{23} = 3.30 \text{ engines}$$

$$\text{Average total inventory} = \frac{81}{23} = 3.52 \text{ engines}$$

> SOLVED PROBLEM 3 <

The following data were reported by the shop floor control system for order processing at the edge grinder. The current date is day 150. The number of remaining operations and the total work remaining include the operation at the edge grinder. All orders are available for processing, and none have been started yet.

Current Order	Processing Time (hr)	Due Date (day)	Remaining Operations	Shop Time Remaining (days)
A101	10	162	10	9
B272	7	158	9	6
C105	15	152	1	1
D707	4	170	8	18
E555	8	154	5	8

a. Specify the priorities for each job if the shop floor control system uses slack per remaining operations (S/RO) or critical ratio (CR).

b. For each priority rule, calculate the average job flow time per job at the edge grinder.

SOLUTION

a. We specify the priorities for each job using the two dispatching rules.

$$S/RO = \frac{(\text{Due date} - \text{Today's date}) - \text{Shop time remaining}}{\text{Number of operations remaining}}$$

$$E555: S/RO = \frac{(154 - 150) - 8}{5} = -0.80 \quad [1]$$

$$B272: S/RO = \frac{(158 - 150) - 6}{9} = 0.22 \quad [2]$$

$$D707: S/RO = \frac{(170 - 150) - 18}{8} = 0.25 \quad [3]$$

$$A101: S/RO = \frac{(162 - 150) - 9}{10} = 0.30 \quad [4]$$

$$C105: S/RO = \frac{(152 - 150) - 1}{1} = 1.00 \quad [5]$$

The sequence of production for S/RO is shown in the preceding brackets.

$$CR = \frac{\text{Due date} - \text{Today's date}}{\text{Shop time remaining}}$$

$$E555: CR = \frac{154 - 150}{8} = 0.50 \quad [1]$$

$$D707: CR = \frac{170 - 150}{18} = 1.11 \quad [2]$$

$$B272: CR = \frac{158 - 150}{6} = 1.33 \quad [3]$$

$$A101: CR = \frac{162 - 150}{9} = 1.33 \quad [4]$$

$$C105: CR = \frac{152 - 150}{1} = 2.00 \quad [5]$$

The sequence of production for CR is shown in the preceding brackets.

b. We are looking for the flow time of a set of jobs at a single machine, so each job's flow time equals the flow time of the job just prior to it in sequence plus its own processing time. Consequently, the average flow times are

$$S/RO: \frac{8 + 15 + 19 + 29 + 44}{5} = 23.0 \text{ hours}$$

$$CR: \frac{8 + 12 + 19 + 29 + 44}{5} = 22.4 \text{ hours}$$

In this example, the average flow time per job is lower for the CR rule, which is not always the case. For example, the critical ratios for B272 and A101 are tied at 1.33. If we arbitrarily assigned A101 before B272, the average flow time would increase to $(8 + 12 + 22 + 29 + 44)/5 = 23.0$ hours.

> SOLVED PROBLEM 4 <

The Rocky Mountain Arsenal, formerly a chemical warfare manufacturing site, is said to be one of the most polluted locations in the United States. Cleanup of chemical waste storage basins will involve two operations.

Operation 1: Drain and dredge basin.

Operation 2: Incinerate materials.

Management estimates that each operation will require the following amounts of time (in days):

	Storage Basin									
	A	**B**	**C**	**D**	**E**	**F**	**G**	**H**	**I**	**J**
Dredge	3	4	3	6	1	3	2	1	8	4
Incinerate	1	4	2	1	2	6	4	1	2	8

Management's objective is to minimize the makespan of the cleanup operations. First, find a schedule that minimizes the makespan. Then, calculate the average job flow time of a storage basin through the two operations. What is the total elapsed time for cleaning all 10 basins? Display the schedule in a Gantt machine chart.

SOLUTION

We can use Johnson's rule to find the schedule that minimizes the total makespan. Four jobs are tied for the shortest process time: A, D, E, and H. E and H are tied for first place, while A and D are tied for last place. We arbitrarily choose to start with basin E, the first on the list for the drain and dredge operation. The 10 steps used to arrive at a sequence are as follows:

1. Select basin E first (tied with basin H); put at the front.   E — — — — — — — — — —

2. Select basin H next; put toward the front.   E H — — — — — — — — —

3. Select basin A next (tied with basin D); put at the end.   E H — — — — — — — — A

4. Put basin D toward the end.   E H — — — — — — — D A

5. Put basin G toward the front.   E H G — — — — — — D A

6. Put basin C toward the end.   E H G — — — — — C D A

7. Put basin I toward the end.   E H G — — — — I C D A

8. Put basin F toward the front.   E H G F — — — I C D A

9. Put basin B toward the front.   E H G F B — — I C D A

10. Put basin J in the remaining space.   E H G F B J — I C D A

Several optimal solutions are available to this problem because of the ties at the start of the scheduling procedure. However, all have the same makespan. The schedule would be as follows:

	Operation 1		Operation 2	
Basin	**Start**	**Finish**	**Start**	**Finish**
E	0	1	1	3
H	1	2	3	4
G	2	4	4	8
F	4	7	8	14
B	7	11	14	18
J	11	15	18	26
I	15	23	26	28
C	23	26	28	30
D	26	32	32	33
A	32	35	35	36
			Total	200

The makespan is 36 days. The average job flow time is the sum of incineration finish times divided by 10, or 200/10 = 20 days. The Gantt machine chart for this schedule is given in Figure 16.7.

Storage basin

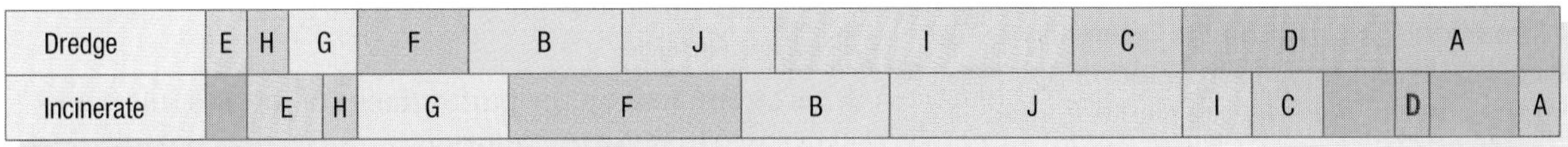

FIGURE **16.7**

> DISCUSSION QUESTIONS <

1. Suppose that two alternative approaches for determining machine schedules are available. One is an optimizing approach that can be run once a week on the computer. The other is a dispatching approach that utilizes priority rules to determine the schedule as it evolves. Discuss the advantages and disadvantages of each approach and the conditions under which each approach is likely to be better.

2. Explain why management should be concerned about priority systems in service and manufacturing organizations.

> PROBLEMS <

Software, such as OM Explorer, Active Models, and POM for Windows, is packaged with every new copy of the textbook. Check with your instructor on how best to use it. In many cases, the instructor wants you to understand how to do the calculations by hand. At most, the software provides a check on your calculations. When calculations are particularly complex and the goal is interpreting the results in making decisions, the software replaces entirely the manual calculations. The software also can be a valuable resource well after your course is completed.

1. Gerald Glynn manages the Michaels Distribution Center. After careful examination of his database information, he has determined the daily requirements for part-time loading dock personnel. The distribution center operates seven days a week, and the daily part-time staffing requirements are

Day	M	T	W	Th	F	S	Su
Requirements	6	3	5	3	7	2	3

Find the minimum number of workers Glynn must hire. Prepare a workforce schedule for these individuals so that each will have two consecutive days off per week and all staffing requirements will be satisfied. Give preference to the S–Su pair in case of a tie.

2. Cara Ryder manages a ski school in a large resort and is trying to develop a schedule for instructors. The instructors receive little salary and work just enough to earn room and board. They do receive free skiing, spending most of their free time tackling the resort's notorious double black diamond slopes. Hence, the instructors work only 4 days a week. One of the lesson packages offered at the resort is a 4-day beginner package. Ryder likes to keep the same instructor with a group over the 4-day period, so she schedules the instructors for 4 consecutive days and then 3 days off. Ryder uses years of experience with demand forecasts provided by management to formulate her instructor requirements for the upcoming month.

Day	M	T	W	Th	F	S	Su
Requirements	7	5	4	5	6	9	8

   a. Determine how many instructors Ryder needs to employ. Give preference to Saturday and Sunday off. (*Hint:* Look for the group of 3 days with lowest requirements.)

   b. Specify the work schedule for each employee. How much slack does your schedule generate for each day?

3. The mayor of Massillon, Ohio, wanting to be environmentally progressive, decided to implement a recycling plan. All residents of the city will receive a special three-part bin to separate their glass, plastic, and aluminum, and the city will be responsible for picking up the materials. A young city and regional planning graduate, Michael Duffy, has been hired to manage the recycling program. After carefully studying the city's population density, Duffy decides that the following numbers of recycling collectors will be needed.

Day	M	T	W	Th	F	S	Su
Requirements	12	7	9	9	5	3	6

The requirements are based on the populations of the various housing developments and subdivisions in the city and surrounding communities. To motivate residents of some areas to have their pickups scheduled on weekends, a special tax break will be given.

   a. Find the minimum number of recycling collectors required if each employee works 5 days a week and has 2 consecutive days off. Give preference to the S–Su pair when that pair is involved in a tie.

   b. Specify the work schedule for each employee. How much slack does your schedule generate for each day?

   c. Suppose that Duffy can smooth the requirements further through greater tax incentives. The requirements then will be eight collectors on Monday and seven on the other days of the week. How many collectors will be needed now? Find the optimal solution in terms of minimal total slack capacity. Does smoothing of requirements have capital investment implications? If so, what are they?

4. The Hickory Company manufactures wooden desks. Management schedules overtime every weekend to reduce the backlog on the most popular models. The automatic routing machine is used to cut certain types of edges on the desktops. The following orders need to be scheduled for the routing machine:

Order	Estimated Machine Time (hr)	Due Date (hr from now)
1	10	12
2	3	8
3	15	18
4	9	20
5	7	21

The due dates reflect the need for the order to be at its next operation.

   a. Develop separate schedules by using the FCFS, SPT, and EDD rules. Compare the schedules on the basis of average flow time, the average early time, and average past due hours for any order.

   b. For each schedule, calculate the average WIP inventory (in orders) and the average total inventory (in orders).

   c. Comment on the performance of the two rules relative to these measures.

5. The drill press is a bottleneck operation in a production system. Currently, five jobs are waiting to be processed. Following are the available operations data. Assume that the current date is week R and that the number of remaining operations and the shop time remaining include the operation at the drill press.

Job	Processing Time	Due Date	Operations Remaining	Shop Time Remaining (wk)
AA	4	10	3	4
BB	8	16	4	6
CC	13	21	10	9
DD	6	23	3	12
EE	2	12	5	3

   a. Specify the priority for each job if the shop floor control system uses each of the following priority rules: SPT, S/RO, EDD, and CR.

   b. For each priority rule, calculate the average flow time per job at the drill press.

   c. Which of these priority rules would work best for priority planning with an MRP system? Why?

TABLE 16.1 | Manufacturing Data

Job	Release Time	Lot Size	Processing Time (hr/unit)	Setup Time (hr)	Due Date
1	9:00 A.M. Monday	50	0.06	4	9:00 P.M. Monday
2	10:00 A.M. Monday	120	0.05	3	10:00 P.M. Monday
3	11:00 A.M. Monday	260	0.03	5	11:00 P.M. Monday
4	12:00 P.M. Monday	200	0.04	2	2:00 A.M. Tuesday

6. The machine shop at Bycraft Enterprises operates 24 hours a day and uses a numerically controlled (NC) welding machine. The load on the machine is monitored, and no more than 24 hours of work is released to the welding operators in one day. The data for a typical set of jobs are shown in Table 16.1. Management has been investigating scheduling procedures that would reduce inventory and increase customer service in the shop. Assume that at 8:00 A.M. on Monday the NC welding machine was idle.

   a. Develop schedules for SPT and EDD priority rules, and draw a Gantt machine chart for each schedule.

   b. For each schedule in part (a), calculate the average past due hours per job and the average flow time per job. Keep in mind that the jobs are available for processing at different times.

   c. Comment on the customer service and inventory performance of the two rules. What trade-offs should management consider in selecting rules for scheduling the welding machine in the future?

7. Refer to the Gantt machine chart in Figure 16.8.

   a. Suppose that a routing requirement is that each job must be processed on machine A first. Can the makespan be improved? If so, draw a Gantt chart with the improved schedule. If not, state why not.

   b. Suppose that the machine sequence has no routing restriction; in other words, jobs can be processed in any sequence on the machines. Can the makespan in the chart be improved in this case? If so, draw a Gantt chart with your schedule. If not, state why not.

8. A manufacturer of sails for small boats has a group of custom sails awaiting the last two processing operations before the sails are sent to the customers. Operation 1 must be performed before operation 2, and the jobs have different time requirements for each operation. The hours required are as follows:

	Job									
	1	2	3	4	5	6	7	8	9	10
Operation 1	1	5	8	3	9	4	7	2	4	9
Operation 2	8	3	1	2	8	6	7	2	4	1

   a. Use Johnson's rule to determine the optimal sequence.

   b. Draw a Gantt chart for each operation.

9. McGee Parts Company is under tremendous pressure to complete a government contract for six orders in 31 working days. The orders are for spare parts for highway maintenance equipment. According to the government contract, a late penalty of $1,000 is imposed each day the order is late. Owing to a nationwide increase in highway construction, McGee Parts has received many orders for spare parts replacement and the shop has been extremely busy. To complete the government contract, the parts must be deburred and heat treated. The production control manager has suggested the following schedule:

	Debur		Heat Treat	
Job	Start	Finish	Start	Finish
1	0	2	2	8
2	2	5	8	13
3	5	12	13	17
4	12	15	17	25
5	15	16	25	30
6	16	24	30	32

   a. Use Johnson's rule to determine the optimal sequence.

   b. Draw a Gantt chart for each operation.

Machine

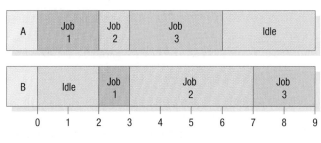

FIGURE 16.8

10. Carolyn Roberts is the operations manager of the machine shop of Reliable Manufacturing. She has to schedule eight jobs that are to be sent to final assembly for an important customer order. Currently, all eight jobs are in department 12 and must be routed to department 22 next. Jason Mangano, supervisor for department 12, is concerned about keeping his WIP inventory low and is adamant about processing the jobs through his department on the basis of shortest processing time. Pat Mooney, supervisor for department 22, pointed out that if Mangano were more flexible the orders could be finished and shipped earlier. The processing times (in days) for each job in each department follow:

				Job				
	1	2	3	4	5	6	7	8
Department 12	2	4	7	5	4	10	8	2
Department 22	3	6	3	8	2	6	6	5

   a. Determine a schedule for the operation in each department. Use SPT for department 12 and the same sequence for department 22. What is the average job flow time for department 12? What is the makespan through both departments? What is the total number of job-days spent in the system?

   b. Find a schedule that will minimize the makespan through both departments, and then calculate the average job flow time for department 12. What is the total number of job-days spent in the system?

   c. Discuss the trade-offs represented by these two schedules. What implications do they have for centralized scheduling?

ADVANCED PROBLEMS

11. Little 6, Inc., an accounting firm, forecasts the following weekly workload during the tax season:

				Day			
	M	T	W	Th	F	S	Su
Personal tax returns	24	14	18	18	10	28	16
Corporate tax returns	18	10	12	15	24	12	4

Corporate tax returns each require 4 hours of an accountant's time, and personal returns each require 90 minutes. During tax season, each accountant can work up to 10 hours per day. However, error rates increase to unacceptable levels when accountants work more than five consecutive days per week.

   a. Create an effective and efficient work schedule.

   b. Assume that Little 6 has three part-time employees available to work three days per week. How could these employees be effectively utilized?

12. Return to Problem 1 and the workforce schedule for part-time loading dock workers. Suppose that each part-time

worker can work only three days, but the days must be consecutive. Devise an approach to this workforce scheduling problem. Your objective is to minimize total slack capacity. What is the minimum number of clerks needed now and what are their schedules?

13. The repair manager at Standard Components needs to develop a priority schedule for repairing eight Dell PCs. Each job requires analysis using the same diagnostic system. Furthermore, each job will require additional processing after the diagnostic evaluation. The manager does not expect any rescheduling delays, and the jobs are to move directly to the next process after the diagnostic work has been completed. The manager has collected the following processing time and scheduling data for each repair job:

Job	Work Time (days)	Due Date (days)	Shop Time Remaining (days)	Operations Remaining
1	1.25	6	2.5	5
2	2.75	5	3.5	7
3	2.50	7	4.0	9
4	3.00	6	4.5	12
5	2.50	5	3.0	8
6	1.75	8	2.5	6
7	2.25	7	3.0	9
8	2.00	5	2.5	3

   a. Compare the relative performance of the FCFS, SPT, EDD, S/RO, and CR rules.

   b. Discuss the selection of one of the rules for this company. What criteria do you consider most important in the selection of a rule in this situation?

14. Penultimate Support Systems makes fairly good speaker and equipment support stands for music groups. The assembly process involves two operations: (1) fabrication, or cutting aluminum tubing to the correct lengths, and (2) assembly, with purchased fasteners and injection-molded plastic parts. Setup time for assembly is negligible. Fabrication setup time and run time per unit, assembly run time per unit, and the production schedule for next week follow. Organize the work to minimize makespan, and create a Gantt chart. Can this work be accomplished within two 40-hour shifts?

		Fabrication		Assembly
Model	Quantity	Setup (hr)	Run Time (hr/unit)	Run Time (hr/unit)
A	200	2	0.050	0.04
B	300	3	0.070	0.10
C	100	1	0.050	0.12
D	250	2	0.064	0.60

15. Eight jobs must be processed on three machines in the sequence M1, M2, and M3. The processing times (in hours) are

	Job							
	1	**2**	**3**	**4**	**5**	**6**	**7**	**8**
Machine 1	2	5	2	3	1	2	4	2
Machine 2	4	1	3	5	5	6	2	1
Machine 3	6	4	5	2	3	2	6	2

Machine M2 is a bottleneck, and management wants to maximize its use. Consequently, the schedule for the eight jobs, through the three machines, was based on the SPT rule on M2. The proposed schedule is 2, 8, 7, 3, 1, 4, 5, and 6.

a. It is now 4 P.M. on Monday. Suppose that processing on M2 is to begin at 7 A.M. on Tuesday. Use the proposed schedule to determine the schedules for M1 and M3 so that job 2 begins processing on M2 at 7 A.M. on Tuesday. Draw Gantt charts for M1, M2, and M3. What is the makespan for the eight jobs?

b. Find a schedule that utilizes M2 better and yields a shorter makespan.

16. The last few steps of a production process require two operations. Some jobs require processing on M1 before processing on M3. Other jobs require processing on M2 before M3. Currently, six jobs are waiting at M1 and four jobs are waiting at M2. The following data have been supplied by the shop floor control system:

	Processing Time (hr)			
Job	**M1**	**M2**	**M3**	**Due Date (hr from now)**
1	6	—	4	13
2	2	—	1	18
3	4	—	7	22
4	5	—	3	16
5	7	—	4	30
6	3	—	1	29
7	—	4	6	42
8	—	2	10	31
9	—	6	9	48
10	—	8	2	40

a. Schedule this shop by using the following rules: SPT, EDD, S/RO, and CR.

b. Discuss the operating implications of each of the schedules you developed in part (a).

> ACTIVE MODEL EXERCISE <

This Active Model appears on the Student CD-ROM. It allows you to evaluate the application of single-dimension priority rules for scheduling jobs at one workstation.

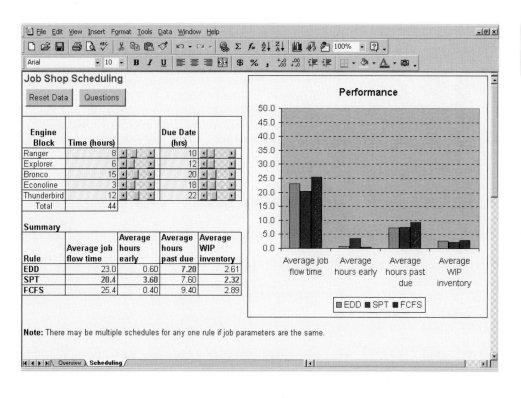

ACTIVE MODEL 16.1

Job Shop Scheduling Using Data from Example 16.2

QUESTIONS

1. Which rule minimizes the average job flow time and the average WIP in the system for this example?

2. Use the scroll bars to change the five processing times and the five due dates. Does the same rule always minimize the average flow time and average WIP?

3. Which rule minimizes the average hours past due for this example?

4. Use the scroll bar to change the processing time for the Thunderbird and to modify the due date for the Thunderbird. Does the same rule always minimize the average hours past due?

5. Which rule minimizes the average hours early for this example?

6. Use the scroll bar to change the processing time for the Econoline and to modify the due date for the Econoline. Does the same rule always minimize the average hours past due?

Food King

Based in Charlotte, North Carolina, the Food King grocery supermarket chain stretches from the Virginias down the East Coast into Florida. As in the rest of the country, the grocery supermarket industry in the Southeast is competitive, with average profit margins running at about 2 percent of revenues. Historically, the overriding competitive priority for all grocery chains was low prices. With profit margins so small, stores were continually looking for ways to reduce costs and utilize facilities efficiently. Several grocery chains still focus on low prices as their main competitive priority.

Food King, however, recently decided to focus its competitive positioning on enhancing the consumer's shopping experience. Food King's target market is the upscale food shopper, who has the following shopping priorities:

1. **Cleanliness.** The facility is clean and orderly, with items well marked and easy to find.

2. **Availability.** The selection of items is broad, and the customer has several choices for any one item.

3. **Timely Service.** The store is open at convenient times, and customers do not have to wait in long checkout lines.

4. **Reasonable Prices.** Although customers are willing to pay a small premium for cleanliness, availability, and good service, prices still must be competitive.

Marty Moyer had been the store manager of the Food King supermarket in Rock Hill, South Carolina, for the past three years having worked his way up from stockboy in this medium-sized facility. Because of his success managing the Rock Hill facility, Moyer was promoted to the store manager's position at the large, flagship Food King store in Columbia. This facility had just instituted around-the-clock hours in response to competitive pressures.

After a month as manager at the Columbia store, Moyer has become familiar with the local market characteristics, store operations, and store personnel. His major challenge for the future is to align the store with the new competitive priorities established for the chain. An area he has identified as a particular concern is the scheduling of stockers and baggers. The cleanliness, availability, and service time priorities put added pressure on Moyer to have the appropriate number of stocking and bagging personnel available. Maintaining a high level of cleanliness requires more stocking personnel to keep the stock orderly on the shelves and the aisles clear and swept. The availability priority requires more frequent replenishment of the shelves because the greater selection of items means less space is allocated to any one brand or item. Finally, the need for fast service requires baggers be available to assist the cashier, especially during peak shopping periods when long waits could occur if cashiers had to both bag and ring up the groceries.

Moyer knows that he cannot solve the cleanliness, availability, and timely service issues just by adding stocking and bagging personnel to the payroll. To make a profit in a low-margin

business environment, he has to control costs so that prices remain competitive. The trick is to develop a work schedule for the stocking and bagging personnel that satisfies competitive requirements, conforms to a reasonable set of work policies, and utilizes the personnel efficiently to minimize labor costs.

Moyer begins to address this problem by collecting information on existing scheduling policies and procedures along with a forecasted level of demand for personnel. The stocking and bagging positions can be filled with either full- or part-time employees. Full-time employees work 8 hours per day, 5 days a week, with two consecutive days off each week. The 8-hour shifts usually are scheduled as consecutive 8-hour blocks of time; however, Moyer can schedule an employee to two 4-hour time blocks (with 4 hours off between them) within a particular day if there is a stocker and a bagger for the 4-hour period between scheduled blocks of time.

All part-time employees are scheduled in 4-hour blocks of time for up to 20 hours per week. Food King limits the number of part-time employees to 50 percent of the total number of full-time employees for each category of worker. Most of the part-time employees are utilized as baggers because they tend to be retired people who have difficulty with the heavy lifting required in stocking shelves. Food King likes to hire retired people because they are dependable, reliable, and more willing to work weekends than are teenagers. Full-time employees earn $5.25 per hour; part-time employees earn only $4.50 per hour.

For scheduling purposes, each day is divided into six 4-hour time blocks beginning with 8:00 A.M. to 12:00 P.M. Demand for stocking and bagging personnel varies quite a bit within a 24-hour period. Moyer developed a forecast of personnel needs by 4-hour time blocks by analyzing customer activity data and supplier delivery schedules. The following table provides estimates of the total number of stockers and baggers required for each 4-hour block of time starting at the time indicated:

Hour	Day						
	M	T	W	Th	F	S	Su
8:00 A.M.	6	8	5	5	8	15	4
12:00 P.M.	6	8	5	5	10	15	6
4:00 P.M.	5	6	5	5	15	15	6
8:00 P.M.	4	4	4	4	8	6	4
12:00 A.M.	4	4	4	4	5	4	4
4:00 A.M.	8	4	4	8	5	4	4

The peak requirements occur during the heavy shopping periods on Friday and Saturday. More stocking personnel are required on Monday and Thursday evenings because of the large number of supplier deliveries on those days.

Moyer wants to determine the number of stocking and bagging personnel needed, the appropriate mix of full-time and part-time employees, and the work schedule for each employee. Going to a 24-hours-a-day operation certainly complicates the scheduling task. He knows that younger, full-time employees probably will be best for the late night and early morning blocks of time. But the younger employees dislike working these hours. Somehow the schedule has to convey fairness for all.

QUESTIONS

1. Translate the four priorities of the shoppers into a set of competitive priorities for operations at the Columbia Food King store.

2. Develop a schedule of full-time and part-time stockers and baggers for Marty Moyer. Explain the strategy you used and the trade-offs you made to satisfy the Columbia store's competitive priorities.

3. What measures would you take to ensure that the schedule is fair to all employees?

Source: This case was prepared by Dr. Brooke Saladin, Wake Forest University, as a basis for classroom discussion.

> SELECTED REFERENCES <

Baker, K. R. *Elements of Sequencing and Scheduling.* Hanover, NH: Baker Press, 2002.

Browne, J. J. "Simplified Scheduling of Routine Work Hours and Days Off." *Industrial Engineering* (December 1979), pp. 27–29.

Browne, J. J., and J. Prop. "Supplement to Scheduling Routine Work Hours." *Industrial Engineering* (July 1989), p. 12.

Dillon, Jeffrey E., and Spyros Kontogiorgis. "US Airways Optimizes the Scheduling of Reserve Flight Crews." *Interfaces* (September–October 1999), pp. 123–131.

Hartvigsen, David. *SimQuick: Process Simulation with Excel,* 2d ed. Upper Saddle River, NJ: Prentice Hall, 2004.

Johnson, S. M. "Optimal Two Stage and Three Stage Production Schedules with Setup Times Included." *Naval Logistics Quarterly,* vol. 1, no. 1 (1954), pp. 61–68.

Kiran, Ali S., and Thomas H. Willingham. "Simulation: Help for Your Scheduling Problems." *APICS—The Performance Advantage* (August 1992), pp. 26–28.

LaForge, R. Lawrence, and Christopher W. Craighead. "Computer-Based Scheduling in Manufacturing Firms: Some Indicators of Successful Practice." *Production and Inventory Management Journal* (First Quarter 2000), pp. 29–34.

Lesaint, David, Christos Voudouris, and Nader Azarmi. "Dynamic Workforce Scheduling for British Telecommunications plc." *Interfaces* (January–February 2000), pp. 45–56.

Metters, Richard, and Vincente Vargas. "A Comparison of Production Scheduling Policies on Costs, Service Levels, and Schedule Changes." *Production and Operations Management,* vol. 17, no. 3 (1999), pp. 76–91.

Pinedo, Michael. *Scheduling: Theory, Algorithms, and Systems,* 2d ed. Upper Saddle River, NJ: Prentice Hall, 2002.

Pinedo, M., and X. Chao. *Operations Scheduling with Applications in Manufacturing and Services.* Boston: McGraw-Hill/Irwin, 1998.

Port, Otis. "Customers Move into the Driver's Seat." *Business Week* (October 4, 1999), pp. 103–106.

Ramani, K. V. "Scheduling Doctors' Activities at a Large Teaching Hospital." *Production and Inventory Management Journal* (First/Second Quarter 2002), pp. 56–62.

Suresh, V., and D. Chaudhuri. "Dynamic Scheduling—A Survey of Research." *International Journal of Production Economics,* vol. 32 (1993), pp. 52–63.

Tibrewala, R. K., D. Philippe, and J. J. Browne. "Optimal Scheduling of Two Consecutive Idle Periods." *Management Science,* vol. 19, no. 1 (1972), pp. 71–75.

Vollmann, Thomas E., William Berry, D. Clay Whybark, and Robert Jacobs. *Manufacturing Planning and Control Systems for Supply Chain Management,* 5th ed. New York: McGraw-Hill/Irwin, 2005.

APPENDIX 1   Normal Distribution

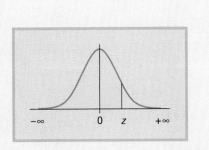

	.00	.01	.02	.03	.04	.05	.06	.07	.08	.09
.0	.5000	.5040	.5080	.5120	.5160	.5199	.5239	.5279	.5319	.5359
.1	.5398	.5438	.5478	.5517	.5557	.5596	.5636	.5675	.5714	.5753
.2	.5793	.5832	.5871	.5910	.5948	.5987	.6026	.6064	.6103	.6141
.3	.6179	.6217	.6255	.6293	.6331	.6368	.6406	.6443	.6480	.6517
.4	.6554	.6591	.6628	.6664	.6700	.6736	.6772	.6808	.6844	.6879
.5	.6915	.6950	.6985	.7019	.7054	.7088	.7123	.7157	.7190	.7224
.6	.7257	.7291	.7324	.7357	.7389	.7422	.7454	.7486	.7517	.7549
.7	.7580	.7611	.7642	.7673	.7704	.7734	.7764	.7794	.7823	.7852
.8	.7881	.7910	.7939	.7967	.7995	.8023	.8051	.8078	.8106	.8133
.9	.8159	.8186	.8212	.8238	.8264	.8289	.8315	.8340	.8365	.8389
1.0	.8413	.8438	.8461	.8485	.8508	.8531	.8554	.8577	.8599	.8621
1.1	.8643	.8665	.8686	.8708	.8729	.8749	.8770	.8790	.8810	.8830
1.2	.8849	.8869	.8888	.8907	.8925	.8944	.8962	.8980	.8997	.9015
1.3	.9032	.9049	.9066	.9082	.9099	.9115	.9131	.9147	.9162	.9177
1.4	.9192	.9207	.9222	.9236	.9251	.9265	.9279	.9292	.9306	.9319
1.5	.9332	.9345	.9357	.9370	.9382	.9394	.9406	.9418	.9429	.9441
1.6	.9452	.9463	.9474	.9484	.9495	.9505	.9515	.9525	.9535	.9545
1.7	.9554	.9564	.9573	.9582	.9591	.9599	.9608	.9616	.9625	.9633
1.8	.9641	.9649	.9656	.9664	.9671	.9678	.9686	.9693	.9699	.9706
1.9	.9713	.9719	.9726	.9732	.9738	.9744	.9750	.9756	.9761	.9767
2.0	.9772	.9778	.9783	.9788	.9793	.9798	.9803	.9808	.9812	.9817
2.1	.9821	.9826	.9830	.9834	.9838	.9842	.9846	.9850	.9854	.9857
2.2	.9861	.9864	.9868	.9871	.9875	.9878	.9881	.9884	.9887	.9890
2.3	.9893	.9896	.9898	.9901	.9904	.9906	.9909	.9911	.9913	.9916
2.4	.9918	.9920	.9922	.9925	.9927	.9929	.9931	.9932	.9934	.9936
2.5	.9938	.9940	.9941	.9943	.9945	.9946	.9948	.9949	.9951	.9952
2.6	.9953	.9955	.9956	.9957	.9959	.9960	.9961	.9962	.9963	.9964
2.7	.9965	.9966	.9967	.9968	.9969	.9970	.9971	.9972	.9973	.9974
2.8	.9974	.9975	.9976	.9977	.9977	.9978	.9979	.9979	.9980	.9981
2.9	.9981	.9982	.9982	.9983	.9984	.9984	.9985	.9985	.9986	.9986
3.0	.9987	.9987	.9987	.9988	.9988	.9989	.9989	.9989	.9990	.9990
3.1	.9990	.9991	.9991	.9991	.9992	.9992	.9992	.9992	.9993	.9993
3.2	.9993	.9993	.9994	.9994	.9994	.9994	.9994	.9995	.9995	.9995
3.3	.9995	.9995	.9995	.9996	.9996	.9996	.9996	.9996	.9996	.9997
3.4	.9997	.9997	.9997	.9997	.9997	.9997	.9997	.9997	.9997	.9998

APPENDIX 2 — Table of Random Numbers

71509	68310	48213	99928	64650	13229	36921	58732	13459	93487
21949	30920	23287	89514	58502	46185	00368	82613	02668	37444
50639	54968	11409	36148	82090	87298	41396	71111	00076	60029
47837	76716	09653	54466	87987	82362	17933	52793	17641	19502
31735	36901	92295	19293	57582	86043	69502	12601	00535	82697
04174	32342	66532	07875	54445	08795	63563	42295	74646	73120
96980	68728	21154	56181	71843	66134	52396	89723	96435	17871
21823	04027	76402	04655	87276	32593	17097	06913	05136	05115
25922	07122	31485	52166	07645	85122	20945	06369	70254	22806
32530	98882	19105	01769	20276	59401	60426	03316	41438	22012
00159	08461	51810	14650	45119	97920	08063	70819	01832	53295
66574	21384	75357	55888	83429	96916	73977	87883	13249	28870
00995	28829	15048	49573	65277	61493	44031	88719	73057	66010
55114	79226	27929	23392	06432	50200	39054	15528	53483	33972
10614	25190	52647	62580	51183	31338	60008	66595	64357	14985
31359	77469	58126	59192	23371	25190	37841	44386	92420	42965
09736	51873	94595	61367	82091	63835	86858	10677	58209	59820
24709	23224	45788	21426	63353	29874	51058	29958	61220	61199
79957	67598	74102	49824	39305	15069	56327	26905	34453	53964
66616	22137	72805	64420	58711	68435	60301	28620	91919	96080
01413	27281	19397	36231	05010	42003	99865	20924	76151	54089
88238	80731	20777	45725	41480	48277	45704	96457	13918	52375
57457	87883	64273	26236	61095	01309	48632	00431	63730	18917
21614	06412	71007	20255	39890	75336	89451	88091	61011	38072
26466	03735	39891	26361	86816	48193	33492	70484	77322	01016
97314	03944	04509	46143	88908	55261	73433	62538	63187	57352
91207	33555	75942	41668	64650	38741	86189	38197	99112	59694
46791	78974	01999	78891	16177	95746	78076	75001	51309	18791
34161	32258	05345	79267	75607	29916	37005	09213	10991	50451
02376	40372	45077	73705	56076	01853	83512	81567	55951	27156
33994	56809	58377	45976	01581	78389	18268	90057	93382	28494
92588	92024	15048	87841	38008	80689	73098	39201	10907	88092
73767	61534	66197	47147	22994	38197	60844	86962	27595	49907
51517	39870	94094	77092	94595	37904	27553	02229	44993	10468
33910	05156	60844	89012	21154	68937	96477	05867	95809	72827
09444	93069	61764	99301	55826	78849	26131	28201	91417	98172
96896	43769	72890	78682	78243	24061	55449	53587	77574	51580
97523	54633	99656	08503	52563	12099	52479	74374	79581	57143
42568	30794	32613	21802	73809	60237	70087	36650	54487	43718
45453	33136	90246	61953	17724	42421	87611	95369	42108	95369
52814	26445	73516	24897	90622	35018	70087	60112	09025	05324
87318	33345	14546	15445	81588	75461	12246	47858	08983	18205
08063	83575	26294	93027	09988	04487	88364	31087	22200	91019
53400	82078	52103	25650	75315	18916	06809	88217	12245	33053
90789	60614	20862	34475	11744	24437	55198	55219	74730	59820
73684	25859	86858	48946	30941	79017	53776	72534	83638	44680
82007	12183	89326	53713	77782	50368	01748	39033	47042	65758
80208	30920	97774	41417	79038	60531	32990	57770	53441	58732
62434	96122	63019	58439	89702	38657	60049	88761	22785	66093
04718	83199	65863	58857	49886	70275	27511	99426	53985	84077

PHOTO CREDITS

NAME INDEX

Page references that contain letters (F.1, G.1, etc.) indicate materials that are in the supplements on the CD packaged with this text.

NAME INDEX

SUBJECT INDEX

Page references that contain letters (F.1, G.1, etc.) indicate materials that are in the supplements on the CD-ROM packaged with this text. Page numbers followed by f have figures. Page numbers followed by t have tables.

SUBJECT INDEX